SELECTED COMMERCIAL STATUTES

ST. PAUL, MINN.
WEST PUBLISHING CO.
1979

TABLE OF CONTENTS

*

UNIFORM COMMERCIAL CODE

The American Law Institute

National Conference of
Commissioners on Uniform State Laws

1978 Official Text
With Comments *
and
Appendix
Showing 1972 Changes

* Comments to Articles 5, 6, 7 and 8 have been omitted.

*

ARTICLE, PART AND SECTION ANALYSIS

ARTICLE 1. GENERAL PROVISIONS

PART 1. SHORT TITLE, CONSTRUCTION, APPLICATION AND SUBJECT MATTER OF THE ACT

PART 2. GENERAL DEFINITIONS AND PRINCIPLES OF INTERPRETATION

ARTICLE 2. SALES

PART 1. SHORT TITLE, GENERAL CONSTRUCTION AND SUBJECT MATTER

ARTICLE, PART AND SECTION ANALYSIS

PART 4. TITLE, CREDITORS AND GOOD FAITH PURCHASERS

PART 5. PERFORMANCE

PART 6. BREACH, REPUDIATION AND EXCUSE

ARTICLE, PART AND SECTION ANALYSIS

ARTICLE 3. COMMERCIAL PAPER

PART 1. SHORT TITLE, FORM AND INTERPRETATION

PART 2. TRANSFER AND NEGOTIATION

PART 3. RIGHTS OF A HOLDER

ARTICLE, PART AND SECTION ANALYSIS

PART 4. LIABILITY OF PARTIES

Section

3—401. Signature.
3—402. Signature in Ambiguous Capacity.
3—403. Signature by Authorized Representative.
3—404. Unauthorized Signatures.
3—405. Impostors; Signature in Name of Payee.
3—406. Negligence Contributing to Alteration or Unauthorized Signature.
3—407. Alteration.
3—408. Consideration.
3—409. Draft Not an Assignment.
3—410. Definition and Operation of Acceptance.
3—411. Certification of a Check.
3—412. Acceptance Varying Draft.
3—413. Contract of Maker, Drawer and Acceptor.
3—414. Contract of Indorser; Order of Liability.
3—415. Contract of Accommodation Party.
3—416. Contract of Guarantor.
3—417. Warranties on Presentment and Transfer.
3—418. Finality of Payment or Acceptance.
3—419. Conversion of Instrument; Innocent Representative.

PART 5. PRESENTMENT, NOTICE OF DISHONOR AND PROTEST

3—501. When Presentment, Notice of Dishonor, and Protest Necessary or Permissible.
3—502. Unexcused Delay; Discharge.
3—503. Time of Presentment.
3—504. How Presentment Made.
3—505. Rights of Party to Whom Presentment Is Made.
3—506. Time Allowed for Acceptance or Payment.
3—507. Dishonor; Holder's Right of Recourse; Term Allowing Re-Presentment.
3—508. Notice of Dishonor.
3—509. Protest; Noting for Protest.
3—510. Evidence of Dishonor and Notice of Dishonor.
3—511. Waived or Excused Presentment, Protest or Notice of Dishonor or Delay Therein.

PART 6. DISCHARGE

3—601. Discharge of Parties.
3—602. Effect of Discharge Against Holder in Due Course.
3—603. Payment or Satisfaction.
3—604. Tender of Payment.
3—605. Cancellation and Renunciation.
3—606. Impairment of Recourse or of Collateral.

ARTICLE 6. BULK TRANSFERS

ARTICLE 7. WAREHOUSE RECEIPTS, BILLS OF LADING AND OTHER DOCUMENTS OF TITLE

PART 1. GENERAL

ARTICLE, PART AND SECTION ANALYSIS

PART 2. WAREHOUSE RECEIPTS: SPECIAL PROVISIONS

PART 3. BILLS OF LADING: SPECIAL PROVISIONS

PART 4. WAREHOUSE RECEIPTS AND BILLS OF LADING: GENERAL OBLIGATIONS

PART 5. WAREHOUSE RECEIPTS AND BILLS OF LADING: NEGOTIATION AND TRANSFER

ARTICLE 8. INVESTMENT SECURITIES

PART 4. REGISTRATION

ARTICLE 9. SECURED TRANSACTIONS; SALES OF ACCOUNTS AND CHATTEL PAPER

PART 1. SHORT TITLE, APPLICABILITY AND DEFINITIONS

PART 2. VALIDITY OF SECURITY AGREEMENT AND RIGHTS OF PARTIES THERETO

PART 3. RIGHTS OF THIRD PARTIES; PERFECTED AND UNPERFECTED SECURITY INTERESTS; RULES OF PRIORITY

ARTICLE 10. EFFECTIVE DATE AND REPEALER

ARTICLE 11. EFFECTIVE DATE AND TRANSITION PROVISIONS

*

UNIFORM COMMERCIAL CODE

TITLE

AN ACT

To be known as the Uniform Commercial Code, Relating to Certain Commercial Transactions in or regarding Personal Property and Contracts and other Documents concerning them, including Sales, Commercial Paper, Bank Deposits and Collections, Letters of Credit, Bulk Transfers, Warehouse Receipts, Bills of Lading, other Documents of Title, Investment Securities, and Secured Transactions, including certain Sales of Accounts, Chattel Paper, and Contract Rights; Providing for Public Notice to Third Parties in Certain Circumstances; Regulating Procedure, Evidence and Damages in Certain Court Actions Involving such Transactions, Contracts or Documents; to Make Uniform the Law with Respect Thereto; and Repealing Inconsistent Legislation.

*

ARTICLE 1

GENERAL PROVISIONS

PART 1. SHORT TITLE, CONSTRUCTION, APPLICATION AND SUBJECT MATTER OF THE ACT

PART 2. GENERAL DEFINITIONS AND PRINCIPLES OF INTERPRETATION

PART 1

SHORT TITLE, CONSTRUCTION, APPLICATION AND SUBJECT MATTER OF THE ACT

§ 1—101. Short Title

This Act shall be known and may be cited as Uniform Commercial Code.

Official Comment

Each Article of the Code (except this Article and Article 10) may also be cited by its own short title. See Sections 2—101, 3—101, 4—101, 5—101, 6—101, 7—101, 8—101 and 9—101.

§ 1—102. Purposes; Rules of Construction; Variation by Agreement

(1) This Act shall be liberally construed and applied to promote its underlying purposes and policies.

(2) Underlying purposes and policies of this Act are

(a) to simplify, clarify and modernize the law governing commercial transactions;

(b) to permit the continued expansion of commercial practices through custom, usage and agreement of the parties;

(c) to make uniform the law among the various jurisdictions.

(3) The effect of provisions of this Act may be varied by agreement, except as otherwise provided in this Act and except that the obligations of good faith, diligence, reasonableness and care prescribed by this Act may not be disclaimed by agreement but the parties may by agreement determine the standards by which the performance of such obligations is to be measured if such standards are not manifestly unreasonable.

(4) The presence in certain provisions of this Act of the words "unless otherwise agreed" or words of similar import does not imply that the effect of other provisions may not be varied by agreement under subsection (3).

(5) In this Act unless the context otherwise requires

(a) words in the singular number include the plural, and in the plural include the singular;

(b) words of the masculine gender include the feminine and the neuter, and when the sense so indicates words of the neuter gender may refer to any gender.

Official Comment

Prior Uniform Statutory Provision: Section 74, Uniform Sales Act; Section 57, Uniform Warehouse Receipts Act; Section 52, Uniform Bills of Lading Act; Section 19, Uniform Stock Transfer Act; Section 18, Uniform Trust Receipts Act.

Changes: Rephrased and new material added.

Purposes of Changes:

1. Subsections (1) and (2) are intended to make it clear that:

This Act is drawn to provide flexibility so that, since it is intended to be a semi-permanent piece of legislation, it will provide its own machinery for expansion of commercial practices. It is intended to make it possible for the law embodied in this Act to be developed by the courts in the light of unforeseen and new circumstances and practices. However, the proper construction of the Act requires that its interpretation and application be limited to its reason.

Courts have been careful to keep broad acts from being hampered in their effects by later acts of limited scope. Pacific Wool Growers v. Draper & Co., 158 Or. 1, 73 P.2d 1391 (1937), and compare Section 1—104. They have recognized the policies embodied in an act as applicable in reason to subject-matter which was not expressly included in the language of the act, Commercial Nat. Bank of New Orleans v. Canal-Louisiana Bank & Trust Co., 239 U.S. 520, 36 S.Ct. 194, 60 L.Ed. 417 (1916) (bona fide purchase policy of Uniform Warehouse Receipts Act extended to case not covered but of equivalent nature). They have done the same where reason and policy so required, even where the subject-matter had been intentionally excluded from the act in general. Agar v. Orda, 264 N.Y. 248, 190 N.E. 479 (1934) (Uniform Sales Act change in seller's remedies applied to contract for sale of choses in action even though the general coverage of that Act was intentionally limited to goods "other than things in action.") They have implemented a statutory policy with liberal and useful remedies not provided in the statutory text. They have disregarded a statutory limitation of remedy where the reason of the limitation did not apply. Fiterman v. J. N. Johnson & Co., 156 Minn. 201, 194 N.W. 399 (1923) (requirement of return of the goods as a condition to rescission for breach of warranty; also, partial rescission allowed). Nothing in this Act stands in the way of the continuance of such action by the courts.

The Act should be construed in accordance with its underlying purposes and policies. The text of each section should be read in the light of the purpose and policy of the rule or principle in question, as also of the Act as a whole, and the application of the language should be construed narrowly or broadly, as the case may be, in conformity with the purposes and policies involved.

2. Subsection (3) states affirmatively at the outset that freedom of contract is a principle of the Code: "the effect" of its provisions may be varied by "agreement." The meaning of the statute itself must be found in its text, including its definitions, and in appropriate extrinsic aids; it cannot be varied by agreement. But the Code seeks to avoid the type of interference with evolutionary growth found in Manhattan Co. v. Morgan, 242 N.Y. 38, 150 N.E. 594 (1926). Thus private parties cannot make an instrument negotiable within the meaning of Article 3 except as provided in Section 3—104; nor can they change the meaning of such terms as "bona fide purchaser," "holder in due course," or "due negotiation," as used in this Act. But an agreement can change the legal consequences which would otherwise flow from the provisions of the Act. "Agreement" here includes the effect given to course of dealing, usage of trade and course of performance by Sec-

tions 1—201, 1—205 and 2—208; the effect of an agreement on the rights of third parties is left to specific provisions of this Act and to supplementary principles applicable under the next section. The rights of third parties under Section 9—301 when a security interest is unperfected, for example, cannot be destroyed by a clause in the security agreement.

This principle of freedom of contract is subject to specific exceptions found elsewhere in the Act and to the general exception stated here. The specific exceptions vary in explicitness: the statute of frauds found in Section 2—201, for example, does not explicitly preclude oral waiver of the requirement of a writing, but a fair reading denies enforcement to such a waiver as part of the "contract" made unenforceable; Section 9—501(3), on the other hand, is quite explicit. Under the exception for "the obligations of good faith, diligence, reasonableness and care prescribed by this Act," provisions of the Act prescribing such obligations are not to be disclaimed. However, the section also recognizes the prevailing practice of having agreements set forth standards by which due diligence is measured and explicitly provides that, in the absence of a showing that the standards manifestly are unreasonable, the agreement controls. In this connection, Section 1—205 incorporating into the agreement prior course of dealing and usages of trade is of particular importance.

3. Subsection (4) is intended to make it clear that, as a matter of drafting, words such as "unless otherwise agreed" have been used to avoid controversy as to whether the subject matter of a particular section does or does not fall within the exceptions to subsection (3), but absence of such words contains no negative implication since under subsection (3) the general and residual rule is that the effect of all provisions of the Act may be varied by agreement.

4. Subsection (5) is modelled on 1 U.S.C. Section 1 and New York General Construction Law Sections 22 and 35.

§ 1—103. Supplementary General Principles of Law Applicable

Unless displaced by the particular provisions of this Act, the principles of law and equity, including the law merchant and the law relative to capacity to contract, principal and agent, estoppel, fraud, misrepresentation, duress, coercion, mistake, bankruptcy, or other validating or invalidating cause shall supplement its provisions.

Official Comment

Prior Uniform Statutory Provision: Sections 2 and 73, Uniform Sales Act; Section 196, Uniform Negotiable Instruments Act; Section 56, Uniform Warehouse Receipts Act; Section 51,

Uniform Bills of Lading Act; Section 18, Uniform Stock Transfer Act; Section 17, Uniform Trust Receipts Act.

Changes: Rephrased, the reference to "estoppel" and "validating" being new.

Purposes of Changes:

1. While this section indicates the continued applicability to commercial contracts of all supplemental bodies of law except insofar as they are explicitly displaced by this Act, the principle has been stated in more detail and the phrasing enlarged to make it clear that the "validating", as well as the "invalidating" causes referred to in the prior uniform statutory provisions, are included here. "Validating" as used here in conjunction with "invalidating" is not intended as a narrow word confined to original validation, but extends to cover any factor which at any time or in any manner renders or helps to render valid any right or transaction.

2. The general law of capacity is continued by express mention to make clear that section 2 of the old Uniform Sales Act (omitted in this Act as stating no matter not contained in the general law) is also consolidated in the present section. Hence, where a statute limits the capacity of a non-complying corporation to sue, this is equally applicable to contracts of sale to which such corporation is a party.

*3. The listing given in this section is merely illustrative; no listing could be exhaustive. Nor is the fact that in some sections particular circumstances have led to express reference to other fields of law intended at any time to suggest the negation of the general application of the principles of this section.

§ 1—104. Construction Against Implicit Repeal

This Act being a general act intended as a unified coverage of its subject matter, no part of it shall be deemed to be impliedly repealed by subsequent legislation if such construction can reasonably be avoided.

Official Comment

Prior Uniform Statutory Provision: None.

Purposes:

To express the policy that no Act which bears evidence of carefully considered permanent regulative intention should lightly be regarded as impliedly repealed by subsequent legislation. This Act, carefully integrated and intended as a uniform codification of permanent character covering an entire "field" of law, is to be regarded as particularly resistant to implied repeal. See Pacific Wool Growers v. Draper & Co., 158 Or. 1, 73 P.2d 1391 (1937).

§ 1—105. Territorial Application of the Act; Parties' Power to Choose Applicable Law

(1) Except as provided hereafter in this section, when a transaction bears a reasonable relation to this state and also to another state or nation the parties may agree that the law either of this state or of such other state or nation shall govern their rights and duties. Failing such agreement this Act applies to transactions bearing an appropriate relation to this state.

(2) Where one of the following provisions of this Act specifies the applicable law, that provision governs and a contrary agreement is effective only to the extent permitted by the law (including the conflict of laws rules) so specified:

Rights of creditors against sold goods. Section 2—402.

Applicability of the Article on Bank Deposits and Collections. Section 4—102.

Bulk transfers subject to the Article on Bulk Transfers. Section 6—102.

Applicability of the Article on Investment Securities. Section 8—106.

Perfection provisions of the Article on Secured Transactions. Section 9—103.

As amended 1972.

See Appendix I for changes made in former text and the reasons for change.

Official Comment

Prior Uniform Statutory Provision: None.

Purposes:

1. Subsection (1) states affirmatively the right of the parties to a multi-state transaction or a transaction involving foreign trade to choose their own law. That right is subject to the firm rules stated in the five sections listed in subsection (2), and is limited to jurisdictions to which the transaction bears a "reasonable relation." In general, the test of "reasonable relation" is similar to that laid down by the Supreme Court in Seeman v. Philadelphia Warehouse Co., 274 U.S. 403, 47 S.Ct. 626, 71 L. Ed. 1123 (1927). Ordinarily the law chosen must be that of a jurisdiction where a significant enough portion of the making or performance of the contract is to occur or occurs. But an agreement as to choice of law may sometimes take effect as a shorthand expression of the intent of the parties as to matters governed by their agreement, even though the transaction has no significant contact with the jurisdiction chosen.

2. Where there is no agreement as to the governing law,

the Act is applicable to any transaction having an "appropriate" relation to any state which enacts it. Of course, the Act applies to any transaction which takes place in its entirety in a state which has enacted the Act. But the mere fact that suit is brought in a state does not make it appropriate to apply the substantive law of that state. Cases where a relation to the enacting state is not "appropriate" include, for example, those where the parties have clearly contracted on the basis of some other law, as where the law of the place of contracting and the law of the place of contemplated performance are the same and are contrary to the law under the Code.

3. Where a transaction has significant contacts with a state which has enacted the Act and also with other jurisdictions, the question what relation is "appropriate" is left to judicial decision. In deciding that question, the court is not strictly bound by precedents established in other contexts. Thus a conflict-of-laws decision refusing to apply a purely local statute or rule of law to a particular multi-state transaction may not be valid precedent for refusal to apply the Code in an analogous situation. Application of the Code in such circumstances may be justified by its comprehensiveness, by the policy of uniformity, and by the fact that it is in large part a reformulation and restatement of the law merchant and of the understanding of a business community which transcends state and even national boundaries. Compare Global Commerce Corp. v. Clark-Babbitt Industries, Inc., 239 F.2d 716, 719 (2d Cir.1956). In particular, where a transaction is governed in large part by the Code, application of another law to some detail of performance because of an accident of geography may violate the commercial understanding of the parties.

4. The Act does not attempt to prescribe choice-of-law rules for states which do not enact it, but this section does not prevent application of the Act in a court of such a state. Common-law choice of law often rests on policies of giving effect to agreements and of uniformity of result regardless of where suit is brought. To the extent that such policies prevail, the relevant considerations are similar in such a court to those outlined above.

5. Subsection (2) spells out essential limitations on the parties' right to choose the applicable law. Especially in Article 9 parties taking a security interest or asked to extend credit which may be subject to a security interest must have sure ways to find out whether and where to file and where to look for possible existing filings.

6. Section 9—103 should be consulted as to the rules for perfection of security interests and the effects of perfection and nonperfection.

§ 1—106. Remedies to Be Liberally Administered

(1) The remedies provided by this Act shall be liberally administered to the end that the aggrieved party may be put in as good a position as if the other party had fully performed

but neither consequential or special nor penal damages may be had except as specifically provided in this Act or by other rule of law.

(2) Any right or obligation declared by this Act is enforceable by action unless the provision declaring it specifies a different and limited effect.

Official Comment

Prior Uniform Statutory Provision: Subsection (1)—none; Subsection (2)—Section 72, Uniform Sales Act.

Changes: Reworded.

Purposes of Changes and New Matter: Subsection (1) is intended to effect three things:

1. First, to negate the unduly narrow or technical interpretation of some remedial provisions of prior legislation by providing that the remedies in this Act are to be liberally administered to the end stated in the section. Second, to make it clear that compensatory damages are limited to compensation. They do not include consequential or special damages, or penal damages; and the Act elsewhere makes it clear that damages must be minimized. Cf. Sections 1—203, 2—706(1), and 2—712(2). The third purpose of subsection (1) is to reject any doctrine that damages must be calculable with mathematical accuracy. Compensatory damages are often at best approximate: they have to be proved with whatever definiteness and accuracy the facts permit, but no more. Cf. Section 2—204(3).

2. Under subsection (2) any right or obligation described in this Act is enforceable by court action, even though no remedy may be expressly provided, unless a particular provision specifies a different and limited effect. Whether specific performance or other equitable relief is available is determined not by this section but by specific provisions and by supplementary principles. Cf. Sections 1—103, 2—716.

3. "Consequential" or "special" damages and "penal" damages are not defined in terms in the Code, but are used in the sense given them by the leading cases on the subject.

Cross References:

Sections 1—103, 1—203, 2—204(3), 2—701, 2—706(1), 2—712(2) and 2—716.

Definitional Cross References:

"Action". Section 1—201.
"Aggrieved party". Section 1—201.
"Party". Section 1—201.
"Remedy". Section 1—201.
"Rights". Section 1—201.

§ 1—107. Waiver or Renunciation of Claim or Right After Breach

Any claim or right arising out of an alleged breach can be discharged in whole or in part without consideration by a written waiver or renunciation signed and delivered by the aggrieved party.

Official Comment

Prior Uniform Statutory Provision: Compare Section 1, Uniform Written Obligations Act; Sections 119(3), 120(2) and 122, Uniform Negotiable Instruments Law.

Purposes:

This section makes consideration unnecessary to the effective renunciation or waiver of rights or claims arising out of an alleged breach of a commercial contract where such renunciation is in writing and signed and delivered by the aggrieved party. Its provisions, however, must be read in conjunction with the section imposing an obligation of good faith. (Section 1—203). There may, of course, also be an oral renunciation or waiver sustained by consideration but subject to Statute of Frauds provisions and to the section of Article 2 on Sales dealing with the modification of signed writings (Section 2—209). As is made express in the latter section this Act fully recognizes the effectiveness of waiver and estoppel.

Cross References:

Sections 1—203, 2—201 and 2—209. And see Section 2—719.

Definitional Cross References:

"Aggrieved party". Section 1—201.

"Rights". Section 1—201.

"Signed". Section 1—201.

"Written". Section 1—201.

§ 1—108. Severability

If any provision or clause of this Act or application thereof to any person or circumstances is held invalid, such invalidity shall not affect other provisions or applications of the Act which can be given effect without the invalid provision or application, and to this end the provisions of this Act are declared to be severable.

Official Comment

This is the model severability section recommended by the National Conference of Commissioners on Uniform State Laws for inclusion in all acts of extensive scope.

Definitional Cross Reference:

"Person". Section 1—201.

§ 1—109. Section Captions

Section captions are parts of this Act.

Official Comment

Prior Uniform Statutory Provision: None.

Purposes:

To make explicit in all jurisdictions that section captions are a part of the text of this Act and not mere surplusage.

PART 2

GENERAL DEFINITIONS AND PRINCIPLES OF INTERPRETATION

§ 1—201. General Definitions

Subject to additional definitions contained in the subsequent Articles of this Act which are applicable to specific Articles or Parts thereof, and unless the context otherwise requires, in this Act:

(1) "Action" in the sense of a judicial proceeding includes recoupment, counterclaim, set-off, suit in equity and any other proceedings in which rights are determined.

(2) "Aggrieved party" means a party entitled to resort to a remedy.

(3) "Agreement" means the bargain of the parties in fact as found in their language or by implication from other circumstances including course of dealing or usage of trade or course of performance as provided in this Act (Sections 1—205 and 2—208). Whether an agreement has legal consequences is determined by the provisions of this Act, if applicable; otherwise by the law of contracts (Section 1—103). (Compare "Contract".)

(4) "Bank" means any person engaged in the business of banking.

(5) "Bearer" means the person in possession of an instrument, document of title, or certificated security payable to bearer or indorsed in blank.

(6) "Bill of lading" means a document evidencing the receipt of goods for shipment issued by a person engaged in the business of transporting or forwarding goods, and includes an airbill. "Airbill" means a document serving for air transportation as a bill of lading does for marine or rail transportation, and includes an air consignment note or air waybill.

(7) "Branch" includes a separately incorporated foreign branch of a bank.

(8) "Burden of establishing" a fact means the burden of persuading the triers of fact that the existence of the fact is more probable than its non-existence.

(9) "Buyer in ordinary course of business" means a person who in good faith and without knowledge that the sale to him is in violation of the ownership rights or security interest of a third party in the goods buys in ordinary course from a person in the business of selling goods of that kind but does not include a pawnbroker. All persons who sell minerals or the like (including oil and gas) at wellhead or minehead shall be deemed to be persons in the business of selling goods of that kind. "Buying" may be for cash or by exchange of other property or on secured or unsecured credit and includes receiving goods or documents of title under a pre-existing contract for sale but does not include a transfer in bulk or as security for or in total or partial satisfaction of a money debt.

(10) "Conspicuous": A term or clause is conspicuous when it is so written that a reasonable person against whom it is to operate ought to have noticed it. A printed heading in capitals (as: NON-NEGOTIABLE BILL OF LADING) is conspicuous. Language in the body of a form is "conspicuous" if it is in larger or other contrasting type or color. But in a telegram any stated term is "conspicuous". Whether a term or clause is "conspicuous" or not is for decision by the court.

(11) "Contract" means the total legal obligation which results from the parties' agreement as affected by this Act and any other applicable rules of law. (Compare "Agreement".)

(12) "Creditor" includes a general creditor, a secured creditor, a lien creditor and any representative of creditors, including an assignee for the benefit of creditors, a trustee in bankruptcy, a receiver in equity and an executor or administrator of an insolvent debtor's or assignor's estate.

(13) "Defendant" includes a person in the position of defendant in a cross-action or counterclaim.

(14) "Delivery" with respect to instruments, documents of title, chattel paper, or certificated securities means voluntary transfer of possession.

(15) "Document of title" includes bill of lading, dock warrant, dock receipt, warehouse receipt or order for the delivery of goods, and also any other document which in the regular course of business or financing is treated as adequately evidencing that the person in possession of it is entitled to receive, hold and dispose of the document and the goods it covers.

To be a document of title a document must purport to be issued by or addressed to a bailee and purport to cover goods in the bailee's possession which are either identified or are fungible portions of an identified mass.

(16) "Fault" means wrongful act, omission or breach.

(17) "Fungible" with respect to goods or securities means goods or securities of which any unit is, by nature or usage of trade, the equivalent of any other like unit. Goods which are not fungible shall be deemed fungible for the purposes of this Act to the extent that under a particular agreement or document unlike units are treated as equivalents.

(18) "Genuine" means free of forgery or counterfeiting.

(19) "Good faith" means honesty in fact in the conduct or transaction concerned.

(20) "Holder" means a person who is in possession of a document of title or an instrument or a certificated investment security drawn, issued, or indorsed to him or his order or to bearer or in blank.

(21) To "honor" is to pay or to accept and pay, or where a credit so engages to purchase or discount a draft complying with the terms of the credit.

(22) "Insolvency proceedings" includes any assignment for the benefit of creditors or other proceedings intended to liquidate or rehabilitate the estate of the person involved.

(23) A person is "insolvent" who either has ceased to pay his debts in the ordinary course of business or cannot pay his debts as they become due or is insolvent within the meaning of the federal bankruptcy law.

(24) "Money" means a medium of exchange authorized or adopted by a domestic or foreign government as a part of its currency.

(25) A person has "notice" of a fact when

(a) he has actual knowledge of it; or

(b) he has received a notice or notification of it; or

(c) from all the facts and circumstances known to him at the time in question he has reason to know that it exists.

A person "knows" or has "knowledge" of a fact when he has actual knowledge of it. "Discover" or "learn" or a word or phrase of similar import refers to knowledge rather than to reason to know. The time and circumstances under which a notice or notification may cease to be effective are not determined by this Act.

(26) A person "notifies" or "gives" a notice or notification to another by taking such steps as may be reasonably required to inform the other in ordinary course whether or not such other actually comes to know of it. A person "receives" a notice or notification when

(a) it comes to his attention; or

(b) it is duly delivered at the place of business through which the contract was made or at any other place held out by him as the place for receipt of such communications.

(27) Notice, knowledge or a notice or notification received by an organization is effective for a particular transaction from the time when it is brought to the attention of the individual conducting that transaction, and in any event from the time when it would have been brought to his attention if the organization had exercised due diligence. An organization exercises due diligence if it maintains reasonable routines for communicating significant information to the person conducting the transaction and there is reasonable compliance with the routines. Due diligence does not require an individual acting for the organization to communicate information unless such communication is part of his regular duties or unless he has reason to know of the transaction and that the transaction would be materially affected by the information.

(28) "Organization" includes a corporation, government or governmental subdivision or agency, business trust, estate, trust, partnership or association, two or more persons having a joint or common interest, or any other legal or commercial entity.

(29) "Party", as distinct from "third party", means a person who has engaged in a transaction or made an agreement within this Act.

(30) "Person" includes an individual or an organization (See Section 1—102).

(31) "Presumption" or "presumed" means that the trier of fact must find the existence of the fact presumed unless and until evidence is introduced which would support a finding of its non-existence.

(32) "Purchase" includes taking by sale, discount, negotiation, mortgage, pledge, lien, issue or re-issue, gift or any other voluntary transaction creating an interest in property.

(33) "Purchaser" means a person who takes by purchase.

(34) "Remedy" means any remedial right to which an aggrieved party is entitled with or without resort to a tribunal.

(35) "Representative" includes an agent, an officer of a corporation or association, and a trustee, executor or administrator of an estate, or any other person empowered to act for another.

(36) "Rights" includes remedies.

(37) "Security interest" means an interest in personal property or fixtures which secures payment or performance of an obligation. The retention or reservation of title by a seller of goods notwithstanding shipment or delivery to the buyer (Section 2—401) is limited in effect to a reservation of a "security interest". The term also includes any interest of a buyer of accounts or chattel paper which is subject to Article 9. The special property interest of a buyer of goods on identification of such goods to a contract for sale under Section 2—401 is not a "security interest", but a buyer may also acquire a "security interest" by complying with Article 9. Unless a lease or consignment is intended as security, reservation of title thereunder is not a "security interest" but a consignment is in any event subject to the provisions on consignment sales (Section 2—326). Whether a lease is intended as security is to be determined by the facts of each case; however, (a) the inclusion of an option to purchase does not of itself make the lease one intended for security, and (b) an agreement that upon compliance with the terms of the lease the lessee shall become or has the option to become the owner of the property for no additional consideration or for a nominal consideration does make the lease one intended for security.

(38) "Send" in connection with any writing or notice means to deposit in the mail or deliver for transmission by any other usual means of communication with postage or cost of transmission provided for and properly addressed and in the case of an instrument to an address specified thereon or otherwise agreed, or if there be none to any address reasonable under the circumstances. The receipt of any writing or notice within the time at which it would have arrived if properly sent has the effect of a proper sending.

(39) "Signed" includes any symbol executed or adopted by a party with present intention to authenticate a writing.

(40) "Surety" includes guarantor.

(41) "Telegram" includes a message transmitted by radio, teletype, cable, any mechanical method of transmission, or the like.

(42) "Term" means that portion of an agreement which relates to a particular matter.

(43) "Unauthorized" signature or indorsement means one made without actual, implied or apparent authority and includes a forgery.

(44) "Value". Except as otherwise provided with respect to negotiable instruments and bank collections (Sections 3—303, 4—208 and 4—209) a person gives "value" for rights if he acquires them

(a) in return for a binding commitment to extend credit or for the extension of immediately available credit whether or not drawn upon and whether or not a charge-back is provided for in the event of difficulties in collection; or

(b) as security for or in total or partial satisfaction of a pre-existing claim; or

(c) by accepting delivery pursuant to a pre-existing contract for purchase; or

(d) generally, in return for any consideration sufficient to support a simple contract.

(45) "Warehouse receipt" means a receipt issued by a person engaged in the business of storing goods for hire.

(46) "Written" or "writing" includes printing, typewriting or any other intentional reduction to tangible form.

Amended in 1962, 1972 and 1977.

See Appendix I for changes made in former text and the reasons for change.

Official Comment

Prior Uniform Statutory Provision, Changes and New Matter:

1. "Action". See similar definitions in Section 191, Uniform Negotiable Instruments Law; Section 76, Uniform Sales Act; Section 58, Uniform Warehouse Receipts Act; Section 53, Uniform Bills of Lading Act. The definition has been rephrased and enlarged.

2. "Aggrieved party". New.

3. "Agreement". New. As used in this Act the word is intended to include full recognition of usage of trade, course of dealing, course of performance and the surrounding circumstances as effective parts thereof, and of any agreement permitted under the provisions of this Act to displace a stated rule of law.

4. "Bank". See Section 191, Uniform Negotiable Instruments Law.

5. "Bearer". From Section 191, Uniform Negotiable Instruments Law. The prior definition has been broadened.

6. "Bill of Lading". See similar definitions in Section 1, Uniform Bills of Lading Act. The definition has been enlarged to include freight forwarders' bills and bills issued by contract carriers as well as those issued by common carriers. The definition of airbill is new.

7. "Branch". New.

8. "Burden of establishing a fact". New.

9. "Buyer in ordinary course of business". From Section 1, Uniform Trust Receipts Act. The definition has been expanded to make clear the type of person protected. Its major significance lies in Section 2—403 and in the Article on Secured Transactions (Article 9).

The reference to minerals and the like makes clear that a buyer in ordinary course buying minerals under the circumstances described takes free of a prior mortgage created by the sellers. See Comment to Section 9—103.

A pawnbroker cannot be a buyer in ordinary course of business because the person from whom he buys goods (or acquires ownership after foreclosing an initial pledge) is typically an ordinary user and not a person engaged in selling goods of that kind.

10. "Conspicuous". New. This is intended to indicate some of the methods of making a term attention-calling. But the test is whether attention can reasonably be expected to be called to it.

11. "Contract". New. But see Sections 3 and 71, Uniform Sales Act.

12. "Creditor". New.

13. "Defendant". From Section 76, Uniform Sales Act. Rephrased.

14. "Delivery". Section 76, Uniform Sales Act, Section 191, Uniform Negotiable Instruments Law, Section 58, Uniform Warehouse Receipts Act and Section 53, Uniform Bills of Lading Act.

15. "Document of title". From Section 76, Uniform Sales Act, but rephrased to eliminate certain ambiguities. Thus, by making it explicit that the obligation or designation of a third party as "bailee" is essential to a document of title, this definition clearly rejects any such result as obtained in Hixson v. Ward, 254 Ill. App. 505 (1929), which treated a conditional sales contract as a document of title. Also the definition is left open so that new types of documents may be included. It is unforeseeable what documents may one day serve the essential purpose now filled by warehouse receipts and bills of lading. Truck transport has already opened up problems which do not fit the patterns of practice resting upon the assumption that a draft can move through banking channels faster than the goods themselves can reach their destination. There lie ahead air transport and such probabilities as teletype transmission of what may some day be regarded commercially as "Documents of Title". The definition is stated in terms of the function of the documents with the intention that any document which gains commercial recognition as accomplishing the desired result shall be included within its scope. Fungible goods are adequately identified within the language of the definition by identification of the mass of which they are a part.

Dock warrants were within the Sales Act definition of document of title apparently for the purpose of recognizing a valid tender by means of such paper. In current commercial practice a dock warrant or receipt is a kind of interim certificate issued by steamship companies upon delivery of the goods at the dock, entitling a designated person to have issued to him at the company's office a bill of lading. The receipt itself is invariably nonnegotiable in form although it may indicate that a negotiable bill is to be forthcoming. Such a document is not within the general compass of the definition, although trade usage may in some cases entitle such paper to be treated as a document of title. If the dock receipt actually represents a storage obligation undertaken by the shipping company, then it is a warehouse receipt within this Section regardless of the name given to the instrument.

The goods must be "described", but the description may be by marks or labels and may be qualified in such a way as to disclaim personal knowledge of the issuer regarding contents or condition. However, baggage and parcel checks and similar "tokens" of storage which identify stored goods only as those received in exchange for the token are not covered by this Article.

The definition is broad enough to include an airway bill.

16. "Fault". From Section 76, Uniform Sales Act.

17. "Fungible". See Sections 5, 6 and 76, Uniform Sales Act; Section 58, Uniform Warehouse Receipts Act. Fungibility of goods "by agreement" has been added for clarity and accuracy. As to securities, see Section 8—107 and Comment.

18. "Genuine". New.

19. "Good faith". See Section 76(2), Uniform Sales Act; Section 58(2), Uniform Warehouse Receipts Act; Section 53(2), Uniform Bills of Lading Act; Section 22(2), Uniform Stock Transfer Act. "Good faith", whenever it is used in the Code, means at least what is here stated. In certain Articles, by specific provision, additional requirements are made applicable. See, e. g., Secs. 2—103(1) (b), 7—404. To illustrate, in the Article on Sales, Section 2—103, good faith is expressly defined as including in the case of a merchant observance of reasonable commercial standards of fair dealing in the trade, so that throughout that Article wherever a merchant appears in the case an inquiry into his observance of such standards is necessary to determine his good faith.

20. "Holder". See similar definitions in Section 191, Uniform Negotiable Instruments Law; Section 58, Uniform Warehouse Receipts Act; Section 53, Uniform Bills of Lading Act.

21. "Honor". New.

22. "Insolvency proceedings". New.

23. "Insolvent". Section 76 (3), Uniform Sales Act. The three tests of insolvency—"ceased to pay his debts in the ordinary course of business," "cannot pay his debts as they become due," and "insolvent within the meaning of the federal bankruptcy law"—are expressly set up as alternative tests and must be approached from a commercial standpoint.

24. "Money". Section 6(5), Uniform Negotiable Instruments Law. The test adopted is that of sanction of government, whether by authorization before issue or adoption afterward, which recognizes the circulating medium as a part of the official currency of that government. The narrow view that money is limited to legal tender is rejected.

25. "Notice". New. Compare N.I.L. Sec. 56. Under the definition a person has notice when he has received a notification of the

fact in question. But by the last sentence the act leaves open the time and circumstances under which notice or notification may cease to be effective. Therefore such cases as Graham v. White-Phillips Co., 296 U.S. 27, 56 S.Ct. 21, 80 L.Ed. 20 (1935), are not overruled.

26. "Notifies". New. This is the word used when the essential fact is the proper dispatch of the notice, not its receipt. Compare "Send". When the essential fact is the other party's receipt of the notice, that is stated. The second sentence states when a notification is received.

27. New. This makes clear that reason to know, knowledge, or a notification, although "received" for instance by a clerk in Department A of an organization, is effective for a transaction conducted in Department B only from the time when it was or should have been communicated to the individual conducting that transaction.

28. "Organization". This is the definition of every type of entity or association, excluding an individual, acting as such. Definitions of "person" were included in Section 191, Uniform Negotiable Instruments Law; Section 76, Uniform Sales Act; Section 58, Uniform Warehouse Receipts Act; Section 53, Uniform Bills of Lading Act; Section 22, Uniform Stock Transfer Act; Section 1, Uniform Trust Receipts Act. The definition of "organization" given here includes a number of entities or associations not specifically mentioned in prior definition of "person", namely, government, governmental subdivision or agency, business trust, trust and estate.

29. "Party". New. Mention of a party includes, of course, a person acting through an agent. However, where an agent comes into opposition or contrast to his principal, particular account is taken of that situation.

30. "Person". See Comment to definition of "Organization". The reference to Section 1—102 is to subsection (5) of that section.

31. "Presumption". New.

32. "Purchase". Section 58, Uniform Warehouse Receipts Act; Section 76, Uniform Sales Act; Section 53, Uniform Bills of Lading Act; Section 22, Uniform Stock Transfer Act; Section 1, Uniform Trust Receipts Act. Rephrased.

33. "Purchaser". Section 58, Uniform Warehouse Receipts Act; Section 76, Uniform Sales Act; Section 53, Uniform Bills of Lading Act; Section 22, Uniform Stock Transfer Act; Section 1, Uniform Trust Receipts Act. Rephrased.

34. "Remedy". New. The purpose is to make it clear that both remedy and rights (as defined) include those remedial rights of "self help" which are among the most important bodies of rights under this Act, remedial rights being those to which an aggrieved party can resort on his own motion.

35. "Representative". New.

36. "Rights". New. See Comment to "Remedy".

37. "Security Interest". See Section 1, Uniform Trust Receipts Act. The present definition is elaborated, in view espe-

cially of the complete coverage of the subject in Article 9. Notice that in view of the Article the term includes the interest of certain outright buyers of certain kinds of property. The last two sentences give guidance on the question whether reservation of title under a particular lease of personal property is or is not a security interest.

38. "Send". New. Compare "notifies".

39. "Signed". New. The inclusion of authentication in the definition of "signed" is to make clear that as the term is used in this Act a complete signature is not necessary. Authentication may be printed, stamped or written; it may be by initials or by thumbprint. It may be on any part of the document and in appropriate cases may be found in a billhead or letterhead. No catalog of possible authentications can be complete and the court must use common sense and commercial experience in passing upon these matters. The question always is whether the symbol was executed or adopted by the party with present intention to authenticate the writing.

40. "Surety". New.

41. "Telegram". New.

42. "Term". New.

43. "Unauthorized". New.

44. "Value". See Sections 25, 26, 27, 191, Uniform Negotiable Instruments Law; Section 76, Uniform Sales Act; Section 53, Uniform Bills of Lading Act; Section 58, Uniform Warehouse Receipts Act; Section 22(1), Uniform Stock Transfer Act; Section 1, Uniform Trust Receipts Act. All the Uniform Acts in the commercial law field (except the Uniform Conditional Sales Act) have carried definitions of "value". All those definitions provided that value was any consideration sufficient to support a simple contract, including the taking of property in satisfaction of or as security for a pre-existing claim. Subsections (a), (b) and (d) in substance continue the definitions of "value" in the earlier acts. Subsection (c) makes explicit that "value" is also given in a third situation: where a buyer by taking delivery under a pre-existing contract converts a contingent into a fixed obligation.

This definition is not applicable to Articles 3 and 4, but the express inclusion of immediately available credit as value follows the separate definitions in those Articles. See Sections 4—208, 4—209, 3—303. A bank or other financing agency which in good faith makes advances against property held as collateral becomes a bona fide purchaser of that property even though provision may be made for charge-back in case of trouble. Checking credit is "immediately available" within the meaning of this section if the bank would be subject to an action for slander of credit in case checks drawn against the credit were dishonored, and when a charge-back is not discretionary with the bank, but may only be made when difficulties in collection arise in connection with the specific transaction involved.

45. "Warehouse receipt". See Section 76(1), Uniform Sales Act; Section 1, Uniform Warehouse Receipts Act. Receipts issued by a field warehouse are in-

cluded, provided the warehouseman and the depositor of the goods are different persons.

46. "Written" or "writing". This is a broadening of the definition contained in Section 191 of the Uniform Negotiable Instruments Law.

§ 1—202. Prima Facie Evidence by Third Party Documents

A document in due form purporting to be a bill of lading, policy or certificate of insurance, official weigher's or inspector's certificate, consular invoice, or any other document authorized or required by the contract to be issued by a third party shall be prima facie evidence of its own authenticity and genuineness and of the facts stated in the document by the third party.

Official Comment

Prior Uniform Statutory Provision: None.

Purposes:

1. This section is designed to supply judicial recognition for documents which have traditionally been relied upon as trustworthy by commercial men.

2. This section is concerned only with documents which have been given a preferred status by the parties themselves who have required their procurement in the agreement and for this reason the applicability of the section is limited to actions arising out of the contract which authorized or required the document. The documents listed are intended to be illustrative and not all inclusive.

3. The provisions of this section go no further than establishing the documents in question as prima facie evidence and leave to the court the ultimate determination of the facts where the accuracy or authenticity of the documents is questioned. In this connection the section calls for a commercially reasonable interpretation.

Definitional Cross References:

"Bill of lading". Section 1—201.

"Contract". Section 1—201.

"Genuine". Section 1—201.

§ 1—203. Obligation of Good Faith

Every contract or duty within this Act imposes an obligation of good faith in its performance or enforcement.

Official Comment

Prior Uniform Statutory Provision: None.

Purposes:

This section sets forth a basic principle running throughout this Act. The principle involved is that in commercial transactions good faith is required in the performance and enforcement of all agreements or duties. Particular applications of this general principle appear in specific provisions of the Act such as the option to accelerate at will (Section 1—208), the right to cure a defective delivery of goods (Section 2—508), the duty of a merchant buyer who has rejected goods to effect salvage operations (Section 2—603), substituted performance (Section 2—614), and failure of presupposed conditions (Section 2—615). The concept, however, is broader than any of these illustrations and applies generally, as stated in this section, to the performance or enforcement of every contract or duty within this Act. It is further implemented by Section 1—205 on course of dealing and usage of trade.

It is to be noted that under the Sales Article definition of good faith (Section 2—103), contracts made by a merchant have incorporated in them the explicit standard not only of honesty in fact (Section 1—201), but also of observance by the merchant of reasonable commercial standards of fair dealing in the trade.

Cross References:

Sections 1—201; 1—205; 1—208; 2—103; 2—508; 2—603; 2—614; 2—615.

Definitional Cross References:

"Contract". Section 1—201.

"Good faith". Section 1—201; 2—103.

§ 1—204. Time; Reasonable Time; "Seasonably"

(1) Whenever this Act requires any action to be taken within a reasonable time, any time which is not manifestly unreasonable may be fixed by agreement.

(2) What is a reasonable time for taking any action depends on the nature, purpose and circumstances of such action.

(3) An action is taken "seasonably" when it is taken at or within the time agreed or if no time is agreed at or within a reasonable time.

Official Comment

Prior Uniform Statutory Provision: None.

Purposes:

1. Subsection (1) recognizes that nothing is stronger evidence of a reasonable time than the fixing of such time by a fair agreement between the parties. However, provision is made for disregarding a clause which whether by inadvertence or overreaching fixes a time so unreasonable that it amounts to eliminating all remedy under the contract. The parties are not required to fix the most reasonable time but may fix any time which is not obviously unfair as judged by the time of contracting.

2. Under the section, the agreement which fixes the time need not be part of the main agreement, but may occur sepa-

rately. Notice also that under the definition of "agreement" (Section 1—201) the circumstances of the transaction, including course of dealing or usages of trade or course of performance may be material. On the question what is a reasonable time these matters will often be important.

Definitional Cross Reference:
"Agreement". Section 1—201.

§ 1—205. Course of Dealing and Usage of Trade

(1) A course of dealing is a sequence of previous conduct between the parties to a particular transaction which is fairly to be regarded as establishing a common basis of understanding for interpreting their expressions and other conduct.

(2) A usage of trade is any practice or method of dealing having such regularity of observance in a place, vocation or trade as to justify an expectation that it will be observed with respect to the transaction in question. The existence and scope of such a usage are to be proved as facts. If it is established that such a usage is embodied in a written trade code or similar writing the interpretation of the writing is for the court.

(3) A course of dealing between parties and any usage of trade in the vocation or trade in which they are engaged or of which they are or should be aware give particular meaning to and supplement or qualify terms of an agreement.

(4) The express terms of an agreement and an applicable course of dealing or usage of trade shall be construed wherever reasonable as consistent with each other; but when such construction is unreasonable express terms control both course of dealing and usage of trade and course of dealing controls usage of trade.

(5) An applicable usage of trade in the place where any part of performance is to occur shall be used in interpreting the agreement as to that part of the performance.

(6) Evidence of a relevant usage of trade offered by one party is not admissible unless and until he has given the other party such notice as the court finds sufficient to prevent unfair surprise to the latter.

Official Comment

Prior Uniform Statutory Provision: No such general provision but see Sections 9(1), 15(5), 18 (2), and 71, Uniform Sales Act.

Purposes: This section makes it clear that:

1. This Act rejects both the "lay-dictionary" and the "con-

veyancer's" reading of a commercial agreement. Instead the meaning of the agreement of the parties is to be determined by the language used by them and by their action, read and interpreted in the light of commercial practices and other surrounding circumstances. The measure and background for interpretation are set by the commercial context, which may explain and supplement even the language of a formal or final writing.

2. Course of dealing under subsection (1) is restricted, literally, to a sequence of conduct between the parties previous to the agreement. However, the provisions of the Act on course of performance make it clear that a sequence of conduct after or under the agreement may have equivalent meaning. (Section 2—208.)

3. "Course of dealing" may enter the agreement either by explicit provisions of the agreement or by tacit recognition.

4. This Act deals with "usage of trade" as a factor in reaching the commercial meaning of the agreement which the parties have made. The language used is to be interpreted as meaning what it may fairly be expected to mean to parties involved in the particular commercial transaction in a given locality or in a given vocation or trade. By adopting in this context the term "usage of trade" this Act expresses its intent to reject those cases which see evidence of "custom" as representing an effort to displace or negate "established rules of law". A distinction is to be drawn between mandatory rules of law such as the Statute of Frauds provisions of Article 2 on Sales whose very office is to control and restrict the actions of the parties, and which cannot be abrogated by agreement, or by a usage of trade, and those rules of law (such as those in Part 3 of Article 2 on Sales) which fill in points which the parties have not considered and in fact agreed upon. The latter rules hold "unless otherwise agreed" but yield to the contrary agreement of the parties. Part of the agreement of the parties to which such rules yield is to be sought for in the usages of trade which furnish the background and give particular meaning to the language used, and are the framework of common understanding controlling any general rules of law which hold only when there is no such understanding.

5. A usage of trade under subsection (2) must have the "regularity of observance" specified. The ancient English tests for "custom" are abandoned in this connection. Therefore, it is not required that a usage of trade be "ancient or immemorial", "universal" or the like. Under the requirement of subsection (2) full recognition is thus available for new usages and for usages currently observed by the great majority of decent dealers, even though dissidents ready to cut corners do not agree. There is room also for proper recognition of usage agreed upon by merchants in trade codes.

6. The policy of this Act controlling explicit unconscionable contracts and clauses (Sections 1—203, 2—302) applies to implicit clauses which rest on usage of trade and carries forward the policy underlying the ancient requirement that a custom

or usage must be "reasonable". However, the emphasis is shifted. The very fact of commercial acceptance makes out a prima facie case that the usage is reasonable, and the burden is no longer on the usage to establish itself as being reasonable. But the anciently established policing of usage by the courts is continued to the extent necessary to cope with the situation arising if an unconscionable or dishonest practice should become standard.

7. Subsection (3), giving the prescribed effect to usages of which the parties "are or should be aware", reinforces the provision of subsection (2) requiring not universality but only the described "regularity of observance" of the practice or method. This subsection also reinforces the point of subsection (2) that such usages may be either general to trade or particular to a special branch of trade.

8. Although the terms in which this Act defines "agreement" include the elements of course of dealing and usage of trade, the fact that express reference is made in some sections to those elements is not to be construed as carrying a contrary intent or implication elsewhere. Compare Section 1—102(4).

9. In cases of a well established line of usage varying from the general rules of this Act where the precise amount of the variation has not been worked out into a single standard, the party relying on the usage is entitled, in any event, to the minimum variation demonstrated. The whole is not to be disregarded because no particular line of detail has been established. In case a dominant pattern has been fairly evidenced, the party relying on the usage is entitled under this section to go to the trier of fact on the question of whether such dominant pattern has been incorporated into the agreement.

10. Subsection (6) is intended to insure that this Act's liberal recognition of the needs of commerce in regard to usage of trade shall not be made into an instrument of abuse.

Cross References:

Point 1: Sections 1—203, 2—104 and 2—202.

Point 2: Section 2—208.

Point 4: Section 2—201 and Part 3 of Article 2.

Point 6: Sections 1—203 and 2—302.

Point 8: Sections 1—102 and 1—201.

Point 9: Section 2—204(3).

Definitional Cross References:

"Agreement". Section 1—201.

"Contract". Section 1—201.

"Party". Section 1—201.

"Term". Section 1—201.

§ 1—206. Statute of Frauds for Kinds of Personal Property Not Otherwise Covered

(1) Except in the cases described in subsection (2) of this section a contract for the sale of personal property is not enforceable by way of action or defense beyond five thousand dollars in amount or value of remedy unless there is some writing

which indicates that a contract for sale has been made between the parties at a defined or stated price, reasonably identifies the subject matter, and is signed by the party against whom enforcement is sought or by his authorized agent.

(2) Subsection (1) of this section does not apply to contracts for the sale of goods (Section 2—201) nor of securities (Section 8—319) nor to security agreements (Section 9—203).

Official Comment

Prior Uniform Statutory Provision: Section 4, Uniform Sales Act (which was based on Section 17 of the Statute of 29 Charles II).

Changes: Completely rewritten by this and other sections.

Purposes: To fill the gap left by the Statute of Frauds provisions for goods (Section 2—201), securities (Section 8—319), and security interests (Section 9—203). The Uniform Sales Act covered the sale of "choses in action"; the principal gap relates to sale of the "general intangibles" defined in Article 9 (Section 9—106) and to transactions excluded from Article 9 by Section 9—104. Typical are the sale of bilateral contracts, royalty rights or the like. The informality normal to such transactions is recognized by lifting the limit for oral transactions to $5,000. In such transactions there is often no standard of practice by which to judge, and values can rise or drop without warning; troubling abuses are avoided when the dollar limit is exceeded by requiring that the subject-matter be reasonably identified in a signed writing which indicates that a contract for sale has been made at a defined or stated price.

Definitional Cross References:

"Action". Section 1—201.
"Agreement". Section 1—201.
"Contract". Section 1—201.
"Contract for sale". Section 2—106.
"Goods". Section 2—105.
"Party". Section 1—201.
"Sale". Section 2—106.
"Signed". Section 1—201.
"Writing". Section 1—201.

§ 1—207. Performance or Acceptance Under Reservation of Rights

A party who with explicit reservation of rights performs or promises performance or assents to performance in a manner demanded or offered by the other party does not thereby prejudice the rights reserved. Such words as "without prejudice", "under protest" or the like are sufficient.

Official Comment

Prior Uniform Statutory Provision: None.

Purposes:

1. This section provides machinery for the continuation of

performance along the lines contemplated by the contract despite a pending dispute, by adopting the mercantile device of going ahead with delivery, acceptance, or payment "without prejudice," "under protest," "under reserve," "with reservation of all our rights," and the like. All of these phrases completely reserve all rights within the meaning of this section. The section therefore contemplates that limited as well as general reservations and acceptance by a party may be made "subject to satisfaction of our purchaser," "subject to acceptance by our customers," or the like.

2. This section does not add any new requirement of language of reservation where not already required by law, but merely provides a specific measure on which a party can rely as he makes or concurs in any interim adjustment in the course of performance. It does not affect or impair the provisions of this Act such as those under which the buyer's remedies for defect survive acceptance without being expressly claimed if notice of the defects is given within a reasonable time. Nor does it disturb the policy of those cases which restrict the effect of a waiver of a defect to reasonable limits under the circumstances, even though no such reservation is expressed.

The section is not addressed to the creation or loss of remedies in the ordinary course of performance but rather to a method of procedure where one party is claiming as of right something which the other feels to be unwarranted.

Cross Reference:

Section 2—607.

Definitional Cross References:

"Party". Section 1—201.
"Rights". Section 1—201.

§ 1—208. Option to Accelerate at Will

A term providing that one party or his successor in interest may accelerate payment or performance or require collateral or additional collateral "at will" or "when he deems himself insecure" or in words of similar import shall be construed to mean that he shall have power to do so only if he in good faith believes that the prospect of payment or performance is impaired. The burden of establishing lack of good faith is on the party against whom the power has been exercised.

Official Comment

Prior Uniform Statutory Provision: None.

Purposes:

The increased use of acceleration clauses either in the case of sales on credit or in time paper or in security transactions has led to some confusion in the cases as to the effect to be given to a clause which seemingly grants the power of an acceleration at the whim and caprice of one party. This Section is intended to make clear that despite language which can be so construed and which further might be held to make the agreement void as against public policy or to make the contract illusory or too indefinite for enforcement, the clause means that the option is to be exercised only in the good faith belief that the prospect of payment or performance is impaired.

Obviously this section has no application to demand instruments or obligations whose very nature permits call at any time with or without reason. This section applies only to an agreement or to paper which in the first instance is payable at a future date.

Definitional Cross References:

"Burden of establishing". Section 1—201.

"Good faith". Section 1—201.

"Party". Section 1—201.

"Term". Section 1—201.

§ 1—209. Subordinated Obligations

An obligation may be issued as subordinated to payment of another obligation of the person obligated, or a creditor may subordinate his right to payment of an obligation by agreement with either the person obligated or another creditor of the person obligated. Such a subordination does not create a security interest as against either the common debtor or a subordinated creditor. This section shall be construed as declaring the law as it existed prior to the enactment of this section and not as modifying it. Added 1966.

Note: *This new section is proposed as an optional provision to make it clear that a subordination agreement does not create a security interest unless so intended.*

Official Comment

Source: New York.

Prior Uniform Statutory Provision: None.

Reason for Change: The drafting history of Article 9 makes it clear that there was no intention to cover agreements by which the rights of one unsecured creditor are subordinated to the rights of another unsecured creditor of a common debtor. Nevertheless, since in insolvency proceedings dividends otherwise payable to a subordinated creditor are turned over to the superior creditor, fears have been expressed that a subordination agreement might be treated as a "security agreement" creating a "security interest" in property of the subordinated creditor, and that inappropriate provisions of Article 9 might be applied. This optional section is intended to allay such fears by making an explicit declaration that a subordination agreement does not of itself create a security interest. Nothing in this section prevents the creation of a security interest in such a case when the parties to the agreement so intend.

Purposes:

1. Billions of dollars of subordinated debt are held by the public and by institutional investors. Commonly, the subordinated debt is subordinated on issue or acquisition and is evidenced by an investment security or by

a negotiable or non-negotiable note. Debt is also sometimes subordinated after it arises, either by agreement between the subordinating creditor and the debtor, by agreement between two creditors of the same debtor, or by agreement of all three parties. The subordinated creditor may be a stockholder or other "insider" interested in the common debtor; the subordinated debt may consist of accounts or other rights to payment not evidenced by any instrument. All such cases are included in the terms "subordinated obligation," "subordination," and "subordinated creditor."

2. Subordination agreements are enforceable between the parties as contracts; and in the bankruptcy of the common debtor dividends otherwise payable to the subordinated creditor are turned over to the superior creditor. This "turn-over" practice has on occasion been explained in terms of "equitable lien," "equitable assignment," or "constructive trust," but whatever the label the practice is essentially an equitable remedy and does not mean that there is a transaction "intended to create a security interest," a "sale of accounts, contract rights or chattel paper," or a "security interest created by contract," within the meaning of Section 9—102. On the other hand, nothing in this section prevents one creditor from assigning his rights to another creditor of the same debtor in such a way as to create a security interest within Article 9, where the parties so intend.

3. The last sentence of this section is intended to negate any implication that the section changes the law. It is intended to be declaratory of pre-existing law. Both the history and the text of Article 9 make it clear that it was not intended to cover subordination agreements. The provisions of Section 9—203 for signature by the "debtor" would be entirely unworkable if read to require signature by public holders of subordinated investment securities. The priorities, filing provisions and remedies on default provided by Article 9 would also be largely inappropriate in many situations. The precautionary language of Section 9—316 preserving subordination of priority by agreement between secured parties points to the conclusion that similar arrangements among unsecured lenders are not covered unless otherwise within the scope of the Article.

4. The enforcement of subordination agreements is largely left to supplementary principles under Section 1—103. If the subordinated debt is evidenced by an investment security, Section 8—202(1) authorizes enforcement against purchasers on terms stated or referred to on the security. If the fact of subordination is noted on a negotiable instrument, a holder under Sections 3—302 and 3—306 is subject to the term because notice precludes him from taking free of the subordination. Sections 3—302(3) (a), 3—306 and 8—317 severely limit the rights of levying creditors of a subordinated creditor in such cases.

Definitional Cross References:

"Agreement". Section 1—201.
"Creditor". Section 1—201.
"Debtor". Section 9—105.
"Person". Section 1—201.
"Rights". Section 1—201.
"Security interest". Section 1—201.

ARTICLE 2

SALES

PART 1. SHORT TITLE, GENERAL CONSTRUCTION AND SUBJECT MATTER

PART 2. FORM, FORMATION AND READJUSTMENT OF CONTRACT

PART 3. GENERAL OBLIGATION AND CONSTRUCTION OF CONTRACT

PART 4. TITLE, CREDITORS AND GOOD FAITH PURCHASERS

PART 5. PERFORMANCE

PART 6. BREACH, REPUDIATION AND EXCUSE

PART 7. REMEDIES

PART 1

SHORT TITLE, GENERAL CONSTRUCTION AND SUBJECT MATTER

§ 2—101. Short Title

This Article shall be known and may be cited as Uniform Commerical Code—Sales.

Official Comment

This Article is a complete revision and modernization of the Uniform Sales Act which was promulgated by the National Conference of Commissioners on Uniform State Laws in 1906 and has been adopted in 34 states and Alaska, the District of Columbia and Hawaii.

The coverage of the present Article is much more extensive than that of the old Sales Act and extends to the various bodies of case law which have been developed both outside of and under the latter.

The arrangement of the present Article is in terms of contract for sale and the various steps of its performance. The legal consequences are stated as following directly from the contract and action taken under it without resorting to the idea of when property or title passed or was to pass as being the determining factor. The purpose is to avoid making practical issues between practical men turn upon the location of an intangible something, the passing of which no man can prove by evidence and to substitute for such abstractions proof of words and actions of a tangible character.

§ 2—102. Scope; Certain Security and Other Transactions Excluded From This Article

Unless the context otherwise requires, this Article applies to transactions in goods; it does not apply to any transaction which although in the form of an unconditional contract to sell or present sale is intended to operate only as a security transaction nor does this Article impair or repeal any statute regulating sales to consumers, farmers or other specified classes of buyers.

Official Comment

Prior Uniform Statutory Provision: Section 75, Uniform Sales Act.

Changes: Section 75 has been rephrased.

Purposes of Changes and New Matter: To make it clear that:

The Article leaves substantially unaffected the law relating to purchase money security such as conditional sale or chattel mortgage though it regulates the general sales aspects of such transactions. "Security transaction" is used in the same sense as in the Article on Secured Transactions (Article 9).

Cross Reference:

Article 9.

Definitional Cross References:

"Contract". Section 1—201.

"Contract for sale". Section 2—106.

"Present sale". Section 2—106.

"Sale". Section 2—106.

§ 2—103. Definitions and Index of Definitions

(1) In this Article unless the context otherwise requires

(a) "Buyer" means a person who buys or contracts to buy goods.

(b) "Good faith" in the case of a merchant means honesty in fact and the observance of reasonable commercial standards of fair dealing in the trade.

(c) "Receipt" of goods means taking physical possession of them.

(d) "Seller" means a person who sells or contracts to sell goods.

(2) Other definitions applying to this Article or to specified Parts thereof, and the sections in which they appear are:

"Acceptance". Section 2—606.
"Banker's credit". Section 2—325.
"Between merchants". Section 2—104.
"Cancellation". Section 2—106(4).

"Commercial unit". Section 2—105.
"Confirmed credit". Section 2—325.
"Conforming to contract". Section 2—106.
"Contract for sale". Section 2—106.
"Cover". Section 2—712.
"Entrusting". Section 2—403.
"Financing agency". Section 2—104.
"Future goods". Section 2—105.
"Goods". Section 2—105.
"Identification". Section 2—501.
"Installment contract". Section 2—612.
"Letter of Credit". Section 2—325.
"Lot". Section 2—105.
"Merchant". Section 2—104.
"Overseas". Section 2—323.
"Person in position of seller". Section 2—707.
"Present sale". Section 2—106.
"Sale". Section 2—106.
"Sale on approval". Section 2—326.
"Sale or return". Section 2—326.
"Termination". Section 2—106.

(3) The following definitions in other Articles apply to this Article:

"Check". Section 3—104.
"Consignee". Section 7—102.
"Consignor". Section 7—102.
"Consumer goods". Section 9—109.
"Dishonor". Section 3—507.
"Draft". Section 3—104.

(4) In addition Article 1 contains general definitions and principles of construction and interpretation applicable throughout this Article.

Official Comment

Prior Uniform Statutory Provision: Subsection (1): Section 76, Uniform Sales Act.

Changes:

The definitions of "buyer" and "seller" have been slightly rephrased, the reference in Section 76 of the prior Act to "any legal successor in interest of such person" being omitted. The definition of "receipt" is new.

Purposes of Changes and New Matter:

1. The phrase "any legal successor in interest of such person" has been eliminated since Section 2—210 of this Article, which limits some types of delegation of performance on assignment of a sales contract, makes it clear that not every such successor can be safely included in the definition. In every ordinary case, however,

such successors are as of course included.

2. "Receipt" must be distinguished from delivery particularly in regard to the problems arising out of shipment of goods, whether or not the contract calls for making delivery by way of documents of title, since the seller may frequently fulfill his obligations to "deliver" even though the buyer may never "receive" the goods. Delivery with respect to documents of title is defined in Article 1 and requires transfer of physical delivery. Otherwise the many divergent incidents of delivery are handled incident by incident.

Cross References:

Point 1: See Section 2—210 and Comment thereon.

Point 2: Section 1—201.

Definitional Cross Reference:

"Person". Section 1—201.

§ 2—104. Definitions: "Merchant"; "Between Merchants"; "Financing Agency"

(1) "Merchant" means a person who deals in goods of the kind or otherwise by his occupation holds himself out as having knowledge or skill peculiar to the practices or goods involved in the transaction or to whom such knowledge or skill may be attributed by his employment of an agent or broker or other intermediary who by his occupation holds himself out as having such knowledge or skill.

(2) "Financing agency" means a bank, finance company or other person who in the ordinary course of business makes advances against goods or documents of title or who by arrangement with either the seller or the buyer intervenes in ordinary course to make or collect payment due or claimed under the contract for sale, as by purchasing or paying the seller's draft or making advances against it or by merely taking it for collection whether or not documents of title accompany the draft. "Financing agency" includes also a bank or other person who similarly intervenes between persons who are in the position of seller and buyer in respect to the goods (Section 2—707).

(3) "Between merchants" means in any transaction with respect to which both parties are chargeable with the knowledge or skill of merchants.

Official Comment

Prior Uniform Statutory Provision: None. But see Sections 15 (2), (5), 16(c), 45(2) and 71, Uniform Sales Act, and Sections 35 and 37, Uniform Bills of Lading Act for examples of the policy expressly provided for in this Article.

Purposes:

1. This Article assumes that transactions between profession-

als in a given field require special and clear rules which may not apply to a casual or inexperienced seller or buyer. It thus adopts a policy of expressly stating rules applicable "between merchants" and "as against a merchant", wherever they are needed instead of making them depend upon the circumstances of each case as in the statutes cited above. This section lays the foundation of this policy by defining those who are to be regarded as professionals or "merchants" and by stating when a transaction is deemed to be "between merchants".

2. The term "merchant" as defined here roots in the "law merchant" concept of a professional in business. The professional status under the definition may be based upon specialized knowledge as to the goods, specialized knowledge as to business practices, or specialized knowledge as to both and which kind of specialized knowledge may be sufficient to establish the merchant status is indicated by the nature of the provisions.

The special provisions as to merchants appear only in this Article and they are of three kinds. Sections 2—201(2), 2—205, 2—207 and 2—209 dealing with the statute of frauds, firm offers, confirmatory memoranda and modification rest on normal business practices which are or ought to be typical of and familiar to any person in business. For purposes of these sections almost every person in business would, therefore, be deemed to be a "merchant" under the language "who . . . by his occupation holds himself out as having knowledge or skill peculiar to the practices . . . involved in the transaction . . ." since the practices involved in the transaction are non-specialized business practices such as answering mail. In this type of provision, banks or even universities, for example, well may be "merchants." But even these sections only apply to a merchant in his mercantile capacity; a lawyer or bank president buying fishing tackle for his own use is not a merchant.

On the other hand, in Section 2—314 on the warranty of merchantability, such warranty is implied only "if the seller is a merchant with respect to goods of that kind." Obviously this qualification restricts the implied warranty to a much smaller group than everyone who is engaged in business and requires a professional status as to particular kinds of goods. The exception in Section 2—402(2) for retention of possession by a merchant-seller falls in the same class; as does Section 2—403(2) on entrusting of possession to a merchant "who deals in goods of that kind".

A third group of sections includes 2—103(1) (b), which provides that in the case of a merchant "good faith" includes observance of reasonable commercial standards of fair dealing in the trade; 2—327(1) (c), 2—603 and 2—605, dealing with responsibilities of merchant buyers to follow seller's instructions, etc.; 2—509 on risk of loss, and 2—609 on adequate assurance of performance. This group of sections applies to persons who are merchants under either the "practices" or the "goods" aspect of the definition of merchant.

3. The "or to whom such knowledge or skill may be attributed by his employment of an agent or broker . . ." clause of the definition of merchant means that even persons such as universities, for example, can come within the definition of merchant if they have regular purchasing departments or business personnel who are familiar with business practices and who are equipped to take any action required.

Cross References:

Point 1: See Sections 1—102 and 1—203.

Point 2: See Sections 2—314, 2—315 and 2—320 to 2—325, of this Article, and Article 9.

Definitional Cross References:

"Bank". Section 1—201.

"Buyer". Section 2—103.

"Contract for sale". Section 2—106.

"Document of title". Section 1—201.

"Draft". Section 3—104.

"Goods". Section 2—105.

"Person". Section 1—201.

"Purchase". Section 1—201.

"Seller". Section 2—103.

§ 2—105. Definitions: Transferability; "Goods"; "Future" Goods; "Lot"; "Commercial Unit"

(1) "Goods" means all things (including specially manufactured goods) which are movable at the time of identification to the contract for sale other than the money in which the price is to be paid, investment securities (Article 8) and things in action. "Goods" also includes the unborn young of animals and growing crops and other identified things attached to realty as described in the section on goods to be severed from realty (Section 2—107).

(2) Goods must be both existing and identified before any interest in them can pass. Goods which are not both existing and identified are "future" goods. A purported present sale of future goods or of any interest therein operates as a contract to sell.

(3) There may be a sale of a part interest in existing identified goods.

(4) An undivided share in an identified bulk of fungible goods is sufficiently identified to be sold although the quantity of the bulk is not determined. Any agreed proportion of such a bulk or any quantity thereof agreed upon by number, weight or other measure may to the extent of the seller's interest in the bulk be sold to the buyer who then becomes an owner in common.

(5) "Lot" means a parcel or a single article which is the subject matter of a separate sale or delivery, whether or not it is sufficient to perform the contract.

(6) "Commercial unit" means such a unit of goods as by commercial usage is a single whole for purposes of sale and division of which materially impairs its character or value on the market or in use. A commercial unit may be a single article (as a machine) or a set of articles (as a suite of furniture or an assortment of sizes) or a quantity (as a bale, gross, or carload) or any other unit treated in use or in the relevant market as a single whole.

Official Comment

Prior Uniform Statutory Provision: Subsections (1), (2), (3) and (4)—Sections 5, 6 and 76, Uniform Sales Act; Subsections (5) and (6)—none.

Changes: Rewritten.

Purposes of Changes and New Matter:

1. Subsection (1) on "goods": The phraseology of the prior uniform statutory provision has been changed so that:

The definition of goods is based on the concept of movability and the term "chattels personal" is not used. It is not intended to deal with things which are not fairly identifiable as movables before the contract is performed.

Growing crops are included within the definition of goods since they are frequently intended for sale. The concept of "industrial" growing crops has been abandoned, for under modern practices fruit, perennial hay, nursery stock and the like must be brought within the scope of this Article. The young of animals are also included expressly in this definition since they, too, are frequently intended for sale and may be contracted for before birth. The period of gestation of domestic animals is such that the provisions of the section on identification can apply as in the case of crops to be planted. The reason of this definition also leads to the inclusion of a wool crop or the like as "goods" subject to identification under this Article.

The exclusion of "money in which the price is to be paid" from the definition of goods does not mean that foreign currency which is included in the definition of money may not be the subject matter of a sales transaction. Goods is intended to cover the sale of money when money is being treated as a commodity but not to include it when money is the medium of payment.

As to contracts to sell timber, minerals, or structures to be removed from the land Section 2—107(1) (Goods to be severed from Realty: recording) controls.

The use of the word "fixtures" is avoided in view of the diversity of definitions of that term. This Article in including within its scope "things attached to realty" adds the further test that they must be capable of severance without material harm thereto. As between the parties any identified things which fall within that definition become "goods" upon the making of the contract for sale.

"Investment securities" are expressly excluded from the coverage of this Article. It is not intended by this exclusion, however, to prevent the application of a particular section of this Article by analogy to securities (as was done with the Original Sales Act in Agar v. Orda, 264 N.Y. 248, 190 N.E. 479, 99 A.L.R. 269 (1934)) when the reason of that section makes such application sensible and the situation involved is not covered by the Article of this Act dealing specifically with such securities (Article 8).

2. References to the fact that a contract for sale can extend to future or contingent goods and that ownership in common follows the sale of a part interest have been omitted here as obvious without need for expression; hence no inference to negate these principles should be drawn from their omission.

3. Subsection (4) does not touch the question of how far an appropriation of a bulk of fungible goods may or may not satisfy the contract for sale.

4. Subsections (5) and (6) on "lot" and "commercial unit" are introduced to aid in the phrasing of later sections.

5. The question of when an identification of goods takes place is determined by the provisions of Section 2—501 and all that this section says is what kinds of goods may be the subject of a sale.

Cross References:

Point 1: Sections 2—107, 2—201, 2—501 and Article 8.

Point 5: Section 2—501.

See also Section 1—201.

Definitional Cross References:

"Buyer". Section 2—103.

"Contract". Section 1—201.

"Contract for sale". Section 2—106.

"Fungible". Section 1—201.

"Money". Section 1—201.

"Present sale". Section 2—106.

"Sale". Section 2—106.

"Seller". Section 2—103.

§ 2—106. Definitions: "Contract"; "Agreement"; "Contract for Sale"; "Sale"; "Present Sale"; "Conforming" to Contract; "Termination"; "Cancellation"

(1) In this Article unless the context otherwise requires "contract" and "agreement" are limited to those relating to the present or future sale of goods. "Contract for sale" includes both a present sale of goods and a contract to sell goods at a future time. A "sale" consists in the passing of title from the seller to the buyer for a price (Section 2—401). A "present sale" means a sale which is accomplished by the making of the contract.

(2) Goods or conduct including any part of a performance are "conforming" or conform to the contract when they are in accordance with the obligations under the contract.

(3) "Termination" occurs when either party pursuant to a power created by agreement or law puts an end to the contract

otherwise than for its breach. On "termination" all obligations which are still executory on both sides are discharged but any right based on prior breach or performance survives.

(4) "Cancellation" occurs when either party puts an end to the contract for breach by the other and its effect is the same as that of "termination" except that the cancelling party also retains any remedy for breach of the whole contract or any unperformed balance.

Official Comment

Prior Uniform Statutory Provision: Subsection (1)—Section 1 (1) and (2), Uniform Sales Act; Subsection (2)—none, but subsection generally continues policy of Sections 11, 44 and 69, Uniform Sales Act; Subsections (3) and (4)—none.

Changes: Completely rewritten.

Purposes of Changes and New Matter:

1. Subsection (1): "Contract for sale" is used as a general concept throughout this Article, but the rights of the parties do not vary according to whether the transaction is a present sale or a contract to sell unless the Article expressly so provides.

2. Subsection (2): It is in general intended to continue the policy of requiring exact performance by the seller of his obligations as a condition to his right to require acceptance. However, the seller is in part safeguarded against surprise as a result of sudden technicality on the buyer's part by the provisions of Section 2—508 on seller's cure of improper tender or delivery. Moreover usage of trade frequently permits commercial leeways in performance and the language of the agreement itself must be read in the light of such custom or usage and also, prior course of dealing, and in a long term contract, the course of performance.

3. Subsections (3) and (4): These subsections are intended to make clear the distinction carried forward throughout this Article between termination and cancellation.

Cross References:

Point 2: Sections 1—203, 1—205, 2—208 and 2—508.

Definitional Cross References:

"Agreement". Section 1—201.
"Buyer". Section 2—103.
"Contract". Section 1—201.
"Goods". Section 2—105.
"Party". Section 1—201.
"Remedy". Section 1—201.
"Rights". Section 1—201.
"Seller". Section 2—103.

§ 2—107. Goods to Be Severed From Realty: Recording

(1) A contract for the sale of minerals or the like (including oil and gas) or a structure or its materials to be removed from realty is a contract for the sale of goods within this Article if

they are to be severed by the seller but until severance a purported present sale thereof which is not effective as a transfer of an interest in land is effective only as a contract to sell.

(2) A contract for the sale apart from the land of growing crops or other things attached to realty and capable of severance without material harm thereto but not described in subsection (1) or of timber to be cut is a contract for the sale of goods within this Article whether the subject matter is to be severed by the buyer or by the seller even though it forms part of the realty at the time of contracting, and the parties can by identification effect a present sale before severance.

(3) The provisions of this section are subject to any third party rights provided by the law relating to realty records, and the contract for sale may be executed and recorded as a document transferring an interest in land and shall then constitute notice to third parties of the buyer's rights under the contract for sale. As amended 1972.

See Appendix I for changes made in former text and the reasons for change.

Official Comment

Prior Uniform Statutory Provision: See Section 76, Uniform Sales Act on prior policy; Section 7, Uniform Conditional Sales Act.

Purposes:

1. Subsection (1). Notice that this subsection applies only if the minerals or structures "are to be severed by the seller". If the buyer is to sever, such transactions are considered contracts affecting land and all problems of the Statute of Frauds and of the recording of land rights apply to them. Therefore, the Statute of Frauds section of this Article does not apply to such contracts though they must conform to the Statute of Frauds affecting the transfer of interests in land.

2. Subsection (2). "Things attached" to the realty which can be severed without material harm are goods within this Article regardless of who is to effect the severance. The word "fixtures" has been avoided because of the diverse definitions of this term, the test of "severance without material harm" being substituted.

The provision in subsection (3) for recording such contracts is within the purview of this Article since it is a means of preserving the buyer's rights under the contract of sale.

3. The security phases of things attached to or to become attached to realty are dealt with in the Article on Secured Transactions (Article 9) and it is to be noted that the definition of goods in that Article differs from the definition of goods in this Article.

However, both Articles treat as goods growing crops and also timber to be cut under a contract of severance.

Cross References:

Point 1: Section 2—201.

Point 2: Section 2—105.

Point 3: Articles 9 and 9—105.

Definitional Cross References:

"Buyer". Section 2—103.

"Contract". Section 1—201.

"Contract for sale". Section 2—106.

"Goods". Section 2—105.

"Party". Section 1—201.

"Present sale". Section 2—106.

"Rights". Section 1—201.

"Seller". Section 2—103.

PART 2

FORM, FORMATION AND READJUSTMENT OF CONTRACT

§ 2—201. Formal Requirements; Statute of Frauds

(1) Except as otherwise provided in this section a contract for the sale of goods for the price of $500 or more is not enforceable by way of action or defense unless there is some writing sufficient to indicate that a contract for sale has been made between the parties and signed by the party against whom enforcement is sought or by his authorized agent or broker. A writing is not insufficient because it omits or incorrectly states a term agreed upon but the contract is not enforceable under this paragraph beyond the quantity of goods shown in such writing.

(2) Between merchants if within a reasonable time a writing in confirmation of the contract and sufficient against the sender is received and the party receiving it has reason to know its contents, it satisfies the requirements of subsection (1) against such party unless written notice of objection to its contents is given within 10 days after it is received.

(3) A contract which does not satisfy the requirements of subsection (1) but which is valid in other respects is enforceable

(a) if the goods are to be specially manufactured for the buyer and are not suitable for sale to others in the ordinary course of the seller's business and the seller, before notice of repudiation is received and under circumstances which reasonably indicate that the goods are for the buyer, has made either a substantial beginning of their manufacture or commitments for their procurement; or

(b) if the party against whom enforcement is sought admits in his pleading, testimony or otherwise in court that a contract for sale was made, but the contract is not enforceable under this provision beyond the quantity of goods admitted; or

(c) with respect to goods for which payment has been made and accepted or which have been received and accepted (Sec. 2—606).

Official Comment

Prior Uniform Statutory Provision: Section 4, Uniform Sales Act (which was based on Section 17 of the Statute of 29 Charles II).

Changes: Completely rephrased; restricted to sale of goods. See also Sections 1—206, 8—319 and 9—203.

Purposes of Changes: The changed phraseology of this section is intended to make it clear that:

1. The required writing need not contain all the material terms of the contract and such material terms as are stated need not be precisely stated. All that is required is that the writing afford a basis for believing that the offered oral evidence rests on a real transaction. It may be written in lead pencil on a scratch pad. It need not indicate which party is the buyer and which the seller. The only term which must appear is the quantity term which need not be accurately stated but recovery is limited to the amount stated. The price, time and place of payment or delivery, the general quality of the goods, or any particular warranties may all be omitted.

Special emphasis must be placed on the permissibility of omitting the price term in view of the insistence of some courts on the express inclusion of this term even where the parties have contracted on the basis of a published price list. In many valid contracts for sale the parties do not mention the price in express terms, the buyer being bound to pay and the seller to accept a reasonable price which the trier of the fact may well be trusted to determine. Again, frequently the price is not mentioned since the parties have based their agreement on a price list or catalogue known to both of them and this list serves as an efficient safeguard against perjury. Finally, "market" prices and valuations that are current in the vicinity constitute a similar check. Thus if the price is not stated in the memorandum it can normally be supplied without danger of fraud. Of course if the "price" consists of goods rather than money the quantity of goods must be stated.

Only three definite and invariable requirements as to the memorandum are made by this subsection. First, it must evidence a contract for the sale of goods; second, it must be "signed", a word which includes any authentication which identifies the party to be charged; and third, it must specify a quantity.

2. "Partial performance" as a substitute for the required memorandum can validate the contract only for the goods which have been accepted or for which pay-

ment has been made and accepted.

Receipt and acceptance either of goods or of the price constitutes an unambiguous overt admission by both parties that a contract actually exists. If the court can make a just apportionment, therefore, the agreed price of any goods actually delivered can be recovered without a writing or, if the price has been paid, the seller can be forced to deliver an apportionable part of the goods. The overt actions of the parties make admissible evidence of the other terms of the contract necessary to a just apportionment. This is true even though the actions of the parties are not in themselves inconsistent with a different transaction such as a consignment for resale or a mere loan of money.

Part performance by the buyer requires the delivery of something by him that is accepted by the seller as such performance. Thus, part payment may be made by money or check, accepted by the seller. If the agreed price consists of goods or services, then they must also have been delivered and accepted.

3. Between merchants, failure to answer a written confirmation of a contract within ten days of receipt is tantamount to a writing under subsection (2) and is sufficient against both parties under subsection (1). The only effect, however, is to take away from the party who fails to answer the defense of the Statute of Frauds; the burden of persuading the trier of fact that a contract was in fact made orally prior to the written confirmation is unaffected. Compare the effect of a failure to reply under Section 2—207.

4. Failure to satisfy the requirements of this section does not render the contract void for all purposes, but merely prevents it from being judicially enforced in favor of a party to the contract. For example, a buyer who takes possession of goods as provided in an oral contract which the seller has not meanwhile repudiated, is not a trespasser. Nor would the Statute of Frauds provisions of this section be a defense to a third person who wrongfully induces a party to refuse to perform an oral contract, even though the injured party cannot maintain an action for damages against the party so refusing to perform.

5. The requirement of "signing" is discussed in the comment to Section 1—201.

6. It is not necessary that the writing be delivered to anybody. It need not be signed or authenticated by both parties but it is, of course, not sufficient against one who has not signed it. Prior to a dispute no one can determine which party's signing of the memorandum may be necessary but from the time of contracting each party should be aware that to him it is signing by the other which is important.

7. If the making of a contract is admitted in court, either in a written pleading, by stipulation or by oral statement before the court, no additional writing is necessary for protection against fraud. Under this section it is no longer possible to admit the contract in court and still treat the Statute as a defense. However, the contract is not thus conclu-

sively established. The admission so made by a party is itself evidential against him of the truth of the facts so admitted and of nothing more; as against the other party, it is not evidential at all.

Cross References:

See Sections 1—201, 2—202, 2—207, 2—209 and 2—304.

Definitional Cross References:

"Action". Section 1—201.

"Between merchants". Section 2—104.

"Buyer". Section 2—103.

"Contract". Section 1—201.

"Contract for sale". Section 2—106.

"Goods". Section 2—105.

"Notice". Section 1—201.

"Party". Section 1—201.

"Reasonable time". Section 1—204.

"Sale". Section 2—106.

"Seller". Section 2—103.

§ 2—202. Final Written Expression: Parol or Extrinsic Evidence

Terms with respect to which the confirmatory memoranda of the parties agree or which are otherwise set forth in a writing intended by the parties as a final expression of their agreement with respect to such terms as are included therein may not be contradicted by evidence of any prior agreement or of a contemporaneous oral agreement but may be explained or supplemented

(a) by course of dealing or usage of trade (Section 1—205) or by course of performance (Section 2—208); and

(b) by evidence of consistent additional terms unless the court finds the writing to have been intended also as a complete and exclusive statement of the terms of the agreement.

Official Comment

Prior Uniform Statutory Provision: None.

Purposes:

1. This section definitely rejects:

(a) Any assumption that because a writing has been worked out which is final on some matters, it is to be taken as including all the matters agreed upon;

(b) The premise that the language used has the meaning attributable to such language by rules of construction existing in the law rather than the meaning which arises out of the commercial context in which it was used; and

(c) The requirement that a condition precedent to the admissibility of the type of evidence specified in paragraph (a) is an original determination by the court that the language used is ambiguous.

2. Paragraph (a) makes admissible evidence of course of dealing, usage of trade and course of performance to explain

or supplement the terms of any writing stating the agreement of the parties in order that the true understanding of the parties as to the agreement may be reached. Such writings are to be read on the assumption that the course of prior dealings between the parties and the usages of trade were taken for granted when the document was phrased. Unless carefully negated they have become an element of the meaning of the words used. Similarly, the course of actual performance by the parties is considered the best indication of what they intended the writing to mean.

3. Under paragraph (b) consistent additional terms, not reduced to writing, may be proved unless the court finds that the writing was intended by both parties as a complete and exclusive statement of all the terms. If the additional terms are such that, if agreed upon, they would certainly have been included in the document in the view of the court, then evidence of their alleged making must be kept from the trier of fact.

Cross References:

Point 3: Sections 1—205, 2—207, 2—302 and 2—316.

Definitional Cross References:

"Agreed" and "agreement". Section 1—201.

"Course of dealing". Section 1—205.

"Parties". Section 1—201.

"Term". Section 1—201.

"Usage of trade". Section 1—205.

"Written" and "writing". Section 1—201.

§ 2—203. Seals Inoperative

The affixing of a seal to a writing evidencing a contract for sale or an offer to buy or sell goods does not constitute the writing a sealed instrument and the law with respect to sealed instruments does not apply to such a contract or offer.

Official Comment

Prior Uniform Statutory Provision: Section 3, Uniform Sales Act.

Changes: Portion pertaining to "seals" rewritten.

Purposes of Changes:

1. This section makes it clear that every effect of the seal which relates to "sealed instruments" as such is wiped out insofar as contracts for sale are concerned. However, the substantial effects of a seal, except extension of the period of limitations, may be had by appropriate drafting as in the case of firm offers (see Section 2—205).

2. This section leaves untouched any aspects of a seal which relate merely to signatures or to authentication of execution and the like. Thus, a statute providing that a purported signature gives prima facie evidence of its own authenticity or that a signature gives prima facie evidence of consideration is still applicable to sales transactions even though a seal may be held to be a signature within the meaning of such a statute. Similarly, the author-

ized affixing of a corporate seal bearing the corporate name to a contractual writing purporting to be made by the corporation may have effect as a signature without any reference to the law of sealed instruments.

Cross Reference:

Point 1: Section 2—205.

Definitional Cross References:

"Contract for sale". Section 2—106.

"Goods". Section 2—105.

"Writing". Section 1—201.

§ 2—204. Formation in General

(1) A contract for sale of goods may be made in any manner sufficient to show agreement, including conduct by both parties which recognizes the existence of such a contract.

(2) An agreement sufficient to constitute a contract for sale may be found even though the moment of its making is undetermined.

(3) Even though one or more terms are left open a contract for sale does not fail for indefiniteness if the parties have intended to make a contract and there is a reasonably certain basis for giving an appropriate remedy.

Official Comment

Prior Uniform Statutory Provision: Sections 1 and 3, Uniform Sales Act.

Changes: Completely rewritten by this and other sections of this Article.

Purposes of Changes:

Subsection (1) continues without change the basic policy of recognizing any manner of expression of agreement, oral, written or otherwise. The legal effect of such an agreement is, of course, qualified by other provisions of this Article.

Under subsection (1) appropriate conduct by the parties may be sufficient to establish an agreement. Subsection (2) is directed primarily to the situation where the interchanged correspondence does not disclose the exact point at which the deal was closed, but the actions of the parties indicate that a binding obligation has been undertaken.

Subsection (3) states the principle as to "open terms" underlying later sections of the Article. If the parties intend to enter into a binding agreement, this subsection recognizes that agreement as valid in law, despite missing terms, if there is any reasonably certain basis for granting a remedy. The test is not certainty as to what the parties were to do nor as to the exact amount of damages due the plaintiff. Nor is the fact that one or more terms are left to be agreed upon enough of itself to defeat an otherwise adequate agreement. Rather, commercial standards on the point of "indefiniteness" are intended to be applied, this Act making provision elsewhere for missing terms needed for performance, open price, remedies and the like.

The more terms the parties leave open, the less likely it is that they have intended to conclude a binding agreement, but their actions may be frequently conclusive on the matter despite the omissions.

Cross References:

Subsection (1): Sections 1—103, 2—201 and 2—302.

Subsection (2): Sections 2—205 through 2—209.

Subsection (3): See Part 3.

Definitional Cross References:

"Agreement". Section 1—201.
"Contract". Section 1—201.
"Contract for sale". Section 2—106.
"Goods". Section 2—105.
"Party". Section 1—201.
"Remedy". Section 1—201.
"Term". Section 1—201.

§ 2—205. Firm Offers

An offer by a merchant to buy or sell goods in a signed writing which by its terms gives assurance that it will be held open is not revocable, for lack of consideration, during the time stated or if no time is stated for a reasonable time, but in no event may such period of irrevocability exceed three months; but any such term of assurance on a form supplied by the offeree must be separately signed by the offeror.

Official Comment

Prior Uniform Statutory Provision: Sections 1 and 3, Uniform Sales Act.

Changes: Completely rewritten by this and other sections of this Article.

Purposes of Changes:

1. This section is intended to modify the former rule which required that "firm offers" be sustained by consideration in order to bind, and to require instead that they must merely be characterized as such and expressed in signed writings.

2. The primary purpose of this section is to give effect to the deliberate intention of a merchant to make a current firm offer binding. The deliberation is shown in the case of an individualized document by the merchant's signature to the offer, and in the case of an offer included on a form supplied by the other party to the transaction by the separate signing of the particular clause which contains the offer. "Signed" here also includes authentication but the reasonableness of the authentication herein allowed must be determined in the light of the purpose of the section. The circumstances surrounding the signing may justify something less than a formal signature or initialing but typically the kind of authentication involved here would consist of a minimum of initialing of the clause involved. A handwritten memorandum on the writer's letterhead purporting in its terms to "confirm" a firm offer already made would be enough to satisfy this section, although not sub-

scribed, since under the circumstances it could not be considered a memorandum of mere negotiation and it would adequately show its own authenticity. Similarly, an authorized telegram will suffice, and this is true even though the original draft contained only a typewritten signature. However, despite settled courses of dealing or usages of the trade whereby firm offers are made by oral communication and relied upon without more evidence, such offers remain revocable under this Article since authentication by a writing is the essence of this section.

3. This section is intended to apply to current "firm" offers and not to long term options, and an outside time limit of three months during which such offers remain irrevocable has been set. The three month period during which firm offers remain irrevocable under this section need not be stated by days or by date. If the offer states that it is "guaranteed" or "firm" until the happening of a contingency which will occur within the three month period, it will remain irrevocable until that event. A promise made for a longer period will operate under this section to bind the offeror only for the first three months of the period but may of course be renewed. If supported by consideration it may continue for as long as the parties specify. This section deals only with the offer which is not supported by consideration.

4. Protection is afforded against the inadvertent signing of a firm offer when contained in a form prepared by the offeree by requiring that such a clause be separately authenticated. If the offer clause is called to the offeror's attention and he separately authenticates it, he will be bound; Section 2—302 may operate, however, to prevent an unconscionable result which otherwise would flow from other terms appearing in the form.

5. Safeguards are provided to offer relief in the case of material mistake by virtue of the requirement of good faith and the general law of mistake.

Cross References:

Point 1: Section 1—102.
Point 2: Section 1—102.
Point 3: Section 2—201.
Point 5: Section 2—302.

Definitional Cross References:

"Goods". Section 2—105.
"Merchant". Section 2—104.
"Signed". Section 1—201.
"Writing". Section 1—201.

§ 2—206. Offer and Acceptance in Formation of Contract

(1) Unless otherwise unambiguously indicated by the language or circumstances

(a) an offer to make a contract shall be construed as inviting acceptance in any manner and by any medium reasonable in the circumstances;

(b) an order or other offer to buy goods for prompt or current shipment shall be construed as inviting acceptance either by a prompt promise to ship or by the prompt or current shipment of conforming or non-conforming goods, but such a shipment of non-conforming goods does not constitute an acceptance if the seller seasonably notifies the buyer that the shipment is offered only as an accommodation to the buyer.

(2) Where the beginning of a requested performance is a reasonable mode of acceptance an offeror who is not notified of acceptance within a reasonable time may treat the offer as having lapsed before acceptance.

Official Comment

Prior Uniform Statutory Provision: Sections 1 and 3, Uniform Sales Act.

Changes: Completely rewritten in this and other sections of this Article.

Purposes of Changes: To make it clear that:

1. Any reasonable manner of acceptance is intended to be regarded as available unless the offeror has made quite clear that it will not be acceptable. Former technical rules as to acceptance, such as requiring that telegraphic offers be accepted by telegraphed acceptance, etc., are rejected and a criterion that the acceptance be "in any manner and by any medium reasonable under the circumstances," is substituted. This section is intended to remain flexible and its applicability to be enlarged as new media of communication develop or as the more time-saving present day media come into general use.

2. Either shipment or a prompt promise to ship is made a proper means of acceptance of an offer looking to current shipment. In accordance with ordinary commercial understanding the section interprets an order looking to current shipment as allowing acceptance either by actual shipment or by a prompt promise to ship and rejects the artificial theory that only a single mode of acceptance is normally envisaged by an offer. This is true even though the language of the offer happens to be "ship at once" or the like. "Shipment" is here used in the same sense as in Section 2—504; it does not include the beginning of delivery by the seller's own truck or by messenger. But loading on the seller's own truck might be a beginning of performance under subsection (2).

3. The beginning of performance by an offeree can be effective as acceptance so as to bind the offeror only if followed within a reasonable time by notice to the offeror. Such a beginning of performance must unambiguously express the offeree's intention to engage himself. For the protection of both parties it is essential that notice follow in due course to constitute acceptance. Nothing in this section however bars the possibility that under the common law performance begun may have an intermediate effect of temporarily barring revocation of the offer, or at the offeror's option, final effect in constituting acceptance.

4. Subsection (1) (b) deals with the situation where a shipment made following an order is shown by a notification of shipment to be referable to that order but has a defect. Such a non-conforming shipment is normally to be understood as intended to close the bargain, even though it proves to have been at the same time a breach. However, the seller by stating that the shipment is non-conforming and is offered only as an accommodation to the buyer keeps the shipment or notification from operating as an acceptance.

Definitional Cross References:

"Buyer". Section 2—103.

"Conforming". Section 2—106.

"Contract". Section 1—201.

"Goods". Section 2—105.

"Notifies". Section 1—201.

"Reasonable time". Section 1—204.

§ 2—207. Additional Terms in Acceptance or Confirmation

(1) A definite and seasonable expression of acceptance or a written confirmation which is sent within a reasonable time operates as an acceptance even though it states terms additional to or different from those offered or agreed upon, unless acceptance is expressly made conditional on assent to the additional or different terms.

(2) The additional terms are to be construed as proposals for addition to the contract. Between merchants such terms become part of the contract unless:

(a) the offer expressly limits acceptance to the terms of the offer;

(b) they materially alter it; or

(c) notification of objection to them has already been given or is given within a reasonable time after notice of them is received.

(3) Conduct by both parties which recognizes the existence of a contract is sufficient to establish a contract for sale although the writings of the parties do not otherwise establish a contract. In such case the terms of the particular contract consist of those terms on which the writings of the parties agree, together with any supplementary terms incorporated under any other provisions of this Act.

Official Comment

Prior Uniform Statutory Provision: Sections 1 and 3, Uniform Sales Act.

Changes: Completely rewritten by this and other sections of this Article.

Purposes of Changes:

1. This section is intended to deal with two typical situations. The one is the written confirmation, where an agreement has been reached either orally or by informal correspondence between the parties and is followed by one or both of the parties sending formal memoranda embodying the terms so far as agreed upon and adding terms not discussed. The other situation is offer and acceptance, in which a wire or letter expressed and intended as an acceptance or the closing of an agreement adds further minor suggestions or proposals such as "ship by Tuesday," "rush," "ship draft against bill of lading inspection allowed," or the like. A frequent example of the second situation is the exchange of printed purchase order and acceptance (sometimes called "acknowledgment") forms. Because the forms are oriented to the thinking of the respective drafting parties, the terms contained in them often do not correspond. Often the seller's form contains terms different from or additional to those set forth in the buyer's form. Nevertheless, the parties proceed with the transaction. [Comment 1 was amended in 1966.]

2. Under this Article a proposed deal which in commercial understanding has in fact been closed is recognized as a contract. Therefore, any additional matter contained in the confirmation or in the acceptance falls within subsection (2) and must be regarded as a proposal for an added term unless the acceptance is made conditional on the acceptance of the additional or different terms. [Comment 2 was amended in 1966.]

3. Whether or not additional or different terms will become part of the agreement depends upon the provisions of subsection (2). If they are such as materially to alter the original bargain, they will not be included unless expressly agreed to by the other party. If, however, they are terms which would not so change the bargain they will be incorporated unless notice of objection to them has already been given or is given within a reasonable time.

4. Examples of typical clauses which would normally "materially alter" the contract and so result in surprise or hardship if incorporated without express awareness by the other party are: a clause negating such standard warranties as that of merchantability or fitness for a particular purpose in circumstances in which either warranty normally attaches; a clause requiring a guaranty of 90% or 100% deliveries in a case such as a contract by cannery, where the usage of the trade allows greater quantity leeways; a clause reserving to the seller the power to cancel upon the buyer's failure to meet any invoice when due; a clause requiring that complaints be made in a time materially shorter than customary or reasonable.

5. Examples of clauses which involve no element of unreasonable surprise and which therefore are to be incorporated in the contract unless notice of objection is seasonably given are: a clause setting forth and perhaps enlarging slightly upon the seller's exemption due to supervening causes beyond his control, similar to those covered

by the provision of this Article on merchant's excuse by failure of presupposed conditions or a clause fixing in advance any reasonable formula of proration under such circumstances; a clause fixing a reasonable time for complaints within customary limits, or in the case of a purchase for sub-sale, providing for inspection by the sub-purchaser; a clause providing for interest on overdue invoices or fixing the seller's standard credit terms where they are within the range of trade practice and do not limit any credit bargained for; a clause limiting the right of rejection for defects which fall within the customary trade tolerances for acceptance "with adjustment" or otherwise limiting remedy in a reasonable manner (see Sections 2—718 and 2—719).

6. If no answer is received within a reasonable time after additional terms are proposed, it is both fair and commercially sound to assume that their inclusion has been assented to. Where clauses on confirming forms sent by both parties conflict each party must be assumed to object to a clause of the other conflicting with one on the confirmation sent by himself. As a result the requirement that there be notice of objection which is found in subsection (2) is satisfied and the conflicting terms do not become a part of the contract. The contract then consists of the terms originally expressly agreed to, terms on which the confirmations agree, and terms supplied by this Act, including subsection (2). The written confirmation is also subject to Section 2—201. Under that section a failure to respond permits enforcement of a prior oral agreement; under this section a failure to respond permits additional terms to become part of the agreement. [Comment 6 was amended in 1966.]

7. In many cases, as where goods are shipped, accepted and paid for before any dispute arises, there is no question whether a contract has been made. In such cases, where the writings of the parties do not establish a contract, it is not necessary to determine which act or document constituted the offer and which the acceptance. See Section 2—204. The only question is what terms are included in the contract, and subsection (3) furnishes the governing rule. [Comment 7 was added in 1966.]

Cross References:

See generally Section 2—302.

Point 5: Sections 2—513, 2—602, 2—607, 2—609, 2—612, 2—614, 2—615, 2—616, 2—718 and 2—719.

Point 6: Sections 1—102 and 2—104.

Definitional Cross References:

"Between merchants". Section 2—104.

"Contract". Section 1—201.

"Notification". Section 1—201.

"Reasonable time". Section 1—204.

"Seasonably". Section 1—204.

"Send". Section 1—201.

"Term". Section 1—201.

"Written". Section 1—201.

§ 2—208. Course of Performance or Practical Construction

(1) Where the contract for sale involves repeated occasions for performance by either party with knowledge of the nature of the performance and opportunity for objection to it by the other, any course of performance accepted or acquiesced in without objection shall be relevant to determine the meaning of the agreement.

(2) The express terms of the agreement and any such course of performance, as well as any course of dealing and usage of trade, shall be construed whenever reasonable as consistent with each other; but when such construction is unreasonable, express terms shall control course of performance and course of performance shall control both course of dealing and usage of trade (Section 1—205).

(3) Subject to the provisions of the next section on modification and waiver, such course of performance shall be relevant to show a waiver or modification of any term inconsistent with such course of performance

Official Comment

Prior Uniform Statutory Provision: No such general provision but concept of this section recognized by terms such as "course of dealing", "the circumstances of the case," "the conduct of the parties," etc., in Uniform Sales Act.

Purposes:

1. The parties themselves know best what they have meant by their words of agreement and their action under that agreement is the best indication of what that meaning was. This section thus rounds out the set of factors which determines the meaning of the "agreement" and therefore also of the "unless otherwise agreed" qualification to various provisions of this Article.

2. Under this section a course of performance is always relevant to determine the meaning of the agreement. Express mention of course of performance elsewhere in this Article carries no contrary implication when there is a failure to refer to it in other sections.

3. Where it is difficult to determine whether a particular act merely sheds light on the meaning of the agreement or represents a waiver of a term of the agreement, the preference is in favor of "waiver" whenever such construction, plus the application of the provisions on the reinstatement of rights waived (see Section 2—209), is needed to preserve the flexible character of commercial contracts and to prevent surprise or other hardship.

4. A single occasion of conduct does not fall within the language of this section but other sections such as the ones on silence after acceptance and

failure to specify particular defects can affect the parties' rights on a single occasion (see Sections 2—605 and 2—607).

Cross References:

Point 1: Section 1—201.

Point 2: Section 2—202.

Point 3: Sections 2—209, 2—601 and 2—607.

Point 4: Sections 2—605 and 2—607.

§ 2—209. Modification, Rescission and Waiver

(1) An agreement modifying a contract within this Article needs no consideration to be binding.

(2) A signed agreement which excludes modification or rescission except by a signed writing cannot be otherwise modified or rescinded, but except as between merchants such a requirement on a form supplied by the merchant must be separately signed by the other party.

(3) The requirements of the statute of frauds section of this Article (Section 2—201) must be satisfied if the contract as modified is within its provisions.

(4) Although an attempt at modification or rescission does not satisfy the requirements of subsection (2) or (3) it can operate as a waiver.

(5) A party who has made a waiver affecting an executory portion of the contract may retract the waiver by reasonable notification received by the other party that strict performance will be required of any term waived, unless the retraction would be unjust in view of a material change of position in reliance on the waiver.

Official Comment

Prior Uniform Statutory Provision: Subsection (1)—Compare Section 1, Uniform Written Obligations Act; Subsections (2) to (5)—none.

Purposes of Changes and New Matter:

1. This section seeks to protect and make effective all necessary and desirable modifications of sales contracts without regard to the technicalities which at present hamper such adjustments.

2. Subsection (1) provides that an agreement modifying a sales contract needs no consideration to be binding.

However, modifications made thereunder must meet the test of good faith imposed by this Act. The effective use of bad faith to escape performance on the original contract terms is barred, and the extortion of a "modification" without legitimate commercial reason is ineffective as a violation of the duty of good faith. Nor can a mere technical consideration support a modification made in bad faith.

The test of "good faith" between merchants or as against

merchants includes "observance of reasonable commercial standards of fair dealing in the trade" (Section 2—103), and may in some situations require an objectively demonstrable reason for seeking a modification. But such matters as a market shift which makes performance come to involve a loss may provide such a reason even though there is no such unforeseen difficulty as would make out a legal excuse from performance under Sections 2—615 and 2—616.

3. Subsections (2) and (3) are intended to protect against false allegations of oral modifications. "Modification or rescission" includes abandonment or other change by mutual consent, contrary to the decision in Green v. Doniger, 300 N.Y. 238, 90 N.E. 2d 56 (1949); it does not include unilateral "termination" or "cancellation" as defined in Section 2—106.

The Statute of Frauds provisions of this Article are expressly applied to modifications by subsection (3). Under those provisions the "delivery and acceptance" test is limited to the goods which have been accepted, that is, to the past. "Modification" for the future cannot therefore be conjured up by oral testimony if the price involved is $500.00 or more since such modification must be shown at least by an authenticated memo. And since a memo is limited in its effect to the quantity of goods set forth in it there is safeguard against oral evidence.

Subsection (2) permits the parties in effect to make their own Statute of Frauds as regards any future modification of the contract by giving effect to a clause in a signed agreement which expressly requires any modification to be by signed writing. But note that if a consumer is to be held to such a clause on a form supplied by a merchant it must be separately signed.

4. Subsection (4) is intended, despite the provisions of subsections (2) and (3), to prevent contractual provisions excluding modification except by a signed writing from limiting in other respects the legal effect of the parties' actual later conduct. The effect of such conduct as a waiver is further regulated in subsection (5).

Cross References:

Point 1: Section 1—203.

Point 2: Sections 1—201, 1—203, 2—615 and 2—616.

Point 3: Sections 2—106, 2—201 and 2—202.

Point 4: Sections 2—202 and 2—208.

Definitional Cross References:

"Agreement". Section 1—201.

"Between merchants". Section 2—104.

"Contract". Section 1—201.

"Notification". Section 1—201.

"Signed". Section 1—201.

"Term". Section 1—201.

"Writing". Section 1—201.

§ 2—210. Delegation of Performance; Assignment of Rights

(1) A party may perform his duty through a delegate unless otherwise agreed or unless the other party has a substantial

interest in having his original promisor perform or control the acts required by the contract. No delegation of performance relieves the party delegating of any duty to perform or any liability for breach.

(2) Unless otherwise agreed all rights of either seller or buyer can be assigned except where the assignment would materially change the duty of the other party, or increase materially the burden or risk imposed on him by his contract, or impair materially his chance of obtaining return performance. A right to damages for breach of the whole contract or a right arising out of the assignor's due performance of his entire obligation can be assigned despite agreement otherwise.

(3) Unless the circumstances indicate the contrary a prohibition of assignment of "the contract" is to be construed as barring only the delegation to the assignee of the assignor's performance

(4) An assignment of "the contract" or of "all my rights under the contract" or an assignment in similar general terms is an assignment of rights and unless the language or the circumstances (as in an assignment for security) indicate the contrary, it is a delegation of performance of the duties of the assignor and its acceptance by the assignee constitutes a promise by him to perform those duties. This promise is enforceable by either the assignor or the other party to the original contract.

(5) The other party may treat any assignment which delegates performance as creating reasonable grounds for insecurity and may without prejudice to his rights against the assignor demand assurances from the assignee (Section 2—609).

Official Comment

Prior Uniform Statutory Provision: None.

Purposes:

1. Generally, this section recognizes both delegation of performance and assignability as normal and permissible incidents of a contract for the sale of goods.

2. Delegation of performance, either in conjunction with an assignment or otherwise, is provided for by subsection (1) where no substantial reason can be shown as to why the delegated performance will not be as satisfactory as personal performance.

3. Under subsection (2) rights which are no longer executory such as a right to damages for breach or a right to payment of an "account" as defined in the Article on Secured Transactions (Article 9) may be assigned although the agreement prohibits assignment. In

such cases no question of delegation of any performance is involved. The assignment of a "contract right" as defined in the Article on Secured Transactions (Article 9) is not covered by this subsection.

4. The nature of the contract or the circumstances of the case, however, may bar assignment of the contract even where delegation of performance is not involved. This Article and this section are intended to clarify this problem, particularly in cases dealing with output requirement and exclusive dealing contracts. In the first place the section on requirements and exclusive dealing removes from the construction of the original contract most of the "personal discretion" element by substituting the reasonably objective standard of good faith operation of the plant or business to be supplied. Secondly, the section on insecurity and assurances, which is specifically referred to in subsection (5) of this section, frees the other party from the doubts and uncertainty which may afflict him under an assignment of the character in question by permitting him to demand adequate assurance of due performance without which he may suspend his own performance. Subsection (5) is not in any way intended to limit the effect of the section on insecurity and assurances and the word "performance" includes the giving of orders under a requirements contract. Of course, in any case where a material personal discretion is sought to be transferred, effective assignment is barred by subsection (2).

5. Subsection (4) lays down a general rule of construction distinguishing between a normal commercial assignment, which substitutes the assignee for the assignor both as to rights and duties, and a financing assignment in which only the assignor's rights are transferred.

This Article takes no position on the possibility of extending some recognition or power to the original parties to work out normal commercial readjustments of the contract in the case of financing assignments even after the original obligor has been notified of the assignment. This question is dealt with in the Article on Secured Transactions (Article 9).

6. Subsection (5) recognizes that the non-assigning original party has a stake in the reliability of the person with whom he has closed the original contract, and is, therefore, entitled to due assurance that any delegated performance will be properly forthcoming.

7. This section is not intended as a complete statement of the law of delegation and assignment but is limited to clarifying a few points doubtful under the case law. Particularly, neither this section nor this Article touches directly on such questions as the need or effect of notice of the assignment, the rights of successive assignees, or any question of the form of an assignment, either as between the parties or as against any third parties. Some of these questions are dealt with in Article 9.

Cross References:

Point 3: Articles 5 and 9.

Point 4: Sections 2—306 and 2—609.

Point 5: Article 9, Sections 9—317 and 9—318.
Point 7: Article 9.

Definitional Cross References:

"Agreement". Section 1—201.
"Buyer". Section 2—103.
"Contract". Section 1—201.
"Party". Section 1—201.
"Rights". Section 1—201.
"Seller". Section 2—103.
"Term". Section 1—201.

PART 3

GENERAL OBLIGATION AND CONSTRUCTION OF CONTRACT

§ 2—301. General Obligations of Parties

The obligation of the seller is to transfer and deliver and that of the buyer is to accept and pay in accordance with the contract.

Official Comment

Prior Uniform Statutory Provision: Sections 11 and 41, Uniform Sales Act.

Changes: Rewritten.

Purposes of Changes:

This section uses the term "obligation" in contrast to the term "duty" in order to provide for the "condition" aspects of delivery and payment insofar as they are not modified by other sections of this Article such as those on cure of tender. It thus replaces not only the general provisions of the Uniform Sales Act on the parties' duties, but also the general provisions of that Act on the effect of conditions. In order to determine what is "in accordance with the contract" under this Article usage of trade, course of dealing and performance, and the general background of circumstances must be given due consideration in conjunction with the lay meaning of the words used to define the scope of the conditions and duties.

Cross References:

Section 1—106. See also Sections 1—205, 2—208, 2—209, 2—508 and 2—612.

Definitional Cross References:

"Buyer". Section 2—103.
"Contract". Section 1—201.
"Party". Section 1—201.
"Seller". Section 2—103.

§ 2—302. Unconscionable Contract or Clause

(1) If the court as a matter of law finds the contract or any clause of the contract to have been unconscionable at the time it was made the court may refuse to enforce the contract, or it may enforce the remainder of the contract without the unconscionable clause, or it may so limit the application of any unconscionable clause as to avoid any unconscionable result.

(2) When it is claimed or appears to the court that the contract or any clause thereof may be unconscionable the parties shall be afforded a reasonable opportunity to present evidence as to its commercial setting, purpose and effect to aid the court in making the determination.

Official Comment

Prior Uniform Statutory Provision: None.

Purposes:

1. This section is intended to make it possible for the courts to police explicitly against the contracts or clauses which they find to be unconscionable. In the past such policing has been accomplished by adverse construction of language, by manipulation of the rules of offer and acceptance or by determinations that the clause is contrary to public policy or to the dominant purpose of the contract. This section is intended to allow the court to pass directly on the unconscionability of the contract or particular clause therein and to make a conclusion of law as to its unconscionability. The basic test is whether, in the light of the general commercial background and the commercial needs of the particular trade or case, the clauses involved are so one-sided as to be unconscionable under the circumstances existing at the time of the making of the contract. Subsection (2) makes it clear that it is proper for the court to hear evidence upon these questions. The principle is one of the prevention of oppression and unfair surprise (Cf. Campbell Soup Co. v. Wentz, 172 F.2d 80, 3d Cir. 1948) and not of disturbance of allocation of risks because of superior bargaining power. The underlying basis of this section is illustrated by the results in cases such as the following:

Kansas City Wholesale Grocery Co. v. Weber Packing Corporation, 93 Utah 414, 73 P.2d 1272 (1937), where a clause limiting time for complaints was held inapplicable to latent defects in a shipment of catsup which could be discovered only by microscopic analysis; Hardy v. General Motors Acceptance Corporation, 38 Ga.App. 463, 144 S.E. 327 (1928), holding that a disclaimer of warranty clause applied only to express warranties, thus letting in a fair implied warranty; Andrews Bros. v. Singer & Co. (1934 CA) 1 K.B. 17, holding that where a car with substantial mileage was delivered instead of a "new" car, a disclaimer of warranties, including those "implied," left unaffected an "express obligation" on the description, even though the Sale of Goods Act called such an implied warranty; New Prague Flouring Mill Co. v. G. A. Spears, 194 Iowa 417, 189 N.W. 815 (1922), holding that a clause permitting the seller, upon the buyer's failure to supply shipping instructions, to cancel, ship, or allow delivery date to be indefinitely postponed 30 days at a time by the inaction, does not indefinitely postpone the date of measuring damages for the buyer's breach, to the seller's advantage; and Kansas Flour Mills Co. v. Dirks, 100 Kan. 376, 164 P. 273 (1917), where under a similar clause in a rising market the court permitted the buyer to measure his damages for non-delivery at the end of only one 30 day postponement; Green v. Arcos, Ltd. (1931 CA) 47 T.L.R. 336, where a blanket clause prohibiting rejection of shipments by the buyer was restricted to apply to shipments where discrepancies represented merely mercantile variations; Meyer v. Packard Cleveland Motor Co., 106 Ohio St. 328, 140 N.E. 118 (1922), in which the court held that a "waiver" of all agreements not specified did not preclude implied warranty of fitness of a rebuilt dump truck for ordinary use as a dump truck; Austin Co. v. J. H. Tillman Co., 104 Or. 541, 209 P. 131 (1922), where a clause limiting the buyer's remedy to return was held to be applicable only if the seller had delivered a machine needed for a construction job which reasonably met the contract description; Bekkevold v. Potts, 173 Minn. 87, 216 N.W. 790, 59 A.L.R. 1164 (1927), refusing to allow warranty of fitness for purpose imposed by law to be negated by clause excluding all warranties "made" by the seller; Robert A. Munroe & Co. v. Meyer (1930) 2 K.B. 312, holding that the warranty of description overrides a clause reading "with all faults and defects" where adulterated meat not up to the contract description was delivered.

2. Under this section the court, in its discretion, may refuse to enforce the contract as a whole if it is permeated by the unconscionability, or it may strike any single clause or group of clauses which are so tainted or which are contrary to the essential purpose of the agreement, or it may simply limit unconscionable clauses so as to avoid unconscionable results.

3. The present section is addressed to the court, and the decision is to be made by it. The commercial evidence referred to in subsection (2) is for the court's consideration, not the jury's. Only the agreement which results from the court's action on these matters is to be submitted to the general triers of the facts.

Definitional Cross Reference:

"Contract". Section 1—201.

§ 2—303. Allocation or Division of Risks

Where this Article allocates a risk or a burden as between the parties "unless otherwise agreed", the agreement may not only shift the allocation but may also divide the risk or burden.

Official Comment

Prior Uniform Statutory Provision: None.

Purposes:

1. This section is intended to make it clear that the parties may modify or allocate "unless otherwise agreed" risks or burdens imposed by this Article as they desire, always subject, of course, to the provisions on unconscionability.

Compare Section 1—102(4).

2. The risk or burden may be divided by the express terms of the agreement or by the attending circumstances, since under the definition of "agreement" in this Act the circumstances surrounding the transaction as well as the express language used by the parties enter into the meaning and substance of the agreement.

Cross References:

Point 1: Sections 1—102, 2—302.

Point 2: Section 1—201.

Definitional Cross References:

"Party". Section 1—201.

"Agreement". Section 1—201.

§ 2—304. Price Payable in Money, Goods, Realty, or Otherwise

(1) The price can be made payable in money or otherwise. If it is payable in whole or in part in goods each party is a seller of the goods which he is to transfer.

(2) Even though all or part of the price is payable in an interest in realty the transfer of the goods and the seller's obligations with reference to them are subject to this Article, but not the transfer of the interest in realty or the transferor's obligations in connection therewith.

Official Comment

Prior Uniform Statutory Provision: Subsections (2) and (3) of Section 9, Uniform Sales Act.

Changes: Rewritten.

Purposes of Changes:

1. This section corrects the phrasing of the Uniform Sales Act so as to avoid misconstruction and produce greater accuracy in commercial result. While it continues the essential intent and purpose of the Uniform Sales Act it rejects any purely verbalistic construction in disregard of the underlying reason of the provisions.

2. Under subsection (1) the provisions of this Article are applicable to transactions where the "price" of goods is payable in something other than money. This does not mean, however, that this whole Article applies automatically and in its entirety simply because an agreed transfer of title to goods is not a gift. The basic purposes and reasons of the Article must always be considered in determining the applicability of any of its provisions.

3. Subsection (2) lays down the general principle that when goods are to be exchanged for realty, the provisions of this Article apply only to those aspects of the transaction which concern the transfer of title to goods but do not affect the transfer of the realty since the detailed regulation of various particular contracts which fall outside the scope of this Article is left to the courts and other legislation. However, the complex-

ities of these situations may be such that each must be analyzed in the light of the underlying reasons in order to determine the applicable principles. Local statutes dealing with realty are not to be lightly disregarded or altered by language of this Article. In contrast, this Article declares definite policies in regard to certain matters legitimately within its scope though concerned with real property situations, and in those instances the provisions of this Article control.

Cross References:

Point 1: Section 1—102.

Point 3: Sections 1—102, 1—103, 1—104 and 2—107.

Definitional Cross References:

"Goods". Section 2—105.

"Money". Section 1—201.

"Party". Section 1—201.

"Seller". Section 2—103.

§ 2—305. Open Price Term

(1) The parties if they so intend can conclude a contract for sale even though the price is not settled. In such a case the price is a reasonable price at the time for delivery if

(a) nothing is said as to price; or

(b) the price is left to be agreed by the parties and they fail to agree; or

(c) the price is to be fixed in terms of some agreed market or other standard as set or recorded by a third person or agency and it is not so set or recorded.

(2) A price to be fixed by the seller or by the buyer means a price for him to fix in good faith.

(3) When a price left to be fixed otherwise than by agreement of the parties fails to be fixed through fault of one party the other may at his option treat the contract as cancelled or himself fix a reasonable price.

(4) Where, however, the parties intend not to be bound unless the price be fixed or agreed and it is not fixed or agreed there is no contract. In such a case the buyer must return any goods already received or if unable so to do must pay their reasonable value at the time of delivery and the seller must return any portion of the price paid on account.

Official Comment

Prior Uniform Statutory Provision: Sections 9 and 10, Uniform Sales Act.

Changes: Completely rewritten.

Purposes of Changes:

1. This section applies when the price term is left open on the making of an agreement which is nevertheless intended by the parties to be a binding agreement. This Article rejects in these instances the formula that "an agreement to agree is unenforceable" if the case falls within subsection (1) of this

section, and rejects also defeating such agreements on the ground of "indefiniteness". Instead this Article recognizes the dominant intention of the parties to have the deal continue to be binding upon both. As to future performance, since this Article recognizes remedies such as cover (Section 2—712), resale (Section 2—706) and specific performance (Section 2—716) which go beyond any mere arithmetic as between contract price and market price, there is usually a "reasonably certain basis for granting an appropriate remedy for breach" so that the contract need not fail for indefiniteness.

2. Under some circumstances the postponement of agreement on price will mean that no deal has really been concluded, and this is made express in the preamble of subsection (1) ("The parties *if they so intend*") and in subsection (4). Whether or not this is so is, in most cases, a question to be determined by the trier of fact.

3. Subsection (2), dealing with the situation where the price is to be fixed by one party rejects the uncommercial idea that an agreement that the seller may fix the price means that he may fix any price he may wish by the express qualification that the price so fixed must be fixed in good faith. Good faith includes observance of reasonable commercial standards of fair dealing in the trade if the party is a merchant. (Section 2—103). But in the normal case a "posted price" or a future seller's or buyer's "given price," "price in effect," "market price," or the like satisfies the good faith requirement.

4. The section recognizes that there may be cases in which a particular person's judgment is not chosen merely as a barometer or index of a fair price but is an essential condition to the parties' intent to make any contract at all. For example, the case where a known and trusted expert is to "value" a particular painting for which there is no market standard differs sharply from the situation where a named expert is to determine the grade of cotton, and the difference would support a finding that in the one the parties did not intend to make a binding agreement if that expert were unavailable whereas in the other they did so intend. Other circumstances would of course affect the validity of such a finding.

5. Under subsection (3), wrongful interference by one party with any agreed machinery for price fixing in the contract may be treated by the other party as a repudiation justifying cancellation, or merely as a failure to take cooperative action thus shifting to the aggrieved party the reasonable leeway in fixing the price.

6. Throughout the entire section, the purpose is to give effect to the agreement which has been made. That effect, however, is always conditioned by the requirement of good faith action which is made an inherent part of all contracts within this Act. (Section 1—203).

Cross References:

Point 1: Sections 2—204(3), 2—706, 2—712 and 2—716.

Point 3: Section 2—103.
Point 5: Sections 2—311 and 2—610.
Point 6: Section 1—203.

Definitional Cross References:

"Agreement". Section 1—201.
"Burden of establishing". Section 1—201.
"Buyer". Section 2—103.
"Cancellation". Section 2—106.
"Contract". Section 1—201.
"Contract for sale". Section 2—106.
"Fault". Section 1—201.
"Goods". Section 2—105.
"Party". Section 1—201.
"Receipt of goods". Section 2—103.
"Seller". Section 2—103.
"Term". Section 1—201.

§ 2—306. Output, Requirements and Exclusive Dealings

(1) A term which measures the quantity by the output of the seller or the requirements of the buyer means such actual output or requirements as may occur in good faith, except that no quantity unreasonably disproportionate to any stated estimate or in the absence of a stated estimate to any normal or otherwise comparable prior output or requirements may be tendered or demanded.

(2) A lawful agreement by either the seller or the buyer for exclusive dealing in the kind of goods concerned imposes unless otherwise agreed an obligation by the seller to use best efforts to supply the goods and by the buyer to use best efforts to promote their sale.

Official Comment

Prior Uniform Statutory Provision: None.

Purposes:

1. Subsection (1) of this section, in regard to output and requirements, applies to this specific problem the general approach of this Act which requires the reading of commercial background and intent into the language of any agreement and demands good faith in the performance of that agreement. It applies to such contracts of nonproducing establishments such as dealers or distributors as well as to manufacturing concerns.

2. Under this Article, a contract for output or requirements is not too indefinite since it is held to mean the actual good faith output or requirements of the particular party. Nor does such a contract lack mutuality of obligation since, under this section, the party who will determine quantity is required to operate his plant or conduct his business in good faith and according to commercial standards of fair dealing in the trade so that his output or requirements will approximate a reasonably foreseeable figure. Reasonable elasticity in the requirements is expressly envisaged by this

section and good faith variations from prior requirements are permitted even when the variation may be such as to result in discontinuance. A shut-down by a requirements buyer for lack of orders might be permissible when a shut-down merely to curtail losses would not. The essential test is whether the party is acting in good faith. Similarly, a sudden expansion of the plant by which requirements are to be measured would not be included within the scope of the contract as made but normal expansion undertaken in good faith would be within the scope of this section. One of the factors in an expansion situation would be whether the market price had risen greatly in a case in which the requirements contract contained a fixed price. Reasonable variation of an extreme sort is exemplified in Southwest Natural Gas Co. v. Oklahoma Portland Cement Co., 102 F.2d 630 (C.C.A. 10, 1939). This Article takes no position as to whether a requirements contract is a provable claim in bankruptcy.

3. If an estimate of output or requirements is included in the agreement, no quantity unreasonably disproportionate to it may be tendered or demanded. Any minimum or maximum set by the agreement shows a clear limit on the intended elasticity. In similar fashion, the agreed estimate is to be regarded as a center around which the parties intend the variation to occur.

4. When an enterprise is sold, the question may arise whether the buyer is bound by an existing output or requirements contract. That question is outside the scope of this Article, and is to be determined on other principles of law. Assuming that the contract continues, the output or requirements in the hands of the new owner continue to be measured by the actual good faith output or requirements under the normal operation of the enterprise prior to sale. The sale itself is not grounds for sudden expansion or decrease.

5. Subsection (2), on exclusive dealing, makes explicit the commercial rule embodied in this Act under which the parties to such contracts are held to have impliedly, even when not expressly, bound themselves to use reasonable diligence as well as good faith in their performance of the contract. Under such contracts the exclusive agent is required, although no express commitment has been made, to use reasonable effort and due diligence in the expansion of the market or the promotion of the product, as the case may be. The principal is expected under such a contract to refrain from supplying any other dealer or agent within the exclusive territory. An exclusive dealing agreement brings into play all of the good faith aspects of the output and requirement problems of subsection (1). It also raises questions of insecurity and right to adequate assurance under this Article.

Cross References:

Point 4: Section 2—210.

Point 5: Sections 1—203 and 2—609.

Definitional Cross References:

"Agreement". Section 1—201.

"Buyer". Section 2—103.
"Contract for sale". Section 2—106.
"Good faith". Section 1—201.
"Goods". Section 2—105.
"Party". Section 1—201.
"Term". Section 1—201.
"Seller". Section 2—103.

§ 2—307. Delivery in Single Lot or Several Lots

Unless otherwise agreed all goods called for by a contract for sale must be tendered in a single delivery and payment is due only on such tender but where the circumstances give either party the right to make or demand delivery in lots the price if it can be apportioned may be demanded for each lot.

Official Comment

Prior Uniform Statutory Provision: Section 45(1), Uniform Sales Act.

Changes: Rewritten and expanded.

Purposes of Changes:

1. This section applies where the parties have not specifically agreed whether delivery and payment are to be by lots and generally continues the essential intent of original Act, Section 45(1) by assuming that the parties intended delivery to be in a single lot.

2. Where the actual agreement or the circumstances do not indicate otherwise, delivery in lots is not permitted under this section and the buyer is properly entitled to reject for a deficiency in the tender, subject to any privilege in the seller to cure the tender.

3. The "but" clause of this section goes to the case in which it is not commercially feasible to deliver or to receive the goods in a single lot as for example, where a contract calls for the shipment of ten carloads of coal and only three cars are available at a given time. Similarly, in a contract involving brick necessary to build a building the buyer's storage space may be limited so that it would be impossible to receive the entire amount of brick at once, or it may be necessary to assemble the goods as in the case of cattle on the range, or to mine them.

In such cases, a partial delivery is not subject to rejection for the defect in quantity alone, if the circumstances do not indicate a repudiation or default by the seller as to the expected balance or do not give the buyer ground for suspending his performance because of insecurity under the provisions of Section 2—609. However, in such cases the undelivered balance of goods under the contract must be forthcoming within a reasonable time and in a reasonable manner according to the policy of Section 2—503 on manner of tender of delivery. This is reinforced by the express provisions of Section 2—608 that if a lot has been accepted on the reasonable assumption that its nonconformity will be cured, the acceptance may be revoked if the cure does not seasonably occur. The section rejects the rule of Kelly Construction Co. v. Hackensack Brick Co., 91 N.J.L. 585, 103 A. 417, 2 A.L.R. 685 (1918) and approves the result in Lynn M. Ranger, Inc. v. Gildersleeve, 106 Conn. 372, 138 A. 142 (1927) in which a contract was made for six carloads of coal then rolling from the mines and consigned to the seller but the seller agreed to divert the carloads to the buyer as soon as the car numbers became known to him. He arranged a diversion of two cars and then notified the buyer who then repudiated the contract. The seller was held to be entitled to his full remedy for the two cars diverted because simultaneous delivery of all of the cars was not contemplated by either party.

4. Where the circumstances indicate that a party has a right to delivery in lots, the price may be demanded for each lot if it is apportionable.

Cross References:

Point 1: Section 1—201.

Point 2: Sections 2—508 and 2—601.

Point 3: Sections 2—503, 2—608 and 2—609.

Definitional Cross References:

"Contract for sale". Section 2—106.

"Goods". Section 2—105.

"Lot". Section 2—105.

"Party". Section 1—201.

"Rights". Section 1—201.

§ 2—308. Absence of Specified Place for Delivery

Unless otherwise agreed

(a) the place for delivery of goods is the seller's place of business or if he has none his residence; but

(b) in a contract for sale of identified goods which to the knowledge of the parties at the time of contracting are in some other place, that place is the place for their delivery; and

(c) documents of title may be delivered through customary banking channels.

Official Comment

Prior Uniform Statutory Provision: Paragraphs (a) and (b)—Section 43(1), Uniform Sales Act; Paragraph (c)—none.

Changes: Slight modification in language.

Purposes of Changes and New Matter:

1. Paragraphs (a) and (b) provide for those noncommercial sales and for those occasional commercial sales where no place or means of delivery has been agreed upon by the parties. Where delivery by carrier is "required or authorized by the agreement", the seller's duties as to delivery of the goods are governed not by this section but by Section 2—504.

2. Under paragraph (b) when the identified goods contracted for are known to both

parties to be in some location other than the seller's place of business or residence, the parties are presumed to have intended that place to be the place of delivery. This paragraph also applies (unless, as would be normal, the circumstances show that delivery by way of documents is intended) to a bulk of goods in the possession of a bailee. In such a case, however, the seller has the additional obligation to procure the acknowledgment by the bailee of the buyer's right to possession.

3. Where "customary banking channels" call only for due notification by the banker that the documents are on hand, leaving the buyer himself to see to the physical receipt of the goods, tender at the buyer's address is not required under paragraph (c). But that paragraph merely eliminates the possibility of a default by the seller if "customary banking channels" have been properly used in giving notice to the buyer. Where the bank has purchased a draft accompanied by documents or has undertaken its collection on behalf of the seller, Part 5 of Article 4 spells out its duties and relations to its customer. Where the documents move forward under a letter of credit the Article on Letters of Credit spells out the duties and relations between the bank, the seller and the buyer.

4. The rules of this section apply only "unless otherwise agreed." The surrounding circumstances, usage of trade, course of dealing and course of performance, as well as the express language of the parties, may constitute an "otherwise agreement".

Cross References:

Point 1: Sections 2—504 and 2—505.

Point 2: Section 2—503.

Point 3: Section 2—512, Articles 4, Part 5, and 5.

Definitional Cross References:

"Contract for sale". Section 2—106.

"Delivery". Section 1—201.

"Document of title". Section 1—201.

"Goods". Section 2—105.

"Party". Section 1—201.

"Seller". Section 2—103.

§ 2—309. Absence of Specific Time Provisions; Notice of Termination

(1) The time for shipment or delivery or any other action under a contract if not provided in this Article or agreed upon shall be a reasonable time.

(2) Where the contract provides for successive performances but is indefinite in duration it is valid for a reasonable time but unless otherwise agreed may be terminated at any time by either party.

(3) Termination of a contract by one party except on the happening of an agreed event requires that reasonable notification be received by the other party and an agreement dis-

pensing with notification is invalid if its operation would be unconscionable.

Official Comment

Prior Uniform Statutory Provision: Subsection (1)—see Sections 43(2), 45(2), 47(1) and 48, Uniform Sales Act, for policy continued under this Article; Subsection (2)—none; Subsection (3)—none.

Changes: Completely different in scope.

Purposes of Changes and New Matter:

1. Subsection (1) requires that all actions taken under a sales contract must be taken within a reasonable time where no time has been agreed upon. The reasonable time under this provision turns on the criteria as to "reasonable time" and on good faith and commercial standards set forth in Sections 1—203, 1—204 and 2—103. It thus depends upon what constitutes acceptable commercial conduct in view of the nature, purpose and circumstances of the action to be taken. Agreement as to a definite time, however, may be found in a term implied from the contractual circumstances, usage of trade or course of dealing or performance as well as in an express term. Such cases fall outside of this subsection since in them the time for action is "agreed" by usage.

2. The time for payment, where not agreed upon, is related to the time for delivery; the particular problems which arise in connection with determining the appropriate time of payment and the time for any inspection before payment which is both allowed by law and demanded by the buyer are covered in Section 2—513.

3. The facts in regard to shipment and delivery differ so widely as to make detailed provision for them in the text of this Article impracticable. The applicable principles, however, make it clear that surprise is to be avoided, good faith judgment is to be protected, and notice or negotiation to reduce the uncertainty to certainty is to be favored.

4. When the time for delivery is left open, unreasonably early offers of or demands for delivery are intended to be read under this Article as expressions of desire or intention, requesting the assent or acquiescence of the other party, not as final positions which may amount without more to breach or to create breach by the other side. See Sections 2—207 and 2—609.

5. The obligation of good faith under this Act requires reasonable notification before a contract may be treated as breached because a reasonable time for delivery or demand has expired. This operates both in the case of a contract originally indefinite as to time and of one subsequently made indefinite by waiver.

When both parties let an originally reasonable time go by in silence, the course of conduct under the contract may be viewed as enlarging the reasonable time for tender or demand of performance. The contract may be terminated by abandonment.

6. Parties to a contract are not required in giving reasonable notification to fix, at peril of breach, a time which is in fact reasonable in the unforeseeable judgment of a later trier of fact. Effective communication of a proposed time limit calls for a response, so that failure to reply will make out acquiescence. Where objection is made, however, or if the demand is merely for information as to when goods will be delivered or will be ordered out, demand for assurances on the ground of insecurity may be made under this Article pending further negotiations. Only when a party insists on undue delay or on rejection of the other party's reasonable proposal is there a question of flat breach under the present section.

7. Subsection (2) applies a commercially reasonable view to resolve the conflict which has arisen in the cases as to contracts of indefinite duration. The "reasonable time" of duration appropriate to a given arrangement is limited by the circumstances. When the arrangement has been carried on by the parties over the years, the "reasonable time" can continue indefinitely and the contract will not terminate until notice.

8. Subsection (3) recognizes that the application of principles of good faith and sound commercial practice normally call for such notification of the termination of a going contract relationship as will give the other party reasonable time to seek a substitute arrangement. An agreement dispensing with notification or limiting the time for the seeking of a substitute arrangement is, of course, valid under this subsection unless the results of putting it into operation would be the creation of an unconscionable state of affairs.

9. Justifiable cancellation for breach is a remedy for breach and is not the kind of termination covered by the present subsection.

10. The requirement of notification is dispensed with where the contract provides for termination on the happening of an "agreed event." "Event" is a term chosen here to contrast with "option" or the like.

Cross References:

Point 1: Sections 1—203, 1—204 and 2—103.

Point 2: Sections 2—320, 2—321, 2—504, and 2—511 through 2—514.

Point 5: Section 1—203.

Point 6: Section 2—609.

Point 7: Section 2—204.

Point 9: Sections 2—106, 2—318, 2—610 and 2—703.

Definitional Cross References:

"Agreement". Section 1—201.

"Contract". Section 1—201.

"Notification". Section 1—201.

"Party". Section 1—201.

"Reasonable time". Section 1—204.

"Termination". Section 2—106.

§ 2—310. Open Time for Payment or Running of Credit; Authority to Ship Under Reservation

Unless otherwise agreed

(a) payment is due at the time and place at which the buyer is to receive the goods even though the place of shipment is the place of delivery; and

(b) if the seller is authorized to send the goods he may ship them under reservation, and may tender the documents of title, but the buyer may inspect the goods after their arrival before payment is due unless such inspection is inconsistent with the terms of the contract (Section 2—513); and

(c) if delivery is authorized and made by way of documents of title otherwise than by subsection (b) then payment is due at the time and place at which the buyer is to receive the documents regardless of where the goods are to be received; and

(d) where the seller is required or authorized to ship the goods on credit the credit period runs from the time of shipment but post-dating the invoice or delaying its dispatch will correspondingly delay the starting of the credit period.

Official Comment

Prior Uniform Statutory Provision: Sections 42 and 47(2), Uniform Sales Act.

Changes: Completely rewritten in this and other sections.

Purposes of Changes: This section is drawn to reflect modern business methods of dealing at a distance rather than face to face. Thus:

1. Paragraph (a) provides that payment is due at the time and place "the buyer is to receive the goods" rather than at the point of delivery except in documentary shipment cases (paragraph (c)). This grants an opportunity for the exercise by the buyer of his preliminary right to inspection before paying even though under the delivery term the risk of loss may have previously passed to him or the running of the credit period has already started.

2. Paragraph (b) while providing for inspection by the buyer before he pays, protects the seller. He is not required to give up possession of the goods until he has received payment, where no credit has been contemplated by the parties. The seller may collect through a bank by a sight draft against an order bill of lading "hold until arrival; inspection allowed." The obligations of the bank under such a provision are set forth in Part 5 of Article 4. In the absence of a credit term,

the seller is permitted to ship under reservation and if he does payment is then due where and when the buyer is to receive the documents.

3. Unless otherwise agreed, the place for the receipt of the documents and payment is the buyer's city but the time for payment is only after arrival of the goods, since under paragraph (b), and Sections 2—512 and 2—513 the buyer is under no duty to pay prior to inspection.

4. Where the mode of shipment is such that goods must be unloaded immediately upon arrival, too rapidly to permit adequate inspection before receipt, the seller must be guided by the provisions of this Article on inspection which provide that if the seller wishes to demand payment before inspection, he must put an appropriate term into the contract. Even requiring payment against documents will not of itself have this desired result if the documents are to be held until the arrival of the goods. But under (b) and (c) if the terms are C.I.F., C.O.D., or cash against documents payment may be due before inspection.

5. Paragraph (d) states the common commercial understanding that an agreed credit period runs from the time of shipment or from that dating of the invoice which is commonly recognized as a representation of the time of shipment. The provision concerning any delay in sending forth the invoice is included because such conduct results in depriving the buyer of his full notice and warning as to when he must be prepared to pay.

Cross References:

Generally: Part 5.

Point 1: Section 2—509.

Point 2: Sections 2—505, 2—511, 2—512, 2—513 and Article 4.

Point 3: Sections 2—308(b), 2—512 and 2—513.

Point 4: Section 2—513(3)(b).

Definitional Cross References:

"Buyer". Section 2—103.

"Delivery". Section 1—201.

"Document of title". Section 1—201.

"Goods". Section 2—105.

"Receipt of goods". Section 2—103.

"Seller". Section 2—103.

"Send". Section 1 201.

"Term". Section 1—201.

§ 2—311. Options and Cooperation Respecting Performance

(1) An agreement for sale which is otherwise sufficiently definite (subsection (3) of Section 2—204) to be a contract is not made invalid by the fact that it leaves particulars of performance to be specified by one of the parties. Any such specification must be made in good faith and within limits set by commercial reasonableness.

(2) Unless otherwise agreed specifications relating to assortment of the goods are at the buyer's option and except as

otherwise provided in subsections (1) (c) and (3) of Section 2—319 specifications or arrangements relating to shipment are at the seller's option.

(3) Where such specification would materially affect the other party's performance but is not seasonably made or where one party's cooperation is necessary to the agreed performance of the other but is not seasonably forthcoming, the other party in addition to all other remedies

(a) is excused for any resulting delay in his own performance; and

(b) may also either proceed to perform in any reasonable manner or after the time for a material part of his own performance treat the failure to specify or to cooperate as a breach by failure to deliver or accept the goods.

Official Comment

Prior Uniform Statutory Provision: None.

Purposes:

1. Subsection (1) permits the parties to leave certain detailed particulars of performance to be filled in by either of them without running the risk of having the contract invalidated for indefiniteness. The party to whom the agreement gives power to specify the missing details is required to exercise good faith and to act in accordance with commercial standards so that there is no surprise and the range of permissible variation is limited by what is commercially reasonable. The "agreement" which permits one party so to specify may be found as well in a course of dealing, usage of trade, or implication from circumstances as in explicit language used by the parties.

2. Options as to assortment of goods or shipping arrangements are specifically reserved to the buyer and seller respectively under subsection (2) where no other arrangement has been made. This section rejects the test which mechanically and without regard to usage or the purpose of the option gave the option to the party "first under a duty to move" and applies instead a standard commercial interpretation to these circumstances. The "unless otherwise agreed" provision of this subsection covers not only express terms but the background and circumstances which enter into the agreement.

3. Subsection (3) applies when the exercise of an option or cooperation by one party is necessary to or materially affects the other party's performance, but it is not seasonably forthcoming; the subsection relieves the other party from the necessity for performance or excuses his delay in performance as the case may be. The contract-keeping party may at his option under this subsection proceed to perform in any commercially reasonable manner

rather than wait. In addition to the special remedies provided, this subsection also reserves "all other remedies". The remedy of particular importance in this connection is that provided for insecurity. Request may also be made pursuant to the obligation of good faith for a reasonable indication of the time and manner of performance for which a party is to hold himself ready.

4. The remedy provided in subsection (3) is one which does not operate in the situation which falls within the scope of Section 2—614 on substituted performance. Where the failure to cooperate results from circumstances set forth in that Section, the other party is under a duty to proffer or demand (as the case may be) substitute performance as a condition to claiming rights against the non-cooperating party.

Cross References:

Point 1: Sections 1—201, 2—204 and 1—203.

Point 3: Sections 1—203 and 2—609.

Point 4: Section 2—614.

Definitional Cross References:

"Agreement". Section 1—201.

"Buyer". Section 2—103.

"Contract for sale". Section 2—106.

"Goods". Section 2—105.

"Party". Section 1—201.

"Remedy". Section 1—201.

"Seasonably". Section 1—204.

"Seller". Section 2—103.

§ 2—312. Warranty of Title and Against Infringement; Buyer's Obligation Against Infringement

(1) Subject to subsection (2) there is in a contract for sale a warranty by the seller that

(a) the title conveyed shall be good, and its transfer rightful; and

(b) the goods shall be delivered free from any security interest or other lien or encumbrance of which the buyer at the time of contracting has no knowledge.

(2) A warranty under subsection (1) will be excluded or modified only by specific language or by circumstances which give the buyer reason to know that the person selling does not claim title in himself or that he is purporting to sell only such right or title as he or a third person may have.

(3) Unless otherwise agreed a seller who is a merchant regularly dealing in goods of the kind warrants that the goods shall be delivered free of the rightful claim of any third person by way of infringement or the like but a buyer who furnishes specifications to the seller must hold the seller harmless against any such claim which arises out of compliance with the specifications.

Official Comment

Prior Uniform Statutory Provision: Section 13, Uniform Sales Act.

Changes: Completely rewritten, the provisions concerning infringement being new.

Purposes of Changes:

1. Subsection (1) makes provision for a buyer's basic needs in respect to a title which he in good faith expects to acquire by his purchase, namely, that he receive a good, clean title transferred to him also in a rightful manner so that he will not be exposed to a lawsuit in order to protect it.

The warranty extends to a buyer whether or not the seller was in possession of the goods at the time the sale or contract to sell was made.

The warranty of quiet possession is abolished. Disturbance of quiet possession, although not mentioned specifically, is one way, among many, in which the breach of the warranty of title may be established.

The "knowledge" referred to in subsection 1(b) is actual knowledge as distinct from notice.

2. The provisions of this Article requiring notification to the seller within a reasonable time after the buyer's discovery of a breach apply to notice of a breach of the warranty of title, where the seller's breach was innocent. However, if the seller's breach was in bad faith he cannot be permitted to claim that he has been misled or prejudiced by the delay in giving notice. In such case the "reasonable" time for notice should receive a very liberal interpretation. Whether the breach by the seller is in good or bad faith Section 2—725 provides that the cause of action accrues when the breach occurs. Under the provisions of that section the breach of the warranty of good title occurs when tender of delivery is made since the warranty is not one which extends to "future performance of the goods."

3. When the goods are part of the seller's normal stock and are sold in his normal course of business, it is his duty to see that no claim of infringement of a patent or trademark by a third party will mar the buyer's title. A sale by a person other than a dealer, however, raises no implication in its circumstances of such a warranty. Nor is there such an implication when the buyer orders goods to be assembled, prepared or manufactured on his own specifications. If, in such a case, the resulting product infringes a patent or trademark, the liability will run from buyer to seller. There is, under such circumstances, a tacit representation on the part of the buyer that the seller will be safe in manufacturing according to the specifications, and the buyer is under an obligation in good faith to indemnify him for any loss suffered.

4. This section rejects the cases which recognize the principle that infringements violate the warranty of title but deny the buyer a remedy unless he

has been expressly prevented from using the goods. Under this Article "eviction" is not a necessary condition to the buyer's remedy since the buyer's remedy arises immediately upon receipt of notice of infringement; it is merely one way of establishing the fact of breach.

5. Subsection (2) recognizes that sales by sheriffs, executors, foreclosing lienors and persons similarly situated are so out of the ordinary commercial course that their peculiar character is immediately apparent to the buyer and therefore no personal obligation is imposed upon the seller who is purporting to sell only an unknown or limited right. This subsection does not touch upon and leaves open all questions of restitution arising in such cases, when a unique article so sold is reclaimed by a third party as the rightful owner.

6. The warranty of subsection (1) is not designated as an "implied" warranty, and hence is not subject to Section 2—316 (3). Disclaimer of the warranty of title is governed instead by subsection (2), which requires either specific language or the described circumstances.

Cross References:

Point 1: Section 2—403.
Point 2: Sections 2—607 and 2—725.
Point 3: Section 1—203.
Point 4: Sections 2—609 and 2—725.
Point 6: Section 2—316.

Definitional Cross References:

"Buyer". Section 2—103.
"Contract for sale". Section 2—106.
"Goods". Section 2—105.
"Person". Section 1—201.
"Right". Section 1—201.
"Seller". Section 2—103.

§ 2—313. Express Warranties by Affirmation, Promise, Description, Sample

(1) Express warranties by the seller are created as follows:

(a) Any affirmation of fact or promise made by the seller to the buyer which relates to the goods and becomes part of the basis of the bargain creates an express warranty that the goods shall conform to the affirmation or promise.

(b) Any description of the goods which is made part of the basis of the bargain creates an express warranty that the goods shall conform to the description.

(c) Any sample or model which is made part of the basis of the bargain creates an express warranty that the whole of the goods shall conform to the sample or model.

(2) It is not necessary to the creation of an express warranty that the seller use formal words such as "warrant" or

"guarantee" or that he have a specific intention to make a warranty, but an affirmation merely of the value of the goods or a statement purporting to be merely the seller's opinion or commendation of the goods does not create a warranty.

Official Comment

Prior Uniform Statutory Provision: Sections 12, 14 and 16, Uniform Sales Act.

Changes: Rewritten.

Purposes of Changes: To consolidate and systematize basic principles with the result that:

1. "Express" warranties rest on "dickered" aspects of the individual bargain, and go so clearly to the essence of that bargain that words of disclaimer in a form are repugnant to the basic dickered terms. "Implied" warranties rest so clearly on a common factual situation or set of conditions that no particular language or action is necessary to evidence them and they will arise in such a situation unless unmistakably negated.

This section reverts to the older case law insofar as the warranties of description and sample are designated "express" rather than "implied".

2. Although this section is limited in its scope and direct purpose to warranties made by the seller to the buyer as part of a contract for sale, the warranty sections of this Article are not designed in any way to disturb those lines of case law growth which have recognized that warranties need not be confined either to sales contracts or to the direct parties to such a contract. They may arise in other appropriate circumstances such as in the case of bailments for hire, whether such bailment is itself the main contract or is merely a supplying of containers under a contract for the sale of their contents. The provisions of Section 2—318 on third party beneficiaries expressly recognize this case law development within one particular area. Beyond that, the matter is left to the case law with the intention that the policies of this Act may offer useful guidance in dealing with further cases as they arise.

3. The present section deals with affirmations of fact by the seller, descriptions of the goods or exhibitions of samples, exactly as any other part of a negotiation which ends in a contract is dealt with. No specific intention to make a warranty is necessary if any of these factors is made part of the basis of the bargain. In actual practice affirmations of fact made by the seller about the goods during a bargain are regarded as part of the description of those goods; hence no particular reliance on such statements need be shown in order to weave them into the fabric of the agreement. Rather, any fact which is to take such affirmations, once made, out of the agreement requires clear affirmative proof. The issue normally is one of fact.

4. In view of the principle that the whole purpose of the law of warranty is to determine

what it is that the seller has in essence agreed to sell, the policy is adopted of those cases which refuse except in unusual circumstances to recognize a material deletion of the seller's obligation. Thus, a contract is normally a contract for a sale of something describable and described. A clause generally disclaiming "all warranties, express or implied" cannot reduce the seller's obligation with respect to such description and therefore cannot be given literal effect under Section 2—316.

This is not intended to mean that the parties, if they consciously desire, cannot make their own bargain as they wish. But in determining what they have agreed upon good faith is a factor and consideration should be given to the fact that the probability is small that a real price is intended to be exchanged for a pseudo-obligation.

5. Paragraph (1) (b) makes specific some of the principles set forth above when a description of the goods is given by the seller.

A description need not be by words. Technical specifications, blueprints and the like can afford more exact description than mere language and if made part of the basis of the bargain goods must conform with them. Past deliveries may set the description of quality, either expressly or impliedly by course of dealing. Of course, all descriptions by merchants must be read against the applicable trade usages with the general rules as to merchantability resolving any doubts.

6. The basic situation as to statements affecting the true essence of the bargain is no different when a sample or model is involved in the transaction. This section includes both a "sample" actually drawn from the bulk of goods which is the subject matter of the sale, and a "model" which is offered for inspection when the subject matter is not at hand and which has not been drawn from the bulk of the goods.

Although the underlying principles are unchanged, the facts are often ambiguous when something is shown as illustrative, rather than as a straight sample. In general, the presumption is that any sample or model just as any affirmation of fact is intended to become a basis of the bargain. But there is no escape from the question of fact. When the seller exhibits a sample purporting to be drawn from an existing bulk, good faith of course requires that the sample be fairly drawn. But in mercantile experience the mere exhibition of a "sample" does not of itself show whether it is merely intended to "suggest" or to "be" the character of the subject-matter of the contract. The question is whether the seller has so acted with reference to the sample as to make him responsible that the whole shall have at least the values shown by it. The circumstances aid in answering this question. If the sample has been drawn from an existing bulk, it must be regarded as describing values of the goods contracted for unless it is accompanied by an unmistakable denial of such responsibility. If, on the other hand, a model of merchandise not on hand is offered, the mercantile presumption that it has become a literal description of the subject matter is not so strong, and particularly so if modification on the buyer's initiative impairs any feature of the model.

7. The precise time when words of description or affirmation are made or samples are shown is not material. The sole question is whether the language or samples or models are fairly to be regarded as part of the contract. If language is used after the closing of the deal (as when the buyer when taking delivery asks and receives an additional assurance), the warranty becomes a modification, and need not be supported by consideration if it is otherwise reasonable and in order (Section 2—209).

8. Concerning affirmations of value or a seller's opinion or commendation under subsection (2), the basic question remains the same: What statements of the seller have in the circumstances and in objective judgment become part of the basis of the bargain? As indicated above, all of the statements of the seller do so unless good reason is shown to the contrary. The provisions of subsection (2) are included, however, since common experience discloses that some statements or predictions cannot fairly be viewed as entering into the bargain. Even as to false statements of value, however, the possibility is left open that a remedy may be provided by the law relating to fraud or misrepresentation.

Cross References:

Point 1: Section 2—316.
Point 2: Sections 1—102(3) and 2—318.
Point 3: Section 2—316(2)(b).
Point 4: Section 2—316.
Point 5: Sections 1—205(4) and 2—314.
Point 6: Section 2—316.
Point 7: Section 2—209.
Point 8: Section 1—103.

Definitional Cross References:

"Buyer". Section 2—103.
"Conforming". Section 2—106.
"Goods". Section 2—105.
"Seller". Section 2—103.

§ 2—314. Implied Warranty: Merchantability; Usage of Trade

(1) Unless excluded or modified (Section 2—316), a warranty that the goods shall be merchantable is implied in a contract for their sale if the seller is a merchant with respect to goods of that kind. Under this section the serving for value of food or drink to be consumed either on the premises or elsewhere is a sale.

(2) Goods to be merchantable must be at least such as

(a) pass without objection in the trade under the contract description; and

(b) in the case of fungible goods, are of fair average quality within the description; and

(c) are fit for the ordinary purposes for which such goods are used; and

(d) run, within the variations permitted by the agreement, of even kind, quality and quantity within each unit and among all units involved; and

(e) are adequately contained, packaged, and labeled as the agreement may require; and

(f) conform to the promises or affirmations of fact made on the container or label if any.

(3) Unless excluded or modified (Section 2—316) other implied warranties may arise from course of dealing or usage of trade.

Official Comment

Prior Uniform Statutory Provision: Section 15(2), Uniform Sales Act.

Changes: Completely rewritten.

Purposes of Changes: This section, drawn in view of the steadily developing case law on the subject, is intended to make it clear that:

1. The seller's obligation applies to present sales as well as to contracts to sell subject to the effects of any examination of specific goods. (Subsection (2) of Section 2—316). Also, the warranty of merchantability applies to sales for use as well as to sales for resale.

2. The question when the warranty is imposed turns basically on the meaning of the terms of the agreement as recognized in the trade. Goods delivered under an agreement made by a merchant in a given line of trade must be of a quality comparable to that generally acceptable in that line of trade under the description or other designation of the goods used in the agreement. The responsibility imposed rests on any merchant-seller, and the absence of the words "grower or manufacturer or not" which appeared in Section 15(2) of the Uniform Sales Act does not restrict the applicability of this section.

3. A specific designation of goods by the buyer does not exclude the seller's obligation that they be fit for the general purposes appropriate to such goods. A contract for the sale of second-hand goods, however, involves only such obligation as is appropriate to such goods for that is their contract description. A person making an isolated sale of goods is not a "merchant" within the meaning of the full scope of this section and, thus, no warranty of merchantability would apply. His knowledge of any defects not apparent on inspection would, however, without need for express agreement and in keeping with the underlying reason of the present section and the pro-

visions on good faith, impose an obligation that known material but hidden defects be fully disclosed.

4. Although a seller may not be a "merchant" as to the goods in question, if he states generally that they are "guaranteed" the provisions of this section may furnish a guide to the content of the resulting express warranty. This has particular significance in the case of second-hand sales, and has further significance in limiting the effect of fine-print disclaimer clauses where their effect would be inconsistent with large-print assertions of "guarantee".

5. The second sentence of subsection (1) covers the warranty with respect to food and drink. Serving food or drink for value is a sale, whether to be consumed on the premises or elsewhere. Cases to the contrary are rejected. The principal warranty is that stated in subsections (1) and (2) (c) of this section.

6. Subsection (2) does not purport to exhaust the meaning of "merchantable" nor to negate any of its attributes not specifically mentioned in the text of the statute, but arising by usage of trade or through case law. The language used is "must be at least such as . . . ," and the intention is to leave open other possible attributes of merchantability.

7. Paragraphs (a) and (b) of subsection (2) are to be read together. Both refer, as indicated above, to the standards of that line of the trade which fits the transaction and the seller's business. "Fair average" is a term directly appropriate to agricultural bulk products and means goods centering around the middle belt of quality, not the least or the worst that can be understood in the particular trade by the designation, but such as can pass "without objection." Of course a fair percentage of the least is permissible but the goods are not "fair average" if they are all of the least or worst quality possible under the description. In cases of doubt as to what quality is intended, the price at which a merchant closes a contract is an excellent index of the nature and scope of his obligation under the present section.

8. Fitness for the ordinary purposes for which goods of the type are used is a fundamental concept of the present section and is covered in paragraph (c). As stated above, merchantability is also a part of the obligation owing to the purchaser for use. Correspondingly, protection, under this aspect of the warranty, of the person buying for resale to the ultimate consumer is equally necessary, and merchantable goods must therefore be "honestly" resalable in the normal course of business because they are what they purport to be.

9. Paragraph (d) on evenness of kind, quality and quantity follows case law. But precautionary language has been added as a reminder of the frequent usages of trade which permit substantial variations both with and without an allowance or an obligation to replace the varying units.

10. Paragraph (e) applies only where the nature of the

goods and of the transaction require a certain type of container, package or label. Paragraph (f) applies, on the other hand, wherever there is a label or container on which representations are made, even though the original contract, either by express terms or usage of trade, may not have required either the labelling or the representation. This follows from the general obligation of good faith which requires that a buyer should not be placed in the position of reselling or using goods delivered under false representations appearing on the package or container. No problem of extra consideration arises in this connection since, under this Article, an obligation is imposed by the original contract not to deliver mislabeled articles, and the obligation is imposed where mercantile good faith so requires and without reference to the doctrine of consideration.

11. Exclusion or modification of the warranty of merchantability, or of any part of it, is dealt with in the section to which the text of the present section makes explicit precautionary references. That section must be read with particular reference to its subsection (4) on limitation of remedies. The warranty of merchantability, wherever it is normal, is so commonly taken for granted that its exclusion from the contract is a matter threatening surprise and therefore requiring special precaution.

12. Subsection (3) is to make explicit that usage of trade and course of dealing can create warranties and that they are implied rather than express warranties and thus subject to exclusion or modification under Section 2—316. A typical instance would be the obligation to provide pedigree papers to evidence conformity of the animal to the contract in the case of a pedigreed dog or blooded bull.

13. In an action based on breach of warranty, it is of course necessary to show not only the existence of the warranty but the fact that the warranty was broken and that the breach of the warranty was the proximate cause of the loss sustained. In such an action an affirmative showing by the seller that the loss resulted from some action or event following his own delivery of the goods can operate as a defense. Equally, evidence indicating that the seller exercised care in the manufacture, processing or selection of the goods is relevant to the issue of whether the warranty was in fact broken. Action by the buyer following an examination of the goods which ought to have indicated the defect complained of can be shown as matter bearing on whether the breach itself was the cause of the injury.

Cross References:

Point 1: Section 2—316.
Point 3: Sections 1—203 and 2—104.
Point 5: Section 2—315.
Point 11: Section 2—316.
Point 12: Sections 1—201, 1—205 and 2—316.

Definitional Cross References:

"Agreement". Section 1—201.
"Contract". Section 1—201.
"Contract for sale". Section 2—106.
"Goods". Section 2—105.
"Merchant". Section 2—104
"Seller". Section 2—103.

§ 2—315. Implied Warranty: Fitness for Particular Purpose

Where the seller at the time of contracting has reason to know any particular purpose for which the goods are required and that the buyer is relying on the seller's skill or judgment to select or furnish suitable goods, there is unless excluded or modified under the next section an implied warranty that the goods shall be fit for such purpose.

Official Comment

Prior Uniform Statutory Provision: Section 15(1), (4), (5), Uniform Sales Act.

Changes: Rewritten.

Purposes of Changes:

1. Whether or not this warranty arises in any individual case is basically a question of fact to be determined by the circumstances of the contracting. Under this section the buyer need not bring home to the seller actual knowledge of the particular purpose for which the goods are intended or of his reliance on the seller's skill and judgment, if the circumstances are such that the seller has reason to realize the purpose intended or that the reliance exists. The buyer, of course, must actually be relying on the seller.

2. A "particular purpose" differs from the ordinary purpose for which the goods are used in that it envisages a specific use by the buyer which is peculiar to the nature of his business whereas the ordinary purposes for which goods are used are those envisaged in the concept of merchantability and go to uses which are customarily made of the goods in question. For example, shoes are generally used for the purpose of walking upon ordinary ground, but a seller may know that a particular pair was selected to be used for climbing mountains.

A contract may of course include both a warranty of merchantability and one of fitness for a particular purpose.

The provisions of this Article on the cumulation and conflict of express and implied warranties must be considered on the question of inconsistency between or among warranties. In such a case any question of fact as to which warranty was intended by the parties to apply must be resolved in favor of the warranty of fitness for particular purpose as against all other warranties except where the buyer has taken upon himself the responsibility of furnishing the technical specifications.

3. In connection with the warranty of fitness for a particular purpose the provisions of this Article on the allocation or division of risks are particularly applicable in any transaction in which the purpose for which the goods are to be used combines requirements both as to the quality of the goods themselves and compliance with certain laws or regulations. How the risks are divided is a question of fact to be determined, where not

expressly contained in the agreement, from the circumstances of contracting, usage of trade, course of performance and the like, matters which may constitute the "otherwise agreement" of the parties by which they may divide the risk or burden.

4. The absence from this section of the language used in the Uniform Sales Act in referring to the seller, "whether he be the grower or manufacturer or not," is not intended to impose any requirement that the seller be a grower or manufacturer. Although normally the warranty will arise only where the seller is a merchant with the appropriate "skill or judgment," it can arise as to nonmerchants where this is justified by the particular circumstances.

5. The elimination of the "patent or other trade name" exception constitutes the major extension of the warranty of fitness which has been made by the cases and continued in this Article. Under the present section the existence of a patent or other trade name and the designation of the article by that name, or indeed in any other definite manner, is only one of the facts to be considered on the question of whether the buyer actually relied on the seller, but it is not of itself decisive of the issue. If the buyer himself is insisting on a particular brand he is not relying on the seller's skill and judgment and so no warranty results. But the mere fact that the article purchased has a particular patent or trade name is not sufficient to indicate nonreliance if the article has been recommended by the seller as adequate for the buyer's purposes.

6. The specific reference forward in the present section to the following section on exclusion or modification of warranties is to call attention to the possibility of eliminating the warranty in any given case. However it must be noted that under the following section the warranty of fitness for a particular purpose must be excluded or modified by a conspicuous writing.

Cross References:

Point 2: Sections 2—314 and 2—317.

Point 3: Section 2—303.

Point 6: Section 2—316.

Definitional Cross References:

"Buyer". Section 2—103.

"Goods". Section 2—105.

"Seller". Section 2—103.

2-316 must be distinguished from 2-719

§ 2—316. Exclusion or Modification of Warranties

(1) Words or conduct relevant to the creation of an express warranty and words or conduct tending to negate or limit warranty shall be construed wherever reasonable as consistent with each other; but subject to the provisions of this Article on parol or extrinsic evidence (Section 2—202) negation or limitation is inoperative to the extent that such construction is unreasonable.

See comment #1

(2) Subject to subsection (3), to exclude or modify the implied warranty of merchantability or any part of it the language must mention merchantability and in case of a writing must be conspicuous, and to exclude or modify any implied warranty of fitness the exclusion must be by a writing and conspicuous. Language to exclude all implied warranties of fitness is sufficient if it states, for example, that "There are no warranties which extend beyond the description on the face hereof."

(3) Notwithstanding subsection (2)

(a) unless the circumstances indicate otherwise, all implied warranties are excluded by expressions like "as is", "with all faults" or other language which in common understanding calls the buyer's attention to the exclusion of warranties and makes plain that there is no implied warranty; and

(b) when the buyer before entering into the contract has examined the goods or the sample or model as fully as he desired or has refused to examine the goods there is no implied warranty with regard to defects which an examination ought in the circumstances to have revealed to him; and

(c) an implied warranty can also be excluded or modified by course of dealing or course of performance or usage of trade.

(4) Remedies for breach of warranty can be limited in accordance with the provisions of this Article on liquidation or limitation of damages and on contractual modification of remedy (Sections 2—718 and 2—719).

Official Comment

Prior Uniform Statutory Provision: None. See sections 15 and 71, Uniform Sales Act.

Purposes:

1. This section is designed principally to deal with those frequent clauses in sales contracts which seek to exclude "all warranties, express or implied." It seeks to protect a buyer from unexpected and unbargained language of disclaimer by denying effect to such language when inconsistent with language of express warranty and permitting the exclusion of implied warranties only by conspicuous language or other circumstances which protect the buyer from surprise.

2. The seller is protected under this Article against false allegations of oral warranties by its provisions on parol and extrinsic evidence and against unauthorized representations by the customary "lack of author-

ity" clauses. This Article treats the limitation or avoidance of consequential damages as a matter of limiting remedies for breach, separate from the matter of creation of liability under a warranty. If no warranty exists, there is of course no problem of limiting remedies for breach of warranty. Under subsection (4) the question of limitation of remedy is governed by the sections referred to rather than by this section.

3. Disclaimer of the implied warranty of merchantability is permitted under subsection (2), but with the safeguard that such disclaimers must mention merchantability and in case of a writing must be conspicuous.

4. Unlike the implied warranty of merchantability, implied warranties of fitness for a particular purpose may be excluded by general language, but only if it is in writing and conspicuous.

5. Subsection (2) presupposes that the implied warranty in question exists unless excluded or modified. Whether or not language of disclaimer satisfies the requirements of this section, such language may be relevant under other sections to the question whether the warranty was ever in fact created. Thus, unless the provisions of this Article on parol and extrinsic evidence prevent, oral language of disclaimer may raise issues of fact as to whether reliance by the buyer occurred and whether the seller had "reason to know" under the section on implied warranty of fitness for a particular purpose.

6. The exceptions to the general rule set forth in paragraphs (a), (b) and (c) of subsection (3) are common factual situations in which the circumstances surrounding the transaction are in themselves sufficient to call the buyer's attention to the fact that no implied warranties are made or that a certain implied warranty is being excluded.

7. Paragraph (a) of subsection (3) deals with general terms such as "as is," "as they stand," "with all faults," and the like. Such terms in ordinary commercial usage are understood to mean that the buyer takes the entire risk as to the quality of the goods involved. The terms covered by paragraph (a) are in fact merely a particularization of paragraph (c) which provides for exclusion or modification of implied warranties by usage of trade.

8. Under paragraph (b) of subsection (3) warranties may be excluded or modified by the circumstances where the buyer examines the goods or a sample or model of them before entering into the contract. "Examination" as used in this paragraph is not synonymous with inspection before acceptance or at any other time after the contract has been made. It goes rather to the nature of the responsibility assumed by the seller at the time of the making of the contract. Of course if the buyer discovers the defect and uses the goods anyway, or if he unreasonably fails to examine the goods before he uses them, resulting injuries may be found to result from his own action rather than proximately from a breach of warranty. See Sections 2—314 and 2—715 and comments thereto.

In order to bring the transaction within the scope of "refused to examine" in paragraph (b), it is not sufficient that the goods are available for inspection. There must in addition be a demand by the seller that the buyer examine the goods fully. The seller by the demand puts the buyer on notice that he is assuming the risk of defects which the examination ought to reveal. The language "refused to examine" in this paragraph is intended to make clear the necessity for such demand.

Application of the doctrine of "caveat emptor" in all cases where the buyer examines the goods regardless of statements made by the seller is, however, rejected by this Article. Thus, if the offer of examination is accompanied by words as to their merchantability or specific attributes and the buyer indicates clearly that he is relying on those words rather than on his examination, they give rise to an "express" warranty. In such cases the question is one of fact as to whether a warranty of merchantability has been expressly incorporated in the agreement. Disclaimer of such an express warranty is governed by subsection (1) of the present section.

The particular buyer's skill and the normal method of examining goods in the circumstances determine what defects are excluded by the examination. A failure to notice defects which are obvious cannot excuse the buyer. However, an examination under circumstances which do not permit chemical or other testing of the goods would not exclude defects which could be ascertained only by such testing. Nor can latent defects be excluded by a simple examination. A professional buyer examining a product in his field will be held to have assumed the risk as to all defects which a professional in the field ought to observe, while a nonprofessional buyer will be held to have assumed the risk only for such defects as a layman might be expected to observe.

9. The situation in which the buyer gives precise and complete specifications to the seller is not explicitly covered in this section, but this is a frequent circumstance by which the implied warranties may be excluded. The warranty of fitness for a particular purpose would not normally arise since in such a situation there is usually no reliance on the seller by the buyer. The warranty of merchantability in such a transaction, however, must be considered in connection with the next section on the cumulation and conflict of warranties. Under paragraph (c) of that section in case of such an inconsistency the implied warranty of merchantability is displaced by the express warranty that the goods will comply with the specifications. Thus, where the buyer gives detailed specifications as to the goods, neither of the implied warranties as to quality will normally apply to the transaction unless consistent with the specifications.

Cross References:

Point 2: Sections 2—202, 2—718 and 2—719.

Point 7: Sections 1—205 and 2—208.

Definitional Cross References:
"Agreement". Section 1—201.
"Buyer". Section 2—103.
"Contract". Section 1—201.
"Course of dealing". Section 1—205.
"Goods". Section 2—105.
"Remedy". Section 1—201.
"Seller". Section 2—103.
"Usage of trade". Section 1—205.

§ 2—317. Cumulation and Conflict of Warranties Express or Implied

Warranties whether express or implied shall be construed as consistent with each other and as cumulative, but if such construction is unreasonable the intention of the parties shall determine which warranty is dominant. In ascertaining that intention the following rules apply:

(a) Exact or technical specifications displace an inconsistent sample or model or general language of description.

(b) A sample from an existing bulk displaces inconsistent general language of description.

(c) Express warranties displace inconsistent implied warranties other than an implied warranty of fitness for a particular purpose.

Official Comment

Prior Uniform Statutory Provision: On cumulation of warranties see Sections 14, 15, and 16, Uniform Sales Act.

Changes: Completely rewritten into one section.

Purposes of Changes:

1. The present section rests on the basic policy of this Article that no warranty is created except by some conduct (either affirmative action or failure to disclose) on the part of the seller. Therefore, all warranties are made cumulative unless this construction of the contract is impossible or unreasonable.

This Article thus follows the general policy of the Uniform Sales Act except that in case of the sale of an article by its patent or trade name the elimination of the warranty of fitness depends solely on whether the buyer has relied on the seller's skill and judgment; the use of the patent or trade name is but one factor in making this determination.

2. The rules of this section are designed to aid in determin-

ing the intention of the parties as to which of inconsistent warranties which have arisen from the circumstances of their transaction shall prevail. These rules of intention are to be applied only where factors making for an equitable estoppel of the seller do not exist and where he has in perfect good faith made warranties which later turn out to be inconsistent. To the extent that the seller has led the buyer to believe that all of the warranties can be performed, he is estopped from setting up any essential inconsistency as a defense.

3. The rules in subsections (a), (b) and (c) are designed to ascertain the intention of the parties by reference to the factor which probably claimed the attention of the parties in the first instance. These rules are not absolute but may be changed by evidence showing that the conditions which existed at the time of contracting make the construction called for by the section inconsistent or unreasonable.

Cross Reference:

Point 1: Section 2—315.

Definitional Cross Reference:

"Party". Section 1—201.

§ 2—318. Third Party Beneficiaries of Warranties Express or Implied

Note: *If this Act is introduced in the Congress of the United States this section should be omitted. (States to select one alternative.)*

Alternative A

A seller's warranty whether express or implied extends to any natural person who is in the family or household of his buyer or who is a guest in his home if it is reasonable to expect that such person may use, consume or be affected by the goods and who is injured in person by breach of the warranty. A seller may not exclude or limit the operation of this section.

Alternative B

A seller's warranty whether express or implied extends to any natural person who may reasonably be expected to use, consume or be affected by the goods and who is injured in person by breach of the warranty. A seller may not exclude or limit the operation of this section.

Alternative C

A seller's warranty whether express or implied extends to any person who may reasonably be expected to use, consume or be affected by the goods and who is injured by breach of the warranty. A seller may not exclude or limit the operation of this section with respect to injury to the person of an individual to whom the warranty extends. As amended 1966.

Official Comment

Prior Uniform Statutory Provision: None.

Purposes:

1. The last sentence of this section does not mean that a seller is precluded from excluding or disclaiming a warranty which might otherwise arise in connection with the sale provided such exclusion or modification is permitted by Section 2—316. Nor does that sentence preclude the seller from limiting the remedies of his own buyer and of any beneficiaries, in any manner provided in Sections 2—718 or 2—719. To the extent that the contract of sale contains provisions under which warranties are excluded or modified, or remedies for breach are limited, such provisions are equally operative against beneficiaries of warranties under this section. What this last sentence forbids is exclusion of liability by the seller to the persons to whom the warranties which he has made to his buyer would extend under this section.

2. The purpose of this section is to give certain beneficiaries the benefit of the same warranty which the buyer received in the contract of sale, thereby freeing any such beneficiaries from any technical rules as to "privity." It seeks to accomplish this purpose without any derogation of any right or remedy resting on negligence. It rests primarily upon the merchant-seller's warranty under this Article that the goods sold are merchantable and fit for the ordinary purposes for which such goods are used rather than the warranty of fitness for a particular purpose. Implicit in the section is that any beneficiary of a warranty may bring a direct action for breach of warranty against the seller whose warranty extends to him [As amended in 1966].

3. The first alternative expressly includes as beneficiaries within its provisions the family, household and guests of the purchaser. Beyond this, the section in this form is neutral and is not intended to enlarge or restrict the developing case law on whether the seller's warranties, given to his buyer who resells, extend to other persons in the distributive chain.

The second alternative is designed for states where the case law has already developed further and for those that desire to expand the class of beneficiaries. The third alternative goes further, following the trend of modern decisions as indicated by Restatement of Torts 2d § 402A (Tentative Draft No. 10, 1965) in extending the rule beyond injuries to the person [As amended in 1966].

Cross References:

Point 1: Sections 2—316, 2—718 and 2—719.

Point 2: Section 2—314.

Definitional Cross References:

"Buyer". Section 2—103.

"Goods". Section 2—105.

"Seller". Section 2—103.

§ 2—319. F.O.B. and F.A.S. Terms

(1) Unless otherwise agreed the term F.O.B. (which means "free on board") at a named place, even though used only in connection with the stated price, is a delivery term under which

(a) when the term is F.O.B. the place of shipment, the seller must at that place ship the goods in the manner provided in this Article (Section 2—504) and bear the expense and risk of putting them into the possession of the carrier; or

(b) when the term is F.O.B. the place of destination, the seller must at his own expense and risk transport the goods to that place and there tender delivery of them in the manner provided in this Article (Section 2—503);

(c) when under either (a) or (b) the term is also F.O.B. vessel, car or other vehicle, the seller must in addition at his own expense and risk load the goods on board. If the term is F.O.B. vessel the buyer must name the vessel and in an appropriate case the seller must comply with the provisions of this Article on the form of bill of lading (Section 2—323).

(2) Unless otherwise agreed the term F.A.S. vessel (which means "free alongside") at a named port, even though used only in connection with the stated price, is a delivery term under which the seller must

(a) at his own expense and risk deliver the goods alongside the vessel in the manner usual in that port or on a dock designated and provided by the buyer; and

(b) obtain and tender a receipt for the goods in exchange for which the carrier is under a duty to issue a bill of lading.

(3) Unless otherwise agreed in any case falling within subsection (1) (a) or (c) or subsection (2) the buyer must seasonably give any needed instructions for making delivery, including when the term is F.A.S. or F.O.B. the loading berth of the vessel and in an appropriate case its name and sailing date. The seller may treat the failure of needed instructions as a failure of cooperation under this Article (Section 2—311). He may also at his option move the goods in any reasonable manner preparatory to delivery or shipment.

(4) Under the term F.O.B. vessel or F.A.S. unless otherwise agreed the buyer must make payment against tender of the required documents and the seller may not tender nor the buyer demand delivery of the goods in substitution for the documents.

Official Comment

Prior Uniform Statutory Provision: None.

Purposes:

1. This section is intended to negate the uncommercial line of decision which treats an "F.O.B." term as "merely a price term." The distinctions taken in subsection (1) handle most of the issues which have on occasion led to the unfortunate judicial language just referred to. Other matters which have led to sound results being based on unhappy language in regard to F.O.B. clauses are dealt with in this Act by Section 2—311(2) (seller's option re arrangements relating to shipment) and Sections 2—614 and 615 (substituted performance and seller's excuse).

2. Subsection (1) (c) not only specifies the duties of a seller who engages to deliver "F.O.B. vessel," or the like, but ought to make clear that no agreement is soundly drawn when it looks to reshipment from San Francisco or New York, but speaks merely of "F.O.B." the place.

3. The buyer's obligations stated in subsection (1) (c) and subsection (3) are, as shown in the text, obligations of cooperation. The last sentence of subsection (3) expressly, though perhaps unnecessarily, authorizes the seller, pending instructions, to go ahead with such preparatory moves as shipment from the interior to the named point of delivery. The sentence presupposes the usual case in which instructions "fail"; a prior repudiation by the buyer, giving notice that breach was intended, would remove the reason for the sentence, and would nor-

mally bring into play, instead, the second sentence of Section 2—704, which duly calls for lessening damages.

4. The treatment of "F.O.B. vessel" in conjunction with F.A. S. fits, in regard to the need for payment against documents, with standard practice and case-law; but "F.O.B. vessel" is a term which by its very language makes express the need for an "on board" document. In this respect, that term is stricter than the ordinary overseas "shipment" contract (C.I.F., etc., Section 2—320).

Cross References:

Sections 2—311(3), 2—323, 2—503 and 2—504.

Definitional Cross References:

"Agreed". Section 1—201.
"Bill of lading". Section 1—201.
"Buyer". Section 2—103.
"Goods". Section 2—105.
"Seasonably". Section 1—204.
"Seller". Section 2—103.
"Term". Section 1—201.

§ 2—320. C.I.F. and C. & F. Terms

(1) The term C.I.F. means that the price includes in a lump sum the cost of the goods and the insurance and freight to the named destination. The term C. & F. or C.F. means that the price so includes cost and freight to the named destination.

(2) Unless otherwise agreed and even though used only in connection with the stated price and destination, the term C.I.F. destination or its equivalent requires the seller at his own expense and risk to

(a) put the goods into the possession of a carrier at the port for shipment and obtain a negotiable bill or bills of lading covering the entire transportation to the named destination; and

(b) load the goods and obtain a receipt from the carrier (which may be contained in the bill of lading) showing that the freight has been paid or provided for; and

(c) obtain a policy or certificate of insurance, including any war risk insurance, of a kind and on terms then current at the port of shipment in the usual amount, in the currency of the contract, shown to cover the same goods covered by the bill of lading and providing for payment of loss to the order of the buyer or for the account of whom it may concern; but the seller may add to the price the amount of the premium for any such war risk insurance; and

(d) prepare an invoice of the goods and procure any other documents required to effect shipment or to comply with the contract; and

(e) forward and tender with commercial promptness all the documents in due form and with any indorsement necessary to perfect the buyer's rights.

(3) Unless otherwise agreed the term C. & F. or its equivalent has the same effect and imposes upon the seller the same obligations and risks as a C.I.F. term except the obligation as to insurance.

(4) Under the term C.I.F. or C. & F. unless otherwise agreed the buyer must make payment against tender of the required documents and the seller may not tender nor the buyer demand delivery of the goods in substitution for the documents.

Official Comment

Prior Uniform Statutory Provision: None.

Purposes: To make it clear that:

1. The C.I.F. contract is not a destination but a shipment contract with risk of subsequent loss or damage to the goods passing to the buyer upon shipment if the seller has properly performed all his obligations with respect to the goods. Delivery to the carrier is delivery to the buyer for purposes of risk and "title". Delivery of possession of the goods is accomplished by delivery of the bill of lading, and upon tender of the required documents the buyer must pay the agreed price without awaiting the arrival of the goods and if they have been lost or damaged after proper shipment he must seek his remedy against the carrier or insurer. The buyer has no right of inspection prior to payment or acceptance of the documents.

2. The seller's obligations remain the same even though the C.I.F. term is "used only in connection with the stated price and destination".

3. The insurance stipulated by the C.I.F. term is for the buyer's benefit, to protect him against the risk of loss or damage to the goods in transit. A clause in a C.I.F. contract "insurance—for the account of sellers" should be viewed in its ordinary mercantile meaning that the sellers must pay for the insurance and not that it is intended to run to the seller's benefit.

4. A bill of lading covering the entire transportation from the port of shipment is explicitly required but the provision on this point must be read in the light of its reason to assure the buyer of as full protection as the conditions of shipment reasonably permit, remembering always that this type of contract is designed to move the goods in the channels commercially available. To enable the buyer to deal with the goods while they are afloat the bill of lading must be one that covers only the quantity of goods called for by the

contract. The buyer is not required to accept his part of the goods without a bill of lading because the latter covers a larger quantity, nor is he required to accept a bill of lading for the whole quantity under a stipulation to hold the excess for the owner. Although the buyer is not compelled to accept either goods or documents under such circumstances he may of course claim his rights in any goods which have been identified to his contract.

5. The seller is given the option of paying or providing for the payment of freight. He has no option to ship "freight collect" unless the agreement so provides. The rule of the common law that the buyer need not pay the freight if the goods do not arrive is preserved.

Unless the shipment has been sent "freight collect" the buyer is entitled to receive documentary evidence that he is not obligated to pay the freight; the seller is therefore required to obtain a receipt "showing that the freight has been paid or provided for." The usual notation in the appropriate space on the bill of lading that the freight has been prepaid is a sufficient receipt, as at common law. The phrase "provided for" is intended to cover the frequent situation in which the carrier extends credit to a shipper for the freight on successive shipments and receives periodical payments of the accrued freight charges from him.

6. The requirement that unless otherwise agreed the seller must procure insurance "of a kind and on terms then current at the port for shipment in the usual amount, in the currency of the contract, sufficiently shown to cover the same goods covered by the bill of lading", applies to both marine and war risk insurance. As applied to marine insurance, it means such insurance as is usual or customary at the port for shipment with reference to the particular kind of goods involved, the character and equipment of the vessel, the route of the voyage, the port of destination and any other considerations that affect the risk. It is the substantial equivalent of the ordinary insurance in the particular trade and on the particular voyage and is subject to agreed specifications of type or extent of coverage. The language does not mean that the insurance must be adequate to cover all risks to which the goods may be subject in transit. There are some types of loss or damage that are not covered by the usual marine insurance and are excepted in bills of lading or in applicable statutes from the causes of loss or damage for which the carrier or the vessel is liable. Such risks must be borne by the buyer under this Article.

Insurance secured in compliance with a C.I.F. term must cover the entire transportation of the goods to the named destination.

7. An additional obligation is imposed upon the seller in requiring him to procure customary war risk insurance at the buyer's expense. This changes the common law on the point. The seller is not required to assume the risk of including in the C.I.F. price the cost of such insurance, since it often fluctuates

rapidly, but is required to treat it simply as a necessary for the buyer's account. What war risk insurance is "current" or usual turns on the standard forms of policy or rider in common use.

8. The C.I.F. contract calls for insurance covering the value of the goods at the time and place of shipment and does not include any increase in market value during transit or any anticipated profit to the buyer on a sale by him.

The contract contemplates that before the goods arrive at their destination they may be sold again and again on C.I.F. terms and that the original policy of insurance and bill of lading will run with the interest in the goods by being transferred to each successive buyer. A buyer who becomes the seller in such an intermediate contract for sale does not thereby, if his sub-buyer knows the circumstances, undertake to insure the goods again at an increased price fixed in the new contract or to cover the increase in price by additional insurance, and his buyer may not reject the documents on the ground that the original policy does not cover such higher price. If such a sub-buyer desires additional insurance he must procure it for himself.

Where the seller exercises an option to ship "freight collect" and to credit the buyer with the freight against the C.I.F. price, the insurance need not cover the freight since the freight is not at the buyer's risk. On the other hand, where the seller prepays the freight upon shipping under a bill of lading requiring prepayment and providing that the freight shall be deemed earned and shall be retained by the carrier "ship and/or cargo lost or not lost," or using words of similar import, he must procure insurance that will cover the freight, because notwithstanding that the goods are lost in transit the buyer is bound to pay the freight as part of the C. I.F. price and will be unable to recover it back from the carrier.

9. Insurance "for the account of whom it may concern" is usual and sufficient. However, for a valid tender the policy of insurance must be one which can be disposed of together with the bill of lading and so must be "sufficiently shown to cover the same goods covered by the bill of lading". It must cover separately the quantity of goods called for by the buyer's contract and not merely insure his goods as part of a larger quantity in which others are interested, a case provided for in American mercantile practice by the use of negotiable certificates of insurance which are expressly authorized by this section. By usage these certificates are treated as the equivalent of separate policies and are good tender under C.I.F. contracts. The term "certificate of insurance", however, does not of itself include certificates or "cover notes" issued by the insurance broker and stating that the goods are covered by a policy. Their sufficiency as substitutes for policies will depend upon proof of an established usage or course of dealing. The present section rejects the English rule that not only brokers' certificates and "cover notes" but also certain forms of American insurance certificates are not

the equivalent of policies and are not good tender under a C.I. F. contract.

The seller's failure to tender a proper insurance document is waived if the buyer refuses to make payment on other and untenable grounds at a time when proper insurance could have been obtained and tendered by the seller if timely objection had been made. Even a failure to insure on shipment may be cured by seasonable tender of a policy retroactive in effect; e. g., one insuring the goods "lost or not lost." The provisions of this Article on cure of improper tender and on waiver of buyer's objections by silence are applicable to insurance tenders under a C.I.F. term. Where there is no waiver by the buyer as described above, however, the fact that the goods arrive safely does not cure the seller's breach of his obligations to insure them and tender to the buyer a proper insurance document.

10. The seller's invoice of the goods shipped under a C.I.F. contract is regarded as a usual and necessary document upon which reliance may properly be placed. It is the document which evidences points of description, quality and the like which do not readily appear in other documents. This Article rejects those statements to the effect that the invoice is a usual but not a necessary document under a C.I.F. term.

11. The buyer needs all of the documents required under a C. I.F. contract, in due form and with necessary endorsements, so that before the goods arrive he may deal with them by negotiating the documents or may obtain prompt possession of the goods after their arrival. If the goods are lost or damaged in transit the documents are necessary to enable him promptly to assert his remedy against the carrier or insurer. The seller is therefore obligated to do what is mercantilely reasonable in the circumstances and should make every reasonable exertion to send forward the documents as soon as possible after the shipment. The requirement that the documents be forwarded with "commercial promptness" expresses a more urgent need for action than that suggested by the phrase "reasonable time".

12. Under a C.I.F. contract the buyer, as under the common law, must pay the price upon tender of the required documents without first inspecting the goods, but his payment in these circumstances does not constitute an acceptance of the goods nor does it impair his right of subsequent inspection or his options and remedies in the case of improper delivery. All remedies and rights for the seller's breach are reserved to him. The buyer must pay before inspection and assert his remedy against the seller afterward unless the nonconformity of the goods amounts to a real failure of consideration, since the purpose of choosing this form of contract is to give the seller protection against the buyer's unjustifiable rejection of the goods at a distant port of destination which would necessitate taking possession of the goods and suing the buyer there.

13. A valid C.I.F. contract may be made which requires

part of the transportation to be made on land and part on the sea, as where the goods are to be brought by rail from an inland point to a seaport and thence transported by vessel to the named destination under a "through" or combination bill of lading issued by the railroad company. In such a case shipment by rail from the inland point within the contract period is a timely shipment notwithstanding that the loading of the goods on the vessel is delayed by causes beyond the seller's control.

14. Although subsection (2) stating the legal effects of the C.I.F. term is an "unless otherwise agreed" provision, the express language used in an agreement is frequently a precautionary, fuller statement of the normal C.I.F. terms and hence not intended as a departure or variation from them. Moreover, the dominant outlines of the C.I.F. term are so well understood commercially that any variation should, whenever reasonably possible, be read as falling within those dominant outlines rather than as destroying the whole meaning of a term which essentially indicates a contract for proper shipment rather than one for delivery at destination. Particularly careful consideration is necessary before a printed form or clause is construed to mean agreement otherwise and where a C.I.F. contract is prepared on a printed form designed for some other type of contract, the C.I.F. terms must prevail over printed clauses repugnant to them.

15. Under subsection (4) the fact that the seller knows at the time of the tender of the documents that the goods have been lost in transit does not affect his rights if he has performed his contractual obligations. Similarly, the seller cannot perform under a C.I.F. term by purchasing and tendering landed goods.

16. Under the C. & F. term, as under the C.I.F. term, title and risk of loss are intended to pass to the buyer on shipment. A stipulation in a C. & F. contract that the seller shall effect insurance on the goods and charge the buyer with the premium (in effect that he shall act as the buyer's agent for that purpose) is entirely in keeping with the pattern. On the other hand, it often happens that the buyer is in a more advantageous position than the seller to effect insurance on the goods or that he has in force an "open" or "floating" policy covering all shipments made by him or to him, in either of which events the C. & F. term is adequate without mention of insurance.

17. It is to be remembered that in a French contract the term "C.A.F." does not mean "Cost and Freight" but has exactly the same meaning as the term "C.I.F." since it is merely the French equivalent of that term. The "A" does not stand for "and" but for "assurance" which means insurance.

Cross References:

Point 4: Section 2—323.

Point 6: Section 2—509(1) (a).

Point 9: Sections 2—508 and 2—605(1) (a).

Point 12: Sections 2—321(3), 2—512 and 2—513(3) and Article 5.

Definitional Cross References:
"Bill of lading". Section 1—201.
"Buyer". Section 2—103.
"Contract". Section 1—201.
"Goods". Section 2—105.
"Rights". Section 1—201.
"Seller". Section 2—103.
"Term". Section 1—201.

§ 2—321. C.I.F. or C. & F.: "Net Landed Weights"; "Payment on Arrival"; Warranty of Condition on Arrival

Under a contract containing a term C.I.F. or C. & F.

(1) Where the price is based on or is to be adjusted according to "net landed weights", "delivered weights", "out turn" quantity or quality or the like, unless otherwise agreed the seller must reasonably estimate the price. The payment due on tender of the documents called for by the contract is the amount so estimated, but after final adjustment of the price a settlement must be made with commercial promptness.

(2) An agreement described in subsection (1) or any warranty of quality or condition of the goods on arrival places upon the seller the risk of ordinary deterioration, shrinkage and the like in transportation but has no effect on the place or time of identification to the contract for sale or delivery or on the passing of the risk of loss.

(3) Unless otherwise agreed where the contract provides for payment on or after arrival of the goods the seller must before payment allow such preliminary inspection as is feasible; but if the goods are lost delivery of the documents and payment are due when the goods should have arrived.

Official Comment

Prior Uniform Statutory Provision: None.

Purposes:

This section deals with two variations of the C.I.F. contract which have evolved in mercantile practice but are entirely consistent with the basic C.I.F. pattern. Subsections (1) and (2), which provide for a shift to the seller of the risk of quality and weight deterioration during shipment, are designed to conform the law to the best mercantile practice and usage without changing the legal consequences of the C.I.F. or C. & F. term as to the passing of marine risks to the buyer at the point of shipment. Subsection (3) provides that where under the contract documents are to be presented for payment after arrival of the goods, this amounts merely to a postponement of the payment under the C.I.F. contract and is not to be confused with the "no arrival, no sale" contract. If the goods are lost, delivery of the documents and payment against them are due when the goods should have arrived. The clause for payment on or after arrival is not to be construed as such a condition precedent to payment that if the goods are lost in transit the buyer need never pay and the seller must bear the loss.

Cross Reference:

Section 2—324.

Definitional Cross References:

"Agreement". Section 1—201.
"Contract". Section 1—201.
"Delivery". Section 1—201.
"Goods". Section 2—105.
"Seller". Section 2—103.
"Term". Section 1—201.

§ 2—322. Delivery "Ex-Ship"

(1) Unless otherwise agreed a term for delivery of goods "ex-ship" (which means from the carrying vessel) or in equivalent language is not restricted to a particular ship and requires delivery from a ship which has reached a place at the named port of destination where goods of the kind are usually discharged.

(2) Under such a term unless otherwise agreed

(a) the seller must discharge all liens arising out of the carriage and furnish the buyer with a direction which puts the carrier under a duty to deliver the goods; and

(b) the risk of loss does not pass to the buyer until the goods leave the ship's tackle or are otherwise properly unloaded.

Official Comment

Prior Uniform Statutory Provision: None.

Purposes:

1. The delivery term, "ex-ship", as between seller and buyer, is the reverse of the f. a. s. term covered.

2. Delivery need not be made from any particular vessel under a clause calling for delivery "ex-ship", even though a vessel on which shipment is to be made originally is named in the contract, unless the agreement by appropriate language, restricts the clause to delivery from a named vessel.

3. The appropriate place and manner of unloading at the port of destination depend upon the nature of the goods and the facilities and usages of the port.

4. A contract fixing a price "ex-ship" with payment "cash against documents" calls only for such documents as are appropriate to the contract. Tender of a delivery order and of a receipt for the freight after the arrival of the carrying vessel is adequate. The seller is not required to tender a bill of lading as a document of title nor is he required to insure the goods for the buyer's benefit, as the goods

are not at the buyer's risk during the voyage.

Cross Reference:

Point 1: Section 2—319(2).

Definitional Cross References:

"Buyer". Section 2—103.
"Goods". Section 2—105.
"Seller". Section 2—103.
"Term". Section 1—201.

§ 2—323. Form of Bill of Lading Required in Overseas Shipment; "Overseas"

(1) Where the contract contemplates overseas shipment and contains a term C.I.F. or C. & F. or F.O.B. vessel, the seller unless otherwise agreed must obtain a negotiable bill of lading stating that the goods have been loaded on board or, in the case of a term C.I.F. or C. & F., received for shipment.

(2) Where in a case within subsection (1) a bill of lading has been issued in a set of parts, unless otherwise agreed if the documents are not to be sent from abroad the buyer may demand tender of the full set; otherwise only one part of the bill of lading need be tendered. Even if the agreement expressly requires a full set

(a) due tender of a single part is acceptable within the provisions of this Article on cure of improper delivery (subsection (1) of Section 2—508); and

(b) even though the full set is demanded, if the documents are sent from abroad the person tendering an incomplete set may nevertheless require payment upon furnishing an indemnity which the buyer in good faith deems adequate.

(3) A shipment by water or by air or a contract contemplating such shipment is "overseas" insofar as by usage of trade or agreement it is subject to the commercial, financing or shipping practices characteristic of international deep water commerce.

Official Comment

Prior Uniform Statutory Provision: None.

Purposes:

1. Subsection (1) follows the "American" rule that a regular bill of lading indicating delivery of the goods at the dock for shipment is sufficient, except under a term "F.O.B. vessel." See Section 2—319 and comment thereto.

2. Subsection (2) deals with the problem of bills of lading covering deep water shipments, issued not as a single bill of lading but in a set of parts, each part referring to the other parts and the entire set constituting in commercial practice and at law a single bill of lading. Commercial practice in international commerce is to accept and pay against presentation of the first

part of a set if the part is sent from overseas even though the contract of the buyer requires presentation of a full set of bills of lading provided adequate indemnity for the missing parts is forthcoming.

This subsection codifies that practice as between buyer and seller. Article 5 (Section 5—113) authorizes banks presenting drafts under letters of credit to give indemnities against the missing parts, and this subsection means that the buyer must accept and act on such indemnities if he in good faith deems them adequate. But neither this subsection nor Article 5 decides whether a bank which has issued a letter of credit is similarly bound. The issuing bank's obligation under a letter of credit is independent and depends on its own terms. See Article 5.

Cross References:

Sections 2—508(2), 5—113.

Definitional Cross References:

"Bill of lading". Section 1—201.
"Buyer". Section 2—103.
"Contract". Section 1—201.
"Delivery". Section 1—201.
"Financing agency". Section 2—104.
"Person". Section 1—201.
"Seller". Section 2—103.
"Send". Section 1—201.
"Term". Section 1—201.

§ 2—324. "No Arrival, No Sale" Term

Under a term "no arrival, no sale" or terms of like meaning, unless otherwise agreed,

(a) the seller must properly ship conforming goods and if they arrive by any means he must tender them on arrival but he assumes no obligation that the goods will arrive unless he has caused the non-arrival; and

(b) where without fault of the seller the goods are in part lost or have so deteriorated as no longer to conform to the contract or arrive after the contract time, the buyer may proceed as if there had been casualty to identified goods (Section 2—613).

Official Comment

Prior Uniform Statutory Provision: None.

Purposes:

1. The "no arrival, no sale" term in a "destination" overseas contract leaves risk of loss on the seller but gives him an exemption from liability for non-delivery. Both the nature of the case and the duty of good faith require that the seller must not interfere with the arrival of the goods in any way. If the circumstances impose upon him the responsibility for making or arranging the shipment, he must have a shipment made despite the exemption clause. Further, the shipment made must be a conforming one, for the exemption under a "no arrival, no sale" term applies only to the hazards of transportation and the goods

must be proper in all other respects.

The reason of this section is that where the seller is reselling goods bought by him as shipped by another and this fact is known to the buyer, so that the seller is not under any obligation to make the shipment himself, the seller is entitled under the "no arrival, no sale" clause to exemption from payment of damages for non-delivery if the goods do not arrive or if the goods which actually arrive are non-conforming. This does not extend to sellers who arrange shipment by their own agents, in which case the clause is limited to casualty due to marine hazards. But sellers who make known that they are contracting only with respect to what will be delivered to them by parties over whom they assume no control are entitled to the full quantum of the exemption.

2. The provisions of this Article on identification must be read together with the present section in order to bring the exemption into application. Until there is some designation of the goods in a particular shipment or on a particular ship as being those to which the contract refers there can be no application of an exemption for their non-arrival.

3. The seller's duty to tender the agreed or declared goods if they do arrive is not impaired because of their delay in arrival or by their arrival after transshipment.

4. The phrase "to arrive" is often employed in the same sense as "no arrival, no sale" and may then be given the same effect. But a "to arrive" term, added to a C.I.F. or C. & F. contract, does not have the full meaning given by this section to "no arrival, no sale". Such a "to arrive" term is usually intended to operate only to the extent that the risks are not covered by the agreed insurance and the loss or casualty is due to such uncovered hazards. In some instances the "to arrive" term may be regarded as a time of payment term, or, in the case of the reselling seller discussed in point 1 above, as negating responsibility for conformity of the goods, if they arrive, to any description which was based on his good faith belief of the quality. Whether this is the intention of the parties is a question of fact based on all the circumstances surrounding the resale and in case of ambiguity the rules of Sections 2—316 and 2—317 apply to preclude dishonor.

5. Paragraph (b) applies where goods arrive impaired by damage or partial loss during transportation and makes the policy of this Article on casualty to identified goods applicable to such a situation. For the term cannot be regarded as intending to give the seller an unforeseen profit through casualty; it is intended only to protect him from loss due to causes beyond his control.

Cross References:

Point 1: Section 1—203.

Point 2: Section 2—501(a) and (c).

Point 5: Section 2—613.

Definitional Cross References:

"Buyer". Section 2—103.

"Conforming". Section 2—106.

"Contract". Section 1—201.
"Fault". Section 1—201.
"Goods". Section 2—105.
"Sale". Section 2—106.
"Seller". Section 2—103.
"Term". Section 1—201.

§ 2—325. "Letter of Credit" Term; "Confirmed Credit"

(1) Failure of the buyer seasonably to furnish an agreed letter of credit is a breach of the contract for sale.

(2) The delivery to seller of a proper letter of credit suspends the buyer's obligation to pay. If the letter of credit is dishonored, the seller may on seasonable notification to the buyer require payment directly from him.

(3) Unless otherwise agreed the term "letter of credit" or "banker's credit" in a contract for sale means an irrevocable credit issued by a financing agency of good repute and, where the shipment is overseas, of good international repute. The term "confirmed credit" means that the credit must also carry the direct obligation of such an agency which does business in the seller's financial market.

Official Comment

Prior Uniform Statutory Provision: None.

Purposes: To express the established commercial and banking understanding as to the meaning and effects of terms calling for "letters of credit" or "confirmed credit":

1. Subsection (2) follows the general policy of this Article and Article 3 (Section 3—802) on conditional payment, under which payment by check or other short-term instrument is not ordinarily final as between the parties if the recipient duly presents the instrument and honor is refused. Thus the furnishing of a letter of credit does not substitute the financing agency's obligation for the buyer's, but the seller must first give the buyer reasonable notice of his intention to demand direct payment from him.

2. Subsection (3) requires that the credit be irrevocable and be a prime credit as determined by the standing of the issuer. It is not necessary, unless otherwise agreed, that the credit be a negotiation credit; the seller can finance himself by an assignment of the proceeds under Section 5—116(2).

3. The definition of "confirmed credit" is drawn on the supposition that the credit is issued by a bank which is not doing direct business in the seller's financial market; there is no intention to require the obligation of two banks both local to the seller.

Cross References:

Sections 2—403, 2—511(3) and 3—802 and Article 5.

Definitional Cross References:

"Buyer". Section 2—103.

"Contract for sale". Section 2—106.

"Draft". Section 3—104.

"Financing agency". Section 2—104.

"Notifies". Section 1—201.
"Overseas". Section 2—323.
"Purchaser". Section 1—201.
"Seasonably". Section 1—204.
"Seller". Section 2—103.
"Term". Section 1—201.

§ 2—326. Sale on Approval and Sale or Return; Consignment Sales and Rights of Creditors

(1) Unless otherwise agreed, if delivered goods may be returned by the buyer even though they conform to the contract, the transaction is

(a) a "sale on approval" if the goods are delivered primarily for use, and

(b) a "sale or return" if the goods are delivered primarily for resale.

(2) Except as provided in subsection (3), goods held on approval are not subject to the claims of the buyer's creditors until acceptance; goods held on sale or return are subject to such claims while in the buyer's possession.

(3) Where goods are delivered to a person for sale and such person maintains a place of business at which he deals in goods of the kind involved, under a name other than the name of the person making delivery, then with respect to claims of creditors of the person conducting the business the goods are deemed to be on sale or return. The provisions of this subsection are applicable even though an agreement purports to reserve title to the person making delivery until payment or resale or uses such words as "on consignment" or "on memorandum". However, this subsection is not applicable if the person making delivery

(a) complies with an applicable law providing for a consignor's interest or the like to be evidenced by a sign, or

(b) establishes that the person conducting the business is generally known by his creditors to be substantially engaged in selling the goods of others, or

(c) complies with the filing provisions of the Article on Secured Transactions (Article 9).

(4) Any "or return" term of a contract for sale is to be treated as a separate contract for sale within the statute of frauds section of this Article (Section 2—201) and as contradicting the sale aspect of the contract within the provisions of this Article on parol or extrinsic evidence (Section 2—202).

Official Comment

Prior Uniform Statutory Provision: Section 19(3), Uniform Sales Act.

Changes: Completely rewritten in this and the succeeding section.

Purposes of Changes: To make it clear that:

1. A "sale on approval" or "sale or return" is distinct from other types of transactions with which they have frequently been confused. The type of "sale on approval," "on trial" or "on satisfaction" dealt with involves a contract under which the seller undertakes a particular business risk to satisfy his prospective buyer with the appearance or performance of the goods in question. The goods are delivered to the proposed purchaser but they remain the property of the seller until the buyer accepts them. The price has already been agreed. The buyer's willingness to receive and test the goods is the consideration for the seller's engagement to deliver and sell. The type of "sale or return" involved herein is a sale to a merchant whose unwillingness to buy is overcome only by the seller's engagement to take back the goods (or any commercial unit of goods) in lieu of payment if they fail to be resold. These two transactions are so strongly delineated in practice and in general understanding that every presumption runs against a delivery to a consumer being a "sale or return" and against a delivery to a merchant for resale being a "sale on approval."

The right to return the goods for failure to conform to the contract does not make the transaction a "sale on approval" or "sale or return" and has nothing to do with this and the following section. The present section is not concerned with remedies for breach of contract. It deals instead with a power given by the contract to turn back the goods even though they are wholly as warranted.

This section nevertheless presupposes that a contract for sale is contemplated by the parties although that contract may be of the peculiar character here described.

Where the buyer's obligation as a buyer is conditioned not on his personal approval but on the article's passing a described objective test, the risk of loss by casualty pending the test is properly the seller's and proper return is at his expense. On the point of "satisfaction" as meaning "reasonable satisfaction" where an industrial machine is involved, this Article takes no position.

2. Pursuant to the general policies of this Act which require good faith not only between the parties to the sales contract, but as against interested third parties, subsection (3) resolves all reasonable doubts as to the nature of the transaction in favor of the general creditors of the buyer. As against such creditors words such as "on consignment" or "on memorandum", with or without words of reservation of title in the seller, are disregarded when the buyer has a place of business at which he deals in goods of the kind involved. A necessary exception is made where the buyer is known to be engaged primarily in selling the goods of others or is selling under a relevant sign law, or the seller complies with the filing provisions of Article 9 as if his interest were a security interest. However, there is no intent in this Section to narrow the

protection afforded to third parties in any jurisdiction which has a selling Factors Act. The purpose of the exception is merely to limit the effect of the present subsection itself, in the absence of any such Factors Act, to cases in which creditors of the buyer may reasonably be deemed to have been misled by the secret reservation.

3. Subsection (4) resolves a conflict in the pre-existing case law by recognition that an "or return" provision is so definitely at odds with any ordinary contract for sale of goods that where written agreements are involved it must be contained in a written memorandum. The "or return" aspect of a sales contract must be treated as a separate contract under the Statute of Frauds section and as contradicting the sale insofar as questions of parol or extrinsic evidence are concerned.

Cross References:

Point 2: Article 9.

Point 3: Sections 2—201 and 2—202.

Definitional Cross References:

"Between merchants". Section 2—104.

"Buyer". Section 2—103.

"Conform". Section 2—106.

"Contract for sale". Section 2—106.

"Creditor". Section 1—201.

"Goods". Section 2—105.

"Sale". Section 2—106.

"Seller". Section 2—103.

§ 2—327. Special Incidents of Sale on Approval and Sale or Return

(1) Under a sale on approval unless otherwise agreed

(a) although the goods are identified to the contract the risk of loss and the title do not pass to the buyer until acceptance; and

(b) use of the goods consistent with the purpose of trial is not acceptance but failure seasonably to notify the seller of election to return the goods is acceptance, and if the goods conform to the contract acceptance of any part is acceptance of the whole; and

(c) after due notification of election to return, the return is at the seller's risk and expense but a merchant buyer must follow any reasonable instructions.

(2) Under a sale or return unless otherwise agreed

(a) the option to return extends to the whole or any commercial unit of the goods while in substantially their original condition, but must be exercised seasonably; and

(b) the return is at the buyer's risk and expense.

Official Comment

Prior Uniform Statutory Provision: Section 19(3), Uniform Sales Act.

Changes: Completely rewritten in preceding and this section.

Purposes of Changes: To make it clear that:

1. In the case of a sale on approval:

If all of the goods involved conform to the contract, the buyer's acceptance of part of the goods constitutes acceptance of the whole. Acceptance of part falls outside the normal intent of the parties in the "on approval" situation and the policy of this Article allowing partial acceptance of a defective delivery has no application here. A case where a buyer takes home two dresses to select one commonly involves two distinct contracts; if not, it is covered by the words "unless otherwise agreed".

2. In the case of a sale or return, the return of any unsold unit merely because it is unsold is the normal intent of the "sale or return" provision, and therefore the right to return for this reason alone is independent of any other action under the contract which would turn on wholly different considerations. On the other hand, where the return of goods is for breach, including return of items resold by the buyer and returned by the ultimate purchasers because of defects, the return procedure is governed not by the present section but by the provisions on the effects and revocation of acceptance.

3. In the case of a sale on approval the risk rests on the seller until acceptance of the goods by the buyer, while in a sale or return the risk remains throughout on the buyer.

4. Notice of election to return given by the buyer in a sale on approval is sufficient to relieve him of any further liability. Actual return by the buyer to the seller is required in the case of a sale or return contract. What constitutes due "giving" of notice, as required in "on approval" sales, is governed by the provisions on good faith and notice. "Seasonable" is used here as defined in Section 1—204. Nevertheless, the provisions of both this Article and of the contract on this point must be read with commercial reason and with full attention to good faith.

Cross References:

Point 1: Sections 2—501, 2—601 and 2—603.

Point 2: Sections 2—607 and 2—608.

Point 4: Sections 1—201 and 1—204.

Definitional Cross References:

"Agreed". Section 1—201.

"Buyer". Section 2—103.

"Commercial unit". Section 2—105.

"Conform". Section 2—106.

"Contract". Section 1—201.

"Goods". Section 2—105.

"Merchant". Section 2—104.

"Notifies". Section 1—201.

"Notification". Section 1—201.

"Sale on approval". Section 2—326.

"Sale or return". Section 2—326.

"Seasonably". Section 1—204.

"Seller". Section 2—103.

§ 2—328. Sale by Auction

(1) In a sale by auction if goods are put up in lots each lot is the subject of a separate sale.

(2) A sale by auction is complete when the auctioneer so announces by the fall of the hammer or in other customary manner. Where a bid is made while the hammer is falling in acceptance of a prior bid the auctioneer may in his discretion reopen the bidding or declare the goods sold under the bid on which the hammer was falling.

(3) Such a sale is with reserve unless the goods are in explicit terms put up without reserve. In an auction with reserve the auctioneer may withdraw the goods at any time until he announces completion of the sale. In an auction without reserve, after the auctioneer calls for bids on an article or lot, that article or lot cannot be withdrawn unless no bid is made within a reasonable time. In either case a bidder may retract his bid until the auctioneer's announcement of completion of the sale, but a bidder's retraction does not revive any previous bid.

(4) If the auctioneer knowingly receives a bid on the seller's behalf or the seller makes or procures such a bid, and notice has not been given that liberty for such bidding is reserved, the buyer may at his option avoid the sale or take the goods at the price of the last good faith bid prior to the completion of the sale. This subsection shall not apply to any bid at a forced sale.

Official Comment

Prior Uniform Statutory Provision: Section 21, Uniform Sales Act.

Changes: Completely rewritten.

Purposes of Changes: To make it clear that:

1. The auctioneer may in his discretion either reopen the bidding or close the sale on the bid on which the hammer was falling when a bid is made at that moment. The recognition of a bid of this kind by the auctioneer in his discretion does not mean a closing in favor of such a bidder, but only that the bid has been accepted as a continuation of the bidding. If recognized, such a bid discharges the bid on which the hammer was falling when it was made.

2. An auction "with reserve" is the normal procedure. The crucial point, however, for determining the nature of an auction is the "putting up" of the goods. This Article accepts the view that the goods may be withdrawn before they are actually "put up," regardless of whether the auction is advertised as one without reserve, without liability on the part of the auction announcer to persons who are present. This is subject to any peculiar facts which might bring the case within the "firm offer" principle of this Article, but an offer

to persons generally would require unmistakable language in order to fall within that section. The prior announcement of the nature of the auction either as with reserve or without reserve will, however, enter as an "explicit term" in the "putting up" of the goods and conduct thereafter must be governed accordingly. The present section continues the prior rule permitting withdrawal of bids in auctions both with and without reserve; and the rule is made explicit that the retraction of a bid does not revive a prior bid.

Cross Reference:

Point 2: Section 2—205.

Definitional Cross References:

"Buyer". Section 2—103.
"Good faith". Section 1—201.
"Goods". Section 2—105.
"Lot". Section 2—105.
"Notice". Section 1—201.
"Sale". Section 2—106.
"Seller". Section 2—103.

PART 4

TITLE, CREDITORS AND GOOD FAITH PURCHASERS

§ 2—401. Passing of Title; Reservation for Security; Limited Application of This Section

Each provision of this Article with regard to the rights, obligations and remedies of the seller, the buyer, purchasers or other third parties applies irrespective of title to the goods except where the provision refers to such title. Insofar as situations are not covered by the other provisions of this Article and matters concerning title become material the following rules apply:

(1) Title to goods cannot pass under a contract for sale prior to their identification to the contract (Section 2—501), and unless otherwise explicitly agreed the buyer acquires by their identification a special property as limited by this Act. Any retention or reservation by the seller of the title (property) in goods shipped or delivered to the buyer is limited in effect to a reservation of a security interest. Subject to these provisions and to the provisions of the Article on Secured Transactions (Article 9), title to goods passes from the seller to the buyer in any manner and on any conditions explicitly agreed on by the parties.

(2) Unless otherwise explicitly agreed title passes to the buyer at the time and place at which the seller completes his performance with reference to the physical delivery of the goods, despite any reservation of a security interest and even though a document of title is to be delivered at a different time or place;

and in particular and despite any reservation of a security interest by the bill of lading

(a) if the contract requires or authorizes the seller to send the goods to the buyer but does not require him to deliver them at destination, title passes to the buyer at the time and place of shipment; but

(b) if the contract requires delivery at destination, title passes on tender there.

(3) Unless otherwise explicitly agreed where delivery is to be made without moving the goods,

(a) if the seller is to deliver a document of title, title passes at the time when and the place where he delivers such documents; or

(b) if the goods are at the time of contracting already identified and no documents are to be delivered, title passes at the time and place of contracting.

(4) A rejection or other refusal by the buyer to receive or retain the goods, whether or not justified, or a justified revocation of acceptance revests title to the goods in the seller. Such revesting occurs by operation of law and is not a "sale".

Official Comment

Prior Uniform Statutory Provision: See generally, Sections 17, 18, 19 and 20, Uniform Sales Act.

Purposes: To make it clear that:

1. This Article deals with the issues between seller and buyer in terms of step by step performance or non-performance under the contract for sale and not in terms of whether or not "title" to the goods has passed. That the rules of this section in no way alter the rights of either the buyer, seller or third parties declared elsewhere in the Article is made clear by the preamble of this section. This section, however, in no way intends to indicate which line of interpretation should be followed in cases where the applicability of "public" regulation depends upon a "sale" or upon location of "title" without further definition. The basic policy of this Article that known purpose and reason should govern interpretation cannot extend beyond the scope of its own provisions. It is therefore necessary to state what a "sale" is and when title passes under this Article in case the courts deem any public regulation to incorporate the defined term of the "private" law.

2. "Future" goods cannot be the subject of a present sale. Before title can pass the goods must be identified in the manner set forth in Section 2—501. The parties, however, have full liberty to arrange by specific terms for the passing of title to goods which are existing.

3. The "special property" of the buyer in goods identified to the contract is excluded from the

definition of "security interest"; its incidents are defined in provisions of this Article such as those on the rights of the seller's creditors, on good faith purchase, on the buyer's right to goods on the seller's insolvency, and on the buyer's right to specific performance or replevin.

4. The factual situations in subsections (2) and (3) upon which passage of title turn actually base the test upon the time when the seller has finally committed himself in regard to specific goods. Thus in a "shipment" contract he commits himself by the act of making the shipment. If shipment is not contemplated subsection (3) turns on the seller's final commitment, i. e. the delivery of documents or the making of the contract.

Cross References:

Point 2: Sections 2—102, 2—501 and 2—502.

Point 3: Sections 1—201, 2—402, 2—403, 2—502 and 2—716.

Definitional Cross References:

"Agreement". Section 1—201.
"Bill of lading". Section 1—201.
"Buyer". Section 2—103.
"Contract". Section 1—201.
"Contract for sale". Section 2—106.
"Delivery". Section 1—201.
"Document of title". Section 1—201.
"Good faith". Section 2—103.
"Goods". Section 2—105.
"Party". Section 1—201.
"Purchaser". Section 1—201.
"Receipt" of goods. Section 2—103.
"Remedy". Section 1—201.
"Rights". Section 1—201.
"Sale". Section 2—106.
"Security interest". Section 1—201.
"Seller". Section 2—103.
"Send". Section 1—201.

§ 2—402. Rights of Seller's Creditors Against Sold Goods

(1) Except as provided in subsections (2) and (3), rights of unsecured creditors of the seller with respect to goods which have been identified to a contract for sale are subject to the buyer's rights to recover the goods under this Article (Sections 2—502 and 2—716).

(2) A creditor of the seller may treat a sale or an identification of goods to a contract for sale as void if as against him a retention of possession by the seller is fraudulent under any rule of law of the state where the goods are situated, except that retention of possession in good faith and current course of trade by a merchant-seller for a commercially reasonable time after a sale or identification is not fraudulent.

(3) Nothing in this Article shall be deemed to impair the rights of creditors of the seller

(a) under the provisions of the Article on Secured Transactions (Article 9); or

(b) where identification to the contract or delivery is made not in current course of trade but in satisfaction of or as security for a pre-existing claim for money, security or the like and is made under circumstances which under any rule of law of the state where the goods are situated would apart from this Article constitute the transaction a fraudulent transfer or voidable preference.

Official Comment

Prior Uniform Statutory Provision: Subsection (2)—Section 26, Uniform Sales Act; Subsections (1) and (3)—none.

Changes: Rephrased.

Purposes of Changes and New Matter: To avoid confusion on ordinary issues between current sellers and buyers and issues in the field of preference and hindrance by making it clear that:

1. Local law on questions of hindrance of creditors by the seller's retention of possession of the goods are outside the scope of this Article, but retention of possession in the current course of trade is legitimate. Transactions which fall within the law's policy against improper preferences are reserved from the protection of this Article.

2. The retention of possession of the goods by a merchant seller for a commercially reasonable time after a sale or identification in current course is exempted from attack as fraudulent. Similarly, the provisions of subsection (3) have no application to identification or delivery made in the current course of trade, as measured against general commercial understanding of what a "current" transaction is.

Definitional Cross References:

"Contract for sale". Section 2—106.
"Creditor". Section 1—201.
"Good faith". Section 2—103.
"Goods". Section 2—105.
"Merchant". Section 2—104.
"Money". Section 1—201.
"Reasonable time". Section 1—204.
"Rights". Section 1—201.
"Sale". Section 2—106.
"Seller". Section 2—103.

§ 2—403. Power to Transfer; Good Faith Purchase of Goods; "Entrusting"

(1) A purchaser of goods acquires all title which his transferor had or had power to transfer except that a purchaser of a limited interest acquires rights only to the extent of the interest purchased. A person with voidable title has power to transfer a good title to a good faith purchaser for value. When goods have been delivered under a transaction of purchase the purchaser has such power even though

(a) the transferor was deceived as to the identity of the purchaser, or

(b) the delivery was in exchange for a check which is later dishonored, or

(c) it was agreed that the transaction was to be a "cash sale", or

(d) the delivery was procured through fraud punishable as larcenous under the criminal law.

(2) Any entrusting of possession of goods to a merchant who deals in goods of that kind gives him power to transfer all rights of the entruster to a buyer in ordinary course of business.

(3) "Entrusting" includes any delivery and any acquiescence in retention of possession regardless of any condition expressed between the parties to the delivery or acquiescence and regardless of whether the procurement of the entrusting or the possessor's disposition of the goods have been such as to be larcenous under the criminal law.

(4) The rights of other purchasers of goods and of lien creditors are governed by the Articles on Secured Transactions (Article 9), Bulk Transfers (Article 6) and Documents of Title (Article 7).

Official Comment

Prior Uniform Statutory Provision: Sections 20(4), 23, 24, 25, Uniform Sales Act; Section 9, especially 9(2), Uniform Trust Receipts Act; Section 9, Uniform Conditional Sales Act.

Changes: Consolidated and rewritten.

Purposes of Changes: To gather together a series of prior uniform statutory provisions and the case-law thereunder and to state a unified and simplified policy on good faith purchase of goods.

1. The basic policy of our law allowing transfer of such title as the transferor has is generally continued and expanded under subsection (1). In this respect the provisions of the section are applicable to a person taking by any form of "purchase" as defined by this Act. Moreover the policy of this Act expressly providing for the application of supplementary general principles of law to sales transactions wherever appropriate joins with the present section to continue unimpaired all rights acquired under the law of agency or of apparent agency or ownership or other estoppel, whether based on statutory provisions or on case law principles. The section also leaves unimpaired the powers given to selling factors under the earlier Factors Acts. In addition subsection (1) provides specifically for the protection of the good faith purchaser for value in a number of specific situations which have been troublesome under prior law.

On the other hand, the contract of purchase is of course limited by its own terms as in a case of pledge for a limited amount or of sale of a fractional interest in goods.

2. The many particular situations in which a buyer in ordinary course of business from a deal-

er has been protected against reservation of property or other hidden interest are gathered by subsections (2)-(4) into a single principle protecting persons who buy in ordinary course out of inventory. Consignors have no reason to complain, nor have lenders who hold a security interest in the inventory, since the very purpose of goods in inventory is to be turned into cash by sale.

The principle is extended in subsection (3) to fit with the abolition of the old law of "cash sale" by subsection (1) (c). It is also freed from any technicalities depending on the extended law of larceny; such extension of the concept of theft to include trick, particular types of fraud, and the like is for the purpose of helping conviction of the offender; it has no proper application to the long-standing policy of civil protection of buyers from persons guilty of such trick or fraud. Finally, the policy is extended, in the interest of simplicity and sense, to any entrusting by a bailor; this is in consonance with the explicit provisions of Section 7—205 on the powers of a warehouseman who is also in the business of buying and selling fungible goods of the kind he warehouses. As to entrusting by a secured party, subsection (2) is limited by the more specific provisions of Section 9—307(1), which deny protection to a person buying farm products from a person engaged in farming operations.

3. The definition of "buyer in ordinary course of business" (Section 1—201) is effective here and preserves the essence of the healthy limitations engrafted by the case-law on the older statutes. The older loose concept of good faith and wide definition of value combined to create apparent good faith purchasers in many situations in which the result outraged common sense; the court's solution was to protect the original title especially by use of "cash sale" or of overtechnical construction of the enabling clauses of the statutes. But such rulings then turned into limitations on the proper protection of buyers in the ordinary market. Section 1—201(9) cuts down the category of buyer in ordinary course in such fashion as to take care of the results of the cases, but with no price either in confusion or in injustice to proper dealings in the normal market.

4. Except as provided in subsection (1), the rights of purchasers other than buyers in ordinary course are left to the Articles on Secured Transactions, Documents of Title, and Bulk Sales.

Cross References:

Point 1: Sections 1—103 and 1—201.

Point 2: Sections 1—201, 2—402, 7—205 and 9—307(1).

Points 3 and 4: Sections 1—102, 1—201, 2—104, 2—707 and Articles 6, 7 and 9.

Definitional Cross References:

"Buyer in ordinary course of business". Section 1—201.

"Good faith". Sections 1—201 and 2—103.

"Goods". Section 2—105.

"Person". Section 1—201.

"Purchaser". Section 1—201.

"Signed". Section 1—201.

"Term". Section 1—201.

"Value". Section 1—201.

PART 5

PERFORMANCE

§ 2—501. Insurable Interest in Goods; Manner of Identification of Goods

(1) The buyer obtains a special property and an insurable interest in goods by identification of existing goods as goods to which the contract refers even though the goods so identified are non-conforming and he has an option to return or reject them. Such identification can be made at any time and in any manner explicitly agreed to by the parties. In the absence of explicit agreement identification occurs

(a) when the contract is made if it is for the sale of goods already existing and identified;

(b) if the contract is for the sale of future goods other than those described in paragraph (c), when goods are shipped, marked or otherwise designated by the seller as goods to which the contract refers;

(c) when the crops are planted or otherwise become growing crops or the young are conceived if the contract is for the sale of unborn young to be born within twelve months after contracting or for the sale of crops to be harvested within twelve months or the next normal harvest season after contracting whichever is longer.

(2) The seller retains an insurable interest in goods so long as title to or any security interest in the goods remains in him and where the identification is by the seller alone he may until default or insolvency or notification to the buyer that the identification is final substitute other goods for those identified.

(3) Nothing in this section impairs any insurable interest recognized under any other statute or rule of law.

Official Comment

Prior Uniform Statutory Provision: See Sections 17 and 19, Uniform Sales Act.

Purposes:

1. The present section deals with the manner of identifying goods to the contract so that an insurable interest in the buyer and the rights set forth in the next section will accrue. Generally speaking, identification may be made in any manner "explicitly agreed to" by the parties. The rules of paragraphs (a), (b) and (c) apply only in the absence of such "explicit agreement".

2. In the ordinary case identification of particular existing goods as goods to which the contract refers is unambiguous and may occur in one of many ways. It is possible, however, for the identification to be tentative or contingent. In view of the limited effect given to identification by this Article, the general policy is to resolve all doubts in favor of identification.

3. The provision of this section as to "explicit agreement" clarifies the present confusion in the law of sales which has arisen from the fact that under prior uniform legislation all rules of presumption with reference to the passing of title or to appropriation (which in turn depended upon identification) were regarded as subject to the contrary intention of the parties or of the party appropriating. Such uncertainty is reduced to a minimum under this section by requiring "explicit agreement" of the parties before the rules of paragraphs (a), (b) and (c) are displaced—as they would be by a term giving the buyer power to select the goods. An "explicit" agreement, however, need not necessarily be found in the terms used in the particular transaction. Thus, where a usage of the trade has previously been made explicit by reduction to a standard set of "rules and regulations" currently incorporated by reference into the contracts of the parties, a relevant provision of those "rules and regulations" is "explicit" within the meaning of this section.

4. In view of the limited function of identification there is no requirement in this section that the goods be in deliverable state or that all of the seller's duties with respect to the processing of the goods be completed in order that identification occur. For example, despite identification the risk of loss remains on the seller under the risk of loss provisions until completion of his duties as to the goods and all of his remedies remain dependent upon his not defaulting under the contract.

5. Undivided shares in an identified fungible bulk, such as grain in an elevator or oil in a storage tank, can be sold. The mere making of the contract with reference to an undivided share in an identified fungible bulk is enough under subsection (a) to effect an identification if there is no explicit agreement otherwise. The seller's duty, however, to segregate and deliver according to the contract is not affected by such an identification but is controlled by other provisions of this Article.

6. Identification of crops under paragraph (c) is made upon planting only if they are to be harvested within the year or within the next normal harvest season. The phrase "next normal harvest season" fairly includes nursery stock raised for normally quick "harvest," but plainly excludes a "timber" crop to which the concept of a harvest "season" is inapplicable.

Paragraph (c) is also applicable to a crop of wool or the young of animals to be born within twelve months after contracting. The product of a lumbering, mining or fishing operation, though seasonal, is not within the concept of "growing". Identification under a contract for all or part of the output of such an operation can be effected early in the operation.

Cross References:

Point 1: Section 2—502.

Point 4: Sections 2—509, 2—510 and 2—703.

Point 5: Sections 2—105, 2—308, 2—503 and 2—509.

Point 6: Sections 2—105(1), 2—107(1) and 2—402.

Definitional Cross References:

"Agreement". Section 1—201.

"Contract". Section 1—201.

"Contract for sale". Section 2—106.

"Future goods". Section 2—105.

"Goods". Section 2—105.

"Notification". Section 1—201.

"Party". Section 1—201.

"Sale". Section 2—106.

"Security interest". Section 1—201.

"Seller". Section 2—103.

§ 2—502. Buyer's Right to Goods on Seller's Insolvency

(1) Subject to subsection (2) and even though the goods have not been shipped a buyer who has paid a part or all of the price of goods in which he has a special property under the provisions of the immediately preceding section may on making and keeping good a tender of any unpaid portion of their price recover them from the seller if the seller becomes insolvent within ten days after receipt of the first installment on their price.

(2) If the identification creating his special property has been made by the buyer he acquires the right to recover the goods only if they conform to the contract for sale.

Official Comment

Prior Uniform Statutory Provision: Compare Sections 17, 18 and 19, Uniform Sales Act.

Purposes:

1. This section gives an additional right to the buyer as a result of identification of the goods to the contract in the manner provided in Section 2—501. The buyer is given a right to the goods on the seller's insolvency occurring within 10 days after he receives the first installment on their price.

2. The question of whether the buyer also acquires a security interest in identified goods and has rights to the goods when insolvency takes place after the ten-day period provided in this section depends upon compliance with the provisions of the Article on Secured Transactions (Article 9).

3. Subsection (2) is included to preclude the possibility of unjust enrichment which exists if the buyer were permitted to recover goods even though they were greatly superior in quality or quantity to that called for by the contract for sale.

Cross References:

Point 1: Sections 1—201 and 2—702.

Point 2: Article 9.

Definitional Cross References:

"Buyer". Section 2—103.

"Conform". Section 2—106.

"Contract for sale". Section 2—106.

"Goods". Section 2—105.

"Insolvent". Section 1—201.

"Right". Section 1—201.

"Seller". Section 2—103.

§ 2—503. Manner of Seller's Tender of Delivery

(1) Tender of delivery requires that the seller put and hold conforming goods at the buyer's disposition and give the buyer any notification reasonably necessary to enable him to take delivery. The manner, time and place for tender are determined by the agreement and this Article, and in particular

(a) tender must be at a reasonable hour, and if it is of goods they must be kept available for the period reasonably necessary to enable the buyer to take possession; but

(b) unless otherwise agreed the buyer must furnish facilities reasonably suited to the receipt of the goods.

(2) Where the case is within the next section respecting shipment tender requires that the seller comply with its provisions.

(3) Where the seller is required to deliver at a particular destination tender requires that he comply with subsection (1) and also in any appropriate case tender documents as described in subsections (4) and (5) of this section.

(4) Where goods are in the possession of a bailee and are to be delivered without being moved

(a) tender requires that the seller either tender a negotiable document of title covering such goods or procure acknowledgment by the bailee of the buyer's right to possession of the goods; but

(b) tender to the buyer of a non-negotiable document of title or of a written direction to the bailee to deliver is sufficient tender unless the buyer seasonably objects, and receipt by the bailee of notification of the buyer's rights fixes those rights as against the bailee and all third persons; but risk of loss of the goods and of any failure by the bailee to honor the non-negotiable document of title or to obey the direction remains on the seller until the buyer has had a reasonable time to present the document or direction, and a refusal by the bailee to honor the document or to obey the direction defeats the tender.

(5) Where the contract requires the seller to deliver documents

(a) he must tender all such documents in correct form, except as provided in this Article with respect to bills of lading in a set (subsection (2) of Section 2—323); and

(b) tender through customary banking channels is sufficient and dishonor of a draft accompanying the documents constitutes non-acceptance or rejection.

Official Comment

Prior Uniform Statutory Provision: See Sections 11, 19, 20, 43 (3) and (4), 46 and 51, Uniform Sales Act.

Changes: The general policy of the above sections is continued and supplemented but subsection (3) changes the rule of prior section 19(5) as to what constitutes a "destination" contract and subsection (4) incorporates a minor correction as to tender of delivery of goods in the possession of a bailee.

Purposes of Changes:

1. The major general rules governing the manner of proper or due tender of delivery are gathered in this section. The term "tender" is used in this Article in two different senses. In one sense it refers to "due tender" which contemplates an offer coupled with a present ability to fulfill all the conditions resting on the tendering party and must be followed by actual performance if the other party shows himself ready to proceed. Unless the context unmistakably indicates otherwise this is the meaning of "tender" in this Article and the occasional addition of the word "due" is only for clarity and emphasis. At other times it is used to refer to an offer of goods or documents under a contract as if in fulfillment of its conditions even though there is a defect when measured against the contract obligation. Used in either sense, however, "tender" connotes such performance by the tendering party as puts the other party in default if he fails to proceed in some manner.

2. The seller's general duty to tender and deliver is laid down in Section 2—301 and more particularly in Section 2—507. The seller's right to a receipt if he demands one and receipts are customary is governed by Section 1—205. Subsection (1) of the present section proceeds to set forth two primary requirements of tender: first, that the seller "put and hold conforming goods at the buyer's disposition" and, second, that he "give the buyer any notice reasonably necessary to enable him to take delivery."

In cases in which payment is due and demanded upon delivery the "buyer's disposition" is qualified by the seller's right to retain control of the goods until payment by the provision of this Article on delivery on condition. However, where the seller is demanding payment on delivery he must first allow the buyer to inspect the goods in order to avoid impairing his tender unless the contract for sale is on C.I.F., C.O.D., cash against documents or similar terms negating the privilege of inspection before payment.

In the case of contracts involving documents the seller can "put and hold conforming goods at the buyer's disposition" under subsection (1) by tendering documents which give the buyer complete control of the goods under the provisions of Article 7 on due negotiation.

3. Under paragraph (a) of subsection (1) usage of the trade and the circumstances of the particular case determine what is a reasonable hour for tender and what constitutes a reasonable period of holding the goods available.

4. The buyer must furnish reasonable facilities for the receipt of the goods tendered by the seller under subsection (1), paragraph (b). This obligation of the buyer is no part of the seller's tender.

5. For the purposes of subsections (2) and (3) there is omitted from this Article the rule under prior uniform legislation that a term requiring the seller to pay the freight or cost of transportation to the buyer is equivalent to an agreement by the seller to deliver to the buyer or at an agreed destination. This omission is with the specific intention of negating the rule, for under this Article the "shipment" contract is regarded as the normal one and the "destination" contract as the variant type. The seller is not obligated to deliver at a named destination and bear the concurrent risk of loss until arrival, unless he has specifically agreed so to deliver or the commercial understanding of the terms used by the parties contemplates such delivery.

6. Paragraph (a) of subsection (4) continues the rule of the prior uniform legislation as to acknowledgment by the bailee. Paragraph (b) of subsection (4) adopts the rule that between the buyer and the seller the risk of loss remains on the seller during a period reasonable for securing acknowledgment of the transfer from the bailee, while as against all other parties the buyer's rights are fixed as of the time the bailee receives notice of the transfer.

7. Under subsection (5) documents are never "required" except where there is an express contract term or it is plainly implicit in the peculiar circumstances of the case or in a usage of trade. Documents may, of course, be "authorized" although not required, but such cases are not within the scope of this subsection. When documents are required, there are three main requirements of this subsection: (1) "All": each required document is essential to a proper tender; (2) "Such": the documents must be the ones actually required by the contract in terms of source and substance; (3) "Correct form": All documents must be in correct form.

When a prescribed document cannot be procured, a question of fact arises under the provision of this Article on substituted performance as to whether the agreed manner of delivery is actually commercially impracticable and whether the substitute is commercially reasonable.

Cross References:

Point 2: Sections 1—205, 2—301, 2—310, 2—507 and 2—513 and Article 7.

Point 5: Sections 2—308, 2—310 and 2—509.

Point 7: Section 2—614(1).

Specific matters involving tender are covered in many additional sections of this Article. See Sections 1—205, 2—301, 2—306 to 2—319, 2—321(3), 2—504, 2—507(2), 2—511(1), 2—513, 2—612 and 2—614.

Definitional Cross References:

"Agreement". Section 1—201.

"Bill of lading". Section 1—201.

"Buyer". Section 2—103.

"Conforming". Section 2—106.

"Contract". Section 1—201.

"Delivery". Section 1—201.

"Dishonor". Section 3—508.

"Document of title". Section 1—201.

"Draft". Section 3—104.

"Goods". Section 2—105.

"Notification". Section 1—201.

"Reasonable time". Section 1—204.

"Receipt" of goods. Section 2—103.

"Rights". Section 1—201.

"Seasonably". Section 1—204.

"Seller". Section 2—103.

"Written". Section 1—201.

§ 2—504. Shipment by Seller

Where the seller is required or authorized to send the goods to the buyer and the contract does not require him to deliver them at a particular destination, then unless otherwise agreed he must

(a) put the goods in the possession of such a carrier and make such a contract for their transportation as may be reasonable having regard to the nature of the goods and other circumstances of the case; and

(b) obtain and promptly deliver or tender in due form any document necessary to enable the buyer to obtain possession of the goods or otherwise required by the agreement or by usage of trade; and

(c) promptly notify the buyer of the shipment.

Failure to notify the buyer under paragraph (c) or to make a proper contract under paragraph (a) is a ground for rejection only if material delay or loss ensues.

Official Comment

Prior Uniform Statutory Provision: Section 46, Uniform Sales Act.

Changes: Rewritten.

Purposes of Changes: To continue the general policy of the prior uniform statutory provision while incorporating certain modifications with respect to the requirement that the contract with the carrier be made expressly on behalf of the buyer and as to the necessity of giving notice of the shipment to the buyer, so that:

1. The section is limited to "shipment" contracts as contrasted with "destination" contracts or contracts for delivery at the place where the goods are locat-

ed. The general principles embodied in this section cover the special cases of F. O. B. point of shipment contracts and C. I. F. and C. & F. contracts. Under the preceding section on manner of tender of delivery, due tender by the seller requires that he comply with the requirements of this section in appropriate cases.

2. The contract to be made with the carrier under paragraph (a) must conform to all express terms of the agreement, subject to any substitution necessary because of failure of agreed facilities as provided in the later provision on substituted performance. However, under the policies of this Article on good faith and commercial standards and on buyer's rights on improper delivery, the requirements of explicit provisions must be read in terms of their commercial and not their literal meaning. This policy is made express with respect to bills of lading in a set in the provision of this Article on form of bills of lading required in overseas shipment.

3. In the absence of agreement, the provision of this Article on options and cooperation respecting performance gives the seller the choice of any reasonable carrier, routing and other arrangements. Whether or not the shipment is at the buyer's expense the seller must see to any arrangements, reasonable in the circumstances, such as refrigeration, watering of live stock, protection against cold, the sending along of any necessary help, selection of specialized cars and the like for paragraph (a) is intended to cover all necessary arrangements whether made by contract with the carrier or otherwise. There is, however, a proper relaxation of such requirements if the buyer is himself in a position to make the appropriate arrangements and the seller gives him reasonable notice of the need to do so. It is an improper contract under paragraph (a) for the seller to agree with the carrier to a limited valuation below the true value and thus cut off the buyer's opportunity to recover from the carrier in the event of loss, when the risk of shipment is placed on the buyer by his contract with the seller.

4. Both the language of paragraph (b) and the nature of the situation it concerns indicate that the requirement that the seller must obtain and deliver promptly to the buyer in due form any document necessary to enable him to obtain possession of the goods is intended to cumulate with the other duties of the seller such as those covered in paragraph (a).

In this connection, in the case of pool car shipments a delivery order furnished by the seller on the pool car consignee, or on the carrier for delivery out of a larger quantity, satisfies the requirements of paragraph (b) unless the contract requires some other form of document.

5. This Article, unlike the prior uniform statutory provision, makes it the seller's duty to notify the buyer of shipment in all cases. The consequences of his failure to do so, however, are limited in that the buyer may reject on this ground only where material delay or loss ensues.

A standard and acceptable manner of notification in open credit shipments is the sending of an invoice and in the case of documentary contracts is the prompt forwarding of the documents as under paragraph (b) of this section. It is also usual to send on a straight bill of lading but this is not necessary to the required notification. However, should such a document prove necessary or convenient to the buyer, as in the case of loss and claim against the carrier, good faith would require the seller to send it on request.

Frequently the agreement expressly requires prompt notification as by wire or cable. Such a term may be of the essence and the final clause of paragraph (c) does not prevent the parties from making this a particular ground for rejection. To have this vital and irreparable effect upon the seller's duties, such a term should be part of the "dickered" terms written in any "form," or should otherwise be called seasonably and sharply to the seller's attention.

6. Generally, under the final sentence of the section, rejection by the buyer is justified only when the seller's dereliction as to any of the requirements of this section in fact is followed by material delay or damage. It rests on the seller, so far as concerns matters not within the peculiar knowledge of the buyer, to establish that his error has not been followed by events which justify rejection.

Cross References:

Point 1: Sections 2—319, 2—320 and 2—503(2).

Point 2: Sections 1—203, 2—323(2), 2—601 and 2—614(1).

Point 3: Section 2—311(2).

Point 5: Section 1—203.

Definitional Cross References:

"Agreement". Section 1—201.
"Buyer". Section 2—103.
"Contract". Section 1—201.
"Delivery". Section 1—201.
"Goods". Section 2—105.
"Notifies". Section 1—201.
"Seller". Section 2—103.
"Send". Section 1—201.
"Usage of trade". Section 1—205.

§ 2—505. Seller's Shipment Under Reservation

(1) Where the seller has identified goods to the contract by or before shipment:

(a) his procurement of a negotiable bill of lading to his own order or otherwise reserves in him a security interest in the goods. His procurement of the bill to the order of a financing agency or of the buyer indicates in addition only the seller's expectation of transferring that interest to the person named.

(b) a non-negotiable bill of lading to himself or his nominee reserves possession of the goods as security but except in a case of conditional delivery (subsection (2) of Section 2—507) a non-negotiable bill of lading naming the buyer as consignee reserves no security interest even though the seller retains possession of the bill of lading.

(2) When shipment by the seller with reservation of a security interest is in violation of the contract for sale it constitutes an improper contract for transportation within the preceding section but impairs neither the rights given to the buyer by shipment and identification of the goods to the contract nor the seller's powers as a holder of a negotiable document.

Official Comment

Prior Uniform Statutory Provision: Section 20(2), (3), (4), Uniform Sales Act.

Changes: Completely rephrased, the "powers" of the parties in cases of reservation being emphasized primarily rather than the "rightfulness" of reservation.

Purposes of Changes: To continue in general the policy of the prior uniform statutory provision with certain modifications of emphasis and language, so that:

1. The security interest reserved to the seller under subsection (1) is restricted to securing payment or performance by the buyer and the seller is strictly limited in his disposition and control of the goods as against the buyer and third parties. Under this Article, the provision as to the passing of interest expressly applies "despite any reservation of security title" and also provides that the "rights, obligations and remedies" of the parties are not altered by the incidence of title generally. The security interest, therefore, must be regarded as a means given to the seller to enforce his rights against the buyer which is unaffected by and in turn does not affect the location of title generally. The rules set forth in subsection (1) are not to be altered by any apparent "contrary intent" of the parties as to passing of title, since the rights and remedies of the parties to the contract of sale, as defined in this Article, rest on the contract and its performance or breach and not on stereotyped presumptions as to the location of title.

This Article does not attempt to regulate local procedure in regard to the effective maintenance of the seller's security interest when the action is in replevin by the buyer against the carrier.

2. Every shipment of identified goods under a negotiable bill of lading reserves a security interest in the seller under subsection (1) paragraph (a).

It is frequently convenient for the seller to make the bill of lading to the order of a nominee such as his agent at destination, the financing agency to which he expects to negotiate the document or the bank issuing a credit to him. In many instances, also, the buyer is made the order party. This Article does not deal directly with the question as to whether a bill of lading made out by the seller to the order of a nominee gives the carrier notice of any rights which the nominee may have so as to limit its freedom or obligation to honor the bill of lading in the hands of the seller as the original shipper if the expected negotiation fails. This is dealt with in the Article on Documents of Title (Article 7).

3. A non-negotiable bill of lading taken to a party other than the buyer under subsection (1) paragraph (b) reserves possession of the goods as security in the seller but if he seeks to withhold the goods improperly the buyer can tender payment and recover them.

4. In the case of a shipment by non-negotiable bill of lading taken to a buyer, the seller, under subsection (1) retains no security interest or possession as against the buyer and by the shipment he *de facto* loses control as against the carrier except where he rightfully and effectively stops delivery in transit. In cases in which the contract gives the seller the right to payment against delivery, the seller, by making an immediate demand for payment, can show that his delivery is conditional, but this does not prevent the buyer's power to transfer full title to a sub-buyer in ordinary course or other purchaser under Section 2—403.

5. Under subsection (2) an improper reservation by the seller which would constitute a breach in no way impairs such of the buyer's rights as result from identification of the goods. The security title reserved by the seller under subsection (1) does not protect his holding of the document or the goods for the purpose of exacting more than is due him under the contract.

Cross References:

Point 1: Section 1—201.

Point 2: Article 7.

Point 3: Sections 2—501(2) and 2—504.

Point 4: Sections 2—403, 2—507(2) and 2—705.

Point 5: Sections 2—310, 2—319(4), 2—320(4), 2—501 and 2—502 and Article 7.

Definitional Cross References:

"Bill of lading". Section 1—201.

"Buyer". Section 2—103.

"Consignee". Section 7—102.

"Contract". Section 1—201.

"Contract for sale". Section 2—106.

"Delivery". Section 1—201.

"Financing agency". Section 2—104.

"Goods". Section 2—105.

"Holder". Section 1—201.

"Person". Section 1—201.

"Security interest". Section 1—201.

"Seller". Section 2—103.

§ 2—506. Rights of Financing Agency

(1) A financing agency by paying or purchasing for value a draft which relates to a shipment of goods acquires to the extent of the payment or purchase and in addition to its own rights under the draft and any document of title securing it any rights of the shipper in the goods including the right to stop delivery and the shipper's right to have the draft honored by the buyer.

(2) The right to reimbursement of a financing agency which has in good faith honored or purchased the draft under commitment to or authority from the buyer is not impaired by subsequent discovery of defects with reference to any relevant document which was apparently regular on its face.

Official Comment

Prior Uniform Statutory Provision: None.

Purposes:

1. "Financing agency" is broadly defined in this Article to cover every normal instance in which a party aids or intervenes in the financing of a sales transaction. The term as used in subsection (1) is not in any sense intended as a limitation and covers any other appropriate situation which may arise outside the scope of the definition.

2. "Paying" as used in subsection (1) is typified by the letter of credit, or "authority to pay" situation in which a banker, by arrangement with the buyer or other consignee, pays on his behalf a draft for the price of the goods. It is immaterial whether the draft is formally drawn on the party paying or his principal, whether it is a sight draft paid in cash or a time draft "paid" in the first instance by acceptance, or whether the payment is viewed as absolute or conditional. All of these cases constitute "payment" under this subsection. Similarly, "purchasing for value" is used to indicate the whole area of financing by the seller's banker, and the principle of subsection (1) is applicable without any niceties of distinction between "purchase," "discount," "advance against collection" or the like. But it is important to notice that the only right to have the draft honored that is acquired is that *against the buyer;* if any right against any one else is claimed it will have to be under some separate obligation of that other person. A letter of credit does not necessarily protect *purchasers* of drafts. See Article 5. And for the relations of the parties to documentary drafts see Part 5 of Article 4.

3. Subsection (1) is made applicable to payments or advances against a draft which "relates to" a shipment of goods and this has been chosen as a term of maximum breadth. In particular the term is intended to cover the case of a draft against an invoice or against a delivery order. Further, it is unnecessary that there be an explicit assignment of the invoice attached to the draft to bring the transaction within the reason of this subsection.

4. After shipment, "the rights of the shipper in the goods" are merely security rights and are subject to the buyer's right to force delivery upon tender of the price. The rights acquired by the financing agency are similarly limited and, moreover, if the agency fails to procure any outstanding negotiable document of title, it may find its exercise of these rights hampered or even defeated by the seller's disposition of the document to a third party. This section does not attempt to create any new rights in the financing agency against the carrier which would force the latter to honor a stop order from the agency, a stranger to the shipment, or any new rights against a holder to whom a document of title has been duly negotiated under Article 7.

Cross References:

Point 1: Section 2—104(2) and Article 4.

Point 2: Part 5 of Article 4, and Article 5.

Point 4: Sections 2—501 and 2—502(1) and Article 7.

Definitional Cross References:

"Buyer". Section 2—103.

"Document of title". Section 1—201.

"Draft". Section 3—104.

"Financing agency". Section 2—104.

"Good faith". Section 2—103.

"Goods". Section 2—105.

"Honor". Section 1—201.

"Purchase". Section 1—201.

"Rights". Section 1—201.

"Value". Section 1—201.

§ 2—507. Effect of Seller's Tender; Delivery on Condition

(1) Tender of delivery is a condition to the buyer's duty to accept the goods and, unless otherwise agreed, to his duty to pay for them. Tender entitles the seller to acceptance of the goods and to payment according to the contract.

(2) Where payment is due and demanded on the delivery to the buyer of goods or documents of title, his right as against the seller to retain or dispose of them is conditional upon his making the payment due.

Official Comment

Prior Uniform Statutory Provision: See Sections 11, 41, 42 and 69, Uniform Sales Act.

Purposes:

1. Subsection (1) continues the policies of the prior uniform statutory provisions with respect to tender and delivery by the seller. Under this Article the same rules in these matters are applied to present sales and to contracts for sale. But the provisions of this subsection must be read within the framework of the other sections of this Article which bear upon the question of delivery and payment.

2. The "unless otherwise agreed" provision of subsection (1) is directed primarily to cases in which payment in advance has been promised or a letter of credit term has been included. Payment "according to the contract" contemplates immediate payment, payment at the end of an agreed credit term, payment by a time acceptance or the like. Under this Act, "contract" means the total obligation in law which results from the parties' agreement including the effect of this Article. In this context, therefore, there must be considered the effect in law of such provisions as those on means and manner of payment and on failure of agreed means and manner of payment.

3. Subsection (2) deals with the effect of a conditional delivery by the seller and in such a situation makes the buyer's "right as against the seller" conditional upon payment. These words are used as words of limitation to conform with the policy set forth in the bona fide purchase sections of this Article. Should the seller after making such a conditional delivery fail

to follow up his rights, the condition is waived. The provision of this Article for a ten day limit within which the seller may reclaim goods delivered on credit to an insolvent buyer is also applicable here.

Cross References:

Point 1: Sections 2—310, 2—503, 2—511, 2—601 and 2—711 to 2—713.

Point 2: Sections 1—201, 2—511 and 2—614.

Point 3: Sections 2—401, 2—403, and 2—702(1) (b).

Definitional Cross References:

"Buyer". Section 2—103.
"Contract". Section 1—201.
"Delivery". Section 1—201.
"Document of title". Section 1—201.
"Goods". Section 2—105.
"Rights". Section 1—201.
"Seller". Section 2—103.

§ 2—508. Cure by Seller of Improper Tender or Delivery; Replacement

(1) Where any tender or delivery by the seller is rejected because non-conforming and the time for performance has not yet expired, the seller may seasonably notify the buyer of his intention to cure and may then within the contract time make a conforming delivery.

(2) Where the buyer rejects a non-conforming tender which the seller had reasonable grounds to believe would be acceptable with or without money allowance the seller may if he seasonably notifies the buyer have a further reasonable time to substitute a conforming tender.

Official Comment

Prior Uniform Statutory Provision: None.

Purposes:

1. Subsection (1) permits a seller who has made a non-conforming tender in any case to make a conforming delivery within the contract time upon seasonable notification to the buyer. It applies even where the seller has taken back the non-conforming goods and refunded the purchase price. He may still make a good tender within the contract period. The closer, however, it is to the contract date, the greater is the necessity for extreme promptness on the seller's part in notifying of his intention to cure, if such notification is to be "seasonable" under this subsection.

The rule of this subsection, moreover, is qualified by its underlying reasons. Thus if, after contracting for June delivery, a buyer later makes known to the seller his need for shipment early in the month and the seller ships accordingly, the "contract time" has been cut down by the supervening modification and the time for cure of tender must be referred to this modified time term.

2. Subsection (2) seeks to avoid injustice to the seller by reason of a surprise rejection by

the buyer. However, the seller is not protected unless he had "reasonable grounds to believe" that the tender would be acceptable. Such reasonable grounds can lie in prior course of dealing, course of performance or usage of trade as well as in the particular circumstances surrounding the making of the contract. The seller is charged with commercial knowledge of any factors in a particular sales situation which require him to comply strictly with his obligations under the contract as, for example, strict conformity of documents in an overseas shipment or the sale of precision parts or chemicals for use in manufacture. Further, if the buyer gives notice either implicitly, as by a prior course of dealing involving rigorous inspections, or expressly, as by the deliberate inclusion of a "no replacement" clause in the contract, the seller is to be held to rigid compliance. If the clause appears in a "form" contract evidence that it is out of line with trade usage or the prior course of dealing and was not called to the seller's attention may be sufficient to show that the seller had reasonable grounds to believe that the tender would be acceptable.

3. The words "a further reasonable time to substitute a conforming tender" are intended as words of limitation to protect the buyer. What is a "reasonable time" depends upon the attending circumstances. Compare Section 2—511 on the comparable case of a seller's surprise demand for legal tender.

4. Existing trade usages permitting variations without rejection but with price allowance enter into the agreement itself as contractual limitations of remedy and are not covered by this section.

Cross References:

Point 2: Section 2—302.
Point 3: Section 2—511.
Point 4: Sections 1—205 and 2—721.

Definitional Cross References:

"Buyer". Section 2—103.
"Conforming". Section 2—106.
"Contract". Section 1—201.
"Money". Section 1—201.
"Notifies". Section 1—201.
"Reasonable time". Section 1—204.
"Seasonably". Section 1—204.
"Seller". Section 2—103.

§ 2—509. Risk of Loss in the Absence of Breach

(1) Where the contract requires or authorizes the seller to ship the goods by carrier

(a) if it does not require him to deliver them at a particular destination, the risk of loss passes to the buyer when the goods are duly delivered to the carrier even though the shipment is under reservation (Section 2—505); but

(b) if it does require him to deliver them at a particular destination and the goods are there duly tendered while in the possession of the carrier, the risk of loss passes to the buyer when the goods are there duly so tendered as to enable the buyer to take delivery.

(2) Where the goods are held by a bailee to be delivered without being moved, the risk of loss passes to the buyer

(a) on his receipt of a negotiable document of title covering the goods; or

(b) on acknowledgment by the bailee of the buyer's right to possession of the goods; or

(c) after his receipt of a non-negotiable document of title or other written direction to deliver, as provided in subsection (4) (b) of Section 2—503.

(3) In any case not within subsection (1) or (2), the risk of loss passes to the buyer on his receipt of the goods if the seller is a merchant; otherwise the risk passes to the buyer on tender of delivery.

(4) The provisions of this section are subject to contrary agreement of the parties and to the provisions of this Article on sale on approval (Section 2—327) and on effect of breach on risk of loss (Section 2—510).

Official Comment

Prior Uniform Statutory Provision: Section 22, Uniform Sales Act.

Changes: Rewritten, subsection (3) of this section modifying prior law.

Purposes of Changes: To make it clear that:

1. The underlying theory of these sections on risk of loss is the adoption of the contractual approach rather than an arbitrary shifting of the risk with the "property" in the goods. The scope of the present section, therefore, is limited strictly to those cases where there has been no breach by the seller. Where for any reason his delivery or tender fails to conform to the contract, the present section does not apply and the situation is governed by the provisions on effect of breach on risk of loss.

2. The provisions of subsection (1) apply where the contract "requires or authorizes" shipment of the goods. This language is intended to be construed parallel to comparable language in the section on shipment by seller. In order that the goods be "duly delivered to the carrier" under paragraph (a) a contract must be entered into with the carrier which will satisfy the requirements of the section on shipment by the seller and the delivery must be made under circumstances which will enable the seller to take any further steps necessary to a due tender. The underlying reason of this subsection does not require that the shipment be made after contracting, but where, for example, the seller buys the goods afloat and later diverts the shipment to the buyer, he must identify the goods to the

contract before the risk of loss can pass. To transfer the risk it is enough that a proper shipment and a proper identification come to apply to the same goods although, aside from special agreement, the risk will not pass retroactively to the time of shipment in such a case.

3. Whether the contract involves delivery at the seller's place of business or at the situs of the goods, a merchant seller cannot transfer risk of loss and it remains upon him until actual receipt by the buyer, even though full payment has been made and the buyer has been notified that the goods are at his disposal. Protection is afforded him, in the event of breach by the buyer, under the next section.

The underlying theory of this rule is that a merchant who is to make physical delivery at his own place continues meanwhile to control the goods and can be expected to insure his interest in them. The buyer, on the other hand, has no control of the goods and it is extremely unlikely that he will carry insurance on goods not yet in his possession.

4. Where the agreement provides for delivery of the goods as between the buyer and seller without removal from the physical possession of a bailee, the provisions on manner of tender of delivery apply on the point of transfer of risk. Due delivery of a negotiable document of title covering the goods or acknowledgment by the bailee that he holds for the buyer completes the "delivery" and passes the risk.

5. The provisions of this section are made subject by subsection (4) to the "contrary agreement" of the parties. This language is intended as the equivalent of the phrase "unless otherwise agreed" used more frequently throughout this Act. "Contrary" is in no way used as a word of limitation and the buyer and seller are left free to readjust their rights and risks as declared by this section in any manner agreeable to them. Contrary agreement can also be found in the circumstances of the case, a trade usage or practice, or a course of dealing or performance.

Cross References:

Point 1: Section 2—510(1).

Point 2: Sections 2—503 and 2—504.

Point 3: Sections 2—104, 2—503 and 2—510.

Point 4: Section 2—503(4).

Point 5: Section 1—201.

Definitional Cross References:

"Agreement". Section 1—201.

"Buyer". Section 2—103.

"Contract". Section 1—201

"Delivery". Section 1—201.

"Document of title". Section 1—201.

"Goods". Section 2—105.

"Merchant". Section 2—104.

"Party". Section 1—201.

"Receipt" of goods. Section 2—103.

"Sale on approval". Section 2—326.

"Seller". Section 2—103.

§ 2—510. Effect of Breach on Risk of Loss

(1) Where a tender or delivery of goods so fails to conform to the contract as to give a right of rejection the risk of their loss remains on the seller until cure or acceptance.

(2) Where the buyer rightfully revokes acceptance he may to the extent of any deficiency in his effective insurance coverage treat the risk of loss as having rested on the seller from the beginning.

(3) Where the buyer as to conforming goods already identified to the contract for sale repudiates or is otherwise in breach before risk of their loss has passed to him, the seller may to the extent of any deficiency in his effective insurance coverage treat the risk of loss as resting on the buyer for a commercially reasonable time.

Official Comment

Prior Uniform Statutory Provision: None.

Purposes: To make clear that:

1. Under subsection (1) the seller by his individual action cannot shift the risk of loss to the buyer unless his action conforms with all the conditions resting on him under the contract.

2. The "cure" of defective tenders contemplated by subsection (1) applies only to those situations in which the seller makes changes in goods already tendered, such as repair, partial substitution, sorting out from an improper mixture and the like since "cure" by repossession and new tender has no effect on the risk of loss of the goods originally tendered. The seller's privilege of cure does not shift the risk, however, until the cure is completed.

Where defective documents are involved a cure of the defect by the seller or a waiver of the defects by the buyer will operate to shift the risk under this section. However, if the goods have been destroyed prior to the cure or the buyer is unaware of their destruction at the time he waives the defect in the documents, the risk of the loss must still be borne by the seller, for the risk shifts only at the time of cure, waiver of documentary defects or acceptance of the goods.

3. In cases where there has been a breach of the contract, if the one in control of the goods is the aggrieved party, whatever loss or damage may prove to be uncovered by his insurance falls upon the contract breaker under subsections (2) and (3) rather than upon him. The word "effective" as applied to insurance coverage in those subsections is used to meet the case of supervening insolvency of the insurer. The "deficiency" referred to in the text means such deficiency in the insurance coverage as exists without subrogation. This section merely distributes the risk of loss as stated and is not in-

tended to be disturbed by any subrogation of an insurer.

Cross Reference:

Section 2—509.

Definitional Cross References:

"Buyer". Section 2—103.

"Conform". Section 2—106.

"Contract for sale". Section 2—106.

"Goods". Section 2—105.

"Seller". Section 2—103.

§ 2—511. Tender of Payment by Buyer; Payment by Check

(1) Unless otherwise agreed tender of payment is a condition to the seller's duty to tender and complete any delivery.

(2) Tender of payment is sufficient when made by any means or in any manner current in the ordinary course of business unless the seller demands payment in legal tender and gives any extension of time reasonably necessary to procure it.

(3) Subject to the provisions of this Act on the effect of an instrument on an obligation (Section 3—802), payment by check is conditional and is defeated as between the parties by dishonor of the check on due presentment.

Official Comment

Prior Uniform Statutory Provision: Section 42, Uniform Sales Act.

Changes: Rewritten by this section and Section 2—507.

Purposes of Changes:

1. The requirement of payment against delivery in subsection (1) is applicable to noncommercial sales generally and to ordinary sales at retail although it has no application to the great body of commercial contracts which carry credit terms. Subsection (1) applies also to documentary contracts in general and to contracts which look to shipment by the seller but contain no term on time and manner of payment, in which situations the payment may, in proper case, be demanded against delivery of appropriate documents.

In the case of specific transactions such as C.O.D. sales or agreements providing for payment against documents, the provisions of this subsection must be considered in conjunction with the special sections of the Article dealing with such terms. The provision that tender of payment is a condition to the seller's duty to tender and complete "any delivery" integrates this section with the language and policy of the section on delivery in several lots which call for separate payment. Finally, attention should be directed to the provision on right to adequate assurance of performance which recognizes, even before the time for tender, an obligation on the buyer not to impair the seller's expectation of receiving payment in due course.

2. Unless there is agreement otherwise the concurrence of the

conditions as to tender of payment and tender of delivery requires their performance at a single place or time. This Article determines that place and time by determining in various other sections the place and time for tender of delivery under various circumstances and in particular types of transactions. The sections dealing with time and place of delivery together with the section on right to inspection of goods answer the subsidiary question as to when payment may be demanded before inspection by the buyer.

3. The essence of the principle involved in subsection (2) is avoidance of commercial surprise at the time of performance. The section on substituted performance covers the peculiar case in which legal tender is not available to the commercial community.

4. Subsection (3) is concerned with the rights and obligations as between the parties to a sales transaction when payment is made by check. This Article recognizes that the taking of a seemingly solvent party's check is commercially normal and proper and, if due diligence is exercised in collection, is not to be penalized in any way. The conditional character of the payment under this section refers only to the effect of the transaction "as between the parties" thereto and does not purport to cut into the law of "absolute" and "conditional" payment as applied to such other problems as the discharge of sureties or the responsibilities of a drawee bank which is at the same time an agent for collection.

The phrase "by check" includes not only the buyer's own but any check which does not effect a discharge under Article 3 (Section 3—802). Similarly the reason of this subsection should apply and the same result should be reached where the buyer "pays" by sight draft on a commercial firm which is financing him.

5. Under subsection (3) payment by check is defeated if it is not honored upon due presentment. This corresponds to the provisions of article on Commercial Paper. (Section 3—802). But if the seller procures certification of the check instead of cashing it, the buyer is discharged. (Section 3—411).

6. Where the instrument offered by the buyer is not a payment but a credit instrument such as a note or a check postdated by even one day, the seller's acceptance of the instrument insofar as third parties are concerned, amounts to a delivery on credit and his remedies are set forth in the section on buyer's insolvency. As between the buyer and the seller, however, the matter turns on the present subsection and the section on conditional delivery and subsequent dishonor of the instrument gives the seller rights on it as well as for breach of the contract for sale.

Cross References:

Point 1: Sections 2—307, 2—310, 2—320, 2—325, 2—503, 2—513 and 2—609.

Point 2: Sections 2—307, 2—310, 2—319, 2—322, 2—503, 2—504 and 2—513.

Point 3: Section 2—614.

Point 5: Article 3, esp. Sections 3—802 and 3—411.

Point 6: Sections 2—507, 2—702, and Article 3.

Definitional Cross References:

"Buyer". Section 2—103.

"Check". Section 3—104.

"Dishonor". Section 3—508.

"Party". Section 1—201.

"Reasonable time". Section 1—204.

"Seller". Section 2—103.

§ 2—512. Payment by Buyer Before Inspection

(1) Where the contract requires payment before inspection non-conformity of the goods does not excuse the buyer from so making payment unless

(a) the non-conformity appears without inspection; or

(b) despite tender of the required documents the circumstances would justify injunction against honor under the provisions of this Act (Section 5—114).

(2) Payment pursuant to subsection (1) does not constitute an acceptance of goods or impair the buyer's right to inspect or any of his remedies.

Official Comment

Prior Uniform Statutory Provision: None, but see Sections 47 and 49, Uniform Sales Act.

Purposes:

1. Subsection (1) of the present section recognizes that the essence of a contract providing for payment before inspection is the intention of the parties to shift to the buyer the risks which would usually rest upon the seller. The basic nature of the transaction is thus preserved and the buyer is in most cases required to pay first and litigate as to any defects later.

2. "Inspection" under this section is an inspection in a manner reasonable for detecting defects in goods whose surface appearance is satisfactory.

3. Clause (a) of this subsection states an exception to the general rule based on common sense and normal commercial practice. The apparent non-conformity referred to is one which is evident in the mere process of taking delivery.

4. Clause (b) is concerned with contracts for payment against documents and incorporates the general clarification and modification of the case law contained in the section on excuse of a financing agency. Section 5—114.

5. Subsection (2) makes explicit the general policy of the Uniform Sales Act that the payment required before inspection in no way impairs the buyer's remedies or rights in the event of a default by the seller. The remedies preserved to the buyer are all of his remedies, which include as a matter of reason the remedy for total non-delivery after payment in advance.

The provision on performance or acceptance under reservation of rights does not apply to the situations contemplated here in which payment is made in due course under the contract and the buyer need not pay "under protest" or the like in order to preserve his rights as to defects discovered upon inspection.

6. This section applies to cases in which the contract requires payment before inspection either by the express agreement of the parties or by reason of the effect in law of that contract. The present section must therefore be considered in conjunction with the provision on right to inspection of goods which sets forth the instances in which the buyer is not entitled to inspection before payment

Cross References:

Point 4: Article 5.
Point 5: Section 1—207.
Point 6: Section 2—513(3).

Definitional Cross References:

"Buyer". Section 2—103.
"Conform". Section 2—106.
"Contract". Section 1—201.
"Financing agency". Section 2—104.
"Goods". Section 2—105.
"Remedy". Section 1—201.
"Rights". Section 1—201.

§ 2—513. Buyer's Right to Inspection of Goods

(1) Unless otherwise agreed and subject to subsection (3), where goods are tendered or delivered or identified to the contract for sale, the buyer has a right before payment or acceptance to inspect them at any reasonable place and time and in any reasonable manner. When the seller is required or authorized to send the goods to the buyer, the inspection may be after their arrival.

(2) Expenses of inspection must be borne by the buyer but may be recovered from the seller if the goods do not conform and are rejected.

(3) Unless otherwise agreed and subject to the provisions of this Article on C.I.F. contracts (subsection (3) of Section 2—321), the buyer is not entitled to inspect the goods before payment of the price when the contract provides

(a) for delivery "C.O.D." or on other like terms; or

(b) for payment against documents of title, except where such payment is due only after the goods are to become available for inspection.

(4) A place or method of inspection fixed by the parties is presumed to be exclusive but unless otherwise expressly agreed it does not postpone identification or shift the place for delivery or for passing the risk of loss. If compliance becomes impossible, inspection shall be as provided in this section unless the place or method fixed was clearly intended as an indispensable condition failure of which avoids the contract.

Official Comment

Prior Uniform Statutory Provision: Section 47(2), (3), Uniform Sales Act.

Changes: Rewritten, Subsections (2) and (3) being new.

Purposes of Changes and New Matter: To correspond in substance with the prior uniform statutory provision and to incorporate in addition some of the results of the better case law so that:

1. The buyer is entitled to inspect goods as provided in subsection (1) unless it has been otherwise agreed by the parties. The phrase "unless otherwise agreed" is intended principally to cover such situations as those outlined in subsections (3) and (4) and those in which the agreement of the parties negates inspection before tender of delivery. However, no agreement by the parties can displace the entire right of inspection except where the contract is simply for the sale of "this thing." Even in a sale of boxed goods "as is" inspection is a right of the buyer, since if the boxes prove to contain some other merchandise altogether the price can be recovered back; nor do the limitations of the provision on effect of acceptance apply in such a case.

2. The buyer's right of inspection is available to him upon tender, delivery or appropriation of the goods with notice to him. Since inspection is available to him on tender, where payment is due against delivery he may, unless otherwise agreed, make his inspection before payment of the price. It is also available to him after receipt of the goods and so may be postponed after receipt for a reasonable time. Failure to inspect before payment does not impair the right to inspect after receipt of the goods unless the case falls within subsection (4) on agreed and exclusive inspection provisions. The right to inspect goods which have been appropriated with notice to the buyer holds whether or not the sale was by sample.

3. The buyer may exercise his right of inspection at any reasonable time or place and in any reasonable manner. It is not necessary that he select the most appropriate time, place or manner to inspect or that his selection be the customary one in the trade or locality. Any reasonable time, place or manner is available to him and the reasonableness will be determined by trade usages, past practices between the parties and the other circumstances of the case.

The last sentence of subsection (1) makes it clear that the place of arrival of shipped goods is a reasonable place for their inspection.

4. Expenses of an inspection made to satisfy the buyer of the seller's performance must be assumed by the buyer in the first instance. Since the rule provides merely for an allocation of expense there is no policy to prevent the parties from providing otherwise in the agreement. Where the buyer would normally bear the expenses of the inspection but the goods are rightly rejected because of what the in-

spection reveals, demonstrable and reasonable costs of the inspection are part of his incidental damage caused by the seller's breach.

5. In the case of payment against documents, subsection (3) requires payment before inspection, since shipping documents against which payment is to be made will commonly arrive and be tendered while the goods are still in transit. This Article recognizes no exception in any peculiar case in which the goods happen to arrive before the documents. However, where by the agreement payment is to await the arrival of the goods, inspection before payment becomes proper since the goods are then "available for inspection."

Where by the agreement the documents are to be held until arrival the buyer is entitled to inspect before payment since the goods are then "available for inspection". Proof of usage is not necessary to establish this right, but if inspection before payment is disputed the contrary must be established by usage or by an explicit contract term to that effect.

For the same reason, that the goods are available for inspection, a term calling for payment against storage documents or a delivery order does not normally bar the buyer's right to inspection before payment under subsection (3) (b). This result is reinforced by the buyer's right under subsection (1) to inspect goods which have been appropriated with notice to him.

6. Under subsection (4) an agreed place or method of inspection is generally held to be intended as exclusive. However, where compliance with such an agreed inspection term becomes impossible, the question is basically one of intention. If the parties clearly intend that the method of inspection named is to be a necessary condition without which the entire deal is to fail, the contract is at an end if that method becomes impossible. On the other hand, if the parties merely seek to indicate a convenient and reliable method but do not intend to give up the deal in the event of its failure, any reasonable method of inspection may be substituted under this Article.

Since the purpose of an agreed place of inspection is only to make sure at that point whether or not the goods will be thrown back, the "exclusive" feature of the named place is satisfied under this Article if the buyer's failure to inspect there is held to be an acceptance with the knowledge of such defects as inspection would have revealed within the section on waiver of buyer's objections by failure to particularize. Revocation of the acceptance is limited to the situations stated in the section pertaining to that subject. The reasonable time within which to give notice of defects within the section on notice of breach begins to run from the point of the "acceptance."

7. Clauses on time of inspection are commonly clauses which limit the time in which the buyer must inspect and give notice of defects. Such clauses are therefore governed by the section of this Article which requires that such a time limitation must be reasonable.

8. Inspection under this Article is not to be regarded as a

"condition precedent to the passing of title" so that risk until inspection remains on the seller. Under subsection (4) such an approach cannot be sustained. Issues between the buyer and seller are settled in this Article almost wholly by special provisions and not by the technical determination of the locus of the title. Thus "inspection as a condition to the passing of title" becomes a concept almost without meaning. However, in peculiar circumstances inspection may still have some of the consequences hitherto sought and obtained under that concept.

9. "Inspection" under this section has to do with the buyer's check-up on whether the seller's performance is in accordance with a contract previously made and is not to be confused with the "examination" of the goods or of a sample or model of them at the time of contracting which may affect the warranties involved in the contract.

Cross References:

Generally: Sections 2—310 (b), 2—321(3) and 2—606(1) (b).

Point 1: Section 2—607.

Point 2: Sections 2—501 and 2—502.

Point 4: Section 2—715.

Point 5: Section 2—321(3).

Point 6: Sections 2—606 to 2—608.

Point 7: Section 1—204.

Point 8: Comment to Section 2—401.

Point 9: Section 2—316(3) (b).

Definitional Cross References:

"Buyer". Section 2—103.

"Conform". Section 2—106.

"Contract". Section 1—201.

"Contract for sale". Section 2—106.

"Document of title". Section 1—201.

"Goods". Section 2—105.

"Party". Section 1—201.

"Presumed". Section 1—201.

"Reasonable time". Section 1—204.

"Rights". Section 1—201.

"Seller". Section 2—103.

"Send". Section 1—201.

"Term". Section 1—201.

§ 2—514. When Documents Deliverable on Acceptance; When on Payment

Unless otherwise agreed documents against which a draft is drawn are to be delivered to the drawee on acceptance of the draft if it is payable more than three days after presentment; otherwise, only on payment.

Official Comment

Prior Uniform Statutory Provision: Section 41, Uniform Bills of Lading Act.

Changes: Rewritten.

Purposes of Changes: To make the provision one of general application so that:

1. It covers any document against which a draft may be drawn, whatever may be the form of the document, and applies to

interpret the action of a seller or consignor insofar as it may affect the rights and duties of any buyer, consignee or financing agency concerned with the paper. Supplementary or corresponding provisions are found in Sections 4—503 and 5—112.

2. An "arrival" draft is a sight draft within the purpose of this section.

Cross References:

Point 1: See Sections 2—502, 2—505(2), 2—507(2), 2—512, 2—513, 2—607 concerning protection of rights of buyer and seller, and 4—503 and 5—112 on delivery of documents.

Definitional Cross References:

"Delivery". Section 1—201.

"Draft". Section 3—104.

§ 2—515. Preserving Evidence of Goods in Dispute

In furtherance of the adjustment of any claim or dispute

(a) either party on reasonable notification to the other and for the purpose of ascertaining the facts and preserving evidence has the right to inspect, test and sample the goods including such of them as may be in the possession or control of the other; and

(b) the parties may agree to a third party inspection or survey to determine the conformity or condition of the goods and may agree that the findings shall be binding upon them in any subsequent litigation or adjustment.

Official Comment

Prior Uniform Statutory Provision: None.

Purposes:

1. To meet certain serious problems which arise when there is a dispute as to the quality of the goods and thereby perhaps to aid the parties in reaching a settlement, and to further the use of devices which will promote certainty as to the condition of the goods, or at least aid in preserving evidence of their condition.

2. Under paragraph (a), to afford either party an opportunity for preserving evidence, whether or not agreement has been reached, and thereby to reduce uncertainty in any litigation and, in turn perhaps, to promote agreement.

Paragraph (a) does not conflict with the provisions on the seller's right to resell rejected goods or the buyer's similar right. Apparent conflict between these provisions which will be suggested in certain circumstances is to be resolved by requiring prompt action by the parties. Nor does paragraph (a) impair the effect of a term for payment before inspection. Short of such defects as amount to fraud or substantial failure of consideration, non-conformity is neither an excuse nor a defense to an action for non-acceptance of documents. Normally, therefore, until the buyer has made payment, inspected and rejected the goods, there is no occasion or use for the rights under paragraph (a).

3. Under paragraph (b), to provide for third party inspection upon the agreement of the parties, thereby opening the door to amicable adjustments based upon the findings of such third parties.

The use of the phrase "conformity or condition" makes it clear that the parties' agreement may range from a complete settlement of all aspects of the dispute by a third party to the use of a third party merely to determine and record the condition of the goods so that they can be resold or used to reduce the stake in controversy. "Conformity", at one end of the scale of possible issues, includes the whole question of interpretation of the agreement and its legal effect, the state of the goods in regard to quality and condition, whether any defects are due to factors which operate at the risk of the buyer, and the degree of non-conformity where that may be material. "Condition", at the other end of the scale, includes nothing but the degree of damage or deterioration which the goods show. Paragraph (b) is intended to reach any point in the gamut which the parties may agree upon.

The principle of the section on reservation of rights reinforces this paragraph in simplifying such adjustments as the parties wish to make in partial settlement while reserving their rights as to any further points. Paragraph (b) also suggests the use of arbitration, where desired, of any points left open, but nothing in this section is intended to repeal or amend any statute governing arbitration. Where any question arises as to the extent of the parties' agreement under the paragraph, the presumption should be that it was meant to extend only to the relation between the contract description and the goods as delivered, since that is what a craftsman in the trade would normally be expected to report upon. Finally, a written and authenticated report of inspection or tests by a third party, whether or not sampling has been practicable, is entitled to be admitted as evidence under this Act, for it is a third party document.

Cross References:

Point 2: Sections 2—513(3), 2—706 and 2—711(2) and Article 5.

Point 3: Sections 1—202 and 1—207.

Definitional Cross References:

"Conform". Section 2—106.

"Goods". Section 2—105.

"Notification". Section 1—201.

"Party". Section 1—201.

PART 6

BREACH, REPUDIATION AND EXCUSE

§ 2—601. Buyer's Rights on Improper Delivery

Subject to the provisions of this Article on breach in installment contracts (Section 2—612) and unless otherwise agreed under the sections on contractual limitations of remedy (Sections 2—718 and 2—719), if the goods or the tender of delivery fail in any respect to conform to the contract, the buyer may

(a) reject the whole; or

(b) accept the whole; or

(c) accept any commercial unit or units and reject the rest.

Official Comment

Prior Uniform Statutory Provision: No one general equivalent provision but numerous provisions, dealing with situations of non-conformity where buyer may accept or reject, including Sections 11, 44 and 69(1), Uniform Sales Act.

Changes: Partial acceptance in good faith is recognized and the buyer's remedies on the contract for breach of warranty and the like, where the buyer has returned the goods after transfer of title, are no longer barred.

Purposes of Changes: To make it clear that:

1. A buyer accepting a non-conforming tender is not penalized by the loss of any remedy otherwise open to him. This policy extends to cover and regulate the acceptance of a part of any lot improperly tendered in any case where the price can reasonably be apportioned. Partial acceptance is permitted whether the part of the goods accepted conforms or not. The only limitation on partial acceptance is that good faith and commercial reasonableness must be used to avoid undue impairment of the value of the remaining portion of the goods. This is the reason for the insistence on the "commercial unit" in paragraph (c). In this respect, the test is not only what unit has been the basis of contract, but whether the partial acceptance produces so materially adverse an effect on the remainder as to constitute bad faith.

2. Acceptance made with the knowledge of the other party is final. An original refusal to accept may be withdrawn by a later acceptance if the seller has indicated that he is holding the tender open. However, if the buyer attempts to accept, either in whole or in part, after his original rejection has caused the seller to arrange for other disposition of the goods, the buyer must answer for any ensuing damage since the next section provides that any exercise of ownership after rejection is wrongful as against the seller. Further, he is liable even though the seller

may choose to treat his action as acceptance rather than conversion, since the damage flows from the misleading notice. Such arrangements for resale or other disposition of the goods by the seller must be viewed as within the normal contemplation of a buyer who has given notice of rejection. However, the buyer's attempts in good faith to dispose of defective goods where the seller has failed to give instructions within a reasonable time are not to be regarded as an acceptance.

Cross References:

Sections 2—602(2) (a), 2—612, 2—718 and 2—719.

Definitional Cross References:

"Buyer". Section 2—103.

"Commercial unit". Section 2—105.

"Conform". Section 2—106.

"Contract". Section 1—201.

"Goods". Section 2—105.

"Installment contract". Section 2—612.

"Rights". Section 1—201.

§ 2—602. Manner and Effect of Rightful Rejection

(1) Rejection of goods must be within a reasonable time after their delivery or tender. It is ineffective unless the buyer seasonably notifies the seller.

(2) Subject to the provisions of the two following sections on rejected goods (Sections 2—603 and 2—604),

(a) after rejection any exercise of ownership by the buyer with respect to any commercial unit is wrongful as against the seller; and

(b) if the buyer has before rejection taken physical possession of goods in which he does not have a security interest under the provisions of this Article (subsection (3) of Section 2—711), he is under a duty after rejection to hold them with reasonable care at the seller's disposition for a time sufficient to permit the seller to remove them; but

(c) the buyer has no further obligations with regard to goods rightfully rejected.

(3) The seller's rights with respect to goods wrongfully rejected are governed by the provisions of this Article on Seller's remedies in general (Section 2—703).

Official Comment

Prior Uniform Statutory Provision: Section 50, Uniform Sales Act.

Changes: Rewritten.

Purposes of Changes: To make it clear that:

1. A tender or delivery of goods made pursuant to a contract of sale, even though wholly

non-conforming, requires affirmative action by the buyer to avoid acceptance. Under subsection (1), therefore, the buyer is given a reasonable time to notify the seller of his rejection, but without such seasonable notification his rejection is ineffective. The sections of this Article dealing with inspection of goods must be read in connection with the buyer's reasonable time for action under this subsection. Contract provisions limiting the time for rejection fall within the rule of the section on "Time" and are effective if the time set gives the buyer a reasonable time for discovery of defects. What constitutes a due "notifying" of rejection by the buyer to the seller is defined in Section 1—201.

2. Subsection (2) lays down the normal duties of the buyer upon rejection, which flow from the relationship of the parties. Beyond his duty to hold the goods with reasonable care for the buyer's [seller's] disposition, this section continues the policy of prior uniform legislation in generally relieving the buyer from any duties with respect to them, except when the circumstances impose the limited obligation of salvage upon him under the next section.

3. The present section applies only to rightful rejection by the buyer. If the seller has made a tender which in all respects conforms to the contract, the buyer has a positive duty to accept and his failure to do so constitutes a "wrongful rejection" which gives the seller immediate remedies for breach. Subsection (3) is included here to emphasize the sharp distinction between the rejection of an improper tender and the non-acceptance which is a breach by the buyer.

4. The provisions of this section are to be appropriately limited or modified when a negotiation is in process.

Cross References:

Point 1: Sections 1—201, 1—204(1) and (3), 2—512(2), 2—513(1) and 2—606(1) (b).

Point 2: Section 2—603(1).

Point 3: Section 2—703.

Definitional Cross References:

"Buyer". Section 2—103.

"Commercial unit". Section 2—105.

"Goods". Section 2—105.

"Merchant". Section 2—104.

"Notifies". Section 1—201.

"Reasonable time". Section 1—204.

"Remedy". Section 1—201.

"Rights". Section 1—201.

"Seasonably". Section 1—204.

"Security interest". Section 1—201.

"Seller". Section 2—103.

§ 2—603. Merchant Buyer's Duties as to Rightfully Rejected Goods

(1) Subject to any security interest in the buyer (subsection (3) of Section 2—711), when the seller has no agent or place of business at the market of rejection a merchant buyer is under a duty after rejection of goods in his possession or control to follow any reasonable instructions received from the seller with respect to the goods and in the absence of such instruc-

tions to make reasonable efforts to sell them for the seller's account if they are perishable or threaten to decline in value speedily. Instructions are not reasonable if on demand indemnity for expenses is not forthcoming.

(2) When the buyer sells goods under subsection (1), he is entitled to reimbursement from the seller or out of the proceeds for reasonable expenses of caring for and selling them, and if the expenses include no selling commission then to such commission as is usual in the trade or if there is none to a reasonable sum not exceeding ten per cent on the gross proceeds.

(3) In complying with this section the buyer is held only to good faith and good faith conduct hereunder is neither acceptance nor conversion nor the basis of an action for damages.

Official Comment

Prior Uniform Statutory Provision: None.

Purposes:

1. This section recognizes the duty imposed upon the merchant buyer by good faith and commercial practice to follow any reasonable instructions of the seller as to reshipping, storing, delivery to a third party, reselling or the like. Subsection (1) goes further and extends the duty to include the making of reasonable efforts to effect a salvage sale where the value of the goods is threatened and the seller's instructions do not arrive in time to prevent serious loss.

2. The limitations on the buyer's duty to resell under subsection (1) are to be liberally construed. The buyer's duty to resell under this section arises from commercial necessity and thus is present only when the seller has "no agent or place of business at the market of rejection". A financing agency which is acting in behalf of the seller in handling the documents rejected by the buyer is sufficiently the seller's agent to lift the burden of salvage resale from the buyer. (See provisions of Sections 4—503 and 5—112 on bank's duties with respect to rejected documents.) The buyer's duty to resell is extended only to goods in his "possession or control", but these are intended as words of wide, rather than narrow, import. In effect, the measure of the buyer's "control" is whether he can practicably effect control without undue commercial burden.

3. The explicit provisions for reimbursement and compensation to the buyer in subsection (2) are applicable and necessary only where he is not acting under instructions from the seller. As provided in subsection (1) the seller's instructions to be "reasonable" must on demand of the buyer include indemnity for expenses.

4. Since this section makes the resale of perishable goods an affirmative duty in contrast to a mere right to sell as under the case law, subsection (3) makes it clear that the buyer is liable only for the exercise of good faith in determining wheth-

er the value of the goods is sufficiently threatened to justify a quick resale or whether he has waited a sufficient length of time for instructions, or what a reasonable means and place of resale is.

5. A buyer who fails to make a salvage sale when his duty to do so under this section has arisen is subject to damages pursuant to the section on liberal administration of remedies.

Cross References:

Point 2: Sections 4—503 and 5—112.

Point 5: Section 1—106. Compare generally section 2—706.

Definitional Cross References:

"Buyer". Section 2—103.

"Good faith". Section 1—201.

"Goods". Section 2—105.

"Merchant". Section 2—104.

"Security interest". Section 1—201.

"Seller". Section 2—103.

§ 2—604. Buyer's Options as to Salvage of Rightfully Rejected Goods

Subject to the provisions of the immediately preceding section on perishables if the seller gives no instructions within a reasonable time after notification of rejection the buyer may store the rejected goods for the seller's account or reship them to him or resell them for the seller's account with reimbursement as provided in the preceding section. Such action is not acceptance or conversion.

Official Comment

Prior Uniform Statutory Provision: None.

Purposes:

The basic purpose of this section is twofold: on the one hand it aims at reducing the stake in dispute and on the other at avoiding the pinning of a technical "acceptance" on a buyer who has taken steps towards realization on or preservation of the goods in good faith. This section is essentially a salvage section and the buyer's right to act under it is conditioned upon (1) non-conformity of the goods, (2) due notification of rejection to the seller under the section on manner of rejection, and (3) the absence of any instructions from the seller which the merchant-buyer has a duty to follow under the preceding section.

This section is designed to accord all reasonable leeway to a rightfully rejecting buyer acting in good faith. The listing of what the buyer may do in the absence of instructions from the seller is intended to be not exhaustive but merely illustrative. This is not a "merchant's" section and the options are pure options given to merchant and non-merchant buyers alike. The merchant-buyer, however, may in some instances be under a duty rather than an option to resell under the provisions of the preceding section.

Cross References:

Sections 2—602(1), and 2—603(1) and 2—706.

Definitional Cross References:

"Buyer". Section 2—103.

"Notification". Section 1—201.

"Reasonable time". Section 1—204.

"Seller". Section 2—103.

§ 2—605. Waiver of Buyer's Objections by Failure to Particularize

(1) The buyer's failure to state in connection with rejection a particular defect which is ascertainable by reasonable inspection precludes him from relying on the unstated defect to justify rejection or to establish breach

(a) where the seller could have cured it if stated seasonably; or

(b) between merchants when the seller has after rejection made a request in writing for a full and final written statement of all defects on which the buyer proposes to rely.

(2) Payment against documents made without reservation of rights precludes recovery of the payment for defects apparent on the face of the documents.

Official Comment

Prior Uniform Statutory Provision: None.

Purposes:

1. The present section rests upon a policy of permitting the buyer to give a quick and informal notice of defects in a tender without penalizing him for omissions in his statement, while at the same time protecting a seller who is reasonably misled by the buyer's failure to state curable defects.

2. Where the defect in a tender is one which could have been cured by the seller, a buyer who merely rejects the delivery without stating his objections to it is probably acting in commercial bad faith and seeking to get out of a deal which has become unprofitable. Subsection (1) (a), following the general policy of this Article which looks to preserving the deal wherever possible, therefore insists that the seller's right to correct his tender in such circumstances be protected.

3. When the time for cure is past, subsection (1) (b) makes it plain that a seller is entitled upon request to a final statement of objections upon which he can rely. What is needed is that he make clear to the buyer exactly what is being sought. A formal demand under paragraph (b) will be sufficient in the case of a merchant-buyer.

4. Subsection (2) applies to the particular case of documents the same principle which the sec-

tion on effects of acceptance applies to the case of goods. The matter is dealt with in this section in terms of "waiver" of objections rather than of right to revoke acceptance, partly to avoid any confusion with the problems of acceptance of goods and partly because defects in documents which are not taken as grounds for rejection are generally minor ones. The only defects concerned in the present subsection are defects in the documents which are apparent on their face. Where payment is required against the documents they must be inspected before payment, and the payment then constitutes acceptance of the documents. Under the section dealing with this problem, such acceptance of the documents does not constitute an acceptance of the goods or impair any options or remedies of the buyer for their improper delivery. Where the documents are delivered without requiring such contemporary action as payment from the buyer, the reason of the next section on what constitutes acceptance of goods, applies. Their acceptance by non-objection is therefore postponed until after a reasonable time for their inspection. In either situation, however, the buyer "waives" only what is apparent on the face of the documents.

Cross References:

Point 2: Section 2—508.

Point 4: Sections 2—512(2), 2—606(1) (b), 2—607(2).

Definitional Cross References:

"Between merchants". Section 2—104.

"Buyer". Section 2—103.

"Seasonably". Section 1—204.

"Seller". Section 2—103.

"Writing" and "written". Section 1—201.

§ 2—606. What Constitutes Acceptance of Goods

(1) Acceptance of goods occurs when the buyer

(a) after a reasonable opportunity to inspect the goods signifies to the seller that the goods are conforming or that he will take or retain them in spite of their nonconformity; or

(b) fails to make an effective rejection (subsection (1) of Section 2—602), but such acceptance does not occur until the buyer has had a reasonable opportunity to inspect them; or

(c) does any act inconsistent with the seller's ownership; but if such act is wrongful as against the seller it is an acceptance only if ratified by him.

(2) Acceptance of a part of any commercial unit is acceptance of that entire unit.

Official Comment

Prior Uniform Statutory Provision: Section 48, Uniform Sales Act.

Changes: Rewritten, the qualification in paragraph (c) and subsection (2) being new; otherwise the general policy of the prior legislation is continued.

Purposes of Changes and New Matter: To make it clear that:

1. Under this Article "acceptance" as applied to goods means that the buyer, pursuant to the contract, takes particular goods which have been appropriated to the contract as his own, whether or not he is obligated to do so, and whether he does so by words, action, or silence when it is time to speak. If the goods conform to the contract, acceptance amounts only to the performance by the buyer of one part of his legal obligation.

2. Under this Article acceptance of goods is always acceptance of identified goods which have been appropriated to the contract or are appropriated by the contract. There is no provision for "acceptance of title" apart from acceptance in general, since acceptance of title is not material under this Article to the detailed rights and duties of the parties. (See Section 2—401). The refinements of the older law between acceptance of goods and of title become unnecessary in view of the provisions of the sections on effect and revocation of acceptance, on effects of identification and on risk of loss, and those sections which free the seller's and buyer's remedies from the complications and confusions caused by the question of whether title has or has not passed to the buyer before breach.

3. Under paragraph (a), payment made after tender is always one circumstance tending to signify acceptance of the goods but in itself it can never be more than one circumstance and is not conclusive. Also, a conditional communication of acceptance always remains subject to its expressed conditions.

4. Under paragraph (c), any action taken by the buyer, which is inconsistent with his claim that he has rejected the goods, constitutes an acceptance. However, the provisions of paragraph (c) are subject to the sections dealing with rejection by the buyer which permit the buyer to take certain actions with respect to the goods pursuant to his options and duties imposed by those sections, without effecting an acceptance of the goods. The second clause of paragraph (c) modifies some of the prior case law and makes it clear that "acceptance" in law based on the wrongful act of the acceptor is acceptance only as against the wrongdoer and then only at the option of the party wronged.

In the same manner in which a buyer can bind himself, despite his insistence that he is rejecting or has rejected the goods, by an act inconsistent with the seller's ownership under paragraph (c), he can obligate himself by a communication of acceptance despite a prior rejection under paragraph (a). However, the sections on buyer's rights on improper delivery and on the effect of rightful rejection, make it clear that after he once rejects a tender, paragraph (a) does not operate in favor of the buyer unless the seller has re-tendered the goods or has taken affirmative action indicating that he is holding the tender open. See also Comment 2 to Section 2—601.

5. Subsection (2) supplements the policy of the section on buyer's rights on improper delivery, recognizing the validity of a partial acceptance but insisting that the buyer exercise this right only as to whole commercial units.

Cross References:

Point 2: Sections 2—401, 2—509, 2—510, 2—607, 2—608 and Part 7.

Point 4: Sections 2—601 through 2—604.

Point 5: Section 2—601.

Definitional Cross References:

"Buyer". Section 2—103.

"Commercial unit". Section 2—105.

"Goods". Section 2—105.

"Seller". Section 2—103.

§ 2—607. Effect of Acceptance; Notice of Breach; Burden of Establishing Breach After Acceptance; Notice of Claim or Litigation to Person Answerable Over

(1) The buyer must pay at the contract rate for any goods accepted.

(2) Acceptance of goods by the buyer precludes rejection of the goods accepted and if made with knowledge of a non-conformity cannot be revoked because of it unless the acceptance was on the reasonable assumption that the non-conformity would be seasonably cured but acceptance does not of itself impair any other remedy provided by this Article for non-conformity.

(3) Where a tender has been accepted

(a) the buyer must within a reasonable time after he discovers or should have discovered any breach notify the seller of breach or be barred from any remedy; and

(b) if the claim is one for infringement or the like (subsection (3) of Section 2—312) and the buyer is sued as a result of such a breach he must so notify the seller within a reasonable time after he receives notice of the litigation or be barred from any remedy over for liability established by the litigation.

(4) The burden is on the buyer to establish any breach with respect to the goods accepted.

(5) Where the buyer is sued for breach of a warranty or other obligation for which his seller is answerable over

(a) he may give his seller written notice of the litigation. If the notice states that the seller may come in and defend and that if the seller does not do so he will be bound in any action against him by his buyer by any determination of fact common to the two litigations, then unless the seller after seasonable receipt of the notice does come in and defend he is so bound.

(b) if the claim is one for infringement or the like (subsection (3) of Section 2—312) the original seller may demand in writing that his buyer turn over to him control of the litigation including settlement or else be barred from any remedy over and if he also agrees to bear all expense and to satisfy any adverse judgment, then unless the buyer after seasonable receipt of the demand does turn over control the buyer is so barred.

(6) The provisions of subsections (3), (4) and (5) apply to any obligation of a buyer to hold the seller harmless against infringement or the like (subsection (3) of Section 2—312).

Official Comment

Prior Uniform Statutory Provision: Subsection (1)—Section 41, Uniform Sales Act; Subsections (2) and (3)—Sections 49 and 69, Uniform Sales Act.

Changes: Rewritten.

Purposes of Changes: To continue the prior basic policies with respect to acceptance of goods while making a number of minor though material changes in the interest of simplicity and commercial convenience so that:

1. Under subsection (1), once the buyer accepts a tender the seller acquires a right to its price on the contract terms. In cases of partial acceptance, the price of any part accepted is, if possible, to be reasonably apportioned, using the type of apportionment familiar to the courts in quantum valebat cases, to be determined in terms of "the contract rate," which is the rate determined from the bargain in fact (the agreement) after the rules and policies of this Article have been brought to bear.

2. Under subsection (2) acceptance of goods precludes their subsequent rejection. Any return of the goods thereafter must be by way of revocation of acceptance under the next section. Revocation is unavailable for a non-conformity known to the buyer at the time of acceptance, except where the buyer has accepted on the reasonable assumption that the non-conformity would be seasonably cured.

3. All other remedies of the buyer remain unimpaired under subsection (2). This is intended to include the buyer's full rights with respect to future installments despite his acceptance of any earlier non-conforming installment.

4. The time of notification is to be determined by applying commercial standards to a merchant buyer. "A reasonable time" for notification from a re-

tail consumer is to be judged by different standards so that in his case it will be extended, for the rule of requiring notification is designed to defeat commercial bad faith, not to deprive a good faith consumer of his remedy.

The content of the notification need merely be sufficient to let the seller know that the transaction is still troublesome and must be watched. There is no reason to require that the notification which saves the buyer's rights under this section must include a clear statement of all the objections that will be relied on by the buyer, as under the section covering statements of defects upon rejection (Section 2—605). Nor is there reason for requiring the notification to be a claim for damages or of any threatened litigation or other resort to a remedy. The notification which saves the buyer's rights under this Article need only be such as informs the seller that the transaction is claimed to involve a breach, and thus opens the way for normal settlement through negotiation.

5. Under this Article various beneficiaries are given rights for injuries sustained by them because of the seller's breach of warranty. Such a beneficiary does not fall within the reason of the present section in regard to discovery of defects and the giving of notice within a reasonable time after acceptance, since he has nothing to do with acceptance. However, the reason of this section does extend to requiring the beneficiary to notify the seller that an injury has occurred. What is said above, with regard to the extended time for reasonable notification from the lay consumer after the injury is also applicable here; but even a beneficiary can be properly held to the use of good faith in notifying, once he has had time to become aware of the legal situation.

6. Subsection (4) unambiguously places the burden of proof to establish breach on the buyer after acceptance. However, this rule becomes one purely of procedure when the tender accepted was non-conforming and the buyer has given the seller notice of breach under subsection (3). For subsection (2) makes it clear that acceptance leaves unimpaired the buyer's right to be made whole, and that right can be exercised by the buyer not only by way of cross-claim for damages, but also by way of recoupment in diminution or extinction of the price.

7. Subsections (3) (b) and (5) (b) give a warrantor against infringement an opportunity to defend or compromise third-party claims or be relieved of his liability. Subsection (5) (a) codifies for all warranties the practice of voucher to defend. Compare Section 3—803. Subsection (6) makes these provisions applicable to the buyer's liability for infringement under Section 2—312.

8. All of the provisions of the present section are subject to any explicit reservation of rights.

Cross References:

Point 1: Section 1—201.
Point 2: Section 2—608.
Point 4: Sections 1—204 and 2—605.

Point 5: Section 2—318.
Point 6: Section 2—717.
Point 7: Sections 2—312 and 3—803.
Point 8: Section 1—207.

Definitional Cross References:

"Burden of establishing". Section 1—201.
"Buyer". Section 2—103.
"Conform". Section 2—106.
"Contract". Section 1—201.
"Goods". Section 2—105.
"Notifies". Section 1—201.
"Reasonable time". Section 1—204.
"Remedy". Section 1—201.
"Seasonably". Section 1—204.

§ 2—608. Revocation of Acceptance in Whole or in Part

(1) The buyer may revoke his acceptance of a lot or commercial unit whose non-conformity substantially impairs its value to him if he has accepted it

(a) on the reasonable assumption that its non-conformity would be cured and it has not been seasonably cured; or

(b) without discovery of such non-conformity if his acceptance was reasonably induced either by the difficulty of discovery before acceptance or by the seller's assurances.

(2) Revocation of acceptance must occur within a reasonable time after the buyer discovers or should have discovered the ground for it and before any substantial change in condition of the goods which is not caused by their own defects. It is not effective until the buyer notifies the seller of it

(3) A buyer who so revokes has the same rights and duties with regard to the goods involved as if he had rejected them.

Official Comment

Prior Uniform Statutory Provision: Section 69(1) (d), (3), (4) and (5), Uniform Sales Act.

Changes: Rewritten.

Purposes of Changes: To make it clear that:

1. Although the prior basic policy is continued, the buyer is no longer required to elect between revocation of acceptance and recovery of damages for breach. Both are now available to him. The non-alternative character of the two remedies is stressed by the terms used in the present section. The section no longer speaks of "rescission," a term capable of ambiguous application either to transfer of title to the goods or to the contract of sale and susceptible also of confusion with cancellation for cause of an executed or executory portion of the contract. The remedy under this section is instead referred to simply as "revocation of acceptance" of goods tendered under a contract for sale and involves no suggestion of "election" of any sort.

2. Revocation of acceptance is possible only where the non-conformity substantially impairs the value of the goods to the buyer. For this purpose the test is not what the seller had reason to know at the time of contracting; the question is whether the non-conformity is such as will in fact cause a substantial impairment of value to the buyer though the seller had no advance knowledge as to the buyer's particular circumstances.

3. "Assurances" by the seller under paragraph (b) of subsection (1) can rest as well in the circumstances or in the contract as in explicit language used at the time of delivery. The reason for recognizing such assurances is that they induce the buyer to delay discovery. These are the only assurances involved in paragraph (b). Explicit assurances may be made either in good faith or bad faith. In either case any remedy accorded by this Article is available to the buyer under the section on remedies for fraud.

4. Subsection (2) requires notification of revocation of acceptance within a reasonable time after discovery of the grounds for such revocation. Since this remedy will be generally resorted to only after attempts at adjustment have failed, the reasonable time period should extend in most cases beyond the time in which notification of breach must be given, beyond the time for discovery of non-conformity after acceptance and beyond the time for rejection after tender. The parties may by their agreement limit the time for notification under this section, but the same sanctions and considerations apply to such agreements as are discussed in the comment on manner and effect of rightful rejection.

5. The content of the notice under subsection (2) is to be determined in this case as in others by considerations of good faith, prevention of surprise, and reasonable adjustment. More will generally be necessary than the mere notification of breach required under the preceding section. On the other hand the requirements of the section on waiver of buyer's objections do not apply here. The fact that quick notification of trouble is desirable affords good ground for being slow to bind a buyer by his first statement. Following the general policy of this Article, the requirements of the content of notification are less stringent in the case of a non-merchant buyer.

6. Under subsection (2) the prior policy is continued of seeking substantial justice in regard to the condition of goods restored to the seller. Thus the buyer may not revoke his acceptance if the goods have materially deteriorated except by reason of their own defects. Worthless goods, however, need not be offered back and minor defects in the articles reoffered are to be disregarded.

7. The policy of the section allowing partial acceptance is carried over into the present section and the buyer may revoke his acceptance, in appropriate cases, as to the entire lot or any commercial unit thereof.

Cross References:

Point 3: Section 2—721.

Point 4: Sections 1—204, 2—602 and 2—607.

Point 5: Sections 2—605 and 2—607.

Point 7: Section 2—601.

Definitional Cross References:

"Buyer". Section 2—103.

"Commercial unit". Section 2—105.

"Conform". Section 2—106.

"Goods". Section 2—105.

"Lot". Section 2—105.

"Notifies". Section 1—201.

"Reasonable time". Section 1—204.

"Rights". Section 1—201.

"Seasonably". Section 1—204.

"Seller". Section 2—103.

§ 2—609. Right to Adequate Assurance of Performance

(1) A contract for sale imposes an obligation on each party that the other's expectation of receiving due performance will not be impaired. When reasonable grounds for insecurity arise with respect to the performance of either party the other may in writing demand adequate assurance of due performance and until he receives such assurance may if commercially reasonable suspend any performance for which he has not already received the agreed return.

(2) Between merchants the reasonableness of grounds for insecurity and the adequacy of any assurance offered shall be determined according to commercial standards.

(3) Acceptance of any improper delivery or payment does not prejudice the aggrieved party's right to demand adequate assurance of future performance.

(4) After receipt of a justified demand failure to provide within a reasonable time not exceeding thirty days such assurance of due performance as is adequate under the circumstances of the particular case is a repudiation of the contract.

Official Comment

Prior Uniform Statutory Provision: See Sections 53, 54(1) (b), 55 and 63(2), Uniform Sales Act.

Purposes:

1. The section rests on the recognition of the fact that the essential purpose of a contract between commercial men is actual performance and they do not bargain merely for a promise, or for a promise plus the right to win a lawsuit and that a continuing sense of reliance and security that the promised performance will be forthcoming when due, is an important feature of the bargain. If either the willingness or the ability of a party to perform declines materially between the time of contracting and the time for performance, the other party is threatened with the loss of a substantial part of what he has bargained for. A seller needs protection not merely against having to deliver on credit to a

shaky buyer, but also against having to procure and manufacture the goods, perhaps turning down other customers. Once he has been given reason to believe that the buyer's performance has become uncertain, it is an undue hardship to force him to continue his own performance. Similarly, a buyer who believes that the seller's deliveries have become uncertain cannot safely wait for the due date of performance when he has been buying to assure himself of materials for his current manufacturing or to replenish his stock of merchandise.

2. Three measures have been adopted to meet the needs of commercial men in such situations. First, the aggrieved party is permitted to suspend his own performance and any preparation therefor, with excuse for any resulting necessary delay, until the situation has been clarified. "Suspend performance" under this section means to hold up performance pending the outcome of the demand, and includes also the holding up of any preparatory action. This is the same principle which governs the ancient law of stoppage and seller's lien, and also of excuse of a buyer from prepayment if the seller's actions manifest that he cannot or will not perform. (Original Act, Section 63 (2).)

Secondly, the aggrieved party is given the right to require adequate assurance that the other party's performance will be duly forthcoming. This principle is reflected in the familiar clauses permitting the seller to curtail deliveries if the buyer's credit becomes impaired, which when held within the limits of reasonableness and good faith actually express no more than the fair business meaning of any commercial contract.

Third, and finally, this section provides the means by which the aggrieved party may treat the contract as broken if his reasonable grounds for insecurity are not cleared up within a reasonable time. This is the principle underlying the law of anticipatory breach, whether by way of defective part performance or by repudiation. The present section merges these three principles of law and commercial practice into a single theory of general application to all sales agreements looking to future performance.

3. Subsection (2) of the present section requires that "reasonable" grounds and "adequate" assurance as used in subsection (1) be defined by commercial rather than legal standards. The express reference to commercial standards carries no connotation that the obligation of good faith is not equally applicable here.

Under commercial standards and in accord with commercial practice, a ground for insecurity need not arise from or be directly related to the contract in question. The law as to "dependence" or "independence" of promises within a single contract does not control the application of the present section.

Thus a buyer who falls behind in "his account" with the seller, even though the items involved have to do with separate and legally distinct contracts, impairs the seller's expectation of due performance. Again, under the same test, a buyer who requires precision parts which he intends to use immediately upon delivery, may have reasonable grounds for insecurity if he discovers that his seller is making defective deliveries of such parts to other buyers with similar needs. Thus, too, in a situation such as arose in Jay Dreher Corporation v. Delco Appliance Corporation, 93 F.2d 275 (C.C.A.2, 1937), where a manufacturer gave a dealer an exclusive franchise for the sale of his product but on two or three occasions breached the exclusive dealing clause, although there was no default in orders, deliveries or payments under the separate sales contract between the parties, the aggrieved dealer would be entitled to suspend his performance of the contract for sale under the present section and to demand assurance that the exclusive dealing contract would be lived up to. There is no need for an explicit clause tying the exclusive franchise into the contract for the sale of goods since the situation itself ties the agreements together.

The nature of the sales contract enters also into the question of reasonableness. For example, a report from an apparently trustworthy source that the seller had shipped defective goods or was planning to ship them would normally give the buyer reasonable grounds for insecurity. But when the buyer has assumed the risk of payment before inspection of the goods, as in a sales contract on C.I.F. or similar cash against documents terms, that risk is not to be evaded by a demand for assurance. Therefore no ground for insecurity would exist under this section unless the report went to a ground which would excuse payment by the buyer.

4. What constitutes "adequate" assurance of due performance is subject to the same test of factual conditions. For example, where the buyer can make use of a defective delivery, a mere promise by a seller of good repute that he is giving the matter his attention and that the defect will not be repeated, is normally sufficient. Under the same circumstances, however, a similar statement by a known corner-cutter might well be considered insufficient without the posting of a guaranty or, if so demanded by the buyer, a speedy replacement of the delivery involved. By the same token where a delivery has defects, even though easily curable, which interfere with easy use by the buyer, no verbal assurance can be deemed adequate which is not accompanied by replacement, repair, money-allowance, or other commercially reasonable cure.

A fact situation such as arose in Corn Products Refining Co. v. Fasola, 94 N.J.L. 181, 109 A. 505 (1920) offers illustration both of reasonable grounds for insecurity and "adequate" assurance. In that case a contract for the sale of oils on 30 days' credit, 2% off for payment within 10 days, provided that credit was to be extended to the buyer only if his financial responsibility was satisfactory to the seller. The buyer had been in the habit of taking advantage of the discount but at the same time that he failed to make his customary 10 day payment, the seller heard rumors, in fact false, that the buyer's financial condition was shaky. Thereupon, the seller demanded cash before shipment or security satisfactory to him. The buyer sent a good credit report from his banker, expressed willingness to make payments when due on the 30 day terms and insisted on further deliveries under the contract. Under this Article the rumors, although false, were enough to make the buyer's financial condition "unsatisfactory" to the seller under the contract clause. Moreover, the buyer's practice of taking the cash discounts is enough, apart from the contract clause, to lay a commercial foundation for suspicion when the practice is suddenly stopped. These matters, however, go only to the justification of the seller's demand for security, or his "reasonable grounds for insecurity".

The adequacy of the assurance given is not measured as in the type of "satisfaction" situation affected with intangibles, such as in personal service cases, cases involving a third party's judgment as final, or cases in which the whole contract is dependent on one party's satisfaction, as in a sale on approval. Here, the seller must exercise good faith and observe commercial standards. This Article thus approves the statement of the court in James B. Berry's Sons Co. of Illinois v. Monark Gasoline & Oil Co., Inc., 32 F.2d 74 (C.C.A.8, 1929), that the seller's satisfaction under such a clause must be based upon reason and must not be arbitrary or capricious; and rejects the purely personal "good faith" test of the Corn Products Refining Co. case, which held that in the seller's sole judgment, if for *any* reason he was dissatisfied, he was entitled to revoke the credit. In the absence of the buyer's failure to take the 2% discount as was his custom, the banker's report given in that case would have been "adequate" assurance under this Act, regardless of the language of the "satisfaction" clause. However, the seller is reasonably entitled to feel insecure at a sudden expansion of the buyer's use of a credit term, and should be entitled either to security or to a satisfactory explanation.

The entire foregoing discussion as to adequacy of assurance by way of explanation is subject to qualification when repeated occasions for the application of this section arise. This Act recognizes that repeated delinquencies must be viewed as cumulative. On the other hand, commercial sense also requires that if repeated claims for assurance are made under this section, the basis for these claims must be increasingly obvious.

5. A failure to provide adequate assurance of performance and thereby to re-establish the security of expectation, results in a breach only "by repudiation" under subsection (4). Therefore, the possibility is continued of retraction of the repudiation under the section dealing with that problem, unless the aggrieved party has acted on the breach in some manner.

The thirty day limit on the time to provide assurance is laid down to free the question of reasonable time from uncertainty in later litigation.

6. Clauses seeking to give the protected party exceedingly wide powers to cancel or readjust the contract when ground for insecurity arises must be read against the fact that good faith is a part of the obligation of the contract and not subject to modification by agreement and includes, in the case of a merchant, the reasonable observance of commercial standards of fair dealing in the trade. Such clauses can thus be effective to enlarge the protection given by the present section to a certain extent, to fix the reasonable time within which requested assurance must be given, or to define adequacy of the assurance in any commercially reasonable fashion. But any clause seeking to set up arbitrary standards for action is ineffective under this Article. Acceleration clauses are treated similarly in the Articles on Commercial Paper and Secured Transactions.

Cross References:

Point 3: Section 1—203.
Point 5: Section 2—611.
Point 6: Sections 1—203 and 1—208 and Articles 3 and 9.

Definitional Cross References:

"Aggrieved party". Section 1—201.
"Between merchants". Section 2—104.
"Contract". Section 1—201.
"Contract for sale". Section 2—106.
"Party". Section 1—201.
"Reasonable time". Section 1—204.
"Rights". Section 1—201.
"Writing". Section 1—201.

§ 2—610. Anticipatory Repudiation

When either party repudiates the contract with respect to a performance not yet due the loss of which will substantially impair the value of the contract to the other, the aggrieved party may

(a) for a commercially reasonable time await performance by the repudiating party; or

(b) resort to any remedy for breach (Section 2—703 or Section 2—711), even though he has notified the repudiating party that he would await the latter's performance and has urged retraction; and

(c) in either case suspend his own performance or proceed in accordance with the provisions of this Article on the seller's right to identify goods to the contract notwithstanding breach or to salvage unfinished goods (Section 2—704).

Official Comment

Prior Uniform Statutory Provision: See Sections 63(2) and 65, Uniform Sales Act.

Purposes: To make it clear that:

1. With the problem of insecurity taken care of by the preceding section and with provision being made in this Article as to the effect of a defective delivery under an installment contract, anticipatory repudiation centers upon an overt communication of intention or an action which renders performance impossible or demonstrates a clear determination not to continue with performance.

Under the present section when such a repudiation substantially impairs the value of the contract, the aggrieved party may at any time resort to his remedies for breach, or he may suspend his own performance while he negotiates with, or awaits performance by, the other party. But if he awaits performance beyond a commercially reasonable time he cannot recover resulting damages which he should have avoided.

2. It is not necessary for repudiation that performance be made literally and utterly impossible. Repudiation can result from action which reasonably indicates a rejection of the continuing obligation. And, a repudiation automatically results under the preceding section on insecurity when a party fails to provide adequate assurance of due future performance within thirty days after a justifiable demand therefor has been made. Under the language of this section, a demand by one or both parties for more than the contract calls for in the way of counter-performance is not in itself a repudiation nor does it invalidate a plain expression of desire for future performance. However, when under a fair reading it amounts to a statement of intention not to perform except on conditions which go beyond the contract, it becomes a repudiation.

3. The test chosen to justify an aggrieved party's action under this section is the same as that in the section on breach in installment contracts—namely the substantial value of the contract. The most useful test of substantial value is to determine whether material inconvenience or injustice will result if the aggrieved party is forced to wait and receive an ultimate tender minus the part or aspect repudiated.

4. After repudiation, the aggrieved party may immediately resort to any remedy he chooses provided he moves in good faith (see Section 1—203). Inaction and silence by the aggrieved party may leave the matter open but it cannot be regarded as misleading the repudiating party. Therefore the aggrieved party is left free to proceed at any time with his options under this section, unless he has taken some positive action which in good faith requires notification to the other party before the remedy is pursued.

Cross References:

Point 1: Sections 2—609 and 2—612.

Point 2: Section 2—609.

Point 3: Section 2—612.

Point 4: Section 1—203.

Definitional Cross References:

"Aggrieved party". Section 1—201.

"Contract". Section 1—201.

"Party". Section 1—201.

"Remedy". Section 1—201.

§ 2—611. Retraction of Anticipatory Repudiation

(1) Until the repudiating party's next performance is due he can retract his repudiation unless the aggrieved party has since the repudiation cancelled or materially changed his position or otherwise indicated that he considers the repudiation final.

(2) Retraction may be by any method which clearly indicates to the aggrieved party that the repudiating party intends to perform, but must include any assurance justifiably demanded under the provisions of this Article (Section 2—609).

(3) Retraction reinstates the repudiating party's rights under the contract with due excuse and allowance to the aggrieved party for any delay occasioned by the repudiation.

Official Comment

Prior Uniform Statutory Provision: None.

Purposes: To make it clear that:

1. The repudiating party's right to reinstate the contract is entirely dependent upon the action taken by the aggrieved party. If the latter has cancelled the contract or materially changed his position at any time after the repudiation, there can be no retraction under this section.

2. Under subsection (2) an effective retraction must be accompanied by any assurances demanded under the section dealing with right to adequate assurance. A repudiation is of course sufficient to give reasonable ground for insecurity and to warrant a request for assurance as an essential condition of the retraction. However, after a timely and unambiguous expression of retraction, a reasonable time for the assurance to be worked out should be allowed by the aggrieved party before cancellation.

Cross Reference:

Point 2: Section 2—609.

Definitional Cross References:

"Aggrieved party". Section 1—201.

"Cancellation". Section 2—106.

"Contract". Section 1—201.

"Party". Section 1—201.

"Rights". Section 1—201.

§ 2—612. "Installment Contract"; Breach

(1) An "installment contract" is one which requires or authorizes the delivery of goods in separate lots to be separately

accepted, even though the contract contains a clause "each delivery is a separate contract" or its equivalent.

(2) The buyer may reject any installment which is non-conforming if the non-conformity substantially impairs the value of that installment and cannot be cured or if the non-conformity is a defect in the required documents; but if the non-conformity does not fall within subsection (3) and the seller gives adequate assurance of its cure the buyer must accept that installment.

(3) Whenever non-conformity or default with respect to one or more installments substantially impairs the value of the whole contract there is a breach of the whole. But the aggrieved party reinstates the contract if he accepts a non-conforming installment without seasonably notifying of cancellation or if he brings an action with respect only to past installments or demands performance as to future installments.

Official Comment

Prior Uniform Statutory Provision: Section 45(2), Uniform Sales Act.

Changes: Rewritten.

Purposes of Changes: To continue prior law but to make explicit the more mercantile interpretation of many of the rules involved, so that:

1. The definition of an installment contract is phrased more broadly in this Article so as to cover installment deliveries tacitly authorized by the circumstances or by the option of either party.

2. In regard to the apportionment of the price for separate payment this Article applies the more liberal test of what can be apportioned rather than the test of what is clearly apportioned by the agreement. This Article also recognizes approximate calculation or apportionment of price subject to subsequent adjustment. A provision for separate payment for each lot delivered ordinarily means that the price is at least roughly calculable by units of quantity, but such a provision is not essential to an "installment contract." If separate acceptance of separate deliveries is contemplated, no generalized contrast between wholly "entire" and wholly "divisible" contracts has any standing under this Article.

3. This Article rejects any approach which gives clauses such as "each delivery is a separate contract" their legalistically literal effect. Such contracts nonetheless call for installment deliveries. Even where a clause speaks of "a separate contract for all purposes", a commercial reading of the language under the section on good faith and commercial standards requires that the singleness of the document and the negotiation, together with the sense of the situation, prevail over any uncommercial and legalistic interpretation.

4. One of the requirements for rejection under subsection

(2) is non-conformity substantially impairing the value of the installment in question. However, an installment agreement may require accurate conformity in quality as a condition to the right to acceptance if the need for such conformity is made clear either by express provision or by the circumstances. In such a case the effect of the agreement is to define explicitly what amounts to substantial impairment of value impossible to cure. A clause requiring accurate compliance as a condition to the right to acceptance must, however, have some basis in reason, must avoid imposing hardship by surprise and is subject to waiver or to displacement by practical construction.

Substantial impairment of the value of an installment can turn not only on the quality of the goods but also on such factors as time, quantity, assortment, and the like. It must be judged in terms of the normal or specifically known purposes of the contract. The defect in required documents refers to such matters as the absence of insurance documents under a C. I. F. contract, falsity of a bill of lading, or one failing to show shipment within the contract period or to the contract destination. Even in such cases, however, the provisions on cure of tender apply if appropriate documents are readily procurable.

5. Under subsection (2) an installment delivery must be accepted if the non-conformity is curable and the seller gives adequate assurance of cure. Cure of non-conformity of an installment in the first instance can usually be afforded by an allowance against the price, or in the case of reasonable discrepancies in quantity either by a further delivery or a partial rejection. This Article requires reasonable action by a buyer in regard to discrepant delivery and good faith requires that the buyer make any reasonable minor outlay of time or money necessary to cure an overshipment by severing out an acceptable percentage thereof. The seller must take over a cure which involves any material burden; the buyer's obligation reaches only to cooperation. Adequate assurance for purposes of subsection (2) is measured by the same standards as under the section on right to adequate assurance of performance.

6. Subsection (3) is designed to further the continuance of the contract in the absence of an overt cancellation. The question arising when an action is brought as to a single installment only is resolved by making such action waive the right of cancellation. This involves merely a defect in one or more installments, as contrasted with the situation where there is a true repudiation within the section on anticipatory repudiation. Whether the non-conformity in any given installment justifies cancellation as to the future depends, not on whether such non-conformity indicates an intent or likelihood that the future deliveries will also be defective, but whether the non-conformity substantially impairs the value of the whole contract. If only the seller's security in regard to future installments is impaired, he has the right to demand adequate assurances of proper future performance but

has not an immediate right to cancel the entire contract. It is clear under this Article, however, that defects in prior installments are cumulative in effect, so that acceptance does not wash out the defect "waived." Prior policy is continued, putting the rule as to buyer's default on the same footing as that in regard to seller's default.

7. Under the requirement of seasonable notification of cancellation under subsection (3), a buyer who accepts a non-conforming installment which substantially impairs the value of the entire contract should properly be permitted to withhold his decision as to whether or not to cancel pending a response from the seller as to his claim for cure or adjustment. Similarly, a seller may withhold a delivery pending payment for prior ones, at the same time delaying his decision as to cancellation. A reasonable time for notifying of cancellation, judged by commercial standards under the section on good faith, extends of course to include the time covered by any reasonable negotiation in good faith. However, during this period the defaulting party is entitled, on request, to know whether the contract is still in effect, before he can be required to perform further.

Cross References:

Point 2: Sections 2—307 and 2—607.

Point 3: Section 1—203.

Point 5: Sections 2—208 and 2—609.

Point 6: Section 2—610.

Definitional Cross References:

"Action". Section 1—201.

"Aggrieved party". Section 1—201.

"Buyer". Section 2—103.

"Cancellation". Section 2—106.

"Conform". Section 2—106.

"Contract". Section 1—201.

"Lot". Section 2—105.

"Notifies". Section 1—201.

"Seasonably". Section 1—204.

"Seller". Section 2—103.

§ 2—613. Casualty to Identified Goods

Where the contract requires for its performance goods identified when the contract is made, and the goods suffer casualty without fault of either party before the risk of loss passes to the buyer, or in a proper case under a "no arrival, no sale" term (Section 2—324) then

(a) if the loss is total the contract is avoided; and

(b) if the loss is partial or the goods have so deteriorated as no longer to conform to the contract the buyer may nevertheless demand inspection and at his option either treat the contract as avoided or accept the goods with due allowance from the contract price for the deterioration or the deficiency in quantity but without further right against the seller.

Official Comment

Prior Uniform Statutory Provision: Sections 7 and 8, Uniform Sales Act.

Changes: Rewritten, the basic policy being continued but the test of a "divisible" or "indivisible" sale or contract being abandoned in favor of adjustment in business terms.

Purposes of Changes:

1. Where goods whose continued existence is presupposed by the agreement are destroyed without fault of either party, the buyer is relieved from his obligation but may at his option take the surviving goods at a fair adjustment. "Fault" is intended to include negligence and not merely wilful wrong. The buyer is expressly given the right to inspect the goods in order to determine whether he wishes to avoid the contract entirely or to take the goods with a price adjustment.

2. The section applies whether the goods were already destroyed at the time of contracting without the knowledge of either party or whether they are destroyed subsequently but before the risk of loss passes to the buyer. Where under the agreement, including of course usage of trade, the risk has passed to the buyer before the casualty, the section has no application. Beyond this, the essential question in determining whether the rules of this section are to be applied is whether the seller has or has not undertaken the responsibility for the continued existence of the goods in proper condition through the time of agreed or expected delivery.

3. The section on the term "no arrival, no sale" makes clear that delay in arrival, quite as much as physical change in the goods, gives the buyer the options set forth in this section.

Cross Reference:

Point 3: Section 2—324.

Definitional Cross References:

"Buyer". Section 2—103.
"Conform". Section 2—106.
"Contract". Section 1—201.
"Fault". Section 1—201.
"Goods". Section 2—105.
"Party". Section 1—201.
"Rights". Section 1—201.
"Seller". Section 2—103.

§ 2—614. Substituted Performance

(1) Where without fault of either party the agreed berthing, loading, or unloading facilities fail or an agreed type of carrier becomes unavailable or the agreed manner of delivery otherwise becomes commercially impracticable but a commercially reasonable substitute is available, such substitute performance must be tendered and accepted.

(2) If the agreed means or manner of payment fails because of domestic or foreign governmental regulation, the seller may withhold or stop delivery unless the buyer provides a means or manner of payment which is commercially a substantial equiva-

lent. If delivery has already been taken, payment by the means or in the manner provided by the regulation discharges the buyer's obligation unless the regulation is discriminatory, oppressive or predatory.

Official Comment

Prior Uniform Statutory Provision: None.

Purposes:

1. Subsection (1) requires the tender of a commercially reasonable substituted performance where agreed to facilities have failed or become commercially impracticable. Under this Article, in the absence of specific agreement, the normal or usual facilities enter into the agreement either through the circumstances, usage of trade or prior course of dealing.

This section appears between Section 2—613 on casualty to identified goods and the next section on excuse by failure of presupposed conditions, both of which deal with excuse and complete avoidance of the contract where the occurrence or non-occurrence of a contingency which was a basic assumption of the contract makes the expected performance impossible. The distinction between the present section and those sections lies in whether the failure or impossibility of performance arises in connection with an incidental matter or goes to the very heart of the agreement. The differing lines of solution are contrasted in a comparison of International Paper Co. v. Rockefeller, 161 App. Div. 180, 146 N.Y.S. 371 (1914) and Meyer v. Sullivan, 40 Cal. App. 723, 181 P. 847 (1919). In the former case a contract for the sale of spruce to be cut from a particular tract of land was involved. When a fire destroyed the trees growing on that tract the seller was held excused since performance was impossible. In the latter case the contract called for delivery of wheat "f.o.b. Kosmos Steamer at Seattle." The war led to cancellation of that line's sailing schedule after space had been duly engaged and the buyer was held entitled to demand substituted delivery at the warehouse on the line's loading dock. Under this Article, of course, the seller would also be entitled, had the market gone the other way, to make a substituted tender in that manner.

There must, however, be a true commercial impracticability to excuse the agreed to performance and justify a substituted performance. When this is the case a reasonable substituted performance tendered by either party should excuse him from strict compliance with contract terms which do not go to the essence of the agreement.

2. The substitution provided in this section as between buyer and seller does not carry over into the obligation of a financing agency under a letter of credit, since such an agency is entitled to performance which is plainly adequate on its face and without need to look into commercial evidence outside of the documents. See Article 5, especially Sections 5—102, 5—103, 5—109, 5—110, 5—114.

3. Under subsection (2) where the contract is still executory on both sides, the seller is permitted to withdraw unless the buyer can provide him with a commercially equivalent return despite the governmental regulation. Where, however, only the debt for the price remains, a larger leeway is permitted. The buyer may pay in the manner provided by the regulation even though this may not be commercially equivalent provided that the regulation is not "discriminatory, oppressive or predatory."

Cross Reference:

Point 2: Article 5.

Definitional Cross References:

"Buyer". Section 2—103.
"Fault". Section 1—201.
"Party". Section 1—201.
"Seller". Section 2—103.

§ 2—615. Excuse by Failure of Presupposed Conditions

Except so far as a seller may have assumed a greater obligation and subject to the preceding section on substituted performance:

(a) Delay in delivery or non-delivery in whole or in part by a seller who complies with paragraphs (b) and (c) is not a breach of his duty under a contract for sale if performance as agreed has been made impracticable by the occurrence of a contingency the non-occurrence of which was a basic assumption on which the contract was made or by compliance in good faith with any applicable foreign or domestic governmental regulation or order whether or not it later proves to be invalid.

(b) Where the causes mentioned in paragraph (a) affect only a part of the seller's capacity to perform, he must allocate production and deliveries among his customers but may at his option include regular customers not then under contract as well as his own requirements for further manufacture. He may so allocate in any manner which is fair and reasonable.

(c) The seller must notify the buyer seasonably that there will be delay or non-delivery and, when allocation is required under paragraph (b), of the estimated quota thus made available for the buyer.

Official Comment

Prior Uniform Statutory Provision: None.

Purposes:

1. This section excuses a seller from timely delivery of goods contracted for, where his performance has become commercially impracticable because of unforeseen supervening circumstances not within the contemplation of the parties at the time

of contracting. The destruction of specific goods and the problem of the use of substituted performance on points other than delay or quantity, treated elsewhere in this Article, must be distinguished from the matter covered by this section.

2. The present section deliberately refrains from any effort at an exhaustive expression of contingencies and is to be interpreted in all cases sought to be brought within its scope in terms of its underlying reason and purpose.

3. The first test for excuse under this Article in terms of basic assumption is a familiar one. The additional test of commercial impracticability (as contrasted with "impossibility," "frustration of performance" or "frustration of the venture") has been adopted in order to call attention to the commercial character of the criterion chosen by this Article.

4. Increased cost alone does not excuse performance unless the rise in cost is due to some unforeseen contingency which alters the essential nature of the performance. Neither is a rise or a collapse in the market in itself a justification, for that is exactly the type of business risk which business contracts made at fixed prices are intended to cover. But a severe shortage of raw materials or of supplies due to a contingency such as war, embargo, local crop failure, unforeseen shutdown of major sources of supply or the like, which either causes a marked increase in cost or altogether prevents the seller from securing supplies necessary to his performance, is within the contemplation of this section. (See Ford & Sons, Ltd., v. Henry Leetham & Sons, Ltd., 21 Com. Cas. 55 (1915, K.B.D.).)

5. Where a particular source of supply is exclusive under the agreement and fails through casualty, the present section applies rather than the provision on destruction or deterioration of specific goods. The same holds true where a particular source of supply is shown by the circumstances to have been contemplated or assumed by the parties at the time of contracting. (See Davis Co. v. Hoffmann-LaRoche Chemical Works, 178 App.Div. 855, 166 N.Y.S. 179 (1917) and International Paper Co. v. Rockefeller, 161 App.Div. 180, 146 N.Y.S. 371 (1914).) There is no excuse under this section, however, unless the seller has employed all due measures to assure himself that his source will not fail. (See Canadian Industrial Alcohol Co., Ltd., v. Dunbar Molasses Co., 258 N.Y. 194, 179 N.E. 383, 80 A.L.R. 1173 (1932) and Washington Mfg. Co. v. Midland Lumber Co., 113 Wash. 593, 194 P. 777 (1921).)

In the case of failure of production by an agreed source for causes beyond the seller's control, the seller should, if possible, be excused since production by an agreed source is without more a basic assumption of the contract. Such excuse should not result in relieving the defaulting supplier from liability nor in dropping into the seller's lap an unearned bonus of damages over. The flexible adjustment machinery of this Article provides the solution under the provision on the obligation of good faith. A condition to his making good the claim of excuse is the turning over to the buyer of his rights against the defaulting source of supply to the extent of the buyer's contract in relation to which excuse is being claimed.

6. In situations in which neither sense nor justice is served by either answer when the issue is posed in flat terms of "excuse" or "no excuse," adjustment under the various provisions of this Article is necessary, especially the sections on good faith, on insecurity and assurance and on the reading of all provisions in the light of their purposes, and the general policy of this Act to use equitable principles in furtherance of commercial standards and good faith.

7. The failure of conditions which go to convenience or collateral values rather than to the commercial practicability of the main performance does not amount to a complete excuse. However, good faith and the reason of the present section and of the preceding one may properly be held to justify and even to require any needed delay involved in a good faith inquiry seeking a readjustment of the contract terms to meet the new conditions.

8. The provisions of this section are made subject to assumption of greater liability by agreement and such agreement is to be found not only in the expressed terms of the contract but in the circumstances surrounding the contracting, in trade usage and the like. Thus the exemptions of this section do not apply when the contingency in question is sufficiently foreshadowed at the time of contracting to be included among the business risks which are fairly to be regarded as part of the dickered terms, either consciously or as a matter of reasonable, commercial interpretation from the circumstances. (See Madeirense Do Brasil, S. A. v. Stulman-Emrick Lumber Co., 147 F.2d 399 (C.C. A., 2 Cir., 1945).) The exemption otherwise present through usage of trade under the present section may also be expressly negated by the language of the agreement. Generally, express agreements as to exemptions designed to enlarge upon or supplant the provisions of this section are to be read in the light of mercantile sense and reason, for this section itself sets up the commercial standard for normal and reasonable interpretation and provides a minimum beyond which agreement may not go.

Agreement can also be made in regard to the consequences of exemption as laid down in paragraphs (b) and (c) and the next section on procedure on notice claiming excuse.

9. The case of a farmer who has contracted to sell crops to be grown on designated land may be regarded as falling either within the section on casualty to identified goods or this section, and he may be excused, when there is a failure of the specific crop, either on the basis of the destruction of identified goods or because of the failure of a basic assumption of the contract.

Exemption of the buyer in the case of a "requirements" contract is covered by the "Output and Requirements" section both as to assumption and allocation of the relevant risks. But when a contract by a manufacturer to buy fuel or raw material makes no specific reference to a particular venture and no such reference may be drawn from the circumstances, commercial understanding views it as a general deal in the general market and not conditioned on any assumption of the continuing operation of the buyer's plant. Even when notice is given by the buyer that the supplies are needed to fill a specific contract of a normal commercial kind, commercial understanding does not see such a supply contract as conditioned on the continuance of the buyer's further contract for outlet. On the other hand, where the buyer's contract is in reasonable commercial understanding conditioned on a definite and specific venture or assumption as, for instance, a war procurement subcontract known to be based on a prime contract which is subject to termination, or a supply contract for a particular construction venture, the reason of the present section may well apply and entitle the buyer to the exemption.

10. Following its basic policy of using commercial practicability as a test for excuse, this section recognizes as of equal significance either a foreign or domestic regulation and disregards any technical distinctions between "law," "regulation," "order" and the like. Nor does it make the present action of the seller depend upon the eventual judicial determination of the legality of the particular governmental action. The seller's good faith belief in the validity of the regulation is the test under this Article and the best evidence of his good faith is the general commercial acceptance of the regulation. However, governmental interference cannot excuse unless it truly "supervenes" in such a manner as to be beyond the seller's assumption of risk. And any action by the party claiming excuse which causes or colludes in inducing the governmental action preventing his performance would be in breach of good faith and would destroy his exemption.

11. An excused seller must fulfill his contract to the extent which the supervening contingency permits, and if the situation is such that his customers are generally affected he must take account of all in supplying one. Subsections (a) and (b), therefore, explicitly permit in any proration a fair and reasonable attention to the needs of regular customers who are probably relying on spot orders for supplies. Customers at different stages of the manufacturing process may be fairly treated by including the seller's manufacturing requirements. A fortiori, the seller may also take account of contracts later in date than the one in question. The fact that such spot orders may be closed at an advanced price causes no difficulty, since any allocation which exceeds normal past requirements will not be reasonable. However, good faith requires, when prices have advanced, that the seller exercise real care in making his allocations, and in case of doubt his contract customers should be favored and supplies prorated evenly among them regardless of price. Save for the extra care thus required by changes in the market, this section seeks to leave every reasonable business leeway to the seller.

Cross References:

Point 1: Sections 2—613 and 2—614.

Point 2: Section 1—102.

Point 5: Sections 1—203 and 2—613.

Point 6: Sections 1—102, 1—203 and 2—609.

Point 7: Section 2—614.

Point 8: Sections 1—201, 2—302 and 2—616.

Point 9: Sections 1—102, 2—306 and 2—613.

Definitional Cross References:

"Between merchants". Section 2—104.

"Buyer". Section 2—103.

"Contract". Section 1—201.

"Contract for sale". Section 2—106.

"Good faith". Section 1—201.

"Merchant". Section 2—104.

"Notifies". Section 1—201.

"Seasonably". Section 1—204.

"Seller". Section 2—103.

§ 2—616. Procedure on Notice Claiming Excuse

(1) Where the buyer receives notification of a material or indefinite delay or an allocation justified under the preceding section he may by written notification to the seller as to any delivery concerned, and where the prospective deficiency substantially impairs the value of the whole contract under the provisions of this Article relating to breach of installment contracts (Section 2—612), then also as to the whole,

(a) terminate and thereby discharge any unexecuted portion of the contract; or

(b) modify the contract by agreeing to take his available quota in substitution.

(2) If after receipt of such notification from the seller the buyer fails so to modify the contract within a reasonable time not exceeding thirty days the contract lapses with respect to any deliveries affected.

(3) The provisions of this section may not be negated by agreement except in so far as the seller has assumed a greater obligation under the preceding section.

Official Comment

Prior Uniform Statutory Provision: None.

Purposes:

This section seeks to establish simple and workable machinery for providing certainty as to when a supervening and excusing contingency "excuses" the delay, "discharges" the contract, or may result in a waiver of the delay by the buyer. When the seller notifies, in accordance with the preceding section, claiming excuse, the buyer may acquiesce, in which case the contract is so modified. No consideration is necessary in a case of this kind to support such a modification. If the buyer does not elect so to modify the contract, he may terminate it and under subsection (2) his silence after receiving the seller's claim of excuse operates as such a termination. Subsection (3) denies effect to any contract clause made in advance of trouble which would require the buyer to stand ready to take delivery whenever the seller is excused from delivery by unforeseen circumstances.

Cross References:

Point 1: Sections 2—209 and 2—615.

Definitional Cross References:

"Buyer". Section 2—103.

"Contract". Section 1—201.

"Installment contract". Section 2—612.

"Notification". Section 1—201.

"Reasonable time". Section 1—204.

"Seller". Section 2—103.

"Termination". Section 2—106.

"Written". Section 1—201.

PART 7

REMEDIES

§ 2—701. Remedies for Breach of Collateral Contracts Not Impaired

Remedies for breach of any obligation or promise collateral or ancillary to a contract for sale are not impaired by the provisions of this Article.

Official Comment

Prior Uniform Statutory Provision: None.

Purposes:

Whether a claim for breach of an obligation collateral to the contract for sale requires separate trial to avoid confusion of issues is beyond the scope of this Article; but contractual arrangements which as a business matter enter vitally into the contract should be considered a part thereof in so far as cross-claims or defenses are concerned.

Definitional Cross References:

"Contract for sale". Section 2—106.

"Remedy". Section 1—201.

§ 2—702. Seller's Remedies on Discovery of Buyer's Insolvency

(1) Where the seller discovers the buyer to be insolvent he may refuse delivery except for cash including payment for all

goods theretofore delivered under the contract, and stop delivery under this Article (Section 2—705).

(2) Where the seller discovers that the buyer has received goods on credit while insolvent he may reclaim the goods upon demand made within ten days after the receipt, but if misrepresentation of solvency has been made to the particular seller in writing within three months before delivery the ten day limitation does not apply. Except as provided in this subsection the seller may not base a right to reclaim goods on the buyer's fraudulent or innocent misrepresentation of solvency or of intent to pay.

(3) The seller's right to reclaim under subsection (2) is subject to the rights of a buyer in ordinary course or other good faith purchaser under this Article (Section 2—403). Successful reclamation of goods excludes all other remedies with respect to them. As amended 1966.

Official Comment

Prior Uniform Statutory Provision: Subsection (1)—Sections 53(1) (b), 54(1) (c) and 57, Uniform Sales Act; Subsection (2) —none; Subsection (3)—Section 76(3), Uniform Sales Act.

Changes: Rewritten, the protection given to a seller who has sold on credit and has delivered goods to the buyer immediately preceding his insolvency being extended.

Purposes of Changes and New Matter: To make it clear that:

1. The seller's right to withhold the goods or to stop delivery except for cash when he discovers the buyer's insolvency is made explicit in subsection (1) regardless of the passage of title, and the concept of stoppage has been extended to include goods in the possession of any bailee who has not yet attorned to the buyer.

2. Subsection (2) takes as its base line the proposition that any receipt of goods on credit by an insolvent buyer amounts to a tacit business misrepresentation of solvency and therefore is fraudulent as against the particular seller. This Article makes discovery of the buyer's insolvency and demand within a ten day period a condition of the right to reclaim goods on this ground. The ten day limitation period operates from the time of receipt of the goods.

An exception to this time limitation is made when a written misrepresentation of solvency has been made to the particular seller within three months prior to the delivery. To fall within the exception the statement of solvency must be in writing, addressed to the particular seller and dated within three months of the delivery.

3. Because the right of the seller to reclaim goods under this section constitutes preferential treatment as against the buyer's other creditors, subsection (3) provides that such reclamation bars all his other remedies as to the goods involved. As amended 1966.

Cross References:

Point 1: Sections 2—401 and 2—705.

Compare Section 2—502.

Definitional Cross References:

"Buyer". Section 2—103.

"Buyer in ordinary course of business". Section 1—201.

"Contract". Section 1—201.

"Good faith". Section 1—201.

"Goods". Section 2—105.

"Insolvent". Section 1—201.

"Person". Section 1—201.

"Purchaser". Section 1—201.

"Receipt" of goods. Section 2—103.

"Remedy". Section 1—201.

"Rights". Section 1—201.

"Seller". Section 2—103.

"Writing". Section 1—201.

§ 2—703. Seller's Remedies in General

Where the buyer wrongfully rejects or revokes acceptance of goods or fails to make a payment due on or before delivery or repudiates with respect to a part or the whole, then with respect to any goods directly affected and, if the breach is of the whole contract (Section 2—612), then also with respect to the whole undelivered balance, the aggrieved seller may

(a) withhold delivery of such goods;

(b) stop delivery by any bailee as hereafter provided (Section 2—705);

(c) proceed under the next section respecting goods still unidentified to the contract;

(d) resell and recover damages as hereafter provided (Section 2—706);

(e) recover damages for non-acceptance (Section 2—708) or in a proper case the price (Section 2—709);

(f) cancel.

Official Comment

Prior Uniform Statutory Provision: No comparable index section. See Section 53, Uniform Sales Act.

Purposes:

1. This section is an index section which gathers together in one convenient place all of the various remedies open to a seller for any breach by the buyer. This Article rejects any doctrine of election of remedy as a fundamental policy and thus the remedies are essentially cumulative in nature and include all of the available remedies for breach. Whether the pursuit of

one remedy bars another depends entirely on the facts of the individual case.

2. The buyer's breach which occasions the use of the remedies under this section may involve only one lot or delivery of goods, or may involve all of the goods which are the subject matter of the particular contract. The right of the seller to pursue a remedy as to all the goods when the breach is as to only one or more lots is covered by the section on breach in installment contracts. The present section deals only with the remedies available after the goods involved in the breach have been determined by that section.

3. In addition to the typical case of refusal to pay or default in payment, the language in the preamble, "fails to make a payment due," is intended to cover the dishonor of a check on due presentment, or the non-acceptance of a draft, and the failure to furnish an agreed letter of credit.

4. It should also be noted that this Act requires its remedies to be liberally administered and provides that any right or obligation which it declares is enforceable by action unless a different effect is specifically prescribed (Section 1—106).

Cross References:

Point 2: Section 2—612.
Point 3: Section 2—325.
Point 4: Section 1—106.

Definitional Cross References:

"Aggrieved party". Section 1—201.
"Buyer". Section 2—103.
"Cancellation". Section 2—106.
"Contract". Section 1—201.
"Goods". Section 2—105.
"Remedy". Section 1—201.
"Seller". Section 2—103.

§ 2—704. Seller's Right to Identify Goods to the Contract Notwithstanding Breach or to Salvage Unfinished Goods

(1) An aggrieved seller under the preceding section may

(a) identify to the contract conforming goods not already identified if at the time he learned of the breach they are in his possession or control;

(b) treat as the subject of resale goods which have demonstrably been intended for the particular contract even though those goods are unfinished.

(2) Where the goods are unfinished an aggrieved seller may in the exercise of reasonable commercial judgment for the purposes of avoiding loss and of effective realization either complete the manufacture and wholly identify the goods to the contract or cease manufacture and resell for scrap or salvage value or proceed in any other reasonable manner.

Official Comment

Prior Uniform Statutory Provision: Sections 63(3) and 64(4), Uniform Sales Act.

Changes: Rewritten, the seller's rights being broadened.

Purposes of Changes:

1. This section gives an aggrieved seller the right at the time of breach to identify to the contract any conforming finished goods, regardless of their resalability, and to use reasonable judgment as to completing unfinished goods. It thus makes the goods available for resale under the resale section, the seller's primary remedy, and in the special case in which resale is not practicable, allows the action for the price which would then be necessary to give the seller the value of his contract.

2. Under this Article the seller is given express power to complete manufacture or procurement of goods for the contract unless the exercise of reasonable commercial judgment as to the facts as they appear at the time he learns of the breach makes it clear that such action will result in a material increase in damages. The burden is on the buyer to show the commercially unreasonable nature of the seller's action in completing manufacture.

Cross References:

Sections 2—703 and 2—706.

Definitional Cross References:

"Aggrieved party". Section 1—201.

"Conforming". Section 2—106.

"Contract". Section 1—201.

"Goods". Section 2—105.

"Rights". Section 1—201.

"Seller". Section 2—103.

§ 2—705. Seller's Stoppage of Delivery in Transit or Otherwise

(1) The seller may stop delivery of goods in the possession of a carrier or other bailee when he discovers the buyer to be insolvent (Section 2—702) and may stop delivery of carload, truckload, planeload or larger shipments of express or freight when the buyer repudiates or fails to make a payment due before delivery or if for any other reason the seller has a right to withhold or reclaim the goods.

(2) As against such buyer the seller may stop delivery until

(a) receipt of the goods by the buyer; or

(b) acknowledgment to the buyer by any bailee of the goods except a carrier that the bailee holds the goods for the buyer; or

(c) such acknowledgment to the buyer by a carrier by reshipment or as warehouseman; or

(d) negotiation to the buyer of any negotiable document of title covering the goods.

(3) (a) To stop delivery the seller must so notify as to enable the bailee by reasonable diligence to prevent delivery of the goods.

(b) After such notification the bailee must hold and deliver the goods according to the directions of the seller but the seller is liable to the bailee for any ensuing charges or damages.

(c) If a negotiable document of title has been issued for goods the bailee is not obliged to obey a notification to stop until surrender of the document.

(d) A carrier who has issued a non-negotiable bill of lading is not obliged to obey a notification to stop received from a person other than the consignor.

Official Comment

Prior Uniform Statutory Provision: Sections 57–59, Uniform Sales Act; see also Sections 12, 14 and 42, Uniform Bills of Lading Act and Sections 9, 11 and 49, Uniform Warehouse Receipts Act.

Changes: This section continues and develops the above sections of the Uniform Sales Act in the light of the other uniform statutory provisions noted.

Purposes: To make it clear that:

1. Subsection (1) applies the stoppage principle to other bailees as well as carriers.

It also expands the remedy to cover the situations, in addition to buyer's insolvency, specified in the subsection. But since stoppage is a burden in any case to carriers, and might be a very heavy burden to them if it covered all small shipments in all these situations, the right to stop for reasons other than insolvency is limited to carload, truckload, planeload or larger shipments. The seller shipping to a buyer of doubtful credit can protect himself by shipping C.O.D.

Where stoppage occurs for insecurity it is merely a suspension of performance, and if assurances are duly forthcoming from the buyer the seller is not entitled to resell or divert.

Improper stoppage is a breach by the seller if it effectively interferes with the buyer's right to due tender under the section on manner of tender of delivery. However, if the bailee obeys an unjustified order to stop he may also be liable to the buyer. The measure of his obligation is dependent on the provisions of the Documents of Title Article (Section 7—303). Subsection 3(b) therefore gives him a right of indemnity as against the seller in such a case.

2. "Receipt by the buyer" includes receipt by the buyer's designated representative, the subpurchaser, when shipment is made direct to him and the buyer himself never receives the goods. It is entirely proper under this

Article that the seller, by making such direct shipment to the sub-purchaser, be regarded as acquiescing in the latter's purchase and as thus barred from stoppage of the goods as against him.

As between the buyer and the seller, the latter's right to stop the goods at any time until they reach the place of final delivery is recognized by this section.

Under subsection (3)(c) and (d), the carrier is under no duty to recognize the stop order of a person who is a stranger to the carrier's contract. But the seller's right as against the buyer to stop delivery remains, whether or not the carrier is obligated to recognize the stop order. If the carrier does obey it, the buyer cannot complain merely because of that circumstance; and the seller becomes obligated under subsection (3) (b) to pay the carrier any ensuing damages or charges.

3. A diversion of a shipment is not a "reshipment" under subsection (2) (c) when it is merely an incident to the original contract of transportation. Nor is the procurement of "exchange bills" of lading which change only the name of the consignee to that of the buyer's local agent but do not alter the destination of a reshipment.

Acknowledgment by the carrier as a "warehouseman" within the meaning of this Article requires a contract of a truly different character from the original shipment, a contract not in extension of transit but as a warehouseman.

4. Subsection (3) (c) makes the bailee's obedience of a notification to stop conditional upon the surrender of any outstanding negotiable document.

5. Any charges or losses incurred by the carrier in following the seller's orders, whether or not he was obligated to do so, fall to the seller's charge.

6. After an effective stoppage under this section the seller's rights in the goods are the same as if he had never made a delivery.

Cross References:

Sections 2—702 and 2—703.

Point 1: Sections 2—503 and 2—609, and Article 7.

Point 2: Section 2—103 and Article 7.

Definitional Cross References:

"Buyer". Section 2—103.

"Contract for sale". Section 2—106.

"Document of title". Section 1—201.

"Goods". Section 2—105.

"Insolvent". Section 1—201.

"Notification". Section 1—201.

"Receipt" of goods. Section 2—103.

"Rights". Section 1—201.

"Seller". Section 2—103.

§ 2—706. Seller's Resale Including Contract for Resale

(1) Under the conditions stated in Section 2—703 on seller's remedies, the seller may resell the goods concerned or the undelivered balance thereof. Where the resale is made in good faith and in a commercially reasonable manner the seller may recover the difference between the resale price and the contract price to-

gether with any incidental damages allowed under the provisions of this Article (Section 2—710), but less expenses saved in consequence of the buyer's breach.

(2) Except as otherwise provided in subsection (3) or unless otherwise agreed resale may be at public or private sale including sale by way of one or more contracts to sell or of identification to an existing contract of the seller. Sale may be as a unit or in parcels and at any time and place and on any terms but every aspect of the sale including the method, manner, time, place and terms must be commercially reasonable. The resale must be reasonably identified as referring to the broken contract, but it is not necessary that the goods be in existence or that any or all of them have been identified to the contract before the breach.

(3) Where the resale is at private sale the seller must give the buyer reasonable notification of his intention to resell.

(4) Where the resale is at public sale

(a) only identified goods can be sold except where there is a recognized market for a public sale of futures in goods of the kind; and

(b) it must be made at a usual place or market for public sale if one is reasonably available and except in the case of goods which are perishable or threaten to decline in value speedily the seller must give the buyer reasonable notice of the time and place of the resale; and

(c) if the goods are not to be within the view of those attending the sale the notification of sale must state the place where the goods are located and provide for their reasonable inspection by prospective bidders; and

(d) the seller may buy.

(5) A purchaser who buys in good faith at a resale takes the goods free of any rights of the original buyer even though the seller fails to comply with one or more of the requirements of this section.

(6) The seller is not accountable to the buyer for any profit made on any resale. A person in the position of a seller (Section 2—707) or a buyer who has rightfully rejected or justifiably revoked acceptance must account for any excess over the amount of his security interest, as hereinafter defined (subsection (3) of Section 2—711).

Official Comment

Prior Uniform Statutory Provision: Section 60, Uniform Sales Act.

Changes: Rewritten.

Purposes of Changes: To simplify the prior statutory provision and to make it clear that:

1. The only condition precedent to the seller's right of resale under subsection (1) is a breach by the buyer within the section on the seller's remedies in general or insolvency. Other meticulous conditions and restrictions of the prior uniform statutory provision are disapproved by this Article and are replaced by standards of commercial reasonableness. Under this section the seller may resell the goods after any breach by the buyer. Thus, an anticipatory repudiation by the buyer gives rise to any of the seller's remedies for breach, and to the right of resale. This principle is supplemented by subsection (2) which authorizes a resale of goods which are not in existence or were not identified to the contract before the breach.

2. In order to recover the damages prescribed in subsection (1) the seller must act "in good faith and in a commercially reasonable manner" in making the resale. This standard is intended to be more comprehensive than that of "reasonable care and judgment" established by the prior uniform statutory provision. Failure to act properly under this section deprives the seller of the measure of damages here provided and relegates him to that provided in Section 2—708.

Under this Article the seller resells by authority of law, in his own behalf, for his own benefit and for the purpose of fixing his damages. The theory of a seller's agency is thus rejected.

3. If the seller complies with the prescribed standard of duty in making the resale, he may recover from the buyer the damages provided for in subsection (1). Evidence of market or current prices at any particular time or place is relevant only on the question of whether the seller acted in a commercially reasonable manner in making the resale.

The distinction drawn by some courts between cases where the title had not passed to the buyer and the seller had resold as owner, and cases where the title had passed and the seller had resold by virtue of his lien on the goods, is rejected.

4. Subsection (2) frees the remedy of resale from legalistic restrictions and enables the seller to resell in accordance with reasonable commercial practices so as to realize as high a price as possible in the circumstances. By "public" sale is meant a sale by auction. A "private" sale may be effected by solicitation and negotiation conducted either directly or through a broker. In choosing between a public and private sale the character of the goods must be considered and relevant trade practices and usages must be observed.

5. Subsection (2) merely clarifies the common law rule that the time for resale is a

reasonable time after the buyer's breach, by using the language "commercially reasonable." What is such a reasonable time depends upon the nature of the goods, the condition of the market and the other circumstances of the case; its length cannot be measured by any legal yardstick or divided into degrees. Where a seller contemplating resale receives a demand from the buyer for inspection under the section of preserving evidence of goods in dispute, the time for resale may be appropriately lengthened.

On the question of the place for resale, subsection (2) goes to the ultimate test, the commercial reasonableness of the seller's choice as to the place for an advantageous resale. This Article rejects the theory that the seller is required to resell at the agreed place for delivery and that a resale elsewhere can be permitted only in exceptional cases.

6. The purpose of subsection (2) being to enable the seller to dispose of the goods to the best advantage, he is permitted in making the resale to depart from the terms and conditions of the original contract for sale to any extent "commercially reasonable" in the circumstances.

7. The provision of subsection (2) that the goods need not be in existence to be resold applies when the buyer is guilty of anticipatory repudiation of a contract for future goods, before the goods or some of them have come into existence. In such a case the seller may exercise the right of resale and fix his damages by "one or more contracts to sell" the quantity of conforming future goods affected by the repudiation. The companion provision of subsection (2) that resale may be made although the goods were not identified to the contract prior to the buyer's breach, likewise contemplates an anticipatory repudiation by the buyer but occurring after the goods are in existence. If the goods so identified conform to the contract, their resale will fix the seller's damages quite as satisfactorily as if they had been identified before the breach.

8. Where the resale is to be by private sale, subsection (3) requires that reasonable notification of the seller's intention to resell must be given to the buyer. The length of notification of a private sale depends upon the urgency of the matter. Notification of the time and place of this type of sale is not required.

Subsection (4) (b) requires that the seller give the buyer reasonable notice of the time and place of a public resale so that he may have an opportunity to bid or to secure the attendance of other bidders. An exception is made in the case of goods "which are perishable or threaten to decline speedily in value."

9. Since there would be no reasonable prospect of competitive bidding elsewhere, subsection (4) requires that a public resale "must be made at a usual place or market for public sale if one is reasonably available;" i. e., a place or market which prospective bidders may reasonably be expected to attend. Such a market may still be "reasonably available" under this subsection, though at a considerable

distance from the place where the goods are located. In such a case the expense of transporting the goods for resale is recoverable from the buyer as part of the seller's incidental damages under subsection (1). However, the question of availability is one of commercial reasonableness in the circumstances and if such "usual" place or market is not reasonably available, a duly advertised public resale may be held at another place if it is one which prospective bidders may reasonably be expected to attend, as distinguished from a place where there is no demand whatsoever for goods of the kind.

Paragraph (a) of subsection (4) qualifies the last sentence of subsection (2) with respect to resales of unidentified and future goods at public sale. If conforming goods are in existence the seller may identify them to the contract after the buyer's breach and then resell them at public sale. If the goods have not been identified, however, he may resell them at public sale only as "future" goods and only where there is a recognized market for public sale of futures in goods of the kind.

The provisions of paragraph (c) of subsection (4) are intended to permit intelligent bidding.

The provision of paragraph (d) of subsection (4) permitting the seller to bid and, of course, to become the purchaser, benefits the original buyer by tending to increase the resale price and thus decreasing the damages he will have to pay.

10. This Article departs in subsection (5) from the prior uniform statutory provision in permitting a good faith purchaser at resale to take a good title as against the buyer even though the seller fails to comply with the requirements of this section.

11. Under subsection (6), the seller retains profit, if any, without distinction based on whether or not he had a lien since this Article divorces the question of passage of title to the buyer from the seller's right of resale or the consequences of its exercise. On the other hand, where "a person in the position of a seller" or a buyer acting under the section on buyer's remedies, exercises his right of resale under the present section he does so only for the limited purpose of obtaining cash for his "security interest" in the goods. Once that purpose has been accomplished any excess in the resale price belongs to the seller to whom an accounting must be made as provided in the last sentence of subsection (6).

Cross References:

Point 1: Sections 2—610, 2—702 and 2—703.

Point 2: Section 1—201.

Point 3: Sections 2—708 and 2—710.

Point 4: Section 2—328.

Point 8: Section 2—104.

Point 9: Section 2—710.

Point 11: Sections 2—401, 2—707 and 2—711(3).

Definitional Cross References:

"Buyer". Section 2—103.

"Contract". Section 1—201.

"Contract for sale". Section 2—106.

"Good faith". Section 2—103.
"Goods". Section 2—105.
"Merchant". Section 2—104.
"Notification". Section 1—201.
"Person in position of seller". Section 2—707.
"Purchase". Section 1—201.
"Rights". Section 1—201.
"Sale". Section 2—106.
"Security interest". Section 1—201.
"Seller". Section 2—103.

§ 2—707. "Person in the Position of a Seller"

(1) A "person in the position of a seller" includes as against a principal an agent who has paid or become responsible for the price of goods on behalf of his principal or anyone who otherwise holds a security interest or other right in goods similar to that of a seller.

(2) A person in the position of a seller may as provided in this Article withhold or stop delivery (Section 2—705) and resell (Section 2—706) and recover incidental damages (Section 2—710).

Official Comment

Prior Uniform Statutory Provision: Section 52(2), Uniform Sales Act.

Changes: Rewritten.

Purposes of Changes: To make it clear that:

In addition to following in general the prior uniform statutory provision, the case of a financing agency which has acquired documents by honoring a letter of credit for the buyer or by discounting a draft for the seller has been included in the term "a person in the position of a seller."

Cross Reference:

Article 5, Section 2—506.

Definitional Cross References:

"Consignee". Section 7—102.
"Consignor". Section 7—102.
"Goods". Section 2—105.
"Security interest". Section 1—201.
"Seller". Section 2—103.

§ 2—708. Seller's Damages for Non-acceptance or Repudiation

(1) Subject to subsection (2) and to the provisions of this Article with respect to proof of market price (Section 2—723), the measure of damages for non-acceptance or repudiation by the buyer is the difference between the market price at the time and place for tender and the unpaid contract price together with any incidental damages provided in this Article (Section 2—710), but less expenses saved in consequence of the buyer's breach.

(2) If the measure of damages provided in subsection (1) is inadequate to put the seller in as good a position as performance would have done then the measure of damages is the profit (including reasonable overhead) which the seller would have made from full performance by the buyer, together with any incidental damages provided in this Article (Section 2—710), due allowance for costs reasonably incurred and due credit for payments or proceeds of resale.

Official Comment

Prior Uniform Statutory Provision: Section 64, Uniform Sales Act.

Changes: Rewritten.

Purposes of Changes: To make it clear that:

1. The prior uniform statutory provision is followed generally in setting the current market price at the time and place for tender as the standard by which damages for non-acceptance are to be determined. The time and place of tender is determined by reference to the section on manner of tender of delivery, and to the sections on the effect of such terms as FOB, FAS, CIF, C & F, Ex Ship and No Arrival, No Sale.

In the event that there is no evidence available of the current market price at the time and place of tender, proof of a substitute market may be made under the section on determination and proof of market price. Furthermore, the section on the admissibility of market quotations is intended to ease materially the problem of providing competent evidence.

2. The provision of this section permitting recovery of expected profit including reasonable overhead where the standard measure of damages is inadequate, together with the new requirement that price actions may be sustained only where resale is impractical, are designed to eliminate the unfair and economically wasteful results arising under the older law when fixed price articles were involved. This section permits the recovery of lost profits in all appropriate cases, which would include all standard priced goods. The normal measure there would be list price less cost to the dealer or list price less manufacturing cost to the manufacturer. It is not necessary to a recovery of "profit" to show a history of earnings, especially if a new venture is involved.

3. In all cases the seller may recover incidental damages.

Cross References:

Point 1: Sections 2—319 through 2—324, 2—503, 2—723 and 2—724.

Point 2: Section 2—709.

Point 3: Section 2—710.

Definitional Cross References:

"Buyer". Section 2—103.

"Contract". Section 1—201.

"Seller". Section 2—103.

§ 2—709. Action for the Price

(1) When the buyer fails to pay the price as it becomes due the seller may recover, together with any incidental damages under the next section, the price

(a) of goods accepted or of conforming goods lost or damaged within a commercially reasonable time after risk of their loss has passed to the buyer; and

(b) of goods identified to the contract if the seller is unable after reasonable effort to resell them at a reasonable price or the circumstances reasonably indicate that such effort will be unavailing.

(2) Where the seller sues for the price he must hold for the buyer any goods which have been identified to the contract and are still in his control except that if resale becomes possible he may resell them at any time prior to the collection of the judgment. The net proceeds of any such resale must be credited to the buyer and payment of the judgment entitles him to any goods not resold.

(3) After the buyer has wrongfully rejected or revoked acceptance of the goods or has failed to make a payment due or has repudiated (Section 2—610), a seller who is held not entitled to the price under this section shall nevertheless be awarded damages for non-acceptance under the preceding section.

Official Comment

Prior Uniform Statutory Provision: Section 63, Uniform Sales Act.

Changes: Rewritten, important commercially needed changes being incorporated.

Purposes of Changes: To make it clear that:

1. Neither the passing of title to the goods nor the appointment of a day certain for payment is now material to a price action.

2. The action for the price is now generally limited to those cases where resale of the goods is impracticable except where the buyer has accepted the goods or where they have been destroyed after risk of loss has passed to the buyer.

3. This section substitutes an objective test by action for the former "not readily resalable" standard. An action for the price under subsection (1) (b) can be sustained only after a "reasonable effort to resell" the goods "at reasonable price" has actually been made or where the circumstances "reasonably indicate" that such an effort will be unavailing.

4. If a buyer is in default not with respect to the price, but on an obligation to make an ad-

vance, the seller should recover not under this section for the price as such, but for the default in the collateral (though coincident) obligation to finance the seller. If the agreement between the parties contemplates that the buyer will acquire, on making the advance, a security interest in the goods, the buyer on making the advance has such an interest as soon as the seller has rights in the agreed collateral. See Section 9—204.

5. "Goods accepted" by the buyer under subsection (1) (a) include only goods as to which there has been no justified revocation of acceptance, for such a revocation means that there has been a default by the seller which bars his rights under this section. "Goods lost or damaged" are covered by the section on risk of loss. "Goods identified to the contract" under subsection (1) (b) are covered by the section on identification and the section on identification notwithstanding breach.

6. This section is intended to be exhaustive in its enumeration of cases where an action for the price lies.

7. If the action for the price fails, the seller may nonetheless have proved a case entitling him to damages for non-acceptance. In such a situation, subsection (3) permits recovery of those damages in the same action.

Cross References:

Point 4: Section 1—106.

Point 5: Sections 2—501, 2—509, 2—510 and 2—704.

Point 7: Section 2—708.

Definitional Cross References:

"Action". Section 1—201.

"Buyer". Section 2—103.

"Conforming". Section 2—106.

"Contract". Section 1—201.

"Goods". Section 2—105.

"Seller". Section 2—103.

2-706
2-708
2-709

§ 2—710. Seller's Incidental Damages

Incidental damages to an aggrieved seller include any commercially reasonable charges, expenses or commissions incurred in stopping delivery, in the transportation, care and custody of goods after the buyer's breach, in connection with return or resale of the goods or otherwise resulting from the breach.

Official Comment

Prior Uniform Statutory Provision: See Sections 64 and 70, Uniform Sales Act.

Purposes: To authorize reimbursement of the seller for expenses reasonably incurred by him as a result of the buyer's breach. The section sets forth the principal normal and necessary additional elements of damage flowing from the breach but intends to allow all commercially reasonable expenditures made by the seller.

Definitional Cross References:

"Aggrieved party". Section 1—201.

"Buyer". Section 2—103.

"Goods". Section 2—105.

"Seller". Section 2—103.

§ 2—711. Buyer's Remedies in General; Buyer's Security Interest in Rejected Goods

(1) Where the seller fails to make delivery or repudiates or the buyer rightfully rejects or justifiably revokes acceptance then with respect to any goods involved, and with respect to the whole if the breach goes to the whole contract (Section 2—612), the buyer may cancel and whether or not he has done so may in addition to recovering so much of the price as has been paid

(a) "cover" and have damages under the next section as to all the goods affected whether or not they have been identified to the contract; or

(b) recover damages for non-delivery as provided in this Article (Section 2—713).

(2) Where the seller fails to deliver or repudiates the buyer may also

(a) if the goods have been identified recover them as provided in this Article (Section 2—502); or

(b) in a proper case obtain specific performance or replevy the goods as provided in this Article (Section 2—716).

(3) On rightful rejection or justifiable revocation of acceptance a buyer has a security interest in goods in his possession or control for any payments made on their price and any expenses reasonably incurred in their inspection, receipt, transportation, care and custody and may hold such goods and resell them in like manner as an aggrieved seller (Section 2—706).

Official Comment

Prior Uniform Statutory Provision: No comparable index section; Subsection (3)—Section 69(5), Uniform Sales Act.

Changes: The prior uniform statutory provision is generally continued and expanded in Subsection (3).

Purposes of Changes and New Matter:

1. To index in this section the buyer's remedies, subsection (1) covering those remedies permitting the recovery of money damages, and subsection (2) covering those which permit reaching the goods themselves. The remedies listed here are those available to a buyer who has not accepted the goods or who has justifiably revoked his acceptance. The remedies available to a buyer with regard to goods finally accepted appear in the section dealing with breach in regard to accepted goods. The buyer's right to proceed as to all goods when the breach is as to only some of the goods is determined by the section on breach in installment contracts and by the section on partial acceptance.

Despite the seller's breach, proper retender of delivery under the section on cure of improper tender or replacement can effectively preclude the buyer's remedies under this section, except for any delay involved.

2. To make it clear in subsection (3) that the buyer may hold and resell rejected goods if he has paid a part of the price or incurred expenses of the type specified. "Paid" as used here includes acceptance of a draft or other time negotiable instrument or the signing of a negotiable note. His freedom of resale is coextensive with that of a seller under this Article except that the buyer may not keep any profit resulting from the resale and is limited to retaining only the amount of the price paid and the costs involved in the inspection and handling of the goods. The buyer's security interest in the goods is intended to be limited to the items listed in subsection (3), and the buyer is not permitted to retain such funds as he might believe adequate for his damages. The buyer's right to cover, or to have damages for non-delivery, is not impaired by his exercise of his right of resale.

3. It should also be noted that this Act requires its remedies to be liberally administered and provides that any right or obligation which it declares is enforceable by action unless a different effect is specifically prescribed (Section 1—106).

Cross References:

Point 1: Sections 2—508, 2—601(c), 2—608, 2—612 and 2—714.

Point 2: Section 2—706.

Point 3: Section 1—106.

Definitional Cross References:

"Aggrieved party". Section 1—201.

"Buyer". Section 2—103.

"Cancellation". Section 2—106.

"Contract". Section 1—201.

"Cover". Section 2—712.

"Goods". Section 2—105.

"Notifies". Section 1—201.

"Receipt" of goods. Section 2—103.

"Remedy". Section 1—201.

"Security interest". Section 1—201.

"Seller". Section 2—103.

§ 2—712. "Cover"; Buyer's Procurement of Substitute Goods

(1) After a breach within the preceding section the buyer may "cover" by making in good faith and without unreasonable delay any reasonable purchase of or contract to purchase goods in substitution for those due from the seller.

(2) The buyer may recover from the seller as damages the difference between the cost of cover and the contract price together with any incidental or consequential damages as hereinafter defined (Section 2—715), but less expenses saved in consequence of the seller's breach.

(3) Failure of the buyer to effect cover within this section does not bar him from any other remedy.

Official Comment

Prior Uniform Statutory Provision: None.

Purposes:

1. This section provides the buyer with a remedy aimed at enabling him to obtain the goods he needs thus meeting his essential need. This remedy is the buyer's equivalent of the seller's right to resell.

2. The definition of "cover" under subsection (1) envisages a series of contracts or sales, as well as a single contract or sale; goods not identical with those involved but commercially usable as reasonable substitutes under the circumstances of the particular case; and contracts on credit or delivery terms differing from the contract in breach, but again reasonable under the circumstances. The test of proper cover is whether at the time and place the buyer acted in good faith and in a reasonable manner, and it is immaterial that hindsight may later prove that the method of cover used was not the cheapest or most effective.

The requirement that the buyer must cover "without unreasonable delay" is not intended to limit the time necessary for him to look around and decide as to how he may best effect cover. The test here is similar to that generally used in this Article as to reasonable time and seasonable action.

3. Subsection (3) expresses the policy that cover is not a mandatory remedy for the buyer. The buyer is always free to choose between cover and damages for non-delivery under the next section.

However, this subsection must be read in conjunction with the section which limits the recovery of consequential damages to such as could not have been obviated by cover. Moreover, the operation of the section on specific performance of contracts for "unique" goods must be considered in this connection for availability of the goods to the particular buyer for his particular needs is the test for that remedy and inability to cover is made an express condition to the right of the buyer to replevy the goods.

4. This section does not limit cover to merchants, in the first instance. It is the vital and important remedy for the consumer buyer as well. Both are free to use cover: the domestic or non-merchant consumer is required only to act in normal good faith while the merchant buyer must also observe all reasonable commercial standards of fair dealing in the trade, since this falls within the definition of good faith on his part.

Cross References:

Point 1: Section 2—706.

Point 2: Section 1—204.

Point 3: Sections 2—713, 2—715 and 2—716.

Point 4: Section 1—203.

Definitional Cross References:

"Buyer". Section 2—103.
"Contract". Section 1—201.
"Good faith". Section 2—103.
"Goods". Section 2—105.
"Purchase". Section 1—201.
"Remedy". Section 1—201.
"Seller". Section 2—103.

§ 2—713. Buyer's Damages for Non-Delivery or Repudiation

(1) Subject to the provisions of this Article with respect to proof of market price (Section 2—723), the measure of damages for non-delivery or repudiation by the seller is the difference between the market price at the time when the buyer learned of the breach and the contract price together with any incidental and consequential damages provided in this Article (Section 2—715), but less expenses saved in consequence of the seller's breach.

(2) Market price is to be determined as of the place for tender or, in cases of rejection after arrival or revocation of acceptance, as of the place of arrival.

Official Comment

Prior Uniform Statutory Provision: Section 67(3), Uniform Sales Act.

Changes: Rewritten.

Purposes of Changes: To clarify the former rule so that:

1. The general baseline adopted in this section uses as a yardstick the market in which the buyer would have obtained cover had he sought that relief. So the place for measuring damages is the place of tender (or the place of arrival if the goods are rejected or their acceptance is revoked after reaching their destination) and the crucial time is the time at which the buyer learns of the breach.

2. The market or current price to be used in comparison with the contract price under this section is the price for goods of the same kind and in the same branch of trade.

3. When the current market price under this section is difficult to prove the section on determination and proof of market price is available to permit a showing of a comparable market price or, where no market price is available, evidence of spot sale prices is proper. Where the unavailability of a market price is caused by a scarcity of goods of the type involved, a good case is normally made for specific performance under this Article. Such scarcity conditions, moreover, indicate that the price has risen and under the section providing for liberal administration of remedies, opinion evidence as to the value of the goods would be admissible in the absence of a market price and a liberal construction of allowable consequential damages should also result.

4. This section carries forward the standard rule that the buyer must deduct from his damages any expenses saved as a result of the breach.

5. The present section provides a remedy which is completely alternative to cover under the preceding section and applies only when and to the extent that the buyer has not covered.

Cross References:

Point 3: Sections 1—106, 2—716 and 2—723.

Point 5: Section 2—712.

Definitional Cross References:

"Buyer". Section 2—103.

"Contract". Section 1—201.

"Seller". Section 2—103.

§ 2—714. Buyer's Damages for Breach in Regard to Accepted Goods

(1) Where the buyer has accepted goods and given notification (subsection (3) of Section 2—607) he may recover as damages for any non-conformity of tender the loss resulting in the ordinary course of events from the seller's breach as determined in any manner which is reasonable.

(2) The measure of damages for breach of warranty is the difference at the time and place of acceptance between the value of the goods accepted and the value they would have had if they had been as warranted, unless special circumstances show proximate damages of a different amount.

(3) In a proper case any incidental and consequential damages under the next section may also be recovered.

Official Comment

Prior Uniform Statutory Provision: Section 69(6) and (7), Uniform Sales Act.

Changes: Rewritten.

Purposes of Changes:

1. This section deals with the remedies available to the buyer after the goods have been accepted and the time for revocation of acceptance has gone by. In general this section adopts the rule of the prior uniform statutory provision for measuring damages where there has been a breach of warranty as to goods accepted, but goes further to lay down an explicit provision as to the time and place for determining the loss.

The section on deduction of damages from price provides an additional remedy for a buyer who still owes part of the purchase price, and frequently the two remedies will be available concurrently. The buyer's failure to notify of his claim under the section on effects of acceptance, however, operates to bar his remedies under either that section or the present section.

2. The "non-conformity" referred to in subsection (1) includes not only breaches of warranties but also any failure of the seller to perform according to his obligations under the contract. In the case of such non-conformity, the buyer is permitted to recover for his loss "in any manner which is reasonable."

3. Subsection (2) describes the usual, standard and reasonable method of ascertaining damages in the case of breach of warranty but it is not intended as an exclusive measure. It departs from the measure of dam-

ages for non-delivery in utilizing the place of acceptance rather than the place of tender. In some cases the two may coincide, as where the buyer signifies his acceptance upon the tender. If, however, the non-conformity is such as would justify revocation of acceptance, the time and place of acceptance under this section is determined as of the buyer's decision not to revoke.

4. The incidental and consequential damages referred to in subsection (3), which will usually accompany an action brought under this section, are discussed in detail in the comment on the next section.

Cross References:

Point 1: Compare Section 2—711; Sections 2—607 and 2—717.

Point 2: Section 2—106.

Point 3: Sections 2—608 and 2—713.

Point 4: Section 2—715.

Definitional Cross References:

"Buyer". Section 2—103.

"Conform". Section 2—106.

"Goods". Section 1—201.

"Notification". Section 1—201.

"Seller". Section 2—103.

§ 2—715. Buyer's Incidental and Consequential Damages

(1) Incidental damages resulting from the seller's breach include expenses reasonably incurred in inspection, receipt, transportation and care and custody of goods rightfully rejected, any commercially reasonable charges, expenses or commissions in connection with effecting cover and any other reasonable expense incident to the delay or other breach.

(2) Consequential damages resulting from the seller's breach include

(a) any loss resulting from general or particular requirements and needs of which the seller at the time of contracting had reason to know and which could not reasonably be prevented by cover or otherwise; and

(b) injury to person or property proximately resulting from any breach of warranty.

Official Comment

Prior Uniform Statutory Provisions: Subsection (2) (b)—Sections 69(7) and 70, Uniform Sales Act.

Changes: Rewritten.

Purposes of Changes and New Matter:

1. Subsection (1) is intended to provide reimbursement for the buyer who incurs reasonable expenses in connection with the handling of rightfully rejected goods or goods whose acceptance may be justifiably revoked, or in connection with effecting cover where the breach of the contract lies in non-conformity or non-delivery of the goods. The incidental damages listed are not intended to be exhaustive but are merely illustrative of the typical kinds of incidental damage.

2. Subsection (2) operates to allow the buyer, in an appropriate case, any consequential damages which are the result of the seller's breach. The "tacit agreement" test for the recovery of consequential damages is rejected. Although the older rule at common law which made the seller liable for all consequential damages of which he had "reason to know" in advance is followed, the liberality of that rule is modified by refusing to permit recovery unless the buyer could not reasonably have prevented the loss by cover or otherwise. Subparagraph (2) carries forward the provisions of the prior uniform statutory provision as to consequential damages resulting from breach of warranty, but modifies the rule by requiring first that the buyer attempt to minimize his damages in good faith, either by cover or otherwise.

3. In the absence of excuse under the section on merchant's excuse by failure of presupposed conditions, the seller is liable for consequential damages in all cases where he had reason to know of the buyer's general or particular requirements at the time of contracting. It is not necessary that there be a conscious acceptance of an insurer's liability on the seller's part, nor is his obligation for consequential damages limited to cases in which he fails to use due effort in good faith.

Particular needs of the buyer must generally be made known to the seller while general needs must rarely be made known to charge the seller with knowledge.

Any seller who does not wish to take the risk of consequential damages has available the section on contractual limitation of remedy.

4. The burden of proving the extent of loss incurred by way of consequential damage is on the buyer, but the section on liberal administration of remedies rejects any doctrine of certainty which requires almost mathematical precision in the proof of loss. Loss may be determined in any manner which is reasonable under the circumstances.

5. Subsection (2) (b) states the usual rule as to breach of warranty, allowing recovery for injuries "proximately" resulting from the breach. Where the injury involved follows the use of goods without discovery of the defect causing the damage, the question of "proximate" cause turns on whether it was reasonable for the buyer to use the goods without such inspection as would have revealed the defects. If it was not reasonable for him to do so, or if he did in fact discover the defect prior to his use, the injury would not proximately result from the breach of warranty.

6. In the case of sale of wares to one in the business of reselling them, resale is one of the requirements of which the seller has reason to know within the meaning of subsection (2) (a).

Cross References:

Point 1: Section 2—608.

Point 3: Sections 1—203, 2—615 and 2—719.

Point 4: Section 1—106.

Definitional Cross References:
"Cover". Section 2—712.
"Goods". Section 1—201.
"Person". Section 1—201.
"Receipt" of goods. Section 2—103.
"Seller". Section 2—103.

§ 2—716. Buyer's Right to Specific Performance or Replevin

(1) Specific performance may be decreed where the goods are unique or in other proper circumstances.

(2) The decree for specific performance may include such terms and conditions as to payment of the price, damages, or other relief as the court may deem just.

(3) The buyer has a right of replevin for goods identified to the contract if after reasonable effort he is unable to effect cover for such goods or the circumstances reasonably indicate that such effort will be unavailing or if the goods have been shipped under reservation and satisfaction of the security interest in them has been made or tendered.

Official Comment

Prior Uniform Statutory Provision: Section 68, Uniform Sales Act.

Changes: Rephrased.

Purposes of Changes: To make it clear that:

1. The present section continues in general prior policy as to specific performance and injunction against breach. However, without intending to impair in any way the exercise of the court's sound discretion in the matter, this Article seeks to further a more liberal attitude than some courts have shown in connection with the specific performance of contracts of sale.

2. In view of this Article's emphasis on the commercial feasibility of replacement, a new concept of what are "unique" goods is introduced under this section. Specific performance is no longer limited to goods which are already specific or ascertained at the time of contracting. The test of uniqueness under this section must be made in terms of the total situation which characterizes the contract. Output and requirements contracts involving a particular or peculiarly available source or market present today the typical commercial specific performance situation, as contrasted with contracts for the sale of heirlooms or priceless works of art which were usually involved in the older cases. However, uniqueness is not the sole basis of the remedy under this section for the relief may also be granted "in other proper circumstances" and inability to cover is strong evidence of "other proper circumstances".

3. The legal remedy of replevin is given the buyer in cases in which cover is reasonably unavailable and goods have been

identified to the contract. This is in addition to the buyer's right to recover identified goods on the seller's insolvency (Section 2—502).

4. This section is intended to give the buyer rights to the goods comparable to the seller's rights to the price.

5. If a negotiable document of title is outstanding, the buyer's right of replevin relates of course to the document not directly to the goods. See Article 7, especially Section 7—602.

Cross References:

Point 3: Section 2—502.
Point 4: Section 2—709.
Point 5: Article 7.

Definitional Cross References:

"Buyer". Section 2—103.
"Goods". Section 1—201.
"Rights". Section 1—201.

§ 2—717. Deduction of Damages From the Price

The buyer on notifying the seller of his intention to do so may deduct all or any part of the damages resulting from any breach of the contract from any part of the price still due under the same contract.

Official Comment

Prior Uniform Statutory Provision: See Section 69(1) (a), Uniform Sales Act.

Purposes:

1. This section permits the buyer to deduct from the price damages resulting from any breach by the seller and does not limit the relief to cases of breach of warranty as did the prior uniform statutory provision. To bring this provision into application the breach involved must be of the same contract under which the price in question is claimed to have been earned.

2. The buyer, however, must give notice of his intention to withhold all or part of the price if he wishes to avoid a default within the meaning of the section on insecurity and right to assurances. In conformity with the general policies of this Article, no formality of notice is required and any language which reasonably indicates the buyer's reason for holding up his payment is sufficient.

Cross Reference:

Point 2: Section 2—609.

Definitional Cross References:

"Buyer". Section 2—103.
"Notifies". Section 1—201.

§ 2—718. Liquidation or Limitation of Damages; Deposits

(1) Damages for breach by either party may be liquidated in the agreement but only at an amount which is reasonable in the light of the anticipated or actual harm caused by the breach, the difficulties of proof of loss, and the inconvenience or nonfeasibility of otherwise obtaining an adequate remedy.

A term fixing unreasonably large liquidated damages is void as a penalty.

(2) Where the seller justifiably withholds delivery of goods because of the buyer's breach, the buyer is entitled to restitution of any amount by which the sum of his payments exceeds

(a) the amount to which the seller is entitled by virtue of terms liquidating the seller's damages in accordance with subsection (1), or

(b) in the absence of such terms, twenty per cent of the value of the total performance for which the buyer is obligated under the contract or $500, whichever is smaller.

(3) The buyer's right to restitution under subsection (2) is subject to offset to the extent that the seller establishes

(a) a right to recover damages under the provisions of this Article other than subsection (1), and

(b) the amount or value of any benefits received by the buyer directly or indirectly by reason of the contract.

(4) Where a seller has received payment in goods their reasonable value or the proceeds of their resale shall be treated as payments for the purposes of subsection (2); but if the seller has notice of the buyer's breach before reselling goods received in part performance, his resale is subject to the conditions laid down in this Article on resale by an aggrieved seller (Section 2—706).

Official Comment

Prior Uniform Statutory Provision: None.

Purposes:

1. Under subsection (1) liquidated damage clauses are allowed where the amount involved is reasonable in the light of the circumstances of the case. The subsection sets forth explicitly the elements to be considered in determining the reasonableness of a liquidated damage clause. A term fixing unreasonably large liquidated damages is expressly made void as a penalty. An unreasonably small amount would be subject to similar criticism and might be stricken under the section on unconscionable contracts or clauses.

2. Subsection (2) refuses to recognize a forfeiture unless the amount of the payment so forfeited represents a reasonable liquidation of damages as determined under subsection (1). A special exception is made in the case of small amounts (20% of the price or $500, whichever is smaller) deposited as security. No distinction is made between cases in which the payment is to be applied on the price and those in which it is intended as security for performance. Sub-

section (2) is applicable to any deposit or down or part payment. In the case of a deposit or turn in of goods resold before the breach, the amount actually received on the resale is to be viewed as the deposit rather than the amount allowed the buyer for the trade in. However, if the seller knows of the breach prior to the resale of the goods turned in, he must make reasonable efforts to realize their true value, and this is assured by requiring him to comply with the conditions laid down in the section on resale by an aggrieved seller.

Cross References:

Point 1: Section 2—302.
Point 2: Section 2—706.

Definitional Cross References:

"Aggrieved party". Section 1—201.
"Agreement". Section 1—201.
"Buyer". Section 2—103.
"Goods". Section 2—105.
"Notice". Section 1—201.
"Party". Section 1—201.
"Remedy". Section 1—201.
"Seller". Section 2—103.
"Term". Section 1—201.

§ 2—719. Contractual Modification or Limitation of Remedy

(1) Subject to the provisions of subsections (2) and (3) of this section and of the preceding section on liquidation and limitation of damages,

(a) the agreement may provide for remedies in addition to or in substitution for those provided in this Article and may limit or alter the measure of damages recoverable under this Article, as by limiting the buyer's remedies to return of the goods and repayment of the price or to repair and replacement of non-conforming goods or parts; and

(b) resort to a remedy as provided is optional unless the remedy is expressly agreed to be exclusive, in which case it is the sole remedy.

(2) Where circumstances cause an exclusive or limited remedy to fail of its essential purpose, remedy may be had as provided in this Act.

(3) Consequential damages may be limited or excluded unless the limitation or exclusion is unconscionable. Limitation of consequential damages for injury to the person in the case of consumer goods is prima facie unconscionable but limitation of damages where the loss is commercial is not.

Official Comment

Prior Uniform Statutory Provision: None.

Purposes:

1. Under this section parties are left free to shape their remedies to their particular requirements and reasonable agreements limiting or modifying remedies are to be given effect.

However, it is of the very essence of a sales contract that at least minimum adequate remedies be available. If the parties intend to conclude a contract for sale within this Article they must accept the legal consequence that there be at least a fair quantum of remedy for breach of the obligations or duties outlined in the contract. Thus any clause purporting to modify or limit the remedial provisions of this Article in an unconscionable manner is subject to deletion and in that event the remedies made available by this Article are applicable as if the stricken clause had never existed. Similarly, under subsection (2), where an apparently fair and reasonable clause because of circumstances fails in its purpose or operates to deprive either party of the substantial value of the bargain, it must give way to the general remedy provisions of this Article.

2. Subsection (1) (b) creates a presumption that clauses prescribing remedies are cumulative rather than exclusive. If the parties intend the term to describe the sole remedy under the contract, this must be clearly expressed.

3. Subsection (3) recognizes the validity of clauses limiting or excluding consequential damages but makes it clear that they may not operate in an unconscionable manner. Actually such terms are merely an allocation of unknown or undeterminable risks. The seller in all cases is free to disclaim warranties in the manner provided in Section 2—316.

Cross References:

Point 1: Section 2—302.
Point 3: Section 2—316.

Definitional Cross References:

"Agreement". Section 1—201.
"Buyer". Section 2—103.
"Conforming". Section 2—106.
"Contract". Section 1—201.
"Goods". Section 2—105.
"Remedy". Section 1—201.
"Seller". Section 2—103.

§ 2—720. Effect of "Cancellation" or "Rescission" on Claims for Antecedent Breach

Unless the contrary intention clearly appears, expressions of "cancellation" or "rescission" of the contract or the like shall not be construed as a renunciation or discharge of any claim in damages for an antecedent breach.

Official Comment

Prior Uniform Statutory Provision: None.

Purpose:

This section is designed to safeguard a person holding a right of action from any unintentional loss of rights by the ill-advised use of such terms as "cancellation", "rescission", or the like. Once a party's rights have accrued they are not to be lightly impaired by concessions made in business decency and without intention to forego them. Therefore, unless the cancellation of a contract expressly declares that it is "without reservation of rights", or the like, it cannot be considered to be a renunciation under this section.

Cross Reference:

Section 1—107.

Definitional Cross References:

"Cancellation". Section 2—106.

"Contract". Section 1—201.

§ 2—721. Remedies for Fraud

Remedies for material misrepresentation or fraud include all remedies available under this Article for non-fraudulent breach. Neither rescission or a claim for rescission of the contract for sale nor rejection or return of the goods shall bar or be deemed inconsistent with a claim for damages or other remedy.

Official Comment

Prior Uniform Statutory Provision: None.

Purposes: To correct the situation by which remedies for fraud have been more circumscribed than the more modern and mercantile remedies for breach of warranty. Thus the remedies for fraud are extended by this section to coincide in scope with those for non-fraudulent breach. This section thus makes it clear that neither rescission of the contract for fraud nor rejection of the goods bars other remedies unless the circumstances of the case make the remedies incompatible.

Definitional Cross References:

"Contract for sale". Section 2—106.

"Goods". Section 1—201.

"Remedy". Section 1—201.

§ 2—722. Who Can Sue Third Parties for Injury to Goods

Where a third party so deals with goods which have been identified to a contract for sale as to cause actionable injury to a party to that contract

(a) a right of action against the third party is in either party to the contract for sale who has title to or a security interest or a special property or an insurable interest in the goods; and if the goods have been destroyed or converted a right of action is also in the party who either bore the risk of loss under the contract for sale or has since the injury assumed that risk as against the other;

(b) if at the time of the injury the party plaintiff did not bear the risk of loss as against the other party to the contract for sale and there is no arrangement between them for disposition of the recovery, his suit or settlement is, subject to his own interest, as a fiduciary for the other party to the contract;

(c) either party may with the consent of the other sue for the benefit of whom it may concern.

Official Comment

Prior Uniform Statutory Provision: None.

Purposes: To adopt and extend somewhat the principle of the statutes which provide for suit by the real party in interest. The provisions of this section apply only after identification of the goods. Prior to that time only the seller has a right of action. During the period between identification and final acceptance (except in the case of revocation of acceptance) it is possible for both parties to have the right of action. Even after final acceptance both parties may have the right of action if the seller retains possession or otherwise retains an interest.

Definitional Cross References:

"Action". Section 1—201.
"Buyer". Section 2—103.
"Contract for sale". Section 2—106.
"Goods". Section 2—105.
"Party". Section 1—201.
"Rights". Section 1—201.
"Security interest". Section 1—201.

§ 2—723. Proof of Market Price: Time and Place

(1) If an action based on anticipatory repudiation comes to trial before the time for performance with respect to some or all of the goods, any damages based on market price (Section 2—708 or Section 2—713) shall be determined according to the price of such goods prevailing at the time when the aggrieved party learned of the repudiation.

(2) If evidence of a price prevailing at the times or places described in this Article is not readily available the price prevailing within any reasonable time before or after the time described or at any other place which in commercial judgment or under usage of trade would serve as a reasonable substitute for

the one described may be used, making any proper allowance for the cost of transporting the goods to or from such other place.

(3) Evidence of a relevant price prevailing at a time or place other than the one described in this Article offered by one party is not admissible unless and until he has given the other party such notice as the court finds sufficient to prevent unfair surprise.

Official Comment

Prior Uniform Statutory Provision: None.

Purposes: To eliminate the most obvious difficulties arising in connection with the determination of market price, when that is stipulated as a measure of damages by some provision of this Article. Where the appropriate market price is not readily available the court is here granted reasonable leeway in receiving evidence of prices current in other comparable markets or at other times comparable to the one in question. In accordance with the general principle of this Article against surprise, however, a party intending to offer evidence of such a substitute price must give suitable notice to the other party.

This section is not intended to exclude the use of any other reasonable method of determining market price or of measuring damages if the circumstances of the case make this necessary.

Definitional Cross References:

"Action". Section 1—201.

"Aggrieved party". Section 1—201.

"Goods". Section 2—105.

"Notifies". Section 1—201.

"Party". Section 1—201.

"Reasonable time". Section 1—204.

"Usage of trade". Section 1—205.

§ 2—724. Admissibility of Market Quotations

Whenever the prevailing price or value of any goods regularly bought and sold in any established commodity market is in issue, reports in official publications or trade journals or in newspapers or periodicals of general circulation published as the reports of such market shall be admissible in evidence. The circumstances of the preparation of such a report may be shown to affect its weight but not its admissibility.

Official Comment

Prior Uniform Statutory Provision: None.

Purposes: To make market quotations admissible in evidence while providing for a challenge of the material by showing the circumstances of its preparation.

No explicit provision as to the weight to be given to market quotations is contained in this section, but such quotations, in the absence of compelling challenge, offer an adequate basis for a verdict.

Market quotations are made admissible when the price or value of goods traded "in any established market" is in issue. The reason of the section does not require that the market be closely organized in the manner of a produce exchange. It is sufficient if transactions in the commodity are frequent and open enough to make a market established by usage in which one price can be expected to affect another and in which an informed report of the range and trend of prices can be assumed to be reasonably accurate.

This section does not in any way intend to limit or negate the application of similar rules of admissibility to other material, whether by action of the courts or by statute. The purpose of the present section is to assure a minimum of mercantile administration in this important situation and not to limit any liberalizing trend in modern law.

Definitional Cross Reference:

"Goods". Section 2—105.

§ 2—725. Statute of Limitations in Contracts for Sale

(1) An action for breach of any contract for sale must be commenced within four years after the cause of action has accrued. By the original agreement the parties may reduce the period of limitation to not less than one year but may not extend it.

(2) A cause of action accrues when the breach occurs, regardless of the aggrieved party's lack of knowledge of the breach. A breach of warranty occurs when tender of delivery is made, except that where a warranty explicitly extends to future performance of the goods and discovery of the breach must await the time of such performance the cause of action accrues when the breach is or should have been discovered.

(3) Where an action commenced within the time limited by subsection (1) is so terminated as to leave available a remedy by another action for the same breach such other action may be commenced after the expiration of the time limited and within six months after the termination of the first action unless the termination resulted from voluntary discontinuance or from dismissal for failure or neglect to prosecute.

(4) This section does not alter the law on tolling of the statute of limitations nor does it apply to causes of action which have accrued before this Act becomes effective.

Official Comment

Prior Uniform Statutory Provision: None.

Purposes: To introduce a uniform statute of limitations for sales contracts, thus eliminating the jurisdictional variations and providing needed relief for concerns doing business on a nationwide scale whose contracts have heretofore been governed by several different periods of limitation depending upon the state in which the transaction occurred. This Article takes sales contracts out of the general laws limiting the time for commencing contractual actions and selects a four year period as the most appropriate to modern business practice. This is within the normal commercial record keeping period.

Subsection (1) permits the parties to reduce the period of limitation. The minimum period is set at one year. The parties may not, however, extend the statutory period.

Subsection (2), providing that the cause of action accrues when the breach occurs, states an exception where the warranty extends to future performance.

Subsection (3) states the saving provision included in many state statutes and permits an additional short period for bringing new actions, where suits begun within the four year period have been terminated so as to leave a remedy still available for the same breach.

Subsection (4) makes it clear that this Article does not purport to alter or modify in any respect the law on tolling of the Statute of Limitations as it now prevails in the various jurisdictions.

Definitional Cross References:

"Action". Section 1—201.

"Aggrieved party". Section 1—201.

"Agreement". Section 1—201.

"Contract for sale". Section 2—106.

"Goods". Section 2—105.

"Party". Section 1—201.

"Remedy". Section 1—201.

"Term". Section 1—201.

"Termination". Section 2—106.

*

ARTICLE 3

COMMERCIAL PAPER

PART 1. SHORT TITLE, FORM AND INTERPRETATION

Section

PART 2. TRANSFER AND NEGOTIATION

PART 3. RIGHTS OF A HOLDER

PART 4. LIABILITY OF PARTIES

PART 5. PRESENTMENT, NOTICE OF DISHONOR AND PROTEST

PART 6. DISCHARGE

PART 1

SHORT TITLE, FORM AND INTERPRETATION

§ 3—101. Short Title

This Article shall be known and may be cited as Uniform Commercial Code—Commercial Paper.

Official Comment

This Article represents a complete revision and modernization of the Uniform Negotiable Instruments Law.

The Comments which follow will point out the respects in which this Article changes the Negotiable Instruments Law, which was promulgated by the National Conference of Commissioners on Uniform State Laws in 1896, and was subsequently enacted in every American jurisdiction. Needless to say, in the 50 odd years of the history of that statute, there have been vast changes in commercial practices relating to the handling of negotiable instruments. The need for revision of this important statute was felt for some years before the present project was undertaken.

It should be noted especially that this Article does not apply in any way to the handling of securities. Article 8 deals with that subject. See Sec. 3—103.

§ 3—102. Definitions and Index of Definitions

(1) In this Article unless the context otherwise requires

(a) "Issue" means the first delivery of an instrument to a holder or a remitter.

(b) An "order" is a direction to pay and must be more than an authorization or request. It must identify the person to pay with reasonable certainty. It may be addressed to one or more such persons jointly or in the alternative but not in succession.

(c) A "promise" is an undertaking to pay and must be more than an acknowledgment of an obligation.

(d) "Secondary party" means a drawer or endorser.

(e) "Instrument" means a negotiable instrument.

(2) Other definitions applying to this Article and the sections in which they appear are:

"Acceptance". Section 3—410.
"Accommodation party". Section 3—415.
"Alteration". Section 3—407.
"Certificate of deposit". Section 3—104.
"Certification". Section 3—411.
"Check". Section 3—104.
"Definite time". Section 3—109.
"Dishonor". Section 3—507.
"Draft". Section 3—104.
"Holder in due course". Section 3—302.
"Negotiation". Section 3—202.
"Note". Section 3—104.
"Notice of dishonor". Section 3—508.
"On demand". Section 3—108.
"Presentment". Section 3—504.
"Protest". Section 3—509.
"Restrictive Indorsement". Section 3—205.
"Signature". Section 3—401.

(3) The following definitions in other Articles apply to this Article:

"Account". Section 4—104.
"Banking Day". Section 4—104.
"Clearing house". Section 4—104.
"Collecting bank". Section 4—105.
"Customer". Section 4—104.
"Depositary Bank". Section 4—105.
"Documentary Draft". Section 4—104.
"Intermediary Bank". Section 4—105.
"Item". Section 4—104.
"Midnight deadline". Section 4—104.
"Payor bank". Section 4—105.

(4) In addition Article 1 contains general definitions and principles of construction and interpretation applicable throughout this Article.

Official Comment

Prior Uniform Statutory Provision: Sections 1(5), 128 and 191, Uniform Negotiable Instruments Law.

Changes: See below.

Purposes of Changes:

1. The definition of "issue" in Section 191 of the original act has been clarified in two respects. The Section 191 definition required that the instrument delivered be "complete in form" inconsistently with the provisions of Sections 14 and 15 (relating to incomplete instruments) of the original act. The "complete in form" language has therefore been deleted. Furthermore the Section 191 definition required that the delivery be "to a person who takes as a holder", thus raising difficulties in the case of the remitter (see Comment 3 to Sec. 3—302) who may not be a party to the instrument and thus not a holder. The definition in subsection (1) (a) of this Section thus provides that the delivery may be to a holder or to a remitter.

2. The definitions of "order" [subsection (b)] and "promise" [subsection (c)] are new, but state principles clearly recognized by the courts. In the case of orders the dividing line between "a direction to pay" and "an authorization or request" may not be self-evident in the occasional unusual, and therefore non-commercial, case. The prefixing of words of courtesy to the direction—as "please pay" or "kindly pay"—should not lead to a holding that the direction has degenerated into a mere request. On the other hand informal language—such as "I wish you would pay"—would not qualify as an order and such an instrument would be non-negotiable. The definition of "promise" is intended to make it clear that a mere I.O.U. is not a negotiable instrument, and to change the result in occasional cases which have held that "Due Currier & Barker seventeen dollars and fourteen cents, value received." and "I borrowed from P. Shemonia the sum of five hundred dollars with four per cent interest; the borrowed money ought to be paid within four months from the above date" were promises sufficient to make the instruments into notes.

3. The last sentence of subsection (1) (b) ("order") permits the order to be addressed to one or more persons (as drawees) in the alternative, recognizing the practice of corporations issuing dividend checks and of other drawers who for commercial convenience name a number of drawees, usually in different parts of the country. The section on presentment provides that presentment may be made to any one of such drawees. Drawees in succession are not permitted because the holder should not be required to make more than one presentment, and upon the first dishonor should have his recourse against the drawer and indorsers.

4. Comments on the definitions indexed follow the sections

in which the definitions are contained.

Cross Reference:

Point 3: Section 3—504(3)(a).

Definitional Cross References:

"Bank". Section 1—201.
"Delivery". Section 1—201.
"Holder". Section 1—201.
"Money". Section 1—201.
"Person". Section 1—201.

§ 3—103. Limitations on Scope of Article

(1) This Article does not apply to money, documents of title or investment securities.

(2) The provisions of this Article are subject to the provisions of the Article on Bank Deposits and Collections (Article 4) and Secured Transactions (Article 9).

Official Comment

Prior Uniform Statutory Provision: None.

Purposes:

1. This Article is restricted to commercial paper—that is to say, to drafts, checks, certificates of deposit and notes as defined in Section 3—104(2). Subsection (1) expressly excludes any money, as defined in this Act (Section 1—201), even though the money may be in the form of a bank note which meets all the requirements of Section 3—104(1). Money is of course negotiable at common law or under separate statutes, but no provision of this Article is applicable to it. Subsection (1) also expressly excludes documents of title and investment securities which fall within Articles 7 and 8, respectively. To this extent the section follows decisions which held that interim certificates calling for the delivery of securities were not negotiable instruments under the original statute. Such paper is now covered under Article 8, but is not within any section of this Article. Likewise, bills of lading, warehouse receipts and other documents of title which fall within Article 7 may be negotiable under the provision of that Article, but are not covered by any section of this Article.

2. Instruments which fall within the scope of this Article may also be subject to other Articles of the Code. Many items in course of bank collection will of course be negotiable instruments, and the same may be true of collateral pledged as security for a debt. In such cases this Article, which is general, is, in case of conflicting provisions, subject to the Articles which deal specifically with the type of transaction or instrument involved: Article 4 (Bank Deposits and Collections) and Article 9 (Secured Transactions). In the case of a negotiable instrument which is subject to Article 4 because it is in course of collection or to Article 9 because it is used as collateral, the provisions of this Article continue to be applicable except insofar as

there may be conflicting provisions in the Bank Collection or Secured Transactions Article.

An instrument which qualifies as "negotiable" under this Article may also qualify as a "security" under Article 8. It will be noted that the formal requisites of negotiability (Section 3—104) go to matters of form exclusively; the definition of "security" on the other hand (Section 8—102) looks principally to the manner in which an instrument is used ("commonly dealt in upon securities exchanges . . . or commonly recognized . . . as a medium for investment"). If an instrument negotiable in form under Section 3—104 is, because of the manner of its use, a "security" under Section 8—102, Article 8 and not this Article applies. See subsection (1) of this Section and Section 8—102(1)(b).

Cross References:

Point 1: Articles 7 and 8; Sections 1—201, 3—104(1) and (2), 3—107.

Point 2: Articles 4 and 9; Sections 3—104 and 8—102.

Definitional Cross References:

"Document of title". Section 1—201.

"Money". Section 1—201.

§ 3—104. Form of Negotiable Instruments; "Draft"; "Check"; "Certificate of Deposit"; "Note"

(1) Any writing to be a negotiable instrument within this Article must

(a) be signed by the maker or drawer; and

(b) contain an unconditional promise or order to pay a sum certain in money and no other promise, order, obligation or power given by the maker or drawer except as authorized by this Article; and

(c) be payable on demand or at a definite time; and

(d) be payable to order or to bearer.

(2) A writing which complies with the requirements of this section is

(a) a "draft" ("bill of exchange") if it is an order;

(b) a "check" if it is a draft drawn on a bank and payable on demand;

(c) a "certificate of deposit" if it is an acknowledgment by a bank of receipt of money with an engagement to repay it;

(d) a "note" if it is a promise other than a certificate of deposit.

(3) As used in other Articles of this Act, and as the context may require, the terms "draft", "check", "certificate of deposit" and "note" may refer to instruments which are not negotiable

within this Article as well as to instruments which are so negotiable.

Official Comment

Prior Uniform Statutory Provision: Sections 1, 5, 10, 126, 184 and 185, Uniform Negotiable Instruments Law.

Changes: Parts of original sections combined and reworded; new provisions; original Section 10 omitted.

Purposes of Changes and New Matter: The changes are intended to bring together in one section related provisions and definitions formerly widely separated.

1. Under subsection (1) (b) any writing, to be a negotiable instrument within this Article, must be payable in money. In a few states there are special statutes, enacted at an early date when currency was less sound and barter was prevalent, which make promises to pay in commodities negotiable. Even under these statutes commodity notes are now little used and have no general circulation. This Article makes no attempt to provide for such paper, as it is a matter of purely local concern. Even if retention of the old statutes is regarded in any state as important, amendment of this section may not be necessary, since "within this Article" in subsection (1) leaves open the possibility that some writings may be made negotiable by other statutes or by judicial decision. The same is true as to any new type of paper which commercial practice may develop in the future.

2. While a writing cannot be made a negotiable instrument within this Article by contract or by conduct, nothing in this section is intended to mean that in a particular case a court may not arrive at a result similar to that of negotiability by finding that the obligor is estopped by his conduct from asserting a defense against a bona fide purchaser. Such an estoppel rests upon ordinary principles of the law of simple contract; it does not depend upon negotiability, and it does not make the writing negotiable for any other purpose. But a contract to build a house or to employ a workman, or equally a security agreement does not become a negotiable instrument by the mere insertion of a clause agreeing that it shall be one.

3. The words "no other promise, order, obligation or power" in subsection (1) (b) are an expansion of the first sentence of the original Section 5. Section 3—112 permits an instrument to carry certain limited obligations or powers in addition to the simple promise or order to pay money. Subsection (1) of this Section is intended to say that it cannot carry others.

4. Any writing which meets the requirements of subsection (1) and is not excluded under Section 3—103 is a negotiable instrument, and all sections of this Article apply to it, even though it may contain additional language beyond that contem-

plated by this section. Such an instrument is a draft, a check, a certificate of deposit or a note as defined in subsection (2). Traveler's checks in the usual form, for instance, are negotiable instruments under this Article when they have been completed by the identifying signature.

5. This Article omits the original Section 10, which provided that the instrument need not follow the language of the act if it "clearly indicates an intention to conform" to it. The provision has served no useful purpose, and it has been an encouragement to bad drafting and to liberality in holding questionable paper to be negotiable. The omission is not intended to mean that the instrument must follow the language of this section, or that one term may not be recognized as clearly the equivalent of another, as in the case of "I undertake" instead of "I promise," or "Pay to holder" instead of "Pay to bearer." It does mean that either the language of the section or a clear equivalent must be found, and that in doubtful cases the decision should be against negotiability.

6. Subsection (3) is intended to make clear the same policy expressed in Section 3—805.

Cross References:

Sections 3—105 through 3—112, 3—401, 3—402 and 3—403.

Point 1: Section 3—107.

Point 3: Section 3—112.

Point 4: Sections 3—103 and 3—805.

Point 6: Section 3—805.

Definitional Cross References:

"Bank". Section 1—201.

"Bearer". Section 1—201.

"Definite time". Section 3—109.

"Money". Section 1—201.

"On demand". Section 3—108.

"Order". Section 3—102.

"Promise". Section 3—102.

"Signed". Section 1—201.

"Term". Section 1—201.

"Writing". Section 1—201.

§ 3—105. When Promise or Order Unconditional

(1) A promise or order otherwise unconditional is not made conditional by the fact that the instrument

(a) is subject to implied or constructive conditions; or

(b) states its consideration, whether performed or promised, or the transaction which gave rise to the instrument, or that the promise or order is made or the instrument matures in accordance with or "as per" such transaction; or

(c) refers to or states that it arises out of a separate agreement or refers to a separate agreement for rights as to prepayment or acceleration; or

(d) states that it is drawn under a letter of credit; or

(e) states that it is secured, whether by mortgage, reservation of title or otherwise; or

(f) indicates a particular account to be debited or any other fund or source from which reimbursement is expected; or

(g) is limited to payment out of a particular fund or the proceeds of a particular source, if the instrument is issued by a government or governmental agency or unit; or

(h) is limited to payment out of the entire assets of a partnership, unincorporated association, trust or estate by or on behalf of which the instrument is issued.

(2) A promise or order is not unconditional if the instrument

(a) states that it is subject to or governed by any other agreement; or

(b) states that it is to be paid only out of a particular fund or source except as provided in this section. As amended 1962.

Official Comment

Prior Uniform Statutory Provision: Section 3, Uniform Negotiable Instruments Law.

Changes: Completely revised.

Purposes of Changes: The section is intended to make it clear that, so far as negotiability is affected, the conditional or unconditional character of the promise or order is to be determined by what is expressed in the instrument itself; and to permit certain specific limitations upon the terms of payment.

1. Paragraph (a) of subsection (1) rejects the theory of decisions which have held that a recital in an instrument that it is given in return for an executory promise gives rise to an implied condition that the instrument is not to be paid if the promise is not performed, and that this condition destroys negotiability. Nothing in the section is intended to imply that language may not be fairly construed to mean what it says, but implications, whether of law or fact, are not to be considered in determining negotiability.

2. Paragraph (b) of subsection (1) is an amplification of Section 3(2) of the original act. The final clause is intended to resolve a conflict in the decisions over the effect of such language as "This note is given for payment as per contract for the purchase of goods of even date, maturity being in conformity with the terms of such contract." It adopts the general commercial understanding that such language is intended as a mere recital of the origin of the instrument and a reference to the transaction for information, but is not meant to condition payment according to the terms of any other agreement.

3. Paragraph (c) of subsection (1) likewise is intended to resolve a conflict, and to reject cases in which a reference to a separate agreement was held to

mean that payment of the instrument must be limited in accordance with the terms of the agreement, and hence was conditioned by it. Such a reference normally is inserted for the purpose of making a record or giving information to anyone who may be interested, and in the absence of any express statement to that effect is not intended to limit the terms of payment. Inasmuch as rights as to prepayment or acceleration has to do with a "speed-up" in payment and since notes frequently refer to separate agreements for a statement of these rights, such reference does not destroy negotiability even though it has mild aspects of incorporation by reference. The general reasoning with respect to subparagraph (c) also applies to a draft which on its face states that it is drawn under a letter of credit (subparagraph (d)). Paragraphs (c) and (d) therefore adopt the position that negotiability is not affected. If the reference goes further and provides that payment must be made according to the terms of the agreement, it falls under paragraph (a) of subsection (2) [As amended 1962].

4. Paragraph (e) of subsection (1) is intended to settle another conflict in the decisions, over the effect of "title security notes" and other instruments which recite the security given. It rejects cases which have held that the mere statement that the instrument is secured, by reservation of title or otherwise, carries the implied condition that payment is to be made only if the security agreement is fully performed. Again such a recital normally is included only for the purpose of making a record or giving information, and is not intended to condition payment in any way. The provision adopts the position of the great majority of the courts.

5. Paragraph (f) of subsection (1) is a rewording of Section 3(1) of the original act.

6. Paragraph (g) of subsection (1) is new. It is intended to permit municipal corporations or other governments or governmental agencies to draw checks or to issue other short-term commercial paper in which payment is limited to a particular fund or to the proceeds of particular taxes or other sources of revenue. The provision will permit some municipal warrants to be negotiable if they are in proper form. Normally such warrants lack the words "order" or "bearer," or are marked "Not Negotiable," or are payable only in serial order, which makes them conditional.

7. Paragraph (h) of subsection (1) is new. It adopts the policy of decisions holding that an instrument issued by an unincorporated association is negotiable although its payment is expressly limited to the assets of the association, excluding the liability of individual members; and recognizing as negotiable an instrument issued by a trust estate without personal liability of the trustee. The policy is extended to a partnership and to any estate. The provision affects only the negotiability of the instrument, and is not intended to change the law of any state as to the liability of a part-

ner, trustee, executor, administrator, or any other person on such an instrument.

8. Paragraph (a) of subsection (2) retains the generally accepted rule that where an instrument contains such language as "subject to terms of contract between maker and payee of this date," its payment is conditioned according to the terms of the agreement and the instrument is not negotiable. The distinction is between a mere recital of the existence of the separate agreement or a reference to it for information, which under paragraph (c) of subsection (1) will not affect negotiability, and any language which, fairly construed, requires the holder to look to the other agreement for the terms of payment. The intent of the provision is that an instrument is not negotiable unless the holder can ascertain all of its essential terms from its face. In the specific instance of rights as to prepayment or acceleration, however, there may be a reference to a separate agreement without destroying negotiability [As amended 1962].

9. Paragraph (b) of subsection (2) restates the last sentence of Section 3 of the original act. As noted above, exceptions are made by paragraphs (g) and (h) of subsection (1) in favor of instruments issued by governments or governmental agencies, or by a partnership, unincorporated association, trust or estate.

Cross Reference:

Section 3—104.

Definitional Cross References:

"Account". Section 4—104.
"Agreement". Section 1—201.
"Instrument". Section 3—102.
"Issue". Section 3—102.
"Order". Section 3—102.
"Promise". Section 3—102.

§ 3—106. Sum Certain

(1) The sum payable is a sum certain even though it is to be paid

(a) with stated interest or by stated installments; or

(b) with stated different rates of interest before and after default or a specified date; or

(c) with a stated discount or addition if paid before or after the date fixed for payment; or

(d) with exchange or less exchange, whether at a fixed rate or at the current rate; or

(e) with costs of collection or an attorney's fee or both upon default.

(2) Nothing in this section shall validate any term which is otherwise illegal.

Official Comment

Prior Uniform Statutory Provision: Sections 2 and 6(5), Uniform Negotiable Instruments Law.

Changes: Reworded.

Purposes of Changes: The new language is intended to clarify doubts arising under the original section as to interest, discounts or additions, exchange, costs and attorney's fees, and acceleration or extension.

1. The section rejects decisions which have denied negotiability to a note with a term providing for a discount for early payment on the ground that at the time of issue the amount payable was not certain. It is sufficient that at any time of payment the holder is able to determine the amount then payable from the instrument itself with any necessary computation. Thus a demand note bearing interest at six per cent is negotiable. A stated discount or addition for early or late payment does not affect the certainty of the sum so long as the computation can be made, nor do different rates of interest before and after default or a specified date. The computation must be one which can be made from the instrument itself without reference to any outside source, and this section does not make negotiable a note payable with interest "at the current rate."

2. Paragraph (d) recognizes the occasional practice of making the instrument payable with exchange deducted rather than added.

3. In paragraph (e) "upon default" is substituted for the language of the original Section 2(5) in order to include any default in payment of interest or installments.

4. The section contains no specific language relating to the effect of acceleration clauses on the certainty of the sum payable. Section 2(3) of the original act contained a saving clause for provisions accelerating principal on default in payment of an installment or of interest, which led to doubt as to the effect of other accelerating provisions. This Article (Section 3—109, Definite Time) broadly validates acceleration clauses; it is not necessary to state the matter in this section as well. The disappearance of the language referred to in old Section 2(3) means merely that it was regarded as surplusage.

5. Most states have usury laws prohibiting excessive rates of interest. In some states there are statutes or rules of law invalidating a term providing for increased interest after maturity, or for costs and attorney's fees. Subsection (2) is intended to make it clear that this section is concerned only with the effect of such terms upon negotiability, and is not meant to change the law of any state as to the validity of the term itself.

Cross References:

Section 3—104.
Point 4: Section 3—109.

Definitional Cross Reference:

"Term". Section 1—201.

§ 3—107. Money

(1) An instrument is payable in money if the medium of exchange in which it is payable is money at the time the instrument is made. An instrument payable in "currency" or "current funds" is payable in money.

(2) A promise or order to pay a sum stated in a foreign currency is for a sum certain in money and, unless a different medium of payment is specified in the instrument, may be satisfied by payment of that number of dollars which the stated foreign currency will purchase at the buying sight rate for that currency on the day on which the instrument is payable or, if payable on demand, on the day of demand. If such an instrument specifies a foreign currency as the medium of payment the instrument is payable in that currency.

Official Comment

Prior Uniform Statutory Provision: Section 6(5), Uniform Negotiable Instruments Law.

Changes: Completely rewritten.

Purposes of Changes and New Matter: To make clear when an instrument is payable in money and to state rules applicable to instruments drawn payable in a foreign currency.

1. The term "money" is defined in Section 1—201 as "a medium of exchange authorized or adopted by a domestic or foreign government as a part of its currency". That definition rejects the narrow view of some early cases that "money" is limited to legal tender. Legal tender acts do no more than designate a particular kind of money which the obligee will be required to accept in discharge of an obligation. It rejects also the contention sometimes advanced that "money" includes any medium of exchange current and accepted in the particular community whether it be gold dust, beaver pelts, or cigarettes in occupied Germany. Such unusual "currency" is necessarily of uncertain and fluctuating value, and an instrument intended to pass generally in commerce as negotiable may not be made payable therein.

The test adopted is that of the sanction of government, which recognizes the circulating medium as a part of the official currency of that government. In particular the provision adopts the position that an instrument expressing the amount to be paid in sterling, francs, lire or other recognized currency of a foreign government is negotiable even though payable in the United States.

2. The provision on "currency" or "current funds" accepts the view of the great majority of the decisions, that "currency" or "current funds" means that the instrument is payable in money.

3. Either the amount to be paid or the medium of payment

may be expressed in terms of a particular kind of money. A draft passing between Toronto and Buffalo may, according to the desire and convenience of the parties, call for payment of 100 United States dollars or of 100 Canadian dollars; and it may require either sum to be paid in either currency. Under this section an instrument in any of these forms is negotiable, whether payable in Toronto or in Buffalo.

4. As stated in the preceding paragraph the intention of the parties in making an instrument payable in a foreign currency may be that the medium of payment shall be either dollars measured by the foreign currency or the foreign currency in which the instrument is drawn. Under subsection (2) the presumption is, unless the instrument otherwise specifies, that the obligation may be satisfied by payment in dollars in an amount determined by the buying sight rate for the foreign currency on the day the instrument becomes payable. Inasmuch as the buying sight rate will fluctuate from day to day, it might be argued that an instrument expressed in a foreign currency but actually payable in dollars is not for a "sum certain". Subsection (2) makes it clear that for the purposes of negotiability under this Article such an instrument, despite exchange fluctuations, is for a sum certain.

Cross References:

Section 3—104.
Point 1: Section 1—201.
Point 4: Section 4—212(6).

Definitional Cross References:

"Instrument". Section 3—102.
"Money". Section 1—201.
"Order". Section 3—102.
"Promise". Section 3—102.
"Purchase". Section 1—201.

§ 3—108. Payable on Demand

Instruments payable on demand include those payable at sight or on presentation and those in which no time for payment is stated.

Official Comment

Prior Uniform Statutory Provision: Section 7, Uniform Negotiable Instruments Law.

Changes: Reworded, final sentence of original section omitted.

Purposes of Changes: Except for the omission of the final sentence this section restates the substance of original Section 7. The final sentence dealt with the status of a person issuing, accepting or indorsing an instrument after maturity and provided that as to such a person the instrument was payable on demand. That language implied that the ordinary rules relating to demand instruments as to due course, holding, presentment, notice of dishonor and so on were applicable. This Article abandons that concept which served no special purpose except to trap the unwary. Under Section 3—302 (Holder in Due Course) and in view of the deletion from this section of the final sentence of original Section 7 there is no longer the possibility that one taking time paper after maturity may acquire due course rights against a post-maturity indorser. Section 3—501(4), however, provides that the indorser after maturity is not entitled to presentment, notice of dishonor or protest.

Cross References:

Sections 3—104, 3—302 and 3—501(4).

Definitional Cross Reference:

"Instrument". Section 3—102.

§ 3—109. Definite Time

(1) An instrument is payable at a definite time if by its terms it is payable

(a) on or before a stated date or at a fixed period after a stated date; or

(b) at a fixed period after sight; or

(c) at a definite time subject to any acceleration; or

(d) at a definite time subject to extension at the option of the holder, or to extension to a further definite time at the option of the maker or acceptor or automatically upon or after a specified act or event.

(2) An instrument which by its terms is otherwise payable only upon an act or event uncertain as to time of occurrence is not payable at a definite time even though the act or event has occurred.

Official Comment

Prior Uniform Statutory Provision: Sections 4 and 17(3), Uniform Negotiable Instruments Law.

Changes: Reworded; new provisions; rule of original Section 4(3) reversed.

Purposes of Changes and New Matter: To remove uncertainties arising under the original section, and to eliminate commercially unacceptable instruments.

1. Subsection (2) reverses the rule of the original Section 4(3) as to instruments payable after events certain to happen but uncertain as to time. Almost the only use of such instruments has been in the anticipation of inheritance or future interests by borrowing on post-obituary notes. These have been much more common in England than in the United States. They are at best questionable paper, not acceptable in general commerce, with no good reason for according them free circulation as negotiable instruments. As in the case of the occasional note payable "one year after the

war" or at a similar uncertain date, they are likely to be made under unusual circumstances suggesting good reason for preserving defenses of the maker. They are accordingly eliminated.

2. With this change "definite time" is substituted for "fixed or determinable future time." The time of payment is definite if it can be determined from the face of the instrument.

3. An undated instrument payable "thirty days after date" is not payable at a definite time, since the time of payment cannot be determined on its face. It is, however, an incomplete instrument within the provisions of Section 3—115 dealing with such instruments and may be completed by dating it. It is then payable at a definite time.

4. Paragraph (c) of subsection (1) resolves a conflict in the decisions on the negotiability of instruments containing acceleration clauses as to the meaning and effect of "on or before a fixed or determinable future time" in the original Section 4 (2). (Instruments expressly stated to be payable "on or before" a given date are dealt with in subsection (1) (a). So far as certainty of time of payment is concerned a note payable at a definite time but subject to acceleration is no less certain than a note payable on demand, whose negotiability never has been questioned. It is in fact more certain, since it at least states a definite time beyond which the instrument cannot run. Objections to the acceleration clause must be based rather on the possibility of abuse by the holder, which has nothing to do with negotiability and is not limited to negotiable instruments. That problem is now covered by Section 1—208.

Subsection (1) (c) is intended to mean that the certainty of time of payment or the negotiability of the instrument is not affected by any acceleration clause, whether acceleration be at the option of the maker or the holder, or automatic upon the occurrence of some event, and whether it be conditional or unrestricted. If the acceleration term itself is uncertain it may fail on ordinary contract principles, but the instrument then remains negotiable and is payable at the definite time.

The effect of acceleration clauses upon a holder in due course is covered by the new definition of the holder in due course (Section 3—302) and by the section on notice to purchaser (subsection (3) of Section 3—304). If the purchaser is not aware of any acceleration, his delay in making presentment may be excused under the section dealing with excused presentment (subsection (1) of Section 3—511).

5. Paragraph (d) of subsection (1) is new. It adopts the generally accepted rule that a clause providing for extension at the option of the holder, even without a time limit, does not affect negotiability since the holder is given only a right which he would have without the clause. If the extension is to be at the option of the maker or acceptor or is to be automatic, a definite time limit must be stated or the time of payment remains uncertain and the instrument is not negotiable. Where such a limit

is stated, the effect upon certainty of time of payment is the same as if the instrument were made payable at the ultimate date with a term providing for acceleration.

The construction and effect of extension clauses is covered by paragraph (f) of Section 3—118 on ambiguous terms and rules of construction, to which reference should be made.

Cross References:

Section 3—104.

Point 3: Section 3—115.

Point 4: Sections 1—208, 3—118(f), 3—304(3), and 3—511(1).

Point 5: Section 3—118(f).

Definitional Cross References:

"Holder". Section 1—201.

"Instrument". Section 3—102.

"Term". Section 1—201.

§ 3—110. Payable to Order

(1) An instrument is payable to order when by its terms it is payable to the order or assigns of any person therein specified with reasonable certainty, or to him or his order, or when it is conspicuously designated on its face as "exchange" or the like and names a payee. It may be payable to the order of

(a) the maker or drawer; or

(b) the drawee; or

(c) a payee who is not maker, drawer or drawee; or

(d) two or more payees together or in the alternative; or

(e) an estate, trust or fund, in which case it is payable to the order of the representative of such estate, trust or fund or his successors; or

(f) an office, or an officer by his title as such in which case it is payable to the principal but the incumbent of the office or his successors may act as if he or they were the holder; or

(g) a partnership or unincorporated association, in which case it is payable to the partnership or association and may be indorsed or transferred by any person thereto authorized.

(2) An instrument not payable to order is not made so payable by such words as "payable upon return of this instrument properly indorsed."

(3) An instrument made payable both to order and to bearer is payable to order unless the bearer words are handwritten or typewritten.

Official Comment

Prior Uniform Statutory Provision: Section 8, Uniform Negotiable Instruments Law.

Changes: Reworded, new provisions.

Purposes of Changes and New Matter: The changes are intended to remove uncertainties arising under the original section.

1. Paragraph (d) of subsection (1) replaces the original subsections (4) and (5). It eliminates the word "jointly," which has carried a possible implication of a right of survivorship. Normally an instrument payable to "A and B" is intended to be payable to the two parties as tenants in common, and there is no survivorship in the absence of express language to that effect. The instrument may be payable to "A or B," in which case it is payable to either A or B individually. It may even be made payable to "A and/or B," in which case it is payable either to A or to B singly, or to the two together. The negotiation, enforcement and discharge of the instrument in all such cases are covered by the section on instruments payable to two or more persons (Sec. 3—116).

2. Paragraph (e) of subsection (1) is intended to change the result of decisions which have held that an instrument payable to the order of the estate of a decedent was payable to bearer, on the ground that the name of the payee did not purport to be that of any person. The intent in such cases is obviously not to make the instrument payable to bearer, but to the order of the representative of the estate. The provision extends the same principle to an instrument payable to the order of "Tilden Trust," or "Community Fund". So long as the payee can be identified, it is not necessary that it be a legal entity; and in each case the instrument is treated as payable to the order of the appropriate representative or his successor.

3. Under paragraph (f) of subsection (1) an instrument may be made payable to the office itself ("Swedish Consulate") or to the officer by his title as such ("Treasurer of City Club"). In either case it runs to the incumbent of the office and his successors. The effect of instruments in such a form is covered by the section on instruments payable with words of description (Sec. 3—117).

4. Vestigial theories relating to the lack of "legal entity" of partnerships and various forms of unincorporated associations —such as labor unions and business trusts—make it the part of wisdom to specify that instruments made payable to such groups are order paper payable as designated and not bearer paper (subsection (1) (g)). As in the case of incorporated associations, any person having authority from the partnership or association to whose order the instrument is payable may indorse or otherwise deal with the instrument.

5. Subsection (2) is intended to change the result of cases

holding that "payable upon return of this certificate properly indorsed" indicated an intention to make the instrument payable to any indorsee and so must be construed as the equivalent of "Pay to order." Ordinarily the purpose of such language is only to insure return of the instrument with indorsement in lieu of a receipt, and the word "order" is omitted with the intention that the instrument shall not be negotiable.

6. Subsection (3) is directed at occasional instruments reading "Pay to the order of John Doe or bearer." Such language usually is found only where the drawer has filled in the name of the payee on a printed form, without intending the ambiguity or noticing the word "bearer." Under such circumstances the name of the specified payee indicates an intent that the order words shall control. If the word "bearer" is handwritten or typewritten, there is sufficient indication of an intent that the instrument shall be payable to bearer. Instruments payable to "order of bearer" are covered not by this section but by the following Section 3—111.

Cross References:

Sections 3—104 and 3—111.

Point 1: Section 3—116.

Points 2, 3 and 4: Section 3—117.

Definitional Cross References:

"Bearer". Section 1—201.

"Conspicuous". Section 1—201.

"Instrument". Section 3—102.

"Negotiation". Section 3—202.

"Person". Section 1—201.

"Term". Section 1—201.

§ 3—111. Payable to Bearer

An instrument is payable to bearer when by its terms it is payable to

(a) bearer or the order of bearer; or

(b) a specified person or bearer; or

(c) "cash" or the order of "cash", or any other indication which does not purport to designate a specific payee.

Official Comment

Prior Uniform Statutory Provision: Section 9, Uniform Negotiable Instruments Law.

Changes: Reworded; original subsections (3) and (5) omitted here but covered by Sections on impostors and signature in name of payee (Section 3—405) and on special and blank indorsements (Section 3—204).

Purposes of Changes: The rewording is intended to remove uncertainties.

1. Language such as "order of bearer" usually results when a printed form is used and the word "bearer" is filled in. Subsection (a) rejects the view that the instrument is payable to order, and adopts the position that "bearer" is the unusual word

and should control. Compare Comment 6 to Section 3—110.

2. Paragraph (c) is reworded to remove any possible implication that "Pay to the order of ———" makes the instrument payable to bearer. It is an incomplete order instrument, and falls under Section 3—115. Likewise "Pay Treasurer of X Corporation" does not mean pay bearer, even though there may be no such officer. Instruments payable to the order of an estate, trust, fund, partnership, unincorporated association or office are covered by the preceding section. This subsection applies only to such language as "Pay Cash," "Pay to the order of cash," "Pay bills payable," "Pay to the order of one keg of nails," or other words which do not purport to designate any specific payee.

3. Under Section 40 of the original Act an instrument payable to bearer on its face remained bearer paper negotiable by delivery although subsequently specially indorsed. It should be noted that Section 3—204 on special indorsement reverses this rule and allows the special indorsement to control.

Cross References:

Sections 3—104, 3—405 and 3—204.

Point 2: Sections 3—110(1) (a) and (f) and 3—115.

Point 3: Section 3—204.

Definitional Cross References:

"Bearer". Section 1—201.
"Instrument". Section 3—102.
"Person". Section 1—201.
"Term". Section 1—201.

§ 3—112. Terms and Omissions Not Affecting Negotiability

(1) The negotiability of an instrument is not affected by

(a) the omission of a statement of any consideration or of the place where the instrument is drawn or payable; or

(b) a statement that collateral has been given to secure obligations either on the instrument or otherwise of an obligor on the instrument or that in case of default on those obligations the holder may realize on or dispose of the collateral; or

(c) a promise or power to maintain or protect collateral or to give additional collateral; or

(d) a term authorizing a confession of judgment on the instrument if it is not paid when due; or

(e) a term purporting to waive the benefit of any law intended for the advantage or protection of any obligor; or

(f) a term in a draft providing that the payee by indorsing or cashing it acknowledges full satisfaction of an obligation of the drawer; or

(g) A statement in a draft drawn in a set of parts (Section 3—801) to the effect that the order is effective only if no other part has been honored.

(2) Nothing in this section shall validate any term which is otherwise illegal. As amended 1962.

Official Comment

Prior Uniform Statutory Provision: Sections 5 and 6, Uniform Negotiable Instruments Law.

Changes: Reworded; new provisions; Subsection (4) of original Section 5 omitted. Subsection (4) of the original Section 6 is now covered by Section 3—113, and Subsection (5) by Section 3—107.

Purposes of Changes and New Matter: The changes are intended to remove uncertainties arising under the original sections. Subsection (4) of the original Section 5 is omitted because it has been important only in connection with bonds and other investment securities now covered by Article 8 of this Act. An option to require something to be done in lieu of payment of money is uncommon and not desirable in commercial paper.

This section permits the insertion of certain obligations and powers in addition to the simple promise or order to pay money. Under Section 3—104, dealing with form of negotiable instruments, the instrument may not contain any other promise, order, obligation or power.

1. Paragraph (b) of subsection (1) permits a clause authorizing the sale or disposition of collateral given to secure obligations either on the instrument or otherwise of an obligor on the instrument upon any default in those obligations, including a default in payment of an installment or of interest. It is not limited, as was the original Section 5(1), to default at maturity. The reference to obligations of an obligor on the instrument is intended to recognize so-called cross collateral provisions that appear in collateral note forms used by banks and others throughout the United States and to permit the use of these provisions without destroying negotiability. Paragraph (c) is new. It permits a clause, apparently not within the original section, containing a promise or power to maintain or protect collateral or to give additional collateral, whether on demand or on some other condition. Such terms frequently are accompanied by a provision for acceleration if the collateral is not given, which is now permitted by the section on what constitutes a definite time. Section 1—208 should be consulted as to the construction to be given such clauses under this Act.

2. As under the original Section 5(2), paragraph (d) is intended to mean that a confession of judgment may be authorized only if the instrument is not paid when due, and that otherwise negotiability is affected. The use of judgment notes is confined to two or three states, and in others

the judgment clauses are made illegal or ineffective either by special statutes or by decision. Subsection (2) is intended to say that any such local rule remains unchanged, and that the clause itself may be invalid, although the negotiability of the instrument is not affected.

3. As in the case of the original Section 5(3), paragraph (e) applies not only to any waiver of the benefits of this Article, such as presentment, notice of dishonor or protest, but also to a waiver of the benefits of any other law such as a homestead exemption. Again subsection (2) is intended to mean that any rule which invalidates the waiver itself is not changed, and that while negotiability is not affected, a waiver of the statute of limitations contained in an instrument may be invalid.

This paragraph is to be read together with subsection (1) of Section 3—104 on form of negotiable instruments. A waiver cannot make the instrument negotiable within this Article where it does not comply with the requirements of that section.

4. Paragraph (f) is new. The effect of a clause of acknowledgment of satisfaction upon negotiability has been uncertain under the original section.

5. **Paragraph (g) is intended to insure that a condition arising from the statement in question will not adversely affect negotiability.**

Cross References:

Sections 3—104 and 3—105.

Point 1: Sections 1—208 and 3—109(1) (c).

Point 3: Section 3—104.

Definitional Cross References:

"Draft". Section 3—104.

"Instrument". Section 3—102.

"On demand". Section 3—108.

"Promise". Section 3—102.

"Term". Section 1—201.

§ 3—113. Seal

An instrument otherwise negotiable is within this Article even though it is under a seal.

Official Comment

Prior Uniform Statutory Provision: Section 6(4), Uniform Negotiable Instruments Law.

Changes: Reworded.

Purposes of Changes: The revised wording is intended to change the result of decisions holding that while a seal does not affect the negotiability of an instrument it may affect it in other respects falling within the statute, such as the conclusiveness of consideration. The section is intended to place sealed instruments on the same footing as any other instruments so far as all sections of this Article are concerned. It does not affect any other statutes or rules of law relating to sealed instruments except insofar as, in the case of negotiable instruments, they are inconsistent with this Article. Thus a sealed instrument which is within this Article may still be subject to a longer statute of limitations than negotiable instruments not under seal, or to such local rules of procedure as that it may be enforced by an action of special assumpsit.

Cross Reference:
Section 3—104.

Definitional Cross Reference:
"Instrument". Section 3—102.

§ 3—114. Date, Antedating, Postdating

(1) The negotiability of an instrument is not affected by the fact that it is undated, antedated or postdated.

(2) Where an instrument is antedated or postdated the time when it is payable is determined by the stated date if the instrument is payable on demand or at a fixed period after date.

(3) Where the instrument or any signature thereon is dated, the date is presumed to be correct.

Official Comment

Prior Uniform Statutory Provision: Sections 6(1), 11, 12 and 17(3), Uniform Negotiable Instruments Law.

Changes: Reworded; new provision; parts of original section 12 omitted.

Purposes of Changes and New Matter: The rewording is intended to remove uncertainties arising under the original sections.

1. The reference to an "illegal or fraudulent purpose" in the original Section 12 is omitted as inaccurate and misleading. Any fraud or illegality connected with the date of an instrument does not affect its negotiability, but is merely a defense under Sections 3—306 and 3—307 to the same extent as any other fraud or illegality. The provision in the same section as to acquisition of title upon delivery is also omitted, as obvious and unnecessary.

2. Subsection (2) is new. An undated instrument payable "thirty days after date" is uncertain as to time of payment, and does not fall within Section 3—109(1) (a) on definite time. It is, however, an incomplete instrument, and the date may be inserted as provided in the section dealing with such instruments (Section 3—115). When the instrument has been dated, this subsection follows decisions under the original Act in providing that the time of payment is to be determined from the stated date, even though the instrument is antedated or postdated. An antedated instrument may thus be due before it is issued. As to the liability of indorsers in such a case, see Section 3—501(4), on indorsement after maturity.

3. Subsection (3) extends the original Section 11 to any signature on an instrument. As to the meaning of "presumed," see Section 1—201.

Cross References:

Point 1: Sections 3—306 and 3—307.

Point 2: Sections 3—109(1)(a), 3—115 and 3—501(4).

Point 3: Section 1—201.

Definitional Cross References:

"Instrument". Section 3—102.
"Issue". Section 3—102.
"On demand". Section 3—108.
"Presumed". Section 1—201.
"Signature". Section 3—401.

§ 3—115. Incomplete Instruments

(1) When a paper whose contents at the time of signing show that it is intended to become an instrument is signed while still incomplete in any necessary respect it cannot be enforced until completed, but when it is completed in accordance with authority given it is effective as completed.

(2) If the completion is unauthorized the rules as to material alteration apply (Section 3—407), even though the paper was not delivered by the maker or drawer; but the burden of establishing that any completion is unauthorized is on the party so asserting.

Official Comment

Prior Uniform Statutory Provision: Sections 13, 14 and 15, Uniform Negotiable Instruments Law.

Changes: Condensed and reworded; original Section 13 and parts of Section 14 omitted; rule of Section 15 reversed.

Purposes of Changes:

1. The original sections were lengthy and confusing. Section 13 is eliminated because it has suggested some uncertain distinction between undated instruments and those incomplete in other respects, and has carried the inference that only a holder may fill in the date. An instrument lacking in an essential date is merely one kind of incomplete instrument, to be treated like any other. The third sentence of Section 14, providing that the instrument must be filled up strictly in accordance with the authority given and within a reasonable time, is eliminated as entirely superfluous, since any authority must always be exercised in accordance with its limitations, and expires within a reasonable time unless a time limit is fixed.

2. The language "signed while still incomplete in any necessary respect" in subsection (1) is substituted for "wanting in any material particular" in the original Section 14, in order to make it entirely clear that a complete writing which lacks an essential element of an instrument and contains no blanks or spaces or anything else to indicate that what is missing is to be supplied, does not fall within the section. "Necessary" means necessary to a complete instrument. It will always include the promise or order, the designation of the payee, and the amount payable. It may include the time of payment where a blank is left for that time to be filled in; but

where it is clear that no time is intended to be stated the instrument is complete, and is payable on demand under Section 3—108. It does not include the date of issue, which under Section 3—114 (1) is not essential, unless the instrument is made payable at a fixed period after that date.

3. This section omits the second sentence of the original Section 14, providing that "a signature on a blank paper delivered by the person making the signature in order that the paper may be converted into a negotiable instrument operates as a prima facie authority to fill it up as such for any amount." This had utility only in connection with the ancient practice of signing blank paper to be filled in later as an acceptance, at a time when communications were slow and difficult. The practice has been obsolete for nearly a century. It affords obvious opportunity for fraud, and should not be encouraged by express sanction in the statute. The omission is not intended, however, to mean that any person may not be authorized to write in an instrument over a signature either before or after delivery.

4. Subsection (2) states the rule generally recognized by the courts, that any unauthorized completion is an alteration of the instrument which stands on the same footing as any other alteration. Reference is therefore made to Section 3—407 where the effect of alteration is stated. Subsection (3) of that section provides that a subsequent holder in due course may in all cases enforce the instrument as completed, and replaces the final sentence of the original Section 14.

5. The language "even though the paper was not delivered" reverses the rule of the original Section 15, which provides that where an incomplete instrument has not been delivered it will not, if completed, be a valid contract in the hands of any holder as against any person whose signature was placed thereon before delivery. Since under this Article (Sections 3—305 and 3—407) neither non-delivery nor unauthorized completion is a defense against a holder in due course, it has always been illogical that the two together should invalidate the instrument in his hands. A holder in due course sees and takes the same paper, whether it was complete when stolen or completed afterward by the thief, and in each case he relies in good faith on the maker's signature. The loss should fall upon the party whose conduct in signing blank paper has made the fraud possible, rather than upon the innocent purchaser. The result is consistent with the theory of decisions holding the drawer of a check stolen and afterwards filled in to be estopped from setting up the non-delivery against an innocent party.

A similar provision protecting a depositary bank which pays an item in good faith is contained in Section 4—401. The policy of that Section should apply in favor of drawees other than banks.

6. The language on burden of establishing unauthorized completion is substituted for the "prima facie authority" of the original section 14. It follows the generally accepted rule that

the full burden of proof by a preponderance of the evidence is upon the party attacking the completed instrument. "Burden of establishing" is defined in Section 1—201.

Cross References:

Point 2: Sections 3—108 and 3—114(1).

Point 4: Section 3—407.

Point 5: Sections 3—305(2), 3—407(3) and 4—401.

Point 6: Section 1—201.

Definitional Cross References:

"Alteration". Section 3—407.

"Burden of establishing". Section 1—201.

"Delivery". Section 1—201.

"Instrument". Section 3—102.

"Party". Section 1—201.

"Signed". Section 1—201.

§ 3—116. Instruments Payable to Two or More Persons

An instrument payable to the order of two or more persons

(a) if in the alternative is payable to any one of them and may be negotiated, discharged or enforced by any of them who has possession of it;

(b) if not in the alternative is payable to all of them and may be negotiated, discharged or enforced only by all of them.

Official Comment

Prior Uniform Statutory Provision: Section 41, Uniform Negotiable Instruments Law.

Changes: Revised in wording and substance.

Purposes of Changes: The changes are intended to make clear the distinction between an instrument payable to "A or B" and one payable to "A and B." The first names either A or B as payee, so that either of them who is in possession becomes a holder as that term is defined in Section 1—201 and may negotiate, enforce or discharge the instrument. The second is payable only to A and B together, and as provided in the original section both must indorse in order to negotiate the instrument, although one may of course be authorized to sign for the other. Likewise both must join in any action to enforce the instrument, and the rights of one are not discharged without his consent by the act of the other.

If the instrument is payable to "A and/or B," it is payable in the alternative to A, or to B, or to A and B together, and it may be negotiated, enforced or discharged accordingly.

Cross Reference:

Section 1—201.

Definitional Cross References:

"Instrument". Section 3—102.

"Person". Section 1—201.

§ 3—117. Instruments Payable With Words of Description

An instrument made payable to a named person with the addition of words describing him

(a) as agent or officer of a specified person is payable to his principal but the agent or officer may act as if he were the holder;

(b) as any other fiduciary for a specified person or purpose is payable to the payee and may be negotiated, discharged or enforced by him;

(c) in any other manner is payable to the payee unconditionally and the additional words are without effect on subsequent parties.

Official Comment

Prior Uniform Statutory Provision: Section 42, Uniform Negotiable Instruments Law.

Changes: Revised and extended.

Purposes of Changes:

1. Subsection (a) extends the policy of the original Section 42, which covered only cashiers and fiscal officers of banks and corporations, to any case where a payee is named with words describing him as agent or officer of another named person. The intent is to include all such descriptions as "John Doe, Treasurer of Town of Framingham," "John Doe, President Home Telephone Co.," "John Doe, Secretary of City Club," or "John Doe, agent of Richard Roe." In all such cases it is commercial understanding that the description is not added for mere identification but for the purpose of making the instrument payable to the principal, and that the agent or officer is named as payee only for convenience in enabling him to cash the check.

2. Subsection (b) covers such descriptions as "John Doe, Trustee of Smithers Trust," "John Doe, Administrator of the Estate of Richard Roe," or "John Doe, Executor under Will of Richard Roe." In such cases the instrument is payable to the individual named, and he may negotiate it, enforce it or discharge it, but he remains subject to any liability for breach of his obligation as a fiduciary. Any subsequent holder of the instrument is put on notice of the fiduciary position, and under the section on notice to purchaser (Section 3—304) is not a holder in due course if he takes with notice that John Doe has negotiated the instrument in payment of or as security for his own debt or in any transaction for his own benefit, or otherwise in breach of duty.

3. Any other words of description, such as "John Doe, 1121 Main Street," "John Doe, Attorney," or "Jane Doe, unremarried widow," are to be treated as mere identification, and not in any respect as a condition of payment. The same is true of any description of the payee as "Treasurer," "President," "Agent," "Trustee," "Executor,"

or "Administrator," which does not name the principal or beneficiary. In all such cases the person named may negotiate, enforce or discharge the instrument if he is otherwise identified, even though he does not meet the description. Any subsequent party dealing with the instrument may disregard the description and treat the paper as payable unconditionally to the individual, and is fully protected in the absence of independent notice of other facts sufficient to affect his position.

Cross Reference:

Point 2: Section 3—304(2).

Definitional Cross References:

"Holder". Section 1—201.
"Instrument". Section 3—102.
"Party". Section 1—201.
"Person". Section 1—201.

§ 3—118. Ambiguous Terms and Rules of Construction

The following rules apply to every instrument:

(a) Where there is doubt whether the instrument is a draft or a note the holder may treat it as either. A draft drawn on the drawer is effective as a note.

(b) Handwritten terms control typewritten and printed terms, and typewritten control printed.

(c) Words control figures except that if the words are ambiguous figures control.

(d) Unless otherwise specified a provision for interest means interest at the judgment rate at the place of payment from the date of the instrument, or if it is undated from the date of issue.

(e) Unless the instrument otherwise specifies two or more persons who sign as maker, acceptor or drawer or indorser and as a part of the same transaction are jointly and severally liable even though the instrument contains such words as "I promise to pay."

(f) Unless otherwise specified consent to extension authorizes a single extension for not longer than the original period. A consent to extension, expressed in the instrument, is binding on secondary parties and accommodation makers. A holder may not exercise his option to extend an instrument over the objection of a maker or acceptor or other party who in accordance with Section 3—604 tenders full payment when the instrument is due.

Official Comment

Prior Uniform Statutory Provision: Sections 17 and 68, Uniform Negotiable Instruments Law.

Changes: Reworded; new provisions; original subsections (3) and (6) of Section 17 omitted. The original Section 17(3) is covered, so far as the question can arise, by Sections 3—109(1) (a) and 3—114 of this Article. The original Section 17(6) is now covered by Section 3—402.

Purposes of Changes and New Matter:

1. The purpose of this section is to protect holders and to encourage the free circulation of negotiable paper by stating rules of law which will preclude a resort to parol evidence for any purpose except reformation of the instrument. Except as to such reformation, these rules cannot be varied by any proof that any party intended the contrary.

2. Subsection (a): The language of the original Section 17 (5) is changed to make it clear that the provision is not limited to ambiguities of phrasing, but extends to any case where the form of the instrument leaves its character as a draft or a note in doubt.

3. Subsection (b): The original Section 17(4) is revised to cover typewriting because of its frequent use in instruments, particularly in promissory notes.

4. Subsection (c): The rewording of the original Section 17(1) is intended to make it clear that figures control only where the words are ambiguous and the figures are not.

5. Subsection (d): The revision of the original Section 17(2) is intended to make it clear that where the instrument provides for payment "with interest" without specifying the rate, the judgment rate of interest of the place of payment is to be taken as intended.

6. Subsection (e): This subsection combines and revises the original Section 17(7) and the last sentence of the original Section 68. The rule applies to any two or more persons who sign in the same capacity, whether as makers, drawers, acceptors or indorsers. It applies only where such parties sign as a part of the same transaction; successive indorsers are, of course, liable severally but not jointly.

7. Subsection (f): This provision is new. It has reference to such clauses as "The makers and indorsers of this note consent that it may be extended without notice to them." Such terms usually are inserted to obtain the consent of the indorsers and any accommodation maker to extension which might otherwise discharge them under Section 3—606 dealing with impairment of recourse or collateral. An extension in accord with these terms binds secondary parties. The holder may not force an extension on a maker or acceptor who makes due tender; the holder is not free to refuse payment and keep interest running on a good note or other instrument by extending it over the objection of a maker or acceptor or other par-

ty who in accordance with Section 3—604 tenders full payment when the instrument is due. Where consent to extension has been given, the subsection provides that unless otherwise specified the consent is to be construed as authorizing only one extension for not longer than the original period of the note.

Cross References:

Sections 3—109, 3—114, 3—402 and 3—606.

Point 7: Sections 3—604 and 3—606.

Definitional Cross References:

"Draft". Section 3—104.
"Holder". Section 1—201.
"Instrument". Section 3—102.
"Issue". Section 3—102.
"Note". Section 3—104.
"Person". Section 1—201.
"Promise". Section 3—102.
"Signed". Section 1—201.
"Term". Section 1—201.

§ 3—119. Other Writings Affecting Instrument

(1) As between the obligor and his immediate obligee or any transferee the terms of an instrument may be modified or affected by any other written agreement executed as a part of the same transaction, except that a holder in due course is not affected by any limitation of his rights arising out of the separate written agreement if he had no notice of the limitation when he took the instrument.

(2) A separate agreement does not affect the negotiability of an instrument.

Official Comment

Prior Uniform Statutory Provision: None.

Purposes: This section is new. It is intended to resolve conflicts as to the effect of a separate writing upon a negotiable instrument.

1. This Article does not attempt to state general rules as to when an instrument may be varied or affected by parol evidence, except to the extent indicated by the comment to the preceding section. This section is limited to the effect of a separate written agreement executed as a part of the same transaction. The separate writing is most commonly an agreement creating or providing for a security interest such as a mortgage, chattel mortgage, conditional sale or pledge. It may, however, be any type of contract, including an agreement that upon certain conditions the instrument shall be discharged or is not to be paid, or even an agreement that it is a sham and not to be enforced at all. Nothing in this section is intended to validate any such agreement which is fraudulent or void as against public policy, as in the case of a note given to deceive a bank examiner.

2. Other parties, such as an accommodation indorser, are not affected by the separate writing unless they were also parties to it as a part of the transaction by which they became bound on the instrument.

3. The section applies to negotiable instruments the ordinary rule that writings executed as a part of the same transaction are to be read together as a single agreement. As between the immediate parties a negotiable instrument is merely a contract, and is no exception to the principle that the courts will look to the entire contract in writing. Accordingly a note may be affected by an acceleration clause, a clause providing for discharge under certain conditions, or any other relevant term in the separate writing. "May be modified or affected" does not mean that the separate agreement must necessarily be given effect. There is still room for construction of the writing as not intended to affect the instrument at all, or as intended to affect it only for a limited purpose such as foreclosure or other realization of collateral. If there is outright contradiction between the two, as where the note is for $1,000 but the accompanying mortgage recites that it is for $2,000, the note may be held to stand on its own feet and not to be affected by the contradiction.

4. Under this Article a purchaser of the instrument may become a holder in due course although he takes it with knowledge that it was accompanied by a separate agreement, if he has no notice of any defense or claim arising from the terms of the agreement. If any limitation in the separate writing in itself amounts to a defense or claim, as in the case of an agreement that the note is a sham and cannot be enforced, a purchaser with notice of it cannot be a holder in due course. The section also covers limitations which do not in themselves give notice of any present defense or claim, such as conditions providing that under certain conditions the note shall be extended for one year. A purchaser with notice of such limitations may be a holder in due course, but he takes the instrument subject to the limitation. If he is without such notice, he is not affected by such a limiting clause in the separate writing.

5. Subsection (2) rejects decisions which have carried the rule that contemporaneous writings must be read together to the length of holding that a clause in a mortgage affecting a note destroyed the negotiability of the note. The negotiability of an instrument is always to be determined by what appears on the face of the instrument alone, and if it is negotiable in itself a purchaser without notice of a separate writing is in no way affected by it. If the instrument itself states that it is subject to or governed by any other agreement, it is not negotiable under this Article; but if it merely refers to a separate agreement or states that it arises out of such an agreement, it is negotiable.

Cross References:

Point 1: Section 3—119.

Point 4: Section 3—304(4)(b).

Point 5: Section 3—105(2) (a) and (1) (c).

Definitional Cross References:

"Agreement". Section 1—201.

"Holder in due course". Section 3—302.

"Instrument". Section 3—102.
"Notice". Section 1—201.
"Rights". Section 1—201.
"Term". Section 1—201.
"Written" and "writing". Section 1—201.

§ 3—120. Instruments "Payable Through" Bank

An instrument which states that it is "payable through" a bank or the like designates that bank as a collecting bank to make presentment but does not of itself authorize the bank to pay the instrument.

Official Comment

Prior Uniform Statutory Provision: None.

Purposes: Insurance, dividend or payroll checks, and occasionally other types of instruments, are sometimes made payable "through" a particular bank. This section states the commercial understanding as to the effect of such language. The bank is not named as drawee, and it is not ordered or even authorized to pay the instrument out of the drawer's account or any other funds of the drawer in its hands. Neither is it required to take the instrument for collection in the absence of special agreement to that effect. It is merely designated as a collecting bank through which presentment is properly made to the drawee.

Definitional Cross References:

"Bank". Section 1—201.
"Collecting bank". Section 4—105.
"Instrument". Section 3—102.
"Presentment". Section 3—504.

§ 3—121. Instruments Payable at Bank

Note: *If this Act is introduced in the Congress of the United States this section should be omitted.*

(States to select either alternative)

Alternative A—

A note or acceptance which states that it is payable at a bank is the equivalent of a draft drawn on the bank payable when it falls due out of any funds of the maker or acceptor in current account or otherwise available for such payment.

Alternative B—

A note or acceptance which states that it is payable at a bank is not of itself an order or authorization to the bank to pay it.

Official Comment

Prior Uniform Statutory Provision: Section 87, Uniform Negotiable Instruments Law.

Changes: Alternative sections offered.

Purposes of Changes: The original section 87 has been amended so extensively that no uniformity has been achieved; and in many parts of the country it has been consistently disregarded in practice.

The original section represents the commercial and banking practice of New York and the surrounding states, according to which a note or acceptance made payable at a bank is treated as the equivalent of a draft drawn on the bank. The bank is not only authorized but ordered to make payment out of the account of the maker or acceptor when the instrument falls due, and it is expected to do so without consulting him. In the western and southern states a contrary understanding prevails. The note or acceptance payable at a bank is treated as merely designating a place of payment, as if the instrument were made payable at the office of an attorney. The bank's only function is to notify the maker or acceptor that the instrument has been presented and to ask for his instructions; and in the absence of specific instructions it is not regarded as required or even authorized to pay. Notwithstanding the original section western and southern banks have consistently followed the practice of asking for instructions and treating a direction not to pay as a revocation, equivalent to a direction to stop payment.

Both practices are well established, and the division is along geographical lines. A change in either practice might lead to undesirable consequences for holders, banks or depositors. The instruments involved are chiefly promissory notes, which infrequently cross state lines. There is no great need for uniformity. This section therefore offers alternative provisions, the first of which states the New York commercial understanding, and the second that of the south and west.

Cross Reference:

Section 3—502.

Definitional Cross References:

"Acceptance". Section 3—410.
"Account". Section 4—104.
"Bank". Section 1—201.
"Draft". Section 3—104.
"Instrument". Section 3—102.
"Note". Section 3—104.
"Order". Section 3—102.

§ 3—122. Accrual of Cause of Action

(1) A cause of action against a maker or an acceptor accrues

(a) in the case of a time instrument on the day after maturity;

(b) in the case of a demand instrument upon its date or, if no date is stated, on the date of issue.

(2) A cause of action against the obligor of a demand or time certificate of deposit accrues upon demand, but demand on a time certificate may not be made until on or after the date of maturity.

(3) A cause of action against a drawer of a draft or an indorser of any instrument accrues upon demand following dishonor of the instrument. Notice of dishonor is a demand.

(4) Unless an instrument provides otherwise, interest runs at the rate provided by law for a judgment

(a) in the case of a maker, acceptor or other primary obligor of a demand instrument, from the date of demand;

(b) in all other cases from the date of accrual of the cause of action. As amended 1962.

Official Comment

Prior Uniform Statutory Provision: None.

Purpose:

1. This section is new. It follows the generally accepted rule that action may be brought on a demand note immediately upon issue, without demand, since presentment is not required to charge the maker under the original Act or under this Article. An exception is made in the case of certificates of deposit for the reason that banking custom and expectation is that demand will be made before any liability is incurred by the bank, and the additional reason that such certificates are issued with the understanding that they will be held for a considerable length of time, which in many instances exceeds the period of the statute of limitations. As to makers and acceptors of time instruments generally, the cause of action accrues on the day after maturity. As to drawers of drafts (including checks) and all indorsers, the cause of action accrues, in conformity with their underlying contract on the instrument (Sections 3—413 and 3—414), only upon demand made, typically in the form of a notice of dishonor, after the instrument has been presented to and dishonored by the person designated on the instrument to pay it.

2. Closely related to the accrual of a cause of action is the question of when interest begins to run where the instrument is blank on the point. A term in the instrument providing for interest controls. (See Section 3—118(d) for the construction of a term which provides for interest but does not specify the rate or the time from which it runs.) In the absence of such a term and except in the case of a maker, acceptor or other primary obligor of a demand instrument subsection (4) states the rule that interest at the judgment rate runs from the date the cause of action accrues. In the case of a primary obligor of a demand instrument, interest runs from the date of demand although the cause of action (subsection (1) (a)) accrues on the stated date of the instrument or

on issue. There has been a conflict in the decisions as to when "legal" interest begins to run on a demand note. Some courts have taken the view that, since the note is due when issued without demand, it should follow that interest runs from the same date. On the other hand it is clear that there is no default until after demand by the holder and thus no reason for the imposition of the penalty on the maker. Subsection (4), therefore, adopts the position of the majority of the courts that on a demand note interest runs only from demand. This same rule is applied to acceptors and other primary obligors on a demand instrument.

Cross References:

Point 1: Sections 3—501, 3—413 and 3—414.

Point 2: Section 3—118(d).

Definitional Cross References:

"Action". Section 1—201.

"Certificate of deposit". Section 3—102.

"Dishonor". Section 3—507.

"Draft". Section 3—104.

"Instrument". Section 3—102.

"Note". Section 3—104.

"Notice of dishonor". Section 3—508.

"On demand". Section 3—108.

PART 2

TRANSFER AND NEGOTIATION

§ 3—201. Transfer: Right to Indorsement

(1) Transfer of an instrument vests in the transferee such rights as the transferor has therein, except that a transferee who has himself been a party to any fraud or illegality affecting the instrument or who as a prior holder had notice of a defense or claim against it cannot improve his position by taking from a later holder in due course.

(2) A transfer of a security interest in an instrument vests the foregoing rights in the transferee to the extent of the interest transferred.

(3) Unless otherwise agreed any transfer for value of an instrument not then payable to bearer gives the transferee the specifically enforceable right to have the unqualified indorsement of the transferor. Negotiation takes effect only when the indorsement is made and until that time there is no presumption that the transferee is the owner.

Official Comment

Prior Uniform Statutory Provision: Sections 27, 49 and 58, Uniform Negotiable Instruments Law.

Changes: Combined and reworded; new provisions.

Purposes of Changes and New Matter: To make it clear that:

1. The section applies to any transfer, whether by a holder or not. Any person who transfers an instrument transfers whatever rights he has in it. The transferee acquires those rights even though they do not amount to "title."

2. The transfer of rights is not limited to transfers for value. An instrument may be transferred as a gift, and the donee acquires whatever rights the donor had.

3. A holder in due course may transfer his rights as such. The "shelter" provision of the last sentence of the original Section 58 is merely one illustration of the rule that anyone may transfer what he has. Its policy is to assure the holder in due course a free market for the paper, and that policy is continued in this section. The provision is not intended and should not be used to permit any holder who has himself been a party to any fraud or illegality affecting the instrument, or who has received notice of any defense or claim against it, to wash the paper clean by passing it into the hands of a holder in due course and then repurchasing it. The operation of the provision is illustrated by the following examples:

(a) A induces M by fraud to make an instrument payable to A, A negotiates it to B, who takes as a holder in due course. After the instrument is overdue B gives it to C, who has notice of the fraud. C succeeds to B's rights as a holder in due course, cutting off the defense.

(b) A induces M by fraud to make an instrument payable to A, A negotiates it to B, who takes as a holder in due course. A then repurchases the instrument from B. A does not succeed to B's rights as a holder in due course, and remains subject to the defense of fraud.

(c) A induces M by fraud to make an instrument payable to A, A negotiates it to B, who takes with notice of the fraud. B negotiates it to C, a holder in due course, and then repurchases the instrument from C. B does not succeed to C's rights as a holder in due course, and remains subject to the defense of fraud.

(d) The same facts as (c), except that B had no notice of the fraud when he first acquired the instrument, but learned of it while he was a holder and with such knowledge negotiated to C. B does not succeed to C's rights as a holder in due course, and his position is not improved by the negotiation and repurchase.

4. The rights of a transferee with respect to collateral for the instrument are determined by Article 9 (Secured Transactions).

5. Subsection (2) restates original Section 27 and is intended to make it clear that a transfer of a limited interest in the instrument passes the rights of the transferor to the extent of the interest given. Thus a transferee for security acquires all such rights subject of course to the provisions of Article 9 (Secured Transactions).

6. Subsection (3) applies only to the transfer for value of an

instrument payable to order or specially indorsed. It has no application to a gift, or to an instrument payable or indorsed to bearer or indorsed in blank. The transferee acquires, in the absence of any agreement to the contrary, the right to have the indorsement of the transferor. This right is now made enforceable by an action for specific performance. Unless otherwise agreed, it is a right to the general indorsement of the transferor with full liability as indorser, rather than to an indorsement without recourse. The question commonly arises where the purchaser has paid in advance and the indorsement is omitted fraudulently or through oversight; a transferor who is willing to indorse only without recourse or unwilling to indorse at all should make his intentions clear. The agreement for the transferee to take less than an unqualified indorsement need not be an express one, and the understanding may be implied from conduct, from past practice, or from the circumstances of the transaction.

7. Subsection (3) follows the second sentence of the original Section 49 in providing that there is no effective negotiation until the indorsement is made. Until that time the purchaser does not become a holder, and if he receives earlier notice of defense against or claim to the instrument he does not qualify as a holder in due course under Section 3—302 (1) (c).

8. The final clause of subsection (3), which is new, is intended to make it clear that the transferee without indorsement of an order instrument is not a holder and so is not aided by the presumption that he is entitled to recover on the instrument provided in Section 3—307(2). The terms of the obligation do not run to him, and he must account for his possession of the unindorsed paper by proving the transaction through which he acquired it. Proof of a transfer to him by a holder is proof that he has acquired the rights of a holder and that he is entitled to the presumption.

Cross References:

Sections 3—202 and 3—416.

Point 5: Article 9.

Point 7: Section 3—302(1) (c).

Point 8: Section 3—307(2).

Definitional Cross References:

"Bearer". Section 1—201.

"Holder". Section 1—201.

"Holder in due course". Section 3—302.

"Instrument". Section 3—102.

"Negotiation". Section 3—202.

"Notice". Section 1—201.

"Party". Section 1—201.

"Presumption". Section 1—201.

"Rights". Section 1—201.

"Security interest". Section 1—201.

§ 3—202. Negotiation

(1) Negotiation is the transfer of an instrument in such form that the transferee becomes a holder. If the instrument is pay-

able to order it is negotiated by delivery with any necessary indorsement; if payable to bearer it is negotiated by delivery.

(2) An indorsement must be written by or on behalf of the holder and on the instrument or on a paper so firmly affixed thereto as to become a part thereof.

(3) An indorsement is effective for negotiation only when it conveys the entire instrument or any unpaid residue. If it purports to be of less it operates only as a partial assignment.

(4) Words of assignment, condition, waiver, guaranty, limitation or disclaimer of liability and the like accompanying an indorsement do not affect its character as an indorsement.

Official Comment

Prior Uniform Statutory Provision: Sections 30, 31 and 32, Uniform Negotiable Instruments Law.

Changes: Combined and reworded; new provisions.

Purposes of Changes and New Matter: To make it clear that:

1. Negotiation is merely a special form of transfer, the importance of which lies entirely in the fact that it makes the transferee a holder as defined in Section 1—201. Any negotiation carries a transfer of rights as provided in the section on transfer (subsections (1) and (2) of Section 3—201).

2. Any instrument which has been specially indorsed can be negotiated only with the indorsement of the special indorsee as provided in Section 3—204 on special indorsement. An instrument indorsed in blank may be negotiated by delivery alone, provided that it bears the indorsement of all prior special indorsees.

3. Subsection (2) follows decisions holding that a purported indorsement on a mortgage or other separate paper pinned or clipped to an instrument is not sufficient for negotiation. The indorsement must be on the instrument itself or on a paper intended for the purpose which is so firmly affixed to the instrument as to become an extension or part of it. Such a paper is called an allonge.

4. The cause of action on an instrument cannot be split. Any indorsement which purports to convey to any party less than the entire amount of the instrument is not effective for negotiation. This is true of either "Pay A one-half," or "Pay A two-thirds and B one-third," and neither A nor B becomes a holder. On the other hand an indorsement reading merely "Pay A and B" is effective, since it transfers the entire cause of action to A and B as tenants in common.

The partial indorsement does, however, operate as a partial assignment of the cause of action. The provision makes no attempt to state the legal effect of such an assignment, which is left to the local law. In a jurisdiction in which a partial assignee has any rights, either at law or in equity, the partial indorsee has such rights; and in any jurisdiction where a partial assignee has no rights the partial indorsee has none.

5. Subsection (4) is intended to reject decisions holding that the addition of such words as "I hereby assign all my right, title and interest in the within note" prevents the signature from operating as an indorsement. Such words usually are added by laymen out of an excess of caution and a desire to indicate formally that the instrument is conveyed, rather than with any intent to limit the effect of the signature.

6. Subsection (4) is also intended to reject decisions which have held that the addition of "I guarantee payment" indicates an intention not to indorse but merely to guarantee. Any signature with such added words is an indorsement, and if it is made by a holder is effective for negotiation; but the liability of the indorser may be affected by the words of guarantee as provided in the section on the contract of a guarantor. (Section 3—416.)

Cross References:

Section 3—417.

Point 1: Sections 1—201 and 3—201(1) and (2).

Point 2: Section 3—204.

Point 6: Section 3—416.

Definitional Cross References:

"Bearer". Section 1—201.

"Delivery". Section 1—201.

"Holder". Section 1—201.

"Instrument". Section 3—102

"Written". Section 1—201.

§ 3—203. Wrong or Misspelled Name

Where an instrument is made payable to a person under a misspelled name or one other than his own he may indorse in that name or his own or both; but signature in both names may be required by a person paying or giving value for the instrument.

Official Comment

Prior Uniform Statutory Provision: Section 43, Uniform Negotiable Instruments Law.

Changes: Reworded.

Purposes of Changes: To make it clear that:

1. The party whose name is wrongly designated or misspelled may make an indorsement effective for negotiation by signing in his true name only. This is not commercially satisfactory, since any subsequent purchaser may be left in doubt as to the state of the title; but whether it is done intentionally or through oversight, the party transfers his rights and is liable on his indorsement, and there is a negotiation if identity exists.

2. He may make an effective indorsement in the wrongly designated or misspelled name only. This again is not commercially satisfactory, since his liability as an indorser may require proof of identity.

3. He may indorse in both names. This is the proper and

desirable form of indorsement, and any person called upon to pay an instrument or under contract to purchase it may protect his interest by demanding indorsement in both names, and is not in default if such demand is refused.

Cross Reference:

Section 3—401(2).

Definitional Cross References:

"Instrument". Section 3—102.
"Person". Section 1—201.
"Signature". Section 3—401.

§ 3—204. Special Indorsement; Blank Indorsement

(1) A special indorsement specifies the person to whom or to whose order it makes the instrument payable. Any instrument specially indorsed becomes payable to the order of the special indorsee and may be further negotiated only by his indorsement.

(2) An indorsement in blank specifies no particular indorsee and may consist of a mere signature. An instrument payable to order and indorsed in blank becomes payable to bearer and may be negotiated by delivery alone until specially indorsed.

(3) The holder may convert a blank indorsement into a special indorsement by writing over the signature of the indorser in blank any contract consistent with the character of the indorsement.

Official Comment

Prior Uniform Statutory Provision: Sections 9(5), 33, 34, 35, 36, and 40, Uniform Negotiable Instruments Law.

Changes: Combined and reworded; rule of Section 40 reversed.

Purposes of Changes:

The last sentence of subsection (1) reverses the rule of the original Section 40, under which an instrument drawn payable to bearer and specially indorsed could be further negotiated by delivery alone. The principle here adopted is that the special indorser, as the owner even of a bearer instrument, has the right to direct the payment and to require the indorsement of his indorsee as evidence of the satisfaction of his own obligation. The special indorsee may of course make it payable to bearer again by himself indorsing in blank.

Cross Reference:

Section 3—202.

Definitional Cross References:

"Bearer". Section 1—201.
"Delivery". Section 1—201.
"Instrument". Section 3—102.
"Person". Section 1—201.
"Signature". Section 3—401.

§ 3—205. Restrictive Indorsements

An indorsement is restrictive which either

(a) is conditional; or

(b) purports to prohibit further transfer of the instrument; or

(c) includes the words "for collection", "for deposit", "pay any bank", or like terms signifying a purpose of deposit or collection; or

(d) otherwise states that it is for the benefit or use of the indorser or of another person.

Official Comment

Prior Uniform Statutory Provision: Sections 36 and 39, Uniform Negotiable Instruments Law.

Changes: Combined and reworded; new provisions.

Purposes of Changes and New Matter:

1. This section is intended to provide a definition of restrictive indorsements which will include the varieties of indorsement described in original Sections 36 and 39. The separate mention of conditional indorsements, those prohibiting transfer, indorsements in the bank deposit or collection process, and other indorsements to a fiduciary, permits separate treatment in subsequent sections where policy so requires.

2. This is part of a series of changes of the prior uniform statutory provisions effected by Sections 3—102, 3—205, 3—206, 3—304, 3—419, 3—603, and in Article 4, Sections 4—203 and 4—205. The purpose of the changes is generally to require a taker or payor under restrictive indorsement to apply or pay value given consistently with the indorsement, but to provide certain exceptions applying to banks in the collection process (other than depositary banks), and to some other takers and payors.

Cross References:

Sections 3—102, 3—202(2), 3—205, 3—206, 3—304, 3—419, 3—603, 4—203 and 4—205.

Definitional Cross References:

"Instrument". Section 3—102.
"Person". Section 1—201.

§ 3—206. Effect of Restrictive Indorsement

(1) No restrictive indorsement prevents further transfer or negotiation of the instrument.

(2) An intermediary bank, or a payor bank which is not the depositary bank, is neither given notice nor otherwise affected by a restrictive indorsement of any person except the bank's immediate transferor or the person presenting for payment.

(3) Except for an intermediary bank, any transferee under an indorsement which is conditional or includes the words "for collection", "for deposit", "pay any bank", or like terms (subparagraphs (a) and (c) of Section 3—205) must pay or apply any value given by him for or on the security of the instrument consistently with the indorsement and to the extent that he does so he becomes a holder for value. In addition such transferee is a holder in due course if he otherwise complies with the requirements of Section 3—302 on what constitutes a holder in due course.

(4) The first taker under an indorsement for the benefit of the indorser or another person (subparagraph (d) of Section 3—205) must pay or apply any value given by him for or on the security of the instrument consistently with the indorsement and to the extent that he does so he becomes a holder for value. In addition such taker is a holder in due course if he otherwise complies with the requirements of Section 3—302 on what constitutes a holder in due course. A later holder for value is neither given notice nor otherwise affected by such restrictive indorsement unless he has knowledge that a fiduciary or other person has negotiated the instrument in any transaction for his own benefit or otherwise in breach of duty (subsection (2) of Section 3—304).

Official Comment

Prior Uniform Statutory Provision: Sections 36, 37, 39 and 47, Uniform Negotiable Instruments Law.

Changes: Completely revised.

Purposes of Changes:

1. Subsections (1) and (2) apply to all four classes of restrictive indorsements defined in Section 3—205. Conditional indorsements and indorsements for deposit or collection, defined in paragraphs (a) and (c) of Section 3—205, are also subject to subsection (3); and trust indorsements as defined in paragraph (d) of Section 3—205 are subject to subsection (4). This section negates the implication which has sometimes been found in the original Sections 37 and 47, that under a restrictive indorsement neither the indorsee nor any subsequent taker from him could become a holder in due course. By omitting the original Section 47, this Article also avoids any implication that a discharge is effective against a holder in due course. See Section 3—602.

2. Under subsection (1) an indorsement reading "Pay A only," or any other indorsement purporting to prohibit further transfer, is without effect for that purpose. Such indorsements have rarely appeared in reported American cases. Ordinarily further negotiation will be contemplated by the indorser, if only for bank collection. The indorsee becomes a holder, and the

indorsement does not of itself give notice to subsequent parties of any defense or claim of the indorser. Hence this section gives such an indorsement the same effect as an unrestricted indorsement.

3. Subsection (2) permits an intermediary bank (Sections 3—102(3) and 4—105) or a payor bank which is not a depositary bank (Sections 3—102(3) and 4—105) to disregard any restrictive indorsement except that of the bank's immediate transferor. Such banks ordinarily handle instruments, especially checks, in bulk and have no practicable opportunity to consider the effect of restrictive indorsements. Subsection (2) does not affect the rights of the restrictive indorser against parties outside the bank collection process or against the first bank in the collection process; such rights are governed by subsections (3) and (4) and Section 3—603.

4. Conditional indorsements are treated by this section like indorsements for deposit or collection. Under subsection (3) any transferee under such an indorsement except an intermediary bank becomes a holder for value to the extent that he acts consistently with the indorsement in paying or applying any value given by him for or on the security of the instrument. Contrary to the original Section 39, subsection (3) permits a transferee under a conditional indorsement to become a holder in due course free of the conditional indorser's claim.

5. Of the indorsements covered by this section those "for collection", "for deposit" and "pay any bank" are overwhelmingly the most frequent. Indorsements "for collection" or "for deposit" may be either special or blank; indorsements "pay any bank" are governed by Section 4—201(2). Instruments so indorsed are almost invariably destined to be lodged in a bank for collection. Subsection (3) requires any transferee other than an intermediary bank to act consistently with the purpose of collection, and Section 3—603 lays down a similar rule for payors not covered by subsection (2).

6. Subsection (4), applying to trust indorsements other than those for deposit or collection (paragraph (d) of Section 3—205) is similar to subsection (3); but in subsection (4) the duty to act consistently with the indorsement is limited to the first taker under it. If an instrument is indorsed "Pay T in trust for B" or "Pay T for B" or "Pay T for account of B" or "Pay T as agent for B," whether B is the indorser or a third person, T is of course subject to liability for any breach of his obligation as fiduciary. But trustees commonly and legitimately sell trust assets in transactions entirely outside the bank collection process; the trustee therefore has power to negotiate the instrument and make his transferee a holder in due course. Whether transferees from T have notice of a breach of trust such as to deny them the status of holders in due course is governed by the section on notice to purchasers (Section 3—304); the trust indorsement does not of itself give such notice. Payors are immunized either by subsection (2) of this section or by Section

3—603: payment to the trustee or to a purchaser from the trustee is "consistent with the terms" of the trust indorsement under Section 3—603(1) (b).

7. Several sections of Article 3 and Article 4 are explicitly made subject to the rules stated in this section. See Sections 3—306, 3—419, 4—203 and 4—205.

Cross References:

Point 1: Sections 3—205 and 3—602.

Point 2: Section 3—205(b).

Point 3: Sections 3—102(3), 3—419(4), 3—603, 4—105, 4—205 (2).

Point 4: Section 3—205(a).

Point 5: Sections 3—205, 3—603 and 4—201.

Point 6: Sections 3—205, 3—304 and 3—603.

Point 7: Sections 3—306, 3—419, 4—203 and 4—205.

Definitional Cross References:

"Bank". Section 1—201.

"Depositary bank". Sections 3—102(3) and 4—105.

"Holder in due course". Section 3—302.

"Intermediary bank". Sections 3—102(3) and 4—105.

"Negotiation". Sections 3—102(2) and 3—202.

"Payor bank". Sections 3—102 (3) and 4—105.

"Restrictive indorsement". Section 3—205.

"Transfer". Section 3—201.

§ 3—207. Negotiation Effective Although It May Be Rescinded

(1) Negotiation is effective to transfer the instrument although the negotiation is

(a) made by an infant, a corporation exceeding its powers, or any other person without capacity; or

(b) obtained by fraud, duress or mistake of any kind; or

(c) part of an illegal transaction; or

(d) made in breach of duty.

(2) Except as against a subsequent holder in due course such negotiation is in an appropriate case subject to rescission, the declaration of a constructive trust or any other remedy permitted by law.

Official Comment

Prior Uniform Statutory Provision: Sections 22, 58 and 59, Uniform Negotiable Instruments Law.

Changes: Completely revised.

Purposes of Changes: To make it clear that:

1. The original Section 22, which covered only negotiation by an infant or a corporation, is extended by this section to include other negotiations which may be rescinded. The provision applies even though the party's lack of capacity, or the illegality, is of a character which goes to the essence of the transaction and makes it entirely void, and even though the party negotiat-

ing has incurred no liability and is entitled to recover the instrument and have his indorsement cancelled.

2. It is inherent in the character of negotiable paper that any person in possession of an instrument which by its terms runs to him is a holder, and that anyone may deal with him as a holder. The principle finds its most extreme application in the well settled rule that a holder in due course may take the paper even from a thief and be protected against the claim of the rightful owner. Where there is actual negotiation, even in an entirely void transaction, it is no less effective. The policy of this provision, as well as of the last sentence of the original Section 59, is that any person to whom an instrument is negotiated is a holder until the instrument has been recovered from his possession; and that any person who negotiates an instrument thereby parts with all his rights in it until such recovery. The remedy of any such claimant is to recover the paper by replevin or otherwise; to impound it or to enjoin its enforcement, collection or negotiation; to recover its proceeds from the holder; or to intervene in any action brought by the holder against the obligor. As provided in the section on the rights of one not a holder in due course (Section 3—306) his claim is not a defense to the obligor unless he himself defends the action.

3. Negotiation under this Article always includes delivery. (Section 3—202, and see Section 1—201(14)). Acquisition of possession by a thief can therefore never be negotiation under this section. But delivery by the thief to another person may be.

4. Nothing in this section is intended to impose any liability on the party negotiating. He may assert any defense available to him under Sections 3—305, 3—306 and 3—307.

5. A holder in due course takes the instrument free from all claims to it on the part of any person (Section 3—305(1)). Against him there can be no rescission or other remedy, even though the prior negotiation may have been fraudulent or illegal in its essence and entirely void. As against any other party the claimant may have any remedy permitted by law. This section is not intended to specify what that remedy may be, or to prevent any court from imposing conditions or limitations such as prompt action or return of the consideration received. All such questions are left to the law of the particular jurisdiction. Subsection (2) of Section 3—207 gives no right where it would not otherwise exist. The section is intended to mean that any remedies afforded by the local law are cut off only by a holder in due course, and that other parties, such as a bona fide purchaser with notice that the instrument is overdue, take it subject to the claim as provided in paragraph (a) of the section on the rights of one not a holder in due course (Section 3—306).

Cross References:

Point 2: Sections 1—201 and 3—306(d).

Point 3: Sections 1—201 and 3—202.

Point 4: Sections 3—305, 3—306 and 3—307.

Point 5: Sections 3—305(1) and 3—306(a).

Definitional Cross References:

"Holder in due course". Section 3—302.

"Instrument". Section 3—102.

"Negotiation". Section 3—202.

"Person". Section 1—201.

"Remedy". Section 1—201.

§ 3—208. Reacquisition

Where an instrument is returned to or reacquired by a prior party he may cancel any indorsement which is not necessary to his title and reissue or further negotiate the instrument, but any intervening party is discharged as against the reacquiring party and subsequent holders not in due course and if his indorsement has been cancelled is discharged as against subsequent holders in due course as well.

Official Comment

Prior Uniform Statutory Provision: Sections 48, 50 and 121, Uniform Negotiable Instruments Law.

Changes: Parts of original sections combined and rephrased.

Purposes of Changes: No change in the substance of the law is intended. "Returned to or reacquired by" is substituted for "negotiated back to" in the original Section 50 in order to make it clear that the section applies to a return by an indorsee who does not himself indorse. "Discharged" is substituted for the original language to make it clear that the discharge of the intervening party is included within the rule of the section on effect of discharge against a holder in due course (Section 3—602) and is not effective against a subsequent holder in due course who takes without notice of it.

The reacquirer may keep the instrument himself or he may further negotiate it. On further negotiation he may or may not cancel intervening indorsements. In any case intervening indorsers are discharged as to the reacquirer, since if he attempted to enforce it against them they would have an action back against him. Where the reacquirer negotiates without cancelling the intervening indorsements, the section provides that such indorsers are discharged except against subsequent holders in due course. The intervening indorser whose indorsement is stricken is, in conformity with Section 3—605, discharged even as against subsequent holders in due course.

Cross References:

Sections 3—602, 3—603(2) and 3—605.

Definitional Cross References:

"Holder in due course". Section 3—302.

"Instrument". Section 3—102.

"Party". Section 1—201.

PART 3

RIGHTS OF A HOLDER

§ 3—301. Rights of a Holder

The holder of an instrument whether or not he is the owner may transfer or negotiate it and, except as otherwise provided in Section 3—603 on payment or satisfaction, discharge it or enforce payment in his own name.

Official Comment

Prior Uniform Statutory Provision: Section 51, Uniform Negotiable Instruments Law.

Changes: Reworded. The provision in the original Section 51 as to discharge by payment is now covered by Section 3—603(1).

Purposes of Changes: The section is revised to state in one provision all the rights of a holder, and to make it clear that every holder has such rights. The only limitations are those found in Section 3—603 on payment or satisfaction. That section provides (with stated exceptions) that payment to a holder discharges the liability of the party paying even though made with knowledge of a claim of another person to the instrument, unless the adverse claimant posts indemnity or procures the issuance of appropriate legal process restraining the payment. Thus payment to a holder in an adverse claim situation would not give discharge if the adverse claimant had followed either of the procedures provided for in the "unless" clause of Section 3—603; nor would a discharge result from payment in two other specific situations described in Section 3—603.

Cross References:

Sections 1—201, 3—307 and 3—603(1).

Definitional Cross References:

"Holder". Section 1—201.
"Instrument". Section 3—102.
"Rights". Section 1—201.

§ 3—302. Holder in Due Course

(1) A holder in due course is a holder who takes the instrument

(a) for value; and

(b) in good faith; and

(c) without notice that it is overdue or has been dishonored or of any defense against or claim to it on the part of any person.

(2) A payee may be a holder in due course.

(3) A holder does not become a holder in due course of an instrument:

(a) by purchase of it at judicial sale or by taking it under legal process; or

(b) by acquiring it in taking over an estate; or

(c) by purchasing it as part of a bulk transaction not in regular course of business of the transferor.

(4) A purchaser of a limited interest can be a holder in due course only to the extent of the interest purchased.

Official Comment

Prior Uniform Statutory Provision: Section 52, Uniform Negotiable Instruments Law.

Changes: Reworded; new provisions.

Purposes of Changes and New Matter: The changes are intended to remove uncertainties arising under the original section.

1. The language "without notice that it is overdue" is substituted for that of the original subsection (2) in order to make it clear that the purchaser of an instrument which is in fact overdue may be a holder in due course if he takes it without notice that it is overdue. Such notice is covered by the section on notice to purchaser (Section 3—304).

2. Subsection (2) is intended to settle the long continued conflict over the status of the payee as a holder in due course. This conflict has turned very largely upon the word "negotiated" in the original Section 52(4), which is now eliminated. The position here taken is that the payee may become a holder in due course to the same extent and under the same circumstances as any other holder. This is true whether he takes the instrument by purchase from a third person or directly from the obligor. All that is necessary is that the payee meet the requirements of this section. In the following cases, among others, the payee is a holder in due course:

a. A remitter, purchasing goods from P, obtains a bank draft payable to P and forwards it to P, who takes it for value, in good faith and without notice as required by this section.

b. The remitter buys the bank draft payable to P, but it is forwarded by the bank directly to P, who takes it in good faith and without notice in payment of the remitter's obligation to him.

c. A and B sign a note as comakers. A induces B to sign by fraud, and without authority from B delivers the note to P, who takes it for value, in good faith and without notice.

d. A defrauds the maker into signing an instrument payable to P. P pays A for it in good faith and without notice, and the maker delivers the instrument directly to P.

e. D draws a check payable to P and gives it to his agent to be delivered to P in payment of D's debt. The agent delivers it to P, who takes it in good faith and without notice in payment of the agent's debt to P. But as to this case see Section 3—304(2), which may apply.

f. D draws a check payable to P but blank as to the amount, and gives it to his agent to be delivered to P. The agent fills in the check with an excessive amount, and P takes it for value, in good faith and without notice.

g. D draws a check blank as to the name of the payee, and gives it to his agent to be filled in with the name of A and delivered to A. The agent fills in the name of P, and P takes the check in good faith, for value and without notice.

3. Subsection (3) is intended to state existing case law. It covers a few situations in which the purchaser takes the instrument under unusual circumstances which indicate that he is merely a successor in interest to the prior holder and can acquire no better rights. (If such prior holder was himself a holder in due course, the purchaser succeeds to that status under Section 3—201 on Transfer.) The provision applies to a purchaser at an execution sale, a sale in bankruptcy or a sale by a state bank commissioner of the assets of an insolvent bank. It applies equally to an attaching creditor or any other person who acquires the instrument by legal process, even under an antecedent claim; and equally to a representative, such as an executor, administrator, receiver or assignee for the benefit of creditors, who takes over the instrument as part of an estate, even though he is representing antecedent creditors.

Subsection (3) (c) applies to bulk purchases lying outside of the ordinary course of business of the seller. It applies, for example, when a new partnership takes over for value all of the assets of an old one after a new member has entered the firm, or to a reorganized or consolidated corporation taking over in bulk the assets of a predecessor. It has particular application to the purchase by one bank of a substantial part of the paper held by another bank which is threatened with insolvency and seeking to liquidate its assets.

4. A purchaser of a limited interest—as a pledgee in a security transaction—may become a holder in due course, but he may enforce the instrument over defenses only to the extent of his interest, and defenses good against the pledgor remain available insofar as the pledgor retains an equity in the instrument. This is merely a special application of the general rule (Section 1—201) that a purchaser of a limited interest acquires rights only to the extent of the interest purchased. Section 27 of the original Act contained a similar provision.

Cross References:

Sections 1—201, 3—303, 3—305 and 3—306.

Point 1: Section 3—304(5).

Point 3: Section 3—201.

Point 4: Section 1—201.

Definitional Cross References:

"Good faith". Section 1—201.

"Holder". Section 1—201.

"Instrument". Section 3—102.

"Notice". Section 1—201.

"Notice of dishonor". Section 3—508.

"Person". Section 1—201.
"Purchase". Section 1—201.
"Purchaser". Section 1—201.
"Value". Section 3—303.

§ 3—303. Taking for Value

A holder takes the instrument for value

(a) to the extent that the agreed consideration has been performed or that he acquires a security interest in or a lien on the instrument otherwise than by legal process; or

(b) when he takes the instrument in payment of or as security for an antecedent claim against any person whether or not the claim is due; or

(c) when he gives a negotiable instrument for it or makes an irrevocable commitment to a third person.

Official Comment

Prior Uniform Statutory Provision: Sections 25, 26, 27 and 54, Uniform Negotiable Instruments Law.

Changes: Combined and reworded; original Section 26 omitted.

Purposes of Changes: The changes are intended to remove uncertainties arising under the original Act.

1. The original Section 26 which had reference to the liability of accommodation parties is omitted as erroneous and misleading, since a holder who does not himself give value cannot qualify as a holder in due course in his own right merely because value has previously been given for the instrument.

2. In this Article value is divorced from consideration (Section 3—408). The latter is important only on the question of whether the obligation of a party can be enforced against him; while value is important only on the question of whether the holder who has acquired that obligation qualifies as a particular kind of holder.

3. Paragraph (a) resolves an apparent conflict between the original Section 54 and the first sentence of the original Section 25, by requiring that the agreed consideration shall actually have been given. An executory promise to give value is not itself value, except as provided in paragraph (c). The underlying reason of policy is that when the purchaser learns of a defense against the instrument or of a defect in the title he is not required to enforce the instrument, but is free to rescind the transaction for breach of the transferor's warranty (Section 3—417). There is thus not the same necessity for giving him the status of a holder in due course, cutting off claims and defenses, as where he has actually paid value. A common illustration is the bank credit not drawn upon, which can be and is revoked when a claim or defense appears.

4. Paragraph (a) limits the language of the original Section

27, eliminating the attaching creditor or any other person who acquires a lien by legal process. Any such lienor has been uniformly held not to be a holder in due course.

5. Paragraph (b) restates the last sentence of the original Section 25. It adopts the generally accepted rule that the holder takes for value when he takes the instrument as security for an antecedent debt, even though there is no extension of time or other concession, and whether or not the debt is due. The provision extends the same rule to any claim against any person; there is no requirement that the claim arise out of contract. In particular the provision is intended to apply to an instrument given in payment of or as security for the debt of a third person, even though no concession is made in return.

6. Paragraph (c) is new, but states generally recognized exceptions to the rule that an executory promise is not value. A negotiable instrument is value because it carries the possibility of negotiation to a holder in due course, after which the party who gives it cannot refuse to pay. The same reasoning applies to any irrevocable commitment to a third person, such as a letter of credit issued when an instrument is taken.

Cross References:

Sections 3—302 and 3—415.
Point 1: Section 3—415.
Point 2: Section 3—408.
Point 3: Section 3—417.

Definitional Cross References:

"Holder". Section 1—201.
"Instrument". Section 3—102.
"Person". Section 1—201.
"Security interest". Section 1—201.

§ 3—304. Notice to Purchaser

(1) The purchaser has notice of a claim or defense if

(a) the instrument is so incomplete, bears such visible evidence of forgery or alteration, or is otherwise so irregular as to call into question its validity, terms or ownership or to create an ambiguity as to the party to pay; or

(b) the purchaser has notice that the obligation of any party is voidable in whole or in part, or that all parties have been discharged.

(2) The purchaser has notice of a claim against the instrument when he has knowledge that a fiduciary has negotiated the instrument in payment of or as security for his own debt or in any transaction for his own benefit or otherwise in breach of duty.

(3) The purchaser has notice that an instrument is overdue if he has reason to know

(a) that any part of the principal amount is overdue or that there is an uncured default in payment of another instrument of the same series; or

(b) that acceleration of the instrument has been made; or

(c) that he is taking a demand instrument after demand has been made or more than a reasonable length of time after its issue. A reasonable time for a check drawn and payable within the states and territories of the United States and the District of Columbia is presumed to be thirty days.

(4) Knowledge of the following facts does not of itself give the purchaser notice of a defense or claim

(a) that the instrument is antedated or postdated;

(b) that it was issued or negotiated in return for an executory promise or accompanied by a separate agreement, unless the purchaser has notice that a defense or claim has arisen from the terms thereof;

(c) that any party has signed for accommodation;

(d) that an incomplete instrument has been completed, unless the purchaser has notice of any improper completion;

(e) that any person negotiating the instrument is or was a fiduciary;

(f) that there has been default in payment of interest on the instrument or in payment of any other instrument, except one of the same series.

(5) The filing or recording of a document does not of itself constitute notice within the provisions of this Article to a person who would otherwise be a holder in due course.

(6) To be effective notice must be received at such time and in such manner as to give a reasonable opportunity to act on it.

Official Comment

Prior Uniform Statutory Provision: Sections 45, 52, 53, 55 and 56, Uniform Negotiable Instruments Law.

Changes: Combined and reworded; new provisions.

Purposes of Changes and New Matter: The original sections are expanded, with the addition of specific provisions intended to remove uncertainties in the existing law.

1. "Notice" is defined in Section 1—201.

2. Paragraph (a) of subsection (1) replaces the provision in the original Section 52(1) requiring that the instrument be "complete and regular on its face." An instrument may be blank as to some unnecessary particular, may contain minor erasures, or even have an obvious change in the date, as where "January 2, 1948" is changed to "January 2, 1949", without even

exciting suspicion. Irregularity is properly a question of notice to the purchaser of something wrong, and is so treated here.

3. "Voidable" obligation in paragraph (b) of subsection (1) is intended to limit the provision to notice of defense which will permit any party to avoid his original obligation on the instrument, as distinguished from a set-off or counterclaim.

4. Notice that one party has been discharged is not notice to the purchaser of an infirmity in the obligation of other parties who remain liable on the instrument. A purchaser with notice that an indorser is discharged takes subject to that discharge as provided in the section on effect of discharge against a holder in due course (Section 3—602) but is not prevented from taking the obligation of the maker in due course. If he has notice that all parties are discharged he cannot be a holder in due course.

5. Subsection (2) follows the policy of Section 6 of the Uniform Fiduciaries Act, and specifies the same elements as notice of improper conduct of a fiduciary. Under paragraph (e) of subsection (4) mere notice of the existence of the fiduciary relation is not enough in itself to prevent the holder from taking in due course, and he is free to take the instrument on the assumption that the fiduciary is acting properly. The purchaser may pay cash into the hands of the fiduciary without notice of any breach of the obligation. Section 3—206 should be consulted for the effect of a restrictive indorsement.

6. Subsection (3) removes an uncertainty in the original Act by providing that reason to know of an overdue installment or other part of the principal amount is notice that the instrument is overdue and thus prevents the purchaser from taking in due course. On the other hand subsection (4) (f) makes notice that interest is overdue insufficient, on the basis of banking and commercial practice, the decisions under the original Act, and the frequency with which interest payments are in fact delayed. Notice of default in payment of any other instrument, except an uncured default in another instrument of the same series, is likewise insufficient.

7. Subsection (3) departs from the original Section 52(2) by providing that the purchaser may take accelerated paper, or a demand instrument on which demand has in fact been made, as a holder in due course if he takes without notice of the acceleration or demand. With this change the original Section 45 is eliminated, as the presumption that any negotiation has taken place before the instrument was in fact overdue is of importance only in aid of a holder in due course. Under this section it is not conclusive that the instrument was in fact overdue when it was negotiated, if the holder takes without notice of that fact.

The "reasonable time after issue" is retained from the original Section 53, but paragraph (c) adds a presumption, as that term is defined in this Act (Section 1—201), that a domestic check is stale after thirty days.

8. Paragraph (a) of subsection (4) rejects decisions holding that an instrument known to be antedated or postdated is not

"regular." Such knowledge does not prevent a holder from taking in due course.

9. Paragraph (b) of subsection (4) is to be read together with the provisions of this Article as to when a promise or order is unconditional and as to other writings affecting the instrument (Sections 3—105 and 3—119). Mere notice of the existence of an executory promise or a separate agreement does not prevent the holder from taking in due course, and such notice may even appear in the instrument itself. If the purchaser has notice of any default in the promise or agreement which gives rise to a defense or claim against the instrument, he is on notice to the same extent as in the case of any other information as to the existence of a defense or claim.

10. Paragraph (d) of subsection (4) follows the policy of the original Section 14, under which any person in possession of an instrument has prima facie authority to fill blanks. It is intended to mean that the holder may take in due course even though a blank is filled in his presence, if he is without notice that the filling is improper. Section 3—407 on alteration should be consulted as to the rights of subsequent holders following such an alteration.

11. Subsection (5) is new. It removes an uncertainty arising under the original Act as to the effect of "constructive notice" through public filing or recording.

12. Subsection (6) is new. It means that notice must be received with a sufficient margin of time to afford a reasonable opportunity to act on it, and that a notice received by the president of a bank one minute before the bank's teller cashes a check is not effective to prevent the bank from becoming a holder in due course. See in this connection the provision on notice to an organization, Sec. 1—201(27).

Cross References:

Sections 3—201 and 3—302.
Point 1: Section 1—201.
Point 4: Section 3—602.
Point 5: Section 3—206.
Point 7: Section 1—201.
Point 9: Sections 3—105(1) (b) and (c) and 3—119.
Point 10: Section 3—407.
Point 12: Section 1—201.

Definitional Cross References:

"Accommodation party". Section 3—415.
"Agreement". Section 1—201.
"Alteration". Section 3—407.
"Bank". Section 1—201.
"Check". Section 3—104.
"Holder in due course". Section 3—302.
"Instrument". Section 3—102.
"Issue". Section 3—102.
"Negotiation". Section 3—202.
"Notice". Section 1—201.
"Party". Section 1—201.
"Person". Section 1—201.
"Presumed". Section 1—201.
"Promise". Section 3—102.
"Purchaser". Section 1—201.
"Reasonable time". Section 1—204.
"Signed". Section 1—201.
"Term". Section 1—201.

§ 3—305. Rights of a Holder in Due Course

To the extent that a holder is a holder in due course he takes the instrument free from

(1) all claims to it on the part of any person; and

(2) all defenses of any party to the instrument with whom the holder has not dealt except

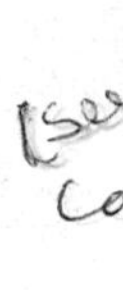

(a) infancy, to the extent that it is a defense to a simple contract; and

(b) such other incapacity, or duress, or illegality of the transaction, as renders the obligation of the party a nullity; and

(c) such misrepresentation as has induced the party to sign the instrument with neither knowledge nor reasonable opportunity to obtain knowledge of its character or its essential terms; and

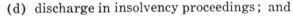

(d) discharge in insolvency proceedings; and

(e) any other discharge of which the holder has notice when he takes the instrument.

Official Comment

Prior Uniform Statutory Provision: Sections 15, 16 and 57, Uniform Negotiable Instruments Law.

Changes: Combined and reworded; new provisions; rule of original Section 15 reversed.

Purposes of Changes and New Matter:

1. The section applies to any person who is himself a holder in due course, and equally to any transferee who acquires the rights of one (Section 3—201). "Takes" is substituted for "holds" in the original Section 57 because a holder in due course may still be subject to any claims or defenses which arise against him after he has taken the instrument.

2. The language "all claims to it on the part of any person" is substituted for "any defect of title of prior parties" in the original Section 57 in order to make it clear that the holder in due course takes the instrument free not only from any claim of legal title but also from all liens, equities or claims of any other kind. This includes any claim for rescission of a prior negotiation, in accordance with the provisions of the section on reacquisition (Section 3—208).

3. "All defenses" includes nondelivery, conditional delivery or delivery for a special purpose. Under this Article such nondelivery or qualified delivery is a defense (Sections 3—306 and 3—307) and the defendant has the full burden of establishing it.

Accordingly the "conclusive presumption" of the third sentence of the original Section 16 is abrogated in favor of a rule of law cutting off the defense.

The effect of this section, together with the sections dealing with incomplete instruments (Section 3—115) and alteration (Section 3—407) is to cut off the defense of nondelivery of an incomplete instrument against a holder in due course, and to change the rule of the original Section 15.

4. Paragraph (a) of subsection (2) is new. It follows the decisions under the original Act in providing that the defense of infancy may be asserted against a holder in due course, even though its effect is to render the instrument voidable but not void. The policy is one of protection of the infant against those who take advantage of him, even at the expense of occasional loss to an innocent purchaser. No attempt is made to state when infancy is available as a defense or the conditions under which it may be asserted. In some jurisdictions it is held that an infant cannot rescind the transaction or set up the defense unless he restores the holder to his former position, which in the case of a holder in due course is normally impossible. In other states an infant who has misrepresented his age may be estopped to assert his infancy. Such questions are left to the local law, as an integral part of the policy of each state as to the protection of infants.

5. Paragraph (b) of subsection (2) is new. It covers mental incompetence, guardianship, ultra vires acts or lack of corporate capacity to do business, any remaining incapacity of married women, or any other incapacity apart from infancy. Such incapacity is largely statutory. Its existence and effect is left to the law of each state. If under the local law the effect is to render the obligation of the instrument entirely null and void, the defense may be asserted against a holder in due course. If the effect is merely to render the obligation voidable at the election of the obligor, the defense is cut off.

6. Duress is a matter of degree. An instrument signed at the point of a gun is void, even in the hands of a holder in due course. One signed under threat to prosecute the son of the maker for theft may be merely voidable, so that the defense is cut off. Illegality is most frequently a matter of gambling or usury, but may arise in many other forms under a great variety of statutes. The statutes differ greatly in their provisions and the interpretations given them. They are primarily a matter of local concern and local policy. All such matters are therefore left to the local law. If under that law the effect of the duress or the illegality is to make the obligation entirely null and void, the defense may be asserted against a holder in due course. Otherwise it is cut off.

7. Paragraph (c) of subsection (2) is new. It follows the great majority of the decisions under the original Act in recognizing the defense of "real" or "essential" fraud, sometimes called fraud in the essence or fraud in the factum, as effective against a holder in due course. The common illustration is that

of the maker who is tricked into signing a note in the belief that it is merely a receipt or some other document. The theory of the defense is that his signature on the instrument is ineffective because he did not intend to sign such an instrument at all. Under this provision the defense extends to an instrument signed with knowledge that it is a negotiable instrument, but without knowledge of its essential terms.

The test of the defense here stated is that of excusable ignorance of the contents of the writing signed. The party must not only have been in ignorance, but must also have had no reasonable opportunity to obtain knowledge. In determining what is a reasonable opportunity all relevant factors are to be taken into account, including the age and sex of the party, his intelligence, education and business experience; his ability to read or to understand English, the representations made to him and his reason to rely on them or to have confidence in the person making them; the presence or absence of any third person who might read or explain the instrument to him, or any other possibility of obtaining independent information; and the apparent necessity, or lack of it, for acting without delay.

Unless the misrepresentation meets this test, the defense is cut off by a holder in due course.

8. Paragraph (d) is also new. It is inserted to make it clear that any discharge in bankruptcy or other insolvency proceedings, as defined in this Article, is not cut off when the instrument is purchased by a holder in due course.

9. Paragraph (e) of subsection (2) is also new. Under the notice to purchaser section of this Article (Section 3—304), notice of any discharge which leaves other parties liable on the instrument does not prevent the purchaser from becoming a holder in due course. The obvious case is that of the cancellation of an indorsement, which leaves the maker and prior indorsers liable. As to such parties the purchaser may be a holder in due course, but he takes the instrument subject to the discharge of which he has notice. If he is without such notice, the discharge is not effective against him (Section 3—602).

Cross References:

Point 1: Section 3—201(1).

Point 2: Section 3—208.

Point 3: Sections 3—115(2), 3—306(c), 3—307(2) and 3—407(3).

Point 9: Sections 3—304(1)(b) and 3—602.

Definitional Cross References:

"Contract". Section 1—201.

"Holder in due course". Section 3—302.

"Insolvency proceedings". Section 1—201.

"Instrument". Section 3—102.

"Notice". Section 1—201.

"Party". Section 1—201.

"Person". Section 1—201.

"Term". Section 1—201.

§ 3—306. Rights of One Not Holder in Due Course

Unless he has the rights of a holder in due course any person takes the instrument subject to

(a) all valid claims to it on the part of any person; and

(b) all defenses of any party which would be available in an action on a simple contract; and

(c) the defenses of want or failure of consideration, non-performance of any condition precedent, non-delivery, or delivery for a special purpose (Section 3—408); and

(d) the defense that he or a person through whom he holds the instrument acquired it by theft, or that payment or satisfaction to such holder would be inconsistent with the terms of a restrictive indorsement. The claim of any third person to the instrument is not otherwise available as a defense to any party liable thereon unless the third person himself defends the action for such party.

Official Comment

Prior Uniform Statutory Provision: Sections 16, 28, 58 and 59, Uniform Negotiable Instruments Law.

Changes: Combined, condensed and reworded.

Purposes of Changes: The changes are intended to remove the following uncertainties arising under the original sections:

1. Any transferee who acquires the rights of a holder in due course under the transfer section of this Article (Section 3—201) is included within the provisions of the preceding Section 305. This section covers any person who neither qualifies in his own right as a holder in due course nor has acquired the rights of one by transfer. In particular the section applies to a bona fide purchaser with notice that the instrument is overdue.

2. "All valid claims to it on the part of any person" includes not only claims of legal title, but all liens, equities, or other claims of right against the instrument or its proceeds. It includes claims to rescind a prior negotiation and to recover the instrument or its proceeds.

3. Paragraph (b) restates the first sentence of the original Section 58.

4. Paragraph (c) condenses the original Sections 16 and 28. Want or failure of consideration is specifically mentioned, as in the original Section 28, in order to make it clear that either is a defense which the defendant has the burden of establishing under the following section of this Article. The language as to an "ascertained or liquidated amount or otherwise" in the original Section 28 is omitted because it is

believed to be superfluous. The third sentence of Section 16 is now covered by the preceding section. The fourth sentence is omitted in favor of the rule stated in the following section, which places the full burden of establishing the defense of non-delivery, conditional delivery or delivery for a special purpose upon the defendant, and makes any presumption unnecessary.

5. Paragraph (d) is substituted for the last sentence of the original Section 59, as a more detailed and explicit statement of the same policy, which is also found in the original Section 22. The contract of the obligor is to pay the holder of the instrument, and the claims of other persons against the holder are generally not his concern. He is not required to set up such a claim as a defense, since he usually will have no satisfactory evidence of his own on the issue; and the provision that he may not do so is intended as much for his protection as for that of the holder. The claimant who has lost possession of an instrument so payable or indorsed that another may become a holder has lost his rights on the instrument, which by its terms no longer runs to him. The provision includes all claims for rescission of a negotiation, whether based in incapacity, fraud, duress, mistake, illegality, breach of trust or duty or any other reason. It includes claims based on conditional delivery or delivery for a special purpose. It includes claims of legal title, lien, constructive trust or other equity against the instrument or its proceeds. The exception made in the case of theft is based on the policy which refuses to aid a proved thief to recover, and refuses to aid him indirectly by permitting his transferee to recover unless the transferee is a holder in due course. The exception concerning restrictive indorsements is intended to achieve consistency with Section 3—603 and related sections.

Nothing in this section is intended to prevent the claimant from intervening in the holder's action against the obligor or defending the action for the latter, and asserting his claim in the course of such intervention or defense. Nothing here stated is intended to prevent any interpleader, deposit in court or other available procedure under which the defendant may bring the claimant into court or be discharged without himself litigating the claim as a defense. Compare Section 3—803 on vouching in other parties alleged to be liable.

Cross References:

Section 3—302.

Point 1: Sections 3—201(1) and 3—305.

Point 2: Section 3—207.

Point 3: Section 3—307(2).

Point 4: Sections 3—305 and 3—307(2).

Point 5: Section 3—803.

Definitional Cross References:

"Action". Section 1—201.

"Contract". Section 1—201.

"Delivery". Section 1—201.

"Holder in due course". Section 3—302.

"Instrument". Section 3—102.

"Party". Section 1—201.

"Person". Section 1—201.

"Rights". Section 1—201.

§ 3—307. Burden of Establishing Signatures, Defenses and Due Course

(1) Unless specifically denied in the pleadings each signature on an instrument is admitted. When the effectiveness of a signature is put in issue

(a) the burden of establishing it is on the party claiming under the signature; but

(b) the signature is presumed to be genuine or authorized except where the action is to enforce the obligation of a purported signer who has died or become incompetent before proof is required.

(2) When signatures are admitted or established, production of the instrument entitles a holder to recover on it unless the defendant establishes a defense.

(3) After it is shown that a defense exists a person claiming the rights of a holder in due course has the burden of establishing that he or some person under whom he claims is in all respects a holder in due course.

Official Comment

Prior Uniform Statutory Provision: Section 59, Uniform Negotiable Instruments Law.

Changes: Reworded; new provisions.

Purposes of Changes and New Matter:

1. Subsection (1) is new, although similar provisions are found in a number of states. The purpose of the requirement of a specific denial in the pleadings is to give the plaintiff notice that he must meet a claim of forgery or lack of authority as to the particular signature, and to afford him an opportunity to investigate and obtain evidence. Where local rules of pleading permit, the denial may be on information and belief, or it may be a denial of knowledge or information sufficient to form a belief. It need not be under oath unless the local statutes or rules require verification. In the absence of such specific denial the signature stands admitted, and is not in issue. Nothing in this section is intended, however, to prevent amendment of the pleading in a proper case.

The question of the burden of establishing the signature arises only when it has been put in issue by specific denial. "Burden of establishing" is defined in the definitions section of this Act (Section 1—201). The burden is on the party claiming under the signature, but he is aided by the presumption that it is genuine or authorized [as] stated in paragraph (b). "Presumption" is also defined in this Act (Section 1—201). It means that until some evidence is introduced which would support a finding that the signature is forged or unauthorized the plaintiff is not required to prove that it is authentic. The presumption rests upon the fact that in ordinary experience forged or unauthorized signatures are very uncommon, and normally any evidence is within the control of the defendant or more accessible to him. He is therefore required to make some sufficient showing of the grounds for his denial before the plaintiff is put to his proof. His evidence need not be sufficient to require a directed verdict in his favor, but it must be enough to support his denial by permitting a finding in his favor. Until he introduces such evidence the presumption requires a finding for the plaintiff. Once such evidence is introduced the burden of establishing the signature by a preponderance of the total evidence is on the plaintiff.

Under paragraph (b) this presumption does not arise where the action is to enforce the obligation of a purported signer who has died or become incompetent before the evidence is required, and so is disabled from obtaining or introducing it. "Action" of course includes a claim asserted against the estate of a deceased or an incompetent.

2. Subsection (2) is substituted for the first clause of the original Section 59. Once signatures are proved or admitted, a holder makes out his case by mere production of the instrument, and is entitled to recover in the absence of any further evidence. The defendant has the burden of establishing any and all defenses, not only in the first instance but by a preponderance of the total evidence. The provision applies only to a holder, as defined in this Act (Section 1—201). Any other person in possession of an instrument must prove his right to it and account for the absence of any necessary indorsement. If he establishes a transfer which gives him the rights of a holder (Section 3—201), this provision becomes applicable, and he is then entitled to recover unless the defendant establishes a defense.

3. Subsection (3) rephrases the last clause of the first sentence of the original Section 59. Until it is shown that a defense exists the issue as to whether the holder is a holder in due course does not arise. In the absence of a defense any holder is entitled to recover and there is no occasion to say that he is deemed prima facie to be a holder in due course. When it is shown that a defense exists the plaintiff may, if he so elects, seek to cut off the defense by establishing that he is himself a holder in due course, or that he has acquired the rights of a prior holder in due course (Section 3—201). On this issue he has the full burden of proof by a preponderance of the total evidence. "In all respects" means that he must sustain this burden by affirmative proof that the instrument was taken for value, that it was taken in good faith, and that it was taken without notice (Section 3—302).

Nothing in this section is intended to say that the plaintiff must necessarily prove that he is a holder in due course. He may elect to introduce no further evidence, in which case a verdict may be directed for the plaintiff or the defendant, or the issue of the defense may be left to the jury, according to the weight and sufficiency of the defendant's evidence. He may elect to rebut the defense itself by proof to the contrary, in which case again a verdict may be directed for either party or the issue may be for the jury. This subsection means only that if the plaintiff claims the rights of a holder in due course against the defense he has the burden of proof upon that issue.

Cross References:

Sections 3—305, 3—306, 3—401, 3—403 and 3—404.

Point 1: Section 1—201.

Point 2: Sections 1—201 and 3—201(1).

Point 3: Sections 3—201(1) and 3—302.

Definitional Cross References:

"Action". Section 1—201.

"Burden of establishing". Section 1—201.

"Defendant". Section 1—201.

"Genuine". Section 1—201.

"Holder". Section 1—201.

"Holder in due course". Section 3—302.

"Instrument". Section 3—102.

"Party". Section 1—201.

"Person". Section 1—201.

"Presumed". Section 1—201.

"Rights". Section 1—201.

"Signature". Section 3—401.

PART 4

LIABILITY OF PARTIES

§ 3—401. Signature

(1) No person is liable on an instrument unless his signature appears thereon.

(2) A signature is made by use of any name, including any trade or assumed name, upon an instrument, or by any word or mark used in lieu of a written signature.

Official Comment

Prior Uniform Statutory Provision: Section 18, Uniform Negotiable Instruments Law.

Changes: Reworded.

Purposes of Changes: To make it clear that:

1. No one is liable on an instrument unless and until he has signed it. The chief application of the rule has been in cases holding that a principal whose name does not appear on an instrument signed by his agent is not liable on the instrument even though the payee knew when it was issued that it was intended to be the obligation of one who did not sign. The exceptions made as to collateral and virtual acceptances by the original Sections 134 and 135 are now abrogated by the definition of an acceptance and the rules governing its operation. An allonge is part of the instrument to which it is affixed. Section 3—202(2).

Nothing in this section is intended to prevent any liability arising apart from the instrument itself. The party who does not sign may still be liable on the original obligation for which the instrument was given, or for breach of any agreement to sign, or in tort for misrepresentation, or even on an oral guaranty of payment where the statute of frauds is satisfied. He may of course be liable under any separate writing. The provision is not intended to prevent an estoppel to deny that the party has signed, as where the instrument is purchased in good faith reliance upon his assurance that a forged signature is genuine.

2. A signature may be handwritten, typed, printed or made in any other manner. It need not be subscribed, and may appear in the body of the instrument, as in the case of "I, John Doe, promise to pay—" without any other signature. It may be made by mark, or even by thumbprint. It may be made in any name, including any trade name or assumed name, however false and fictitious, which is adopted for the purpose. Parol evidence is admissible to identify the signer, and when he is identified the signature is effective.

This section is not intended to affect any local statute or rule of law requiring a signature by mark to be witnessed, or any signature to be otherwise authenticated, or requiring any form of proof. It is to be read together with the provision under which a person paying or giving value for the instrument may require indorsement in both the right name and the wrong one; and with the provision that the absence of an indorsement in the right name may make an instrument so irregular as to call its ownership into question and put a purchaser upon notice which will prevent his taking as a holder in due course.

Cross References:

Sections 3—202(2), 3—402 through 3—406.

Point 1: Section 3—410.

Point 2: Section 3—203.

Definitional Cross References:

"Person". Section 1—201.

"Instrument". Section 3—102.

"Signed". Section 1—201.

"Written". Section 1—201.

§ 3—402. Signature in Ambiguous Capacity

Unless the instrument clearly indicates that a signature is made in some other capacity it is an indorsement.

Official Comment

Prior Uniform Statutory Provision: Sections 17(6) and 63, Uniform Negotiable Instruments Law.

Changes: Combined and reworded.

Purposes of Changes: The revised language is intended to say that any ambiguity as to the capacity in which a signature is made must be resolved by a rule of law that it is an indorsement. Parol evidence is not admissible to show any other capacity, except for the purpose of reformation of the instrument as it may be permitted under the rules of the particular jurisdiction. The question is to be determined from the face of the instrument alone, and unless the instrument itself makes it clear that he has signed in some other capacity the signer must be treated as an indorser.

The indication that the signature is made in another capacity must be clear without reference to anything but the instrument. It may be found in the language used. Thus if John Doe signs after "I, John Doe, promise to pay," he is clearly a maker; and "John Doe, witness" is not liable at all. The capacity may be found in any clearly evidenced purpose of the signature, as where a drawee signing in an unusual place on the paper has no visible reason to sign at all unless he is an acceptor. It may be found in usage or custom. Thus by long established practice judicially noticed or otherwise established a signature in the lower right hand corner of an instrument indicates an intent to sign as the maker of a note or the drawer of a draft. Any similar clear indication of an intent to sign in some other capacity may be enough to remove the signature from the application of this section.

Cross Reference:

Section 3—401.

Definitional Cross References:

"Instrument". Section 3—102.
"Signature". Section 3—401.

§ 3—403. Signature by Authorized Representative

(1) A signature may be made by an agent or other representative, and his authority to make it may be established as in other cases of representation. No particular form of appointment is necessary to establish such authority.

(2) An authorized representative who signs his own name to an instrument

(a) is personally obligated if the instrument neither names the person represented nor shows that the representative signed in a representative capacity;

(b) except as otherwise established between the immediate parties, is personally obligated if the instrument names the person represented but does not show that the representative signed in a representative capacity, or if the instrument does not name the person represented but does show that the representative signed in a representative capacity.

(3) Except as otherwise established the name of an organization preceded or followed by the name and office of an authorized individual is a signature made in a representative capacity.

Official Comment

Prior Uniform Statutory Provision: Sections 19, 20 and 21, Uniform Negotiable Instruments Law.

Changes: Combined and reworded; original Section 21 omitted.

Purposes of Changes:

1. The definition of "representative" in this Act (Section 1—201) includes an officer of a corporation or association, a trustee, an executor or administrator of an estate, or any person empowered to act for another. It is not intended to mean that a trust or an estate is necessarily a legal entity with the capacity to issue negotiable instruments, but merely that if it can issue them they may be signed by the representative.

The power to sign for another may be an express authority, or it may be implied in law or in fact, or it may rest merely upon apparent authority. It may be established as in other cases of representation, and when relevant parol evidence is admissible to prove or to deny it.

2. Subsection (2) applies only to the signature of a representative whose authority to sign for another is established. If he is not authorized his signature has the effect of an unauthorized signature (Section 3—404). Even though he is authorized the principal is not liable on the instrument, under the provisions (Section 3—401) relating to signatures, unless the instrument names him and clearly shows that the signature is made on his behalf.

3. Assuming that Peter Pringle is a principal and Arthur Adams is his agent, an instrument might, for example, bear the following signatures affixed by the agent—

(a) "Peter Pringle", or
(b) "Arthur Adams", or
(c) "Peter Pringle by Arthur Adams, Agent", or
(d) "Arthur Adams, Agent", or
(e) "Peter Pringle
Arthur Adams".

A signature in form (a) does not bind Adams if authorized (Sections 3—401 and 3—404).

A signature as in (b) personally obligates the agent and parol evidence is inadmissible under subsection (2) (a) to disestablish his obligation.

The unambiguous way to make the representation clear is to sign as in (c). Any other definite indication is sufficient, as where the instrument reads "Peter Pringle promises to pay" and it is signed "Arthur Adams, Agent." Adams is not bound if he is authorized (Section 3—404).

Subsection 2(b) adopts the New York (minority) rule of Megowan v. Peterson, 173 N.Y. 1 (1902), in such a case as (d); and adopts the majority rule in such a case as (e). In both cases the section admits parol evidence in litigation between the immediate parties to prove signature by the agent in his representative capacity. [Paragraph 3 was amended in 1966].

4. The original Section 21, covering signatures by "procuration," is omitted. It was based

on English practice under which the words "per procuration" added to any signature are understood to mean that the signer is acting under a power of attorney which the holder is free to examine. The holder is thus put on notice of the limited authority, and there can be no apparent authority extending beyond the power of attorney. This meaning of "per procuration" is almost unknown in the United States, and the words are understood by the ordinary banker or attorney to be merely the equivalent of "by." The omission is not intended to suggest that a signature "by procuration" can no longer have the effect which it had under the original Section 21, in any case where a party chooses to use the expression.

Cross References:

Point 1: Section 1—201.

Point 2: Sections 3—401(1), 3—404 and 3—405.

Definitional Cross References:

"Instrument". Section 3—102.

"Person". Section 1—201.

"Representative". Section 1—201.

"Signature". Section 3—401.

§ 3—404. Unauthorized Signatures

(1) Any unauthorized signature is wholly inoperative as that of the person whose name is signed unless he ratifies it or is precluded from denying it; but it operates as the signature of the unauthorized signer in favor of any person who in good faith pays the instrument or takes it for value.

(2) Any unauthorized signature may be ratified for all purposes of this Article. Such ratification does not of itself affect any rights of the person ratifying against the actual signer.

Official Comment

Prior Uniform Statutory Provision: Section 23, Uniform Negotiable Instruments Law.

Changes: Reworded; new provisions.

Purpose of Changes and New Matter: The changes are intended to remove uncertainties arising under the original section:

1. "Unauthorized signature" is a defined term (Section 1—201). It includes both a forgery and a signature made by an agent exceeding his actual or apparent authority.

2. The final clause of subsection (1) is new. It states the generally accepted rule that the unauthorized signature, while it is wholly inoperative as that of the person whose name is signed, is effective to impose liability upon the actual signer or to transfer any rights that he may have in the instrument. His liability is not in damages for breach of a warranty of his authority, but is full liability on the instrument in the capacity in which he has signed. It is, however, limited to parties who take or pay the instrument in good faith; and one

who knows that the signature is unauthorized cannot recover from the signer on the instrument.

3. Subsection (2) is new. It settles the conflict which has existed in the decisions as to whether a forgery may be ratified. A forged signature may at least be adopted; and the word "ratified" is used in order to make it clear that the adoption is retroactive, and that it may be found from conduct as well as from express statements. Thus it may be found from the retention of benefits received in the transaction with knowledge of the unauthorized signature; and although the forger is not an agent, the ratification is governed by the same rules and principles as if he were.

This provision makes ratification effective only for the purposes of this Article. The unauthorized signature becomes valid so far as its effect as a signature is concerned. The ratification relieves the actual signer from liability on the signature. It does not of itself relieve him from liability to the person whose name is signed. It does not in any way affect the criminal law. No policy of the criminal law requires that the person whose name is forged shall not assume liability to others on the instrument; but he cannot affect the rights of the state. While the ratification may be taken into account with other relevant facts in determining punishment, it does not relieve the signer of criminal liability.

4. The words "or is precluded from denying it" are retained in subsection (1) to recognize the possibility of an estoppel against the person whose name is signed, as where he expressly or tacitly represents to an innocent purchaser that the signature is genuine; and to recognize the negligence which precludes a denial of the signature.

Cross References:

Sections 3—307, 3—401, 3—403 and 3—405.

Point 1: Section 1—201.

Point 4: Section 3—406.

Definitional Cross References:

"Good faith". Section 1—201.
"Instrument". Section 3—102.
"Person". Section 1—201.
"Rights". Section 1—201.
"Signature". Section 3—401.
"Signed". Section 1—201.
"Unauthorized signature". Section 1—201.
"Value". Section 3—303.

§ 3—405. Impostors; Signature in Name of Payee

(1) An indorsement by any person in the name of a named payee is effective if

(a) an impostor by use of the mails or otherwise has induced the maker or drawer to issue the instrument to him or his confederate in the name of the payee; or

(b) a person signing as or on behalf of a maker or drawer intends the payee to have no interest in the instrument; or

(c) an agent or employee of the maker or drawer has supplied him with the name of the payee intending the latter to have no such interest.

(2) Nothing in this section shall affect the criminal or civil liability of the person so indorsing.

wexler case + padded payroll

Official Comment

Prior Uniform Statutory Provision: Section 9(3), Uniform Negotiable Instruments Law.

Changes: Reworded; new provisions.

Purposes of Changes and New Matter:

1. This section enlarges the original subsection to include additional situations which it has not been held to cover. The words "fictitious or nonexisting person" have been eliminated as misleading, since the existence or nonexistence of the named payee is not decisive and is important only as it may bear on the intent that he shall have no interest in the instrument. The instrument is not made payable to bearer and indorsements are still necessary to negotiation. The section however recognizes as effective indorsement of the types of paper covered no matter by whom made. This solution is thought preferable to making such instruments bearer paper; on the face of things they are payable to order and a subsequent taker should require what purports to be a regular chain of indorsements. On the other hand it is thought to be unduly restrictive to require that the actual indorsement be made by the impostor or other fraudulent actor. In most cases the person whose fraud procured the instrument to be issued will himself indorse; when some other third person indorses it will most probably be a case of theft or a second independent fraud superimposed upon the original fraud. In neither case does there seem to be sufficient reason to reverse the rule of the section. To recapitulate: the instrument does not become bearer paper, a purportedly regular chain in indorsements is required, but any person—first thief, second impostor or third murderer—can effectively indorse in the name of the payee.

2. Subsection (1) (a) is new. It rejects decisions which distinguish between face-to-face imposture and imposture by mail and hold that where the parties deal by mail the dominant intent of the drawer is to deal with the name rather than with the person so that the resulting instrument may be negotiated only by indorsement of the payee whose name has been taken in vain. The result of the distinction has been under some prior law, to throw the loss in the mail imposture forward to a subsequent holder or to the drawee. Since the maker or drawer believes the two to be one and the same, the two intentions cannot be separated, and the "dominant intent" is a fiction. The position here taken is that the loss, regardless of the type of fraud which the particular impostor has commit-

ted, should fall upon the maker or drawer.

"Impostor" refers to impersonation, and does not extend to a false representation that the party is the authorized agent of the payee. The maker or drawer who takes the precaution of making the instrument payable to the principal is entitled to have his indorsement.

3. Subsection (1) (b) restates the substance of the original subsection 9(3). The test stated is not whether the named payee is "fictitious," but whether the signer intends that he shall have no interest in the instrument. The following situations illustrate the application of the subsection.

a. The drawer of a check, for his own reasons, makes it payable to P knowing that P does not exist.

b. The drawer makes the check payable in the name of P. A person named P exists, but the drawer does not know it.

c. The drawer makes the check payable to P, an existing person whom he knows, intending to receive the money himself and that P shall have no interest in the check.

d. The treasurer of a corporation draws its check payable to P, who to the knowledge of the treasurer does not exist.

e. The treasurer of a corporation draws its check payable to P. P exists but the treasurer has fraudulently added his name to the payroll intending that he shall not receive the check.

f. The president and the treasurer of a corporation both sign its check payable to P. P does not exist. The treasurer knows it but the president does not.

g. The same facts as f, except that P exists and the treasurer knows it, but intends that P shall have no interest in the check.

In all the cases stated an indorsement by any person in the name of P is effective.

4. Paragraph (c) is new. It extends the rule of the original Subsection 9(3) to include the padded payroll cases, where the drawer's agent or employee prepares the check for signature or otherwise furnishes the signing officer with the name of the payee. The principle followed is that the loss should fall upon the employer as a risk of his business enterprise rather than upon the subsequent holder or drawee. The reasons are that the employer is normally in a better position to prevent such forgeries by reasonable care in the selection or supervision of his employees, or, if he is not, is at least in a better position to cover the loss by fidelity insurance; and that the cost of such insurance is properly an expense of his business rather than of the business of the holder or drawee.

The provision applies only to the agent or employee of the drawer, and only to the agent or employee who supplies him with the name of the payee. The following situations illustrate its application.

a. An employee of a corporation prepares a padded payroll for its treasurer, which includes the name of P. P does not exist, and the employee knows it, but the treasurer does not. The treasurer draws the corporation's check payable to P.

b. The same facts as a, except that P exists and the employee knows it but intends him to have no interest in the check. In both cases an indorsement by any person in the name of P is effective and the loss falls on the corporation.

5. The section is not intended to affect criminal liability for forgery or any other crime, or civil liability to the drawer or to any other person. It is to be read together with the section under which an unauthorized signer is personally liable on the signature to any person who takes the instrument in good faith (3—404 (1)).

Cross References:

Sections 3—401, 3—403, 3—404 and 3—406.

Point 5: Section 3—404(1).

Definitional Cross References:

"Instrument". Section 3—102.
"Issue". Section 3—102.
"Person". Section 1—201.
"Signature". Section 3—401.

§ 3—406. Negligence Contributing to Alteration or Unauthorized Signature

Any person who by his negligence substantially contributes to a material alteration of the instrument or to the making of an unauthorized signature is precluded from asserting the alteration or lack of authority against a holder in due course or against a drawee or other payor who pays the instrument in good faith and in accordance with the reasonable commercial standards of the drawee's or payor's business.

Official Comment

Prior Uniform Statutory Provision: None.

Purposes:

1. This section is new. It adopts the doctrine of Young v. Grote, 4 Bing. 253 (1827), which held that a drawer who so negligently draws an instrument as to facilitate its material alteration is liable to a drawee who pays the altered instrument in good faith. It should be noted that the rule as stated in the section requires that the negligence "substantially" contribute to the alteration.

2. The section extends the above principle to the protection of a holder in due course and of payors who may not technically be drawees. It rejects decisions which have held that the maker of a note owes no duty of care to the holder because at the time the instrument is drawn there is no contract between them. By drawing the instrument and "setting it afloat upon a sea of strangers" the maker or drawer voluntarily enters into a relation with later holders which justifies his responsibility. In this respect an instrument so negligently drawn as to facilitate alteration does not differ in principle from an instrument containing blanks which may be filled.

The holder in due course under the rules governing alteration (Section 3—407) may enforce the altered instrument according to its original tenor. Where negligence of the obligor has substantially contributed to the alteration, this section gives the holder the alternative right to enforce the instrument as altered.

3. No attempt is made to define negligence which will contribute to an alteration. The question is left to the court or the jury upon the circumstances of the particular cases. Negligence usually has been found where spaces are left in the body of the instrument in which words or figures may be inserted. No unusual precautions are required, and the section is not intended to change decisions holding that the drawer of a bill is under no duty to use sensitized paper, indelible ink or a protectograph; or that it is not negligence to leave spaces between the lines or at the end of the instrument in which a provision for interest or the like can be written.

4. The section applies only where the negligence contributes to the alteration. It must afford an opportunity of which advantage is in fact taken. The section approves decisions which have refused to hold the drawer responsible where he has left spaces in a check but the payee erased all the writing with chemicals and wrote in an entirely new check.

5. This section does not make the negligent party liable in tort for damages resulting from the alteration. Instead it estops him from asserting it against the holder in due course or drawee. The reason is that in the usual case the extent of the loss, which involves the possibility of ultimate recovery from the wrongdoer, cannot be determined at the time of litigation, and the decision would have to be made on the unsatisfactory basis of burden of proof. The holder or drawee is protected by an estoppel, and the task of pursuing the wrongdoer is left to the negligent party. Any amount in fact recovered from the wrongdoer must be held for the benefit of the negligent party under ordinary principles of equity.

6. The section protects parties who act not only in good faith, (Section 1—201) but also in observance of the reasonable standards of their business. Thus any bank which takes or pays an altered check which ordinary banking standards would require it to refuse cannot take advantage of the estoppel.

7. The section applies the same rule to negligence which contributes to a forgery or other unauthorized signature, as defined in this Act (Section 1—201). The most obvious case is that of the drawer who makes use of a signature stamp or other automatic signing device and is negligent in looking after it. The section extends, however, to cases where the party has notice that forgeries of his signature have occurred and is negligent in failing to prevent further forgeries by the same person. It extends to negligence which contributes to a forgery of the signature of another, as in the case where a check is negligently mailed to the wrong person having the same name as the payee. As in the case of alteration, no

attempt is made to specify what is negligence, and the question is one for the court or the jury on the facts of the particular case.

Cross References:

Sections 3—401 and 3—404.
Point 2: Section 3—407(3).
Point 6: Section 1—201.
Point 7: Section 1—201.

Definitional Cross References:

"Alteration". Section 3—407.
"Good faith". Section 1—201.
"Holder in due course". Section 3—302.
"Instrument". Section 3—102.
"Person". Section 1—201.
"Unauthorized signature". Section 1—201.

§ 3—407. Alteration

(1) Any alteration of an instrument is material which changes the contract of any party thereto in any respect, including any such change in

(a) the number or relations of the parties; or

(b) an incomplete instrument, by completing it otherwise than as authorized; or

(c) the writing as signed, by adding to it or by removing any part of it.

(2) As against any person other than a subsequent holder in due course.

(a) alteration by the holder which is both fraudulent and material discharges any party whose contract is thereby changed unless that party assents or is precluded from asserting the defense;

(b) no other alteration discharges any party and the instrument may be enforced according to its original tenor, or as to incomplete instruments according to the authority given.

(3) A subsequent holder in due course may in all cases enforce the instrument according to its original tenor, and when an incomplete instrument has been completed, he may enforce it as completed.

Official Comment

Prior Uniform Statutory Provision: Sections 14, 15, 124 and 125, Uniform Negotiable Instruments Law.

Changes: Combined and reworded; new provisions; rule of original Section 15 reversed.

Purposes of Changes and New Matter: The changes are intended to remove uncertainties arising under the original sections, and to modify the rules as to discharge:

1. Subsection (1) substitutes a general definition for the list

of illustrations in the original Section 125. Any alteration is material only as it may change the contract of a party to the instrument; and the addition or deletion of words which do not in any way affect the contract of any previous signer is not material. But any change in the contract of a party, however slight, is a material alteration; and the addition of one cent to the amount payable, or an advance of one day in the date of payment, will operate as a discharge if it is fraudulent.

Specific mention is made of a change in the number or relations of the parties in order to make it clear that any such change is material only if it changes the contract of one who has signed. The addition of a co-maker or a surety does not change in most jurisdictions the contract of one who has already signed as maker and should not be held material as to him. The addition of the name of an alternative payee is material, since it changes his obligation. Paragraph (c) makes special mention of a change in the writing signed in order to cover occasional cases of addition of sticker clauses, scissoring or perforating instruments where the separation is not authorized.

2. Paragraph (b) of subsection (1) is to be read together with Section 3—115 on incomplete instruments. Where an instrument contains blanks or is otherwise incomplete, it may be completed in accordance with the authority given and is then valid and effective as completed. If the completion is unauthorized and has the effect of changing the contract of any previous signer, this provision follows the generally accepted rule in treating it as a material alteration which may operate as a discharge.

3. Subsection (2) modifies the very rigorous rule of the original Section 124. The changes made are as follows:

a. A material alteration does not discharge any party unless it is made by the holder. Spoliation by any meddling stranger does not affect the rights of the holder. It is of course intended that the acts of the holder's authorized agent or employee, or of his confederates, are to be attributed to him.

b. A material alteration does not discharge any party unless it is made for a fraudulent purpose. There is no discharge where a blank is filled in the honest belief that it is as authorized; or where a change is made with a benevolent motive such as a desire to give the obligor the benefit of a lower interest rate. Changes favorable to the obligor are unlikely to be made with any fraudulent intent; but if such an intent is found the alteration may operate as a discharge.

c. The discharge is a personal defense of the party whose contract is changed by the alteration, and anyone whose contract is not affected cannot assert it. The contract of any party is necessarily affected, however, by the discharge of any party against whom he has a right of recourse on the instrument. Assent to the alteration given before or after it is made will prevent the party from asserting the discharge. "Or is precluded from asserting the defense" is added in paragraph (a) to recognize the possibility of an estoppel or other ground barring the defense which does not rest on assent.

d. If the alteration is not material or if it is not made for a fraudulent purpose there is no discharge, and the instrument may be enforced according to its original tenor. Where blanks are filled or an incomplete instrument is otherwise completed there is no original tenor, but the instrument may be enforced according to the authority in fact given.

4. Subsection (3) combines the final sentences of the original Sections 14 and 124, and provides that a subsequent holder in due course takes free of the discharge in all cases. The provision is merely one form of the general rule governing the effect of discharge against a holder in due course (Section 3—602). The holder in due course may enforce the instrument according to its original tenor. In this connection reference should be made to the section giving the holder in due course the right, where the maker's or drawer's negligence has substantially contributed to the alteration, to enforce the instrument in its altered form (Section 3—406). Reference should also be made to Section 4—401 covering a bank's right to charge its customer's account in the case of altered instruments.

Where blanks are filled or an incomplete instrument is otherwise completed, this subsection follows the original Section 14 in placing the loss upon the party who left the instrument incomplete and permitting the holder to enforce it in its completed form. As indicated in the comment to Section 3—115 on incomplete instruments, this result is intended even though the instrument was stolen from the maker or drawer and completed after the theft; and the effect of this subsection, together with the section on incomplete instruments is to reverse the rule of the original Section 15.

There is no inconsistency between subsection (3) and paragraph (b) of subsection (2). The holder in due course may elect to enforce the instrument either as provided in that paragraph or as provided in subsection (3).

It should be noted that a purchaser who takes the instrument with notice of any material alteration, including the unauthorized completion of an incomplete instrument, takes with notice of a claim or defense and cannot be a holder in due course (Section 3—304).

Cross References:

Sections 3—305, 3—306 and 3—307.

Point 2: Section 3—115.

Point 4: Sections 3—115, 3—304(2), 3—602 and 4—401.

Definitional Cross References:

"Contract". Section 1—201.

"Holder". Section 1—201.

"Holder in due course". Section 3—302.

"Instrument". Section 3—102.

"Party". Section 1—201.

"Person". Section 1—201.

"Signed". Section 1—201.

"Writing". Section 1—201.

§ 3—408. Consideration

Want or failure of consideration is a defense as against any person not having the rights of a holder in due course (Section 3—305), except that no consideration is necessary for an instrument or obligation thereon given in payment of or as security for an antecedent obligation of any kind. Nothing in this section shall be taken to displace any statute outside this Act under which a promise is enforceable notwithstanding lack or failure of consideration. Partial failure of consideration is a defense pro tanto whether or not the failure is in an ascertained or liquidated amount.

Official Comment

Prior Uniform Statutory Provision: Sections 24, 25 and 28, Uniform Negotiable Instruments Law.

Changes: Combined and reworded.

Purposes of Changes:

1. "Consideration" is distinguished from "value" throughout this Article. "Consideration" refers to what the obligor has received for his obligation, and is important only on the question of whether his obligation can be enforced against him.

2. The "except" clause is intended to remove the difficulties which have arisen where a note or a draft, or an indorsement of either, is given as payment or as security for a debt already owed by the party giving it, or by a third person. The provision is intended to change the result of decisions holding that where no extension of time or other concession is given by the creditor the new obligation fails for lack of legal consideration. It is intended also to mean that an instrument given for more or less than the amount of a liquidated obligation does not fail by reason of the common law rule that an obligation for a lesser liquidated amount cannot be consideration for the surrender of a greater.

3. With respect to the necessity or sufficiency of consideration other obligations on an instrument are subject to the ordinary rules of contract law relating to contracts not under seal. Promissory estoppel or any other equivalent or substitute for consideration is to be recognized as in other contract cases. The provision of the original Section 28 as to absence or failure of consideration is now covered by the section dealing with the rights of one not a holder in due course; and the "presumption" of consideration in the original Section 24 is replaced by the provision relating to the burden of establishing defenses.

Cross References:

Point 1: Section 3—303.

Point 3: Sections 3—306(c) and 3—307(2).

Definitional Cross References:

"Holder in due course". Section 3—302.

"Instrument". Section 3—102.

"Person". Section 1—201.

"Rights". Section 1—201.

§ 3—409. Draft Not an Assignment

(1) A check or other draft does not of itself operate as an assignment of any funds in the hands of the drawee available for its payment, and the drawee is not liable on the instrument until he accepts it.

(2) Nothing in this section shall affect any liability in contract, tort or otherwise arising from any letter of credit or other obligation or representation which is not an acceptance.

Official Comment

Prior Uniform Statutory Provision: Sections 127 and 189, Uniform Negotiable Instruments Law.

Changes: Combined and reworded; new provisions.

Purposes of Changes and New Matter:

The two original sections are combined, brought forward to appear in connection with acceptance, and reworded to remove uncertainties.

1. As under the original sections, a check or other draft does not of itself operate as an assignment in law or equity. The assignment may, however, appear from other facts, and particularly from other agreements, express or implied; and when the intent to assign is clear the check may be the means by which the assignment is effected.

2. The language of the original Section 189, that the drawee is not liable "to the holder", is changed as inaccurate and not intended. The drawee is not liable on the instrument until he accepts; but he remains subject to any other liability to the holder. In this connection reference should be made to Section 4—302 on the payor bank's liability for late return. Such a bank if it does not either make prompt settlement or return on an item received by it will become liable to a holder of the item.

3. Subsection (2) is new. It is intended to make it clear that this section does not in any way affect any liability which may arise apart from the instrument itself. The drawee who fails to accept may be liable to the drawer or to the holder for breach of the terms of a letter of credit or any other agreement by which he is obligated to accept. He may be liable in tort or upon any other basis because of his representation that he has accepted, or that he intends to accept. The section leaves unaffected any liability of any kind apart from the instrument.

Cross References:

Sections 3—410, 3—411, 3—412 and 3—415.

Point 2: Section 4—302.

Definitional Cross References:

"Acceptance". Section 3—410.
"Check". Section 3—104.
"Contract". Section 1—201.
"Draft". Section 3—104.
"Instrument". Section 3—102.
"Letter of credit". Section 5—104.

§ 3—410. Definition and Operation of Acceptance

(1) Acceptance is the drawee's signed engagement to honor the draft as presented. It must be written on the draft, and may consist of his signature alone. It becomes operative when completed by delivery or notification.

(2) A draft may be accepted although it has not been signed by the drawer or is otherwise incomplete or is overdue or has been dishonored.

(3) Where the draft is payable at a fixed period after sight and the acceptor fails to date his acceptance the holder may complete it by supplying a date in good faith.

Official Comment

Prior Uniform Statutory Provision: Sections 132, 133, 134, 135, 136, 137, 138, 161–170, and 191, Uniform Negotiable Instruments Law.

Changes: Combined, reworded; original Sections 134, 135, 137 and 161–170 eliminated.

Purposes of Changes:

1. The original Sections 161–170 providing for acceptance for honor are omitted from this Article. This ancient practice developed at a time when communications were slow, and particularly in overseas transactions there might be a delay of several months before the drawer could be notified of dishonor by nonacceptance and take steps to protect his credit. The need for intervention by a third party has passed with the development of the cable transfer, the letter of credit, and numerous other devices by which a substitute arrangement is promptly made. The practice has been obsolete for many years, and the sections are therefore eliminated.

2. Under Section 3—417 a person obtaining acceptance gives a warranty against alteration of the instrument before acceptance.

3. Subsection (1) adopts the rule of Section 17 of the English Bills of Exchange Act that the acceptance must be written on the draft. It eliminates the original Sections 134 and 135, providing for "virtual" acceptance by a written promise to accept drafts to be drawn, and "collateral" acceptance by a separate writing. Both have been anomalous exceptions to the policy that no person is liable on an instrument unless his signature appears on it. Both are derived from a line of early American cases decided at a time when difficulties of communication, particularly overseas, might leave the holder in doubt for a long period whether the draft was accepted. Such conditions have long since ceased to exist, and the "virtual" or "collateral" acceptance is now almost entirely obsolete. Good commercial and banking practice does not sanction acceptance by any separate writing because of the dangers and uncertainties arising when it becomes separated from the draft. The instru-

ment is now forwarded to the drawee for his acceptance upon it, or reliance is placed upon the obligation of the separate writing itself, as in the case of a letter of credit.

Nothing in this section is intended to eliminate any liability of the drawee in contract, tort or otherwise arising from the separate writing or any other obligation or representation, as provided in Section 3—409.

Subsection (1) likewise eliminates the original section 137, providing for acceptance by delay or refusal to return the instrument but the drawee may be liable for a conversion of the instrument under Section 3—419.

4. Subsection (1) states the generally recognized rule that the mere signature of the drawee on the instrument is a sufficient acceptance. Customarily the signature is written vertically across the face of the instrument; but since the drawee has no reason to sign for any other purpose his signature in any other place, even on the back of the instrument, is sufficient. It need not be accompanied by such words as "Accepted," "Certified," or "Good." It must not, however, bear any words indicating an intent to refuse to honor the bill; and nothing in this provision is intended to change such decisions as Norton v. Knapp, 64 Iowa 112, 19 N.W. 867 (1884), holding that the drawee's signature accompanied by the words "Kiss my foot" is not an acceptance.

5. The final sentence of subsection (1) expressly states the generally recognized rule, implied in the definition of acceptance in the original Section 191, that an acceptance written on the draft takes effect when the drawee notifies the holder or gives notice according to his instructions. Acceptance is thus an exception to the usual rule that no obligation on an instrument is effective until delivery.

6. Subsection (3) changes the last sentence of the original Section 138. The purpose of the provision is to provide a definite date of payment where none appears on the instrument. An undated acceptance of a draft payable "thirty days after sight" is incomplete; and unless the acceptor himself writes in a different date the holder is authorized to complete the acceptance according to the terms of the draft by supplying a date of presentment. Any date which the holder chooses to write in is effective providing his choice of date is made in good faith. Any different agreement not written on the draft is not effective, and parol evidence is not admissible to show it.

Cross References:

Sections 3—411, 3—412 and 3—418.

Point 2: Section 3—417.

Point 3: Sections 3—401(1), 3—409(2) and 3—419.

Point 6: Section 3—412.

Definitional Cross References:

"Delivery". Section 1—201.

"Dishonor". Section 3—507.

"Draft". Section 3—104.

"Good faith". Section 1—201.

"Holder". Section 1—201.

"Honor". Section 1—201.

"Notification". Section 1—201.

"Presentment". Section 3—504.
"Signature". Section 3—401.
"Signed". Section 1—201.
"Written". Section 1—201.

§ 3—411. Certification of a Check

(1) Certification of a check is acceptance. Where a holder procures certification the drawer and all prior indorsers are discharged.

(2) Unless otherwise agreed a bank has no obligation to certify a check.

(3) A bank may certify a check before returning it for lack of proper indorsement. If it does so the drawer is discharged.

Official Comment

Prior Uniform Statutory Provision: Sections 187 and 188, Uniform Negotiable Instruments Law.

Changes: Combined and reworded; new provisions.

Purposes of Changes and New Matter:

1. The second sentence of subsection (1) continues the rule of original Section 188 that, while certification procured by a holder discharges the drawer and other prior parties, certification procured by the drawer leaves him liable. Under this provision any certification procured by a holder discharges the drawer and prior indorsers. Any indorsement made after a certification so procured remains effective; and where it is intended that any indorser shall remain liable notwithstanding certification, he may indorse with the words "after certification" to make his liability clear.

2. Subsection (2) is new. It states the generally recognized rule that in the absence of agreement a bank is under no obligation to certify a check, because it is a demand instrument calling for payment rather than acceptance. The bank may be liable for breach of any agreement with the drawer, the holder, or any other person by which it undertakes to certify. Its liability is not on the instrument, since the drawee is not so liable until acceptance (Section 3—409(1)). Any liability is for breach of the separate agreement.

3. Subsection (3) is new. It recognizes the banking practice of certifying a check which is returned for proper indorsement in order to protect the drawer against a longer contingent liability. It is consistent with the provision of Section 3—410(2) permitting certification although the check has not been signed or is otherwise incomplete.

Cross References:

Sections 3—412, 3—413, 3—417 and 3—418.

Point 2: Section 3—409(1).

Point 3: Section 3—410(2).

Definitional Cross References:

"Acceptance". Section 3—410.

"Bank". Section 1—201.

"Check". Section 3—104.

"Holder". Section 1—201

§ 3—412. Acceptance Varying Draft

(1) Where the drawee's proffered acceptance in any manner varies the draft as presented the holder may refuse the acceptance and treat the draft as dishonored in which case the drawee is entitled to have his acceptance cancelled.

(2) The terms of the draft are not varied by an acceptance to pay at any particular bank or place in the United States, unless the acceptance states that the draft is to be paid only at such bank or place.

(3) Where the holder assents to an acceptance varying the terms of the draft each drawer and indorser who does not affirmatively assent is discharged. As amended 1962.

Official Comment

Prior Uniform Statutory Provision: Sections 139, 140, 141 and 142, Uniform Negotiable Instruments Law.

Changes: Combined and reworded; law changed as to qualified acceptances.

Purposes of Changes:

1. The section applies to conditional acceptances, acceptances for part of the amount, acceptances to pay at a different time from that required by the draft, or to the acceptance of less than all of the drawees, all of which are covered by the original Section 141. It applies to any other engagement changing the essential terms of the draft.

2. Where the drawee offers such a varied engagement the holder has an election. He may reject the offer, insist on acceptance of the draft as presented, and treat the refusal to give it as a dishonor. In that event the drawee is not bound by his engagement, and is entitled to have it cancelled. After any necessary notice of dishonor and protest the holder may have his recourse against the drawer and indorsers.

If the holder elects to accept the offer, this section does not invalidate the drawee's varied engagement. It remains his effective obligation, which the holder may enforce against him. By his assent, however, the holder discharges any drawer or indorser who does not also assent. The rule of the original Section 142 is changed to require that the assent of the drawer or indorser be affirmatively expressed. Mere failure to object within a reasonable time is not assent which will prevent the discharge.

3. The rule of original Section 140 that an acceptance to pay at a particular place is an unqualified acceptance is modified by the provision of subsection (2) that the terms of the draft are not

varied by an acceptance to pay at any particular bank or place in the United States unless the acceptance states that the draft is to be paid only at such bank or place. Section 3—504(4) provides that a draft accepted payable at a bank in the United States must be presented at the bank designated [As amended 1962].

Cross References:

Sections 3—410 and 3—413.
Point 3: Section 3—504(4).

Definitional Cross References:

"Acceptance". Section 3—410.
"Bank". Section 1—201.
"Dishonor". Section 3—507.
"Draft". Section 3—104.
"Holder". Section 1—201.
"Term". Section 1—201.
"Written". Section 1—201.

§ 3—413. Contract of Maker, Drawer and Acceptor

(1) The maker or acceptor engages that he will pay the instrument according to its tenor at the time of his engagement or as completed pursuant to Section 3—115 on incomplete instruments.

(2) The drawer engages that upon dishonor of the draft and any necessary notice of dishonor or protest he will pay the amount of the draft to the holder or to any indorser who takes it up. The drawer may disclaim this liability by drawing without recourse.

(3) By making, drawing or accepting the party admits as against all subsequent parties including the drawee the existence of the payee and his then capacity to indorse.

Official Comment

Prior Uniform Statutory Provision: Sections 60, 61 and 62, Uniform Negotiable Instruments Law.

Changes: Combined and reworded.

Purposes of Changes:

The original sections are combined for convenience and condensed to avoid duplication of language. This section should be read in connection with the sections on incomplete instruments (3—115), negligence contributing to alteration or unauthorized signature (3—406), alteration (3—407), acceptances varying a draft (3—412) and finality of payment or acceptance (3—418). Thus a maker who signs an incomplete note engages under this section to pay it according to its tenor at the time he signs it, but by virtue of Sections 3—115 and 3—407 the note may thereafter be completed and enforced against him. In the same way, if the maker's negligence substantially contributes to alteration of the instrument, he will become liable on his note as altered under Section 3—406. When a holder assents to an acceptance varying a draft (Section 3—412) he can of course hold the acceptor only according to the form of acceptance to which the holder agreed. Section 3—418 applies the rule of Price v. Neal both to acceptance and payment; thus an acceptor may not, after acceptance, assert that the drawer's signature is unauthorized.

Subsection (1) applies to all drafts (including checks) the rule that the acceptance relates to the instrument as it was at the time of its acceptance and not (in case of alteration before acceptance) to its original tenor. The cases on this point under the original act (all of which involved checks) have been in conflict. It should be noted that under Section 3—417 a person who obtains acceptance warrants to the acceptor that the instrument has not been materially altered.

Except as indicated in the foregoing comment the section makes no change in substance from the provision of the original act.

Cross References:

Sections 3—115, 3—406, 3—407, 3—412, 3—417 and 3—418.

Definitional Cross References:

"Contract". Section 1—201.
"Dishonor". Section 3—507.
"Draft". Section 3—104.
"Holder". Section 1—201.
"Instrument". Section 3—102.
"Notice of dishonor". Section 3—508.
"Party". Section 1—201.
"Protest". Section 3—509.

§ 3—414. Contract of Indorser; Order of Liability

(1) Unless the indorsement otherwise specifies (as by such words as "without recourse") every indorser engages that upon dishonor and any necessary notice of dishonor and protest he will pay the instrument according to its tenor at the time of his indorsement to the holder or to any subsequent indorser who takes it up, even though the indorser who takes it up was not obligated to do so.

(2) Unless they otherwise agree indorsers are liable to one another in the order in which they indorse, which is presumed to be the order in which their signatures appear on the instrument.

Official Comment

Prior Uniform Statutory Provision: Sections 38, 44, 66, 67 and 68, Uniform Negotiable Instruments Law.

Changes: Combined and reworded.

Purposes of Changes:

1. Subsection (1) states the contract of indorsement—that if the instrument is dishonored and any protest or notice of dishonor which may be necessary under Section 3—501 is given, the indorser will pay the instrument. The indorser's engagement runs to any holder (whether or not for value) and to any indorser subsequent to him who has taken the instrument up.

An indorser may disclaim his liability on the contract of indorsement, but only if the indorsement itself so specifies. Since the disclaimer varies the written contract of indorsement, the disclaimer itself must be written on the instrument and cannot be proved by parol. The customary manner of disclaiming the indorser's liability under this section is to indorse "without recourse". Apart from such a disclaimer all indorsers incur this liability, without regard to whether or not the indorser transferred the instrument for value or received consideration for his indorsement.

Original Section 44, permitting a representative to indorse in such terms as to exclude personal liability, is omitted as unnecessary and included in the broader right to disclaim any liability. No change in the law is intended by this omission.

2. In addition to his liability on the contract of indorsement, an indorser, if a transferor, gives the warranties stated in Section 3—417.

3. As in the case of acceptor's liability (Section 3—413), this section conditions the indorser's liability on the tenor of the instrument at the time of his indorsement. Thus if a person indorses an altered instrument he assumes liability as indorser on the instrument as altered.

4. Subsection (2) is intended to clarify existing law under original Section 68.

The section states two presumptions: One is that the indorsers are liable to one another in the order in which they have in fact indorsed. The other is that they have in fact indorsed in the order in which their names appear. Parol evidence is admissible to show that they have indorsed in another order, or that they have otherwise agreed as to their liability to one another.

The last sentence of the original Section 68 is now covered by Section 3—118(e) (Ambiguous Terms and Rules of Construction).

Cross References:

Point 1: Section 3—501.
Point 2: Section 3—417.
Point 3: Section 3—413.
Point 4: Section 3—118(e).

Definitional Cross References:

"Contract". Section 1—201.
"Dishonor". Section 3—507.
"Holder". Section 1—201.
"Instrument". Section 3—102.
"Notice of dishonor". Section 3—508.
"Presumed". Section 1—201.
"Protest". Section 3—509.
"Signature". Section 3—401.

§ 3—415. Contract of Accommodation Party

(1) An accommodation party is one who signs the instrument in any capacity for the purpose of lending his name to another party to it.

(2) When the instrument has been taken for value before it is due the accommodation party is liable in the capacity in

which he has signed even though the taker knows of the accommodation.

(3) As against a holder in due course and without notice of the accommodation oral proof of the accommodation is not admissible to give the accommodation party the benefit of discharges dependent on his character as such. In other cases the accommodation character may be shown by oral proof.

(4) An indorsement which shows that it is not in the chain of title is notice of its accommodation character.

(5) An accommodation party is not liable to the party accommodated, and if he pays the instrument has a right of recourse on the instrument against such party.

Official Comment

Prior Uniform Statutory Provision: Sections 28, 29 and 64, Uniform Negotiable Instruments Law.

Changes: Combined and reworded; new provisions.

Purposes of Changes and New Matter: To make it clear that:

1. Subsection (1) recognizes that an accommodation party is always a surety (which includes a guarantor), and it is his only distinguishing feature. He differs from other sureties only in that his liability is on the instrument and he is a surety for another party to it. His obligation is therefore determined by the capacity in which he signs. An accommodation maker or acceptor is bound on the instrument without any resort to his principal, while an accommodation indorser may be liable only after presentment, notice of dishonor and protest. The subsection recognizes the defenses of a surety in accordance with the provisions subjecting one not a holder in due course to all simple contract defenses, as well as his rights against his principal after payment. Under subsection (3) except as against a holder in due course without notice of the accommodation, parol evidence is admissible to prove that the party has signed for accommodation. In any case, however, under subsection (4) an indorsement which is not in the chain of title (the irregular or anomalous indorsement) is notice to all subsequent takers of the instrument of the accommodation character of the indorsement.

2. Subsection (1) eliminates the language of the old Section 29 requiring that the accommodation party sign the instrument "without receiving value therefor." The essential characteristic is that the accommodation party is a surety, and not that he has signed gratuitously. He may be a paid surety, or receive other compensation from the party accommodated. He may even receive it from the payee, as where A and B buy goods and it is understood that A is to pay for all of them and that B is to sign a note only as a surety for A.

3. The obligation of the accommodation party is supported by any consideration for which the instrument is taken before it is due. Subsection (2) is intended to change occasional decisions holding that there is no sufficient consideration where an accommodation party signs a note after it is in the hands of a holder who has given value. The party is liable to the holder in such a case even though there is no extension of time or other concession. This is consistent with the provision as to antecedent obligations as consideration (Section 3—408). The limitation to "before it is due" is one of suretyship law, by which the obligation of the surety is terminated at the time limit unless in the meantime the obligation of the principal has become effective.

4. As a surety the accommodation party is not liable to the party accommodated; but he is otherwise liable on the instrument in the capacity in which he has signed. This general statement of the rule makes unnecessary the detailed provisions of the original Section 64, which is therefore eliminated, without any change in substance.

5. Subsection (5) is intended to change the result of such decisions as Quimby v. Varnum, 190 Mass. 211, 76 N.E. 671 (1906), which held that an accommodation indorser who paid the instrument could not maintain an action on it against the accommodated party since he had no "former rights" to which he was remitted. Under ordinary principles of suretyship the accommodation party who pays is subrogated to the rights of the holder paid, and should have his recourse on the instrument.

Cross References:

Sections 3—305, 3—408, 3—603, 3—604 and 3—606.

Point 1: Section 3—306(b).

Point 3: Section 3—408.

Definitional Cross References:

"Holder in due course". Section 3—302.

"Instrument". Section 3—102.

"Notice". Section 1—201.

"Party". Section 1—201.

"Presentment". Section 3—504.

"Signed". Section 1—201.

"Writing". Section 1—201.

§ 3—416. Contract of Guarantor

(1) "Payment guaranteed" or equivalent words added to a signature mean that the signer engages that if the instrument is not paid when due he will pay it according to its tenor without resort by the holder to any other party.

(2) "Collection guaranteed" or equivalent words added to a signature mean that the signer engages that if the instrument is not paid when due he will pay it according to its tenor, but only after the holder has reduced his claim against the maker or acceptor to judgment and execution has been returned unsatisfied, or after the maker or acceptor has become insolvent

or it is otherwise apparent that it is useless to proceed against him.

(3) Words of guaranty which do not otherwise specify guarantee payment.

(4) No words of guaranty added to the signature of a sole maker or acceptor affect his liability on the instrument. Such words added to the signature of one of two or more makers or acceptors create a presumption that the signature is for the accommodation of the others.

(5) When words of guaranty are used presentment, notice of dishonor and protest are not necessary to charge the user.

(6) Any guaranty written on the instrument is enforcible notwithstanding any statute of frauds.

stop

Official Comment

Prior Uniform Statutory Provision: None.

Purposes: The section is new. It states the commercial understanding as to the meaning and effect of words of guaranty added to a signature.

An indorser who guarantees payment waives not only presentment, notice of dishonor and protest, but also all demand upon the maker or drawee. Words of guaranty do not affect the character of the indorsement as an indorsement (Section 3—202 (4)); but the liability of the indorser becomes indistinguishable from that of a co-maker. A guaranty of collection likewise waives formal presentment, notice of dishonor and protest, but requires that the holder first proceed against the maker or acceptor by suit and execution, or show that such proceeding would be useless.

Subsection (6) is concerned chiefly with the type of statute of frauds which provides that no promise to answer for the debt, default or miscarriage of another is enforceable unless it is evidenced by a writing which states the consideration for the promise. It is unusual to state any consideration when a guaranty is added to a signature on a negotiable instrument, which in itself sufficiently shows the nature of the transaction; and such statutes have commonly been held not to apply to such guaranties.

Cross References:

Sections 3—202(4) and 3—415.

Definitional Cross References:

"Holder". Section 1—201.
"Insolvent". Section 1—201.
"Instrument". Section 3—102.
"Notice of dishonor". Section 3—508.
"Party". Section 1—201.
"Presumption". Section 1—201.
"Protest". Section 3—509.
"Signature". Section 3—401.
"Written". Section 1—201

§ 3—417. Warranties on Presentment and Transfer

(1) Any person who obtains payment or acceptance and any prior transferor warrants to a person who in good faith pays or accepts that

(a) he has a good title to the instrument or is authorized to obtain payment or acceptance on behalf of one who has a good title; and

(b) he has no knowledge that the signature of the maker or drawer is unauthorized, except that this warranty is not given by a holder in due course acting in good faith

(i) to a maker with respect to the maker's own signature; or

(ii) to a drawer with respect to the drawer's own signature, whether or not the drawer is also the drawee; or

(iii) to an acceptor of a draft if the holder in due course took the draft after the acceptance or obtained the acceptance without knowledge that the drawer's signature was unauthorized; and

(c) the instrument has not been materially altered, except that this warranty is not given by a holder in due course acting in good faith

(i) to the maker of a note; or

(ii) to the drawer of a draft whether or not the drawer is also the drawee; or

(iii) to the acceptor of a draft with respect to an alteration made prior to the acceptance if the holder in due course took the draft after the acceptance, even though the acceptance provided "payable as originally drawn" or equivalent terms; or

(iv) to the acceptor of a draft with respect to an alteration made after the acceptance.

(2) Any person who transfers an instrument and receives consideration warrants to his transferee and if the transfer is by indorsement to any subsequent holder who takes the instrument in good faith that

(a) he has a good title to the instrument or is authorized to obtain payment or acceptance on behalf of one who has a good title and the transfer is otherwise rightful; and

(b) all signatures are genuine or authorized; and

(c) the instrument has not been materially altered; and

(d) no defense of any party is good against him; and

(e) he has no knowledge of any insolvency proceeding instituted with respect to the maker or acceptor or the drawer of an unaccepted instrument.

(3) By transferring "without recourse" the transferor limits the obligation stated in subsection (2) (d) to a warranty that he has no knowledge of such a defense.

(4) A selling agent or broker who does not disclose the fact that he is acting only as such gives the warranties provided in this section, but if he makes such disclosure warrants only his good faith and authority.

Official Comment

Prior Uniform Statutory Provision: Sections 65 and 69, Uniform Negotiable Instruments Law.

Changes: Combined and reworded; new provisions added.

Purposes of Changes and New Matter:

1. The obligations imposed by this section are stated in terms of warranty. Warranty terms, which are not limited to sale transactions, are used with the intention of bringing in all the usual rules of law applicable to warranties, and in particular the necessity of reliance in good faith and the availability of all remedies for breach of warranty, such as rescission of the transaction or an action for damages. Like other warranties, those stated in this section may be disclaimed by agreement between the immediate parties. In the case of an indorser, disclaimer of his liability as a transferor, to be effective, must appear in the form of the indorsement, and no parol proof of "agreement otherwise" is admissible. For corresponding warranties in the case of items in the bank collection process, Section 4—207 should be consulted.

2. Subsection (1) is new. It is intended to state the undertaking to a party who accepts or pays of one who obtains payment or acceptance or of any prior transferor. It is closely connected with the following section on the finality of acceptance or payment (Section 3—418), and should be read together with it.

3. Subsection (1) (a) retains the generally accepted rule that the party who accepts or pays does not "admit" the genuineness of indorsements, and may recover from the person presenting the instrument when they turn out to be forged. The justification for the distinction between forgery of the signature of the drawer and forgery of an indorsement is that the drawee is in a position to verify the drawer's signature by comparison with one in his hands, but has ordinarily no opportunity to verify an indorsement.

4. Subsection (1) (b) recognizes and deals with competing equities of parties accepting or

paying instruments bearing unauthorized maker's or drawer's signatures and those obtaining acceptances or receiving payment. The warranties prescribed and exceptions thereto follow closely principles established at common law, particularly, those under Price v. Neal, 3 Burr. 1354 (1762).

The basic warranty that the person obtaining payment or acceptance and any prior transferor warrants that he has no knowledge that the signature of the maker or drawer is unauthorized stems from the general principle that one who presents an instrument knowing that the signature of the maker or drawer is forged or unauthorized commits an obvious fraud upon the party to whom presentment is made. However, few cases present this simple fact situation. If the signature of a maker or drawer has been forged, the parties include the dishonest forger himself and usually one or more innocent holders taking from him. Frequently, the state of knowledge of a holder is difficult to determine and sometimes a holder takes such a forged instrument in perfect good faith but subsequently learns of the forgery. Since in different fact situations holders have equities of varying strength, it is necessary to have some exceptions to the basic warranty.

The exceptions apply only in favor of a holder in due course and, within the provisions of Section 3—201, to all subsequent transferees from a holder in due course. Since a condition of the status of a holder in due course under Section 3—302(1) (a) is that the holder takes the instrument without notice of any defense against it, this condition presupposes that at the time of taking such a holder had no knowledge of the unauthorized signature. Consequently, the warranty of subsection (1) (b) is pertinent in the case of a holder in due course only in the relatively few cases where he acquires knowledge of the forgery after the taking but before the presentment. In this situation the holder in due course must continue to act in good faith to be exempted from the basic warranty.

The first exemption from the warranty by such a holder, made by subparagraph (i), is that the warranty does not run to a maker of a note with respect to the maker's own signature. This codifies the rule of Price v. Neal, and related cases. Since a maker of a note is presumed to know his own signature, if he fails to detect a forgery of his own signature and pays the note, under the Price v. Neal principle he should not be permitted to recover such payment from a holder in due course acting in good faith. Similarly, under subparagraph (ii) a drawer of a draft is presumed to know his own signature and if he fails to detect a forgery of his signature and pays a draft he may not recover that payment from a holder in due course acting in good faith. This rule applies if the drawer pays the instrument as drawer and also if he pays the instrument as drawee in a case where he is both drawer and drawee.

Under the principle of Price v. Neal a drawee of a draft is presumed to know the signature of his customer, the drawer. However, under subsection (1) (b) and subparagraph (iii) of this subsection this presumption is not strong enough to deprive such a drawee (either in accepting or paying an instrument) of the warranty of no knowledge of the unauthorized drawer's signature, unless the holder in due course took the instrument and became such a holder after the drawee's acceptance; or obtained the acceptance without knowledge that the drawer's signature was unauthorized. In the former case, the holder taking after and thereby presumably in reliance on the acceptance should be protected as against the drawee who accepted without detecting the unauthorized signature. In the latter case the holder, having no knowledge of the unauthorized signature at the time of the drawee's acceptance, would not be charged with this warranty and would be entitled to enforce such acceptance under Section 3—418, even if thereafter he acquired knowledge of the unauthorized signature prior to enforcement of the acceptance. Such right of the holder to enforce the acceptance would be valueless if immediately upon enforcing it and obtaining payment the holder became obligated to return the payment by reason of breach of the warranty of no knowledge at the time of payment.

5. Subsection (1) (c) retains the common law rule, followed by several decisions under the original Act, which has permitted a party paying a materially altered instrument in good faith to recover, and a party who accepts such an instrument to avoid such acceptance. As in the case of subsection (1) (b) this warranty is not imposed against a holder in due course acting in good faith in favor of a maker of a note or a drawer of a draft on the ground that such maker or drawer should know the form and amount of the note or draft which he has signed. The exception made by subparagraph (iii) in the case of a holder in due course of a draft accepted after the alteration follows the decisions in National City Bank of Chicago v. National Bank of Republic of Chicago, 300 Ill. 103, 132 N.E. 832, 22 A.L.R. 1153 (1921), and Wells Fargo Bank & Union Trust Company v. Bank of Italy, 214 Cal. 156, 4 P.2d 781 (1931), and is based on the principle that an acceptance is an undertaking relied upon in good faith by an innocent party. The attempt to avoid this result by certifying checks "payable as originally drawn" leaves the subsequent purchaser in uncertainty as to the amount for which the instrument is certified, and so defeats the entire purpose of certification, which is to obtain the definite obligation of the bank to honor a definite instrument. Subparagraph (iii) accordingly provides that such language is not sufficient to impose on the holder in due course the warranty of no material alteration where the holder took the draft after the acceptance and presumably in reliance on it.

Subparagraph (iv) of subsection (1) (c) exempts a holder in due course from the warranty of no material alteration to the acceptor of a draft with respect to an alteration made after the acceptance. A drawee accepting a draft has an opportunity of ascertaining the form and particularly the amount of the draft accepted. If, thereafter, the draft is materially altered and is thereupon presented for payment to the acceptor, the acceptor has the necessary information in its records to verify the form and particularly the amount of the draft. If in spite of this available information it pays the draft, there is as much reason to leave the responsibility for such payment upon the acceptor (as against a holder in due course acting in good faith) as there is in the case of a maker or drawer paying a materially altered note or draft.

6. Under Section 3—201 parties taking from or holding under a holder in due course, within the limits of that section, will have the same rights under Section 3—417(1) as a holder in due course. Of course such parties claiming under a holder in due course must act in good faith and be free from fraud, illegality and notice as provided in Section 3—201.

7. The liabilities imposed by subsection (2) in favor of the immediate transferee apply to all persons who transfer an instrument for consideration whether or not the transfer is accompanied by indorsement. Any consideration sufficient to support a simple contract will support those warranties.

8. Subsection (2) changes the original Section 65 to extend the warranties of any *indorser* beyond the immediate transferee in all cases. Where there is an indorsement the warranty runs with the instrument and the remote holder may sue the indorser-warrantor directly and thus avoid a multiplicity of suits which might be interrupted by the insolvency of an intermediate transferor. The language of subsections (2) (b) and (2) (c) is substituted for "genuine and what it purports to be" in the original Section 65(1). The language of subsection (2) (a) is substituted for that of Section 65(2) in order to cover the case of the agent who transfers for another.

9. Subsection (2) (d) resolves a conflict in the decisions as to whether the transferor warrants that there are no defenses to the instrument good against him. The position taken is that the buyer does not undertake to buy an instrument incapable of enforcement, and that in the absence of contrary understanding the warranty is implied. Even where the buyer takes as a holder in due course who will cut off the defense, he still does not undertake to buy a lawsuit with the necessity of proving his status. Subsection (3) however provides that an indorsement "without recourse" limits the (2) (d) warranty to one that the indorser has no knowledge of such defenses. With this exception the liabilities of a "without recourse" indorser under this section are the same as those of any other transferor. Under Section 3—414 "without recourse" in an indorsement is effective to disclaim the general contract of the indorser stated in that section.

10. Subsection (2) (e) is substituted for Section 65(4). The transferor does not warrant

against difficulties of collection, apart from defenses, or against impairment of the credit of the obligor or even his insolvency in the commercial sense. The buyer is expected to determine such questions for himself before he takes the obligation. If insolvency proceedings as defined in this Act (Section 1—201) have been instituted against the party who is expected to pay and the transferor knows it, the concealment of that fact amounts to a fraud upon the buyer, and the warranty against knowledge of such proceedings is provided accordingly.

11. Subsection (4) is substituted for Section 69 of the original Act. It applies only to a selling agent, as distinguished from an agent for collection. It follows the rule generally accepted that an agent who makes the disclosure warrants his good faith and authority and may not by contract assume a lesser warranty.

Cross References:

Sections 3—404, 3—405, 3—406, 3—414 and 4—207.

Point 1: Section 4—207.

Point 2: Section 3—418.

Point 4: Sections 3—201, 3—302 and 3—418.

Point 9: Section 3—414.

Point 10: Section 1—201.

Definitional Cross References:

"Acceptance". Section 3—410.

"Alteration". Section 3—407.

"Bank". Section 1—201.

"Draft". Section 3—104.

"Genuine". Section 1—201.

"Good faith". Section 1—201.

"Holder in due course". Section 3—302.

"Instrument". Section 3—102.

"Note". Section 3—104.

"Party". Section 1—201.

"Person". Section 1—201.

"Signature". Section 3—401.

"Term". Section 1—201.

§ 3—418. Finality of Payment or Acceptance

Except for recovery of bank payments as provided in the Article on Bank Deposits and Collections (Article 4) and except for liability for breach of warranty on presentment under the preceding section, payment or acceptance of any instrument is final in favor of a holder in due course, or a person who has in good faith changed his position in reliance on the payment.

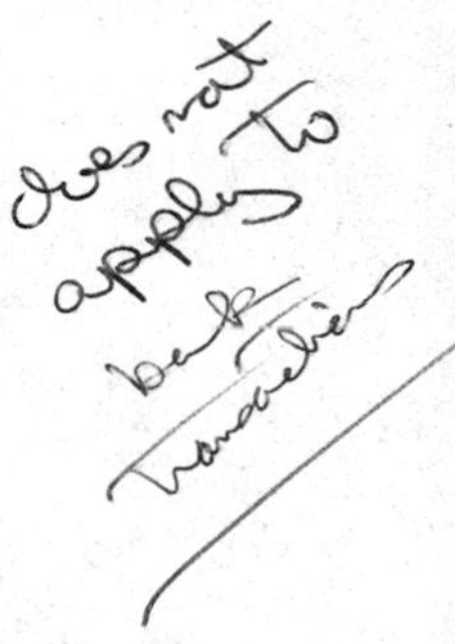

Official Comment

Prior Uniform Statutory Provision: Section 62, Uniform Negotiable Instruments Law.

Changes: Completely restated.

Purposes of Changes:

The rewording is intended to remove a number of uncertainties arising under the original section.

1. The section follows the rule of Price v. Neal, 3 Burr. 1354 (1762), under which a drawee who accepts or pays an instrument on which the signature of the drawer is forged is bound on his acceptance and

cannot recover back his payment. Although the original Act is silent as to payment, the common law rule has been applied to it by all but a very few jurisdictions. The traditional justification for the result is that the drawee is in a superior position to detect a forgery because he has the maker's signature and is expected to know and compare it; a less fictional rationalization is that it is highly desirable to end the transaction on an instrument when it is paid rather than reopen and upset a series of commercial transactions at a later date when the forgery is discovered.

The rule as stated in the section is not limited to drawees, but applies equally to the maker of a note or to any other party who pays an instrument.

2. The section follows the decisions under the original Act applying the rule of Price v. Neal to the payment of overdrafts, or any other payment made in error as to the state of the drawer's account. The same argument for finality applies, with the additional reason that the drawee is responsible for knowing the state of the account before he accepts or pays.

3. The section follows decisions under the original Act, in making payment or acceptance final only in favor of a holder in due course, or a transferee who has the rights of a holder in due course under the shelter principle. If no value has been given for the instrument the holder loses nothing by the recovery of the payment or the avoidance of the acceptance, and is not entitled to profit at the expense of the drawee; and if he has given only an executory promise or credit he is not compelled to perform it after the forgery or other reason for recovery is discovered. If he has taken the instrument in bad faith or with notice he has no equities as against the drawee.

4. The section rejects decisions under the original Act permitting recovery on the basis of mere negligence of the holder in taking the instrument. If such negligence amounts to a lack of good faith as defined in this Act (Section 1—201) or to notice under the rules (Section 3—304) relating to notice to a purchaser of an instrument, the holder is not a holder in due course and is not protected; but otherwise the holder's negligence does not affect the finality of the payment or acceptance.

5. This section is to be read together with the preceding section, which states the warranties given by the person obtaining acceptance or payment. It is also limited by the bank collection provision (Section 4—301) permitting a payor bank to recover a payment improperly paid if it returns the item or sends notice of dishonor within the limited time provided in that section. But notice that the latter right is sharply limited in time, and terminates in any case when the bank has made final payment, as defined in Section 4—213.

Cross References:

Sections 3—302, 3—303 and 3—417.

Point 2: Section 3—201(1).

Point 4: Sections 1—201, 3—302 and 3—304.

Point 5: Sections 3—417, 4—213 and 4—301.

Definitional Cross References:

"Acceptance". Section 3—410.

"Account". Section 4—104.

"Bank". Section 1—201.

"Holder in due course". Section 3—302.

"Instrument". Section 3—102.

"Presentment". Section 3—504.

§ 3—419. Conversion of Instrument; Innocent Representative

(1) An instrument is converted when

(a) a drawee to whom it is delivered for acceptance refuses to return it on demand; or

(b) any person to whom it is delivered for payment refuses on demand either to pay or to return it; or

(c) it is paid on a forged indorsement.

(2) In an action against a drawee under subsection (1) the measure of the drawee's liability is the face amount of the instrument. In any other action under subsection (1) the measure of liability is presumed to be the face amount of the instrument.

(3) Subject to the provisions of this Act concerning restrictive indorsements a representative, including a depositary or collecting bank, who has in good faith and in accordance with the reasonable commercial standards applicable to the business of such representative dealt with an instrument or its proceeds on behalf of one who was not the true owner is not liable in conversion or otherwise to the true owner beyond the amount of any proceeds remaining in his hands.

(4) An intermediary bank or payor bank which is not a depositary bank is not liable in conversion solely by reason of the fact that proceeds of an item indorsed restrictively (Sections 3—205 and 3—206) are not paid or applied consistently with the restrictive indorsement of an indorser other than its immediate transferor.

Official Comment

Prior Uniform Statutory Provision: Section 137, Uniform Negotiable Instruments Law.

Changes: Rule changed; new provisions.

Purposes of Changes and New Matter: To remove difficulties arising under the original section, and to cover additional situations:

1. The provision of the original Section 137 that refusal to

return a bill presented for acceptance is deemed to be acceptance has led to difficulties. If the bill is accepted it is not dishonored, and the holder is left without recourse against the drawer and indorsers when he has most need for immediate recourse. The drawee does not in fact accept and does everything he can to display an intention not to accept; and the "acceptance" is useless to the holder for any purpose other than an action against the drawee, since he has nothing that he can negotiate. The original rule has therefore been changed (see Section 3—410).

2. A negotiable instrument is the property of the holder. It is a mercantile specialty which embodies rights against other parties, and a thing of value. This section adopts the generally recognized rule that a refusal to return it on demand is a conversion. The provision is not limited to drafts presented for acceptance, but extends to any instrument presented for payment, including a note presented to the maker. The action is not on the instrument, but in tort for its conversion.

The detention of an instrument voluntarily delivered is not wrongful unless and until there is demand for its return. Demand for a return at a particular time may, however, be made at the time of delivery; or it may be implied under the circumstances or understood as a matter of custom. If the holder is to call for the instrument and fails to do so, he is to be regarded as extending the time. "Refuses" is meant to cover any intentional failure to return the instrument, including its intentional destruction. It does not cover a negligent loss or destruction, or any other unintentional failure to return. In such a case the party may be liable in tort for any damage sustained as a result of his negligence, but he is not liable as a converter under this section.

3. Subsection (1) (c) is new. It adopts the prevailing view of decisions holding that payment on a forged indorsement is not an acceptance, but that even though made in good faith it is an exercise of dominion and control over the instrument inconsistent with the rights of the owner, and results in liability for conversion.

4. Subsection (2) is new. It adopts the rule generally applied to the conversion of negotiable instruments, that the obligation of any party on the instrument is presumed, in the sense that the term is defined in this Act (Section 1—201), to be worth its face value. Evidence is admissible to show that for any reason such as insolvency or the existence of a defense the obligation is in fact worth less, or even that it is without value. In the case of the drawee, however, the presumption is replaced by a rule of absolute liability.

5. Subsection (3), which is new, is intended to adopt the rule of decisions which has held that a representative, such as a broker or depositary bank, who deals with a negotiable instrument for his principal in good

faith is not liable to the true owner for conversion of the instrument or otherwise, except that he may be compelled to turn over to the true owner the instrument itself or any proceeds of the instrument remaining in his hands. The provisions of subsection (3) are, however, subject to the provisions of this Act concerning restrictive indorsements (Sections 3—205, 3—206 and related sections).

6. The provisions of this section are not intended to eliminate any liability on warranties of presentment and transfer (Section 3—417). Thus a collecting bank might be liable to a drawee bank which had been subject to liability under this section, even though the collecting bank might not be liable directly to the owner of the instrument.

Cross References:

Sections 3—409, 3—410, 3—411 and 3—603.

Point 4: Section 1—201.

Point 5: Sections 1—201, 3—205 and 3—206.

Point 6: Section 3—417.

Definitional Cross References:

"Acceptance". Section 3—410.

"Action". Section 1—201.

"Bank". Section 1—201.

"Collecting bank". Sections 3—102 and 4—105.

"Depositary bank". Sections 3—102 and 4—105.

"Good faith". Section 1—201.

"Instrument". Section 3—102.

"Intermediary bank". Sections 3—102 and 4—105.

"On demand". Section 3—108.

"Person". Section 1—201.

"Presumed". Section 1—201.

"Representative". Section 1—201.

PART 5

PRESENTMENT, NOTICE OF DISHONOR AND PROTEST

§ 3—501. When Presentment, Notice of Dishonor, and Protest Necessary or Permissible

(1) Unless excused (Section 3—511) presentment is necessary to charge secondary parties as follows:

(a) presentment for acceptance is necessary to charge the drawer and indorsers of a draft where the draft so provides, or is payable elsewhere than at the residence or place of business of the drawee, or its date of payment depends upon such presentment. The holder may at his option present for acceptance any other draft payable at a stated date;

(b) presentment for payment is necessary to charge any indorser;

(c) in the case of any drawer, the acceptor of a draft payable at a bank or the maker of a note payable at a bank, presentment for payment is necessary, but failure to make presentment discharges such drawer, acceptor or maker only as stated in Section 3—502(1) (b).

(2) Unless excused (Section 3—511)

(a) notice of any dishonor is necessary to charge any indorser;

(b) in the case of any drawer, the acceptor of a draft payable at a bank or the maker of a note payable at a bank, notice of any dishonor is necessary, but failure to give such notice discharges such drawer, acceptor or maker only as stated in Section 3—502(1) (b).

(3) Unless excused (Section 3—511) protest of any dishonor is necessary to charge the drawer and indorsers of any draft which on its face appears to be drawn or payable outside of the states, territories, dependencies and possessions of the United States, the District of Columbia and the Commonwealth of Puerto Rico. The holder may at his option make protest of any dishonor of any other instrument and in the case of a foreign draft may on insolvency of the acceptor before maturity make protest for better security.

(4) Notwithstanding any provision of this section, neither presentment nor notice of dishonor nor protest is necessary to charge an indorser who has indorsed an instrument after maturity. As amended 1966.

Official Comment

Prior Uniform Statutory Provision: Sections 70, 89, 118, 129, 143, 144, 150, 151, 152, 157, 158 and 186, Uniform Negotiable Instruments Law.

Changes: Combined and simplified.

Purposes of Changes:

1. Part 5 simplifies the requirements of the original Act as to presentment for acceptance or payment, notice of dishonor and protest. This section assembles in one place all provisions as to when any such proceeding is necessary. It eliminates some of the requirements and simplifies others. The effect of unexcused delay in any such proceeding as a discharge is covered by the next section, and the sections following prescribe the details of the proceedings.

2. The words "Necessary to charge" are retained from the original Act. They mean that the necessary proceeding is a condition precedent to any right of action against the drawer or indorser. He is not liable and cannot be sued without the proceedings however long delayed.

Under some circumstances delay is excused. If it is not excused it may operate as a discharge under the next section. Under some circumstances the proceeding may be entirely excused and the drawer or indorser is then liable as if the proceeding had been duly taken. Section 3—511 states the circumstances under which delay may be excused or the proceeding entirely excused.

3. Subsection (1) (a) retains the substance of the original Sections 143, 144 and 150. The last sentence of the subsection states the rule of the decisions both at common law and under the original Act, that the holder may at his option present any time draft for acceptance, and is not required to wait until the due date to know whether the drawee will accept it; but that if he does make presentment and acceptance is refused he must give notice of dishonor. There is no similar right to present for acceptance a draft payable on demand, since a demand draft entitles the holder to immediate payment but not to acceptance.

4. Subsections (1) (b) and (1) (c) on presentment for payment follow Section 70 of the original Act with one important change. Under the original Act and under this section ((1) (b)) presentment for payment is necessary (unless excused) to charge any drawer. Under the original Act drawers of drafts other than checks were wholly discharged by a failure to make due presentment but drawers of checks (Section 70 in conjunction with Section 186) were discharged only "to the extent of the loss caused by the delay"—that is to say, when insolvency of the drawee bank occurred after the time when presentment was due. The check rule of the original Act (somewhat modified—see Section 3—502(1) (b) and Comment thereto) is by subsection (1) (c) extended to all drawers, and also to the acceptors and makers of domiciled—"payable at a bank"—drafts and notes. Thus drawers of drafts other than checks are not, as they were under Section 70, wholly discharged by failure to make due presentment but, like drawers of checks, are discharged only as they may have suffered loss as provided in Section 3—502(1) (b). As to domiciled paper original Section 70 provided that ability and willingness to pay at the place named at maturity were "equivalent to a tender of payment"—that is to say would stop the running of interest, but had no other effect. Accordingly cases have held that makers and acceptors of domiciled paper were not discharged to any extent by the holder's failure to make presentment even when the obligor had funds available in the paying bank on the date for presentment and the bank subsequently failed. Subsection (1) (c) applies the check rule to such makers and acceptors; the "tender" language of Section 70 is eliminated; and the result in the cases referred to in the preceding sentence is reversed. Under this section as under the original act presentment for payment is not necessary to charge primary parties (makers and acceptors of undomiciled paper).

5. Under subsection (2) the rules as to necessity of notice of dishonor run parallel with the

rules as to necessity of presentment stated in subsection (1).

6. Under the original Sections 129 and 152 protest is required in the case of every "foreign draft", defined as a draft which on its face is not both drawn and payable "within this state." The result has been that upon dishonor in New York a check which appears on its face to be drawn in Jersey City must be protested in order to sue the drawer or any indorser. This has led to great inconvenience and expense of protest fees. The only function of protest is that of proof of dishonor, and it adds nothing to notice of dishonor as such.

Subsection (3) eliminates the requirement of protest except upon dishonor of a draft which on its face appears to be either drawn or payable outside of the states, territories, dependencies and possessions of the United States, the District of Columbia and the Commonwealth of Puerto Rico. The requirement is left as to such international drafts because it is generally required by foreign law, which this Article cannot affect. The formalities of protest are covered by Section 3—509 on protest, and substitutes for protest as proof of dishonor are provided for in Section 3—510 on evidence of dishonor and of notice. [This paragraph was amended in 1966].

This provision retains from the original Section 118 the rule permitting the holder at his option to make protest of any dishonor of any other instrument. Even where not required protest may have definite convenience where process does not run to another state and the taking of depositions is a slow and expensive matter. Even where the instrument is drawn and payable entirely within a state there may be convenience in saving the trip of a witness from Buffalo to New York to testify to dishonor, where the substitute evidence of dishonor and notice of dishonor cannot be relied on. Either required or optional protest is presumptive evidence of dishonor. (Section 3—510.)

7. The permissible "protest for better security" of original Section 158 is retained in the case of a foreign draft, as the practice is common in certain foreign countries.

8. Under the final sentence of Section 7 of the original Act an instrument indorsed when overdue became payable on demand as to the indorser. That language has been deleted from this Article—see Section 3—108 and Comment. It meant, among other things and in view of the provisions of the original Act as to demand paper, that such an indorser was discharged unless the instrument was presented for payment within a reasonable time after his indorsement. Presentment of overdue paper for the purpose of charging an indorser is unusual and not an expected commercial practice; the rule has been little more than a trap for those not familiar with the Act. Subsection (4), reversing the original Act, provides that as to indorsers after maturity neither presentment nor notice of dishonor nor protest is necessary; like primary parties therefore they will remain liable on the instrument for the period of the applicable statute of limitations.

Cross References:

Point 1: Sections 3—502 through 3—508.

Point 2: Sections 3—413, 3—414 and 3—511.

Point 3: Sections 3—413, 3—414 and 3—511.

Point 4: Section 3—502.

Point 6: Sections 3—413, 3—414, 3—509, 3—510 and 3—511.

Point 8: Section 3—108.

Definitional Cross References:

"Acceptance". Section 3—410.

"Bank". Section 1—201.

"Certificate of deposit". Section 3—104.

"Dishonor". Section 3—507.

"Draft". Section 3—104.

"Holder". Section 1—201.

"Instrument". Section 3—102.

"Note". Section 3—104.

"Notice of dishonor". Section 3—508.

"Party". Section 1—201.

"Presentment". Section 3—504.

"Protest". Section 3—509.

"Secondary party". Section 3—102.

"Signature". Section 3—401.

§ 3—502. Unexcused Delay; Discharge

(1) Where without excuse any necessary presentment or notice of dishonor is delayed beyond the time when it is due

(a) any indorser is discharged; and

(b) any drawer or the acceptor of a draft payable at a bank or the maker of a note payable at a bank who because the drawee or payor bank becomes insolvent during the delay is deprived of funds maintained with the drawee or payor bank to cover the instrument may discharge his liability by written assignment to the holder of his rights against the drawee or payor bank in respect of such funds, but such drawer, acceptor or maker is not otherwise discharged.

(2) Where without excuse a necessary protest is delayed beyond the time when it is due any drawer or indorser is discharged.

Official Comment

Prior Uniform Statutory Provision: Sections 7, 70, 89, 144, 150, 152 and 186, Uniform Negotiable Instruments Law.

Changes: Combined and simplified.

Purposes of Changes:

This section is the complement of the preceding section. It covers in one section widely scattered provisions of the original Act:

1. The circumstances under which presentment or notice of dishonor or protest or delay therein are excused are stated in Section 3—511. When not excused delay operates as a discharge as provided in this section.

2. Subsection (1) (b) applies to any drawer, as well as to the makers and acceptors of drafts and notes payable at a bank, the rule of the original Section 186 providing for discharge only where the drawer of a check has sustained loss through the delay. This section expressly limits the rule to loss sustained through insolvency of the drawee or payor which was the only type of loss to which the Section 186 rule has ever been applied in the cases arising under it.

The purpose of the rule is to avoid hardship upon the holder through complete discharge, and unjust enrichment of the drawer or other party who normally has received goods or other consideration for the issue of the instrument. He is "deprived of funds" in any case where bank failure or other insolvency of the drawee or payor has prevented him from receiving the benefit of funds which would have paid the instrument if it had been duly presented.

The original language discharging the drawer "to the extent of the loss caused by the delay" has not worked out satisfactorily in the decided cases, since the amount of the loss caused by the failure of a bank is almost never ascertainable at the time of suit and may not be ascertained until some years later. The decisions have turned upon burden of proof, and the drawer has seldom succeeded in proving his discharge. Subsection (1) (b) therefore substitutes a right to discharge liability by written assignment to the holder of rights against the drawee or payor as to the funds which cover the particular instrument. The assignment is intended to give the holder an effective right to claim against the drawee or payor.

3. Subsection (2) retains the rule of the original Section 152, that any unexcused delay of a required protest is a complete discharge of all drawers and indorsers.

Cross References:

Point 1: Section 3—511(1).
Point 2: Section 3—501.
Point 3: Section 3—509.

Definitional Cross References:

"Bank". Section 1—201.
"Draft". Section 3—104.
"Holder". Section 1—201.
"Insolvent". Section 1—201.
"Instrument". Section 3—102.
"Note". Section 3—104.
"Notice of dishonor". Section 3—508.
"Payor bank". Section 4—105.
"Presentment". Section 3—504.
"Protest". Section 3—509.
"Rights". Section 1—201.
"Signature". Section 3—401.
"Written". Section 1—201.

§ 3—503. Time of Presentment

(1) Unless a different time is expressed in the instrument the time for any presentment is determined as follows:

(a) where an instrument is payable at or a fixed period after a stated date any presentment for acceptance must be made on or before the date it is payable;

(b) where an instrument is payable after sight it must either be presented for acceptance or negotiated within a reasonable time after date or issue whichever is later;

(c) where an instrument shows the date on which it is payable presentment for payment is due on that date;

(d) where an instrument is accelerated presentment for payment is due within a reasonable time after the acceleration;

(e) with respect to the liability of any secondary party presentment for acceptance or payment of any other instrument is due within a reasonable time after such party becomes liable thereon.

(2) A reasonable time for presentment is determined by the nature of the instrument, any usage of banking or trade and the facts of the particular case. In the case of an uncertified check which is drawn and payable within the United States and which is not a draft drawn by a bank the following are presumed to be reasonable periods within which to present for payment or to initiate bank collection:

(a) with respect to the liability of the drawer, thirty days after date or issue whichever is later; and

(b) with respect to the liability of an indorser, seven days after his indorsement.

(3) Where any presentment is due on a day which is not a full business day for either the person making presentment or the party to pay or accept, presentment is due on the next following day which is a full business day for both parties.

(4) Presentment to be sufficient must be made at a reasonable hour, and if at a bank during its banking day.

Official Comment

Prior Uniform Statutory Provision: Sections 71, 72, 75, 85, 86, 144, 145, 146, 186 and 193, Uniform Negotiable Instruments Law.

Changes: Combined and simplified; new provisions.

Purposes of Changes and New Matter:

1. This section states in one place all of the rules applicable to the time of presentment. Excused delay is covered by Section 3—511 on waiver and excuse, and the effect of unexcused delay by Section 3—502 on discharge.

The original Section 86, as to the determination of the time of payment by calculation from the day the time is to run, is omitted as superfluous. It states a rule universally applied to all time calculations in the law of contracts, and has no special application to negotiable instruments. No change in the law is intended.

2. Subsection (1) contains new provisions stating the commercial understanding as to the presentment of instruments payable after sight, and of accelerated paper.

3. Subsection (2) retains the substance of the original Section 193 as to the determination of a reasonable time. It provides specific time limits which are presumed, as that term is defined in this Act (Section 1—201), to be reasonable for uncertified checks drawn and payable within the continental limits of the United States. The court-made time limit of one day after the receipt of the instrument found in decisions under the original Act has proved to be too short a time for some holders, such as the department store or other large business clearing many checks through its books shortly after the first of the month, as well as the farmer or other individual at a distance from a bank.

The time limit provided differs as to drawer and indorser. The drawer, who has himself issued the check and normally expects to have it paid and charged to his account is reasonably required to stand behind it for a longer period, especially in view of the protection now provided by Federal Deposit Insurance. The thirty days specified coincides with the time after which a purchaser has notice that a check has become stale (Section 3—304(3) (c)). The indorser, who has normally merely received the check and passed it on, and does not expect to have to pay it, is entitled to know more promptly whether it is to be dishonored, in order that he may have recourse against the person with whom he has dealt.

4. Subsection (3) replaces the original Sections 85 and 146. It is intended to make allowance for the increasing practice of closing banks or businesses on Saturday or other days of the week. It is not intended to mean that any drawee or obligor can avoid dishonor of instruments by extended closing.

5. Subsection (4) eliminates the provision of the original Section 75 permitting presentment "at any hour before the bank is closed" if the drawer has no funds in the bank. The change is made to avoid inconvenience to the bank.

"Banking day" is defined in Section 4—104.

Cross References:

Point 1: Sections 3—501, 3—502, 3—505, 3—506 and 3—511.

Point 3: Sections 1—201 and 3—304(3) (c).

Point 5: Section 4—104.

Definitional Cross References:

"Acceptance". Section 3—410.

"Bank". Section 1—201.

"Banking day". Section 4—104.

"Check". Section 3—104.

"Draft". Section 3—104.

"Instrument". Section 3—102.

"Issue". Section 3—102.

"Party". Section 1—201.

"Person". Section 1—201.

"Presentment". Section 3—504.

"Presumed". Section 1—201.
"Reasonable time". Section 1—204.
"Secondary party". Section 3—102.
"Usage of trade". Section 1—205.

§ 3—504. How Presentment Made

(1) Presentment is a demand for acceptance or payment made upon the maker, acceptor, drawee or other payor by or on behalf of the holder.

(2) Presentment may be made

(a) by mail, in which event the time of presentment is determined by the time of receipt of the mail; or

(b) through a clearing house; or

(c) at the place of acceptance or payment specified in the instrument or if there be none at the place of business or residence of the party to accept or pay. If neither the party to accept or pay nor anyone authorized to act for him is present or accessible at such place presentment is excused.

(3) It may be made

(a) to any one of two or more makers, acceptors, drawees or other payors; or

(b) to any person who has authority to make or refuse the acceptance or payment.

(4) A draft accepted or a note made payable at a bank in the United States must be presented at such bank.

(5) In the cases described in Section 4—210 presentment may be made in the manner and with the result stated in that section. As amended 1962.

Official Comment

Prior Uniform Statutory Provision: Sections 72, 73, 77, 78 and 145, Uniform Negotiable Instruments Law.

Changes: Combined and simplified.

Purposes of Changes:

1. This section is intended to simplify the rules as to how presentment is made and to make it clear that any demand upon the party to pay is a presentment no matter where or how. Former technical requirements of exhibition of the instrument and the like are not required unless insisted upon by the party to pay (Section 3—505).

2. Paragraph (a) of subsection (2) authorizes presentment by mail directly to the obligor. The presentment is sufficient

and the instrument is dishonored by non-acceptance or non-payment even though the party making presentment may be liable for improper collection methods. "Through a clearing-house" means that presentment is not made when the demand reaches the clearing-house, but when it reaches the obligor. Section 4—210 should also be consulted for the methods of presenting which may properly be employed by a collecting bank. Subsection (5) of this section makes it clear that presentment made under Section 4—210 is proper presentment.

3. Paragraph (a) of subsection (3) eliminates the requirement of the original Sections 78 and 145(1) that presentment be made to each of two or more makers, acceptors or drawees unless they are partners or one has authority to act for the others. The holder is entitled to expect that any one of the named parties will pay or accept, and should not be required to go to the trouble and expense of making separate presentment to a number of them.

4. Section 3—412 provides that an acceptance made payable at a bank in the United States does not vary the draft. Subsection (4) of this section makes it clear that a draft so accepted must be presented at the bank so designated. The same rule is applied to notes made payable at a bank. The rule of the subsection is in conformity with the provisions of Section 3—501 on presentment and Section 3—502 on the effect of failure to make presentment with reference to domiciled paper [This paragraph was amended in 1962].

Cross References:

Point 1: Sections 3—501, 3—502, 3—505 and 3—511.

Point 2: Section 4—210.

Point 5: Sections 3—412, 3—501 and 3—502.

Definitional Cross References:

"Acceptance". Section 3—410.
"Bank". Section 1—201.
"Clearing house". Section 4—104.
"Draft". Section 3—104.
"Holder". Section 1—201.
"Instrument". Section 3—102.
"Note". Section 3—104.
"Party". Section 1—201.
"Person". Section 1—201.

§ 3—505. Rights of Party to Whom Presentment Is Made

(1) The party to whom presentment is made may without dishonor require

(a) exhibition of the instrument; and

(b) reasonable identification of the person making presentment and evidence of his authority to make it if made for another; and

(c) that the instrument be produced for acceptance or payment at a place specified in it, or if there be none at any place reasonable in the circumstances; and

(d) a signed receipt on the instrument for any partial or full payment and its surrender upon full payment.

(2) Failure to comply with any such requirement invalidates the presentment but the person presenting has a reasonable time in which to comply and the time for acceptance or payment runs from the time of compliance.

Official Comment

Prior Uniform Statutory Provision: Section 74, Uniform Negotiable Instruments Law.

Changes: Expanded and modified.

Purposes of Changes: To supplement the provisions as to how presentment is made, by permitting the party to whom it is made to insist on additional requirements:

1. In the first instance a mere demand for acceptance or payment is sufficient presentment, and if the payment is unqualifiedly refused nothing more is required. The party to whom presentment is made may, however, require exhibition of the instrument, its production at the proper place, identification of the party making presentment, and a signed receipt on the instrument, or its surrender on full payment. Failure to comply with any such requirement invalidates the presentment and means that the instrument is not dishonored. The time for presentment is, however, extended to give the person presenting a reasonable opportunity to comply with the requirements.

2. "Reasonable identification" means identification reasonable under all the circumstances. If the party on whom demand is made knows the person making presentment, no requirement of identification is reasonable, while if the circumstances are suspicious a great deal may be required. The requirement applies whether the instrument presented is payable to order or to bearer.

Cross References:

Point 1: Sections 3—504 and 3—506.

Definitional Cross References:

"Acceptance". Section 3—410.
"Dishonor". Section 3—507.
"Instrument". Section 3—102.
"Party". Section 1—201.
"Person". Section 1—201.
"Presentment". Section 3—504.
"Reasonable time". Section 1—204.
"Signed". Section 1—201.

§ 3—506. Time Allowed for Acceptance or Payment

(1) Acceptance may be deferred without dishonor until the close of the next business day following presentment. The holder may also in a good faith effort to obtain acceptance and without either dishonor of the instrument or discharge of secondary parties allow postponement of acceptance for an additional business day.

(2) Except as a longer time is allowed in the case of documentary drafts drawn under a letter of credit, and unless an earlier time is agreed to by the party to pay, payment of an instrument may be deferred without dishonor pending reasonable examination to determine whether it is properly payable, but payment must be made in any event before the close of business on the day of presentment.

Official Comment

Prior Uniform Statutory Provision: Section 136, Uniform Negotiable Instruments Law.

Changes: Expanded.

Purposes of Changes: The original section covered only the time allowed to the drawee on presentment for acceptance. This section also covers the time allowed on presentment for payment.

Section 5—112 (Time Allowed for Honor) states the time, longer than here provided, during which a bank to which drafts are presented under a letter of credit may defer payment or acceptance without dishonor of the drafts. As to drafts drawn under a letter of credit Section 5—112 of course controls.

Section 4—301 on deferred posting should be consulted for the right of a payor bank to recover tentative settlements made by it on the day an item is received. That right does not survive final payment (Section 4—213).

Cross References:

Sections 4—301 and 5—112.

Definitional Cross References:

"Acceptance". Section 3—410.
"Dishonor". Section 3—507.
"Documentary draft". Sections 3—102 and 4—104.
"Instrument". Section 3—102.
"Letter of credit". Section 5—103.
"Party". Section 1—201.
"Presentment". Section 3—504.

§ 3—507. Dishonor; Holder's Right of Recourse; Term Allowing Re-Presentment

(1) An instrument is dishonored when

(a) a necessary or optional presentment is duly made and due acceptance or payment is refused or cannot be obtained within the prescribed time or in case of bank collections the instrument is seasonably returned by the midnight deadline (Section 4—301); or

(b) presentment is excused and the instrument is not duly accepted or paid.

(2) Subject to any necessary notice of dishonor and protest, the holder has upon dishonor an immediate right of recourse against the drawers and indorsers.

(3) Return of an instrument for lack of proper indorsement is not dishonor.

(4) A term in a draft or an indorsement thereof allowing a stated time for re-presentment in the event of any dishonor of the draft by nonacceptance if a time draft or by nonpayment if a sight draft gives the holder as against any secondary party bound by the term an option to waive the dishonor without affecting the liability of the secondary party and he may present again up to the end of the stated time.

Official Comment

Prior Uniform Statutory Provision: Sections 83 and 149, Uniform Negotiable Instruments Law.

Changes: Reworded.

Purposes of Changes:

1. The language of the section is changed in accordance with the provisions of the preceding section as to the time allowed for acceptance or payment.

2. Subsection (3) is new. It states general banking and commercial understanding. The time within which a payor bank must return items, and the methods of returning, are stated in Section 4—301. Under Section 3—411 (3) a bank may certify an item so returned.

Cross References:

Point 1: Sections 3—503, 3—504, 3—505, 3—508 and 4—301.

Point 2: Sections 3—411(3), 4—301.

Definitional Cross References:

"Acceptance". Section 3—410.
"Bank". Section 1—201.
"Draft". Section 3—104.
"Holder". Section 1—201.
"Instrument". Section 3—102.
"Midnight deadline". Section 4—104.
"Notice of dishonor". Section 3—508.
"Presentment". Section 3—504.
"Protest". Section 3—509.
"Right". Section 1—201.
"Seasonably". Section 1—204.
"Secondary party". Section 3—102.
"Term". Section 1—201.

§ 3—508. Notice of Dishonor

(1) Notice of dishonor may be given to any person who may be liable on the instrument by or on behalf of the holder or any party who has himself received notice, or any other party who can be compelled to pay the instrument. In addition an agent or bank in whose hands the instrument is dishonored may give notice to his principal or customer or to another agent or bank from which the instrument was received.

(2) Any necessary notice must be given by a bank before its midnight deadline and by any other person before midnight of

the third business day after dishonor or receipt of notice of dishonor.

(3) Notice may be given in any reasonable manner. It may be oral or written and in any terms which identify the instrument and state that it has been dishonored. A misdescription which does not mislead the party notified does not vitiate the notice. Sending the instrument bearing a stamp, ticket or writing stating that acceptance or payment has been refused or sending a notice of debit with respect to the instrument is sufficient.

(4) Written notice is given when sent although it is not received.

(5) Notice to one partner is notice to each although the firm has been dissolved.

(6) When any party is in insolvency proceedings instituted after the issue of the instrument notice may be given either to the party or to the representative of his estate.

(7) When any party is dead or incompetent notice may be sent to his last known address or given to his personal representative.

(8) Notice operates for the benefit of all parties who have rights on the instrument against the party notified.

Official Comment

Prior Uniform Statutory Provision: Sections 90 through 108, Uniform Negotiable Instruments Law.

Changes: Combined and simplified.

Purposes of Changes: To simplify notice of dishonor and eliminate many of the detailed requirements of the original Act:

1. Notice is normally given by the holder or by an indorser who has himself received notice. Subsection (1) is intended to encourage and facilitate notice of dishonor by permitting any party who may be compelled to pay the instrument to notify any party who may be liable on it. Thus an indorser may notify another indorser who is not liable to the one who gives notice, even when the latter has not received notice from any other party to the instrument.

2. Except as to collecting banks, as to whom Section 4—212 controls, the time within which necessary notice must be given is extended to three days after dishonor or receipt of notice from another party. In the case of individuals the one-day time limit of the original Act has proved too short in many cases. It is extended to give the party a margin of time within which to ascertain what is required of him and get out an ordinary business letter. This time leeway eliminates the elab-

orate provisions as to the time of mailing in the original Sections 103 and 104.

3. Subsection (3) retains the substance of the original Sections 95 and 96. The provision approves the bank practice of returning the instrument bearing a stamp, ticket or other writing, or a notice of debit of the account, as sufficient notice. Subsection (4) retains the substance of the original Section 105.

4. Subsection (7) permits notice to be sent to the last known address of a party who is dead or incompetent rather than to his personal representative. The provision is intended to save time, as the name of the personal representative often cannot easily be ascertained, and mail addressed to the original party will reach the representative.

Cross References:

Sections 3—501, 3—507 and 3—511.

Point 2: Section 4—212.

Definitional Cross References:

"Acceptance". Section 3—410.
"Bank". Section 1—201.
"Customer". Section 4—104.
"Dishonor". Section 3—507.
"Holder". Section 1—201.
"Insolvency proceedings". Section 1—201.
"Instrument". Section 3—102.
"Issue". Section 3—102.
"Midnight deadline". Section 4—104.
"Notifies". Section 1—201.
"Party". Section 1—201.
"Person". Section 1—201.
"Representative". Section 1—201.
"Rights". Section 1—201.
"Send". Section 1—201.
"Written" and "writing". Section 1—201.

§ 3—509. Protest; Noting for Protest

(1) A protest is a certificate of dishonor made under the hand and seal of a United States consul or vice consul or a notary public or other person authorized to certify dishonor by the law of the place where dishonor occurs. It may be made upon information satisfactory to such person.

(2) The protest must identify the instrument and certify either that due presentment has been made or the reason why it is excused and that the instrument has been dishonored by nonacceptance or nonpayment.

(3) The protest may also certify that notice of dishonor has been given to all parties or to specified parties.

(4) Subject to subsection (5) any necessary protest is due by the time that notice of dishonor is due.

(5) If, before protest is due, an instrument has been noted for protest by the officer to make protest, the protest may be made at any time thereafter as of the date of the noting.

Official Comment

Prior Uniform Statutory Provision: Sections 153, 154, 155, 156, 158 and 160, Uniform Negotiable Instruments Law.

Changes: Combined and simplified.

Purposes of Changes:

1. Protest is not necessary except on drafts drawn or payable outside of the United States. Section 3—501(3) which also permits the holder at his option to make protest on dishonor of any other instrument. This section is intended to simplify either necessary or optional protest when it is made.

2. "Protest" has been used to mean the act of making protest, and sometimes loosely to refer to the entire process of presentment, notice of dishonor and protest. In this Article it is given its original, technical meaning, that of the official certificate of dishonor.

3. Subsection (1) adds to the notary public the United States consul or vice consul, and any other person authorized to certify dishonor by the law of the place where dishonor occurs. It eliminates the requirement of the original Section 156 that protest must be made at the place of dishonor. It eliminates also the provision of the original Section 154 permitting protest by "any respectable resident of the place where the bill is dishonored, in the presence of two or more credible witnesses." This has at least left uncertainty as to the identity and credibility of the persons certifying, and has almost never been used. Any necessary delay in finding the proper officer to make protest is excused under Section 3—511.

4. "Information satisfactory to such person" does away with the requirement occasionally stated, that the person making protest must certify as of his own knowledge. The requirement has been more honored in the breach than in the observance, and in practice protest has been made upon hearsay which the officer regards as reliable, upon the admission of the person who has dishonored, or at most upon re-presentment, which is only indirect proof of the original dishonor. There is seldom any possible motive for false protest, and the basis on which it is made is never questioned. Subsection (1) leaves to the certifying officer the responsibility for determining whether he has satisfactory information. The provision is not intended to affect any personal liability of the officer for making a false certificate.

5. The protest need not be in any particular form, so long as it certifies the matters stated in Subsection (2). It need not be annexed to the instrument, and may be forwarded separately; but annexation may identify the instrument. If the instrument is lost, destroyed, or wrongfully withheld, protest is still sufficient if it identifies the instrument; but the owner must prove his rights as in any action under this Article on a lost, destroyed or stolen instrument (Section 3—804).

6. Subsection (3) recognizes the practice of including in the protest a certification that notice of dishonor has been given to all parties or to specified parties. The next section makes such a certification presumptive evidence that the notice has been given.

7. Protest is normally forwarded with notice of dishonor. Subsection (4) extends the time for making a necessary protest to coincide with the time for giving notice of dishonor. Any delay due to circumstances beyond the holder's control is excused under Section 3—511 on waiver or excuse. Any protest which is not necessary but merely optional with the holder may be made at any time before it is used as evidence.

8. Subsection (5) retains from the original Section 155 the provision permitting the officer to note the protest and extend it formally later.

Cross References:

Point 1: Sections 3—501(3) and 3—511.

Point 3: Section 3—511(1).

Point 5: Section 3—804.

Point 6: Section 3—510(a).

Point 7: Sections 3—508(2) and 3—511(1).

Definitional Cross References:

"Dishonor". Section 3—507.

"Instrument". Section 3—102.

"Notice of dishonor". Section 3—508.

"Party". Section 1—201.

"Person". Section 1—201.

"Presentment". Section 3—504.

§ 3—510. Evidence of Dishonor and Notice of Dishonor

The following are admissible as evidence and create a presumption of dishonor and of any notice of dishonor therein shown:

(a) a document regular in form as provided in the preceding section which purports to be a protest;

(b) the purported stamp or writing of the drawee, payor bank or presenting bank on the instrument or accompanying it stating that acceptance or payment has been refused for reasons consistent with dishonor;

(c) any book or record of the drawee, payor bank, or any collecting bank kept in the usual course of business which shows dishonor, even though there is no evidence of who made the entry.

Official Comment

Prior Uniform Statutory Provision: None.

Purposes: This section is new. It states the effect of protest as evidence, and provides two substitutes for protest as proof of dishonor:

1. Paragraph (a) states the generally accepted rule that a protest is not only admissible as

evidence, but creates a presumption, as that term is defined in this Act (Section 1—201), of the dishonor which it certifies. The rule is extended to include the giving of any notice of dishonor certified by the protest. The provision also relieves the holder of the necessity of proving that a document regular in form which purports to be a protest is authentic, or that the person making it was qualified. Nothing in the provision is intended to prevent the obligor from overthrowing the presumption by evidence that there was in fact no dishonor, that notice was not given, or that the protest is not authentic or not made by a proper officer.

2. Paragraph (b) recognizes as the full equivalent of protest the stamp, ticket or other writing of the drawee, payor or presenting bank. The drawee's statement that payment is refused on account of insufficient funds always has been commercially acceptable as full proof of dishonor. It should be satisfactory evidence in any court. It is therefore made admissible, and creates a presumption of dishonor. The provision applies only where the stamp or writing states reasons for refusal which are consistent with dishonor. Thus the following reasons for refusal are not evidence of dishonor, but of justifiable refusal to pay or accept:

Indorsement missing
Signature missing
Signature illegible
Forgery
Payee altered
Date altered
Post dated
Not on us

On the other hand the following reasons are satisfactory evidence of dishonor, consistent with due presentment, and are within this provision:

Not sufficient funds
Account garnisheed
No account
Payment stopped

3. Paragraph (c) recognizes as the full equivalent of protest any books or records of the drawee, payor bank or any collecting bank kept in its usual course of business, even though there is no evidence of who made the entries. The provision, as well as that of paragraph (b), rests upon the inherent improbability that bank records, or those of the drawee, will show any dishonor which has not in fact occurred, or that the holder will attempt to proceed on the basis of dishonor if he could in fact have obtained payment.

Cross References:

Sections 3—501 and 3—508.
Point 1: Section 1—201.

Definitional Cross References:

"Acceptance". Section 3—410.
"Collecting bank". Section 4—105.
"Dishonor". Section 3—507.
"Instrument". Section 3—102.
"Notice of dishonor". Section 3—508.
"Payor bank". Section 4—105.
"Presumption". Section 1—201.
"Protest." Section 3—509.
"Writing". Section 1—201.

§ 3—511. Waived or Excused Presentment, Protest or Notice of Dishonor or Delay Therein

(1) Delay in presentment, protest or notice of dishonor is excused when the party is without notice that it is due or when the delay is caused by circumstances beyond his control and he exercises reasonable diligence after the cause of the delay ceases to operate.

(2) Presentment or notice or protest as the case may be is entirely excused when

(a) the party to be charged has waived it expressly or by implication either before or after it is due; or

(b) such party has himself dishonored the instrument or has countermanded payment or otherwise has no reason to expect or right to require that the instrument be accepted or paid; or

(c) by reasonable diligence the presentment or protest cannot be made or the notice given.

(3) Presentment is also entirely excused when

(a) the maker, acceptor or drawee of any instrument except a documentary draft is dead or in insolvency proceedings instituted after the issue of the instrument; or

(b) acceptance or payment is refused but not for want of proper presentment.

(4) Where a draft has been dishonored by nonacceptance a later presentment for payment and any notice of dishonor and protest for nonpayment are excused unless in the meantime the instrument has been accepted.

(5) A waiver of protest is also a waiver of presentment and of notice of dishonor even though protest is not required.

(6) Where a waiver of presentment or notice or protest is embodied in the instrument itself it is binding upon all parties; but where it is written above the signature of an indorser it binds him only.

Official Comment

Prior Uniform Statutory Provision: Sections 79, 80, 81, 82, 109, 111, 112, 113, 114, 115, 116, 130, 147, 148, 150, 151, 159, Uniform Negotiable Instruments Law.

Changes: Combined and simplified.

Purposes of Changes: This section combines widely scattered sections of the original act, and is intended to simplify the rules as to when presentment, notice or protest is excused:

1. The single term "excused" is substituted for "excused," "dispensed with," "not necessary," "not required," as used variously in the original act. No change in meaning is intended.

2. Subsection (1) combines provisions found in the original Sections 81, 113, 147 and 159. Delay in making presentment either for payment or for acceptance, in giving notice of dishonor or in making protest is excused when the party has acted with reasonable diligence and the delay is not his fault. This is true where an instrument has been accelerated without his knowledge, or demand has been made by a prior holder immediately before his purchase. It is true under any other circumstances where the delay is beyond his control. The words "not imputable to his default, misconduct or negligence" found in the original Sections 81, 113 and 159 are omitted as superfluous, but no change in substance is intended.

3. Any waived presentment, notice or protest is excused, as under the original Sections 82, 109, 110 and 111. The waiver may be express or implied, oral or written, and before or after the proceeding waived is due. It may be, and often is, a term of the instrument when it is issued. Subsection (5) retains as standard commercial usage the meaning attached by the original Section 111 to "protest waived."

4. Paragraph (b) of subsection (2) combines the substance of provisions found in the original Sections 79, 80, 114, 115 and 130. A party who has no right to require or reason to expect that the instrument will be honored is not entitled to presentment, notice or protest. This is of course true where he has himself dishonored the instrument or has countermanded payment. It is equally true, for example, where he is an accommodated party and has himself broken the accommodation agreement.

5. Paragraph (c) of subsection (2) combines provisions found in the original Sections 82 (1), 112 and 159. The excuse is established only by proof that reasonable diligence has been exercised without success, or that reasonable diligence would in any case have been unsuccessful.

6. Paragraph (a) of subsection (3) is new. It excuses presentment in situations where immediate payment or acceptance is impossible or so unlikely that the holder cannot reasonably be expected to make presentment. He is permitted instead to have his immediate recourse upon the drawer or indorser, and let the latter file any necessary claim in probate or insolvency proceedings. The exception for the documentary draft is to preserve any profit on the resale of goods for the creditors of the drawee if his representative can find the funds to pay.

7. Paragraph (b) of subsection (3) extends the original Section 148(3) to include any case where payment or acceptance is definitely refused and the refusal is not on the ground that there has been no proper presentment. The purpose of presentment is to

determine whether or not the maker, acceptor or drawee will pay or accept; and when that question is clearly determined the holder is not required to go through a useless ceremony. The provision applies to a definite refusal stating no reasons.

8. Subsection (4) retains the rule of the original Sections 116 and 151.

9. Subsection (6) retains the rule of original Section 110.

Cross References:

Sections 3—501, 3—502, 3—503, 3—507 and 3—509.

Definitional Cross References:

"Acceptance". Section 3—410.
"Dishonor". Section 3—507.
"Documentary draft". Section 4—104.
"Draft". Section 3—104.
"Insolvency proceedings". Section 1—201.
"Instrument". Section 3—102.
"Issue". Section 3—102.
"Notice of dishonor". Section 3—508.
"Party". Section 1—201.
"Presentment". Section 3—504.
"Protest". Section 3—509.
"Right". Section 1—201.

PART 6

DISCHARGE

§ 3—601. Discharge of Parties

(1) The extent of the discharge of any party from liability on an instrument is governed by the sections on

(a) payment or satisfaction (Section 3—603); or

(b) tender of payment (Section 3—604); or

(c) cancellation or renunciation (Section 3—605); or

(d) impairment of right of recourse or of collateral (Section 3—606); or

(e) reacquisition of the instrument by a prior party (Section 3—208); or

(f) fraudulent and material alteration (Section 3—407); or

(g) certification of a check (Section 3—411); or

(h) acceptance varying a draft (Section 3—412); or

(i) unexcused delay in presentment or notice of dishonor or protest (Section 3—502).

(2) Any party is also discharged from his liability on an instrument to another party by any other act or agreement with such party which would discharge his simple contract for the payment of money.

(3) The liability of all parties is discharged when any party who has himself no right of action or recourse on the instrument

(a) reacquires the instrument in his own right; or

(b) is discharged under any provision of this Article, except as otherwise provided with respect to discharge for impairment of recourse or of collateral (Section 3—606).

Official Comment

Prior Uniform Statutory Provision: Sections 119, 120 and 121, Uniform Negotiable Instruments Law.

Changes: Portions of original sections combined and reworded; new provisions.

Purposes of Changes:

1. Subsection (1) contains an index referring to all of the sections of this Article which provide for the discharge of any party. The list is exclusive so far as the provisions of this Article are concerned, but it is not intended to prevent or affect any discharge arising apart from this statute, as for example a discharge in bankruptcy or a statutory provision for discharge if the instrument is negotiated in a gaming transaction.

2. A negotiable instrument is in itself merely a piece of paper bearing a writing, and strictly speaking is incapable of being discharged. The parties are rather discharged from liability on their contracts on the instrument. The language of the original Section 119 as to discharge of the instrument itself has left uncertainties as to the effect of the discharge upon the rights of a subsequent holder in due course. It is therefore eliminated, and this section now distinguishes instead between the discharge of a single party and the discharge of all parties.

So far as the discharge of any one party is concerned a negotiable instrument differs from any other contract only in the special rules arising out of its character to which paragraphs (a) to (i) of subsection (1) are an index, and in the effect of the discharge against a subsequent holder in due course (Section 3—602). Subsection (2) therefore retains from the original Section 119(4) the provision for discharge by "any other act which will discharge a simple contract for the payment of money," and specifically recognizes the possibility of a discharge by agreement.

The discharge of any party is a defense available to that party as provided in sections on rights of those who are and are not holders in due course (Sections 3—305 and 3—306). He has the burden of establishing the defense (Section 3—307).

3. Subsection (3) substitutes for the "discharge of the instrument" the discharge of all parties from liability on their contracts on the instrument. It covers a part of the substance of the orig-

inal Section 119(1), (2) and (5), the original Section 120(1) and (3), and the original Section 121 (1) and (2). It states a general principle in lieu of the original detailed provisions. The principle is that all parties to an instrument are discharged when no party is left with rights against any other party on the paper.

When any party reacquires the instrument in his own right his own liability is discharged; and any intervening party to whom he was liable is also discharged as provided in Section 3—208 on reacquisition. When he is left with no right of action against an intervening party and no right of recourse against any prior party, all parties are obviously discharged. The instrument itself is not necessarily extinct, since it may be reissued or renegotiated with a new and further liability; and if it subsequently reaches the hands of a holder in due course without notice of the discharge he may still enforce it as provided in Section 3—602 on effect of discharge against a holder in due course.

Under Section 3—606 on impairment of recourse or collateral, the discharge of any party discharges those who have a right of recourse against him, except in the case of a release with reservation of rights or a failure to give notice of dishonor. A discharge of one who has himself no right of action or recourse on the instrument may thus discharge all parties. Again the instrument itself is not necessarily extinct, and if it is negotiated to a subsequent holder in due course without notice of the discharge he may enforce it as provided in Section 3—602 on effect of discharge against a holder in due course.

4. The language "any party who has himself no right of action or recourse on the instrument" is substituted for "principal debtor," which is not defined by the original Act and has been misleading. This Article also omits the original Section 192, defining the "person primarily liable." Under Section 3—415 on accommodation parties an accommodation maker or acceptor, although he is primarily liable on the instrument in the sense that he is obligated to pay it without recourse upon another, has himself a right of recourse against the accommodated payee; and his reacquisition or discharge leaves the accommodated party liable to him. The accommodated payee, although he is not primarily liable to others, has no right of action or recourse against the accommodation maker, and his reacquisition or discharge may discharge all parties.

Cross References:

Sections 3—406, 3—411, 3—412, 3—509, 3—603, 3—604 and 3—605.

Point 2: Sections 3—305, 3—306, 3—307 and 3—602.

Point 3: Sections 3—208, 3—602 and 3—606.

Point 4: Section 3—415.

Definitional Cross References:

"Action". Section 1—201.

"Agreement". Section 1—201.

"Alteration". Section 3—407.

"Certification". Section 3—411.

"Check". Section 3—104.

"Contract". Section 1—201.
"Draft". Section 3—104.
"Instrument". Section 3—102.
"Money". Section 1—201.
"Notice of dishonor". Section 3—508.
"Party". Section 1—201.
"Presentment". Section 3—504.
"Rights". Section 1—201.

§ 3—602. Effect of Discharge Against Holder in Due Course

No discharge of any party provided by this Article is effective against a subsequent holder in due course unless he has notice thereof when he takes the instrument.

Official Comment

Prior Uniform Statutory Provision: None.

Purposes:

The section is intended to remove an uncertainty as to which the original Act is silent. It rests on the principle that any discharge of a party provided under any section of this Article is a personal defense of the party, which is cut off when a subsequent holder in due course takes the instrument without notice of the defense. Thus where an instrument is paid without surrender such a subsequent purchase cuts off the defense. This section applies only to discharges arising under the provisions of this Article, and it has no application to any discharge arising apart from it, such as a discharge in bankruptcy.

Under Section 3—304(1) (b) on notice to purchaser it is possible for a holder to take the instrument in due course even though he has notice that one or more parties have been discharged, so long as any party remains undischarged. Thus he may take with notice that an indorser of a note has been released, and still be a holder in due course as to the liability of the maker. In that event, the holder in due course is subject to the defense of the discharge of which he had notice when he took the instrument.

Cross References:

Sections 3—302, 3—304, 3—305 and 3—601.

Definitional Cross References:

"Holder in due course". Section 3—302.
"Instrument". Section 3—102.
"Notice". Section 1—201.
"Party". Section 1—201.

§ 3—603. Payment or Satisfaction

(1) The liability of any party is discharged to the extent of his payment or satisfaction to the holder even though it is made with knowledge of a claim of another person to the instrument unless prior to such payment or satisfaction the person making the claim either supplies indemnity deemed adequate by the

bond

party seeking the discharge or enjoins payment or satisfaction by order of a court of competent jurisdiction in an action in which the adverse claimant and the holder are parties. This subsection does not, however, result in the discharge of the liability

(a) of a party who in bad faith pays or satisfies a holder who acquired the instrument by theft or who (unless having the rights of a holder in due course) holds through one who so acquired it; or

(b) of a party (other than an intermediary bank or a payor bank which is not a depositary bank) who pays or satisfies the holder of an instrument which has been restrictively indorsed in a manner not consistent with the terms of such restrictive indorsement.

(2) Payment or satisfaction may be made with the consent of the holder by any person including a stranger to the instrument. Surrender of the instrument to such a person gives him the rights of a transferee (Section 3—201).

Official Comment

Prior Uniform Statutory Provision: Sections 51, 88, 119, 121 and 171–177, Uniform Negotiable Instruments Law.

Changes: Parts of original sections combined and reworded; law changed.

Purposes of Changes: This section changes the law as follows:

1. It eliminates the "payment in due course" found in the original Sections 51, 88 and 119. "Payment in due course" discharged all parties where it was made by one who has no right of recourse on the instrument; but this is true of any other discharge of such a party, and is now covered by Section 3—601(3) on discharge of parties. Such payment was effective as a discharge against a subsequent purchaser; but since it is made at or after maturity of the instrument a purchaser with notice of that fact cannot be a holder in due course, and one who takes without notice of the payment and the maturity should be protected against failure to take up the instrument. The matter is now covered by Section 3—602.

2. The original Sections 171–177 provide for payment of a draft "for honor" after protest. The practice originated at a time when communications were slow and difficult, and in overseas transactions there might be a delay of several months before the drawer could act upon any dishonor. It provided a method by which a third party might intervene to protect the credit of the drawer and at the same time preserve his own rights. Cable, telegraph and telephone have made the practice obsolete for nearly a century, and it is today almost entirely unknown. It has been replaced by the cable transfer, the letter of credit and nu-

merous other devices by which a substitute arrangement is promptly made. "Payment for honor" is therefore eliminated; and subsection (2) now provides that any person may pay with the consent of the holder.

3. Payment to the holder discharges the party who makes it from his own liability on the instrument, and a part payment discharges him pro tanto. The same is true of any other satisfaction. Subsection (1) changes the law by eliminating the requirement of the original Section 88 that the payment be made in good faith and without notice that the title of the holder is defective. It adopts as a general principle the position that a payor is not required to obey an order to stop payment received from an indorser. However, this general principle is qualified by the provisions of subsection (1) (a) and (b) respecting persons who acquire an instrument by theft, or through a restrictive indorsement (Section 3—205). These provisions are thus consistent with Section 3—306 covering the rights of one not a holder in due course.

When the party to pay is notified of an adverse claim to the instrument he has normally no means of knowing whether the assertion is true. The "unless" clause of subsection (1) follows statutes which have been passed in many states on adverse claims to bank deposits. The paying party may pay despite notification of the adverse claim unless the adverse claimant supplies indemnity deemed adequate by the paying party or procures the issuance of process restraining payment in an action in which the adverse claimant and the holder of the instrument are both parties. If the paying party chooses to refuse payment and stand suit, even though not indemnified or enjoined, he is free to do so, although, under Section 3—306(d) on the rights of one not a holder in due course, except where theft or taking through a restrictive indorsement is alleged the payor must rely on the third party claimant to litigate the issue and may not himself defend on such a ground. His contract is to pay the holder of the instrument, and he performs it by making such payment. Except in cases of theft or restrictive indorsement there is no good reason to put him to inconvenience because of a dispute between two other parties unless he is indemnified or served with appropriate process.

4. With the elimination of "payment for honor", subsection (2) provides that with the consent of the holder payment may be made by anyone, including a stranger. The subsection omits the provision of the original Section 121 by which the payor is "remitted to his former rights". It rejects such decisions as Quimby v. Varnum, 190 Mass. 211, 76 N.E. 671 (1906), holding that an irregular indorser who makes payment cannot recover on the instrument. The same result is reached under Section 3—415(5) on accommodation parties. Upon payment and surrender of the paper the payor succeeds to the rights of the holder, subject to

the limitation found in Section 3—201 on transfer that one who has himself been a party to any fraud or illegality affecting the instrument or who as a prior holder had notice of a defense or claim against it cannot improve his position by taking from a later holder in due course.

5. Payment discharges the liability of the person making it. It discharges the liability of other parties only as

a. The discharge of the payor discharges others who have a right of recourse against him under Section 3—606; or

b. Reacquisition of the instrument discharges intervening parties under Section 3—208 on reacquisition; or

c. The discharge of one who has himself no right of recourse on the instrument discharges all parties under Section 3—601 on discharge of parties.

Cross References:

Sections 3—604 and 3—606.

Point 1: Section 3—601(3).

Point 3: Sections 3—205 and 3—306(d).

Point 4: Sections 3—201 and 3—415(5).

Point 5: Sections 3—606, 3—208, 3—601.

Definitional Cross References:

"Action". Section 1—201.

"Holder". Section 1—201.

"Instrument". Section 3—102.

"Order". Section 3—102.

"Party". Section 1—201.

"Person". Section 1—201.

"Rights". Section 1—201.

§ 3—604. Tender of Payment

(1) Any party making tender of full payment to a holder when or after it is due is discharged to the extent of all subsequent liability for interest, costs and attorney's fees.

(2) The holder's refusal of such tender wholly discharges any party who has a right of recourse against the party making the tender.

(3) Where the maker or acceptor of an instrument payable otherwise than on demand is able and ready to pay at every place of payment specified in the instrument when it is due, it is equivalent to tender.

Official Comment

Prior Uniform Statutory Provision: Sections 70 and 120, Uniform Negotiable Instruments Law.

Changes: Parts of original sections combined and reworded; new provisions.

Purposes of Changes and New Matter:

1. Subsection (1) is new. It states the generally accepted rule as to the effect of tender.

2. Subsection (2) rewords the original subsection 120(4). The

party discharged is one who has a right of recourse against the party making tender, whether the latter be a prior party or a subsequent one who has been accommodated.

3. Subsection (3) rewords the final clause of the first sentence of the original Section 70. Where the instrument is payable at any one of two or more specified places, the maker or acceptor must be able and ready to pay at each of them. The language in original Section 70 was taken to mean that makers and acceptors of notes and drafts payable at a bank were not discharged by failure of a holder to make due presentment of such paper at the designated bank. This Article reverses that rule. See Sections 3—501 on necessity of presentment, 3—504 on how presentment is made, and 3—502 on effect of delay in presentment.

Cross References:

Section 3—601.

Point 3: Sections 3—501, 3—502 and 3—504.

Definitional Cross References:

"Holder". Section 1—201.

"Instrument". Section 3—102.

"On demand". Section 3—108.

"Party". Section 1—201.

"Right". Section 1—201.

§ 3—605. Cancellation and Renunciation

(1) The holder of an instrument may even without consideration discharge any party

(a) in any manner apparent on the face of the instrument or the indorsement, as by intentionally cancelling the instrument or the party's signature by destruction or mutilation, or by striking out the party's signature; or

(b) by renouncing his rights by a writing signed and delivered or by surrender of the instrument to the party to be discharged.

(2) Neither cancellation nor renunciation without surrender of the instrument affects the title thereto.

Official Comment

Prior Uniform Statutory Provision: Sections 48, 119(3), 120(2), 122 and 123, Uniform Negotiable Instruments Law.

Changes: Combined and reworded.

Purposes of Changes:

1. The original Act does not state how cancellation is to be effected, except as to striking indorsements under the original Section 48. It must be done in such a manner as to be apparent on the face of the instrument, and the methods stated, which are supported by the decisions, are exclusive.

2. Subsection (1) (b) restates the original Section 122. The provision as to "discharge

of the instrument" is now covered by discharge, Section 3—601(3); that as to subsequent holders in due course by Section 3—602 on effect of discharge against a holder in due course.

3. Subsection (2) is new. It is intended to make it clear that the striking of an indorsement, or any other cancellation or renunciation, does not affect the title.

Cross References:

Point 2: Sections 3—601 and 3—602.

Definitional Cross References:

"Holder". Section 1—201.
"Instrument". Section 3—102.
"Party". Section 1—201.
"Rights". Section 1—201.
"Signature". Section 3—401.
"Signed". Section 1—201.
"Writing". Section 1—201.

§ 3—606. Impairment of Recourse or of Collateral

(1) The holder discharges any party to the instrument to the extent that without such party's consent the holder

(a) without express reservation of rights releases or agrees not to sue any person against whom the party has to the knowledge of the holder a right of recourse or agrees to suspend the right to enforce against such person the instrument or collateral or otherwise discharges such person, except that failure or delay in effecting any required presentment, protest or notice of dishonor with respect to any such person does not discharge any party as to whom presentment, protest or notice of dishonor is effective or unnecessary; or

(b) unjustifiably impairs any collateral for the instrument given by or on behalf of the party or any person against whom he has a right of recourse.

(2) By express reservation of rights against a party with a right of recourse the holder preserves

(a) all his rights against such party as of the time when the instrument was originally due; and

(b) the right of the party to pay the instrument as of that time; and

(c) all rights of such party to recourse against others.

Official Comment

Prior Uniform Statutory Provision: Section 120, Uniform Negotiable Instruments Law.

Changes: Reworded; new provisions.

Purposes of Changes and New Matter: To make it clear that:

1. The words "any party to the instrument" remove an uncertainty arising under the original section. The suretyship

defenses here provided are not limited to parties who are "secondarily liable," but are available to any party who is in the position of a surety, having a right of recourse either on the instrument or dehors it, including an accommodation maker or acceptor known to the holder to be so.

2. Consent may be given in advance, and is commonly incorporated in the instrument; or it may be given afterward. It requires no consideration, and operates as a waiver of the consenting party's right to claim his own discharge.

3. The words "to the knowledge of the holder" exclude the latent surety, as for example the accommodation maker where there is nothing on the instrument to show that he has signed for accommodation and the holder is ignorant of that fact. In such a case the holder is entitled to proceed according to what is shown by the face of the paper or what he otherwise knows, and does not discharge the surety when he acts in ignorance of the relation.

4. This section retains the right of the holder to release one party, or to postpone his time of payment, while expressly reserving rights against others. Subsection (2), which is new, states the generally accepted rule as to the effect of such an express reservation of rights. [Comment 4 was amended in 1966].

5. Paragraph (b) of subsection (1) is new. The suretyship defense stated has been generally recognized as available to indorsers or accommodation parties. As to when a holder's actions in dealing with collateral may be "unjustifiable", the section on rights and duties with respect to collateral in the possession of a secured party (Section 9—207) should be consulted.

Cross Reference:

Point 5: Section 9—207.

Definitional Cross References:

"Agreement". Section 1—201.
"Holder". Section 1—201.
"Instrument". Section 3—102.
"Notice of dishonor". Section 3—508.
"Party". Section 1—201.
"Person". Section 1—201.
"Rights". Section 1—201.

PART 7

ADVICE OF INTERNATIONAL SIGHT DRAFT

§ 3—701. Letter of Advice of International Sight Draft

(1) A "letter of advice" is a drawer's communication to the drawee that a described draft has been drawn.

(2) Unless otherwise agreed when a bank receives from another bank a letter of advice of an international sight draft the drawee bank may immediately debit the drawer's account

and stop the running of interest pro tanto. Such a debit and any resulting credit to any account covering outstanding drafts leaves in the drawer full power to stop payment or otherwise dispose of the amount and creates no trust or interest in favor of the holder.

(3) Unless otherwise agreed and except where a draft is drawn under a credit issued by the drawee, the drawee of an international sight draft owes the drawer no duty to pay an unadvised draft but if it does so and the draft is genuine, may appropriately debit the drawer's account.

Official Comment

Prior Uniform Statutory Provision: None.

Purposes: To recognize and clarify, in law, certain established practices of international banking.

1. Checks drawn by one international bank on the account it carries (in a currency foreign to itself) in another international bank are still handled under practices which reflect older conditions, but which have a real, continuing reason in the typical, European rule that a bank paying a check in good faith and in ordinary course can charge its depositor's account notwithstanding forgery of a necessary indorsement. To decrease the risk that forgery will prove successful, the practice is to send a letter of advice that a draft has been drawn and will be forthcoming. Subsection 3 recognizes that a drawer who sends no such letter forfeits any rights for improper dishonor, while still permitting the drawee to protect his delinquent drawer's credit.

2. Subsection (2) clears up for American courts, the meaning of another international practice: that of charging the drawer's account on receipt of the letter of advice. This practice involves no conception of trust or the like and the rule of Section 3—409(1) (Draft not an assignment) still applies. The debit has to do with the payment of interest only. The section recognizes the fact.

Cross Reference:

Point 2: Section 3—409(1).

Definitional Cross References:

"Account". Section 4—104.
"Bank". Section 1—201.
"Credit". Section 5—103.
"Draft". Section 3—104.
"Genuine". Section 1—201.
"Holder". Section 1—201.

PART 8
MISCELLANEOUS

§ 3—801. Drafts in a Set

(1) Where a draft is drawn in a set of parts, each of which is numbered and expressed to be an order only if no other part has been honored, the whole of the parts constitutes one draft but a taker of any part may become a holder in due course of the draft.

(2) Any person who negotiates, indorses or accepts a single part of a draft drawn in a set thereby becomes liable to any holder in due course of that part as if it were the whole set, but as between different holders in due course to whom different parts have been negotiated the holder whose title first accrues has all rights to the draft and its proceeds.

(3) As against the drawee the first presented part of a draft drawn in a set is the part entitled to payment, or if a time draft to acceptance and payment. Acceptance of any subsequently presented part renders the drawee liable thereon under subsection (2). With respect both to a holder and to the drawer payment of a subsequently presented part of a draft payable at sight has the same effect as payment of a check notwithstanding an effective stop order (Section 4—407).

(4) Except as otherwise provided in this section, where any part of a draft in a set is discharged by payment or otherwise the whole draft is discharged.

Official Comment

Prior Uniform Statutory Provision: Sections 178–183, Uniform Negotiable Instruments Law.

Changes: Combined and reworded.

Purposes of Changes:

The revised language makes no important change in substance, and is intended only as a clarification and supplementation of the original sections:

1. Drafts in a set customarily contain such language as "Pay ——— this first of exchange (second unpaid)," with equivalent language in the second part. Today a part also commonly bears conspicuous indication of its number. At least the first factor is necessary to notify the holder of his rights, and is therefore necessary in order to make this section apply. Subsection (1) so provides, thus stating in the statute a matter left previously to a commercial practice long uniform but expensive to establish in court.

2. The final sentence of subsection (3) is new. Payment of the part of the draft subsequent-

ly presented is improper and the drawee may not charge it to the account of the drawer, but some one has probably been unjustly enriched on the total transaction, at the expense of the drawee. So the drawee is like a bank which has paid a check over an effective stop payment order, and is subrogated as provided in that situation. Section 4—407.

3. A statement in a draft drawn in a set of parts to the effect that the order is effective only if no other part has been honored does not render the draft nonnegotiable as conditional. See Section 3—112(1)(g).

Cross References:

Point 2: Section 4—407.
Point 3: Section 3—112.

Definitional Cross References:

"Acceptance". Section 3—410.
"Check". Section 3—104.
"Draft". Section 3—104.
"Holder". Section 1—201.
"Holder in due course". Section 3—302.
"Honor". Section 1—201.
"Person". Section 1—201.
"Rights". Section 1—201.

§ 3—802. Effect of Instrument on Obligation for Which It Is Given

(1) Unless otherwise agreed where an instrument is taken for an underlying obligation

(a) the obligation is pro tanto discharged if a bank is drawer, maker or acceptor of the instrument and there is no recourse on the instrument against the underlying obligor; and

(b) in any other case the obligation is suspended pro tanto until the instrument is due or if it is payable on demand until its presentment. If the instrument is dishonored action may be maintained on either the instrument or the obligation; discharge of the underlying obligor on the instrument also discharges him on the obligation.

(2) The taking in good faith of a check which is not postdated does not of itself so extend the time on the original obligation as to discharge a surety.

Official Comment

Prior Uniform Statutory Provision: None.

Purposes:

1. The section is new. It is intended to settle conflicts as to the effect of an instrument as payment of the obligation for which it is given.

2. Where a holder procures certification of a check the drawer is discharged under Section 3—411 on check certification.

Thereafter the original obligation is regarded as paid, and the holder must look to the certifying bank. The circumstances may indicate a similar intent in other transactions, and the question may be one of fact for the jury. Subsection (1) (a) states a rule discharging the obligation pro tanto when the instrument taken carries the obligation of a bank as drawer, maker or acceptor and there is no recourse on the instrument against the underlying obligor.

3. It is commonly said that a check or other negotiable instrument is "conditional payment." By this it is normally meant that taking the instrument is a surrender of the right to sue on the obligation until the instrument is due, but if the instrument is not paid on due presentment the right to sue on the obligation is "revived." Subsection (1) (b) states this result in terms of suspension of the obligation, which is intended to include suspension of the running of the statute of limitations. On dishonor of the instrument the holder is given his option to sue either on the instrument or on the underlying obligation. If, however, the original obligor has been discharged on the instrument (see Section 3—601) he is also discharged on the original obligation.

4. Subsection (2) is intended to remove any implication that a check given in payment of an obligation discharges a surety. The check is taken as a means of immediate payment; the thirty day period for presentment specified in Section 3—503 does not affect the surety's liability.

Cross References:

Point 2: Sections 1—201, 3—411 and 3—601.

Point 4: Section 3—503.

Definitional Cross References:

"Action". Section 1—201.
"Bank". Section 1—201.
"Check". Section 3—104.
"Dishonor". Section 3—507.
"Good faith". Section 1—201.
"Instrument". Section 3—102.
"On demand". Section 3—108.
"Presentment". Section 3—504.

§ 3—803. Notice to Third Party

Where a defendant is sued for breach of an obligation for which a third person is answerable over under this Article he may give the third person written notice of the litigation, and the person notified may then give similar notice to any other person who is answerable over to him under this Article. If the notice states that the person notified may come in and defend and that if the person notified does not do so he will in any action against him by the person giving the notice be bound by any determination of fact common to the two litigations, then unless after seasonable receipt of the notice the person notified does come in and defend he is so bound.

Official Comment

Prior Uniform Statutory Provisions: None.

Purposes:

The section is new. It is intended to supplement, not to displace existing procedures for interpleader or joinder of parties.

The section conforms to the analogous provision in Section 2—607. It extends to such liabilities as those arising from forged indorsements even though not "on the instrument," and is intended to make it clear that the notification is not effective until received. In Hartford Accident & Indemnity Co. v. First Nat. Bank & Trust Co., 281 N.Y. 162, 22 N.E.2d 324, 123 A.L.R. 1149 (1939), the common-law doctrine of "vouching in" was held inapplicable where the party notified had no direct liability to the party giving the notice. In that case the drawer of a check, sued by the payee whose indorsement had been forged, gave notice to a collecting bank. In a second action the drawee was held liable to the drawer; but in an action by the drawee for judgment over against the collecting bank the determinations of fact in the first action were held not conclusive. This section does not disturb this result; the section is limited to cases where the person notified is "answerable over" to the person giving the notice.

Cross Reference:

Section 2—607.

Definitional Cross References:

"Action". Section 1—201.
"Defendant". Section 1—201.
"Instrument". Section 3—102.
"Notifies". Section 1—201.
"Person". Section 1—201.
"Right". Section 1—201.
"Seasonably". Section 1—204.
"Written". Section 1—201.

§ 3—804. Lost, Destroyed or Stolen Instruments

The owner of an instrument which is lost, whether by destruction, theft or otherwise, may maintain an action in his own name and recover from any party liable thereon upon due proof of his ownership, the facts which prevent his production of the instrument and its terms. The court may require security indemnifying the defendant against loss by reason of further claims on the instrument.

Official Comment

Prior Uniform Statutory Provision: None.

Purposes:

This section is new. It is intended to provide a method of recovery on instruments which are lost, destroyed or stolen. The plaintiff who claims to be the owner of such an instrument is not a holder as that term is defined in this Act, since he is not in possession of the paper, and he does not have the holder's prima facie right to recover under the section on the burden of establishing signatures. He must prove his case. He must establish the terms of the instrument and his ownership, and must account for its absence.

If the claimant testifies falsely, or if the instrument subsequently turns up in the hands of a holder in due course, the obligor may be subjected to double liability. The court is therefore authorized to require security indemnifying the obligor against loss by reason of such possibilities. There may be cases in which so much time has elapsed, or there is so little possible doubt as to the destruction of the instrument and its ownership that there is no good reason to require the security. The requirement is therefore not an absolute one, and the matter is left to the discretion of the court.

Cross References:

Sections 1—201 and 3—307.

Definitional Cross References:

"Action". Section 1—201.
"Defendant". Section 1—201.
"Instrument". Section 3—102.
"Party". Section 1—201.
"Term". Section 1—201.

§ 3—805. Instruments Not Payable to Order or to Bearer

This Article applies to any instrument whose terms do not preclude transfer and which is otherwise negotiable within this Article but which is not payable to order or to bearer, except that there can be no holder in due course of such an instrument.

Official Comment

Prior Uniform Statutory Provision: None.

Purposes:

This section covers the "non-negotiable instrument." As it has been used by most courts, this term has been a technical one of art. It does not refer to a writing, such as a note containing an express condition, which is not negotiable and is entirely outside of the scope of this Article and to be treated as a simple contract. It refers to a particular type of instrument which meets all requirements as to form of a negotiable instrument except that it is not payable to order or to bearer. The typical example is the check reading merely "Pay John Doe."

Such a check is not a negotiable instrument under this Article. At the same time it is still a check, a mercantile specialty which differs in many respects from a simple contract. Commercial and banking practice treats it as a check, and a long line of decisions before and after the original Act have made it clear that it is subject to the law merchant as distinguished from ordinary contract law. Although the Negotiable Instruments Law has been held by its terms not to apply to such "non-negotiable instruments" it has been recognized as a codification and restatement of the law merchant, and has in fact been applied to them by analogy.

Thus the holder of the check reading "Pay A" establishes his case by production of the instrument and proof of signatures; and the burden of proving want of consideration or any other defense is upon the obligor. Such a check passes by indorsement and delivery without words of assignment, and the indorser undertakes greater liabilities than those of an assignor. This section resolves a conflict in the decisions as to the extent of that undertaking by providing in effect that the indorser of such an instrument is not distinguished from any indorser of a negotiable instrument. The indorser is entitled to presentment, notice of dishonor and protest, and the procedure and liabilities in bank collection are the same. The rules as to alteration, the filling of blanks, accommodation parties, the liability of signing agents, discharge, and the like are those applied to negotiable instruments.

In short, the "non-negotiable instrument" is treated as a negotiable instrument, so far as its form permits. Since it lacks words of negotiability there can be no holder in due course of such an instrument, and any provision of any section of this Article peculiar to a holder in due course cannot apply to it. With this exception, such instruments are covered by all sections of this Article.

Cross Reference:

Section 3—104.

Definitional Cross References:

"Bearer". Section 1—201.

"Holder in due course". Section 3—302.

"Instrument". Section 3—102.

"Term". Section 1—201.

*

ARTICLE 4

BANK DEPOSITS AND COLLECTIONS

PART 1. GENERAL PROVISIONS AND DEFINITIONS

PART 2. COLLECTION OF ITEMS: DEPOSITARY AND COLLECTING BANKS

PART 3. COLLECTION OF ITEMS: PAYOR BANKS

PART 4. RELATIONSHIP BETWEEN PAYOR BANK AND ITS CUSTOMER

PART 5. COLLECTION OF DOCUMENTARY DRAFTS

PART 1

GENERAL PROVISIONS AND DEFINITIONS

§ 4—101. Short Title

This Article shall be known and may be cited as Uniform Commercial Code—Bank Deposits and Collections.

Official Comment

The tremendous number of checks handled by banks and the country-wide nature of the bank collection process require uniformity in the law of bank collections. Individual Federal Reserve banks process as many as 1,000,000 items a day; large metropolitan banks average 300,000 a day; banks with less than $5,000,000 on deposit handle from 1,000 to 2,000 daily. There is needed a uniform statement of the principal rules of the bank collection process with ample provision for flexibility to meet the needs of the large volume handled and the changing needs and conditions that are bound to come with the years.

The American Bankers Association Bank Collection Code, enacted in eighteen states, has stated many of the bank collection rules that have developed, and more recently Deferred Posting statutes have developed and varied further rules. With items flowing in great volume not only in and around metropolitan and smaller centers but also continuously across state lines and back and forth across the entire country, a proper situation exists for uniform rules that will state in modern concepts at least some of the rights of the parties and in addition aid this flow and not interfere with its progress.

This Article adopts many of the rules of the American Bankers Association Code that are still in current operation, the principles and rules of the Deferred Posting and other statutes, codifies some rules established by court decisions and in addition states certain patterns and procedures that exist even though not heretofore covered by statute.

§ 4—102. Applicability

(1) To the extent that items within this Article are also within the scope of Articles 3 and 8, they are subject to the provisions of those Articles. In the event of conflict the provisions of this Article govern those of Article 3 but the provisions of Article 8 govern those of this Article.

(2) The liability of a bank for action or non-action with respect to any item handled by it for purposes of presentment, payment or collection is governed by the law of the place where the bank is located. In the case of action or non-action by or at a branch or separate office of a bank, its liability is governed by the law of the place where the branch or separate office is located.

Official Comment

Prior Uniform Statutory Provision: None.

Purposes:

1. The rules governing negotiable instruments, their transfer, and the contracts of the parties thereto apply to the items collected through banking channels wherever no specific provision is found in this Article. In the case of conflict, this Article governs. See Section 3—103(2).

Bonds and like instruments constituting investment securities under Article 8 may also be handled by banks for collection purposes. Various sections of

Article 8 prescribe rules of transfer some of which (see Sections 8—304 and 8—306) may conflict with provisions of this Article (Sections 4—205 and 4—207). In the case of conflict, Article 8 governs.

Section 4—208 deals specifically with overlapping problems and possible conflicts between this Article and Article 9. However, similar reconciling provisions are not necessary in the case of Articles 5 and 7. Sections 4—301 and 4—302 are consistent with Section 5—112. In the case of Article 7 documents of title frequently accompany items but they are not themselves items. See Section 4—104(g).

2. Subsection (2) is designed to state a workable rule for the solution of otherwise vexatious problems of the conflicts of laws:

a. The routine and mechanical nature of bank collections makes it imperative that one law govern the activities of one office of a bank. The requirement found in some cases that to hold an indorser notice must be given in accordance with the law of the place of indorsement, since that method of notice became an implied term of the indorser's contract, is more theoretical than practical.

b. Adoption of what is in essence a tort theory of the conflict of laws is consistent with the general theory of this Article that the basic duty of a collecting bank is one of good faith and the exercise of ordinary care. Justification lies in the fact that, in using an ambulatory instrument, the drawer, payee, and indorsers must know that action will be taken with respect to it in other jurisdictions. This is especially pertinent with respect to the law of the place of payment.

c. The phrase "action or non-action with respect to any item handled by it for purposes of presentment, payment or collection" is intended to make the conflicts rule of subsection (2) apply from the inception of the collection process of an item through all phases of deposit, forwarding, presentment, payment and remittance or credit of proceeds. Specifically the subsection applies to the initial act of a depositary bank in receiving an item and to the incidents of such receipt. The conflicts rule of Weissman v. Banque de Bruxelles, 254 N.Y. 488, 173 N.E. 835 (1930), is rejected. The subsection applies to questions of possible vicarious liability of a bank for action or non-action of sub-agents (see Section 4—202(3)) and tests these questions by the law of the state of the location of the bank which uses the sub-agent. The conflicts rule of St. Nicholas Bank of New York v. State Nat. Bank, 128 N.Y. 26, 27 N.E. 849, 13 L.R.A. 241 (1891), is rejected. The subsection applies to action or non-action of a payor bank in connection with handling an item (see Sections 4—213(1), 4—301, 4—302, 4—303) as well as action or non-action of a collecting bank (Sections 4—201 through 4—214); to action or non-action of a bank which suspends payment or is affected by another bank suspending payment (Section 4—214); to action or non-action of a bank with respect to an item under the rules of Part 4 of Article 4.

d. Where subsection (2) makes this Article applicable, Section 4—103(1) leaves open the possibility of an agreement with respect to applicable law. Such freedom of agreement follows the general policy of Section 1—105.

Cross References:

Sections 1—105; 3—103(2) and Article 3; all sections of Article 4; 5—112; Article 7; 8—304 and 8—306; Article 9.

Definitional Cross References:

"Bank". Section 1—201.
"Branch". Section 1—201.
"Item". Section 4—104.

§ 4—103. Variation by Agreement; Measure of Damages; Certain Action Constituting Ordinary Care

(1) The effect of the provisions of this Article may be varied by agreement except that no agreement can disclaim a bank's responsibility for its own lack of good faith or failure to exercise ordinary care or can limit the measure of damages for such lack or failure; but the parties may by agreement determine the standards by which such responsibility is to be measured if such standards are not manifestly unreasonable.

(2) Federal Reserve regulations and operating letters, clearing house rules, and the like, have the effect of agreements under subsection (1), whether or not specifically assented to by all parties interested in items handled.

(3) Action or non-action approved by this Article or pursuant to Federal Reserve regulations or operating letters constitutes the exercise of ordinary care and, in the absence of special instructions, action or non-action consistent with clearing house rules and the like or with a general banking usage not disapproved by this Article, prima facie constitutes the exercise of ordinary care.

(4) The specification or approval of certain procedures by this Article does not constitute disapproval of other procedures which may be reasonable under the circumstances.

(5) The measure of damages for failure to exercise ordinary care in handling an item is the amount of the item reduced by an amount which could not have been realized by the use of ordinary care, and where there is bad faith it includes other damages, if any, suffered by the party as a proximate consequence.

Official Comment

Prior Uniform Statutory Provision: None; but see Sections 5 and 6 of the American Bankers Association Bank Collection Code.

Purposes:

1. Section 1—102 states the general principles and rules for variation of the effect of this Act by agreement and the limitations to this power. Section 4—103 states the specific rules for variation of Article 4 by agreement and also certain standards of ordinary care. In view of the technical complexity of the field of bank collections, the enormous number of items handled by banks, the certainty that there will be variations from the normal in each day's work in each bank, the certainty of changing conditions and the possibility of developing improved methods of collection to speed the process, it would be unwise to freeze present methods of operation by mandatory statutory rules. This section, therefore, permits within wide limits variation of provisions of the Article by agreement.

2. Subsection (1) confers blanket power to vary all provisions of the Article by agreements of the ordinary kind. The agreements may not disclaim a bank's responsibility for its own lack of good faith or failure to exercise ordinary care and may not limit the measure of damages for such lack or failure, but this subsection like Section 1—102(3) approves the practice of parties determining by agreement the standards by which such responsibility is to be measured. In the absence of a showing that the standards manifestly are unreasonable, the agreement controls. Owners of items and other interested parties are not affected by agreements under this subsection unless they are parties to the agreement or are bound by adoption, ratification, estoppel or the like.

As here used "agreement" has the meaning given to it by Section 1—201(3). The agreement may be direct, as between the owner and the depositary bank; or indirect, as where the owner authorizes a particular type of procedure and any bank in the collection chain acts pursuant to such authorization. It may be with respect to a single item; or to all items handled for a particular customer, e. g., a general agreement between the depositary bank and the customer at the time a deposit account is opened. Legends on deposit tickets, collection letters and acknowledgments of items, coupled with action by the affected party constituting acceptance, adoption, ratification, estoppel or the like, are agreements if they meet the tests of the definition of "agreement". See Section 1—201(3). First Nat. Bank of Denver v. Federal Reserve Bank, 6 F.2d 339 (8th Cir.1925) (deposit slip); Jefferson County Bldg. Ass'n v. Southern Bank & Trust Co., 225 Ala. 25, 142 So. 66 (1932) (signature card and deposit slip); Semingson v. Stock Yards Nat.

Bank, 162 Minn. 424, 203 N.W. 412 (1925) (passbook); Farmers State Bank v. Union Nat. Bank, 42 N.D. 449, 454, 173 N.W. 789, 790 (1919) (acknowledgment of receipt of item).

3. Subsection (1) (subject to its limitations with respect to good faith and ordinary care) goes far to meet the requirements of flexibility. However, it does not by itself confer fully effective flexibility. When it is recognized that banks handle probably 25,000,000 items every business day and that the parties interested in each item include the owner of the item, the drawer (if it is a check), all non-bank indorsers, the payor bank and from one to five or more collecting banks, it is obvious that it is impossible, practically, to obtain direct agreements from all of these parties on all items. *En masse,* the interested parties constitute virtually every adult person and business organization in the United States. On the other hand they may become bound to agreements on the principle that collecting banks acting as agents have authority to make binding agreements with respect to items being handled. This conclusion was assumed but was not flatly decided in Federal Reserve Bank of Richmond v. Malloy, 264 U.S. 160, at 167, 44 S.Ct. 296, at 298, 68 L. Ed. 617, 31 A.L.R. 1261 (1924).

To meet this problem subsection (2) provides that official or quasi-official rules of collection, that is Federal Reserve regulations and operating letters, clearing house rules, and the like, have the effect of agreements under subsection (1), whether or not specifically assented to by all parties interested in items handled. Consequently, such official or quasi-official rules may, standing by themselves but subject to the good faith and ordinary care limitations, vary the effect of the provisions of Article 4.

Federal Reserve regulations. Various sections of the Federal Reserve Act (12 U.S.C.A. § 221 et seq.) authorize the Board of Governors of the Federal Reserve System to direct the Federal Reserve banks to exercise bank collection functions. For example, Section 16 (12 U.S.C.A. § 248(o)) authorizes the Board to require each Federal Reserve bank to exercise the functions of a clearing house for its members and Section 13 (12 U.S.C.A. § 342) authorizes each Federal Reserve bank to receive deposits from non-member banks solely for the purposes of exchange or of collection. Under this statutory authorization the Board has issued Regulation J (Check Clearing and Collection), which has been infrequently amended over the many years during which it has been in force. (Regulation G, issued under comparable statutory authority, covers the handling of "non-cash items"). Where regulations issued by the Board in pursuance of its statutory mandate may be said to have some force of law and constitute an effective means of maintaining flexibility, it is appropriate to provide that such regulations may vary this Article even though not specifically assented to by all parties interested in items handled.

Federal Reserve operating letters. The regulations of the Federal Reserve Board authorize the Federal Reserve banks to promulgate rules covering operating details. Regulation J, for example, provides that each bank may promulgate rules "not inconsistent with the terms of the law or of this regulation governing the sorting, listing, packaging and transmission of items and other details of its check clearing and collection operation. Such rules . . . shall be set forth . . . in . . . letters of instructions to . . . member and nonmember clearing banks." The term "operating letters" means these "letters of instructions", sometimes called "operating circulars", issued by the Federal Reserve banks under appropriate regulation of the Board. This Article recognizes such "operating letters" issued pursuant to the regulations and concerned with operating details as appropriate means, within their proper sphere, to vary the effect of the Article.

Clearing House Rules. Local clearing houses have long issued rules governing the details of clearing; hours of clearing, media of remittance, time for return of mis-sent items and the like. The case law has recognized such rules, within their proper sphere, as binding on affected parties and as appropriate sources for the courts to look to in filling out details of bank collection law. Subsection (2) in recognizing clearing house rules as a means of preserving flexibility continues the sensible approach indicated in the cases. Included in the term "clearing houses" are county and regional clearing houses as well as those within a single city or town. There is, of course, no intention of authorizing a local clearing house or a group of clearing houses to rewrite the basic law generally. The term "clearing house rules" should be understood in the light of functions the clearing houses have exercised in the past.

And the like. This phrase is to be construed in the light of the foregoing. "Federal Reserve regulations and operating letters" cover rules and regulations issued by public or quasi-public agencies under statutory authority. "Clearing house rules" cover rules issued by a group of banks which have associated themselves to perform through a clearing house some of their collection, payment and clearing functions. Other such agencies or associations may be established in the future whose rules and regulations could be appropriately looked on as constituting means of avoiding absolute statutory rigidity. The phrase "and the like" leaves open such possibilities of future development. An agreement between a number of banks or even all the banks in an area simply because they are banks, would not of itself, by virtue of the phrase "and the like," meet the purposes and objectives of subsection (2).

4. Under this Article banks come under the general obligations of the use of good faith and the exercise of ordinary care. "Good faith" is defined in this Act (Section 1—201(19)) as "honesty in fact in the con-

duct or transaction concerned." The term "ordinary care" is not defined and is here used with its normal tort meaning and not in any special sense relating to bank collections. No attempt is made in the Article to define *in toto* what constitutes ordinary care or lack of it. Section 4—202 states respects in which collecting banks must use ordinary care. Subsection (3) of 4—103 provides that action or non-action approved by the Article or pursuant to Federal Reserve regulations or operating letters constitutes the exercise of ordinary care. Where Federal Reserve regulations and operating letters are issued pursuant to statutory mandate as indicated above, they constitute an affirmative standard of ordinary care equally with the provisions of Article 4 itself.

Subsection (3) further provides that, absent special instructions, action or non-action consistent with clearing house rules and the like or with a general banking usage not disapproved by the Article, prima facie constitutes the exercise of ordinary care. Clearing house rules and the phrase "and the like" have the significance set forth above in these Comments. The term "general banking usage" is not defined but should be taken to mean a general usage common to banks in the area concerned. See Section 1—205(2). Where the adjective "general" is used, the intention is to require a usage broader than a mere practice between two or three banks but it is not intended to require anything as broad as a country-wide usage. A usage followed generally throughout a state, a substantial portion of a state, a metropolitan area or the like would certainly be sufficient. Consistently with the principle of Section 1—205(3), action or non-action consistent with clearing house rules or the like or with such banking usages prima facie constitutes the exercise of ordinary care. However, the phrase "in the absence of special instructions" affords owners of items an opportunity to prescribe other standards and where there may be no direct supervision or control of clearing houses or banking usages by official supervisory authorities, the confirmation of ordinary care by compliance with these standards is *prima facie* only, thus conferring on the courts the ultimate power to determine ordinary care in any case where it should appear desirable to do so. The *prima facie* rule does, however, impose on the party contesting the standards to establish that they are unreasonable, arbitrary or unfair.

5. Subsection (4), in line with the flexible approach required for the bank collection process is designed to make clear that a novel procedure adopted by a bank is not to be considered unreasonable merely because that procedure is not specifically contemplated by this Article or by agreement, or because it has not yet been generally accepted as a bank usage. Changing conditions constantly call for new procedures and someone has to use the new procedure first. If such a procedure when called in question is

found to be reasonable under the circumstances, provided, of course, that it is not inconsistent with any provision of the Article or other law or agreement, the bank which has followed the new procedure should not be found to have failed in the exercise of ordinary care.

6. Subsection (5) sets forth a rule for determining the measure of damages which, under subsection (1), cannot be limited by agreement. In the absence of bad faith the maximum recovery is the amount of the item concerned. When it is established that some part or all of the item could not have been collected even by the use of ordinary care the recovery is reduced by the amount which would have been in any event uncollectible. This limitation on recovery follows the case law. Finally, when bad faith is established the rule opens to allow the recovery of other damages, whose "proximateness" is to be tested by the ordinary rules applied in comparable cases. Of course, it continues to be as necessary under subsection (5) as it has been under ordinary common law principles that, before the damage rule of the subsection becomes operative, liability of the bank and some loss to the customer or owner must be established.

Cross References:

Sections 1—102(3), 1—203, 1—205 and 4—202.

Definitional Cross References:

"Bank". Section 1—201.
"Good faith". Section 1—201.
"Item". Section 4—104.
"Usage". Section 1—205.

§ 4—104. Definitions and Index of Definitions

(1) In this Article unless the context otherwise requires

(a) "Account" means any account with a bank and includes a checking, time, interest or savings account;

(b) "Afternoon" means the period of a day between noon and midnight;

(c) "Banking day" means that part of any day on which a bank is open to the public for carrying on substantially all of its banking functions;

(d) "Clearing house" means any association of banks or other payors regularly clearing items;

(e) "Customer" means any person having an account with a bank or for whom a bank has agreed to collect items and includes a bank carrying an account with another bank;

(f) "Documentary draft" means any negotiable or non-negotiable draft with accompanying documents, securities or other papers to be delivered against honor of the draft;

(g) "Item" means any instrument for the payment of money even though it is not negotiable but does not include money;

(h) "Midnight deadline" with respect to a bank is midnight on its next banking day following the banking day on which it receives the relevant item or notice or from which the time for taking action commences to run, whichever is later;

(i) "Properly payable" includes the availability of funds for payment at the time of decision to pay or dishonor;

(j) "Settle" means to pay in cash, by clearing house settlement, in a charge or credit or by remittance, or otherwise as instructed. A settlement may be either provisional or final;

(k) "Suspends payments" with respect to a bank means that it has been closed by order of the supervisory authorities, that a public officer has been appointed to take it over or that it ceases or refuses to make payments in the ordinary course of business.

(2) Other definitions applying to this Article and the sections in which they appear are:

"Collecting bank"	Section 4—105.
"Depositary bank"	Section 4—105.
"Intermediary bank"	Section 4—105.
"Payor bank"	Section 4—105.
"Presenting bank"	Section 4—105.
"Remitting bank"	Section 4—105.

(3) The following definitions in other Articles apply to this Article:

"Acceptance"	Section 3—410.
"Certificate of deposit"	Section 3—104.
"Certification"	Section 3—411.
"Check"	Section 3—104.
"Draft"	Section 3—104.
"Holder in due course"	Section 3—302.
"Notice of dishonor"	Section 3—508.
"Presentment"	Section 3—504.
"Protest"	Section 3—509.
"Secondary party"	Section 3—102.

(4) In addition Article 1 contains general definitions and principles of construction and interpretation applicable throughout this Article.

Official Comment

Prior Uniform Statutory Provision: None.

Purposes:

1. Subsection (1) (c): "Banking Day". Under this definition that part of a business day when a bank is open only for limited functions, e. g., on Saturday evenings to receive deposits and cash checks, but with loan, bookkeeping and other departments closed, is not part of a banking day.

2. Subsection (1) (d): "Clearing House". Occasionally express companies, governmental agencies and other non-banks deal directly with a clearing house; hence the definition does not limit the term to an association of banks.

3. Subsection (1) (e): "Customer". It is to be noted that this term includes a bank carrying an account with another bank as well as the more typical non-bank customer or depositor.

4. Subsection (1) (g): The word "item" is chosen because it is "banking language" and includes non-negotiable as well as negotiable paper calling for money and also similar paper governed by the Article on Investment Securities (Article 8) as well as that governed by the Article on Commercial Paper (Article 3).

5. Subsection (1) (h): "Midnight Deadline". The use of this phrase is an example of the more mechanical approach used in this Article. Midnight is selected as a termination point or time limit to obtain greater uniformity and definiteness than would be possible from other possible termination points, such as the close of the banking day or business day.

6. Subsection (1) (j): The term "settle" is a new term in bank collection language that has substantial importance throughout Article 4. In the American Bankers Association Bank Collection Code, in deferred posting statutes, in Federal Reserve regulations and operating letters, in clearing house rules, in agreements between banks and customers and in legends on deposit tickets and collection letters, there is repeated reference to "conditional" or "provisional" credits or payments. Tied in with this concept of credits or payments being in some way tentative, has been a related but somewhat different problem as to when an item is "paid" or "finally paid" either to determine the relative priority of the item as against attachments, stop payment orders and the like or in insolvency situations. There has been extensive litigation in the various states on these problems. To a substantial extent the confusion, the litigation and even the resulting court decisions fail to take into account that in the collection process some debits or credits are provisional or tentative and others are final and that very many debits or credits are provisional or tentative for awhile but later become final. Similarly, some cases fail to recognize that within a single bank, particularly a payor bank, each item goes

through a series of processes and that in a payor bank most of these processes are preliminary to the basic act of payment or "final payment".

The term "settle" is used as a convenient term to characterize a broad variety of conditional, provisional, tentative and also final payments of items. Such a comprehensive term is needed because it is frequently difficult or unnecessary to determine whether a particular action is tentative or final or when a particular credit shifts from the tentative class to the final class. Therefore, its use throughout the Article indicates that in that particular context it is unnecessary or unwise to determine whether the debit or the credit or the payment is tentative or final. However, when qualified by the adjective "provisional" its tentative nature is intended, and when qualified by the adjective "final" its permanent nature is intended.

Examples of the various types of settlement contemplated by the term include payments in cash; the efficient but somewhat complicated process of payment through the adjustment and offsetting of balances through clearing houses; debit or credit entries in accounts between banks; the forwarding of various types of remittance instruments, sometimes to cover a particular item but more frequently to cover an entire group of items received on a particular day.

7. Subsection (1) (k): "Suspends payments". This term is designed to afford an objective test to determine when a bank is no longer operating as a part of the banking system.

Definitional Cross References:

"Bank". Section 1—201.
"Documents". Section 1—201.
"Money". Section 1—201.
"Negotiable". Section 3—104.
"Notice". Section 1—201.
"Person". Section 1—201.
"Securities". Section 8—102.

§ 4—105. "Depositary Bank"; "Intermediary Bank"; "Collecting Bank"; "Payor Bank"; "Presenting Bank"; "Remitting Bank"

In this Article unless the context otherwise requires:

(a) "Depositary bank" means the first bank to which an item is transferred for collection even though it is also the payor bank;

(b) "Payor bank" means a bank by which an item is payable as drawn or accepted;

(c) "Intermediary bank" means any bank to which an item is transferred in course of collection except the depositary or payor bank;

(d) "Collecting bank" means any bank handling the item for collection except the payor bank;

(e) "Presenting bank" means any bank presenting an item except a payor bank;

(f) "Remitting bank" means any payor or intermediary bank remitting for an item.

Official Comment

Prior Uniform Statutory Provision: None.

Purposes:

1. The definitions in general exclude a bank to which an item is issued, as such bank does not take by transfer except in the particular case covered where the item is issued to a payee for collection, as where a corporation is transferring balances from one account to another. Thus, the definition of "depositary bank" does not include the bank to which a check is made payable where a check is given in payment of a mortgage. Such a bank has the status of a payee under Article 3 on Commercial Paper and not that of a collecting bank.

2. The term payor bank includes a drawee bank and also a bank at which an item is payable if the item constitutes an order on the bank to pay, for it is then "payable by" the bank. If the "at" item is not an order in the particular state (See Section 3—121), then the bank is not a payor, but will be a presenting or collecting bank.

3. Items are sometimes drawn or accepted "payable through" a particular bank. Under this Section and Section 3—120 the "payable through" bank (if it in fact handles the item) will be a collecting (and often a presenting) bank; it is not a "payor bank."

4. The term intermediary bank includes the last bank in the collection process where the payor is not a bank. Usually the last bank is also a presenting bank.

Cross References:

Article 3, especially Sections 3—120 and 3—121.

Definitional Cross References:

"Bank". Section 1—201.
"Customer". Section 4—104.
"Item". Section 4—104.

§ 4—106. Separate Office of a Bank

A branch or separate office of a bank [maintaining its own deposit ledgers] is a separate bank for the purpose of computing the time within which and determining the place at or to which action may be taken or notices or orders shall be given under this Article and under Article 3. As amended 1962.

Note: *The brackets are to make it optional with the several states whether to require a branch to maintain its own deposit ledgers in order to be considered to be a* *separate bank for certain purposes under Article 4. In some states "maintaining its own deposit ledgers" is a satisfactory test. In others branch banking practices are such that this test would not be suitable.*

Official Comment

Prior Uniform Statutory Provision: None; but see Section 1, American Bankers Association Bank Collection Code.

Purposes:

1. A rule with respect to the status of a branch or separate office of a bank as a part of any statute on bank collections is highly desirable if not absolutely necessary. However, practices in the operations of branches and separate offices vary substantially in the different states and it has not been possible to find any single rule that is logically correct, fair in all situations and workable under all different types of practices.

2. In many states and for many purposes a branch or separate office of the bank needs to be treated as a separate bank. Many branches function as separate banks in the handling and payment of items and require time for doing so similar to that of a separate bank. This is particularly true where branch banking is permitted throughout a state or in different towns and cities. Similarly, where there is this separate functioning a particular branch or separate office is the only proper place for various types of action to be taken or orders or notices to be given. Examples include the drawing of a check on a particular branch by a customer whose account is carried at that branch; the presentment of that same check at that branch; the issuance of an order to the branch to stop payment on the check.

3. Section 1 of the American Bankers Association Bank Collection Code provides simply: "A branch or office of any such bank shall be deemed a bank." Although this rule appears to be brief and simple, as applied to particular sections of the ABA Code it produces illogical and, in some cases, unreasonable results. For example, under Section 11 of the ABA Code it seems anomalous for one branch of a bank to have charged an item to the account of the drawer and another branch to have the power to elect to treat the item as dishonored. Similar logical problems would flow from applying the same rule to Article 4. Warranties by one branch to another branch under Section 4—207 (each considered a separate bank) do not make sense.

4. Assuming that it is not desirable to make each branch a separate bank for all purposes, this Section provides that a branch or separate office is a separate bank for certain purposes. In so doing the single legal entity of the bank as a whole is preserved, thereby carrying with it the liability of the institution as a whole on such obligations as it may be under. On the other hand, where the

Article provides a number of time limits for different types of action by banks, if a branch functions as a separate bank, it should have the time limits available to a separate bank. Similarly if in its relations to customers a branch functions as a separate bank, notices and orders with respect to accounts of customers of the branch should be given at the branch. For example, whether a branch has notice sufficient to affect its status as a holder in due course of an item taken by it should depend upon what notice that branch has received with respect to the item. Similarly the receipt of a stop payment order at one branch should not be notice to another branch so as to impair the right of the second branch to be a holder in due course of the item, although in circumstances in which ordinary care requires the communication of a notice or order to the proper branch of a bank, such notice or order would be effective at such proper branch from the time it was or should have been received. See Section 1—201(27).

5. Whether a branch functions as a separate bank may vary depending upon the type of activity taking place and upon practices in the different states. If the activity is that of a payor bank paying items, a branch will usually function as a separate bank if it maintains its own deposit ledgers. Similarly whether a branch functions as a separate bank in the collection of items usually depends also on whether it maintains its own deposit ledgers. Conversely, if a particular bank having branches does all of its bookkeeping at its head office, the branches of that bank do not usually function as separate banks either in the payment or collection of items.

On the other hand, in its relations to customers a branch may function as a separate bank regardless of whether it maintains its own deposit ledgers. Checks may be drawn on a particular branch and notices and stop orders delivered to that branch even though all the bookkeeping is done at the head office or another branch.

Where the words "maintaining its own deposit ledgers" are bracketed, the option is given to each state enacting the Code to include these words as a test of separateness. In those states where the maintenance by a branch of its own deposit ledgers will serve as a satisfactory standard, the bracketed words should be retained. In those states where these words will cause more problems than benefits, they may be deleted. Insofar as this latter rule allows extra time to banks maintaining branches where such extra time is not needed, it is not ideal. However, it has not been found possible to find a rule that will meet this problem and will work in all cases. Further, it is highly unlikely that large banks maintaining branches will needlessly take advantage of extra time under this rule.

Cross References:

Sections 3—504, 4—102(2).

Definitional Cross References:

"Bank". Section 1—201.
"Branch". Section 1—201.

§ 4—107. Time of Receipt of Items

(1) For the purpose of allowing time to process items, prove balances and make the necessary entries on its books to determine its position for the day, a bank may fix an afternoon hour of 2 P.M. or later as a cut-off hour for the handling of money and items and the making of entries on its books.

(2) Any item or deposit of money received on any day after a cut-off hour so fixed or after the close of the banking day may be treated as being received at the opening of the next banking day.

Official Comment

Prior Uniform Statutory Provision: None.

Purposes:

1. After an item has been received by a bank it goes through a series of processes varying with the type of item that it is. It moves from the teller's window, branch office, or mail desk at which it is received through settlement and proving departments until it is forwarded or presented to a clearing house or another bank, if it is a transit item, or until it reaches the bookkeeping department, if the bank receiving it is the payor bank. In addition, in order that the books of the bank always remain in balance while items are moving through it, the amount of each item is included in lists or proofs of debits or credits several times as it progresses through the bank. The running of proofs, the making of debit and credit entries in subsidiary and general ledgers and the striking of a general balance for each day requires a considerable amount of time. If these processes are to be completed on any particular day during normal working hours without the employment of night forces, a number of banks have found it necessary to establish a "cut-off hour" to allow time to obtain final figures to be incorporated into the bank's position for the day. Subsection (1) approves a cut-off hour of this type provided it is not earlier than 2 P. M. Subsection (2) provides that if such a cut-off hour is fixed, items received after the cut-off hour may be treated as being received at the opening of the next banking day. Where the number of items received either through the mail or over the counter tends to taper off radically as the afternoon hours progress, a 2 P. M. cut-off hour does not involve a large portion of the items received but at the same time permits a bank using such a cut-off hour to leave its doors open later in the afternoon without forcing into the evening the completion of its settling and proving process.

2. The alternative provision in Subsection (2) that items or deposits received after the close of the banking day may be treated as received at the opening of the next banking day is impor-

tant in cases where a bank closes at twelve or one o'clock, e. g., on a Saturday, but continues to receive some items by mail or over the counter if, for example, it opens Saturday evening for the limited purpose of receiving deposits and cashing checks.

Definitional Cross References:

"Afternoon". Section 4—104.

"Bank". Section 1—201.

"Banking day". Section 4—104.

"Item". Section 4—104.

"Money". Section 1—201.

§ 4—108. Delays

(1) Unless otherwise instructed, a collecting bank in a good faith effort to secure payment may, in the case of specific items and with or without the approval of any person involved, waive, modify or extend time limits imposed or permitted by this Act for a period not in excess of an additional banking day without discharge of secondary parties and without liability to its transferor or any prior party.

(2) Delay by a collecting bank or payor bank beyond time limits prescribed or permitted by this Act or by instructions is excused if caused by interruption of communication facilities, suspension of payments by another bank, war, emergency conditions or other circumstances beyond the control of the bank provided it exercises such diligence as the circumstances require.

Official Comment

Prior Uniform Statutory Provision: None.

Purposes:

1. Sections 4—202(2), 4—212, 4—301 and 4—302 prescribe various time limits for the handling of items. These are the limits of time within which a bank, in fulfilment of its obligation to exercise ordinary care, must handle items entrusted to it for collection or payment. Under Section 4—103 they may be varied by agreement or by Federal Reserve regulations or operating letters, clearing house rules, or the like.

2. Subsection (1) of this section permits a limited extension of these time limits in special cases. It permits collecting banks to grant, within a rather narrow field, an additional banking day and to do so with or without the approval of any interested party. Such one-day extension can only be granted in a good faith effort to secure payment and only with respect to specific items. It cannot be exercised if the customer instructs otherwise. Thus limited the escape provision should afford a limited degree of flexibility in special cases but should not interfere with the overall requirement and objective of speedy collections.

3. Notice that an extension granted under Subsection (1) is "without discharge of secondary parties". It therefore extends

also the times for presentment or payment, as the case may be, specified in Article 3. See Sections 3—503 and 3—506. Where this Article and Article 3 conflict, this Article controls. See Sections 3—103(2) and 4—102(1).

4. Subsection (2) is another escape clause from time limits. This clause operates not only with respect to time limits imposed by the article itself but also time limits imposed by special instructions, by agreement or by Federal Reserve regulations or operating letters, clearing house rules or the like. The latter time limits are "permitted" by the Code. This clause operates, however, only in the types of situation specified. Examples of these situations include blizzards, floods, or hurricanes, and other "Act of God" events or conditions, and wrecks or disasters, interfering with mails; suspension of payments by another bank; abnormal operating conditions such as substantial increased volume or substantial shortage of personnel during war or emergency situations. When delay is sought to be excused under this subsection the bank must "exercise such diligence as the circumstances require" and it has the burden of proof. See Section 4—202(2).

Cross References:

Sections 3—103(2), 3—503, 3—506, 4—102(1), 4—103, 4—104, 4—202(2), 4—212, 4—213, 4—301, 4—302.

Definitional Cross References:

"Bank". Section 1—201.

"Banking day". Section 4—104.

"Collecting bank". Section 4—105.

"Good faith". Section 1—201.

"Item". Section 4—104.

"Party". Section 1—201.

§ 4—109. Process of Posting

The "process of posting" means the usual procedure followed by a payor bank in determining to pay an item and in recording the payment including one or more of the following or other steps as determined by the bank:

(a) verification of any signature;

(b) ascertaining that sufficient funds are available;

(c) affixing a "paid" or other stamp;

(d) entering a charge or entry to a customer's account;

(e) correcting or reversing an entry or erroneous action with respect to the item.

Added 1962.

Official Comment

Prior Uniform Statutory Provisions: None.

Purposes:

Completion of the "process of posting" is one of the measuring points for determining when an item is finally paid (subsection (1) (c) of Section 4—213) and when knowledge, notice, stop order, legal process and set-off come too late to affect a payor bank's right or duty to pay an item (subsection (1) (d) of Section 4—303). This Section defines what is meant by the "process of posting". It is the "usual procedure followed by a payor bank in determining to pay an item and in recording the payment . . .". It involves the two basic elements of some decision to pay and some recording of the payment with a listing of some of the typical steps that might be involved. Procedures followed by banks in determining to pay an item and in recording the payment vary. Examples of some of these procedures will illustrate what is meant by completion of the "process of posting".

Example 1. A payor bank receives an item through the clearing on Monday morning. It is sorted under the name of the customer on Monday and under deferred posting routines (Section 4—301) reaches the bookkeeper for that customer on Tuesday morning. The bookkeeper examines the signature, verifies there are sufficient funds and decides at 11 a. m. on Tuesday to pay the item. A debit entry for or including the amount of the item is entered in the customer's account at 12 noon on Tuesday. The process of posting is completed at 12 noon on Tuesday.

Example 2. A payor bank with branches receives an item through the clearing on Monday morning. One branch does all the bookkeeping for itself and nine other branches. The item is sent to that branch and a provisional debit is entered to the customer's account for the amount of the item on Monday. After this entry is made the item is sent to the branch where the customer transacts business and at this branch a clerk verifies the signature on Tuesday, e. g. at 12 noon. If the clerk determines the signature is valid and makes a decision to pay, the process of posting is completed at 12 noon on Tuesday because there has been both a charge to the customer's account and a determination to pay. If, however, the clerk determines the signature is not valid or that the item should not be paid for some other reason, the item is then returned to the presenting bank through the clearing house and an offsetting credit entry is made in the customer's account by the bookkeeping branch. In this case there has been no determination to pay the item, no completion of the process of posting and no payment of the item.

Example 3. A payor bank receives in the mail on Monday an item drawn upon it. The item is sorted and otherwise processed on Monday and during Monday night is provisionally recorded on tape by an electronic computer as charged to the customer's account. On Tuesday a clerk examines the signature on the item and makes other checks to determine finally whether the item should be paid. If the clerk determines the signature is valid and makes a decision to pay and all processing of this item is complete, e. g., at 12 noon on Tuesday, the "process of posting" is completed at that time. If, however, the clerk determines the signature is not valid or that the item should not be paid for some other reason, the item is returned to the presenting bank and in the regular Tuesday night run of the computer the debit to the customer's account for the item is reversed or an offsetting credit entry is made. In this case, as in Example 2, there has been no determination to pay the item, no completion of the process of posting and no payment of the item.

Cross References:

Sections 4—213(1) (c), 4—303 (1) (d).

Definitional Cross References:

"Account". Section 4—104(1) (a).

"Customer". Section 4—104 (1) (e).

"Item". Section 4—104(1) (g).

"Payor bank". Section 4—105 (b).

PART 2

COLLECTION OF ITEMS: DEPOSITARY AND COLLECTING BANKS

§ 4—201. Presumption and Duration of Agency Status of Collecting Banks and Provisional Status of Credits; Applicability of Article; Item Indorsed "Pay Any Bank"

(1) Unless a contrary intent clearly appears and prior to the time that a settlement given by a collecting bank for an item is or becomes final (subsection (3) of Section 4—211 and Sections 4—212 and 4—213) the bank is an agent or sub-agent of the owner of the item and any settlement given for the item is provisional. This provision applies regardless of the form of indorsement or lack of indorsement and even though credit given for the item is subject to immediate withdrawal as of right or is in fact withdrawn; but the continuance of ownership of an item by its owner and any rights of the owner to proceeds of the item are subject to rights of a collecting bank such as those resulting from outstanding advances on the item and valid rights of setoff. When an item is handled by banks for purposes of presentment, payment and collection, the relevant provisions of this Article apply even though action of parties clearly establishes that a particular bank has purchased the item and is the owner of it.

(2) After an item has been indorsed with the words "pay any bank" or the like, only a bank may acquire the rights of a holder

(a) until the item has been returned to the customer initiating collection; or

(b) until the item has been specially indorsed by a bank to a person who is not a bank.

Official Comment

Prior Uniform Statutory Provision: None; but see Sections 2 and 4 of the American Bankers Association Bank Collection Code.

Purposes:

1. This section states certain basic rules and presumptions of the bank collection process. One basic rule, appearing in the last sentence of subsection (1), is that, to the extent applicable, the provisions of the Article govern without regard to whether a bank handling an item owns the item or is an agent for collection. Historically, much time has been spent and effort expended in determining or attempting to determine whether a bank was a purchaser of an item or merely an agent for collection. See discussion of this subject and cases cited in 11 A.L.R. 1043, 16 A.L.R. 1084, 42 A.L.R. 492, 68 A.L.R. 725, 99 A.L.R. 486. See also Section 4 of the American Bankers Association Bank Collection Code. The general approach of Article 4, similar to that of other articles, is to provide, within reasonable limits, rules or answers to major problems known to exist in the bank collection process without regard to questions of status and ownership but to keep general principles such as status and ownership available to cover residual areas not covered by specific rules. In line with this approach, the last sentence of subsection (1) says in effect that Article 4 applies to practically every item moving through banks for the purpose of presentment, payment or collection.

2. Within this general rule of broad coverage, the first two sentences of subsection (1) state a rule of status in terms of a strong presumption. "Unless a contrary intent clearly appears" the status of a collecting bank is that of an agent or sub-agent for the owner of the item. Although as indicated in Comment 1 it is much less important under Article 4 to determine status than has been the case heretofore, such status may have importance in some residual areas not covered by specific rules. Further, where status has been considered so important in the past, to omit all reference to it might cause confusion. The presumption of agency "applies regardless of the form of indorsement or lack of indorsement and even though credit given for the item is subject to immediate withdrawal as of right or is in fact withdrawn". Thus questions heretofore litigated as to whether ordinary indorsements "for deposit", "for collection" or in blank have the effect of creating an agency status or a purchase, no longer have significance in varying the prima facie rule of agency. Similarly, the nature of the credit given for an item or whether it is subject to immediate withdrawal as of right or is in fact withdrawn, do not re-

but the general presumption. See A.L.R. references supra in Comment 1.

A contrary intent can rebut the presumption but this must be clear. An example of a clear contrary intent would be if collateral papers established or the item bore a legend stating that the item was sold absolutely to the depositary bank.

3. The prima facie agency status of collecting banks is consistent with prevailing law and practice today. Section 2 of the American Bankers Association Bank Collection Code so provides. Legends on deposit tickets, collection letters and acknowledgments of items and Federal Reserve operating letters consistently so provide. The status is consistent with rights of chargeback (Section 4—212 and Section 11 of the ABA Code) and risk of loss in the event of insolvency (Section 4—214 and Section 13 of the ABA Code).

4. Affirmative statement of a prima facie agency status for collecting banks requires certain limitations and qualifications. Under current practices substantially all bank collections sooner or later merge into bank credits, at least if collection is effected. Usually, this takes place within a few days of the initiation of collection. An intermediary bank receives final collection and evidences the result of its collection by a "credit" on its books to the depositary bank. The depositary bank evidences the results of its collection by a "credit" in the account of its customer. As used in these instances the term "credit" clearly indicates a debtor-creditor relationship. At some stage in the bank collection process the agency status of a collecting bank changes to that of debtor, a debtor of its customer. Usually at about the same time it also becomes a creditor for the amount of the item, a creditor of some intermediary, payor or other bank. Thus the collection is completed, all agency aspects are terminated and the identity of the item has become completely merged in bank accounts, that of the customer with the depositary bank and that of one bank with another.

Although Section 4—213(1) provides that an item is finally paid when the payor bank takes certain action with respect to the item such final payment of the item may or may not result in the simultaneous *final settlement* for the item in the case of all prior parties. If a series of provisional debits and credits for the item have been entered in accounts between banks, the final payment of the item by the payor bank may result in the automatic firming up of all these provisional debits and credits under Section 4—213 (2), and the consequent receipt of final settlement for the item by each collecting bank and the customer of the depositary bank simultaneously with such action of the payor bank. However, if the payor bank or some intermediary bank accounts for the item with a remittance draft, the next prior bank usually does not receive final settlement for the item until such remittance draft finally clears. See Section 4—211(3) (a). The first sentence of subsection (1) provides that the agency status of a collecting bank (whether intermediary or depositary) continues until the settlement *given by it for the item* is or becomes final, referring to Sections 4—211(3), 4—212, and 4—213. In the case of the series of provisional credits covered by Section 4—213(2), this could be simultaneously with the final payment of the item by the payor bank. In cases where remittance drafts are used or in straight non-cash collections, this would not be until the times specified in Sections 4—211(3) and 4—213(3).

A number of practical results flow from this rule continuing the agency status of a collecting bank until its settlement for the item is or becomes final, some of which are specifically set forth in this Article. One is that risk of loss continues in the owner of the item rather than the agent bank. See Section 4—212. Offsetting rights favorable to the owner are that pending such final settlement, the owner has the preference rights of Section 4—214 and the direct rights of Section 4—302 against the payor bank. It also follows from this rule that the dollar limitations of Federal Deposit Insurance are measured by the claim of the owner of the item rather than that of the collecting bank.

5. In those cases where some period of time elapses between the final payment of the item by the payor bank and the time that the settlement of the collecting bank is or becomes final, e. g., where the payor bank or an intermediary bank accounts for the item with a remittance draft or in straight non-cash collections, the continuance of the agency status of the collecting bank necessarily carries with it the continuance of the owner's status as principal. The second sentence of subsection (1) provides that whatever rights the owner has to proceeds of the item are subject to the rights of collecting banks for outstanding advances on the item and other valid rights, if any. The rule provides a sound rule to govern cases of attempted attachment of proceeds of a non-cash item in the hands of the payor bank as property of the absent owner. If a collecting bank has made an advance on an item which is still outstanding, its right to obtain reimbursement for this advance should be superior to the rights of the owner to the proceeds or to the rights of a creditor of the owner. The phrase "other valid rights, if any" is broad enough to cover legitimate rights of set-off of accounts between banks without attempting to provide that all set-offs may be valid. An intentional crediting of proceeds of an item to the account of a prior bank known to be insolvent, for the purpose of acquiring a right of set-off, would not produce a valid set-off. See 8 Zollman, Banks and Banking (1936) Sec. 5443.

6. This section and Article 4 as a whole represent an intentional abandonment of the approach to bank collection problems appearing in Section 4 of the American Bankers Association Bank Collection Code. Where the tremendous volume of items handled makes impossible the examination by all banks of all indorsements on all items and where in fact this examination is not made, except perhaps by depositary banks, it is unrealistic

to base the rights and duties of all banks in the collection chain on variations in the form of indorsements. It is anomalous to provide throughout the ABA Code that the prima facie status of collecting banks is that of agent or sub-agent but in Section 4 to provide that subsequent holders (sub-agents) shall have the right to rely on the presumption that the bank of deposit (the primary agent) is the owner of the item. It is unrealistic, particularly in this background, to base rights and duties on status of agent or owner. This Section 4—201 makes the pertinent provisions of Article 4 applicable to substantially all items handled by banks for presentment, payment or collection, recognizes the prima facie status of most banks as agents, and then seeks to state appropriate limits and some attributes to the general rules and presumptions so expressed.

7. Subsection (2) protects the ownership rights with respect to an item indorsed "pay any bank or banker" or in similar terms of a customer initiating collection or of any bank acquiring a security interest under Section 4—208, in the event the item is subsequently acquired under improper circumstances by a person who is not a bank and transferred by that person to another person, whether or not a bank. Upon return to the customer initiating collection of an item so indorsed, the indorsement may be cancelled (Section 3—208). A bank holding an item so indorsed may transfer the item out of banking channels by special indorsement; however, under Section 4—103 (5), such bank would be liable to the owner of the item for any loss resulting therefrom if the transfer had been made in bad faith or with lack of ordinary care. If briefer and more simple forms of bank indorsements are developed under Section 4—206 (e. g., the use of bank transit numbers in lieu of present lengthy forms of bank indorsements), a depositary bank having the transit number "X100" could make subsection (2) operative by indorsements such as "Pay any bank—X100".

Cross References:

Sections 3—206, 3—208, 4—103, 4—206, 4—208, 4—212, 4—213, 4—214 and 4—302.

Definitional Cross References:

"Bank". Section 1—201.
"Collecting bank". Section 4—105.
"Customer". Section 4—104.
"Depositary bank". Section 4—105.
"Holder". Section 1—201.
"Item". Section 4—104.
"Indorsements". Sections 3—202, 3—204, 3—205 and 3—206.
"Person". Section 1—201.
"Settle". Section 4—104.

§ 4—202. Responsibility for Collection; When Action Seasonable

(1) A collecting bank must use ordinary care in

(a) presenting an item or sending it for presentment; and

(b) sending notice of dishonor or non-payment or returning an item other than a documentary draft to the bank's transferor [or directly to the depositary bank under subsection (2) of Section 4—212] (*see note to Section 4—212*) after learning that the item has not been paid or accepted, as the case may be; and

(c) settling for an item when the bank receives final settlement; and

(d) making or providing for any necessary protest; and

(e) notifying its transferor of any loss or delay in transit within a reasonable time after discovery thereof.

(2) A collecting bank taking proper action before its midnight deadline following receipt of an item, notice or payment acts seasonably; taking proper action within a reasonably longer time may be seasonable but the bank has the burden of so establishing.

(3) Subject to subsection (1) (a), a bank is not liable for the insolvency, neglect, misconduct, mistake or default of another bank or person or for loss or destruction of an item in transit or in the possession of others.

Official Comment

Prior Uniform Statutory Provision: None; but see Sections 5 and 6, American Bankers Association Bank Collection Code.

Purposes:

1. Subsection (1) states the basic responsibilities of a collecting bank. Of course, under Section 1—203 a collecting bank is subject to the standard requirement of good faith. By subsection (1) it must also use ordinarv care in the exercise of its basic collection tasks. By Section 4—103(1) neither requirement may be disclaimed.

2. If the bank makes presentment itself, subsection 1(a) requires ordinary care with respect both to the time and manner of presentment. (Sections 3—503, 3—504, 4—210.) If it forwards the item to be presented the subsection requires ordinary care with respect to routing (Section 4—204), and also in the selection of intermediary banks or other agents.

3. Subsection (1) describes *types* of basic action with respect to which a collecting bank must use ordinary care. Subsection (2) deals with the *time* for taking action. It first prescribes the general standard for seasonable action, namely, for items received on Monday, proper action (such as forwarding or presenting) on Monday or Tuesday is seasonable. Although under current "production line" operations banks customarily move items along on regular schedules substantially briefer than two days, the subsection states an outside time within which a bank may know it has acted seasonably. To provide flexibility from this standard norm, the subsection further states that action within

a reasonably longer time may be seasonable but the bank has the burden of proof. In the case of time items, action after the midnight deadline, but sufficiently in advance of maturity for proper presentation, is a clear example of a "reasonably longer time" that is seasonable. The standard of requiring action not later than Tuesday in the case of Monday items is also subject to possibilities of variation under the general provisions of Section 4—103, or under the special provisions regarding time of receipt of items (Section 4—107), and regarding delays (Section 4—108). This subsection (2) deals only with collecting banks. The time limits applicable to payor banks appear in Sections 4—301 and 4—302.

4. At common law the so-called New York collection rule subjected the initial collecting bank to liability for the actions of subsequent banks in the collection chain; the so-called Massachusetts rule was that each bank, subject to the duty of selecting proper intermediaries, was liable only for its own negligence. Subsection (3) adopts the Massachusetts rule. But since this is stated to be subject to subsection (1) (a) a collecting bank remains responsible for using ordinary care in selecting properly qualified intermediary banks and agents and in giving proper instructions to them.

Cross References:

Sections 1—203, 4—103, 4—107, 4—108, 4—301, and 4—302.

Definitional Cross References:

"Collecting bank". Section 4—105.

"Depositary bank". Section 4—105.

"Documentary draft". Section 4—104.

"Item". Section 4—104.

"Midnight deadline". Section 4—104.

"Presentment". Article 3, Part 5.

"Protest". Section 3—509.

§ 4—203. Effect of Instructions

Subject to the provisions of Article 3 concerning conversion of instruments (Section 3—419) and the provisions of both Article 3 and this Article concerning restrictive indorsements only a collecting bank's transferor can give instructions which affect the bank or constitute notice to it and a collecting bank is not liable to prior parties for any action taken pursuant to such instructions or in accordance with any agreement with its transferor.

Official Comment

Prior Uniform Statutory Provision: None; but see Section 2 of the American Bankers Association Bank Collection Code.

Purposes:

This Section adopts a "chain of command" theory which renders it unnecessary for an intermediary or collecting bank to determine whether its transferor is "authorized" to give the instructions. Equally the bank is not put on notice of any "revocation of authority" or "lack of authority" by notice received from any other person. The desirability of speed in the collection process and the fact that, by reason of advances made, the transferor may have the paramount interest in the item requires the rule.

The Section is made subject to the provisions of Article 3 concerning conversion of instruments (Section 3—419) and other provisions of Article 3 and this Article concerning restrictive indorsements (Sections 3—205, 3—206, 3—419, 3—603, 4—205). Of course instructions from or an agreement with its transferor does not relieve a collecting bank of its general obligation to exercise good faith and ordinary care. See Section 4—103(1). If in any particular case a bank has exercised good faith and ordinary care and is relieved of responsibility by reason of instructions of or an agreement with its transferor, the owner of the item may still have a remedy for loss against the transferor (another bank) if such transferor has given wrongful instructions.

The rules of the Section are applied only to collecting banks. Payor banks always have the problem of making proper payment of an item; whether such payment is proper should be based upon all of the rules of Articles 3 and 4 and all of the facts of any particular case, and should not be dependent exclusively upon instructions from or an agreement with a person presenting the item.

Cross References:

Sections 3—205, 3—206, 3—419, 3—603, 4—103(1) and 4—205.

Definitional Cross References:

"Collecting bank". Section 4—105.

"Restrictive indorsement". Section 3—205.

§ 4—204. Methods of Sending and Presenting; Sending Direct to Payor Bank

(1) A collecting bank must send items by reasonably prompt method taking into consideration any relevant instructions, the nature of the item, the number of such items on hand, and the cost of collection involved and the method generally used by it or others to present such items.

(2) A collecting bank may send

(a) any item direct to the payor bank;

(b) any item to any non-bank payor if authorized by its transferor; and

(c) any item other than documentary drafts to any non-bank payor, if authorized by Federal Reserve regulation or operating letter, clearing house rule or the like.

(3) Presentment may be made by a presenting bank at a place where the payor bank has requested that presentment be made. As amended 1962.

Official Comment

Prior Uniform Statutory Provision: None; but see Section 6, American Bankers Association Bank Collection Code.

Purposes:

1. Subsection (1) prescribes the general standards applicable to proper sending or forwarding of items. Because of the many types of methods available and the desirability of preserving flexibility any attempt to prescribe limited or precise methods is avoided.

2. Subsection (2) (a) codifies the practice of direct mail, express, messenger or like presentment to payor banks. The practice is now country-wide and is justified by the need for speed, the general responsibility of banks, Federal Deposit Insurance protection and other reasons.

3. Full approval of the practice of direct sending is limited to cases where a bank is a payor. Where non-bank drawees or payors may be of unknown responsibility, substantial risks may be attached to placing in their hands the instruments calling for payments from them. This is obviously so in the case of documentary drafts. However, in some cities practices have long existed under clearing house procedures to forward certain types of items to certain non-bank payors. Examples include insurance loss drafts drawn by field agents on home offices. For the purpose of leaving the door open to legitimate practices of this kind, subsection (2) (c) affirmatively approves direct sending of any item other than documentary drafts to any non-bank payor, if authorized by Federal Reserve regulation or operating letter, clearing house rule or the like.

On the other hand subsection (2) (b) approves sending any item direct to a non-bank payor if authorized by a collecting bank's transferor. This permits special instructions or agreements out of the norm and is consistent with the "chain of command" theory of Section 4—203. However, if a transferor other than the owner of the item, e. g., a prior collecting bank, authorizes a direct sending to a non-bank payor, such transferor assumes responsibility for the propriety or impropriety of such authorization.

4. Section 3—504 states how presentment is made and subsection (2) of that Section affirmatively approves three specific methods by which presentment may be made. The methods so specified are permissive and do not foreclose other possible methods. However, in view of the substantial increase in recent years of presentment at centralized bookkeeping centers and electronic processing centers maintained or used by payor banks, many of which are at locations other than the banks themselves, subsection (3) specifically approves presentment by a presenting bank at any place requested by the payor

bank. [This paragraph was added in 1962].

Cross References:

Sections 3—504, 4—501 and 4—502.

Definitional Cross References:

"Collecting bank". Section 4—105.

"Documentary draft". Section 4—104.

"Item". Section 4—104.

"Payor bank". Section 4—105.

"Presenting bank". Section 4—105.

§ 4—205. Supplying Missing Indorsement; No Notice from Prior Indorsement

(1) A depositary bank which has taken an item for collection may supply any indorsement of the customer which is necessary to title unless the item contains the words "payee's indorsement required" or the like. In the absence of such a requirement a statement placed on the item by the depositary bank to the effect that the item was deposited by a customer or credited to his account is effective as the customer's indorsement.

(2) An intermediary bank, or payor bank which is not a depositary bank, is neither given notice nor otherwise affected by a restrictive indorsement of any person except the bank's immediate transferor.

Official Comment

Prior Uniform Statutory Provision: None.

Purposes:

1. Subsection (1) is designed to speed up collections by eliminating any necessity to return to a non-bank depositor any items he may have failed to indorse.

2. For the purpose of permitting items to move rapidly through banking channels, intermediary banks and payor banks which are not also depositary banks are permitted to ignore restrictive indorsements of any person except the bank's immediate transferor. However, depositary banks may not so ignore restrictive indorsements. If an owner of an item indorses it "for deposit" or "for collection" he usually does so in the belief such indorsement will guard against further negotiation of the item to a holder in due course by a finder or a thief. This belief is reasonably justified if at least one bank in any chain of banks collecting the item has a responsibility to act consistently with the indorsement.

Cross References:

Sections 3—205, 3—206, 3—419, 3—603 and 4—203.

Definitional Cross References:

"Collecting bank." Section 4—105.

"Customer." Section 4—104.

"Depositary bank". Section 4—105.

"Intermediary bank." Section 4—105.

"Item." Section 4—104.

"Payor bank." Section 4—105.

"Restrictive indorsement." Section 3—205.

§ 4—206. Transfer Between Banks

Any agreed method which identifies the transferor bank is sufficient for the item's further transfer to another bank.

Official Comment

Prior Uniform Statutory Provision: None.

Purposes:

This section is designed to permit the simplest possible form of transfer from one bank to another, once an item gets in the bank collection chain, provided only identity of the transferor bank is preserved. This is important for tracing purposes and if recourse is necessary. However, since the responsibilities of the various banks appear in the Article it becomes unnecessary to have liability or responsibility depend on more formal indorsements. Simplicity in the form of transfer is conducive to speed. Where the transfer is between banks this section takes the place of the more formal requirements of Section 3—202.

Cross References:

Sections 3—201, 3—202.

Definitional Cross References:

"Bank". Section 1—201.
"Item". Section 4—104.

§ 4—207. Warranties of Customer and Collecting Bank on Transfer or Presentment of Items; Time for Claims

(1) Each customer or collecting bank who obtains payment or acceptance of an item and each prior customer and collecting bank warrants to the payor bank or other payor who in good faith pays or accepts the item that

(a) he has a good title to the item or is authorized to obtain payment or acceptance on behalf of one who has a good title; and

(b) he has no knowledge that the signature of the maker or drawer is unauthorized, except that this warranty is not given by any customer or collecting bank that is a holder in due course and acts in good faith

(i) to a maker with respect to the maker's own signature; or

(ii) to a drawer with respect to the drawer's own signature, whether or not the drawer is also the drawee; or

(iii) to an acceptor of an item if the holder in due course took the item after the acceptance or obtained the acceptance without knowledge that the drawer's signature was unauthorized; and

(c) the item has not been materially altered, except that this warranty is not given by any customer or collecting bank that is a holder in due course and acts in good faith

(i) to the maker of a note; or

(ii) to the drawer of a draft whether or not the drawer is also the drawee; or

(iii) to the acceptor of an item with respect to an alteration made prior to the acceptance if the holder in due course took the item after the acceptance, even though the acceptance provided "payable as originally drawn" or equivalent terms; or

(iv) to the acceptor of an item with respect to an alteration made after the acceptance.

(2) Each customer and collecting bank who transfers an item and receives a settlement or other consideration for it warrants to his transferee and to any subsequent collecting bank who takes the item in good faith that

(a) he has a good title to the item or is authorized to obtain payment or acceptance on behalf of one who has a good title and the transfer is otherwise rightful; and

(b) all signatures are genuine or authorized; and

(c) the item has not been materially altered; and

(d) no defense of any party is good against him; and

(e) he has no knowledge of any insolvency proceeding instituted with respect to the maker or acceptor or the drawer of an unaccepted item.

In addition each customer and collecting bank so transferring an item and receiving a settlement or other consideration engages that upon dishonor and any necessary notice of dishonor and protest he will take up the item.

(3) The warranties and the engagement to honor set forth in the two preceding subsections arise notwithstanding the absence of indorsement or words of guaranty or warranty in the transfer or presentment and a collecting bank remains liable for their breach despite remittance to its transferor. Damages for breach of such warranties or engagement to honor shall not exceed the consideration received by the customer or collecting bank responsible plus finance charges and expenses related to the item, if any.

(4) Unless a claim for breach of warranty under this section is made within a reasonable time after the person claiming

learns of the breach, the person liable is discharged to the extent of any loss caused by the delay in making claim.

Official Comment

Prior Uniform Statutory Provision: None; but see American Bankers Association Bank Collection Code, Section 4.

Purposes:

1. Subject to certain exceptions peculiar to the bank collection process and except that they apply only to customers and collecting banks, the warranties and engagements to honor in this section are identical in substance with those provided in the Article on Commercial Paper (Article 3). See Sections 3—414, 3—417. For a more complete explanation of the purposes of these warranties and engagements see the Comments to Sections 3—414 and 3—417.

2. In addition to imposing upon customers and collecting banks the warranties and engagements imposed by the original Sections 65 and 66 of the Uniform Negotiable Instruments Law and those of Sections 3—414 and 3—417 of Article 3, with some variations, this Section 4—207 is intended to give the effect presently obtained in bank collections by the words "prior indorsements guaranteed" in collection transfers and presentments between banks. The warranties and engagements arise automatically as a part of the bank collection process. Receipt of a settlement or other consideration by a customer or collecting bank is a requirement but any settlement is sufficient regardless of whether the settlement is concurrent with the transfer, as in the case of a cash item, or delayed, as in the case of a non-cash straight collection item. Further, the warranties and engagements run with the item with the result that a collecting bank may sue a remote prior collecting bank or a remote customer and thus avoid multiplicity of suits. This section is also intended to make it clear that the so-called equitable defense of "payment over" does not apply to a collecting bank and that no statute of frauds provision will defeat recovery. Subsections (2) and (3) indicate that these results are intended notwithstanding the absence of indorsement or words of guarantee or warranty in a transfer or presentment. Consequently, if for purposes of simplification or the speeding up of the bank collection process, banks desire to cut down the length or size of indorsements (Section 4—206), they may do so and the standard warranties and engagements to honor still apply.

3. With respect to the exceptions to the warranties in favor of a holder in due course specified in sub-paragraphs (b) and (c) of subsection (1), collecting banks usually have holder in due course status (Sections 4—208, 4—209). However, if in any case there is a holder in due course but a subsequent collecting bank does not have holder in due course status (e. g., in a straight non-cash collection where no settlement of any kind is made until the bank itself receives final settlement) the bank still has the

benefit of the exceptions (if it acts in good faith) under the shelter provisions of Section 3—201. It is to be noted that these shelter provisions, by virtue of successive transfers, benefit not only the immediate transferee from a holder in due course but also subsequent transferees.

4. In this section as in Section 3—417, the (a), (b) and (c) warranties to transferees and collecting banks under subsection (2) are in general similar to the (a), (b) and (c) warranties to payors under subsection (1); but the warranties to payors are less inclusive because of exceptions reflecting the rule of Price v. Neal, 3 Burr. 1354 (1762), and related principles. See Comment to Section 3—417. Thus collecting banks are given not only all the warranties given to payors by subsection (1), without those exceptions, but also the (d) and (e) warranties of subsection (2).

5. The last sentence of subsection (3) provides that damages for breach of warranties or the engagement to honor shall not exceed the consideration received by the customer or collecting bank responsible "plus finance charges and expenses related to the item, if any". The "expenses" referred to in this phrase may be ordinary collecting expenses and in appropriate cases could also include such expenses as attorneys fees. "Finance charges" are also referred to because in some cases interest or a finance charge is charged by the collecting bank for the time that the bank's advance on the item is outstanding prior to receipt of proceeds of collection. An example of this type of case would be where a bank undertakes a foreign collection in South America or Europe and makes an advance on the item at the time of receipt but may not receive proceeds of the foreign collection for three months or more.

Cross References:

Sections 3—201, 3—414, 3—417, 3—418, 4—206, 4—208, 4—209 and 4—406.

Definitional Cross References:

"Collecting bank". Section 4—105.

"Customer". Section 4—104.

"Draft". Section 3—104.

"Genuine". Section 1—201.

"Good faith". Section 1—201.

"Holder". Section 1—201.

"Holder in due course". Section 3—302.

"Insolvency proceedings". Section 1—201.

"Item". Section 4—104.

"Party". Section 1—201.

"Payor bank". Section 4—105.

"Person". Section 1—201.

"Presentment". Section 3—504.

"Protest". Section 3—509.

"Unauthorized signature". Section 1—201.

§ 4—208. Security Interest of Collecting Bank in Items, Accompanying Documents and Proceeds

(1) A bank has a security interest in an item and any accompanying documents or the proceeds of either

(a) in case of an item deposited in an account to the extent to which credit given for the item has been withdrawn or applied;

(b) in case of an item for which it has given credit available for withdrawal as of right, to the extent of the credit given whether or not the credit is drawn upon and whether or not there is a right of charge-back; or

(c) if it makes an advance on or against the item.

(2) When credit which has been given for several items received at one time or pursuant to a single agreement is withdrawn or applied in part the security interest remains upon all the items, any accompanying documents or the proceeds of either. For the purpose of this section, credits first given are first withdrawn.

(3) Receipt by a collecting bank of a final settlement for an item is a realization on its security interest in the item, accompanying documents and proceeds. To the extent and so long as the bank does not receive final settlement for the item or give up possession of the item or accompanying documents for purposes other than collection, the security interest continues and is subject to the provisions of Article 9 except that

(a) no security agreement is necessary to make the security interest enforceable (subsection (1)(a) of Section 9—203); and

(b) no filing is required to perfect the security interest; and

(c) the security interest has priority over conflicting perfected security interests in the item, accompanying documents or proceeds.

Official Comment

Prior Uniform Statutory Provision: None; but see American Bankers Association Bank Collection Code, Section 2.

Purposes:

1. Subsection (1) states a rational rule for the interest of a bank in an item. The customer of the depositary bank is normally the owner of the item and the several collecting banks are his agents (Section 4—201). A collecting agent may properly make advances on the security of paper held by him for collection, and

when he does acquires at common law a possessory lien for his advances. Subsection (1) applies an analogous principle to a bank in the collection chain which extends credit on items in the course of collection. The bank has a security interest to the extent stated in this section. To the extent of its security interest it is a holder for value (Sections 3—303, 4—209) and a holder in due course if it satisfies the other requirements for that status (Section 3—302). Subsection (1) does not derogate from the banker's general common-law lien or right of set-off against indebtedness owing in deposit accounts. See Section 1—103. Rather subsection (1) specifically implements and extends the principle as a part of the bank collection process.

2. Subsection (2) spreads the security interest of the bank over all items in a single deposit or received under a single agreement and a single giving of credit. It also adopts the "first-in, first-out" rule.

3. Collection statistics establish that in excess of ninety-nine per cent of items handled for collection are in fact collected. The first sentence of subsection (3) reflects the fact that in such normal case the bank's security interest is self-liquidating. The remainder of the subsection correlates the security interest with the provisions of Article 9, particularly for use in the cases of non-collection where the security interest may be important.

Cross References:

Sections 3—302, 3—303, 4—201, 4—209, 9—203(1) (b) and 9—302.

Definitional Cross References:

"Account". Section 4—104.
"Agreement". Section 1—201.
"Bank". Section 1—201.
"Item". Section 4—104.
"Security interest". Section 1—201.
"Settlement". Section 4—104.

§ 4—209. When Bank Gives Value for Purposes of Holder in Due Course

For purposes of determining its status as a holder in due course, the bank has given value to the extent that it has a security interest in an item provided that the bank otherwise complies with the requirements of Section 3—302 on what constitutes a holder in due course.

Official Comment

Prior Uniform Statutory Provision: Negotiable Instruments Law, Section 27.

Purpose:

The section completes the thought of the previous section and makes clear that a security interest in an item is "value" for the purpose of determining the holder's status as a holder in due course. The provision is in accord with the prior law (N.I.L. Section 27) and with Article 3 (Section 3—303). The section does not prescribe a security interest under Section 4—208 as a test of "value" generally because the meaning of "value" under other Articles is adequately defined in Section 1—201.

Cross References:

Sections 1—201, 3—302, 3—303 and 4—208.

Definitional Cross References:

"Bank". Section 1—201.

"Holder in due course". Section 3—302.

"Item". Section 4—104.

"Security interest". Section 1—201.

§ 4—210. Presentment by Notice of Item Not Payable by, Through or at a Bank; Liability of Secondary Parties

(1) Unless otherwise instructed, a collecting bank may present an item not payable by, through or at a bank by sending to the party to accept or pay a written notice that the bank holds the item for acceptance or payment. The notice must be sent in time to be received on or before the day when presentment is due and the bank must meet any requirement of the party to accept or pay under Section 3—505 by the close of the bank's next banking day after it knows of the requirement.

(2) Where presentment is made by notice and neither honor nor request for compliance with a requirement under Section 3—505 is received by the close of business on the day after maturity or in the case of demand items by the close of business on the third banking day after notice was sent, the presenting bank may treat the item as dishonored and charge any secondary party by sending him notice of the facts.

Official Comment

Prior Uniform Statutory Provision: None.

Purposes:

1. This section codifies a practice extensively followed in presentation of trade acceptances and documentary and other drafts drawn on non-bank payors. It imposes a duty on the payor to respond to the notice of the item if the item is not to be considered dishonored. Notice of such a dishonor charges parties secondarily liable. Presentment under this Secticn is good presentment under Article 3. See Section 3—504(5).

2. A drawee not receiving notice is not, of course, liable to the drawer for wrongful dishonor.

3. A bank so presenting an instrument must be sufficiently close to the drawee to be able to exhibit the instrument on the day it is requested to do so or the next business day at the latest.

Cross References:

Sections 3—501 through 3—508, 4—501 and 4—502.

Definitional Cross References:

"Acceptance". Section 3—410.

"Banking day". Section 4—104.

"Collecting bank". Section 4—105.
"Item". Section 4—104.
"Party". Section 1—201.
"Presentment". Section 3—504.
"Secondary party". Section 3—102.
"Send". Section 1—201.

§ 4—211. Media of Remittance; Provisional and Final Settlement in Remittance Cases

(1) A collecting bank may take in settlement of an item

(a) a check of the remitting bank or of another bank on any bank except the remitting bank; or

(b) a cashier's check or similar primary obligation of a remitting bank which is a member of or clears through a member of the same clearing house or group as the collecting bank; or

(c) appropriate authority to charge an account of the remitting bank or of another bank with the collecting bank; or

(d) if the item is drawn upon or payable by a person other than a bank, a cashier's check, certified check or other bank check or obligation.

(2) If before its midnight deadline the collecting bank properly dishonors a remittance check or authorization to charge on itself or presents or forwards for collection a remittance instrument of or on another bank which is of a kind approved by subsection (1) or has not been authorized by it, the collecting bank is not liable to prior parties in the event of the dishonor of such check, instrument or authorization.

(3) A settlement for an item by means of a remittance instrument or authorization to charge is or becomes a final settlement as to both the person making and the person receiving the settlement

(a) if the remittance instrument or authorization to charge is of a kind approved by subsection (1) or has not been authorized by the person receiving the settlement and in either case the person receiving the settlement acts seasonably before its midnight deadline in presenting, forwarding for collection or paying the instrument or authorization,—at the time the remittance instrument or authorization is finally paid by the payor by which it is payable;

(b) if the person receiving the settlement has authorized remittance by a non-bank check or obligation or by a cashier's check or similar primary obligation of or a check upon the payor or other remitting bank which is not of a kind approved by subsection (1) (b),—at the time of the receipt of such remittance check or obligation; or

(c) if in a case not covered by sub-paragraphs (a) or (b) the person receiving the settlement fails to seasonably present, forward for collection, pay or return a remittance instrument or authorization to it to charge before its midnight deadline,—at such midnight deadline.

Official Comment

Prior Uniform Statutory Provision: None; but see Sections 9 and 10, American Bankers Association Bank Collection Code.

Purposes:

1. Subsection (1) states various types of remittance instruments and authorities to charge which may be received by a collecting bank in a settlement for an item, without the collecting bank being responsible if such form of remittance is not itself paid. The action of the collecting bank in receiving these provisional forms of remittance is approved and the risk that they are not paid is placed on the owner of the item, and not on the collecting bank. Justification for these results lies in the fact that with the tremendous volume of items collected it is simply not mechanically feasible to remit or pay in money or other forms of technical "legal tender". Since it is not feasible for banks to perform their collection functions except with the use of these provisional remittances, they should not be penalized for acting in the only way they can act.

2. The first approved form of provisional remittance having these results is a check of the remitting bank or of another bank on any bank except the remitting bank (subsection (1) (a)). A check on the remitting bank itself is not approved because this would merely be substituting for the original item another item on the same payor.

3. A cashier's check or similar primary obligation of the remitting bank which is a member of or clears through a member of the same clearing house or group as the collecting bank is approved by subsection (1) (b) because this is just as speedy and effective a means of settlement through a clearing house as any other type of instrument or a check on another bank. On the other hand such cashier's checks or primary obligations are not approved for use, at the owner's risk, outside a single clearing house or clearing area because when so used they do not constitute a means of final settlement but merely substitute one item on the remitting bank for another one on the same bank. To the remitting bank they may have benefit in maintaining "float" or having the use of money even though drawn against, but this is

not looked upon as sound practice.

4. Subsection (1) (d) recognizes and approves the general and consistent practice of collecting banks to accept cashier's checks, certified checks or other bank checks or obligations as a proper means of remittance from non-bank payors, with the owner of the original item carrying the risk of non-payment of these bank instruments rather than the collecting bank, to the extent there is any risk. Here again this rule and practice is justified by the fact that payment in money for all practical purposes is no longer feasible and consequently is not used except in rare instances. Subsection (1) (d) recognizes the standard medium that is used.

5. This section does not purport to deal with all kinds of settlements for items. It does not purport to deal with settlements for "cash items" (described in Comments to Section 4—212), settlements merely by debits and credits in accounts between banks (Section 4—213) or settlements through clearing houses. The section is limited to those situations where a collecting or payor bank or a non-bank payor receives an item and accounts for it by "remitting" or "sending back" something for the item, usually some form of a remittance instrument, order or authorization. Some specific rules are needed for remittance cases because of time required to process the remittance instrument.

Failure to mention in subsection (1) entries in accounts between banks and clearing house settlements carries no implication of impropriety of these types of provisional or final settlement. Approval of these means of settlement is evidenced by the definition of "settle" in Section 4—104(j), provision for charge-back and refund in Section 4—212, and provisions regarding settlements becoming final (Section 4—213). Further, the specific listing in subsection (1) of certain usual types of remittances does not imply that all other types of remittances are improper (Section 4—103(4)).

6. Subsection (2) provides that if a remittance is one of the kinds approved by subsection (1) and the collecting bank receiving the item acts seasonably in handling it before the bank's midnight deadline, the bank is not liable to prior parties in the event of dishonor. The subsection also provides for an additional situation. If without any authorization whatsoever the payor or remitting bank or person remits with an improper remittance instrument, the collecting bank should not be penalized where it is without fault. Nevertheless, the owner of the item may not be served if the collecting bank rejects the improper instrument. In many cases the best course would be to collect the instrument as rapidly as possible. Subsection (2) provides that if this is done the collecting bank is not responsible in the event of dishonor.

7. Subsection (3) complements subsections (1) and (2) by providing when a settlement by means of a remittance instrument or authorization to charge becomes final. Subparagraph (a) provides that in situations speci-

fied in subsection (2) the settlement becomes final at the time the remittance instrument or authorization is finally paid by the payor by which it is payable. The standards determining this final payment are those prescribed in Section 4—213. Conversely, under subparagraph (b) if the person receiving the settlement has authorized remittance by certain specified media not approved by subsection (1) the settlement becomes final at the time of receipt of such check or obligation. In this event the person receiving the settlement assumes the risk that the remittance instrument is not itself paid. A prior course of dealing of receiving unapproved forms of remittances from the payor or remitting person in question would be the equivalent of an authorization and effective as such. Subparagraph (c) provides for most, if not all, remaining remittance situations. Here settlement becomes final at the midnight deadline of the person receiving the remittance.

Subsection (3) provides that the times of final settlement prescribed apply both to the person making and the person receiving the settlement. Further, by use of the term "person", these rules also apply to non-bank payors of items and non-bank customers for whom items are being collected, as well as to collecting and payor banks.

8. When settlement is by credit in an account with another bank Section 4—213 controls.

Cross Reference:

Section 4—213.

Definitional Cross References:

"Account". Section 4—104.
"Bank". Section 1—201.
"Clearing house". Section 4—104.
"Collecting bank". Section 4—105.
"Item". Section 4—104.
"Midnight deadline". Section 4—104.
"Money". Section 1—201.
"Payor bank." Section 4—105.
"Person". Section 1—201.
"Remitting bank". Section 4—105.
"Settle". Section 4—104.

§ 4—212. Right of Charge-Back or Refund

(1) If a collecting bank has made provisional settlement with its customer for an item and itself fails by reason of dishonor, suspension of payments by a bank or otherwise to receive a settlement for the item which is or becomes final, the bank may revoke the settlement given by it, charge back the amount of any credit given for the item to its customer's account or obtain refund from its customer whether or not it is able to return the items if by its midnight deadline or within a longer reasonable time after it learns the facts it returns the item or sends notification of the facts. These rights to revoke, charge-back and obtain refund terminate if and when a settlement for the item received by the bank is or becomes final (subsection (3) of Section 4—211 and subsections (2) and (3) of Section 4—213).

[(2) Within the time and manner prescribed by this section and Section 4—301, an intermediary or payor bank, as the case may be, may return an unpaid item directly to the depositary bank and may send for collection a draft on the depositary bank and obtain reimbursement. In such case, if the depositary bank has received provisional settlement for the item, it must reimburse the bank drawing the draft and any provisional credits for the item between banks shall become and remain final.]

> **Note:** *Direct returns is recognized as an innovation that is not yet established bank practice, and therefore, Paragraph 2 has been bracketed. Some lawyers have doubts whether it should be included in legislation or left to development by agreement.*

(3) A depositary bank which is also the payor may charge-back the amount of an item to its customer's account or obtain refund in accordance with the section governing return of an item received by a payor bank for credit on its books. (Section 4—301).

(4) The right to charge-back is not affected by

(a) prior use of the credit given for the item; or

(b) failure by any bank to exercise ordinary care with respect to the item but any bank so failing remains liable.

(5) A failure to charge-back or claim refund does not affect other rights of the bank against the customer or any other party.

(6) If credit is given in dollars as the equivalent of the value of an item payable in a foreign currency the dollar amount of any charge-back or refund shall be calculated on the basis of the buying sight rate for the foreign currency prevailing on the day when the person entitled to the charge-back or refund learns that it will not receive payment in ordinary course.

Official Comment

Prior Uniform Statutory Provision: None; but see Sections 2 and 11, American Bankers Association Bank Collection Code.

Purposes:

1. Under current bank practice, in a major portion of cases banks make provisional settlement for items when they are first received and then await subsequent determination of whether the item will be finally paid. This is the principal characteristic of what are referred to in banking parlance as "cash items". Statistically, this practice of settling provisionally first and then awaiting final payment is justified because more than ninety-nine per cent of such cash items are finally paid, with the

result that in this great preponderance of cases it becomes unnecessary for the banks making the provisional settlements to make any further entries. In due course the provisional settlements become final simply with the lapse of time. However, in those cases where the item being collected is not finally paid or where for various reasons the bank making the provisional settlement does not itself receive final payment, under the American Bankers Association Bank Collection Code, under Federal Reserve Regulations and operating letters and under various types of agreements between banks and between customers and banks, provision is made for the reversal of the provisional settlements, charge-back of provisional credits and the right to obtain refund. Subsection (1) codifies and simplifies the statement of these rights.

2. Various causes of a bank not receiving final payment, with the resulting right of charge-back or refund, are stated or suggested in subsection (1). These include dishonor of the original item; dishonor of a remittance instrument given for it; reversal of a provisional credit for the item; suspension of payments by another bank. The causes stated are illustrative; the right of charge-back or refund is stated to exist whether the failure to receive final payment in ordinary course arises through one of them "or otherwise".

3. The right of charge-back or refund exists if a collecting bank has made a provisional settlement for an item with its customer but terminates if and when a settlement received by the bank for the item is or becomes final. If the bank fails to receive such a final settlement the right of charge-back or refund must be exercised promptly after the bank learns the facts. The right exists (if so promptly exercised) whether or not the bank is able to return the item.

4. Subsection (2) is an affirmative provision for so-called "direct returns". This is a new practice that is currently in the process of developing in a few sections of the country. Its purpose is to speed up the return of unpaid items by avoiding handling by one or more intermediate banks. The subsection is bracketed because the practice is not yet well established and some bankers and bank lawyers would prefer to let the practice develop by agreement. The contention is made that substantive rights between banks may be affected, e. g. available set-offs, but proponents contend advantages of direct returns outweigh possible detriments. However, if the subsection were omitted, the election to use direct returns would be on the depositary bank and it would probably be necessary for that bank to specifically authorize direct returns with each outgoing letter. This is a cumbersome way of meeting the problem. If the subsection is retained the payor bank, unless it has been specifically directed otherwise, will have the right to make the decision whether it will return an unpaid item directly. Since the subsection is permissive and its inclusion tends toward greater flexibility, its retention is recommended.

5. The rule of subsection (4) relating to charge-back (as distinguished from claim for refund) applies irrespective of the cause of the nonpayment, and of the person ultimately liable for nonpayment. Thus charge-back is permitted even where nonpayment results from the depositary bank's own negligence. Any other rule would result in litigation based upon a claim for wrongful dishonor of other checks of the customer, with potential damages far in excess of the amount of the item. Any other rule would require a bank to determine difficult questions of fact. The customer's protection is found in the general obligation of good faith (Sections 1—203 and 4—103). If bad faith is established the customer's recovery "includes other damages, if any, suffered by the party as a proximate consequence" (Section 4—103(5); see also Section 4—402).

6. It is clear that the charge-back does not relieve the bank from any liability for failure to exercise ordinary care in handling the item. The measure of damages for such failure is stated in Section 4—103(5).

7. Subsection (6) states a rule fixing the time for determining the rate of exchange if there is a charge-back or refund of a credit given in dollars for an item payable in a foreign currency. Compare Section 3—107(2). Fixing such a rule is desirable to avoid disputes. If in any case the parties wish to fix a different time for determining the rate of exchange, they may do so by agreement.

Cross References:

Sections 1—203, 3—107, 4—103, 4—211(3), 4—213(2) and (3), 4—402.

Definitional Cross References:

"Account". Section 4—104.
"Collecting bank". Section 4—105.
"Customer". Section 4—104.
"Depositary bank". Section 4—105.
"Intermediary bank". Section 4—105.
"Item". Section 4—104.
"Midnight deadline". Section 4—104.
"Payor bank". Section 4—105.
"Send". Section 1—201.
"Settlement". Section 4—104.
"Suspension of payment". Section 4—104.

§ 4—213. Final Payment of Item by Payor Bank; When Provisional Debits and Credits Become Final; When Certain Credits Become Available for Withdrawal

(1) An item is finally paid by a payor bank when the bank has done any of the following, whichever happens first:

(a) paid the item in cash; or

(b) settled for the item without reserving a right to revoke the settlement and without having such right under statute, clearing house rule or agreement; or

(c) completed the process of posting the item to the indicated account of the drawer, maker or other person to be charged therewith; or

(d) made a provisional settlement for the item and failed to revoke the settlement in the time and manner permitted by statute, clearing house rule or agreement.

Upon a final payment under subparagraphs (b), (c) or (d) the payor bank shall be accountable for the amount of the item.

(2) If provisional settlement for an item between the presenting and payor banks is made through a clearing house or by debits or credits in an account between them, then to the extent that provisional debits or credits for the item are entered in accounts between the presenting and payor banks or between the presenting and successive prior collecting banks seriatim, they become final upon final payment of the item by the payor bank.

(3) If a collecting bank receives a settlement for an item which is or becomes final (subsection (3) of Section 4—211, subsection (2) of Section 4—213) the bank is accountable to its customer for the amount of the item and any provisional credit given for the item in an account with its customer becomes final.

(4) Subject to any right of the bank to apply the credit to an obligation of the customer, credit given by a bank for an item in an account with its customer becomes available for withdrawal as of right

(a) in any case where the bank has received a provisional settlement for the item,—when such settlement becomes final and the bank has had a reasonable time to learn that the settlement is final;

(b) in any case where the bank is both a depositary bank and a payor bank and the item is finally paid,—at the opening of the bank's second banking day following receipt of the item.

(5) A deposit of money in a bank is final when made but, subject to any right of the bank to apply the deposit to an obligation of the customer, the deposit becomes available for withdrawal as of right at the opening of the bank's next banking day following receipt of the deposit.

Official Comment

Prior Uniform Statutory Provisions: None; but see Section 11, American Bankers Association Bank Collection Code.

Purposes:

1. By the definition and use of the term "settle" (Section 4—104 (j)) this Article recognizes that

various debits or credits, remittances, settlements or payments given for an item may be either provisional or final, that settlements sometimes are provisional and sometimes are final and sometimes are provisional for awhile but later become final. Subsection (1) of Section 4—213 defines when settlement for an item or other action with respect to it constitutes final payment.

Final payment of an item is important for a number of reasons. It is one of several factors determining the relative priorities between items and notices, stop-orders, legal process and set-offs (Section 4—303). It is the "end of the line" in the collection process and the "turn around" point commencing the return flow of proceeds. It is the point at which many provisional settlements become final. See Section 4—213(2). Final payment of an item by the payor bank fixes preferential rights under Section 4—214(1) and (2).

2. If an item being collected moves through several states, e. g., is deposited for collection in California, moves through two or three California banks to the Federal Reserve Bank of San Francisco, to the Federal Reserve Bank of Boston, to a payor bank in Maine, the collection process involves the eastward journey of the item from California to Maine and the westward journey of the proceeds from Maine to California. Subsection (1) adopts the basic policy that final payment occurs at some point in the processing of the item by the payor bank. This policy recognizes that final payment does not take place, in such hypothetical case, on the journey of the item eastward. It also adopts the view that neither does final payment occur on the journey westward because what in fact is journeying westward are *proceeds* of the item. Because the true tests of final payment are the same in all cases and to avoid the confusion resulting from variable standards, the rule basing final payment exclusively on action of the payor bank is not affected by whether payment is made by a remittance draft or whether such draft is itself paid. Consequently, subsection (1) rejects those cases which base time of payment of the item in remittance cases on whether the remittance draft was *accepted* by the presenting bank; Page v. Holmes-Darst Coal Co., 269 Mich. 159, 256 N.W. 840 (1934); Tobiason v. First State Bank of Ashby, 173 Minn. 533, 217 N.W. 934 (1928); Bohlig v. First Nat. Bank in Wadena, 233 Minn. 523, 48 N.W.2d 445 (1951); Dewey v. Margolis & Brooks, 195 N.C. 307, 142 S.E. 22 (1928); Texas Electric Service Co. v. Clark, 47 S.W.2d 483 (Tex.Civ. App.1932); cf. Ellis Way Drug Co. v. McLean, 176 Miss. 830, 170 So. 288 (1936); 2 Paton's Digest 1332; or whether the remittance draft was itself *paid*; Cleve v. Craven Chemical Co., 18 F.2d 711 (4th Cir. 1927); Holdingford Milling Co. v. Hillman Farmers' Cooperative Creamery, 181 Minn. 212, 231 N.W. 928 (1930); or upon an election of a collecting bank under Section 11 of the American Bankers Association Bank Collection Code; United States Pipe & Foundry Co. v. City of Hornell, 146 Misc. 812, 263 N.Y.S. 89 (1933); Jones v. Board of Education, 242 App.Div. 17,

272 N.Y.S. 5 (1934); Matter of State Bank of Binghamton, 156 Misc. 353, 281 N.Y.S. 706 (1935); cf. Malcolm, Inc. v. Burlington City Loan & Trust Co., 115 N.J. Eq. 227, 170 A. 32 (1934). Of course, the time of payment of the remittance draft will be governed by subsection (1) but payment or nonpayment of the remittance draft will not change the time of payment of the original item.

3. In fixing the point of time within the payor bank when an item is finally paid, subsection (1) recognizes and is framed on the basis that in a payor bank an item goes through a series of processes before its handling is completed. The item is received first from the clearing house or over the counter or through the mail. When received over the counter, the bank may receipt for it in some way by making a notation in the customer's passbook or by receipting a duplicate deposit slip. After the initial receipt the item moves to the sorting and proving departments. When sorted and proved it may be photographed. Still later it moves to the bookkeeping department where it is examined for form and signature and compared against the ledger account of the customer to whom it is to be charged. If it is in good form and there are funds to cover it, it is posted to the drawer's account, either immediately or at a later time. If paid, it is so marked and filed with other items of the same customer. This process may take either a few hours or substantially all of the day of receipt and of the next banking day.

Within this period of processing by the payor bank subsection (1) first recognizes two types of overt external acts constituting final payment. Traditionally and under various decisions payment in cash of an item by a payor bank has been considered final payment. Chambers v. Miller, 13 C.B.N.S. 125 (Eng.1862); Fidelity & Casualty Co. of New York v. Planenscheck, 200 Wis. 304, 309, 227 N.W. 387, 389, 71 A.L.R. 331 (1929); see Bellevue Bank of Allen Kimberly & Co. v. Security Nat. Bank of Sioux City, 168 Iowa 707, 712, 150 N.W. 1076, 1077 (1915); 1 Paton's Digest 1066. Subsection (1) (a) first recognizes and provides that payment of an item in cash by a payor bank is final payment.

4. Section 4–104(j) defines "settle" as meaning "to pay in cash, by clearing house settlement, in a charge or credit or by remittance, or otherwise as instructed. A settlement may be either provisional or final;" Subsection (1) (b) of Section 4—213 provides that an item is finally paid by a payor bank when the bank has "settled for the item without reserving a right to revoke the settlement and without having such right under statute, clearing house rule or agreement". Subsection (1) (b) provides in effect that if the payor bank finally settles for an item this constitutes final payment of the item. The subsection operates if nothing has occurred and no situation exists making the settlement provisional. If at the time of settlement the payor bank reserves a right to revoke the settlement, the settlement is provisional. In the alternative, if under statute, clearing house rule

or agreement, a right of revocation of the settlement exists the settlement is provisional. Conversely, if there is an absence of a reservation of the right to revoke and also an absence of a right to revoke under statute, clearing house rule or agreement, the settlement is final and such final settlement constitutes final payment of the item.

A primary example of a statutory right on the part of the payor bank to revoke a settlement is the right to revoke conferred by Section 4—301. The underlying theory and reason for deferred posting statutes (Section 4—301) is to require a settlement on the date of receipt of an item but to keep that settlement provisional with the right to revoke prior to the midnight deadline. In any case where Section 4—301 is applicable, any settlement by the payor bank is provisional solely by virtue of the statute, subsection (1) (b) of Section 4—213 does not operate and such provisional settlement does not constitute final payment of the item.

A second important example of a right to revoke a settlement is that arising under clearing house rules. It is very common for clearing house rules to provide that items exchanged and settled for in a clearing, (e. g., before 10:00 a.m. on Monday) may be returned and the settlements revoked up to but not later than 2:00 p.m. on the same day (Monday) or under deferred posting at some hour on the next business day (e. g., 2:00 p.m. Tuesday). Under this type of rule the Monday morning settlement is provisional and being provisional does not constitute a final payment of the item.

An example of a reservation of a right to revoke a settlement is where the payor bank is also the depositary bank and has signed a receipt or duplicate deposit ticket or has made an entry in a passbook acknowledging receipt, for credit to the account of A, of a check drawn on it by B. If the receipt, deposit ticket, passbook or other agreement with A is to the effect that any credit so entered is provisional and may be revoked pending the time required by the payor bank to process the item to determine if it is in good form and there are funds to cover it, such reservation or agreement keeps the receipt or credit provisional and avoids it being either final settlement or final payment.

In other ways the payor bank may keep settlements provisional: by general or special agreement with the presenting party or bank; by simple reservation at the time the settlement is made; or otherwise. Thus a payor bank (except in the case of statutory provisions) has control whether a settlement made by it is provisional or final, by participating in general agreements or clearing house rules or by special agreement or reservation. If it fails to keep a settlement provisional and if no applicable statute keeps the settlement provisional, its settlement is final and, unless the item had previously been paid by one of the other methods prescribed in subsection (1), such final settlement constitutes final payment. In this manner payor banks may without difficulty avoid the effect of such cases as: Cohen v. First Nat. Bank of Nogales, 22 Ariz. 394, 400, 198 P. 122, 124, 15 A.L.R. 701 (1921); Briviesca v. Coronado, 19 Cal.2d 244, 120 P.2d 649 (1941); White Brokerage Co. v. Cooperman, 207 Minn. 239, 290 N.W. 790 (1940); Scotts Bluff County v. First Nat. Bank of Gering, 115 Neb. 273, 212 N.W. 617 (1927); Provident Savings Bank & Trust Co. v. Hildebrand, 49 Ohio App. 207, 196 N.E. 790, 791 (1934); Schaer v. First Nat. Bank of Brenham, 132 Tex. 499, 124 S.W.2d 108 (1939) (bill of exchange); Union State Bank of Lancaster v. Peoples State Bank of Lancaster, 192 Wis. 28, 33, 211 N.W. 931, 933 (1927); 1 Paton's Digest 1067.

5. If a payor bank has not previously paid an item in cash or finally settled for it, certain internal acts or procedures will produce final payment of the item. Exclusive of the external acts of payment in cash or final settlement, the key point at which the decision of the bank to pay or dishonor is made is when the bookkeeper for the drawer's account determines or verifies that the check is in good form and that there are sufficient funds in the drawer's account to cover it. Previous steps in the processing of an item are preliminary to this vital step and in no way indicate a decision to pay. However, a more tangible measuring point is desirable than a mere examination of the account of the person to be charged. The mechanical step that usually indicates that the examination has been completed and the decision to pay has been made is the posting of the item to the account to be charged. Therefore, subsection (1) (c) adopts as the third measuring point the completion of the process of posting. The phrase "completed the process of posting" is used rather than simple "posting" because under current machine operations posting is a process and something more than simply making entries on the customer's ledger. Subsection (1) follows fairly closely the New York statute, 37 McKinney's Consolidated Laws of New York, Negotiable Instruments, Art. 19–A, Sec. 350–b as amended by L.1950, C. 153, Sec. 1. However, subsections (1) (a) and (b) furnish more precise rules for determining "final settlement" by the payor bank than does the New York statute in using the term "irrevocable credit", the definition of which is not helpful.

6. Subsection (1) (d) covers the situation where the payor bank makes a provisional settlement for an item, which settlement becomes final at a later time by reason of the failure of the payor bank to revoke it in the time and manner permitted by statute, clearing house rule or agreement. An example of this type of situation is the clearing house settlement referred to in Comment 4. In the illustration there given if the time limit for the return of items received in the Monday morning clearing is 2:00 p. m. on Tuesday and the provisional settlement has not been revoked at that time in a manner permitted by the clearing house rules, the provisional settlement made on Monday morning becomes final at 2:00 p. m. on Tuesday. Subsection (1) (d) provides specifi-

cally that in this situation the item is finally paid at 2:00 p. m. Tuesday. If on the other hand a payor bank receives an item in the mail on Monday and makes some provisional settlement for the item on Monday, it has until midnight on Tuesday to return the item or give notice and revoke any settlement under Section 4—301. In this situation subsection (1) (d) of Section 4—213 provides that if the provisional settlement made on Monday is not revoked before midnight on Tuesday as permitted by Section 4—301, the item is finally paid at midnight on Tuesday even if the process of posting the item to the account of the drawer has not been completed at that time.

7. Subsection (1) provides that an item is finally paid by the payor bank when any one of the four events set forth in subparagraphs (a), (b), (c) and (d) have occurred, whichever happens first, and then provides that upon a final payment under subparagraphs (b), (c) or (d) the payor bank shall be accountable for the amount of the item. It is not made accountable if it has paid the item in cash because such payment is itself a sufficient accounting. The term "accountable" is used as imposing a duty to account, which duty is met if and when a settlement for the item satisfactorily clears. The fact that determination of the time of final payment is based exclusively upon action of the payor bank is not detrimental to the interests of owners of items or collecting banks because of the general obligations of payors to honor or dishonor and the time limits for action imposed by Sections 4—301 and 4—302.

8. Subsection (2) states the country-wide usage that when the item is finally paid by the payor bank under subsection (1) this final payment automatically without further action "firms up" other provisional settlements made for it. However, the subsection makes clear that this "firming up" occurs only where the settlement between the presenting and payor banks was made either through a clearing house or by debits and credits in accounts between them. It does not take place where the payor bank remits for the item with some form of remittance instrument. Further, the "firming up" continues only to the extent that provisional debits and credits are entered seriatim in accounts between banks which are successive to the presenting bank. The automatic "firming up" is broken at any time that any collecting bank remits for the item with a remittance draft, because final payment to the remittee then usually depends upon final payment of the remittance draft.

9. Subsection (3) states the general rule that if a collecting bank receives settlement for an item which is or becomes final, the bank is accountable to its customer for the amount of the item. One means of accounting is to remit to its customer the amount it has received on the item. If previously it gave to its customer a provisional credit for the item in an account its receipt of final settlement for the item "firms up" this provisional credit and makes it final. When this credit given by it so

becomes final, in the usual case its agency status terminates and it becomes a debtor to its customer for the amount of the item. See Section 4—201(1). If the accounting is by a remittance instrument or authorization to charge further time will usually be required to complete its accounting (Section 4—211).

10. Subsection (4) states when certain credits given by a bank to its customer become available for withdrawal as of right. Subsection (4) (a) deals with the situation where a bank has given a credit (usually provisional) for an item to its customer and in turn has received a provisional settlement for the item from an intermediary or payor bank to which it has forwarded the item. In this situation before the provisional credit entered by the collecting bank in the account of its customer becomes available for withdrawal as of right, it is not only necessary that the provisional settlement received by the bank for the item becomes final but also that the collecting bank has a reasonable time to learn that this is so. Hence, subsection (4) (a) imposes both of these conditions. If the provisional settlement received is a provisional debit or credit in an account with the intermediary or payor bank or a remittance instrument on some bank other than the collecting bank itself, the collecting bank will usually learn that this debit or credit is final or that the remittance instrument has been paid merely by not learning the opposite within a reasonable time. How much time is "reasonable" for these purposes will of course depend on the distance the item has to travel and the number of banks through which it must pass (having in mind not only travel time by regular lines of transmission but also the successive midnight deadlines of the several banks) and other pertinent facts. Also, if the provisional settlement received is some form of a remittance instrument or authorization to charge, the "reasonable" time depends on the identity and location of the payor of the remittance instrument, the means for clearing such instrument and other pertinent facts.

11. Subsection (4) (b) deals with the situation of a bank which is both a depositary bank and a payor bank. The subsection recognizes that where A and B are both customers of a depositary-payor bank and A deposits B's check on the depositary-payor in A's account on Monday, time must be allowed to permit the check under the deferred posting rules of Section 4--301 to reach the bookkeeper for B's account at some time on Tuesday, and if there are insufficient funds in B's account to reverse or charge back the provisional credit in A's account. Consequently this provisional credit in A's account does not become available for withdrawal as of right until the opening of business on Wednesday. If it is determined on Tuesday that there are insufficient funds in B's account to pay the check the credit to A's account can be reversed on Tuesday. On the other hand if the item is in fact paid on Tuesday, the rule of subsection (4) (b) is desirable to avoid uncertainty and possible

disputes between the bank and its customer as to exactly what hour within the day the credit is available.

12. Subsection (5) recognizes that even when A makes a deposit of cash in his account on Monday it takes some period of time to record that cash deposit and communicate it to A's bookkeeper (the bookkeeper handling A's account) so that A's bookkeeper has a record of it when she considers whether there are available funds to pay A's check. Where as indicated in Comment 5 A's bookkeeper is the particular employee in the bank to determine, in most cases and subject to supervisory control, whether the item may be paid, the effectiveness of a deposit of cash as a basis for paying a check must of necessity rest upon when the record of that deposit reaches such bookkeeper rather than when it passes through the teller's window. Consequently, although the bank is charged with responsibility for cash deposited from the moment it is received on Monday the cash is not effective as a basis for paying checks until the opening of business on Tuesday.

Cross References:

Sections 3—418, 4—107, 4—201, 4—211, 4—212, 4—214, 4—301, 4—302, and 4—303.

Definitional Cross References:

"Account". Section 4—104.
"Agreement". Section 1—201.
"Banking day". Section 4—104.
"Clearing house". Section 4—104.
"Collecting bank". Section 4—105.
"Customer". Section 4—104.
"Depositary bank". Section 4—105.
"Item". Section 4—104.
"Money". Section 1—201.
"Notice". Section 1—201.
"Payor bank". Section 4—105.
"Presenting bank". Section 4—105.
"Settlement". Section 4—104.

§ 4—214. Insolvency and Preference

(1) Any item in or coming into the possession of a payor or collecting bank which suspends payment and which item is not finally paid shall be returned by the receiver, trustee or agent in charge of the closed bank to the presenting bank or the closed bank's customer.

(2) If a payor bank finally pays an item and suspends payments without making a settlement for the item with its customer or the presenting bank which settlement is or becomes final, the owner of the item has a preferred claim against the payor bank.

(3) If a payor bank gives or a collecting bank gives or receives a provisional settlement for an item and thereafter suspends payments, the suspension does not prevent or interfere with the settlement becoming final if such finality occurs automatically up-

on the lapse of certain time or the happening of certain events (subsection (3) of Section 4—211, subsections (1) (d), (2) and (3) of Section 4—213).

(4) If a collecting bank receives from subsequent parties settlement for an item which settlement is or becomes final and suspends payments without making a settlement for the item with its customer which is or becomes final, the owner of the item has a preferred claim against such collecting bank.

Official Comment

Prior Uniform Statutory Provision: None; but see Section 13, American Bankers Association Bank Collection Code.

Purposes:

1. The underlying purpose of the provisions of this section is not to confer upon banks, holders of items or anyone else preferential positions in the event of bank failures over general depositors or any other creditors of the failed banks. The purpose is to fix as definitely as possible the cut-off point of time for the completion or cessation of the collection process in the case of items that happen to be in such process at the time a particular bank suspends payments. It must be remembered that in bank collections as a whole and in the handling of items by an individual bank, items go through a whole series of processes. It must also be remembered that at any particular point of time a particular bank (at least one of any size) is functioning as a depositary bank for some items, as an intermediary bank for others, as a presenting bank for still others and as a payor bank for still others, and that when it suspends payments it will have close to its normal load of items working through its various processes. For the convenience of receivers, owners of items, banks, and in fact substantially everyone concerned, it is recognized that at the particular moment of time that a bank suspends payment, a certain portion of the items being handled by it have progressed far enough in the bank collection process that it is preferable to permit them to continue the remaining distance, rather than to send them back and reverse the many entries that have been made or the steps that have been taken with respect to them. Therefore, having this background and these purposes in mind, the section states what items must be turned backward at the moment suspension intervenes and what items have progressed far enough that the collection process with respect to them continues, with the resulting necessary statement of rights of various parties flowing from this prescription of the cut-off time.

2. The rules stated are similar to those stated in the American Bankers Association Bank Collection Code, but with the abandonment of any theory of trust. Although for practical purposes Federal Deposit Insurance affects materially the result of bank failures on holders

of items and banks, no attempt is made to vary the rules of the section by reason of such insurance.

3. It is recognized that in view of Jennings v. United States Fidelity & Guaranty Co., 294 U.S. 216, 55 S.Ct. 394, 79 L.Ed. 869, 99 A.L.R. 1248 (1935), amendment of the National Bank Act would be necessary to have this section apply to national banks. But there is no reason why it should not apply to others. See Section 1—108.

Cross References:

Sections 1—108, 4—211(3) and 4—213.

Definitional Cross References:

"Collecting bank". Section 4—105.

"Customer". Section 4—104.

"Item". Section 4—104.

"Payor bank". Section 4—105.

"Presenting bank". Section 4—105.

"Settlement". Section 4—104.

"Suspends payment". Section 4—104.

PART 3

COLLECTION OF ITEMS: PAYOR BANKS

§ 4—301. Deferred Posting; Recovery of Payment by Return of Items; Time of Dishonor

(1) Where an authorized settlement for a demand item (other than a documentary draft) received by a payor bank otherwise than for immediate payment over the counter has been made before midnight of the banking day of receipt the payor bank may revoke the settlement and recover any payment if before it has made final payment (subsection (1) of Section 4—213) and before its midnight deadline it

(a) returns the item; or

(b) sends written notice of dishonor or nonpayment if the item is held for protest or is otherwise unavailable for return.

(2) If a demand item is received by a payor bank for credit on its books it may return such item or send notice of dishonor and may revoke any credit given or recover the amount thereof withdrawn by its customer, if it acts within the time limit and in the manner specified in the preceding subsection.

(3) Unless previous notice of dishonor has been sent an item is dishonored at the time when for purposes of dishonor it is returned or notice sent in accordance with this section.

(4) An item is returned:

(a) as to an item received through a clearing house, when it is delivered to the presenting or last collecting bank or to the clearing house or is sent or delivered in accordance with its rules; or

(b) in all other cases, when it is sent or delivered to the bank's customer or transferor or pursuant to his instructions.

Official Comment

Prior Uniform Statutory Provision: None; but see American Bankers Association Model Deferred Posting Statute.

Purposes:

1. Deferred posting and delayed returns is that practice whereby a payor bank sorts and proves items received by it on the day they are received, e. g. Monday, but does not post the items to the customer's account or return "not good" items until the next day, e. g. Tuesday. The practice typifies "production line" methods currently used in bank collection and is based upon the necessity of an even flow of items through payor banks on a day by day basis in a manner which can be handled evenly by employee personnel without abnormal peak load periods, night work, and other practices objectionable to personnel. Since World War II statutes authorizing deferred posting and delayed returns have been passed in almost all of the forty-eight states. This section codifies the content of these statutes and approves the practice.

2. The time limits for action imposed by Subsection (1) are adopted by Subsection (2) for cases where the payor bank is also the depositary bank, but in this case the requirement of a settlement on the day of receipt is omitted.

3. Subsection (3) fixes a base point from which to measure the time within which notice of dishonor must be given. See Section 3—508.

4. Subsection (4) leaves banks free to agree upon the manner of returning items but establishes a precise time when an item is "returned". For definition of "sent" as used in subsections (a) and (b) see Section 1—201(38).

5. Obviously the section assumes that the item has not been "finally paid" under Section 4—213(1). If it has been, this section has no operation.

Cross References:

Sections 3—508, 4—213, 4—302.

Definitional Cross References:

"Banking day". Section 4—104.

"Clearing house". Section 4—104.

"Collecting bank". Section 4—105.

"Customer". Section 4—104.

"Documentary draft". Section 4—104.

"Item". Section 4—104.

"Midnight deadline". Section 4—104.

"Notice of dishonor". Section 3—508.

"Payor bank". Section 4—105.

"Presenting bank". Section 4—105.

"Sent". Section 1—201(38).

"Settlement". Section 4—104.

§ 4—302. Payor Bank's Responsibility for Late Return of Item

In the absence of a valid defense such as breach of a presentment warranty (subsection (1) of Section 4—207), settlement effected or the like, if an item is presented on and received by a payor bank the bank is accountable for the amount of

(a) a demand item other than a documentary draft whether properly payable or not if the bank, in any case where it is not also the depositary bank, retains the item beyond midnight of the banking day of receipt without settling for it or, regardless of whether it is also the depositary bank, does not pay or return the item or send notice of dishonor until after its midnight deadline; or

(b) any other properly payable item unless within the time allowed for acceptance or payment of that item the bank either accepts or pays the item or returns it and accompanying documents.

Official Comment

Prior Uniform Statutory Provision: None; but see American Bankers Association Model Deferred Posting Statute.

Purposes:

Under Section 4—301, time limits are prescribed within which a payor bank must take action if it receives an item payable by it. Section 4—302 states the rights of the customer if the payor bank fails to take the action required within the time limits prescribed.

Cross Reference:

Section 4—301.

Definitional Cross References:

"Acceptance". Section 3—410.

"Banking day". Section 4—104.

"Customer". Section 4—104.

"Depositary bank". Section 4—105.

"Documentary draft". Section 4—104.

"Item". Section 4—104.

"Midnight deadline". Section 4—104.

"Notice of dishonor". Section 3—508.

"Payor bank". Section 4—105.

"Properly payable". Section 4—104.

"Settle". Section 4—104.

§ 4—303. When Items Subject to Notice, Stop-Order, Legal Process or Setoff; Order in Which Items May Be Charged or Certified

(1) Any knowledge, notice or stop-order received by, legal process served upon or setoff exercised by a payor bank, wheth-

er or not effective under other rules of law to terminate, suspend or modify the bank's right or duty to pay an item or to charge its customer's account for the item, comes too late to so terminate, suspend or modify such right or duty if the knowledge, notice, stop-order or legal process is received or served and a reasonable time for the bank to act thereon expires or the setoff is exercised after the bank has done any of the following:

(a) accepted or certified the item;

(b) paid the item in cash;

(c) settled for the item without reserving a right to revoke the settlement and without having such right under statute, clearing house rule or agreement;

(d) completed the process of posting the item to the indicated account of the drawer, maker or other person to be charged therewith or otherwise has evidenced by examination of such indicated account and by action its decision to pay the item; or

(e) become accountable for the amount of the item under subsection (1) (d) of Section 4—213 and Section 4—302 dealing with the payor bank's responsibility for late return of items.

(2) Subject to the provisions of subsection (1) items may be accepted, paid, certified or charged to the indicated account of its customer in any order convenient to the bank.

Official Comment

Prior Uniform Statutory Provision: None.

Purposes:

1. The comments to Section 4—213 describe the process through which an item passes in the payor bank. Prior to this process or at any time while it is going on, the payor bank may receive knowledge or a legal notice affecting the item, such as knowledge or a notice that the drawer has filed a petition in bankruptcy or made an assignment for the benefit of creditors; may receive an order of the drawer stopping payment on the item; may have served on it an attachment of the account of the drawer; or the bank itself may exercise a right of setoff against the drawer's account. Each of these events affects the account of the drawer and may eliminate or freeze all or part of whatever balance is available to pay the item. Subsection (1) states the rule for determining the relative priorities between these various legal events and the item.

2. The rule is that if any one of several things has been done to the item or if it has reached any one of several stages in its processing at the time

the knowledge, notice, stop-order or legal process is received or served and a reasonable time for the bank to act thereon expires or the setoff is exercised, the knowledge, notice, stop-order, legal process or setoff comes too late, the item has priority and a charge to the customer's account may be made and is effective. Certain of the tests determining the priority status of the item are the same as for final payment under Section 4—213(1), but additional tests apply in the context of the present section. The first event mentioned, namely, acceptance, means formal acceptance as that term is used and defined in Section 3—410. Certification is the type of certification defined in Section 3—411. Payment of the item in cash under Section 4—213(1) (a), final settlement for the item under Section 4—213(1) (b) and completion of the process of posting under Section 4—213(1) (c) all constitute final payment of the item and confer priority. After a cash payment, final settlement or the completion of the process of posting, any knowledge, notice, stop-order, legal process or setoff comes too late and cannot interfere with either the payment of the item or a charge to the customer's account based upon such payment.

3. The sixth event conferring priority is stated by the language "or otherwise has evidenced by examination of such indicated account and by action its decision to pay the item." This general "omnibus" language is necessary to pick up other possible types of action impossible to specify particularly but where the bank has examined the account to see if there are sufficient funds and has taken some action indicating an intention to pay. An example is what has sometimes been called "sight posting" where the bookkeeper examines the account and makes a decision to pay but postpones posting. The clause should be interpreted in the light of Nineteenth Ward Bank v. First Nat. Bank of South Weymouth, 184 Mass. 49, 67 N.E. 670 (1903). It is not intended to refer to various preliminary acts in no way close to a true decision of the bank to pay the item, such as receipt of the item over the counter for deposit, entry of a provisional credit in a passbook, or the making of a provisional settlement for the item through the clearing house, by entries in accounts, remittance or otherwise. All actions of this type are provisional and none of them evidences the bank's decision to pay the item. In this Section as in Section 4—213 reasoning such as appears in Cohen v. First Nat. Bank of Nogales, 22 Ariz. 394, 400, 198 P. 122, 124, 15 A.L.R. 701 (1921); Briviesca v. Coronado, 19 Cal.2d 244, 120 P.2d 649 (1941); White Brokerage Co. v. Cooperman, 207 Minn. 239, 290 N.W. 790 (1940); Scotts Bluff County v. First Nat. Bank of Gering, 115 Neb. 273, 212 N.W. 617, 618 (1927); Provident Savings Bank & Trust Co. v. Hildebrand, 49 Ohio App. 207, 196 N.E. 790, 791 (1934); Schaer v. First Nat. Bank of Brenham, 132 Tex. 499, 124 S.W.2d 108 (1939) (bill of exchange); Union State Bank of Lancaster v. People's State Bank of Lancaster, 192 Wis. 28, 33, 211 N.W. 931, 933 (1927); 1 Paton's Digest 1067, is rejected.

4. The seventh and last event conferring priority for an item and a charge to the customer's account based upon the item is stated by the language "become accountable for the amount of the item under subsection (1) (d) of Section 4—213 and Section 4—302 dealing with the payor bank's responsibility for late return of items". Under Section 4—213(1) (d) if a payor bank makes a provisional settlement for an item and fails to revoke the settlement in the time and manner permitted by statute, clearing house rule or agreement, such combination of events constitutes final payment of the item. Under Section 4—302 a payor bank may also become accountable for the amount of an item in certain other situations even though there has been no provisional settlement for the item or such action as constitutes final payment under Section 4—213(1). Expiration of the deadlines under Sections 4—213(1) (d) or 4—302 with resulting accountability by the payor bank for the amount of the item, establish priority of the item over notices, stop-orders, legal process or setoff.

5. In the case of knowledge, notice, stop-orders and legal process the effective time for determining whether they were received too late to affect the payment of an item and a charge to the customer's account by reason of such payment, is receipt plus a reasonable time for the bank to act on any of these communications. Usually a relatively short time is required to communicate to the bookkeeping department advice of one of these events but certainly some time is necessary. Compare Sections 1—201(27) and 4—403. In the case of setoff the effective time is when the setoff is actually made.

6. As between one item and another no priority rule is stated, other than the convenience of the bank. This rule is justified because of the impossibility of stating a rule that would be fair in all cases, having in mind the almost infinite number of combinations of large and small checks in relation to the available balance on hand in the drawer's account; the possible methods of receipt; and other difficulties. Further, where the drawer has drawn all the checks, he should have funds available to meet all of them and has no basis for urging one should be paid before another; and the holders have no direct right against the payor bank in any event, unless of course, the bank has accepted, certified or finally paid a particular item, or has become liable for it under Section 4—302. Under subsection (2) the bank obviously has the right to pay items for which it is itself liable ahead of those for which it is not.

Cross References:

Sections 3—410, 3—411, 4—213(1), 4—301, and 4—302.

Definitional Cross References:

"Accepted". Section 3—410.
"Account". Section 4—104.
"Agreement". Section 1—201.
"Certified". Section 3—411.
"Clearing house". Section 4—104.
"Customer". Section 4—104.
"Item". Section 4—104.
"Notice". Section 1—201.
"Payor bank". Section 4—105.
"Settle". Section 4—104.

PART 4

RELATIONSHIP BETWEEN PAYOR BANK AND ITS CUSTOMER

§ 4—401. When Bank May Charge Customer's Account

(1) As against its customer, a bank may charge against his account any item which is otherwise properly payable from that account even though the charge creates an overdraft.

(2) A bank which in good faith makes payment to a holder may charge the indicated account of its customer according to

(a) the original tenor of his altered item; or

(b) the tenor of his completed item, even though the bank knows the item has been completed unless the bank has notice that the completion was improper.

Official Comment

Prior Uniform Statutory Provision: None.

Purposes:

1. It is fundamental that upon proper payment of a draft the drawee may charge the account of the drawer. This is true even though the draft is an overdraft since the draft itself authorizes the payment for the drawer's account and carries an implied promise to reimburse the drawee.

2. Subsection (2) parallels the provision which protects a holder in due course against discharge by reason of alteration and permits him to enforce the instrument according to its original tenor. Section 3—407(3). It adopts the rule of cases extending the same protection to a drawee who pays in good faith. The subsection also follows the policy of Sections 3—115 and 3—407(3) by protecting the drawee who pays a completed instrument in good faith according to the instrument as completed.

Cross References:

Sections 3—115 and 3—407.

Definitional Cross References:

"Account". Section 4—104.
"Bank". Section 1—201.
"Customer". Section 4—104.
"Good faith". Section 1—201.
"Holder". Section 1—201.
"Item". Section 4—104.
"Properly payable". Section 4—104.

§ 4—402. Bank's Liability to Customer for Wrongful Dishonor

A payor bank is liable to its customer for damages proximately caused by the wrongful dishonor of an item. When the dishonor occurs through mistake liability is limited to actual damages proved. If so proximately caused and proved damages may include damages for an arrest or prosecution of the customer or other consequential damages. Whether any consequential damages are proximately caused by the wrongful dishonor is a question of fact to be determined in each case.

Official Comment

Prior Uniform Statutory Provision: None.

Purposes:

1. This section is new to the Uniform Laws, although similar statutory provisions are in existence in twenty-three jurisdictions.

2. The liability of the drawee for dishonor has sometimes been stated as one for breach of contract, sometimes as for negligence or other breach of a tort duty, and sometimes as for defamation. This section does not attempt to specify a theory. "Wrongful dishonor" excludes any permitted or justified dishonor, as where the drawer has no credit extended by the drawee, or where the draft lacks a necessary indorsement or is not properly presented.

3. This section rejects decisions which have held that where the dishonored item has been drawn by a merchant, trader or fiduciary he is defamed in his business, trade or profession by a reflection on his credit and hence that substantial damages may be awarded on the basis of defamation "per se" without proof that damage has occurred. The merchant, trader and fiduciary are placed on the same footing as any other drawer and in all cases of dishonor by mistake damages recoverable are limited to those actually proved.

4. Wrongful dishonor is different from "failure to exercise ordinary care in handling an item", and the measure of damages is that stated in this section, not that stated in Section 4—103(5).

5. The fourth sentence of the section rejects decisions holding that as a matter of law the dishonor of a check is not the "proximate cause" of the arrest and prosecution of the customer, and leaves to determination in each case as a question of fact whether the dishonor is or may be the "proximate cause".

Definitional Cross References:

"Bank". Section 1—201.
"Customer". Section 4—104.
"Item". Section 4—104.

§ 4—403. Customer's Right to Stop Payment; Burden of Proof of Loss

(1) A customer may by order to his bank stop payment of any item payable for his account but the order must be received at such time and in such manner as to afford the bank a reason-

able opportunity to act on it prior to any action by the bank with respect to the item described in Section 4—303.

(2) An oral order is binding upon the bank only for fourteen calendar days unless confirmed in writing within that period. A written order is effective for only six months unless renewed in writing.

(3) The burden of establishing the fact and amount of loss resulting from the payment of an item contrary to a binding stop payment order is on the customer.

Official Comment

Prior Uniform Statutory Provision: None.

Purposes:

1. This section is new. It is intended to replace separate statutes in twenty-nine states which regulate stop-payment orders.

2. The position taken by this section is that stopping payment is a service which depositors expect and are entitled to receive from banks notwithstanding its difficulty, inconvenience and expense. The inevitable occasional losses through failure to stop should be borne by the banks as a cost of the business of banking.

3. Subsection (1) follows the decisions holding that a payee or indorsee has no right to stop payment. This is consistent with the provision governing payment or satisfaction. See Section 3—603. The sole exception to this rule is found in Section 4—405 on payment after notice of death, by which any person claiming an interest in the account can stop payment.

4. Payment is commonly stopped only on checks; but the right to stop payment is not limited to checks, and extends to any item payable by any bank. Where the maker of a note payable at a bank is in a position analogous to that of a drawer (Section 3—121) he may stop payment of the note. By analogy the rule extends to drawees other than banks.

5. There is no right to stop payment after certification of a check or other acceptance of a draft, and this is true no matter who procures the certification. See Sections 3—411 and 4—303. The acceptance is the drawee's own engagement to pay, and he is not required to impair his credit by refusing payment for the convenience of the drawer.

6. Normally a direction to stop payment is first given by telephone. Notwithstanding statutes which require a written order, banks customarily accept such directions, and have been held to waive the writing. Subsection (2) is intended to protect both parties by making the oral direction effective for only a short time during which the drawer must confirm it in writing, and by eliminating thereafter any claim of waiver by acceptance of the oral direction.

7. The existing statutes all specify a time limit after which

any direction to stop payment becomes ineffective unless it is renewed in writing; and the majority of them have specified six months. The purpose of the provision is, of course, to facilitate stopping payment by clearing the records of the drawee of accumulated unrevoked stop orders, as where the drawer has found a lost instrument or has settled his controversy with the payee, but has failed to notify the drawee. The last sentence of subsection (2), together with the second clause in Section 4—404, rejects the reasoning of such cases as Goldberg v. Manufacturers Trust Company, 199 Misc. 167, 102 N.Y.S.2d 144 (1951).

8. A payment in violation of an effective direction to stop payment is an improper payment, even though it is made by mistake or inadvertence. Any agreement to the contrary is invalid under Section 4—103(1) if in paying the item over the stop payment order the bank has failed to exercise ordinary care. The drawee is, however, entitled to subrogation to prevent unjust enrichment (Section 4—407); retains common-law defenses, e. g., that by conduct in recognizing the payment the customer has ratified the bank's action in paying over a stop payment order (Section 1—103); and retains common-law rights, e. g., to recover money paid under a mistake (Section 1—103) in cases where the payment is not made final by Section 3—418. It has sometimes been said that payment cannot be stopped against a holder in due course, but the statement is inaccurate. The payment can be stopped but the drawer remains liable on the instrument to the holder in due course (Sections 3—305, 3—413) and the drawee, if he pays, becomes subrogated to the rights of the holder in due course against the drawer. Section 4—407. Any defenses available against a holder in due course remain available to the drawer, but other defenses are cut off to the same extent as if the holder himself were bringing the action.

Cross References:

Point 3: Sections 3—603(1), 4—405.

Point 4: Section 3—121.

Point 5: Sections 3—411 and 4—303.

Point 8: Sections 3—305, 3—413, 3—418, 4—103 and 4—407.

Definitional Cross References:

"Account". Section 4—104.

"Bank". Section 1—201.

"Burden of establishing". Section 1—201.

"Customer". Section 4—104.

"Item". Section 4—104.

"Send". Section 1—201.

§ 4—404. Bank Not Obligated to Pay Check More Than Six Months Old

A bank is under no obligation to a customer having a checking account to pay a check, other than a certified check, which is presented more than six months after its date, but it may charge its customer's account for a payment made thereafter in good faith.

Official Comment

Prior Uniform Statutory Provision: None.

Purposes:

This section incorporates a type of statute adopted in twenty-six jurisdictions. The time limit is set at six months because banking and commercial practice regards a check outstanding for longer than that period as stale, and a bank will normally not pay such a check without consulting the depositor. It is therefore not required to do so, but is given the option to pay because it may be in a position to know, as in the case of dividend checks, that the drawer wants payment made.

Certified checks are excluded from the section because they are the primary obligation of the certifying bank (Sections 3—411 and 3—413), which obligation runs direct to the holder of the check. The customer's account was charged when the check was certified.

Cross References:

Sections 3—411 and 3—413.

Definitional Cross References:

"Account". Section 4—104.
"Bank". Section 1—201.
"Check". Section 3—104.
"Customer". Section 4—104.
"Good faith". Section 1—201.
"Present". Section 3—504.

§ 4—405. Death or Incompetence of Customer

(1) A payor or collecting bank's authority to accept, pay or collect an item or to account for proceeds of its collection if otherwise effective is not rendered ineffective by incompetence of a customer of either bank existing at the time the item is issued or its collection is undertaken if the bank does not know of an adjudication of incompetence. Neither death nor incompetence of a customer revokes such authority to accept, pay, collect or account until the bank knows of the fact of death or of an adjudication of incompetence and has reasonable opportunity to act on it.

(2) Even with knowledge a bank may for 10 days after the date of death pay or certify checks drawn on or prior to that date unless ordered to stop payment by a person claiming an interest in the account.

Official Comment

Prior Uniform Statutory Provision: None.

Purposes:

1. This section is new, although similar statutory provisions are in existence in seven states.

2. Subsection (1) follows existing decisions which hold that a drawee (payor) bank is not

liable for the payment of a check before it has notice of the death or incompetence of the drawer. The justice and necessity of the rule are obvious. A check is an order to pay which the bank must obey under penalty of possible liability for dishonor. Further, with the tremendous volume of items handled any rule which required banks to verify the continued life and competency of drawers would be completely unworkable.

One or both of these same reasons apply to other phases of the bank collection and payment process and the rule is made wide enough to apply to these other phases. It applies to all kinds of "items"; to "customers" who own items as well as "customers" who draw or make them; to the function of collecting items as well as the function of accepting or paying them; to the carrying out of instructions to account for proceeds even though these may involve transfers to third parties; to depositary and intermediary banks as well as payor banks; and to incompetency existing at the time of the issuance of an item or the commencement of the collection or payment process as well as to incompetency occurring thereafter. Further, the requirement of actual knowledge makes inapplicable the rule of some cases that an adjudication of incompetency is constructive notice to all the world because obviously it is as impossible for banks to keep posted on such adjudications (in the absence of actual knowledge) as it is to keep posted as to death of immediate or remote customers.

3. Subsection (2) provides a limited period after death during which a bank may continue to pay checks (as distinguished from other items) even though it has notice. The purpose of the provision, as of the existing statutes, is to permit holders of checks drawn and issued shortly before death to cash them without the necessity of filing a claim in probate. The justification is that such checks normally are given in immediate payment of an obligation, that there is almost never any reason why they should not be paid, and that filing in probate is a useless formality, burdensome to the holder, the executor, the court and the bank.

This section does not prevent an executor or administrator from recovering the payment from the holder of the check. It is not intended to affect the validity of any gift causa mortis or other transfer in contemplation of death, but merely to relieve the bank of liability for the payment.

4. Any surviving relative, creditor or other person who claims an interest in the account may give a direction to the bank not to pay checks, or not to pay a particular check. Such notice has the same effect as a direction to stop payment. The bank has no responsibility to determine the validity of the claim or even whether it is "colorable". But obviously anyone who has an interest in the estate, including the person named as executor in a will, even if the will has not yet been admitted to probate, is entitled to claim an interest in the account.

Definitional Cross References:

"Accept". Section 3—410.
"Bank". Section 1—201.
"Certify". Section 3—411.
"Check". Section 3—104.
"Customer". Section 4—104.
"Depositary bank". Section 4—105.
"Item". Section 4—104.
"Payor bank". Section 4—105.

§ 4—406. Customer's Duty to Discover and Report Unauthorized Signature or Alteration

(1) When a bank sends to its customer a statement of account accompanied by items paid in good faith in support of the debit entries or holds the statement and items pursuant to a request or instructions of its customer or otherwise in a reasonable manner makes the statement and items available to the customer, the customer must exercise reasonable care and promptness to examine the statement and items to discover his unauthorized signature or any alteration on an item and must notify the bank promptly after discovery thereof.

(2) If the bank establishes that the customer failed with respect to an item to comply with the duties imposed on the customer by subsection (1) the customer is precluded from asserting against the bank

(a) his unauthorized signature or any alteration on the item if the bank also establishes that it suffered a loss by reason of such failure; and

(b) an unauthorized signature or alteration by the same wrongdoer on any other item paid in good faith by the bank after the first item and statement was available to the customer for a reasonable period not exceeding fourteen calendar days and before the bank receives notification from the customer of any such unauthorized signature or alteration.

(3) The preclusion under subsection (2) does not apply if the customer establishes lack of ordinary care on the part of the bank in paying the item(s).

(4) Without regard to care or lack of care of either the customer or the bank a customer who does not within one year from the time the statement and items are made available to the customer (subsection (1)) discover and report his unauthorized signature or any alteration on the face or back of the item or does not within 3 years from that time discover and report any unauthorized indorsement is precluded from asserting against the bank such unauthorized signature or indorsement or such alteration.

(5) If under this section a payor bank has a valid defense against a claim of a customer upon or resulting from payment of an item and waives or fails upon request to assert the defense the bank may not assert against any collecting bank or other prior party presenting or transferring the item a claim based upon the unauthorized signature or alteration giving rise to the customer's claim.

Official Comment

Prior Uniform Statutory Provision: None.

Purposes:

1. This section is new to Uniform Laws. It is to replace statutes in forty jurisdictions dealing with the general subject of a depositor's duty to discover and report forgeries and alterations. In these statutes there is substantial variation in rules prescribed as to the following matters: application of the statute to unauthorized signatures, raised checks or altered checks; inclusion of special provisions with respect to fictitious payees; periods of time prescribed for termination of right of customer to assert claims against bank; time when limitation period begins to run; restriction of rights of customer stated in terms of liability for loss, preclusion of rights or limitations on time in which suits may be brought.

2. Subsection (1) states the general duty of a customer to exercise reasonable care and promptness to examine his bank statements and items to discover his unauthorized signature or any alteration and to promptly notify the bank if he discovers an unauthorized signature or alteration. This duty becomes operative when the bank does any one of three things with respect to the statement of account and supporting items paid in good faith. The first action is the sending of the statement and items to the customer. The sending may be either by mailing or any other action within the definition of "send" (Section 1—201). The second action is the holding of such statement and items available for the customer pursuant to a request for instructions of the customer. The third action is stated as "or otherwise in a reasonable manner makes the statement and items available to the customer." Such wider residual language is desirable to cover unusual situations. An example might be where the bank knows a customer has left a former address but does not know any new address to which to send the statement or item or to obtain instructions from the customer. The third residual type of action, however, must be "reasonable" and any court has the power to determine that a particular action or practice of a bank, other than sending statements and items or holding them pursuant to instructions, is not reasonable.

3. Subsection (2) states the effect of a failure of a customer to comply with subsection (1). The first effect stated in subparagraph (a) is that he is precluded from asserting against the

bank his unauthorized signature and alteration if the bank establishes that it suffered a loss by reason of the customer's failure. The bank has the burden of establishing that it suffered some loss.

Under subparagraph (b) if, after the first item and statement becomes available plus a reasonable period not exceeding fourteen calendar days, the bank pays in good faith any other item on which there is an unauthorized signature or alteration by the same wrongdoer, which payment is prior to receipt by the bank of notification of such unauthorized signature or alteration on the first item, the customer is precluded from asserting the additional unauthorized signature or alteration. This rule follows substantial case law that payment of an additional item or items bearing an unauthorized signature or alteration by the same wrongdoer is a loss suffered by the bank traceable to the customer's failure to exercise reasonable care in examining his statement and notifying the bank of objections to it. One of the most serious consequences of failure of the customer to comply with the requirements of subsection (1) is the opportunity presented to the wrongdoer to repeat his misdeeds. Conversely, one of the best ways to keep down losses in this type of situation is for the customer to promptly examine his statement and notify the bank of an unauthorized signature or alteration so that the bank will be alerted to stop paying further items. Hence, the rule of subparagraph (b) is prescribed and to avoid dispute a specific time limit for action by the customer is designated, namely fourteen calendar days.

4. The two effects on the customer of his failure to comply with subsection (1) (subparagraphs (a) and (b) of subsection (2)) are stated in terms of preclusion from asserting a claim against the bank. However, these two effects occur only if the customer has failed to exercise reasonable care and promptness in examining his statement and items and notifying the bank and as to this question of fact the burden is upon the bank to establish such failure. Further, even if the bank succeeds in establishing that the customer has failed to exercise ordinary care, if in turn the customer succeeds in establishing that the bank failed to exercise ordinary care in paying the item(s) the preclusion rule does not apply. This distribution of the burden of establishing between the customer and the bank provides reasonable equality of treatment and requires each person asserting the negligence to establish such negligence rather than requiring either person to establish that his entire course of conduct constituted ordinary care.

5. Whether the preclusion rule of subsection (2) operates or does not operate depends upon determinations as to ordinary care of the customer and possibly of the bank. However, subsection (4) places an absolute time limit on the right of a customer to make claim for payment of altered or forged paper without regard to care or lack of care of either the customer or

the bank. In the case of alteration or the unauthorized signature of the customer himself the absolute time limit is one year. In the case of unauthorized indorsements it is three years. This recognizes that there is little excuse for a customer not detecting an alteration of his own check or a forgery of his own signature. However, he does not know the signatures of indorsers and may be delayed in learning that indorsements are forged. The three year absolute time limit on the discovery of forged indorsements should be ample, because in the great preponderance of cases the customer will learn of the forged indorsements within this time and if in any exceptional case he does not, the balance in favor of a mechanical termination of the liability of the bank outweighs what few residuary risks the customer may still have. In thirteen of the existing statutes there are limitations on the liability of a bank for payment of items bearing forged indorsements which limitation periods range from thirty days to two years. In the remaining twenty-seven no provision is made for forged indorsements.

6. Nothing in this section is intended to affect any decision holding that a customer who has notice of something wrong with an indorsement must exercise reasonable care to investigate and to notify the bank. It should be noted that under the rules relating to impostors and signatures in the name of the payee (Section 3—405) certain forged indorsements on which the bank has paid the item in good faith may be treated as effective notwithstanding such discovery and notice. If the alteration or forgery results from the drawer's negligence the drawee who pays in good faith is also protected. Section 3—406.

7. The forty existing statutes on the subject as well as Section 4—406 evidence a public policy in favor of imposing on customers the duty of prompt examination of their bank statements and the notification of banks of forgeries and alterations and in favor of reasonable time limitations on the responsibility of banks for payment of forged or altered items. In two New York cases, however, it has been held that a payor bank may waive defenses of the kind prescribed by the section and ignore the public policy indicated by these defenses and recover the full amount of a forged or altered item from a collecting bank. Fallick v. Amalgamated Bank of New York, 232 App.Div. 127, 249 N.Y.S. 238 (1st Dep't 1931); National Surety Corp. v. Federal Reserve Bank of New York, 188 Misc. 207, 70 N.Y.S.2d 636 (1946), affirmed without opinion 188 Misc. 213, 70 N.Y.S.2d 642 (1946). Subsection (5) is intended to reject the holding of these and like cases. Although the principle of subsection (5) might well be applied to other types of claims of customers against banks and defenses to these claims, the rule of the subsection is limited to defenses of a payor bank under this section. No present need is known to give the rule wider effect.

Cross References:

Sections 3—404, 3—405, 3—406, 3—407, 3—417 and 4—207.

Definitional Cross References:

"Alteration". Section 3—407.
"Bank". Section 1—201.
"Collecting bank". Section 4—105.
"Customer". Section 4—104.
"Good faith". Section 1—201.
"Indorsement". Section 3—204.
"Item". Section 4—104.
"Payor bank". Section 4—105.
"Send". Section 1—201.
"Unauthorized signature". Section 1—201.

§ 4—407. Payor Bank's Right to Subrogation on Improper Payment

If a payor bank has paid an item over the stop payment order of the drawer or maker or otherwise under circumstances giving a basis for objection by the drawer or maker, to prevent unjust enrichment and only to the extent necessary to prevent loss to the bank by reason of its payment of the item, the payor bank shall be subrogated to the rights

(a) of any holder in due course on the item against the drawer or maker; and

(b) of the payee or any other holder of the item against the drawer or maker either on the item or under the transaction out of which the item arose; and

(c) of the drawer or maker against the payee or any other holder of the item with respect to the transaction out of which the item arose.

Official Comment

Prior Uniform Statutory Provision: None.

Purposes:

1. Section 4—403 states that a stop payment order is binding on a bank. If a bank pays an item over such a stop order it is prima facie liable, but under subsection (3) of 4—403 the burden of establishing the fact and amount of loss from such payment is on the customer. A defense frequently interposed by a bank in an action against it for wrongful payment over a stop-order is that the drawer or maker suffered no loss because he would have been liable to a holder in due course in any event. On this argument some cases have held that payment cannot be stopped against a holder in due course. Payment can be stopped, but if it is, the drawer or maker is liable and the sound rule is that the bank is subrogated to the rights of the holder in due course. The preamble and subsection (a) of this section state this rule.

2. Subsection (b) also subrogates the bank to the rights of the payee or other holder against the drawer or maker ei-

ther on the item or under the transaction out of which it arose. It may well be that the payee is not a holder in due course but still has good rights against the drawer. These may be on the check but also may not be as, for example, where the drawer buys goods from the payee and the goods are partially defective so that the payee is not entitled to the full price, but the goods are still worth a portion of the contract price. If the drawer retains the goods he is obligated to pay a part of the agreed price. If the bank has paid the check it should be subrogated to this claim of the payee against the drawer.

3. Subsection (c) subrogates the bank to the rights of the drawer or maker against the payee or other holder with respect to the transaction out of which the item arose. If, for example, the payee was a fraudulent salesman inducing the drawer to issue his check for defective securities, and the bank pays the check over a stop order but reimburses the drawer for such payment, the bank should have a basis for getting the money back from the fraudulent salesman.

4. The limitations of the preamble prevent the bank itself from getting any double recovery or benefits out of its subrogation rights conferred by the section.

5. The spelling out of the affirmative rights of the bank in this section does not destroy other existing rights (Section 1—103). Among others these may include the defense of a payor bank that by conduct in recognizing the payment a customer has ratified the bank's action in paying in disregard of a stop payment order or rights to recover money paid under a mistake.

Cross Reference:

Section 4—403.

Definitional Cross References:

"Holder". Section 1—201.

"Holder in due course". Section 3—302.

"Item". Section 4—104.

"Payor bank". Section 4—105.

PART 5

COLLECTION OF DOCUMENTARY DRAFTS

§ 4—501. Handling of Documentary Drafts; Duty to Send for Presentment and to Notify Customer of Dishonor

A bank which takes a documentary draft for collection must present or send the draft and accompanying documents for presentment and upon learning that the draft has not been paid or accepted in due course must seasonably notify its customer of such fact even though it may have discounted or bought the draft or extended credit available for withdrawal as of right.

Official Comment

Prior Uniform Statutory Provision: None.

Purposes:

To state the duty of a bank handling a documentary draft for a customer. "Documentary draft" is defined in Section 4—104. Notice that the duty stated exists even when the bank has bought the draft. This is because to the customer the draft normally represents an underlying commercial transaction, and if that is not going through as planned he should know it promptly.

Cross References:

In Article 4: Sections 4—201, 4—202, 4—203, 4—204 and 4—210.

In Article 5: Sections 5—110, 5—111, 5—112 and 5—113.

Definitional Cross References:

"Documentary draft". Sections 4—104, 5—103.

§ 4—502. Presentment of "On Arrival" Drafts

When a draft or the relevant instructions require presentment "on arrival", "when goods arrive" or the like, the collecting bank need not present until in its judgment a reasonable time for arrival of the goods has expired. Refusal to pay or accept because the goods have not arrived is not dishonor; the bank must notify its transferor of such refusal but need not present the draft again until it is instructed to do so or learns of the arrival of the goods.

Official Comment

Prior Uniform Statutory Provision: None.

Purposes:

The section is designed to establish a definite rule for "on arrival" drafts. The term includes not only drafts drawn payable "on arrival" but also drafts forwarded with instructions to present "on arrival". The term refers to the arrival of the relevant goods. Unless a bank has actual knowledge of the arrival of the goods, as for example, when it is the "notify" party on the bill of lading, the section only requires the exercise of such judgment in estimating time as a bank may be expected to have. Commonly the buyer-drawee will want the goods and will therefore call for the documents and take up the draft when they do arrive.

Cross References:

In Article 4: Sections 4—202 and 4—203.

In Article 5: Section 5—112.

Definitional Cross References:

"Collecting bank". Section 4—105.

§ 4—503. Responsibility of Presenting Bank for Documents and Goods; Report of Reasons for Dishonor; Referee in Case of Need

Unless otherwise instructed and except as provided in Article 5 a bank presenting a documentary draft

(a) must deliver the documents to the drawee on acceptance of the draft if it is payable more than three days after presentment; otherwise, only on payment; and

(b) upon dishonor, either in the case of presentment for acceptance or presentment for payment, may seek and follow instructions from any referee in case of need designated in the draft or if the presenting bank does not choose to utilize his services it must use diligence and good faith to ascertain the reason for dishonor, must notify its transferor of the dishonor and of the results of its effort to ascertain the reasons therefor and must request instructions.

But the presenting bank is under no obligation with respect to goods represented by the documents except to follow any reasonable instructions seasonably received; it has a right to reimbursement for any expense incurred in following instructions and to prepayment of or indemnity for such expenses.

Official Comment

Prior Uniform Statutory Provision: Section 131(3), Uniform Negotiable Instruments Law.

Changes: Completely rewritten and enlarged.

Purposes:

1. To state the rules governing, in the absence of instructions, the duty of the presenting bank in case either of honor or of dishonor of a documentary draft. The section should be read in connection with Section 2—514 on when documents are deliverable on acceptance, when on payment.

2. If the draft is drawn under a letter of credit, Article 5 controls. See Sections 5—109 through 5—114.

Cross References:

Point 1. Section 2—514; see also Section 4—504.

Point 2. Article 5, especially Sections 5—109 through 5—114.

Definitional Cross References:

"Documentary draft". Sections 4—104, 5—103.

"Presenting bank". Section 4—105.

§ 4—504. Privilege of Presenting Bank to Deal With Goods; Security Interest for Expenses

(1) A presenting bank which, following the dishonor of a documentary draft, has seasonably requested instructions but does not receive them within a reasonable time may store, sell, or otherwise deal with the goods in any reasonable manner.

(2) For its reasonable expenses incurred by action under subsection (1) the presenting bank has a lien upon the goods or their proceeds, which may be foreclosed in the same manner as an unpaid seller's lien.

Official Comment

Prior Uniform Statutory Provision: None.

Purposes:

To give the presenting bank, after dishonor, a privilege to deal with the goods in any commercially reasonable manner pending instructions from its transferor and, if still unable to communicate with its principal after a reasonable time, a right to realize its expenditures as if foreclosing on an unpaid seller's lien (Section 2—706). The provision includes situations in which storage of goods or other action becomes commercially necessary pending receipt of any requested instructions, even if the requested instructions are later received.

The "reasonable manner" referred to means one reasonable in the light of business factors and the judgment of a business man.

Cross References:

Sections 4—503 and 2—706.

Definitional Cross References:

"Presenting bank". Section 4—105.

"Documentary draft". Sections 4—104, 5—103.

ARTICLE 5

LETTERS OF CREDIT

Section

§ 5—101. Short Title

This Article shall be known and may be cited as Uniform Commercial Code—Letters of Credit.

§ 5—102. Scope

(1) This Article applies

(a) to a credit issued by a bank if the credit requires a documentary draft or a documentary demand for payment; and

(b) to a credit issued by a person other than a bank if the credit requires that the draft or demand for payment be accompanied by a document of title; and

(c) to a credit issued by a bank or other person if the credit is not within subparagraphs (a) or (b) but conspicuously states that it is a letter of credit or is conspicuously so entitled.

(2) Unless the engagement meets the requirements of subsection (1), this Article does not apply to engagements to make advances or to honor drafts or demands for payment, to authorities to pay or purchase, to guarantees or to general agreements.

(3) This Article deals with some but not all of the rules and concepts of letters of credit as such rules or concepts have developed prior to this act or may hereafter develop. The fact that this Article states a rule does not by itself require, imply or negate application of the same or a converse rule to a situation not provided for or to a person not specified by this Article.

§ 5—103. Definitions

(1) In this Article unless the context otherwise requires

(a) "Credit" or "letter of credit" means an engagement by a bank or other person made at the request of a customer and of a kind within the scope of this Article (Section 5—102) that the issuer will honor drafts or other demands for payment upon compliance with the conditions specified in the credit. A credit may be either revocable or irrevocable. The engagement may be either an agreement to honor or a statement that the bank or other person is authorized to honor.

(b) A "documentary draft" or a "documentary demand for payment" is one honor of which is conditioned upon the presentation of a document or documents. "Document" means any paper including document of title, security, invoice, certificate, notice of default and the like.

(c) An "issuer" is a bank or other person issuing a credit.

(d) A "beneficiary" of a credit is a person who is entitled under its terms to draw or demand payment.

(e) An "advising bank" is a bank which gives notification of the issuance of a credit by another bank.

(f) A "confirming bank" is a bank which engages either that it will itself honor a credit already issued by another bank or that such a credit will be honored by the issuer or a third bank.

(g) A "customer" is a buyer or other person who causes an issuer to issue a credit. The term also includes a bank which procures issuance or confirmation on behalf of that bank's customer.

(2) Other definitions applying to this Article and the sections in which they appear are:

"Notation of Credit".	Section 5—108.
"Presenter".	Section 5—112(3).

(3) Definitions in other Articles applying to this Article and the sections in which they appear are:

"Accept" or "Acceptance".	Section 3—410.
"Contract for sale".	Section 2—106.
"Draft".	Section 3—104.
"Holder in due course".	Section 3—302.
"Midnight deadline".	Section 4—104.
"Security".	Section 8—102.

(4) In addition, Article 1 contains general definitions and principles of construction and interpretation applicable throughout this Article.

§ 5—104. Formal Requirements; Signing

(1) Except as otherwise required in subsection (1) (c) of Section 5—102 on scope, no particular form of phrasing is required for a credit. A credit must be in writing and signed by the issuer and a confirmation must be in writing and signed by the confirming bank. A modification of the terms of a credit or confirmation must be signed by the issuer or confirming bank.

(2) A telegram may be a sufficient signed writing if it identifies its sender by an authorized authentication. The authentication may be in code and the authorized naming of the issuer in an advice of credit is a sufficient signing.

§ 5—105. Consideration

No consideration is necessary to establish a credit or to enlarge or otherwise modify its terms.

§ 5—106. Time and Effect of Establishment of Credit

(1) Unless otherwise agreed a credit is established

(a) as regards the customer as soon as a letter of credit is sent to him or the letter of credit or an authorized written advice of its issuance is sent to the beneficiary; and

(b) as regards the beneficiary when he receives a letter of credit or an authorized written advice of its issuance.

(2) Unless otherwise agreed once an irrevocable credit is established as regards the customer it can be modified or revoked only with the consent of the customer and once it is established as regards the beneficiary it can be modified or revoked only with his consent.

(3) Unless otherwise agreed after a revocable credit is established it may be modified or revoked by the issuer without notice to or consent from the customer or beneficiary.

(4) Notwithstanding any modification or revocation of a revocable credit any person authorized to honor or negotiate under the terms of the original credit is entitled to reimbursement for or honor of any draft or demand for payment duly honored or negotiated before receipt of notice of the modification or revocation and the issuer in turn is entitled to reimbursement from its customer.

§ 5—107. Advice of Credit; Confirmation; Error in Statement of Terms

(1) Unless otherwise specified an advising bank by advising a credit issued by another bank does not assume any obligation to honor drafts drawn or demands for payment made under the credit but it does assume obligation for the accuracy of its own statement.

(2) A confirming bank by confirming a credit becomes directly obligated on the credit to the extent of its confirmation as though it were its issuer and acquires the rights of an issuer.

(3) Even though an advising bank incorrectly advises the terms of a credit it has been authorized to advise the credit is established as against the issuer to the extent of its original terms.

(4) Unless otherwise specified the customer bears as against the issuer all risks of transmission and reasonable translation or interpretation of any message relating to a credit.

§ 5—108. "Notation Credit"; Exhaustion of Credit

(1) A credit which specifies that any person purchasing or paying drafts drawn or demands for payment made under it must note the amount of the draft or demand on the letter or advice of credit is a "notation credit".

(2) Under a notation credit

(a) a person paying the beneficiary or purchasing a draft or demand for payment from him acquires a right to honor only if the appropriate notation is made and by transferring or forwarding for honor the documents under the credit such a person warrants to the issuer that the notation has been made; and

(b) unless the credit or a signed statement that an appropriate notation has been made accompanies the draft or demand for payment the issuer may delay honor until evidence of notation has been procured which is satisfactory to it but its obligation and that of its customer continue for a reasonable time not exceeding thirty days to obtain such evidence.

(3) If the credit is not a notation credit

(a) the issuer may honor complying drafts or demands for payment presented to it in the order in which they are presented and is discharged pro tanto by honor of any such draft or demand;

(b) as between competing good faith purchasers of complying drafts or demands the person first purchasing has priority over a subsequent purchaser even though the later purchased draft or demand has been first honored.

§ 5—109. Issuer's Obligation to Its Customer

(1) An issuer's obligation to its customer includes good faith and observance of any general banking usage but unless otherwise agreed does not include liability or responsibility

(a) for performance of the underlying contract for sale or other transaction between the customer and the beneficiary; or

(b) for any act or omission of any person other than itself or its own branch or for loss or destruction of a draft, demand or document in transit or in the possession of others; or

(c) based on knowledge or lack of knowledge of any usage of any particular trade.

(2) An issuer must examine documents with care so as to ascertain that on their face they appear to comply with the terms of the credit but unless otherwise agreed assumes no liability or responsibility for the genuineness, falsification or effect of any document which appears on such examination to be regular on its face.

(3) A non-bank issuer is not bound by any banking usage of which it has no knowledge.

§ 5—110. Availability of Credit in Portions; Presenter's Reservation of Lien or Claim

(1) Unless otherwise specified a credit may be used in portions in the discretion of the beneficiary.

(2) Unless otherwise specified a person by presenting a documentary draft or demand for payment under a credit relinquishes upon its honor all claims to the documents and a person by transferring such draft or demand or causing such presentment authorizes such relinquishment. An explicit reservation of claim makes the draft or demand non-complying.

§ 5—111. Warranties on Transfer and Presentment

(1) Unless otherwise agreed the beneficiary by transferring or presenting a documentary draft or demand for payment war-

rants to all interested parties that the necessary conditions of the credit have been complied with. This is in addition to any warranties arising under Articles 3, 4, 7 and 8.

(2) Unless otherwise agreed a negotiating, advising, confirming, collecting or issuing bank presenting or transferring a draft or demand for payment under a credit warrants only the matters warranted by a collecting bank under Article 4 and any such bank transferring a document warrants only the matters warranted by an intermediary under Articles 7 and 8.

§ 5—112. Time Allowed for Honor or Rejection; Withholding Honor or Rejection by Consent; "Presenter"

(1) A bank to which a documentary draft or demand for payment is presented under a credit may without dishonor of the draft, demand or credit

(a) defer honor until the close of the third banking day following receipt of the documents; and

(b) further defer honor if the presenter has expressly or impliedly consented thereto.

Failure to honor within the time here specified constitutes dishonor of the draft or demand and of the credit [except as otherwise provided in subsection (4) of Section 5—114 on conditional payment].

Note: *The bracketed language in the last sentence of subsection (1) should be included only if the optional provisions of Section 5—114(4) and (5) are included.*

(2) Upon dishonor the bank may unless otherwise instructed fulfill its duty to return the draft or demand and the documents by holding them at the disposal of the presenter and sending him an advice to that effect.

(3) "Presenter" means any person presenting a draft or demand for payment for honor under a credit even though that person is a confirming bank or other correspondent which is acting under an issuer's authorization.

§ 5—113. Indemnities

(1) A bank seeking to obtain (whether for itself or another) honor, negotiation or reimbursement under a credit may give an indemnity to induce such honor, negotiation or reimbursement.

(2) An indemnity agreement inducing honor, negotiation or reimbursement

(a) unless otherwise explicitly agreed applies to defects in the documents but not in the goods; and

(b) unless a longer time is explicitly agreed expires at the end of ten business days following receipt of the documents by the ultimate customer unless notice of objection is sent before such expiration date. The ultimate customer may send notice of objection to the person from whom he received the documents and any bank receiving such notice is under a duty to send notice to its transferor before its midnight deadline.

§ 5—114. Issuer's Duty and Privilege to Honor; Right to Reimbursement

(1) An issuer must honor a draft or demand for payment which complies with the terms of the relevant credit regardless of whether the goods or documents conform to the underlying contract for sale or other contract between the customer and the beneficiary. The issuer is not excused from honor of such a draft or demand by reason of an additional general term that all documents must be satisfactory to the issuer, but an issuer may require that specified documents must be satisfactory to it.

(2) Unless otherwise agreed when documents appear on their face to comply with the terms of a credit but a required document does not in fact conform to the warranties made on negotiation or transfer of a document of title (Section 7—507) or of a certificated security (Section 8—306) or is forged or fraudulent or there is fraud in the transaction

(a) the issuer must honor the draft or demand for payment if honor is demanded by a negotiating bank or other holder of the draft or demand which has taken the draft or demand under the credit and under circumstances which would make it a holder in due course (Section 3—302) and in an appropriate case would make it a person to whom a document of title has been duly negotiated (Section 7—502) or a bona fide purchaser of a certificated security (Section 8—302); and

(b) in all other cases as against its customer, an issuer acting in good faith may honor the draft or demand for payment despite notification from the customer of fraud, forgery or other defect not apparent on the face of the documents but a court of appropriate jurisdiction may enjoin such honor.

(3) Unless otherwise agreed an issuer which has duly honored a draft or demand for payment is entitled to immediate reimbursement of any payment made under the credit and to be put in effectively available funds not later than the day before maturity of any acceptance made under the credit.

[(4) When a credit provides for payment by the issuer on receipt of notice that the required documents are in the possession of a correspondent or other agent of the issuer

(a) any payment made on receipt of such notice is conditional; and

(b) the issuer may reject documents which do not comply with the credit if it does so within three banking days following its receipt of the documents; and

(c) in the event of such rejection, the issuer is entitled by charge back or otherwise to return of the payment made.]

[(5) In the case covered by subsection (4) failure to reject documents within the time specified in sub-paragraph (b) constitutes acceptance of the documents and makes the payment final in favor of the beneficiary.]

Note: *Subsections (4) and (5) are bracketed as optional. If they are included the bracketed language in the last sentence of Section 5—112(1) should also be included.*

Amended in 1977.

§ 5—115. Remedy for Improper Dishonor or Anticipatory Repudiation

(1) When an issuer wrongfully dishonors a draft or demand for payment presented under a credit the person entitled to honor has with respect to any documents the rights of a person in the position of a seller (Section 2—707) and may recover from the issuer the face amount of the draft or demand together with incidental damages under Section 2—710 on seller's incidental damages and interest but less any amount realized by resale or other use or disposition of the subject matter of the transaction. In the event no resale or other utilization is made the documents, goods or other subject matter involved in the transaction must be turned over to the issuer on payment of judgment.

(2) When an issuer wrongfully cancels or otherwise repudiates a credit before presentment of a draft or demand for payment drawn under it the beneficiary has the rights of a seller after anticipatory repudiation by the buyer under Section 2—610 if he learns of the repudiation in time reasonably to avoid procurement of the required documents. Otherwise the beneficiary has an immediate right of action for wrongful dishonor.

§ 5—116. Transfer and Assignment

(1) The right to draw under a credit can be transferred or assigned only when the credit is expressly designated as transferable or assignable.

(2) Even though the credit specifically states that it is nontransferable or nonassignable the beneficiary may before performance of the conditions of the credit assign his right to proceeds. Such an assignment is an assignment of a contract right

under Article 9 on Secured Transactions and is governed by that Article except that

(a) the assignment is ineffective until the letter of credit or advice of credit is delivered to the assignee which delivery constitutes perfection of the security interest under Article 9; and

(b) the issuer may honor drafts or demands for payment drawn under the credit until it receives a notification of the assignment signed by the beneficiary which reasonably identifies the credit involved in the assignment and contains a request to pay the assignee; and

(c) after what reasonably appears to be such a notification has been received the issuer may without dishonor refuse to accept or pay even to a person otherwise entitled to honor until the letter of credit or advice of credit is exhibited to the issuer.

(3) Except where the beneficiary has effectively assigned his right to draw or his right to proceeds, nothing in this section limits his right to transfer or negotiate drafts or demands drawn under the credit. Amended in 1972.

See Appendix for changes made in former text and the reasons for change.

§ 5—117. Insolvency of Bank Holding Funds for Documentary Credit

(1) Where an issuer or an advising or confirming bank or a bank which has for a customer procured issuance of a credit by another bank becomes insolvent before final payment under the credit and the credit is one to which this Article is made applicable by paragraphs (a) or (b) of Section 5—102(1) on scope, the receipt or allocation of funds or collateral to secure or meet obligations under the credit shall have the following results:

(a) to the extent of any funds or collateral turned over after or before the insolvency as indemnity against or specifically for the purpose of payment of drafts or demands for payment drawn under the designated credit, the drafts or demands are entitled to payment in preference over depositors or other general creditors of the issuer or bank; and

(b) on expiration of the credit or surrender of the beneficiary's rights under it unused any person who has given such funds or collateral is similarly entitled to return thereof; and

(c) a charge to a general or current account with a bank if specifically consented to for the purpose of indemnity against or payment of drafts or demands for payment drawn under the designated credit falls under the same rules as if the funds had been drawn out in cash and then turned over with specific instructions.

(2) After honor or reimbursement under this section the customer or other person for whose account the insolvent bank has acted is entitled to receive the documents involved.

ARTICLE 6

BULK TRANSFERS

Section

§ 6—101. Short Title

This Article shall be known and may be cited as Uniform Commercial Code—Bulk Transfers.

§ 6—102. "Bulk Transfers"; Transfers of Equipment; Enterprises Subject to This Article; Bulk Transfers Subject to This Article

(1) A "bulk transfer" is any transfer in bulk and not in the ordinary course of the transferor's business of a major part of the materials, supplies, merchandise or other inventory (Section 9—109) of an enterprise subject to this Article.

(2) A transfer of a substantial part of the equipment (Section 9—109) of such an enterprise is a bulk transfer if it is made in connection with a bulk transfer of inventory, but not otherwise.

(3) The enterprises subject to this Article are all those whose principal business is the sale of merchandise from stock, including those who manufacture what they sell.

(4) Except as limited by the following section all bulk transfers of goods located within this state are subject to this Article.

§ 6—103. Transfers Excepted From This Article

The following transfers are not subject to this Article:

(1) Those made to give security for the performance of an obligation;

(2) General assignments for the benefit of all the creditors of the transferor, and subsequent transfers by the assignee thereunder;

(3) Transfers in settlement or realization of a lien or other security interests;

(4) Sales by executors, administrators, receivers, trustees in bankruptcy, or any public officer under judicial process;

(5) Sales made in the course of judicial or administrative proceedings for the dissolution or reorganization of a corporation and of which notice is sent to the creditors of the corporation pursuant to order of the court or administrative agency;

(6) Transfers to a person maintaining a known place of business in this State who becomes bound to pay the debts of the transferor in full and gives public notice of that fact, and who is solvent after becoming so bound;

(7) A transfer to a new business enterprise organized to take over and continue the business, if public notice of the transaction is given and the new enterprise assumes the debts of the transferor and he receives nothing from the transaction except an interest in the new enterprise junior to the claims of creditors;

(8) Transfers of property which is exempt from execution.

Public notice under subsection (6) or subsection (7) may be given by publishing once a week for two consecutive weeks in a newspaper of general circulation where the transferor had its principal place of business in this state an advertisement including the names and addresses of the transferor and transferee and the effective date of the transfer.

§ 6—104. Schedule of Property, List of Creditors

(1) Except as provided with respect to auction sales (Section 6—108), a bulk transfer subject to this Article is ineffective against any creditor of the transferor unless:

(a) The transferee requires the transferor to furnish a list of his existing creditors prepared as stated in this section; and

(b) The parties prepare a schedule of the property transferred sufficient to identify it; and

(c) The transferee preserves the list and schedule for six months next following the transfer and permits inspection of either or both and copying therefrom at all reasonable hours by any creditor of the transferor, or files the list and schedule in (a public office to be here identified).

(2) The list of creditors must be signed and sworn to or affirmed by the transferor or his agent. It must contain the names and business addresses of all creditors of the transferor, with the amounts when known, and also the names of all persons who are known to the transferor to assert claims against him even though such claims are disputed. If the transferor is the obligor of an outstanding issue of bonds, debentures or the like as to which there is an indenture trustee, the list of creditors need include only the name and address of the indenture trustee and the aggregate outstanding principal amount of the issue.

(3) Responsibility for the completeness and accuracy of the list of creditors rests on the transferor, and the transfer is not rendered ineffective by errors or omissions therein unless the transferee is shown to have had knowledge.

§ 6—105. Notice to Creditors

In addition to the requirements of the preceding section, any bulk transfer subject to this Article except one made by auction sale (Section 6—108) is ineffective against any creditor of the transferor unless at least ten days before he takes possession of the goods or pays for them, whichever happens first, the transferee gives notice of the transfer in the manner and to the persons hereafter provided (Section 6—107).

[§ 6—106. Application of the Proceeds

In addition to the requirements of the two preceding sections:

(1) Upon every bulk transfer subject to this Article for which new consideration becomes payable except those made by sale at auction it is the duty of the transferee to assure that such consideration is applied so far as necessary to pay those debts of the transferor which are either shown on the list furnished by the transferor (Section 6–104) or filed in writing in the place stated in the notice (Section 6–107) within thirty days after the mailing of such notice. This duty of the transferee runs to all the holders of such debts, and may be enforced by any of them for the benefit of all.

(2) If any of said debts are in dispute the necessary sum may be withheld from distribution until the dispute is settled or adjudicated.

(3) If the consideration payable is not enough to pay all of the said debts in full distribution shall be made pro rata.]

Note: *This section is bracketed to indicate division of opinion as to whether or not it is a wise provision, and* *to suggest that this is a point on which State enactments may differ without serious damage to the principle of uniformity.*

In any State where this section is omitted, the following parts of sections, also bracketed in the text, should also be omitted, namely:

Section 6–107(2) (e).
6–108(3) (c).
6–109(2).

In any State where this section is enacted, these other provisions should be also.

Optional Subsection (4)

[(4) The transferee may within ten days after he takes possession of the goods pay the consideration into the (specify court) in the county where the transferor had its principal place of business in this state and thereafter may discharge his duty under this section by giving notice by registered or certified mail to all the persons to whom the duty runs that the consideration has been paid into that court and that they should file their claims there. On motion of any interested party, the court may order the distribution of the consideration to the persons entitled to it.]

Note: *Optional subsection (4) is recommended for those states which do not have a general statute providing for payment of money into court.*

§ 6—107. The Notice

(1) The notice to creditors (Section 6—105) shall state:

(a) that a bulk transfer is about to be made; and

(b) the names and business addresses of the transferor and transferee, and all other business names and addresses used by the transferor within three years last past so far as known to the transferee; and

(c) whether or not all the debts of the transferor are to be paid in full as they fall due as a result of the transaction, and if so, the address to which creditors should send their bills.

(2) If the debts of the transferor are not to be paid in full as they fall due or if the transferee is in doubt on that point then the notice shall state further:

(a) the location and general description of the property to be transferred and the estimated total of the transferor's debts;

(b) the address where the schedule of property and list of creditors (Section 6—104) may be inspected;

(c) whether the transfer is to pay existing debts and if so the amount of such debts and to whom owing;

(d) whether the transfer is for new consideration and if so the amount of such consideration and the time and place of payment; [and]

[(e) if for new consideration the time and place where creditors of the transferor are to file their claims.]

(3) The notice in any case shall be delivered personally or sent by registered or certified mail to all the persons shown on the list of creditors furnished by the transferor (Section 6—104) and to all other persons who are known to the transferee to hold or assert claims against the transferor.

Note: *The words in brackets are optional. See Note under § 6—106.*

§ 6—108. Auction Sales; "Auctioneer"

(1) A bulk transfer is subject to this Article even though it is by sale at auction, but only in the manner and with the results stated in this section.

(2) The transferor shall furnish a list of his creditors and assist in the preparation of a schedule of the property to be sold, both prepared as before stated (Section 6—104).

(3) The person or persons other than the transferor who direct, control or are responsible for the auction are collectively called the "auctioneer". The auctioneer shall:

(a) receive and retain the list of creditors and prepare and retain the schedule of property for the period stated in this Article (Section 6—104);

(b) give notice of the auction personally or by registered or certified mail at least ten days before it occurs to all persons shown on the list of creditors and to all other persons who are known to him to hold or assert claims against the transferor; [and]

[(c) assure that the net proceeds of the auction are applied as provided in this Article (Section 6—106).]

(4) Failure of the auctioneer to perform any of these duties does not affect the validity of the sale or the title of the purchasers, but if the auctioneer knows that the auction constitutes a bulk transfer such failure renders the auctioneer liable to the creditors of the transferor as a class for the sums owing to them from the transferor up to but not exceeding the net proceeds of the auction. If the auctioneer consists of several persons their liability is joint and several.

Note: *The words in brackets are optional. See Note under § 6—106.*

§ 6—109. What Creditors Protected; [Credit for Payment to Particular Creditors]

(1) The creditors of the transferor mentioned in this Article are those holding claims based on transactions or events

occurring before the bulk transfer, but creditors who become such after notice to creditors is given (Sections 6—105 and 6—107) are not entitled to notice.

[(2) Against the aggregate obligation imposed by the provisions of this Article concerning the application of the proceeds (Section 6—106 and subsection (3) (c) of 6—108) the transferee or auctioneer is entitled to credit for sums paid to particular creditors of the transferor, not exceeding the sums believed in good faith at the time of the payment to be properly payable to such creditors.]

Note: *The words in brackets are optional. See Note under § 6—106.*

§ 6—110. Subsequent Transfers

When the title of a transferee to property is subject to a defect by reason of his non-compliance with the requirements of this Article, then:

(1) a purchaser of any of such property from such transferee who pays no value or who takes with notice of such non-compliance takes subject to such defect, but

(2) a purchaser for value in good faith and without such notice takes free of such defect.

§ 6—111. Limitation of Actions and Levies

No action under this Article shall be brought nor levy made more than six months after the date on which the transferee took possession of the goods unless the transfer has been concealed. If the transfer has been concealed, actions may be brought or levies made within six months after its discovery.

Note to Article 6: *Section 6—106 is bracketed to indicate division of opinion as to whether or not it is a wise provision, and to suggest that this is a point on which State enactments may differ without serious damage to the principle of uniformity.*

In any State where Section 6—106 is not enacted, the following parts of sections, also bracketed in the text, should also be omitted, namely:

Sec. 6—107(2)(e).
6—108(3)(c).
6—109(2).

In any State where Section 6—106 is enacted, these other provisions should be also.

ARTICLE 7

WAREHOUSE RECEIPTS, BILLS OF LADING AND OTHER DOCUMENTS OF TITLE

PART 1. GENERAL

Section

7—101. Short Title.
7—102. Definitions and Index of Definitions.
7—103. Relation of Article to Treaty, Statute, Tariff, Classification or Regulation.
7—104. Negotiable and Non-Negotiable Warehouse Receipt, Bill of Lading or Other Document of Title.
7—105. Construction Against Negative Implication.

PART 2. WAREHOUSE RECEIPTS: SPECIAL PROVISIONS

7—201. Who May Issue a Warehouse Receipt; Storage Under Government Bond.
7—202. Form of Warehouse Receipt; Essential Terms; Optional Terms.
7—203. Liability for Non-Receipt or Misdescription.
7—204. Duty of Care; Contractual Limitation of Warehouseman's Liability.
7—205. Title Under Warehouse Receipt Defeated in Certain Cases.
7—206. Termination of Storage at Warehouseman's Option.
7—207. Goods Must Be Kept Separate; Fungible Goods.
7—208. Altered Warehouse Receipts.
7—209. Lien of Warehouseman.
7—210. Enforcement of Warehouseman's Lien.

PART 3. BILLS OF LADING: SPECIAL PROVISIONS

7—301. Liability for Non-Receipt or Misdescription; "Said to Contain"; "Shipper's Load and Count"; Improper Handling.
7—302. Through Bills of Lading and Similar Documents.
7—303. Diversion; Reconsignment; Change of Instructions.
7—304. Bills of Lading in a Set.
7—305. Destination Bills.
7—306. Altered Bills of Lading.
7—307. Lien of Carrier.
7—308. Enforcement of Carrier's Lien.
7—309. Duty of Care; Contractual Limitation of Carrier's Liability.

PART 4. WAREHOUSE RECEIPTS AND BILLS OF LADING: GENERAL OBLIGATIONS

7—401. Irregularities in Issue of Receipt or Bill or Conduct of Issuer.
7—402. Duplicate Receipt or Bill; Overissue.

PART 1

GENERAL

§ 7—101. Short Title

This Article shall be known and may be cited as Uniform Commercial Code—Documents of Title.

§ 7—102. Definitions and Index of Definitions

(1) In this Article, unless the context otherwise requires:

(a) "Bailee" means the person who by a warehouse receipt, bill of lading or other document of title acknowledges possession of goods and contracts to deliver them.

(b) "Consignee" means the person named in a bill to whom or to whose order the bill promises delivery.

(c) "Consignor" means the person named in a bill as the person from whom the goods have been received for shipment.

(d) "Delivery order" means a written order to deliver goods directed to a warehouseman, carrier or other person who in the ordinary course of business issues warehouse receipts or bills of lading.

(e) "Document" means document of title as defined in the general definitions in Article 1 (Section 1—201).

(f) "Goods" means all things which are treated as movable for the purposes of a contract of storage or transportation.

(g) "Issuer" means a bailee who issues a document except that in relation to an unaccepted delivery order it means the person who orders the possessor of goods to deliver. Issuer includes any person for whom an agent or employee purports to act in issuing a document if the agent or employee has real or apparent authority to issue documents, notwithstanding that the issuer received no goods or that the goods were misdescribed or that in any other respect the agent or employee violated his instructions.

(h) "Warehouseman" is a person engaged in the business of storing goods for hire.

(2) Other definitions applying to this Article or to specified Parts thereof, and the sections in which they appear are:

"Duly negotiate". Section 7—501.

"Person entitled under the document". Section 7—403(4).

(3) Definitions in other Articles applying to this Article and the sections in which they appear are:

"Contract for sale". Section 2—106.

"Overseas". Section 2—323.

"Receipt" of goods. Section 2—103.

(4) In addition Article 1 contains general definitions and principles of construction and interpretation applicable throughout this Article.

§ 7—103. Relation of Article to Treaty, Statute, Tariff, Classification or Regulation

To the extent that any treaty or statute of the United States, regulatory statute of this State or tariff, classification or regulation filed or issued pursuant thereto is applicable, the provisions of this Article are subject thereto.

§ 7—104. Negotiable and Non-Negotiable Warehouse Receipt, Bill of Lading or Other Document of Title

(1) A warehouse receipt, bill of lading or other document of title is negotiable

(a) if by its terms the goods are to be delivered to bearer or to the order of a named person; or

(b) where recognized in overseas trade, if it runs to a named person or assigns.

(2) Any other document is non-negotiable. A bill of lading in which it is stated that the goods are consigned to a named person is not made negotiable by a provision that the goods are to be delivered only against a written order signed by the same or another named person.

§ 7—105. Construction Against Negative Implication

The omission from either Part 2 or Part 3 of this Article of a provision corresponding to a provision made in the other Part does not imply that a corresponding rule of law is not applicable.

PART 2

WAREHOUSE RECEIPTS: SPECIAL PROVISIONS

§ 7—201. Who May Issue a Warehouse Receipt; Storage Under Government Bond

(1) A warehouse receipt may be issued by any warehouseman.

(2) Where goods including distilled spirits and agricultural commodities are stored under a statute requiring a bond against withdrawal or a license for the issuance of receipts in the nature of warehouse receipts, a receipt issued for the goods has like effect as a warehouse receipt even though issued by a person who is the owner of the goods and is not a warehouseman.

§ 7—202. Form of Warehouse Receipt; Essential Terms; Optional Terms

(1) A warehouse receipt need not be in any particular form.

(2) Unless a warehouse receipt embodies within its written or printed terms each of the following, the warehouseman is liable for damages caused by the omission to a person injured thereby:

(a) the location of the warehouse where the goods are stored;

(b) the date of issue of the receipt;

(c) the consecutive number of the receipt;

(d) a statement whether the goods received will be delivered to the bearer, to a specified person, or to a specified person or his order;

(e) the rate of storage and handling charges, except that where goods are stored under a field warehousing arrangement a statement of that fact is sufficient on a non-negotiable receipt;

(f) a description of the goods or of the packages containing them;

(g) the signature of the warehouseman, which may be made by his authorized agent;

(h) if the receipt is issued for goods of which the warehouseman is owner, either solely or jointly or in common with others, the fact of such ownership; and

(i) a statement of the amount of advances made and of liabilities incurred for which the warehouseman claims a lien or security interest (Section 7—209). If the precise amount of such advances made or of such liabilities incurred is, at the time of the issue of the receipt, unknown to the warehouseman or to his agent who issues it, a statement of the fact that advances have been made or liabilities incurred and the purpose thereof is sufficient.

(3) A warehouseman may insert in his receipt any other terms which are not contrary to the provisions of this Act and do not impair his obligation of delivery (Section 7—403) or his duty of care (Section 7—204). Any contrary provisions shall be ineffective.

§ 7—203. Liability for Non-Receipt or Misdescription

A party to or purchaser for value in good faith of a document of title other than a bill of lading relying in either case upon the description therein of the goods may recover from the issuer damages caused by the non-receipt or misdescription of the goods, except to the extent that the document conspicuously indicates that the issuer does not know whether any part or all of the goods in fact were received or conform to the description, as where the description is in terms of marks or labels or kind, quantity or condition, or the receipt or description is qualified by "contents, condition and quality unknown", "said to contain" or the like, if such indication be true, or the party or purchaser otherwise has notice.

§ 7—204. Duty of Care; Contractual Limitation of Warehouseman's Liability

(1) A warehouseman is liable for damages for loss of or injury to the goods caused by his failure to exercise such care in regard to them as a reasonably careful man would exercise under like circumstances but unless otherwise agreed he is not liable for damages which could not have been avoided by the exercise of such care.

(2) Damages may be limited by a term in the warehouse receipt or storage agreement limiting the amount of liability in case of loss or damage, and setting forth a specific liability per article or item, or value per unit of weight, beyond which the warehouseman shall not be liable; provided, however, that such liability may on written request of the bailor at the time of signing such storage agreement or within a reasonable time after receipt of the warehouse receipt be increased on part or all of the goods thereunder, in which event increased rates may be charged based on such increased valuation, but that no such increase shall be permitted contrary to a lawful limitation of liability contained in the warehouseman's tariff, if any. No such limitation is effective with respect to the warehouseman's liability for conversion to his own use.

(3) Reasonable provisions as to the time and manner of presenting claims and instituting actions based on the bailment may be included in the warehouse receipt or tariff.

(4) This section does not impair or repeal . . .

Note: *Insert in subsection (4) a reference to any statute which imposes a higher responsibility upon the warehouseman or invalidates contractual limitations which would be permissible under this Article.*

§ 7—205. Title Under Warehouse Receipt Defeated in Certain Cases

A buyer in the ordinary course of business of fungible goods sold and delivered by a warehouseman who is also in the business of buying and selling such goods takes free of any claim under a warehouse receipt even though it has been duly negotiated.

§ 7—206. Termination of Storage at Warehouseman's Option

(1) A warehouseman may on notifying the person on whose account the goods are held and any other person known to claim an interest in the goods require payment of any charges and removal of the goods from the warehouse at the termination of the period of storage fixed by the document, or, if no period is fixed, within a stated period not less than thirty days after the notification. If the goods are not removed before the date specified in the notification, the warehouseman may sell them in accordance with the provisions of the section on enforcement of a warehouseman's lien (Section 7—210).

(2) If a warehouseman in good faith believes that the goods are about to deteriorate or decline in value to less than the amount of his lien within the time prescribed in subsection (1) for notification, advertisement and sale, the warehouseman may specify in the notification any reasonable shorter time for removal of the goods and in case the goods are not removed, may sell them at public sale held not less than one week after a single advertisement or posting.

(3) If as a result of a quality or condition of the goods of which the warehouseman had no notice at the time of deposit the goods are a hazard to other property or to the warehouse or to persons, the warehouseman may sell the goods at public or private sale without advertisement on reasonable notification to all persons known to claim an interest in the goods. If the warehouseman after a reasonable effort is unable to sell the goods he may dispose of them in any lawful manner and shall incur no liability by reason of such disposition.

(4) The warehouseman must deliver the goods to any person entitled to them under this Article upon due demand made at any time prior to sale or other disposition under this section.

(5) The warehouseman may satisfy his lien from the proceeds of any sale or disposition under this section but must hold the balance for delivery on the demand of any person to whom he would have been bound to deliver the goods.

§ 7—207. Goods Must Be Kept Separate; Fungible Goods

(1) Unless the warehouse receipt otherwise provides, a warehouseman must keep separate the goods covered by each receipt so as to permit at all times identification and delivery of those goods except that different lots of fungible goods may be commingled.

(2) Fungible goods so commingled are owned in common by the persons entitled thereto and the warehouseman is severally liable to each owner for that owner's share. Where because of overissue a mass of fungible goods is insufficient to meet all the receipts which the warehouseman has issued against it, the persons entitled include all holders to whom overissued receipts have been duly negotiated.

§ 7—208. Altered Warehouse Receipts

Where a blank in a negotiable warehouse receipt has been filled in without authority, a purchaser for value and without notice of the want of authority may treat the insertion as authorized. Any other unauthorized alteration leaves any receipt enforceable against the issuer according to its original tenor.

§ 7—209. Lien of Warehouseman

(1) A warehouseman has a lien against the bailor on the goods covered by a warehouse receipt or on the proceeds thereof in his possession for charges for storage or transportation (including demurrage and terminal charges), insurance, labor, or charges present or future in relation to the goods, and for expenses necessary for preservation of the goods or reasonably incurred in their sale pursuant to law. If the person on whose account the goods are held is liable for like charges or expenses in relation to other goods whenever deposited and it is stated in the receipt that a lien is claimed for charges and expenses in relation to other goods, the warehouseman also has a lien against him for such charges and expenses whether or not the other goods have been delivered by the warehouseman. But against a person to whom a negotiable warehouse receipt is duly negotiated a warehouseman's lien is limited to charges in an amount or at a rate specified on the receipt or if no charges are so speci-

fied then to a reasonable charge for storage of the goods covered by the receipt subsequent to the date of the receipt.

(2) The warehouseman may also reserve a security interest against the bailor for a maximum amount specified on the receipt for charges other than those specified in subsection (1), such as for money advanced and interest. Such a security interest is governed by the Article on Secured Transactions (Article 9).

(3) (a) A warehouseman's lien for charges and expenses under subsection (1) or a security interest under subsection (2) is also effective against any person who so entrusted the bailor with possession of the goods that a pledge of them by him to a good faith purchaser for value would have been valid but is not effective against a person as to whom the document confers no right in the goods covered by it under Section 7—503.

(b) A warehouseman's lien on household goods for charges and expenses in relation to the goods under subsection (1) is also effective against all persons if the depositor was the legal possessor of the goods at the time of deposit. "Household goods" means furniture, furnishings and personal effects used by the depositor in a dwelling.

(4) A warehouseman loses his lien on any goods which he voluntarily delivers or which he unjustifiably refuses to deliver. (As amended in 1966.)

§ 7—210. Enforcement of Warehouseman's Lien

(1) Except as provided in subsection (2), a warehouseman's lien may be enforced by public or private sale of the goods in block or in parcels, at any time or place and on any terms which are commercially reasonable, after notifying all persons known to claim an interest in the goods. Such notification must include a statement of the amount due, the nature of the proposed sale and the time and place of any public sale. The fact that a better price could have been obtained by a sale at a different time or in a different method from that selected by the warehouseman is not of itself sufficient to establish that the sale was not made in a commercially reasonable manner. If the warehouseman either sells the goods in the usual manner in any recognized market therefor, or if he sells at the price current in such market at the time of his sale, or if he has otherwise sold in conformity with commercially reasonable practices among dealers in the type of goods sold, he has sold in a commercially reasonable manner. A sale of more goods than apparently necessary to be offered to insure satisfaction of the obligation is not commercially reasonable except in cases covered by the preceding sentence.

(2) A warehouseman's lien on goods other than goods stored by a merchant in the course of his business may be enforced only as follows:

(a) All persons known to claim an interest in the goods must be notified.

(b) The notification must be delivered in person or sent by registered or certified letter to the last known address of any person to be notified.

(c) The notification must include an itemized statement of the claim, a description of the goods subject to the lien, a demand for payment within a specified time not less than ten days after receipt of the notification, and a conspicuous statement that unless the claim is paid within that time the goods will be advertised for sale and sold by auction at a specified time and place.

(d) The sale must conform to the terms of the notification.

(e) The sale must be held at the nearest suitable place to that where the goods are held or stored.

(f) After the expiration of the time given in the notification, an advertisement of the sale must be published once a week for two weeks consecutively in a newspaper of general circulation where the sale is to be held. The advertisement must include a description of the goods, the name of the person on whose account they are being held, and the time and place of the sale. The sale must take place at least fifteen days after the first publication. If there is no newspaper of general circulation where the sale is to be held, the advertisement must be posted at least ten days before the sale in not less than six conspicuous places in the neighborhood of the proposed sale.

(3) Before any sale pursuant to this section any person claiming a right in the goods may pay the amount necessary to satisfy the lien and the reasonable expenses incurred under this section. In that event the goods must not be sold, but must be retained by the warehouseman subject to the terms of the receipt and this Article.

(4) The warehouseman may buy at any public sale pursuant to this section.

(5) A purchaser in good faith of goods sold to enforce a warehouseman's lien takes the goods free of any rights of persons against whom the lien was valid, despite noncompliance by the warehouseman with the requirements of this section.

(6) The warehouseman may satisfy his lien from the proceeds of any sale pursuant to this section but must hold the balance, if any, for delivery on demand to any person to whom he would have been bound to deliver the goods.

(7) The rights provided by this section shall be in addition to all other rights allowed by law to a creditor against his debtor.

(8) Where a lien is on goods stored by a merchant in the course of his business the lien may be enforced in accordance with either subsection (1) or (2).

(9) The warehouseman is liable for damages caused by failure to comply with the requirements for sale under this section and in case of willful violation is liable for conversion. As amended in 1962.

PART 3

BILLS OF LADING: SPECIAL PROVISIONS

§ 7—301. Liability for Non-Receipt or Misdescription; "Said to Contain"; "Shipper's Load and Count"; Improper Handling

(1) A consignee of a non-negotiable bill who has given value in good faith or a holder to whom a negotiable bill has been duly negotiated relying in either case upon the description therein of the goods, or upon the date therein shown, may recover from the issuer damages caused by the misdating of the bill or the non-receipt or misdescription of the goods, except to the extent that the document indicates that the issuer does not know whether any part or all of the goods in fact were received or conform to the description, as where the description is in terms of marks or labels or kind, quantity, or condition or the receipt or description is qualified by "contents or condition of contents of packages unknown", "said to contain", "shipper's weight, load and count" or the like, if such indication be true.

(2) When goods are loaded by an issuer who is a common carrier, the issuer must count the packages of goods if package freight and ascertain the kind and quantity if bulk freight. In such cases "shipper's weight, load and count" or other words indicating that the description was made by the shipper are ineffective except as to freight concealed by packages.

(3) When bulk freight is loaded by a shipper who makes available to the issuer adequate facilities for weighing such freight, an issuer who is a common carrier must ascertain the kind and quantity within a reasonable time after receiving the written request of the shipper to do so. In such cases "shipper's weight" or other words of like purport are ineffective.

(4) The issuer may by inserting in the bill the words "shipper's weight, load and count" or other words of like purport indicate that the goods were loaded by the shipper; and if such statement be true the issuer shall not be liable for damages caused by the improper loading. But their omission does not imply liability for such damages.

(5) The shipper shall be deemed to have guaranteed to the issuer the accuracy at the time of shipment of the description, marks, labels, number, kind, quantity, condition and weight, as furnished by him; and the shipper shall indemnify the issuer against damage caused by inaccuracies in such particulars. The right of the issuer to such indemnity shall in no way limit his responsibility and liability under the contract of carriage to any person other than the shipper.

§ 7—302. Through Bills of Lading and Similar Documents

(1) The issuer of a through bill of lading or other document embodying an undertaking to be performed in part by persons acting as its agents or by connecting carriers is liable to anyone entitled to recover on the document for any breach by such other persons or by a connecting carrier of its obligation under the document but to the extent that the bill covers an undertaking to be performed overseas or in territory not contiguous to the continental United States or an undertaking including matters other than transportation this liability may be varied by agreement of the parties.

(2) Where goods covered by a through bill of lading or other document embodying an undertaking to be performed in part by persons other than the issuer are received by any such person, he is subject with respect to his own performance while the goods are in his possession to the obligation of the issuer. His obligation is discharged by delivery of the goods to another such person pursuant to the document, and does not include liability for breach by any other such persons or by the issuer.

(3) The issuer of such through bill of lading or other document shall be entitled to recover from the connecting carrier or such other person in possession of the goods when the breach of the obligation under the document occurred, the amount it may be required to pay to anyone entitled to recover on the document therefor, as may be evidenced by any receipt, judgment, or transcript thereof, and the amount of any expense reasonably incurred by it in defending any action brought by anyone entitled to recover on the document therefor.

§ 7—303. Diversion; Reconsignment; Change of Instructions

(1) Unless the bill of lading otherwise provides, the carrier may deliver the goods to a person or destination other than that stated in the bill or may otherwise dispose of the goods on instructions from

(a) the holder of a negotiable bill; or

(b) the consignor on a non-negotiable bill notwithstanding contrary instructions from the consignee; or

(c) the consignee on a non-negotiable bill in the absence of contrary instructions from the consignor, if the goods have arrived at the billed destination or if the consignee is in possession of the bill; or

(d) the consignee on a non-negotiable bill if he is entitled as against the consignor to dispose of them.

(2) Unless such instructions are noted on a negotiable bill of lading, a person to whom the bill is duly negotiated can hold the bailee according to the original terms.

§ 7—304. Bills of Lading in a Set

(1) Except where customary in overseas transportation, a bill of lading must not be issued in a set of parts. The issuer is liable for damages caused by violation of this subsection.

(2) Where a bill of lading is lawfully drawn in a set of parts, each of which is numbered and expressed to be valid only if the goods have not been delivered against any other part, the whole of the parts constitute one bill.

(3) Where a bill of lading is lawfully issued in a set of parts and different parts are negotiated to different persons, the title of the holder to whom the first due negotiation is made prevails as to both the document and the goods even though any later holder may have received the goods from the carrier in good faith and discharged the carrier's obligation by surrender of his part.

(4) Any person who negotiates or transfers a single part of a bill of lading drawn in a set is liable to holders of that part as if it were the whole set.

(5) The bailee is obliged to deliver in accordance with Part 4 of this Article against the first presented part of a bill of lading lawfully drawn in a set. Such delivery discharges the bailee's obligation on the whole bill.

§ 7—305. Destination Bills

(1) Instead of issuing a bill of lading to the consignor at the place of shipment a carrier may at the request of the consignor procure the bill to be issued at destination or at any other place designated in the request.

(2) Upon request of anyone entitled as against the carrier to control the goods while in transit and on surrender of any outstanding bill of lading or other receipt covering such goods, the issuer may procure a substitute bill to be issued at any place designated in the request.

§ 7—306. Altered Bills of Lading

An unauthorized alteration or filling in of a blank in a bill of lading leaves the bill enforceable according to its original tenor.

§ 7—307. Lien of Carrier

(1) A carrier has a lien on the goods covered by a bill of lading for charges subsequent to the date of its receipt of the goods for storage or transportation (including demurrage and terminal charges) and for expenses necessary for preservation of the goods incident to their transportation or reasonably incurred in their sale pursuant to law. But against a purchaser for value of a negotiable bill of lading a carrier's lien is limited to charges stated in the bill or the applicable tariffs, or if no charges are stated then to a reasonable charge.

(2) A lien for charges and expenses under subsection (1) on goods which the carrier was required by law to receive for transportation is effective against the consignor or any person entitled to the goods unless the carrier had notice that the consignor lacked authority to subject the goods to such charges and expenses. Any other lien under subsection (1) is effective against the consignor and any person who permitted the bailor to have control or possession of the goods unless the carrier had notice that the bailor lacked such authority.

(3) A carrier loses his lien on any goods which he voluntarily delivers or which he unjustifiably refuses to deliver.

§ 7—308. Enforcement of Carrier's Lien

(1) A carrier's lien may be enforced by public or private sale of the goods, in block or in parcels, at any time or place and on any terms which are commercially reasonable, after notifying all persons known to claim an interest in the goods. Such notification must include a statement of the amount due, the nature of the proposed sale and the time and place of any public sale. The fact that a better price could have been obtained by a sale at a different time or in a different method from that selected by the carrier is not of itself sufficient to establish that the sale was not made in a commercially reasonable manner. If the carrier either sells the goods in the usual manner in any recognized market therefor or if he sells at the price current in such market at the time of his sale or if he has otherwise sold in conformity with commercially reasonable practices among dealers in the type of goods sold he has sold in a commercially reasonable manner. A sale of more goods than apparently necessary to be offered to ensure satisfaction of the obligation is not commercially reasonable except in cases covered by the preceding sentence.

(2) Before any sale pursuant to this section any person claiming a right in the goods may pay the amount necessary to satisfy the lien and the reasonable expenses incurred under this section. In that event the goods must not be sold, but must be retained by the carrier subject to the terms of the bill and this Article.

(3) The carrier may buy at any public sale pursuant to this section.

(4) A purchaser in good faith of goods sold to enforce a carrier's lien takes the goods free of any rights of persons against whom the lien was valid, despite noncompliance by the carrier with the requirements of this section.

(5) The carrier may satisfy his lien from the proceeds of any sale pursuant to this section but must hold the balance, if any, for delivery on demand to any person to whom he would have been bound to deliver the goods.

(6) The rights provided by this section shall be in addition to all other rights allowed by law to a creditor against his debtor.

(7) A carrier's lien may be enforced in accordance with either subsection (1) or the procedure set forth in subsection (2) of Section 7—210.

(8) The carrier is liable for damages caused by failure to comply with the requirements for sale under this section and in case of willful violation is liable for conversion.

§ 7—309. Duty of Care; Contractual Limitation of Carrier's Liability

(1) A carrier who issues a bill of lading whether negotiable or non-negotiable must exercise the degree of care in relation to the goods which a reasonably careful man would exercise under like circumstances. This subsection does not repeal or change any law or rule of law which imposes liability upon a common carrier for damages not caused by its negligence.

(2) Damages may be limited by a provision that the carrier's liability shall not exceed a value stated in the document if the carrier's rates are dependent upon value and the consignor by the carrier's tariff is afforded an opportunity to declare a higher value or a value as lawfully provided in the tariff, or where no tariff is filed he is otherwise advised of such opportunity; but no such limitation is effective with respect to the carrier's liability for conversion to its own use.

(3) Reasonable provisions as to the time and manner of presenting claims and instituting actions based on the shipment may be included in a bill of lading or tariff.

PART 4

WAREHOUSE RECEIPTS AND BILLS OF LADING: GENERAL OBLIGATIONS

§ 7—401. Irregularities in Issue of Receipt or Bill or Conduct of Issuer

The obligations imposed by this Article on an issuer apply to a document of title regardless of the fact that

(a) the document may not comply with the requirements of this Article or of any other law or regulation regarding its issue, form or content; or

(b) the issuer may have violated laws regulating the conduct of his business; or

(c) the goods covered by the document were owned by the bailee at the time the document was issued; or

(d) the person issuing the document does not come within the definition of warehouseman if it purports to be a warehouse receipt.

§ 7—402. Duplicate Receipt or Bill; Overissue

Neither a duplicate nor any other document of title purporting to cover goods already represented by an outstanding document of the same issuer confers any right in the goods, except as provided in the case of bills in a set, overissue of documents for fungible goods and substitutes for lost, stolen or destroyed documents. But the issuer is liable for damages caused by his overissue or failure to identify a duplicate document as such by conspicuous notation on its face.

§ 7—403. Obligation of Warehouseman or Carrier to Deliver; Excuse

(1) The bailee must deliver the goods to a person entitled under the document who complies with subsections (2) and (3), unless and to the extent that the bailee establishes any of the following:

(a) delivery of the goods to a person whose receipt was rightful as against the claimant;

(b) damage to or delay, loss or destruction of the goods for which the bailee is not liable [, but the burden of establishing negligence in such cases is on the person entitled under the document];

Note: *The brackets in (1) (b) indicate that State enactments may differ on this point without serious damage to the principle of uniformity.*

(c) previous sale or other disposition of the goods in lawful enforcement of a lien or on warehouseman's lawful termination of storage;

(d) the exercise by a seller of his right to stop delivery pursuant to the provisions of the Article on Sales (Section 2—705);

(e) a diversion, reconsignment or other disposition pursuant to the provisions of this Article (Section 7—303) or tariff regulating such right;

(f) release, satisfaction or any other fact affording a personal defense against the claimant;

(g) any other lawful excuse.

(2) A person claiming goods covered by a document of title must satisfy the bailee's lien where the bailee so requests or where the bailee is prohibited by law from delivering the goods until the charges are paid.

(3) Unless the person claiming is one against whom the document confers no right under Sec. 7—503(1), he must surrender for cancellation or notation of partial deliveries any outstanding negotiable document covering the goods, and the bailee must cancel the document or conspicuously note the partial delivery thereon or be liable to any person to whom the document is duly negotiated.

(4) "Person entitled under the document" means holder in the case of a negotiable document, or the person to whom delivery is to be made by the terms of or pursuant to written instructions under a non-negotiable document.

§ 7—404. No Liability for Good Faith Delivery Pursuant to Receipt or Bill

A bailee who in good faith including observance of reasonable commercial standards has received goods and delivered or otherwise disposed of them according to the terms of the document of title or pursuant to this Article is not liable therefor. This rule applies even though the person from whom he received the goods had no authority to procure the document or to dispose of the goods and even though the person to whom he delivered the goods had no authority to receive them.

PART 5

WAREHOUSE RECEIPTS AND BILLS OF LADING: NEGOTIATION AND TRANSFER

§ 7—501. Form of Negotiation and Requirements of "Due Negotiation"

(1) A negotiable document of title running to the order of a named person is negotiated by his indorsement and delivery. After his indorsement in blank or to bearer any person can negotiate it by delivery alone.

(2) (a) A negotiable document of title is also negotiated by delivery alone when by its original terms it runs to bearer.

(b) When a document running to the order of a named person is delivered to him the effect is the same as if the document had been negotiated.

(3) Negotiation of a negotiable document of title after it has been indorsed to a specified person requires indorsement by the special indorsee as well as delivery.

(4) A negotiable document of title is "duly negotiated" when it is negotiated in the manner stated in this section to a holder who purchases it in good faith without notice of any defense against or claim to it on the part of any person and for value, unless it is established that the negotiation is not in the regular course of business or financing or involves receiving the document in settlement or payment of a money obligation.

(5) Indorsement of a non-negotiable document neither makes it negotiable nor adds to the transferee's rights.

(6) The naming in a negotiable bill of a person to be notified of the arrival of the goods does not limit the negotiability of the bill nor constitute notice to a purchaser thereof of any interest of such person in the goods.

§ 7—502. Rights Acquired by Due Negotiation

(1) Subject to the following section and to the provisions of Section 7—205 on fungible goods, a holder to whom a negotiable document of title has been duly negotiated acquires thereby:

(a) title to the document;

(b) title to the goods;

(c) all rights accruing under the law of agency or estoppel, including rights to goods delivered to the bailee after the document was issued; and

(d) the direct obligation of the issuer to hold or deliver the goods according to the terms of the document free of any defense or claim by him except those arising under the terms of the document or under this Article. In the case of a delivery order the bailee's obligation accrues only upon acceptance and the obligation acquired by the holder is that the issuer and any indorser will procure the acceptance of the bailee.

(2) Subject to the following section, title and rights so acquired are not defeated by any stoppage of the goods represented by the document or by surrender of such goods by the bailee, and are not impaired even though the negotiation or any prior negotiation constituted a breach of duty or even though any person has been deprived of possession of the document by misrepresentation, fraud, accident, mistake, duress, loss, theft or conversion, or even though a previous sale or other transfer of the goods or document has been made to a third person.

§ 7—503. Document of Title to Goods Defeated in Certain Cases

(1) A document of title confers no right in goods against a person who before issuance of the document had a legal interest or a perfected security interest in them and who neither

(a) delivered or entrusted them or any document of title covering them to the bailor or his nominee with actual or apparent authority to ship, store or sell or with power to obtain delivery under this Article (Section 7—403) or with power of disposition under this Act (Sections 2—403 and 9—307) or other statute or rule of law; nor

(b) acquiesced in the procurement by the bailor or his nominee of any document of title.

(2) Title to goods based upon an unaccepted delivery order is subject to the rights of anyone to whom a negotiable warehouse receipt or bill of lading covering the goods has been duly negotiated. Such a title may be defeated under the next section to the same extent as the rights of the issuer or a transferee from the issuer.

(3) Title to goods based upon a bill of lading issued to a freight forwarder is subject to the rights of anyone to whom a bill issued by the freight forwarder is duly negotiated; but delivery by the carrier in accordance with Part 4 of this Article pursuant to its own bill of lading discharges the carrier's obligation to deliver.

§ 7—504. Rights Acquired in the Absence of Due Negotiation; Effect of Diversion; Seller's Stoppage of Delivery

(1) A transferee of a document, whether negotiable or nonnegotiable, to whom the document has been delivered but not duly negotiated, acquires the title and rights which his transferor had or had actual authority to convey.

(2) In the case of a non-negotiable document, until but not after the bailee receives notification of the transfer, the rights of the transferee may be defeated

(a) by those creditors of the transferor who could treat the sale as void under Section 2—402; or

(b) by a buyer from the transferor in ordinary course of business if the bailee has delivered the goods to the buyer or received notification of his rights; or

(c) as against the bailee by good faith dealings of the bailee with the transferor.

(3) A diversion or other change of shipping instructions by the consignor in a non-negotiable bill of lading which causes the bailee not to deliver to the consignee defeats the consignee's title to the goods if they have been delivered to a buyer in ordinary course of business and in any event defeats the consignee's rights against the bailee.

(4) Delivery pursuant to a non-negotiable document may be stopped by a seller under Section 2—705, and subject to the requirement of due notification there provided. A bailee honoring the seller's instructions is entitled to be indemnified by the seller against any resulting loss or expense.

§ 7—505. Indorser Not a Guarantor for Other Parties

The indorsement of a document of title issued by a bailee does not make the indorser liable for any default by the bailee or by previous indorsers.

§ 7—506. Delivery Without Indorsement: Right to Compel Indorsement

The transferee of a negotiable document of title has a specifically enforceable right to have his transferor supply any necessary indorsement but the transfer becomes a negotiation only as of the time the indorsement is supplied.

§ 7—507. Warranties on Negotiation or Transfer of Receipt or Bill

Where a person negotiates or transfers a document of title for value otherwise than as a mere intermediary under the next following section, then unless otherwise agreed he warrants to his immediate purchaser only in addition to any warranty made in selling the goods

(a) that the document is genuine; and

(b) that he has no knowledge of any fact which would impair its validity or worth; and

(c) that his negotiation or transfer is rightful and fully effective with respect to the title to the document and the goods it represents.

§ 7—508. Warranties of Collecting Bank as to Documents

A collecting bank or other intermediary known to be entrusted with documents on behalf of another or with collection of a draft or other claim against delivery of documents warrants by such delivery of the documents only its own good faith and authority. This rule applies even though the intermediary has purchased or made advances against the claim or draft to be collected.

§ 7—509. Receipt or Bill: When Adequate Compliance With Commercial Contract

The question whether a document is adequate to fulfill the obligations of a contract for sale or the conditions of a credit is governed by the Articles on Sales (Article 2) and on Letters of Credit (Article 5).

PART 6

WAREHOUSE RECEIPTS AND BILLS OF LADING: MISCELLANEOUS PROVISIONS

§ 7—601. Lost and Missing Documents

(1) If a document has been lost, stolen or destroyed, a court may order delivery of the goods or issuance of a substitute document and the bailee may without liability to any person comply with such order. If the document was negotiable the claimant must post security approved by the court to indemnify any person who may suffer loss as a result of non-surrender of the document. If the document was not negotiable, such security may be required at the discretion of the court. The court may also in its discretion order payment of the bailee's reasonable costs and counsel fees.

(2) A bailee who without court order delivers goods to a person claiming under a missing negotiable document is liable to any person injured thereby, and if the delivery is not in good faith becomes liable for conversion. Delivery in good faith is not conversion if made in accordance with a filed classification or tariff or, where no classification or tariff is filed, if the claimant posts security with the bailee in an amount at least double the value of the goods at the time of posting to indemnify any person injured by the delivery who files a notice of claim within one year after the delivery.

§ 7—602. Attachment of Goods Covered by a Negotiable Document

Except where the document was originally issued upon delivery of the goods by a person who had no power to dispose of them, no lien attaches by virtue of any judicial process to goods in the possession of a bailee for which a negotiable document of title is outstanding unless the document be first surrendered to the bailee or its negotiation enjoined, and the bailee shall not be compelled to deliver the goods pursuant to process until the document is surrendered to him or impounded by the court. One who purchases the document for value without notice of the process or injunction takes free of the lien imposed by judicial process.

§ 7—603. Conflicting Claims; Interpleader

If more than one person claims title or possession of the goods, the bailee is excused from delivery until he has had a reasonable time to ascertain the validity of the adverse claims or to bring an action to compel all claimants to interplead and may compel such interpleader, either in defending an action for non-delivery of the goods, or by original action, whichever is appropriate.

*

ARTICLE 8

INVESTMENT SECURITIES

PART 1. SHORT TITLE AND GENERAL MATTERS

PART 2. ISSUE—ISSUER

PART 3. TRANSFER

PART 1

SHORT TITLE AND GENERAL MATTERS

§ 8—101. Short Title

This Article shall be known and may be cited as Uniform Commercial Code—Investment Securities.

§ 8—102. Definitions and Index of Definitions

(1) In this Article, unless the context otherwise requires:

(a) A "certificated security" is a share, participation, or other interest in property of or an enterprise of the issuer or an obligation of the issuer which is

(i) represented by an instrument issued in bearer or registered form;

(ii) of a type commonly dealt in on securities exchanges or markets or commonly recognized in any area in which it is issued or dealt in as a medium for investment; and

(iii) either one of a class or series or by its terms divisible into a class or series of shares, participations, interests, or obligations.

(b) An "uncertificated security" is a share, participation, or other interest in property or an enterprise of the issuer or an obligation of the issuer which is

(i) not represented by an instrument and the transfer of which is registered upon books maintained for that purpose by or on behalf of the issuer;

(ii) of a type commonly dealt in on securities exchanges or markets; and

(iii) either one of a class or series or by its terms divisible into a class or series of shares, participations, interests, or obligations.

(c) A "security" is either a certificated or an uncertificated security. If a security is certificated, the terms "security" and "certificated security" may mean either the intangible interest, the instrument representing that interest, or both, as the context requires. A writing that is a certificated security is governed by this Article and not by Article 3, even though it also meets the requirements of that Article. This Article does not apply to money. If a certificated security has been retained by or surrendered to the issuer or its transfer agent for reasons other than registration of transfer, other temporary purpose, payment, exchange, or acquisition by the issuer, that security shall be treated as an uncertificated security for purposes of this Article.

(d) A certificated security is in "registered form" if

(i) it specifies a person entitled to the security or the rights it represents; and

(ii) its transfer may be registered upon books maintained for that purpose by or on behalf of the issuer, or the security so states.

(e) A certificated security is in "bearer form" if it runs to bearer according to its terms and not by reason of any indorsement.

(2) A "subsequent purchaser" is a person who takes other than by original issue.

(3) A "clearing corporation" is a corporation registered as a "clearing agency" under the federal securities laws or a corporation:

(a) at least 90 percent of whose capital stock is held by or for one or more organizations, none of which, other than a national securities exchange or association, holds in excess of 20 percent of the capital stock of the corporation, and each of which is

(i) subject to supervision or regulation pursuant to the provisions of federal or state banking laws or state insurance laws,

(ii) a broker or dealer or investment company registered under the federal securities laws, or

(iii) a national securities exchange or association registered under the federal securities laws; and

(b) any remaining capital stock of which is held by individuals who have purchased it at or prior to the time of their taking office as directors of the corporation and who have purchased only so much of the capital stock as is necessary to permit them to qualify as directors.

(4) A "custodian bank" is a bank or trust company that is supervised and examined by state or federal authority having supervision over banks and is acting as custodian for a clearing corporation.

(5) Other definitions applying to this Article or to specified Parts thereof and the sections in which they appear are:

"Adverse claim".	Section 8—302.
"Bona fide purchaser".	Section 8—302.
"Broker".	Section 8—303.
"Debtor".	Section 9—105.
"Financial intermediary".	Section 8—313.
"Guarantee of the signature".	Section 8—402.
"Initial transaction statement".	Section 8—408.
"Instruction".	Section 8—308.

"Intermediary bank".	Section 4—105.
"Issuer".	Section 8—201.
"Overissue".	Section 8—104.
"Secured Party".	Section 9—105.
"Security Agreement".	Section 9—105.

(6) In addition, Article 1 contains general definitions and principles of construction and interpretation applicable throughout this Article.

Amended in 1962, 1973 and 1977.

§ 8—103. Issuer's Lien

A lien upon a security in favor of an issuer thereof is valid against a purchaser only if:

(a) the security is certificated and the right of the issuer to the lien is noted conspicuously thereon; or

(b) the security is uncertificated and a notation of the right of the issuer to the lien is contained in the initial transaction statement sent to the purchaser or, if his interest is transferred to him other than by registration of transfer, pledge, or release, the initial transaction statement sent to the registered owner or the registered pledgee.

Amended in 1977.

§ 8—104. Effect of Overissue; "Overissue"

(1) The provisions of this Article which validate a security or compel its issue or reissue do not apply to the extent that validation, issue, or reissue would result in overissue; but if:

(a) an identical security which does not constitute an overissue is reasonably available for purchase, the person entitled to issue or validation may compel the issuer to purchase the security for him and either to deliver a certificated security or to register the transfer of an uncertificated security to him, against surrender of any certificated security he holds; or

(b) a security is not so available for purchase, the person entitled to issue or validation may recover from the issuer the price he or the last purchaser for value paid for it with interest from the date of his demand.

(2) "Overissue" means the issue of securities in excess of the amount the issuer has corporate power to issue.

Amended in 1977.

§ 8—105. Certificated Securities Negotiable; Statements and Instructions Not Negotiable; Presumptions

(1) Certificated securities governed by this Article are negotiable instruments.

(2) Statements (Section 8—408), notices, or the like, sent by the issuer of uncertificated securities and instructions (Section 8—308) are neither negotiable instruments nor certificated securities.

(3) In any action on a security:

(a) unless specifically denied in the pleadings, each signature on a certificated security, in a necessary indorsement, on an initial transaction statement, or on an instruction, is admitted;

(b) if the effectiveness of a signature is put in issue, the burden of establishing it is on the party claiming under the signature, but the signature is presumed to be genuine or authorized;

(c) if signatures on a certificated security are admitted or established, production of the security entitles a holder to recover on it unless the defendant establishes a defense or a defect going to the validity of the security;

(d) if signatures on an initial transaction statement are admitted or established, the facts stated in the statement are presumed to be true as of the time of its issuance; and

(e) after it is shown that a defense or defect exists, the plaintiff has the burden of establishing that he or some person under whom he claims is a person against whom the defense or defect is ineffective (Section 8—202).

Amended in 1977.

§ 8—106. Applicability

The law (including the conflict of laws rules) of the jurisdiction of organization of the issuer governs the validity of a security, the effectiveness of registration by the issuer, and the rights and duties of the issuer with respect to:

(a) registration of transfer of a certificated security;

(b) registration of transfer, pledge, or release of an uncertificated security; and

(c) sending of statements of uncertificated securities.

Amended in 1977.

§ 8—107. Securities Transferable; Action for Price

(1) Unless otherwise agreed and subject to any applicable law or regulation respecting short sales, a person obligated to transfer securities may transfer any certificated security of the specified issue in bearer form or registered in the name of the transferee, or indorsed to him or in blank, or he may transfer an equivalent uncertificated security to the transferee or a person designated by the transferee.

(2) If the buyer fails to pay the price as it comes due under a contract of sale, the seller may recover the price of:

(a) certificated securities accepted by the buyer;

(b) uncertificated securities that have been transferred to the buyer or a person designated by the buyer; and

(c) other securities if efforts at their resale would be unduly burdensome or if there is no readily available market for their resale.

Amended in 1977.

§ 8—108. Registration of Pledge and Release of Uncertificated Securities

A security interest in an uncertificated security may be evidenced by the registration of pledge to the secured party or a person designated by him. There can be no more than one registered pledge of an uncertificated security at any time. The registered owner of an uncertificated security is the person in whose name the security is registered, even if the security is subject to a registered pledge. The rights of a registered pledgee of an uncertificated security under this Article are terminated by the registration of release.

Added in 1977.

PART 2

ISSUE—ISSUER

§ 8—201. "Issuer"

(1) With respect to obligations on or defenses to a security, "issuer" includes a person who:

(a) places or authorizes the placing of his name on a certificated security (otherwise than as authenticating trustee, registrar, transfer agent, or the like) to evidence that it represents a share, participation, or other interest in his property or in an enterprise, or to evidence his duty to perform an obligation represented by the certificated security;

(b) creates shares, participations, or other interests in his property or in an enterprise or undertakes obligations, which shares, participations, interests, or obligations are uncertificated securities;

(c) directly or indirectly creates fractional interests in his rights or property, which fractional interests are represented by certificated securities; or

(d) becomes responsible for or in place of any other person described as an issuer in this section.

(2) With respect to obligations on or defenses to a security, a guarantor is an issuer to the extent of his guaranty, whether or not his obligation is noted on a certificated security or on statements of uncertificated securities sent pursuant to Section 8—408.

(3) With respect to registration of transfer, pledge, or release (Part 4 of this Article), "issuer" means a person on whose behalf transfer books are maintained.

Amended in 1977.

§ 8—202. Issuer's Responsibility and Defenses; Notice of Defect or Defense

(1) Even against a purchaser for value and without notice, the terms of a security include:

(a) if the security is certificated, those stated on the security;

(b) if the security is uncertificated, those contained in the initial transaction statement sent to such purchaser or, if his interest is transferred to him other than by registration of transfer, pledge, or release, the initial transaction statement sent to the registered owner or registered pledgee; and

(c) those made part of the security by reference, on the certificated security or in the initial transaction statement, to another instrument, indenture, or document or to a constitution, statute, ordinance, rule, regulation, order or the like, to the extent that the terms referred to do not conflict with the terms stated on the certificated security or contained in the statement. A reference under this paragraph does not of itself charge a purchaser for value with notice of a defect going to the validity of the security, even though the certificated security or statement expressly states that a person accepting it admits notice.

(2) A certificated security in the hands of a purchaser for value or an uncertificated security as to which an initial transaction statement has been sent to a purchaser for value, other than a security issued by a government or governmental agency or unit, even though issued with a defect going to its validity, is valid with respect to the purchaser if he is without notice of the particular defect unless the defect involves a violation of constitutional provisions, in which case the security is valid with respect to a subsequent purchaser for value and without notice of the defect. This subsection applies to an issuer that is a government or governmental agency or unit only if either there has been substantial compliance with the legal requirements governing the issue or the issuer has received a substantial consideration for the issue as a whole or for the particular security and a stated purpose of the issue is one for which the issuer has power to borrow money or issue the security.

(3) Except as provided in the case of certain unauthorized signatures (Section 8—205), lack of genuineness of a certificated security or an initial transaction statement is a complete defense, even against a purchaser for value and without notice.

(4) All other defenses of the issuer of a certificated or uncertificated security, including nondelivery and conditional delivery of a certificated security, are ineffective against a purchaser for value who has taken without notice of the particular defense.

(5) Nothing in this section shall be construed to affect the right of a party to a "when, as and if issued" or a "when distributed" contract to cancel the contract in the event of a material

change in the character of the security that is the subject of the contract or in the plan or arrangement pursuant to which the security is to be issued or distributed.

Amended in 1977.

§ 8—203. Staleness as Notice of Defects or Defenses

(1) After an act or event creating a right to immediate performance of the principal obligation represented by a certificated security or that sets a date on or after which the security is to be presented or surrendered for redemption or exchange, a purchaser is charged with notice of any defect in its issue or defense of the issuer if:

- (a) the act or event is one requiring the payment of money, the delivery of certificated securities, the registration of transfer of uncertificated securities, or any of these on presentation or surrender of the certificated security, the funds or securities are available on the date set for payment or exchange, and he takes the security more than one year after that date; and
- (b) the act or event is not covered by paragraph (a) and he takes the security more than 2 years after the date set for surrender or presentation or the date on which performance became due.

(2) A call that has been revoked is not within subsection (1).

Amended in 1977.

§ 8—204. Effect of Issuer's Restrictions on Transfer

A restriction on transfer of a security imposed by the issuer, even if otherwise lawful, is ineffective against any person without actual knowledge of it unless:

- (a) the security is certificated and the restriction is noted conspicuously thereon; or
- (b) the security is uncertificated and a notation of the restriction is contained in the initial transaction statement sent to the person or, if his interest is transferred to him other than by registration of transfer, pledge, or release, the initial transaction statement sent to the registered owner or the registered pledgee.

Amended in 1977.

§ 8—205. Effect of Unauthorized Signature on Certificated Security or Initial Transaction Statement

An unauthorized signature placed on a certificated security prior to or in the course of issue or placed on an initial transaction statement is ineffective, but the signature is effective in favor of a purchaser for value of the certificated security or a purchaser for value of an uncertificated security to whom the initial transaction statement has been sent, if the purchaser is without notice of the lack of authority and the signing has been done by:

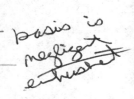

(a) an authenticating trustee, registrar, transfer agent, or other person entrusted by the issuer with the signing of the security, of similar securities, or of initial transaction statements or the immediate preparation for signing of any of them; or

(b) an employee of the issuer, or of any of the foregoing, entrusted with responsible handling of the security or initial transaction statement.

Amended in 1977.

§ 8—206. Completion or Alteration of Certificated Security or Initial Transaction Statement

(1) If a certificated security contains the signatures necessary to its issue or transfer but is incomplete in any other respect:

(a) any person may complete it by filling in the blanks as authorized; and

(b) even though the blanks are incorrectly filled in, the security as completed is enforceable by a purchaser who took it for value and without notice of the incorrectness.

(2) A complete certificated security that has been improperly altered, even though fraudulently, remains enforceable, but only according to its original terms.

(3) If an initial transaction statement contains the signatures necessary to its validity, but is incomplete in any other respect:

(a) any person may complete it by filling in the blanks as authorized; and

(b) even though the blanks are incorrectly filled in, the statement as completed is effective in favor of the person to whom it is sent if he purchased the security referred to therein for value and without notice of the incorrectness.

(4) A complete initial transaction statement that has been improperly altered, even though fraudulently, is effective in favor of a purchaser to whom it has been sent, but only according to its original terms.

Amended in 1977.

§ 8—207. Rights and Duties of Issuer With Respect to Registered Owners and Registered Pledgees

(1) Prior to due presentment for registration of transfer of a certificated security in registered form, the issuer or indenture trustee may treat the registered owner as the person exclusively entitled to vote, to receive notifications, and otherwise to exercise all the rights and powers of an owner.

(2) Subject to the provisions of subsections (3), (4), and (6), the issuer or indenture trustee may treat the registered owner of an uncertificated security as the person exclusively entitled to vote, to receive notifications, and otherwise to exercise all the rights and powers of an owner.

(3) The registered owner of an uncertificated security that is subject to a registered pledge is not entitled to registration of transfer prior to the due presentment to the issuer of a release instruction. The exercise of conversion rights with respect to a convertible uncertificated security is a transfer within the meaning of this section.

(4) Upon due presentment of a transfer instruction from the registered pledgee of an uncertificated security, the issuer shall:

(a) register the transfer of the security to the new owner free of pledge, if the instruction specifies a new owner (who may be the registered pledgee) and does not specify a pledgee;

(b) register the transfer of the security to the new owner subject to the interest of the existing pledgee, if the instruction specifies a new owner and the existing pledgee; or

(c) register the release of the security from the existing pledge and register the pledge of the security to the other pledgee, if the instruction specifies the existing owner and another pledgee.

(5) Continuity of perfection of a security interest is not broken by registration of transfer under subsection (4)(b) or by registration of release and pledge under subsection (4)(c), if the security interest is assigned.

(6) If an uncertificated security is subject to a registered pledge:

(a) any uncertificated securities issued in exchange for or distributed with respect to the pledged security shall be registered subject to the pledge;

(b) any certificated securities issued in exchange for or distributed with respect to the pledged security shall be delivered to the registered pledgee; and

(c) any money paid in exchange for or in redemption of part or all of the security shall be paid to the registered pledgee.

(7) Nothing in this Article shall be construed to affect the liability of the registered owner of a security for calls, assessments, or the like.

Amended in 1977.

§ 8—208. Effect of Signature of Authenticating Trustee, Registrar, or Transfer Agent

(1) A person placing his signature upon a certificated security or an initial transaction statement as authenticating trustee, registrar, transfer agent, or the like, warrants to a purchaser for value of the certificated security or a purchaser for value of an uncertificated security to whom the initial transaction statement has been sent, if the purchaser is without notice of the particular defect, that:

(a) the certificated security or initial transaction statement is genuine;

(b) his own participation in the issue or registration of the transfer, pledge, or release of the security is within his capacity and within the scope of the authority received by him from the issuer; and

(c) he has reasonable grounds to believe the security is in the form and within the amount the issuer is authorized to issue.

(2) Unless otherwise agreed, a person by so placing his signature does not assume responsibility for the validity of the security in other respects.

Amended in 1962 and 1977.

PART 3

TRANSFER

§ 8—301. Rights Acquired by Purchaser

(1) Upon transfer of a security to a purchaser (Section 8—313), the purchaser acquires the rights in the security which his transferor had or had actual authority to convey unless the purchaser's rights are limited by Section 8—302(4).

(2) A transferee of a limited interest acquires rights only to the extent of the interest transferred. The creation or release of a security interest in a security is the transfer of a limited interest in that security.

Amended in 1977.

§ 8—302. "Bona Fide Purchaser"; "Adverse Claim"; Title Acquired by Bona Fide Purchaser

(1) A "bona fide purchaser" is a purchaser for value in good faith and without notice of any adverse claim:

(a) who takes delivery of a certificated security in bearer form or in registered form, issued or indorsed to him or in blank;

(b) to whom the transfer, pledge, or release of an uncertificated security is registered on the books of the issuer; or

(c) to whom a security is transferred under the provisions of paragraph (c), (d)(i), or (g) of Section 8—313(1).

(2) "Adverse claim" includes a claim that a transfer was or would be wrongful or that a particular adverse person is the owner of or has an interest in the security.

(3) A bona fide purchaser in addition to acquiring the rights of a purchaser (Section 8—301) also acquires his interest in the security free of any adverse claim.

(4) Notwithstanding Section 8—301(1), the transferee of a particular certificated security who has been a party to any fraud or illegality affecting the security, or who as a prior holder of that certificated security had notice of an adverse claim, cannot improve his position by taking from a bona fide purchaser.

Amended in 1977.

§ 8—303. "Broker"

"Broker" means a person engaged for all or part of his time in the business of buying and selling securities, who in the transaction concerned acts for, buys a security from, or sells a security to, a customer. Nothing in this Article determines the capacity in which a person acts for purposes of any other statute or rule to which the person is subject.

§ 8—304. Notice to Purchaser of Adverse Claims

(1) A purchaser (including a broker for the seller or buyer, but excluding an intermediary bank) of a certificated security is charged with notice of adverse claims if:

(a) the security, whether in bearer or registered form, has been indorsed "for collection" or "for surrender" or for some other purpose not involving transfer; or

(b) the security is in bearer form and has on it an unambiguous statement that it is the property of a person other than the transferor. The mere writing of a name on a security is not such a statement.

(2) A purchaser (including a broker for the seller or buyer, but excluding an intermediary bank) to whom the transfer, pledge, or release of an uncertificated security is registered is charged with notice of adverse claims as to which the issuer has a duty under Section 8—403(4) at the time of registration and which are noted in the initial transaction statement sent to the purchaser or, if his interest is transferred to him other than by registration of transfer, pledge, or release, the initial transaction statement sent to the registered owner or the registered pledgee.

(3) The fact that the purchaser (including a broker for the seller or buyer) of a certificated or uncertificated security has notice that the security is held for a third person or is registered in the name of or indorsed by a fiduciary does not create a duty of inquiry into the rightfulness of the transfer or constitute constructive notice of adverse claims. However, if the purchaser (excluding an intermediary bank) has knowledge that the proceeds are being used or the transaction is for the individual benefit of the fiduciary or otherwise in breach of duty, the purchaser is charged with notice of adverse claims.

Amended in 1977.

§ 8—305. Staleness as Notice of Adverse Claims

An act or event that creates a right to immediate performance of the principal obligation represented by a certificated security or sets a date on or after which a certificated security is to be presented or surrendered for redemption or exchange does not itself constitute any notice of adverse claims except in the case of a transfer:

(a) after one year from any date set for presentment or surrender for redemption or exchange; or

(b) after 6 months from any date set for payment of money against presentation or surrender of the security if funds are available for payment on that date.

Amended in 1977.

§ 8—306. Warranties on Presentment and Transfer of Certificated Securities; Warranties of Originators of Instructions

(1) A person who presents a certificated security for registration of transfer or for payment or exchange warrants to the issuer that he is entitled to the registration, payment, or exchange. But, a purchaser for value and without notice of adverse claims who receives a new, reissued, or re-registered certificated security on registration of transfer or receives an initial transaction statement confirming the registration of transfer of an equivalent uncertificated security to him warrants only that he has no knowledge of any unauthorized signature (Section 8—311) in a necessary indorsement.

(2) A person by transferring a certificated security to a purchaser for value warrants only that:

(a) his transfer is effective and rightful;

(b) the security is genuine and has not been materially altered; and

(c) he knows of no fact which might impair the validity of the security.

(3) If a certificated security is delivered by an intermediary known to be entrusted with delivery of the security on behalf of another or with collection of a draft or other claim against delivery, the intermediary by delivery warrants only his own good faith and authority, even though he has purchased or made advances against the claim to be collected against the delivery.

(4) A pledgee or other holder for security who redelivers a certificated security received, or after payment and on order of the debtor delivers that security to a third person, makes only the warranties of an intermediary under subsection (3).

(5) A person who originates an instruction warrants to the issuer that:

(a) he is an appropriate person to originate the instruction; and

(b) at the time the instruction is presented to the issuer he will be entitled to the registration of transfer, pledge, or release.

(6) A person who originates an instruction warrants to any person specially guaranteeing his signature (subsection 8—312 (3)) that:

(a) he is an appropriate person to originate the instruction; and

(b) at the time the instruction is presented to the issuer

(i) he will be entitled to the registration of transfer, pledge, or release; and

(ii) the transfer, pledge, or release requested in the instruction will be registered by the issuer free from all liens, security interests, restrictions, and claims other than those specified in the instruction.

(7) A person who originates an instruction warrants to a purchaser for value and to any person guaranteeing the instruction (Section 8—312(6)) that:

(a) he is an appropriate person to originate the instruction;

(b) the uncertificated security referred to therein is valid; and

(c) at the time the instruction is presented to the issuer

(i) the transferor will be entitled to the registration of transfer, pledge, or release;

(ii) the transfer, pledge, or release requested in the instruction will be registered by the issuer free from all liens, security interests, restrictions, and claims other than those specified in the instruction; and

(iii) the requested transfer, pledge, or release will be rightful.

(8) If a secured party is the registered pledgee or the registered owner of an uncertificated security, a person who originates an instruction of release or transfer to the debtor or, after payment and on order of the debtor, a transfer instruction to a third person, warrants to the debtor or the third person only that he is an appropriate person to originate the instruction and, at the time the instruction is presented to the issuer, the transferor will be entited to the registration of release or transfer. If a transfer instruction to a third person who is a purchaser for value is originated on order of the debtor, the debtor makes to the purchaser the warranties of paragraphs (b), (c)(ii) and (c)(iii) of subsection (7).

(9) A person who transfers an uncertificated security to a purchaser for value and does not originate an instruction in connection with the transfer warrants only that:

(a) his transfer is effective and rightful; and

(b) the uncertificated security is valid.

(10) A broker gives to his customer and to the issuer and a purchaser the applicable warranties provided in this section and has the rights and privileges of a purchaser under this section. The warranties of and in favor of the broker, acting as an agent are in addition to applicable warranties given by and in favor of his customer.

Amended in 1962 and 1977.

§ 8—307. Effect of Delivery Without Indorsement; Right to Compel Indorsement

If a certificated security in registered form has been delivered to a purchaser without a necessary indorsement he may become a bona fide purchaser only as of the time the indorsement is supplied; but against the transferor, the transfer is complete upon delivery and the purchaser has a specifically enforceable right to have any necessary indorsement supplied.

Amended in 1977.

§ 8—308. Indorsements; Instructions

(1) An indorsement of a certificated security in registered form is made when an appropriate person signs on it or on a separate document an assignment or transfer of the security or a power to assign or transfer it or his signature is written without more upon the back of the security.

(2) An indorsement may be in blank or special. An indorsement in blank includes an indorsement to bearer. A special indorsement specifies to whom the security is to be transferred, or who has power to transfer it. A holder may convert a blank indorsement into a special indorsement.

(3) An indorsement purporting to be only of part of a certificated security representing units intended by the issuer to be separately transferable is effective to the extent of the indorsement.

(4) An "instruction" is an order to the issuer of an uncertificated security requesting that the transfer, pledge, or release from pledge of the uncertificated security specified therein be registered.

(5) An instruction originated by an appropriate person is:

(a) a writing signed by an appropriate person; or

(b) a communication to the issuer in any form agreed upon in a writing signed by the issuer and an appropriate person.

If an instruction has been originated by an appropriate person but is incomplete in any other respect, any person may complete it as authorized and the issuer may rely on it as completed even though it has been completed incorrectly.

(6) "An appropriate person" in subsection (1) means the person specified by the certificated security or by special indorsement to be entitled to the security.

(7) "An appropriate person" in subsection (5) means:

(a) for an instruction to transfer or pledge an uncertificated security which is then not subject to a registered pledge, the registered owner; or

(b) for an instruction to transfer or release an uncertificated security which is then subject to a registered pledge, the registered pledgee.

(8) In addition to the persons designated in subsections (6) and (7), "an appropriate person" in subsections (1) and (5) includes:

(a) if the person designated is described as a fiduciary but is no longer serving in the described capacity, either that person or his successor;

(b) if the persons designated are described as more than one person as fiduciaries and one or more are no longer serving in the described capacity, the remaining fiduciary or fiduciaries, whether or not a successor has been appointed or qualified;

(c) if the person designated is an individual and is without capacity to act by virtue of death, incompetence, infancy, or otherwise, his executor, administrator, guardian, or like fiduciary;

(d) if the persons designated are described as more than one person as tenants by the entirety or with right of survivorship and by reason of death all cannot sign, the survivor or survivors;

(e) a person having power to sign under applicable law or controlling instrument; and

(f) to the extent that the person designated or any of the foregoing persons may act through an agent, his authorized agent.

(9) Unless otherwise agreed, the indorser of a certificated security by his indorsement or the originator of an instruction by his origination assumes no obligation that the security will be honored by the issuer but only the obligations provided in Section 8—306.

(10) Whether the person signing is appropriate is determined as of the date of signing and an indorsement made by or an instruction originated by him does not become unauthorized for the purposes of this Article by virtue of any subsequent change of circumstances.

(11) Failure of a fiduciary to comply with a controlling instrument or with the law of the state having jurisdiction of the fiduciary relationship, including any law requiring the fiduciary to obtain court approval of the transfer, pledge, or release, does not render his indorsement or an instruction originated by him unauthorized for the purposes of this Article.

Amended in 1962 and 1977.

§ 8—309. Effect of Indorsement Without Delivery

An indorsement of a certificated security, whether special or in blank, does not constitute a transfer until delivery of the certificated security on which it appears or, if the indorsement is on a separate document, until delivery of both the document and the certificated security.

Amended in 1977.

§ 8—310. Indorsement of Certificated Security in Bearer Form

An indorsement of a certificated security in bearer form may give notice of adverse claims (Section 8—304) but does not otherwise affect any right to registration the holder possesses.

Amended in 1977.

§ 8—311. Effect of Unauthorized Indorsement or Instruction

Unless the owner or pledgee has ratified an unauthorized indorsement or instruction or is otherwise precluded from asserting its ineffectiveness:

(a) he may assert its ineffectiveness against the issuer or any purchaser, other than a purchaser for value and without notice of adverse claims, who has in good faith received a new, reissued, or re-registered certificated security on registration of transfer or received an initial transaction statement confirming the registration of transfer, pledge, or release of an equivalent uncertificated security to him; and

(b) an issuer who registers the transfer of a certificated security upon the unauthorized indorsement or who registers the transfer, pledge, or release of an uncertificated security upon the unauthorized instruction is subject to liability for improper registration (Section 8—404).

Amended in 1977.

§ 8—312. Effect of Guaranteeing Signature, Indorsement or Instruction

(1) Any person guaranteeing a signature of an indorser of a certificated security warrants that at the time of signing:

(a) the signature was genuine;

(b) the signer was an appropriate person to indorse (Section 8—308); and

(c) the signer had legal capacity to sign.

(2) Any person guaranteeing a signature of the originator of an instruction warrants that at the time of signing:

(a) the signature was genuine;

(b) the signer was an appropriate person to originate the instruction (Section 8—308) if the person specified in the instruction as the registered owner or registered pledgee of the uncertificated security was, in fact, the registered owner or registered pledgee of the security, as to which fact the signature guarantor makes no warranty;

(c) the signer had legal capacity to sign; and

(d) the taxpayer identification number, if any, appearing on the instruction as that of the registered owner or registered pledgee was the taxpayer identification number of the signer or of the owner or pledgee for whom the signer was acting.

(3) Any person specially guaranteeing the signature of the originator of an instruction makes not only the warranties of a signature guarantor (subsection (2)) but also warrants that at the time the instruction is presented to the issuer:

(a) the person specified in the instruction as the registered owner or registered pledgee of the uncertificated security will be the registered owner or registered pledgee; and

(b) the transfer, pledge, or release of the uncertificated security requested in the instruction will be registered by the issuer free from all liens, security interests, restrictions, and claims other than those specified in the instruction.

(4) The guarantor under subsections (1) and (2) or the special guarantor under subsection (3) does not otherwise warrant the rightfulness of the particular transfer, pledge, or release.

(5) Any person guaranteeing an indorsement of a certificated security makes not only the warranties of a signature guarantor under subsection (1) but also warrants the rightfulness of the particular transfer in all respects.

(6) Any person guaranteeing an instruction requesting the transfer, pledge, or release of an uncertificated security makes not only the warranties of a special signature guarantor under subsection (3) but also warrants the rightfulness of the particular transfer, pledge, or release in all respects.

(7) No issuer may require a special guarantee of signature (subsection (3)), a guarantee of indorsement (subsection (5)), or a guarantee of instruction (subsection (6)) as a condition to registration of transfer, pledge, or release.

(8) The foregoing warranties are made to any person taking or dealing with the security in reliance on the guarantee, and the guarantor is liable to the person for any loss resulting from breach of the warranties.

Amended in 1977.

§ 8—313. When Transfer to Purchaser Occurs; Financial Intermediary as Bona Fide Purchaser; "Financial Intermediary"

(1) Transfer of a security or a limited interest (including a security interest) therein to a purchaser occurs only:

(a) at the time he or a person designated by him acquires possession of a certificated security;

(b) at the time the transfer, pledge, or release of an uncertificated security is registered to him or a person designated by him;

(c) at the time his financial intermediary acquires possession of a certificated security specially indorsed to or issued in the name of the purchaser;

(d) at the time a financial intermediary, not a clearing corporation, sends him confirmation of the purchase and also by book entry or otherwise identifies as belonging to the purchaser

(i) a specific certificated security in the financial intermediary's possession;

(ii) a quantity of securities that constitute or are part of a fungible bulk of certificated securities in the financial intermediary's possession or of uncertificated securities registered in the name of the financial intermediary; or

(iii) a quantity of securities that constitute or are part of a fungible bulk of securities shown on the account of the financial intermediary on the books of another financial intermediary;

(e) with respect to an identified certificated security to be delivered while still in the possession of a third person, not a financial intermediary, at the time that person acknowledges that he holds for the purchaser;

(f) with respect to a specific uncertificated security the pledge or transfer of which has been registered to a third person, not a financial intermediary, at the time that person acknowledges that he holds for the purchaser;

(g) at the time appropriate entries to the account of the purchaser or a person designated by him on the books of a clearing corporation are made under Section 8—320;

(h) with respect to the transfer of a security interest where the debtor has signed a security agreement containing a description of the security, at the time a written notification, which, in the case of the creation of the security interest, is signed by the debtor (which may be a copy of the security agreement) or which, in the case of the release or assignment of the security interest created pursuant to this paragraph, is signed by the secured party, is received by

(i) a financial intermediary on whose books the interest of the transferor in the security appears;

(ii) a third person, not a financial intermediary, in possession of the security, if it is certificated;

(iii) a third person, not a financial intermediary, who is the registered owner of the security, if it is uncertificated and not subject to a registered pledge; or

(iv) a third person, not a financial intermediary, who is the registered pledgee of the security, if it is uncertificated and subject to a registered pledge;

(i) with respect to the transfer of a security interest where the transferor has signed a security agreement containing a description of the security, at the time new value is given by the secured party; or

(j) with respect to the transfer of a security interest where the secured party is a financial intermediary and the security has already been transferred to the financial intermediary under paragraphs (a), (b), (c), (d), or (g), at the time the transferor has signed a security agreement containing a description of the security and value is given by the secured party.

(2) The purchaser is the owner of a security held for him by a financial intermediary, but cannot be a bona fide purchaser of a security so held except in the circumstances specified in paragraphs (c), (d)(i), and (g) of subsection (1). If a secur-

ity so held is part of a fungible bulk, as in the circumstances specified in paragraphs (d)(ii) and (d)(iii) of subsection (1), the purchaser is the owner of a proportionate property interest in the fungible bulk.

(3) Notice of an adverse claim received by the financial intermediary or by the purchaser after the financial intermediary takes delivery of a certificated security as a holder for value or after the transfer, pledge, or release of an uncertificated security has been registered free of the claim to a financial intermediary who has given value is not effective either as to the financial intermediary or as to the purchaser. However, as between the financial intermediary and the purchaser the purchaser may demand transfer of an equivalent security as to which no notice of adverse claim has been received.

(4) A "financial intermediary" is a bank, broker, clearing corporation, or other person (or the nominee of any of them) which in the ordinary course of its business maintains security accounts for its customers and is acting in that capacity. A financial intermediary may have a security interest in securities held in account for its customer.

Amended in 1962 and 1977.

§ 8—314. Duty to Transfer, When Completed

(1) Unless otherwise agreed, if a sale of a security is made on an exchange or otherwise through brokers:

(a) the selling customer fulfills his duty to transfer at the time he:

(i) places a certificated security in the possession of the selling broker or a person designated by the broker;

(ii) causes an uncertificated security to be registered in the name of the selling broker or a person designated by the broker;

(iii) if requested, causes an acknowledgment to be made to the selling broker that a certificated or uncertificated security is held for the broker; or

(iv) places in the possession of the selling broker or of a person designated by the broker a transfer instruction for an uncertificated security, providing the issuer does not refuse to register the requested transfer if the instruction is presented to the issuer for registration within 30 days thereafter; and

(b) the selling broker, including a correspondent broker acting for a selling customer, fulfills his duty to transfer at the time he:

(i) places a certificated security in the possession of the buying broker or a person designated by the buying broker;

(ii) causes an uncertificated security to be registered in the name of the buying broker or a person designated by the buying broker;

(iii) places in the possession of the buying broker or of a person designated by the buying broker a transfer instruction for an uncertificated security, providing the issuer does not refuse to register the requested transfer if the instruction is presented to the issuer for registration within 30 days thereafter; or

(iv) effects clearance of the sale in accordance with the rules of the exchange on which the transaction took place.

(2) Except as provided in this section or unless otherwise agreed, a transferor's duty to transfer a security under a contract of purchase is not fulfilled until he:

(a) places a certificated security in form to be negotiated by the purchaser in the possession of the purchaser or of a person designated by the purchaser;

(b) causes an uncertificated security to be registered in the name of the purchaser or a person designated by the purchaser; or

(c) if the purchaser requests, causes an acknowledgment to be made to the purchaser that a certificated or uncertificated security is held for the purchaser.

(3) Unless made on an exchange, a sale to a broker purchasing for his own account is within subsection (2) and not within subsection (1).

Amended in 1977.

§ 8—315. Action Against Transferee Based Upon Wrongful Transfer

(1) Any person against whom the transfer of a security is wrongful for any reason, including his incapacity, as against anyone except a bona fide purchaser, may:

(a) reclaim possession of the certificated security wrongfully transferred;

(b) obtain possession of any new certificated security representing all or part of the same rights;

(c) compel the origination of an instruction to transfer to him or a person designated by him an uncertificated security constituting all or part of the same rights; or

(d) have damages.

(2) If the transfer is wrongful because of an unauthorized indorsement of a certificated security, the owner may also reclaim or obtain possession of the security or a new certificated security, even from a bona fide purchaser, if the ineffectiveness of the purported indorsement can be asserted against him under the provisions of this Article on unauthorized indorsements (Section 8—311).

(3) The right to obtain or reclaim possession of a certificated security or to compel the origination of a transfer instruction may be specifically enforced and the transfer of a certificated or uncertificated security enjoined and a certificated security impounded pending the litigation.

Amended in 1977.

§ 8—316. Purchaser's Right to Requisites for Registration of Transfer, Pledge, or Release on Books

Unless otherwise agreed, the transferor of a certificated security or the transferor, pledgor, or pledgee of an uncertificated security on due demand must supply his purchaser with any proof of his authority to transfer, pledge, or release or with any other requisite necessary to obtain registration of the transfer, pledge, or release of the security; but if the transfer, pledge, or release is not for value, a transferor, pledgor, or pledgee need not do so unless the purchaser furnishes the necessary expenses. Failure within a reasonable time to comply with a demand made gives the purchaser the right to reject or rescind the transfer, pledge, or release.

Amended in 1977.

§ 8—317. Creditors' Rights

(1) Subject to the exceptions in subsections (3) and (4), no attachment or levy upon a certificated security or any share or other interest represented thereby which is outstanding is valid until the security is actually seized by the officer making the attachment or levy, but a certificated security which has been surrendered to the issuer may be reached by a creditor by legal process at the issuer's chief executive office in the United States.

(2) An uncertificated security registered in the name of the debtor may not be reached by a creditor except by legal process at the issuer's chief executive office in the United States.

(3) The interest of a debtor in a certificated security that is in the possession of a secured party not a financial intermediary or in an uncertificated security registered in the name of a secured party not a financial intermediary (or in the name of a nominee of the secured party) may be reached by a creditor by legal process upon the secured party.

(4) The interest of a debtor in a certificated security that is in the possession of or registered in the name of a financial intermediary or in an uncertificated security registered in the name of a financial intermediary may be reached by a creditor by legal process upon the financial intermediary on whose books the interest of the debtor appears.

(5) Unless otherwise provided by law, a creditor's lien upon the interest of a debtor in a security obtained pursuant to subsection (3) or (4) is not a restraint on the transfer of the security, free of the lien, to a third party for new value; but in the event of a transfer, the lien applies to the proceeds of the transfer in the hands of the secured party or financial intermediary, subject to any claims having priority.

(6) A creditor whose debtor is the owner of a security is entitled to aid from courts of appropriate jurisdiction, by injunction or otherwise, in reaching the security or in satisfying the claim by means allowed at law or in equity in regard to property that cannot readily be reached by ordinary legal process.

Amended in 1977.

§ 8—318. No Conversion by Good Faith Conduct

An agent or bailee who in good faith (including observance of reasonable commercial standards if he is in the business of buying, selling, or otherwise dealing with securities) has received certificated securities and sold, pledged, or delivered them or has sold or caused the transfer or pledge of uncertificated securities over which he had control according to the instructions of his principal, is not liable for conversion or for participation in breach of fiduciary duty although the principal had no right so to deal with the securities.

Amended in 1977.

§ 8—319. Statute of Frauds

A contract for the sale of securities is not enforceable by way of action or defense unless:

(a) there is some writing signed by the party against whom enforcement is sought or by his authorized agent or broker, sufficient to indicate that a contract has been made for sale of a stated quantity of described securities at a defined or stated price;

(b) delivery of a certificated security or transfer instruction has been accepted, or transfer of an uncertificated security has been registered and the transferee has failed to send written objection to the issuer within 10 days after receipt of the initial transaction statement confirming the registration, or payment has been made, but the contract is enforceable under this provision only to the extent of the delivery, registration, or payment;

(c) within a reasonable time a writing in confirmation of the sale or purchase and sufficient against the sender under paragraph (a) has been received by the party against whom enforcement is sought and he has failed to send written objection to its contents within 10 days after its receipt; or

(d) the party against whom enforcement is sought admits in his pleading, testimony, or otherwise in court that a contract was made for the sale of a stated quantity of described securities at a defined or stated price.

Amended in 1977.

§ 8—320. Transfer or Pledge Within Central Depository System

(1) In addition to other methods, a transfer, pledge, or release of a security or any interest therein may be effected by the making of appropriate entries on the books of a clearing corporation

reducing the account of the transferor, pledgor, or pledgee and increasing the account of the transferee, pledgee, or pledgor by the amount of the obligation or the number of shares or rights transferred, pledged, or released, if the security is shown on the account of a transferor, pledgor, or pledgee on the books of the clearing corporation; is subject to the control of the clearing corporation; and

(a) if certificated,

(i) is in the custody of the clearing corporation, another clearing corporation, a custodian bank, or a nominee of any of them; and

(ii) is in bearer form or indorsed in blank by an appropriate person or registered in the name of the clearing corporation, a custodian bank, or a nominee of any of them; or

(b) if uncertificated, is registered in the name of the clearing corporation, another clearing corporation, a custodian bank, or a nominee of any of them.

(2) Under this section entries may be made with respect to like securities or interests therein as a part of a fungible bulk and may refer merely to a quantity of a particular security without reference to the name of the registered owner, certificate or bond number, or the like, and, in appropriate cases, may be on a net basis taking into account other transfers, pledges, or releases of the same security.

(3) A transfer under this section is effective (Section 8—313) and the purchaser acquires the rights of the transferor (Section 8—301). A pledge or release under this section is the transfer of a limited interest. If a pledge or the creation of a security interest is intended, the security interest is perfected at the time when both value is given by the pledgee and the appropriate entries are made (Section 8—321). A transferee or pledgee under this section may be a bona fide purchaser (Section 8—302).

(4) A transfer or pledge under this section is not a registration of transfer under Part 4.

(5) That entries made on the books of the clearing corporation as provided in subsection (1) are not appropriate does not affect the validity or effect of the entries or the liabilities or obligations of the clearing corporation to any person adversely affected thereby.

Added in 1962; amended in 1977.

§ 8—321. Enforceability, Attachment, Perfection and Termination of Security Interests

(1) A security interest in a security is enforceable and can attach only if it is transferred to the secured party or a person designated by him pursuant to a provision of Section 8—313(1).

(2) A security interest so transferred pursuant to agreement by a transferor who has rights in the security to a transferee who has given value is a perfected security interest, but a security interest that has been transferred solely under paragraph (i) of Section 8—313(1) becomes unperfected after 21 days unless, within that time, the requirements for transfer under any other provision of Section 8—313(1) are satisfied.

(3) A security interest in a security is subject to the provisions of Article 9, but:

(a) no filing is required to perfect the security interest; and

(b) no written security agreement signed by the debtor is necessary to make the security interest enforceable, except as provided in paragraph (h), (i), or (j) of Section 8—313(1). The secured party has the rights and duties provided under Section 9—207, to the extent they are applicable, whether or not the security is certificated, and, if certificated, whether or not it is in his possession.

(4) Unless otherwise agreed, a security interest in a security is terminated by transfer to the debtor or a person designated by him pursuant to a provision of Section 8—313(1). If a security is thus transferred, the security interest, if not terminated, becomes unperfected unless the security is certificated and is delivered to the debtor for the purpose of ultimate sale or exchange or presentation, collection, renewal, or registration of transfer. In that case, the security interest becomes unperfected after 21 days unless, within that time, the security (or securities for which it has been exchanged) is transferred to the secured party or a person designated by him pursuant to a provision of Section 8—313(1).

Added in 1977.

PART 4

REGISTRATION

§ 8—401. Duty of Issuer to Register Transfer, Pledge, or Release

(1) If a certificated security in registered form is presented to the issuer with a request to register transfer or an instruction is presented to the issuer with a request to register transfer, pledge, or release, the issuer shall register the transfer, pledge, or release as requested if:

(a) the security is indorsed or the instruction was originated by the appropriate person or persons (Section 8—308);

(b) reasonable assurance is given that those indorsements or instructions are genuine and effective (Section 8—402);

(c) the issuer has no duty as to adverse claims or has discharged the duty (Section 8—403);

(d) any applicable law relating to the collection of taxes has been complied with; and

(e) the transfer, pledge, or release is in fact rightful or is to a bona fide purchaser.

(2) If an issuer is under a duty to register a transfer, pledge, or release of a security, the issuer is also liable to the person presenting a certificated security or an instruction for registration or his principal for loss resulting from any unreasonable delay in registration or from failure or refusal to register the transfer, pledge, or release.

Amended in 1977.

§ 8—402. Assurance that Indorsements and Instructions Are Effective

(1) The issuer may require the following assurance that each necessary indorsement of a certificated security or each instruction (Section 8—308) is genuine and effective:

(a) in all cases, a guarantee of the signature (Section 8—312(1) or (2)) of the person indorsing a certificated security or originating an instruction including, in the case of an instruction, a warranty of the taxpayer identification number or, in the absence thereof, other reasonable assurance of identity;

(b) if the indorsement is made or the instruction is originated by an agent, appropriate assurance of authority to sign;

(c) if the indorsement is made or the instruction is originated by a fiduciary, appropriate evidence of appointment or incumbency;

(d) if there is more than one fiduciary, reasonable assurance that all who are required to sign have done so; and

(e) if the indorsement is made or the instruction is originated by a person not covered by any of the foregoing, assurance appropriate to the case corresponding as nearly as may be to the foregoing.

(2) A "guarantee of the signature" in subsection (1) means a guarantee signed by or on behalf of a person reasonably believed by the issuer to be responsible. The issuer may adopt standards with respect to responsibility if they are not manifestly unreasonable.

(3) "Appropriate evidence of appointment or incumbency" in subsection (1) means:

(a) in the case of a fiduciary appointed or qualified by a court, a certificate issued by or under the direction or supervision of that court or an officer thereof and dated within 60 days before the date of presentation for transfer, pledge, or release; or

(b) in any other case, a copy of a document showing the appointment or a certificate issued by or on behalf of a person reasonably believed by the issuer to be responsible or, in the absence of that document or certificate, other evidence reasonably deemed by the issuer to be appropriate. The issuer may adopt standards with respect to the evidence if they are not manifestly unreasonable. The issuer is not charged with notice of the contents of any document obtained pursuant to this paragraph (b) except to the extent that the contents relate directly to the appointment or incumbency.

(4) The issuer may elect to require reasonable assurance beyond that specified in this section, but if it does so and, for a purpose other than that specified in subsection (3)(b), both requires and obtains a copy of a will, trust, indenture, articles of

co-partnership, by-laws, or other controlling instrument, it is charged with notice of all matters contained therein affecting the transfer, pledge, or release.

Amended in 1977.

§ 8—403. Issuer's Duty as to Adverse Claims

(1) An issuer to whom a certificated security is presented for registration shall inquire into adverse claims if:

(a) a written notification of an adverse claim is received at a time and in a manner affording the issuer a reasonable opportunity to act on it prior to the issuance of a new, reissued, or re-registered certificated security, and the notification identifies the claimant, the registered owner, and the issue of which the security is a part, and provides an address for communications directed to the claimant; or

(b) the issuer is charged with notice of an adverse claim from a controlling instrument it has elected to require under Section 8–402(4).

(2) The issuer may discharge any duty of inquiry by any reasonable means, including notifying an adverse claimant by registered or certified mail at the address furnished by him or, if there be no such address, at his residence or regular place of business that the certificated security has been presented for registration of transfer by a named person, and that the transfer will be registered unless within 30 days from the date of mailing the notification, either:

(a) an appropriate restraining order, injunction, or other process issues from a court of competent jurisdiction; or

(b) there is filed with the issuer an idemnity bond, sufficient in the issuer's judgment to protect the issuer and any transfer agent, registrar, or other agent of the issuer involved from any loss it or they may suffer by complying with the adverse claim.

(3) Unless an issuer is charged with notice of an adverse claim from a controlling instrument which it has elected to require under Section 8—402(4) or receives notification of an adverse claim under subsection (1), if a certificated security presented for registration is indorsed by the appropriate person or

persons the issuer is under no duty to inquire into adverse claims. In particular:

(a) an issuer registering a certificated security in the name of a person who is a fiduciary or who is described as a fiduciary is not bound to inquire into the existence, extent, or correct description of the fiduciary relationship; and thereafter the issuer may assume without inquiry that the newly registered owner continues to be the fiduciary until the issuer receives written notice that the fiduciary is no longer acting as such with respect to the particular security;

(b) an issuer registering transfer on an indorsement by a fiduciary is not bound to inquire whether the transfer is made in compliance with a controlling instrument or with the law of the state having jurisdiction of the fiduciary relationship, including any law requiring the fiduciary to obtain court approval of the transfer; and

(c) the issuer is not charged with notice of the contents of any court record or file or other recorded or unrecorded document even though the document is in its possession and even though the transfer is made on the indorsement of a fiduciary to the fiduciary himself or to his nominee.

(4) An issuer is under no duty as to adverse claims with respect to an uncertificated security except:

(a) claims embodied in a restraining order, injunction, or other legal process served upon the issuer if the process was served at a time and in a manner affording the issuer a reasonable opportunity to act on it in accordance with the requirements of subsection (5);

(b) claims of which the issuer has received a written notification from the registered owner or the registered pledgee if the notification was received at a time and in a manner affording the issuer a reasonable opportunity to act on it in accordance with the requirements of subsection (5);

(c) claims (including restrictions on transfer not imposed by the issuer) to which the registration of transfer to the present registered owner was subject and were so noted in the initial transaction statement sent to him; and

(d) claims as to which an issuer is charged with notice from a controlling instrument it has elected to require under Section 8—402(4).

(5) If the issuer of an uncertificated security is under a duty as to an adverse claim, he discharges that duty by:

(a) including a notation of the claim in any statements sent with respect to the security under Sections 8—408 (3), (6), and (7); and

(b) refusing to register the transfer or pledge of the security unless the nature of the claim does not preclude transfer or pledge subject thereto.

(6) If the transfer or pledge of the security is registered subject to an adverse claim, a notation of the claim must be included in the initial transaction statement and all subsequent statements sent to the transferee and pledgee under Section 8—408.

(7) Notwithstanding subsections (4) and (5), if an uncertificated security was subject to a registered pledge at the time the issuer first came under a duty as to a particular adverse claim, the issuer has no duty as to that claim if transfer of the security is requested by the registered pledgee or an appropriate person acting for the registered pledgee unless:

(a) the claim was embodied in legal process which expressly provides otherwise;

(b) the claim was asserted in a written notification from the registered pledgee;

(c) the claim was one as to which the issuer was charged with notice from a controlling instrument it required under Section 8—402(4) in connection with the pledgee's request for transfer; or

(d) the transfer requested is to the registered owner.

Amended in 1977.

§ 8—404. Liability and Non-Liability for Registration

(1) Except as provided in any law relating to the collection of taxes, the issuer is not liable to the owner, pledgee, or any other person suffering loss as a result of the registration of a transfer, pledge, or release of a security if:

(a) there were on or with a certificated security the necessary indorsements or the issuer had received an instruction originated by an appropriate person (Section 8—308); and

(b) the issuer had no duty as to adverse claims or has discharged the duty (Section 8—403).

(2) If an issuer has registered a transfer of a certificated security to a person not entitled to it, the issuer on demand shall deliver a like security to the true owner unless:

(a) the registration was pursuant to subsection (1);

(b) the owner is precluded from asserting any claim for registering the transfer under Section 8—405(1); or

(c) the delivery would result in overissue, in which case the issuer's liability is governed by Section 8—104.

(3) If an issuer has improperly registered a transfer, pledge, or release of an uncertificated security, the issuer on demand from the injured party shall restore the records as to the injured party to the condition that would have obtained if the improper registration had not been made unless:

(a) the registration was pursuant to subsection (1); or

(b) the registration would result in overissue, in which case the issuer's liability is governed by Section 8—104.

Amended in 1977.

§ 8—405. Lost, Destroyed, and Stolen Certificated Securities

(1) If a certificated security has been lost, apparently destroyed, or wrongfully taken, and the owner fails to notify the issuer of that fact within a reasonable time after he has notice of it and the issuer registers a transfer of the security before receiving notification, the owner is precluded from asserting against the issuer any claim for registering the transfer under Section 8—404 or any claim to a new security under this section.

(2) If the owner of a certificated security claims that the security has been lost, destroyed, or wrongfully taken, the issuer shall issue a new certificated security or, at the option of the issuer, an equivalent uncertificated security in place of the original security if the owner:

(a) so requests before the issuer has notice that the security has been acquired by a bona fide purchaser;

(b) files with the issuer a sufficient indemnity bond; and

(c) satisfies any other reasonable requirements imposed by the issuer.

(3) If, after the issue of a new certificated or uncertificated security, a bona fide purchaser of the original certificated security presents it for registration of transfer, the issuer shall register the transfer unless registration would result in overissue, in which event the issuer's liability is governed by Section 8—104. In addition to any rights on the indemnity bond, the issuer may recover the new certificated security from the person to whom it was issued or any person taking under him except a bona fide purchaser or may cancel the uncertificated security unless a bona fide purchaser or any person taking under a bona fide purchaser is then the registered owner or registered pledgee thereof.

Amended in 1977.

§ 8—406. Duty of Authenticating Trustee, Transfer Agent, or Registrar

(1) If a person acts as authenticating trustee, transfer agent, registrar, or other agent for an issuer in the registration of transfers of its certificated securities or in the registration of transfers, pledges, and releases of its uncertificated securities, in the issue of new securities, or in the cancellation of surrendered securities:

(a) he is under a duty to the issuer to exercise good faith and due diligence in performing his functions; and

(b) with regard to the particular functions he performs, he has the same obligation to the holder or owner of a certificated security or to the owner or pledgee of an uncertificated security and has the same rights and privileges as the issuer has in regard to those functions.

(2) Notice to an authenticating trustee, transfer agent, registrar or other agent is notice to the issuer with respect to the functions performed by the agent.

Amended in 1977.

§ 8—407. Exchangeability of Securities

(1) No issuer is subject to the requirements of this section unless it regularly maintains a system for issuing the class of securities involved under which both certificated and uncertificated securities are regularly issued to the category of own-

ers, which includes the person in whose name the new security is to be registered.

(2) Upon surrender of a certificated security with all necessary indorsements and presentation of a written request by the person surrendering the security, the issuer, if he has no duty as to adverse claims or has discharged the duty (Section 8–403), shall issue to the person or a person designated by him an equivalent uncertificated security subject to all liens, restrictions, and claims that were noted on the certificated security.

(3) Upon receipt of a transfer instruction originated by an appropriate person who so requests, the issuer of an uncertificated security shall cancel the uncertificated security and issue an equivalent certificated security on which must be noted conspicuously any liens and restrictions of the issuer and any adverse claims (as to which the issuer has a duty under Section 8—403 (4)) to which the uncertificated security was subject. The certificated security shall be registered in the name of and delivered to:

(a) the registered owner, if the uncertificated security was not subject to a registered pledge; or

(b) the registered pledgee, if the uncertificated security was subject to a registered pledge.

Added in 1977.

§ 8—408. Statements of Uncertificated Securities

(1) Within 2 business days after the transfer of an uncertificated security has been registered, the issuer shall send to the new registered owner and, if the security has been transferred subject to a registered pledge, to the registered pledgee a written statement containing:

(a) a description of the issue of which the uncertificated security is a part;

(b) the number of shares or units transferred;

(c) the name and address and any taxpayer identification number of the new registered owner and, if the security has been transferred subject to a registered pledge, the name and address and any taxpayer identification number of the registered pledgee;

(d) a notation of any liens and restrictions of the issuer and any adverse claims (as to which the issuer has a duty under Section 8—403(4)) to which the uncertificated security is or may be subject at the time of registration or a statement that there are none of those liens, restrictions, or adverse claims; and

(e) the date the transfer was registered.

(2) Within 2 business days after the pledge of an uncertificated security has been registered, the issuer shall send to the registered owner and the registered pledgee a written statement containing:

(a) a description of the issue of which the uncertificated security is a part;

(b) the number of shares or units pledged;

(c) the name and address and any taxpayer identification number of the registered owner and the registered pledgee;

(d) a notation of any liens and restrictions of the issuer and any adverse claims (as to which the issuer has a duty under Section 8—403(4)) to which the uncertificated security is or may be subject at the time of registration or a statement that there are none of those liens, restrictions, or adverse claims; and

(e) the date the pledge was registered.

(3) Within 2 business days after the release from pledge of an uncertificated security has been registered, the issuer shall send to the registered owner and the pledgee whose interest was released a written statement containing:

(a) a description of the issue of which the uncertificated security is a part;

(b) the number of shares or units released from pledge;

(c) the name and address and any taxpayer identification number of the registered owner and the pledgee whose interest was released;

(d) a notation of any liens and restrictions of the issuer and any adverse claims (as to which the issuer has a duty under Section 8–403(4)) to which the uncertificated security is or may be subject at the time of registration or a statement that there are none of those liens, restrictions, or adverse claims; and

(e) the date the release was registered.

(4) An "initial transaction statement" is the statement sent to:

(a) the new registered owner and, if applicable, to the registered pledgee pursuant to subsection (1);

(b) the registered pledgee pursuant to subsection (2); or

(c) the registered owner pursuant to subsection (3).

Each initial transaction statement shall be signed by or on behalf of the issuer and must be identified as "Initial Transaction Statement".

(5) Within 2 business days after the transfer of an uncertificated security has been registered, the issuer shall send to the former registered owner and the former registered pledgee, if any, a written statement containing:

(a) a description of the issue of which the uncertificated security is a part;

(b) the number of shares or units transferred;

(c) the name and address and any taxpayer identification number of the former registered owner and of any former registered pledgee; and

(d) the date the transfer was registered.

(6) At periodic intervals no less frequent than annually and at any time upon the reasonable written request of the registered owner, the issuer shall send to the registered owner of each uncertificated security a dated written statement containing:

(a) a description of the issue of which the uncertificated security is a part;

(b) the name and address and any taxpayer identification number of the registered owner;

(c) the number of shares or units of the uncertificated security registered in the name of the registered owner on the date of the statement;

(d) the name and address and any taxpayer identification number of any registered pledgee and the number of shares or units subject to the pledge; and

(e) a notation of any liens and restrictions of the issuer and any adverse claims (as to which the issuer has a duty under Section 8—403(4)) to which the uncertificated security is or may be subject or a statement that there are none of those liens, restrictions, or adverse claims.

(7) At periodic intervals no less frequent than annually and at any time upon the reasonable written request of the registered pledgee, the issuer shall send to the registered pledgee of each uncertificated security a dated written statement containing:

(a) a description of the issue of which the uncertificated security is a part;

(b) the name and address and any taxpayer identification number of the registered owner;

(c) the name and address and any taxpayer identification number of the registered pledgee;

(d) the number of shares or units subject to the pledge; and

(e) a notation of any liens and restrictions of the issuer and any adverse claims (as to which the issuer has a duty under Section 8–403(4)) to which the uncertificated security is or may be subject or a statement that there are none of those liens, restrictions, or adverse claims.

(8) If the issuer sends the statements described in subsections (6) and (7) at periodic intervals no less frequent than quarterly, the issuer is not obliged to send additional statements upon request unless the owner or pledgee requesting them pays to the issuer the reasonable cost of furnishing them.

(9) Each statement sent pursuant to this section must bear a conspicuous legend reading substantially as follows: "This statement is merely a record of the rights of the addressee as of the time of its issuance. Delivery of this statement, of itself, confers no rights on the recipient. This statement is neither a negotiable instrument nor a security."

Added in 1977.

ARTICLE 9

SECURED TRANSACTIONS; SALES OF ACCOUNTS AND CHATTEL PAPER

PART 1. SHORT TITLE, APPLICABILITY AND DEFINITIONS

PART 2. VALIDITY OF SECURITY AGREEMENT AND RIGHTS OF PARTIES THERETO

PART 3. RIGHTS OF THIRD PARTIES; PERFECTED AND UNPERFECTED SECURITY INTERESTS; RULES OF PRIORITY

PART 4. FILING

PART 1

SHORT TITLE, APPLICABILITY AND DEFINITIONS

§ 9—101. Short Title

This Article shall be known and may be cited as Uniform Commercial Code—Secured Transactions.

Official Comment

This Article sets out a comprehensive scheme for the regulation of security interests in personal property and fixtures. It supersedes prior legislation dealing with such security devices as chattel mortgages, conditional sales, trust receipts, factor's liens and assignments of accounts receivable (see Note to Section 9—102).

Consumer installment sales and consumer loans present special problems of a nature which makes special regulation of them inappropriate in a general commercial codification. Many states now regulate such loans and sales under small loan acts, retail installment selling acts and the like. The National Conference of Commissioners on Uniform State Laws has proposed a Uniform Consumer Credit Code dealing with this subject. While this Article applies generally to security interests in consumer goods, it is not designed to supersede such regulatory legislation (see Notes to Sections 9—102 and 9—203). Nor is this Article designed as a substitute for small loan acts or retail installment selling acts in any state which does not presently have such legislation.

Pre-Code law recognized a wide variety of security devices, which came into use at various times to make possible different types of secured financing. Differences between one device and another persisted, in formal requisites, in the secured party's rights against the debtor and third parties, in the debtor's rights against the secured party, and in filing requirements, although many of those differences no longer served any useful function. Thus an unfiled chattel mortgage was by the law of many states "void" against creditors generally; a conditional sale, often available as a substitute for the chattel mortgage, was in some states valid against all creditors without filing, and in states where filing is required was, if unfiled, void only against lien creditors. The recognition of so many separate security devices had the result that half a dozen filing systems covering chattel security devices might be maintained within a state, some on a county basis, others on a state-wide basis, each of which had to be separately checked to determine a debtor's status.

Nevertheless, despite the great number of security devices there remained gaps in the structure. In many states, for example, a security interest could not be taken in inventory or a stock in trade although there was a real need for such financing. It was often baffling to try to maintain a technically valid security interest when financing a manufacturing process, where the collateral starts out as raw materials, becomes work in process and ends as finished goods. Furthermore, it was by no means clear, even to specialists, how under pre-Code law a security interest might be taken in many kinds of intangible property—such as television or motion picture rights—which have come to be an important source of commercial collateral.

While the chattel mortgage was adaptable for use in almost any situation where goods are collateral, there were limitations, sometimes highly technical, on the use of other devices, such as the conditional sale and particularly the trust receipt. The cases are many in which a security transaction described by the parties as a conditional sale or a trust receipt was later determined by a court to be something else, usually a chattel mortgage. The consequence of such a determination was typically to void the security interest against creditors because the security agreement was not filed *as a chattel mortgage* (even though it may have been filed as a conditional sale or a trust receipt). The already mentioned difficulty of financing on the security of inventory has been got around to some extent by the device known as "field warehousing" as well as by the use of the trust receipt. After 1940 a number of states generally authorized inventory financing by enacting statutes, similar although not uniform, known as "factor's lien" acts. Also after 1940 the increasingly important business of lending against accounts receivable inspired new statutes in that field in more than thirty states.

The growing complexity of financing transactions forced legislatures to keep piling new statutory provisions on top of our inadequate and already sufficiently complicated nineteenth-century structure of security law. The results of this continuing development were increasing costs to both parties and increasing uncertainty as to their rights and the rights of third parties dealing with them.

The aim of this Article is to provide a simple and unified structure within which the immense variety of present-day secured financing transactions can go forward with less cost and with greater certainty.

Under this Article the traditional distinctions among security devices, based largely on form, are not retained; the Article applies to all transactions intended to create security interests in personal property and fixtures, and the single term "security interest" substitutes for the variety of descriptive terms which had grown up at common law and under a hundred-year accretion of statutes. This does not mean that the old forms may not be used, and Section 9—102 (2) makes it clear that they may be.

This Article does not determine whether "title" to collateral is in the secured party or in the debtor and adopts neither a "title theory" nor a "lien theory" of security interests. Rights, obligations and remedies under the Article do not depend on the location of title (Section 9—202). The location of title may become important for other purposes—as, for example, in determining the incidence of taxation—and in such a case the parties are left free to contract as they will. In this connection the use of a form which has traditionally been regarded as determinative of title (e. g., the conditional sale) could reasonably be regarded as evidencing the parties' intention with respect to title to the collateral.

Under the Article distinctions based on form (except as between pledge and non-possessory interests) are no longer controlling. For some purposes there are distinctions based on the type of property which constitutes the collateral—industrial and commercial equipment, business inventory, farm products, consumer goods, accounts receivable, documents of title and other intangibles—and, where appropriate, the Article states special rules applicable to financing transactions involving a particular type of property. Despite the statutory simplification a greater degree of flexibility in the financing transaction is allowed than is possible under existing law.

The scheme of the Article is to make distinctions, where distinctions are necessary, along functional rather than formal lines.

This has made possible a radical simplification in the formal requisites for creation of a security interest.

A more rational filing system replaces the present system of different files for each security device which is subject to filing requirements. Thus not only is the information contained in the files made more accessible but the cost of procuring credit information, and, incidentally, of maintaining the files, is greatly reduced.

The Article's flexibility and simplified formalities should make it possible for new forms of secured financing, as they develop, to fit comfortably under its provisions, thus avoiding the necessity, so apparent in recent years, of year by year passing new statutes and tinkering with the old ones to allow legitimate business transactions to go forward.

The rules set out in this Article are principally concerned with the limits of the secured party's protection against purchasers from and creditors of the debtor. Except for procedure on default, freedom of contract prevails between the immediate parties to the security transaction.

§ 9—102. Policy and Subject Matter of Article

(1) Except as otherwise provided in Section 9—104 on excluded transactions, this Article applies

(a) to any transaction (regardless of its form) which is intended to create a security interest in personal property or fixtures including goods, documents, instruments, general intangibles, chattel paper or accounts; and also

(b) to any sale of accounts or chattel paper.

(2) This Article applies to security interests created by contract including pledge, assignment, chattel mortgage, chattel trust, trust deed, factor's lien, equipment trust, conditional sale, trust receipt, other lien or title retention contract and lease or consignment intended as security. This Article does not apply to statutory liens except as provided in Section 9—310.

(3) The application of this Article to a security interest in a secured obligation is not affected by the fact that the obligation is itself secured by a transaction or interest to which this Article does not apply. Amended in 1972.

See Appendix I for changes made in former text and the reasons for change.

Note: *The adoption of this Article should be accompanied by the repeal of existing statutes dealing with conditional sales, trust receipts, factor's liens where the factor is given a non-possessory lien, chattel mortgages, crop mortgages, mortgages on railroad equipment, as-*

signment of accounts and generally statutes regulating security interests in personal property.

Where the state has a retail installment selling act or small loan act, that legislation should be carefully examined to determine what changes in those acts are needed to conform them to this Article. This Article primarily sets out rules defining rights of a secured party against persons dealing with the debtor; it does not prescribe regulations and controls which may be necessary to curb abuses arising in the small loan business or in the financing of consumer purchases on credit. Accordingly there is no intention to repeal existing regulatory acts in those fields by enactment or re-enactment of Article 9. See Section 9—203(4) and the Note thereto.

Official Comment

Prior Uniform Statutory Provision: None.

Purposes:

The main purpose of this Section is to bring all consensual security interests in personal property and fixtures under this Article, except for certain types of transactions excluded by Section 9—104. In addition certain sales of accounts and chattel paper are brought within this Article to avoid difficult problems of distinguishing between transactions intended for security and those not so intended. As to security interests in fixtures created under the law applicable to real estate, see Section 9—313(1).

1. Except for sales of accounts and chattel paper, the principal test whether a transaction comes under this Article is: is the transaction intended to have effect as security? For example, Section 9—104 excludes certain transactions where the security interest (such as an artisan's lien) arises under statute or common law by reason of status and not by consent of the parties. Transactions in the form of consignments or leases are subject to this Article if the understanding of the parties or the effect of the arrangement shows that a security interest was intended. (As to consignments the provisions of Sections 2—326, 9—114 and 9—408 should be consulted.) When it is found that a security interest as defined in Section 1—201(37) was intended, this Article applies regardless of the form of the transaction or the name by which the parties may have christened it. The list of traditional security devices in subsection (2) is illustrative only; other old devices, as well as any new ones which the ingenuity of lawyers may invent, are included, so long as the requisite intent is found. The controlling definition is that contained in subsection (1).

The Article does not in terms abolish existing security devices.

The conditional sale or bailment-lease, for example, is not prohibited; but even though it is used, the rules of this Article govern.

2. If an obligation is to repay money lent and is not part of chattel paper, it is either an instrument or a general intangible. A sale of an instrument or general intangible is not within this Article, but a transfer intended to have effect as security for an obligation of the transferor is covered by subsection 1(a). In either case the nature of the transaction is not affected by the fact that collateral is transferred with the instrument or general intangible. Such a transfer is treated as a transfer by operation of law, whether or not it is articulated in the agreement.

An assignment of accounts or chattel paper as security for an obligation is covered by subsection (1) (a). Commercial financing on the basis of accounts and chattel paper is often so conducted that the distinction between a security transfer and a sale is blurred, and a sale of such property is therefore covered by subsection (1) (b) whether intended for security or not, unless excluded by Section 9—104. The buyer then is treated as a secured party, and his interest as a security interest. See Sections 9—105(1) (m), 1—201(37). Certain sales which have nothing to do with commercial financing transactions are excluded by Section 9—104(f); compare Spurlin v. Sloan, 368 S.W.2d 314 (Ky. 1963). See also Section 9—302 (1) (e), exempting from filing casual or isolated assignments, and Section 9—302(2), preserving the perfected status of a security interest against the original debtor when a secured party assigns his interest.

3. In general, problems of choice of law in this Article as to the validity of security agreements are governed by Section 1—105. Problems of choice of law as to perfection of security interests and the effect of perfection or non-perfection thereof, including rules requiring reperfection, are governed by Section 9—103.

4. An illustration of subsection (3) is as follows:

The owner of Blackacre borrows $10,000 from his neighbor, and secures his note by a mortgage on Blackacre. This Article is not applicable to the creation of the real estate mortgage. Nor is it applicable to a sale of the note by the mortgagee, even though the mortgage continues to secure the note. However, when the mortgagee pledges the note to secure his own obligation to X, this Article applies to the security interest thus created, which is a security interest in an instrument even though the instrument is secured by a real estate mortgage. This Article leaves to other law the question of the effect on rights under the mortgage of delivery or non-delivery of the mortgage or of recording or non-recording of an assignment of the mortgagee's interest. See Section 9—104(j). But under Section 3—304(5) recording of the assignment does not of itself prevent X from holding the note in due course.

5. While most sections of this Article apply to a security interest without regard to the nature of the collateral or its use, some sections state special rules with reference to particular types of collateral. An index of sections where such special rules are stated follows:

ACCOUNTS

Section	
9—102(1)(b)	Sale of accounts subject to Article
9—103(1)	When Article applies; conflict of laws rules
9—104(f)	Certain sales of accounts excluded from Article
9—106	Definitions
9—205	Permissible for debtor to make collections
9—206(1)	Agreement not to assert defenses against assignee
9—301(1)(d)	Unperfected security interest subordinate to certain transferees
9—302(1)(e)	What assignments need not be filed
9—306(5)	Rule when goods whose sale gave rise to an account return to seller's possession
9—318(1)	Rights of assignee subject to defenses
9—318(2)	Modification of contract after assignment of contract right
9—318(3)	When account debtor may pay assignor
9—318(4)	Term prohibiting assignment ineffective
9—401	Place of filing
9—502	Collection rights of secured party
9—504(2)	Rights on default where underlying transaction was sale of accounts or contract rights

CHATTEL PAPER

9—102(1)(b)	Sale subject to Article
9—104(f)	Certain sales excluded from Article
9—105(1)(b)	Definition
9—205	Permissible for debtor to make collections
9—206(1)	Agreement not to assert defenses against assignee
9—207(1)	Duty of secured party in possession to preserve rights against prior parties
9—301(1)(c)	Unperfected security interest subordinate to certain transferees
9—304(1)	Perfection by filing
9—305	When possession by secured party perfects security interest
9—306(5)	Rule when goods whose sale results in chattel paper return to seller's possession
9—308	When purchasers of chattel paper have priority over security interest
9—318(1)	Rights of assignee subject to defenses
9—318(3)	When account debtor may pay assignor

Section	
9—502	Collection rights of secured party
9—504(2)	Rights on default where underlying transaction was sale

DOCUMENTS AND INSTRUMENTS

9—105(1)(e)	Definition of document (and see 1—201)
9—105(1)(g)	Definition of instrument
9—206(1)	Rule where buyer of goods signs both negotiable instrument and security agreement
9—207(1)	Duty of secured party in possession of instrument to preserve rights against prior parties
9—301(1)(c)	Unperfected security interest subordinate to certain transferees
9—302(1)(b) and (f)	What interests need not be filed
9—304(1)	How security interest can be perfected
9—304(2, 3)	Perfection of security interest in goods in possession of issuer of negotiable document or of other bailee
9—304(4, 5)	Perfection of security interest in instruments or negotiable documents without filing or transfer of possession
9—305	When possession by secured party perfects security interest
9—308	When purchasers of instruments have priority over security interest
9—309	When purchasers of negotiable instruments or negotiable documents have priority over security interest
9—501(1)	Rights on default where collateral is documents
9—502	Collection rights of secured party

GENERAL INTANGIBLES

9—103(2)	When Article applies; conflict of laws rules
9—105	Obligor is "account debtor"
9—106	Definition
9—301(1)(d)	Unperfected security interest subordinate to certain transferees
9—318(1)	Rights of assignee subject to defenses
9—318(3)	When account debtor may pay assignor
9—502	Collection rights of secured party

GOODS

(See also Consumer Goods, Equipment, Farm Products, Inventory)

9—103	When Article applies with regard to goods of a type normally used in more than one jurisdiction; goods covered by certificate of title; conflict of laws rules
9—105(1)(h)	Definition

Section	
9—109	Classification of goods as consumer goods, equipment, farm products and inventory
9—203	Formal requisites of security agreement covering certain types of goods (crops or timber)
9—204	Validity of after-acquired property clause covering certain types of goods (crops, consumer goods)
9—205	Permissible for debtor to accept returned goods
9—206(2)	When security agreement can limit or modify warranties on sale
9—301(1)(c)	Unperfected security interest subordinate to certain transferees
9—304(2, 3)	Perfection of security interest in goods in possession of issuer of negotiable document or of other bailee
9—304(5)	Perfection of security interest without filing or transfer of possession where goods in possession of certain bailees
9—305	When possession by secured party perfects security interest
9—306(5)	Rule when goods whose sale gave rise to account or chattel paper return to seller's possession
9—307	When buyers of goods from debtor take free of security interest
9—313	Goods which are or become fixtures
9—314	Goods affixed to other goods
9—315	Goods commingled in a product
9—401(1)	Place of filing for fixtures
9—402	Form of financing statement covering fixtures
9—504(1)	Sale of goods by secured party after default subject to Article 2 (Sales)

CONSUMER GOODS

9—109(1)	Definition
9—203(2)	Transaction, although subject to this Article, may also be subject to certain regulatory statutes
9—204(2)	Validity of after-acquired property clause
9—206(1)	Buyer's agreement not to assert defenses against an assignee subject to statute or decision which establishes rule for buyers of consumer goods
9—302(1)(d)	When filing not required
9—307(2)	When buyers from debtor take free of security interest
9—401(1)(a)	Place of filing
9—505(1)	Secured party's duty to dispose of repossessed consumer goods
9—507(1)	Secured party's liability for improper disposition of consumer goods after default

EQUIPMENT

Section	
9—103(2)	When Article applies with regard to certain types of equipment normally used in more than one jurisdiction; conflict of laws rules
9—109(2)	Definition
9—302(1)(c)	When filing not required to perfect security interest in certain farm equipment
9—307(2)	When buyers of certain farm equipment from debtor take free of security interest
9—401(1)	Place of filing for equipment used in farming operation
9—503	Secured party's right after default to remove or to render equipment unusable

FARM PRODUCTS

9—109(3)	Definition
9—203(1)(b)	Formal requisites of security agreement covering crops
9—307	When a buyer of farm products takes free of security interest
9—312(2)	Priority of secured party who gives new value to enable debtor to produce crops
9—401(1)	Place of filing
9—402(1) and (3)	Form of financing statement covering crops

INVENTORY

9—103(3)	When Article applies with regard to certain types of inventory normally used in more than one jurisdiction; conflict of laws rules
9—109(4)	Definition
9—114	Consigned goods
9—306(5)	Rule where goods whose sale gave rise to account or chattel paper return to seller's possession
9—307(1)	When buyers from debtor take free of security interest
9—312(3), 9—304(5)	When purchase money security interest takes priority over conflicting security interest
9—408	Financing statements covering consigned or leased goods

Cross References:

Sections 9—103 and 9—104.

Point 1: Section 2—326.

Point 2: Section 1—105.

Definitional Cross References:

"Account". Section 9—106.

"Chattel paper". Section 9—105.

"Contract". Section 1—201.

"Document". Section 9—105.

"General intangibles". Section 9—106.

"Goods". Section 9—105.

"Instrument". Section 9—105.

"Security interest". Section 1—201.

§ 9—103. Perfection of Security Interest in Multiple State Transactions

(1) Documents, instruments and ordinary goods.

(a) This subsection applies to documents and instruments and to goods other than those covered by a certificate of title described in subsection (2), mobile goods described in subsection (3), and minerals described in subsection (5).

(b) Except as otherwise provided in this subsection, perfection and the effect of perfection or non-perfection of a security interest in collateral are governed by the law of the jurisdiction where the collateral is when the last event occurs on which is based the assertion that the security interest is perfected or unperfected.

(c) If the parties to a transaction creating a purchase money security interest in goods in one jurisdiction understand at the time that the security interest attaches that the goods will be kept in another jurisdiction, then the law of the other jurisdiction governs the perfection and the effect of perfection or non-perfection of the security interest from the time it attaches until thirty days after the debtor receives possession of the goods and thereafter if the goods are taken to the other jurisdiction before the end of the thirty-day period.

(d) When collateral is brought into and kept in this state while subject to a security interest perfected under the law of the jurisdiction from which the collateral was removed, the security interest remains perfected, but if action is required by Part 3 of this Article to perfect the security interest,

(i) if the action is not taken before the expiration of the period of perfection in the other jurisdiction or the end of four months after the collateral is brought into this state, whichever period first expires, the security interest becomes unperfected at the end of that period and is thereafter deemed to have been unperfected as against a person who became a purchaser after removal;

(ii) if the action is taken before the expiration of the period specified in subparagraph (i), the security interest continues perfected thereafter;

(iii) for the purpose of priority over a buyer of consumer goods (subsection (2) of Section 9—307), the period of the effectiveness of a filing in the jurisdiction from which the collateral is removed is governed by the rules with respect to perfection in subparagraphs (i) and (ii).

(2) Certificate of title.

(a) This subsection applies to goods covered by a certificate of title issued under a statute of this state or of another jurisdiction under the law of which indication of a security interest on the certificate is required as a condition of perfection.

(b) Except as otherwise provided in this subsection, perfection and the effect of perfection or non-perfection of the security interest are governed by the law (including the conflict of laws rules) of the jurisdiction issuing the certificate until four months after the goods are removed from that jurisdiction and thereafter until the goods are registered in another jurisdiction, but in any event not beyond surrender of the certificate. After the expiration of that period, the goods are not covered by the certificate of title within the meaning of this section.

(c) Except with respect to the rights of a buyer described in the next paragraph, a security interest, perfected in another jurisdiction otherwise than by notation on a certificate of title, in goods brought into this state and thereafter covered by a certificate of title issued by this state is subject to the rules stated in paragraph (d) of subsection (1).

(d) If goods are brought into this state while a security interest therein is perfected in any manner under the law of the jurisdiction from which the goods are removed and a certificate of title is issued by this state and the certificate does not show that the goods are subject to the security interest or that they may be subject to security interests not shown on the certificate, the security interest is subordinate to the rights of a buyer of the goods who is not in the business of selling goods of that kind to the extent that he gives value and receives delivery of the goods after issuance of the certificate and without knowledge of the security interest.

(3) Accounts, general intangibles and mobile goods.

(a) This subsection applies to accounts (other than an account described in subsection (5) on minerals) and general intangibles (other than uncertificated securities) and to goods which are mobile and which are of a type normally used in more than one jurisdiction, such as motor vehicles, trailers, rolling stock, airplanes, shipping containers, road building and construction machinery and commercial harvesting machinery and the like, if the goods are equipment or are inventory leased or held for lease by the debtor to others, and are not covered by a certificate of title described in subsection (2).

(b) The law (including the conflict of laws rules) of the jurisdiction in which the debtor is located governs the perfection and the effect of perfection or non-perfection of the security interest.

(c) If, however, the debtor is located in a jurisdiction which is not a part of the United States, and which does not provide for perfection of the security interest by filing or recording in that jurisdiction, the law of the jurisdiction in the United States in which the debtor has its major executive office in the United States governs the perfection and the effect of perfection or non-perfection of the security interest through filing. In the alternative, if the debtor is located in a jurisdiction which is not a part of the United States or Canada and the collateral is accounts or general intangibles for money due or to become due, the security interest may be perfected by notification to the account debtor. As used in this paragraph, "United States" includes its territories and possessions and the Commonwealth of Puerto Rico.

(d) A debtor shall be deemed located at his place of business if he has one, at his chief executive office if he has more than one place of business, otherwise at his residence. If, however, the debtor is a foreign air carrier under the Federal Aviation Act of 1958, as amended, it shall be deemed located at the designated office of the agent upon whom service of process may be made on behalf of the foreign air carrier.

(e) A security interest perfected under the law of the jurisdiction of the location of the debtor is perfected until the expiration of four months after a change of the debtor's location to another jurisdiction, or until perfection would have ceased by the law of the first jurisdiction, whichever period first expires. Unless perfected in the new jurisdiction before the end of that period, it becomes unperfected thereafter and is deemed to have been unperfected as against a person who became a purchaser after the change.

(4) Chattel paper.

The rules stated for goods in subsection (1) apply to a possessory security interest in chattel paper. The rules stated for accounts in subsection (3) apply to a non-possessory security interest in chattel paper, but the security interest may not be perfected by notification to the account debtor.

(5) Minerals.

Perfection and the effect of perfection or non-perfection of a security interest which is created by a debtor who has an interest in minerals or the like (including oil and gas) before extraction and which attaches thereto as extracted, or which attaches to an account resulting from the sale thereof at the wellhead or minehead are governed by the law (including the conflict of laws rules) of the jurisdiction wherein the wellhead or minehead is located.

(6) Uncertificated securities.

The law (including the conflict of laws rules) of the jurisdiction of organization of the issuer governs the perfection and the effect of perfection or non-perfection of a security interest in uncertificated securities.

Amended in 1972 and 1977.

See Appendix I for changes made in former text and the reasons for change.

Official Comment

Prior Uniform Statutory Provisions: Paragraph 1(d): Section 14, Uniform Conditional Sales Act.

Purposes:

1. The general rules on choice of law between the original parties in Section 1—105 apply to this Article. However, when conflicting claims to collateral arise, the question depends on *perfection* of security interests, and thus on the effect of perfection or non-perfection. These problems are dealt with in this section. The general rule (paragraph (1) (b)) is that these questions are governed by the law of the jurisdiction where the collateral is when the last event occurs on which is based the assertion that the security interest is perfected or unperfected. This event will frequently be the filing. If the last event is not filing and perfection is through filing, the filing required is in the jurisdiction where the collateral is when the last event occurs; prior filing in another jurisdiction is not effective and is not saved by the four-month rule discussed below, which applies only when the security interest was *perfected* in the jurisdiction from which the collateral was removed. If the security interest was perfected in one jurisdiction and then removed to another jurisdiction, maintenance of perfection in the latter jurisdiction or failure to do so is the "last event" to which the basic rule refers.

There are, however, exceptions to this basic rule:

2. If the parties to a transaction creating a purchase money security interest in goods understand when the security interest attaches that the collateral will be kept in another jurisdiction, the law of that jurisdiction governs perfection and the effect of perfection or non-perfection until 30 days after the debtor receives possession of the goods (paragraph (1) (c)). A filing in that jurisdiction perfects the security interest even before the goods are removed. The 30-day period is not

a period of grace during which filing is unnecessary or has retroactive effect, but merely states the period during which the other jurisdiction is the place of filing. The effect of late filing is governed by other provisions, such as Sections 9—301 and 9—312.

3. If the goods reach that jurisdiction within the 30 days, the effectiveness of the filing in that jurisdiction continues without interruption. If the collateral is not kept in that jurisdiction before the end of the 30-day period, paragraph (1) (c) ceases to be applicable and thereafter the law of the jurisdiction where the collateral is controls perfection. A failure of the collateral to reach the intended destination jurisdiction before the expiration of the 30-day period because of a conflicting claim or otherwise may cause disappointment of expectations that the law of the destination jurisdiction will govern continuously, and caution may dictate filing both in that jurisdiction and in the jurisdiction where the security interest attaches.

This section uses the concepts that goods are "kept" in a state or "brought" into a state, and related terms. These concepts imply a stopping place of a permanent nature in the state, not merely transit or storage intended to be transitory.

4.(a) Where the collateral is an automobile or other goods covered by a certificate of title issued by any state and the security interest is perfected by notation on the certificate of title, perfection is controlled by the certificate of title rather than by the law of the state wherein the security interest attached (subsection (2)).

(b) It has long been hoped that "exclusive certificate of title laws" would provide a sure means of controlling property interests in goods like automobiles, which because of their nature cannot readily be controlled by local or statewide filing alone. In theory the certificate of title should control the property interests in the vehicle wherever the vehicle may be. However, two circumstances operate to prevent the perfect operation of the certificate of title device:

First, some states have never adopted certificate of title laws. This results in a problem in the issuance of a certificate of title when the vehicle moves from a non-certificate to a certificate state, because the certificate-issuing officer is in no position to conduct a complete search to ascertain the condition of the title in a state of origin which requires no filing or in which filing could be in any one or more of several localities. Also, it seems that when a vehicle moves from a certificate to a non-certificate state, the officers issuing a new registration for the vehicle are not always meticulous to notify secured parties shown on the certificate to give them a chance to perfect their security interests in the non-certificate state when a new registration is issued. Moreover, some vehicles like mobile homes are not always registered and title certificates are not always issued even in a state which may have certificate laws applicable thereto, because the certificate laws may apply only if the mobile homes use the highways.

Registration plates of a mobile home having a certificate could be removed and there would be nothing visible to show that a certificate had ever been issued for it.

Second, various fraudulent devices based on allegations of loss of the certificate of title enable a dishonest person to obtain both an original and a duplicate of title; to have a security interest shown on only one thereof; and then to effect a transfer into a new state on the basis of the clean certificate, no matter how diligent the officers in the second state may be.

Given these practical problems, the choice of applicable rules of law after interstate removals of vehicles subject to certificate of title laws is most difficult. This Article provides the rules set forth below.

(c) The security interest perfected by notation on a certificate of title will be recognized without limit as to time; but, of course, perfection by this method ceases if the certificate of title is surrendered (paragraph (2) (b)). Since the secured party ordinarily holds the certificate, surrender thereof could not occur without his action in the matter in some respect. If the vehicle is reregistered in another jurisdiction while the secured party still holds the certificate, a danger of deception to third parties arises. The section provides that the certificate ceases to control after 4 months following removal if reregistration has occurred, but during the 4 months the secured party has the same protection for cases of interstate removal as is set forth in paragraph (1) (d) of the section and Comment 7, subject to additional limitation if the reregistration also involves a new "clean" certificate of title in the removal jurisdiction and a non-professional buyer buys while that new certificate is outstanding. See paragraph (2) (d) and Comment 4 (e).

(d) If a vehicle not described in the preceding paragraph (i. e., not covered by a certificate of title) is removed to a certificate state and a certificate is issued therefor, the holder of a security interest has the same 4-month protection, subject to the provision discussed in the next paragraph of Comment.

(e) Where "this state" issues a certificate of title on collateral that has come from another state subject to a security interest perfected in any manner, problems will arise if this state, from whatever cause, fails to show on its certificate the security interest perfected in the other jurisdiction. This state will have every reason, nevertheless, to make its certificate of title reliable to the type of person who most needs to rely on it. Paragraph (2) (d) of the section therefore provides that the security interest perfected in the other jurisdiction is subordinate to the rights of a limited class of persons buying the goods while there is a clean certificate of title issued by this state, without knowledge of the security interest perfected in the other jurisdiction. The limited class are buyers who are non-professionals, i. e., not dealers and not secured parties, because these are ordinarily professionals. The protective rule mentioned does not apply if this state adopts a device used under some certificate of title laws, namely, stating on the certificate of title that the vehicle may be subject to security interests not shown on the certificate, where the collateral came from a non-certificate state.

In any event the security interest perfected out of state becomes unperfected unless reperfected in this state under the usual 4-month rule (paragraph (2) (d) of the section). States which place a cautionary statement on a certificate of title coming from a non-certificate state make provision to reissue the certificate without the caution after four months.

One difficulty is that no state's certificate of title law makes any provision by which a foreign security interest may be reperfected in that state, without the cooperation of the owner or other person holding the certificate in temporarily surrendering the certificate. But that cooperation is not likely to be forthcoming from an owner who wrongfully procured the issuance of a new certificate not showing the out-of-state security interest, or from a local secured party finding himself in a priority contest with the out-of-state secured party. The only solution for the out-of-state secured party under present certificate of title laws seems to be reperfect by possession, i. e., by repossessing the goods.

5. The general rules of the section based on location of the collateral could not be applied to certain types of intangible collateral which have no location in any realistic sense, or to certain movable chattels which have no permanent location.

(a) For accounts and general intangibles there is no indispensable or symbolic document which represents the underlying claim, whose endorsement or delivery is the one effectual means of transfer. There is a considerable body of case law dealing with the situs of choses in action such as these. This case law is in the highest degree confused, contradictory and uncertain: it affords no base on which to build a statutory rule.

An account arises typically out of a sale; the contract of sale may be executed in State A, the goods shipped from a warehouse in State B to buyer (account debtor) in State C. The account may then be assigned to an assignee in State D. The seller-assignor may keep his principal records in State E. Under the non-notification system of accounts financing, the seller-assignor, despite the assignment, bills and collects from the account debtor; under notification financing the account debtor makes payment to the assignee, but the bills may be prepared and sent out by either assignor or assignee. The contacts of the transaction are with many jurisdictions: to which one is it appropriate to look for the governing law? Even more complicated situations may be anticipated when the collateral consists of novel or uncommon types of personal property, which fall within the definition of general intangibles.

If we bear in mind that our principal question is where certain financing statements shall be filed, two things become clear. *First*: since the purpose of filing is to allow subsequent creditors of the *debtor-assignor* to determine the true status of his affairs, the place chosen must be one which such creditors would normally associate with the assignor; thus the place of business of the assignee and the places of business or residences of the various account debtors must be rejected in ordinary situations. *Second:* the place chosen must be one which can be determined with the least possible risk of error. The place chosen by subsection (3) is the debtor's location, which is ordinarily the location of its chief executive office. This concept is discussed below.

(b) Another class of collateral for which a special rule is stated in subsection (3) is mobile goods of types which are normally moved for use from one jurisdiction to another. Such goods are generally classified as equipment; sometimes they may be classified as inventory, for example, goods leased by a professional lessor. Subsection (3) provides that a security interest in such equipment or inventory is subject to this Article when the debtor's location, i. e., ordinarily its chief executive office, is in this state.

While automobiles are obviously mobile goods, they will in most cases be covered by subsection (2) of this section and therefore excluded from subsection (3) by paragraph (a) thereof. If an automobile is not covered by a certificate of title and is classified as equipment or as inventory under lease, it will be subject to subsection (3). Automobiles and other mobile goods which are classified as consumer goods are not subject to subsection (3).

The rule of subsection (3) applies to goods of a type "normally used" in more than one jurisdiction; there is no requirement that particular goods be in fact used out of state. Thus, if an enterprise whose chief executive office is in State X keeps in State Y goods of the type covered by subsection (3), the rule of subsection (3) requires filing in State X even though the goods never leave State Y.

(c) "Chief executive office" does not mean the place of incorporation; it means the place from which in fact the debtor manages the main part of this business operations. This is the place where persons dealing with the debtor would normally look for credit information, and is the appropriate place for filing. The term "chief executive office" is not defined in this Section or elsewhere in this Act. Doubt may arise as to which is the "chief executive office" of a multi-state enterprise, but it would be rare that there could be more than two possibilities. A secured party in such a case may easily protect himself at no great additional burden by filing in each possible place. The subsection states a rule which will be simple to apply in most cases, and which makes it possible to dispense with much burdensome and useless filing.

(d) If the location of the debtor is moved after a security interest has been perfected in another jurisdiction, the secured party has four months within which to refile, unless the perfection in the original jurisdiction would have expired earlier (paragraph (3)(e)).

(e) Under subsection (3) each state other than that of the debtor's location in effect disclaims jurisdiction over certain accounts and general intangibles which, by common law rules, might be held to be within its jurisdiction; in the same way there is a disclaimer of jurisdiction over mobile chattels, even though they may be physically located within the state much of the time. If the jurisdiction whose law controls under this rule is a United States jurisdiction or has enacted legislation permitting perfection of the security interest by filing or recording in that jurisdiction, the law of that jurisdiction will be recognized in the disclaiming jurisdiction as perfecting the security interest. The jurisdiction of the debtor's location may not, however, have such legislation. For example, mobile equipment is used in New York; the debtor's chief place of business is in a Canadian jurisdiction which will not permit or recognize filing as to property not physically located therein. Paragraph (3)(c) solves this difficulty by permitting perfection through filing in the jurisdiction in the United States in which the debtor has its major executive office in the United States. Where the debtor is not located in the United States or Canada and the collateral is accounts or general intangibles for money due or to become due, the secured party may alternatively perfect by notification to account debtors.

(f) A sentence in paragraph (3)(d) provides a special rule for security interests in airplanes owned by a foreign air carrier. Without that sentence subsection (3) might refer such a case to the law of a foreign nation whose law is difficult or impossible to ascertain. The sentence clears up such doubts by treating as the location of the carrier the office designated for service of process in the United States under the Federal Aviation Act of 1958. To the extent that it is applicable, the Convention on the International Recognition of Rights in Aircraft (Geneva Convention) supersedes state legislation on this subject, as set forth in Section 9—302(3), but some nations are not parties to that Convention.

6. Subsection (4) deals with chattel paper, a semi-intangible security interest which may be perfected either by possession or by filing (Sections 9—304(1), 9—305). As to possessory security, subsection (4) provides that chattel paper shall be subject to the same rule as goods in subsection (1). As to non-possessory security, subsection (4) provides that it shall be subject to the same rule as the intangibles under subsection (3), except that notification to the account

debtor is ruled out as an optional means of perfection under paragraph (3) (c). The reason for this is that a different alternative, possession, is available for chattel paper.

7. In addition to the foregoing rules defining which jurisdiction governs perfection of a security interest in the first instance, "this state" (i.e., a destination state after removal) adds its own rules requiring reperfection following removal of collateral other than that described in subsections (2), (3), and (5). "This state" will for four months recognize perfection under the law of the jurisdiction from which the collateral came, unless the remaining period of effectiveness of the perfection in that jurisdiction was less than four months (paragraph (1)(d)). After the four month period or the remaining period of effectiveness, whichever is shorter, the secured party must comply with perfection requirements in this state. This rule differs from the former rule of Section 14 of the Uniform Conditional Sales Act. Under that section a conditional seller was required to file within 10 days after he "received notice" that the goods had been removed into this state. Apparently, under the Uniform Conditional Sales Act, if the seller never "received notice" his interest continued or became perfected in this state without filing. Paragraph (1)(d) proceeds on the theory that not only the secured party whose collateral has been removed but also creditors of and purchasers from the debtor "in this state" should be considered.

The four-month period is long enough for a secured party to discover in most cases that the collateral has been removed and refile in this state; thereafter, if he has not done so, his interest, although originally perfected in the jurisdiction from which the collateral was removed, is subject to defeat here by purchasers of the collateral. Compare the situation arising under Section 9—403(2) when a filing lapses.

It should be noted that a "purchaser" includes a secured party. Section 1—201(32) and (33). The rights of a purchaser with a security interest against an unperfected security interest are governed by Section 9—312.

In case of delay beyond the four-month period, there is no "relation back"; and this is also true where the security interest is perfected for the first time in this state.

If the removal occurs within a short period, like two weeks, before the lapse of the filing in the original state, the secured party has only that period, not the full four months, to reperfect in "this state". But ordinarily he would have filed a continuation statement in the original jurisdiction; and he may do so to avoid lapse and allow himself the full four months if he is searching for the collateral and needs more time.

Paragraph (1)(d) does not apply to the case of goods removed from one filing district to another within this state (see subsection (3) of Section 9—401), but only to property brought into this state from another jurisdiction.

8. Subsection (5) deals with problems relating to the financing of minerals (including oil and gas) as these products come from the ground. In some cases rights in oil and gas in the ground have been split into a large variety of interests. As the oil or gas issues from the ground, it may be encumbered by the group of persons having interests therein. Or the product may be sold at minehead or wellhead and the resulting accounts assigned. The question arises as to the place of filing. The usual rule of this section in subsection (2) would make the place to search for encumbrances on the accounts the locations of the respective assignors; but the assignors might be a number of individuals located throughout the country. To avoid the difficult problems of search thus created, subsection (5) provides that the place for filing with respect to security interests in the minerals as they issue from the ground at minehead or wellhead or in the accounts arising out of the sale of the minerals at minehead or wellhead shall be in the state where the minehead or wellhead is located. Section 9—401 similarly provides that the the place to file within the state is in the real property records in the county where the minehead or wellhead is located. These rules conform to pre-Code practice and to practice which seems to have continued in the early Code period before express provision was made for these situations.

The term "at wellhead" is intended to encompass arrangements based on sale of the product as soon as it issues from the ground and is measured, without technical distinctions as to whether title passes at the "Christmas tree" or the far side of a gathering tank or at some other point. The term "at minehead" is a comparable concept.

Cross References:

Sections 1—105, 9—302 and 9—401.

Definitional Cross References:

"Accounts". Section 9—106.
"Attaches". Section 9—203.
"Chattel Paper". Section 9—105.
"Collateral". Section 9—105.
"Consumer Goods". Section 9—109.
"Debtor". Section 9—105.
"Document". Section 9—105.
"Equipment". Section 9—109.
"General intangibles". Section 9—106.
"Goods". Section 9—105.
"Instrument". Section 9—109.
"Purchase money security interest". Section 9—107.
"Purchaser". Section 1—201 (33).
"Security interest". Section 1—201(37).

§ 9—104. Transactions Excluded From Article

This Article does not apply

(a) to a security interest subject to any statute of the United States, to the extent that such statute governs the rights of parties to and third parties affected by transactions in particular types of property; or

(b) to a landlord's lien; or

(c) to a lien given by statute or other rule of law for services or materials except as provided in Section 9—310 on priority of such liens; or

(d) to a transfer of a claim for wages, salary or other compensation of an employee; or

(e) to a transfer by a government or governmental subdivision or agency; or

(f) to a sale of accounts or chattel paper as part of a sale of the business out of which they arose, or an assignment of accounts or chattel paper which is for the purpose of collection only, or a transfer of a right to payment under a contract to an assignee who is also to do the performance under the contract or a transfer of a single account to an assignee in whole or partial satisfaction of a preexisting indebtedness; or

(g) to a transfer of an interest in or claim in or under any policy of insurance, except as provided with respect to proceeds (Section 9—306) and priorities in proceeds (Section 9—312); or

(h) to a right represented by a judgment (other than a judgment taken on a right to payment which was collateral); or

(i) to any right of set-off; or

(j) except to the extent that provision is made for fixtures in Section 9—313, to the creation or transfer of an interest in or lien on real estate, including a lease or rents thereunder; or

(k) to a transfer in whole or in part of any claim arising out of tort; or

(*l*) to a transfer of an interest in any deposit account (subsection (1) of Section 9—105), except as provided with respect to proceeds (Section 9—306) and priorities in proceeds (Section 9—312).

Amended in 1972.

See Appendix I for changes made in former text and the reasons for change.

Official Comment

Prior Uniform Statutory Provisions: None.

Purposes:

To exclude certain security transactions from this Article.

1. Where a federal statute regulates the incidents of security interests in particular types of property, those security interests are of course governed by the federal statute and excluded from this Article. The Ship Mortgage Act, 1920, is an example of such a federal act. The present provisions of the Federal Aviation Act of 1958 (49 U.S.C. § 1403 et seq.) call for registration of title to and liens upon aircraft with the Civil Aeronautics Administrator and such registration is recognized as equivalent to filing under this Article (Section 9—302(3)); but to the extent that the Federal Aviation Act does not regulate the rights of parties to and third parties affected by such transactions, security interests in aircraft remain subject to this Article.

Although the Federal Copyright Act contains provisions permitting the mortgage of a copyright and for the recording of an assignment of a copyright (17 U.S.C. §§ 28, 30) such a statute would not seem to contain sufficient provisions regulating the rights of the parties and third parties to exclude security interests in copyrights from the provisions of this Article. Compare Republic Pictures Corp. v. Security-First National Bank of Los Angeles, 197 F.2d 767 (9th Cir.1952). Compare also with respect to patents, 35 U.S.C. § 47. The filing provisions under these Acts, like the filing provisions of the Federal Aviation Act, are recognized as the equivalent to filing under this Article. Section 9—302(3) and (4).

Even such a statute as the Ship Mortgage Act is far from a comprehensive regulation of all aspects of ship mortgage financing. That Act contains provisions on formal requisites, on recordation and on foreclosure but not much more. If problems arise under a ship mortgage which are not covered by the Act, the federal admiralty court must decide whether to improvise an answer under "federal law" or to follow the law of some state with which the mortgage transaction has appropriate contacts. The exclusionary language in paragraph (a) is that this Article does not apply to such security interest "to the extent" that the federal statute governs the rights of the parties. Thus if the federal statute contained no relevant provision, this Article could be looked to for an answer.

2. Except for fixtures (Section 9—313), the Article applies only to security interests in personal property. The exclusion of landlord's liens by paragraph (b) and of leases and other interests in or liens on real estate by paragraph (j) merely reiterates the limitations on coverage already made explicit in Section 9—102(3). See Comment 4 to that section.

3. In all jurisdictions liens are given suppliers of many types of services and materials either by statute or by common law. It was thought to be both inappropriate and unnecessary for this Article to attempt a general codification of that lien structure which is in considerable part determined by local conditions and which is far removed from ordinary commercial financing. Moreover, federal law may displace state law in situations such as admiralty liens. Paragraph (c) therefore excludes statutory liens from the Article. Section 9—310 states a rule for determining priorities between such liens and the consensual security interests covered by this Article.

4. In many states assignments of wage claims and the like are regulated by statute. Such assignments present important social problems whose solution should be a matter of local regulation. Paragraph (d) therefore excludes them from this Article.

5. Certain governmental borrowings include collateral in the form of assignments of water, electricity or sewer charges, rents on dormitories or industrial buildings, tools, etc. Since these assignments are usually governed by special provisions of law, these governmental transfers are excluded from this Article.

6. In general sales as well as security transfers of accounts and chattel paper are within the Article (see Section 9—102). Paragraph (f) excludes from the Article certain transfers of such intangibles which, by their nature, have nothing to do with commercial financing transactions.

Similarly, this paragraph excludes from the Article such transactions as that involved in Lyon v. Ty-Wood Corporation, 212 Pa.Super. 69, 239 A.2d 819 (1968) and Spurlin v. Sloan, 368 S.W.2d 314 (Ky.1963).

7. Rights under life insurance and other policies, and deposit accounts, are often put up as collateral. Such transactions are often quite special, do not fit easily under a general commercial statute and are adequately covered by existing law. Paragraphs (g) and (*l*) make appropriate exclusions, but provision is made for coverage of deposit accounts and certain insurance money as proceeds.

8. The remaining exclusions go to other types of claims which do not customarily serve as commercial collateral: judgments under paragraph (h), set-offs under paragraph (i) and tort claims under paragraph (k).

Cross References:

Point 1: Section 9—302(3).

Point 2: Sections 9—102(3) and 9—313.

Point 3: Sections 9—102(2) and 9—310.

Point 6: Section 9—102.

Definitional Cross References:

"Account". Section 9—106.

"Chattel paper". Section 9—105.

"Contract". Section 1—201.

"Deposit account". Section 9—105.

"Party". Section 1—201.

"Rights". Section 1—201.

"Security interest". Section 1—201.

§ 9—105. Definitions and Index of Definitions

(1) In this Article unless the context otherwise requires:

(a) "Account debtor" means the person who is obligated on an account, chattel paper or general intangible;

(b) "Chattel paper" means a writing or writings which evidence both a monetary obligation and a security interest in or a lease of specific goods, but a charter or other contract involving the use or hire of a vessel is not chattel paper. When a transaction is evidenced both by such a security agreement or a lease and by an instrument or a series of instruments, the group of writings taken together constitutes chattel paper;

(c) "Collateral" means the property subject to a security interest, and includes accounts and chattel paper which have been sold;

(d) "Debtor" means the person who owes payment or other performance of the obligation secured, whether or not he owns or has rights in the collateral, and includes the seller of accounts or chattel paper. Where the debtor and the owner of the collateral are not the same person, the term "debtor" means the owner of the collateral in any provision of the Article dealing with the collateral, the obligor in any provision dealing with the obligation, and may include both where the context so requires;

(e) "Deposit account" means a demand, time, savings, passbook or like account maintained with a bank, savings and loan association, credit union or like organization, other than an account evidenced by a certificate of deposit;

(f) "Document" means document of title as defined in the general definitions of Article 1 (Section 1—201), and a receipt of the kind described in subsection (2) of Section 7—201;

(g) "Encumbrance" includes real estate mortgages and other liens on real estate and all other rights in real estate that are not ownership interests;

(h) "Goods" includes all things which are movable at the time the security interest attaches or which are fixtures (Section 9—313), but does not include money, documents, instruments, accounts, chattel paper, general intangibles, or minerals or the like (including oil and gas) before extraction. "Goods" also includes standing timber which is to be cut and removed under a conveyance or contract for sale, the unborn young of animals, and growing crops;

(i) "Instrument" means a negotiable instrument (defined in Section 3—104), or a certificated security (defined in Section 8—102) or any other writing which evidences a right to the payment of money and is not itself a security agreement or lease and is of a type which is in ordinary course of business transferred by delivery with any necessary indorsement or assignment;

(j) "Mortgage" means a consensual interest created by a real estate mortgage, a trust deed on real estate, or the like;

(k) An advance is made "pursuant to commitment" if the secured party has bound himself to make it, whether or not a subsequent event of default or other event not within his control has relieved or may relieve him from his obligation;

(*l*) "Security agreement" means an agreement which creates or provides for a security interest;

(m) "Secured party" means a lender, seller or other person in whose favor there is a security interest, including a person to whom accounts or chattel paper have been sold. When the holders of obligations issued under an indenture of trust, equipment trust agreement or the like are represented by a trustee or other person, the representative is the secured party;

(n) "Transmitting utility" means any person primarily engaged in the railroad, street railway or trolley bus business, the electric or electronics communications transmission business, the transmission of goods by pipeline, or the transmission or the production and transmission of electricity, steam, gas or water, or the provision of sewer service.

(2) Other definitions applying to this Article and the sections in which they appear are:

"Account".	Section 9—106.
"Attach".	Section 9—203.
"Construction mortgage".	Section 9—313(1).
"Consumer goods".	Section 9—109(1).
"Equipment".	Section 9—109(2).
"Farm products".	Section 9—109(3).

"Fixture".	Section 9—313(1).
"Fixture filing".	Section 9—313(1).
"General intangibles".	Section 9—106.
"Inventory".	Section 9—109(4).
"Lien creditor".	Section 9—301(3).
"Proceeds".	Section 9—306(1).
"Purchase money security interest".	Section 9—107.
"United States".	Section 9—103.

(3) The following definitions in other Articles apply to this Article:

"Check".	Section 3—104.
"Contract for sale".	Section 2—106.
"Holder in due course".	Section 3—302.
"Note".	Section 3—104.
"Sale".	Section 2—106.

(4) In addition Article 1 contains general definitions and principles of construction and interpretation applicable throughout this Article.

Amended in 1966, 1972 and 1977.

See Appendix I for changes made in former text and the reasons for change.

Official Comment

Prior Uniform Statutory Provisions: Various.

Purposes:

1. **General.** It is necessary to have a set of terms to describe the parties to a secured transaction, the agreement itself, and the property involved therein; but the selection of the set of terms applicable to any one of the existing forms (e. g., mortgagor and mortgagee) might carry to some extent the implication that the existing law referable to that form was to be used for the construction and interpretation of this Article. Since it is desired to avoid any such implication, a set of terms has been chosen which have no common law or statutory roots tying them to a particular form.

In place of such terms as "chattel mortgage," "conditional sale," "assignment of accounts receivable," "trust receipt," etc., this Article substitutes the general term "security agreement" defined in paragraph (1) (*l*). In place of "mortgagor," "mortgagee," "conditional vendee," "conditional vendor," etc., this Article substitutes "debtor", defined in paragraph (1) (d), and "secured party", defined in paragraph (1) (m). The property subject to the security agreement is "collateral", defined in paragraph (1) (c). The interest in the collateral which is conveyed by the debtor to the secured party is a "security interest", defined in Section 1—201 (37).

2. **Parties.** The parties to the security agreement are the "debtor" and the "secured party."

"Debtor": In all but a few cases the person who owes the debt and the person whose property secures the debt will be the same. Occasionally, one person furnishes security for another's debt, and sometimes property is transferred subject to a secured debt of the transferor which the transferee does not assume; in such cases, under the second sentence of the definition, the term "debtor" may, depending upon the context, include either or both such persons. Section 9—112 sets out special rules which are applicable where collateral is owned by a person who does not owe a debt.

"Secured Party": The term includes any person in whose favor there is a security interest (defined in Section 1—201). The term is used equally to refer to a person who as a seller retains a lien on or title to goods sold, to a person whose interest arises initially from a loan transaction, and to an assignee of either. Note that a seller is a "secured party" in relation to his customer; the seller becomes a "debtor" if he assigns the chattel paper as collateral. This is also true of a lender who assigns the debt as collateral. With the exceptions stated in Section 9—104(f) the Article applies to any sale of accounts or chattel paper: the term "secured party" includes an assignee of such intangibles whether by sale or for security, to distinguish him from the payee of the account, for example, who becomes a "debtor" by pledging the account as security for a loan.

On the applicability of the terms "debtor" and "secured party" to consignments and leases see Section 9—408 and Comment thereto.

"Account debtor": Where the collateral is an account, chattel paper or general intangible the original obligor is called the "account debtor", defined in paragraph (1) (a).

3. **Property subject to the security agreement.** "Collateral", defined in paragraph (1) (c), is a general term for the tangible and intangible property subject to a security interest. For some purposes the Code makes distinctions between different types of collateral and therefore further classification of collateral is necessary. Collateral which consists of tangible property is "goods", defined in paragraph (1) (h); and "goods" are again subdivided in Section 9—109. For purposes of this Article all intangible collateral fits one of five categories, two of which, "accounts", and "general intangibles" are defined in the following Section 9—106; the other three, "documents", "instruments" and "chattel paper", are defined in paragraphs (1) (f), (1) (i) and (1) (b) of this section.

"Goods": the definition in paragraph (1) (h) is similar to that contained in Section 2—105 except that the Sales Article definition refers to "time of identification to the contract for sale", while this definition refers to "the time the security interest attaches".

For the treatment of fixtures, Section 9—313 should be consulted. It will be noted that the treatment of fixtures under Section 9—313 does not at all points conform to their treatment under Section 2—107 (goods to be severed from realty). Section 2—107 relates to sale of such goods; Section 9—313 to security interests in them. The discrepancies between the two sections arise from the differences in the types of interest covered. A comparable discrepancy exists as to minerals. In the case of timber, both sections treat it as goods if it is to be severed under a contract of sale, but not otherwise.

If in any state minerals before severance are deemed to be personal property, they fall outside the Article's definition of "goods" and would therefore fall in the catch-all definition, "general intangibles", in Section 9—106. The special provisions of Section 9—103(5) would not apply and those of Section 9—103(3) would apply. The resulting problems should be considered locally.

For the purpose of this Article, goods are classified as "consumer goods", "equipment", "farm products", and "inventory"; those terms are defined in Section 9—109. When the general term "goods" is used in this Article, it includes, as may be appropriate in the context, the subclasses of goods defined in Section 9—109.

"Instrument": the term as defined in paragraph (1) (i) includes not only negotiable instruments and certificated securities but also any other intangibles evidenced by writings which are in ordinary course of business transferred by delivery. As in the case of chattel paper "delivery" is only the minimum stated and may be accompanied by other steps.

If a writing is itself a security agreement or lease with respect to specific goods it is not an instrument although it otherwise meets the term of the definition. See Comment below on "chattel paper".

The fact that an instrument is secured by collateral, whether the collateral be other instruments, documents, goods, accounts or general intangibles, does not change the character of the principal obligation as an instrument or convert the combination of instrument and collateral into a separate Code classification of personal property. The single qualification to this principle is that an instrument which is secured by chattel paper is itself part of the chattel paper, while also retaining its identity as an instrument.

"Document": See the Comments under Sections 1—201(15) and 7—201.

"Chattel paper": To secure his own financing a secured party may wish to borrow against or sell the security agreement itself along with his interest in the collateral which he has received from his debtor. Since the refinancing of paper secured by specific goods presents some problems of its own, the term "chattel paper" is used to describe this kind of collateral. The Comments under Section 9—308 further describe this concept.

Charters of vessels are excluded from the definition of chattel paper because they fit under the definition of accounts. See Comment to Section 9—106. The term "charter" as used herein and in Section 9—106 includes bareboat charters, time charters, successive voyage charters, contracts of affreightment, contracts of carriage, and all other arrangements for use of vessels.

4. The following transactions illustrate the use of the term "chattel paper" and some of the other terms defined in this section.

A dealer sells a tractor to a farmer on conditional sales contract or purchase money security interest. The conditional sales contract is a "security agreement", the farmer is the "debtor", the dealer is the "secured party" and the tractor is the type of "collateral" defined in Section 9—109 as "equipment". But now the dealer transfers the contract to his bank, either by outright sale or to secure a loan. Since the conditional sales contract is a security agreement relating to specific equipment, the conditional sales contract is now the type of collateral called "chattel paper". In this transaction between the dealer and his bank, the bank is the "secured party", the dealer is the "debtor", and the farmer is the "account debtor".

Under the definition of "security interest" in Section 1—201(37) a lease does not create a security interest unless intended as security. Whether or not the lease itself is a security agreement, it is chattel paper when transferred if it relates to specific goods. Thus, if the dealer enters into a straight lease of the tractor to the farmer (not intended as security), and then arranges to borrow money on the security of the lease, the lease is chattel paper.

Security agreements of the type formerly known as chattel mortgages and conditional sales contracts are frequently executed in connection with a negotiable note or a series of such notes. Under the definitions in paragraphs (1) (b) and (1) (i) the rules applicable to chattel paper, rather than those relating to instruments, are applicable to the group of writings (contract plus note) taken together.

5. **Miscellaneous definitions.**

"Deposit account" is a type of collateral excluded from this Article under Section 9—104(*l*), except when it constitutes proceeds of other collateral under Section 9—306.

The terms "encumbrance" and "mortgage" are defined for use in the section on fixtures, Section 9—113.

The term "transmitting utility" is defined to designate a special class of debtors for whom separate filing rules are provided in Part 4, thus obviating all local filing and particularly the several local filings that would be necessary under the usual rules of Section 9—401 for the fixture collateral of a far-flung public utility debtor. See Comments under Sections 9—401 and 9—403.

The term "pursuant to commitment" is defined for use in the rules relating to priority of future advances in Sections 9—301 (4), 9—307(3), and 9—312(7).

6. Comments to the definitions indexed in subsections (2) and (3) follow the sections in which the definitions are contained.

Cross References:

Point 2: Sections 9—104(f) and 9—112.

Point 3: Sections 2—105, 2—107, 9—106, 9—109, 9—303 and 9—313.

Definitional Cross References:

"Account". Section 9—106.

"Agreement". Section 1—201.

"Document of title". Sections 1—201, 7—201.

"General intangibles". Section 9—106.

"Holder". Section 1—201.

"Money". Section 1—201.

"Negotiable instrument". Section 3—104.

"Person". Section 1—201.

"Representative". Section 1—201.

"Rights". Section 1—201.

"Security". Section 8—102.

"Security interest". Section 1—201.

"Writing". Section 1—201.

§ 9—106. Definitions: "Account"; "General Intangibles"

"Account" means any right to payment for goods sold or leased or for services rendered which is not evidenced by an instrument or chattel paper, whether or not it has been earned by performance. "General intangibles" means any personal property (including things in action) other than goods, accounts, chattel paper, documents, instruments, and money. All rights to payment earned or unearned under a charter or other contract involving the use or hire of a vessel and all rights incident to the charter or contract are accounts. Amended in 1966, 1972.

See Appendix I for changes made in former text and the reasons for change.

Official Comment

Prior Uniform Statutory Provision: None.

Purposes:

The terms defined in this section round out the classification of intangibles: see the definitions of "document", "chattel paper" and "instrument" in Section 9—105. Those three terms cover the various categories of commercial paper which are either negotiable or to a greater or less extent dealt with as if negotiable. The term "account" covers most choses in action which may be the subject of commercial financing transactions but which are not evidenced by an indispensable writing. The term "general intangibles" brings under this Article miscellaneous types of contractual rights and other personal property which are used or may become customarily used as commercial security. Examples are goodwill, literary rights and rights to performance. Other examples are copyrights, trademarks and patents, except to the extent that they may be excluded by Section 9—104(a). This Article solves the problems of filing of security interests in these types of intangibles (Sections 9—103(3) and 9—401). Note that this catch-all definition does not apply to money or to types of intangibles which are specifically excluded from the coverage of the Article (Section 9—104) and note also that under Section 9—302 filing under a federal statute may satisfy the filing requirements of this Article.

A right to the payment of money is frequently buttressed by ancillary covenants to insure the preservation of collateral, such as covenants in a purchase agreement, note or mortgage requiring insurance on the collateral or forbidding removal of the collateral; or covenants to preserve creditworthiness of the promisor, such as covenants restricting dividends, etc. While these miscellaneous ancillary rights might conceivably be thought to fall within the definition of "general intangibles", it is not the intention of the Code to treat them separately and require the perfection of assignment thereof by filing in the manner required for perfection of an assignment of general intangibles. Whatever perfection is required for the perfection of an assignment of the right to the payment of money will also carry these ancillary rights.

Similarly, when the right to the payment of money is not yet earned by performance, there are frequently ancillary rights designed to assure that an assignee may complete the performance and crystallize the right to payment of money. Such rights are frequently present in a "maintenance" lease where the lessor has continuing duties to perform, or in a ship charter. These ancillary rights, if considered in the abstract, might be thought to be "general intangibles", since they do not themselves involve the payment of money; but it is not the intent of the Code to split up the rights to the payment of money and its ancillary supports, and thereby multiply the problem of perfection of assignments. Therefore, all rights of the lessor in a lease are to be perfected as "chattel paper", and all rights of the owner in a ship charter are to be perfected as "accounts".

"Account" is defined as a right to payment for goods sold or leased or services rendered; the ordinary commercial account receivable. In some special cases a right to receive money not yet earned by performance crystallizes not into an account but into a general intangible, for it is a right to payment of money that is not "for goods sold or leased or for services rendered." Examples of such rights are the right to receive payment of a loan not evidenced by an instrument or chattel paper; a right to receive partial refund of purchase prices paid by reason of retroactive volume discounts; rights to receive payment under licenses of patents and copyrights, exhibition contracts, etc.

This Article rejects any lingering common law notion that only rights already earned can be assigned. In the triangular arrangement following assignment, there is reason to allow the original parties—assignor and account debtor—more flexibility in modifying the underlying contract before performance than after performance (see Section 9—318). It will, however, be found that in most situations the same rules apply to accounts both before and after performance.

Cross References:

Sections 9—103(2), 9—104, 9—302(3), 9—318 and 9—401.

Definitional Cross References:

"Chattel paper". Section 9—105.

"Contract". Section 1—201.

"Document". Section 9—105.

"Goods". Section 9—105.

"Instrument". Section 9—105.

§ 9—107. Definitions: "Purchase Money Security Interest"

A security interest is a "purchase money security interest" to the extent that it is

(a) taken or retained by the seller of the collateral to secure all or part of its price; or

(b) taken by a person who by making advances or incurring an obligation gives value to enable the debtor to acquire rights in or the use of collateral if such value is in fact so used.

Official Comment

Prior Uniform Statutory Provision: None.

Purposes:

1. Under existing rules of law and under this Article purchase money obligations often have priority over other obligations. Thus a purchase money obligation has priority over an interest acquired under an after-acquired property clause (Section 9—312 (3) and (4)); where filing is required a grace period of ten days is allowed against creditors and transferees in bulk (Section 9—301(2)); and in some instances filing may not be necessary (Section 9—302(1) (d)).

Under this section a seller has a purchase money security interest if he retains a security interest in the goods; a financing agency has a purchase money security interest when it advances money to the seller, taking back an assignment of chattel paper, and also when it makes advances to the buyer (e. g., on chattel mortgage) to enable him to buy, and he uses the money for that purpose.

2. When a purchase money interest is claimed by a secured

party who is not a seller, he must of course have given present consideration. This section therefore provides that the purchase money party must be one who gives value "by making advances or incurring an obligation": the quoted language excludes from the purchase money category any security interest taken as security for or in satisfaction of a pre-existing claim or antecedent debt.

Cross References:

Point 1: Sections 9—301, 9—302 and 9—312.

Point 2: Section 9—108.

Definitional Cross References:

"Collateral". Section 9—105.

"Debtor". Section 9—105.

"Person". Section 1—201.

"Rights". Section 1—201.

"Security interest". Section 1—201.

"Value". Section 1—201

§ 9—108. When After-Acquired Collateral Not Security for Antecedent Debt

Where a secured party makes an advance, incurs an obligation, releases a perfected security interest, or otherwise gives new value which is to be secured in whole or in part by after-acquired property his security interest in the after-acquired collateral shall be deemed to be taken for new value and not as security for an antecedent debt if the debtor acquires his rights in such collateral either in the ordinary course of his business or under a contract of purchase made pursuant to the security agreement within a reasonable time after new value is given.

Official Comment

Prior Uniform Statutory Provision: None.

Purposes:

1. Many financing transactions contemplate that the collateral will include both the debtor's existing assets and also assets thereafter acquired by him in the operation of his business. This Article generally validates such after-acquired property interests (see Section 9—204 and Comment) although they may be subordinated to later purchase money interests under Section 9—312(3) and (4).

Interests in after-acquired property have never been considered as involving transfers of property for antecedent debt merely because of the after-acquired feature, nor should they be so considered. The section makes explicit what has been true under the case law: an after-acquired property interest is not, by virtue of that fact alone, security for a pre-existing claim. This rule is of importance principally in insolvency proceedings under the federal Bankruptcy Act or state statutes which make certain transfers for antecedent debt voidable as preferences. The determination of when a transfer is for antecedent debt is largely left by the Bankruptcy Act to state law.

Two tests must be met under this section for an interest in after-acquired property to be one not taken for an antecedent debt. *First:* the secured party must, at the inception of the transaction, have given new value in some form. *Second:* the after-acquired property must come in either in the ordinary course of the debtor's business or as an acquisition which is made under a contract of purchase entered into within a reasonable time after the giving of new value and pursuant to the security agreement. The reason for the first test needs no comment. The second is in line with limitations which judicial construction has placed on the operation of after-acquired property clauses. Their coverage has been in many cases restricted to subsequent ordinary course acquisitions: this Article does not go so far (see Section 9—204 and Comment), but it does deny present value status to out of ordinary course acquisitions not made pursuant to the original loan agreement. This solution gives the secured party full protection as to the collateral which he may be reasonably thought to have contracted for; it gives other creditors the possibility, under the law of preferences, of subjecting to their claims windfall or uncontemplated acquisitions shortly before bankruptcy.

2. The term "value" is defined in Section 1—201(44) and discussed in the accompanying Comment. In this section and in other sections of this Article the term "new value" is used but is left without statutory definition. The several illustrations of "new value" given in the text of this section (making an advance, incurring an obligation, releasing a perfected security interest) as well as the "purchase money security interest" definition in Section 9—107 indicate the nature of the concept. In other situations it is left to the courts to distinguish between "new" and "old" value, between present considerations and antecedent debt.

Cross References:

Point 1: Sections 9—204 and 9—312.

Point 2: Section 9—107.

Definitional Cross References:

"Collateral". Section 9—105.

"Contract". Section 1—201.

"Debtor". Section 9—105.

"Purchase". Section 1—201.

"Rights". Section 1—201.

"Secured party". Section 9—105.

"Security agreement". Section 9—105.

"Security interest". Section 1—201.

"Value". Section 1—201.

§ 9—109. Classification of Goods: "Consumer Goods"; "Equipment"; "Farm Products"; "Inventory"

Goods are

(1) "consumer goods" if they are used or bought for use primarily for personal, family or household purposes;

(2) "equipment" if they are used or bought for use primarily in business (including farming or a profession) or by a debtor who is a non-profit organization or a governmental subdivision or agency or if the goods are not included in the definitions of inventory, farm products or consumer goods;

(3) "farm products" if they are crops or livestock or supplies used or produced in farming operations or if they are products of crops or livestock in their unmanufactured states (such as ginned cotton, wool-clip, maple syrup, milk and eggs), and if they are in the possession of a debtor engaged in raising, fattening, grazing or other farming operations. If goods are farm products they are neither equipment nor inventory;

(4) "inventory" if they are held by a person who holds them for sale or lease or to be furnished under contracts of service or if he has so furnished them, or if they are raw materials, work in process or materials used or consumed in a business. Inventory of a person is not to be classified as his equipment.

Official Comment

Prior Uniform Statutory Provision: None.

Purposes:

1. This section classifies goods as consumer goods, equipment, farm products and inventory. The classification is important in many situations: it is relevant, for example, in determining the rights of persons who buy from a debtor goods subject to a security interest (Section 9—307), in certain questions of priority (Section 9—312), in determining the place of filing (Section 9—401) and in working out rights after default (Part 5). Comment 5 to Section 9—102 contains an index of the special rules applicable to different classes of collateral.

2. The classes of goods are mutually exclusive; the same property cannot at the same time and as to the same person be both equipment and inventory, for example. In borderline cases—a physician's car or a farmer's jeep which might be either consumer goods or equipment—the principal use to which the property is put should be considered as determinative. Goods can fall into different classes at different times; a radio is inventory in the hands of a dealer and consumer goods in the hands of a householder.

3. The principal test to determine whether goods are inventory is that they are held for immediate or ultimate sale. Implicit in the definition is the criterion that the prospective sale is in the ordinary course of business. Machinery used in manufacturing, for example, is equipment and not inventory even though it is the continuing policy of the enterprise to sell machinery when it becomes obsolete.

Goods to be furnished under a contract of service are inventory even though the arrangement under which they are furnished is not technically a sale. When an enterprise is engaged in the business of leasing a stock of products to users (for example, the fleet of cars owned by a car rental agency), that stock is also included within the definition of "inventory". It should be noted that one class of goods which is not held for disposition to a purchaser or user is included in inventory: "Materials used or consumed in a business". Examples of this class of inventory are fuel to be used in operations, scrap metal produced in the course of manufacture, and containers to be used to package the goods. In general it may be said that goods used in a business are equipment when they are fixed assets or have, as identifiable units, a relatively long period of use; but are inventory, even though not held for sale, if they are used up or consumed in a short period of time in the production of some end product.

4. Goods are "farm products" only if they are in the possession of a debtor engaged in farming operations. Animals in a herd of livestock are covered whether they are acquired by purchase or result from natural increase. Products of crops or livestock remain farm products so long as they are in the possession of a debtor engaged in farming operations and have not been subjected to a manufacturing process. The terms "crops", "livestock" and "farming operations" are not defined; however, it is obvious from the text that "farming operations" includes raising livestock as well as crops; similarly, since eggs are products of livestock, livestock includes fowl.

When crops or livestock or their products come into the possession of a person not engaged in farming operations they cease to be "farm products". If they come into the possession of a marketing agency for sale or distribution or of a manufacturer or processor as raw materials, they become inventory.

Products of crops or livestock, even though they remain in the possession of a person engaged in farming operations, lose their status as farm products if they are subjected to a manufacturing process. What is and what is not a manufacturing operation is not determined by this Article. At one end of the scale some processes are so closely connected with farming—such as pasteurizing milk or boiling sap to produce maple syrup or maple sugar—that they would not rank as manufacturing. On the other hand an extensive canning operation would be manufacturing. The line is one for the courts to draw. After farm products have been subjected to a manufacturing operation, they become inventory if held for sale.

Note that the buyer in ordinary course who under Section 9—307 takes free of a security interest in goods held for sale does not include one who buys farm products from a person engaged in farming operations.

5. The principal definition of equipment is a negative one: goods used in a business (including farming or a profession) which are not inventory and not farm products. Trucks, rolling stock, tools, machinery are typical. It will be noted furthermore that any goods which are not covered by one of the other definitions in this section are to be treated as equipment.

Cross References:

Point 1: Sections 9—102, 9—307, 9—312, 9—401 and Part 5.

Point 3: Section 9—307.

Point 4: Section 9—307.

Definitional Cross References:

"Contract". Section 1—201.

"Debtor". Section 9—105.

"Goods". Section 9—105.

"Organization". Section 1—201.

"Person". Section 1—201.

"Sale". Sections 2—106 and 9—105.

§ 9—110. Sufficiency of Description

For the purposes of this Article any description of personal property or real estate is sufficient whether or not it is specific if it reasonably identifies what is described.

Official Comment

Prior Uniform Statutory Provision: None.

Purposes:

The requirement of description of collateral (see Section 9—203 and Comment thereto) is evidentiary. The test of sufficiency of a description laid down by this section is that the description do the job assigned to it—that it make possible the identification of the thing described. Under this rule courts should refuse to follow the holdings, often found in the older chattel mortgage cases, that descriptions are insufficient unless they are of the most exact and detailed nature, the so-called "serial number" test. The same test of reasonable identification applies where a description of real estate is required in a financing statement. See Section 9—402.

Cross References:

Sections 9—203 and 9—402.

§ 9—111. Applicability of Bulk Transfer Laws

The creation of a security interest is not a bulk transfer under Article 6 (see Section 6—103).

Official Comment

Prior Uniform Statutory Provision: None.

Purposes:

The bulk transfer laws, which have been almost everywhere

enacted, were designed to prevent a once prevalent type of fraud which seems to have flourished particularly in the retail field: the owner of a debt-burdened enterprise would sell it to an unwary purchaser and then remove himself, with the purchase price and his other assets, beyond the reach of process. The creditors would find themselves with no recourse unless they could establish that the purchaser assumed existing debts. The bulk transfer laws, which require advance notice of sale to all known creditors, seem to have been successful in preventing such frauds.

There has been disagreement whether the bulk transfer laws should be applied to security as well as to sale transactions. In most states security transactions have not been covered; in a few states the opposite result has been reached either by judicial construction or by express statutory provision. Whatever the reasons may be, it seems to be true that the bulk transfer type of fraud has not often made its appearance in the security field: it may be that lenders of money are more inclined to investigate a potential borrower than are purchasers of retail stores to determine the true state of their vendor's affairs. Since compliance with the bulk transfer laws is onerous and expensive, legitimate financing transactions should not be required to comply when there is no reason to believe that other creditors will be prejudiced.

This section merely reiterates the provisions of Article 6 on Bulk Transfers which provides in Section 6—103(1) that transfers "made to give security for the performance of an obligation" are not subject to that Article.

Cross Reference:

Section 6—103(1).

Definitional Cross Reference:

"Security interest". Section 1—201.

§ 9—112. Where Collateral Is Not Owned by Debtor

Unless otherwise agreed, when a secured party knows that collateral is owned by a person who is not the debtor, the owner of the collateral is entitled to receive from the secured party any surplus under Section 9—502(2) or under Section 9—504 (1), and is not liable for the debt or for any deficiency after resale, and he has the same right as the debtor

(a) to receive statements under Section 9—208;

(b) to receive notice of and to object to a secured party's proposal to retain the collateral in satisfaction of the indebtedness under Section 9—505;

(c) to redeem the collateral under Section 9—506;

(d) to obtain injunctive or other relief under Section 9—507(1); and

(e) to recover losses caused to him under Section 9—208 (2).

Official Comment

Prior Uniform Statutory Provision: None.

Purposes:

Under the definition of Section 9—105, in any provisions of the Article dealing with the collateral the term "debtor" means the owner of the collateral even though he is not the person who owes payment or performance of the obligation secured. The section covers several situations in which the implications of this definition are specifically set out.

The duties which this section imposes on a secured party toward such an owner of collateral are conditioned on the secured party's knowledge of the true state of facts. Short of such knowledge he may continue to deal exclusively with the person who owes the obligation. Nor does the section suggest that the secured party is under any duty of inquiry. It does not purport to cut across the law of conversion or of ultra vires. Whether a person who does not own property has authority to encumber it for his own debts and whether a person is free to encumber his property as collateral for the debts of another, are matters to be decided under other rules of law and are not covered by this section.

The section does not purport to be an exhaustive treatment of the subject. It isolates certain problems which may be expected to arise and states rules as to them. Others will no doubt arise: their solution is left to the courts.

Cross References:

Sections 9—105, 9—208 and Part 5.

Definitional Cross References:

"Collateral". Section 9—105.

"Debtor". Section 9—105.

"Notice". Section 1—201.

"Person". Section 1—201.

"Receive notice". Section 1—201.

"Right". Section 1—201.

"Secured party". Section 9—105.

§ 9—113. Security Interests Arising Under Article on Sales

A security interest arising solely under the Article on Sales (Article 2) is subject to the provisions of this Article except that to the extent that and so long as the debtor does not have or does not lawfully obtain possession of the goods

(a) no security agreement is necessary to make the security interest enforceable; and

(b) no filing is required to perfect the security interest; and

(c) the rights of the secured party on default by the debtor are governed by the Article on Sales (Article 2).

Official Comment

Prior Uniform Statutory Provision: None.

Purposes:

1. Under the provisions of Article 2 on Sales, a seller of goods may reserve a security interest (see, e. g., Sections 2—401 and 2—505); and in certain circumstances, whether or not a security interest is reserved, the seller has rights of resale and stoppage under Sections 2—703, 2—705 and 2—706 which are similar to the rights of a secured party. Similarly, under such sections as Sections 2—506, 2—707 and 2—711, a financing agency, an agent, a buyer or another person may have a security interest or other right in goods similar to that of a seller. The use of the term "security interest" in the Sales Article is meant to bring the interests so designated within this Article. This section makes it clear, however, that such security interests are exempted from certain provisions of this Article. Compare Section 4—208(3), making similar special provisions for security interests arising in the bank collection process.

2. The security interests to which this section applies commonly arise by operation of law in the course of a sales transaction. Since the circumstances under which they arise are defined in the Sales Article, there is no need for the "security agreement" defined in Section 9—105(1) (*l*) and required by Section 9—203(1) and paragraph (a) dispenses with such requirements. The requirement of filing may be inapplicable under Sections 9—302(1) (a) and (b), 9—304 and 9—305, where the goods are in the possession of the secured party or of a bailee other than the debtor. To avoid difficulty in the residual cases, as for example where a bailee does not receive notification of the secured party's interest until after the security interest arises, paragraph (b) dispenses with any filing requirement. Finally, paragraph (c) makes inapplicable the default provisions of Part 5 of this Article, since the Sales Article contains detailed provisions governing stoppage of delivery and resale after breach. See Sections 2—705, 2—706, 2—707(2) and 2—711(3).

3. These limitations on the applicability of this Article to security interests arising under the Sales Article are appropriate only so long as the debtor does not have or lawfully obtain possession of the goods. Compare Section 56(b) of the Uniform Sales Act. A secured party who wishes to retain a security interest after the debtor lawfully obtains possession must comply fully with all the provisions of this Article and ordinarily must

file a financing statement to perfect his interest. This is the effect of the "except" clause in the preamble to this section. Note that in the case of a buyer who has a security interest in rejected goods under Section 2—711(3), the buyer is the "secured party" and the seller is the "debtor".

4. This section applies only to a "security interest". The definition of "security interest" in Section 1—201(37) expressly excludes the special property interest of a buyer of goods on identification under Section 2—401(1). The seller's interest after identification and before delivery may be more than a security interest by virtue of explicit agreement under Section 2—401(1) or 2—501(1), by virtue of the provisions of Section 2—401(2), (3) or (4), or by virtue of substitution pursuant to Section 2—501(2). In such cases, Article 9 is inapplicable by the terms of Section 9—102 (1) (a).

5. Where there is a "security interest", this section applies only if the security interest arises "solely" under the Sales Article. Thus Section 1—201(37) permits a buyer to acquire by agreement a security interest in goods not in his possession or control; such a security interest does not impair his rights under the Sales Article, but any rights based on the security agreement are fully subject to this Article without regard to the limitations of this section. Similarly, a seller who reserves a security interest by agreement does not lose his rights under the Sales Article, but rights other than those conferred by the Sales Article depend on full compliance with this Article.

Cross References:

Point 1: Sections 2—401, 2—505, 2—506, 2—705, 2—706, 2—707, 2—711(3), 4—208(3).

Point 2: Sections 2—705, 2—706, 2—707(2), 2—711(3), 9—203(1), 9—302(1) (a) and (b), 9—304, 9—305 and Part 5.

Point 3: Section 2—711(3).

Point 4: Sections 2—401, 2—501 and 9—102(1) (a).

Definitional Cross References:

"Debtor". Section 9—105.

"Goods". Section 9—105.

"Rights". Section 1—201.

"Secured party". Section 9—105.

"Security agreement". Section 9—105.

"Security interest". Section 1—201.

§ 9—114. Consignment

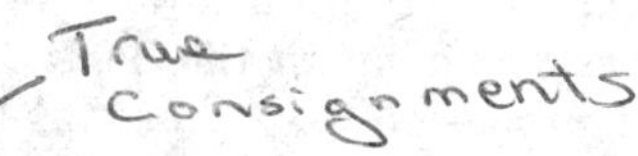

(1) A person who delivers goods under a consignment which is not a security interest and who would be required to file under this Article by paragraph (3) (c) of Section 2—326 has priority over a secured party who is or becomes a creditor of the consignee and who would have a perfected security interest in the goods if they were the property of the consignee, and also has

priority with respect to identifiable cash proceeds received on or before delivery of the goods to a buyer, if

(a) the consignor complies with the filing provision of the Article on Sales with respect to consignments (paragraph (3) (c) of Section 2—326) before the consignee receives possession of the goods; and

(b) the consignor gives notification in writing to the holder of the security interest if the holder has filed a financing statement covering the same types of goods before the date of the filing made by the consignor; and

(c) the holder of the security interest receives the notification within five years before the consignee receives possession of the goods; and

(d) the notification states that the consignor expects to deliver goods on consignment to the consignee, describing the goods by item or type.

(2) In the case of a consignment which is not a security interest and in which the requirements of the preceding subsection have not been met, a person who delivers goods to another is subordinate to a person who would have a perfected security interest in the goods if they were the property of the debtor. Added in 1972.

protects creditors

See Appendix I for reasons for adoption of this new section.

Official Comment

Prior Uniform Statutory Provisions: None.

Purposes:

1. This section requires that where goods are furnished to a merchant under the arrangement known as consignment rather than in a security transaction, the consignor must, in order to protect his position as against an inventory secured party of the consignee, give to that party the same notice and at the same time that he would give to that party if that party had filed first with respect to inventory and if the consignor were furnishing the goods under an inventory security agreement instead of under a consignment.

For the distinction between true consignment and security arrangements, see Section 1—201 (37). For the assimilation of consignments under certain circumstances to goods on sale or return and the requirement of filing in the case of consignments, see Section 2—326.

The requirements of notice in this section conform closely to the concepts and the language of Section 9—312(3), which should be consulted together with the relevant Comments.

Except in the limited cases of identifiable cash proceeds received on or before delivery of the goods to a buyer, no attempt has been made to provide rules as to perfection of a claim to proceeds of consignments (compare Section 9—306) or the priority thereof (compare Section 9—312). It is believed that under many true consignments the consignor acquires a claim for an agreed amount against the consignee at the moment of sale, and does not look to the proceeds of sale. In contrast to the assumption of this Article that rights to proceeds of security interests under Section 9—306 represent the presumed intent of the parties (compare Section 9—203(3)), the Article goes on the assumption that if consignors intend to claim the proceeds of sale, they will do so by expressly contracting for them and will perfect their security interests therein.

Cross References:

Sections 2—326 and 9—312(3).

Definitional Cross References:

"Consignment". Section 1—201(37).

"Debtor". Section 9—105.

"Goods". Section 9—105.

"Notification". Section 1—201 (26).

"Proceeds". Section 9—306.

"Security interest". Section 1—201(37).

PART 2

VALIDITY OF SECURITY AGREEMENT AND RIGHTS OF PARTIES THERETO

§ 9—201. General Validity of Security Agreement

Except as otherwise provided by this Act a security agreement is effective according to its terms between the parties, against purchasers of the collateral and against creditors. Nothing in this Article validates any charge or practice illegal under any statute or regulation thereunder governing usury, small loans, retail installment sales, or the like, or extends the application of any such statute or regulation to any transaction not otherwise subject thereto.

Official Comment

Prior Uniform Statutory Provisions: Section 4, Uniform Conditional Sales Act; Section 3, Uniform Trust Receipts Act.

Purposes:

This section states the general validity of a security agreement. In general the security agreement is effective between the parties; it is likewise effective against third parties. Exceptions to this general rule arise where there is a specific provision in any Article of this Act, for example, where Article 1 invalidates a disclaimer of the obligations of good faith, etc. (Section 1—102(3)), or this Article subordinates the security interest because it has not been perfected (Section 9—301) or for other reasons (see Section 9—312 on priorities) or defeats the security interest where certain types of claimants are involved (for example Section 9—307 on buyers of goods). As pointed out in the Note to Section 9—102, there is no intention that the enactment of this Article should repeal retail installment selling acts or small loan acts. Nor of course are the usury laws of any state repealed. These are mentioned in the text of Section 9—201 as examples of applicable laws, outside this Code entirely, which might invalidate the terms of a security agreement.

Cross References:

Sections 1—102(3), 9—301, 9—307 and 9—312.

Definitional Cross References:

"Collateral". Section 9—105.
"Creditor". Section 1—201.
"Party". Section 1—201.
"Purchaser". Section 1—201.
"Security agreement". Section 9—105.

§ 9—202. Title to Collateral Immaterial

Each provision of this Article with regard to rights, obligations and remedies applies whether title to collateral is in the secured party or in the debtor.

Official Comment

Prior Uniform Statutory Provision: None.

Purposes:

The rights and duties of the parties to a security transaction and of third parties are stated in this Article without reference to the location of "title" to the collateral. Thus the incidents of a security interest which secures the purchase price of goods are the same under this Article whether the secured party appears to have retained title or the debtor appears to have obtained title and then conveyed it or a lien to the secured party. This Article in no way determines which line of interpretation (title theory v. lien theory or retained title v. conveyed title) should be followed in cases where the applicability of some other rule of law depends upon who has title. Thus if a revenue law imposes a tax on the "legal" owner of goods or if a corporation law makes a vote of the stockholders prerequisite to a corporation "giving" a security interest but not if it acquires property "subject" to a security interest, this Article does not attempt to define whether the secured party is a "legal" owner or whether the transaction "gives" a security interest for the purpose of such laws. Other rules of law or the agreement of the parties determine the location of "title" for such purposes.

Petitions for reclamation brought by a secured party in his debtor's insolvency proceedings have often been granted or denied on a title theory: where the secured party has title, reclamation will be granted; where he has "merely a lien", reclamation may be denied. For the treatment of such petitions under this Article, see Point 1 of Comment to Section 9—507.

Cross References:

Sections 2—401 and 2—507.

Definitional Cross References:

"Collateral". Section 9—105.
"Debtor". Section 9—105.
"Remedy". Section 1—201.
"Rights". Section 1—201.
"Secured party". Section 9—105.

§ 9—203. Attachment and Enforceability of Security Interest; Proceeds; Formal Requisites

(1) Subject to the provisions of Section 4—208 on the security interest of a collecting bank, Section 8—321 on security interests in securities and Section 9—113 on a security interest arising under the Article on Sales, a security interest is not enforceable against the debtor or third parties with respect to the collateral and does not attach unless:

(a) the collateral is in the possession of the secured party pursuant to agreement, or the debtor has signed a security agreement which contains a description of the collateral and in addition, when the security interest covers crops growing or to be grown or timber to be cut, a description of the land concerned;

(b) value has been given; and

(c) the debtor has rights in the collateral.

(2) A security interest attaches when it becomes enforceable against the debtor with respect to the collateral. Attachment occurs as soon as all of the events specified in subsection (1) have taken place unless explicit agreement postpones the time of attaching.

(3) Unless otherwise agreed a security agreement gives the secured party the rights to proceeds provided by Section 9—306.

(4) A transaction, although subject to this Article, is also subject to ....*, and in the case of conflict between the provisions of this Article and any such statute, the provisions of such statute control. Failure to comply with any applicable statute has only the effect which is specified therein.

Amended in 1972 and 1977.

See Appendix I for changes made in former text and the reasons for change.

Note: *At * in subsection (4) insert reference to any local statute regulating small loans, retail installment sales and the like.*

The foregoing subsection (4) is designed to make it clear that certain transactions, although subject to this Article, must also comply with other applicable legislation.

This Article is designed to regulate all the "security" aspects of transactions within its scope. There is, however, much regulatory legislation, particularly in the consumer field, which supplements this Article and should not be repealed by its enactment. Examples are small loan acts, retail installment selling acts and the like. Such acts may provide for licensing and rate regulation and may prescribe particular forms of contract. Such provisions should remain in force despite the enactment of this Article. On the other hand if a retail installment selling act contains provisions on filing, rights on default, etc., such provisions should be repealed as inconsistent with this Article except that inconsistent provisions as to deficiencies, penalties, etc., in the Uniform Consumer Credit Code and other recent related legislation should remain because those statutes were drafted after the substantial enactment of the Article and with the intention of modifying certain provisions of this Article as to consumer credit.

Official Comment

Prior Uniform Statutory Provision: Section 2, Uniform Trust Receipts Act.

Purposes:

1. Subsection (1) states three basic prerequisites to the existence of a security interest: agreement, value, and collateral. In addition, the agreement must be in writing unless the collateral is in the possession of the secured party (including an agent on his behalf—see Comment 2 to Section 9—305). When all of these elements exist, the security agreement becomes enforceable between the parties and is said to "attach". Perfection of a security interest (see Section 9—303) will in many cases depend on the additional step of filing a financing statement (see Section 9—302) or possession of the collateral (Sections 9—304 (1) and 9—305). Section 9—301 states who will take priority over a security interest which has attached but which has not been perfected. Subsection (2) states a rule of construction under which the security interest, unless postponed by explicit agreement, attaches automatically when the stated events have occurred.

2. As to the type of description of collateral in a written security agreement which will satisfy the requirements of this sec-

tion, see Section 9—110 and Comment thereto.

In the case of crops growing or to be grown or timber to be cut the best identification is by describing the land, and subsection (1) (a) requires such a description.

3. One purpose of the formal requisites stated in subsection (1) (a) is evidentiary. The requirement of written record minimizes the possibility of future dispute as to the terms of a security agreement and as to what property stands as collateral for the obligation secured. Where the collateral is in the possession of the secured party, the evidentiary need for a written record is much less than where the collateral is in the debtor's possession; customarily, of course, as a matter of business practice the written record will be kept, but, in this Article as at common law, the writing is not a formal requisite. Subsection (1) (a), therefore, dispenses with the written agreement—and thus with signature and description—if the collateral is in the secured party's possession.

4. The definition of "security agreement" (Section 9—105) is "an agreement which creates or provides for a security interest". Under that definition the requirement of this section that the debtor sign a security agreement is not intended to reject, and does not reject, the deeply rooted doctrine that a bill of sale although absolute in form may be shown to have been in fact given as security. Under this Article as under prior law a debtor may show by parol evidence that a transfer purporting to be absolute was in fact for security and may then, on payment of the debt, assert his fundamental right to return of the collateral and execution of an acknowledgment of satisfaction.

5. The formal requisite of a writing stated in this section is not only a condition to the enforceability of a security interest against third parties, it is in the nature of a Statute of Frauds. Unless the secured party is in possession of the collateral, his security interest, absent a writing which satisfies paragraph (1) (a), is not enforceable even against the debtor, and cannot be made so on any theory of equitable mortgage or the like. If he has advanced money, he is of course a creditor and, like any creditor, is entitled after judgment to appropriate process to enforce his claim against his debtor's assets; he will not, however, have against his debtor the rights given a secured party by Part 5 of this Article on Default. The theory of equitable mortgage, insofar as it has operated to allow creditors to enforce informal security agreements against debtors, may well have developed as a necessary escape from the elaborate requirements of execution, acknowledgment and the like which the nineteenth century chattel mortgage acts vainly relied on as a deterrent to fraud. Since this Article reduces formal requisites to a minimum, the doctrine is no longer necessary or useful. More harm than good would result from allowing creditors to establish a secured status

by parol evidence after they have neglected the simple formality of obtaining a signed writing.

6. Subsection (4) states that the provisions of regulatory statutes covering the field of consumer finance prevail over the provisions of this Article in case of conflict. The second sentence of the subsection is added to make clear that no doctrine of total voidness for illegality is intended: failure to comply with the applicable regulatory statute has whatever effect may be specified in that statute, but no more.

Cross References:

Sections 4—208 and 9—113.
Point 1: Section 9—110.
Point 5: Part 5.

Definitional Cross References:

"Collateral". Section 9—105.
"Debtor". Section 9—105.
"Party". Section 1—201.
"Proceeds". Section 9—306.
"Secured party". Section 9—105.
"Security agreement". Section 9—105.
"Security interest". Section 1—201.
"Signed". Section 1—201.

§ 9—204. After-Acquired Property; Future Advances

(1) Except as provided in subsection (2), a security agreement may provide that any or all obligations covered by the security agreement are to be secured by after-acquired collateral.

(2) No security interest attaches under an after-acquired property clause to consumer goods other than accessions (Section 9—314) when given as additional security unless the debtor acquires rights in them within ten days after the secured party gives value.

(3) Obligations covered by a security agreement may include future advances or other value whether or not the advances or value are given pursuant to commitment (subsection (1) of Section 9—105). Amended in 1972.

See Appendix I for changes made in former text and the reasons for change.

Official Comment

Prior Uniform Statutory Provision: None.

Purposes:

1. Subsection (1) makes clear that a security interest arising by virtue of an after-acquired property clause has equal status with a security interest in collateral in which the debtor has rights at the time value is given under the security agreement. That is to say: the security interest in after-acquired property is not merely an "equitable" interest; no further action by the secured party—such as the taking of a supplemental agreement covering the new collateral—is required. This does not however

mean that the interest is proof against subordination or defeat: Section 9—108 should be consulted on when a security interest in after-acquired collateral is not security for antecedent debt, and Section 9—312(3) and (4) on when such a security interest may be subordinated to a conflicting purchase money security interest in the same collateral.

2. This Article accepts the principle of a "continuing general lien". It rejects the doctrine —of which the judicial attitude toward after-acquired property interests was one expression— that there is reason to invalidate as a matter of law what has been variously called the floating charge, the free-handed mortgage and the lien on a shifting stock. This Article validates a security interest in the debtor's existing and future assets, even though (see Section 9—205) the debtor has liberty to use or dispose of collateral without being required to account for proceeds or substitute new collateral. (See further, however, Section 9—306 on Proceeds and Comment thereto.)

The widespread nineteenth century prejudice against the floating charge was based on a feeling, often inarticulate in the opinions, that a commercial borrower should not be allowed to encumber all his assets present and future, and that for the protection not only of the borrower but of his other creditors a cushion of free assets should be preserved. That inarticulate premise has much to recommend it. This Article decisively rejects it not on the ground that it was wrong in policy but on the ground that it was not effective. In pre-Code law there was a multiplication of security devices designed to avoid the policy: field warehousing, trust receipts, factor's lien acts and so on. The cushion of free assets was not preserved. In almost every state it was possible before the Code for the borrower to give a lien on everything he held or would have. There have no doubt been sufficient economic reasons for the change. This Article, in expressly validating the floating charge, merely recognizes an existing state of things. The substantive rules of law set forth in the balance of the Article are designed to achieve the protection of the debtor and the equitable resolution of the conflicting claims of creditors which the old rules no longer give.

Notice that the question of assignment of future accounts is treated like any other case of after-acquired property: no periodic list of accounts is required by this Act. Where less than all accounts are assigned such a list may of course be necessary to permit identification of the particular accounts assigned.

3. Subsection (1) has been already referred to in connection with after-acquired property. It also serves to validate the so-called "cross-security" clause under which collateral acquired at any time may secure advances whenever made.

4. Subsection (2) limits the operation of the after-acquired property clause against consumers. No such interest can be claimed as additional security in consumer goods (defined in Section 9—109), except accessions (see Section 9—314), acquired more than ten days after the giving of value.

5. Under subsection (3) collateral may secure future as well as present advances when the security agreement so provides. At common law and under chattel mortgage statutes there seems to have been a vaguely articulated prejudice against future advance agreements comparable to the prejudice against after-acquired property interests. Although only a very few jurisdictions went to the length of invalidating interests claimed by virtue of future advances, judicial limitations severely restricted the usefulness of such arrangements. A common limitation was that an interest claimed in collateral existing at the time the security transaction was entered into for advances made thereafter was good only to the extent that the original security agreement specified the amount of such later advances and even the times at which they should be made. In line with the policy of this Article toward after-acquired property interests this subsection validates the future advance interest, provided only that the obligation be covered by the security agreement.

The effect of after-acquired property and future advance clauses in the security agreement should not be confused with the use of financing statements in notice filing. The references to after-acquired property clauses and future advance clauses in Section 9—204 are limited to security agreements. This section follows Section 9—203, the section requiring a written security agreement, and its purpose is to make clear that confirmatory agreements are not necessary where the basic agreement has the clauses mentioned. This section has no reference to the operation of financing statements. The filing of a financing statement is effective to perfect security interests as to which the other required elements for perfection exist, whether the security agreement involved is one existing at the date of filing with an after-acquired property clause or a future advance clause, or whether the applicable security agreement is executed later. Indeed, Section 9—402(1) expressly contemplates that a financing statement may be filed when there is no security agreement. There is no need to refer to after-acquired property or future advances in the financing statement.

As in the case of interests in after-acquired collateral, a security interest based on future advances may be subordinated to conflicting interests in the same collateral. See Sections 9—301(4); 9—307(3); 9—312(3), (4) and (7).

Cross References:

Point 1: Sections 9—108 and 9—312.

Point 2: Sections 9—205 and 9—306.

Point 4: Sections 9—109 and 9—314.

Point 5: Section 9—301(4); 9—307(3); 9—312(3), (4), and (7).

Definitional Cross References:

"Account". Section 9—106.

"Agreement". Section 1—201.

"Collateral". Section 9—105.

"Consumer goods". Section 9—109.

"Contract". Section 1—201.

"Debtor". Section 9—105.

"Purchase". Section 1—201.

"Pursuant to commitment". Section 9—105.

"Rights". Section 1—201.

"Secured party". Section 9—105.

"Security agreement". Section 9—105.

"Security interest". Section 1—201.

"Value". Section 1—201.

§ 9—205. Use or Disposition of Collateral Without Accounting Permissible

A security interest is not invalid or fraudulent against creditors by reason of liberty in the debtor to use, commingle or dispose of all or part of the collateral (including returned or repossessed goods) or to collect or compromise accounts or chattel paper, or to accept the return of goods or make repossessions, or to use, commingle or dispose of proceeds, or by reason of the failure of the secured party to require the debtor to account for proceeds or replace collateral. This section does not relax the requirements of possession where perfection of a security interest depends upon possession of the collateral by the secured party or by a bailee. Amended in 1972.

See Appendix I for changes made in former text and the reasons for change.

Official Comment

Prior Uniform Statutory Provision: None.

Purposes:

1. This Article expressly validates the floating charge or lien on a shifting stock. (See Sections 9—201, 9—204, and Comment to Section 9—204.) This section provides that a security interest is not invalid or fraudulent by reason of liberty in the debtor to dispose of the collateral without being required to account for proceeds or substitute new collateral. It repeals the rule of Benedict v. Ratner, 268 U.S. 353, 45 S.Ct. 566, 69 L.Ed. 991 (1925), and other cases which held such arrangements void as a matter of law because the debtor was given unfettered dominion or control over the collateral. The principal effect of the Benedict rule has been, not to discourage or eliminate security transactions in inventory and accounts receivable—on the contrary such trans-

actions have vastly increased in volume—but rather to force financing arrangements in this field toward a self-liquidating basis. Furthermore, several lower court cases drew implications from Justice Brandeis' opinion in Benedict v. Ratner which required lenders operating in this field to observe a number of needless and costly formalities: for example it was thought necessary for the debtor to make daily remittances to the lender of all collections received, even though the amount remitted is immediately returned to the debtor in order to keep the loan at an agreed level.

2. The Benedict rule was, in the accounts receivable field, repealed in many of the state accounts receivable statutes enacted after 1943, and, in the inventory field, by some of the factor's lien statutes. (Benedict v. Ratner purported to state the law of New York and not a rule of federal bankruptcy law. Since its acceptance is a matter of state law, it can of course be rejected by state statute.)

3. The requirement of "policing" is the substance of the Benedict rule. While this section repeals Benedict in matters of form, the filing requirements (Section 9—302) give other creditors the opportunity to ascertain from public sources whether property of their debtor or prospective debtor is subject to secured claims, and the provisions about proceeds (Section 9—306(4)) enable creditors to claim collections which were made by the debtor more than 10 days before insolvency proceedings and commingled or deposited in a bank account before institution of the insolvency proceedings. The repeal of the Benedict rule under this section must be read in the light of these provisions.

4. Other decisions reaching results like that in the Benedict case, but relating to other aspects of dominion (of which Lee v. State Bank & Trust Co., 54 F.2d 518 (2d Cir. 1931), is an example) are likewise rejected.

5. Nothing in Section 9—205 prevents such "policing" or dominion as the secured party and the debtor may agree upon; business and not legal reasons will determine the extent to which strict accountability, segregation of collections, daily reports and the like will be employed.

6. The last sentence is added to make clear that the section does not mean that the holder of an unfiled security interest, whose perfection depends on possession of the collateral by the secured party or by a bailee (such as a field warehouseman), can allow the debtor access to and control over the goods without thereby losing his perfected interest. The common law rules on the degree and extent of possession which are necessary to perfect a pledge interest or to constitute a valid field warehouse are not relaxed by this or any other section of this Article.

Cross References:

Point 1: Sections 9—201 and 9—204.

Point 3: Sections 9—302 and 9—306(4).

Point 6: Sections 9—304 and 9—305.

Definitional Cross References:

"Account". Section 9—106.

"Chattel paper". Section 9—105.

"Collateral". Section 9—105.

"Creditor". Section 1—201.

"Debtor". Section 9—105.

"Goods". Section 9—105.

"Proceeds". Section 9—306.

"Secured party". Section 9—105.

"Security interest". Section 1—201.

§ 9—206. Agreement Not to Assert Defenses Against Assignee; Modification of Sales Warranties Where Security Agreement Exists

(1) Subject to any statute or decision which establishes a different rule for buyers or lessees of consumer goods, an agreement by a buyer or lessee that he will not assert against an assignee any claim or defense which he may have against the seller or lessor is enforceable by an assignee who takes his assignment for value, in good faith and without notice of a claim or defense, except as to defenses of a type which may be asserted against a holder in due course of a negotiable instrument under the Article on Commercial Paper (Article 3). A buyer who as part of one transaction signs both a negotiable instrument and a security agreement makes such an agreement.

(2) When a seller retains a purchase money security interest in goods the Article on Sales (Article 2) governs the sale and any disclaimer, limitation or modification of the seller's warranties. Amended in 1962.

Official Comment

Prior Uniform Statutory Provision: Section 2, Uniform Conditional Sales Act.

Purposes:

1. Clauses are frequently inserted in installment purchase contracts under which the conditional vendee agrees not to assert defenses against an assignee of the contract. These clauses have led to litigation and their present status under the case law is in confusion. In some jurisdictions they have been held void as attempts to create negotiable instruments outside the framework of Article 3 or on grounds of public policy; in others they have been allowed to operate to cut off at least defenses based on breach of warranty. Under subsection (1) such clauses in a security agreement are validated outside the consumer field, but only as to defenses which could be cut off if a negotiable instrument were used. This limitation is important since if the clauses were allowed to have full effect as typically drafted, they would operate to cut off real as well as

personal defenses. The execution of a negotiable note in connection with a security agreement is given like effect as the execution of an agreement containing a waiver of defense clause. The same rules are made applicable to leases as to security agreements, whether or not the lease is intended as security.

2. This Article takes no position on the controversial question whether a buyer of consumer goods may effectively waive defenses by contractual clause or by execution of a negotiable note. In some states such waivers have been invalidated by statute. In other states the course of judicial decision has rendered them ineffective or unreliable—courts have found that the assignee is not protected against the buyer's defense by a clause in the contract or that the holder of a note, by reason of his too close connection with the underlying transaction, does not have the rights of a holder in due course. This Article neither adopts nor rejects the approach taken in such statutes and decisions, except that the validation of waivers in subsection (1) is expressly made "subject to any statute or decision" which may restrict the waiver's effectiveness in the case of a buyer of consumer goods.

3. Subsection (2) makes clear, as did Section 2 of the Uniform Conditional Sales Act, that purchase money security transactions are sales, and warranty rules for sales are applicable. It also prevents a buyer from inadvertently abandoning his warranties by a "no warranties" term in the security agreement when warranties have already been created under the sales arrangement. Where the sales arrangement and the purchase money security transaction are evidenced by only one writing, that writing may disclaim, limit or modify warranties to the extent permitted by Article 2.

Cross References:

Point 1: Section 3—305.

Point 2: Section 9—203(2).

Point 3: Sections 2—102 and 2—316.

Definitional Cross References:

"Agreement". Section 1—201.

"Consumer goods". Section 9—109.

"Good faith". Section 1—201.

"Goods". Section 9—105.

"Holder". Section 1—201.

"Holder in due course". Sections 3—302 and 9—105.

"Negotiable instrument". Section 3—104.

"Notice". Section 1—201.

"Purchase money security interest". Section 9—107.

"Sale". Sections 2—106 and 9—105.

"Security agreement". Section 9—105.

"Security interest". Section 1—201.

"Value". Section 1—201.

§ 9—207. Rights and Duties When Collateral is in Secured Party's Possession

(1) A secured party must use reasonable care in the custody and preservation of collateral in his possession. In the case of an instrument or chattel paper reasonable care includes taking necessary steps to preserve rights against prior parties unless otherwise agreed.

(2) Unless otherwise agreed, when collateral is in the secured party's possession

(a) reasonable expenses (including the cost of any insurance and payment of taxes or other charges) incurred in the custody, preservation, use or operation of the collateral are chargeable to the debtor and are secured by the collateral;

(b) the risk of accidental loss or damage is on the debtor to the extent of any deficiency in any effective insurance coverage;

(c) the secured party may hold as additional security any increase or profits (except money) received from the collateral, but money so received, unless remitted to the debtor, shall be applied in reduction of the secured obligation;

(d) the secured party must keep the collateral identifiable but fungible collateral may be commingled;

(e) the secured party may repledge the collateral upon terms which do not impair the debtor's right to redeem it.

(3) A secured party is liable for any loss caused by his failure to meet any obligation imposed by the preceding subsections but does not lose his security interest.

(4) A secured party may use or operate the collateral for the purpose of preserving the collateral or its value or pursuant to the order of a court of appropriate jurisdiction or, except in the case of consumer goods, in the manner and to the extent provided in the security agreement.

Official Comment

Prior Uniform Statutory Provision: None.

Purposes:

1. Subsection (1) states the duty to preserve collateral imposed on a pledge at common law. See Restatement of Security, §§ 17, 18. In many cases a secured party having collateral in his possession may satisfy this duty by notifying the debtor of

any act which must be taken and allowing the debtor to perform such act himself. If the secured party himself takes action, his reasonable expenses may be added to the secured obligation.

Under Section 1—102(3) the duty to exercise reasonable care may not be disclaimed by agreement, although under that section the parties remain free to determine by agreement, in any manner not manifestly unreasonable, what shall constitute reasonable care in a particular case.

2. Subsection (2) states rules, which follow common law precedents, and which apply, unless there is agreement otherwise, in typical situations during the period while the secured party is in possession of the collateral.

3. The right of a secured party holding instruments or documents to have them indorsed or transferred to him or his order is dealt with in the relevant sections of Articles 3 (Commercial Paper), 7 (Warehouse Receipts, Bills of Lading and Other Documents) and 8 (Investment Securities). (Sections 3—201, 7—506, 8—307.)

4. This section applies when the secured party has possession of the collateral before default, as a pledgee, and also when he has taken possession of the collateral after default. See Section 9—501(1) and (2). Subsection (4) permits operation of the collateral in the circumstances stated, and subsection (2) (a) authorizes payment of or provision for expenses of such operation. Agreements providing for such operation are common in trust indentures securing corporate bonds and are particularly important when the collateral is a going business. Such an agreement cannot of course disclaim the duty of care established by subsection (1), nor can it waive or modify the rights of the debtor contrary to Section 9—501(3).

Cross References:

Point 1: Section 1—102(3).

Point 3: Sections 3—201, 7—506 and 8—307.

Point 4: Section 9—501(2) and Part 5.

Definitional Cross References:

"Chattel paper". Section 9—105.

"Collateral". Section 9—105.

"Debtor". Section 9—105.

"Instrument". Section 9—105.

"Money". Section 1—201.

"Party". Section 1—201.

"Secured party". Section 9—105.

"Security interest". Section 1—201.

§ 9—208. Request for Statement of Account or List of Collateral

(1) A debtor may sign a statement indicating what he believes to be the aggregate amount of unpaid indebtedness as of a specified date and may send it to the secured party with a request that the statement be approved or corrected and returned

to the debtor. When the security agreement or any other record kept by the secured party identifies the collateral a debtor may similarly request the secured party to approve or correct a list of the collateral.

(2) The secured party must comply with such a request within two weeks after receipt by sending a written correction or approval. If the secured party claims a security interest in all of a particular type of collateral owned by the debtor he may indicate that fact in his reply and need not approve or correct an itemized list of such collateral. If the secured party without reasonable excuse fails to comply he is liable for any loss caused to the debtor thereby; and if the debtor has properly included in his request a good faith statement of the obligation or a list of the collateral or both the secured party may claim a security interest only as shown in the statement against persons misled by his failure to comply. If he no longer has an interest in the obligation or collateral at the time the request is received he must disclose the name and address of any successor in interest known to him and he is liable for any loss caused to the debtor as a result of failure to disclose. A successor in interest is not subject to this section until a request is received by him.

(3) A debtor is entitled to such a statement once every six months without charge. The secured party may require payment of a charge not exceeding $10 for each additional statement furnished.

Official Comment

Prior Uniform Statutory Provision: None.

Purposes:

1. To provide a procedure whereby a debtor may obtain from the secured party a statement of the amount due on the obligation and in some cases a statement of the collateral.

2. The financing statement required to be filed under this Article (see Section 9—402) may disclose only that a secured party may have a security interest in specified types of collateral owned by the debtor. Unless a copy of the security agreement itself is filed as the financing statement third parties are told neither the amount of the obligation secured nor which particular assets are covered. Since subsequent creditors and purchasers may legitimately need more detailed information, it is necessary to provide a procedure under which the secured party will be required to make disclosure. On the other hand, the secured party should not be under a duty to disclose details of business operations to any casual inquirer or competitor who asks for them. This section gives the right to demand dis-

closure only to the debtor, who will typically request a statement in connection with negotiations with subsequent creditors and purchasers, or for the purpose of establishing his credit standing and proving which of his assets are free of the security interest. The secured party is further protected against onerous requests by the provisions that he need furnish a statement of collateral only when his own records identify the collateral and that if he claims all of a particular type of collateral owned by the debtor he is not required to approve an itemized list.

Cross Reference:

Point 2: Section 9—402.

Definitional Cross References:

"Collateral". Section 9—105.
"Debtor". Section 9—105.
"Good faith". Section 1—201.
"Know". Section 1—201.
"Person". Section 1—201.
"Receive". Section 1—201.
"Secured party". Section 9—105.
"Security agreement". Section 9—105.
"Security interest". Section 1—201.
"Send". Section 1—201.
"Written". Section 1—201.

PART 3

RIGHTS OF THIRD PARTIES; PERFECTED AND UNPERFECTED SECURITY INTERESTS; RULES OF PRIORITY

§ 9—301. Persons Who Take Priority Over Unperfected Security Interests; Rights of "Lien Creditor"

(1) Except as otherwise provided in subsection (2), an unperfected security interest is subordinate to the rights of

(a) persons entitled to priority under Section 9—312;

(b) a person who becomes a lien creditor before the security interest is perfected;

(c) in the case of goods, instruments, documents, and chattel paper, a person who is not a secured party and who is a transferee in bulk or other buyer not in ordinary course of business or is a buyer of farm products in ordinary course of business, to the extent that he gives value and receives delivery of the collateral without knowledge of the security interest and before it is perfected;

(d) in the case of accounts and general intangibles, a person who is not a secured party and who is a transferee to the extent that he gives value without knowledge of the security interest and before it is perfected.

(2) If the secured party files with respect to a purchase money security interest before or within ten days after the debtor receives possession of the collateral, he takes priority over the rights of a transferee in bulk or of a lien creditor which arise between the time the security interest attaches and the time of filing.

(3) A "lien creditor" means a creditor who has acquired a lien on the property involved by attachment, levy or the like and includes an assignee for benefit of creditors from the time of assignment, and a trustee in bankruptcy from the date of the filing of the petition or a receiver in equity from the time of appointment.

(4) A person who becomes a lien creditor while a security interest is perfected takes subject to the security interest only to the extent that it secures advances made before he becomes a lien creditor or within 45 days thereafter or made without knowledge of the lien or pursuant to a commitment entered into without knowledge of the lien. Amended in 1972.

See Appendix I for changes made in former text and the reasons for change.

Official Comment

Prior Uniform Statutory Provision: Sections 8(2) and 9(2) (b), Uniform Trust Receipts Act; Section 5, Uniform Conditional Sales Act.

Purposes:

1. This section lists the classes of persons who take priority over an unperfected security interest. As in Section 60 of the Federal Bankruptcy Act, the term "perfected" is used to describe a security interest in personal property which cannot be defeated in insolvency proceedings or in general by creditors. A security interest is "perfected" when the secured party has taken whatever steps are necessary to give him such an interest. These steps are explained in the five following sections (9—302 through 9—306).

2. Section 9—312 states general rules for the determination of priorities among conflicting security interests and in addition refers to other sections which state special rules of priority in a variety of situations. The interests given priority under Section 9—312 and the other sections therein cited take such priority in general even over a perfected security interest. *A fortiori* they take priority over an unperfected security interest, and paragraph (1) (a) of this section so states.

3. Paragraph (1) (b) provides that an unperfected secur-

ity interest is subordinate to the rights of lien creditors. The section rejects the rule applied in many jurisdictions in pre-Code law that an unperfected security interest is subordinated to all creditors, but requires the lien obtained by legal proceedings to attach to the collateral before the security interest is perfected. The section subordinates the unperfected security interest but does not subordinate the secured debt to the lien.

4. Paragraphs (1) (c) and (1) (d) deal with purchasers (other than secured parties) of collateral who would take subject to a perfected security interest but who are by these subsections given priority over an unperfected security interest. In the cases of goods and of intangibles of the type whose transfer is effected by physical delivery of the representative piece of paper (instruments, documents and chattel paper) the purchaser who takes priority must both give value and receive delivery of the collateral without knowledge of the existing security interest and before perfection (paragraph (1) (c)). Thus even if the purchaser gave value without knowledge and before perfection, he would take subject to the security interest if perfection occurred before physical delivery of the collateral to him. The paragraph (1) (c) rule is obviously not appropriate where the collateral consists of intangibles and there is no representative piece of paper whose physical delivery is the only or the customary method of transfer. Therefore with respect to such intangibles (accounts and general intangibles), paragraph (1) (d) gives priority to any transferee who has given value without knowledge and before perfection of the security interest.

The term "buyer in ordinary course of business" referred to in paragraph (1) (c) is defined in Section 1—201(9).

Other secured parties are excluded from paragraphs (1) (c) and (1) (d) because their priorities are covered in Section 9—312 (see point 2 of this Comment).

5. Except to the extent provided in subsection (2), this Article does not permit a secured party to file or take possession after another interest has received priority under subsection (1) and thereby protect himself against the intervening interest.

A few chattel mortgage statutes did have grace periods, i. e., a filing within x days after the mortgage was given related back to the day the mortgage was given. The Uniform Conditional Sales Act had a ten-day period which cut off all intervening interests. The Uniform Trust Receipts Act had a thirty-day period but did not cut off the interest of a purchaser who took delivery before the filing.

Subsection (2) gives a grace period for perfection by filing as to purchase money security interests only (that term is defined in Section 9—107). The grace period runs for ten days after the debtor receives possession of the collateral but operates to cut off only the interests of intervening lien creditors or bulk purchasers.

6. Subsection (3) defines "lien creditor", following in substance the provisions of the Uniform Trust Receipts Act.

7. Subsection (4) deals with the question whether advances under an existing security interest in collateral, made after rights of lien creditors have attached to that collateral, will take precedence over rights of lien creditors. See related problems in Sections 9—307(3) and 9—312(7). In this section, because of the impact of the rule chosen on the question whether the security interest for future advances is "protected" under Sections 6323(c) (2) and (d) of the Internal Revenue Code as amended by the Federal Tax Lien Act of 1966, the priority of the security interest for future advances over a judgment lien is made absolute for 45 days regardless of knowledge of the secured party concerning the judgment lien. If, however, the advance is made after the 45 days, the advance will not have priority unless it was made or committed without knowledge of the lien obtained by legal proceedings. The importance of the rule chosen for actual conflicts between secured parties making subsequent advances and judgment lien creditors may not be great; but the rule chosen for the first 45 days is important in effectuating the intent of the Federal Tax Lien Act of 1966.

Cross References:

Section 9—312.

Point 1: Sections 9—302 through 9—306.

Point 7: Sections 9—204, 9—307(3) and 9—312(7).

Definitional Cross References:

"Account". Section 9—106.

"Buyer in ordinary course of business". Section 1—201.

"Chattel paper". Section 9—105.

"Collateral". Section 9—105.

"Creditor". Section 1—201.

"Delivery". Section 1—201.

"Document". Section 9—105.

"General intangibles". Section 9—106.

"Goods". Section 9—105.

"Instrument". Section 9—105.

"Knowledge". Section 1—201.

"Person". Section 1—201.

"Purchase money security interest". Section 9—107.

"Pursuant to commitment". Section 9—105.

"Representative". Section 1—201.

"Rights". Section 1—201.

"Secured party". Section 9—105.

"Security interest". Section 1—201.

"Value". Section 1—201.

§ 9—302. When Filing Is Required to Perfect Security Interest; Security Interests to Which Filing Provisions of This Article Do Not Apply

(1) A financing statement must be filed to perfect all security interests except the following:

(a) a security interest in collateral in possession of the secured party under Section 9—305;

(b) a security interest temporarily perfected in instruments or documents without delivery under Section 9—304 or in proceeds for a 10 day period under Section 9—306;

(c) a security interest created by an assignment of a beneficial interest in a trust or a decedent's estate;

(d) a purchase money security interest in consumer goods; but filing is required for a motor vehicle required to be registered; and fixture filing is required for priority over conflicting interests in fixtures to the extent provided in Section 9—313;

(e) an assignment of accounts which does not alone or in conjunction with other assignments to the same assignee transfer a significant part of the outstanding accounts of the assignor;

(f) a security interest of a collecting bank (Section 4—208) or in securities (Section 8—321) or arising under the Article on Sales (see Section 9—113) or covered in subsection (3) of this section;

(g) an assignment for the benefit of all the creditors of the transferor, and subsequent transfers by the assignee thereunder.

(2) If a secured party assigns a perfected security interest, no filing under this Article is required in order to continue the perfected status of the security interest against creditors of and transferees from the original debtor.

(3) The filing of a financing statement otherwise required by this Article is not necessary or effective to perfect a security interest in property subject to

(a) a statute or treaty of the United States which provides for a national or international registration or a national or international certificate of title or which specifies a place of filing different from that specified in this Article for filing of the security interest; or

(b) the following statutes of this state; [list any certificate of title statute covering automobiles, trailers, mobile homes, boats, farm tractors, or the like, and any central filing statute *.]; but during any period in which collateral is inventory held for sale by a person who is in the business of selling goods of that kind, the filing provisions of this Article (Part 4) apply to a security interest in that collateral created by him as debtor; or

(c) a certificate of title statute of another jurisdiction under the law of which indication of a security interest on the certificate is required as a condition of perfection (subsection (2) of Section 9—103).

(4) Compliance with a statute or treaty described in subsection (3) is equivalent to the filing of a financing statement under this Article, and a security interest in property subject to the statute or treaty can be perfected only by compliance therewith except as provided in Section 9—103 on multiple state transactions. Duration and renewal of perfection of a security interest perfected by compliance with the statute or treaty are governed by the provisions of the statute or treaty; in other respects the security interest is subject to this Article.

Amended in 1972 and 1977.

See Appendix I for changes made in former text and the reasons for change.

* **Note:** *It is recommended that the provisions of certificate of title acts for perfection of security interests by notation on the certificates should be amended to exclude coverage of inventory held for sale.*

Official Comment

Prior Uniform Statutory Provision: Section 5, Uniform Conditional Sales Act; Section 8, Uniform Trust Receipts Act.

Purposes:

1. Subsection (1) states the general rule that to perfect a security interest under this Article a financing statement must be filed. Paragraphs (1) (a) through (1) (g) exempt from the filing requirement the transactions described. Subsection (3) further sets out certain transactions to which the filing provisions of this Article do not apply, but it does not defer to another state statute on the filing of inventory security interests. The cases recognized are those where suitable alternative systems for giving public notice of a security interest are available. Subsection (4) states the consequences of such other form of notice.

Section 9—303 states the time when a security interest is perfected by filing or otherwise. Part 4 of the Article deals with the mechanics of filing: place of filing, form of financing statement and so on.

2. As at common law, there is no requirement of filing when the secured party has possession of the collateral in a pledge transaction (paragraph (1) (a)), Section 9—305 should be consulted on what collateral may be pledged and on the requirements of possession.

3. Under this Article, as under the Uniform Trust Receipts Act, filing is not effective to perfect a security interest in instruments. See Section 9—304(1).

4. Where goods subject to a security interest are left in the debtor's possession, the only per-

manent exception from the general filing requirement is that stated in paragraph (1) (d): purchase money security interests in consumer goods. For temporary exceptions, see Sections 9—304(5) (a) and 9—306.

In many jurisdictions under prior law security interests in consumer goods under conditional sale or bailment leases were not subject to filing requirements. Paragraph (1) (d) follows the policy of those jurisdictions. The paragraph changes prior law in jurisdictions where all conditional sales and bailment leases were subject to a filing requirement, except that filing is required for purchase money security interests in consumer fixtures to attain priority under Section 9—313 against real estate interests.

Although the security interests described in paragraph (1) (d) are perfected without filing, Section 9—307(2) provides that unless a financing statement is filed certain buyers may take free of the security interest even though perfected. See that section and the Comment thereto.

On filing for security interests in motor vehicles under certificate of title laws see subsection (3) of this section.

5. A financing statement must be filed to perfect a security interest in accounts except for the transactions described in paragraphs (1) (e) and (g). It should be noted that this Article applies to sales of accounts and chattel paper as well as to transfers thereof for security (Section 9—102(1) (b)); the filing requirement of this section applies both to sales and to transfers thereof for security. In this respect this Article follows many of the pre-Code statutes regulating assignments of accounts receivable.

Over forty jurisdictions had enacted accounts receivable statutes. About half of these statutes required filing to protect or perfect assignments; of the remainder, one was a so-called "book-marking" statute and the others validated assignments without filing. This Article adopts the filing requirement, on the theory that there is no valid reason why public notice is less appropriate for assignments of accounts than for any other type of nonpossessory interest. Section 9—305, furthermore, excludes accounts from the types of collateral which may be the subject of a possessory security interest: filing is thus the only means of perfection contemplated by this Article. See Section 9—306 on accounts as proceeds.

The purpose of the subsection (1) (e) exemption is to save from *ex post facto* invalidation casual or isolated assignments: some accounts receivable statutes were so broadly drafted that all assignments, whatever their character or purpose, fell within their filing provisions. Under such statutes many assignments which no one would think of filing might have been subject to invalidation. The paragraph (1) (e) exemption goes to that type of assignment. Any person who regularly takes assignments of any debtor's accounts should file. In this connection Section 9—104 (f) which excludes certain transfers of accounts from the Article should be consulted.

Assignments of interests in trusts and estates are not required to be filed because they are often not thought of as collateral comparable to the types dealt with by this Article. Assignments for the benefit of creditors are not required to be filed because they are not financing transactions and the debtor will not ordinarily be engaging in further credit transactions.

6. With respect to the paragraph (1) (f) exemptions, see the sections cited therein and Comments thereto.

7. The following example will explain the operation of subsection (2): Buyer buys goods from seller who retains a security interest in them which he perfects. Seller assigns the perfected security interest to X. The security interest, in X's hands and without further steps on his part, continues perfected against *Buyer's* transferees and creditors. If, however, the assignment from Seller to X was itself intended for security (or was a sale of accounts or chattel paper), X must take whatever steps may be required for perfection in order to be protected against *Seller's* transferees and creditors.

8. Subsection (3) exempts from the filing provisions of this Article transactions as to which an adequate system of filing, state or federal, has been set up outside this Article and subsection (4) makes clear that when such a system exists perfection of a relevant security interest can be had only through compliance with that system (i. e., filing under this Article is not a permissible alternative).

Examples of the type of federal statute referred to in paragraph (3) (a) are the provisions of 17 U.S.C. §§ 28, 30 (copyrights), 49 U.S.C. § 1403 (aircraft), 49 U.S.C. § 20(c) (railroads). The Assignment of Claims Act of 1940, as amended, provides for notice to contracting and disbursing officers and to sureties on bonds but does not establish a national filing system and therefore is not within the scope of paragraph (3) (a). An assignee of a claim against the United States, who must of course comply with the Assignment of Claims Act, must also file under this Article in order to perfect his security interest against creditors and transferees of his assignor.

Some states have enacted central filing statutes with respect to security transactions in kinds of property which are of special importance in the local economy. Subsection (3) adopts such statutes as the appropriate filing system for such property.

In addition to such central filing statutes many states have enacted certificate of title laws covering motor vehicles and the like. Subsection (3) exempts transactions covered by such laws from the filing requirements of this Article.

For a discussion of the operation of state motor vehicle certificate of title laws in interstate contexts, see Comment 4 to Section 9—103.

9. Perfection of a security interest under a state or federal statute of the type referred to in subsection (3) has all the consequences of perfection under the provisions of this Article, Subsection (4).

Cross References:

Point 1: Section 9—303 and Part 4.

Point 2: Section 9—305.

Point 3: Section 9—304(1).

Point 4: Section 9—307(2).

Point 5: Sections 9—102(1)(b), 9—104(f) and 9—305.

Point 6: Sections 4—208 and 9—113.

Definitional Cross References:

"Account". Section 9—106.

"Collateral". Section 9—105.

"Consumer goods". Section 9—109.

"Creditor". Section 1—201.

"Debtor". Section 9—105.

"Delivery". Section 1—201.

"Document". Section 9—105.

"Equipment". Section 9—109.

"Fixture". Section 9—313.

"Fixture filing". Section 9—313.

"Instrument". Section 9—105.

"Inventory". Section 9—109.

"Proceeds". Section 9—306.

"Purchase". Section 1—201.

"Purchase money security interest". Section 9—107.

"Sale". Sections 2—106 and 9—105.

"Secured party". Section 9—105.

"Security interest". Section 1—201.

§ 9—303. When Security Interest Is Perfected; Continuity of Perfection

(1) A security interest is perfected when it has attached and when all of the applicable steps required for perfection have been taken. Such steps are specified in Sections 9—302, 9—304, 9—305 and 9—306. If such steps are taken before the security interest attaches, it is perfected at the time when it attaches.

(2) If a security interest is originally perfected in any way permitted under this Article and is subsequently perfected in some other way under this Article, without an intermediate period when it was unperfected, the security interest shall be deemed to be perfected continuously for the purposes of this Article.

Official Comment

Prior Uniform Statutory Provision: None.

Purposes:

1. The term "attach" is used in this Article to describe the

point at which property becomes subject to a security interest. The requisites for attachment are stated in Section 9—203. When it attaches a security interest may be either perfected or unperfected: "Perfected" means that the secured party has taken all the steps required by this Article as specified in the several sections listed in subsection (1). A perfected security interest may still be or become subordinate to other interests (see Section 9—312) but in general after perfection the secured party is protected against creditors and transferees of the debtor and in particular against any representative of creditors in insolvency proceedings instituted by or against the debtor. Subsection (1) states the truism that the time of perfection is when the security interest has attached and any necessary steps for perfection (such as taking possession or filing) have been taken. If the steps for perfection have been taken in advance (as when the secured party files a financing statement before giving value or before the debtor acquires rights in the collateral), then the interest is perfected automatically when it attaches.

2. The following example will illustrate the operation of subsection (2): A bank which has issued a letter of credit honors drafts drawn under the credit and receives possession of the negotiable bill of lading covering the goods shipped. Under Sections 9—304(2) and 9—305 the bank now has a perfected security interest in the document and the goods. The bank releases the bill of lading to the debtor for the purpose of procuring the goods from the carrier and selling them. Under Section 9—304(5) the bank continues to have a perfected security interest in the document and goods for 21 days. The bank files before the expiration of the 21 day period. Its security interest now continues perfected for as long as the filing is good. The goods are sold by the debtor. The bank continues to have a security interest in the proceeds of the sale to the extent stated in Section 9—306.

If the successive stages of the bank's security interest succeed each other without an intervening gap, the security interest is "continuously perfected" and the date of perfection is when the interest first became perfected (i. e., in the example given, when the bank received possession of the bill of lading against honor of the drafts). If, however, there is a gap between stages—for example, if the bank does not file until after the expiration of the 21 day period specified in Section 9—304(5), the collateral still being in the debtor's possession—then, the chain being broken, the perfection is no longer continuous. The date of perfection would now be the date of filing (after expiration of the 21 day period); the bank's interest might now become subject to attack under Section 60 of the Federal Bankruptcy Act and would be subject to any interests arising during the gap period which under Section 9—301 take priority over an unperfected security interest.

The rule of subsection (2) would also apply to the case of collateral brought into this state subject to a security interest which became perfected in another state or jurisdiction. See Section 9—103(1) (d).

Cross References:

Sections 9—302, 9—304, 9—305 and 9—306.

Point 1: Sections 9—204 and 9—312.

Point 2: Sections 9—103(1) (d) and 9—301.

Definitional Cross References:

"Attach". Section 9—203.

"Security interest". Section 1—201.

§ 9—304. Perfection of Security Interest in Instruments, Documents, and Goods Covered by Documents; Perfection by Permissive Filing; Temporary Perfection Without Filing or Transfer of Possession

possession or filing

(1) A security interest in chattel paper or negotiable documents may be perfected by filing. A security interest in money or instruments (other than certificated securities or instruments which constitute part of chattel paper) can be perfected only by the secured party's taking possession, except as provided in subsections (4) and (5) of this section and subsections (2) and (3) of Section 9—306 on proceeds.

(2) During the period that goods are in the possession of the issuer of a negotiable document therefor, a security interest in the goods is perfected by perfecting a security interest in the document, and any security interest in the goods otherwise perfected during such period is subject thereto.

(3) A security interest in goods in the possession of a bailee other than one who has issued a negotiable document therefor is perfected by issuance of a document in the name of the secured party or by the bailee's receipt of notification of the secured party's interest or by filing as to the goods.

(4) A security interest in instruments (other than certificated securities) or negotiable documents is perfected without filing or the taking of possession for a period of 21 days from the time it attaches to the extent that it arises for new value given under a written security agreement.

(5) A security interest remains perfected for a period of 21 days without filing where a secured party having a perfected

security interest in an instrument (other than a certificated security), a negotiable document or goods in possession of a bailee other than one who has issued a negotiable document therefor

(a) makes available to the debtor the goods or documents representing the goods for the purpose of ultimate sale or exchange or for the purpose of loading, unloading, storing, shipping, transshipping, manufacturing, processing or otherwise dealing with them in a manner preliminary to their sale or exchange, but priority between conflicting security interests in the goods is subject to subsection (3) of Section 9—312; or

(b) delivers the instrument to the debtor for the purpose of ultimate sale or exchange or of presentation, collection, renewal or registration of transfer.

(6) After the 21 day period in subsections (4) and (5) perfection depends upon compliance with applicable provisions of this Article.

Amended in 1972 and 1977.

See Appendix I for changes made in former text and the reasons for change.

Official Comment

Prior Uniform Statutory Provision: Sections 3 and 8(1), Uniform Trust Receipts Act.

Purposes:

1. For most types of property, filing and taking possession are alternative methods of perfection. For some types of intangibles (i. e., accounts and general intangibles) filing is the only available method (see Section 9—305 and point 1 of Comment thereto). With respect to instruments subsection (1) provides that, except for the cases of "temporary perfection" covered in subsections (4) and (5), taking possession is the only available method; this provision follows the Uniform Trust Receipts Act. The rule is based on the thought that where the collateral consists of instruments, it is universal practice for the secured party to take possession of them in pledge; any surrender of possession to the debtor is for a short time; therefore it would be unwise to provide the alternative of perfection for a long period by filing which, since it in no way corresponds with commercial practice, would serve no useful purpose.

For similar reasons, filing is not permitted as to money. Perfection of security interests in certificated securities, which are covered by the definition of instruments, is governed by Section 8—321 and, therefore, excluded from this section.

Subsection (1) further provides that filing is available as a method of perfection for security interests in chattel paper and negotiable documents, which also come within Section 9—305 on perfection by possession. Chattel paper is sometimes delivered to the assignee, sometimes left in the hands of the assignor for collection; subsection (1) allows the assignee to perfect his interest by filing in the latter case. Negotiable documents may be, and usually are, delivered to the secured party; subsection (1) follows the Uniform Trust Receipts Act in allowing filing as an alternative method of perfection. Perfection of an interest in goods through a non-negotiable document is covered in subsection (3).

2. Subsection (2), following prior law and consistently with the provisions of Article 7, takes the position that, so long as a negotiable document covering goods is outstanding, title to the goods is, so to say, locked up in the document and the proper way of dealing with such goods is through the document. Perfection therefore is to be made with respect to the document and, when made, automatically carries over to the goods. Any interest perfected directly in the goods while the document is outstanding (for example, a chattel mortgage type of security interest on goods in a warehouse) is subordinated to an outstanding negotiable document.

3. Subsection (3) takes a different approach to the problem of goods covered by a non-negotiable document or otherwise in the possession of a bailee who has not issued a negotiable document. Here title to the goods is not looked on as being locked up in the document and the secured party may perfect his interest directly in the goods by filing as to them. The subsection states two other methods of perfection: issuance of the document in the secured party's name (as consignee of a straight bill of lading or the person to whom delivery would be made under a non-negotiable warehouse receipt) and receipt of notification of the secured party's interest by the bailee which, under Section 9—305, is looked on as equivalent to taking possession by the secured party.

4. Subsections (4) and (5) follow the Uniform Trust Receipts Act in giving perfected status to security interests in instruments (other than certificated securities, which are governed by Section 8—321) and documents for a short period although there has been no filing and the collateral is in the debtor's possession. The period of 21 days is chosen to conform to the provisions of Section 60 of the Federal Bankruptcy Act. There are a variety of legitimate reasons—some of them are described in subsections (5) (a) and (5) (b) —why such collateral has to be temporarily released to a debtor and no useful purpose would be served by cluttering the files with records of such exceedingly short term transactions. Under subsection (4) the 21 day perfection runs from the date of attachment; there is no limitation on the purpose for which the debtor is in possession but the secured party must have given new value under a written security agreement. Under subsection (5) the 21 day perfection runs from the date a secured party who already has a perfected security interest turns over the collateral to the debtor (an example is a bank which has acquired a bill of lading by

honoring drafts drawn under a letter of credit and subsequently turns over the bill of lading to its customer); there is no new value requirement but the turnover must be for one or more of the purposes stated in subsections (5) (a) and (5) (b). Note that while subsection (4) is restricted to instruments and *negotiable* documents, subsection (5) extends to goods covered by non-negotiable documents as well. Thus the letter of credit bank referred to in the example could make a subsection (5) turn-over without regard to the form of the bill of lading, provided that, in the case of a non-negotiable document, it had previously perfected its interest under one of the methods stated in subsection (3). But note that the discussion of subsection (5) in this Comment deals only with perfection. Priority of a security interest in inventory after surrender of the document depends on compliance with the requirements of Section 9—312(3) on notice to prior inventory financer.

Finally, it should be noted that the 21 days applies only to the documents and to the goods obtained by surrender thereof. If the goods are sold, the security interest will continue in proceeds for only 10 days under Section 9—306, unless a further perfection occurs as to the security interest in proceeds.

Cross References:

Article 7 and Sections 9—303, 9—305 and 9—312(3).

Definitional Cross References:

"Chattel paper". Section 9—105.
"Debtor". Section 9—105.
"Document". Section 9—105.
"Goods". Section 9—105.
"Instrument". Section 9—105.
"Receives" notification. Section 1—201.
"Sale". Sections 2—106 and 9—105.
"Secured party". Section 9—105.
"Security agreement". Section 9—105.
"Security interest". Section 1—201.
"Value". Section 1—201.
"Written". Section 1—201.

§ 9—305. When Possession by Secured Party Perfects Security Interest Without Filing

A security interest in letters of credit and advices of credit (subsection (2)(a). of Section 5—116), goods, instruments (other than certificated securities), money, negotiable documents, or chattel paper may be perfected by the secured party's taking possession of the collateral. If such collateral other than goods covered by a negotiable document is held by a bailee, the secured party is deemed to have possession from the time the bailee receives notification of the secured party's interest. A security interest is perfected by possession from the time possession is taken without a relation back and continues only so long as possession is retained, unless otherwise specified in this Article. The security interest may be otherwise perfected as provided in this Article before or after the period of possession by the secured party.

Amended in 1972 and 1977.

See Appendix I for changes made in former text and the reasons for change.

Official Comment

Prior Uniform Statutory Provision: None.

Purposes:

1. As under the common law of pledge, no filing is required by this Article to perfect a security interest where the secured party has possession of the collateral. Compare Section 9—302(1) (a). This section permits a security interest to be perfected by transfer of possession only when the collateral is goods, instruments (other than certificated securities, which are governed by Section 8—321), documents or chattel paper: that is to say, accounts and general intangibles are excluded. See Section 5—116 for the special case of assignments of letters and advices of credit. A security interest in accounts and general intangibles—property not ordinarily represented by any writing whose delivery operates to transfer the claim—may under this Article be perfected only by filing, and this rule would not be affected by the fact that a security agreement or other writing described the assignment of such collateral as a "pledge". Section 9—302(1) (e) exempts from filing certain assignments of accounts which are out of the ordinary course of financing: such exempted assignments are perfected when they attach under Section 9—303(1); they do not fall within this section.

2. Possession may be by the secured party himself or by an agent on his behalf: it is of course clear, however, that the debtor or a person controlled by him cannot qualify as such an agent for the secured party. See also the last sentence of Section 9—205. Where the collateral (except for goods covered by a negotiable document) is held by a bailee, the time of perfection of the security interest, under the second sentence of the section, is when the bailee receives notification of the secured party's interest: this rule rejects the common law doctrine that it is necessary for the bailee to attorn to the secured party or acknowledge that he now holds on his behalf.

3. The third sentence of the section rejects the "equitable pledge" theory of relation back, under which the taking possession was deemed to relate back to the date of the original security agreement. The relation back theory has had little vitality since the 1938 revision of the Federal Bankruptcy Act, which introduced in Section 60a provisions designed to make such interests voidable as preferences in bankruptcy proceedings. This section now brings state law into conformity with the overriding federal policy: where a pledge transaction is contemplated, perfection dates

only from the time possession is taken, although a security interest may attach, unperfected, before that under the rules stated in Section 9—204. The only exception to this rule is the short twenty-one day period of perfection provided in Section 9—304 (4) and (5) during which a debtor may have possession of specified collateral in which there is a perfected security interest.

Cross References:

Sections 5—116, 9—204, 9—302, 9—303 and 9—304.

Definitional Cross References:

"Chattel paper". Section 9—105.

"Collateral". Section 9—105.

"Documents". Section 9—105.

"Goods". Section 9—105.

"Instruments". Section 9—105.

"Receives" notification. Section 1—201.

"Secured party". Section 9—105.

"Security interest". Section 1—201.

§ 9—306. "Proceeds"; Secured Party's Rights on Disposition of Collateral

(1) "Proceeds" includes whatever is received upon the sale, exchange, collection or other disposition of collateral or proceeds. Insurance payable by reason of loss or damage to the collateral is proceeds, except to the extent that it is payable to a person other than a party to the security agreement. Money, checks, deposit accounts, and the like are "cash proceeds". All other proceeds are "non-cash proceeds".

(2) Except where this Article otherwise provides, a security interest continues in collateral notwithstanding sale, exchange or other disposition thereof unless the disposition was authorized by the secured party in the security agreement or otherwise, and also continues in any identifiable proceeds including collections received by the debtor.

(3) The security interest in proceeds is a continuously perfected security interest if the interest in the original collateral was perfected but it ceases to be a perfected security interest and becomes unperfected ten days after receipt of the proceeds by the debtor unless

(a) a filed financing statement covers the original collateral and the proceeds are collateral in which a security interest may be perfected by filing in the office or offices where the financing statement has been filed and, if the proceeds are acquired with cash proceeds, the description of collateral in the financing statement indicates the types of property constituting the proceeds; or

(b) a filed financing statement covers the original collateral and the proceeds are identifiable cash proceeds; or

(c) the security interest in the proceeds is perfected before the expiration of the ten day period.

Except as provided in this section, a security interest in proceeds can be perfected only by the methods or under the circumstances permitted in this Article for original collateral of the same type.

(4) In the event of insolvency proceedings instituted by or against a debtor, a secured party with a perfected security interest in proceeds has a perfected security interest only in the following proceeds:

(a) in identifiable non-cash proceeds and in separate deposit accounts containing only proceeds;

(b) in identifiable cash proceeds in the form of money which is neither commingled with other money nor deposited in a deposit account prior to the insolvency proceedings;

(c) in identifiable cash proceeds in the form of checks and the like which are not deposited in a deposit account prior to the insolvency proceedings; and

(d) in all cash and deposit accounts of the debtor in which proceeds have been commingled with other funds, but the perfected security interest under this paragraph (d) is

(i) subject to any right to set-off; and

(ii) limited to an amount not greater than the amount of any cash proceeds received by the debtor within ten days before the institution of the insolvency proceedings less the sum of (I) the payments to the secured party on account of cash proceeds received by the debtor during such period and (II) the cash proceeds received by the debtor during such period to which the secured party is entitled under paragraphs (a) through (c) of this subsection (4).

(5) If a sale of goods results in an account or chattel paper which is transferred by the seller to a secured party, and if the

goods are returned to or are repossessed by the seller or the secured party, the following rules determine priorities:

(a) If the goods were collateral at the time of sale, for an indebtedness of the seller which is still unpaid, the original security interest attaches again to the goods and continues as a perfected security interest if it was perfected at the time when the goods were sold. If the security interest was originally perfected by a filing which is still effective, nothing further is required to continue the perfected status; in any other case, the secured party must take possession of the returned or repossessed goods or must file.

(b) An unpaid transferee of the chattel paper has a security interest in the goods against the transferor. Such security interest is prior to a security interest asserted under paragraph (a) to the extent that the transferee of the chattel paper was entitled to priority under Section 9—308.

(c) An unpaid transferee of the account has a security interest in the goods against the transferor. Such security interest is subordinate to a security interest asserted under paragraph (a).

(d) A security interest of an unpaid transferee asserted under paragraph (b) or (c) must be perfected for protection against creditors of the transferor and purchasers of the returned or repossessed goods.

Amended in 1972.

See Appendix I for changes made in former text and the reasons for change.

Official Comment

Prior Uniform Statutory Provision: Section 10, Uniform Trust Receipts Act.

Purposes:

1. This section states a secured party's right to the proceeds received by a debtor on disposition of collateral and states when his interest in such proceeds is perfected.

It makes clear that insurance proceeds from casualty loss of collateral are proceeds within the meaning of this section.

As to the proceeds of consigned goods, see Section 9—114 and the Comment thereto.

2. (a) Whether a debtor's sale of collateral was authorized or unauthorized, prior law generally gave the secured party a claim to the proceeds. Sometimes it was said that the security interest attached to the

"property" received in substitution; sometimes it was said the debtor held the proceeds as "trustee" or "agent" for the secured party. Whatever the formulation of the rule, the secured party, if he could identify the proceeds, could reclaim them or their equivalent from the debtor or his trustee in bankruptcy. This section provides new rules for insolvency proceedings. Paragraphs 4(a) through (c) substitute specific rules of identification for general principles of tracing. Paragraph 4(d) limits the security interest in proceeds not within these rules to an amount of the debtor's cash and deposit accounts not greater than cash proceeds received within ten days of insolvency proceedings less the cash proceeds during this period already paid over and less the amounts for which the security interest is recognized under paragraphs 4 (a) through (c).

(b) Subsections (2) and (3) make clear that the four-month period for calculating a voidable preference in bankruptcy begins with the date of the secured party's obtaining the security interest in the original collateral and not with the date of his obtaining control of the proceeds. The interest in the proceeds "continues" as a perfected interest if the original interest was perfected; but the interest ceases to be perfected after the expiration of ten days unless a filed financing statement covered the original collateral and the proceeds are collateral of a type as to which a security interest could be perfected by a filing in the same office or unless the secured party perfects his interest in the proceeds themselves—i. e., by filing a financing statement covering them or by taking possession. See Section 9—312(6) and Comment thereto for priority of rights in proceeds perfected by a filing as to original collateral.

(c) Where cash proceeds are covered into the debtor's checking account and paid out in the operation of the debtor's business, recipients of the funds of course take free of any claim which the secured party may have in them as proceeds. What has been said relates to payments and transfers in ordinary course. The law of fraudulent conveyances would no doubt in appropriate cases support recovery of proceeds by a secured party from a transferee out of ordinary course or otherwise in collusion with the debtor to defraud the secured party.

3. In most cases when a debtor makes an unauthorized disposition of collateral, the security interest, under prior law and under this Article, continues in the original collateral in the hands of the purchaser or other transferee. That is to say, since the transferee takes subject to the security interest, the secured party may repossess the collateral from him or in an appropriate case maintain an action for conversion. Subsection (2) codifies this rule. The secured party may claim both proceeds and collateral, but may of course have only one satisfaction.

In many cases a purchaser or other transferee of collateral will take free of a security interest: in such cases the secured party's only right will be to proceeds. The transferee will take free whenever the disposition was authorized; the authorization may be contained in the security agreement or otherwise given. The right to proceeds, either under the rules of this section or under specific mention thereof in a security agreement or financing statement does not in itself constitute an authorization of sale.

Section 9—301 states when transferees take free of unperfected security interests. Sections 9—307 on goods, 9—308 on chattel paper and instruments and 9—309 on negotiable instruments, negotiable documents and securities state when purchasers of such collateral take free of a security interest even though perfected and even though the disposition was not authorized.

4. Subsection (5) states rules to determine priorities when collateral which has been sold is returned to the debtor: for example goods returned to a department store by a dissatisfied customer. The most typical problems involve sale and return of inventory, but the subsection can also apply to equipment. Under the rule of Benedict v. Ratner, failure to segregate such returned goods sometimes led to invalidation of the entire security arrangement. This Article rejects the Benedict v. Ratner line of cases (see Section 9—205 and Comment). Subsection (5) (a) of this section reinforces the rule of Section 9—205: as between secured party and debtor (and debtor's trustee in bankruptcy) the original security interest continues on the returned goods. Whether or not the security interest in the returned goods is perfected depends upon factors stated in the text.

Paragraphs (5) (b), (c) and (d) deal with a different aspect of the returned goods situation. Assume that a dealer has sold an automobile and transferred the chattel paper or the account arising on the sale to Bank X (which had not previously financed the car as inventory). Thereafter the buyer of the automobile rightfully rescinds the sale, say for breach of warranty, and the car is returned to the dealer. Paragraph (5) (b) gives the bank as transferee of the chattel paper or the account a security interest in the car against the dealer. For protection against dealer's creditors or purchasers from him (other than buyers in the ordinary course of business, see Section 9—307), Bank X as the transferee, under paragraph (5) (d), must perfect its interest by taking possession of the car or by filing as to it. Perfection of his original interest in the chattel paper or the account does not automatically carry over to the returned car, as it does under paragraph (5) (a) where the secured party originally financed the dealer's inventory.

In the situation covered by (5) (b) and (5) (c) a secured party who financed the inventory and a secured party to whom the chattel paper or the account was transferred may both claim the returned goods—the inventory financer under paragraph (5)(a), the transferee under paragraphs (5)(b) and (5)(c). With respect to chattel paper, Section 9—308 regulates the priorities. With respect to an account, paragraph (5)(c) subordinates the security interest of the transferee of the account to that of the inventory financer. However, if the inventory security interest was unperfected, the transferee's interest could become entitled to priority under the rules stated in Section 9—312(5).

In cases of repossession by the dealer and also in cases where the chattel was returned to the dealer by the voluntary act of the account debtor, the dealer's position may be that of a mere custodian; he may be an agent for resale, but without any other obligation to the holder of the chattel paper; he may be obligated to repurchase the chattel, the chattel paper or the account from the secured party or to hold it as collateral for a loan secured by a transfer of the chattel paper or the account.

If the dealer thereafter sells the chattel to a buyer in ordinary course of business in any of the foregoing cases, the buyer is fully protected under Section 2—403(2) as well as under Section 9—307(1), whichever is technically applicable.

Cross References:

Sections 9—307, 9—308 and 9—309.

Point 3: Sections 1—205 and 9—301.

Point 4: Sections 2—403(2), 9—205 and 9—312.

Definitional Cross References:

"Account". Section 9—106.

"Bank". Section 1—201.

"Chattel paper". Section 9—105.

"Check". Sections 3—104 and 9—105.

"Collateral". Section 9—105.

"Creditors". Section 1—201.

"Debtor". Section 9—105.

"Deposit account". Section 9—105.

"Goods". Section 9—105.

"Insolvency proceedings". Section 1—201.

"Money". Section 1—201.

"Purchaser". Section 1—201.

"Sale". Sections 2—106 and 9—105.

"Secured party". Section 9—105.

"Security agreement". Section 9—105.

"Security interest". Section 1—201.

§ 9—307. Protection of Buyers of Goods

(1) A buyer in ordinary course of business (subsection (9) of Section 1—201) other than a person buying farm products from a person engaged in farming operations takes free of a security interest created by his seller even though the security interest is perfected and even though the buyer knows of its existence.

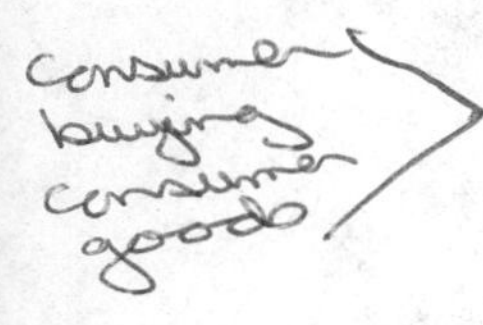

(2) In the case of consumer goods, a buyer takes free of a security interest even though perfected if he buys without knowledge of the security interest, for value and for his own personal, family or household purposes unless prior to the purchase the secured party has filed a financing statement covering such goods.

(3) A buyer other than a buyer in ordinary course of business (subsection (1) of this section) takes free of a security interest to the extent that it secures future advances made after the secured party acquires knowledge of the purchase, or more than 45 days after the purchase, whichever first occurs, unless made pursuant to a commitment entered into without knowledge of the purchase and before the expiration of the 45 day period. Amended in 1972.

See Appendix I for changes made in former text and the reasons for change.

Official Comment

Prior Uniform Statutory Provision: Section 9, Uniform Conditional Sales Act; Section 9(2), Uniform Trust Receipts Act.

Purposes:

1. This section states when buyers of goods take free of a security interest even though perfected. A buyer who takes free of a perfected security interest of course takes free of an unperfected one. Section 9—301 should be consulted to determine what purchasers, in addition to the buyers covered in this section, take free of an unperfected security interest.

Article 2 (Sales) states general rules on purchase of goods from a seller with defective or voidable title (Section 2—403).

2. The definition of "buyer in ordinary course of business" in Section 1—201(9) restricts the application of subsection (1) to buyers (except pawnbrokers) "from a person in the business of selling goods of that kind": thus the subsection applies, in the terminology of this Article, primarily to inventory. Subsection (1) further excludes from its operation buyers of "farm products", defined in Section 9—109 (3), from a person engaged in farming operations. The buyer in ordinary course of business is defined as one who buys "in good faith and without knowledge that the sale to him is in violation of the ownership rights or security interest of a third party." This section provides that such a buyer takes free of a security interest, even though perfected, and although he knows the security interest exists. Reading the two provisions together, it results that the buyer takes free if he merely knows that there is a security interest which covers the goods but takes subject if he knows, in addition, that the sale is in violation of some term in the security agreement not

waived by the words or conduct of the secured party.

The limitations which this section imposes on the persons who may take free of a security interest apply of course only to unauthorized sales by the debtor. If the secured party has authorized the sale in the security agreement or otherwise, the buyer takes free without regard to the limitations of this section. Section 9—306 states the right of a secured party to the proceeds of a sale, authorized or unauthorized.

3. Subsection (2) deals with buyers of "consumer goods" (defined in Section 9—109). Under Section 9—301(1) (d) no filing is required to perfect a purchase money interest in consumer goods subject to this subsection except motor vehicles required to be registered; filing is required to perfect security interests in such goods other than purchase money interests and, for motor vehicles, even in the case of purchase money interests. (The special case of fixtures has added complications that are apart from the point of this discussion.)

Under subsection (2) a buyer of consumer goods takes free of a security interest even though perfected a) if he buys without knowledge of the security interest, b) for value, c) for his own personal, family, or household purposes and d) before a financing statement is filed.

As to purchase money security interests which are perfected without filing under Section 9—302(1) (d): A secured party may file a financing statement (although filing is not required for perfection). If he does file, all buyers take subject to the security interest. If he does not file, a buyer who meets the qualifications stated in the preceding paragraph takes free of the security interest.

As to security interests which can be perfected only by filing under Section 9—302: This category includes all non-purchase money interests, and all interests, whether or not purchase money, in motor vehicles, as well as interests which may be and are filed, though filing was not required for perfection under Section 9—302. (Note that under Section 9—302(3) the filing provisions of this Article do not apply when a state has enacted a certificate of title law. Thus where motor vehicles are concerned, in a state having such a certificate of title law, perfection will be under that law.) So long as the security interest remains unperfected, not only the buyers described in subsection (2) but the purchasers described in Section 9—301 will take free of the interest. After a financing statement has been filed or after compliance with the certificate of title law all subsequent buyers, under the rule of subsection (2), are subject to the security interest.

4. Although a buyer is of course subject to the Code's system of notice from filing or possession, subsection (3) makes clear that he will not be subject to future advances under a security interest after the secured party has knowledge that the

buyer has purchased the collateral and in any event after 45 days after the purchase unless the advances were made pursuant to a commitment entered into before the expiration of the 45 days and without knowledge of the purchase. Of course, a buyer in ordinary course who takes free of the security interest under subsection (1) is not subject to any future advances. Compare Sections 9—301(4) and 9—312 (7).

Cross References:

Point 1: Sections 2—403 and 9—301.

Point 2: Section 9—306.

Point 3: Sections 9—301 and 9—302.

Point 4: Sections 9—301(4) and 9—312(7).

Definitional Cross References:

"Buyer in ordinary course of business". Section 1—201.

"Consumer goods". Section 9—109.

"Goods". Section 9—105.

"Knows" and "Knowledge". Section 1—201.

"Person". Section 1—201.

"Purchase". Section 1—201.

"Pursuant to commitment". Section 9—105.

"Secured party". Section 9—105.

"Security interest". Section 1—201.

"Value". Section 1—201.

§ 9—308. Purchase of Chattel Paper and Instruments

A purchaser of chattel paper or an instrument who gives new value and takes possession of it in the ordinary course of his business has priority over a security interest in the chattel paper or instrument

(a) which is perfected under Section 9—304 (permissive filing and temporary perfection) or under Section 9—306 (perfection as to proceeds) if he acts without knowledge that the specific paper or instrument is subject to a security interest; or

(b) which is claimed merely as proceeds of inventory subject to a security interest (Section 9—306) even though he knows that the specific paper or instrument is subject to the security interest.

Amended in 1972.

See Appendix I for changes made in former text and the reasons for change.

Official Comment

Prior Uniform Statutory Provision: Sections 9(a) and 10 of Uniform Trust Receipts Act.

Purposes:

1. Chattel paper is defined (Section 9—105) as "a writing or writings which evidence both a monetary obligation and a security interest in or a lease of specific goods". Such paper has become an important class of collateral in financing arrangements,

which may—as in the automobile and some other fields—follow an earlier financing arrangement covering inventory or which may begin with the chattel paper itself.

Arrangements where the chattel paper is delivered to the secured party who then makes collections, as well as arrangements where the debtor, whether or not he is left in possession of the paper, makes the collections, are both widely used, and are known respectively as notification (or "direct collection") and non-notification (or "indirect collection") arrangements. In the automobile field, for example, when a car is sold to a consumer buyer under an installment purchase agreement and the resulting chattel paper is assigned, the assignee usually takes possession, the obligor is notified of the assignment and is directed to make payments to the assignee. In the furniture field, for an example on the other hand, the chattel paper may be left in the dealer's hands or delivered to the assignee; in either case the obligor may not be notified, and payments are made to the dealer-assignor who receives them under a duty to remit to his assignee. The widespread use of both methods of dealing with chattel paper is recognized by the provisions of this Article, which permit perfection of a chattel paper security interest either by filing or by taking possession.

2. Although perfection by filing is permitted as to chattel paper, certain purchasers of chattel paper allowed to remain in the debtor's possession take free of the security interest despite the filing.

Clause (b) of the section deals with the case where the security interest in the chattel paper is claimed merely as proceeds—i. e., on behalf of an inventory financer who has not by some new transaction with the debtor acquired a specific interest in the chattel paper. In that case a purchaser, even though he knows of the inventory financer's proceeds interest, takes priority provided he gives new value and takes possession of the paper in the ordinary course of his business.

The same basic rule applies in favor of a purchaser of other instruments who claims priority against a proceeds interest therein of which he has knowledge. Thus a purchaser of a negotiable instrument might prevail under clause (b) even though his knowledge of the conflicting proceeds claim precluded his having holder in due course status under Section 9—309.

3. Clause (a) deals with the case where the non-possessory security interest in the chattel paper is more than a mere claim to proceeds—i. e., exists in favor of a secured party who has given value against the paper, whether or not he financed the inventory whose sale gave rise to it. In this case the purchaser, to take priority, must not only give new value and take possession in the ordinary course of his business; he must also take without knowledge of the existing security interest. Thus a secured party,

who has a specific interest in the chattel paper and not merely a claim to proceeds, and who wishes to leave the paper in the debtor's possession can, because of the knowledge requirement, protect himself against purchasers by stamping or noting on the paper the fact that it has been assigned to him.

4. It should be noted that under Section 9—304(1) a security interest in an instrument, negotiable or non-negotiable, cannot be perfected by filing (except where the instrument constitutes part of chattel paper). Thus the only types of perfected non-possessory security interest that can arise in an instrument are the temporary 21 day perfection provided for in Section 9—304(4) and (5) or the 10 day perfection in proceeds of Section 9—306. Where such a perfected interest exists in a non-negotiable instrument, purchasers will take free if they qualify under clause (a) of the section.

Cross References:

Point 1: Sections 9—304(1) and 9—305.

Point 2: Section 9—306.

Point 4: Sections 9—304 and 9—306.

Definitional Cross References:

"Chattel paper". Section 9—105.

"Instrument". Section 9—105.

"Inventory". Section 9—109.

"Knowledge". Section 1—201.

"Proceeds". Section 9—306.

"Purchaser". Section 1—201.

"Security interest". Section 1—201.

"Value". Section 1—201.

§ 9—309. Protection of Purchasers of Instruments, Documents, and Securities

Nothing in this Article limits the rights of a holder in due course of a negotiable instrument (Section 3—302) or a holder to whom a negotiable document of title has been duly negotiated (Section 7—501) or a bona fide purchaser of a security (Section 8—302) and the holders or purchasers take priority over an earlier security interest even though perfected. Filing under this Article does not constitute notice of the security interest to such holders or purchasers.

Amended in 1977.

Official Comment

Prior Uniform Statutory Provision: Section 9(a), Uniform Trust Receipts Act.

Purposes:

1. Under this Article as at common law and under prior statutes the rights of purchasers of negotiable paper, including negotiable documents of title and investment securities, are determined by the rules of holding in due course and the like which are applicable to the type of pa-

per concerned. (Articles 3, 7, and 8.) This section, as did Section 9(a) of the Uniform Trust Receipts Act, makes explicit the rule which was implicitly but universally recognized under the earlier statutes.

2. Under Section 9—304(1) filing is ineffective to perfect a security interest in instruments (including securities) except those instruments which are part of chattel paper, and of course is ineffective to constitute notice to subsequent purchasers. Although filing is permissible as a method of perfection for a security interest in documents, this section follows the policy of the Uniform Trust Receipts Act in providing that the filing does not constitute notice to purchasers.

Cross References:

Articles 3, 7, and 8 and Sections 9—304(1) and 9—308.

Definitional Cross References:

"Bona fide purchaser". Section 8—302.

"Document of title". Section 1—201.

"Duly negotiated". Section 7—501.

"Holder". Section 1—201.

"Holder in due course". Sections 3—302 and 9—105.

"Negotiable instrument". Sections 3—104 and 9—105.

"Notice". Section 1—201.

"Purchaser". Section 1—201.

"Security". Sections 8—102 and 9—105.

"Security interest". Section 1—201.

§ 9—310. Priority of Certain Liens Arising by Operation of Law

When a person in the ordinary course of his business furnishes services or materials with respect to goods subject to a security interest, a lien upon goods in the possession of such person given by statute or rule of law for such materials or services takes priority over a perfected security interest unless the lien is statutory and the statute expressly provides otherwise.

Official Comment

Prior Uniform Statutory Provision: Section 11, Uniform Trust Receipts Act.

Purposes:

1. To provide that liens securing claims arising from work intended to enhance or preserve the value of the collateral take priority over an earlier security interest even though perfected.

2. Apart from the Uniform Trust Receipts Act which had a section similar to this one, there was generally no specific statutory rule as to priority between security devices and liens for services or materials. Under chattel mortgage or conditional sales law many decisions made the priority of such liens turn on whether the secured party did or did not have "title". This section changes such rules and makes the lien for services or materials prior in all cases

where they are furnished in the ordinary course of the lienor's business and the goods involved are in the lienor's possession. Some of the statutes creating such liens expressly make the lien subordinate to a prior security interest. This section does not repeal such statutory provisions. If the statute creating the lien is silent, even though it has been construed by decision to make the lien subordinate to the security interest, this section provides a rule of interpretation that the lien should take priority over the security interest.

Cross References:

Sections 9—102(2), 9—104(c) and 9—312(1).

Definitional Cross References:

"Goods". Section 9—105.

"Person". Section 1—201.

"Security interest". Section 1—201.

§ 9—311. Alienability of Debtor's Rights: Judicial Process

The debtor's rights in collateral may be voluntarily or involuntarily transferred (by way of sale, creation of a security interest, attachment, levy, garnishment or other judicial process) notwithstanding a provision in the security agreement prohibiting any transfer or making the transfer constitute a default.

Official Comment

Prior Uniform Statutory Provision: None.

Purposes:

1. To make clear that in all security transactions under this Article, the debtor has an interest (whether legal title or an equity) which he can dispose of and which his creditors can reach.

2. Some jurisdictions have held that when a mortgagee or conditional seller has "title" to the collateral, creditors may not proceed against the mortgagor's or vendee's interest by levy, attachment or other judicial process. This section changes those rules by providing that in all security interests the debtor's interest in the collateral remains subject to claims of creditors who take appropriate action. It is left to the law of each state to determine the form of "appropriate process".

3. Where the security interest is in inventory, difficult problems arise with reference to attachment and levy. Assume that a debt of $100,000 is secured by inventory worth twice that amount. If by attachment or levy certain units of the inventory are seized, the determination of the debtor's equity in the units seized is not a simple matter. The section leaves the solution of this problem to the courts. Procedures such as marshalling may be appropriate.

Cross References:

Sections 9—301(4), 9—307(3) and 9—312(7).

Definitional Cross References:
"Collateral". Section 9—105.
"Debtor". Section 9—105.
"Rights". Section 1—201.
"Sale". Sections 2—106 and 9—105.
"Security agreement". Section 9—105.
"Security interest". Section 1—201.

§ 9—312. Priorities Among Conflicting Security Interests in the Same Collateral

(1) The rules of priority stated in other sections of this Part and in the following sections shall govern when applicable: Section 4—208 with respect to the security interests of collecting banks in items being collected, accompanying documents and proceeds; Section 9—103 on security interests related to other jurisdictions; Section 9—114 on consignments.

(2) A perfected security interest in crops for new value given to enable the debtor to produce the crops during the production season and given not more than three months before the crops become growing crops by planting or otherwise takes priority over an earlier perfected security interest to the extent that such earlier interest secures obligations due more than six months before the crops become growing crops by planting or otherwise, even though the person giving new value had knowledge of the earlier security interest.

(3) A perfected purchase money security interest in inventory has priority over a conflicting security interest in the same inventory and also has priority in identifiable cash proceeds received on or before the delivery of the inventory to a buyer if

(a) the purchase money security interest is perfected at the time the debtor receives possession of the inventory; and

(b) the purchase money secured party gives notification in writing to the holder of the conflicting security interest if the holder had filed a financing statement covering the same types of inventory (i) before the date of the filing made by the purchase money secured party, or (ii) before the beginning of the 21 day period where the purchase money security interest is temporarily perfected without filing or possession (subsection (5) of Section 9—304); and

(c) the holder of the conflicting security interest receives the notification within five years before the debtor receives possession of the inventory; and

(d) the notification states that the person giving the notice has or expects to acquire a purchase money security interest in inventory of the debtor, describing such inventory by item or type.

(4) A purchase money security interest in collateral other than inventory has priority over a conflicting security interest in the same collateral or its proceeds if the purchase money security interest is perfected at the time the debtor receives possession of the collateral or within ten days thereafter.

(5) In all cases not governed by other rules stated in this section (including cases of purchase money security interests which do not qualify for the special priorities set forth in subsections (3) and (4) of this section), priority between conflicting security interests in the same collateral shall be determined according to the following rules:

(a) Conflicting security interests rank according to priority in time of filing or perfection. Priority dates from the time a filing is first made covering the collateral or the time the security interest is first perfected, whichever is earlier, provided that there is no period thereafter when there is neither filing nor perfection.

(b) So long as conflicting security interests are unperfected, the first to attach has priority.

(6) For the purposes of subsection (5) a date of filing or perfection as to collateral is also a date of filing or perfection as to proceeds.

(7) If future advances are made while a security interest is perfected by filing, the taking of possession, or under Section 8—321 on securities, the security interest has the same priority for the purposes of subsection (5) with respect to the future advances as it does with respect to the first advance. If a commitment is made before or while the security interest is so perfected, the security interest has the same priority with respect to advances made pursuant thereto. In other cases a perfected security interest has priority from the date the advance is made.
Amended in 1972 and 1977.

See Appendix I for changes made in former text and the reasons for change.

Official Comment

Prior Uniform Statutory Provision: None.

Purposes:

1. In a variety of situations two or more people may claim an interest in the same property. The several sections specified in subsection (1) contain rules for determining priorities between security interests and such other claims in the situations covered in those sections. For cases not covered in those sections this section states general rules of priority between conflicting security interests.

2. Subsection (2) gives priority to a new value security interest in crops based on a current crop production loan over an earlier security interest in the crop which secured obligations (such as rent, interest or mortgage principal amortization) due more than six months before the crops become growing crops. This priority is not affected by the fact that the person making the crop loan knew of the earlier security interest.

3. Subsections (3) and (4) give priority to a purchase money security interest (defined in Section 9—107) under certain conditions over non-purchase money interests, which in this context will usually be interests asserted under after-acquired property clauses. See Section 9—204 on the extent to which after-acquired property interests are validated and Section 9—108 on when a security interest in after-acquired property is deemed taken for new value.

Prior law, under one or another theory, usually contrived to protect purchase money interests over after-acquired property interests (to the extent to which the after-acquired property interest was recognized at all). For example, in the field of industrial equipment financing it was possible, by manipulation of title theory, for the purchase money financer of new equipment (under conditional sale or equipment trust) to protect himself against the claims of prior mortgagees or bondholders under an after-acquired clause in the mortgage or trust indenture: the result was arrived at on the theory that since "title" to the equipment was never in the vendee or lessee there was nothing for the lien of the mortgage to attach to. While this Article broadly validates the after-acquired property interest, it also recognizes as sound the preference which prior law gave to the purchase money interest. That policy is carried out in subsections (3) and (4).

Subsection (4) states a general rule applicable to all types of collateral except inventory: the purchase money interest takes priority if it is perfected when the debtor receives possession of the collateral or within ten days thereafter. As to the ten day grace period, compare Section 9—301(2). The perfection requirement means that the purchase money secured party either has filed a financing statement before that time or has a temporarily perfected interest in goods covered by documents under Section 9—304(4) and (5) (which is continued in a perfected status by filing before the expiration of the 21 day period specified in that section). There is no requirement that the purchase money secured party be without notice or knowledge of the other interest; he takes priority although he knows of it or it has been filed.

Under subsection (3) the same rule of priority, but without the ten day grace period for filing, applies to a purchase money security interest in inventory, with the additional requirement that the purchase money secured party give notification, as stated in subsection (3), to any other secured party who filed earlier for the same item or type of inventory. The reason for the additional requirement of notification is that typically the arrangement between an inventory secured party and his debtor will require the secured party to make periodic advances against incoming inventory or periodic releases of old inventory as new inventory is received. A fraudulent debtor may apply to the secured party for advances even though he has already given a security interest in the inventory to another secured party. The notification requirement protects the inventory financer in such a situation: if he has received notification, he will presumably not make an advance; if he has not received notification (or if the other interest does not qualify as a purchase money interest), any advance he may make will have priority. Since an arrangement for periodic advances against incoming property is unusual outside the inventory field, no notification requirement is included in subsection (4).

Where the purchase money inventory financing began by possession of a negotiable document of title by the secured party, he must in order to retain priority give the notice required by subsection (3) at or before the usual time, i. e., when the debtor gets possession of the inventory, even though his security interest remains perfected for 21 days under Section 9—304(5).

When under these rules the purchase money secured party has priority over another secured party, the question arises whether this priority extends to the proceeds of the original collateral. Under subsection (4) which deals with non-inventory collateral and where there was no ordinary expectation that the goods would be sold, the section gives an affirmative answer. In the case of inventory collateral under subsection (3), where it was expected that the goods would be sold and where financing frequently is based on the resulting accounts, chattel paper, or other proceeds, the subsection gives an answer limited to the preservation of the purchase money priority only in so far as the proceeds are cash received on or before the delivery of the inventory to a buyer, that is, without the creation of an intervening account to which conflicting rights might attach. The conflicting rights to proceeds consisting of accounts are governed by subsection (5). See Comment 8.

The foregoing rules applicable to purchase money security interests in inventory apply also to the rights in consigned merchandise. See Section 9—114.

4. Subsection (5) states a rule for determining priority between conflicting security interests in cases not covered in the sections referred to in subsection (1) or in subsections (2), (3) and (4) of this section. Note that subsection (5) applies to cases of purchase money security interests which do not qualify for the special priorities set forth in subsections (3) and (4).

There is a single priority rule based on precedence in the time as of which the competing parties either filed their security interests or perfected their security interests. The form of the claim to priority, i. e., filing or perfection, may shift from time to time, and the rank will be based on the first filing or perfection so long as there is no intervening period without filing or perfection. Filing may occur as to particular collateral before the collateral comes into existence. Under the standards of Section 9—203 perfection cannot occur as to particular collateral until the collateral itself (and not prior collateral) comes into existence and the debtor has rights therein; but under subsection (6) of this section the secured party's priority may date from his time of perfection as to the prior collateral, if perfection or filing has been continuously maintained. Subsection (6) provides that a date of filing or perfection as to original collateral is also a date of filing or perfection as to proceeds. This rule should also be read with Section 9—306, which makes it unnecessary to claim proceeds expressly in a financing statement and provides in effect that a filing as to original collateral is also a filing as to proceeds (with exceptions therein stated). Thus, if a financing statement is filed covering inventory, then (subject to the exception involving multistate problems) this filing is also a filing as to the resulting accounts and constitutes the date of filing as to the accounts.

The party who may have had a prior security interest in inventory or may have had the only such security interest does not automatically for that reason have priority as to the accounts. His claim to accounts may or may not have priority over competing filed claims to accounts. The priority is based on precedence as to the accounts under the rules stated in the preceding paragraph.

5. The operation of this section is illustrated by the examples set forth under this and the succeeding Points.

Example 1. A files against X (debtor) on February 1. B files against X on March 1. B makes a non-purchase money advance against certain collateral on April 1. A makes an advance against the same collateral on

May 1. A has priority even though B's advance was made earlier and was perfected when made. It makes no difference whether or not A knew of B's interest when he made his advance.

The problem stated in the example is peculiar to a notice filing system under which filing may be made before the security interest attaches (see Section 9—402). The Uniform Trust Receipts Act, which first introduced such a filing system, contained no hint of a solution and case law under it was unpredictable. This Article follows several of the accounts receivable statutes in determining priority by order of filing. The justification for the rule lies in the necessity of protecting the filing system—that is, of allowing the secured party who has first filed to make subsequent advances without each time having, as a condition of protection, to check for filings later than his. Note, however, that his protection is not absolute: if, in the example, B's advance creates a purchase money security interest, he has priority under subsection (4), or, in the case of inventory, under subsection (3) provided he has properly notified A. (See further Example 3 below.)

Example 2. A and B make non-purchase money advances against the same collateral. The collateral is in the debtor's possession and neither interest is perfected when the second advance is made. Whichever secured party first perfects his interest (by taking possession of the collateral or by filing) takes priority and it makes no difference whether or not he knows of the other interest at the time he perfects his own.

This result may be regarded as an adoption, in this type of situation, of the idea, deeply rooted at common law, of a race of diligence among creditors. Subsection (5) (b) adds the thought that so long as neither of the interests is perfected, the one which first attached (i. e., under the advance first made) has priority. The last mentioned rule may be thought to be of merely theoretical interest, since it is hard to imagine a situation where the case would come into litigation without either A or B having perfected his interest. If neither interest had been perfected at the time of the filing of a petition in bankruptcy, of course neither would be good against the trustee in bankruptcy.

Example 3. A has a temporarily perfected (21 day) security interest, unfiled, in a negotiable document in the debtor's possession under Section 9—304 (4) or (5). On the fifth day B files and thus perfects a security interest in the same document. On the tenth day A files. A has priority, whether or not he knows of B's interest when he files, because he perfected first and has maintained continuous perfection or filing.

6. The application of the priority rules to after-acquired property must be considered separately for each item of collateral. Priority does not depend

only on time of perfection, but may also be based on priority in filing before perfection.

Example 4. On February 1 A makes advances to X under a security agreement which covers "all the machinery in X's plant" and contains an after-acquired property clause. A promptly files his financing statement. On March 1 X acquires a new machine, B makes an advance against it and files his financing statement. On April 1 A, under the original security agreement, makes an advance against the machine acquired March 1. If B's advance creates a purchase money security interest, he has priority under subsection (4) (provided he filed before X received possession of the machine or within ten days thereafter). If B's advance, although he gave new value, did not create a purchase money interest, A has priority as to both of his advances by virtue of his priority in filing, although the parties perfected simultaneously on March 1 as to the new machine.

The application of the priority rules to proceeds presents special features discussed in Comment 8.

7. The application of the priority rules to future advances is complicated. In general, since any secured party must operate in reference to the Code's system of notice, he takes subject to future advances under a priority security interest while it is perfected through filing or possession, whether the advances are committed or non-committed, and to any advances subsequently made "pursuant to commitment" (Section 9—105) during that period. In the rare case when a future advance is made without commitment while the security interest is perfected temporarily without either filing or possession, the future advance has priority from the date it is made. These rules are more liberal toward the priority of future advances than the corresponding rules applicable to an intervening buyer (Section 9—307(3)) because of the different characteristics of the intervening party. Compare the corresponding rule applicable to an intervening judgment creditor. (Section 9—301(4)).

Example 5. On February 1 A makes an advance against machinery in the debtor's possession and files his financing statement. On March 1 B makes an advance against the same machinery and files his financing statement. On April 1 A makes a further advance, under the original security agreement, against the same machinery (which is covered by the original financing statement and thus perfected when made). A has priority over B both as to the February 1 and as to the April 1 advance and it makes no difference whether or not A knows of B's intervening advance when he makes his second advance.

A wins, as to the April 1 advance, because he first filed even though B's interest attached, and indeed was perfected, before the April 1 advance. The same rule would apply if either A or B had perfected through possession.

Section 9–204(3) and the Comment thereto should be consulted for the validation of future advances.

The same result would be reached even though A's April 1 advance was not under the original security agreement, but was under a new security agreement under A's same financing statement or during the continuation of A's possession.

8. The application of the priority rules of subsections (5) and (6) to proceeds is shown by the following examples:

Example 6. A files a financing statement covering a described type of inventory then owned or thereafter acquired. B subsequently takes a purchase money security interest in certain inventory described in A's financing statement and achieves priority over A under subsection (3) as to this inventory. This inventory is then sold, producing proceeds.

If the proceeds of the inventory are instruments or chattel paper, the rights of A and B on the one hand and any adverse claimant to these proceeds on the other are governed by Sections 9—308 and 9—309. If the proceeds are cash, subsection (3) indicates that B's priority as to the inventory carries over to the cash. Proceeds which are accounts constitute different collateral and the priorities as to the original collateral do not control the priority as to the accounts. Under Sections 9—306 and 9—312(6), A's first filing as to the inventory constitutes a first filing as to the accounts, provided that the same filing office would be appropriate for filing as to accounts under the rules of Section 9—306(3). Therefore, A has priority as to the accounts.

Many parties financing inventory are quite content to protect their first security interest in the inventory itself, realizing that when inventory is sold, someone else will be financing the accounts and the priority for inventory will not run forward to the accounts. Indeed, the cash supplied by the accounts financer will be used to pay the inventory financing. In some situations, the party financing the inventory on a purchase money basis makes contractual arrangements that the proceeds of accounts financing by another be devoted to paying off the first inventory security interest.

Example 7. In the foregoing case, if B had filed directly as to accounts, the date of that filing as to accounts would be compared with the date of A's first filing as to the inventory, and the first-to-file rule would prevail.

Subsection (6) provides that a filing as to original collateral determines the date of a filing as to the proceeds thereof. This rule implies, of course, that the filing as to the original collateral is effective as to proceeds under the rule of Section 9—306(3).

Example 8. If C had filed as to accounts in Example 6 above before either A or B had filed as to inventory, C's first filing as to accounts would have priority over the filings of A and B, which would also constitute filings as to accounts under the rule just mentioned. A's and B's position as to the inventory gives them no automatic claim to the proceeds of the inventory consisting of accounts against someone who has filed earlier as to accounts. If, on the other hand, either A's or B's filings as to the inventory constituted good filings as to accounts and these filings preceded C's direct filings as to accounts, A or B would outrank C as to the accounts.

If the filings as to inventory were not effective under subsection (6) for filing as to accounts because a filing for accounts would have to be in a different filing office under Section 9—103 (3), these inventory filings would nevertheless be effective for 10 days as to accounts. If the perfection of the security interest in accounts was continued within the 10 days by appropriate filings, then A and B's interests in the accounts would date from the date of filing as to inventory.

Cross References:

Sections 9—204(1) and 9—303.

Point 1: Sections 4—208, 9—114, 9—301, 9—304, 9—306, 9—307, 9—308, 9—309, 9—310, 9—313, 9—314, 9—315 and 9—316.

Point 3: Sections 9—108, 9—204, 9—304(4) and (5).

Points 4 to 7: Sections 9—204, 9—301(4), 9—304(4) and (5), 9—306, 9—307(3) and 9—402(1).

Point 8: Sections 9—103(6) and 9—306(3).

Definitional Cross References:

"Chattel paper". Section 9—105.

"Collateral". Section 9—105.

"Collecting bank". Section 4—105.

"Debtor". Section 9—105.

"Documents". Section 9—105.

"Give notice". Section 1—201.

"Goods". Section 9—105.

"Instruments". Section 9—105.

"Inventory". Section 9—109.

"Knowledge". Section 1—201.

"Person". Section 1—201.

"Proceeds". Section 9—306.

"Purchase money security interest". Section 9—107.

"Pursuant to commitment". Section 9—105.

"Receives" notification. Section 1—201.

"Secured party". Section 9—105.

"Security". Sections 8—102 and 9—105.

"Security interest". Section 1—201.

"Value". Section 1—201.

§ 9—313. Priority of Security Interests in Fixtures

(1) In this section and in the provisions of Part 4 of this Article referring to fixture filing, unless the context otherwise requires

(a) goods are "fixtures" when they become so related to particular real estate that an interest in them arises under real estate law

(b) a "fixture filing" is the filing in the office where a mortgage on the real estate would be filed or recorded of a financing statement covering goods which are or are to become fixtures and conforming to the requirements of subsection (5) of Section 9—402

(c) a mortgage is a "construction mortgage" to the extent that it secures an obligation incurred for the construction of an improvement on land including the acquisition cost of the land, if the recorded writing so indicates.

(2) A security interest under this Article may be created in goods which are fixtures or may continue in goods which become fixtures, but no security interest exists under this Article in ordinary building materials incorporated into an improvement on land.

(3) This Article does not prevent creation of an encumbrance upon fixtures pursuant to real estate law.

(4) A perfected security interest in fixtures has priority over the conflicting interest of an encumbrancer or owner of the real estate where

(a) the security interest is a purchase money security interest, the interest of the encumbrancer or owner arises before the goods become fixtures, the security interest is perfected by a fixture filing before the goods become fixtures or within ten days thereafter, and the debtor has an interest of record in the real estate or is in possession of the real estate; or

(b) the security interest is perfected by a fixture filing before the interest of the encumbrancer or owner is of record, the security interest has priority over any conflicting interest of a predecessor in title of the encumbrancer or owner, and the debtor has an interest of record in the real estate or is in possession of the real estate; or

(c) the fixtures are readily removable factory or office machines or readily removable replacements of domestic appliances which are consumer goods, and before the goods become fixtures the security interest is perfected by any method permitted by this Article; or

(d) the conflicting interest is a lien on the real estate obtained by legal or equitable proceedings after the security interest was perfected by any method permitted by this Article.

(5) A security interest in fixtures, whether or not perfected, has priority over the conflicting interest of an encumbrancer or owner of the real estate where

(a) the encumbrancer or owner has consented in writing to the security interest or has disclaimed an interest in the goods as fixtures; or

(b) the debtor has a right to remove the goods as against the encumbrancer or owner. If the debtor's right terminates, the priority of the security interest continues for a reasonable time.

(6) Notwithstanding paragraph (a) of subsection (4) but otherwise subject to subsections (4) and (5), a security interest in fixtures is subordinate to a construction mortgage recorded before the goods become fixtures if the goods become fixtures before the completion of the construction. To the extent that it is given to refinance a construction mortgage, a mortgage has this priority to the same extent as the construction mortgage.

(7) In cases not within the preceding subsections, a security interest in fixtures is subordinate to the conflicting interest of an encumbrancer or owner of the related real estate who is not the debtor.

(8) When the secured party has priority over all owners and encumbrancers of the real estate, he may, on default, subject to the provisions of Part 5, remove his collateral from the real estate but he must reimburse any encumbrancer or owner of the real estate who is not the debtor and who has not otherwise agreed for the cost of repair of any physical injury, but not for any diminution in value of the real estate caused by the absence of the goods removed or by any necessity of replacing them. A person entitled to reimbursement may refuse permission to remove until the secured party gives adequate security for the performance of this obligation. Amended in 1972.

See Appendix I for changes made in former text and the reasons for change.

Official Comment

Prior Uniform Statutory Provision: Section 7, Uniform Conditional Sales Act.

Purposes:

1. Section 9—313 deals with the problem that certain goods which are the subject of chattel financing become so affixed or otherwise so related to real estate that they become part of the real estate, and that chattel interests would be subordinate to real estate interests except as protected by the priorities regulated by the section. These goods are called "fixtures". Some fixtures also retain their chattel nature in that a chattel financing with respect to them may exist and may continue to be recognized, if notice thereof is given to real estate interests in accordance with this section. But this concept does not apply if the goods are integrally incorporated into the real estate.

The term "fixture filing" has been introduced and defined. It emphasizes that when a filing is intended to give the priority advantages herein discussed against real estate interests, the filing must (except as stated below) be for record in the real estate records and indexed therein, so that it will be found in a real estate search.

Since the determination in advance of judicial decision of the question whether goods have become fixtures is a difficult one, no inference may be drawn from a fixture filing that the secured party concedes that the goods are or will become fixtures. The fixture filing may be merely precautionary.

2. "Fixture" is defined to include any goods which become so related to particular real estate that an interest in them arises under real estate law and therefore, goods integrally incorporated into the real estate are clearly fixtures. But under subsection (2) no security interest exists under Article 9 in ordinary building materials incorporated into an improvement on land.

Goods may be technically "ordinary building materials," e. g., window glass, but if they are incorporated into a structure which as a whole has not become an integral part of the real estate, the rules applicable to the ordinary building materials follow the rules applicable to the structure itself. The outstanding examples presenting this kind of problem are the modern "mobile homes" and the modern prefabricated steel buildings usable as warehouses, garages, factories, etc. In the case of the mobile homes, most of them are erected on leased land and the right of the debtor under a mobile home purchase contract to remove the goods as lessee will make clear that his secured party ordinarily has a similar right. See paragraph (5) (b).

In cases where mobile homes or prefabricated steel buildings are erected by a person having an ownership interest in the land, the question into which category the buildings fall is one determined by local law. In general, the governing local law will not be that applicable in determining whether goods have become real property between landlord and tenant, or between mortgagor and mortgagee, or between grantor and grantee, but rather that applicable in a three-party situation, determining whether chattel financing can survive as against parties who acquire rights through the affixation of the goods to the real estate.

The assertion that no security interest exists in ordinary building materials is only for the operation of the priority provisions of this section. It is without prejudice to any rights which the secured party may have against the debtor himself if he incorporated the goods into real estate or against any party guilty of wrongful incorporation thereof in violation of the secured party's rights.

3. Under these concepts the section recognizes three categories of goods: (1) those which retain their chattel character entirely and are not part of the real estate; (2) ordinary building materials which have become an integral part of the real estate and cannot retain their chattel character for purposes of finance; and (3) an intermediate class which has become real estate for certain purposes, but as to which chattel financing may be preserved. This third and intermediate class is the primary subject of this section. The demarcation between these classifications is not delineated by this section.

4. In considering fixture priority problems, there will always first be a preliminary question whether real estate interests per se have an interest in the goods as part of real estate. If not, it is immaterial, so far as concerns real estate parties as such, whether a chattel security interest is perfected or unperfected. In no event does a real estate party acquire an interest in a "pure" chattel just because a security interest therein is unperfected. If on the other hand real estate law gives real estate parties an interest in the goods, a conflict arises and this section states the priorities.

(a) The principal exception to the general rule of priority stated in Comment 4(b) based on time of filing or recording is a priority given in paragraph (4)(a) to purchase money security interests in fixtures as against *prior* recorded real estate interests, provided that the purchase money security interest is filed as a fixture filing in the real estate records before the goods become fixtures or within 10 days thereafter. This priority corresponds to one given in Section 9—312(4), and the 10 days of grace represents a reduction of the purchase money priority as against prior interests in the real estate under the present Section 9—313, where the purchase money priority exists even though the security interest is *never* filed.

It should be emphasized that this purchase money priority with the 10-day grace period for filing is limited to rights against *prior* real estate interests. There is no such priority with the 10-day grace period as against subsequent real estate interests. The fixture security interest can defeat subsequent real estate interests only if it is filed first and prevails under the usual conveyancing rule recognized in paragraph (4) (b).

(b) The general principle of priority announced in this section is set forth in paragraph (4) (b). It is basically that a fixture filing gives to the fixture security interest priority as against other real estate interests according to the usual priority rule of conveyancing, that is, the first to file or record prevails. An apparent limitation to this principle set forth in paragraph (4) (b), namely that the secured party must have had priority over any interest of a predecessor in title of the conflicting encumbrancer or owner, is not really a limitation, but is an expression of the usual rule that a person must be entitled to transfer what he has. Thus, if the fixture security interest is subordinate to a mortgage, it is subordinate to an interest of an assignee of the mortgage even though the assignment is a later recorded instrument. Similarly if the fixture security interest is subordinate to the rights of an owner, it is subordinate to a subsequent grantee of the owner and likewise subordinate to a subsequent mortgagee of the owner.

(c) A qualification to the rule based on priority of filing or recording is paragraph (4) (d), where priority based on precedence in filing or recording is preserved, but there is no requirement that as against a judgment lienor of the real estate, the prior filing of the fixture security interest must be in the real estate records. The fixture security interest if perfected first should prevail even though not filed or recorded in real estate records, because generally a judgment creditor is not a reliance creditor who would have searched records. Thus, even a prior filing in the chattel records protects the priority of a fixture security interest against a subsequent judgment lien.

It is hoped that this rule will have the effect of preserving a fixture security interest so filed against invalidation by a trustee in bankruptcy. That would, of course, be the result under Section 60a of the Bankruptcy Act if the time of perfection of the fixture security interest were measured by the judgment creditor test applicable to personal property. It would not be the result if the time of perfection were measured by the purchaser test applicable to real estate. Since the fixture security interest arises against the goods in their capacity as chattels, the bankruptcy courts should apply the judgment creditor test. The effectiveness of the drafting to achieve its purpose cannot be known certainly until the courts adjudicate the question or until it is settled by amendment to Section 60a of the Bankruptcy Act.

The phrase "lien by legal or equitable proceedings" is suggested by Section 70c of the Bankruptcy Act, and is intended to encompass all liens on real estate obtained by any of the creditor action therein described.

(d) A special exception to the usual rule of priority based on precedence in time is the one of paragraph (4) (c) in favor of holders of security interests in factory and office machines, and in certain replacement domestic appliances, as discussed below. This is not as broad an exception as it might seem. To repeat, a fixture conflict is not reached if the goods are held as a matter of local law not to have become part of the real estate, which will frequently be the holding for goods of these types. If the opposite is held, the rule of paragraph (4) (c) operates only if the fixture security interest is perfected before the goods become fixtures. Having been perfected, it would of course have priority over subsequent real estate interests under the rule of paragraph (4) (b). Since it would in almost all cases be a purchase money security interest, it would also have priority over other real estate interests under the purchase-money priority of paragraph (4) (a), discussed in paragraph (a) above. The rule is stated separately because the permitted perfection is by any method permitted by the Article, and not exclusively by fixture filing in the real estate records. This rule is made necessary by the confusions of the law as to whether certain machinery and appliances become fixtures.

As an additional point, in the case of machinery, the separate statement of this rule makes clear that it is not overridden by the construction mortgage priority of subsection (6) discussed in Comment 4(e) below, as would have been true if reliance had been solely on the purchase money priority. Factory and office machines are not always financed as part of a construction mortgage, and the mortgagee should be alert to conflicting chattel financing of these machines.

As to appliances, the rule stated is limited to readily removable replacements, not original installations, of appliances which are consumer goods in the hands of the debtor (Section 9—109). To facilitate financing of original appliances in new dwellings as part of the real estate financing of the dwellings, no special priority is given to chattel financing of original appliances. The section leaves to other law of the state the question whether original installations are fixtures to which the protection accorded by this section to construction mortgages would be applicable. Likewise, it is recognized that (when not supplied by tenants) appliances in commercial apartment buildings are intended as permanent improvements, and no special rule is stated for appliances in that case. The special priority rule here stated in favor of chattel financing is limited to situations where the installation of appliances may not be intended to be permanent, i. e., replacement appliances used by the debtor or his family (consumer goods). The principal effect of the rule is to make clear that a secured party financing occasional replacements of domestic appliances in noncommercial owner-occupied contexts need not concern himself with real estate descriptions or records; indeed, for a purchase-money replacement of consumer goods, perfection without any filing will be possible. (The priority of the construction mortgage has no application to replacement appliances.)

(e) The purchase money priority presents a difficult problem in relation to construction mortgages. The latter will ordinarily have been recorded even before the commencement of delivery of materials to the job, and therefore would be prior in rank to the fixture security interests were it not for the problem of the purchase money priority. Subsection (6) expressly gives priority to the construction mortgage recorded before the filing of the fixture security interest, but this priority of a construction mortgage applies only during the construction period leading to the completion of the improvement. As to additions to the building made long after completion of the improvement, the construction priority will not apply simply because the additions are financed by the real estate mortgagee under an open end clause of his construction mortgage. In such case, the applicable principles will be those of paragraphs (4) (a) and (4) (b). A refinancing of a construction mortgage has the same priority as the mortgage itself.

The phrase "an obligation incurred for the construction of an improvement" covers both optional advances and advances pursuant to commitment, and both types of advances have the same priority under the section.

5. The section makes it impossible for a fixture supplier to retain a security interest against a contractor, to the possible surprise and deception of real estate interests, unless the debtor has an interest of record in the real estate. See paragraphs (4) (a) and (b).

On the other hand, these paragraphs do recognize that fixture filing may be necessary when the debtor is in possession of the real estate (e. g., a lessee) even without an interest of record. This possibility of a filing against a debtor who is not in the real estate chain of title makes it necessary to require the furnishing of the name of a record owner in such cases. See Sections 9—402(3), item 3; 9—402(5); 9—403(7).

6. The status of fixtures installed by tenants (as well as such persons as licensees and holders of easements) is defined by paragraph (5) (b) to the effect that if the debtor (tenant or other interest mentioned) has the right to remove the fixture as against a real estate interest, the secured party has priority over that real estate interest.

7. Real estate lenders and title companies will have little difficulty in locating relevant fixture security interests applicable to particular parcels of real estate because of the provisions as to real estate descrip-

tion in fixture filings, the indexing thereof, and other related provisions in Part 4 of Article 9.

8. Real estate lending is typically long-term, and is usually done by institutional investors who can afford to take a long view of the matter rather than concentrating on the results of any particular case. It is apparent that the rule which permits and encourages purchase money fixture financing, which in contrast is typically short-term, will result in the modernization and improvement of real estate rather than in its deterioration and will on balance benefit long-term real estate lenders. Because of the short-term character of the chattel financing, it will rarely produce any conflict in fact with the real estate lender. The contrary rule would chill the availability of short-term credit for modernization of real estate by installation of new fixtures and in the long run could not help real estate lenders.

9. Subsection (8) is an important departure from Section 7 of the Uniform Conditional Sales Act and from much other conditional sales legislation. Under the Uniform Conditional Sales Act a conditional vendor could not sever and remove the affixed chattel if a "material injury to the freehold" would result. The courts of various jurisdictions were in sharp disagreement on the meaning of "material injury"; some held that only physical injury was meant; others adopted the so-called "institutional theory" and denied removal whenever the "going value" of the structure would be materially diminished by the removal. Under these rules the conditional vendor either could not remove at all, or, if he could, could damage the structure on removal without becoming accountable to the real estate claimant. The situation was complicated by the fact that it became increasingly difficult to predict what types of goods the courts in a given jurisdiction would hold not subject to removal.

Subsection (8) abandons the "material injury to the freehold" rule. Instead a secured party entitled to priority may in all cases sever and remove his collateral, subject, however, to a duty to reimburse any real estate claimant (other than the debtor himself) for any physical injury caused by the removal. The right to reimbursement is implemented by the last sentence of subsection (8) which gives the real estate claimant a statutory right to security or indemnity failing which he may refuse permission to remove. The subsection (8) rule thus accomplishes two things: it puts an end to the uncertainty which has grown up under the "material injury" rule, while at the same time it protects the real estate claimant under the reimbursement provisions.

Cross References:

Sections 2—107, 9—102(1), 9—104(j) and 9—312(1), and Parts 4 and 5.

Definitional Cross References:

"Collateral". Section 9—105.
"Contract". Section 1—201.
"Creditor". Section 1—201.
"Debtor". Section 9—105.
"Encumbrance". Section 9—105.
"Goods". Section 9—105.
"Knowledge". Section 1—201.
"Mortgage". Section 9—105.
"Person". Section 1—201.
"Purchase". Section 1—201.
"Purchaser". Section 1—201.
"Secured party". Section 9—105.
"Security interest". Section 1—201.
"Value". Section 1—201.
"Writing". Section 1—201.

§ 9—314. Accessions

(1) A security interest in goods which attaches before they are installed in or affixed to other goods takes priority as to the goods installed or affixed (called in this section "accessions") over the claims of all persons to the whole except as stated in subsection (3) and subject to Section 9—315(1).

(2) A security interest which attaches to goods after they become part of a whole is valid against all persons subsequently acquiring interests in the whole except as stated in subsection (3) but is invalid against any person with an interest in the whole at the time the security interest attaches to the goods who has not in writing consented to the security interest or disclaimed an interest in the goods as part of the whole.

(3) The security interests described in subsections (1) and (2) do not take priority over

(a) a subsequent purchaser for value of any interest in the whole; or

(b) a creditor with a lien on the whole subsequently obtained by judicial proceedings; or

(c) a creditor with a prior perfected security interest in the whole to the extent that he makes subsequent advances

if the subsequent purchase is made, the lien by judicial proceedings obtained or the subsequent advance under the prior perfected security interest is made or contracted for without knowledge of the security interest and before it is perfected. A purchaser of the whole at a foreclosure sale other than the holder of a perfected security interest purchasing at his own foreclosure sale is a subsequent purchaser within this section.

(4) When under subsections (1) or (2) and (3) a secured party has an interest in accessions which has priority over the claims of all persons who have interests in the whole, he may

on default subject to the provisions of Part 5 remove his collateral from the whole but he must reimburse any encumbrancer or owner of the whole who is not the debtor and who has not otherwise agreed for the cost of repair of any physical injury but not for any diminution in value of the whole caused by the absence of the goods removed or by any necessity for replacing them. A person entitled to reimbursement may refuse permission to remove until the secured party gives adequate security for the performance of this obligation.

Official Comment

Prior Uniform Statutory Provision: None.

Purposes:

1. To state when a secured party claiming an interest in goods installed in or affixed to other goods is entitled to priority over a party with a security interest in the whole.

2. This section changes prior law in that the secured party claiming an interest in a part (e. g., a new motor in an old car) is entitled to priority and has a right to remove even though under other rules of law the part now belongs to the whole.

3. This section does not apply to goods which, for example, are so commingled in a manufacturing process that their original identity is lost. That type of situation is covered in Section 9—315. Section 9—315 should also be consulted for the effect of a financing statement which claims both component parts and the resulting product.

Cross References:

Sections 9—203(1), 9—303 and 9—312(1) and Part 5.
Point 3: Section 9—315.

Definitional Cross References:

"Collateral". Section 9—105.
"Creditor". Section 1—201.
"Debtor". Section 9—105.
"Goods". Section 9—105.
"Knowledge". Section 1—201.
"Person". Section 1—201.
"Purchaser". Section 1—201.
"Secured party". Section 9—105.
"Security interest". Section 1—201.
"Value". Section 1—201.
"Writing". Section 1—201.

§ 9—315. Priority When Goods Are Commingled or Processed

(1) If a security interest in goods was perfected and subsequently the goods or a part thereof have become part of a product or mass, the security interest continues in the product or mass if

(a) the goods are so manufactured, processed, assembled or commingled that their identity is lost in the product or mass; or

(b) a financing statement covering the original goods also covers the product into which the goods have been manufactured, processed or assembled.

In a case to which paragraph (b) applies, no separate security interest in that part of the original goods which has been manufactured, processed or assembled into the product may be claimed under Section 9—314.

(2) When under subsection (1) more than one security interest attaches to the product or mass, they rank equally according to the ratio that the cost of the goods to which each interest originally attached bears to the cost of the total product or mass.

Official Comment

Prior Uniform Statutory Provision: None.

Purposes:

1. To state when a secured party whose collateral contributes to a product has priority over others who have conflicting claims in the same product.

2. This section changes the law in some jurisdictions where a security interest in goods (e. g., raw materials) was lost when the goods lost their identity by being commingled or processed. Under this section the security interest continues in the resulting mass or product in the cases stated in subsection (1).

3. This section applies not only to cases where flour, sugar and eggs are commingled into cake mix or cake, but also to cases where components are assembled into a machine. In the latter case a secured party is put to an election at the time of filing, by the last sentence of subsection (1), whether to claim under this section or to claim a security interest in one component under Section 9—314.

4. Subsection (2) is new and is needed because under subsection (1) it is possible to have more than one secured party claiming an interest in a product. The rule stated treats all such interests as being of equal priority entitled to share ratably in the product.

Cross References:

Sections 9—203(1), 9—303, 9—312(1) and 9—314.

Definitional Cross References:

"Goods". Section 9—105.

"Security interest". Section 1—201.

§ 9—316. Priority Subject to Subordination

Nothing in this Article prevents subordination by agreement by any person entitled to priority.

Official Comment

Prior Uniform Statutory Provision: None.

Purposes:

The several preceding sections deal elaborately with questions of priority. This section is inserted to make it entirely clear that a person entitled to priority may effectively agree to subordinate his claim. Only the person entitled to priority may make such an agreement: his rights cannot be adversely affected by an agreement to which he is not a party.

Cross References:

Sections 1—102 and 9—312 (1).

Definitional Cross References:

"Agreement". Section 1—201.
"Person". Section 1—201.

§ 9—317. Secured Party Not Obligated on Contract of Debtor

The mere existence of a security interest or authority given to the debtor to dispose of or use collateral does not impose contract or tort liability upon the secured party for the debtor's acts or omissions.

Official Comment

Prior Uniform Statutory Provision: Section 12, Uniform Trust Receipts Act.

Purposes:

There were a few common law decisions, mostly in cases involving trust receipts, which suggested, if they did not hold, that a secured party who gave his debtor liberty of sale might be liable (for example, for breach of warranty) on the debtor's contracts of sale. The theory was grounded on the law of agency; the debtor being regarded as selling agent for the secured party as principal. This section rejects that theory. Section 12 of the Uniform Trust Receipts Act provided that the entruster was not subject to liability, merely because of his status as entruster, on sale of the goods subject to trust receipt. This section adopts the policy of the prior act and states it in general terms.

Cross Reference:

Section 2—210(4).

Definitional Cross References:

"Collateral". Section 9—105.
"Contract". Section 1—201.
"Debtor". Section 9—105.
"Secured party". Section 9—105.
"Security interest". Section 1—201.

§ 9—318. Defenses Against Assignee; Modification of Contract After Notification of Assignment; Term Prohibiting Assignment Ineffective; Identification and Proof of Assignment

Ertel- p. 989

(1) Unless an account debtor has made an enforceable agreement not to assert defenses or claims arising out of a sale as provided in Section 9—206 the rights of an assignee are subject to

(a) all the terms of the contract between the account debtor and assignor and any defense or claim arising therefrom; and

(b) any other defense or claim of the account debtor against the assignor which accrues before the account debtor receives notification of the assignment.

(2) So far as the right to payment or a part thereof under an assigned contract has not been fully earned by performance, and notwithstanding notification of the assignment, any modification of or substitution for the contract made in good faith and in accordance with reasonable commercial standards is effective against an assignee unless the account debtor has otherwise agreed but the assignee acquires corresponding rights under the modified or substituted contract. The assignment may provide that such modification or substitution is a breach by the assignor.

(3) The account debtor is authorized to pay the assignor until the account debtor receives notification that the amount due or to become due has been assigned and that payment is to be made to the assignee. A notification which does not reasonably identify the rights assigned is ineffective. If requested by the account debtor, the assignee must seasonably furnish reasonable proof that the assignment has been made and unless he does so the account debtor may pay the assignor.

(4) A term in any contract between an account debtor and an assignor is ineffective if it prohibits assignment of an account or prohibits creation of a security interest in a general intangible for money due or to become due or requires the account debtor's consent to such assignment or security interest. Amended in 1972.

See Appendix I for changes made in former text and the reasons for change.

Official Comment

Prior Uniform Statutory Provision: Section 9(3), Uniform Trust Receipts Act.

Purposes:

1. Subsection (1) makes no substantial change in prior law. An assignee has traditionally been subject to defenses or set-offs existing before an account debtor is notified of the assignment. When the account debtor's defenses on an assigned claim arise from the contract between him and the assignor, it makes no difference whether the breach giving rise to the defense occurs before or after the account debtor is notified of the assignment (paragraph (1) (a)). The account debtor may also have claims against the assignor which arise independently of that contract: an assignee is subject to all such claims which accrue before, and free of all those which accrue after, the account debtor is notified (paragraph (1) (b)). The account debtor may waive his right to assert claims or defenses against an assignee to the extent provided in Section 9—206.

2. Prior law was in confusion as to whether modification of an executory contract by account debtor and assignor without the assignee's consent was possible after notification of an assignment. Subsection (2) makes good faith modifications by assignor and account debtor without the assignee's consent effective against the assignee even after notification. This rule may do some violence to accepted doctrines of contract law. Nevertheless it is a sound and indeed a necessary rule in view of the realities of large scale procurement. When for example it becomes necessary for a government agency to cut back or modify existing contracts, comparable arrangements must be made promptly in hundreds and even thousands of subcontracts lying in many tiers below the prime contract. Typically the right to payments under these subcontracts will have been assigned. The government, as sovereign, might have the right to amend or terminate existing contracts apart from statute. This subsection gives the prime contractor (the account debtor) the right to make the required arrangements directly with his subcontractors without undertaking the task of procuring assents from the many banks to whom rights under the contracts may have been assigned. Assignees are protected by the provision which gives them automatically corresponding rights under the modified or substituted contract. Notice that subsection (2) applies only so far as the right to payment has not been earned by performance, and therefore its application ends entirely when the work is done or the goods furnished.

3. Subsection (3) clarifies the right of an account debtor to make payment to his seller-assignor in an "indirect collection" situation (see Comment to Section 9—308). So long as the assignee permits the assignor to collect claims or leaves him in

possession of chattel paper which does not indicate that payment is to be made at some place other than the assignor's place of business, the account debtor may pay the assignor even though he may know of the assignment. In such a situation an assignee who wants to take over collections must notify the account debtor to make further payments to him.

4. Subsection (4) breaks sharply with the older contract doctrines by denying effectiveness to contractual terms prohibiting assignment of sums due and to become due under contracts of sale, construction contracts and the like. Under the rule as stated, an assignment would be effective even if made to an assignee who took with full knowledge that the account debtor had sought to prohibit or restrict assignment of the claims.

It is only for the past hundred years that our law has recognized the possibility of assigning choses in action. The history of this development, at law and equity, is in broad outline well known. Lingering traces of the absolute common law prohibition have survived almost to our own day.

There can be no doubt that a term prohibiting assignment of proceeds was effective against an assignee with notice through the nineteenth century and well into the twentieth. Section 151 of the Restatement of Contracts (1932) so states the law without qualification, but the changing character of the law is shown in the proposed Section 154 of the Restatement, Second, Contracts.

The original rule of law has been progressively undermined by a process of erosion which began much earlier than the cited section of the Restatement of Contracts would suggest. The cases are legion in which courts have construed the heart out of prohibitory or restrictive terms and held the assignment good. The cases are not lacking where courts have flatly held assignments valid without bothering to construe away the prohibition. See 4 Corbin on Contracts (1951) §§ 872, 873. Such cases as Allhusen v. Caristo Const. Corp., 303 N.Y. 446, 103 N.E.2d 891 (1952), are rejected by this subsection.

This gradual and largely unacknowledged shift in legal doctrine has taken place in response to economic need: as accounts and other rights under contracts have become the collateral which secures an ever increasing number of financing transactions, it has been necessary to reshape the law so that these intangibles, like negotiable instruments and negotiable documents of title, can be freely assigned.

Subsection (4) thus states a rule of law which is widely recognized in the cases and which corresponds to current business practices. It can be regarded as a revolutionary departure only by those who still cherish the hope that we may yet return to the views entertained some two hundred years ago by the Court of King's Bench.

5. The Federal Assignment of Claims Act of 1940—to which

of course this section is subject—requires that assignments of claims against the United States be filed as provided in that Act. Many large business enterprises, situated like the United States in that claims against them are held by hundreds or thousands of subcontractors or suppliers, often require in their contract or purchase order forms that assignments against them be filed in a prescribed way. Subsection (3) requires reasonable identification of the account assigned and recognizes the right of an account debtor to require reasonable proof of the making of the assignment and to that extent validates such requirements in contracts or purchase order forms. If the notification does not contain such reasonable identification or if such reasonable proof is not furnished on request, the account debtor may disregard the assignment and make payment to the assignor. What is "reasonable" is not left to the arbitrary decision of the account debtor; if there is doubt as to the adequacy either of a notification or of proof submitted after request, the account debtor may not be safe in disregarding it unless he has notified the assignee with commercial promptness as to the respects in which identification or proof is considered defective.

6. If the thing to be assigned is the beneficiary's right under a letter of credit, Section 5—116 should be consulted.

Cross References:

Point 1: Section 9—206.

Point 3: Sections 9—205 and 9—308.

Point 4: Section 2—210(2) and (3).

Point 6: Section 5—116.

Definitional Cross References:

"Account". Section 9—106.

"Account debtor". Section 9—105.

"Agreement". Section 1—201.

"Contract". Section 1—201.

"Good faith". Section 1—201.

"Party". Section 1—201.

"Receives" notification. Section 1—201.

"Rights". Section 1—201.

"Sale". Sections 2—106 and 9—105.

"Seasonably". Section 1—204.

"Term". Section 1—201.

PART 4

FILING

§ 9—401. Place of Filing; Erroneous Filing; Removal of Collateral

First Alternative Subsection (1)

(1) The proper place to file in order to perfect a security interest is as follows:

(a) when the collateral is timber to be cut or is minerals or the like (including oil and gas) or accounts subject to subsection (5) of Section 9—103, or when the financing statement is filed as a fixture filing (Section 9—313) and the collateral is goods which are or are to become fixtures, then in the office where a mortgage on the real estate would be filed or recorded;

(b) in all other cases, in the office of the [Secretary of State].

Second Alternative Subsection (1)

(1) The proper place to file in order to perfect a security interest is as follows:

(a) when the collateral is equipment used in farming operations, or farm products, or accounts or general intangibles arising from or relating to the sale of farm products by a farmer, or consumer goods, then in the office of the .... in the county of the debtor's residence or if the debtor is not a resident of this state then in the office of the .... in the county where the goods are kept, and in addition when the collateral is crops growing or to be grown in the office of the .... in the county where the land is located;

(b) when the collateral is timber to be cut or is minerals or the like (including oil and gas) or accounts subject to subsection (5) of Section 9—103, or when the financing statement is filed as a fixture filing (Section 9—313) and the collateral is goods which are or are to become fixtures, then in the office where a mortgage on the real estate would be filed or recorded;

(c) in all other cases, in the office of the [Secretary of State].

Third Alternative Subsection (1) = Ohio

(1) The proper place to file in order to perfect a security interest is as follows:

(a) when the collateral is equipment used in farming operations, or farm products, or accounts or general intangibles arising from or relating to the sale of farm products by a farmer, or consumer goods, then in the office of the ...... in the county of the debtor's residence or if the debtor is not a resident of this state then in the office of the .... in the county where the goods are kept, and in addition when the collateral is crops growing or to be grown in the office of the ...... in the county where the land is located;

(b) when the collateral is timber to be cut or is minerals or the like (including oil and gas) or accounts subject to subsection (5) of Section 9—103, or when the financing statement is filed as a fixture filing (Section 9—313) and the collateral is goods which are or are to become fixtures, then in the office where a mortgage on the real estate would be filed or recorded;

(c) in all other cases, in the office of the [Secretary of State] and in addition, if the debtor has a place of business in only one county of this state, also in the office of ...... of such county, or, if the debtor has no place of business in this state, but resides in the state, also in the office of ...... of the county in which he resides.

Note: *One of the three alternatives should be selected as subsection (1).*

(2) A filing which is made in good faith in an improper place or not in all of the places required by this section is nevertheless effective with regard to any collateral as to which the filing complied with the requirements of this Article and is also effective with regard to collateral covered by the financing statement against any person who has knowledge of the contents of such financing statement.

(3) A filing which is made in the proper place in this state continues effective even though the debtor's residence or place of business or the location of the collateral or its use, whichever controlled the original filing, is thereafter changed.

Alternative Subsection (3)

[(3) A filing which is made in the proper county continues effective for four months after a change to another county of the debtor's residence or place of business or the location of the collateral, whichever controlled the original filing. It becomes ineffective thereafter unless a copy of the financing statement signed by the secured party is filed in the new county within said period. The security interest may also be perfected in the new county after the expiration of the four-month period; in such case perfection dates from the time of perfection in the new county. A change in the use of the collateral does not impair the effectiveness of the original filing.]

(4) The rules stated in Section 9—103 determine whether filing is necessary in this state.

(5) Notwithstanding the preceding subsections, and subject to subsection (3) of Section 9—302, the proper place to file in order to perfect a security interest in collateral, including fixtures, of a transmitting utility is the office of the [Secretary of State]. This filing constitutes a fixture filing (Section 9—313) as to the collateral described therein which is or is to become fixtures.

(6) For the purposes of this section, the residence of an organization is its place of business if it has one or its chief executive office if it has more than one place of business. Amended in 1962 and 1972.

See Appendix I for changes made in former text and the reasons for change.

Note: *Subsection (6) should be used only if the state chooses the Second or Third Alternative Subsection (1).*

Official Comment

Prior Uniform Statutory Provision: Section 4, Uniform Trust Receipts Act; Sections 6 and 7, Uniform Conditional Sales Act.

Purposes:

1. Under chattel mortgage acts, the Uniform Conditional Sales Act and other conditional sales legislation the geographical unit for filing or recording was local: the county or township in which the mortgagor or vendee resided or in which the goods sold or mortgaged were kept. The Uniform Trust Receipts Act used the state as the geographical filing unit: under that Act statements of trust receipt financing were filed with an official in the state capital and were not filed locally. The state-wide filing system of the Trust Receipts Act has been followed in

many accounts receivable and factor's lien acts.

Both systems have their advocates and both their own advantages and drawbacks. The principal advantage of state-wide filing is ease of access to the credit information which the files exist to provide. Consider for example the national distributor who wishes to have current information about the credit standing of the thousands of persons he sells to on credit. The more completely the files are centralized on a state-wide basis, the easier and cheaper it becomes to procure credit information; the more the files are scattered in local filing units, the more burdensome and costly. On the other hand, it can be said that most credit inquiries about local businesses, farmers and consumers come from local sources; convenience is served by having the files locally available and there is not great advantage in centralized filing.

This section does not attempt to resolve the controversy between the advocates of a completely centralized state-wide filing system and those of a large degree of local autonomy. Instead the section is drafted in a series of alternatives; local considerations of policy will determine the choice to be made.

2. Fortunately there is general agreement that the proper filing place for security interests in fixtures is in the office where a mortgage on the real estate concerned would be filed or recorded, and paragraph (1) (a) in the First Alternative and paragraph (1) (b) in the Second and Third Alternatives so provide. This provision follows the Uniform Conditional Sales Act. Note that there is no requirement for an additional filing with the chattel records.

3. In states where it is felt wise to preserve local filing for transactions of essentially local interest, either the Second or Third Alternative of subsection (1) should be adopted. Paragraph (1) (a) in both alternatives provides county (township, etc.) filing for consumer goods transactions and for agricultural transactions (farm equipment, farm products, farm accounts and crops). Note that the subsection departs from Section 6 of the Uniform Conditional Sales Act and adopts instead the policy of many chattel mortgage acts in selecting the county of the debtor's residence, rather than the county where the goods are located, as the normal filing place. Where, however, the debtor is an out-of-state resident, the filing must of necessity be in the county where the goods are, and the subsection so provides. Though not expressly stated, it is evident that filing for an assignment of accounts arising from the sale of farm products by a farmer who is not a resident must be in the county where the debtor keeps his farm products. In the case of crops growing or to be grown, where the land is in one county and the debtor's residence in another, filing must be made in both counties. Neither this filing for crops in the county where the land is nor the requirements that the

security agreement (Section 9—203(1)(a)) and the financing statement (Section 9—402(1) and (3)) contain a description of the real estate point to the conclusion that a financing statement for a security interest in crops must be filed in the real estate records. This Article follows pre-Code law which recognized such a financing as a chattel mortgage. The policy of the subsection is to require filing in the place or places where a creditor would normally look for information concerning interests created by the debtor.

For some incorporated farmers, reference to residence is an anomaly. Therefore subsection (6) provides that the residence of an organization is its place of business, or its chief executive office if it has more than one place of business. Compare Section 9—103(3), which reaches essentially the same concept as a definition of the "location" of a debtor.

4. It is thought that sound policy requires a state-wide filing system for all transactions except the essentially local ones covered in paragraph (1) (a) of the Second and Third Alternatives and land-related transactions covered in paragraph (1) (b) of the Second and Third Alternatives. Paragraph (1) (c) so provides in both alternatives, as does paragraph (1) (b) in the First Alternative. In a state which has adopted either the Second or Third Alternative, central filing would be required when the collateral was goods except consumer goods, farm equipment or farm products (including crops), or was documents or chattel paper or was accounts or general intangibles, unless related to a farm. Note that the filing provisions of this Article do not apply to instruments (see Section 9—304).

If the Third Alternative subsection (1) is adopted, then local filing, in addition to the central filing, is required in all the cases stated in the preceding paragraph, with respect to any debtor whose places of business within the state are all within a single county (township, etc.) or a debtor who is not engaged in business. The last event test stated in Section 9—103(1) (b) and Comment thereto applies to determine whether local filing is required under the present section, as well as to determine in which state filing is required.

In states where the arguments for a completely centralized set of files (except for fixtures) prevail, the First Alternative subsection (1) should be adopted. That alternative provides for exclusive central filing of all security interests except those in fixtures.

5. When a secured party has in good faith attempted to comply with the filing requirements but has not done so correctly, subsection (2) makes his filing effective in so far as it was proper, and also makes it good for all collateral covered by the financing statement against any person who actually knows the contents of the improperly filed statement. The subsection rejects the occasional decisions that an

improperly filed record is ineffective to give notice even to a person who knows of it. But if the Third Alternative subsection (1) is adopted, the requirements of paragraph (1) (c) are not complied with unless there is filing in both offices specified; filing in only one of two required places is not effective except as against one with actual knowledge of the contents of the defective financing statement.

6. Subsection (3) deals with change of residence or place of business or the location or use of the goods *after* a proper filing has been made. The subsection is important only when local filing is required, and covers only changes between local filing units in the state. For changes of location between states see Section 9—103(1) (d).

Subsection (3) is presented in alternative forms. Under the first no new filing is required in the county to which the collateral has been removed. Under alternative subsection (3) the original filing lapses four months after the change in location; this is basically the same rule that is applied by Section 9—103(1) (d) to the case of collateral brought into the state subject to a security interest which attached elsewhere.

7. The usual filing rules do not apply well for a transmitting utility (defined in Section 9—105). Many pre-Code statutes provided special filing rules for railroads and in some cases for other public utilities to avoid the requirements for filing with legal descriptions in every county in which such debtors had property. The Code recreates and broadens these provisions by subsection (5) of this section, which provides that for transmitting utilities the filing need only be in the office of the Secretary of State. The nature of the debtor will inform persons searching the record as to where to make a search.

Cross References:

Sections 9—302, 9—304 and 9—307(2).

Point 2: Section 9—313.

Point 6: Section 9—103(3).

Point 7: Sections 9—402(5) and 9—403(6).

Definitional Cross References:

"Account". Section 9—106.

"Collateral". Section 9—105.

"Consumer goods". Section 9—109.

"Debtor". Section 9—105.

"Equipment". Section 9—109.

"Farm products". Section 9—109.

"Financing statement". Section 9—402.

"Fixture filing". Section 9—313.

"Good faith". Section 1—201.

"Goods". Section 9—105.

"Knowledge". Section 1—201.

"Person". Section 1—201.

"Secured party". Section 9—105.

"Security interest". Section 1—201.

"Signed". Section 1—201.

"Transmitting utility". Section 9—105.

§ 9—402. Formal Requisites of Financing Statement; Amendments; Mortgage as Financing Statement

(1) A financing statement is sufficient if it gives the names of the debtor and the secured party, is signed by the debtor, gives an address of the secured party from which information concerning the security interest may be obtained, gives a mailing address of the debtor and contains a statement indicating the types, or describing the items, of collateral. A financing statement may be filed before a security agreement is made or a security interest otherwise attaches. When the financing statement covers crops growing or to be grown, the statement must also contain a description of the real estate concerned. When the financing statement covers timber to be cut or covers minerals or the like (including oil and gas) or accounts subject to subsection (5) of Section 9—103, or when the financing statement is filed as a fixture filing (Section 9—313) and the collateral is goods which are or are to become fixtures, the statement must also comply with subsection (5). A copy of the security agreement is sufficient as a financing statement if it contains the above information and is signed by the debtor. A carbon, photographic or other reproduction of a security agreement or a financing statement is sufficient as a financing statement if the security agreement so provides or if the original has been filed in this state.

(2) A financing statement which otherwise complies with subsection (1) is sufficient when it is signed by the secured party instead of the debtor if it is filed to perfect a security interest in

(a) collateral already subject to a security interest in another jurisdiction when it is brought into this state, or when the debtor's location is changed to this state. Such a financing statement must state that the collateral was brought into this state or that the debtor's location was changed to this state under such circumstances; or

(b) proceeds under Section 9—306 if the security interest in the original collateral was perfected. Such a financing statement must describe the original collateral; or

(c) collateral as to which the filing has lapsed; or

(d) collateral acquired after a change of name, identity or corporate structure of the debtor (subsection (7)).

(3) A form substantially as follows is sufficient to comply with subsection (1):

Name of debtor (or assignor) ....
Address ....
Name of secured party (or assignee) ....
Address ....

1. This financing statement covers the following types (or items) of property:

   (Describe) ....

2. (If collateral is crops) The above described crops are growing or are to be grown on:

   (Describe Real Estate) ....

3. (If applicable) The above goods are to become fixtures on *

   (Describe Real Estate) .... and this financing statement is to be filed [for record] in the real estate records. (If the debtor does not have an interest of record) The name of a record owner is ....

4. (If products of collateral are claimed) Products of the collateral are also covered.

(use whichever is applicable)

....
Signature of Debtor (or Assignor)

....
Signature of Secured Party (or Assignee)

(4) A financing statement may be amended by filing a writing signed by both the debtor and the secured party. An amendment does not extend the period of effectiveness of a financing statement. If any amendment adds collateral, it is effective as to the added collateral only from the filing date of the amendment. In this Article, unless the context otherwise requires, the term "financing statement" means the original financing statement and any amendments.

(5) A financing statement covering timber to be cut or covering minerals or the like (including oil and gas) or accounts subject to subsection (5) of Section 9—103, or a financing statement filed as a fixture filing (Section 9—313) where the debtor is not a transmitting utility, must show that it covers this type of

* Where appropriate substitute either "The above timber is standing on . . . ." or "The above minerals or the like (including oil and gas) or accounts will be financed at the wellhead or minehead of the well or mine located on . . . ."

collateral, must recite that it is to be filed [for record] in the real estate records, and the financing statement must contain a description of the real estate [sufficient if it were contained in a mortgage of the real estate to give constructive notice of the mortgage under the law of this state]. If the debtor does not have an interest of record in the real estate, the financing statement must show the name of a record owner.

(6) A mortgage is effective as a financing statement filed as a fixture filing from the date of its recording if

(a) the goods are described in the mortgage by item or type; and

(b) the goods are or are to become fixtures related to the real estate described in the mortgage; and

(c) the mortgage complies with the requirements for a financing statement in this section other than a recital that it is to be filed in the real estate records; and

(d) the mortgage is duly recorded.

No fee with reference to the financing statement is required other than the regular recording and satisfaction fees with respect to the mortgage.

(7) A financing statement sufficiently shows the name of the debtor if it gives the individual, partnership or corporate name of the debtor, whether or not it adds other trade names or names of partners. Where the debtor so changes his name or in the case of an organization its name, identity or corporate structure that a filed financing statement becomes seriously misleading, the filing is not effective to perfect a security interest in collateral acquired by the debtor more than four months after the change, unless a new appropriate financing statement is filed before the expiration of that time. A filed financing statement remains effective with respect to collateral transferred by the debtor even though the secured party knows of or consents to the transfer.

(8) A financing statement substantially complying with the requirements of this section is effective even though it contains minor errors which are not seriously misleading. Amended in 1972.

See Appendix I for changes made in former text and the reasons for change.

Note: *Language in brackets is optional.*

Note: *Where the state has any special recording system for real estate other than the usual grantor-grantee index (as, for instance, a tract system or a title registration or Torrens system) local adaptations of subsection (5) and Section 9—403(7) may be necessary. See Mass.Gen.Laws Chapter 106, Section 9—409.*

Official Comment

Prior Uniform Statutory Provision: Sections 13(3), 13(4), Uniform Trust Receipts Act.

Purposes:

1. Subsection (1) sets out the simple formal requisites of a financing statement under this Article. These requirements are: (1) signature of the debtor; (2) addresses of both parties; (3) a description of the collateral by type or item.

Where the collateral is crops growing or to be grown or when the financing statement is filed as a fixture filing (Section 9—313) or when the collateral is timber to be cut or minerals or the like (including oil and gas) financed at wellhead or minehead or accounts resulting from the sale thereof, the financing statement must also contain a description of the lands concerned. On description generally, see Section 9—110 and Comment 5 to the present section. An important distinction must be drawn, however, between the function of the description of land in reference to crops and its function in the other cases mentioned. For crops it is merely part of the description of the crops concerned, and the security interest in crops is a Code security interest, like the pre-Code "crop mortgage" which was a *chattel* mortgage. In contrast, in the other cases mentioned the function of the description of land is to have the financing statement filed in the county where the land is situated and in the realty records, as distinguished from the chattel records. Subsection (3) suggests a form which complies with the statutory requirements and makes clear that for the types of collateral mentioned other than crops, the financing statement containing a description of the land concerned is to go in the realty records. Note also subsection (5) on the adequacy of the description of land where the filing is to be in the real estate records. See also Section 9—403 (7) on the indexing of these filings in the real estate records.

A copy of the security agreement may be filed in place of a separate financing statement, if it contains the required information and signature.

2. This section adopts the system of "notice filing" which proved successful under the Uniform Trust Receipts Act. What is required to be filed is not, as under chattel mortgage and conditional sales acts, the security agreement itself, but only a simple notice which may be filed before the security interest attaches or thereafter. The

notice itself indicates merely that the secured party who has filed may have a security interest in the collateral described. Further inquiry from the parties concerned will be necessary to disclose the complete state of affairs. Section 9—208 provides a statutory procedure under which the secured party, at the debtor's request, may be required to make disclosure. Notice filing has proved to be of great use in financing transactions involving inventory, accounts and chattel paper, since it obviates the necessity of refiling on each of a series of transactions in a continuing arrangement where the collateral changes from day to day. Where other types of collateral are involved, the alternative procedure of filing a signed copy of the security agreement may prove to be the simplest solution. Sometimes more than one copy of a financing statement or of a security agreement used as a financing statement is needed for filing. In such a case the section permits use of a carbon copy or photographic copy of the paper, including signatures.

However, even in the case of filings that do not necessarily involve a series of transactions the financing statement is effective to encompass transactions under a security agreement not in existence and not contemplated at the time the notice was filed, if the description of collateral in the financing statement is broad enough to encompass them. Similarly, the financing statement is valid to cover after-acquired property and future advances under security agreements whether or not mentioned in the financing statement.

3. This section departs from the requirements of many pre-Code chattel mortgage statutes that the instrument filed be acknowledged or witnessed or accompanied by affidavits of good faith. Those requirements did not seem to have been successful as a deterrent to fraud; their principal effect was to penalize good faith mortgagees who had inadvertently failed to comply with the statutory niceties. They are here abandoned in the interest of a simplified and workable filing system.

4. Subsection (2) allows the secured party to file a financing statement signed only by himself where the filing is required by any of the events listed, each of which occurs after the commencement of the financing, and therefore under circumstances where the cooperation of the debtor is not certain. Section 9—401(3), alternative provision, contains similar permission on removal between counties in this state. The secured party should not be penalized for failure to make a timely filing by reason of difficulty in procuring the signature of a possibly reluctant or hostile debtor. Financing statements filed under this subsection must explain the circumstances under which they are filed with the signature of the secured party rather than that of the debtor.

In contrast to the signatures on original financing statements, an amendment to a financing statement must be signed by both parties, to preclude either from adversely affecting the interests of the other.

The reference in subsection (4) to an amendment which "adds collateral" refers to additional types of collateral. A security interest on additional units of a type of collateral already described can be created under an after-acquired property clause or a new security agreement. See Comment 5 to Section 9—204. On priorities in such cases see Section 9—312 and Comments thereto.

5. A description of real estate must be sufficient to identify it. See Section 9—110. This formulation rejects the view that the real estate description must be by metes and bounds, or otherwise conforming to traditional real estate practice in conveyancing, but of course the incorporation of such a description by reference to the recording data of a deed, mortgage or other instrument containing the description should suffice under the most stringent standards. The proper test is that a description of real estate must be sufficient so that the fixture financing statement will fit into the real estate search system and the financing statement be found by a real estate searcher. Optional language has been added by which the test of adequacy of the description is whether it would be adequate in a mortgage of the real estate. As suggested in the Note, more detail may be required if there is a tract indexing system or a land registration system.

Where the debtor does not have an interest of record in the real estate, a fixture financing statement must show the name of a record owner, and Section 9—403 (7) requires the financing statement to be indexed in the name of that owner. Thus the fixture financing statement will fit into the real estate search system.

6. A real estate mortgage may provide that it constitutes a security agreement with respect to fixtures (or other goods) in conformity with this Article. Combined mortgages on real estate and chattels are common and useful for certain purposes. This section goes further and makes provision that the recording of the real estate mortgage (if it complies with the requirements of a financing statement) shall constitute the filing of a financing statement as to the fixtures (but not, of course, as to the other goods). Section 9—403(6) makes the usual five-year maximum life for financing statements inapplicable to real estate mortgages which operate as financing statements under Section 9—402 (6), and they are effective for the duration of the real estate recording.

Of course, if a combined mortgage covers chattels which are not fixtures, a regular chattel filing is necessary, and subsection (6) is inapplicable to such chattels. Likewise, filing as a "fixture filing" provided in Section 9—401 does not apply to true chattels.

7. Subsection (7) undertakes to deal with some of the problems as to who is the debtor. In the case of individuals, it

contemplates filing only in the individual name, not in a trade name. In the case of partnerships it contemplates filing in the partnership name, not in the names of any of the partners, and not in any other trade names. Trade names are deemed to be too uncertain and too likely not to be known to the secured party or person searching the record, to form the basis for a filing system. However, provision is made in Section 9—403 (5) for indexing in a trade name if the secured party so desires.

Subsection (7) also deals with the case of a change of name of a debtor and provides some guidelines when mergers or other changes of corporate structure of the debtor occur with the result that a filed financing statement might become seriously misleading. Not all cases can be imagined and covered by statutes in advance; however, the principle sought to be achieved by the subsection is that after a change which would be seriously misleading, the old financing statement is not effective as to new collateral acquired more than four months after the change, unless a new appropriate financing statement is filed before the expiration of the four months. The old financing statement, if legally still valid under the circumstances, would continue to protect collateral acquired before the change and, if still operative under the particular circumstances, would also protect collateral acquired within the four months. Obviously, the subsection does not undertake to state whether the old security agreement continues to operate between the secured party and the party surviving the corporate change of the debtor.

8. Subsection (7) also deals with a different problem, namely whether a new filing is necessary where the collateral has been transferred from one debtor to another. This question has been much debated both in pre-Code law and under the Code. This Article now answers the question in the negative. Thus, any person searching the condition of the ownership of a debtor must make inquiry as to the debtor's source of title, and must search in the name of a former owner if circumstances seem to require it.

9. Subsection (8) is in line with the policy of this Article to simplify formal requisites and filing requirements and is designed to discourage the fanatical and impossibly refined reading of such statutory requirements in which courts have occasionally indulged themselves. As an example of the sort of reasoning which this subsection rejects, see General Motors Acceptance Corporation v. Haley, 329 Mass. 559, 109 N.E.2d 143 (1952).

Cross References:

Point 1: Section 9—110.
Point 2: Section 9—208.
Point 4: Sections 9—103, 9—306 and 9—401(3).
Point 5: Section 9—110.
Point 6: Section 9—403(6).
Point 7: Section 9—403(8).
Point 8: Section 9—311.

Definitional Cross References:

"Collateral". Section 9—105.
"Debtor". Section 9—105.
"Fixture". Section 9—313.
"Fixture filing". Section 9—313.
"Goods". Section 9—105.
"Party". Section 1—201.
"Proceeds". Section 9—306.
"Secured party". Section 9—105.
"Security agreement". Section 9—105.
"Security interest". Section 1—201.
"Signed". Section 1—201.
"Transmitting utility". Section 9—105.

§ 9—403. What Constitutes Filing; Duration of Filing; Effect of Lapsed Filing; Duties of Filing Officer

(1) Presentation for filing of a financing statement and tender of the filing fee or acceptance of the statement by the filing officer constitutes filing under this Article.

(2) Except as provided in subsection (6) a filed financing statement is effective for a period of five years from the date of filing. The effectiveness of a filed financing statement lapses on the expiration of the five year period unless a continuation statement is filed prior to the lapse. If a security interest perfected by filing exists at the time insolvency proceedings are commenced by or against the debtor, the security interest remains perfected until termination of the insolvency proceedings and thereafter for a period of sixty days or until expiration of the five year period, whichever occurs later. Upon lapse the security interest becomes unperfected, unless it is perfected without filing. If the security interest becomes unperfected upon lapse, it is deemed to have been unperfected as against a person who became a purchaser or lien creditor before lapse.

(3) A continuation statement may be filed by the secured party within six months prior to the expiration of the five year period specified in subsection (2). Any such continuation statement must be signed by the secured party, identify the original statement by file number and state that the original statement is still effective. A continuation statement signed by a person other than the secured party of record must be accompanied by a separate written statement of assignment signed by the secured party of record and complying with subsection (2) of Section 9—405, including payment of the required fee. Upon timely filing of the continuation statement, the effectiveness of the original statement is continued for five years after the last date to which the filing was effective whereupon it lapses in the same manner as provided in subsection (2) unless another continua-

tion statement is filed prior to such lapse. Succeeding continuation statements may be filed in the same manner to continue the effectiveness of the original statement. Unless a statute on disposition of public records provides otherwise, the filing officer may remove a lapsed statement from the files and destroy it immediately if he has retained a microfilm or other photographic record, or in other cases after one year after the lapse. The filing officer shall so arrange matters by physical annexation of financing statements to continuation statements or other related filings, or by other means, that if he physically destroys the financing statements of a period more than five years past, those which have been continued by a continuation statement or which are still effective under subsection (6) shall be retained.

(4) Except as provided in subsection (7) a filing officer shall mark each statement with a file number and with the date and hour of filing and shall hold the statement or a microfilm or other photographic copy thereof for public inspection. In addition the filing officer shall index the statement according to the name of the debtor and shall note in the index the file number and the address of the debtor given in the statement.

(5) The uniform fee for filing and indexing and for stamping a copy furnished by the secured party to show the date and place of filing for an original financing statement or for a continuation statement shall be $.......... if the statement is in the standard form prescribed by the [Secretary of State] and otherwise shall be $.........., plus in each case, if the financing statement is subject to subsection (5) of Section 9—402, $....... The uniform fee for each name more than one required to be indexed shall be $.......... The secured party may at his option show a trade name for any person and an extra uniform indexing fee of $.......... shall be paid with respect thereto.

(6) If the debtor is a transmitting utility (subsection (5) of Section 9—401) and a filed financing statement so states, it is effective until a termination statement is filed. A real estate mortgage which is effective as a fixture filing under subsection (6) of Section 9—402 remains effective as a fixture filing until the mortgage is released or satisfied of record or its effectiveness otherwise terminates as to the real estate.

(7) When a financing statement covers timber to be cut or covers minerals or the like (including oil and gas) or accounts subject to subsection (5) of Section 9—103, or is filed as a fixture filing, [it shall be filed for record and] the filing officer shall index it under the names of the debtor and any owner of record

shown on the financing statement in the same fashion as if they were the mortgagors in a mortgage of the real estate described, and, to the extent that the law of this state provides for indexing of mortgages under the name of the mortgagee, under the name of the secured party as if he were the mortgagee thereunder, or where indexing is by description in the same fashion as if the financing statement were a mortgage of the real estate described. Amended in 1972.

See Appendix I for changes made in former text and the reasons for change.

Note: *In states in which writings will not appear in the real estate records and indices unless actually recorded the bracketed language in subsection (7) should be used.*

Official Comment

Prior Uniform Statutory Provision: Sections 13(3), 13(4), Uniform Trust Receipts Act; Section 10, Uniform Conditional Sales Act.

Purposes:

1. Prior law was not always clear whether a mortgage filed for record gave constructive notice from the time of presentation to the filing officer or only from the time of indexing. Subsection (1) adopts the former position.

2. Prior statutes have usually limited the effectiveness of a filing to a specified period of time after which refiling is necessary. Subsection (2) follows the same policy, establishing five years as the filing period, with an exception for the cases mentioned in subsection (6). Subsection (3) provides for the filing of one or more continuation statements (which need be signed only by the secured party) if it is desired to continue the effectiveness of the original filing.

The theory of this Article is that the public files of financing statements are self-clearing, because the filing officer may automatically discard each financing statement after a period of five years plus the year after lapse required by subsection (3), unless a continuation statement is filed, or the financing statement is still effective under subsection (6). This theory materially lessens the tension that would otherwise exist to have the files cleared by termination statements under Section 9—404. Similarly, a person searching the files need not go back past this five years plus one year; and if the indices are arranged by years, he has a limited and defined search problem. The section asks the filing officer to attach financing statements whose life has been continued by continuation statements to the latter statements, so that anything contained in the files of old years can be discarded.

Subsection (6) provides certain special filing rules, namely, filings against transmitting utilities (Section 9—105), for which financing statements are filed in the office of the [Secretary of State]; and real estate mortgages which serve as fixture financing statements and which are filed in the real estate records. In both of these cases the financing statement is valid for the life of the obligations secured. No confusion as to the required scope of search should result, because of the special nature of the filings involved.

3. Under subsection (2) the security interest becomes unperfected when filing lapses. Thereafter, the interest of the secured party is subject to defeat by purchasers and lienors even though before lapse the conflicting interest may have been junior. Compare the situation arising under Section 9—103(1) (d) when a perfected security interest under the law of another jurisdiction is not perfected in this state within four months after the property is brought into this state.

Thus if A and B both make non-purchase money advances against the same collateral, and both perfect security interests by filing, A who files first is entitled to priority under Section 9—312(5). But if no continuation statement is filed, A's filing may lapse first. So long as B's interest remains perfected thereafter, he is entitled to priority over A's unperfected interest. This rule avoids the circular priority which arose under some prior statutes, under which A was subordinate to the debtor's trustee in bankruptcy, A retained priority over B, and B's interest was valid against the trustee in bankruptcy. In re Andrews, 172 F.2d 996 (7th Cir. 1949).

4. Subsection (7) makes clear that the filings in real estate records (Sections 9—401 and 9—402 (3) and (5)) shall be indexed in the real estate records, where they will be found by a real estate searcher. Where the debtor is not an owner of record, the financing statement must show the name of an owner of record, and the statement is to be indexed in his name. See Sections 9—313(4) (b) and (c); 9—402(3); 9—402(5).

Cross References:

Point 3: Sections 9—103(3), 9—301 and 9—312(5).

Point 4: Sections 9—313(4) (b) and (c), 9—401(1), 9—402 (3) and (5), and 9—405(2).

Definitional Cross References:

"Debtor". Section 9—105.

"Financing statement". Section 9—402.

"Fixture". Section 9—313.

"Fixture filing". Section 9—313.

"Secured party". Section 9—105.

"Security interest". Section 1—201.

"Transmitting utility". Section 9—105.

§ 9—404. Termination Statement

(1) If a financing statement covering consumer goods is filed on or after ...., then within one month or within ten days following written demand by the debtor after there is no outstanding secured obligation and no commitment to make advances, incur obligations or otherwise give value, the secured party must file with each filing officer with whom the financing statement was filed, a termination statement to the effect that he no longer claims a security interest under the financing statement, which shall be identified by file number. In other cases whenever there is no outstanding secured obligation and no commitment to make advances, incur obligations or otherwise give value, the secured party must on written demand by the debtor send the debtor, for each filing officer with whom the financing statement was filed, a termination statement to the effect that he no longer claims a security interest under the financing statement, which shall be identified by file number. A termination statement signed by a person other than the secured party of record must be accompanied by a separate written statement of assignment signed by the secured party of record complying with subsection (2) of Section 9—405, including payment of the required fee. If the affected secured party fails to file such a termination statement as required by this subsection, or to send such a termination statement within ten days after proper demand therefor, he shall be liable to the debtor for one hundred dollars, and in addition for any loss caused to the debtor by such failure.

(2) On presentation to the filing officer of such a termination statement he must note it in the index. If he has received the termination statement in duplicate, he shall return one copy of the termination statement to the secured party stamped to show the time of receipt thereof. If the filing officer has a microfilm or other photographic record of the financing statement, and of any related continuation statement, statement of assignment and statement of release, he may remove the originals from the files at any time after receipt of the termination statement, or if he has no such record, he may remove them from the files at any time after one year after receipt of the termination statement.

(3) If the termination statement is in the standard form prescribed by the [Secretary of State], the uniform fee for filing and indexing the termination statement shall be $......, and otherwise shall be $......, plus in each case an additional

fee of $...... for each name more than one against which the termination statement is required to be indexed. Amended in 1972.

See Appendix I for changes made in former text and the reasons for change.

Note: *The date to be inserted should be the effective date of the revised Article 9.*

Official Comment

Prior Uniform Statutory Provision: Section 12, Uniform Conditional Sales Act.

Purposes:

1. To provide a procedure for noting discharge of the secured obligation on the records and for noting that a financing arrangement has been terminated.

Since most financing statements expire in five years unless a continuation statement is filed (Section 9—403), no compulsion is placed on the secured party to file a termination statement unless demanded by the debtor, except in the case of consumer goods. Because many consumers will not realize the importance of clearing the situation as it appears on file, an affirmative duty is put on the secured party in that case. But many purchase money security interests in consumer goods will not be filed, except for motor vehicles (Section 9—302(1) (d)); and in the case of motor vehicles a certificate of title law may control instead of the provisions of Article 9.

2. This section adds to the usual provisions one covering the problem which arises because a secured party under a notice filing system may file notice of an intention to make advances which may never be made. Under this section a debtor may require a secured party to send a termination statement when there is no outstanding obligation and no commitment to make future advances.

Cross Reference:

Point 2: Section 9—402(1).

Definitional Cross References:

"Consumer goods". Section 9—109.

"Debtor". Section 9—105.

"Financing statement". Section 9—402.

"Person". Section 1—201.

"Secured party". Section 9—105.

"Security interest". Section 1—201.

"Send". Section 1—201.

"Value". Section 1—201.

"Written". Section 1—201.

§ 9—405. Assignment of Security Interest; Duties of Filing Officer; Fees

(1) A financing statement may disclose an assignment of a security interest in the collateral described in the financing statement by indication in the financing statement of the name and

address of the assignee or by an assignment itself or a copy thereof on the face or back of the statement. On presentation to the filing officer of such a financing statement the filing officer shall mark the same as provided in Section 9—403(4). The uniform fee for filing, indexing and furnishing filing data for a financing statement so indicating an assignment shall be $...... if the statement is in the standard form prescribed by the [Secretary of State] and otherwise shall be $......, plus in each case an additional fee of $...... for each name more than one against which the financing statement is required to be indexed.

(2) A secured party may assign of record all or part of his rights under a financing statement by the filing in the place where the original financing statement was filed of a separate written statement of assignment signed by the secured party of record and setting forth the name of the secured party of record and the debtor, the file number and the date of filing of the financing statement and the name and address of the assignee and containing a description of the collateral assigned. A copy of the assignment is sufficient as a separate statement if it complies with the preceding sentence. On presentation to the filing officer of such a separate statement, the filing officer shall mark such separate statement with the date and hour of the filing. He shall note the assignment on the index of the financing statement, or in the case of a fixture filing, or a filing covering timber to be cut, or covering minerals or the like (including oil and gas) or accounts subject to subsection (5) of Section 9—103, he shall index the assignment under the name of the assignor as grantor and, to the extent that the law of this state provides for indexing the assignment of a mortgage under the name of the assignee, he shall index the assignment of the financing statement under the name of the assignee. The uniform fee for filing, indexing and furnishing filing data about such a separate statement of assignment shall be $...... if the statement is in the standard form prescribed by the [Secretary of State] and otherwise shall be $......, plus in each case an additional fee of $...... for each name more than one against which the statement of assignment is required to be indexed. Notwithstanding the provisions of this subsection, an assignment of record of a security interest in a fixture contained in a mortgage effective as a fixture filing (subsection (6) of Section 9–402) may be made only by an assignment of the mortgage in the manner provided by the law of this state other than this Act.

(3) After the disclosure or filing of an assignment under this section, the assignee is the secured party of record. Amended in 1972.

See Appendix I for changes made in former text and the reasons for change.

Official Comment

Prior Uniform Statutory Provision: None.

Purposes:

This section provides a permissive device whereby a secured party who has assigned all or part of his interest may have the assignment noted of record. Note that under Section 9—302 (2) no filing of such an assignment is required as a condition of continuing the perfected status of the security interest against creditors and transferees of the original debtor. A secured party who has assigned his interest might wish to have the fact noted of record, so that inquiries concerning the transaction would be addressed not to him but to the assignee (see Point 2 of Comment to Section 9—402). After a secured party has assigned his rights of record, the assignee becomes the "secured party of record" and may file a continuation statement under Section 9—403, a termination statement under Section 9—404, or a statement of release under Section 9—406.

Where a mortgage of real estate is effective as a financing statement filed as a fixture filing (Section 9—402(6)), then an assignment of record of the security interest may be made only in the manner in which an assignment of the mortgage may be made under the local state law.

Cross References:

Sections 9—302(2) and 9—402 through 9—406.

Definitional Cross References:

"Collateral". Section 9—105.

"Debtor". Section 9—105.

"Financing statement". Section 9—402.

"Rights". Section 1—201.

"Secured party". Section 9—105.

"Signed". Section 1—201.

"Written". Section 1—201.

§ 9—406. Release of Collateral; Duties of Filing Officer; Fees

A secured party of record may by his signed statement release all or a part of any collateral described in a filed financing statement. The statement of release is sufficient if it contains a description of the collateral being released, the name and address of the debtor, the name and address of the secured party, and the file number of the financing statement. A statement of release signed by a person other than the secured party of record must be accompanied by a separate written statement of assignment signed by the secured party of record and complying with subsection (2) of Section 9—405, including payment of the required fee. Upon presentation of such a statement of release to the filing officer he shall mark the statement with the hour and date of filing and shall note the same upon the margin of the index of the filing of the financing statement. The uniform fee for filing and noting such a statement of release shall be $...... if the statement is in the standard form prescribed by the [Secretary of State] and otherwise shall be $......, plus in each case an additional fee of $...... for each name more than one against which the statement of release is required to be indexed. Amended in 1972.

See Appendix I for changes made in former text and the reasons for change.

Official Comment

Prior Uniform Statutory Provision: None.

Purposes:

Like the preceding section, this section provides a permissive device for noting of record any release of collateral. There is no requirement that such a statement be filed when collateral is released (cf. Section 9—404 on Termination Statements). It is merely a method of making the record reflect the true state of affairs so that fewer inquiries will have to be made by persons who consult the files.

If the statement of release is not signed by the secured party of record, the assignment procedure of Section 9—405(2) must be followed.

Cross Reference:

Section 9—404.

Definitional Cross References:

"Collateral". Section 9—105.

"Debtor". Section 9—105.

"Financing statement". Section 9—402.

"Secured party". Section 9—105.

"Signed". Section 1—201.

[§ 9—407. Information From Filing Officer]

[(1) If the person filing any financing statement, termination statement, statement of assignment, or statement of release, furnishes the filing officer a copy thereof, the filing officer shall upon request note upon the copy the file number and date and hour of the filing of the original and deliver or send the copy to such person.]

[(2) Upon request of any person, the filing officer shall issue his certificate showing whether there is on file on the date and hour stated therein, any presently effective financing statement naming a particular debtor and any statement of assignment thereof and if there is, giving the date and hour of filing of each such statement and the names and addresses of each secured party therein. The uniform fee for such a certificate shall be $...... if the request for the certificate is in the standard form prescribed by the [Secretary of State] and otherwise shall be $...... Upon request the filing officer shall furnish a copy of any filed financing statement or statement of assignment for a uniform fee of $...... per page.] Amended in 1972.

See Appendix I for changes made in former text and the reasons for change.

Note: *This section is proposed as an optional provision to require filing officers to furnish certificates. Local law and practices should be consulted with regard to the advisability of adoption.*

Official Comment

Prior Uniform Statutory Provision: None.

Purposes:

1. Subsection (1) requires the filing officer upon request to return to the secured party a copy of the financing statement on which the material data concerning the filing are noted. Receipt of such a copy will assure the secured party that the mechanics of filing have been complied with. Note, however, that under Section 9—403(1) the secured party does not bear the risk that the filing officer will not properly perform his duties: under that section the secured party has complied with the filing requirements when he presents his financing statement for filing and the filing fee has been tendered or the statement accepted by the filing officer.

2. Subsection (2) requires the filing officer on request to issue to any person who has tendered the proper fee his certificate as to what filings have been made against any particular debtor and to furnish copies of such filed financing statements. In view of the centralized filing system adopted by this Article (see Section 9—401 and Comment thereto), this provision is of obvious convenience to a person who wishes to know what the files contain but who cannot conveniently consult files located in the state capital.

Cross References:

Point 1: Section 9—403(1).
Point 2: Section 9—401.

Definitional Cross References:

"Debtor". Section 9—105.

"Financing statement". Section 9—402.

"Person". Section 1—201.

"Secured party". Section 9—105.

"Send". Section 1—201.

§ 9—408. Financing Statements Covering Consigned or Leased Goods

A consignor or lessor of goods may file a financing statement using the terms "consignor," "consignee," "lessor," "lessee" or the like instead of the terms specified in Section 9—402. The provisions of this Part shall apply as appropriate to such a financing statement but its filing shall not of itself be a factor in determining whether or not the consignment or lease is intended as security (Section 1—201(37)). However, if it is determined for other reasons that the consignment or lease is so intended, a security interest of the consignor or lessor which attaches to the consigned or leased goods is perfected by such filing. Added in 1972.

See Appendix I for reasons for adoption of this new section.

Official Comment

Prior Uniform Statutory Provisions: None.

Purposes:

1. Where filing is required under Sections 2—326(3) and 9—114 for a consignment which is not a security interest (Section 1—201(37)), this section authorizes the appropriate adaptations of terminology.

Apart from the rules in Part 4, the rules of this article using the terms "debtor" and "secured party" will not apply to consignments if they are not security interests. Section 9—114 on consignments essentially parallels Section 9—312(3) on inventory priorities, and the latter rule therefore does not apply to consignments. Section 2—326 states the rights of creditors of a consignee who has not filed or otherwise complied with subsection (3), and Section 9—301 on unperfected security interests is therefore not applicable. Section 2—326 and the law of consignments supply rules which are provided by Section 9—311 for security interests and that section is therefore not applicable to consignments. For reasons indicated in the Comment to Section 9—114, Section 9—306 on proceeds is inapplicable to consignments. An equivalent to the protection of a buyer in ordinary course of business against a security interest under Section 9—307(1) is provided against consignments by Section 2—403(2) and (3).

2. If a lease is actually intended as security (Section 1—201(37)), this Article applies in full. But this question of intention is a doubtful one, and the lessor may choose to file for safety even while contending that the lease is a true lease for which no filing is required. This section authorizes filing with appropriate changes of terminology, and without affecting the substantive question of classification of the lease.

If the lease is a true lease, none of the provisions of the Article is applicable to the lease as an interest in the chattel. Note, however, that the Article may be applicable to the lease in its aspect as chattel paper. See Section 9—105(b).

PART 5

DEFAULT

§ 9—501. Default; Procedure When Security Agreement Covers Both Real and Personal Property

(1) When a debtor is in default under a security agreement, a secured party has the rights and remedies provided in this Part and except as limited by subsection (3) those provided in the security agreement. He may reduce his claim to judgment, foreclose or otherwise enforce the security interest by any available judicial procedure. If the collateral is documents the secured party may proceed either as to the documents or as to the goods covered thereby. A secured party in possession has the rights, remedies and duties provided in Section 9—207. The rights and remedies referred to in this subsection are cumulative.

(2) After default, the debtor has the rights and remedies provided in this Part, those provided in the security agreement and those provided in Section 9—207.

(3) To the extent that they give rights to the debtor and impose duties on the secured party, the rules stated in the subsections referred to below may not be waived or varied except as provided with respect to compulsory disposition of collateral (subsection (3) of Section 9—504 and Section 9—505) and with respect to redemption of collateral (Section 9—506) but the parties may by agreement determine the standards by which the fulfillment of these rights and duties is to be measured if such standards are not manifestly unreasonable:

(a) subsection (2) of Section 9—502 and subsection (2) of Section 9—504 insofar as they require accounting for surplus proceeds of collateral;

(b) subsection (3) of Section 9—504 and subsection (1) of Section 9—505 which deal with disposition of collateral;

(c) subsection (2) of Section 9—505 which deals with acceptance of collateral as discharge of obligation;

(d) Section 9—506 which deals with redemption of collateral; and

(e) subsection (1) of Section 9—507 which deals with the secured party's liability for failure to comply with this Part.

(4) If the security agreement covers both real and personal property, the secured party may proceed under this Part as to the personal property or he may proceed as to both the real and the personal property in accordance with his rights and remedies in respect of the real property in which case the provisions of this Part do not apply.

(5) When a secured party has reduced his claim to judgment the lien of any levy which may be made upon his collateral by virtue of any execution based upon the judgment shall relate back to the date of the perfection of the security interest in such collateral. A judicial sale, pursuant to such execution, is a foreclosure of the security interest by judicial procedure within the meaning of this section, and the secured party may purchase at the sale and thereafter hold the collateral free of any other requirements of this Article. Amended in 1972.

See Appendix I for changes made in former text and the reasons for change.

Official Comment

Prior Uniform Statutory Provision: Section 6, Uniform Trust Receipts Act; Sections 16 through 26, Uniform Conditional Sales Act.

Purposes:

1. The rights of the secured party in the collateral after the debtor's default are of the essence of a security transaction. These are the rights which distinguish the secured from the unsecured lender. This section and the following six sections state those rights as well as the limitations on their free exercise which legislative policy requires for the protection not only of the defaulting debtor but of other creditors. But subsections (1) and (2) make it clear that the statement of rights and remedies in this Part does not exclude other remedies provided by agreement.

2. Following default and the taking possession of the collateral by the secured party, there is nc longer any distinction between the security interest which before default was non-possessory and that which was possessory under a pledge. Therefore no general distinction is taken in this Part between the rights of a non-possessory secured party and those of a pledgee; the latter, being in possession of the collateral at default, will of course not have to avail himself

of the right to take possession under Section 9—503.

3. Section 9—207 states rights, remedies and duties with respect to collateral in the secured party's possession. That section applies not only to the situation where he is in possession before default, as a pledgee, but also, by subsections (1) and (2) of this section, to the secured party in possession after default. Nevertheless the relations of the parties have been changed by default, and Section 9—207 as it applies after default must be read together with this Part. In particular, agreements permitted under Section 9—207 cannot waive or modify the rights of the debtor contrary to subsection (3) of this section.

4. Section 1—102(3) states rules to determine which provisions of this Act are mandatory and which may be varied by agreement. In general, provisions which relate to matters which come up between immediate parties may be varied by agreement. In the area of rights after default our legal system has traditionally looked with suspicion on agreements designed to cut down the debtor's rights and free the secured party of his duties: no mortgage clause has ever been allowed to clog the equity of redemption. The default situation offers great scope for overreaching; the suspicious attitude of the courts has been grounded in common sense.

Subsection (3) of this section contains a codification of this long-standing and deeply rooted attitude: the specified rights of the debtor and duties of the secured party may not be waived or varied except as stated. Provisions not specified in subsection (3) are subject to the general rules stated in Section 1—102 (3).

5. The collateral for many corporate security issues consists of both real and personal property. In the interest of simplicity and speed subsection (4) permits, although it does not require, the secured party to proceed as to both real and personal property in accordance with his rights and remedies in respect of the real property. Except for the permission so granted, this Act leaves to other state law all questions of procedure with respect to real property. For example, this Act does not determine whether the secured party can proceed against the real estate alone and later proceed in a separate action against the personal property in accordance with his rights and remedies against the real estate. By such separate actions the secured party "proceeds as to both," and this Part does not apply in either action. But subsection (4) does give him an option to proceed under this Part as to the personal property.

6. Under subsection (1) a secured party is entitled to reduce his claim to judgment or to foreclose his interest by any available procedure, outside this Article, which state law may provide. The first sentence of subsection (5) makes clear that any judgment lien which the secured party may acquire against the collateral is, so to say, a contin-

uation of his original interest (if perfected) and not the acquisition of a new interest or a transfer of property to satisfy an antecedent debt. The judgment lien is therefore stated to relate back to the date of perfection of the security interest. The second sentence of the subsection makes clear that a judicial sale following judgment, execution and levy is one of the methods of foreclosure contemplated by subsection (1); such a sale is governed by other law and not by this Article and the restrictions which this Article imposes on the right of a secured party to buy in the collateral at a sale under Section 9—504 do not apply.

Cross References:

Point 2: Section 9—503.
Point 3: Section 9—207.
Point 4: Section 1—102(3).
Point 5: Sections 9—102(1) and 9—104(j).
Point 6: Section 9—504.

Definitional Cross References:

"Agreement". Section 1—201.
"Collateral". Section 9—105.
"Debtor". Section 9—105.
"Documents". Section 9—105.
"Goods". Section 9—105.
"Remedy". Section 1—201.
"Rights". Section 1—201.
"Secured party". Section 9—105.
"Security agreement". Section 9—105.
"Security interest". Section 1—201.

§ 9—502. Collection Rights of Secured Party

(1) When so agreed and in any event on default the secured party is entitled to notify an account debtor or the obligor on an instrument to make payment to him whether or not the assignor was theretofore making collections on the collateral, and also to take control of any proceeds to which he is entitled under Section 9—306.

(2) A secured party who by agreement is entitled to charge back uncollected collateral or otherwise to full or limited recourse against the debtor and who undertakes to collect from the account debtors or obligors must proceed in a commercially reasonable manner and may deduct his reasonable expenses of realization from the collections. If the security agreement secures an indebtedness, the secured party must account to the debtor for any surplus, and unless otherwise agreed, the debtor is liable for any deficiency. But, if the underlying transaction was a sale of accounts or chattel paper, the debtor is entitled to any surplus or is liable for any deficiency only if the security agreement so provides. Amended in 1972.

See Appendix I for changes made in former text and the reasons for change.

Official Comment

Prior Uniform Statutory Provision: None.

Purposes:

1. The assignee of accounts, chattel paper, or instruments holds as collateral property which is not only the most liquid asset of the debtor's business but also property which may be collected without any interruption of the business, assuming it to continue after default. The situation is far different from that where the collateral is inventory or equipment, whose removal may bring the business to a halt. Furthermore the problems of valuation and identification, present where the collateral is tangible chattels, do not arise so sharply on the assignment of intangibles. Considerations, similar although not identical, apply to assignments of general intangibles, which are also covered by the rule of the section. Consequently, this section recognizes the fact that financing by assignment of intangibles lacks many of the complexities which arise after default in other types of financing, and allows the assignee to liquidate in the regular course of business by collecting whatever may become due on the collateral, whether or not the method of collection contemplated by the security arrangement before default was direct (i. e., payment by the account debtor to the assignee, "notification" financing) or indirect (i. e., payment by the account debtor to the assignor, "non-notification" financing). By agreement, of course, the secured party may have the right to give notice and to make collections before default.

2. In one form of accounts receivable financing, which is found in the "factoring" arrangements which are common in the textile industry, the assignee assumes the credit risk—that is, he buys the account under an agreement which does not provide for recourse or charge-back against the assignor in the event the account proves uncollectible. Under such an arrangement, neither the debtor nor his creditors have any legitimate concern with the disposition which the assignee makes of the accounts. Under another form of accounts receivable financing, however, the assignee does not assume the credit risk and retains a right of full or limited recourse or charge-back for uncollectible accounts. In such a case both debtor and creditors have a right that the assignee not dump the accounts, if the result will be to increase a possible deficiency claim or to reduce a possible surplus.

3. Where an assignee has a right of charge-back or a right of recourse, subsection (2) provides that liquidation must be made with due regard to the interest of the assignor and of his other creditor—"in a commercially reasonable manner" (compare Section 9—504 and see Section 9—507(2))—and the proceeds allocated to the expenses of realization and to the indebt-

edness. If the "charge-back" provisions of the assignment arrangement provide only for "charge-back" of bad accounts against a reserve, the debtor's claim to surplus and his liability for a deficiency are limited to the amount of the reserve.

4. Financing arrangements of the type dealt with by this section are between business men. The last sentence of subsection (2) therefore preserves freedom of contract, and the subsection recognizes that there may be a true sale of accounts or chattel paper although recourse exists. The determination whether a particular assignment constitutes a sale or a transfer for security is left to the courts. Note that, under Section 9—102, this Article applies both to sales and to security transfers of such intangibles.

Cross References:

Sections 9—205 and 9—306.

Point 3: Sections 9—504 and 9—507(2).

Point 4: Sections 9—102(1)(b) and 9—104(f).

Definitional Cross References:

"Account". Section 9—106.

"Account debtor". Section 9—105.

"Agreement". Section 1—201.

"Chattel paper". Section 9—105.

"Collateral". Section 9—105.

"Debtor". Section 9—105.

"Instrument". Section 9—105.

"Notify". Section 1—201.

"Proceeds". Section 9—306.

"Secured party". Section 9—105.

"Security agreement". Section 9—105.

§ 9—503. Secured Party's Right to Take Possession After Default

Unless otherwise agreed a secured party has on default the right to take possession of the collateral. In taking possession a secured party may proceed without judicial process if this can be done without breach of the peace or may proceed by action. If the security agreement so provides the secured party may require the debtor to assemble the collateral and make it available to the secured party at a place to be designated by the secured party which is reasonably convenient to both parties. Without removal a secured party may render equipment unusable, and may dispose of collateral on the debtor's premises under Section 9—504.

Official Comment

Prior Uniform Statutory Provision: Section 6, Uniform Trust Receipts Act; Sections 16 and 17, Uniform Conditional Sales Act.

Purposes:

Under this Article the secured party's right to possession of the collateral (if he is not already in possession as pledgee) accrues on default unless otherwise agreed in the security agreement. This Article follows the provisions of the earlier uniform legislation in allowing the secured party in most cases to take possession without the issuance of judicial process. In the case of collateral such as heavy equipment, the physical removal from the debtor's plant and the storage of the equipment pending resale may be exceedingly expensive and in some cases impractical. The section therefore provides that in lieu of removal the lender may render equipment unusable or dispose of collateral on the debtor's premises. The authorization to render equipment unusable or to dispose of collateral without removal would not justify unreasonable action by the secured party, since, under Section 9—504(3), all his actions in connection with disposition must be taken in a "commercially reasonable manner".

Cross Reference:

Section 9—504.

Definitional Cross References:

"Action". Section 1—201.
"Collateral". Section 9—105.
"Debtor". Section 9—105.
"Equipment". Section 9—109.
"Rights". Section 1—201.
"Secured party". Section 9—105.
"Security agreement". Section 9—105.

§ 9—504. Secured Party's Right to Dispose of Collateral After Default; Effect of Disposition

(1) A secured party after default may sell, lease or otherwise dispose of any or all of the collateral in its then condition or following any commercially reasonable preparation or processing. Any sale of goods is subject to the Article on Sales (Article 2). The proceeds of disposition shall be applied in the order following to

(a) the reasonable expenses of retaking, holding, preparing for sale or lease, selling, leasing and the like and, to the extent provided for in the agreement and not prohibited by law, the reasonable attorneys' fees and legal expenses incurred by the secured party;

(b) the satisfaction of indebtedness secured by the security interest under which the disposition is made;

(c) the satisfaction of indebtedness secured by any subordinate security interest in the collateral if written notification of demand therefor is received before distribution of the proceeds is completed. If requested by the secured party, the holder of a subordinate security interest must seasonably furnish reasonable proof of his interest, and unless he does so, the secured party need not comply with his demand.

(2) If the security interest secures an indebtedness, the secured party must account to the debtor for any surplus, and, unless otherwise agreed, the debtor is liable for any deficiency. But if the underlying transaction was a sale of accounts or chattel paper, the debtor is entitled to any surplus or is liable for any deficiency only if the security agreement so provides.

(3) Disposition of the collateral may be by public or private proceedings and may be made by way of one or more contracts. Sale or other disposition may be as a unit or in parcels and at any time and place and on any terms but every aspect of the disposition including the method, manner, time, place and terms must be commercially reasonable. Unless collateral is perishable or threatens to decline speedily in value or is of a type customarily sold on a recognized market, reasonable notification of the time and place of any public sale or reasonable notification of the time after which any private sale or other intended disposition is to be made shall be sent by the secured party to the debtor, if he has not signed after default a statement renouncing or modifying his right to notification of sale. In the case of consumer goods no other notification need be sent. In other cases notification shall be sent to any other secured party from whom the secured party has received (before sending his notification to the debtor or before the debtor's renunciation of his rights) written notice of a claim of an interest in the collateral. The secured party may buy at any public sale and if the collateral is of a type customarily sold in a recognized market or is of a type which is the subject of widely distributed standard price quotations he may buy at private sale.

(4) When collateral is disposed of by a secured party after default, the disposition transfers to a purchaser for value all of the debtor's rights therein, discharges the security interest under which it is made and any security interest or lien subordinate thereto. The purchaser takes free of all such rights and interests even though the secured party fails to comply with the requirements of this Part or of any judicial proceedings

(a) in the case of a public sale, if the purchaser has no knowledge of any defects in the sale and if he does not buy in collusion with the secured party, other bidders or the person conducting the sale; or

(b) in any other case, if the purchaser acts in good faith.

(5) A person who is liable to a secured party under a guaranty, indorsement, repurchase agreement or the like and who receives a transfer of collateral from the secured party or is sub-

rogated to his rights has thereafter the rights and duties of the secured party. Such a transfer of collateral is not a sale or disposition of the collateral under this Article. Amended in 1972.

See Appendix I for changes made in former text and the reasons for change.

Official Comment

Prior Uniform Statutory Provision: Section 6, Uniform Trust Receipts Act; Sections 19, 20, 21, and 22, Uniform Conditional Sales Act.

Purposes:

1. The Uniform Trust Receipts Act provides that an entruster in possession after default holds the collateral with the rights and duties of a pledgee, and, in particular, that he may sell such collateral at public or private sale with a right to claim deficiency and a duty to account for any surplus. The Uniform Conditional Sales Act insisted on a sale at public auction with elaborate provisions for the giving of notice of sale. This section follows the more liberal provisions of the Trust Receipts Act. Although public sale is recognized, it is hoped that private sale will be encouraged where, as is frequently the case, private sale through commercial channels will result in higher realization on collateral for the benefit of all parties. The only restriction placed on the secured party's method of disposition is that it must be commercially reasonable. In this respect this section follows the provisions of the section on resale by a seller following a buyer's rejection of goods (Section 2—706). Subsection (1) does not restrict disposition to sale: the collateral may be sold, leased, or otherwise disposed of—subject of course to the general requirement of subsection (2) that all aspects of the disposition be "commercially reasonable". Section 9—507(2) states some tests as to what is "commercially reasonable".

2. Subsection (1) in general follows prior law in its provisions for the application of proceeds and for the debtor's right to surplus and liability for deficiency. Under paragraph (1)(c) the secured party, after paying expenses of retaking and disposition and his own debt, is required to pay over remaining proceeds to the extent necessary to satisfy the holder of any junior security interest in the same collateral if the holder of the junior interest has made a written demand and furnished on request reasonable proof of his interest: this provision is necessary in view of the fact that under subsection (4) the junior interest is discharged by the disposition. Since the requirement is conditioned on written demand, it should not result in undue burden on the secured party making the disposition. It should be noted also that under Section 9—112 where the secured party knows that the collateral is owned by a person who is not the debtor, the owner of the collat-

eral and not the debtor is entitled to any surplus.

3. In any security transaction the debtor (or the owner of the collateral if other than the debtor: see Section 9—112) is entitled to any surplus which results from realization on the collateral; the debtor will also, unless otherwise agreed, be liable for any deficiency. Subsection (2) so provides. Since this Article covers sales of certain intangibles as well as transfers for security, the subsection also provides that apart from agreement the right to surplus or liability for deficiency does not accrue where the transaction between debtor and secured party was a sale and not a security transaction.

4. Subsection (4) provides that a purchaser for value from a secured party after default takes free of any rights of the debtor and of the holders of junior security interests and liens, even though the secured party has not complied with the requirements of this Part or of any judicial proceedings. This subsection follows a similar provision in the Uniform Trust Receipts Act and in the section of this Act on resale by a seller (Section 2—706). Where the purchaser for value has bought at a public sale he is protected under paragraph (a) if he has no knowledge of any defects in the sale and was not guilty of collusive practices. Where the purchaser for value has bought at a private sale he must, to receive the protection of paragraph (b), qualify in all respects as a purchaser in good faith. Thus while the purchaser at a private sale is required to proceed in the exercise of good faith, the purchaser at public sale is protected so long as he is not actively in bad faith, and is put under no duty to inquire into the circumstances of the sale.

5. Both the Uniform Trust Receipts Act and the Uniform Conditional Sales Act required a waiting period after repossession and before sale (five days in the Trust Receipts Act, ten days in the Conditional Sales Act). Under subsection (3), the secured party in most cases is required to give reasonable notification of disposition to the debtor unless the debtor has after default signed a statement renouncing or modifying his right to notification of sale.

The secured party must also (except for consumer goods) give notice to any other secured parties who have in writing given notice of a claim of an interest in the collateral. This latter notice must be given before the debtor renounces his rights or before the secured party gives his notification to the debtor. Compare Section 9—505(2). Except for the requirement of notification there is no statutory period during which the collateral must be held before disposition. "Reasonable notification" is not defined in this Article; at a minimum it must be sent in such time that persons entitled to receive it will have sufficient time to take appropriate steps to protect their interests by taking part in the sale or other disposition if they so desire.

6. Section 19 of the Uniform Conditional Sales Act required that sale be made not more than thirty days after possession taken by the conditional vendor. The Uniform Trust Receipts Act contained no comparable provision. Here again this Article follows the Trust Receipts Act, and no period is set within which the disposition must be made, except in the case of consumer goods which under Section 9—505(1) must in certain instances be sold within ninety days after the secured party has taken possession. The failure to prescribe a statutory period during which disposition must be made is in line with the policy adopted in this Article to encourage disposition by private sale through regular commercial channels. It may, for example, be wise not to dispose of goods when the market has collapsed, or to sell a large inventory in parcels over a period of time instead of in bulk. Note, however, that under subsection (3) every aspect of the sale or other disposition of the collateral must be commercially reasonable; this specifically includes method, manner, time, place and terms. See Section 9—507(2). Under that provision a secured party who without proceeding under Section 9—505(2) held collateral a long time without disposing of it, thus running up large storage charges against the debtor, where no reason existed for not making a prompt sale, might well be found not to have acted in a "commercially reasonable" manner. See also Section 1—203 on the general obligation of good faith.

Cross References:

Point 1: Sections 2—706 and 9—507(2).

Point 2: Section 9—112.

Point 3: Sections 9—102(1)(b) and 9—112.

Point 4: Section 2—706.

Point 6: Sections 9—505 and 9—507(2).

Definitional Cross References:

"Account". Section 9—106.

"Agreement". Section 1—201.

"Chattel paper". Section 9—105.

"Collateral". Section 9—105.

"Consumer goods". Section 9—109.

"Contract". Section 1—201.

"Debtor". Section 9—105.

"Financing statement". Section 9—402.

"Gives" notification. Section 1—201.

"Good faith". Section 1—201.

"Goods". Section 9—105.

"Knowledge". Section 1—201.

"Person". Section 1—201.

"Proceeds". Section 9—306.

"Purchaser". Section 1—201.

"Receives" notification. Section 1—201.

"Rights". Section 1—201.

"Sale". Sections 2—106 and 9—105.

"Secured party". Section 9—105.

"Security agreement". Section 9—105.

"Security interest". Section 1—201.

"Send". Section 1—201.

"Term". Section 1—201.

"Value". Section 1—201.

"Written". Section 1—201.

§ 9—505. Compulsory Disposition of Collateral; Acceptance of the Collateral as Discharge of Obligation

(1) If the debtor has paid sixty per cent of the cash price in the case of a purchase money security interest in consumer goods or sixty per cent of the loan in the case of another security interest in consumer goods, and has not signed after default a statement renouncing or modifying his rights under this Part a secured party who has taken possession of collateral must dispose of it under Section 9—504 and if he fails to do so within ninety days after he takes possession the debtor at his option may recover in conversion or under Section 9—507(1) on secured party's liability.

(2) In any other case involving consumer goods or any other collateral a secured party in possession may, after default, propose to retain the collateral in satisfaction of the obligation. Written notice of such proposal shall be sent to the debtor if he has not signed after default a statement renouncing or modifying his rights under this subsection. In the case of consumer goods no other notice need be given. In other cases notice shall be sent to any other secured party from whom the secured party has received (before sending his notice to the debtor or before the debtor's renunciation of his rights) written notice of a claim of an interest in the collateral. If the secured party receives objection in writing from a person entitled to receive notification within twenty-one days after the notice was sent, the secured party must dispose of the collateral under Section 9—504. In the absence of such written objection the secured party may retain the collateral in satisfaction of the debtor's obligation. Amended in 1972.

See Appendix I for changes made in former text and the reasons for change.

Official Comment

Prior Uniform Statutory Provision: Section 23, Uniform Conditional Sales Act.

Purposes:

1. Experience has shown that the parties are frequently better off without a resale of the collateral; hence this section sanctions an alternative arrangement. In lieu of resale or other disposition, the secured party may propose under subsection (2) that he keep the collateral as his own, thus discharging the obligation and abandoning any claim for a deficiency. This right may not be exercised in the case of consumer goods where the debtor has paid 60% of the

price or obligation and thus has a substantial equity, and may be exercised in other cases only on notification to the debtor, unless the debtor has signed after default a statement renouncing or modifying his rights under this section, and (except in the case of consumer goods) to any other secured party who has given written notice of a claim of an interest in the collateral. In the latter case, notice must be given before the secured party receives the debtor's renunciation or before he sends his notice to the debtor. The secured party may keep the goods in lieu of sale on failure of anyone receiving notification to object within twenty-one days.

2. When an objection is received by the secured party he must then proceed to dispose of the collateral in accordance with Section 9—504, and on failure to do so would incur the liabilities set out in Section 9—507. In the case of consumer goods where 60% of the price or obligation has been paid the disposition must be made within 90 days after possession taken. For failure to make the sale within the 90-day period the secured party is liable in conversion or alternatively may incur the liabilities set out in Section 9—507.

In the absence of objection the secured party is bound by his notice.

3. After default (but not before) a consumer-debtor who has paid 60% of the cash price may sign a written renunciation of his rights to require resale of the collateral.

Cross References:

Sections 9—504 and 9—507(1).

Definitional Cross References:

"Collateral". Section 9—105.
"Consumer goods". Section 9—109.
"Debtor". Section 9—105.
"Knows". Section 1—201.
"Notice". Section 1—201.
"Person". Section 1—201.
"Purchase money security interest". Section 9—107.
"Receives" notification. Section 1—201.
"Rights". Section 1—201.
"Secured party". Section 9—105.
"Security interest". Section 1—201.
"Send". Section 1—201.
"Signed". Section 1—201.
"Written". Section 1—201.

§ 9—506. Debtor's Right to Redeem Collateral

At any time before the secured party has disposed of collateral or entered into a contract for its disposition under Section 9—504 or before the obligation has been discharged under Section 9—505(2) the debtor or any other secured party may unless otherwise agreed in writing after default redeem the collateral by tendering fulfillment of all obligations secured by the collateral as well as the expenses reasonably incurred by the secured party in retaking, holding and preparing the collateral for disposition, in arranging for the sale, and to the extent provided in the agreement and not prohibited by law, his reasonable attorneys' fees and legal expenses.

Official Comment

Prior Uniform Statutory Provision: Section 18, Uniform Conditional Sales Act.

Purposes:

Except in the case stated in Section 9—505(1) (consumer goods) the secured party is not required to dispose of collateral within any stated period of time. Under this section so long as the secured party has not disposed of collateral in his possession or contracted for its disposition, and so long as his right to retain it has not become fixed under Section 9—505(2), the debtor or another secured party may redeem. The debtor must tender fulfillment of all obligations secured, plus certain expenses: if the agreement contains a clause accelerating the entire balance due on default in one installment, the entire balance would have to be tendered. "Tendering fulfillment" obviously means more than a new promise to perform the existing promise; it requires payment in full of all monetary obligations then due and performance in full of all other obligations then matured. If unmatured obligations remain, the security interest continues to secure them as if there had been no default.

Under Section 9—504 the secured party may make successive sales of parts of the collateral in his possession. The fact that he may have sold or contracted to sell part of the collateral would not affect the debtor's right under this section to redeem what was left. In such a case, of course, in calculating the amount required to be tendered the debtor would receive credit for net proceeds of the collateral sold.

Cross References:

Sections 9—504 and 9—505.

Definitional Cross References:

"Agreement". Section 1—201.
"Collateral". Section 9—105.
"Contract". Section 1—201.
"Debtor". Section 9—105.
"Secured party". Section 9—105.
"Writing". Section 1—201.

§ 9—507. Secured Party's Liability for Failure to Comply With This Part

(1) If it is established that the secured party is not proceeding in accordance with the provisions of this Part disposition may be ordered or restrained on appropriate terms and conditions. If the disposition has occurred the debtor or any person entitled to notification or whose security interest has been made known to the secured party prior to the disposition has a right to recover from the secured party any loss caused by a failure

to comply with the provisions of this Part. If the collateral is consumer goods, the debtor has a right to recover in any event an amount not less than the credit service charge plus ten per cent of the principal amount of the debt or the time price differential plus 10 per cent of the cash price.

(2) The fact that a better price could have been obtained by a sale at a different time or in a different method from that selected by the secured party is not of itself sufficient to establish that the sale was not made in a commercially reasonable manner. If the secured party either sells the collateral in the usual manner in any recognized market therefor or if he sells at the price current in such market at the time of his sale or if he has otherwise sold in conformity with reasonable commercial practices among dealers in the type of property sold he has sold in a commercially reasonable manner. The principles stated in the two preceding sentences with respect to sales also apply as may be appropriate to other types of disposition. A disposition which has been approved in any judicial proceeding or by any bona fide creditors' committee or representative of creditors shall conclusively be deemed to be commercially reasonable, but this sentence does not indicate that any such approval must be obtained in any case nor does it indicate that any disposition not so approved is not commercially reasonable.

Official Comment

Prior Uniform Statutory Provision: None.

Purposes:

1. The principal limitation on the secured party's right to dispose of collateral is the requirement that he proceed in good faith (Section 1—203) and in a commercially reasonable manner. See Section 9—504. In the case where he proceeds, or is about to proceed, in a contrary manner, it is vital both to the debtor and other creditors to provide a remedy for the failure to comply with the statutory duty. This remedy will be of particular importance when it is applied prospectively before the unreasonable disposition has been concluded. This section therefore provides that a secured party proposing to dispose of collateral in an unreasonable manner, may, by court order, be restrained from doing so, and such an order might appropriately provide either that he proceed with the sale or other disposition under specified terms and conditions, or that the sale be made by a representative of creditors where insolvency proceedings have been instituted. The section further provides for damages where the unreasonable disposition has been concluded, and, in the case of consumer goods, states a minimum recovery.

A case may be put in which the liquidation value of an insolvent estate would be enhanced by disposing of all the debtor's property (including that subject to a security interest) in the liquidation proceeding and in which, if a secured party repossesses and sells that part of the property which he holds as collateral, the remainder will have little or no resale value. In such a case the question may arise whether a particular court has the power to control the manner of disposition, although reasonable in other respects, in order to preserve the estate for the benefit of creditors. Such a power is no doubt inherent in a Federal bankruptcy court, and perhaps also in other courts of equity administering insolvent estates. Traditionally it was not exercised where the secured party claimed under a title retention device, such as conditional sale or trust receipt. See In re Lake's Laundry, Inc., 79 F.2d 326 (2d Cir. 1935) and the remarks of Clark, J., concurring, in In re White Plains Ice Service, Inc., 109 F.2d 913 (2d Cir. 1940). It has been held that distinctions in results based on these distinctions in form have been made obsolete by this Article. In re Yale Express System, Inc., 370 F.2d 433 (2d Cir. 1966), 384 F.2d 990 (2d Cir. 1967).

2. In view of the remedies provided the debtor and other creditors in subsection (1) when a secured party does not dispose of collateral in a commercially reasonable manner, it is of great importance to make clear what types of disposition are to be considered commercially reasonable, and in an appropriate case to give the secured party means of getting, by court order or negotiation with a creditors' committee or a representative of creditors, approval of a proposed method of disposition as a commercially reasonable one. Subsection (2) states rules to assist in the determination, and provides for such advance approval in appropriate situations. One recognized method of disposing of repossessed collateral is for the secured party to sell the collateral to or through a dealer—a method which in the long run may realize better average returns since the secured party does not usually maintain his own facilities for making such sales. Such a method of sale, fairly conducted, is recognized as commercially reasonable under the second sentence of subsection (2). However, none of the specific methods of disposition set forth in subsection (2) is to be regarded as either required or exclusive, provided only that the disposition made or about to be made by the secured party is commercially reasonable.

Cross References:

Point 1: Sections 1—203, 9—202 and 9—504.

Definitional Cross References:

"Collateral". Section 9—105.
"Consumer goods". Section 9—109.
"Creditor". Section 1—201.

"Debtor". Section 9—105.
"Knows". Section 1—201.
"Notification". Section 1—201.
"Person". Section 1—201.
"Representative". Section 1—201.
"Rights". Section 1—201.
"Secured party". Section 9—105.
"Security interest". Section 1—201.

ARTICLE 10

EFFECTIVE DATE AND REPEALER

See Article 11 for Transition Provisions for those jurisdictions adopting the 1972 amendments.

§ 10—101. Effective Date

This Act shall become effective at midnight on December 31st following its enactment. It applies to transactions entered into and events occurring after that date.

Official Comment

This effective date is suggested so that there may be ample time for all those who will be affected by the provisions of the Code to become familiar with them.

§ 10—102. Specific Repealer; Provision for Transition

(1) The following acts and all other acts and parts of acts inconsistent herewith are hereby repealed:

(Here should follow the acts to be specifically repealed including the following:

Uniform Negotiable Instruments Act
Uniform Warehouse Receipts Act
Uniform Sales Act
Uniform Bills of Lading Act
Uniform Stock Transfer Act
Uniform Conditional Sales Act
Uniform Trust Receipts Act
Also any acts regulating:
Bank collections
Bulk sales
Chattel mortgages
Conditional sales
Factor's lien acts
Farm storage of grain and similar acts
Assignment of accounts receivable)

(2) Transactions validly entered into before the effective date specified in Section 10—101 and the rights, duties and interests flowing from them remain valid thereafter and may be terminated, completed, consummated or enforced as required or permitted by any statute or other law amended or repealed by this Act as though such repeal or amendment had not occurred.

Note

Subsection (1) should be separately prepared for each state. The foregoing is a list of statutes to be checked.

Official Comment

Subsection (1) provides for the repeal of present uniform and other acts superseded by this Act. Subsection (2) provides for the transition to the Code.

§ 10—103. General Repealer

Except as provided in the following section, all acts and parts of acts inconsistent with this Act are hereby repealed.

Official Comment

This section provides for the repeal of all other legislation inconsistent with this Act.

§ 10—104. Laws Not Repealed

[(1)] The Article on Documents of Title (Article 7) does not repeal or modify any laws prescribing the form or contents of documents of title or the services or facilities to be afforded by bailees, or otherwise regulating bailees' businesses in respects not specifically dealt with herein; but the fact that such laws are violated does not affect the status of a document of title which otherwise complies with the definition of a document of title (Section 1—201).

[(2) This Act does not repeal ....
....*, cited as the Uniform Act for the Simplification of Fiduciary Security Transfers, and if in any respect there is any inconsistency between that Act and the Article of this Act on investment securities (Article 8) the provisions of the former Act shall control.] As amended 1962.

Note: *At * in subsection (2) insert the statutory reference to the Uniform Act for the Simplification of Fiduciary Security Transfers if such Act has previously been enacted. If it has not been enacted, omit subsection (2).*

Official Comment

This section subordinates the Article of this Act on Documents of Title (Article 7) to the more specialized regulations of particular classes of bailees under other legislation and international treaties. Particularly, the provisions of that Article are superseded by applicable inconsistent provisions regarding the obligation of carriers and the limitation of their liability found in federal legislation dealing with transportation by water (including the Harter Act, Act of February 13, 1893, 27 Stat. 445, and the Carriage of Goods by Sea Act, Act of April 16, 1936, 49 Stat. 1207); the Warsaw Convention on International Air Transportation, 49 Stat. 3000, and Section 20(11) of the Interstate Commerce Act, Act of February 20, 1887, 24 Stat. 386, as amended. The Documents of Title provisions of this Act supplement such legislation largely in matters other than obligation of the bailee, e. g., form and effects of negotiation, procedure in the case of lost documents, effect of overissue, possibility of rapid transmission.

Doubts have been expressed whether Article 8 provides as complete protection on transfers of securities by fiduciaries as the Uniform Act for the Simplification of Fiduciary Security Transfers. The Editorial Board entirely favors the policy of simplifying fiduciary security transfers and believes that Article 8 soundly implements this policy. However, since the shorter Simplification Act has been so widely enacted and has been working satisfactorily, the Editorial Board recommends that it be retained [As amended in 1962].

Cross Reference:

Section 7—103.

*

ARTICLE 11

EFFECTIVE DATE AND TRANSITION PROVISIONS

This material has been numbered Article 11 to distinguish it from Article 10, the transition provision of the 1962 Code, which may still remain in effect in some states to cover transition problems from pre-Code law to the original Uniform Commercial Code. Adaptation may be necessary in particular states. The terms "[old Code]" and "[new Code]" and "[old U.C.C.]" and "[new U.C.C.]" are used herein, and should be suitably changed in each state.

This draft was prepared by the Reporters and has not been passed upon by the Review Committee, the Permanent Editorial Board, the American Law Institute, or the National Conference of Commissioners on Uniform State Laws. It is submitted as a working draft which may be adapted as appropriate in each state. The "Discussions" in Appendix II were written by the Reporters to assist in understanding the purpose of the drafts.

Section

§ 11—101. Effective Date

This Act shall become effective at 12:01 A.M. on ______, 19__.

§ 11—102. Preservation of Old Transition Provision

The provisions of [here insert reference to the original transition provision in the particular state] shall continue to apply to [the new U.C.C.] and for this purpose the [old U.C.C. and new U.C.C.] shall be considered one continuous statute.

§ 11—103. Transition to [New Code]—General Rule

Transactions validly entered into after [effective date of old U.C.C.] and before [effective date of new U.C.C.], and which were subject to the provisions of [old U.C.C.] and which would be subject to this Act as amended if they had been entered into after the effective date of [new U.C.C.] and the rights, duties and interests flowing from such transactions remain valid after the latter date and may be terminated, completed, consummated or enforced as required or permitted by the [new U.C.C.]. Security interests arising out of such transactions which are perfected when [new U.C.C.] becomes effective shall remain perfected until they lapse as provided in [new U.C.C.], and may be continued as permitted by [new U.C.C.], except as stated in Section 11—105.

§ 11—104. Transition Provision on Change of Requirement of Filing

A security interest for the perfection of which filing or the taking of possession was required under [old U.C.C.] and which attached prior to the effective date of [new U.C.C.] but was not perfected shall be deemed perfected on the effective date of [new U.C.C.] if [new U.C.C.] permits perfection without filing or authorizes filing in the office or offices where a prior ineffective filing was made.

§ 11—105. Transition Provision on Change of Place of Filing

(1) A financing statement or continuation statement filed prior to [effective date of new U.C.C.] which shall not have lapsed prior to [the effective date of new U.C.C.] shall remain effective for the period provided in the [old Code], but not less than five years after the filing.

(2) With respect to any collateral acquired by the debtor subsequent to the effective date of [new U.C.C.], any effective financing statement or continuation statement described in this section shall apply only if the filing or filings are in the office or offices that would be appropriate to perfect the security interests in the new collateral under [new U.C.C.].

(3) The effectiveness of any financing statement or continuation statement filed prior to [effective date of new U.C.C.] may

be continued by a continuation statement as permitted by [new U.C.C.], except that if [new U.C.C.] requires a filing in an office where there was no previous financing statement, a new financing statement conforming to Section 11—106 shall be filed in that office.

(4) If the record of a mortgage of real estate would have been effective as a fixture filing of goods described therein if [new U.C.C.] had been in effect on the date of recording the mortgage, the mortgage shall be deemed effective as a fixture filing as to such goods under subsection (6) of Section 9—402 of the [new U.C.C.] on the effective date of [new U.C.C.].

§ 11—106. Required Refilings

(1) If a security interest is perfected or has priority when this Act takes effect as to all persons or as to certain persons without any filing or recording, and if the filing of a financing statement would be required for the perfection or priority of the security interest against those persons under [new U.C.C.], the perfection and priority rights of the security interest continue until 3 years after the effective date of [new U.C.C.]. The perfection will then lapse unless a financing statement is filed as provided in subsection (4) or unless the security interest is perfected otherwise than by filing.

(2) If a security interest is perfected when [new U.C.C.] takes effect under a law other than [U.C.C.] which requires no further filing, refiling or recording to continue its perfection, perfection continues until and will lapse 3 years after [new U.C.C.] takes effect, unless a financing statement is filed as provided in subsection (4) or unless the security interest is perfected otherwise than by filing, or unless under subsection (3) of Section 9—302 the other law continues to govern filing.

(3) If a security interest is perfected by a filing, refiling or recording under a law repealed by this Act which required further filing, refiling or recording to continue its perfection, perfection continues and will lapse on the date provided by the law so repealed for such further filing, refiling or recording unless a financing statement is filed as provided in subsection (4) or unless the security interest is perfected otherwise than by filing.

(4) A financing statement may be filed within six months before the perfection of a security interest would otherwise lapse. Any such financing statement may be signed by either the debtor or the secured party. It must identify the security agreement,

statement or notice (however denominated in any statute or other law repealed or modified by this Act), state the office where and the date when the last filing, refiling or recording, if any, was made with respect thereto, and the filing number, if any, or book and page, if any, of recording and further state that the security agreement, statement or notice, however denominated, in another filing office under the [U.C.C.] or under any statute or other law repealed or modified by this Act is still effective. Section 9—401 and Section 9—103 determine the proper place to file such a financing statement. Except as specified in this subsection, the provisions of Section 9—403(3) for continuation statements apply to such a financing statement.

§ 11—107. Transition Provisions as to Priorities

Except as otherwise provided in [Article 11], [old U.C.C.] shall apply to any questions of priority if the positions of the parties were fixed prior to the effective date of [new U.C.C.]. In other cases questions of priority shall be determined by [new U.C.C.].

§ 11—108. Presumption that Rule of Law Continues Unchanged

Unless a change in law has clearly been made, the provisions of [new U.C.C.] shall be deemed declaratory of the meaning of the [old U.C.C.].

APPENDIX I

1972 OFFICIAL TEXT SHOWING CHANGES MADE IN FORMER TEXT OF ARTICLE 9, SECURED TRANSACTIONS, AND OF RELATED SECTIONS AND REASONS FOR CHANGES

GENERAL COMMENT ON THE APPROACH OF THE REVIEW COMMITTEE FOR ARTICLE 9 *

Article 9 of the Uniform Commercial Code was the first integration of the badly fragmented field of chattel security. It was, therefore, the most innovative of the articles of the Code, and many persons have indicated their belief that it is the Code's most valuable article.

Nevertheless, the fact that it was a first integration of complex problems led to some imperfection of the drafting. The Reporters have reported to the Committee many instances in which the drafting could be improved for clarity or to answer questions that can be posed that are not now clearly answered. Yet the outstanding result of Article 9 in practice has been that it has been gratifyingly successful; that no errors with serious consequences have been disclosed; and that the demands for change have been in relatively narrow areas. The Committee has therefore felt that it is not its responsibility, consistent with the terms of creation of the Permanent Editorial Board, to seek perfection where the Code appears to be working satisfactorily without significant problems in practice, for to do so would run the risk of opening up still further problems.

The Committee has in mind that at a minimum the changes finally adopted by it, the Permanent Editorial Board and the sponsoring organizations will take several years to enact in the 51 jurisdictions which have now adopted the Code, and that it

* The Review Committee for Article 9 prepared the following document to aid understanding of its recommendations. The discussion is by topics rather than by section as in the Reasons for Change and in the Comments. This document has not been approved by the Permanent Editorial Board for the Uniform Commercial Code or by the Council of the American Law Institute. This document is in the form approved at the last meeting of the Committee in October, 1970. Where the Permanent Editorial Board recommended changes in the statutory text which are inconsistent with the Committee's discussion, that fact is noted in footnotes.

would be a great mistake to introduce serious non-uniformity into any fundamental aspect of operations under Article 9. The Code must remain uniform in its day-to-day impact and operation even if there should be a significant period which may elapse before the Committee's ultimate proposals are adopted in all enacting jurisdictions. Thus the proposed changes must be compatible in operation with the existing Code, and the Committee has eschewed amendment merely for the sake of theoretical improvement where there was no pressing problem illustrated by non-uniform amendment or by substantial demand for change.

The proposed changes have been limited to Article 9 except in a few instances where an individual section of Article 1, 2 or 5 had to be changed to correspond with the changes in Article 9.

The Review Committee has not sought herein to follow the Permanent Editorial Board's past practice of commenting individually on non-uniform amendments, but has proposed a revision in depth of Article 9 to take into account the amendments and also criticisms that might lead to non-uniform amendments. To the extent that the Committee has not incorporated amendments in its proposals in exact words or in substance, they should be deemed disapproved as merely stylistic or mere matters of detail, or because the problem was handled in some other fashion, or because the Committee disagreed as a matter of policy.

There will be Reasons for Change and revised Comments to the sections changed. In addition, because the proposed changes in any given section may be related to several different problems, and the solution to one problem involves changes in more than one section, there is set forth below a Description of Proposed Changes from the 1962 Text, with Reasons Therefor, arranged by topic.[1]

[1] The Committee has had a difficult judgmental task in determining the length and the amount of detail in this Statement. To outline the problems considered in full detail with discussion of arguments pro and con and other possible solutions would have expanded this Statement to the length of a treatise. The Committee has sought to find an appropriate middle ground in succinct statements of the difficulties of the existing Code and the intended operation of suggested solutions. These should be understandable to persons basically familiar with the concepts of Article 9. There is an extensive literature in which the reader can find most of the problems discussed in more detail. It would not be possible in this Statement to cite all of the worthwhile discussions, but mention may be made of Gilmore, Security Interests in Personal Property (2 volumes, 1965); Coogan, Hogan and Vagts, Secured Transactions under the Uniform Commercial Code (2 volumes, 1963); Hawkland, A Transactional Guide to the Uniform Commercial Code (ALI–ABA Joint Committee on Continuing Legal Education, 2 volumes, 1964, (hereinafter referred to as ALI–ABA Joint Committee);

ARTICLE 9—1972 CHANGES

The topics discussed are the following:

A. Fixtures

B. Crops and Farm Products

C. Timber

D. Oil, Gas and Minerals

E. Intangibles, Proceeds and Priorities

F. Conflict of Laws

G. Motor Vehicles and Related Problems of Perfection

H. Matters of Scope

I. Filing

J. Default

A. Fixtures

A—1. Section 9—313 deals with the problem that certain goods which are the subject of chattel financing become so affixed or otherwise so related to real estate that they become part of the real estate, and the chattel interests would be subordinate to real estate interests except as protected by the priorities regulated by the section. Such goods are called "fixtures." Some fixtures also retain their chattel nature in that a chattel financing with respect to them may exist and may continue to be recognized. But this concept does not apply if the goods are integrally incorporated into the real estate.

A—2. Existing Section 9—313 states that the rules of the Section do not apply to goods incorporated in the structure in the manner of lumber, etc. This formulation of the problem would lead to the conclusion that these goods integrally incorporated into real estate are not fixtures. In contrast, the Committee's proposal defines "fixture" to include any goods which become so

Spivack, Secured Transactions (ALI–ABA Joint Committee, 1960); Davenport and Henson, Secured Transactions—ii, (ALI–ABA Joint Committee, 1966); and Uniform Commercial Code Handbook, (American Bar Ass'n, 1964). There have been published transcripts of three discussions in which various members of the Committee, Reporters, Consultants and other specialists have discussed in depth some of the problems here considered: A Practical Approach to Article 9 of the Uniform Commercial Code, 19 Bus. Law. 20 (1963); Advanced ALI–ABA Course of Study on Banking and Secured Transactions Under The Uniform Commercial Code (ALI–ABA Joint Committee, 1968); Problems of Lenders, Borrowers and Sellers Under the Uniform Commercial Code (1968). The extensive and valuable discussions of some of these problems in periodic legal literature may be located through the usual indices and also through Ezer, Uniform Commercial Code Bibliography and Supplements (ALI–ABA Joint Committee, 1966, 1967 and 1969).

related to particular real estate that an interest in them arises under real estate law and therefore, goods integrally incorporated into the real estate are clearly fixtures. This usage, in the Committee's opinion, conforms more clearly to pre-Code usage in most states than does the existing Section 9—313, and therefore permits a less confusing reference to pre-Code cases. There is no practical difference, however, because the Committee's proposal, like the existing Section 9—313, provides in substance that no security interest exists under Article 9 in ordinary building materials incorporated into an improvement on land.

A—3. Thus both the existing section and the Committee proposal recognize three categories of goods: (1) those which retain their chattel character entirely and are not part of the real estate; (2) ordinary building materials which have become an integral part of the real estate and cannot retain their chattel character for purposes of finance; and (3) the intermediate class which has become real estate for certain purposes, but as to which chattel financing may be preserved. This third and intermediate class is the primary subject of Section 9—313. The demarcation between these classifications is not delineated by this section.

A—4. Goods may be technically "ordinary building materials," e. g., window glass, but if they are incorporated into a structure which as a whole has not become an integral part of the real estate, the rules applicable to the ordinary building materials follow the rules applicable to the structure itself. The outstanding examples presenting this kind of problem are the modern "mobile homes" and the modern prefabricated steel buildings usable as warehouses, garages, factories, etc. In the case of the mobile homes, most of them are erected on leased land and the right of the debtor under a mobile home purchase contract to remove the goods as lessee will make clear that his secured party ordinarily has a similar right. See proposed paragraph (5)(b) of Section 9—313. In cases where mobile homes or prefabricated steel buildings are erected by a person having an ownership interest in the land, the question into which category the buildings fall is one determined by local law. In general, the governing local law will not be that applicable in determining whether goods have become real property between landlord and tenant, or between mortgagor and mortgagee, or between grantor and grantee, but rather that applicable in a three-party situation, determining whether chattel financing can survive as against parties who acquire rights through the affixation of the goods to the real estate.

A—5. The assertion that no security interest exists in ordinary building materials is only for the operation of the priority provisions of this section. It is without prejudice to any rights which the secured party may have against the debtor himself if he incorporated the goods into real estate or against any party guilty of wrongful incorporation thereof in violation of the secured party's rights.

A—6. In considering fixture priority problems, there will always first be a preliminary question whether real estate interests per se have an interest in the goods as part of real estate. If not, it is immaterial, so far as concerns real estate parties, as such, whether a chattel security interest is perfected or unperfected. In no event does a real estate party acquire an interest in a "pure" chattel just because a security interest therein is unperfected. If on the other hand real estate law gives real estate parties an interest in the goods, a conflict arises and this section states the priorities.

A—7. The general principle of priority announced in the proposed Section 9—313 is set forth in paragraph (4)(b). It is basically that a fixture filing gives to the fixture security interest priority as against other real estate interests according to the usual priority rule of conveyancing, that is, the first to file or record prevails. An apparent limitation to this principle set forth in paragraph (4)(b), namely that the secured party must have had priority over any interest of a predecessor in title of the conflicting encumbrancer or owner, is not really a limitation, but is an expression of the usual rule that a person must be entitled to transfer what he has. Thus, if the fixture security interest is subordinate to a mortgage, it is subordinate to an interest of an assignee of the mortgage even though the assignment is a later recorded instrument. Similarly if the fixture security interest is subordinate to the rights of an owner, it is subordinate to a subsequent grantee of the owner and likewise subordinate to a subsequent mortgagee of the owner.

A—8. A qualification of the rule based on priority of filing or recording is paragraph (4)(d), where rules of priority in filing or recording are preserved, but there is no requirement that as against a judgment lienor of the real estate, the prior filing of the fixture security interest must be in the real estate records. The Committee thought that the fixture security interest if perfected first should prevail even though not filed or recorded in real estate records, because a judgment creditor is not [2] a reliance creditor who would have searched records. Thus, even a prior filing in the chattel records should protect the priority of a fixture security interest against a subsequent judgment lien.

It is hoped that this rule will also have the effect of preserving a fixture security interest against invalidation by a trustee in bankruptcy. That would, of course, be the result under Section 60a of the Bankruptcy Act if the time of perfection of the fixture security interest were measured by the judgment creditor test applicable to personal property. It would not be the result if the time of perfection were measured by the purchaser test applicable to real estate. It is hoped that since the fixture security interest arises against the goods in their capacity as chattels, the bankruptcy courts will apply the judgment creditor test. But the effectiveness of the Committee's drafting to achieve its purpose cannot be known certainly until the courts adjudicate the question or until it is settled by amendment to Section 60a of the Bankruptcy Act.

The phrase "lien by legal or equitable proceedings" is taken from Section 70c of the Bankruptcy Act, and is intended to encompass all of the three ways in which judgment liens are there described.

It has been suggested that a fixture security interest perfected against lien creditors but subordinate to other real estate interests might be vulnerable to attack under Section 70e of the Bankruptcy Act. The interpretation involved is in dispute among bankruptcy scholars. In any event, those concerned with the question can avoid the issue by not taking advantage of the proposed statutory sanction of a filing in other than the real estate records.

It was also suggested that paragraph (4)(d) should provide for a 10-day grace period like those in Sections 9—301(2) and 9—312(4). But the Committee thought the practical need for such a provision was slight and did not justify the resulting complexities.

A—9. A special exception to the usual rule of priority based on time is the one of paragraph (4)(c) in favor of holders of security interests in factory and office machines, and in certain replacement domestic appliances, as discussed below. This is not as broad an exception as it might seem. To repeat, a fixture con-

[2] It has since been pointed out that in Pennsylvania, because of the use of the confession of judgment to obtain a real estate lien, the judgment creditor may be a reliance creditor.

flict is reached only if the goods are held as a matter of local law to have become part of the real estate. If so, the rule of paragraph (4)(c) operates only if the fixture security interest is perfected before the goods become fixtures. Having been perfected, it would of course have priority over subsequent real estate interests under the rule of paragraph (4)(b). Since it would in almost all cases be a purchase money security interest, it would also have priority over other real estate interests under the purchase-money priority of paragraph (4)(a), to be discussed in paragraph A—11. The rule is stated separately because the permitted perfection is by any method permitted by the article, and not exclusively by fixture filing in the real estate records. This rule is made necessary by the confusions of the law as to whether certain machinery and appliances become fixtures.

As an additional point, in the case of machinery, the separate statement of this rule makes clear that it is not overridden by the construction mortgage priority of subsection (6), as would have been true if reliance had been solely on the purchase money priority. The Committee considers that factory and office machines are not always financed as part of a construction mortgage, and that it is reasonable to expect the mortgagee to be alert to conflicting chattel financing of these machines.

A—10. As to appliances, the rule stated is limited to readily removable replacements, not original installations of appliances. To facilitate financing of original appliances in new dwellings as part of the real estate financing of the dwellings, no special priority is given to chattel financing of the appliances. The section leaves to other law of the state the question whether original installations are fixtures to which the protection accorded by this section to construction mortgages would be applicable. Likewise, it is recognized that (when not supplied by tenants) appliances in commercial apartment buildings are intended as permanent improvements, and no special rule is stated for appliances in that case. The special priority rule here stated in favor of chattel financing is limited to situations where the installation of appliances may not be intended to be permanent, i. e., replacement appliances in apartment units that are likely to be owner-occupied—those with not more than four family units.[3] The principal effect of the rule is to make clear that a

[3] The Permanent Editorial Board revised the Committee's draft to limit this rule, so far as it concerns replacement appliances, to consumer goods, i. e., those used for the buyer's personal or family purposes. The reference to buildings of four units or less was eliminated.

secured party financing occasional replacements of domestic appliances in dwellings, duplexes or similar units need not concern himself with real estate descriptions or records but may perfect by ordinary chattel filing; indeed, a purchase-money replacement in the buyer's own dwelling will be consumer goods, and perfection without filing will be possible. (The priority against the construction mortgage has no application to replacement appliances.)

A—11. The principal exception to the rule of priority based on time of filing or recording is a priority given in paragraph (4)(a) to purchase money security interests in fixtures as against *prior* recorded real estate interests, provided that the purchase money security interest is filed as a fixture filing in the real estate records before the goods become fixtures or within 10 days thereafter. This priority corresponds to one given in Section 9—312(4), and the 10 days of grace represents a reduction of the purchase money priority as against prior interests in the real estate under the present Section 9—313, where the purchase money priority exists even though the security interest is *never* filed.

It should be emphasized that this purchase money priority with the 10-day grace period for filing is limited to rights against *prior* real estate interests. There is no such priority with the 10-day grace period as against subsequent real estate interests. The fixture security interest can defeat subsequent real estate interests only if it is filed first and prevails under the usual conveyancing rule recognized in paragraph (4)(b).

A—12. The purchase money priority presents a difficult problem in relation to construction mortgages. The latter will ordinarily have been recorded even before the commencement of delivery of materials to the job, and therefor will be "prior" as against the fixture security interests. Present Section 9—313 (4) seeks to work this out by treating each advance under a construction mortgage as a separate subsequent loan, but then gets into difficulties of language as to the times of actual advance and the times of commitment. The Committee's proposal is far more favorable to real estate interests, because it provides that the purchase money priority does not apply as against construction mortgages. The latter will ordinarily be recorded before the filing of the fixture security interest, and therefore will have priority over the latter under the basic rule of paragraph (4)(b), and subsection (6) expressly states this subordination. It is the Committee's intention that the priority of a construction mortgage shall apply only during the construction period leading to the completion of the improvement; and that as to additions to the building made long after completion of the improvement, the construction priority will not apply simply because the additions are financed by the real estate mortgagee under an open end clause of his construction mortgage. In such case, the applicable principles will be those of paragraphs (4)(a) and (4)(b). The Committee has further provided that a refinancing of a construction mortgage has the same priority as the mortgage itself. The phrase "an obligation incurred for the construction of an improvement" is intended to cover both optional advances and advances pursuant to commitment, and to include advances for incidental expenses such as financing and title costs.[4]

A—13. The term "fixture filing" has been introduced and defined. It helps to emphasize a point that was intended but not clearly set forth in the existing Code—that when a filing is intended to give the priority advantages herein discussed against real estate interests, the filing must be for record in the real estate records and indexed therein, so that it will be found in a real estate search (except as stated in paragraphs A—8 to A—10).

A—14. The prior uniform provisions seemed to make it possible for a fixture supplier to retain a security interest against a contractor, to the possible surprise and deception of real estate interests. Proposed Section 9—313(4)(a) and (b) preclude such retention by a fixture supplier by denying priority to the security interest unless the debtor has an interest of record in the real estate.

A—15. The status of fixtures installed by tenants (as well as such persons as licensees and holders of easements) is unclear under the present Code. The Committee's proposal in paragraph (5)(b) is that if the debtor (tenant or other interest mentioned) has the right to remove the fixture as against a real estate interest, the secured party has priority over that real estate interest.

A—16. The Committee proposes a change in Section 9—302(1)(d) so that there will be no exception of fixtures from the rule that a purchase money security interest in consumer goods is perfected without filing, and thus good against lien creditors and the trustee in bankruptcy. See paragraph A—8. The fixture security interest would no longer have to be filed in all cases, but only in cases (for goods other than replacement appliances) in which priority against real estate parties is desired.

[4] The Permanent Editorial Board changed the text of Section 9—313(1)(c) to make clear that the term "construction mortgage" may cover land acquisition costs.

A—17. In summary, effort has been made by a fresh approach to provide substantive rules that should satisfy the legitimate interests of all parties. In the Committee's opinion, there remains a necessity to preserve the possibility of purchase money fixture financing notwithstanding the existence of mortgages on the real property. Real estate lending is typically long-term, and is usually done by institutional investors who can afford to take a long view of the matter rather than concentrating on the results of any particular case.

It is apparent that a rule which permits and encourages purchase money fixture financing, which in contrast is typically short term, will result in the modernization and improvement of real estate rather than in its deterioration and will on balance benefit long-term real estate lenders. Because of the short-term character of the chattel financing, it will rarely produce any conflict in fact with the real estate lender. The contrary rule would chill the availability of short-term credit for modernization of real estate by installation of new fixtures and in the long run could not help real estate lenders.

The reported difficulty in locating relevant fixture security interests applicable to particular parcels of real estate has been cured by new provisions as to real estate description in fixture filings, the indexing thereof, and other related provisions in Part 4 of Article 9.

The weightiest objection to present Section 9—313 was to the possibility that fixtures constituting material portions of the value of a building might come into the building subject to fixture security interests which might have priority over the rights of a construction mortgagee. The proposed treatment reverses the position of the existing Code and accords priority to the construction mortgagee.

The draft does not go as far as some of the non-uniform amendments, which would subject fixture filing to the burden of obtaining full "legal descriptions" of real estate and would deny fixture security interests priority against existing real estate parties who had not consented thereto, thus negating the purchase money concept. The Committee's changes move very substantially toward the views which gave rise to such amendments, but do not go all the way.

B. Crops and Farm Products

B—1. In contrast with dissatisfaction with the Code's classification of timber, discussed in Section C, no difficulty seems to have arisen with respect to the recognition in Section 2—107 and in the definition of goods in Section 9—105(1) that growing crops are goods and therefore chattels. This still leaves a possibility that real estate parties such as mortgagees or grantees may have some interest in them. Section 2—107(3) recognizes that a contract for sale of growing crops may have to be recorded in realty records for protection of the buyer against real estate rights, and the Committee has found no indication that this provision declaratory of the pre-Code law has caused any difficulty. Thus no change is proposed.

B—2. The assumption that crops are chattels was carried through in pre-Code law by the treatment of crop mortgages as chattel mortgages. In some states description of the land was required, not for the purpose of placing the crop mortgages into the real estate records, but primarily for identification.

B—3. The Code carries through this treatment. It treats an encumbrance of growing crops as a Code security interest for which a financing statement is required for perfection. A description of the land in the security agreement is required in Section 9—203(1)(a) and a requirement of description of the land in the financing statement is set forth in Section 9—402(1) and (3). Alternatives (2) and (3) of Section 9—401(1) add to the usual rule that a filing for farm products be at the residence of the debtor an additional rule that there be a filing on growing crops in the county where the land is situated, but these provisions do not indicate that the filing in the latter county should be in the real estate records. This is clear from two circumstances: The name of the applicable office is left blank in these two Alternatives of Section 9—401(1) rather than being specified (as is true for fixtures) as the office where a mortgage on the real estate concerned would be filed or recorded. Also, Alternative (1) for Section 9—401(1) contemplates filing for crops only in the office of the Secretary of State, and this could not be intended as a real estate filing.

B—4. Several states have departed from the Official Text by making it clear that the filing of a crop mortgage should be treated as a real estate filing and there is logic to this. But the Official Text seems to have worked satisfactorily without extensive criticism in other states, and the Committee has determined not to make so extensive a change in theory and practice as to require crop mortgages to be filed or recorded in the real estate records. To have made the change would have required the real estate on which crops are growing to be described with a particularity suitable for real estate records, as set forth in proposed

Section 9—402(5). But practice in crop mortgages has never been to require particularity in describing land on which crops are growing, and a substantial change in practice would have been required.

B—5. There may nevertheless be rights of real property mortgagees or grantees in growing crops if Code security interests in the crops have not been properly filed, comparable to the rights referred to in Section 2—107(3). The Committee has not thought it possible in the Uniform Code to deal with the diversity of existing state law on the interrelation of chattel security interests in growing crops and real estate interests.

B—6. Existing Section 9—204(4)(a) provides that no security interest in crops attaches under an after-acquired property clause to crops which become such more than one year after the security agreement, unless the agreement involves certain real estate transactions. The obvious purpose of this provision was to protect a necessitous farmer from encumbering his crops for many years in the future. The provision does not work because there is no corresponding limit on the scope of a *financing statement* covering crops, and under the Code's notice-filing rules the priority position of a security arrangement covering successive crops would be as effectively protected by the filing of a first financing statement whether the granting clause as to successive crops was in one security agreement with an after-acquired property clause or in a succession of security agreements. On the other hand the section does require an annual security agreement for crops even when the encumbrance on crops is agreed to as part of a long-term financing covering farm machinery and other assets. The provision thus appears to be meaningless in operation except to cause unnecessary paperwork, but it does introduce some element of uncertainty as to its purpose. The Committee proposes to eliminate it. See also the next paragraph.

B—7. The priority provision of Section 9—312(2) seems related to the same thinking as discussed in the preceding paragraph, and was intended perhaps to permit enabling crop financing, notwithstanding the existence of prior crop financing. However, subsection (2) is severely limited by a provision that the priority granted to current enabling financing applies only as against earlier interests which are six months or more in default. In the absence of any demand therefor, it would be inappropriate to attempt to create a revolutionary change in crop financing with a broad enabling priority to finance current crops. Such an attempt would probably be ineffectual in any event because lenders on machinery and real estate who claim crops could readily provide that it would be an event of default for the debtor to finance under the proposed enabling priority. The Committee has determined therefore to leave subsection (2) unchanged, even while recognizing that it is of little practical effect.

B—8. Several states have indicated their dissatisfaction with existing Section 9—302(1)(c), which provides a non-filing rule for purchase money security interests in farm equipment having a purchase price of $2500 or less, by reducing the amount. Authors on farm problems have suggested that the section is disadvantageous rather than advantageous to a farmer, because it in effect makes his farm machinery useless as collateral in view of prospective lenders' fear that there may be unfiled perfected security interests. The $2500 amount cannot be dismissed by lenders as immaterial, because substantial aggregates of collateral could have been financed by separate purchase money transactions each of which was no greater than $2500.

The Committee proposes that Section 9—302(1)(c) be eliminated. This makes unnecessary the reference to farm equipment in Section 9—307(2), which deals with the rights of certain buyers against perfected but unfiled security interests.

B—9. A comparable problem exists with respect to the provision of Section 9—307(1) which makes inapplicable to farm products the usual rule of that section protecting a buyer in ordinary course of trade who buys goods from a person engaged in selling goods of that kind and permitting him to take free of any security interest created by his seller. The existing section reflects pre-Code practice in distinguishing between a farmer's inventory and inventory of any other kind of businessman, but it must be seriously questioned whether the pre-Code practice is still sound under modern conditions. Feelings run strong on this issue, as evidenced by the fact that the New Mexico legislature amended other sections of the Code to make sure that waiver would not nullify the rule excluding farm products from Section 9—307(1), as had been held in *Clovis National Bank v. Thomas*, 425 P.2d 776 (N.M.1967). The federal government, an important farm lender, likewise insists on the preservation of its security interest on farm products as against buyers or auctioneers, in reliance on a federal rule independent of the state rule embodied in Section 9—307(1). See U. S. v. McCleskey Mills, Inc., 409 F.2d 1216 (5th Cir. 1969). On the other hand, strong representations have been made to the Committee by food processers and by authors who have written on farm problems under the Code that the inapplicability of Section 9—307(1) to farm products is anomalous and unfair. Georgia has amended the section to protect auctioneers of livestock. Recognizing that the Committee's recommendation is unlikely to induce the removal of the exception for farm products from Section 9—307(1) in all enacting jurisdictions, the Committee nevertheless recommends it as an optional amendment.[5] The Committee considered various possibilities, such as distinguishing between the first buyer and sub-buyers or between a buyer of an entire annual crop and multiple buyers of milk, eggs and the like. But no solution was found. Differences of opinion on basic policy seem to be so sharp that they are unlikely to be resolved by an appeal to the goal of uniformity.

B—10. There has been criticism of the unreality of the present Code's requiring filing against farmers at the "residence". This concept is most unsatisfactory for the reality of the modern corporate farm. The Committee proposes a new Section 9—401(6) to the effect that the residence of an organization is its place of business if it has one, or its chief executive office if it has more than one place of business. The rule is thus very similar in result to the rule as to the location of a debtor in proposed Section 9—103(3), although the latter rule starts as a matter of form with the assumption that the debtor has a place of business, with resort to residence as an exception, while the rule in Section 9—401(6) starts with residence, with the place of business as an exception for the corporate case. See paragraphs F—11 and F—12.

C. Timber

C—1. In contrast with its treatment of growing crops as chattels (paragraphs B—1 to 4 of this Statement), the present Code treats timber as real estate until cut. Section 2—107; note the omission of timber from the definition of "goods" in Section 9—105(1). This treatment has proved to be unsatisfactory, and many of the important timber-cutting states have changed it to provide that timber to be cut under a conveyance or contract for sale is "goods". One reason for this is to facilitate loans by banks on timber to be cut without complying with restrictions relating to real estate mortgages.

C—2. The Committee has decided to recommend adoption of this view. See proposed changes in Section 2—107 and the defi-

[5] The Permanent Editorial Board deleted the committee's optional recommendation. For states that are determined to change the present policy, it is recommended that this be done by deleting the words in Section 9—307 (1): "other than a person buying farm products from a person engaged in farming operations."

nition of "goods" in Section 9—105(1). The assertion in Section 9—204(2) that the debtor has no rights in timber until it is cut is proposed to be deleted together with the remainder of that subsection. See paragraph E—18 of this Statement.

C—3. Corresponding changes have been made in Section 9—401 (1) and in Section 9—402(1) and (3) to recognize a Code filing as to timber before it is cut, to require that filing to be in the real estate records of the county wherein is the land on which the timber is growing, and a new provision (Section 9—403(7)) requires the indexing thereof in real estate records. These requirements conform to the requirements for fixture filing (paragraph A—10 of this Statement). In contrast to growing crops (paragraph B—3 of this Statement), the Committee considers that standing timber has been traditionally a part of the real estate and it could not be assumed that it would normally be cut at any specific time of maturity. Therefore, the filing of security interests thereon has to be in real estate records. This filing will conform to the practice of recording timber deeds in real estate records.

D. Oil, Gas and Minerals

D—1. In general, the existing Code treats oil, gas and minerals as part of the real estate until they have been extracted from the land. See Section 2—107 and the definition of "goods" in Section 9—105(1). There is no provision for filing a security interest against minerals to be effective prior to their extraction from the land, because the Code does not recognize such a security interest and therefore there is no provision for a description of the land in a financing statement covering minerals.

In contrast, the Code requires a description of the land in a security agreement covering minerals to be extracted (Section 9—203(1)(b)). Though this has caused no particular difficulty, it is incongruous and the Committee proposes to delete it.

D—2. Various requests have been made that the Committee clarify the question whether well-drilling equipment is on the one hand fixtures or on the other hand mobile equipment of the kind referred to in Section 9—103. The Committee has sought to avoid encumbering the Code with details in response to inquiries of this nature. It seems fairly clear that well casings and related material that are removable are neither fixtures nor mobile equipment.

D—3. The most significant problems in reference to minerals relate to the split ownership characteristic of oil and gas drilling and the practice of selling the product at wellhead, with the proceeds of the resulting receivable being distributed pursuant to a division order and the proceeds being sometimes repledged to the holder of the oil and gas mortgage. Since the holders of fractional interests in a well or of production payments with respect thereto may be investors living anywhere, the problem of search to determine whether they have encumbered the receivables under the "chief place of business" rule of present Section 9—103 (1) or "location" rule of proposed Section 9—103(3) is a cumbersome one. It is proposed that all filings with respect to these receivables be authorized and required in the county where the well is, thus conforming to much pre-Code practice which assumed that everything related to sales at wellhead should be filed (if at all) in the real estate records in the county where the well is located. See proposed Sections 9—103(5) and 9—401(1).

The term "at wellhead" is intended to encompass all arrangements intended to cover sale of the product when it issues from the ground and is measured, without technical distinctions as to whether title passes at the "Christmas tree" or the far side of a gathering tank or some other point. "At minehead" is a comparable concept.

It is essential to note that this special rule is applicable only to security interests created by persons who have interests in the production from the well which attach when the mineral is extracted, not to buyers of the production who may have an underlying security interest on their inventory which may happen to attach to the mineral as inventory or at the wellhead or minehead when that is where the buyer acquires rights therein.

D—4. A related problem is whether, where the form of contract of sale at wellhead results in the minerals being sold by the persons who had the fractional interests, the purchaser of the product is protected from any encumbrances of the product, pursuant to Section 9—307(1) protecting buyers in ordinary course of business. The Committee has proposed in Section 1—201(9) to clarify the fact that buyers of minerals at wellhead or minehead are buyers in ordinary course of business because all persons who regularly sell the product under those circumstances are deemed to be engaged in selling goods of that kind, even though realistically the sellers may merely be investors.

E. Intangibles, Proceeds and Priorities

The Code has six classifications of intangibles, of which three are semi-intangibles embodied in pieces of paper, namely, documents, instruments and chattel paper (all defined in Section 9—105).

There are also three classifications of completely intangible rights, namely, accounts, contract rights and general intangibles (all defined in Section 9—106).

Proposals as to Semi-Intangibles

E—1. As to the classifications of semi-intangibles, experience has been generally satisfactory and few specific changes are proposed by the Committee.

E—2. A new rule is proposed in Section 9—103(4) as to the jurisdiction in which to file a financing statement relating to chattel paper, thus curing an omission in the present Code. See paragraphs F—14–15 of this Statement.

E—3. Another problem is the classification of money, which is frequently proceeds of original collateral and in some types of financing is itself original collateral. In the absence of an express specification, it could be argued that money is a general intangible, which would permit filing for a security interest therein. While this result would be so obviously unsound that it is doubted that a court would reach that result under the existing Code, it has been thought wise to provide expressly in Section 9—106 that the term "general intangibles" does not include money.

E—4. Sections 9—304(1) and 9—305 have been amended to state specifically that money may be pledged.

E—5. Section 9—304(1) makes clear that as to negotiable instruments, a non-possessory perfection of a security interest is not permitted except for temporary periods without either filing or possession under Sections 9—304(4) and (5). No doubt the failure of Section 9—304(1) to refer to temporary perfection for 10 days under the proceeds provisions of Sections 9—306(2) and (3) is a mere inadvertence of the present Code which the Committee proposes to correct, since this temporary perfection is also clearly contemplated. However, the present Section 9—306(2) and (3) go further and seemingly would permit perfection by filing continued indefinitely as to negotiable instruments which constitute proceeds of original collateral in which a security interest had been perfected by a filed financing statement which also claimed proceeds. The Committee considers this to be an error of the present Code and proposes to rectify it by providing in Section 9—306(3) that a security interest in proceeds does not persist beyond 10 days unless the security interest could have been directly filed against the proceeds as independent collateral. See also paragraphs E—22–23 of this Statement for other applications of this proposal.

E—6. The foregoing discussion should not apply to negotiable instruments which are essentially cash payment, i. e., money and checks. The proceeds security interest should apply to these cash proceeds so long as they are identifiable, and the proposed revision of Section 9—306(3) so provides.

E—7. The Committee considers that another anomaly exists between Sections 9—308 and 9—309. Under the present Code, a purchaser of negotiable instruments prevails against a conflicting proceeds claim thereto only if the purchaser is a holder in due course, which means that he cannot have notice of the conflicting claim to the instrument as proceeds of prior collateral. In contrast, the purchaser of chattel paper may under the second sentence of Section 9—308 defeat a claim to the chattel paper as proceeds of prior collateral even though the purchaser of the chattel paper knows that the specific paper is subject to the proceeds security interest. Thus, the holder of a negotiable note which is not part of chattel paper is governed by less favorable rules than the holder of an equally negotiable note which is part of chattel paper, or than the holder of non-negotiable chattel paper. The Committee has sought to remedy this by rewriting Section 9—308 so that the rights therein conferred on holders of chattel paper and non-negotiable instruments also apply to holders of negotiable instruments. Thus, holders of negotiable instruments which are proceeds may be protected under Section 9—309 if they are holders in due course, and if they do not qualify as holders in due course, they may nevertheless have the rights provided in clause (b) of Section 9—308. Section 9—308 has also been reorganized for clarity.

Proposals as to Intangibles

E—8. As to pure intangibles, i. e., intangibles not embodied in a piece of paper, the Committee considered the question whether three categories are necessary. The Committee concluded that the category "contract rights" is not necessary and proposes to eliminate the definition thereof from Section 9—106 and the references thereto in other sections. The Committee proposes to broaden the term "accounts" to include rights which under the present Code would be "contract rights" since there had not yet been complete performance by the person to whom the monetary obligation is owing.

The elimination of the term "contract rights" avoids the risk of inadvertent error where a financing statement is filed as to "accounts" and the designation turns out to be inapplicable because performance has not been completed, so that the collateral is at the stage of "contract rights."

E—9. This elimination also avoids proceeds problems and possible resulting priority questions where collateral was originally a "contract right" and after performance it became an "account." As a conforming change the Committee proposes to eliminate the statement in Section 9—306(1) that an account is proceeds of a contract right.

E—10. The only place in the 1962 Code where the concept of "contract right" was used to contrast with the concept of "account" was in Section 9—318(2). The Committee proposes to rewrite this subsection to draw the distinction between a right to money not yet completed by performance and a right so completed, without having to preserve the term "contract right" just for this purpose.

E—11. As to the substantive standard of Section 9—318(2) respecting the power of the debtor and assignor to modify a contract before performance to the prejudice of the assignee, the Committee has given consideration to the non-uniform New York amendment which limited the rights of the original parties so to do to cases where the assignee was not materially prejudiced. The Permanent Editorial Board in its Report No. 2 took the position that this New York change merely articulates a condition already included in the requirement of good faith contained in the Official Text. The Committee has considered Professor Gilmore's view that the change goes beyond articulation of the meaning implied in the term "good faith" (2 Gilmore, Security Interests in Personal Property, 1117—21 (1965) and his view disapproving the New York change on substantive grounds. The Committee adheres to the views expressed by the Permanent Editorial Board that the term "good faith" so limits the extent of the permissible change as not to make desirable adoption of the New York amendment.

E—12. The elimination of the term "contract right" requires the re-editing of the 1966 change approved by the Permanent Editorial Board in Section 9—106. The purpose of this change was to choose a single classification of intangibles for ship charters and all related rights. The classification chosen was "contract rights." With the elimination of this term, Section 9—106 has to be re-written to place all these rights in the category "accounts."

E—13. The term "account debtor" is defined in Section 9—105 (1)(a) as a person who is obligated not merely on an account but also on chattel paper, general intangibles (and under the present Code, contract rights). Present Section 9—318(3) speaks of account debtors and, therefore, would apply to the debtors under all of these types of intangibles, but its scope in protecting an account debtor who pays without notice that his obligation has been assigned is limited by the phrase "that the *account* has been assigned." The Committee proposes changes in Section 9—318(3) to afford the intended protection to all account debtors without limitation by the term "account."

E—14. The Committee considered the suggestion that there is not reason for distinguishing between "accounts" and "general intangibles," both of which are defined in Section 9—106. To eliminate the two separate terms would cause great drafting difficulty in preserving Article 9's present useful distinction in the inclusion in its scope of the sale of monetary obligations represented by accounts, contract rights and chattel paper and in the exclusion from its scope of the sale of non-monetary rights known as general intangibles. Therefore, the Committee proposes to retain the two terms.

E—15. A more limited suggestion is to rectify the definitions of "accounts" and "general intangibles." It has been pointed out that some obligations for payment of money are not accounts, but are general intangibles, because the definition of "account" is limited to rights to payment for goods sold or leased or for services rendered. Thus, rights to payments constituting royalties for use of patents, copyrights, etc., or for exhibition rights to moving pictures and television, seemingly constitute general intangibles rather than accounts. A potential source of error by inadvertence thus arises. The Committee nevertheless concluded that it would be undesirable to broaden the definition of accounts to include all rights for the payment of money, because too many standard forms of agreement use the term "accounts" and reflect intention of the parties to include only traditional accounts arising from the sale of goods or services, and not miscellaneous rights for the payment of money.

Attachment and Perfection

E—16. The Code has two important concepts, attachment of security interests and perfection thereof. Attachment is in a sense defined in present Section 9—204. In general, it means the time when a security interest becomes enforceable between the primary parties because there is agreement, value has been furnished, and the debtor has rights in the collateral to which the agreement can apply.

The term "perfection" is not defined by the Code. In general, it means the point at which a security interest becomes good against third parties when there is also attachment. The additional requirements for perfection beyond the requirements for attachment are set forth in Sections 9—302 to 9—305. It would be unwise to attempt a formal definition of perfection, because of the subtlety of the problems involved in rights against many groups of third persons.

E—17. The Committee deemed the existing treatment of the concept of attachment in Section 9—203 and Section 9—204 (which also affects perfection, as indicated) to be unsatisfactory. Section 9—203 contains a statute of frauds which must be satisfied in order that the security interest be enforceable against the debtor or third parties, yet the combined treatments of attachment and perfection indicate that there could be perfection without compliance with the statute of frauds. This obvious anomaly would be corrected by proposed revisions of these sections. The three elements of attachment have been transferred to Section 9—203 from Section 9—204 and there combined with the requirement of a writing (except when the secured party is in possession), which thus becomes part of the concept of attachment.

E—18. The Committee proposes to eliminate from Section 9—204 existing subsection (2) which states various times at which the debtor acquires right in certain kinds of collateral. Some of these statements, notably the statement in paragraph (d) that the debtor has no rights in an account until it comes into existence, have played an unfortunate part in confusing the application of bankruptcy law to Code security interests. None of them seems to serve any purpose.

Proceeds

E—19. Existing Section 9—203 provides that the word "proceeds" is a sufficient description in a security agreement of collateral constituting proceeds. This seems to imply that a claim to proceeds must be based on a term in a security agreement. Yet Section 9—306(2) contemplates that the secured party will have a right in proceeds following sale of original collateral, and this right is not made dependent on the existence of a term in the security agreement. The Committee proposes to resolve this apparent inconsistency by deleting the provision in Section 9—203 and substituting proposed Section 9—203(3) to the effect that a reference to proceeds is not necessary in the security agreement to give the secured party the automatic rights provided by Section 9—306.

The Committee does not consider that this converts the security interest in proceeds into a non-contractual or statutory lien presenting problems under the Bankruptcy Act, for the security interest is still an aspect of the basically contractual security interest under the security agreement.[6]

E—20. Another anomaly appears in the provisions of present Section 9—306(3)(a) that the 10-day right to proceeds recognized by subsection (3) may be continued without further perfection if the filed financing statement covering the original collateral also covers proceeds. The form of financing statement set forth in Section 9—402(3) makes provision for a claim to proceeds, and the forms prescribed by most state filing officials contain a box by which a claim to proceeds may be made simply by checking the box. The claim is almost universally made in the case of inventory which is to be sold or receivables which are to be collected, thus producing proceeds; and the claim is very frequently made routinely in the cases of other collateral. There was deleted from Section 9—306 in the prior history of the Code a statement that a claim to proceeds constituted permission to sell, and a court has recently held that such a claim does not constitute permission to sell. Vermilion County Production Credit v. Izzard, 111 Ill.App.2d 190 (1969).

E—21. Since the claim to proceeds is routinely made, there seems to be no reason that it be required to be made in the financing statement in order to continue the perfection of the security interest in proceeds. If there is a claim to proceeds as presumed intent of the security agreement, notice of the claim comes from the claim to the original collateral claimed in the financing statement, and nothing is accomplished by the routine checking of a box. Many privately printed forms have the box checked in the print itself. The Committee therefore proposes in Section 9—306(3) to eliminate any requirement for claiming proceeds specifically.

E—22. A problem appears as to whether perfection by filing as to original collateral automatically perfects as to *all types* of proceeds. One such problem has already been discussed, namely whether the claim to proceeds perfected by filing as to original collateral negates the basic provision of the Code that one can-

[6] The Permanent Editorial Board amended the text of Section 9—203(3) to make it clear that the assertion thereof is a matter of presumed intent and is "unless otherwise agreed."

not file as to instruments. See paragraph E—5 of this Statement. A provision has been added to Section 9—306(3) making it clear that the proceeds claim does not permit filing as to instruments.

E—23. A similar problem arises when the appropriate place for filing as to accounts resulting from sale of inventory collateral under Section 9—103 is in another state where the debtor is located. The revision of Section 9—306(3) makes it clear that the perfection of the security interest in the accounts as proceeds will not last more than 10 days unless there is a filing as to the accounts in the appropriate jurisdiction.

E—24. Another problem is whether the extension to proceeds of the filed security interest in original collateral (perfected by checking a box as in the existing Code or automatically perfected as in the Committee's proposal, paragraph E—21 of this Statement) really serves the intended function of public notice of the security interest. Under the existing Section 9—306 the security interest in proceeds extends without limit through cash in the debtor's hand to repeated cycles of the business so long as the proceeds can be traced, unless sometimes terminated by priority rules like those in Sections 9—308 and 9—309 or by receipt of the cash by the secured party. See In re Platt, 58 Berks Co.L.J., 275, 6 UCC Rep. 275, 281 (Referee, E.D.Pa.1966), aff'd 257 F.Supp. 478 (E.D.Pa.1966). Thus a financing statement on automobiles could theoretically operate to perfect a security interest in an oil painting traded in for an automobile or bought with the cash proceeds thereof. Several possibilities of limiting the notice as to a security interest in proceeds resulting from a filing as to original collateral present themselves. The Committee has determined not to limit the proceeds claim applicable to direct trade-ins, but to limit the claim to proceeds which have been acquired through cash proceeds to cases where the description of collateral in the financing statement indicates the types of property constituting these remote proceeds. See the proposed revision of Section 9—306(3).

E—25. Several cases have held that the proceeds of insurance on destroyed or damaged collateral are not proceeds of the collateral within the meaning of Section 9—306(1). The Committee considers the result of these cases to be unsatisfactory and proposes to revise Section 9—306(1) to make clear that insurance proceeds are proceeds. But a possibility exists that, under a contract with an insurer through a co-insurance clause or a loss payable clause, a junior secured party will be entitled to receive the insurance proceeds, and the revision has been so drafted that the Code's proceeds rules will not operate to disturb contractual arrangements.

E—26. Proceeds frequently find their way to bank or deposit accounts, and Section 9—306(4)(b) expressly contemplates that the secured party will have a security interest in the proceeds so deposited. But existing Section 9—104(k) provides that Article 9 does not apply to deposit accounts and similar accounts. The Committee proposes to amend the treatment in Section 9—104 so that it is not inconsistent with the recognition of proceeds security interests in these accounts, and to add in Section 9—105 a new definition of "deposit account" to cover all the types of accounts intended to be covered by these provisions.

E—27. Section 9—306(4) deals with cash proceeds, and is intended to substitute for difficult problems of tracing a provision that the secured party has a perfected security interest in cash proceeds (and deposit accounts derived therefrom) received within ten days before the institution of insolvency proceedings by or against the debtor, less the cash proceeds paid over to the debtor within the ten days. In the study of this subsection in connection with adoption of the Code in California, certain imperfections in the drafting were pointed out, and California amended the provision. The Committee recommends adoption of a clarifying amendment based on the California amendment. No significant change of substance is intended.

Priorities between Security Interests

E—28. In many ways Article 9 facilitates the perfection of security interests. This ease of perfection brings to the fore numerous problems of priority between security interests, or between secured parties and other persons. Each proposed change may affect priority problems by affecting the time or the method by which perfection is achieved, as in the proposed limitations of perfection as to proceeds, paragraphs E—5, 22, 23 of this Statement. Certain priority problems are discussed elsewhere in this statement—in Part A as to Fixtures; in Part E as to Sections 9—308 and 9—309; and in Part I as to the effect of lapse.

Some of the major problems of priorities are discussed in the following paragraphs.

A number of problems relate to the purchase money priority as to inventory in Section 9—312(3).

E—29. The existing Section 9—312(3) does not state how often the notification by the purchase-money financer to earlier financers of record must be given. The Committee's revision will make the notice effective for five years, by analogy to the duration of a financing statement.

E—30. The existing subsection requires notice to any secured party known to the purchase money secured party, regardless of perfection by the former. This emphasis on knowledge is inconsistent with the general disregard of knowledge as an operative fact in priority issues between secured parties in Article 9. It is also an ineffective provision, because if the purchase money secured party fails to give the necessary notice to obtain priority over the earlier unperfected secured party under subsection (3), the purchase money secured party will nevertheless obtain priority under Section 9—312(5) as the first to file or perfect. Finally, the existing subsection might be read to deny the contemplated priority to the purchase money secured party against another secured party to whom he has given proper notice unless he also gave notice to all other persons entitled to notice. The Committee proposes a revised Section 9—312(3) to rectify these points.

E—31. Under the existing Code there is uncertainty as to the relationship of Section 9—312(3) to the period of temporary perfection for 21 days of an interest in inventory without either filing or possession under Section 9—304(5), typically coming through release of a document of title to the debtor following a documentary draft or letter of credit transaction. One could conceivably take the view that the security interest under Section 9—304(5) has priority against an earlier filed security interest during the 21 days. If so, one would then have to decide either (a) that the security interest, if filed before the end of the 21 days, continued to have priority without a notice; or (b) that the notice under Section 9—312(3) had to be given before the end of the 21 days; or (c) that the priority reversed after the 21 days. None of these results seems consistent with the obvious purpose of Section 9—312(3) to permit a first-filed inventory financer to rely on his priority in making advances unless he receives notice of a competing purchase money security interest before the debtor receives the inventory. Accordingly, the Committee's proposed revision of Sections 9—304(5) and 9—312(3) requires the notice to be given before the debtor receives the inventory, and if this is done, the purchase money security interest obtains a priority and retains it so long as the interest remains perfected. The Committee's inquiry to several leading banks engaged in foreign trade indicated that this rule would not seriously inconvenience them, and the rule will certainly clarify the position of these banks and all other lenders when acting as general inventory financers.

E—32. The existing Code leaves it uncertain whether the filing required of a consignor under Section 2—326(3) includes a required notice to prior inventory financers of the consignees under Section 9—312(3). An underlying inventory financer assured of his first-filed position could as readily be deceived by consigned merchandise as he could by new inventory subject to the purchase money inventory financing priority, in the absence of notice. Accordingly, the Committee proposes a new Section 9—114 to require the consignor to give the same notices as a purchase money secured party, to attain priority against earlier-filed security interests in inventory of the debtor. These provisions are limited to true consignments. The usual rules apply to consignments that are deemed to be security interests. See Section 1—201(37).

E—33. Another group of priority problems relates to the basic priority rules of Section 9—312(5). This subsection contains two principal rules. Paragraph (a) is a first-to-file rule where both competing security interests are perfected by filing. Paragraph (b) is a first-to-perfect rule when either of the security interests is or both of them are perfected otherwise than by filing. A traffic rule is provided by existing Section 9—312(6) to the effect that a continuously perfected security interest shall be treated for the purpose of the foregoing rules as if at all times perfected in the manner it was first perfected. The problems raised have been the subject of an enormous legal literature. They are complicated by the unforeseeable effect of the temporary perfection of security interests in proceeds under Section 9—306 without filing, and by speculation as to whether a secured party could claim that his security interest was originally perfected without filing under this rule even though the security interest in proceeds was claimed in his filing as to the original collateral. They are further complicated by the question whether different rules would apply when a financing statement was drawn to cover, e. g., inventory and its proceeds (which would include accounts) and when it was drawn to cover inventory and accounts.

E—34. The Committee is convinced that to settle these questions the present paragraphs (a) and (b) of Section 9—312(5) must be replaced by a single rule. The Committee proposes a revised Section 9—312(5) and the elimination of existing Section 9—312(6). Together with this treatment should be noted the fact that an interest in proceeds automatically arises from a filed security interest in original collateral under the proposed revision of Section 9—306(3), subject to the limitations therein stated and discussed in paragraphs E—5, 22, 23 of this Statement. New proposed Section 9—312(6) makes it clear that subject to these limitations the filing as to original collateral constitutes a filing as to proceeds.

E—35. The new rule ranks conflicting perfected security interests by their priority in time, dating back to the respective times when without interruption the security interests were either perfected or were the subjects of appropriate filings.

E—36. Perhaps the most debated subject under Article 9 has been the question whether between conflicting security interests a priority as to original collateral confers a priority as to proceeds. On this topic the discussions as to proceeds (paragraphs E—19–21, E—24, of this Statement) and as to rules of Sections 9—312(5) and (6) (paragraphs E—33–34) are relevant. See also the following paragraphs E—37–38.

E—37. In the case of collateral other than inventory, e. g., equipment, assume that A has a prior purchase money security interest and B, although he was the first to file, has a junior security interest. If the equipment was sold and proceeds resulted, it seems clear that the policy favoring the purchase money secured party in Section 9—312(4) should give A the first claim to the proceeds. This is so even though the security interests will have been perfected simultaneously when the proceeds arose and the debtor acquired rights therein. The present Code does not provide for this result clearly, if at all, and the Committee proposes an amendment to Section 9—312(4) to accomplish it.

E—38. Proper policy is much less clear when the collateral involved is inventory and proceeds consisting of accounts. (Policy as to other types of receivables as proceeds is expressed in Sections 9—308 and 9—309. See paragraph E—7 of this Statement.) Accounts may be financed by some financers without prior involvement in the inventory, and some have argued that one who provides financing at the early inventory stage of the cycle of a business, which involves greater risk, is certainly to be preferred to one who provides financing only at the later stage of the cycle, and that a prior or only claim to inventory must therefore carry through to accounts as proceeds. But others feel that accounts financing is overall more important than inventory financing, and the desirable rule is one which makes accounts financing certain as to its legal position. Even if both competing financers are involved in the inventory, a purchase money priority in inventory may not represent the order of priority in time on accounts, which may be far more important than inventory financing in the particular case. A suggestion that the purchase money priority carry through to accounts if the notice provided by Section 9—312(3) has been given to accounts financers has seeming merit, but in the Committee's view it has two major difficulties: (a) The purchase-money priority as to inventory would be difficult to trace into accounts if the affected inventory was only part of the goods sold. (b) Accounts financing is intricate, and not easily or safely terminated on receipt of an inventory purchase-money notice. Prevailing practice seems to be for accounts financers to require covenants against competitive inventory financing, and to declare a default unless any inventory financier giving a purchase-money notice agrees not to assert a claim to the accounts. The Committee believes that where a financing statement as to accounts financing is filed first (with or without related inventory financing), the security interest in accounts should not be defeated by any subsequent claim to accounts as proceeds of an inventory security interest which was filed later. This result is accomplished by the absence in Section 9—312(3) of any priority rule carrying forward the purchase-money priority to proceeds which are accounts in contrast to the proposed addition to Section 9—312(4) (paragraph E—37); by the revised priority rule in Section 9—312(5); and by proposed Section 9—312(6) to the effect that a date of filing as to original collateral also defines the date of filing as to proceeds. Correspondingly, a financing statement as to inventory (carrying with it a claim to proceeds) which is filed first will under the same provisions have priority over a later-filed security interest in accounts.

Priority of Future Advances

E—39. Certain recent cases in lower courts raised the question whether a single financing statement would be effective to perfect more than one advance on the collateral described, when the later advances were not under a future advance clause of a single security agreement but were under later security agreements and were not contemplated at the time of the original agreement. Some of the reasoning makes the matter depend on whether the original debt was fully paid off or was still in existence at the time of the later advances. Coin-O-Matic Service Co. v. Rhode Island Hospital Trust Co., 3 UCC Rep. 1112 (Super. Ct.R.I.1966); In re Merriman, 4 UCC Rep. 234 (Referee, S.D. Ohio 1967). In another case, in which the point was not directly involved, Safe Deposit Bank & Trust Co. v. Berman, 393 F.2d 401 (1st Cir. 1968), the court cited In re Rivet, 4 CCH Instal.

Credit Guide Par. 97,858, 4 UCC Rep. 1087 (Referee, E.D.Mich. 1967), which was in harmony with the first two cases cited but was subsequently reversed (see paragraph E—40). The Committee disapproves this line of cases, and believes that an appropriate financing statement may perfect security interests securing advances made under agreements not contemplated at the time of the filing of the financing statement, even if the advances then contemplated have been fully paid in the interim. Under the notice-filing procedures of the Code, the filing of a financing statement is effective to perfect security interests as to which the other required elements for perfection exist, whether the security agreement involved is one existing at the date of the filing with an after-acquired property clause or a future advance clause, or whether the applicable security agreement is executed later. Indeed, Section 9—402(1) expressly contemplates that a financing statement may be filed when there is no security agreement. In the Committee's opinion, the references to after-acquired property clauses and future advance clauses in Section 9—204 are limited to security agreements. This section follows Section 9—203, the section requiring a written security agreement, and its purpose is to make clear that confirmatory agreements are not necessary where the basic agreement has the clauses mentioned. The section has no reference to the operation of *financing statements* under the Code's notice filing system.

E—40. The Committee considered drafting a provision emphasizing its disagreement with the *Coin-O-Matic* line of cases, but concluded that the existing Code is clear enough, and should not be disturbed just to overrule some lower court cases. The *Rivet* case, cited by the First Circuit, has since been reversed by In re Rivet, 6 UCC Rep. 460 (E.D.Mich.1969).

E—41. The priority of future advances against an intervening party has been the subject of much discussion and disagreement.

E—42. Where both interests are filed security interests, the first-to-file rule of present Section 9—312(5)(a) or the corresponding proposed revision is clearly applicable.

E—43. While, under the existing Code, the position of an intervening pledgee in reference to a subsequent advance by an earlier-filed secured party is debatable, the proposed unified priority rule of Section 9—312(5)(a) (paragraph E—35 of this Statement) would indicate that the subsequent advances by the first-filed party have priority, and subsequent advances under a security interest perfected by possession likewise have priority over an intervening filed security interest. These priority rules are expressly stated in proposed Section 9—312(7). That proposal also deals with the rare case of the priority position of a subsequent advance made by a secured party whose security interest is temporarily perfected without either filing or possession, against an intervening secured party. Since there is no notice by the usual methods of filing or possession of the existence of the security interest, the subsequent advances rank only from the actual date of making unless made pursuant to commitment.

E—44. In the Committee's view different problems exist with reference to the status of subsequent advances when the intervening party is a judgment creditor. He is not directly part of the Code's system of priorities. There should be a limit on the power of a debtor and secured party to squeeze out a judgment creditor who has successfully levied on a valuable equity subject to a security interest, through later enlargement of the security interest by an additional advance, unless that advance was committed in advance. Accordingly, the Committee proposes to clarify the present uncertain state of the law by a new Section 9—301 (4) providing that a lien creditor does not take subject to a future advance made more than 45 days after he becomes a lien creditor unless it is made "pursuant to commitment." [7] A definition of the quoted phrase is proposed in Section 9—105(1). The 45-day period corresponds to a similar protection of advances made after the filing of tax liens in the Federal Tax Lien Act of 1966.

E—45. A similar problem arises where the intervening party is a buyer of the collateral subject to the security interest. While buyers must necessarily take subject to rights of secured parties, the Committee feels that the buyer should take subject to future advances only to the extent that they are given pursuant to commitment or within the period of 45 days after the purchase but not later than the time that the secured party acquires knowledge of the purchase. The Committee has so proposed in Section 9—307(3).

Effect of Knowledge on Priorities of Lien Creditors and Buyers

E—46. Although knowledge of unperfected security interests does not in general affect the rights of other secured parties, knowledge of unperfected security interests does under Section 9—301 preclude the attainment of priority by lien creditors and

[7] The Permanent Editorial Board amended Section 9—301(4) to continue the priority of the subsequent advances beyond the 45 days and until the secured party acquires knowledge of the judgment lien.

buyers (other than buyers in ordinary course of trade protected by Section 9—307(1)).

E—47. This result as to judgment creditors was severely criticized in California, which totally eliminated the element of knowledge, and gave priority to a person who became a lien creditor before the security interest was perfected, subject to a 10-day grace period. The Committee recommends the California change in Section 9—301(1)(b) but without the grace period, and a conforming change in Section 9—301(3). The Committee considered an intermediate position, making the decisive time for the existence of knowledge the point at which the creditor gave credit, not the point at which he became a lien creditor. But that position was severely criticized as inappropriate for tort creditors and as encouraging a race of diligence.

E—48. Similar considerations might be argued to be applicable to buyers referred to in Section 9—301(1)(c) and (d). However, there seems to be no criticism of these provisions or demand for change, and the Committee has concluded not to recommend any change.

Circular Priority

E—49. The elimination of the element of knowledge from Section 9—301(1)(b) (paragraph E—47) removes one possibility of circular priority. Other such possibilities are resolved by the proposals as to lapse (paragraphs F—23 and I—7). But circular priority can still arise in other situations. The Committee considered a general provision on the subject, but decided that the situations were too infrequent and diverse and the proper solutions too unclear.

F. Conflict of Laws

F—1. Section 9—103 dealing with interstate problems of perfection has occasioned much discussion, and the relationship between subsections (3) and (4) has been criticized as unclear by several courts. The committee has been aided by discussion with Professor Willis L. M. Reese, the Reporter of the Restatement Second of Conflict of Laws, who recently completed his work on cognate material. The Committee proposes a complete revision of Section 9—103, and related changes in Sections 1—105 and 9—102.

F—2. Section 9—103 was drafted in the light of the uncertainty whether the Code would be widely adopted, and the emphasis was on conflicting rules of law and a desire to make the Code rules applicable where such a result was justified under general principles. Today, when 51 jurisdictions have adopted the Code, situations of actual conflict in rules of law within the ambit of the Code will be few, and the emphasis may shift to the question of certainty as to where to file in order to perfect security interests.

Scheme of the Section

F—3. Section 9—102(1), basically intended as a scope provision on the coverage of Article 9, seems to deal with conflict of laws matters by its phrase "so far as concerns any personal property and fixtures within the jurisdiction of this state." The Committee proposes to delete this phrase and a related cross-reference, thus making Section 9—102 silent on conflicts of laws problems.

F—4. The Committee proposes to delete references to "validity" of a security interest appearing sometimes but not consistently in existing Section 9—103.

F—5. The effect of the foregoing changes will be to have questions as to the creation and validity of security interests determined according to the conflict of laws rules in Section 1—105. The cross-reference in that section to Article 9 should be amended to exclude the reference to Section 9—102. Questions as to perfection and the effect of perfection or non-perfection of security interests—i. e., questions as to the rights of third parties—will be determined by Section 9—103.

F—6. The basic rule of proposed Section 9—103, expressed in paragraph (1)(b), is believed to be that intended but not articulated in the existing section, namely, that perfection and the effect of perfection or non-perfection of a security interest are governed by the law (including the conflict of law rules) of the jurisdiction where the collateral is when a conflicting claim comes into existence.[8] That state will ordinarily look for this purpose to the law of the state where the collateral was when the events claimed to constitute perfection occurred, but the section provides special rules in the cases discussed in the next ten paragraphs.

[8] The text being submitted in the present printing changes this formulation to refer to the law of the jurisdiction where the collateral is when the last event occurs on which is based the assertion that the security interest is perfected.

Special Rules as to Jurisdiction Controlling Perfection The 10-Day [9] Rule

F—7. The relationship of the 30-day removal period in existing Section 9—103(3) to the four month removal period in that subsection is imperfectly stated. Paragraph (1)(c) of the revision limits the provision to purchase money security interests in goods and changes the 30 days to 10 days after the debtor receives possession, conforming to Sections 9—301(2) and 9—312(4).[9] The revision also makes clear that the function of the period is to have perfection controlled by the law of the state into which the parties intend to remove the collateral within that period, rather than the law of the state where the collateral is when the security interest attaches. The four month period discussed below is irrelevant to this purpose, and is placed in paragraph (1)(d). During the 10-day period,[9] perfection is fully governed by the law of the state to which the parties intend to remove the collateral, whether or not it is removed to that state within the 10 days.[9] If it is so taken, then perfection continues to be governed by the law of that state. If it is not so taken, the question of perfection reverts at the end of the 10 days [9] to the state where the collateral then is.

Paragraph (1)(c) described in this paragraph does not apply to the cases described in the next two paragraphs.

Motor Vehicles

F—8. Paragraph (2)(b), which to some extent covers the same ground as the existing subsection (4), excludes from the general rule of paragraph (1)(b) collateral covered by a certificate of title. Paragraph (2)(d) is a partial limitation on paragraph (2)(b). These paragraphs are discussed in the treatment of motor vehicles, Part G of this Statement.

Intangibles and Mobile Goods

F—9. Subsection (3) covers essentially the same ground as existing subsections (1) and (2). They are intended to determine the jurisdiction whose law governs perfection in the case of intangibles which have no location in fact, and mobile chattels which have no permanent location. Several substantial changes have been made therein as described in paragraphs F—10 to F—16 below.

[9] The Permanent Editorial Board changed the 10 days back to 30 days.

F—10. The existing subsection (1) provides that a financing statement covering accounts shall be filed in the jurisdiction where the assignor keeps his records concerning them. Existing subsection (2) provides that a financing statement covering general intangibles shall be filed in the jurisdiction of the chief place of business of the debtor. The use of separate tests for accounts and general intangibles has been criticized, because many groups of receivables may include items falling into both categories. See paragraph E—15 of this Statement. Moreover, in the type of accounts financing known as factoring, the assignment is without recourse and the debtor may keep no records concerning the accounts after transfer. A debtor's place of business may be objectively more ascertainable than the place where he keeps accounts, and will not be confused by questions on the latter test arising from remote access computer operations. Accordingly, the Committee proposes to combine the two tests into the place of business test applicable to general intangibles. See also the next paragraph.

F—11. The Committee recommends that the place of business used where there is more than one be redesignated "chief executive office" instead of "chief place of business." This will emphasize that what is intended is the executive office rather than either a statutory office or the site of the largest plant. While occasional situations of uncertainty could still arise, it is doubtful that there could be more than two possibilities in any case, and it would be easy to play safe by filing in both. See proposed paragraph (3)(d).

F—12. Provision has also been added to paragraph (3)(d) covering cases where the debtor is an individual or otherwise has no place of business, in which case his location is deemed to be his residence.

F—13. The coverage of the proposed subsection (3) would be extended to cover containers used on vehicles. The coverage would extend to inventory held for lease as well as inventory out on lease, thus accepting a California amendment designed to achieve consistency with the definition of inventory in Section 9—109(4).

F—14. The coverage of subsection (3) would be extended by proposed subsection (4) to cover perfection of non-possessory security interests in chattel paper. The existing Code has no express provision as to the jurisdiction within which to file for chattel paper, thus presumably referring the matter to the phrase in existing Section 9—102: " . . . this Article applies so far as concerns any . . . property . . . within the jurisdiction of this state. . . . " But location is an unsatisfactory test for a filing as to chattel paper, because the paper's location is not visible to a prospective searcher for filings, it is readily transportable, and there may be more than one executed copy of the chattel paper.

F—15. The Committee considered whether proposed subsection (3) should govern the state of perfection of security interests in chattel paper completely, as it does in the case of general intangibles and accounts, but concluded to draw a distinction between the conflict of laws rule for non-possessory perfection of a security interest in chattel paper (to which Section 9—103(3) is proposed to be made applicable) and the rule for pledge or possessory perfection thereof (which is left to the general principles of subsection (1), which prescribes the law of the state where the chattel paper is in fact). The basis for the distinction was the fact that in a non-possessory perfection the problem is essentially similar to that applicable to accounts and general intangibles, but with a possessory perfection there are frequently local transactions between a local unit of a debtor and a local financer, and in that event the governing considerations should not be referred to the law of a possibly remote jurisdiction where the chief executive office of the debtor might be.

F—16. The coverage of subsection (3) on its face applies even to foreign airplanes, in contradiction to the rules provided by the Geneva Convention, to which the United States and many important foreign countries are parties. This contradiction is recognized in existing Comment 6. The textual problem would be avoided by the Committee proposal to create an exemption from the Code's filing rules for matters controlled by treaty. See paragraph G—4 of this Statement.

F—17. Since the place of filing under subsection (3) is independent of the location of the collateral, it is not affected by the 10-day rule [9] (paragraph F—7, supra) or the four-month rule (paragraph F—19, infra). The only occasion for refiling in cases subject to subsection (3) would be in cases of removal of the debtor's location, for which the Committee proposes a new paragraph (3)(e) providing for refiling within four months after removal, in keeping with the comparable rule applicable to removal of collateral (paragraph F—19, infra). The Committee reaffirms the Permanent Editorial Board's rejection in Report No. 2

[9] The Permanent Editorial Board changed the 10 days back to 30 days.

of the New York subsection (6) denying the need to refile on removal of the chief place of business.[10]

F—18. Proposed paragraph (3)(c) covers the ground of existing optional subsection (5) and the third sentence of existing subsection (2). It covers the case where the jurisdiction of the location of the debtor is not a domestic jurisdiction and does not provide for filing as to the collateral. In that case, perfection by filing "in this state" is authorized if this state bears an appropriate relation to the transaction.[11] Perfection by notification to the account debtor is also authorized, except in a case of chattel paper covered by subsection (4). The Committee reaffirms the Permanent Editorial Board's rejection in Report No. 2 of the New York amendment proposing perfection without filing or notification.

The Four Months Rule on Removals

F—19. To the rules which indicate the jurisdiction whose law governs perfection and the effect of perfection or non-perfection in the first instance (paragraphs F—3 to F—16, supra) the state whose law governs under paragraphs (1)(b) and (2)(b) (paragraph F—6, supra) adds its own local rule requiring refiling within a stated period. A provision of this kind appears in existing subsection (3) and the Committee proposes refinements thereof in proposed paragraphs (1)(a) and (2)(c). The 10-day rule (formerly 30 days) [12] has been removed from these provisions and placed in paragraph (1)(c), paragraph F—7, supra, to avoid any possible reading that the two provisions are somehow interconnected. The debated question under the existing section as to the relationship between the four months rule of existing subsection (3) and the certificate of title provisions of existing subsection (4) is answered by provisions that proposed subsection (1) does not apply to goods covered by subsection (2). On subsection (2) see paragraphs G—10 to G—15 of this statement.

F—20. The state whose law controls the conflict and adds its local rule of refiling is referred to in the draft as "this state." If the litigation were to arise in a forum in another jurisdiction

10 The provision of New York's subsection (6) dealing with removal of the place where the records of accounts are kept becomes unnecessary under the Committee's proposal to eliminate this rule as to the place of filing for accounts.

11 The Permanent Editorial Board changed Section 9—103(3)(c) to provide for filing against a foreign debtor on this set of facts in the jurisdiction where its major executive office in the United States is located.

12 The Permanent Editorial Board changed the 10 days back to 30 days.

which recognized that the law of the state where the conflict arose controlled, it would read the Code as if it were situated in "this state."

F—21. Proposed paragraph (1) (d) refines the rule requiring refiling within four months of removal into "this state" to cover the case where the existing filing in another jurisdiction would remain effective for less than four months. The period allowed within which to refile in "this state" is the shorter of the remaining period of effectiveness in the original jurisdiction or four months, whichever period first expires. If the secured party could not locate the removed collateral in time to refile in the new jurisdiction in a shortened period, he could file a continuation statement in the original jurisdiction, thus giving himself the full four months to locate the collateral and refile in the removal jurisdiction.

F—22. Existing subsection (3) has been construed by some to require some affirmative act of reperfection in the removal state, even though the original security interest was perfected without filing (e. g., a purchase money security interest in consumer goods under Section 9—302(1)). The proposed revision makes clear that no affirmative act of perfection is needed under such circumstances. On the other hand, existing subsection (3) fails to deal with filing which achieves a status beyond perfection under Section 9—307(2) for purchase money security interests in consumer goods, and the proposed paragraph (1) (d) (iii) treats this point expressly in a manner comparable to the rules described in the preceding paragraph.

F—23. The effect of lapse after four months of a security interest perfected without local filing on rights arising within the four months is not specifically covered in the present Code, but is referred to in existing Comment 7 to Section 9—103. Subparagraph (1) (d) (i) of the proposed revision makes clear that after lapse the security interest is deemed unperfected as against a person who became a purchaser after the removal. First National Bank of Bay Shore v. Stamper, 93 N.J.Super. 150, 225 A.2d 162 (1966) held in substance that a buyer during the four month period was a converter of the car, at the suit of a bank whose security interest was perfected in the state from which the car was removed. The case entirely fails to consider the effect of the subsequent lapse of the security interest of the bank for failure to reperfect after the four months. While technically the conversion was complete at the moment of purchase, it is to be hoped that the proposed clarification of the effect of lapse will cause similar cases to be analyzed in the future in terms of priority, not of conversion. (Other aspects of the *Stamper* case are discussed in paragraph G—15 of this Statement).

F—24. Terms like "removed" and "kept" in Section 9—103 imply an idea of permanence, not just passing through the jurisdiction. They thus embody the same concept as the phrase "kept in this state" in present Section 9—103(3).

F—25. New subsection (5) relating to oil, gas and mineral financing, is discussed in paragraph D—4 of this Statement.

G. Motor Vehicles and Related Problems of Perfection

The integration of the provisions of Section 9—302 as to motor vehicles and related types of collateral has been much criticized, and has led to numerous non-uniform amendments.

G—1. Paragraphs (c) and (d) of Section 9—302(1) provide that filing is required for motor vehicles required to be licensed, notwithstanding the absence of a filing requirement for purchase-money security interests in consumer goods. (The Committee proposes to omit paragraph (c) relating to farm equipment. See paragraph B—8 of this Statement.) The term "required to be licensed" is not as clear as it might be and the Committee proposes to change it to "required to be registered."

G—2. The Committee considered changing the word "motor vehicle" to "vehicle" or "collateral," but concluded to leave this to the developing policy of individual states. Over-the-road commercial trailers and semi-trailers are not involved, because the paragraph applies only to consumer goods; but public policy and administration by motor vehicle commissioners may vary as to such items as boat trailers and mobile homes. Public policy as to mobile homes ought not now to be frozen in a uniform Code. As they get larger, they cease to be mobile and are not regularly moved over the highways; thus it is not clear that registration like other trailers is the appropriate legal scheme.

G—3. The present formal inconsistency between the required filing for motor vehicles in subsection (1) and the declared inapplicability of the Code's filing requirements to certificated vehicles in subsection (3)(b) would be resolved in proposed revised subsection (3), which makes it clear that it overrides filing requirements of subsection (1).

G—4. The existing and the proposed revised subsection (3) recognize other state and federal schemes for filed public notice in lieu of Code filing. The Committee proposes an additional category of a filing scheme adopted under a treaty to which the United States is a party, which is intended to refer particularly to the Convention on the International Recognition of Rights in Aircraft (Geneva Convention). (See paragraph F—16 of this Statement.)

G—5. Existing subsection (3) provides two alternatives. Alternative A was intended to refer to "complete" certificate of title laws for motor vehicles or the like. Alternative B was intended to apply to certificate of title laws which were not mandatory but permissive at least in part, and to convert them into mandatory laws by force of the Code (except as to inventory security interests, see the next paragraphs). Neither form of drafting has proved to be satisfactory. Many states have chosen to make express references to their statutes intended to be described, instead of leaving the matter to the Code's effort at a universal description. Moreover, permissive certificate of title laws have been replaced in general by "complete" laws, and the device of Alternative B is no longer necessary. The Committee therefore submits a revision of subsection (3) which recognizes that each state will list its own statutes intended to be covered. There will be great diversity because of the existence of central filing statutes in some states for cattle and the like; and because there is considerable variation as to the applicability of the certificate of title device to boats and boat trailers, mobile homes, farm tractors, construction machinery and the like.

G—6. The Committee has revised subsection (4), partly for clarity, into new subsections (3) and (4).

G—7. The revision also covers a point which is dealt with in the existing section only in Alternative B for subsection (3), namely, that Code filing should be required for security interests in inventory, because there is no reason that the Code's carefully worked out provisions for inventory to protect buyers in Section 9—307(1) and as to rights to proceeds in Section 9—306 should be confused by perfection under a certificate of title or other non-Code system. While the Code's sponsoring organizations cannot amend certificate of title laws, it is to be hoped that certificate of title laws will be amended or construed so that the Code filing system for inventory will be exclusive and will not be duplicated by the certificate of title system. There are indications in recent case law that the courts are already so construing certificate of title laws.

G—8. The requirement in proposed paragraph (3)(b) for Code filing for security interests in inventory is limited to inventory situations controlled by state law. It is to be hoped that a state will avoid double filing by avoiding any requirement that inventory security interests created by dealers be shown on certificates of title. The Code cannot change the provisions of the Federal Aviation Act requiring all security interests in aircraft (including inventory security interests) to be filed under the federal system and making that system exclusive. Fortunately, it has been held that Section 9—307(1) of the Code should apply to the rights of buyers in ordinary course of airplane inventory, although the federal system lacks a provision comparable to that section. Northern Illinois Corp. v. Bishop Distributing Co., 284 F.Supp. 121 (W.D.Mich.1969).

G—9. The proposed revisions of subsections (3) and (4) of Section 9—302, like the existing subsections, apply only to "property subject to" the statutes referred to. Hence the substitute forms of public notice recognized in subsection (3) do not apply to the perfection of security interests in proceeds other than such property. Such security interests must be perfected under Code rules. Compare the proposed revision of Section 9—306(3), discussed in paragraphs E—5, 22, 23 of this Statement.

G—10. The above discussion of Section 9—302 does not deal with the conflict of law problems arising from the use of certificates of title. These problems are covered by existing Sections 9—103(3) and (4), the interrelationship of which has caused much confusion and criticism; and by revisions proposed in new Section 9—103(2).

G—11. Proposed paragraph (2)(b) deals with collateral covered by a certificate of title. In general, a security interest perfected by notation on a certificate of title continues perfected so long as the certificate is outstanding or until the collateral is registered in another jurisdiction, notwithstanding removing the collateral into another state and keeping it there for more than four months. The Committee thus affirms In re White, 266 F.Supp. 863 (N.D. N.Y.1967), and later cases in their interpretation of the relationship between the certificate of title provision of existing subsection (4) and the four months rule of existing subsection (3).

G—12. If, however, reregistration occurs in another jurisdiction to which the collateral is removed while a certificate of title is left outstanding the security interest perfected by notation on the certificate of title remains perfected for four months after removal under Section 9—103(2)(c). This provision adopts the four months of proposed Section 9—103(1)(c), discussed in paragraphs F—19-21 of this Statement, for there is no reason why rights on removal of collateral perfected on a certificate of title should receive less favorable treatment than rights in collateral otherwise perfected.

G—13. Under the Uniform Certificate of Title Act and the Uniform Vehicle Code the four month period of continued perfection after removal commences from the time the first certificate of title is issued in the state to which the collateral is removed, not from the time of removal. The Committee has chosen to commence the four months with removal, to keep the periods of Sections 9—103(1)(d) and 9—103(2) consistent. It is hoped that if the Committee's recommendations are approved, the National Conference of Commissioners on Uniform State Laws will conform its Uniform Act, and that the National Committee on Uniform Traffic Laws and Ordinance will conform its Uniform Vehicle Code.

G—14. Possibilities exist that a certificate of title may be issued in a state to which collateral is removed, and that because of fraudulent affidavits or other fraudulent devices the certificate will fail to disclose a security interest perfected in another state, whether that state does or does not have a certificate of title law. Suppose under these circumstances that rights of a third party arise in reliance on the "clean" local certificate of title. What protection should the issuing state give to rights which arose in reliance on its own certificate of title as against rights which were perfected elsewhere but not shown thereon? The Committee treats this problem in proposed Section 9—103(2)(d).

G—15. The Committee believes that more protection should be given to the local "clean" certificate of title than was accorded in First National Bank of Bay Shore v. Stamper, 93 N.J.Super. 150, 225 A.2d 162 (1966). The court there felt that it was required to recognize a security interest perfected in New York for four months after removal of the car into New Jersey, even though a New Jersey buyer had innocently bought the car within the period in reliance on a New Jersey certificate of title not showing the security interest. The court gave weight to the four month provision of existing Section 9—103(3) rather than to the condition of the New Jersey title under existing Section 9—103 (4). It reasoned that Section 9—103(4) provides that perfection is governed by the law of the jurisdiction which issued the certificate, and that New Jersey recognizes foreign security interests after removal within the limits set by Section 9—103(3). This reasoning gives no scope to the introduction to Section 9—103 (4): "Notwithstanding subsections (2) and (3)." (The lapse aspect of the *Stamper* case is discussed in paragraph F—23 of this Statement.)

The Committee's structure in its proposed Section 9—103(2) (b) follows the structure of existing Section 9—103(4) and thus would not in itself preclude the *Stamper* reading. But the Committee believes that consumer buyers who give value and take delivery without knowledge of the security interest in situations like *Stamper* should be protected in their reliance on local clean certificates of title. Its proposed Section 9—103(2)(d) so provides.

G—16. The Committee's proposed treatment does not apply to rights acquired while a distinctive certificate of title is outstanding as described in this paragraph.

The Uniform Certificate of Title Act and Uniform Vehicle Code provide that where the vehicle comes from a state which did not require that security interests be noted on a certificate of title, the local certificate first issued shall be distinctive and shall contain the legend: "This vehicle may be subject to an undisclosed lien." If the Department receives no notice of a security interest within four months after issuance of such a certificate of title, such a certificate may be reissued without the legend. Other certificate of title laws contain comparable provisions.

H. Scope Questions

H—1. Several questions have been raised as to the status of security interests in beneficial interests in trusts and estates. These are typically not commercial collateral, and a requirement of filing with respect thereto seems inappropriate and might act as an entrapment of secured parties who would fail to analyze the collateral as a general intangible. It would be possible to exclude this kind of collateral from Article 9 by a provision in Section 9—104, but the Committee recommends leaving this collateral subject to the general rules of security law provided by Article 9 but with an exclusion from filing by a provision in Section 9—302(1).

H—2. Certain receipts issued by large grain dealers do not literally qualify as "documents" under Article 9, because the definition in Section 9—105(1) refers back to the definition of "document of title" in Section 1—201 (which requires issuance by a bailee) rather than to the provision in Section 7—201(2) which makes receipts issued by owners under specified conditions substantially the equivalent of warehouse receipts. The Committee proposes to clarify this by amendment of the definition in Section 9—105(1) to refer to both earlier sections.

H—3. When the Code was drafted, railway equipment trusts were excluded from Article 9 by Section 9—104(e) in response to the argument that they were extremely specialized securities and the market in them should not be disturbed by new rules of law. The exclusion has subsequently been criticized as unsound. Opinion among railway authorities whom the Committee consulted was divided, but few of those suggesting retention had any specific reason therefor. The Committee proposes to delete the exclusion. The effect will be that railway equipment trusts will become subject to the general rules of security law provided by Article 9. It should be noted, however, that these rules are almost always subject to agreement of the parties. Ordinarily filing under Article 9 will not be required by reason of Section 9—302(3), because filing is controlled by Section 20(c) of the Interstate Commerce Act.

I. Filing Problems

Substantial changes have been made in Part 4 of Article 9 dealing with filing. The purpose of some of these appears in the discussions of Fixtures, Timber and Oil, Gas and Minerals in Parts A, C and D of this Statement.

I—1. Far-flung railroad and other public utility corporations may have signalling systems or other chattels strung along their rights of way, and the chattels may be encumbered with a combined real estate and chattel indenture on the whole utility plant. Where the chattels are non-fixtures, the Code would require one or at most two chattel filings. But where the chattels may be fixtures, the Code would require filing in each county where the chattels exist, and with a fixture filing including real estate descriptions. This is clearly unduly onerous. Numerous states have attempted to relieve against the burden by a variety of non-uniform amendments to various sections. The Committee has accepted from some of these amendments the concept of "transmitting utility," for which it proposes a definition in Section 9—105. It proposes a Section 9—401(5) making all filings for transmitting utilities in the office of the Secretary of State. This filing constitutes a fixture filing (id.) but need not contain a description of the real estate (Proposed Section 9—402(5)).

I—2. There has been much criticism of the provision in Section 9—403(2) which terminates the effectiveness of a financing statement which states a maturity date 60 days after the stated maturity date. There seems to be no reason why a stated maturity date should terminate the effectiveness any sooner than a financing statement which does not state the date. Even though the transaction has a maturity date, the application of this provision can be avoided simply by not stating the maturity date in the financing statement. The requirement of a financing statement and the form in Section 9—401(1) and (3) do not require the maturity date to be stated even if there is one. The Committee therefore proposes to eliminate the special rule in Section 9—403(2) applicable when a maturity date is stated, and to leave all financing statements operative for five years.

I—3. There has been some objection to the five year period, on the theory that where the duration of a transaction is longer than five years, the financing statement should be good for the duration of the transaction. The Committee has accepted this view in the cases of real estate mortgages which constitute fixture security interests and transmitting utilities (Proposed Section 9—403(6)).

I—4. The Committee has chosen, however, not to recommend this change generally, or in accordance with suggestions that it be made for all combined real estate and chattel mortgages, or all combined mortgages of corporations, or of listed corporations. The burden of chattel filing, even fixture filing, is not too great in other than transmitting utility situations. The theory of the provisions for effectiveness of financing statements under the present Code is that (except for the two cases just mentioned which involve filing in offices other than the usual offices), they last for five years unless continuation statements are filed, and that the files are therefore self-clearing. A filing officer who arranges his filings by years can clear the filings of any year automatically after five years. This would not be possible if there were exceptional cases running more than five years. Moreover, searchers would have to go back to the effective date of the Code if there could be valid long-term filings.

I—5. This operating scheme raises operating questions when effectiveness of the financing statement has been extended by continuation statements, and the Committee has proposed in Section 9—403(3) that the filing officer should work out a physical annexation of the financing statement to the continuation statement to insure the preservation of those from an earlier year whose vitality has been continued.

I—6. Other detailed suggestions have been made in Section 9—403 designed to permit preservation of microfilm instead of the actual financing statements, and on the other hand to preserve the record of filings beyond the point where termination statements have been filed. Evidence of a perfection of a security interest in the past may be necessary for some time after the termination because of litigation involving bankruptcy preferences, fraudulent conveyances, or other related types of issues.

I—7. The Code's provisions as to the effect of lapse have occasioned debate. Existing Section 9—403(2) provides that upon lapse the security interest becomes unperfected, but this statement does not explicitly indicate the result when there was a right junior to the lapsed security interest. It has been argued that since the junior party was charged with notice of the lapsed security interest, he should remain junior. Comment 3 to Section 9—403 and a corresponding Comment to Section 9—103 take the position, however, that the holder of a junior security interest defeats the holder of a lapsed security interest (see also paragraph F—23 of this Statement), but neither Comment deals with the position of a buyer who bought before the lapse. The Committee proposes in Sections 9—103(1)(d)(i) and 9—403(2) to make clear that after the lapse purchasers—i. e., buyers and secured parties—have priority over the lapsed security interest. The negative inference is that judgment lienors remain subordinate.[13]

I—8. To avoid the question whether a financing statement may lapse during a bankruptcy or other insolvency proceeding, the Committee has proposed in Section 9—403(2) that the financing statement does not lapse during the proceeding and that the secured party has a minimum of 60 days after termination of the proceeding within which to refile under Article 9. Refiling, however, requires a new financing statement signed by the debtor; to avoid this, the secured party may file a continuation statement before the end of the five-year period.

I—9. A perpetual question has existed whether in filing against sole proprietorships or partnership debtors one may use a trade name, or whether the individual name of a proprietor is required, and whether the names of partners are required to be shown as debtors. There is substantial lack of uniformity in state instructions to filing officers with respect to these matters. The Committee hopes to clarify these issues by its proposed Section 9—402(7) that one files against a partnership by the name in which it is known and that one files against an individual by his individual name. Neither the names of partners nor a trade name for individuals or partnerships need be shown. The Committee has considered the California provision that a trade name should be shown, but it seems to create too great a risk of insufficient filing, because a secured party may not know of a trade name sometimes informally used by a debtor. Trade name statutes

[13] In the case of Section 9—403(2), the Permanent Editorial Board extended this rule to judgment lienors.

vary so widely in scope and in the effects of compliance or noncompliance that it has not seemed feasible to tie any requirements as to trade names to the existence of such statutes.

I—10. There is presently much difference in view as to whether a secured party is under a duty to refile where he knows of and particularly where he has consented to a debtor's transfer of the property to a new debtor. The Committee has sought to standardize practices in these respects by proposing in Section 9—402(7) that no refiling is necessary following a transfer of the collateral by the debtor. This provision is, of course, limited to the continued perfection of the security interest as to collateral transferred by the original debtor. If additional collateral is assigned after the transfer, even though the mechanism is an after-acquired property clause under a security agreement which the new debtor has assumed, it seems clear that a secured party could not be safe without a filing against the new debtor.

I—11. A similar question arises with respect to the debtor's change of name. The Committee has sought to settle the matter by proposing in Section 9—402(7) that the filing is not effective as to new collateral after four months after the change of name unless the financing statement is refiled. The provision is so drafted that it will also apply to certain corporate readjustments.

I—12. As to all of these problems of filing, the Committee is desirous of avoiding loss of security interests on mere technicalities. Accordingly, the Committee proposes to take existing Section 9—402(5) as to minor errors that are not seriously misleading, move it to the end of Section 9—402 as subsection (8), and to make it clearly applicable to all provisions of that section.

I—13. Title companies have complained with some justice that practices are too loose in the use of the term "fixture" in financing statements as a catchall phrase as in descriptions like "all machinery, equipment, tools and fixtures situated at 14 Digby Road, Chicago." This leads to a question whether a fixture filing is intended and whether a possible objection to the title to the real estate mentioned should be noted. This complaint, coupled with the fact that the Committee's proposals make clear that a fixture filing should be indexed in the real estate records, has induced the Committee to propose blanks in the sample form in Section 9—402(3) for designating unmistakably when a financing statement is intended to be filed as a fixture filing, and to require a statement to that effect in filings covered by Section 9—402(5).

I—14. After considering developing practice and the needs of filing officers for uniformity, the Committee proposes adoption of a non-uniform amendment made in some states which differentiates in the filing fees between financing statements in a form prescribed by the state filing officer and filing statements in other forms. Section 9—403(5). See also Section 9—404(3).

I—15. It is proposed to amend subsection (1) of Section 9—402 so that only the debtor need sign a financing statement. However, subsection (4) would be amended to require both parties to sign an amendment to a financing statement, thus precluding the possibility that either party could unilaterally prejudice the secured party's rights under a filed financing statement.

J. Default

J—1. Existing Section 9—501(3)(c) permits variation of the provisions of Section 9—505(1) with respect to compulsory disposition of collateral, but not the provisions of Section 9—505(2) or 9—504(3). This could be construed to mean that where the secured party proposes to retain the collateral in satisfaction of the obligation under Section 9—505(2), or fixes a time of sale under Section 9—504(3), a debtor who acquiesces cannot waive the thirty day waiting period of Section 9—505(2) or the reasonable notification of Section 9—504(3). Such a result could not be justified. Accordingly, the Committee proposes to amend Section 9—501(3)(c) to extend the authorization of waivers to all of section 9—505 and to Section 9—504(3).

J—2. In the Committee's opinion the secured party's thirty day wait under Section 9—505(2) before he can retain the collateral in satisfaction of the obligation is too long. Moreover, an extra time is involved because of the secured party's uncertainty as to when the debtor "receives notification." These circumstances, coupled with the fact that the waiting period may be wasted if objection is received from the debtor or other party entitled to receive notification, probably defeat the intended purpose of the scheme, which is (at least in part) to avoid the creation of a deficiency. It takes longer to clear title by taking the goods in satisfaction of the obligation than it does to sell. In the process of sale, a deficiency is frequently established. If the program of Section 9—505(2) were made expeditious, deficiencies might sometimes be avoided. Accordingly, the Committee proposes that the waiting period be cut down to twenty-one days after the mailing of the notice.

J—3. A related difficulty in Section 9—505(2) on accepting collateral in satisfaction of the obligation in lieu of sale and in Section 9—504(3) on sale, is the persons entitled to receive notice. Both sections now require notice (except in the case of consumer goods) not only to every other secured party who has filed a financing statement "in this state" but also to every other secured party known to the secured party giving the notice. These requirements put on the secured party the necessity of searching the record in every case and of keeping a record of every telephone call by a person claiming an interest, and determining whether such person is entitled to notice. In the Committee's opinion, this burden simply is not justified in the light of the few cases in which there will be junior security interests on file and even fewer cases in which there will be an equity for the junior party to be protected. The Committee proposes instead that the only persons (other than the debtor) who need be given notice under each section are those who have given the secured party written notice of their claims of interests in the collateral.

Amendments to Article 1

§ 1—105. Territorial Application of the Act; Parties' Power to Choose Applicable Law

(1) Except as provided hereafter in this section, when a transaction bears a reasonable relation to this state and also to another state or nation the parties may agree that the law either of this state or of such other state or nation shall govern their rights and duties. Failing such agreement this Act applies to transactions bearing an appropriate relation to this state.

(2) Where one of the following provisions of this Act specifies the applicable law, that provision governs and a contrary agreement is effective only to the extent permitted by the law (including the conflict of laws rules) so specified:

Rights of creditors against sold goods. Section 2—402.

Applicability of the Article on Bank Deposits and Collections. Section 4—102.

Bulk transfers subject to the Article on Bulk Transfers. Section 6—102.

Applicability of the Article on Investment Securities. Section 8—106.

[Policy and scope of the Article on Secured Transactions. Sections 9—102 and 9—103.]

Perfection provisions of the Article on Secured Transactions, Section 9—103.

Reasons for 1972 Change

The reference to Section 9—102 has been deleted and a change made in Section 9—102 deleting any reference therein to conflict of law problems, because there is no reason why the general principles of the present section should not be applicable to the choice of law problems within its scope. Section 9—103 continues to govern choice of law questions as to perfection of security interests and the effect of perfection and non-perfection thereof. The usual rule is that perfection is governed by the law of the jurisdiction in which the collateral is when the last event occurs on which is based the assertion that the security interest is perfected or unperfected. Section 9—103 contains special rules for the cases of intangibles which have no situs, certain types of movable goods, goods which the parties intended at the inception of the transaction to be kept in another jurisdiction, goods subject to certificate of title laws, and certain other cases. Section 9—103 also contains local law rules as to reperfection of security interests when collateral is moved from one jurisdiction to another.

§ 1—201. General Definitions [Unchanged except for definitions (9) and (37)]

(9) "Buyer in ordinary course of business" means a person who in good faith and without knowledge that the sale to him is in violation of the ownership rights or security interest of a third party in the goods buys in ordinary course from a person in the business of selling goods of that kind but does not include a pawnbroker. All persons who sell minerals or the like (including oil and gas) at wellhead or minehead shall be deemed to be persons in the business of selling goods of that kind. "Buying" may be for cash or by exchange of other property or on secured or unsecured credit and includes receiving goods or documents of title under a pre-existing contract for sale but does not include a transfer in bulk or as security for or in total or partial satisfaction of a money debt.

(37) "Security interest" means an interest in personal property or fixtures which secures payment or performance of an obligation. The retention or reservation of title by a seller of goods notwithstanding shipment or delivery to the buyer (Section 2—401) is limited in effect to a reservation of a "security interest". The term also includes any interest of a buyer of accounts[,] or chattel paper[, or contract rights] which is subject to Article 9. The special property interest of a buyer of

goods on identification of such goods to a contract for sale under Section 2—401 is not a "security interest", but a buyer may also acquire a "security interest" by complying with Article 9. Unless a lease or consignment is intended as security, reservation of title thereunder is not a "security interest" but a consignment is in any event subject to the provisions on consignment sales (Section 2—326). Whether a lease is intended as security is to be determined by the facts of each case; however, (a) the inclusion of an option to purchase does not of itself make the lease one intended for security, and (b) an agreement that upon compliance with the terms of the lease the lessee shall become or has the option to become the owner of the property for no additional consideration or for a nominal consideration does make the lease one intended for security.

Reasons for 1972 Change of Definitions (9) and (37)

(9) The new language fits in with changes as to minerals in Section 9—103 which are explained in the references to minerals in the Reasons for Change and Comments to that section.

(37) The omission of the term "contract rights" conforms to the elimination of that term from Article 9. See Reasons for Change under Section 9—106.

Amendment to Article 2

§ 2—107. Goods to Be Severed From Realty: Recording

(1) A contract for the sale of [timber,] minerals or the like (including oil and gas) or a structure or its materials to be removed from realty is a contract for the sale of goods within this Article if they are to be severed by the seller but until severance a purported present sale thereof which is not effective as a transfer of an interest in land is effective only as a contract to sell.

(2) A contract for the sale apart from the land of growing crops or other things attached to realty and capable of severance without material harm thereto but not described in subsection (1) or of timber to be cut is a contract for the sale of goods within this Article whether the subject matter is to be severed by the buyer or by the seller even though it forms part of the realty at the time of contracting, and the parties can by identification effect a present sale before severance.

(3) The provisions of this section are subject to any third party rights provided by the law relating to realty records, and the contract for sale may be executed and recorded as a docu-

ment transferring an interest in land and shall then constitute notice to third parties of the buyer's rights under the contract for sale.

Reasons for 1972 Change

Several timber-growing states have changed the 1962 Code to make timber to be cut under a contract of severance goods, regardless of the question who is to sever them. The section is revised to adopt this change. Financing of the transaction is facilitated if the timber is treated as goods instead of real estate. A similar change is made in the definition of "goods" in Section 9—105. To protect persons dealing with timberlands, filing on timber to be cut is required in Part 4 of Article 9 to be made in real estate records in a manner comparable to fixture filing.

Amendment to Article 5

§ 5—116. Transfer and Assignment

(1) The right to draw under a credit can be transferred or assigned only when the credit is expressly designated as transferable or assignable.

(2) Even though the credit specifically states that it is nontransferable or nonassignable the beneficiary may before performance of the conditions of the credit assign his right to proceeds. Such an assignment is an assignment of [a contract right] an account under Article 9 on Secured Transactions and is governed by that Article except that

(a) the assignment is ineffective until the letter of credit or advice of credit is delivered to the assignee which delivery constitutes perfection of the security interest under Article 9; and

(b) the issuer may honor drafts or demands for payment drawn under the credit until it receives a notification of the assignment signed by the beneficiary which reasonably identifies the credit involved in the assignment and contains a request to pay the assignee; and

(c) after what reasonably appears to be such a notification has been received the issuer may without dishonor refuse to accept or pay even to a person otherwise entitled to honor until the letter of credit or advice of credit is exhibited to the issuer.

(3) Except where the beneficiary has effectively assigned his right to draw or his right to proceeds, nothing in this section limits his right to transfer or negotiate drafts or demands drawn under the credit.

Reasons for 1972 Change

The change conforms to the deletion of the defined term "contract right" from Article 9.

ARTICLE 9

SECURED TRANSACTIONS; SALES OF ACCOUNTS[, CONTRACT RIGHTS] AND CHATTEL PAPER

PART 1

SHORT TITLE, APPLICABILITY AND DEFINITIONS

§ 9—102. Policy and [Scope] Subject Matter of Article

(1) Except as otherwise provided [in Section 9—103 on multiple state transactions and] in Section 9—104 on excluded transactions, this Article applies [so far as concerns any personal property and fixtures within the jurisdiction of this state]

(a) to any transaction (regardless of its form) which is intended to create a security interest in personal property or fixtures including goods, documents, instruments, general intangibles, chattel paper or accounts [or contract rights]; and also

(b) to any sale of accounts [contract rights] or chattel paper.

(2) This Article applies to security interests created by contract including pledge, assignment, chattel mortgage, chattel trust, trust deed, factor's lien, equipment trust, conditional sale, trust receipt, other lien or title retention contract and lease or consignment intended as security. This Article does not apply to statutory liens except as provided in Section 9—310.

(3) The application of this Article to a security interest in a secured obligation is not affected by the fact that the obligation is itself secured by a transaction or interest to which this Article does not apply.

Note: *The adoption of this Article should be accompanied by the repeal of existing statutes dealing with conditional sales, trust receipts, factor's liens where the factor is given a non-possessory lien, chattel mortgages, crop mortgages, mortgages on railroad equipment, assignment of accounts and generally statutes regulating security interests in personal property.*

Where the state has a retail installment selling act or small loan act, that legislation should be carefully examined to determine what changes in those acts are needed to conform them to this Article. This Article primarily sets out rules defining rights of a secured party against persons dealing with the debtor; it does not prescribe regulations and controls which may be necessary to curb abuses arising in the small loan business or in the financing of consumer purchases on credit. Accordingly there is no intention to repeal existing regulatory acts in those fields [.] *by enactment or re-enactment of Article 9. See Section 9—203(4) and the Note thereto.*

Reasons for 1972 Change

The omissions in the first paragraph of subsection (1) make applicable the general choice of law principles of Section 1—105 (except for special rules stated in Section 9—103), instead of an incomplete statement in this section.

The omission is clause (1) (b) conforms to the elimination of the term "contract rights" from the Article. See Reasons for Change under Section 9—106.

[§ 9—103. Accounts, Contract Rights, General Intangibles and Equipment Relating to Another Jurisdiction; and Incoming Goods Already Subject to a Security Interest]

[(1) If the office where the assignor of accounts or contract rights keeps his record concerning them is in this state, the validity and perfection of a security interest therein and the possibility and effect of proper filing is governed by this Article; otherwise by the law (including the conflict of laws rules) of the jurisdiction where such office is located.]

[(2) If the chief place of business of a debtor is in this state, this Article governs the validity and perfection of a security interest and the possibility and effect of proper filing with regard to general intangibles or with regard to goods of a type which are normally used in more than one jurisdiction (such as automotive equipment, rolling stock, airplanes, road building equipment, commercial harvesting equipment, construction machinery and the like) if such goods are classified as equipment or classified as inventory by reason of their being leased by the debtor to others. Otherwise, the law (including the conflict of laws rules) of the jurisdiction where such chief place of business is located shall govern. If the chief place of business is located in a jurisdiction which does not provide for perfection of the security interest by filing or recording in that jurisdiction, then the security interest may be perfected by filing in this state. [For the purpose of determining the validity and perfection of a security interest in an airplane, the chief place of business of a debtor who is a foreign air carrier under the Federal Aviation Act of 1958, as amended, is the designated office of the agent upon whom service of process may be made on behalf of the debtor.]]

[(3) If personal property other than that governed by subsections (1) and (2) is already subject to a security interest when it is brought into this state, the validity of the security interest in this state is to be determined by the law (including the conflict of laws rules) of the jurisdiction where the property was when the security interest attached. However, if the parties to the transaction understood at the time that the security interest attached that the property would be kept in this state and it was brought into this state within 30 days after the security interest attached for purposes other than transportation through this state, then the validity of the security interest in this state is to be determined by the law of this state. If the security interest was already perfected under the law of the jurisdiction where the property was when the security interest attached and before being brought into this state, the security interest continues perfected in this state for four months and also thereafter if within the four month period it is perfected in this state. The security interest may also be perfected in this state after the expiration of the four month period; in such case perfection dates from the time of perfection in this state. If the security interest was not perfected under the law of the jurisdiction where the property was when the security interest attached and before being brought into this state, it may be perfected in this state; in such case perfection dates from the time of perfection in this state.]

[(4) Notwithstanding subsections (2) and (3), if personal property is covered by a certificate of title issued under a statute of this state or any other jurisdiction which requires indication on a certificate of title of any security interest in the property as a condition of perfection, then the perfection is governed by the law of the jurisdiction which issued the certificate.]

[[(5) Notwithstanding subsection (1) and Section 9—302, if the office where the assignor of accounts or contract rights keeps his records concerning them is not located in a jurisdiction which is a part of the United States, its territories or possessions, and the accounts or contract rights are within the jurisdiction of this state or the transaction which creates the security interest otherwise bears an appropriate relation to this state, this Article governs the validity and perfection of the security interest and the security interest may only be perfected by notification to the account debtor.]]

§ 9—103. Perfection of Security Interests in Multiple State Transactions

(1) Documents, instruments and ordinary goods.

(a) This subsection applies to documents and instruments and to goods other than those covered by a certificate of title described in subsection (2), mobile goods described in subsection (3), and minerals described in subsection (5).

(b) Except as otherwise provided in this subsection, perfection and the effect of perfection or non-perfection of a security interest in collateral are governed by the law of the jurisdiction where the collateral is when the last event occurs on which is based the assertion that the security interest is perfected or unperfected.

(c) If the parties to a transaction creating a purchase money security interest in goods in one jurisdiction understand at the time that the security interest attaches that the goods will be kept in another jurisdiction, then the law of the other jurisdiction governs the perfection and the effect of perfection or non-perfection of the security interest from the time it attaches until thirty days after the debtor receives possession of the goods and thereafter if the goods are taken to the other jurisdiction before the end of the thirty-day period.

(d) When collateral is brought into and kept in this state while subject to a security interest perfected under the law of the jurisdiction from which the collateral was removed, the security interest remains perfected, but if action is required by Part 3 of this Article to perfect the security interest,

(i) if the action is not taken before the expiration of the period of perfection in the other jurisdiction or the end of four months after the collateral is brought into this state, whichever period first expires, the security interest becomes unperfected at the end of that period and is thereafter deemed to have been unperfected as against a person who became a purchaser after removal;

(ii) if the action is taken before the expiration of the period specified in subparagraph (i), the security interest continues perfected thereafter;

(iii) for the purpose of priority over a buyer of consumer goods (subsection (2) of Section 9—307), the period of the effectiveness of a filing in the jurisdiction from which the collateral is removed is governed by the rules with respect to perfection in subparagraphs (i) and (ii).

(2) Certificate of title.

(a) This subsection applies to goods covered by a certificate of title issued under a statute of this state or of another jurisdiction under the law of which indication of a security interest on the certificate is required as a condition of perfection.

(b) Except as otherwise provided in this subsection, perfection and the effect of perfection or non-perfection of the security interest are governed by the law (including the conflict of laws rules) of the jurisdiction issuing the certificate until four months after the goods are removed from that jurisdiction and thereafter until the goods are registered in another jurisdiction, but in any event not beyond surrender of the certificate. After the expiration of that period, the goods are not covered by the certificate of title within the meaning of this section.

(c) Except with respect to the rights of a buyer described in the next paragraph, a security interest, perfected in another jurisdiction otherwise than by notation on a certificate of title, in goods brought into this state and thereafter covered by a certificate of title issued by this state is subject to the rules stated in paragraph (d) of subsection (1).

(d) If goods are brought into this state while a security interest therein is perfected in any manner under the law of the jurisdiction from which the goods are removed and a certificate of title is issued by this state and the certificate does not show that the goods are subject to the security interest or that they may be subject to security interests not shown on the certificate, the security interest is subordinate to the rights of a buyer of the goods who is not in the business of selling goods of that kind to the extent that he gives value and receives delivery of the goods after issuance of the certificate and without knowledge of the security interest.

(3) Accounts, general intangibles and mobile goods.

(a) This subsection applies to accounts (other than an account described in subsection (5) on minerals) and general intangibles and to goods which are mobile and which are of a type normally used in more than one jurisdiction, such as motor vehicles, trailers, rolling stock, airplanes, shipping containers, road building and construction machinery and commercial harvesting machinery and the like, if the goods are equipment or are inventory leased or held for lease by the debtor to others, and are not covered by a certificate of title described in subsection (2).

(b) The law (including the conflict of laws rules) of the jurisdiction in which the debtor is located governs the perfection and the effect of perfection or non-perfection of the security interest.

(c) If, however, the debtor is located in a jurisdiction which is not a part of the United States, and which does not provide for perfection of the security interest by filing or recording in that jurisdiction, the law of the jurisdiction in the United States in which the debtor has its major executive office in the United States governs the perfection and the effect of perfection or non-perfection of the security interest through filing. In the alternative, if the debtor is located in a jurisdiction which is not a part of the United States or Canada and the collateral is accounts or general intangibles for money due or to become due, the security interest may be perfected by notification to the account debtor. As used in this paragraph, "United States" includes its territories and possessions and the Commonwealth of Puerto Rico.

(d) A debtor shall be deemed located at his place of business if he has one, at his chief executive office if he has more than one place of business, otherwise at his residence. If, however, the debtor is a foreign air carrier under the Federal Aviation Act of 1958, as amended, it shall be deemed located at the designated office of the agent upon whom service of process may be made on behalf of the foreign air carrier.

(e) A security interest perfected under the law of the jurisdiction of the location of the debtor is perfected until the expiration of four months after a change of the debtor's location to another jurisdiction, or until perfection would have ceased by the law of the first jurisdiction, whichever period first expires. Unless perfected in the new jurisdiction before the end of that period, it becomes unperfected thereafter and is deemed to have been unperfected as against a person who became a purchaser after the change.

(4) Chattel paper.

The rules stated for goods in subsection (1) apply to a possessory security interest in chattel paper. The rules stated for accounts in subsection (3) apply to a non-possessory security interest in chattel paper, but the security interest may not be perfected by notification to the account debtor.

(5) Minerals.

Perfection and the effect of perfection or non-perfection of a security interest which is created by a debtor who has an interest in minerals or the like (including oil and gas) before extraction and which attaches thereto as extracted, or which attaches to an account resulting from the sale thereof at the wellhead or minehead are governed by the law (including the conflict of laws rules) of the jurisdiction wherein the wellhead or minehead is located.

Reasons for 1972 Change

The section has been completely rewritten to clarify the relationship of its several provisions to each other and to other sections defining the applicable law. Now that the Code has been adopted in all states but Louisiana and also adopted in the District of Columbia and the Virgin Islands, the emphasis in the revision has been to make clear where perfection of a security interest must take place, rather than on problems of actual conflicts of rules of law.

1. The section now concerns itself exclusively with perfection of security interests and the effect of perfection or non-perfection thereof. The 1962 Code has several references to the "validity" of a security agreement, and these have been deleted. Likewise, a deletion has been made from Section 9—102 of the language which went beyond that section's basic function of defining the scope of Article 9 and purported to state a choice of law rule. These two changes make it clear that Article 9 does not govern problems of

choice of law between the original parties, and that this question is governed by the general choice of law provision in Section 1—105.

2. While most of the substantive materials of the section are in the 1962 Text, the statement thereof and their relationship to each other were not clear. In the revision they are clarified according to the following structure:

The basic rule of this section is that the controlling law, as to perfection of the security interests and the effect of perfection or non-perfection, is the law of the jurisdiction where the collateral is when the last event occurs on which is based the assertion that the security interest is perfected or unperfected (paragraph (1) (b)). There are certain exceptions: (i) In the case of a purchase money security interest in goods, where the parties intended to remove the collateral to another jurisdiction within 30 days after the debtor received possession of the goods, the law of the latter jurisdiction will govern the initial perfection until the expiration of the 30-day period, and thereafter if the goods are removed to the other jurisdiction before the end of the period (paragraph (1) (c)). (ii) Where the collateral is covered by a certificate of title, perfection will be governed by the law of the issuing jurisdiction (subsection (2)). (iii) If the collateral is certain mobile goods or certain intangibles, perfection will be governed by the law of the jurisdiction wherein is located the debtor (subsection (3)).

Where the collateral has been removed from the jurisdiction whose law first governed, the jurisdiction into which it is removed (i. e., "this state") adds a local requirement of re-perfection to the requirements of the state from which the collateral was removed—i. e., refiling is required within 4 months after removal, or within any lesser period during which perfection would have continued in the other jurisdiction (paragraphs (1) (d) and (2) (c)).

3. The two former rules for determining place of perfection as to intangibles (namely, for accounts, the office where the records were kept concerning the accounts; and for general intangibles, the chief place of business of the debtor) have been consolidated into the rule that the filing is at the debtor's location. That location will ordinarily be the office designated in the 1962 Text as "chief place of business," now redesignated as "chief executive office." A new provision (paragraph (3) (e)) has been added to cover the case where that office moves from one jurisdiction to another.

A principal objection to the original rule that the place for filing as to accounts was the place where the debtor kept his records with respect to them was that persons seeking to search records might not know where this place might be, in the case of a far-flung debtor or of multicorporate enterprises with central accounting. Where the debtor assigned his accounts without recourse, as in factoring, he might keep few records with respect to them. Moreover, it was thought undesirable to have one rule for accounts and another rule for general intangibles, because in many financing situations both types of receivables may be involved. See discussion in Reasons for Change to Section 9—106. Therefore, it was decided to adopt for both types of intangibles the rule heretofore applicable to general intangibles.

§ 9—104. Transactions Excluded From Article

This Article does not apply

(a) to a security interest subject to any statute of the United States [such as the Ship Mortgage Act, 1920,] to the extent that such statute governs the rights of parties to and third parties affected by transactions in particular types of property; or

(b) to a landlord's lien; or

(c) to a lien given by statute or other rule of law for services or materials except as provided in Section 9—310 on priority of such liens; or

(d) to a transfer of a claim for wages, salary or other compensation of an employee; or

[(e) to an equipment trust covering railway rolling stock; or]

(e) to a transfer by a government or governmental subdivision or agency; or

(f) to a sale of accounts [, contract rights] or chattel paper as part of a sale of the business out of which they arose, or an assignment of accounts [, contract rights] or chattel paper which is for the purpose of collection only, or a transfer of a [contract] right to payment under a contract to an assignee who is also to do the performance under the contract or a transfer of a single account to an assignee in whole or partial satisfaction of a preexisting indebtedness; or

(g) to a transfer of an interest in or claim in or under any policy of insurance, except as provided with respect to proceeds (Section 9—306) and priorities in proceeds (Section 9—312); or

(h) to a right represented by a judgment (other than a judgment taken on a right to payment which was collateral); or

(i) to any right of set-off; or

(j) except to the extent that provision is made for fixtures in Section 9—313, to the creation or transfer of an interest in or lien on real estate, including a lease or rents thereunder; or

(k) to a transfer in whole or in part of [any of the following:] any claim arising out of tort; [any deposit, savings, passbook or like account maintained with a bank, savings and loan association, credit union or like organization.]; or

(*l*) to a transfer of an interest in any deposit account (subsection (1) of Section 9—105), except as provided with respect to proceeds (Section 9—306) and priorities in proceeds (Section 9—312).

Reasons for 1972 Change

Former paragraph (e), excluding railway equipment trusts from the coverage of Article 9, has been deleted. The whole thrust of Article 9 is to eliminate differences based on the form of a transaction, and the equipment trust serves the same function as other purchase money forms of financing. In fact, a form known as the "New York equipment trust" comes closer to a conditional sale contract then it does to a Pennsylvania equipment trust, and thus the former exclusion left substantial uncertainty. Railway financing on rolling stock will continue to be exempt from the filing provisions of Article 9 by virture of Section 9—302(3) and (4). Thus, the principal purpose of the former exclusion will be retained. There is, however, no reason why the other provisions of Article 9 by virtue of Section 9—302(3) and (4). closure, etc., should not be available to the parties to railway financing, since these problems are not adequately covered in any other statutes.

A new paragraph (e) has been added to make clear that this Article does not apply to security interests created by governmental debtors.

Other changes reflect the elimination of the term "contract rights" and the fact that, while transfers of claims under insurance policies and deposit accounts are in general excluded from the Article by this section, proceeds claims thereto are subject to Section 9—306.

§ 9—105. Definitions and Index of Definitions

(1) In this Article unless the context otherwise requires:

(a) "Account debtor" means the person who is obligated on an account, chattel paper[, contract right] or general intangible;

(b) "Chattel paper" means a writing or writings which evidence both a monetary obligation and a security interest in or a lease of specific goods, but a charter or other contract involving the use or hire of a vessel is not chattel paper. When a transaction is evidenced both by such a security agreement or a lease and by an instrument or a series of instruments, the group of writings taken together constitutes chattel paper;

(c) "Collateral" means the property subject to a security interest, and includes accounts[, contract rights] and chattel paper which have been sold;

(d) "Debtor" means the person who owes payment or other performance of the obligation secured, whether or not he owns or has rights in the collateral, and includes the seller of accounts[, contract rights] or chattel paper. Where the debtor and the owner of the collateral are not the same person, the term "debtor" means the owner of the collateral in any provision of the Article dealing with the collateral, the obligor in any provision dealing with the obligation, and may include both where the context so requires;

(e) "Deposit account" means a demand, time, savings, passbook or like account maintained with a bank, savings and loan association, credit union or like organization, other than an account evidenced by a certificate of deposit;

(f) [(e)] "Document" means document of title as defined in the general definitions of Article 1 (Section 1—201) [;], and a receipt of the kind described in subsection (2) of Section 7—201;

(g) "Encumbrance" includes real estate mortgages and other liens on real estate and all other rights in real estate that are not ownership interests.

(h) [(f)] "Goods" includes all things which are movable at the time the security interest attaches or which are fixtures (Section 9—313), but does not include money, documents, instruments, accounts, chattel paper, general intangibles, [contract rights and other things in action,] or minerals or the like (including oil and gas) before extraction. "Goods" also includes standing timber which is to be cut and removed under a conveyance or contract for sale, the unborn young of animals, and growing crops.

(i) [(g)] "Instrument" means a negotiable instrument (defined in Section 3—104), or a security (defined in Section 8—102) or any other writing which evidences a right to the payment of money and is not itself a security agreement or lease and is of a type which is in ordinary course of business transferred by delivery with any necessary indorsement or assignment;

(j) "Mortgage" means a consensual interest created by a real estate mortgage, a trust deed on real estate, or the like;

(k) An advance is made "pursuant to commitment" if the secured party has bound himself to make it, whether or not a subsequent event of default or other event not within his control has relieved or may relieve him from his obligation.

(*l*) [(h)] "Security agreement" means an agreement which creates or provides for a security interest;

(m) [(i)] "Secured party" means a lender, seller or other person in whose favor there is a security interest, including a person to whom accounts[, contract rights] or chattel paper have been sold. When the holders of obligations issued under an indenture of trust, equipment trust agreement or the like are represented by a trustee or other person, the representative is the secured party;

(n) "Transmitting utility" means any person primarily engaged in the railroad, street railway or trolley bus business, the electric or electronics communications transmission business, the transmission of goods by pipeline, or the transmission or the production and transmission of electricity, steam, gas or water, or the provision of sewer service.

(2) Other definitions applying to this Article and the sections in which they appear are:

"Account". Section 9—106.

"Attach". Section 9—203.
"Construction mortgage". Section 9—313(1).
"Consumer goods". Section 9—109(1).
["Contract right". Section 9—106.]
"Equipment". Section 9—109(2).
"Farm products". Section 9—109(3).
"Fixture". Section 9—313.
"Fixture filing". Section 9—313.
"General intangibles". Section 9—106.
"Inventory". Section 9—109(4).
"Lien creditor". Section 9—301(3).
"Proceeds". Section 9—306(1).
"Purchase money security interest". Section 9—107.
"United States". Section 9—103.

(3) The following definitions in other Articles apply to this Article:

"Check". Section 3—104.
"Contract for sale". Section 2—106.
"Holder in due course". Section 3—302.
"Note". Section 3—104.
"Sale". Section 2—106.

(4) In addition Article 1 contains general definitions and principles of construction and interpretation applicable throughout this Article.

Reasons for 1972 Change

A definition of "transmitting utility" has been added to identify a class of debtor with special filing problems on far-flung properties, for which special filing rules are stated in Part 4.

A definition of "deposit account" has been added to facilitate references to such accounts in the section on proceeds (Section 9—306).

A definition of "pursuant to commitment" has been added as the basis for use of this concept in Sections 9—301, 9—307, and 9—312.

Definitions of "encumbrance" and "mortgage" have been added as the basis for the use thereof in Section 9—313.

The definition of "document" has been amended to include therein the kind of receipt issued by a person who is not technically a warehouseman, as described in Section 7—201(2).

The exclusion of "other things in action" from the definition of "goods" has been deleted as unnecessary. "General intangibles", which under Section 9—106 includes "things in action", are themselves excluded from the definition of goods.

Other minor changes reflect the elimination of the classification "contract right" in Section 9—106.

§ 9—106. Definitions: "Account"; ["Contract Right";] "General Intangibles"

"Account" means any right to payment for goods sold or leased or for services rendered which is not evidenced by an instrument or chattel paper[.], whether or not it has been earned by performance. ["Contract right" means any right to payment under a contract not yet earned by performance and not evidenced by an instrument or chattel paper.] "General intangibles" means any personal property (including things in action) other than goods, accounts, [contract rights,] chattel paper, documents, [and] instruments, and money. All rights to payment earned or unearned under a charter or other contract involving the use or hire of a vessel and all rights incident to the charter or contract are [contract rights and neither] accounts [nor general intangibles].

Reasons for 1972 Change

The term "contract right" has been eliminated as unnecessary. As indicated by a sentence now being eliminated from Section 9—306(1), "contract right" was thought of as an "account" before the right to payment became unconditional by performance by the creditor. But the distinction between "account" and "contract right" was not used in the Article except in subsection (2) to Section 9—318 on the right of original parties to modify an assigned contract, and that subsection has been redrafted to preserve the distinction without needing the term "contract right". The term has been troublesome in creating a "proceeds" problem where a contract right becomes an "account" by performance; in the Code's former denial that there could be any right in an account until it came into existence (former Section 9—204 (2) (d)), notwithstanding a security interest in the preexisting contract right; and in the danger of inadequate description in financing statements by claiming "accounts" or "general intangibles" when before performance they should have been described as "contract rights"; and in other respects.

"Money" is expressly excluded from the catch-all definition, "general intangible", to preclude any possible reading that a security interest in money may be perfected by filing.

The other changes are conforming changes.

§ 9—114. Consignment

(1) A person who delivers goods under a consignment which is not a security interest and who would be required to file under this Article by paragraph (3) (c) of Section 2—326 has priority over a secured party who is or becomes a creditor of the consignee and who would have a perfected security interest in the goods if they were the property of the consignee, and also has priority with respect to identifiable cash proceeds received on or before delivery of the goods to a buyer, if

(a) the consignor complies with the filing provision of the Article on Sales with respect to consignments (paragraph (3) (c) of Section 2—326) before the consignee receives possession of the goods; and

(b) the consignor gives notification in writing to the holder of the security interest if the holder has filed a financing statement covering the same types of goods before the date of the filing made by the consignor; and

(c) the holder of the security interest receives the notification within five years before the consignee receives possession of the goods; and

(d) the notification states that the consignor expects to deliver goods on consignment to the consignee, describing the goods by item or type.

(2) In the case of a consignment which is not a security interest and in which the requirements of the preceding subsection have not been met, a person who delivers goods to another is subordinate to a person who would have a perfected security interest in the goods if they were the property of the debtor.

Reasons for 1972 Adoption of New Section

An uncertainty has existed under the 1962 Code whether the filing rule in Section 2—326(3) applicable to true consignments requires only filing under Part 4 of Article 9 or also requires notice to prior inventory secured parties of the debtor under Section 9—312(3). The new Section 9—114 accepts the latter view, and provides in substance that, in order to protect his ownership of the consigned goods, the consignor must give the same notice to an inventory secured party of the debtor that he would have to give if his transaction with the consignee was in the form of a security transaction instead of in the form of a consignment. This new section follows closely the language of Section 9—312(3).

PART 2

VALIDITY OF SECURITY AGREEMENT AND RIGHTS OF PARTIES THERETO

§ 9—203. Attachment and Enforceability of Security Interest; Proceeds; Formal Requisites

[(1) Subject to the provisions of Section 4—208 on the security interest of a collecting bank and Section 9—113 on a security interest arising under the Article on Sales, a security interest is not enforceable against the debtor or third parties unless

(a) the collateral is in the possession of the secured party; or

(b) the debtor has signed a security agreement which contains a description of the collateral and in addition, when the security interest covers crops or oil, gas or minerals to be extracted or timber to be cut, a description of the land concerned. In describing collateral, the word "proceeds" is sufficient without further description to cover proceeds of any character.]

(1) Subject to the provisions of Section 4—208 on the security interest of a collecting bank and Section 9—113 on a security interest arising under the Article on Sales, a security interest is not enforceable against the debtor or third parties with respect to the collateral and does not attach unless

(a) the collateral is in the possession of the secured party pursuant to agreement, or the debtor has signed a security agreement which contains a description of the collateral and in addition, when the security interest covers crops growing or to be grown or timber to be cut, a description of the land concerned; and

(b) value has been given; and

(c) the debtor has rights in the collateral.

(2) A security interest attaches when it becomes enforceable against the debtor with respect to the collateral. Attachment occurs as soon as all of the events specified in subsection (1) have taken place unless explicit agreement postpones the time of attaching.

(3) Unless otherwise agreed a security agreement gives the secured party the rights to proceeds provided by Section 9—306.

(4) [(2)] A transaction, although subject to this Article, is also subject to ....*, and in the case of conflict between the provisions of this Article and any such statute, the provisions of such statute control. Failure to comply with any applicable statute has only the effect which is specified therein.

Note: *At * in subsection (4) insert reference to any local statute regulating small loans, retail installment sales and the like.*

The foregoing subsection (4) is designed to make it clear that certain transactions, although subject to this Article, must also comply with other applicable legislation.

This Article is designed to regulate all the "security" aspects of transactions within its scope. There is, however, much regulatory legislation, particularly in the consumer field, which supplements this Article and should not be repealed by its enactment. Examples are small loan acts, retail installment selling acts and the like. Such acts may provide for licensing and rate regulation and may prescribe particular forms of contract. Such provisions should remain in force despite the enactment of this Article. On the other hand if a retail installment selling act contains provisions on filing, rights on default, etc., such provisions should be repealed as inconsistent with this Article[.] *except that inconsistent provisions as to deficiencies, penalties, etc., in the Uniform Consumer Credit Code and other recent related legislation should remain because those statutes were drafted after the substantial enactment of the Article and with the intention of modifying certain provisions of this Article as to consumer credit.*

Reasons for 1972 Change

Subsection (1) has been revised to incorporate into the concept of enforceability of a security interest the elements of agreement, value, and rights in the collateral, which formerly were stated in Section 9—204. These are combined with the requirement of written agreement (unless the security interest is evidenced by possession of the collateral by the secured party), and the security interest is said to "attach" when all of the events specified have occurred. This drafting cures the former anomaly that a security interest could attach and be perfected, and yet be unenforceable against anyone for lack of a written security agreement.

The requirement that a security agreement covering oil, gas or minerals to be extracted contain a description of the land concerned has been eliminated since the Article does not recognize a security interest in such collateral until it has been extracted from the land.

The former reference to proceeds in subsection (1) has been eliminated and new subsection (3) added to make clear that claims to proceeds under Section 9—306 do not require a statement in the security agreement, for it is assumed that the parties so intend unless otherwise agreed.

§ 9—204. [When Security Interest Attaches;] After-Acquired Property; Future Advances

[(1) A security interest cannot attach until there is agreement (subsection (3) of Section 1—201) that it attach and value is given and the debtor has rights in the collateral. It attaches as soon as all of the events in the preceding sentence have taken place unless explicit agreement postpones the time of attaching.]

[(2) For the purposes of this section the debtor has no rights

(a) in crops until they are planted or otherwise become growing crops, in the young of livestock until they are conceived;

(b) in fish until caught, in oil, gas or minerals until they are extracted, in timber until it is cut;

(c) in a contract right until the contract has been made;

(d) in an account until it comes into existence.]

[(3) Except as provided in subsection (4) a security agreement may provide that collateral, whenever acquired, shall secure all obligations covered by the security agreement.]

[(4) No security interest attaches under an after-acquired property clause

(a) to crops which become such more than one year after the security agreement is executed except that a security interest in crops which is given in conjunction with a lease or a land purchase or improvement transaction evidenced by a contract, mortgage or deed of trust may if so agreed attach to crops to be grown on the land concerned during the period of such real estate transaction;

(b) to consumer goods other than accessions (Section 9—314) when given as additional security unless the debtor acquires rights in them within ten days after the secured party gives value.]

(1) Except as provided in subsection (2), a security agreement may provide that any or all obligations covered by the security agreement are to be secured by after-acquired collateral.

(2) No security interest attaches under an after-acquired property clause to consumer goods other than accessions (Section 9—314) when given as additional security unless the debtor acquires rights in them within ten days after the secured party gives value.

(3) (5) Obligations covered by a security agreement may include future advances or other value whether or not the advances or value are given pursuant to commitment (subsection (1) of Section 9—105).

Reasons for 1972 Change

Former subsection (1) has been eliminated. The term "attach" has been moved to Section 9—203 and related to the concept of enforceability of the security interest between the parties to the security agreement contained in that section.

Former subsection (2) has been eliminated as unnecessary and in some cases confusing. Its operation appeared to be arbitrary, and it is believed that the questions considered are best left to the courts.

Former subsections (3) and (5), now subsections (1) and (3), have been rewritten for clarity.

Former subsection (4) is redesignated (2), and clause (a) thereof relating to crops eliminated. That clause provided that no security interest in crops attaches under an after-acquired property clause to crops which become such more than one year after the security agreement, unless the agreement involved certain real estate transactions. The obvious purpose of this provision was to protect a necessitous farmer from encumbering his crops for many years in the future. The provision did not work because there was no corresponding limit on the scope of a financing statement covering crops, and under the Code's notice-filing rules the priority position of a security arrangement covering successive crops would be as effectively protected by the filing of a first financing statement whether the granting clause as to successive crops was in one security agreement with an after-acquired property clause or in a succession of security agreements. On the other hand the clause did require an annual security agreement for crops even when the encumbrance on crops was agreed to as part of a long-term financing covering farm machinery and other assets. The provision thus appeared to be meaningless in operation except to cause unnecessary paperwork, but it did introduce some element of uncertainty as to its purpose.

§ 9—205. Use or Disposition of Collateral Without Accounting Permissible

A security interest is not invalid or fraudulent against creditors by reason of liberty in the debtor to use, commingle or dispose of all or part of the collateral (including returned or repossessed goods) or to collect or compromise accounts [contract rights] or chattel paper, or to accept the return of goods or make repossessions, or to use, commingle or dispose of proceeds, or by reason of the failure of the secured party to require the debtor to account for proceeds or replace collateral. This section does not relax the requirements of possession where perfection of a security interest depends upon possession of the collateral by the secured party or by a bailee.

Reasons for 1972 Change

The change reflects the deletion of the defined term "contract right" from the Article.

PART 3

RIGHTS OF THIRD PARTIES; PERFECTED AND UNPERFECTED SECURITY INTERESTS; RULES OF PRIORITY

§ 9—301. Persons Who Take Priority Over Unperfected Security Interests; Right of "Lien Creditor"

(1) Except as otherwise provided in subsection (2), an unperfected security interest is subordinate to the rights of

(a) persons entitled to priority under Section 9—312;

(b) a person who becomes a lien creditor [without knowledge of the security interest and] before [it] the security interest is perfected;

(c) in the case of goods, instruments, documents, and chattel paper, a person who is not a secured party and who is a transferee in bulk or other buyer not in ordinary course of business, or is a buyer of farm products in ordinary course of business, to the extent that he gives value and receives delivery of the collateral without knowledge of the security interest and before it is perfected;

(d) in the case of accounts [, contract rights,] and general intangibles, a person who is not a secured party and who is a transferee to the extent that he gives value without knowledge of the security interest and before it is perfected.

(2) If the secured party files with respect to a purchase money security interest before or within ten days after the debtor receives possession of the collateral [comes into possession of the debtor], he takes priority over the rights of a transferee in bulk or of a lien creditor which arise between the time the security interest attaches and the time of filing.

(3) A "lien creditor" means a creditor who has acquired a lien on the property involved by attachment, levy or the like and includes an assignee for benefit of creditors from the time of assignment, and a trustee in bankruptcy from the date of the filing of the petition or a receiver in equity from the time of appointment. [Unless all the creditors represented had knowledge of the security interest such a representative of creditors is a lien

creditor without knowledge even though he personally has knowledge of the security interest.]

(4) A person who becomes a lien creditor while a security interest is perfected takes subject to the security interest only to the extent that it secures advances made before he becomes a lien creditor or within 45 days thereafter or made without knowledge of the lien or pursuant to a commitment entered into without knowledge of the lien.

Reasons for 1972 Change

Paragraph (1) (b) has been amended to eliminate the element of knowledge in the conditions under which a lien creditor may defeat an unperfected security interest. Knowledge of the security interest will no longer subordinate the lien creditor to the unfiled security interest. The former section denied the lien creditor priority even though he had no knowledge when he got involved by extending credit, if he acquired knowledge while attempting to extricate himself. It was completely inconsistent in spirit with the rules of priority between security interests, where knowledge plays a very minor role.

The change in subsection (2) is made to conform the language to that of the related provision in Section 9—312(4).

The second sentence of subsection (3) is deleted because the question of knowledge has been eliminated from paragraph (1) (b).

New subsection (4) deals with the question of the extent to which advances made under a perfected security interest after the rights of a lien creditor have attached to the collateral will come ahead of the position of the lien creditor. This subsection should be read with Section 9—307(3) (which deals with the same problem in the case of an intervening buyer) and Section 9—312(7) (which deals with the same problem in the case of a secured party), and paragraph (5) of Reasons for Change under Section 9—312.

In the case of the lien creditors dealt with by this subsection, the rule chosen is crucial to the priority of the security interest for advances over a federal tax lien for 45 days after the tax lien has been filed, as contemplated under section 6323(c) (2) and (d) of the Internal Revenue Code of 1954 as amended by the Federal Tax Lien Act of 1966. The actual importance of the priority rule chosen between a secured party and possible lien creditors during the 45 days is believed to be slight; but the rule chosen is essential to give the secured party the protection against Federal tax liens believed to have been intended by the Federal Tax Lien Act of 1966, the operation of which is made to depend on state law. The rule of state law was not certain before this revision. Accordingly, the priority of the security interest for future advances over the judgment lien has to be absolute for the 45 days, without regard to any knowledge of the secured party that the judgment lien exists. After the 45 days the priority of the security interest depends on the secured party's lack of knowledge of the lien at the time he makes the subsequent advance or commits to do so.

§ 9—302. When Filing Is Required to Perfect Security Interest; Security Interests to Which Filing Provisions of This Article Do Not Apply

(1) A financing statement must be filed to perfect all security interests except the following:

(a) a security interest in collateral in possession of the secured party under Section 9—305;

(b) a security interest temporarily perfected in instruments or documents without delivery under Section 9—304 or in proceeds for a 10 day period under Section 9—306;

[(c) a purchase money security interest in farm equipment having a purchase price not in excess of $2500; but filing is required for a fixture under Section 9—313 or for a motor vehicle required to be licensed;]

(c) a security interest created by an assignment of a beneficial interest in a trust or a decedent's estate;

(d) a purchase money security interest in consumer goods; but filing is required [for a fixture under Section 9—313 or for a motor vehicle required to be licensed;] for a motor vehicle required to be registered; and fixture filing is required for priority over conflicting interests in fixtures to the extent provided in Section 9—313;

(e) an assignment of accounts [or contract rights] which does not alone or in conjunction with other assignments to the same assignee transfer a significant part of the outstanding accounts [or contract rights] of the assignor;

(f) a security interest of a collecting bank (Section 4—208) or arising under the Article on Sales (see Section 9—113) or covered in subsection (3) of this section;

(g) an assignment for the benefit of all the creditors of the transferor, and subsequent transfers by the assignee thereunder.

(2) If a secured party assigns a perfected security interest, no filing under this Article is required in order to continue the perfected status of the security interest against creditors of and transferees from the original debtor.

[(3) The filing provisions of this Article do not apply to a security interest in property subject to a statute

(a) of the United States which provides for a national registration or filing of all security interests in such property; or

Note: *States to select either Alternative A or Alternative B.*

Alternative A—

(b) of this state which provides for central filing of, or which requires indication on a certificate of title of, such security interests in such property.

Alternative B—

(b) of this state which provides for central filing of security interests in such property, or in a motor vehicle which is not inventory held for sale for which a certificate of title is required under the statutes of this state if a notation of such a security interest can be indicated by a public official on a certificate or a duplicate thereof.]

[(4) A security interest in property covered by a statute described in subsection (3) can be perfected only by registration or filing under that statute or by indication of the security interest on a certificate of title or duplicate thereof by a public official.]

(3) The filing of a financing statement otherwise required by this Article is not necessary or effective to perfect a security interest in property subject to

(a) a statute or treaty of the United States which provides for a national or international registration or a national or international certificate of title or which specifies a place of filing different from that specified in this Article for filing of the security interest; or

(b) the following statutes of this state; [[list any certificate of title statute covering automobiles, trailers, mobile homes, boats, farm tractors, or the like, and any central filing statute*.]]; but during any period in which collateral is inventory held for sale by a person who is in the business of selling goods of that kind, the filing provisions of this Article (Part 4) apply to a security interest in that collateral created by him as debtor; or

(c) a certificate of title statute of another jurisdiction under the law of which indication of a security interest on the certificate is required as a condition of perfection (subsection (2) of Section 9—103).

(4) Compliance with a statute or treaty described in subsection (3) is equivalent to the filing of a financing statement under this Article, and a security interest in property subject to the statute or treaty can be perfected only by compliance therewith except as provided in Section 9—103 on multiple state transactions. Duration and renewal of perfection of a security interest perfected by compliance with the statute or treaty are governed by the provisions of the statute or treaty; in other respects the security interest is subject to this Article.

* **Note:** *It is recommended that the provisions of certificate of title acts for perfection of security interests by notation on the certificates should be amended to exclude coverage of inventory held for sale.*

Reasons for 1972 Change

Former paragraph (1) (c), which created a nonfiling rule for purchase money security interests in certain farm equipment, has been eliminated. The analogy drawn in the 1962 Code of farm equipment to consumer goods (for which a similar nonfiling rule is provided in paragraph (1) (d)) is believed to be inappropriate. The effect of the rule was to make farmers' equipment unavailable to them as collateral for loans from some lenders.

A new paragraph (1) (c) exempts from filing rules security interests created by assignments of beneficial interests in trusts and estates, because these assignments are not ordinarily thought of as subject to this Article, and a filing rule might operate to defeat many assignments.

The requirement of filing for purchase-money security interests in consumer goods which are fixtures has been made applicable only for priority against real estate interests (Section 9—313).

A new paragraph (1) (g) has been added exempting from filing assignments for the benefit of creditors because they are not financing transactions.

Former subsections (3) and (4) have been rewritten into new subsections (3) and (4). The alternatives of former subsection (3) had proved unacceptable formulations in many states. The states adopted non-uniform amendments to use language more closely geared to their certificate of title laws than the uniform alternatives. It is believed that the simplest thing is to have each state specify its statutes intended to be applicable as it adopts the revised Article 9.

Former Alternative B to subsection (3) has been abandoned as no longer serving any purpose: it had been an attempt to convert obsolete non-mandatory certificate of title laws into laws under which notation on the certificate of title was the necessary method of perfection of a security interest.

Subsection (3) continues to carry the thought that was formerly only in Alternative B—namely, that the certificate of title procedure does not control the perfection of inventory or "floor plan" security interests, but instead normal Code filing rules are applicable. Non-uniform variations to the contrary under some state laws are believed to increase operating burdens and it is hoped that the states will abandon them.

References to federal statutes have been broadened to include treaties.

§ 9—304. Perfection of Security Interest in Instruments, Documents, and Goods Covered by Documents; Perfection by Permissive Filing; Temporary Perfection Without Filing or Transfer of Possession

(1) A security interest in chattel paper or negotiable documents may be perfected by filing. A security interest in money or instruments (other than instruments which constitute part of chattel paper) can be perfected only by the secured party's taking possession, except as provided in subsections (4) and (5) of this section and subsections (2) and (3) of Section 9—306 on proceeds.

(2) During the period that goods are in the possession of the issuer of a negotiable document therefor, a security interest in the goods is perfected by perfecting a security interest in the document, and any security interest in the goods otherwise perfected during such period is subject thereto.

(3) A security interest in goods in the possession of a bailee other than one who has issued a negotiable document therefor

is perfected by issuance of a document in the name of the secured party or by the bailee's receipt of notification of the secured party's interest or by filing as to the goods.

(4) A security interest in instruments or negotiable documents is perfected without filing or the taking of possession for a period of 21 days from the time it attaches to the extent that it arises for new value given under a written security agreement.

(5) A security interest remains perfected for a period of 21 days without filing where a secured party having a perfected security interest in an instrument, a negotiable document or goods in possession of a bailee other than one who has issued a negotiable document therefor

(a) makes available to the debtor the goods or documents representing the goods for the purpose of ultimate sale or exchange or for the purpose of loading, unloading, storing, shipping, transshipping, manufacturing, processing or otherwise dealing with them in a manner preliminary to their sale or exchange, [;or] but priority between conflicting security interests in the goods is subject to subsection (3) of Section 9—312; or

(b) delivers the instrument to the debtor for the purpose of ultimate sale or exchange or of presentation, collection, renewal or registration of transfer.

(6) After the 21 day period in subsections (4) and (5) perfection depends upon compliance with applicable provisions of this Article.

Reasons for 1972 Change

The change in subsection (1) corrects an inadvertent omission in the 1962 Text, and makes clear that a security interest in money cannot be perfected by filing.

A provision has been added to subsection (5) making it clear that the 21-day period referred to therein deals only with perfection, but that there must be compliance with the notice provisions of Section 9—312(3) in order to achieve priority over earlier inventory financers. Corresponding clarifying changes have been made in Section 9—312(3).

§ 9—305. When Possession by Secured Party Perfects Security Interest Without Filing

A security interest in letters of credit and advices of credit (subsection (2) (a) of Section 5—116), goods, instruments, money, negotiable documents or chattel paper may be perfected by the secured party's taking possession of the collateral. If such collateral other than goods covered by a negotiable document is held by a bailee, the secured party is deemed to have possession from the time the bailee receives notification of the secured party's interest. A security interest is perfected by possession from the time possession is taken without relation back and continues only so long as possession is retained, unless otherwise specified in this Article. The security interest may be otherwise perfected as provided in this Article before or after the period of possession by the secured party.

Reasons for 1972 Change

The change corresponds to the change in Section 9-304 to clarify the special position of money.

§ 9—306. "Proceeds"; Secured Party's Rights on Disposition of Collateral

(1) ["Proceeds" includes whatever is received when collateral or proceeds is sold, exchanged, collected or otherwise disposed of. The term also includes the account arising when the right to payment is earned under a contract right.]
"Proceeds" includes whatever is received upon the sale, exchange, collection or other disposition of collateral or proceeds. Insurance payable by reason of loss or damage to the collateral is proceeds, except to the extent that it is payable to a person other than a party to the security agreement. Money, checks, deposit accounts, and the like are "cash proceeds". All other proceeds are "non-cash proceeds".

(2) Except where this Article otherwise provides, a security interest continues in collateral notwithstanding sale, exchange or other disposition thereof [by the debtor] unless [his action was] the disposition was authorized by the secured party in the security agreement or otherwise, and also continues in any identifiable proceeds including collections received by the debtor.

(3) The security interest in proceeds is a continuously perfected security interest if the interest in the original collateral was perfected but it ceases to be a perfected security interest and becomes unperfected ten days after receipt of the proceeds by the debtor unless

[(a) a filed financing statement covering the original collateral also covers proceeds; or]

(a) a filed financing statement covers the original collateral and the proceeds are collateral in which a security interest may be perfected by filing in the office or offices where the financing statement has been filed and, if the proceeds are acquired with cash proceeds, the description of collateral in the financing statement indicates the types of property constituting the proceeds; or

(b) a filed financing statement covers the original collateral and the proceeds are identifiable cash proceeds; or

(c) [(b)] the security interest in the proceeds is perfected before the expiration of the ten day period.

Except as provided in this section, a security interest in proceeds can be perfected only by the methods or under the circumstances permitted in this Article for original collateral of the same type.

(4) In the event of insolvency proceedings instituted by or against a debtor, a secured party with a perfected security interest in proceeds has a perfected security interest only in the following proceeds:

(a) in identifiable non-cash proceeds[;] and in separate deposit accounts containing only proceeds;

(b) in identifiable cash proceeds in the form of money which is [not] neither commingled with other money [or] nor deposited in a [bank] deposit account prior to the insolvency proceedings;

(c) in identifiable cash proceeds in the form of checks and the like which are not deposited in a [bank] deposit account prior to the insolvency proceedings; and

(d) in all cash and [bank] deposit accounts of the debtor [if other cash] in which proceeds have been commingled with other funds, [or deposited in a bank account,] but the perfected security interest under this paragraph (d) is

(i) subject to any right of set-off; and

(ii) limited to an amount not greater than the amount of any cash proceeds received by the debtor within ten days before the institution of the insolvency proceedings [and commingled or deposited in a bank account prior to the insolvency proceedings less the amount of cash proceeds received by the debtor and paid over to the secured party during the ten day period,] less the sum of (I) the payments to the secured party on account of cash proceeds received by the debtor during such period and (II) the cash proceeds received by the debtor during such period to which the secured party is entitled under paragraphs (a) through (c) of this subsection (4).

(5) If a sale of goods results in an account or chattel paper which is transferred by the seller to a secured party, and if the goods are returned to or are repossessed by the seller or the secured party, the following rules determine priorities:

(a) If the goods were collateral at the time of sale, for an indebtedness of the seller which is still unpaid, the original security interest attaches again to the goods and continues as a perfected security interest if it was perfected at the time when the goods were sold. If the security interest was originally perfected by a filing which is still effective, nothing further is required to continue the perfected status; in any other case, the secured party must take possession of the returned or repossessed goods or must file.

(b) An unpaid transferee of the chattel paper has a security interest in the goods against the transferor. Such security interest is prior to a security interest asserted under paragraph (a) to the extent that the transferee of the chattel paper was entitled to priority under Section 9—308.

(c) An unpaid transferee of the account has a security interest in the goods against the transferor. Such security interest is subordinate to a security interest asserted under paragraph (a).

(d) A security interest of an unpaid transferee asserted under paragraph (b) or (c) must be perfected for protection against creditors of the transferor and purchasers of the returned or repossessed goods.

Reasons for 1972 Change

The first sentence of subsection (1) is rewritten for clarity.

The former second sentence of subsection (1) is omitted consistently with the abandonment of the term "contract right" in Section 9—106.

The new second sentence of subsection (1) is intended to overrule various cases to the effect that proceeds of insurance on collateral are not proceeds of the collateral. The "except" clause is intended to say that if the insurance contract specifies the person to whom the insurance is payable, the concept of "proceeds" will not interfere with performance of the contract.

Heretofore an apparent inconsistency and ambiguity has existed between the last sentence of Section 9—203(1) (b) of the 1962 Code, which indicated that a claim to proceeds had to be an express term of a security agreement, and Section 9—306(2), which indicated that a right to proceeds was automatic without reference to a term of a security agreement. This ambiguity has been clarified in favor of an automatic right to proceeds, on the theory that this is the intent of the parties, unless otherwise agreed. Further, there has been eliminated the requirement of claiming proceeds in a financing statement, which had resulted in a checking of a box on each financing statement in order to claim proceeds. Instead, the filed claim to the original collateral is treated as constituting automatically a filing as to proceeds. To this principle, a limitation has been stated: Where the filing as to the original collateral is an inappropriate means of perfection as to proceeds of certain types, or is made at a place that is inappropriate as to such proceeds, the filed claim to the original collateral perfects the claim to proceeds for only 10 days. One example of this is negotiable instruments as proceeds, as to which filing is inappropriate under Section 9—304(1). Another example is the case of accounts as proceeds of inventory, as to which under the rules of Section 9—103 the state of filing for the accounts might be different from the state of filing for the inventory.

The revised subsection (4) is a clarification based on the California revision. It makes clear that the claim to cash allowed in insolvency is exclusive of any other claim based on tracing.

§ 9—307. Protection of Buyers of Goods

(1) A buyer in ordinary course of business (subsection (9) of Section 1—201) other than a person buying farm products from a person engaged in farming operations takes free of a security interest created by his seller even though the security interest is perfected and even though the buyer knows of its existence.

(2) In the case of consumer goods [and in the case of farm equipment having an original purchase price not in excess of $2500 (other than fixtures, see Section 9—313)], a buyer takes free of a security interest even though perfected if he buys with-

out knowledge of the security interest, for value and for his own personal, family or household purposes [or his own farming operations] unless prior to the purchase the secured party has filed a financing statement covering such goods.

(3) A buyer other than a buyer in ordinary course of business (subsection (1) of this section) takes free of a security interest to the extent that it secures future advances made after the secured party acquires knowledge of the purchase, or more than 45 days after the purchase, whichever first occurs, unless made pursuant to a commitment entered into without knowledge of the purchase and before the expiration of the 45 day period.

Reasons for 1972 Change

The change in subsection (2) is a conforming change made necessary by the deletion of Section 9—302(1) (c) of the 1962 Code, which provided in substance that a purchase money security interest in farm equipment having an original purchase price not in excess of $2500 need not be filed. The omission of that provision in Subsection 9—302(1) makes any corresponding reference unnecessary in the present section.

Subsection (3) is one of three new provisions clarifying the extent to which future advances under a security interest may outrank an intervening right. See Sections 9—301(4) and 9—312(7) and paragraph (5) of Reasons for Change under Section 9—312.

§ 9—308. Purchase of Chattel Paper and [Non-Negotiable] Instruments

[A purchaser of chattel paper or a non-negotiable instrument who gives new value and takes possession of it in the ordinary course of his business and without knowledge that the specific paper or instrument is subject to a security interest has priority over a security interest which is perfected under Section 9—304 (permissive filing and temporary perfection). A purchaser of chattel paper who gives new value and takes possession of it in the ordinary course of his business has priority over a security interest in chattel paper which is claimed merely as proceeds of inventory subject to a security interest (Section 9—306), even though he knows that the specific paper is subject to the security interest.]

A purchaser of chattel paper or an instrument who gives new value and takes possession of it in the ordinary course of his business has priority over a security interest in the chattel paper or instrument

(a) which is perfected under Section 9—304 (permissive filing and temporary perfection) or under Section 9—306 (perfection as to proceeds) if he acts without knowledge that the specific paper or instrument is subject to a security interest; or

(b) which is claimed merely as proceeds of inventory subject to a security interest (Section 9—306) even though he knows that the specific paper or instrument is subject to the security interest.

Reasons for 1972 Change

The section has been rewritten for clarity.

Another purpose of the changes is to make the rules of this section applicable to negotiable instruments. Heretofore, the holder of a negotiable instrument was under some circumstances in a less protected position against competing claims than the holder of chattel paper. The holder of a negotiable instrument had protection only if he achieved the holder in due course status referred to in Section 9—309, which status would not be achieved if the holder had knowledge of a conflicting proceeds claim. In contrast, the holder of chattel paper who met the stated conditions was protected under the second sentence of Section 9—308 of the 1962 Code even if he had knowledge of the conflicting proceeds claim. Under the changes, the holder of a negotiable instrument who may not qualify as holder in due course may nevertheless qualify for the protections of this section.

§ 9—312. Priorities Among Conflicting Security Interests in the Same Collateral

[(1) The rules of priority stated in the following sections shall govern where applicable: Section 4—208 with respect to the security interest of collecting banks in items being collected, accompanying documents and proceeds; Section 9—301 on certain priorities; Section 9—304 on goods covered by documents; Section 9—306 on proceeds and repossessions; Section 9—307 on buyers of goods; Section 9—308 on possessory against non-possessory interests in chattel paper or non-negotiable instruments; Section 9—309 on security interests in negotiable instruments, documents or securities; Section 9—310 on priorities between perfected security interests and liens by operation of law; Section 9—313 on security interests in fixtures as against interests in real estate; Section 9—314 on security interests in accessions as against interest in goods; Section 9—315 on conflicting security interests where goods lose their identity or become part of a product; and Section 9—316 on contractual subordination.]

(1) The rules of priority stated in other sections of this Part and in the following sections shall govern when applicable: Section 4—208 with respect to the security interests of collecting banks in items being collected, accompanying documents and proceeds; Section 9—103 on security interests related to other jurisdictions; Section 9—114 on consignments.

(2) A perfected security interest in crops for new value given to enable the debtor to produce the crops during the production season and given not more than three months before the crops become growing crops by planting or otherwise takes priority over an earlier perfected security interest to the extent that such earlier interest secures obligations due more than six months before the crops become growing crops by planting or otherwise, even though the person giving new value had knowledge of the earlier security interest.

[(3) A purchase money security interest in inventory collateral has priority over a conflicting security interest in the same collateral if

(a) the purchase money security interest is perfected at the time the debtor receives possession of the collateral; and

(b) any secured party whose security interest is known to the holder of the purchase money security interest or who, prior to the date of the filing made by the holder of the purchase money security interest, had filed a financing statement covering the same items or type of inventory, has received notification of the purchase money security interest before the debtor receives possession of the collateral covered by the purchase money security interest; and

(c) such notification states that the person giving the notice has or expects to acquire a purchase money security interest in inventory of the debtor, describing such inventory by item or type.]

(3) A perfected purchase money security interest in inventory has priority over a conflicting security interest in the same inventory and also has priority in identifiable cash proceeds received on or before the delivery of the inventory to a buyer if

(a) the purchase money security interest is perfected at the time the debtor receives possession of the inventory; and

(b) the purchase money secured party gives notification in writing to the holder of the conflicting security interest if the holder had filed a financing statement covering the same types of inventory (i) before the date of the filing made by the purchase money secured party, or (ii) before the beginning of the 21 day period where the purchase money security interest is temporarily perfected without filing or possession (subsection (5) of Section 9—304); and

(c) the holder of the conflicting security interest receives the notification within five years before the debtor receives possession of the inventory; and

(d) the notification states that the person giving the notice has or expects to acquire a purchase money security interest in inventory of the debtor, describing such inventory by item or type.

(4) A purchase money security interest in collateral other than inventory has priority over a conflicting security interest in the same collateral or its proceeds if the purchase money security interest is perfected at the time the debtor receives possession of the collateral or within ten days thereafter.

(5) In all cases not governed by other rules stated in this section (including cases of purchase money security interests which do not qualify for the special priorities set forth in subsections (3) and (4) of this section), priority between conflicting security interests in the same collateral shall be determined [as follows:

(a) in the order of filing if both are perfected by filing, regardless of which security interest attached first under Section 9—204(1) and whether it attached before or after filing;

(b) in the order of perfection unless both are perfected by filing, regardless of which security interest attached first under Section 9—204(1) and, in the case of a filed security interest, whether it attached before or after filing; and

(c) in the order of attachment under Section 9—204(1) so long as neither is perfected.]

according to the following rules:

(a) Conflicting security interests rank according to priority in time of filing or perfection. Priority dates from the time a filing is first made covering the collateral or the time the security interest is first perfected, whichever is earlier, provided that there is no period thereafter when there is neither filing nor perfection.

(b) So long as conflicting security interests are unperfected, the first to attach has priority.

[(6) For the purpose of the priority rules of the immediately preceding subsection, a continuously perfected security interest shall be treated at all times as if perfected by filing if it was originally so perfected and it shall be treated at all times as if perfected otherwise than by filing if it was originally perfected otherwise than by filing.]

(6) For the purposes of subsection (5) a date of filing or perfection as to collateral is also a date of filing or perfection as to proceeds.

(7) If future advances are made while a security interest is perfected by filing or the taking of possession, the security interest has the same priority for the purposes of subsection (5) with respect to the future advances as it does with respect to the first advance. If a commitment is made before or while the security interest is so perfected, the security interest has the same priority with respect to advances made pursuant thereto. In other cases a perfected security interest has priority from the date the advance is made.

Reasons for 1972 Change

(1) The change in subsection (1) is primarily a simplification of statement.

(2) Changes have been made in subsection (3) to answer unresolved questions under the 1962 Code.

(a) One change answers the question how often a notice must be given under that subsection. The period of five years has been chosen by analogy to the duration of a financing statement.

(b) Another change answers the question of the priority status of the security interest in inventory temporarily perfected for 21 days without filing or perfection in a situation which begins with release of a pledged document under Section 9—304(5). The answer provided is the usual rule that the purchase-money claimant to preserve his priority resulting from the document must give the required notice before the debtor receives possession of the inventory. If the secured party fails to give timely notice, he loses his priority under this subsection.

(c) One of the most widely discussed questions under the 1962 Code was the question of the priority between a person claiming accounts as proceeds of inventory and a person claiming the accounts by direct filing with respect thereto. One issue was whether the special position of an inventory financer as a purchase money financer or as the first financer in the business cycle of the debtor gave him any special position as to accounts resulting from the inventory. In general, as revised, a negative answer has been given, and a prior right to inventory does not confer a prior right to any proceeds except identifiable cash proceeds received on or before the delivery of the inventory (i. e., without the intervention of an account). Other aspects of this issue are discussed under subsection (5) of this section.

(3) A different answer has been given in subsection (4) relating to purchase money security interests in collateral other than inventory. Here, where it is not ordinarily expected that the collateral will be sold and that proceeds will result, it seems appropriate to give the party having a purchase money security interest in the original collateral an equivalent priority in its proceeds. The 1962 Code was unclear on this point.

(4) Existing subsection (5) contains two principal rules. Paragraph (a) is a first-to-file rule where both competing security interests are perfected by filing. Paragraph (b) is a first-to-perfect rule when either of the security interests is or both of them are perfected otherwise than by filing. A traffic rule is provided by existing subsection (6) to the effect that a continuously perfected security interest shall be treated for the purpose of the foregoing rules as if at all times perfected in the manner it was first perfected. The problems raised have been the subject of an enormous legal literature. They are complicated by the unforeseeable effect of the temporary perfection of security interest in proceeds without filing under Section 9—306, and by speculation as to whether a secured party could claim that his security interest was originally perfected without filing under this rule even though the security interest in proceeds was claimed in his filing as to the original collateral. They are further com-

plicated by the question whether different rules would apply when a financing statement was drawn to cover, e. g., inventory and its proceeds (which would include accounts) and when it was drawn to cover inventory and accounts.

To settle these questions it is proposed to replace the present paragraphs (a) and (b) of subsection (5) by a single rule, subsection (5), and to eliminate existing subsection (6). Together with this treatment should be noted the fact that a filing as to proceeds automatically arises from a filed security interest in original collateral under the proposed revision of Section 9—306(3), subject to limitations therein discussed. New proposed subsection (6) makes it clear that subject to these limitations the time of filing or perfection as to original collateral is the time of filing or perfection as to proceeds.

The rule of proposed subsection (5) ranks conflicting perfected security interests by their priority in time, dating back to the respective times when without interruption the security interests were either perfected or were the subjects of appropriate filings.

Perhaps the most debated subject under Article 9 has been the question whether between conflicting security interests a priority as to original collateral confers a priority as to proceeds. As indicated above, in the case of collateral other than inventory, e. g., equipment, it seems clear that the policy favoring the purchase money secured party in Section 9—312 (4) should give him the first claim to the proceeds. This is so even though the security interests will have been perfected simultaneously when the proceeds arise and the debtor acquires rights therein.

Proper policy is much less clear when the collateral involved is inventory and proceeds consisting of accounts. (Policy as to other types of receivables as proceeds is expressed in Sections 9—308 and 9—309). Accounts financing is more important in the economy than the financing of the kinds of inventory that produce accounts, and the desirable rule is one which makes accounts financing certain as to its legal position. Therefore, the rule proposed is that where a financing statement as to accounts is filed first (with or without related inventory financing), the security interest in accounts should not be defeated by any subsequent claim to accounts as proceeds of a security interest in inventory filed later. There is therefore no provision in Section 9—312(3) carrying forward to accounts any priority right in inventory, and proposed subsections (5) and (6) adhere firmly to the principle that a date of filing as to original collateral also defines the date of filing as to proceeds. Correspondingly, a financing statement as to inventory (carrying with it a claim to proceeds) which is filed first will under the same provisions have priority over a later-filed security interest in accounts.

(5) The priority of future advances against an intervening party has been the subject of much discussion and disagreement. Where both interests are filed security interests, the first-to-file rule of present Section 9—312(5) (a) or the corresponding proposed revision is clearly applicable. Under the 1962 Code, the position of an intervening pledgee in reference to a subsequent advance by an earlier-filed secured party is debatable. The proposed unified priority rule of subsection 9—312(5) would indicate that subsequent advances by the first-filed party have priority, and subsequent advances under a security interest perfected by possession likewise have priority over an intervening filed security interest. These priority rules are expressly stated in proposed subsection (7). That proposal also deals with the rare case of the priority position of a subsequent advance made by a secured party whose security interest is temporarily perfected without either filing or possession, against an intervening secured party. Since there is no notice by the usual methods of filing or possession of the existence of the security interest, the subsequent advances rank only from the actual date of making unless made pursuant to commitment.

Different but related problems exist with reference to the status of subsequent advances when the intervening party is a judgment creditor. He is not directly part of the Code's system of priorities. It seems unfair to make it possible for a debtor and secured party with knowledge of the judgment lien to squeeze out a judgment creditor who has successfully levied on a valuable equity subject to a security interest, by permitting later enlargement of the security interest by an additional advance, unless that advance was committed in advance without such knowledge. Proposed Section 9—301(4) provides that a lien creditor does not take subject to a subsequent advance unless it is given or committed without knowledge, but there is an exception protecting future advances within 45 days after the levy regardless of knowledge. The 45-day period corresponds to a provision on protection of advances made after the filing of tax liens in the Federal Tax Lien Act of 1966.

A similar problem arises where the intervening party is a buyer of the collateral subject to the security interest. While buyers must necessarily take subject to rights of secured parties, the buyer should take subject to subsequent advances only to the extent that they are given "pursuant to commitment" or within the period of 45 days after the purchase but not later than the time that the secured party acquires knowledge of the purchase. It is so proposed in Section 9—307(3). A definition of the quoted phrase appears in Section 9—105.

§ 9—313. Priority of Security Interests in Fixtures

[(1) The rules of this section do not apply to goods incorporated into a structure in the manner of lumber, bricks, tile, cement, glass, metal work and the like and no security interest in them exists under this Article unless the structure remains personal property under applicable law. The law of this state other than this Act determines whether and when other goods become fixtures. This Act does not prevent creation of an encumbrance upon fixtures or real estate pursuant to the law applicable to real estate.]

[(2) A security interest which attaches to goods before they become fixtures takes priority as to the goods over the claims of all persons who have an interest in the real estate except as stated in subsection (4).]

[(3) A security interest which attaches to goods after they become fixtures is valid against all persons subsequently acquiring interests in the real estate except as stated in subsection (4) but is invalid against any person with an interest in the real estate at the time the security interest attaches to the goods who has not in writing consented to the security interest or disclaimed an interest in the goods as fixtures.]

[(4) The security interests described in subsections (2) and (3) do not take priority over

(a) a subsequent purchaser for value of any interest in the real estate; or

(b) a creditor with a lien on the real estate subsequently obtained by judicial proceedings; or

(c) a creditor with a prior encumbrance of record on the real estate to the extent that he makes subsequent advances

if the subsequent purchase is made, the lien by judicial proceedings is obtained, or the subsequent advance under the prior encumbrance is made or contracted for without knowledge of the security interest and before it is perfected. A purchaser of the real estate at a foreclosure sale other than an encumbrancer purchasing at his own foreclosure sale is a subsequent purchaser within this section.]

(1) In this section and in the provisions of Part 4 of this Article referring to fixture filing, unless the context otherwise requires

(a) goods are "fixtures" when they become so related to particular real estate that an interest in them arises under real estate law

(b) a "fixture filing" is the filing in the office where a mortgage on the real estate would be filed or recorded of a financing statement covering goods which are or are to become fixtures and conforming to the requirements of subsection (5) of Section 9—402

(c) a mortgage is a "construction mortgage" to the extent that it secures an obligation incurred for the construction of an improvement on land including the acquisition cost of the land, if the recorded writing so indicates.

(2) A security interest under this Article may be created in goods which are fixtures or may continue in goods which become fixtures, but no security interest exists under this Article in ordinary building materials incorporated into an improvement on land.

(3) This Article does not prevent creation of an encumbrance upon fixtures pursuant to real estate law.

(4) A perfected security interest in fixtures has priority over the conflicting interest of an encumbrancer or owner of the real estate where

(a) the security interest is a purchase money security interest, the interest of the encumbrancer or owner arises before the goods become fixtures, the security interest is perfected by a fixture filing before the goods become fixtures or within ten days thereafter, and the debtor has an interest of record in the real estate or is in possession of the real estate; or

(b) the security interest is perfected by a fixture filing before the interest of the encumbrancer or owner is of record, the security interest has priority over any conflicting interest of a predecessor in title of the encumbrancer or owner, and the debtor has an interest of record in the real estate or is in possession of the real estate; or

(c) the fixtures are readily removable factory or office machines or readily removable replacements of domestic appliances which are consumer goods, and before the goods become fixtures the security interest is perfected by any method permitted by this Article; or

(d) the conflicting interest is a lien on the real estate obtained by legal or equitable proceedings after the security interest was perfected by any method permitted by this Article.

(5) A security interest in fixtures, whether or not perfected, has priority over the conflicting interest of an encumbrancer or owner of the real estate where

(a) the encumbrancer or owner has consented in writing to the security interest or has disclaimed an interest in the goods as fixtures; or

(b) the debtor has a right to remove the goods as against the encumbrancer or owner. If the debtor's right terminates, the priority of the security interest continues for a reasonable time.

(6) Notwithstanding paragraph (a) of subsection (4) but otherwise subject to subsections (4) and (5), a security interest in fixtures is subordinate to a construction mortgage recorded before the goods become fixtures if the goods become fixtures before the completion of the construction. To the extent that it is given to refinance a construction mortgage, a mortgage has this priority to the same extent as the construction mortgage.

(7) In cases not within the preceding subsections, a security interest in fixtures is subordinate to the conflicting interest of an encumbrancer or owner of the related real estate who is not the debtor.

(8) [(5)] When [under subsections (2) or (3) or (4) a] the secured party has priority over [the claims of all persons who have interests in] all owners and encumbrancers of the real estate, he may, on default, subject to the provisions of Part 5, remove his collateral from the real estate but he must reimburse any encumbrancer or owner of the real estate who is not the debtor and who has not otherwise agreed for the cost of repair of any physical injury, but not for any diminution in value of the real estate caused by the absence of the goods removed or by any necessity of replacing them. A person entitled to reimbursement may refuse permission to remove until the secured party gives adequate security for the performance of this obligation.

Reasons for 1972 Change

As the Code came to be widely enacted, the real estate bar came to realize the impact of the fixture provisions on real estate financing and real estate titles. They apparently had not fully appreciated the impact of these provisions of Article 9 on real estate matters during the enactment of the Code, because of the commonly-held assumption that Article 9 was concerned only with chattel security matters.

The treatment of fixtures in pre-Code law had varied widely from state to state. The treatment in Article 9 was based generally on prior treatment in the Uniform Conditional Sales Act, which, however, had been enacted in only a dozen states. In other states the word "fixture" had come to mean that a former chattel had become real estate for all purposes and that any chattel rights therein were lost. For lawyers trained in such states the Code provisions seemed to be extreme. Some sections of the real estate bar began attempting with some success to have Section 9—313 amended to bring it closer to the pre-Code law in their states. In some states, such as California and Iowa, Section 9—313 simply was not enacted.

Even supporters of Article 9 and of its fixture provisions came to recognize that there were some ambiguities in Section 9—313, particularly in its application to construction mortgages, and also in its failure to make it clear that filing of fixture security interests was to be in real estate records where they could be found by a standard real estate search.

Section 9—313 and related provisions of Part 4 have been redrafted to meet the legitimate criticisms and to make a substantial shift in the law in favor of construction mortgages. The specific changes are described in the 1972 Comments to Section 9—313, and the Comments to the several sections of Part 4.

§ 9—318. Defenses Against Assignee; Modification of Contract After Notification of Assignment; Term Prohibiting Assignment Ineffective; Identification and Proof of Assignment

(1) Unless an account debtor has made an enforceable agreement not to assert defenses or claims arising out of a sale as

provided in Section 9—206 the rights of an assignee are subject to

(a) all the terms of the contract between the account debtor and assignor and any defense or claim arising therefrom; and

(b) any other defense or claim of the account debtor against the assignor which accrues before the account debtor receives notification of the assignment.

(2) So far as the right to payment or a part thereof under an assigned contract has not been fully earned by performance, [right has not already become an account,] and notwithstanding notification of the assignment, any modification of or substitution for the contract made in good faith and in accordance with reasonable commercial standards is effective against an assignee unless the account debtor has otherwise agreed but the assignee acquires corresponding rights under the modified or substituted contract. The assignment may provide that such modification or substitution is a breach by the assignor.

(3) The account debtor is authorized to pay the assignor until the account debtor receives notification that the [account] amount due or to become due has been assigned and that payment is to be made to the assignee. A notification which does not reasonably identify the rights assigned is ineffective. If requested by the account debtor, the assignee must seasonably furnish reasonable proof that the assignment has been made and unless he does so the account debtor may pay the assignor.

(4) A term in any contract between an account debtor and an assignor [which] is ineffective if it prohibits assignment of an account [or contract right to which they are parties is ineffective] or prohibits creation of a security interest in a general intangible for money due or to become due or requires the account debtor's consent to such assignment or security interest.

Reasons for 1972 Change

The principal changes conform to the elimination of the term "contract right" in Section 9—106.

Minor changes in subsections (3) and (4) eliminate technical difficulties in the 1962 Code which arose out of the fact that the term "account debtor" used in these subsections is defined to include debtors under general intangibles and chattel paper, and is therefore broader than the term "account" heretofore used in these subsections. Subsection (4) is broadened to apply to general intangibles for money due as well as to accounts.

PART 4

FILING

§ 9—401. Place of Filing; Erroneous Filing; Removal of Collateral

First Alternative Subsection (1)

(1) The proper place to file in order to perfect a security interest is as follows:

(a) when the collateral is timber to be cut or is minerals or the like (including oil and gas) or accounts subject to subsection (5) of Section 9—103, or when the financing statement is filed as a fixture filing (Section 9—313) and the collateral is goods which [at the time the security interest attaches] are or are to become fixtures, then in the office where a mortgage on the real estate [concerned] would be filed or recorded;

(b) in all other cases, in the office of the [[Secretary of State]].

Second Alternative Subsection (1)

(1) The proper place to file in order to perfect a security interest is as follows:

(a) when the collateral is equipment used in farming operations, or farm products, or accounts [, contract rights] or general intangibles arising from or relating to the sale of farm products by a farmer, or consumer goods, then in the office of the .... in the county of the debtor's residence or if the debtor is not a resident of this state then in the office of the .... in the county where the goods are kept, and in addition when the collateral is crops growing or to be grown in the office of the .... in the county where the land [on which the crops are growing or to be grown] is located;

(b) when the collateral is [goods which at the time the security interest attaches are or are to become fixtures] timber to be cut or is minerals or the like (including oil and gas) or accounts subject to subsection (5) of Section 9—103, or when the financing statement is filed as a fixture filing (Section 9—313) and the collateral is goods which are or are to be become fixtures, then in the office where a mortgage on the real estate [concerned] would be filed or recorded;

(c) in all other cases, in the office of the [[Secretary of State]].

Third Alternative Subsection (1)

(1) The proper place to file in order to perfect a security interest is as follows:

(a) when the collateral is equipment used in farming operations, or farm products, or accounts [, contract rights] or general intangibles arising from or relating to the sale of farm products by a farmer, or consumer goods, then in the office of the .... in the county of the debtor's residence or if the debtor is not a resident of this state then in the office of the .... in the county where the goods are kept, and in addition when the collateral is crops growing or to be grown in the office of the ...... in the county where the land [on which the crops are growing or to be grown] is located;

(b) when the collateral is [goods which at the time the security interest attaches are or are to become fixtures] timber to be cut or is minerals or the like (including oil and gas) or accounts subject to subsection (5) of Section 9—103, or when the financing statement is filed as a fixture filing (Section 9—313) and the collateral is goods which are or are to become fixtures, then in the office where a mortgage on the real estate [concerned] would be filed or recorded;

(c) in all other cases, in the office of the [[Secretary of State]] and in addition, if the debtor has a place of business in only one county of this state, also in the office of ...... of such county, or, if the debtor has no place of business in this state, but resides in the state, also in the office of ...... of the county in which he resides.

Note: *One of the three alternatives should be selected as subsection (1).*

(2) A filing which is made in good faith in an improper place or not in all of the places required by this section is nevertheless effective with regard to any collateral as to which the filing complied with the requirements of this Article and is also effective with regard to collateral covered by the financing statement against any person who has knowledge of the contents of such financing statement.

(3) A filing which is made in the proper place in this state continues effective even though the debtor's residence or place of business or the location of the collateral or its use, whichever controlled the original filing, is thereafter changed.

Language in double brackets is Alternative Subsection (3)

[[(3) A filing which is made in the proper county continues effective for four months after a change to another county of the debtor's residence or place of business or the location of the collateral, whichever controlled the original filing. It becomes ineffective thereafter unless a copy of the financing statement signed by the secured party is filed in the new county within said period. The security interest may also be perfected in the new county after the expiration of the four-month period; in such case perfected dates from the time of perfection in the new county. A change in the use of the collateral does not impair the effectiveness of the original filing.]]

(4) [If collateral is brought into this state from another jurisdiction, the] The rules stated in Section 9—103 determine whether filing is necessary in this state.

(5) Notwithstanding the preceding subsections, and subject to subsection (3) of Section 9—302, the proper place to file in order to perfect a security interest in collateral, including fixtures, of a transmitting utility is the office of the [[Secretary of State]]. This filing constitutes a fixture filing (Section 9—313) as to the collateral described therein which is or is to become fixtures.

(6) For the purposes of this section, the residence of an organization is its place of business if it has one or its chief executive office if it has more than one place of business.

Note: *Subsection (6) should be used only if the state chooses the Second or Third Alternative Subsection (1).*

Reasons for 1972 Change

The several alternatives for subsection (1) have been rewritten to provide for filing in the real estate records of security interests intended to give a priority as a "fixture filing" under Section 9—313.

This requirement for filing in real estate records applies only if the priority advantages of Section 9—313 are desired. If the secured party is not concerned about priority against real estate parties, he can file for a fixture as for an ordinary chattel, in the chattel records, omitting the filing in the real estate records, and he will have a security interest perfected against everyone but real estate parties. In the case of a purchase money security interest in consumer goods, he need not file at all. See Section 9—313(1) (d). For the question of the effect of the regular chattel filing in lieu of fixture filing in the event of the debtor's bankruptcy, see Comment 4(c) to Section 9—313.

This requirement for filing in real estate records applies also to timber to be cut and to minerals or the like (including oil and gas) financed at the wellhead or minehead or accounts resulting from the sale thereof.

This filing is not merely in the *office* where a mortgage of real estate would be recorded, but it is intended that it be filed *in the real estate records*. This is made clear by the model form in Section 9—402(3) which recites that the financing statement is to be filed for record in the real estate records, the required recital in Section 9—402(5), and the provision of Section 9—403(7) requiring the indexing thereof in the real estate records. Thus, it is intended that these filings will be readily disclosed on any real estate search and they can be treated like any real estate encumbrance so disclosed.

A new subsection (5) makes clear that a financing statement filed against a "transmitting utility" (Section 9—105) need be filed only in the office of the [Secretary of State] and not locally. Special provision had to be made for filing where these far-flung utilities were debtors. If the problem were only on non-fixtures, not more than one local filing would have been necessary under any of the alternative versions of subsection (1), but the problem was more difficult in the case of fixtures, where the standard rule would require filing with real estate descriptions in every county where there were fixtures.

There has been some difficulty in the concept that one files against farmers at their residences, in view of the number of incorporated farms. A new subsection (6) is therefore added to define the residence of an organization. Subsection (6) is also needed if the provision of the Third Alternative Subsection (1) for double filing against local business debtors is adopted.

§ 9—402. Formal Requisites of Financing Statement; Amendments; Mortgage as Financing Statement

(1) A financing statement is sufficient if it gives the names of the debtor and the secured party, is signed by the debtor [and the secured party], gives an address of the secured party from which information concerning the security interest may be obtained, gives a mailing address of the debtor and contains a statement indicating the types, or describing the items, of collateral. A financing statement may be filed before a security agreement is made or a security interest otherwise attaches. When the financing statement covers crops growing or to be grown [or goods which are or are to become fixtures], the statement must also contain a description of the real estate concerned. When the financing statement covers timber to be cut or covers minerals or the like (including oil and gas) or accounts subject to subsection (5) of Section 9—103, or when the financing statement is filed as a fixture filing (Section 9—313) and the collateral is goods which are or are to become fixtures, the statement must also comply with subsection (5). A copy of the security agreement is sufficient as a financing statement if it contains the above information and is signed by [both parties.] the debtor. A carbon, photographic or other reproduction of a security agreement or a financing statement is sufficient as a financing statement if the security agreement so provides or if the original has been filed in this state.

(2) A financing statement which otherwise complies with subsection (1) is sufficient [although] when it is signed [only] by the secured party instead of the debtor if it is filed to perfect a security interest in

(a) collateral already subject to a security interest in another jurisdiction when it is brought into this state, or when the debtor's location is changed to this state. Such a financing statement must state that the collateral was brought into this state or that the debtor's location was changed to this state under such circumstances; or

(b) proceeds under Section 9—306 if the security interest in the original collateral was perfected. Such a financing statement must describe the original collateral; or

(c) collateral as to which the filing has lapsed; or

(d) collateral acquired after a change of name, identity or corporate structure of the debtor (subsection (7)).

(3) A form substantially as follows is sufficient to comply with subsection (1):

Name of debtor (or assignor) ....
Address ....
Name of secured party (or assignee) ....
Address ....

1. This financing statement covers the following types (or items) of property:
   (Describe) ....
2. (If collateral is crops) The above described crops are growing or are to be grown on:
   (Describe Real Estate) ....

[3. (If collateral is goods which are or are to become fixtures) The above described goods are affixed or to be affixed to:
   (Describe Real Estate) ....]

3. (If applicable) The above goods are to become fixtures on*

* Where appropriate substitute either "The above timber is standing on . . . ." or "The above minerals or the like (including oil and gas) or accounts will be financed at the wellhead or minehead of the well or mine located on . . . ."

   (Describe Real Estate) ....
   and this financing statement is to be filed [[for record]] in the real estate records. (If the debtor does not have an interest of record) The name of a record owner is ....

4. (If [proceeds or] products of collateral are claimed) [Proceeds—] Products of the collateral are also covered.

(use whichever is applicable)

....
Signature of Debtor (or Assignor)

....
Signature of Secured Party (or Assignee)

(4) A financing statement may be amended by filing a writing signed by both the debtor and the secured party. An amend-

ment does not extend the period of effectiveness of a financing statement. [The term "financing statement" as used in this Article means the original financing statement and any amendments but if] If any amendment adds collateral, it is effective as to the added collateral only from the filing date of the amendment. In this Article, unless the context otherwise requires, the term "financing statement" means the original financing statement and any amendments.

(5) A financing statement covering timber to be cut or covering minerals or the like (including oil and gas) or accounts subject to subsection (5) of Section 9—103, or a financing statement filed as a fixture filing (Section 9—313) where the debtor is not a transmitting utility, must show that it covers this type of collateral, must recite that it is to be filed [[for record]] in the real estate records, and the financing statement must contain a description of the real estate [[sufficient if it were contained in a mortgage of the real estate to give constructive notice of the mortgage under the law of this state]]. If the debtor does not have an interest of record in the real estate, the financing statement must show the name of a record owner.

(6) A mortgage is effective as a financing statement filed as a fixture filing from the date of its recording if (a) the goods are described in the mortgage by item or type, (b) the goods are or are to become fixtures related to the real estate described in the mortgage, (c) the mortgage complies with the requirements for a financing statement in this section other than a recital that it is to be filed in the real estate records, and (d) the mortgage is duly recorded. No fee with reference to the financing statement is required other than the regular recording and satisfaction fees with respect to the mortgage.

(7) A financing statement sufficiently shows the name of the debtor if it gives the individual, partnership or corporate name of the debtor, whether or not it adds other trade names or the names of partners. Where the debtor so changes his name or in the case of an organization its name, identity or corporate structure that a filed financing statement becomes seriously misleading, the filing is not effective to perfect a security interest in collateral acquired by the debtor more than four months after the change, unless a new appropriate financing statement is filed before the expiration of that time. A filed financing statement remains effective with respect to collateral transferred by the debtor even though the secured party knows of or consents to the transfer.

(8) [(5)] A financing statement substantially complying with the requirements of this section is effective even though it contains minor errors which are not seriously misleading.

Note: *Language in double brackets is optional.*

Note: *Where the state has any special recording system for real estate other than the usual grantor-grantee index (as, for instance, a tract system or a title registration or Torrens system) local adaptations of subsection (5) and Section 9—403(7) may be necessary. See Mass. Gen. Laws Chapter 106, Section 9—409.*

Reasons for 1972 Change

Certain changes are conforming changes to new requirements of Section 9—401 that certain financing statements covering such collateral as timber and minerals be filed in the real estate records. Persons interested in real estate have complained with some justice that the provisions of the 1962 Code failed in several ways to tie the fixture filings to the real estate search system. Among these was the absence of clear specification that the fixture security interest was to be indexed in the real estate records. On this point, a responsive change has been made in Section 9—403. Other objections related to the adequacy of the real estate description and to the fact that the debtor might not be an owner of an interest of record in the real estate. The optional language in subsection (5) is designed to meet the objection as to real estate descriptions but without imposing on a fixture-secured party the duty of obtaining a "legal description" unless the state's recording system requires it. While no doubt a full "legal description" is proper practice in conveyancing, it is believed that something significantly less, like a street address, would be adequate in most states, and would frequently be a guide to a recorded map. Where a state has a tract index system or other special system not dependent on a grantor-grantee index, special adaptations may be required and no attempt is made in the Code to deal with all such situations.

Another objection of real estate parties has been that the name of the debtor might not be in the real estate chain of title and there have been numerous non-uniform amendments to Sections 9—401, 9—402, or 9—403 designed to require the showing of the name of the record owners of the real estate in the financing statement. Since Section 9-313(4) (a) and (b) permit fixture filing against persons in possession of the real estate who do not have interests of record, Section 9—402 requires the naming of an owner of record of the real estate in such cases, and Section 9—403(7) requires indexing the fixture filing against the name.

Subsection (6) makes it possible for a real estate mortgage to serve as a financing statement, and a related change in Section 9—403(6) makes it unnecessary to file continuation statements for such a financing statement.

Subsection (1) has been changed to require only the signature of the debtor rather than that of the secured party. The requirement of signatures of secured parties has sometimes misled secured parties, who are accustomed to pre-Code practice and real estate practice under which only the debtor, not the secured party, need sign such instruments as chattel mortgages and real estate mortgages. Thus, when the security agreement was used as the financing statement, it might have been defective under the 1962 Code for failure to have the signature of the secured party. This change also fits in with the provisions of Section 9—403(6), under which a real estate mortgage (customarily signed only by the debtor) may be effective as a financing statement.

Changes in the form of financing statement in subsection (3) conform to the foregoing and are also intended to have the secured party make clear when a financing statement is intended to be filed in real estate records. This had been a matter of some concern when the parties used the term "fixture" loosely in their description of goods.

Certain of the changes in Section 9—402 are not related to real estate filings. The changes in paragraph (2) (a) conform to Section 9—103(3), which requires refiling when the debtor's location changes. Additions in subsections (2) (d) and (7) relating to the problem of the name of the debtor against which a filing should be made and the effect of transfer are discussed in the related Comments.

§ 9—403. What Constitutes Filing; Duration of Filing; Effect of Lapsed Filing; Duties of Filing Officer

(1) Presentation for filing of a financing statement and tender of the filing fee or acceptance of the statement by the filing officer constitutes filing under this Article.

<u>(2) Except as provided in subsection (6) a</u> [(2) A] filed financing statement [which states a maturity date of the obligation secured of five years or less is effective until such maturity date and thereafter for a period of sixty days. Any other filed financ-

ing statement] is effective for a period of five years from the date of filing. The effectiveness of a filed financing statement lapses [on the expiration of such sixty day period after a stated maturity date or] on the expiration of [such five] the five year period [, as the case may be] unless a continuation statement is filed prior to the lapse. If a security interest perfected by filing exists at the time insolvency proceedings are commenced by or against the debtor, the security interest remains perfected until termination of the insolvency proceedings and thereafter for a period of sixty days or until expiration of the five year period, whichever occurs later. Upon [such] lapse the security interest becomes unperfected, unless it is perfected without filing. If the security interest becomes unperfected upon lapse, it is deemed to have been unperfected as against a person who became a purchaser or lien creditor before lapse. [A filed financing statement which states that the obligation secured is payable on demand is effective for five years from the date of filing.]

(3) A continuation statement may be filed by the secured party [(i) within six months before and sixty days after a stated maturity date of five years or less, and (ii) otherwise] within six months prior to the expiration of the five year period specified in subsection (2). Any such continuation statement must be signed by the secured party, identify the original statement by file number and state that the original statement is still effective. A continuation statement signed by a person other than the secured party of record must be accompanied by a separate written statement of assignment signed by the secured party of record and complying with subsection (2) of Section 9—405, including payment of the required fee. Upon timely filing of the continuation statement, the effectiveness of the original statement is continued for five years after the last date to which the filing was effective whereupon it lapses in the same manner as provided in subsection (2) unless another continuation statement is filed prior to such lapse. Succeeding continuation statements may be filed in the same manner to continue the effectiveness of the original statement. Unless a statute on disposition of public records provides otherwise, the filing officer may remove a lapsed statement from the files and destroy it[.] immediately if he has retained a microfilm or other photographic record, or in other cases after one year after the lapse. The filing officer shall so arrange matters by physical annexation of financing statements to continuation statements or other related filings, or by other means, that if he physically destroys the financing statements of a period more than five years past, those which

have been continued by a continuation statement or which are still effective under subsection (6) shall be retained.

(4) Except as provided in subsection (7) a [(4) A] filing officer shall mark each statement with a [consecutive] file number and with the date and hour of filing and shall hold the statement or a microfilm or other photographic copy thereof for public inspection. In addition the filing officer shall index the statements according to the name of the debtor and shall note in the index the file number and the address of the debtor given in the statement.

[(5) The uniform fee for filing, indexing and furnishing filing data for an original or a continuation statement shall be $......]

(5) The uniform fee for filing and indexing and for stamping a copy furnished by the secured party to show the date and place of filing for an original financing statement or for a continuation statement shall be $.......... if the statement is in the standard form prescribed by the [[Secretary of State]] and otherwise shall be $........, plus in each case, if the financing statement is subject to subsection (5) of Section 9—402, $......... The uniform fee for each name more than one required to be indexed shall be $........... The secured party may at his option show a trade name for any person and an extra uniform indexing fee of $.......... shall be paid with respect thereto.

(6) If the debtor is a transmitting utility (subsection (5) of Section 9—401) and a filed financing statement so states, it is effective until a termination statement is filed. A real estate mortgage which is effective as a fixture filing under subsection (6) of Section 9—402 remains effective as a fixture filing until the mortgage is released or satisfied of record or its effectiveness otherwise terminates as to the real estate.

(7) When a financing statement covers timber to be cut or covers minerals or the like (including oil and gas) or accounts subject to subsection (5) of Section 9—103, or is filed as a fixture filing, [[it shall be filed for record and]] the filing officer shall index it under the names of the debtor and any owner of record shown on the financing statement in the same fashion as if they were the mortgagors in a mortgage of the real estate described, and, to the extent that the law of this state provides for indexing of mortgages under the name of the mortgagee, under the name of the secured party as if he were the mortgagee thereunder, or where indexing is by description in the same fashion as if the financing statement were a mortgage of the real estate described.

Note: *In states in which writings will not appear in the real estate records and indices unless actually recorded the bracketed language in subsection (7) should be used.*

Reasons for 1972 Change

The change in subsection (2) makes every financing statement (except those described in subsection (6)), effective for a full five years, thus changing the rule of the 1962 Code that a financing statement which showed a maturity less than 5 years was effective only for the period until maturity plus 60 days. This limitation could have been easily evaded simply by not showing a maturity, even though there was one. The change facilitates renewals or extensions up to a maximum combined duration of five years, without the danger of the financing statement ceasing to be effective.

Subsection (2) also recognizes that financing statements might expire during an insolvency proceeding. While the prevailing line of decisions is to the effect that the situation is frozen at the moment of bankruptcy without an obligation to refile, there are contrary decisions, and this situation might prove an inadvertent trap to a secured party who failed to refile or file a continuation statement during a bankruptcy. The change continues the validity of the financing statement until the end of the insolvency proceedings and for 60 days thereafter, or until the expiration of the five-year period, whichever is later. Ordinarily, if the secured party expects that the secured debt may continue in existence after the end of the insolvency proceedings, he should file a continuation statement on the normal schedule, to preserve the filing for use at the end of the insolvency proceeding and to preclude any discontinuity of the filings.

Subsection (2) also clarifies the effect of lapse, a matter on which there has been some dispute among writers on the subject. Compare also Section 9—103(1) (d).

Subsection (5) is intended to adopt non-uniform amendments made in some states giving the filing officer authority to charge extra fees if the financing statement does not conform to a uniform prescribed size and content. It also permits the secured party to show a trade name at his option and to have it indexed for an extra fee.

New subsection (6) deals with transmitting utilities (Sections 9—105 and 9—401(5)) and also with real estate mortgages which are effective as financing statements under Section 9—402(6). In these special cases a financing statement is good indefinitely and its validity is not limited to five years. The filing in real estate records of a financing statement which is also a real estate mortgage will give notice to persons searching the record as to this continuing validity and will not interfere with the purpose of the Code's standard rule of five-year validity for financing statements. The name of a transmitting utility should give equivalent notice in filings against that kind of company.

The purpose of the standard rule is to permit the files to be self-clearing, so that whether or not termination statements have been filed, the filing officer can clear the files after a suitable period after the five-year validity expires, unless the duration of the financing statement has been continued by a continuation statement.

Various technical changes in this section are designed to facilitate the handling of financing statements by filing officers in reference to the use of microfilm, etc., and to carry out the principle of the self-clearing nature of the files after five years.

New subsection (7) deals with a point in reference to fixtures on which the 1962 Code was properly subject to criticism, namely, that it was not explicitly stated that the fixture filing in the county where a real estate mortgage would be recorded was intended to be made and be indexed in the *real estate records*. This principle is now stated and is also made applicable to timber to be cut and to minerals and the like (including oil and gas) financed at the wellhead or minehead or accounts resulting from the sale thereof.

The other minor changes coordinate with the addition of subsection (7) to Section 9—402.

§ 9—404. Termination Statement

(1) If a financing statement covering consumer goods is filed on or after ...., then within one month or within ten days following written demand by the debtor after there is no outstanding secured obligation and no commitment to make advances, incur obligations or otherwise give value, the secured party must file with each filing officer with whom the financing statement was filed, a termination statement to the effect that he no longer claims a security interest under the financing statement, which shall be identified by file number. In other cases whenever [Whenever] there is no outstanding secured obligation and no commitment to make advances, incur obligations or otherwise give value, the secured party must on written demand by the debtor send the debtor, for each filing officer with whom the financing statement was filed, a termination statement to the effect that he no longer claims a security inter-

est under the financing statement, which shall be identified by file number. A termination statement signed by a person other than the secured party of record must [include or] be accompanied by [the assignment or] a separate written statement of assignment signed by the secured party of record [that he has assigned the security interest to the signer of the termination statement. and] complying with subsection (2) of Section 9—405, including payment of the required fee. [The uniform fee for filing and indexing such an assignment or statement thereof shall be $.........] If the affected secured party fails to file such a termination statement as required by this subsection, or to send such a termination statement within ten days after proper demand therefor he shall be liable to the debtor for one hundred dollars, and in addition for any loss caused to the debtor by such failure.

(2) On presentation to the filing officer of such a termination statement he must note it in the index. [The filing officer shall remove from the files, mark "terminated" and send or deliver to the secured party the financing statement and any continuation statement, statement of assignment or statement of release pertaining thereto.] If he has received the termination statement in duplicate, he shall return one copy of the termination statement to the secured party stamped to show the time of receipt thereof. If the filing officer has a microfilm or other photographic record of the financing statement, and of any related continuation statement, statement of assignment and statement of release, he may remove the originals from the files at any time after receipt of the termination statement, or if he has no such record, he may remove them from the files at any time after one year after receipt of the termination statement.

(3) If the termination statement is in the standard form prescribed by the [[Secretary of State]], the uniform fee for filing and indexing [a] the termination statement [including sending or delivering the financing statement] shall be $........, and otherwise shall be $........, plus in each case an additional fee of $........ for each name more than one against which the termination statement is required to be indexed.

Note: *The date to be inserted should be the effective date of the revised Article 9.*

Reasons for 1972 Change

The additions to subsection (1) require the filing of termination statements in the case of consumer goods even without a demand by the consumer. It is believed that consumers will frequently not understand the importance of making demand in order to clear the files. The scope of the change is not as great as might first appear, because (1) filing is not required for purchase money security interests in consumer goods, except in the case of motor vehicles (Section 9—302(1)(d)); and (2) perfection of security interests in most motor vehicles is governed by certificate of title laws, not by the provisions of Article 9.

The other changes are purely formal and tie in with corresponding changes in filing mechanics in other sections.

§ 9—405. Assignment of Security Interest; Duties of Filing Officer; Fees

(1) A financing statement may disclose an assignment of a security interest in the collateral described in the financing statement by indication in the financing statement of the name and address of the assignee or by an assignment itself or a copy thereof on the face or back of the statement. [Either the original secured party or the assignee may sign this statement as the secured party.] On presentation to the filing officer of such a financing statement the filing officer shall mark the same as provided in Section 9—403(4). The uniform fee for filing, indexing and furnishing filing data for a financing statement so indicating an assignment shall be $........ if the statement is in the standard form prescribed by the [[Secretary of State]] and otherwise shall be $........, plus in each case an additional fee of $...... for each name more than one against which the financing statement is required to be indexed.

(2) A secured party may assign of record all or part of his rights under a financing statement by the filing in the place where the original financing statement was filed of a separate written statement of assignment signed by the secured party of record and setting forth the name of the secured party of record and the debtor, the file number and the date of filing of the financing statement and the name and address of the assignee and containing a description of the collateral assigned. A copy of the assignment is sufficient as a separate statement if it complies with the preceding sentence. On presentation to the filing officer of such a separate statement, the filing officer shall mark such separate statement with the date and hour of the filing. He shall note the assignment on the index of the financing statement, or in the case of a fixture filing, or a filing covering timber to be cut, or covering minerals or the like (including oil and gas or ac-

counts subject to subsection (5) of Section 9—103, he shall index the assignment under the name of the assignor as grantor and, to the extent that the law of this state provides for indexing the assignment of a mortgage under the name of the assignee, he shall index the assignment of the financing statement under the name of the assignee. The uniform fee for filing, indexing and furnishing filing data about such a separate statement of assignment shall be $...... if the statement is in the standard form prescribed by the [[Secretary of State]] and otherwise shall be $......, plus in each case an additional fee of $...... for each name more than one against which the statement of assignment is required to be indexed. Notwithstanding the provisions of this subsection, an assignment of record of a security interest in a fixture contained in a mortgage effective as a fixture filing (subsection (6) of Section 9—402) may be made only by an assignment of the mortgage in the manner provided by the law of this state other than this Act.

(3) After the disclosure or filing of an assignment under this section, the assignee is the secured party of record.

Reasons for 1972 Change

The changes are all conforming changes connecting with changes in mechanics in other sections of Part 4; with the addition of timber and minerals or the like (including oil and gas) at wellhead or minehead and accounts resulting from the sale thereof to the groups of collateral which must be filed and indexed in the real estate records; and with the provision (Section 9—402(6)) that a mortgage of real estate may act as a financing statement of fixtures.

§ 9—406. Release of Collateral; Duties of Filing Officer; Fees

A secured party of record may by his signed statement release all or a part of any collateral described in a filed financing statement. The statement of release is sufficient if it contains a description of the collateral being released, the name and address of the debtor, the name and address of the secured party, and the file number of the financing statement. A statement of release signed by a person other than the secured party of record must be accompanied by a separate written statement of assignment signed by the secured party of record and complying with subsection (2) of Section 9—405, including payment of the required fee. Upon presentation of such a statement of release to the filing officer he shall mark the statement with the hour and date of filing and shall note the same upon the margin of the index of the filing of the financing statement. The uniform fee for filing and noting such a statement of release shall be $...... if the statement is in the standard form prescribed by the [[Secretary of State]] and otherwise shall be $........, plus in each case an additional fee of $........ for each name more than one against which the statement of release is required to be indexed.

Reasons for 1972 Change

The changes are merely conforming changes to changes in other sections.

[[§ 9—407. Information From Filing Officer]]

[[(1) If the person filing any financing statement, termination statement, statement of assignment, or statement of release, furnishes the filing officer a copy thereof, the filing officer shall upon request note upon the copy the file number and date and hour of the filing of the original and deliver or send the copy to such person.]]

[[(2) Upon request of any person, the filing officer shall issue his certificate showing whether there is on file on the date and hour stated therein, any presently effective financing statement naming a particular debtor and any statement of assignment thereof and if there is, giving the date and hour of filing of each such statement and the names and addresses of each secured party therein. The uniform fee for such a certificate shall be $........ [plus $........ for each financing statement and for each statement of assignment reported therein.] if the request for the certificate is in the standard form prescribed by the [[Secretary of State]] and otherwise shall be $........ [plus $........ for each financing statement and for each statement of assignment reported therein.] Upon request the filing officer shall furnish a copy of any filed financing statement or statement of assignment for a uniform fee of $........ per page.]]

Reasons for 1972 Change

The change in this optional section is merely a conforming change to the changes in other sections.

Note: *This section is proposed as an optional provision to require filing officers to furnish certificates. Local law and practices should be consulted with regard to the advisability of adoption.*

§ 9—408. Financing Statements Covering Consigned or Leased Goods

A consignor or lessor of goods may file a financing statement using the terms "consignor," "consignee," "lessor," "lessee" or the like instead of the terms specified in Section 9—402. The provisions of this Part shall apply as appropriate to such a financing statement but its filing shall not of itself be a factor in determining whether or not the consignment or lease is intended as security (Section 1—201(37)). However, if it is determined for other reasons that the consignment or lease is so intended, a security interest of the consignor or lessor which attaches to the consigned or leased goods is perfected by such filing.

Reasons for 1972 Adoption of New Section

This new section adapts the filing system of the Article to consignments and leases. Filing of consignments is required under certain conditions (Sections 2—326(3), 9—114). Filing of true leases which are not security interests (Section 1—201(37)) is not required; but because the question whether a lease is a true lease may be a close one, filing is permitted for leases.

PART 5

DEFAULT

§ 9—501. Default; Procedure When Security Agreement Covers Both Real and Personal Property

(1) When a debtor is in default under a security agreement, a secured party has the rights and remedies provided in this Part and except as limited by subsection (3) those provided in the security agreement. He may reduce his claim to judgment, foreclose or otherwise enforce the security interest by any available judicial procedure. If the collateral is documents the secured party may proceed either as to the documents or as to the goods covered thereby. A secured party in possession has the rights,

remedies and duties provided in Section 9—207. The rights and remedies referred to in this subsection are cumulative.

(2) After default, the debtor has the rights and remedies provided in this Part, those provided in the security agreement and those provided in Section 9—207.

(3) To the extent that they give rights to the debtor and impose duties on the secured party, the rules stated in the subsections referred to below may not be waived or varied except as provided with respect to compulsory disposition of collateral (subsection (3) of Section 9—504 and [(subsection (1) of] Section 9—505) and with respect to redemption of collateral (Section 9—506) but the parties may by agreement determine the standards by which the fulfillment of these rights and duties is to be measured if such standards are not manifestly unreasonable:

(a) subsection (2) of Section 9—502 and subsection (2) of Section 9—504 insofar as they require accounting for surplus proceeds of collateral;

(b) subsection (3) of Section 9—504 and subsection (1) of Section 9—505 which deal with disposition of collateral;

(c) subsection (2) of Section 9—505 which deals with acceptance of collateral as discharge of obligation;

(d) Section 9—506 which deals with redemption of collateral; and

(e) subsection (1) of Section 9—507 which deals with the secured party's liability for failure to comply with this Part.

(4) If the security agreement covers both real and personal property, the secured party may proceed under this Part as to the personal property or he may proceed as to both the real and the personal property in accordance with his rights and remedies in respect of the real property in which case the provisions of this Part do not apply.

(5) When a secured party has reduced his claim to judgment the lien of any levy which may be made upon his collateral by virtue of any execution based upon the judgment shall relate back to the date of the perfection of the security interest in such collateral. A judicial sale, pursuant to such execution, is a foreclosure of the security interest by judicial procedure within the meaning of this section, and the secured party may purchase at the sale and thereafter hold the collateral free of any other requirements of this Article.

Reasons for 1972 Change

The change is purely technical, to clear up an ambiguity as to whether a debtor could after default agree on the time within which a sale might be held or the time after which a secured party might keep the goods in lieu of a sale.

§ 9—502. Collection Rights of Secured Party

(1) When so agreed and in any event on default the secured party is entitled to notify an account debtor or the obligor on an instrument to make payment to him whether or not the assignor was theretofore making collections on the collateral, and also to take control of any proceeds to which he is entitled under Section 9—306.

(2) A secured party who by agreement is entitled to charge back uncollected collateral or otherwise to full or limited recourse against the debtor and who undertakes to collect from the account debtors or obligors must proceed in a commercially reasonable manner and may deduct his reasonable expenses of realization from the collections. If the security agreement secures an indebtedness, the secured party must account to the debtor for any surplus, and unless otherwise agreed, the debtor is liable for any deficiency. But, if the underlying transaction was a sale of accounts [, contract rights,] or chattel paper, the debtor is entitled to any surplus or is liable for any deficiency only if the security agreement so provides.

Reasons for 1972 Change

The change is only the deletion of the term "contract rights", which is being eliminated as a defined term under the Article.

§ 9—504. Secured Party's Right to Dispose of Collateral After Default; Effect of Disposition

(1) A secured party after default may sell, lease or otherwise dispose of any or all of the collateral in its then condition or following any commercially reasonable preparation or processing. Any sale of goods is subject to the Article on Sales (Article 2). The proceeds of disposition shall be applied in the order following to

(a) the reasonable expenses of retaking, holding, preparing for sale or lease, selling, leasing and the like and, to the extent provided for in the agreement and not prohibited by law, the reasonable attorneys' fees and legal expenses incurred by the secured party;

(b) the satisfaction of indebtedness secured by the security interest under which the disposition is made;

(c) the satisfaction of indebtedness secured by any subordinate security interest in the collateral if written notification of demand therefor is received before distribution of the proceeds is completed. If requested by the secured party, the holder of a subordinate security interest must seasonably furnish reasonable proof of his interest, and unless he does so, the secured party need not comply with his demand.

(2) If the security interest secures an indebtedness, the secured party must account to the debtor for any surplus, and, unless otherwise agreed, the debtor is liable for any deficiency. But if the underlying transaction was a sale of accounts [, contract rights,] or chattel paper, the debtor is entitled to any surplus or is liable for any deficiency only if the security agreement so provides.

(3) Disposition of the collateral may be by public or private proceedings and may be made by way of one or more contracts. Sale or other disposition may be as a unit or in parcels and at any time and place and on any terms but every aspect of the disposition including the method, manner, time, place and terms must be commercially reasonable. Unless collateral is perishable or threatens to decline speedily in value or is of a type customarily sold on a recognized market, reasonable notification of the time and place of any public sale or reasonable notification of the time after which any private sale or other intended disposition is to be made shall be sent by the secured party to the debtor, <u>if he has not signed after default a statement renouncing or modifying his right to notification of sale. In the case of consumer goods no other notification need be sent. In other cases notification shall be sent to any other secured party from whom the secured party has received (before sending his notification to the debtor or before the debtor's renunciation of his rights) written notice of a claim of an interest in the collateral</u> [and except in the case of consumer goods to any other person who has a security interest in the collateral and who has duly filed a financing statement indexed in the name of the debtor in this state or who is known by the secured party to have a security interest in the collateral]. The secured party may buy at any public sale and if the collateral

is of a type customarily sold in a recognized market or is of a type which is the subject of widely distributed standard price quotations he may buy at private sale.

(4) When collateral is disposed of by a secured party after default, the disposition transfers to a purchaser for value all of the debtor's rights therein, discharges the security interest under which it is made and any security interest or lien subordinate thereto. The purchaser takes free of all such rights and interests even though the secured party fails to comply with the requirements of this Part or of any judicial proceedings

(a) in the case of a public sale, if the purchaser has no knowledge of any defects in the sale and if he does not buy in collusion with the secured party, other bidders or the person conducting the sale; or

(b) in any other case, if the purchaser acts in good faith.

(5) A person who is liable to a secured party under a guaranty, indorsement, repurchase agreement or the like and who receives a transfer of collateral from the secured party or is subrogated to his rights has thereafter the rights and duties of the secured party. Such a transfer of collateral is not a sale or disposition of the collateral under this Article.

Reasons for 1972 Change

Under the 1962 Code the secured party giving notice of sale had to notify (except in the case of consumer goods) not only every other person who had duly filed a financing statement indexed in the name of the debtor in the state and who still had a security interest in the collateral, but also any other person known by the secured party to have an interest in the collateral. This meant that the secured party had to search the records in every case of notice of sale, to ascertain whether there were any other secured parties with financing statements that might be deemed to cover the collateral in question. Moreover, he ran the risk that some informal communication by letter, or even orally, might be deemed to have given him knowledge of the interest of that other party. These burdens of searching the record and of checking the secured party's files were greater than the circumstances called for because as a practical matter there would seldom be a junior secured party who really had an interest needing protection in the case of a foreclosure sale. Therefore, a change is made requiring notice to persons other than the debtor only if such persons had notified the secured party in writing of their claim of an interest in the collateral before he sent his notification to the debtor or before the debtor's renunciation of his rights. Express provision is made to recognize the right of a debtor to renounce or modify his right to notice after, but not before, default. A corresponding change is made in Section 9—505.

§ 9—505. Compulsory Disposition of Collateral; Acceptance of the Collateral as Discharge of Obligation

(1) If the debtor has paid sixty per cent of the cash price in the case of a purchase money security interest in consumer goods or sixty per cent of the loan in the case of another security interest in consumer goods, and has not signed after default a statement renouncing or modifying his rights under this Part a secured party who has taken possession of collateral must dispose of it under Section 9—504 and if he fails to do so within ninety days after he takes possession the debtor at his option may recover in conversion or under Section 9—507(1) on secured party's liability.

(2) In any other case involving consumer goods or any other collateral a secured party in possession may, after default, propose to retain the collateral in satisfaction of the obligation. Written notice of such proposal shall be sent to the debtor [and except in the case of consumer goods to any other secured party who has a security interest in the collateral and who has duly filed a financing statement indexed in the name of the debtor in this state or is known by the secured party in possession to have a security interest in it. If the debtor or other person entitled to receive notification objects in writing within thirty days from the receipt of the notification or if any other secured party objects in writing thirty days after the secured party obtains possession the secured party must dispose of the collateral under Section 9—504.] if he has not signed after default a statement renouncing or modifying his rights under this subsection. In the case of consumer goods no other notice need be given. In other cases notice shall be sent to any other secured party from whom the secured party has received (before sending his notice to the debtor or before the debtor's renunciation of his rights) written notice of a claim of an interest in the collateral. If the secured party receives objection in writing from a person entitled to receive notification within twenty-one days after the notice was sent, the secured party must dispose of the collateral under Section 9—504. In the absence of such written objection the se-

cured party may retain the collateral in satisfaction of the debtor's obligation.

Reasons for 1972 Change

Under subsection (2) of this section the secured party may in lieu of sale give notice to the debtor and certain other persons that he proposes to retain the collateral in lieu of sale. Under the 1962 Code the other persons were the same as those who were entitled to notice of sale under Section 9—504(3), and such other persons are limited by the change in the same fashion as they were limited in Section 9—504(3) and for the same reasons. See the Reasons for Change under Section 9—504.

ARTICLE 11

EFFECTIVE DATE AND TRANSITION PROVISIONS

Notes

This material has been numbered Article 11 to distinguish it from Article 10, the transition provision of the 1962 Code, which may still remain in effect in some states to cover transition problems from pre-Code law to the original Uniform Commercial Code. Adaptation may be necessary in particular states. The terms "[old Code]" and "[new Code]" and "[old U.C.C.]" and "[new U.C.C.]" are used herein, and should be suitably changed in each state.

This draft was prepared by the Reporters and has not been passed upon by the Review Committee, the Permanent Editorial Board, the American Law Institute, or the National Conference of Commissioners on Uniform State Laws. It is submitted as a working draft which may be adapted as appropriate in each state. The "Discussions" were written by the Reporters to assist in understanding the purpose of the drafts.

§ 11—101. Effective Date

This Act shall become effective at 12:01 A.M. on ______, 19__.

Discussion

An effective date substantially after enactment is advisable to allow ample time for refilings as required.

§ 11—102. Preservation of Old Transition Provision

The provisions of [here insert reference to the original transition provision in the particular state] shall continue to apply to [the new U.C.C.] and for this purpose the [old U.C.C. and new U.C.C.] shall be considered one continuous statute.

Discussion

This section may be necessary in states in which the U.C.C. has only recently been effective. It preserves the principle of Section 10—102(2) of the 1962 Code that pre-Code transactions continue to be governed by pre-Code law. A different principle is set forth in this Article 11 for transition problems between the [old Code] and the [new Code], because the changes are not nearly as great. That principle is that the [new Code] governs (with minor exceptions).

§ 11—103. Transition to [New Code]—General Rule

Transactions validly entered into after [effective date of old U.C.C.] and before [effective date of new U.C.C.], and which were subject to the provisions of [old U.C.C.] and which would be subject to this Act as amended if they had been entered into after the effective date of [new U.C.C.] and the rights, duties and interests flowing from such transactions remain valid after the latter date and may be terminated, completed, consummated or enforced as required or permitted by the [new U.C.C.]. Security interests arising out of such transactions which are perfected when [new U.C.C. becomes effective shall remain perfected until they lapse as provided in [new U.C.C.], and may be continued as permitted by [new U.C.C.], except as stated in Section 11—105.

Discussion

This makes the [new Code] applicable to existing security interests, e. g., the revised notice provisions of Part 5 will apply to existing security interests. This would be so even if a 30-day notice period concerning retention of the collateral in lieu of sale were running on the effective date of the [new Code].

Suppose that a security interest attached in State A and the secured party filed in State B and assumed that he had 30 days to have the goods reach State B, in a non-purchase money case, under Section 9—103(3) of the [old Code]. Section 9—103(1) (c) of the [new Code] limits the 30-day provision on intended removals to purchase money cases. So long as an ample period of waiting and familiarization is allowed under Section 11—101, this should cause no practical problem.

The "except" clause at the end is necessary because of the possibility that new financing statements would have to be filed in different offices.

§ 11—104. Transition Provision on Change of Requirement of Filing

A security interest for the perfection of which filing or the taking of possession was required under [old U.C.C.] and which attached prior to the effective date of [new U.C.C.] but was not perfected shall be deemed perfected on the effective date of [new U.C.C.] if [new U.C.C.] permits perfection without filing or authorizes filing in the office or offices where a prior ineffective filing was made.

Discussion

This covers the case of a purchase money security interest in consumer goods, which would not have had to be filed under the original Code if the goods had not been fixtures. Under the [new Code] the security interest will be perfected without filing, subject to the rights of real estate parties. Section 9—301(1) (d).

This also covers the case of factory or office machinery or replacement consumer goods appliances where the filing of a financing statement under the original Code in the regular chattel files was invalid because the goods were fixtures, but under the [new Code] that filing would be proper.

Under the [old Code] the status of assignments of revenues and similar collateral for governmental obligations was unclear. Section 9—104(e) of the [new Code] will make clear that Article 9 does not apply to these transfers. Section 11—108 of this draft may apply on the theory that the changes made by the [new Code] are considered to be merely declaratory. If this does not dispose of the matter, and if it might sometime be held that an assignment by a municipality had been ineffective for lack of filing, this provision would then apply from the effective date of the [new Code].

§ 11—105. Transition Provision on Change of Place of Filing

(1) A financing statement or continuation statement filed prior to [effective date of new U.C.C.] which shall not have laps-

ed prior to [the effective date of new U.C.C.] shall remain effective for the period provided in the [old Code], but not less than five years after the filing.

(2) With respect to any collateral acquired by the debtor subsequent to the effective date of [new U.C.C.], any effective financing statement or continuation statement described in this section shall apply only if the filing or filings are in the office or offices that would be appropriate to perfect the security interests in the new collateral under [new U.C.C.].

(3) The effectiveness of any financing statement or continuation statement filed prior to [effective date of new U.C.C.] may be continued by a continuation statement as permitted by [new U.C.C.], except that if [new U.C.C.] requires a filing in an office where there was no previous financing statement, a new financing statement conforming to Section 11—106 shall be filed in that office.

(4) If the record of a mortgage of real estate would have been effective as a fixture filing of goods described therein if [new U.C.C.] had been in effect on the date of recording the mortgage, the mortgage shall be deemed effective as a fixture filing as to such goods under subsection (6) of Section 9—402 of the [new U.C.C.] on the effective date of [new U.C.C.].

Discussion

Subsection (1): All existing financing statements with a duration of less than 5 years are extended to the full 5 years. In the case of transmitting utilities for which a special rule of longer validity had been provided, the special rule will be continued.

Subsection (2) makes clear that all existing financing statements and continuations on the effective date remain valid for the remainder of the five years *as to existing collateral*, even though the appropriate place for filing may have changed under the new rules for accounts, general intangibles, etc. The existing filings also apply to new collateral acquired after the effective date, unless the appropriate filing place is different under the new rules. In that case there will have to be a new filing on the effective date to catch new collateral.

Subsection (3): A continuation statement may be filed after the effective date, but if the appropriate places under the new rules are different, the filing should be a financing statement.

Subsection (4) retroactively validates real estate mortgage recording as fixture filing.

§ 11—106. Required Refilings

(1) If a security interest is perfected or has priority when this Act takes effect as to all persons or as to certain persons without any filing or recording, and if the filing of a financing statement would be required for the perfection or priority of the security interest against those persons under [new U.C.C.], the perfection and priority rights of the security interest continue until 3 years after the effective date of [new U.C.C.]. The perfection will then lapse unless a financing statement is filed as provided in subsection (4) or unless the security interest is perfected otherwise than by filing.

(2) If a security interest is perfected when [new U.C.C.] takes effect under a law other than [U.C.C.] which requires no further filing, refiling or recording to continue its perfection, perfection continues until and will lapse 3 years after [new U.C.C.] takes effect, unless a financing statement is filed as provided in subsection (4) or unless the security interest is perfected otherwise than by filing, or unless under subsection (3) of Section 9—302 the other law continues to govern filing.

(3) If a security interest is perfected by a filing, refiling or recording under a law repealed by this Act which required further filing, refiling or recording to continue its perfection, perfection continues and will lapse on the date provided by the law so repealed for such further filing, refiling or recording unless a financing statement is filed as provided in subsection (4) or unless the security interest is perfected otherwise than by filing.

(4) A financing statement may be filed within six months before the perfection of a security interest would otherwise lapse. Any such financing statement may be signed by either the debtor or the secured party. It must identify the security agreement, statement or notice (however denominated in any statute or other law repealed or modified by this Act), state the office where and the date when the last filing, refiling or recording, if any, was made with respect thereto, and the filing number, if any, or book and page, if any, of recording and further state that the security agreement, statement or notice, however denominated, in another filing office under the [U.C.C.] or under any statute or other law repealed or modified by this Act is still effective. Section 9—401 and Section 9—103 determine the proper place to file such a financing statement. Except as specified in this subsection, the provisions of Section 9—403(3) for continuation statements apply to such a financing statement.

Discussion

Subsection (1) covers farm equipment perfected without filing. The three-year period ought to cover most existing transactions. It also applies to equipment trusts, and would appear to allow three years for filing. But generally filing under Article 9 for equipment trusts is excluded by Section 9—302(3), and the old pre-amendment filing under the Interstate Commerce Act will continue to serve the purpose.

Subsection (2) covers transmitting utility statutes and the like which were *outside the Code*, and provided for indefinite duration. It allows three years for refiling. But perfection under a certificate of title law or the like continues to be effective.

Some states dealt with transmitting utilities by *internal amendment* of the Code to permit filing which was good indefinitely. Section 11—105(1) operates to validate those filings indefinitely even though they may not have been in the Secretary of State's office.

Similarly, Section 11—105(1) would preserve the effect of Ohio's present Section 9—403(2), which in effect makes financing statements related to combined real estate and chattel mortgages good for the duration of the real estate mortgage, whether or not the chattels are fixtures.

Subsection (3) covers the case (if any) where a prior transmitting utility provision outside the Code had a filing of limited duration.

Subsection (4) covers a case where an ordinary continuation statement cannot be filed because the original filing was a non-Code filing or was a Code filing in a different filing office. It was thought advisable to use the concept of financing statement rather than the concept of continuation statement for these fact situations.

§ 11—107. Transition Provisions as to Priorities

Except as otherwise provided in [Article 11], [old U.C.C.] shall apply to any questions of priority if the positions of the parties were fixed prior to the effective date of [new U.C.C.]. In other cases questions of priority shall be determined by [new U.C.C.].

Discussion

Most questions of priority can be broken down to questions between two parties, and the rule is that the [new Code] applies unless the rights of both parties were fixed under the [old Code].

If a creditor acquires knowledge of an unfiled security interest before the effective date of the [new Code], but gets his judgment after the effective date, the rule of the [new Code] governs, since he has no rights until after judgment and levy.

§ 11—108. Presumption that Rule of Law Continues Unchanged

Unless a change in law has clearly been made, the provisions of [new U.C.C.] shall be deemed declaratory of the meaning of the [old U.C.C.].

Discussion

This asserts that the new Code is declaratory, except where a change is clearly intended. This is an effort to minimize transitional problems.

UNIFORM CONSUMER CREDIT CODE

OFFICIAL 1974 TEXT

WITH COMMENTS

TABLE OF CONTENTS

Part 2

SCOPE AND JURISDICTION

Part 3

DEFINITIONS

Article 2

FINANCE CHARGES AND RELATED PROVISIONS

Part 1

GENERAL PROVISIONS

Part 2

CONSUMER CREDIT SALES: MAXIMUM FINANCE CHARGES

Part 3

CONSUMER LOANS: SUPERVISED LENDERS

Part 4

CONSUMER LOANS: MAXIMUM FINANCE CHARGES

Part 5

CONSUMER CREDIT TRANSACTIONS: OTHER CHARGES AND MODIFICATIONS

Part 6

OTHER CREDIT TRANSACTIONS

Article 3

REGULATION OF AGREEMENTS AND PRACTICES

Part 1

GENERAL PROVISIONS

Part 2

DISCLOSURE

Part 2

CONSUMER CREDIT INSURANCE

Part 3

PROPERTY AND LIABILITY INSURANCE

Article 5

REMEDIES AND PENALTIES

Part 1

LIMITATIONS ON CREDITORS' REMEDIES

Part 2

CONSUMERS' REMEDIES

Part 3

CRIMINAL PENALTIES

Article 6

ADMINISTRATION

Part 1

POWERS AND FUNCTIONS OF ADMINISTRATOR

Part 2

NOTIFICATION AND FEES

Part 3

COUNCIL OF ADVISORS ON CONSUMER CREDIT

Part 4

ADMINISTRATIVE PROCEDURE AND JUDICIAL REVIEW

Article 7

[Reserved for Future Use]

Article 8

[Reserved for Future Use]

Article 9

EFFECTIVE DATE AND REPEALER

PREFATORY NOTE

In promulgating the Uniform Consumer Credit Code (the "U3C") in 1968 (the "1968 Text"), the National Conference of Commissioners on Uniform State Laws proposed a completely new approach to the law governing consumer credit.

Enactment of the Code would abolish the crazy-quilt, patchwork welter of prior laws on consumer credit and replace them by a single new comprehensive law providing a modern, theoretically and pragmatically consistent structure of legal regulation designed to provide an adequate volume of credit at reasonable cost under conditions fair to both consumers and creditors. Upon its enactment, no longer would credit regulation within a State consist of a number of separate uncoordinated statutes governing the activities of different types of creditors in disparate ways.

All creditors dealing with consumers would be covered by the same statute. Under this Act, the total consumer credit process —from advertising through collection—would be within the scope of regulation, with variations in the law based on functional differences in the kinds of transactions rather than on the kinds of creditors involved. Whether a consumer is financing an automobile with a sales finance company or borrowing money from a consumer finance or small loan company, certain basic protections would apply across-the-board to safeguard the consumer.

Thus the Conference has chosen to approach consumer credit in much the same way it did so successfully with respect to secured transactions under Article 9 of the Uniform Commercial Code: function should prevail over form.

Nine States have now adopted the U3C: Oklahoma and Utah in 1969, and Colorado, Idaho, Indiana, and Wyoming in 1971, all in substantially the form of the 1968 Text; Kansas in 1973 in substantially that of the U3C Committee's Working Redraft No. 4; and Iowa and Maine in 1974 in substantially that of the Committee's Working Redraft No. 4 or 5. The Code has had an impact on the development of consumer credit law far beyond those States in which it has been adopted. Many provisions of the Federal Truth in Lending Act and Federal Reserve Board Regulation Z are traceable to the U3C. The National Consumer Act and, later, the Model Consumer Credit Act, although taking extreme consumer positions, follow the structure of the U3C. In 1971 Congress enacted for the District of Columbia comprehensive consumer credit legislation drawn in large part from the U3C. In 1972 Wisconsin enacted similar legislation based on the U3C and the National Consumer Act. Adaptations of U3C provisions have been enacted widely in the credit laws of many States; the home solicitation sale provisions are perhaps the best illustration.

Revision of the 1968 Text

Events occurring after promulgation of the 1968 Text have made it desirable to revise it. Experience in the States which enacted the Code has proved that the Code works and that both consumers and creditors are pleased with it, but this experience has also turned up a few unforeseen problems of the kind that come to light only after a law has been in effect. The revision has dealt with these matters as well as with some of the variations from the 1968 Text that were enacted in several of the States.[1]

The late 1960's and early 1970's have seen a number of important legislative and judicial developments in consumer credit. Information gained from legal services attorneys has thrown new light on the needs of poverty-level consumers, but has also revealed that those needs cannot be met solely by consumer credit legislation of general application. The National Consumer Law Center has produced a number of legislative proposals. The United States Supreme Court revolutionized debtor-creditor law in its *Sniadach* [2] decision in 1969. Developments at both the federal level (Consumer Credit Protection Act, Regulation Z, Fair Credit Reporting Act) and the state level (Wisconsin Consumer Act) have invited a review of the U3C. Then, too, new ways of granting consumer credit appeared on the scene during this period. The concept of a nation-wide credit card was in its infancy when the 1968 Text was being prepared in the 1960's; today it is a reality.

A major factor calling for a review of the U3C is the Report of the National Commission on Consumer Finance ("NCCF"). This landmark study, the product of three years of work by a

1 See Report No. 1 of the U3C Committee which contains comments of the Committee on the desirability of the variations in State enactments of the 1968 Text.

2 Sniadach v. Family Finance Corp. (1969) 89 S.Ct. 1820, 395 U.S. 337, 23 L.Ed.2d 349.

federally sponsored Commission, is the first comprehensive examination in the United States of the whole field of consumer finance. The recommendations of the Commission reflect both objectivity and understanding of the complex consumer credit process.

The National Commission on Consumer Finance was authorized under Title IV, Section 404(a) of the Consumer Credit Protection Act to ". . . study and appraise the functioning and structure of the consumer finance industry, as well as consumer credit transactions generally." It issued its Report on December 31, 1972, four weeks after the U3C Committee's Working Redraft No. 4 was published. The Report contains some 100 recommendations intended to improve the consumer credit marketplace, over 40 of which were intended exclusively for implementation by federal statute, *e. g.*, amendments to the Truth in Lending Act and to the Bankruptcy Act. Of the 60 or so recommendations requiring State action, at least 15 related to matters entirely outside the scope of the U3C, *e. g.*, bank branching and enforcement of antitrust laws. Thus only about 45 recommendations required consideration by the U3C Committee.

Of these 45 recommendations, the U3C Committee's Working Redraft No. 4 anticipated over half. The Committee's Working Redraft No. 5 and this Act substantially implement the National Commission's recommendations regarding co-signer agreements, door-to-door sales, buyer's claims and defenses in credit card and other consumer credit transactions, deficiency judgments, "sewer service," limitations on garnishment, debt collection practices, and State enforcement of the Federal Truth in Lending Act. Thus, this Act reflects a conscious and, it is believed, successful effort to incorporate into a single comprehensive code the majority of the recommendations of the National Commission on Consumer Finance that were intended for implementation by state action.

Price of Credit

A basic issue in any regulation in this area is the price of credit. In simplest terms, consumers want credit at the lowest possible prices, and creditors want to supply credit but can and will do so only if they may reasonably expect repayment of principal plus an adequate return on credit extended. In a free economy the prices of goods, services and land traditionally have been controlled by free operation of the market place. To some extent this principle has also extended to the price of credit but for a variety of historical reasons since before the time of Christ, societies have attempted to control the price of credit by executive or legislative fiat. Invariably these attempts have either dried up "legal" or legitimate credit or significantly reduced the amount of credit which would have been available in a free economy. Invariably, too, consumers have been losers by this process.

For hundreds of years in England [3] and in the American colonies and in most of the States, general usury statutes prescribed such low maximum ceilings that they materially interfered with the extension and free flow of credit. In many areas general usury statutes have prevented entirely or reduced substantially the extension of credit with the result that either the courts or legislatures found it necessary to provide a proliferation of exceptions to these statutes. The basic premises of the 1968 Text were that (1) in the business area general usury statutes should be terminated completely and control of the price of credit left solely to the free operation of the market place; (2) although in the consumer credit area the operation of the same free enterprise principles is equally warranted, many consumers do not have equal bargaining power with creditors and traditionally have been protected by governmental controls, including maximum rates, and the U3C should provide recommended maximum rates in a standard form more simple and understandable than a hodge podge of exceptions to general usury statutes; and (3) any rate structure provided should be of the maximum ceiling variety and not a specification of actual rates to be charged as in the regulation of public utilities.

The U3C Committee's Working Redrafts Nos. 1 through 5 [4] and this Act reflect the belief, strongly buttressed by the NCCF Report, that these basic premises are sound and reaffirm them. The proposed specific ceiling rates are socially and economically sound and fit with the other provisions of the U3C and the approach used in drafting it.

This Act makes no change in the specific maximum rates included in the 1968 Text. Empirical evidence developed since 1968 and cited in the U3C Committee's Report No. 1 strongly supports the wisdom of the basic principles adopted and the specific rates suggested. Although the 1968 Text's maximum rates were lowered in some enacting States, in all these States consumer credit

---

[3] England repealed its usury laws in 1854.

[4] The U3C Committee's Working Redrafts Nos. 1 and 2 were internal; its Working Redrafts Nos. 3, 4, and 5 were distributed widely.

has been extended in most cases at rates below the ceilings permitted by the U3C. Five of the six enacting States studied in the Committee's Report No. 1 lowered the maximum ceiling on revolving sale credit from 24% per annum to 18%; however, this change is rejected because the cost studies referred to in the Committee's comment in its Report No. 1 consistently establish that in the case of substantially all sellers, the cost of extending revolving consumer sales credit exceeds 18% per year. For the reasons stated in Report No. 1, reduction in this ceiling rate is believed to be economically unsound.

The extensive studies and findings reported in Chapters 6, 7 and 8 of the NCCF Report clearly support the reasonableness of the U3C maximum ceilings. If anything, the NCCF Report indicates that if the U3C ceilings are open to criticism, the ground should be that they are too low at least for small, short term extensions of credit.

The United States is now experiencing serious inflation. In attempting to combat this inflation the federal government has imposed price controls and ceilings on some goods and services. Opinions may differ as to whether these controls or ceilings were or were not desirable, but there can be little doubt that they not only have not controlled prices significantly but also have caused severe dislocations in the supplies of some goods and services. The difficulties coming to light in these attempts to control prices of goods and services extend equally to attempts to control the price of credit by legislation. General usury statutes and other state laws limiting rates on home mortgages below free market rates have drastically reduced the availability of mortgage funds, the volume of home construction, and employment in the building trades.

Competition and Freedom of Entry

In advocating primary reliance on the market place to control the price of credit, the National Conference has recognized the fundamental importance of competition to permit market forces to operate most effectively, a recognition consistent with the conclusions of the National Commission on Consumer Finance. In moving away from the segmented controls of particular types of credit grantors in consumer credit laws prior to the U3C to a single comprehensive statute dealing with consumer credit generally, it is believed that competition has been and will be enhanced. In the U3C Committee's Working Redrafts Nos. 3 through 5 and in this Act, this comprehensive approach has been continued and strengthened by eliminating the separation and duplication in the treatment of sales credit and loans provided in the 1968 Text.

Licensing is a means of providing governmental control of particular kinds of activity, but it restricts freedom of entry into markets and inhibits competition. The 1968 Text avoided the extension of licensing requirements and also sought to diminish existing licensing requirements.

However, the small loan industry, accustomed to licensing under pre-Code law, in no way objected to licensing and entirely approved of its continuance under the U3C. Moreover, banks and thrift institutions contended that since they could not open offices without the approval of supervisory authorities and since all their activities were regulated and subject to close supervision and examination, small loan lenders should be subject to similar requirements. Consumer comment received on this issue favored increasing rather than decreasing licensing requirements. In response to these various views, the U3C Committee's Working Redrafts Nos. 3 through 5 and this Act have added in Section 2.302 the requirement that licensees obtain a separate license for each place of business where loans are made.

As in the 1968 Text, any lender making loans at a rate in excess of 18% per annum either must be a bank, thrift institution or other supervised financial organization (subsection (41) of Section 1.301) or obtain a license under Section 2.302. On the other hand, this Act avoids imposing on sellers or other types of organizations not engaged in lending any requirement to obtain a license, whether the business carried on is direct or through the use of credit cards. (See subsections (12), (15), (25), and (39) of Section 1.301 and Sections 2.301 and 2.302.)

Consumer Oriented Changes and Additions

Another basic issue in the regulation of consumer credit is adequate protection of consumers from creditor practices and agreements that are abusive or have a potential for abuse. Drawing upon the sources referred to in this Prefatory Note, a substantial number of consumer oriented changes from the 1968 Text have been included in this Act. It is believed that each change or addition has merit and will provide additional protection to consumers but will not interfere with the extension of consumer credit or with legitimate practices of the great majority of creditors.

In making these consumer oriented changes, the necessary relationship between these changes and the U3C rate structure has not been forgotten. In the language of the National Commission on Consumer Finance:

> Recommendations regarding remedies are inextricably interwoven with Commission recommendations on rates and availability...... It is imperative that the relationship be realistically assessed—the higher the rate the fewer the remedies needed and vice versa. States may decide to narrow or broaden Commission recommendations on remedies and contract provisions. But they should recognize that modifications are likely to affect the cost and availability of consumer credit.[5]

A summary of many of these changes and additions follows.

(1) Holder in Due Course; Sales Related Loans; Credit Cards

A major controversial area in consumer credit has been that related to the holder in due course doctrine as applied to outright transfers of retail paper, to sales related loans and to credit card transactions. Traditionally banks and others made credit judgments on purchases of consumer paper solely on the basis of the credit of the buyer and without regard to any aspects of the sale transaction being financed. Insulation of creditors from claims and defenses arising out of sale transactions was obtained in different ways: by use of negotiable notes generating the rights of a holder in due course, or by provisions in contracts freeing assignees of rights under contracts from claims or defenses of buyers against sellers. Banks and others have attempted to preserve these longstanding principles. They have argued that they are lenders of money, not sellers of goods or services, that buyers have the right and responsibility of picking sellers, and that buyers should look solely to sellers for cure of violations of sales contracts, breaches of warranty, and the like.

On the other hand, consumer advocates contend that financing institutions often have close relations with sellers from whom notes and rights under sales contracts are acquired, that these institutions are better able than consumers to police sellers and to require of them reasonable standards of performance. Consequently, consumer advocates contend that creditors acquiring sales paper should *not* be free from claims and defenses of buyers against sellers. Consumer advocates have no difficulty in providing examples of hardships suffered by aggrieved buyers when faced with contentions by assignees of their contracts that the

5 NCCF Report, p. 24.

assignees know nothing about the details of the sales and should not be affected by claims or defenses buyers might have against sellers, and that buyers are still obligated to make their instalment payments.

For upward of 20 years, this underlying dispute has existed and waxed more intense. The issue has been tested in courts, with a number of courts deciding in consumer cases that waiver of defense clauses included in instalment contracts signed by buyers were not effective as contrary to public policy. Legislatures took up the issue and in a number of States enacted statutes prohibiting the use of negotiable notes in consumer sale transactions or limiting or prohibiting waiver of defense clauses in retail instalment sale contracts, and sometimes both. These statutes varied in terms of dollar amounts involved and types of transactions to which they applied.

Recognizing the existence of the controversy and that the underlying issue had not been finally resolved, the 1968 Text by Section 2.403 prohibited the taking of negotiable notes in consumer sale and lease transactions and by Section 2.404 provided alternative provisions relating to the effectiveness of waiver of defense clauses. Of the six enacting States covered by Report No. 1, all enacted the prohibition of negotiable notes in Section 2.403 of the 1968 Text, two States prohibited the waiver of defense clauses, one State took no action on the subject, and three States elected to permit these clauses with restrictions.

In Section 3.307 of this Act, the prohibition of the use of negotiable instruments in consumer sales and leases is continued and strengthened. In Section 3.404, the consumer position is substantially adopted by deleting entirely Alternative B of the 1968 Text and by strengthening the 1968 Alternative A provisions prohibiting waiver of defense clauses. It is believed that on this issue consumers have the stronger case. However, this decision reinforces the need to retain the proposed rate ceilings, since the findings of the National Commission on Consumer Finance show that restrictions on holders' rights tend to increase finance charges and reduce the availability of credit.

In more recent years, another issue has developed which is different from but closely related to transfers of sale paper. That issue is the further contention by consumers that even if the transaction is exclusively in the form of a loan but if proceeds of the loan are used to purchase goods or services, at least under certain circumstances, lenders should be subject to defenses of buyers against sellers. Banks, consumer finance companies and other lenders have objected to this type of provision even more strenuously than to provisions prohibiting waiver of defense clauses in assigned instalment sale contracts.

Notwithstanding objections of this kind by lenders, a number of legislatures have enacted provisions of this type. Section 3.405 of this Act includes such a provision, but is limited to certain prescribed situations where the relationship between the lender and the seller is close and the lender either acts in a manner or receives benefits of a kind that ties the lender closely not only to the seller but to the particular sale transaction.

Inevitably, the argument and debate with respect to these two issues led to argument and debate of the same underlying issues when goods or services are purchased with the aid of a three party credit card issued by a bank or other financing agency. Again banks have argued strenuously that in issuing credit cards and making payments to sellers upon use of the cards by the cardholders, the bank knows nothing about the sellers or the sale transactions and should be completely insulated in its rights against its cardholders from any claims or defenses the cardholder buyers might have against the sellers. Banks have further argued that making them in any way subject to claims or defenses cardholders might have against sellers could seriously interfere with the acceptability and convenience of credit cards (and, by extension, the development of the electronic funds transfer system), because not only would banks be more hesitant to issue cards but sellers would also be more reluctant to make sales in reliance on credit cards.

On the other hand, consumer advocates have contended that banks issuing credit cards are better equipped to police sellers than are consumers, banks may in agreements with sellers obtain charge back agreements from them if merchandise risks or claims arise, and in any event, as between cardholders and card-issuing banks, merchandise risks of this kind should be borne by the banks.

On this third and latest issue, argument and debate again have been intense. However, in California and in the Fair Credit Billing Act passed by the Senate as S.2101 in the summer of 1973, a compromise solution was worked out which bids fair to provide a resolution of this third issue. The compromise solution is that the card issuing bank is subject to any claims or defenses the cardholder may have against the seller only if (1) the customer makes a good faith attempt to resolve a disagreement with the seller, (2) the credit card transaction involves more than $50, and (3) both the residence of the cardholder and the place where the sale or lease occurred are [in the same State or] within 100 miles of each other.

If the card-issuing bank is subject to claims or defenses under this solution, it may have to rely upon rights of charge-back against the seller.

The rationale of this compromise as to amount is that in smaller transactions of $50 or less, the credit card should be looked upon as basically the equivalent of cash and the transaction should have all the finality of a cash transaction.

The rationale for the geographic distinction is that the normal area for use of a credit card as a credit instrument is reasonably proximate to the residence of the cardholder and consequently card-issuing banks should be subject to claims and defenses of the cardholder against the seller only if a transaction and the seller are in this not too large area. A further reason is that any policing of merchants by banks could not reasonably be expected for unlimited geographic distances. Consequently, if and to the extent a cardholder uses his credit card in another State or at a location some distance from his residence, sellers, card-issuing banks and others in the credit card mechanism should not have to worry about credit cards giving to cardholders undue advantages in merchandise disputes by being able to withhold payments from the banks and in turn forcing banks to charge back items to sellers requiring sellers to seek collection from cardholders in distant places.

Section 3.403 of this Act adopts this basic compromise solution. Further, in each of Sections 3.403, 3.404, and 3.405 the extent to which card-issuing banks, lenders and finance companies may be subject to claims and defenses of buyers against sellers is limited to the amount outstanding for the particular transaction at the time the bank or other lender first receives notice of the dispute. Suggestions that card-issuing banks and other lenders should be responsible for the original amount of the transaction and even for product liability that might arise out of the transaction are rejected as neither feasible nor reasonable.

(2) Territorial Reach of Protection

Additional protection is afforded to residents of the enacting State with respect to mail order loans by applying the limitations on finance charges and related provisions to these transactions and giving the Administrator power over them as though the loans were entered into in the enacting State. Also prohibitions of other types of agreements limiting the jurisdiction of the enacting state have been added. See Section 1.201.

(3) Vendor's Single Interest Insurance

The conditions under which a creditor may make an additional charge for vendor's single interest insurance have been more clearly specified and tightened. See Section 2.501.

(4) Notice to Consumers of Precautions and Rights

In certain types of closed-end credit transactions, the creditor is required to furnish the consumer with a copy of the basic contract documents and to advise the consumer of this right, of the wisdom of not signing without reading, and of the right to prepay and possible right to receive a refund. See Section 3.203.

(5) Receipts, Statements and Evidence of Payment

Provisions that consumers are entitled to receipts, statements as to dates and amounts of payments, and evidence of payment in various situations have been added. See Section 3.206.

(6) Notice to Co-Signers

Provisions requiring notice to co-signers and other sureties as to the nature of their obligations have been inserted in accordance with NCCF recommendations. See Section 3.208.

(7) Restrictions on Security and its Enforcement

A potential loophole in the restrictions on security interests that might allow a creditor to take security in a wife's goods for the husband's debt has been eliminated by extending the restriction to property generally rather than only to property of the consumer. See Section 3.301. In addition, enforcement of security interests in property, exempt from execution under a judgment, to secure loans has been restricted. See Section 5.116.

(8) Revocable Deductions from Earnings

Better to assure that an authorized deduction from earnings is revocable both in law and in fact, provisions have been added to give the consumer notice of the revocable nature of any authorization of deductions. See Section 3.305.

(9) Referral Sales and Leases

Restrictions on referral sales and leases have been tightened so as to cover both referral arrangements that are not specifically bargained for in a contract sense and arrangements financed by other than the seller or lessor. In addition to the sanction provided in the section dealing with referrals, a private right of action by the consumer for violation of the prohibition is created better to deter this conduct. See Sections 3.309 and 5.201.

(10) Home Solicitation Sales

The provisions with respect to home solicitation sales have been widened to cover transactions at any residence, not just the residence of the buyer, and have been tightened to prevent evasion by the seller or lessor arranging to have someone else do the financing or by too free use of the emergency exception, and by assuring the buyer a copy of the "buyer's right to cancel" at the time he signs the agreement. Further protection to the consumer is also afforded by prohibition of any cancellation fee and clarification of the right to cancel even though goods sold have received the ordinary use or consumption contemplated by the transaction. Provisions are added that compliance with Federal Trade Commission notice requirements meets U3C requirements in this regard. See Article 3, Part 5.

(11) Refunds of Separate Charges for Insurance

To restrict the creditor's right to withhold a refund until the maturity of a contract, provisions have been added entitling a consumer to a refund at his option rather than a credit in the event of a required rebate of any separate charge for insurance. See Section 4.108.

(12) Deficiency Judgments

Following the NCCF recommendation, restrictions on deficiency judgments have been increased to apply to transactions up to $1,750 rather than $1,000 and have been widened to apply to loans in which the lender is subject to claims and defenses arising from sales as well as to consumer credit sales. See Section 5.103.

(13) Garnishment

Also following an NCCF recommendation, provisions for special court relief from garnishments after judgment on normally non-exempt earnings have been added. See Section 5.105.

(14) Unconscionability

Provisions for court determination of unconscionability in an action by the consumer have been widened to cover, in addition to a consumer credit transaction, (a) a transaction that a consumer is led to believe will give rise to a consumer credit transaction so that, for example, a seller cannot bind the consumer to a short term sale contract payable in a lump sum on the assurance he will secure financing, and then inform the consumer that financing is unavailable and keep the down payment or goods traded upon the consumer's default, (b) inducing a transaction by unconscionable conduct; and (c) unconscionable collection practices. In addition, factors that may be considered in determining unconscionability are spelled out and a provision allowing recovery of attorney's fees is included. See Section 5.108.

(15) Default

Provisions have been added that restrict the unfettered right of the creditor to determine what constitutes a default; that require as a condition to acceleration of debt or enforcement of security interest that the consumer be given notice of his right within a reasonable time to cure a default consisting of the failure to make a required payment; that further clarify the conditions under which self-help repossession is permissible; that control venue in suits against a consumer to collect; that specify what a creditor's petition or complaint must contain to establish his claim; and that provide for relief from default judgments for cause, including sewer service. See Sections 5.109 through 5.115.

(16) Consumers' Remedies

The consumer is given a right of action to recover actual damages and a penalty for the violation of all provisions of the Act which do not have an express or implicit sanction, and even for some provisions that do, better to guard against *in terrorem* uses of prohibited agreements and practices and better to assure compliance with the law. Although the question of the availability of a class action in general is left to other law, the right to recover a penalty is expressly made not enforceable in a class action. In addition, recovery of a penalty is authorized in cases of excess charges or failure to refund within a reasonable time after demand (and a presumption as to reasonable time is created), and the amount of the penalty is not tied to the excess charge, which might permit only a low recovery and therefore establish an inadequate incentive when the excess charge is small. Finally, the voidness penalty for making supervised loans without a necessary license has been deleted as unworkable, and the allowance of attorney's fees has been liberalized and clarified. See Section 5.201.

(17) Administrator's Powers

The rule making power of the Administrator has been expanded; his investigatory powers are increased; his ability to use the device of an assurance of discontinuance has been clarified; his ability to obtain injunctions or other appropriate relief has been clarified; and his powers to sue on behalf of consumers have been clarified. See Sections 6.104, 6.106, 6.109, 6.110, 6.111, 6.112, and 6.113.

Alternative Methods of Computing Finance Charges—Open-End Credit

Another issue that has caused concern in recent years is the appropriate method for computing finance charges on open-end credit. This issue is a product of evolutionary development of practices during the last 25 or more years and of the failure of protagonists for different views to recognize or openly discuss the basic questions involved. This Act deals with this problem in realistic terms.

Four general approaches in imposing finance charges have been used although there have been many variants particularly with regard to the average daily balance method.

The method used by a number of large retailers when they first established revolving accounts was the "ending balance method." The finance charge was computed on the balance in the account at the close of the monthly billing cycle (the "ending balance"). This balance reflected all amounts owed through the date the balance was determined and took into account all purchases and payments through that date.

The previous balance method is the one used by most retailers and until the advent of the modern computer was by far the prevailing method. The finance charge is computed on the same balance as under the ending balance method but the billing of the charge is deferred until the close of the next billing cycle for that customer. At the close of the cycle when the charge is billed, the balance is the "previous balance," that is the previous month's ending balance brought forward as the beginning balance of the current cycle. The billing of the finance charge is deferred to give the customer the opportunity to avoid a finance charge by paying the full amount before the next cycle's billing date. If he makes only a partial payment the finance charge is computed on the full amount of the previous balance. It is this feature which has chagrined consumer advocates who have felt that the finance charge should reflect payments made during the cycle for which the bill was received. The deferral feature of the previous balance method was designed to accommodate customers who wanted the option of using their revolving accounts like the formerly common 30-day charge accounts. Merchants found that the lack of opportunity to avoid finance charges made the ending balance system unattractive both to themselves and to consumers and led many merchants to change from the ending balance method to the previous balance method.

The adjusted balance method provides for the calculation of the finance charge on an amount equal to the previous balance minus all payments and credits during the current cycle but excludes any purchases made during the current cycle. The primary user of this method is a major retailer who did not offer revolving credit until many years after these accounts had become popular.

The average daily balance method requires computer technology and could not be utilized until recent years. The cost of this technology makes this method unavailable to many credit grantors. Under this method the finance charge is computed on the sum of the balances outstanding each day during the billing cycle, divided by the number of days in the cycle. Purchases may or may not be included in the daily balance from the day they are made and there may or may not be an optional feature permitting the customer to avoid finance charges by full payment.

Against this evolutionary background in the retail area, another important factor—the bank credit card—has become involved in the controversy. A cardinal principle has been that if and when a bank lends money, it is entitled to a return or interest on the money loaned from the date of the loan until the loan is paid. In various ways this principle has been followed in both closed-end and open-end credit, but one major exception has developed. When banks moved into the credit card field in the 1960's, they recognized that if credit cards were to be used in the purchase of goods and services, banks would be competing with retailers already extending credit for these same purposes. Consequently, to develop a credit card program that would be competitive with retailers, banks modelled their operations closely on revolving credit techniques of retailers and contrary to the usual principle of banking, provided for free periods to cardholders either under the previous balance or adjusted balance methods. Hence, in bank credit card operations under which banks pay to retailers the dollar amount, less a "merchant discount," of credit card purchases within a few days from the date of purchase and hence at that time advance actual funds for the account of cardholders, but make no charge to cardholders for the credit advanced for the same 30–60 day free period allowed by retailers, the basic principle of charging interest for the full period on which funds are outstanding has been abandoned, the loss of interest being compensated for by the merchant discount charged the retailer.

Against this background, both retailers and banks have vehemently contended that the previous balance method of computing finance charges is justified, legitimate, and proper and should not be outlawed. On the other hand, consumer advocates have urged the mandatory imposition of the adjusted balance method. In support of this position, they contend that it is unfair to them if they have to pay finance charges computed on balances existing at the beginning of a cycle, if these balances have been reduced by payments made during the cycle. Based upon varying possible fact situations, consumer advocates cite "horror stories" of very high percentage rates in finance charges (computed by the actuarial method) that may result if the previous balance method is utilized. In advancing these arguments, however, these advocates never suggest that if the previous balance is reduced by payments made during the cycle, it should also be increased by additional purchases made and charged to the account during the cycle. In other words, these advocates are happy to have, in both retail and bank credit card operations, the continuance of a 30–60 day free period but make the essentially one-sided argument that if the previous balance method is used, it should be reduced by payments made during the cycle.

Computation of finance charges on the average daily balances outstanding in the account of a customer during the cycle for which a bill is rendered is a legitimate, proper method. This Act authorizes the use of this method in Section 2.202(2)(a). However, since the previous balance vs. the adjusted balance argument continues, both in the Congress in its consideration of S.2101 and throughout the country in state legislatures, Section 2.202(2)(b) of this Act provides alternative language for each of the previous balance and adjusted balance methods to permit legislatures to adopt whichever form they approve. Although a strenuous effort was made in the consideration of S.2101 to prohibit the use of the previous balance method, this effort failed in the Senate and, as S.2101 now stands, the previous balance method will continue to be permissible.

Changes in Provisions for Deferrals and Rebates—Sections 2.503 and 2.510

A widespread if not the prevailing practice in the credit industry is to compute both deferrals and rebates by the sum of the balances method. This practice permits single computations in precomputed transactions involving both one or more deferrals and a subsequent rebate. Subsection (6) of Section 3.210 of the 1968 Text in requiring separate calculations of deferrals and rebates casts doubt on this industry practice.

The revisions of Sections 2.503 and 2.510 of this Act are designed to provide affirmatively for this industry practice which simplifies computations and not only does not prejudice consumers but also reduces their costs. A further revision of Section 2.510 requires the use of the actuarial method of calculating refunds upon prepayment of transactions involving a large number of payments when the sum of the balances method produces higher costs to consumers.

Federal Preemption of Disclosure

Increasingly in the last decade the Congress has interested itself in various aspects of consumer credit. Particularly in the case of the Consumer Credit Protection Act (of which the Truth in Lending Act is a part) enacted in 1968 and in amendments of that Act enacted since 1968, Congress has moved into a major area of consumer credit: disclosures to be made to consumers. In that Act the Congress took pains to recognize that other areas of consumer credit continued to be subject to state law and, even in the case of disclosure, made provision for determinations by the Board of Governors of the Federal Reserve System that state law was sufficiently identical with the federal Act to warrant States applying for and obtaining exemptions from the application of the federal Act. Under these provisions, four or more States have applied for and obtained exemptions.

However, States seeking exemption found that state laws with respect to disclosure must be identical not only to the Truth in Lending Act but also to Regulation Z issued under that Act.

PREFATORY NOTE

Entirely aside from these efforts on the part of the Congress and certain States to preserve States' rights and some measure of state control over consumer credit, actual experience from 1968 to the present time has demonstrated that in substantially all cases, creditors engaging in consumer credit look to the federal law and Regulation Z as the controlling law in the area of disclosure. Creditors have found that any additional provisions of state law on the subject constitute a nuisance in attempts to comply with federal law and frequently add confusion in these efforts to comply. Further, in those States obtaining exemptions from the Federal Reserve Board, state officials charged with the duty of enforcing state statutes and regulations designed to parallel the federal Act and Regulation Z find the task of keeping state law parallel onerous and troublesome.

Against this background, this Act evidences the conclusion that the Congress has preempted the field of disclosure and any attempt of States to remain in the field by enacting statutes and regulations of their own cause substantially more harm than good. Consequently, this Act contains few substantive disclosure provisions and in Section 3.201 provides simply that a person upon whom the federal Act imposes duties or obligations shall make or give to the consumer the disclosures required of him by the federal Act and in all respects comply with that Act. Section 3.201 allows the Administrator to enforce the disclosure provisions of the Truth in Lending Act and Regulation Z as state law. Other tracking sections of this Act include Sections 1.102 (2); 1.202(5); 1.301(1); 1.301(33); 1.302; 2.201(4); 2.401 (4); 2.501(1); 2.501(2); 3.209; 3.501; 5.107; 5.203; 5.302; and 6.102(3).

In adopting this basic approach the National Conference recognizes that in some States problems of delegation of legislative power may arise. However, in the ever increasing complexity of areas in which both the federal government and individual States have enacted legislation, solutions of this type are increasingly common and have been sustained. See, *e. g.*, incorporation of definition of "taxable income": by reference to Federal Internal Revenue Code, approved in City National Bank of Clinton v. Iowa State Tax Commission, 251 Iowa 603, 102 N.W.2d 381 (1960); incorporation by state legislatures of Federal Insurance Contributions Act for coverage of state and local governmental employees under Social Security; enactment of state War Emergency Acts as enforcement measures in aid of federal legislation creating the Office of Price Administration and providing for the regulation of prices during war time, approved in People v. Mailman, 182 Misc. 870 (1944); affirmed on appeal 293 N.Y. 887 (1944); incorporation of state law in Federal Assimilative Crimes Act of 1948, 17 U.S.C. § 13, approved in United States v. Sharpnack (1958) 78 S.Ct. 291, 355 U.S. 286, 2 L.Ed.2d 282. In any event, whatever difficulties may be involved, the course adopted in this Act and the abandonment of any effort to duplicate disclosure requirements by substantive provisions seem preferable to the alternative of attempting to establish and maintain parallel federal and state legislation on the subject.

Changes Resulting from Special Problems of Particular Types of Creditors

In a few instances particular types of creditors presented special problems which they considered deserved clarification of or changes from the 1968 Text. In the instances set forth below some adaptations to solve these special problems appear to be justified.

At the request of credit unions, subsection (6) of Section 1.202 has been added so that in any State enacting the U3C it will be optional with the enacting State whether ceilings on rates or limits on loan maturities provided in the U3C will be applicable to credit unions or whether these rates and maturities will be governed by other laws of the State or the United States enacted specifically for credit unions.

A widespread practice of some oil companies operating directly or through franchised filling stations is to avoid the usual revolving credit feature in their credit card agreements which gives the customer the option of paying in full or in instalments. Instead, these companies customarily require full payment of the amount of each billing statement but provide for and assess charges if payments are delinquent. Section 2.601 makes clear that transactions of this kind are not consumer credit transactions governed by the U3C; however, to make equally clear that consumer credit transactions are involved if charges for delinquency are imposed but delinquencies are ignored in practice; the definitions of "finance charge" in Section 1.301(20) and "open-end credit" in Section 1.301(28) have been revised or added.

In many States special statutes have been passed providing for insurance premium financing. To provide for the particular needs of this type of financing a definition of an "insurance premium loan" and some substantive provisions have been added and appear in this Act. See Sections 1.301(22), 2.302(2), 2.401 (6), 3.207, 5.110(3) and 5.111(4). These provisions together with other general provisions of the U3C make these special statutes unnecessary and permit their repeal.

In the States that have enacted the U3C and in other States that have considered it, supervised financial organizations, *e. g.*, banks, thrift institutions and the like, have argued that they are currently supervised by agencies to whom various types of fees and charges must be paid and that they should not be required to pay the same fees as other creditors to finance the administration of the U3C. This Act reflects the belief that all creditors extending consumer credit in a State enacting the U3C are governed by the U3C and should share in financing the cost of its administration, but, responding to these arguments of supervised financial organizations, a new subsection (4) of Section 6.203 reduces by 50% the standard volume fees payable by these organizations.

Refinements and Clarifications

In addition to the above changes and additions, this Act includes many clarifications and refinements and much simplification and improvement of language. Not the least of these has been the reorganization of Articles 2 and 3 to eliminate much of the duplication in these two Articles in the 1968 Text. Although these two Articles have been substantially shortened by the changes, no important distinctions between sales credit and loans have been ignored; rather, they have been clarified, particularly in the case of credit cards. Sections referring specifically to credit cards include: Sections 1.301(12), (15), (17), (24), (25), (28), and (39) and 3.403.

*

UNIFORM CONSUMER CREDIT CODE

AN ACT

Relating to certain consumer and other credit transactions and constituting the uniform consumer credit code; consolidating and revising certain aspects of the law relating to consumer and other loans, consumer and other sales of goods, services and interests in land, and consumer leases; revising the law relating to usury; relating certain practices relating to insurance in consumer credit transactions; providing for administrative regulation of certain consumer and other credit transactions; imposing fees making uniform the law with respect thereto; and repealing inconsistent legislation.

COMMENT

The long title of the Code should be adapted to the constitutional and statutory requirements and practices of the enacting State.

The concept of the Code is that "credit transactions" is a single subject of the law notwithstanding its many facets.

ARTICLE 1

GENERAL PROVISIONS AND DEFINITIONS

PART 1

SHORT TITLE, CONSTRUCTION, GENERAL PROVISIONS

Section 1.101 [Short Title]

This Act shall be known and may be cited as Uniform Consumer Credit Code.

Section 1.102 [Purposes; Rules of Construction]

(1) This Act shall be liberally construed and applied to promote its underlying purposes and policies.

(2) The underlying purposes and policies of this Act are:

(a) to simplify, clarify, and modernize the law governing consumer credit and usury;

(b) to provide rate ceilings to assure an adequate supply of credit to consumers;

(c) to further consumer understanding of the terms of credit transactions and to foster competition among suppliers of consumer credit so that consumers may obtain credit at reasonable cost;

(d) to protect consumers against unfair practices by some suppliers of consumer credit, having due regard for the interests of legitimate and scrupulous creditors;

(e) to permit and encourage the development of fair and economically sound consumer credit practices;

(f) to conform the regulation of disclosure in consumer credit transactions to the Federal Truth in Lending Act; and

(g) to make uniform the law, including administrative rules, among the various jurisdictions.

(3) A reference to a requirement imposed by this Act includes reference to a related rule of the Administrator adopted pursuant to this Act.

COMMENT

Under Section 3.201, a creditor must make disclosure in consumer credit sales and consumer loans in accordance with the Federal Truth in Lending Act, defined in Section 1.302 as including Regulation Z. If a creditor fails to comply, he has violated this Act as well as the Federal Act, and the Administrator may proceed against him pursuant to Section 6.104(2).

Section 1.103 [Supplementary General Principles of Law Applicable]

Unless displaced by the particular provisions of this Act, the Uniform Commercial Code and the principles of law and equity, including the law relative to capacity to contract, principal and agent, estoppel, fraud, misrepresentation, duress, coercion, mistake, bankruptcy, or other validating or invalidating cause supplement its provisions. In the event of inconsistency between the Uniform Commercial Code and this Act the provisions of this Act control.

COMMENT

The Uniform Commercial Code is referred to in the Comments as UCC.

Many transactions are subject both to this Act and to other bodies of law, particularly the UCC. In the event of inconsistency between this Act and the UCC the provisions of this Act control. See, *e. g.*, UCC Sections 9–201 and 9–203. In other cases the provisions of this Act are supplemented by the UCC and other principles. In general such principles have not been repeated in this Act. There are exceptions, *e. g.*, the duty of good faith in UCC Section 1–203 is repeated and defined in Section 1.110.

See Note following Section 9.-103 as to UCC amendments possibly needed.

Section 1.104 [Construction Against Implicit Repeal]

This Act being a general act intended as a unified coverage of its subject matter, no part of it shall be construed to be impliedly repealed by subsequent legislation if that construction can reasonably be avoided.

Section 1.105 [Severability]

If any provision of this Act or the application thereof to any person or circumstances is held invalid, the invalidity does not affect other provisions or applications of this Act which can be given effect without the invalid provision or application, and to this end the provisions of this Act are severable.

Section 1.106 [Adjustment of Dollar Amounts]

(1) From time to time the dollar amounts in this Act designated as subject to change shall change, as provided in this section, according to and to the extent of changes in the Consumer Price Index for Urban Wage Earners and Clerical Workers: U.S. City Average, All Items, 1967 = 100, compiled by the Bureau of Labor Statistics, United States Department of Labor, and hereafter referred to as the Index. The Index for December of the year preceding the year in which this Act becomes effective is the Reference Base Index.

(2) The designated dollar amounts shall change on July 1 of each even-numbered year if the percentage of change, calculated to the nearest whole percentage point, between the Index at the end of the preceding year and the Reference Base Index is ten per cent or more, but

(a) the portion of the percentage change in the Index in excess of a multiple of ten per cent shall be disregarded and the dollar amounts shall change only in multiples of ten per cent of the amounts appearing in this Act on the date of enactment; and

(b) the dollar amounts shall not change if the amounts required by this section are those currently in effect pursuant to this Act as a result of earlier application of this section.

(3) If the Index is revised, the percentage of change pursuant to this section shall be calculated on the basis of the revised Index. If a revision of the Index changes the Reference Base Index, a revised Reference Base Index shall be determined by multiplying the Reference Base Index then applicable by the rebasing factor furnished by the Bureau of Labor Statistics. If the Index is superseded, the Index referred to in this section is the one represented by the Bureau of Labor Statistics as reflecting most accurately changes in the purchasing power of the dollar for consumers.

(4) The Administrator shall adopt a rule announcing

(a) on or before April 30 of each year in which dollar amounts are to change, the changes in dollar amounts required by subsection (2); and

(b) promptly after the changes occur, changes in the Index required by subsection (3) including, if applicable, the numerical equivalent of the Reference Base Index under a revised Reference Base Index and the designation or title of any index superseding the Index.

(5) A person does not violate this Act with respect to a transaction otherwise complying with this Act if he relies on dollar amounts either determined according to subsection (2) or appearing in the last rule of the Administrator announcing the then current dollar amounts.

COMMENT

1. Under this section the dollar amounts designated as subject to change will automatically change on July 1 of each even-numbered year if the change in the Consumer Price Index is great enough. Assume that a state enacts the Uniform Consumer Credit Code and establishes the effective date as July 1, 1974. In this case the Consumer Price Index for December, 1973, is the Reference Base Index. For ease of illustration, assume that the Index is 100. The $300 figure appearing in Section 2.-201(2)(a)(i) will be used as an illustrative dollar amount.

CASE 1: The Index for December, 1975 is 107. The change from the Reference Base Index of 100 is an increase of 7%. Since the change is less than 10%, no change in dollar amounts occurs.

CASE 2: The Index for December, 1977 is 112. The change from the Reference Base Index of 100 is an increase of 12%. Since this is more than 10%, a change occurs. The portion of the 12% in excess of 10% is disregarded; hence, an increase of 10% is indicated. 10% of $300 is $30. The dollar amount is $330, effective July 1, 1978.

CASE 3: The Index for December, 1979 is 118. The change from the Reference Base Index of 100 is an increase of 18%. The portion of 18% in excess of 10% is disregarded; hence, an increase of 10% is indicated. However, the $300 amount changed to $330 in 1978 (see CASE 2). Since the amount currently in effect ($330) is still the correct amount under this section, no change occurs.

CASE 4: The Index for December, 1981 is 122. The change from the Reference Base Index of 100 is an increase of 22%. The portion of 22% in excess of a multiple of 10% (here 20%) is disregarded and a 20% increase is indicated. 20% of $300 is $60. The dollar amount is $360, effective July 1, 1982.

CASE 5: The Index for December, 1983 is 117. The change from the Reference Base Index of 100 is an increase of 17%. The portion of 17% in excess of 10% is disregarded and a 10% increase is indicated. 10% of 300 is $30. The dollar amount is $330, effective July 1, 1984, a decrease from the $360 amount in effect since 1982 (see CASE 4).

CASE 6: In 1985, the Bureau of Labor Statistics (BLS) revises the Index, changing coverage components and selecting a new base period. If only the coverage or components were changed, the revised Index should be used for subsequent calculations. However, if a new base period is selected (1983—84=100), an equivalent on the scale of the revised Index must be assigned to the Reference Base Index (December, 1973). The rebasing factor supplied by the BLS is .6454545. Therefore, the Revised Reference Base Index is (100) x (.6454545) = 64.5.

A comparison of the revised Index for December 1985 (103.-4) with the Revised Reference Base Index (64.5) shows that the change from the Revised Reference Base Index is an increase of 60.3%.

$$\frac{103.4-64.5}{64.5} = .603 = 60.3\%$$

Under subsection (2) 60.3% becomes 60%, and an increase of that percentage is indicated. The dollar amount is $480, effective July 1, 1986.

2. The provisions for adjustment of dollar amounts never permit the maximum rate of finance charge to rise above 36%. To reflect the needs of high-risk consumers for greater amounts of credit as a result of rising prices, the maximum rate permitted is extended to larger amounts of credit. Were this not done automatically, inflation would push creditors' operating costs against a fixed rate ceiling, gradually lessening their ability to provide small amounts of credit to high-risk consumers.

The change in maximum rates permitted by a 10% increase in the dollar amounts is shown below for various amounts financed payable in 12 monthly installments.

Amount financed	Maximum rates prior to adjustment	Maximum rates after 10% increase in dollar amounts
$ 100	36.00%	36.00%
300	36.00	36.00
500	33.02	33.75
1,000	28.05	28.64
1,500	25.10	25.80
3,000	20.73	21.22
5,000	18.58	18.92

---

3. Subsection (1) specifies the Index for the December preceding the year in which the Act is to take effect as the Reference Base Index. Hence, changes in the Index that have occurred since promulgation of this Act but before the December preceding the effective date will not require immediate changes in dollar amounts from those specified in the U3C upon enactment.

Section 1.107 [Waiver; Agreement to Forego Rights; Settlement of Claims]

(1) Except as otherwise permitted in this Act, a consumer may waive or agree to forego rights or benefits under this Act only in settlement of a bona fide dispute.

(2) A claim by a consumer against a creditor for an excess charge, any other violation of this Act, a civil penalty, or a claim against a consumer for a default or breach of a duty imposed by this Act, if disputed in good faith, may be settled by agreement.

(3) A claim against a consumer, whether or not disputed, may be settled for less value than the amount claimed.

(4) A settlement in which the consumer waives or agrees to forego rights or benefits under this Act is invalid if the court as a matter of law finds the settlement to have been unconscionable at the time it was made. The competence of the consumer, any deception or coercion practiced upon him, the nature and extent of the legal advice received by him, and the value of the consideration are relevant to the issue of unconscionability.

COMMENT

Unlike UCC Section 1–102(3) which broadly permits variation by agreement, this Act starts from the premise that a consumer may not in general waive or agree to forego rights or benefits under this Act. Compare UCC Section 9–501(3). If not specifically provided for in the Act, waiver or agreement to forego must be part of a settlement, and settlements are subject to review as provided for in this section.

Section 1.108 [Effect of Act on Powers of Organizations]

(1) This Act prescribes maximum charges for all creditors, except lessors and those excluded (Section 1.202), extending credit in consumer credit transactions (subsection (13) of Section 1.301), and displaces existing limitations on the powers of those creditors based on maximum charges.

(2) With respect to sellers of goods or services, small loan companies, licensed lenders, consumer and sales finance companies, industrial banks and loan companies, and commercial banks and trust companies, this Act displaces existing limitations on their powers based solely on amount or duration of credit.

(3) Except as provided in subsection (1) [and in the Article on Effective Date and Repealer (Article 9)], this Act does not

displace limitations on powers of credit unions, savings banks, savings and loan associations, or other thrift institutions whether organized for the profit of shareholders or as mutual organizations.

(4) Except as provided in subsections (1) and (2) [and in the Article on Effective Date and Repealer (Article 9)], this Act does not displace:

(a) limitations on powers of supervised financial organizations (subsection (41) of Section 1.301) with respect to the amount of a loan to a single borrower, the ratio of a loan to the value of collateral, the duration of a loan secured by an interest in land, or other similar restrictions designed to protect deposits, or

(b) limitations on powers an organization is authorized to exercise under the laws of this State or the United States.

COMMENT

1. The bracketed language in subsections (3) and (4) should be included and the brackets omitted if the enacting State adds to the Article on Effective Date and Repealer (Article 9) provisions displacing limitations on powers of the kinds of organizations enumerated in subsections (3) and (4).

2. This section states the policy of this Act regarding the displacement of laws regulating suppliers of consumer credit and should be read as a guide for the preparation of the repealer provisions of Section 9.103, along with the explanatory note following that section.

3. This Act displaces existing usury laws; in addition, subsection (1) displaces existing limitations on maximum charges for all suppliers of consumer credit except lessors and those excluded under Section 1.202. In other respects, this Act differentiates among creditors depending on their status as either being or not being supervised financial organizations as defined in Section 1.301(41), and among supervised financial organizations depending on whether they are (1) commercial or industrial banks or trust companies, or (2) thrift institutions such as credit unions, savings banks and savings and loan associations whether mutual or not.

4. Subsection (2) frees commercial and industrial banks and trust companies and all creditors other than thrift institutions from existing limitations on their powers based solely on the amount or duration of credit they may extend, such as the typical $5,000 or $7,500 limit on the amount, and the typical 36-month or 60-month limit on the maturity, of a personal loan by a commercial or industrial bank or trust company.

5. Subsection (3) retains all existing limitations on powers of thrift institutions, other than those based on maximum charges, on the theory that those limitations may be required for the protection of their depositors or shareholders.

6. Except for limitations based on maximum charges, and limitations based solely on amount or duration of credit, subsection (4)(a) retains as to all supervised financial organizations existing limitations and restrictions of the kinds enumerated designed to protect deposits such as the typical limitation to 10% of capital and surplus funds on bank loans to a single borrower. Subject to the same exceptions, subsection (4)(b) retains as to all organizations existing limitations on the powers they are authorized by law to exercise.

Section 1.109 [Transactions Subject to Act by Agreement]

Parties to a credit transaction or modification thereof that is not a consumer credit transaction (subsection (13) of Section 1.-301) may agree in a writing signed by them that the transaction is subject to the provisions of this Act applying to consumer credit transactions. If the parties so agree the transaction is a consumer credit transaction for the purposes of this Act.

COMMENT

This section permits creditors, by inserting an appropriate clause in a contract, to be certain that the transaction is a consumer credit transaction for the purposes of this Act.

Section 1.110 [Obligation of Good Faith]

(1) Every contract or duty within this Act imposes an obligation of good faith in its performance or enforcement.

(2) "Good faith" means honesty in fact in the conduct or transaction concerned.

COMMENT

This section is derived from UCC Sections 1–201(19) and 1–203.

PART 2

SCOPE AND JURISDICTION

Section 1.201 [Territorial Application]

(1) Except as otherwise provided in this section, this Act applies to a consumer credit transaction entered into in this State. For the purposes of this Act, a consumer credit transaction is entered into in this State if:

(a) pursuant to other than open-end credit, either a signed writing evidencing the obligation or offer of the consumer is received by the creditor in this State, or the creditor induces the consumer who is a resident of this State to enter into the transaction by face-to-face solicitation in this State; or

(b) pursuant to open-end credit, either the consumer's communication or his indication of intention to establish the open-end credit arrangement is received by the creditor in this State or, if no communication or indication of intention is given by the consumer before the first transaction, the creditor's communication notifying the consumer of the privilege of using the arrangement is mailed in this State.

(2) With respect to a consumer loan to which this Act does not otherwise apply, if a consumer who is a resident of this State, pursuant to solicitation in this State, sends a signed writing evidencing the obligation or offer of the consumer to a creditor in another state and receives the cash proceeds of the loan in this State:

(a) the creditor may not contract for or receive charges exceeding those permitted by the Article on Finance Charges and Related Provisions (Article 2); and

(b) the provisions on Powers and Functions of Administrator (Part 1) of the Article on Administration (Article 6) apply as though the loan were entered into in this State.

(3) The Part on Limitations on Creditors' Remedies (Part 1) of the Article on Remedies and Penalties (Article 5) applies to actions or other proceedings brought in this State to enforce rights arising from consumer credit transactions or extortionate extensions of credit, wherever entered into.

(4) Except as provided in subsection (2), a consumer credit transaction to which this Act does not apply entered into with a

person who is a resident of this State at the time of the transaction is valid and enforceable in this State to the extent that it is valid and enforceable under the laws of another jurisdiction, but:

(a) a creditor may not collect through actions or other proceedings in this State an amount exceeding the total amount permitted if the Article on Finance Charges and Related Provisions (Article 2) were applicable; and

(b) a creditor may not enforce rights against the consumer in this State with respect to the provisions of agreements that violate the provisions on Limitations on Agreements and Practices (Part 3) and Limitations on Consumers' Liabilities (Part 4) of the Article on Regulation of Agreements and Practices (Article 3).

(5) Except as provided in subsections (2), (3), and (4), a consumer credit transaction entered into in another jurisdiction is valid and enforceable in this State according to its terms to the extent that it is valid and enforceable under the laws of the other jurisdiction.

(6) For the purposes of this Act, the residence of a consumer is the address given by him as his residence in a writing signed by him in connection with a consumer credit transaction until he notifies the creditor of a different address as his residence, and is then the different address.

(7) Notwithstanding other provisions of this section:

(a) except as provided in subsection (3), this Act does not apply if the consumer is not a resident of this State at the time of a consumer credit transaction and the parties have agreed that the law of his residence applies; and

(b) this Act applies if the consumer is a resident of this State at the time of a consumer credit transaction and the parties have agreed that the law of his residence applies.

(8) Each of the following agreements or provisions of an agreement by a consumer who is a resident of this State at the time of a consumer credit transaction is invalid with respect to the transaction:

(a) that the law of another jurisdiction apply;

(b) that the consumer consents to be subject to the process of another jurisdiction;

(c) that the consumer appoints an agent to receive service of process;

(d) that fixes venue; and

(e) that the consumer consents to the jurisdiction of the court that does not otherwise have jurisdiction.

(9) The following provisions of this Act specify the applicable law governing certain cases:

(a) applicability (Section 6.102) of the Part on Powers and Functions of Administrator (Part 1) of the Article on Administration (Article 6); and

(b) applicability (Section 6.201) of the Part on Notification and Fees (Part 2) of the Article on Administration (Article 6).

COMMENT

1. This section enables the enacting State to apply this Act for the protection of its own consumer residents in multi-state transactions to the extent consistent with the need for workable operating procedures on the part of creditors. The territorial applicability of the Act varies with the kind of protection safeguard involved. The major substantive protective provisions in this Act are those on rate ceilings (Parts 2 and 4 of Article 2), disclosure (Part 2 of Article 3), limitations on agreements and practices (Part 3 of Article 3), home solicitation sales (Part 5 of Article 3), limitations on consumers' liabilities (Part 4 of Article 3), and limitations on creditors' remedies (Part 1 of Article 5). Except for the disclosure provisions, this section allows the enacting State to apply all of these protective provisions to its own consumer residents when enforcement actions are brought against them in the enacting State.

In the case of a consumer who was a resident when the agreement was made, subsection (4) prohibits the creditor from collecting through actions total amounts including charges to the extent that the charges exceed those permitted by Article 2 and from enforcing rights in violation of the provisions on limitations on agreements and practices of Part 3 of Article 3 and limitations on consumers' liabilities of Part 4 of Article 3. The home solicitation provisions apply to residents because subsection (1) makes this Act apply if the buyer's agreement or offer to purchase is received by the seller in this State and a home solicitation sale is defined in Section 3.501 as one in which the buyer's agreement or offer to purchase is received by the seller, who personally solicits the sale, at a residence. Under subsection (3) a creditor is subject to the limitations on his remedies provided by Part 1 of Article 5 in actions he brings in the enacting State against all persons, whether or not they were residents at the time the credit agreement was made.

2. Subsection (1) serves as a general residual provision governing those matters not specifically

treated elsewhere in the section and controls the applicability of the disclosure provisions. Under this subsection the creditor has a measure of control over the applicability of the Act with respect to the disclosure requirements and can arrange his interstate operations in a manner which minimizes the operational difficulties arising from the variations in the disclosure requirements of the different state laws. This flexibility on the part of creditors with respect to the applicability of the disclosure provisions offers no threat to consumers because the Federal Consumer Credit Protection Act [15 U.S.C. § 1601 et seq.] assures consumers that disclosure requirements will be substantially similar in all states.

3. Creditors falling within the supervised lender category (Part 3 of Article 2) need be licensed only in the State where the loan is entered into, that is, where the debtor's writing is received [Subsection (1)]. However, in the case of a mail order loan to a consumer residing in an enacting State, even if the debtor's writing is received by the creditor in another State, the creditor may not exceed the rate ceilings of the enacting State and the Administrator may go into the creditor's State and investigate potential violations pursuant to Part 1 of Article 6 [Subsection (2)]. Of course, the general rule of subsection (1) that a transaction is entered into in the State where the consumer's writing is received yields whenever the creditor attempts to evade the Act by engaging in face-to-face solicitation in the State of the consumer's residence but contrives to have the consumer's writing sent the creditor in another State [Subsection (1)(a)].

4. The danger that creditors may be able to induce consumers to agree that the applicable law will be that of a creditors' haven that has no effective consumer credit protection has led to invalidating choice of law agreements except where the law chosen is that of the State of the consumer's residence [Subsections (7) and (8)]. Subsection (9) specifies the applicable law governing the powers of the Administrator and the notification and fees requirements.

Section 1.202 [Exclusions]

This Act does not apply to:

(1) extensions of credit to organizations;

(2) except as otherwise provided in the Article on Insurance (Article 4), the sale of insurance if the insured is not obligated to pay instalments of the premium and the insurance may terminate or be cancelled after non-payment of an instalment of the premium;

(3) transactions under public utility or common carrier tariffs if a subdivision or agency of this State or of the United States regulates the charges for the services involved, the

charges for delayed payment, and any discount allowed for early payment;

(4) transactions in securities or commodities accounts with a broker-dealer registered with the Securities and Exchange Commission; [or]

(5) except with respect to the provisions on compliance with the Federal Truth in Lending Act (Section 3.201), [civil liability for violation of disclosure provisions (Section 5.203), criminal penalties for disclosure violations (Section 5.302)], and powers and functions of the Administrator with respect to disclosure violations (Part 1 of Article 6), pawnbrokers who are licensed and whose rates and charges are regulated under or pursuant to ordinances or other statutes [; or

(6) ceilings on rates or limits on loan maturities of credit extended by a credit union organized under the laws of this State or of the United States if these ceilings or limits are established by these laws or by applicable regulations].

Note 1. If the enacting State wishes to apply for an exemption from the Federal Truth in Lending Act, the brackets before and after Sections 5.203 and 5.302 should be deleted and those sections enacted, and the brackets in subsection (5) preceding and following references to those sections should be omitted; otherwise, delete the brackets and the language enclosed within them, and delete the references to Sections 5.203 and 5.302 in the Table of Articles, Parts, and Sections.

Note 2. If subsection (6) is included by the enacting State, delete "[or]" at the end of subsection (4), the opening bracket at the end of subsection (5), and the closing bracket at the end of subsection (6). If subsection (6) is not included by the enacting State, delete the brackets before and after "or" at the end of subsection (4).

COMMENT

The Consumer Credit Protection Act, 15 U.S.C. §§ 1601 et seq., will hereafter be referred to as "CCPA." Regulation Z, 12 CFR §§ 226 et seq., will hereafter be referred to as "Regulation Z."

Subsection (1) excludes transactions in which credit is extended to organizations (Section 1.301(29)). Subsection (2) makes clear that sales of insurance are not consumer credit transactions if no credit (Section 1.301(16)) has been extended. However, loans to purchase insurance are covered if they qualify as consumer loans (Section 1.301(15)), and insurance provided in connection with consumer credit transactions is regulated by Article 4. Subsection (3) is derived from CCPA Section 104(4), 15 U.S.C. § 1603(4). Subsection (4) is derived from CCPA Section 104(2), 15 U.S.C. § 1603(2); this provision excludes stock broker loans from coverage of the Act. Subsection (5) excludes pawnbrokers from coverage of the Act, except for certain disclosure requirements, if local or state laws provide for licensing and regulation of rates and charges. Since the CCPA applies to pawnbrokers engaging in consumer credit transactions, this Act supplements the coverage of the CCPA in this respect by allowing the Administrator to consider a violation of the CCPA as a violation of this Act (Section 3.201) and to act against the violator (Section 6.104(2)). Subsection (6) is an optional provision allowing states to continue the relatively low rate limitations, as well as loan maturities, that have traditionally applied to the credit unions.

Other transactions are inferentially excluded by the definitions of the three key transactions covered by the Act, "consumer credit sale" (Section 1.301(12)), "consumer lease" (Section 1.301(14)), and "consumer loan" (Section 1.-301(15)). With respect to sales and loans, these definitions exclude: sales (paragraph (a)(i)) and loans (paragraph (a)) made by creditors not regularly engaged in these transactions; sales (paragraph (a)(ii)) and loans (paragraph (a)(i)) to organizations; sales (paragraph (a)(iii)) and loans (paragraph (a)(ii)) for business purposes; sales (paragraph (a)(iv)) and loans (paragraph (a)(iii)) in which there is neither a requirement for payment of a finance charge nor for payment in instalments; sales (paragraph (a)(v)) and loans (paragraph (a)(iv)), other than real property transactions, in which the amount financed exceeds $25,000; and sales (paragraph (b)(ii)) and loans (paragraph (b)(ii)) which are real property transactions in which the finance charge is 12 per cent or less. The definition of "consumer lease" (Section 1.301(14)) excludes: leases by lessors not regularly engaged in leasing, leases made to organizations, leases for business purposes (paragraph (a)(i)); leases in which the amount payable exceeds $25,000 (paragraph (a)(ii)); and leases for a term of 4 months or less (paragraph (a)(iii)).

Section 1.203 [Jurisdiction [and Service of Process]]

[(1)] The [ ] court of this State may exercise jurisdiction over any creditor with respect to any conduct of the creditor subject to this Act or with respect to any claim arising from a transaction subject to this Act.

[(2) In addition to any other method provided by [rule] [statute], personal jurisdiction over a creditor may be acquired in a civil action or proceeding instituted in the [ ] court by service of process in the manner provided in this section. If a creditor is not a resident of this State or is a corporation not authorized to do business in this State and engages in any conduct in this State subject to this Act or in a transaction subject to this Act, he may designate an agent upon whom service of process may be made in this State. The agent shall be a resident of this State or a corporation authorized to do business in this State. The designation shall be in a writing and filed with the Secretary of State. If a designation is not made and filed or if process cannot be served in this State upon the designated agent, process may be served upon the Secretary of State, but service upon him is not effective unless the plaintiff or petitioner forthwith mails a copy of the process and pleading by registered or certified mail to the defendant or respondent at his last reasonably ascertainable address. An affidavit of compliance with this section shall be filed with the clerk of the court on or before the return day of the process, if any, or within any further time the court allows.]

Note: If the enacting State has an adequate long arm statute, the bracketed words "and Service of Process" in the section heading, the bracketed "(1)," and all of subsection (2) may be omitted.

COMMENT

Without limiting the jurisdiction of other courts over creditors, this section specifically grants that jurisdiction to a specified court. It also provides a method of obtaining personal jurisdiction over creditors by service of process.

PART 3

DEFINITIONS

Section 1.301 [General Definitions]

(1) "Actuarial method" means the method of allocating payments made on a debt between the amount financed and the finance charge pursuant to which a payment is applied first to the accumulated finance charge and any remainder is subtracted from, or any deficiency is added to, the unpaid balance of the amount financed. The Administrator may adopt rules not inconsistent with the Federal Truth in Lending Act further defining the term and prescribing its application.

(2) "Administrator" means the Administrator designated in the Article (Article 6) on Administration (Section 6.103).

(3) "Agreement" means the bargain of the parties in fact as found in their language or by implication from other circumstances including course of dealing, usage of trade, or course of performance.

(4) "Agricultural purpose" means a purpose related to the production, harvest, exhibition, marketing, transportation, processing, or manufacture of agricultural products by a natural person who cultivates, plants, propagates, or nurtures the agricultural products. "Agricultural products" includes agricultural, horticultural, viticultural, and dairy products, livestock, wildlife, poultry, bees, forest products, fish and shellfish, and products thereof, including processed and manufactured products, and products raised or produced on farms and processed or manufactured products thereof.

(5) "Amount financed" means the total of the following items:

(a) in the case of a sale, the cash price of the goods, services, or interest in land, less the amount of any down payment made in cash or in property traded in, and the amount actually paid or to be paid by the seller pursuant to an agreement with the buyer to discharge a security interest in, a lien on, or a debt with respect to property traded in;

(b) in case of a loan, the net amount paid to, receivable by, or paid or payable for the account of the debtor, plus the amount of any discount excluded from the finance charge (paragraph (b) (iii) of subsection (20)); and

(c) in the case of a sale or loan, to the extent that payment is deferred and the amount is not otherwise included and is authorized and disclosed to the consumer as required by law:

(i) amounts actually paid or to be paid by the creditor for registration, certificate of title, or license fees, and

(ii) permitted additional charges (Section 2.501).

(6) "Billing cycle" means the time interval between periodic billing statement dates.

(7) "Card issuer" means a person who issues a credit card.

(8) "Cardholder" means a person to whom a credit card is issued or who has agreed with the card issuer to pay obligations arising from the issuance to or use of the card by another person.

(9) "Cash price" of goods, services, or an interest in land means the price at which they are offered for sale by the seller to cash buyers in the ordinary course of business and may include (a) the cash price of accessories or services related to the sale, such as delivery, installation, alterations, modifications, and improvements, and (b) taxes to the extent imposed on a cash sale of the goods, services, or interest in land. The cash price stated by the seller to the buyer in a disclosure statement required by law is presumed to be the cash price.

(10) "Conspicuous":

A term or clause is "conspicuous" when it is so written that a reasonable person against whom it is to operate ought to have noticed it. Whether or not a term or clause is conspicuous is for decision by the court.

(11) "Consumer" means the buyer, lessee, or debtor to whom credit is granted in a consumer credit transaction.

(12) "Consumer credit sale":

(a) Except as provided in paragraph (b), "consumer credit sale" means a sale of goods, services, or an interest in land in which:

(i) credit is granted either pursuant to a seller credit card or by a seller who regularly engages as a seller in credit transactions of the same kind;

(ii) the buyer is a person other than an organization;

(iii) the goods, services, or interest in land are purchased primarily for a personal, family, household, or agricultural purpose;

(iv) the debt is payable in instalments or a finance charge is made; and

(v) with respect to a sale of goods or services, the amount financed does not exceed $25,000.

(b) A "consumer credit sale" does not include:

(i) a sale in which the seller allows the buyer to purchase goods or services pursuant to a lender credit card, or

(ii) unless the sale is made subject to this Act by agreement (Section 1.109), a sale of an interest in land if the finance charge does not exceed 12 per cent per year calculated according to the actuarial method on the assumption that the debt will be paid according to the agreed terms and will not be paid before the end of the agreed term.

(c) The amount of $25,000 in paragraph (a)(v) is subject to change pursuant to the provisions on adjustment of dollar amounts (Section 1.106).

(13) "Consumer credit transaction" means a consumer credit sale or consumer loan or a refinancing or consolidation thereof, or a consumer lease.

(14) "Consumer lease":

(a) "Consumer lease" means a lease of goods:

(i) which a lessor regularly engaged in the business of leasing makes to a person, except an organization, who takes under the lease primarily for a personal, family, household, or agricultural purpose;

(ii) in which the amount payable under the lease does not exceed $25,000;

(iii) which is for a term exceeding four months; and

(iv) which is not made pursuant to a lender credit card.

(b) The amount of $25,000 in paragraph (a)(ii) is subject to change pursuant to the provisions on adjustment of dollar amounts (Section 1.106).

(15) "Consumer loan":

(a) Except as provided in paragraph (b), "consumer loan" means a loan made by a creditor regularly engaged in the business of making loans in which:

(i) the debtor is a person other than an organization;

(ii) the debt is incurred primarily for a personal, family, household, or agricultural purpose;

(iii) the debt is payable in instalments or a finance charge is made; and

(iv) the amount financed does not exceed $25,000 or the debt, other than one incurred primarily for an agricultural purpose, is secured by an interest in land.

(b) A "consumer loan" does not include:

(i) a sale or lease in which the seller or lessor allows the buyer or lessee to purchase or lease pursuant to a seller credit card, or

(ii) unless the loan is made subject to this Act by agreement (Section 1.109), a loan secured by an interest in land if the security interest is bona fide and not for the purpose of circumvention or evasion of this Act and the finance charge does not exceed 12 per cent per year calculated according to the actuarial method on the assumption that the debt will be paid according to the agreed terms and will not be paid before the end of the agreed term.

(c) A loan that would be a consumer loan if the lender were regularly engaged in the business of making loans is a consumer loan if the loan is arranged for a commission or other compensation by a person regularly engaged in the business of arranging those loans and the lender is not regularly engaged in the business of making loans. The arranger is deemed to be the creditor making the loan.

(d) The amount of $25,000 in paragraph (a)(iv) is subject to change pursuant to the provisions on adjustment of dollar amounts (Section 1.106).

(16) "Credit" means the right granted by a creditor to a consumer to defer payment of debt, to incur debt and defer its payment, or to purchase property or services and defer payment therefor.

(17) "Credit card" means a card or device issued under an arrangement pursuant to which a card issuer gives to a card-

holder the privilege of obtaining credit from the card issuer or other person in purchasing or leasing property or services, obtaining loans, or otherwise. A transaction is "pursuant to a credit card" only if credit is obtained according to the terms of the arrangement by transmitting information contained on the card or device orally, in writing, by mechanical or electronic methods, or in any other manner. A transaction is not "pursuant to a credit card" if the card or device is used solely in that transaction to:

(a) identify the cardholder or evidence his credit-worthiness and credit is not obtained according to the terms of the arrangement;

(b) obtain a guarantee of payment from the cardholder's deposit account, whether or not the payment results in a credit extension to the cardholder by the card issuer; or

(c) effect an immediate transfer of funds from the cardholder's deposit account by electronic or other means, whether or not the transfer results in a credit extension to the cardholder by the card issuer.

(18) "Creditor" means the person who grants credit in a consumer credit transaction or, except as otherwise provided, an assignee of a creditor's right to payment, but use of the term does not in itself impose on an assignee any obligation of his assignor. In case of credit granted pursuant to a credit card, "creditor" means the card issuer and not another person honoring the credit card.

(19) "Earnings" means compensation paid or payable by an employer to an employee or for his account for personal services rendered or to be rendered by him, whether denominated as wages, salary, commission, bonus, or otherwise, and includes periodic payments pursuant to a pension, retirement, or disability program.

(20) "Finance charge":

(a) Except as provided in paragraph (b), "finance charge" means the sum of all charges payable directly or indirectly by the consumer and imposed directly or indirectly by the creditor as an incident to or as a condition of the extension of credit, including any of the following types of charges which are applicable:

(i) interest or any amount payable under a point, discount, or other system of charges, however denominated;

(ii) time-price differential, credit service, service, carrying, or other charge, however denominated;

(iii) premium or other charge for any guarantee or insurance protecting the creditor against the consumer's default or other credit loss; and

(iv) charges incurred for investigating the collateral or credit-worthiness of the consumer or for commissions or brokerage for obtaining the credit, irrespective of the person to whom the charges are paid or payable, unless the creditor had no notice of the charges when the credit was granted.

(b) The term does not include:

(i) charges as a result of default or delinquency if made for actual unanticipated late payment, delinquency, default, or other like occurrence, unless the parties agree that these charges are finance charges; a charge is not made for actual unanticipated late payment, delinquency, default or other like occurrence if imposed on an account that is or may be debited from time to time for purchases or other debts and, under its terms, payment in full or of a specified amount is required when billed, and in the ordinary course of business the consumer is permitted to continue to have purchases or other debts debited to the account after imposition of the charge;

(ii) additional charges (Section 2.501) or deferral charges (Section 2.503); or

(iii) a discount, if a creditor purchases or satisfies obligations of a cardholder pursuant to a credit card and the purchase or satisfaction is made at less than the face amount of the obligation.

(21) "Goods" includes goods not in existence at the time the transaction is entered into and merchandise certificates, but excludes money, chattel paper, documents of title, and instruments.

(22) "Insurance premium loan" means a consumer loan that (a) is made for the sole purpose of financing the payment by or on behalf of an insured of the premium on one or more policies or contracts issued by or on behalf of an insurer, (b) is secured by an assignment by the insured to the lender of the unearned premium on the policy or contract, and (c) contains an authorization to cancel the policy or contract financed.

(23) Except as otherwise provided, "lender" includes an assignee of a lender's right to payment, but use of the term does not in itself impose on an assignee any obligation of the lender.

(24) "Lender credit card" means a credit card issued by a supervised lender.

(25) "Loan":

(a) Except as provided in paragraph (b), "loan" includes:

(i) the creation of debt by the lender's payment of or agreement to pay money to the debtor or to a third person for the account of the debtor;

(ii) the creation of debt pursuant to a lender credit card in any manner, including a cash advance or the card issuer's honoring a draft or similar order for the payment of money drawn or accepted by the debtor, paying or agreeing to pay the debtor's obligation, or purchasing or otherwise acquiring the debtor's obligation from the obligee or his assignees;

(iii) the creation of debt by a cash advance to a debtor pursuant to a seller credit card;

(iv) the creation of debt by a credit to an account with the lender upon which the debtor is entitled to draw immediately; and

(v) the forbearance of debt arising from a loan.

(b) "Loan" does not include:

(i) a card issuer's payment or agreement to pay money to a third person for the account of a debtor if the debt of the debtor arises from a sale or lease and results from use of a seller credit card; or

(ii) the forbearance of debt arising from a sale or lease.

(26) "Merchandise certificate" means a writing not redeemable in cash and usable in its face amount in lieu of cash in exchange for goods or services.

(27) "Official fees" means:

(a) fees and charges prescribed by law which actually are or will be paid to public officials for determining the existence of or for perfecting, releasing, terminating, or satisfying a security interest related to a consumer credit transaction; or

(b) premiums payable for insurance in lieu of perfecting a security interest otherwise required by the creditor in connection with the transaction, if the premium does not exceed the fees and charges described in paragraph (a) which would otherwise be payable.

(28) "Open-end credit" means an arrangement pursuant to which:

(a) a creditor may permit a consumer, from time to time, to purchase or lease on credit from the creditor or pursuant to a credit card, or to obtain loans from the creditor or pursuant to a credit card;

(b) the amounts financed and the finance and other appropriate charges are debited to an account;

(c) the finance charge, if made, is computed on the account periodically; and

(d) either the consumer has the privilege of paying in full or in instalments or the creditor periodically imposes charges computed on the account for delaying payment and permits the consumer to continue to purchase or lease on credit.

(29) "Organization" means a corporation, government or governmental subdivision or agency, trust, estate, partnership, cooperative, or association.

(30) "Payable in instalments" means that payment is required or permitted by agreement to be made in more than four periodic payments, excluding a downpayment. If any periodic payment other than the downpayment under an agreement requiring or permitting two or more periodic payments is more than twice the amount of any other periodic payment, excluding a downpayment, a consumer credit transaction is "payable in instalments."

(31) "Person" includes a natural person or an individual, and an organization.

(32) "Person related to" with respect to an individual means (a) the spouse of the individual, (b) a brother, brother-in-law, sister, sister-in-law of the individual, (c) an ancestor or lineal descendant of the individual or his spouse, and (d) any other relative, by blood or marriage, of the individual or his spouse who shares the same home with the individual. "Person related to" with respect to an organization means (a) a person directly or indirectly controlling, controlled by, or under common control with the organization, (b) an officer or director of the organiza-

tion or a person performing similar functions with respect to the organization or to a person related to the organization, (c) the spouse of a person related to the organization, and (d) a relative by blood or marriage of a person related to the organization who shares the same home with him.

(33) "Precomputed consumer credit transaction" means a consumer credit transaction, other than a consumer lease, in which the debt is a sum comprising the amount financed and the amount of the finance charge computed in advance. A disclosure required by the Federal Truth in Lending Act does not in itself make a finance charge or transaction precomputed.

(34) "Presumed" or "presumption" means that the trier of fact must find the existence of the fact presumed unless and until evidence is introduced which would support a finding of its non-existence.

(35) "Sale of goods" includes an agreement in the form of a bailment or lease of goods if the bailee or lessee pays or agrees to pay as compensation for use a sum substantially equivalent to or in excess of the aggregate value of the goods involved and it is agreed that the bailee or lessee will become, or for no other or a nominal consideration has the option to become, the owner of the goods upon full compliance with the terms of the agreement.

(36) "Sale of an interest in land" includes a lease in which the lessee has an option to purchase the interest and all or a substantial part of the rental or other payments previously made by him are applied to the purchase price.

(37) "Sale of services" means furnishing or agreeing to furnish services and includes making arrangements to have services furnished by another.

(38) "Seller" includes, except as otherwise provided, an assignee of the seller's right to payment, but use of the term does not in itself impose on an assignee any obligation of the seller.

(39) "Seller credit card" means either:

(a) a credit card issued primarily for the purpose of giving the cardholder the privilege of using the card to purchase or lease property or services from the card issuer, persons related to the card issuer, or persons licensed or franchised to do business under the card issuer's business or trade name or designation, or both from any of these persons and from other persons; or

(b) a credit card issued by a person except a supervised lender primarily for the purpose of giving the cardholder the privilege of using the credit card to purchase or lease property or services from at least 100 persons not related to the card issuer.

(40) "Services" includes (a) work, labor, and other personal services, (b) privileges with respect to transportation, hotel and restaurant accommodations, education, entertainment, recreation, physical culture, hospital accommodations, funerals, cemetery accommodations, and the like, and (c) insurance.

(41) "Supervised financial organization" means a person, except an insurance company or other organization primarily engaged in an insurance business:

(a) organized, chartered, or holding an authorization certificate under laws of this State or of the United States that authorizes the person to make loans and to receive deposits, including a savings, share, certificate or deposit account, and

(b) subject to supervision by an official or agency of this State or of the United States.

(42) "Supervised lender" means a person authorized to make or take assignments of supervised loans, under a license issued by the Administrator (Section 2.301) or as a supervised financial organization (subsection (41)).

(43) "Supervised loan" means a consumer loan, including a loan made pursuant to open-end credit, in which the rate of the finance charge, calculated according to the actuarial method, exceeds 18 per cent per year.

COMMENT

Subsection (1):

This subsection is derived from CCPA Section 107(a)(1)(A), 15 U.S.C. § 1606(a)(1)(A), and from Supplement I to Regulation Z(a). The intent is that with respect to the meaning and application of the defined term the Administrator will maintain by rule consistency between this Act and the Federal Truth in Lending Act.

The assumption underlying the actuarial method is that a periodic payment is applied first to the accumulated unpaid finance charge. If the payment exceeds the unpaid accumulated finance charge, the remainder of the payment is applied to reduce the unpaid balance of the amount financed.

To illustrate the application of this method assume that the amount financed on a four-month contract is $500, and that the finance charge is $12.56. Four monthly payments of $128.14 are contemplated. Thus the amount financed ($500) plus the finance charge ($12.56) equals the original unpaid balance ($512.56), which is divided into four equal monthly payments, the first payment being one month from date of contract. The application of the actual method is demonstrated below:

(A) Unpaid balance of amount financed		(B) Monthly rate		(C) Application of payment — Finance charge		(D) Application of payment — Amount financed		(E) Total monthly payment (C) + (D)
500.00	×	1%	=	5.00		123.14		128.14
376.86	×	1%	=	3.77		124.37		128.14
252.49	×	1%	=	2.52		125.62		128.14
126.87	×	1%	=	1.27		126.87		128.14
				12.56	+	500.00	=	512.56

Rate disclosure involves finding that rate which will generate the stated finance charge when applied to the unpaid balances of the amount financed according to the actuarial method. A monthly rate of 1% produces a finance charge of $12.56, the difference between the sum of the monthly payments and the amount financed. The annual percentage rate would be twelve times the monthly rate, or 12%. In mathematical literature this is generally referred to as the nominal annual rate.

Note the application of the actuarial method. In the first month the first $5 (1% x $500) of the monthly payment of $128.-14 is applied to the finance charge, leaving a balance of $123.14. This remainder is then applied to reduce the unpaid balance of the amount financed from $500 to $376.86. The same process is repeated in subsequent months.

Subsection (3):

This definition is derived from UCC Section 1–201(3). The terms "course of dealing," "usage of trade," and "course of performance" should be given the same meanings under this Act as under the UCC with allowance for the different context, *e. g.*, consumer compared to commercial, and "course of performance" should apply to lessors and lenders as well as to sellers.

Subsection (4):

This definition is identical to that in Regulation Z Section 226.-2(c). The definition of "agricultural products" is derived from the Agricultural Marketing Act of 1946, 7 U.S.C. § 1626. Though the definition of "agricultural products" is broad, the operative definition is "agricultural purpose" and this is narrowed by the requirement that the person dealing with agricultural products be one who cultivates, plants, propagates, or nurtures the agricultural products.

Subsection (5):

The term "amount financed", means the amount of credit extended to the consumer and includes not only the net price in sales and the net amount advanced in loans but also other amounts such as official fees, insurance charges, and other additional charges (Section 2.501) to the extent that payment is deferred. An advance payment of finance charge or a required compensating balance is deducted from the "net amount paid" under paragraph (b) of this subsection. The term is a key definition in Parts 2 (maximum finance charges, sales) and 4 (maximum finance charges, loans) of Article 2 for it determines the amount on which the finance charge is imposed. This definition is in harmony with Regulation Z Sections 226.2(d), 226.-4(b), and 226.8(c)(7) and (d)(1).

The reference in paragraph (b) to Section 1.301(20)(b)(iii) relates to the practice of credit card issuers of paying sellers honoring credit cards less than the face amount of the cardholder's obligation. Paragraph (b) makes clear that this discount is a part of the amount financed even though the amount of the discount is not paid to the seller for the cardholder's account. Since the seller absorbs the discount in the price of his product, the amount of the discount redounds to the cardholder's benefit and is properly included in the amount financed. That is, the cardholder would pay the same price for the product purchased whether he pays cash or uses a credit card. However, if the goods are sold at one price pursuant to credit cards and at a lower price for cash, then the lower price would be the cash price pursuant to Section 1.301(9) and the differential would be a finance charge pursuant to Section 1.301(20) and not part of the amount financed. The discount problem need only be specially treated when use of the credit card results in a loan, as in the case of lender credit cards (Section 1.301(25)(a)(ii)), for in the case of sales pursuant to seller credit cards (Section 1.301(12)(a)(i)) the cash price of the property or services sold includes the discount, if any, which is thereby included in the amount financed.

Subsection (6):

This definition is derived from Regulation Z Section 226.2(g). See also Sections 2.202(3) and 2.-401(1).

Subsection (7):

This definition is derived from Regulation Z Section 226.13(a)(3).

Subsection (8):

This definition is derived from Regulation Z Section 226.13(a)(4).

Subsection (9):

For either rate ceilings or disclosure provisions to be meaningful in credit sales, the amount financed on which finance charges are imposed must include a true cash price. See Regulation Z Section 226.2(i). If a seller sells an item in ordinary course for $97 for cash but sells the same item for $100 to buyers wishing to pay in instalments, the $3 differential is not part of a true cash price but is a finance charge (Section 1.301(20)) imposed by the seller. Nothing in this definition prevents sellers from selling both for cash and on time for the same price. For purposes of this definition it does not matter whether the charges enumerated in (a) and (b) are included in the cash price or separately stated, for in either case the amount financed, on which the finance charge is based, will include both the cash price and the enumerated charges. See Section 1.301(5).

Subsection (10):

This definition is derived from UCC Section 1–201(10), but the specific examples set out in the UCC provision are omitted. Here, as under the UCC, the issue is whether attention can reasonably be expected to be called to a term, and this is a question of law and not fact.

Subsection (12):

Since most of the operative provisions of the Act apply to consumer credit sales, consumer leases, or consumer loans, the definitions of these terms are the key scope definitions of the Act. The definition of consumer credit sale substantially tracks with the coverage of credit sales in Regulation Z Sections 226.2(k) and (m), and 226.3(c). The requirement that a sale either be payable in instalments (Section 1.-301(30)) or subject to a finance charge excludes a great mass of transactions, *e. g.*, the 30-day retail charge account and the short-term credit furnished by professional people and artisans on a one-payment basis in connection with sales of their services for which no charge for credit is made.

Sales or leases pursuant to a lender credit card give rise to loans (Section 1.301(25)(a)(ii)) as between the card issuer and cardholder. Consumer credit sales of land are covered for rate regulation and other purposes so long as the finance charge is in excess of 12%, but the provisions on compliance with the Truth in Lending Act (Section 3.201) apply to land sales whatever the rate of finance charge. See the Comment to Section 1.301(15) "consumer loan" for discussion of the Act's policy with regard to land transactions.

Subsection (14):

Leasing has become a popular alternative to credit sales as a means of distributing goods to consumers and merits inclusion in a comprehensive consumer credit code. The four month term requirement in paragraph (a)(iii) excludes from the Act the innumerable hourly, daily, or weekly rental or hire agreements typically involving automobiles, trailers, home repair tools, sick room equipment, and the like. If the transaction, though in form a lease, is in substance a sale within the meaning of Section 1.-301(35), it is treated as a sale for all purposes in this Act and the provisions on consumer leases are inapplicable. The Act requires disclosure of the elements of the consumer lease transaction (Section 3.202); places limits on advertising respecting consumer leases (Section 3.209); contains a number of limitations on agreements and practices applicable to consumer leases (Part 3 of Article 3) and on the lessee's liability (Part 4 of Article 3, notably Section 3.401); regulates insurance provided in relation to consumer lease transactions (Article 4); makes provisions for remedies and penalties in consumer lease transactions (Article 5); and gives the Administrator powers over consumer lease transactions (Article 6). Since a finance charge is not made in the usual consumer lease transaction, the rate ceiling provisions of the Act (Article 2) are inapplicable.

Subsection (15):

See Comment to Section 1.-301(12) "consumer credit sale." Sales pursuant to seller credit cards are classified as credit sales and not loans (Section 1.-301(25)(b)(i)).

With respect to this Act's treatment of real property transactions, the 12% cut-off was chosen as a convenient line of demarcation between two dissimilar transactions—the home mortgage and the high rate, "small loan" type of real estate loan. The exclusion of the home mortgage was made because the problems of home financing are sufficiently different to justify separate statutory treatment. On the other hand, the high rate second mortgage transaction has been a major source of consumer complaint and merits full coverage by this Act. Since the Truth in Lending Act applies to real estate credit without regard to the rate of finance charge, the provision on compliance with Truth in Lending (Section 3.201) applies to all consumer real estate transactions without regard to the rate of the finance charge.

Paragraph (c) applies to transactions in which a professional arranger places loans for a lender not ordinarily engaged in the business of making loans and collects a commission for arranging the loan. The arranger is considered to be the creditor making the loan for purposes of compliance with the provisions on authority to make supervised loans (Section 2.301).

Subsection (16):

Credit is extended either when one who owes a debt is allowed to defer payment of the obligation or when one is given the right to incur an obligation in the future and to defer its payment. A commitment by a creditor to advance funds on request, as in the case of a letter of credit, is an example of the latter case. The original U3C definition of "credit" appearing in the 1968 Text, which did not contain the last clause in the present definition, was adopted by CCPA Section 103(e), 15 U.S.C. § 1602(e). For its definition of "credit," Regulation Z Section 226.2(1) added the last clause to this definition, and the definition in the U3C 1974 Text was modified to conform to Regulation Z.

Subsection (17):

The meanings of "credit card" and "pursuant to a credit card" are broadly defined to allow for continuing technological developments in this area. The term "credit card" is defined to encompass the varied arrangements under which creditors equip consumers with some form of "card or device" that enables them to obtain credit from the issuing creditor or others. A "credit card" may be conceived of in its broadest sense as a repository of information, and a transaction is "pursuant to a credit card" when credit is obtained in accordance with the arrangement under which the card was issued by the transmission of some information on the card. Hence, a cardholder who telephones an airline and buys a ticket by giving the agent his credit card number or a cardholder who communicates the requisite information to a seller by using a device which gives off an electronic impulse is each engaging in a transaction "pursuant to a credit card" so long as they are acting within the terms of the arrangement. However, a creditor who himself extends credit to a consumer relying on the consumer's credit card issued by another creditor merely as an identification or verification of credit-worthiness of the consumer has not extended credit "pursuant to a credit card."

Moreover, use of a credit card to obtain a guarantee of payment or to effect an immediate transfer from the cardholder's deposit account is not "pursuant to a credit card" whether or not the payment or transfer results in a credit extension to the cardholder by the card issuer.

Subsection (18):

Though assignees take all rights conferred by this Act on creditors, they are liable for the obligations imposed on creditors by this Act only with respect to occurrences after assignment unless the Act provides otherwise. Various provisions of the Act apply specifically to assignees of credit grantors, *e. g.*, Sections 5.201(2), [5.203(4)], 5.301(2), 6.102(2). The second sentence makes clear that in credit card transactions the person honoring the credit card is not granting credit unless he is also the card issuer. However, even though the person honoring a credit card may not be a creditor, he does "participate in consumer credit transactions" under Section 6.102(1) and is under the jurisdiction of the Administrator.

Subsection (19):

This definition varies from that found in CCPA Section 302, 15 U.S.C. § 1672, in that "by an employer to an employee" is added, thereby restricting this definition to the employment relationship in contrast to the broad coverage of the federal act which would include sums owed to independent contractors.

Subsection (20):

This definition, together with the provisions on "additional charges" (Section 2.501), is substantially similar to the concept of finance charge embodied in Regulation Z Section 226.4. In general, charges "incident to or as a condition of the extension of credit" are finance charges, whatever the parties call them, if imposed by the creditor on the consumer, unless the charge is excluded by paragraph (b) as a default or delinquency charge, an additional or deferral charge, or a credit card discount.

True default or delinquency charges are not finance charges and are separately regulated by Section 2.502. The test prescribed by Regulation Z Section 226.4(c) and Interpretation 226.-

401 is adopted in paragraph (b)(i) for determining when a charge is a true default or delinquency charge. In some instances this will leave the question of the applicability of the Act to depend on the factual determination whether a given charge is (1) a true late charge, which would make the Act inapplicable if there is no provision either for payment in instalments or a finance charge, or (2) a finance charge, which would make the Act applicable even though there is no provision for payment in instalments (Section 1.-301(12)(a)(iv)). An example is the case in which an oil company extends 30-day credit with no right to defer payment further and imposes a charge for late payment but does not require surrender of the credit card if full payment is not made by the consumer when billed. In such a case paragraph (b)(i) allows the creditor to avoid any uncertainty about the applicability of the Act by obtaining the consumer's agreement that the charge should be considered a finance charge.

For a discussion of the reason for the exclusion in paragraph (b)(iii) of the credit card discount, see the Comment to Section 1.301(5) "amount financed."

Subsection (22):

The financing of the premium for an insurance policy or contract is a loan whether made directly between lender and insured or arranged by an insurance agent or broker. An "insurance premium loan" includes neither the sale of insurance if the insured is not obligated to pay instalments of the premium and the insurance may terminate or be cancelled after non-payment of the premium (subsection (2) of Section 1.202), nor the provision of insurance in connection with a consumer credit transaction when the charge for the insurance is a permitted "additional charge" (paragraph (e) of subsection (1), and subsection (2) of Section 2.-501).

Subsection (23):

See Comment to Section 1.-301(18) "creditor."

Subsection (24):

The bank credit card is the most common lender credit card; however, licensed lenders (Section 2.301) can also issue lender credit cards.

Subsection (25):

The distinction between loans and sales is basic to the applicability of the rate ceiling provisions (Parts 2 and 4 of Article 2), the licensing provisions (Part 3 of Article 2), provisions relating to credit cards (Section 1.-301(24) "lender credit card" and (39) "seller credit card"), and other provisions of the Act. The traditional concept of a loan as an advance of money or a commitment to advance money is continued in paragraph (a)(i) and (iv). The development of the credit card has blurred somewhat accepted boundaries between loans and sales and has necessitated a clarification of the rules in this regard. See the discussion of this matter in Comment to Section 1.301(39) "seller credit card." Use of a lender credit card, whether for purchases or cash advances, results in a loan. The arrangement for the card issuer's payment to the person honoring the credit card may take different forms. It does not matter under paragraph (a)(ii) whether the arrangement calls for the third party to be the payee of a draft drawn by the cardholder on the card issuer, for the card issuer to take an assignment of the debt from the third party, or for the card issuer merely to pay to the third party the discounted amount of the cardholder's obligation. Each of these methods is sufficiently similar in function to be treated alike by this section.

Under this Act forbearance of debt is characterized on the basis of the nature of the original debt. Thus forbearance of debt arising from sales or leases is not a loan transaction within this Act (paragraph (b)(ii)). Sellers and lessors can enter into refinancings to meet the needs of consumers without having these transactions classified as loans resulting in the applicability of the licensing provisions and other provisions of the Act designed to regulate lenders.

Occasionally seller credit card issuers may allow their cardholders to obtain nominal cash advances pursuant to their credit card. An example is an automobile rental company which extends to its cardholders as a convenience the privilege of obtaining cash advances up to $40 in emergency situations. This is a loan transaction under paragraph (a)(iii), and if the finance charge exceeds 18% (Section 2.-401(1)) the licensing provisions of Part 3 of Article 2 apply.

Subsection (26):

"Merchandise certificate" primarily means the kind of scrip issued by merchants to facilitate the purchase on credit of a number of relatively small items so that a separate contract or agreement is not required for each item purchased; it does not include a trading stamp redeemable only at a stamp redemption center.

Subsection (27):

This definition is derived from Regulation Z Section 226.4(b)(1) and (2).

Subsection (28):

The problem arises how the Act applies to a transaction in which a seller credit card issuer allows a cardholder to make purchases and add them to an account payable at a fixed time after billing with no right to defer payment further and with a charge imposed for late payment. If the charge imposed is a "true" late payment under Section 1.-301(20)(b)(i), the transaction is not a consumer credit sale because there is neither a finance charge nor the privilege of paying in instalments (Section 1.-301(12)(a)(iv)). The Act's only coverage of such a case is a limit on the amount of the late charge (Section 2.601(2)). If the late charge is in fact a finance charge under the test set out in Section 1.301(20)(b)(i), the transaction is a consumer credit sale and the Act applies fully. The last "or" clause in paragraph (d) directs that such a transaction be treated as open-end credit. A similar result is reached by Regulation Z

Section 226.2(r) and Interpretation 226.401.

Subsection (30):

Two guiding principles in determining the scope of the Act are: (1) The Act should not apply to the myriad credit transactions in which no finance charge is made and no substantial period of credit extension is involved. The old-fashioned 30-day department store charge account is an example. (2) The Act should apply to credit extended over a substantial period of time even though the creditor does not separately state a finance charge. The transactions of the credit jeweler who "buries" his finance charge and sells his merchandise for the same price on a 12-month instalment contract as for cash is an example. The drafting technique by which these ends are attained is the definition of consumer credit sales (Section 1.301(12)(a)(iv)) and consumer loans (Section 1.301(15)(a)(iii)) as transactions in which either a finance charge is made or which are payable in instalments. In the definition of "payable in instalments," the Act adopts the more-than-four-payment rule as the dividing line for transactions meriting coverage by the Act. This test has been incorporated into Regulation Z Section 226.2(k) and was sustained in Mourning v. Family Publications Serv., Inc., 411 U.S. 356, 93 S.Ct. 1652, 36 L.Ed.2d 318 (1973). A consumer transaction is payable in instalments if the consumer has the option either of paying the debt in full within a given period of time without a finance charge or of paying the balance in instalments plus a finance charge.

Subsection (33):

A credit transaction is precomputed whether the finance charge is "added-on" to the amount financed or, as is common in loan situations, the "discount" method is used and the finance charge is deducted from the face amount of the credit at the time of the credit extension. In both transactions the debt is expressed as a sum comprising the amount financed and the amount of the finance charge. If a loan transaction involves a principal of $2,000 repayable in 12 monthly instalments at an interest rate of 10% on the declining balance, the transaction is not precomputed even though the creditor must for purposes of the Federal Truth in Lending Act disclose a sum including both the $2,000 and the amount of the finance charge the debtor would pay if each instalment were paid on time.

Subsection (34):

This definition is derived from UCC Section 1–201(31).

Subsection (35):

This definition is derived from Regulation Z Section 226.2(n).

Subsection (36):

This definition parallels that in subsection (35).

Subsection (38):

See definition of "creditor" in subsection (18).

Subsection (39):

Seller credit cards are issued primarily for the purpose of enabling cardholders to purchase property or services. Paragraph

(a) applies to cards issued by card issuers who are themselves involved in the selling process either as retailers or as distributors who license or franchise retailers. So long as the card is issued for the purpose of purchasing from the issuer, a person related to the issuer, or a licensee or franchisee of the issuer, the card falls within paragraph (a) even though it may also be honored by sellers having no relation to the card issuer. For example, an oil distributor may issue a card for the purpose of allowing cardholders to buy petroleum products from independently owned franchisees of the issuer; the card falls within paragraph (a) even though it may also be honored by hotels, motels, and other service stations unrelated to the card issuer.

Paragraph (b) covers credit cards issued for the purpose of enabling cardholders to purchase from sellers unrelated to the card issuer. "Travel and entertainment" credit cards are the stereotype. The requirement that the card be honored by at least 100 unrelated retailers is designed to assure that this kind of card will be issued for bona fide sales purposes by entities large enough to be visible to the Administrator and will not be used as a subterfuge for masking unlicensed loans.

Although lender credit cards (Section 1.301(24)) are also used for purchasing property or services, they are increasingly utilized for cash loans. By classifying the use of credit cards issued by banks and licensed lenders as creating loans (Section 1.301(25)(a)(ii)), whether the card was used for purchases or cash advanced, the Act recognizes that credit card transactions are but one of many ways in which banks and other financial institutions extend credit and that it is not operationally desirable to introduce regulatory distinctions that would force these institutions to treat sales and loans pursuant to credit cards differently for purposes of maximum charges and other provisions of the Act.

Subsection (40):

The retail instalment sales acts often excluded from the definition of services those furnished by members of professions—physicians, dentists, and the like. This Act makes no such exclusion, but the definition of consumer credit sale in Section 1.301(12) excludes the usual arrangement that professional men use in selling their services in that they usually do not enter into instalment contracts with their patients or clients and do not impose finance charges. However, this Act does apply to the so-called "credit dentist" who sells his services on instalment contract with or without provision for a finance charge.

Subsection (41):

This definition defines the class of lender which may engage in the business of making supervised loans or taking assignments of such loans for collection without first being licensed under the Act by the Administrator. Sections 2.301 and 2.302. If a lender of this class is subject to supervision by an official or agency other than the Administrator, the powers of examination, investigation, and enforcement under this Act may be exercised by that official or agency. Section 6.105. This class of lender typically includes persons authorized to make loans and receive deposits or their equivalents, such as commercial banks, savings banks, savings and loan associations, and credit unions.

Subsection (43):

Although all persons making consumer loans (Section 1.301(15)) are regulated by this Act, those making high rate loans must either be licensed by the Administrator or be supervised financial organizations (Section 2.301). This Act has settled on the 18% finance charge rate as the dividing line, above which a creditor's right to operate may be conditioned on meeting the tests of Section 2.302(2) for licensing or qualifying as a supervised financial organization.

Section 1.302 [Definition: "Federal Truth in Lending Act"]

In this Act, as applicable, "Federal Truth in Lending Act" means Title I of the Consumer Credit Protection Act (Public Law 90–321; 82 Stat. 146; 15 U.S.C. § 1601 et seq.; as amended), except for the provisions concerning issuance, liability of holders, and fraudulent use of credit cards (Sections 132–134, as added by Public Law 90–321; 84 Stat. 1126; 15 U.S.C. §§ 1642–1644), and includes regulations issued by the Board of Governors of the Federal Reserve System pursuant to that Act except those relating to the excepted provisions.

COMMENT

See Comment to Section 1.102.

Section 1.303 [Other Defined Terms]

Other defined terms in this Act and the sections in which they appear are:

"Closing costs" Section 2.501(1)
"Computational period" Section 2.503(1)
"Deferral" Section 2.503(1)
"Deferral period" Section 2.503(1)
"Disposable earnings" Section 5.105
"Garnishment" Section 5.105
"Home solicitation sale" Section 3.501
"Interval" Section 2.503(1)
"Periodic balance" Section 2.503(1)
"Pursuant to a credit card" Section 1.301(17)
"Residence" Section 1.201(6)
"Rule of 78" Section 2.503(1)
"Standard deferral" Section 2.503(1)
"Sum of the balances method" Section 2.503(1)
"Transaction" Section 2.503(1)

ARTICLE 2

FINANCE CHARGES AND RELATED PROVISIONS

PART 1

GENERAL PROVISIONS

Section 2.101 [Short Title]

This Article shall be known and may be cited as Uniform Consumer Credit Code—Finance Charges and Related Provisions.

Section 2.102 [Scope]

Part 2 of this Article applies to consumer credit sales. Parts 3 and 4 apply to consumer loans, including loans made by supervised lenders. Part 5 applies to other charges and modifications with respect to consumer credit transactions. Part 6 applies to other credit transactions.

PART 2

CONSUMER CREDIT SALES: MAXIMUM FINANCE CHARGES

Section 2.201 [Finance Charge for Consumer Credit Sales Not Pursuant to Open-End Credit]

(1) With respect to a consumer credit sale, except a sale pursuant to open-end credit, a creditor may contract for and receive a finance charge not exceeding that permitted in this section.

(2) The finance charge, calculated according to the actuarial method, may not exceed the equivalent of the greater of either of the following:

(a) the total of:

(i) 36 per cent per year on that part of the unpaid balances of the amount financed which is $300 or less;

(ii) 21 per cent per year on that part of the unpaid balances of the amount financed which exceeds $300 but does not exceed $1,000; and

(iii) 15 per cent per year on that part of the unpaid balances of the amount financed which exceeds $1,000; or

(b) 18 per cent per year on the unpaid balances of the amount financed.

(3) This section does not limit or restrict the manner of calculating the finance charge whether by way of add-on, discount, single annual percentage rate, or otherwise, so long as the rate of the finance charge does not exceed that permitted by this section. The finance charge may be contracted for and earned at the single annual percentage rate that would earn the same finance charge as the graduated rates when the debt is paid according to the agreed terms and the calculations are made according to the actuarial method. If the sale is a precomputed consumer credit transaction:

(a) the finance charge may be calculated on the assumption that all scheduled payments will be made when due, and

(b) the effect of prepayment is governed by the provisions on rebate upon prepayment (Section 2.510).

(4) For purposes of this section, the term of a sale agreement commences with the date the credit is granted or, if goods are

delivered or services performed ten days or more after that date, with the date of commencement of delivery or performance. Any month may be counted as 1/12th of a year, but a day is counted as 1/365th of a year. Subject to classifications and differentiations the seller may reasonably establish, a part of a month in excess of 15 days may be treated as a full month if periods of 15 days or less are disregarded and that procedure is not consistently used to obtain a greater yield than would otherwise be permitted. The Administrator may adopt rules not inconsistent with the Federal Truth in Lending Act with respect to treating as regular other minor irregularities in amount or time.

(5) Subject to classifications and differentiations the seller may reasonably establish, he may make the same finance charge on all amounts financed within a specified range. A finance charge so made does not violate subsection (2) if:

(a) when applied to the median amount within each range, it does not exceed the maximum permitted by subsection (2), and

(b) when applied to the lowest amount within each range, it does not produce a rate of finance charge exceeding the rate calculated according to paragraph (a) by more then eight per cent of the rate calculated according to paragraph (a).

(6) Notwithstanding subsection (2), the seller may contract for and receive a minimum finance charge of not more than $5 when the amount financed does not exceed $75, or $7.50 when the amount financed exceeds $75.

(7) The amounts of $300 and $1,000 in subsection (2) are subject to change pursuant to the provisions on adjustment of dollar amounts (Section 1.106).

COMMENT

1. *Purpose of rate ceilings provisions.* The purpose of this section and subsection (2) of Section 2.401 (Finance Charge for Consumer Loans) is to set ceilings and not to fix rates. Even under present statutes, considerable rate competition exists. The intent of this Act is to provide even more effective competition. Therefore, while this section sets rate ceilings, several sections are designed to generate sufficient competition to set rates. In addition, other provisions have been omitted by design, because they would have tended to restrict competition. Other provisions related to this section include:

(1) Disclosure of the finance charge both in dollar amounts

and as annual percentages, as required by the Federal Truth in Lending Act and Section 3.201, is designed to facilitate comparative shopping. This is the most effective means of limiting prices. For most goods and services offered for sale in competitive markets, disclosure of the price generally has been deemed sufficient to regulate prices.

(2) The absence of special rate ceilings according to the type of credit grantors, type of item financed, or the form of credit extension is by design. Segmentation of the market for credit by differentiated rate ceilings tends to reduce competition and introduce regidities into the market that benefit a few suppliers at the expense of others and work to the disadvantage of consumers.

(3) Greater freedom of entry to the credit field is fostered by several provisions, as well as by several deliberate omissions. Open-end credit may be offered both in connection with consumer credit sales, consumer loans, and supervised loans. No type of credit grantor is limited by this Act in the amount of credit that may be extended. By design the license required to make supervised loans is made readily accessible to those showing financial responsibility, character, and fitness. Provisions for minimum financial assets and for a showing of convenience and advantage have been deliberately omitted, since their inclusion would tend to restrict competition and require establishment of rates, rather than ceilings.

Because of the different cost structures that will be developed as a result of this Act, comparison of these rate ceilings cannot be made to existing rate ceilings. In this respect, the rate ceilings in this section are intimately related to other parts of the Act which provide for limitations on agreements and practices (Article 3, Part 3), limitations on creditors' remedies (Article 5, Part 1), limitations on consumers' liabilities (Article 3, Part 4), and consumers' remedies (Article 5, Part 2). These provisions will tend to raise operating costs of credit grantors above current levels. Other things being equal, these provisions would require higher rate ceilings than now exist to assure the same availability of credit to consumers. If they were not provided, the least credit-worthy consumers now in the market would be relegated to the illegal market.

The rate ceiling declines with the amount of credit granted by design. There are substantial fixed costs in granting consumer instalment credit. Up to a point the relative amount of fixed costs declines as the amount of credit granted increases. The present rate structure is designed not to restrict the amount of credit granted in any size category. Consequently, any changes in the rate ceilings provided would require a complete re-evaluation of the gradation in the rate structure, as well as of the other provisions of this Act which are closely related in an economic sense to rate ceilings.

2. *Explanation of operation of rate ceilings.* This explanation of maximum rates applies equally to finance charges made under Section 2.201 (finance charge for consumer credit sales not pursuant to open-end credit) and under subsection (2) of Section 2.401 (finance charge for consumer loans).

(1) *Other than precomputed transactions*: With respect to other than precomputed transactions the graduated rates permitted are calculated on unpaid principal balances. For example, Table A below illustrates the calculation of the monthly finance charge at the graduated rates on unpaid principal balances of various dollar amounts up to $1,500.

(2) *Precomputed transactions*: With respect to precomputed transactions, the graduated rates permitted are calculated on the periodic declining unpaid balances. The provisions for graduated rates should not be construed as requiring simultaneous liquidation of different portions of the original unpaid balance. Thus, the 21% annual rate permitted on unpaid balances exceeding $300, but not exceeding $1,000, does not apply to the initial unpaid balance in that range for the scheduled maturity of the transaction, but only to the extent that periodic declining unpaid balances fall within the range from $300.-01 to $1,000.

The operation of this principle with respect to a precomputed transaction involving a $1,500 principal amount to be repaid in twelve months is illustrated in Table A below. The table shows the total dollar charge, the monthly payments and the charge earned each month when the rates stated in Sections 2.201 and 2.-401(2) are computed on the unpaid balance as of each scheduled payment date and each payment is applied first to the earned charge and then to principal. It also shows the unpaid balances which result from applying the rates stated in Sections 2.201 and 2.401(2) and the parts of each unpaid balance to which each rate applies each month. The total dollar charge so computed is $211.71, but three cents is waived rather than increase the final payment.

3. *Explanation of subsection (5).* With respect to Sections 2.-201(5) and 2.401(5), the variation permitted is limited to 8% of the rate of the finance charge and does not permit an eight percentage point variation. For example, if a credit grantor were to levy an annual add-on finance charge of $10 per $100 of initial unpaid balance, under the provisions of this section he could establish the following maximum range for one-year contracts:

Amount Financed	Finance Charge
$92.45–$107.55	$10.00

The median amount financed is $100; that is, this amount is $7.-55 from both the upper and lower limits of the specified range. Alternatively, it is just halfway between $92.45 and $107.55.

The specified range is limited by the 8% requirement. On one-year contracts the add-on finance charge results in an actuarial rate of 17.972%. Sections 2.-201(5)(b) and 2.401(5)(b) specify that the yield on the lowest amount within the range may not be more than 8% higher than the yield provided on the median amount. Thus the yield on the lowest amount may not exceed 19.40% [17.972 + (.08 × 17.-972) = 19.4098]. It follows that the lower amount must be such that the $10 credit service charge produces an annual rate not in excess of 19.40%. Interpolation from annuity tables shows that the lower amount must be about $92.45. Since the median is halfway between the upper and lower limits, the upper amount must be $107.55. These are close approximations; in actual practice precise limits can be determined.

To gain the convenience of using a single dollar amount of finance charge for a specified range of amounts financed the credit grantor must under-charge for amounts financed above the median. Thus the $10 finance charge is about $0.76 less than the $10.76 finance charge that could have been received by precise application of an add-on rate of $10 per $100 per annum on the initial unpaid balance. These results are summarized below for one-year monthly instalment contracts.

(A) Amount financed	(B) Actual finance charge	(C) Accurate finance charge	(D) Dollar difference (C) — (B)	(E) Annual percentage rate
$107.55	$10.00	$10.755	−$0.755	16.74%
$100.00	$10.00	$10.00	0.00	17.97%
$ 92.45	$10.00	$ 9.245	+$0.755	19.40%

The 8% variation is derived from Regulation Z Section 226.5(c).

TABLE A

Amortization Schedule for $1,500 to be paid in 12 equal and consecutive monthly instalments of Principal Amount and Finance Charge combined with the charge computed at maximum graduated rates authorized by Sections 2.201 and 2.401(2)—36% per year on that part of the unpaid balances not exceeding $300, plus 21% per year on that part of the unpaid balances exceeding $300 but not exceeding $1,000, plus 15% per year on that part of the unpaid balances exceeding $1,000, yields $211.68.

	Unpaid Principal Balances Outstanding During Month				Application of $142.64 Monthly Payments	
Mo.	36%	21%	15%	Total	Charges	Principal
1	$300.00	$700.00	$500.00	$1500.00	$27.50	$ 115.14
2	300.00	700.00	384.86	1384.86	26.06	116.58
3	300.00	700.00	268.28	1268.28	24.60	118.04
4	300.00	700.00	150.24	1150.24	23.13	119.51
5	300.00	700.00	30.73	1030.73	21.63 *	121.01
6	300.00	609.72	. . .	909.72	19.67	122.97
7	300.00	486.75	. . .	786.75	17.52	125.12
8	300.00	361.63	. . .	661.63	15.33	127.31
9	300.00	234.32	. . .	534.32	13.10	129.54
10	300.00	104.78	. . .	404.78	10.83	131.81
11	272.97	. . .	. . .	272.97	8.19	134.45
12	138.52	. . .	. . .	138.52	4.12 **	138.52
	TOTALS				$211.68	$1500.00

* Finance Charge rates are applied to parts of Unpaid Principal Balances scheduled to be outstanding. For example, the Finance Charge on $1030.73 is computed as follows:

1/12 × 36% on	$ 300.00	=	$ 9.00
1/12 × 21% on	700.00	=	12.25
1/12 × 15% on	30.73	=	.38
	$1030.73		$21.63

** The charge earned the last month is $4.15, but three cents is waived and applied to principal to make the final payment equal to the others.

For purposes of disclosure under the Truth in Lending Act the credit grantor must determine the single annual percentage rate, which, when applied according to the actuarial method, earns the same dollar amount of finance charge that is produced by the graduated rates. Table B shows that an annual rate of 25.10% applied monthly to the periodic declining unpaid balances produces the same total dollar charge of $211.68 calculated by application of graduated rates in Table A.

TABLE B

Amortization Schedule for $1500 to be paid in 12 equal and consecutive monthly instalments of Principal Amount and Finance Charge combined showing that the Single Annual Percentage Rate of 25.10% computed by the Actuarial Method yields $211.68.

Mo.	Unpaid Principal Balances	Application of $142.64 Monthly Payments Charges	Principal
1	$1500.00	$ 31.38	$ 111.26
2	1388.74	29.05	113.59
3	1275.15	26.67	115.97
4	1159.18	24.25	118.39
5	1040.79	21.77	120.87
6	919.92	19.24	123.40
7	796.52	16.66	125.98
8	670.54	14.03	128.61
9	541.93	11.34	131.30
10	410.63	8.59	134.05
11	276.58	5.79	136.85
12	139.73	2.91 *	139.73
TOTALS	....	$211.68	$1500.00

* The charge earned the last month is $2.92 but 1 cent is waived and applied to principal to make the final payment equal to the others.

This Act is intended to give creditors the following choice in making their charges under Sections 2.201 and 2.401(2).

(1) The contract may be precomputed to include the dollar finance charge for payment according to schedule. In the example shown, the dollar finance charge of $211.68 would be added to the original unpaid principal, making a total of $1,711.68 to be repaid in twelve monthly instalments of $142.64.

A precomputed transaction is subject to delinquency charges pursuant to Section 2.502 or deferral charges pursuant to Section 2.503 in case of delinquency or deferral and to rebate for prepayment pursuant to Section 2.510 in case of prepayment in full.

(2) The contract need not be precomputed, but may provide for: (a) the addition of finance charges, computed on unpaid balances of the principal amount, at the rates specified in Sections 2.201 and 2.401(2); in this case there is no rebate for prepayment in full because charges are collected only as earned, and there are no separate charges for default or deferment; or (b) not more than the maximum single annual percentage rate computed on actual unpaid balances for the actual time outstanding. The single annual percentage is the rate which yields the charge for payment according to schedule when the rate is computed according to the actuarial method. In the example, the rate is 25.10%. In this case there is no rebate for

prepayment in full because the charges are collected only as earned, and there are no separate charges for default or deferment.

4. *Explanation of Section 2.-201(6).* Subsection (6) of this section permits minimum charges equal to finance charges for which the CCPA (15 U.S.C. § 1601 et seq.) requires no annual percentage rate disclosure. The CCPA does not set limits on the amounts of minimum charges, but does require annual percentage rate disclosure when the minimum charges exceed those permitted by subsection (6). Subsection (6) also sets limits on the amounts of minimum charges.

5. *Operation of 18% APR finance charge ceiling.* According to tables furnished by Financial Publishing Company, the 18% APR finance charge ceiling rate on unpaid balances of the amount financed permitted by subsection (2)(b) yields a greater finance charge than the sliding scale ceiling rates of 36%, 21% and 15% when applied to unpaid balances of the amount financed on amounts equal to or exceeding the following for the respective following number of equal monthly instalments (the corresponding Total of Payments, Finance Charge and amount of equal monthly instalments is set out below):

No. of Monthly Instalments	Unpaid Balance of Amount to be Financed	Total of Payments	Finance Charge	Amount of Monthly Instalments
3	$5,190.00	$5,346.51	$ 156.51	$1,782.17
6	5,853.00	6,164.16	311.16	1,027.36
9	5,953.00	6,408.45	455.45	712.15
12	6,016.00	6,618.72	602.72	551.56
15	6,011.00	6,757.50	746.50	450.50
18	5,985.00	6,874.02	889.02	381.89
24	5,906.00	7,076.64	1170.64	294.86
30	5,800.00	7,245.60	1445.60	241.52
36	5,695.00	7,412.40	1717.40	205.90
42	5,594.00	7,581.00	1987.00	180.50
48	5,491.00	7,742.88	2251.88	161.31
54	5,393.00	7,907.76	2514.76	146.44
60	5,301.00	8,077.20	2776.20	134.62
66	5,209.00	8,242.74	3033.74	124.89
72	5,121.00	8,410.32	3289.32	116.81
78	5,041.00	8,587.02	3546.02	110.09
84	4,958.00	8,754.48	3796.48	104.22
90	4,882.00	8,929.80	4047.80	99.22
96	4,810.00	9,108.48	4298.48	94.88
102	4,741.00	9,289.14	4548.14	91.07
108	4,676.00	9,473.76	4797.76	87.72
114	4,615.00	9,662.64	5047.64	84.76
120	4,554.00	9,848.40	5294.40	82.07

Section 2.202 [Finance Charge for Consumer Credit Sales Pursuant to Open-End Credit]

(1) With respect to a consumer credit sale pursuant to open-end credit, a creditor may contract for and receive a finance charge not exceeding that permitted in this section.

(2) For each billing cycle a finance charge may be made which is a percentage of an amount not exceeding the greatest of:

(a) the average daily balance of the open-end account in the billing cycle for which the charge is made, which is the sum of the amount unpaid each day during that cycle, divided by the number of days in that cycle; the amount unpaid on a day is determined by adding to any balance unpaid as of the beginning of that day all purchases and other debits and deducting all payments and other credits made or received as of that day;

(b) the balance of the open-end account at the beginning of the first day of the billing cycle [after deducting all payments and credits made in the cycle except credits attributable to purchases charged to the account during the cycle]; or

(c) the median amount within a specified range including the balance of the open-end account not exceeding that permitted by paragraph (a) or (b); a finance charge may be made pursuant to this paragraph only if the creditor, subject to classifications and differentiations he may reasonably establish, makes the same charge on all balances within the specified range and if the percentage when applied to the median amount within the range does not produce a charge exceeding the charge resulting from applying that percentage to the lowest amount within the range by more than eight per cent of the charge on the median amount.

(3) If the billing cycle is monthly, the finance charge may not exceed an amount equal to two per cent of that part of the maximum amount pursuant to subsection (2) which is $500 or less and one and one-half per cent of that part of the maximum amount which is more than $500. If the billing cycle is not monthly, the maximum charge for the billing cycle shall bear the same relation to the applicable monthly maximum charge as the number of days in the billing cycle bears to 365 divided by 12. A billing cycle is monthly if the closing date of the cycle is the same date each month or does not vary by more than four

days from the regular date. Without regard to the length of the billing cycle, the finance charge may be computed at a daily rate that does not exceed 1/365ths of 12 times the monthly charge permitted by this section for a billing cycle that is monthly.

(4) If the finance charge determined pursuant to subsection (3) is less than 50 cents, a finance charge may be made which does not exceed 50 cents if the billing cycle is monthly or longer, or the pro rata part of 50 cents which bears the same relation to 50 cents as the number of days in the billing cycle bears to 365 divided by 12 if the billing cycle is shorter than monthly.

(5) The amounts of $500 in subsection (3) are subject to change pursuant to the provisions on adjustment of dollar amounts (Section 1.106).

COMMENT

1. See Comment 1 to Section 2.201 for an explanation of the theory of rate regulation adopted by the Act.

2. Subsection (2) allows the creditor an option with respect to the balance on which the finance charge is imposed. The Federal Truth in Lending Act requires the creditor to disclose the method of determining the balance on which the finance charge is imposed (Regulation Z Section 226.-7(a)(2) and (b)(8)). The average daily balance method authorized by paragraph (a) of subsection (2) is that commonly utilized by creditors employing electronic data processing equipment. Paragraph (b) of subsection (2), read with the bracketed material included, states the adjusted balance method under which the balance at the beginning of the cycle is reduced by all payments and credits during the cycle. Although under this method the balance is adjusted downward by payments and credits during the cycle, it is not adjusted upward by new purchases made within the cycle. The except clause is necessary to prevent the beginning balance from being reduced by returns of merchandise attributable to purchases made within the cycle the amounts of which had not been included in that balance. Paragraph (b) of subsection (2), read without the bracketed material, states the previous or beginning balance method under which the opening balance is neither decreased by payments or credits during the billing cycle nor increased by new purchases made during that period. Either the previous balance or the adjusted balance method is usable by a creditor with a manual system of entries. The brackets in paragraph (b) of subsection (2) acknowledge the as yet unresolved controversy in the Congress and the state legislatures about the comparative merit of the previous and adjusted balance methods.

3. See Comment 3 to Section 2.201 for a discussion of the median amount method of computing the balance on which the finance

charge is imposed under paragraph (c) of subsection (2). The "classifications and differentiations" language in paragraph (c) is intended to give the seller some flexibility in using this method of determining the finance charge. The creditor need not use this method for all his customers nor need he use it for all his transactions with one customer, but he may classify his transactions and customers on reasonable bases.

4. In requiring a complex disclosure procedure if the maximum charge exceeds 50¢ per month (CCPA Section 127(b)(6), 15 U.S.C. § 1637(b)(6)), Congress indirectly recognized the fairness of the 50¢ minimum figure. This Act adopts the 50¢ limit in recognition of this Congressional guidance as well as the difficulties inherent in disclosing the annual percentage rate of a higher charge.

PART 3

CONSUMER LOANS: SUPERVISED LENDERS

Section 2.301 [Authority to Make Supervised Loans]

Unless a person is a supervised financial organization or has obtained a license from the Administrator authorizing him so to do, he may not engage in the business of:

(1) making supervised loans, or

(2) taking assignments of and undertaking direct collection of payments from or enforcement of rights against consumers arising from supervised loans, but he may collect and enforce for three months without a license if he promptly applies for a license and his application has not been denied.

COMMENT

1. Since supervised financial organizations are already subject to supervision by a state or federal official or agency, such organizations are not required to obtain a license under this Act from the Administrator, but their powers may be limited by statutes other than this Act. Section 1.108. Other persons making supervised loans in this State or taking assignments of supervised loans for collection or enforcement in this State must obtain a license from the Administrator.

2. Out-of-state lenders who make loans through the mail normally will not be subject to the licensing requirement if the evidence of debt is received by the lender out of the enacting State; however, in such a case the lender may not exceed the rate ceilings of the enacting State and the Administrator may go into the lender's State and investigate potential violations pursuant to Part 1 of Article 6. See Section 1.-201(1) and (2). An out-of-state lender who opens a loan office in this State at which evidence of debt for supervised loans is received must be licensed in this State.

3. If an unlicensed assignee not previously engaged in this State in the business of making collections or enforcing rights under the paper assigned to him undertakes collection or enforcement of rights, subsection (2) gives him a 3-month grace period during which he can operate before obtaining a license.

Section 2.302 [License to Make Supervised Loans]

(1) The Administrator shall receive and act on all applications for licenses to make supervised loans under this Act. Applications shall be in the form and filed in the manner prescribed by the Administrator and contain or be accompanied by the information the Administrator requires by rule.

(2) The Administrator may not issue a license unless upon investigation he finds that the financial responsibility, character, and fitness of the applicant, and of the members thereof if the applicant is a partnership or association or of the officers and directors thereof if the applicant is a corporation, warrant belief that the business will be operated honestly and fairly within the purposes of this Act. In determining the financial responsibility of an applicant proposing to engage in making insurance premium loans, the Administrator shall consider the liabilities the lender may incur for erroneous cancellation of insurance.

(3) Upon written request, the applicant is entitled to a hearing on the question of his qualifications for a license if (a) the Administrator notifies the applicant in writing that his application has been denied, or (b) the Administrator does not issue a license within 60 days after the application for the license was filed. A request for a hearing may not be made more than 15 days after the Administrator mails a writing to the applicant notifying him that the application has been denied and stating in substance the Administrator's findings supporting denial of the application.

(4) The Administrator shall issue additional licenses to the same licensee upon compliance with all the provisions of this Act governing issuance of a single license. A separate license is required for each place of business. Each license remains in full force and effect until surrendered, suspended, or revoked.

(5) A licensee may not change the location of any place of business without giving the Administrator at least 15 days prior written notice.

(6) A licensee may conduct the business of making supervised loans only at or from a place of business for which he holds a license and only under the name in the license. Credit granted pursuant to a lender credit card does not violate this subsection.

COMMENT

1. This section is intimately related to the provisions on maximum finance charges (Parts 2 and 4 of Article 2) and disclosure (Part 2 of Article 3). A major objective of this Act is to facilitate entry into the cash loan field so that the resultant rate competition fostered by disclosure will generally force rates below the permitted maximum charges. To this end this section adopts a test of "financial responsibility, character and fitness" rather than the test of "convenience and advantage" often used in prior small loan laws. Competition is further encouraged by the absence of licensing requirements in consumer credit sales (Section 2.201)

and in consumer loans not made by supervised lenders (subsection (1) of Section 2.401).

2. A secondary purpose is to reduce the likelihood of establishing localized monopolies in the granting of cash credit. Such monopolies tend to push rates charged to maximum permitted levels and to establish conditions under which some share of the anticipated monopoly profits are devoted to direct or indirect pressures to obtain the license.

3. This section does not apply to supervised financial organizations. Their authority to open new offices at which they may receive deposits and make loans is found not in this Act but in the statutes otherwise governing those organizations.

4. If increased competition should cause the development of undesirable credit practices, these practices are subject to controls by the Administrator's powers to revoke or suspend a license (Section 2.303), and by the other powers of the Administrator (Article 6) as well as by the provisions on remedies and penalties available to aggrieved consumers (Article 5).

5. Licensees must obtain a license for each place of business and may do business only at these locations. A lender credit card issuer does not conduct business at a place where a third person honors its card within the meaning of the section. There is no requirement that the license be renewed annually or that the licensee pay a fee for a license. Income for the operation of the office of the Administrator is derived from general appropriations rather than from the licensing of supervised lenders. Annual fees are required by Section 6.203 of all persons required to file notification under Section 6.202, not just licensees. This includes all persons making consumer credit sales, consumer leases, or consumer loans and certain persons taking assignments of and undertaking direct collection of payments from or enforcement of rights against debtors arising from such sales, leases, or loans.

Section 2.303 [Revocation or Suspension of License]

(1) The Administrator may issue to a person licensed to make supervised loans an order to show cause why his license with respect to one or more specific places of business should not be suspended for a period not in excess of six months or be revoked. The order shall set a place for a hearing and a time therefor that is no less than ten days from the date of the order. After the hearing the Administrator shall revoke or suspend the license or, if there are mitigating circumstances, may accept an assurance of discontinuance (Section 6.109) and allow retention of the license, if he finds that:

(a) the licensee has repeatedly and intentionally violated this Act or any rule or order lawfully made pursuant to this Act, or has violated an assurance of discontinuance; or

(b) facts or conditions exist which clearly would have justified the Administrator in refusing to grant a license for that place or those places of business were these facts or conditions known to exist at the time the application for the license was made.

(2) A revocation or suspension of a license is not lawful unless the Administrator, before instituting proceedings, gives notice to the licensee of the facts or conduct which warrant the intended action, and the licensee is afforded an opportunity to show compliance with all lawful requirements for retention of the license.

(3) If the Administrator finds that probable cause for revocation of a license exists and that enforcement of this Act requires immediate suspension of the license pending investigation, he, after a hearing upon five days' written notice, may enter an order suspending the license for not more than 30 days.

(4) Whenever the Administrator revokes or suspends a license, he shall enter an order to that effect and forthwith notify the licensee of the revocation or suspension. Within five days after entry of the order he shall deliver to the licensee a copy of the order and the findings supporting the order.

(5) A person holding a license to make supervised loans may relinquish the license by notifying the Administrator in writing of its relinquishment, but the relinquishment does not affect his liability for acts previously committed.

(6) Revocation, suspension, or relinquishment of a license does not impair or affect the obligation of any preexisting lawful contract between the licensee and any consumer.

(7) The administrator may reinstate a license, terminate a suspension, or grant a new license to a person whose license has been revoked or suspended if no fact or condition then exists which clearly would have justified the Administrator in refusing to grant a license.

COMMENT

This section provides the Administrator with a range of alternatives in cases in which creditors violate the Act. If after a noticed hearing the Administrator finds repeated and intentional violations, he may revoke the license, suspend the license for up to six months, or, if mitigating circumstances warrant, accept an assurance of discontinuance. Subsequent violation of the assurance of discontinuance may be a basis for revocation or suspension.

Section 2.304 [Records; Annual Reports]

(1) Every licensee shall maintain records in conformity with generally accepted accounting principles and practices in a manner that will enable the Administrator to determine whether the licensee is complying with this Act. The record keeping system of a licensee is sufficient if he makes the required information reasonably available. The records need not be kept in the place of business where supervised loans are made, if the Administrator is given free access to the records wherever located. The records pertaining to any loan need not be preserved for more than two years after making the final entry relating to the loan, but in the case of open-end credit the two years are measured from the date of each entry.

(2) On or before April 15 each year every licensee shall file with the Administrator a composite annual report in the form prescribed by the Administrator relating to all supervised loans made by him. The Administrator shall consult with comparable officials in other states for the purpose of making the kinds of information required in annual reports uniform among the states. Information contained in annual reports shall be confidential and may be published only in composite form.

COMMENT

1. This section seeks to give to the licensee wide discretion in the method of keeping records. No rigid requirements are imposed with respect to the method of record keeping. Instead, records are acceptable if kept in accordance with generally accepted accounting principles, and if they enable the Administrator to determine whether the licensee is complying with the Act. Modern techniques frequently require that records be kept in one central place, which in the case of multi-state lenders may be outside the State. This section allows central record keeping and allows records to be kept anywhere so long as the Administrator is given free access to them. See Section 2.305(2).

2. Licensees are required to file composite annual reports; information need not be given as to individual loan outlets. This allows the Administrator to compile statistics to aid him in his duties and to provide the Legislature with information necessary for a proper evaluation of the effectiveness of the Act. This section provides for confidential treatment by the Administrator of information contained in annual reports. The Administrator may not publish information concerning individual lenders; all information published must be in composite form.

Section 2.305 [Examinations and Investigations]

(1) The Administrator shall examine periodically at intervals he deems appropriate the loans, business, and records of every licensee. In addition, for the purpose of discovering violations of this Act or securing information lawfully required, the Administrator or the official or agency to whose supervision the organization is subject (Section 6.105) at any time may investigate the loans, business, and records of any lender. For these purposes he shall have free and reasonable access to the offices, places of business, and records of the lender.

(2) If the lender's records are located outside this State, the lender at his option shall make them available to the Administrator at a convenient location within this State, or pay the reasonable and necessary expenses for the Administrator or his representative to examine them where they are located. The Administrator may designate representatives, including comparable officials of the state in which the records are located, to inspect them on his behalf.

(3) For purposes of this section, the Administrator may administer oaths or affirmations, and upon request of a party or his own motion may subpoena witnesses, compel their attendance, adduce evidence, and require the production of any matter which is relevant to the investigation, including the existence, description, nature, custody, condition, and location of any books, documents, or other tangible things and the identity and location of persons having knowledge of relevant facts, or any other matter reasonably calculated to lead to the discovery of admissible evidence.

(4) Upon failure without lawful excuse to obey a subpoena or to give testimony and upon reasonable notice to all persons affected thereby, the Administrator may apply to the [ ] court for an order compelling compliance.

COMMENT

1. This section provides for periodic examinations of supervised lenders but there is no requirement of annual examinations. The Administrator may tailor his examination policy as he sees fit. With respect to other lenders who are not supervised lenders, the Act does not provide for periodic examinations; however, for the purpose of discovering violations of the Act or securing necessary information, investigations may be made by the Administrator, or in the case of supervised financial organizations, by the appropriate supervisory authority. Under Section 6.106 the Administrator has general authority to investigate any person

who he has cause to believe has engaged in an act which is subject to action by the Administrator. The power of the Administrator with respect to lenders is somewhat broader than his general authority in that investigations can be made without cause to believe a violation has occurred and are not restricted to the purpose of discovering violations.

2. Lenders are authorized to maintain records outside the State. The lender is given the option of making the records available to the Administrator within the State or paying the expenses of the Administrator to have them examined outside the State. Where records are kept outside the State the Act authorizes the examination to be made by officials of the state in which the records are kept. In that case these officials act as agents of the Administrator.

3. For the purpose of facilitating investigations, the Administrator is given wide powers, including the subpoena power and the power to require the giving of testimony under oath. These powers are similar to those given to the Administrator by Section 6.106. The Administrator may apply to the appropriate court for an order compelling compliance with his orders.

Section 2.306 [Application of [Administrative Procedure Act] [Part on Administrative Procedure and Judicial Review] to Part]

Except as otherwise provided, the [State Administrative Procedure Act] [Part on Administrative Procedure and Judicial Review (Part 4) of the Article on Administration (Article 6)] applies to and governs all administrative action taken by the Administrator pursuant to this Part.

COMMENT

If the State has an adequate State administrative procedure act reference should be made to it in this section. Otherwise Part 4 of Article 6 should be enacted and referred to here. Brackets and bracketed language in the section and its caption should be retained or deleted dependent upon which course is followed. See Comment to Section 6.401.

Section 2.307 [Restrictions on Interest in Land as Security]

(1) A lender may contract for an interest in land as security, except to secure a supervised loan in which the amount financed is $1,000 or less. A security interest taken in violation of this section is unenforceable to the extent of that loan.

(2) The amount of $1,000 in subsection (1) is subject to change pursuant to the provisions on adjustment of dollar amounts (Section 1.106).

COMMENT

This section continues the policy recognized in a number of states of denying the lender in relatively small loan transactions the great leverage that results from a security interest in land. See Section 3.301 and the Comment thereto.

Section 2.308 [Regular Schedule of Payments; Maximum Loan Term]

(1) Supervised loans, not made pursuant to open-end credit and in which the amount financed is $1,000 or less, shall be scheduled to be payable in substantially equal instalments at substantially equal periodic intervals except to the extent that the schedule of payments is adjusted to the seasonal or irregular income of the debtor, and

(a) over a period not exceeding 37 months if the amount financed exceeds $300, or

(b) over a period not exceeding 25 months if the amount financed is $300 or less..

(2) The amounts of $300 and $1,000 in subsection (1) are subject to change pursuant to the provisions on adjustment of dollar amounts (Section 1.106).

COMMENT

This provision is similar to that commonly found in small loan laws requiring equal payments and a maximum loan term. Balloon payments are not permitted in supervised loans of $1,000 or less unless appropriate to meet the debtor's needs with respect to seasonal or irregular income. See Section 3.308.

Section 2.309 [No Other Business for Purpose of Evasion]

A supervised lender may not carry on other business for the purpose of evasion or violation of this Act at a location where he makes supervised loans.

COMMENT

Some supervised lenders legitimately engage in transactions on their premises other than loaning money. For example, commercial banks typically sell their customers a variety of services with no purpose of violating provisions on maximum charges or other provisions of this Act. On the other hand, tie-in sales of goods or services in connection with loans are flagrant violations of this Act because they are carried on to evade rate ceilings.

PART 4

CONSUMER LOANS: MAXIMUM FINANCE CHARGES

Section 2.401 [Finance Charge for Consumer Loans]

(1) With respect to a consumer loan, including a loan pursuant to open-end credit, a lender who is not a supervised lender may contract for and receive a finance charge, calculated according to the actuarial method, not exceeding 18 per cent per year. With respect to a consumer loan made pursuant to open-end credit, the finance charge shall be deemed not to exceed 18 per cent per year if the finance charge contracted for and received does not exceed a charge for each monthly billing cycle which is one and one-half per cent of the average daily balance of the open-end account in the billing cycle for which the charge is made. The average daily balance of the open-end account is the sum of the amount unpaid each day during that cycle divided by the number of days in the cycle. The amount unpaid on a day is determined by adding to any balance unpaid as of the beginning of that day all purchases, loans, and other debits and deducting all payments and other credits made or received as of that day. If the billing cycle is not monthly, the finance charge shall be deemed not to exceed 18 per cent per year if the finance charge contracted for and received does not exceed a percentage which bears the same relation to one and one-half per cent as the number of days in the billing cycle bears to 365 divided by 12. A billing cycle is monthly if the closing date of the cycle is the same date each month or does not vary by more than four days from the regular date.

(2) With respect to a consumer loan, including a loan pursuant to open-end credit, a supervised lender may contract for and receive a finance charge, calculated according to the actuarial method, not exceeding the equivalent of the greater of either of the following:

(a) the total of:

(i) 36 per cent per year on that part of the unpaid balances of the amount financed which is $300 or less;

(ii) 21 per cent per year on that part of the unpaid balances of the amount financed which exceeds $300 but does not exceed $1,000; and

(iii) 15 per cent per year on that part of the unpaid balances of the amount financed which exceeds $1,000; or

(b) 18 per cent per year on the unpaid balances of the amount financed.

(3) This section does not limit or restrict the manner of calculating the finance charge, whether by way of add-on, discount, single annual percentage rate, or otherwise, so long as the rate of the finance charge does not exceed that permitted by this section. The finance charge may be contracted for and earned at the single annual percentage rate that would earn the same finance charge as the graduated rates when the debt is paid according to the agreed terms and the calculations are made according to the actuarial method. If the loan is a precomputed consumer credit transaction:

(a) the finance charge may be calculated on the assumption that all scheduled payments will be made when due, and

(b) the effect of prepayment is governed by the provisions on rebate upon prepayment (Section 2.510).

(4) Except as provided in subsection (6), the term of a loan for purposes of this section commences on the day the loan is made. Any month may be counted as 1/12th of a year, but a day is counted as 1/365th of a year. Subject to classifications and differentiations the lender may reasonably establish, a part of a month in excess of 15 days may be treated as a full month if periods of 15 days or less are disregarded and that procedure is not consistently used to obtain a greater yield than would otherwise be permitted. The Administrator may adopt rules not inconsistent with the Federal Truth in Lending Act with respect to treating as regular other minor irregularities in amount or time.

(5) Subject to classifications and differentiations the lender may reasonably establish, he may make the same finance charge on all amounts financed within a specified range. A finance charge so made does not violate subsection (1) or (2) if:

(a) when applied to the median amount within each range, it does not exceed the maximum permitted by the applicable subsection, and

(b) when applied to the lowest amount within each range, it does not produce a rate of finance charge exceeding the rate calculated according to paragraph (a) by more than eight per cent of the rate calculated according to paragraph (a).

(6) With respect to an insurance premium loan, the term of the loan commences on the earliest inception date of a policy or contract of insurance payment of the premium on which is financed by the loan.

(7) The amounts of $300 and $1,000 in subsection (2) are subject to change pursuant to the provisions on adjustment of dollar amounts (Section 1.106).

COMMENT

1. For an extensive explanation of the purposes and operation of the rate ceilings provisions of this Act, see the Comment to Section 2.201. Subsection (1) sets the ceilings for all consumer loans not made by supervised lenders at 18% per annum, and this ceiling applies to open-end credit as well as to closed-end credit. The operation of open-end credit is such that a creditor cannot know whether he is exceeding a rate ceiling stated in terms of a rate calculated according to the actuarial method unless he calculates the rate on daily balances. In "deeming" that 1½% per month on the average daily balance is the equivalent of 18% per year, this subsection allows the creditor to use a somewhat simplified method of calculation.

2. The ceilings for loans by supervised lenders in subsection (2) also apply to open-end credit. This enables supervised lenders to serve the needs of higher risk consumers by the use of credit cards and other open-end credit plans.

Lenders are not required to use a graduated rate, but may find it more economical to use a single annual rate provided that it does not exceed the rate ceiling specified. Lenders may not levy delinquency charges (Section 2.502) and deferral charges (Section 2.503) on open-end credit accounts. By the same token a debtor is not entitled to rebates upon prepayment with respect to open-end accounts since at the time of his prepayment there will be no unearned prepaid finance charges on the open-end account.

3. Subsection (6) makes specific provision for the time a loan commences with respect to an insurance premium loan. The term commences when the insurance first covers the consumer whether or not the loan proceeds have as yet been paid over by the creditor for the insurance.

PART 5

CONSUMER CREDIT TRANSACTIONS: OTHER CHARGES AND MODIFICATIONS

Section 2.501 [Additional Charges]

(1) In addition to the finance charge permitted by the parts of this Article on maximum finance charges for consumer credit sales and consumer loans (Parts 2 and 4), a creditor may contract for and receive the following additional charges:

(a) official fees and taxes;

(b) charges for insurance as described in subsection (2);

(c) annual charges, payable in advance, for the privilege of using a credit card which entitles the cardholder to purchase or lease goods or services from at least 100 persons not related to the card issuer, under an arrangement pursuant to which the debts resulting from the purchases or leases are payable to the card issuer;

(d) with respect to a debt secured by an interest in land, the following "closing costs," if they are bona fide, reasonable in amount, and not for the purpose of circumvention or evasion of this Act:

(i) fees or premiums for title examination, abstract of title, title insurance, surveys, or similar purposes,

(ii) fees for preparation of a deed, settlement statement, or other documents, if not paid to the creditor or a person related to the creditor,

(iii) escrows for future payments of taxes, including assessments for improvements, insurance, and water, sewer and land rents, and

(iv) fees for notarizing deeds and other documents, if not paid to the creditor or a person related to the creditor; and

(e) charges for other benefits, including insurance, conferred on the consumer, if the benefits are of value to him and if the charges are reasonable in relation to the benefits, are of a type that is not for credit, and are authorized as permissible additional charges by rule adopted by the Administrator.

(2) An additional charge may be made for insurance written in connection with the transaction:

(a) with respect to insurance against loss of or damage to property, or against liability arising out of the ownership or use of property, if the creditor furnishes a clear, conspicuous, and specific statement in writing to the consumer setting forth the cost of the insurance if obtained from or through the creditor and stating that the consumer may choose the person through whom the insurance is to be obtained;

(b) with respect to consumer credit insurance providing life, accident, or health coverage, if the insurance coverage is not required by the creditor, and this fact is clearly and conspicuously disclosed in writing to the consumer, and if, in order to obtain the insurance in connection with the extension of credit, the consumer gives specific, dated, and separately signed affirmative written indication of his desire to do so after written disclosure to him of the cost thereof; and

(c) with respect to vendor's single interest insurance, but only (i) to the extent that the insurer has no right of subrogation against the consumer, and (ii) to the extent that the insurance does not duplicate the coverage of other insurance under which loss is payable to the creditor as his interest may appear, against loss of or damage to property for which a separate charge is made to the consumer pursuant to paragraph (a), and (iii) if a clear, conspicuous, and specific statement in writing is furnished by the creditor to the consumer setting forth the cost of the insurance if obtained from or through the creditor and stating that the consumer may choose the person through whom the insurance is to be obtained.

COMMENT

1. The two categories of charges a creditor is permitted to make at the inception of a credit extension are finance charges (Section 1.301(20)) and additional charges as enumerated in this section. In general, the charges designated as additional charges fall roughly into three classes: (1) those that would likely have been incurred had there been no credit extension (*e. g.*, closing costs); (2) those closely related to the extension of credit but providing valuable subsidiary benefits to the consumer (*e. g.*, the front-end credit card charge; life, accident, health, and property insurance); and (3) those ultimately payable to third par-

ties with no portion of the charge returnable to the creditor by commission or otherwise (*e. g.*, taxes; official fees for perfecting security interests). These classes are nonexclusive; for instance property insurance would sometimes fall within class (1) and closing costs fit into class (3) as well as in (1). Paragraph (e) of subsection (1) provides the Administrator with the flexibility needed to allow him to deal with new kinds of charges as new credit transactions evolve.

2. Though this section coincides with Regulation Z Section 226.4(a) in excluding premiums for insurance from the finance charge under certain stated conditions, it varies from Regulation Z Section 226.4(e) in that it does not include appraisal fees and credit report charges as additional charges. Section 1.301 (20)(a)(iv) expressly designates these charges as part of the finance charge. Another variation from Truth in Lending is the treatment of vendor's single interest insurance (V.S.I.). Federal Reserve Interpretation 226.404 allows exclusion of the premium for V.S.I. insurance from the finance charge. Paragraph (c) of subsection (2) adopts a more sophisticated test and allows the premium to be treated as an additional charge in limited situations in which the vendor's single interest coverage does not duplicate the coverage of other insurance under which loss is payable to the creditor as his interest may appear, against loss of or damage to property for which a separate charge is made to the consumer. In this case, the charge is sufficiently beneficial to the consumer to justify classifying the premium as an additional charge.

Section 2.502 [Delinquency Charges]

(1) With respect to a precomputed consumer credit transaction, the parties may contract for a delinquency charge on any instalment not paid in full within ten days after its due date, as originally scheduled or as deferred, in an amount, not exceeding $5, which is not more than five per cent of the unpaid amount of the instalment.

(2) A delinquency charge under subsection (1) may be collected only once on an instalment however long it remains in default. No delinquency charge may be collected with respect to a deferred instalment unless the instalment is not paid in full within ten days after its deferred due date. A delinquency charge may be collected at the time it accrues or at any time thereafter.

(3) A delinquency charge under subsection (1) may not be collected on an instalment paid in full within ten days after its scheduled or deferred instalment due date even though an earlier maturing instalment or a delinquency or deferral charge on

an earlier instalment has not been paid in full. For purposes of this subsection a payment is deemed to have been applied first to any instalment due in the computational period (paragraph (a) of subsection (1) of Section 2.503) in which it is received and then to delinquent instalments and charges.

(4) If two instalments or parts thereof of a precomputed consumer loan are in default for ten days or more, the lender may elect to convert the loan from a precomputed loan to one in which the finance charge is based on unpaid balances. In this event he shall make a rebate pursuant to the provisions on rebate upon prepayment (Section 2.510) as if the date of prepayment were one day before the maturity date of a delinquent instalment, and thereafter may make a finance charge as authorized by the provisions on finance charge for consumer loans by lenders not supervised lenders (subsection (1) of Section 2.401) or finance charge for consumer loans by supervised lenders (subsection (2) of Section 2.401), whichever is appropriate. The amount of the rebate shall not be reduced by the amount of any permitted minimum charge (Section 2.510). If the creditor proceeds under this subsection, any delinquency or deferral charges made with respect to instalments due at or after the maturity date of the first delinquent instalment shall be rebated, and no further delinquency or deferral charges shall be made.

(5) The amount of $5 in subsection (1) is subject to change pursuant to the provisions on adjustment of dollar amounts (Section 1.106).

COMMENT

1. If a consumer is late in making a payment under a precomputed credit transaction, the creditor would receive no income for the period of delay unless a delinquency charge were permitted. The alternative of not permitting delinquency charges is rejected because the result would be to enforce a lower effective ceiling on finance charge rates for delinquent consumers than for consumers who pay promptly. Delinquency charges are inapplicable to open-end credit plans under which the finance charge continues to accumulate through any period of delay thus compensating the creditor for this period.

2. The principal consumer abuse at which the section is aimed is that of precluding multiple delinquency charges stemming from a single delayed payment. Under law before this Act if the consumer's payments were due on the first of the month and the January payment of $100 was not made until the 15th, the creditor could assess a late payment of $5 (assuming that to be the correct figure under state law) and allocate the $100 payment received

on February 1st, $95 to the February payment and $5 to the unpaid delinquency charge, thus causing the consumer to be delinquent in February as well. If the consumer made his $100 payment on time for each of the remaining months of the contract, he would incur a delinquency charge for each month remaining on the contract because of the rule allowing the creditor to allocate current payments to unpaid charges incurred in past periods. Subsection (3) meets this problem by compelling the creditor to apply the full $100 payment received on February 1 to the payment due that month. Hence, the creditor could collect the delinquency charge only for January if all other payments were made on time.

Section 2.503 [Deferral Charges]

(1) In this section and in the provisions on rebate upon prepayment (Section 2.510) the following defined terms apply with respect to a precomputed consumer credit transaction:

(a) "Computational period" means (i) the interval between scheduled due dates of instalments under the transaction if the intervals are substantially equal or, (ii) if the intervals are not substantially equal, one month if the smallest interval between the scheduled due dates of instalments under the transaction is one month or more, and, otherwise, one week.

(b) "Deferral" means a postponement of the scheduled due date of an instalment as originally scheduled or as previously deferred.

(c) "Deferral period" means a period in which no instalment is scheduled to be paid by reason of a deferral.

(d) The "interval" between specified dates means the interval between them including one or the other but not both of them; if the interval between the date of a transaction and the due date of the first scheduled instalment does not exceed one month by more than 15 days when the computational period is one month, or does not exceed 11 days when the computational period is one week, the interval may be considered by the creditor as one computational period.

(e) "Periodic balance" means the amount scheduled to be outstanding on the last day of a computational period before deducting the instalment, if any, scheduled to be paid on that day.

(f) "Standard deferral" means a deferral with respect to a transaction made as of the due date of an instalment as scheduled before the deferral by which the due dates of that instalment and all subsequent instalments as scheduled before the deferral are deferred for a period equal to the deferral period. A standard deferral may be for one or more full computational periods or a portion of one computational period or a combination of any of these.

(g) "Sum of the balances method," also known as the "Rule of 78," means a method employed with respect to a transaction to determine the portion of the finance charge attributable to a period of time before the scheduled due date of the final instalment of the transaction. The amount so attributable is determined by multiplying the finance charge by a fraction the numerator of which is the sum of the periodic balances included within the period and the denominator of which is the sum of all periodic balances under the transaction. According to the sum of the balances method the portion of the finance charge attributable to a specified computational period is the difference between the portions of the finance charge attributable to the periods of time including and excluding, respectively, the computational period, both determined according to the sum of the balances method.

(h) "Transaction" means a precomputed consumer credit transaction unless the context otherwise requires.

(2) Before or after default in payment of a scheduled instalment of a transaction, the parties to the transaction may agree in writing to a deferral of all or part of one or more unpaid instalments and the creditor may make at the time of deferral and receive at that time or at any time thereafter a deferral charge not exceeding that provided in this section.

(3) A standard deferral may be made with respect to a transaction as of the due date, as originally scheduled or as deferred pursuant to a standard deferral, of an instalment with respect to which no delinquency charge (Section 2.502) has been made or, if made, is deducted from the deferral charge computed according to this subsection. The deferral charge for a standard deferral may equal but not exceed the portion of the finance charge attributable to the computational period immediately preceding the due date of the earliest maturing instalment deferred as determined according to the sum of the balances method multiplied by the whole or fractional number of computational periods in the deferral period, counting each day as 1/30th of a month without regard to differences in lengths of months when the

computational period is one month or as 1/7th of a week when the computational period is one week. A deferral charge computed according to this subsection is earned pro rata during the deferral period and is fully earned on the last day of the deferral period.

(4) With respect to a transaction as to which a creditor elects not to make and does not make a standard deferral or a deferral charge for a standard deferral, a deferral charge computed according to this subsection may be made as of the due date, as scheduled originally or as deferred pursuant to either subsection (3) or this subsection, of an instalment with respect to which no delinquency charge (Section 2.502) has been made or, if made, is deducted from the deferral charge computed according to this subsection. A deferral charge pursuant to this subsection may equal but not exceed the rate of finance charge required to be disclosed to the consumer pursuant to law applied to each amount deferred for the period for which it is deferred computed without regard to differences in lengths of months, but proportionately for a part of a month, counting each day as 1/30th of a month or as 1/7th of a week. A deferral charge computed according to this subsection is earned pro rata with respect to each amount deferred during the period for which it is deferred.

(5) In addition to the deferral charge permitted by this section, a creditor may make and receive appropriate additional charges (Section 2.501), and any amount of these charges which is not paid may be added to the deferral charge computed according to subsection (3) or to the amount deferred for the purpose of computing the deferral charge computed according to subsection (4).

(6) The parties may agree in writing at the time of a transaction that, if an instalment is not paid within ten days after its due date, the creditor may unilaterally grant a deferral and make charges as provided in this section. A deferral charge may not be made for a period after the date that the creditor elects to accelerate the maturity of the transaction.

COMMENT

1. The definitions in subsection (1) apply to Section 2.510 as well. See subsection (3) of Section 2.510.

2. These definitions and the other provisions of this section can be illustrated more readily than explained.

Assume the loan transaction specified in the example in Comment 2 to Section 2.201, and that the loan is made on July 1, 1974.

It is then a "precomputed consumer credit transaction" (subsections (13) and (33) of Section 1.301), *e. g.*, a "consumer loan" (subsection (15) of Section 1.301), of which the "amount financed" (subsection (5) of Section 1.301) is $1500, the "finance charge" (subsection (20) of Section 1.301) is $211.68, computed at an annual percentage rate of 25.10%, and the "total of payments" is $1711.68 and is payable in 12 equal monthly instalments of $142.64 each beginning on Aug. 1, 1974, and ending on July 1, 1975.

The "computational period" (paragraph (a) of subsection (1) of this section) is one month. The "periodic balances" (paragraph (e) of subsection (1) of this section) of, and other calculations applicable to, the transaction are:

Col. 1	Col. 2	Col. 3	Col. 4	Col. 5	Col. 6
Inst. No.	Inst. Due Date & Last Day of Each Comptnl. Period	Periodic Balances	Col. 3 ÷ by $11,125.92	Sum of Periodic Balances	Col. 5 ÷ by $11,125.92
1	Aug. 1, 1974	$ 1,711.68	12/78	$ 1,711.68	12/78
2	Sept. 1, 1974	1,569.04	11/78	3,280.72	23/78
3	Oct. 1, 1974	1,426.40	10/78	4,707.12	33/78
4	Nov. 1, 1974	1,283.76	9/78	5,990.88	42/78
5	Dec. 1, 1974	1,141.12	8/78	7,132.00	50/78
6	Jan. 1, 1975	998.48	7/78	8,130.48	57/78
7	Feb. 1, 1975	855.84	6/78	8,986.32	63/78
8	Mar. 1, 1975	713.20	5/78	9,699.52	68/78
9	Apr. 1, 1975	570.56	4/78	10,270.08	72/78
10	May 1, 1975	427.92	3/78	10,698.00	75/78
11	June 1, 1975	285.28	2/78	10,983.28	77/78
12	July 1, 1975	142.64	1/78	11,125.92	78/78
78		$11,125.92	78/78		

Col. 4 sets forth the fraction of the finance charge earned in each computational period as computed according to the "sum of the balances method" (paragraph (g) of subsection (1) of this section).

Col. 6 sets forth the fraction of the finance charge earned at the end of each computational period, also computed according to the sum of the balances method.

It will be noted that the fractions in Col. 4 and Col. 6, respectively, express more simply the fractions:

$$\frac{\text{Perodic balance}}{\text{Sum of all periodic balances under the transaction}}$$

and

$$\frac{\text{Sum of all periodic balances including computational period}}{\text{Sum of all periodic balances under the transaction}}$$

According to the "sum of the balances method" (paragraph (g) of subsection (1) of this section) the portion of the finance charge attributable to a period of time prior to the scheduled due date of the final instalment of the transaction is determined by multiplying the finance charge by a fraction the numerator of which is the sum of the periodic balances included within the period and the denominator is the total of all periodic balances under the transaction. Accordingly, in the assumed example, the portions of the total finance charge of $211.-68 attributable to the periods ending, respectively, on Jan. 1, 1975, and Feb. 1, 1975, are 57/78ths and 63/78ths. Moreover, according to the "sum of the balances method" (the last sentence of paragraph (g) of subsection (1) of this section), the portion of the finance charge attributable to a specified computational period is the difference between the portions of the finance charge attributable to the periods of time including and excluding, respectively, that computational period; accordingly, in the assumed example the portion of the finance charge of $211.68 attributable to the computational period ending on Feb. 1, 1975, is 6/78ths (*i. e.*, 63/78ths minus 57/78ths) of $211.68, or $16.28.

3. Assume, further, that the consumer has paid the first 6 instalments, and that the parties have agreed to the deferral of the 7th instalment of $142.64 originally scheduled to be payable on Feb. 1, 1975, by 6 months until Aug. 1, 1975, or its equivalent, a deferral of the 7th and each of the five subsequent instalments of $142.64 each by one month each so that the 12th instalment originally scheduled for July, 1975 is payable on Aug. 1, 1975. The deferral is then a "standard deferral" (paragraph (f) of subsection (1) of this section) and the maximum deferral charge under subsection (3) of this section is $16.28, the finance charge so attributable to the computational period ending on Feb. 1, 1975, since the number of computational periods in the deferral period, the period in which no instalment is scheduled to be paid by reason of the deferral (paragraph (c) of subsection (1) of Section 2.503), is one.

The method of calculating deferral charges prescribed in subsection (3) of this section is that prescribed in the small loan laws of many States, *e. g.*, New York Banking Law § 352(d)(4).

Were the deferral charge to be computed by the application of the annual percentage rate of 25.-10% (or 2.09 1/6% per month) to each amount deferred for the period of its deferral, as provided in U3C (1968 Draft) Sections 2.-204(1) and 3.204(1) or subsection (4) of this section, the deferral charge would be $142.64 × 6 × .0209 1/6 = $17.90, or $1.62 more than the deferral charge of $16.28 as calculated according to subsection (3) of this section.

4. Under subsection (4) of this section if the creditor elects not to make and does not make a "standard deferral" (paragraph (f) of subsection (1) of this section) or a deferral charge for a standard deferral, the maximum

deferral charge may be computed at the rate of finance charge applying to the transaction, *i. e.*, the rate required to be disclosed to the consumer pursuant to law and, in the assumed example, 25.10% per annum upon each amount deferred for the period it is deferred.

5. Under subsection (2) of this section, the agreement of the parties for deferral and for deferral charges must be in writing and may be made before or after default in the payment of a scheduled instalment and the deferral charge may be made and received by the creditor at the time of or after the deferral.

"Before" in subsection (2) means either "at the time of the transaction" as provided in subsection (6), or later at any time before default. However, if the agreement is made at the time of the transaction or before the default, the creditor may not make the deferral until 10 days after default. In both cases, the deferral charge begins to accrue on the due date of the instalment which is in default or unpaid.

6. Under subsection (5) of this section, the creditor may make and receive appropriate additional charges (Section 2.501) and add them to the deferral charges computed according to subsection (3) or to the amount deferred for the computation of the deferral charges computed according to subsection (4).

7. Under subsection (6) of this section, the parties may agree in writing at the time of a precomputed consumer credit transaction that the creditor may unilaterally grant a deferral and make deferral charges as provided in this section if an instalment is not paid within 10 days after its due date. No deferral charge may be made for a period after the creditor elects to accelerate the maturity of a transaction.

Section 2.504 [Finance Charge on Refinancing]

With respect to a consumer credit transaction except a consumer lease, the creditor by agreement with the consumer may refinance the unpaid balance and contract for and receive a finance charge based on the amount financed resulting from the refinancing at a rate not exceeding that permitted by the provisions on finance charge for consumer credit sales other than open-end credit (Section 2.201) if a consumer credit sale is refinanced, or for consumer loans (subsection (1) or (2) of Section 2.401, whichever is appropriate) if a consumer loan is refinanced. For the purpose of determining the finance charge permitted, the amount financed resulting from the refinancing comprises the following:

(1) if the transaction was not precomputed, the total of the unpaid balance and the accrued charges on the date of the refinancing, or, if the transaction was precomputed, the amount

which the consumer would have been required to pay upon prepayment pursuant to the provisions on rebate upon prepayment (Section 2.510) on the date of refinancing, but for the purpose of computing this amount no minimum charge is permitted; and

(2) appropriate additional charges (Section 2.501), payment of which is deferred.

COMMENT

This section provides the method of obtaining the amount financed on which the finance charge is based when a consumer credit sale or consumer loan is refinanced, and sets the ceiling for the charge. In the refinancing of a precomputed transaction the balance owing is treated as though it is prepaid and the consumer is credited with all refunds computed, except that minimum charges permitted under Section 2.510(2) for prepayments of precomputed transactions are not allowed in refinancing in order to remove any incentive the creditor may have to "flip" the consumer through repeated refinancings. A finance charge is then calculated on an amount financed which is the balance owing less refunds. If the refinanced transaction is not precomputed no refunds need be credited to the consumer, and the amount financed is found merely by taking the unpaid balance and accrued charges at the date of refinancing.

Section 2.505 [Finance Charge on Consolidation]

(1) In this section, "consumer credit transaction" does not include a consumer lease.

(2) If a consumer owes an unpaid balance to a creditor with respect to a consumer credit transaction and becomes obligated on another consumer credit transaction with the same creditor, the parties may agree to a consolidation resulting in a single schedule of payments. If the previous consumer credit transaction was not precomputed, the parties may agree to add the unpaid amount of the amount financed and accrued charges on the date of consolidation to the amount financed with respect to the subsequent consumer credit transaction. If the previous consumer credit transaction was precomputed, the parties may agree to refinance the unpaid balance pursuant to the provisions on refinancing (Section 2.504) and to consolidate the amount financed resulting from the refinancing by adding it to the amount financed with respect to the subsequent consumer credit transaction. In either case the creditor may contract for and receive a finance charge as provided in subsection (3) based on the aggregate amount financed resulting from the consolidation.

(3) If the debts consolidated arise exclusively from consumer credit sales, the transaction is a consolidation with respect to a consumer credit sale and the creditor may make a finance charge not exceeding that permitted by the provisions on finance charge for consumer credit sales other than open-end credit (Section 2.201). If the debts consolidated include a debt arising from a prior or contemporaneous consumer loan, the transaction is a consolidation with respect to a consumer loan and the creditor may make a finance charge not exceeding that permitted by the provisions on finance charge for consumer loans by lenders not supervised lenders (subsection (1) of Section 2.401) or for consumer loans by supervised lenders (subsection (2) of Section 2.401), whichever is appropriate.

(4) If a consumer owes an unpaid balance to a creditor with respect to a consumer credit transaction arising out of a consumer credit sale, and becomes obligated on another consumer credit transaction arising out of another consumer credit sale by the same seller, the parties may agree to a consolidation resulting in a single schedule of payments either pursuant to subsection (2) or by adding together the unpaid balances with respect to the two sales.

COMMENT

This section permits two methods of consolidating balances arising from different transactions. Subsection (2) permits the familiar "rewrite:" the old balance is refinanced under Section 2.504 and added to the amount financed under the new transaction. The finance charge is based on the aggregate amounts financed. Under subsection (4) no refinancing entailing a refund of finance charge is involved. The balances owing are simply added together and made payable on one schedule of payments. This usually means that the maturity of the first transaction is extended.

Section 2.506 [Advances to Perform Covenants of Consumer]

(1) If the agreement with respect to a consumer credit transaction other than a consumer lease contains covenants by the consumer to perform certain duties pertaining to insuring or preserving collateral and the creditor pursuant to the agreement pays for performance of the duties on behalf of the consumer, he may add the amounts paid to the debt. Within a reasonable time after advancing any sums, he shall state to the consumer in writing the amount of sums advanced, any charges with respect to this amount, and any revised payment schedule and, if the

duties of the consumer performed by the creditor pertain to insurance, a brief description of the insurance paid for by the creditor including the type and amount of coverages. Further information need not be given.

(2) A finance charge may be made for sums advanced pursuant to subsection (1) at a rate not exceeding the rate of finance charge required to be stated to the consumer pursuant to law in a disclosure statement, but with respect to open-end credit the amount of the advance may be added to the unpaid balance of the debt and the creditor may make a finance charge not exceeding that permitted by the appropriate provisions on finance charge for consumer credit sales pursuant to open-end credit (Section 2.202) or for consumer loans (subsection (1) or (2) of Section 2.401), whichever is appropriate.

COMMENT

If the agreement so provides the creditor may add to the debt sums that he pays for the performance of duties on behalf of the consumer. If he does so he must disclose the details of the transaction to the consumer. If the original transaction was made pursuant to open-end credit, the creditor may add the amount of the advance to the unpaid balance of the account. In other cases the creditor may make a finance charge on these additional amounts at a rate not in excess of the rate disclosed to the consumer for the original transaction. Normally he would compute this charge for the remaining period of the credit term, and increase the amounts of the consumer's remaining payments accordingly.

Alternative A:

Section 2.507 [Attorney's Fees]

With respect to a consumer credit transaction, the agreement may not provide for payment by the consumer of attorney's fees. A provision in violation of this section is unenforceable.

COMMENT

This Act not only places limitations on the amount that a creditor may charge a consumer for credit at the time the agreement is entered into (Parts 2 and 4 of Article 2) but also on the amount that he may charge a defaulting consumer for collecting from him (*e. g.*, this section and Section 3.402). In providing that no charge may be made for attorney's fees, this section reflects a policy decision to follow some small loan acts in treating this expense, like other collection costs, as part of the creditor's cost of doing business, rather than as a charge to be imposed on the defaulting consumer. The provisions made in this Act for rate ceilings and additional charges are generous enough to justify this treatment of attorney's fees and collection costs as part of general overhead.

Alternative B:

Section 2.507 [Attorney's Fees]

(1) With respect to a consumer loan in which the finance charge calculated according to the actuarial method is more than 18 per cent per year, the agreement may not provide for payment by the consumer of attorney's fees:

(a) if the loan is not pursuant to open-end credit and the amount financed is $1,000 or less; or

(b) if the loan is pursuant to open-end credit and the balance of the account at the time of default is $1,000 or less.

A provision in violation of this subsection is unenforceable.

(2) With respect to any other consumer credit transaction, the agreement may provide for payment by the consumer of reasonable attorney's fees not in excess of 15 per cent of the unpaid debt after default and referral to an attorney not a salaried employee of the creditor. A provision in violation of this subsection is unenforceable.

(3) The amounts of $1,000 in subsection (1) are subject to change pursuant to the provisions on adjustment of dollar amounts (Section 1.106).

COMMENT

This Act not only places limitations on the amount that a creditor may charge a consumer for credit at the time the agreement is entered into (*e. g.*, Parts 2 and 4 of Article 2) but also on the amount that he may charge a defaulting consumer for collecting from him (*e. g.*, this section and Section 3.402). In providing in subsection (1) that no charge may be made for attorney's fees in supervised loans of $1,000 or less this section follows some small loan acts in treating this expense, like other collection costs, as part of the creditor's cost of doing business, rather than as a charge to be imposed on the defaulting consumer. Subsection (2) reflects a policy decision in other consumer transactions of treating attorney's fees not as part of the creditor's general overhead to be indirectly borne by all of his customers but as a charge to be imposed, at least in part, on the defaulting consumer who gives rise to the expense. This section allows the parties to agree that upon default and referral of the claim to an attorney a charge can be made. However, the charge may not exceed 15%

of the unpaid debt at the time of default for reasonable attorney's fees actually incurred. There is no requirement that the attorney must file suit against the consumer to earn the fee.

Section 2.508 [Conversion to Open-End Credit]

The parties may agree at or within ten days before the time of conversion to add the unpaid balance of a consumer credit transaction, except a consumer lease, not made pursuant to open-end credit to the consumer's open-end credit account with the creditor. The unpaid balance so added is an amount equal to the amount financed determined according to the provisions on finance charge on refinancing (Section 2.504).

COMMENT

The parties may agree to add a closed-end consumer loan or consumer credit sale to an open-end credit account. This section provides that the loan or sale is treated as refinanced at the time of the conversion and the unpaid balance resulting from the refinancing is added to the open-end credit account. Since the agreement must be entered into within 10 days prior to the time of conversion, a clause in the original credit agreement would not be effective to authorize a conversion occurring more than 10 days after the agreement.

Section 2.509 [Right to Prepay]

Subject to the provisions on rebate upon prepayment (Section 2.510), the consumer may prepay in full the unpaid balance of a consumer credit transaction, except a consumer lease, at any time without penalty.

COMMENT

This section does not apply to real property credit transactions in which the finance charge does not exceed 12% because these are not consumer credit transactions. Sections 1.301(12) and 1.301(15). Nor does the consumer have the right to receive a rebate upon making a partial prepayment without the consent of the creditor. Application of the provisions on rebate upon prepayment (Section 2.510) is not the exaction of a penalty by a creditor within the meaning of this section.

Section 2.510 [Rebate Upon Prepayment]

(1) Except as otherwise provided in this section, upon prepayment in full of a precomputed consumer credit transaction, the creditor shall rebate to the consumer an amount not less

than the unearned portion of the finance charge computed according to this section. If the rebate otherwise required is less than $1, no rebate need be made.

(2) Upon prepayment of a consumer credit transaction, whether or not precomputed, except a consumer lease or one pursuant to open-end credit, the creditor may collect or retain a minimum charge not exceeding $5 in a transaction which had an amount financed of $75 or less, or not exceeding $7.50 in a transaction which had an amount financed of more than $75, if the minimum charge was contracted for and the finance charge earned at the time of prepayment is less than the minimum charge contracted for.

(3) In the following subsections these terms have the meanings ascribed to them in subsection (1) of Section 2.503: computational period, deferral, deferral period, periodic balance, standard deferral, sum of the balances method, and transaction.

(4) If, with respect to a transaction payable according to its original terms in no more than [48] instalments, the creditor has made either:

(a) no deferral or deferral charge, the unearned portion of the finance charge is no less than the portion thereof attributable according to the sum of the balances method to the period from the first day of the computational period following that in which prepayment occurs to the scheduled due date of the final instalment of the transaction; or

(b) a standard deferral and a deferral charge pursuant to the provisions on a standard deferral, the unpaid balance of the transaction includes any unpaid portions of the deferral charge and any appropriate additional charges incident to the deferral, and the unearned portion of the finance charge is no less than the portion thereof attributable according to the sum of the balances method to the period from the first day of the computational period following that in which prepayment occurs except that the numerator of the fraction is the sum of the periodic balances, after rescheduling to give effect to any standard deferral, scheduled to follow the computational period in which prepayment occurs. A separate rebate of the deferral charge is not required unless the unpaid balance of the transaction is paid in full during the deferral period, in which event the creditor shall also rebate the unearned portion of the deferral charge.

(5) In lieu of computing a rebate of the unearned portion of the finance charge as provided in subsection (4) of this section, the creditor:

(a) shall, with respect to a transaction payable according to its original terms in more than [48] instalments, and a transaction payable according to its original terms in no more than [48] instalments as to which the creditor has made a deferral other than a standard deferral, and

(b) may, in other cases,

recompute or redetermine the earned finance charge by applying, according to the actuarial method, the annual percentage rate of finance charge required to be disclosed to the consumer pursuant to law to the actual unpaid balances of the amount financed for the actual time that the unpaid balances were outstanding as of the date of prepayment, giving effect to each payment, including payments of any deferral and delinquency charges, as of the date of the payment. The Administrator shall adopt rules to simplify the calculation of the unearned portion of the finance charge, including allowance of the use of tables or other methods derived by application of a percentage rate which deviates by not more than one-half of one per cent from the rate of the finance charge required to be disclosed to the consumer pursuant to law, and based on the assumption that all payments were made as originally scheduled or as deferred.

(6) Except as otherwise provided in subsection (5), this section does not preclude the collection or retention by the creditor of delinquency charges (Section 2.502).

(7) If the maturity is accelerated for any reason and judgment is entered, the consumer is entitled to the same rebate as if payment had been made on the date judgment is entered.

(8) Upon prepayment in full of a precomputed consumer credit transaction by the proceeds of consumer credit insurance (Section 4.103), the consumer or his estate is entitled to the same rebate as though the consumer had prepaid the agreement on the date the proceeds of insurance are paid to the creditor, but no later than 20 business days after satisfactory proof of loss is furnished to the creditor.

COMMENT

1. This section uses terms defined in Section 2.503. For illustrations of those terms, see the Comment to that section.

2. Upon prepayment in full of a precomputed consumer credit transaction, subsection (1) of this section requires the creditor

to rebate to the consumer the unearned portion of the finance charge computed according to this section if the rebate amounts to $1 or more.

3. Subsection (2) of this section permits the creditor to collect or retain specified minimum charges upon prepayment of any consumer credit transaction, whether or not precomputed, if the minimum charge is contracted for and if the finance charge earned at the time of prepayment is less than the minimum charge. The permitted minimum charges specified ($5 if the amount financed is $75 or less, or $7.50 if the amount financed is more than $75) are those for which Regulation Z Section 226.8(b)(2) requires no annual percentage rate disclosure.

4. Subsection (4) of this section prescribes a method for computing the unearned portion of the finance charge and hence the rebate upon prepayment of a transaction payable according to its original terms in no more than [48] instalments as to which the creditor has made either no deferral or a "standard deferral" and a deferral charge according to the provisions applying to a standard deferral.

Assume the transactions described in Comment 2 to Section 2.201 and in Comments 2 and 3 to Section 2.503. Assume, further, that the consumer has paid not only $855.84, the total of the first six monthly instalments payable before the deferral, but also the deferral charge of $16.28, calculated according to subsection (3) of Section 2.503, $285.28, the total of the 7th and 8th instalments of $142.64 each payable as deferred on Mar. 1 and Apr. 1, 1975, and has prepaid on Apr. 15, 1975, $570.56, the then unpaid balance of his "total of payments." His total payments then aggregate $1,727.96. Then:

(1) According to subsection (4) of this section, the fraction of the finance charge of $211.68 to be used to determine the rebate is the fraction of which the numerator is the sum of periodic balances as rescheduled pursuant to the deferral, viz., $1,426.40 (the total of $570.56, $427.92, $285.28, and $142.64 payable as deferred on the 1st days of May, June, July, and August, 1975, respectively) divided by $11,125.92 (the sum of all the periodic balances under the original transaction). The fraction then is $1,426.40/$11,125.92, or dividing both numerator and denominator by $142.64 (the amount of each instalment), 10/78. The rebate, the unearned portion of the total finance charge of $211.68, is $211.68 × 10/78 = $27.14.

(2) Deducting $27.14 from $1,727.96, the total paid on the transaction by the consumer, produces $1,700.82 as its net cost to the consumer.

Make the same assumptions as above, except that the deferral charge has been computed according to U3C (1968 Draft) Sections 2.204(1) and 3.204(1) or according to subsection (4) of Section 2.503 of this Act. His total payments then aggregate $1,729.58, the total of $1,711.68 (12 payments of $142.64 each) and the deferral charge of $17.90 calculated according to subsection (4) of Section 2.503. Then were the unearned portions of the finance charge and the deferral charge to be computed separately as formerly required by U3C (1968 Text) Sections 2.210(6) and 3.210(6):

(1) The unearned portion of the finance charge would have been computed without regard to the deferral, *i. e.*, as the fraction of which the numerator is $855.-84 (the total of the four prepaid periodic balances of $427.92, $285.28, and $142.64, and $00., as originally scheduled) and the denominator is $11,125.92 (the total of the 12 periodic balances as originally scheduled), or $855.-84/$11,125.92, or, dividing both the numerator and the denominator by $142.64 (the amount of each instalment), 6/78. The rebate, the unearned portion of the finance charge of $211.68, is $211.68 × 6/78 = $16.28.

(2) As noted in Comment 3 to Section 2.503, the deferral charge, calculated as provided in U3C (1968 Draft) Sections 2.204(1) and 3.204(1), was $17.90. The unearned portion of that deferral charge is the fraction of which the numerator is four (the number of instalments remaining to earn the deferral charge) and the denominator is six (the number of instalments deferred). The unearned portion of the deferral charge of $17.90 is $17.-90 × 4/6 = $11.93.

(3) Deducting $28.21, the total of (a) $16.28, the unearned portion of the finance charge, and (b) $11.93, the unearned portion of the deferral charge, from $1,729.58, the total paid by the consumer, produces $1,701.37 as the net cost of the transaction to the consumer.

Consequently, the methods of calculating deferral charges according to subsection (3) of Section 2.503 of this Act and rebate of unearned finance charge according to subsection (4) of this Section not only permit more simple calculations, but also produce a lower cost to the consumer than under the corresponding provisions of the 1968 Draft of the U3C, viz. under the illustrations above, $1,700.82 as compared to $1,701.37.

5. Subsection (4) of this section permits the "sum of the balances method" or the "Rule of 78 method" of calculating the unearned portion of the finance charge when the transaction according to its original terms was payable in no more than [48] instalments and when there has been either no deferral or a "standard deferral." It thus permits under those circumstances the relatively simple method of calculating rebate upon prepayment commonly provided for in "small loan" acts.

6. Subsection (5) requires the unearned finance charge to be calculated as the excess of this charge over that earned according to the actuarial method (subsection (1) of Section 1.301) before the computational period following that in which prepayment occurs:

(1) when the transaction according to the original terms was payable in more than [48] instalments; or

(2) when there has been a deferral other than a standard deferral with respect to a transaction payable according to its original terms in no more than [48] instalments.

Subsection (5) also gives the creditor the option of using the actuarial method in all other cases.

The [48] instalment provision recognizes that the calculation of rebates according to the actuarial method produces a higher rebate to the consumer than the sum of the balances method particularly in the case of a transaction payable in a large number of instalments and prepaid shortly after the date of its inception.

Subsection (5) also requires the Administrator to adopt rules to simplify the calculation of the unearned portion of the finance charge, including allowance of the use of tables or other methods.

7. Except as provided in subsection (5), subsection (6) of this section does not preclude collection or retention of delinquency charges (Section 2.502).

8. Subsection (7) of this section entitles the consumer to the same rebate calculated as of the date of entry of judgment if maturity is accelerated and judgment is entered.

9. Subsection (8) of this section provides for a rebate computed according to this section if a precomputed consumer credit transaction is prepaid by proceeds of consumer credit insurance calculated as of the date of payment of the proceeds to the creditor, but no later than 20 days after satisfactory proof of loss is furnished to him.

NOTE

The following Administrator's rule is suggested to carry out the direction in the last sentence of subsection (5):

In accordance with the provisions of the last sentence of subsection (5) of Section 2.510, the creditor may calculate the unearned portion of the finance charge as follows:

(1) The unearned portion of the finance charge shall be no less than the excess of the finance charge over the portion thereof attributable according to the actuarial method at, as the creditor elects, either the rate required to be disclosed to the consumer pursuant to law or at that rate rounded to the nearest 1/2 of 1%, to the period before the first day of the computational period following that in which prepayment occurs, determined without regard to any deferral.

(2) Each instalment which was payable as originally scheduled or as deferred before the date of prepayment and which either was paid before its due date as so scheduled or deferred or as to which a delinquency charge was made pursuant to the provisions on delinquency charges (Section 2.502) shall be considered as having been paid on its due date as so scheduled or deferred.

(3) The amount of any deferral charge earned at the date of prepayment shall also be computed. If the deferral charge earned is less than the deferral charge paid, the difference shall be add-

ed to the unearned portion of the finance charge. If any part of a deferral charge has been earned but has not been paid, that part shall be subtracted from the unearned portion of the finance charge or shall be added to the unpaid balance.

(4) This rule does not preclude the collection or retention by the creditor of delinquency or deferral charges.

PART 6

OTHER CREDIT TRANSACTIONS

Section 2.601 [Charges for Other Credit Transactions]

(1) Except as provided in subsection (2), with respect to a credit transaction other than a consumer credit transaction, the parties may contract for payment by the debtor of any finance or other charge.

(2) With respect to a credit transaction which would be a consumer credit transaction if a finance charge were made, a charge for delinquency may not exceed amounts allowed for finance charges for consumer credit sales pursuant to open-end credit (Section 2.202).

COMMENT

1. An economic fundamental of this Act is that too low a rate ceiling prevents both consumer and commercial debtors who need credit from getting credit at reasonable rates from legitimate creditors. Because basic usury laws had that effect, the legislatures in almost all the States have enacted myriad exceptions to the usury statutes for consumer and commercial transactions such as small, industrial and instalment loan laws and prohibitions against a defense of usury by a corporation. The sale of goods, services, or interests in land on credit, whether in a consumer or commercial context, has been held by the courts of most of the States to be exempt from their usury laws under the time-price doctrine. That doctrine has been recognized and limited by the legislatures of most States which have enacted laws regulating consumer instalment sales.

This Act repeals the general usury statute as well as the exceptions to it, sets reasonable ceilings on all consumer credit rates, and in this section leaves the finance charge and other charges in transactions other than consumer credit transactions, such as:

(a) A transaction by a seller or lender not regularly engaged in similar credit transactions,

(b) A transaction over $25,000 in amount not involving real property,

(c) A transaction in which an organization is the debtor, and

(d) A transaction for a business purpose,

basically to the agreement of the parties. In all these types of transactions except the first, which is usually a family transaction or may be within subsection (15)(c) of Section 1.301, the debtors are usually sophisticated enough to take care of themselves in negotiating credit charges. It is difficult to impose an arbitrary rate ceiling for these transactions that will be high enough to allow for high risk business transactions without setting a limit that is so high as to be virtually meaningless. This Act contemplates the repeal of the general usury statute in any State which enacts it; hence the need for the time-price doctrine is eliminated in any such State. Given the basic philosophy of this Act, it should not be interpreted as rejecting the time-price doctrine in either its consumer or commercial context in any State which has not enacted the Act or which continues to have a general usury statute.

2. Some transactions involving open accounts are not consumer credit transactions within this Act because there is neither provision for a finance charge nor for payment in instalments (Sections 1.301(12) and 1.-301(15)). Some oil company credit card accounts are examples. Subsection (2) limits delinquency charges in such cases to amounts allowed by finance charge ceilings in open-end credit.

ARTICLE 3

REGULATION OF AGREEMENTS AND PRACTICES

PART 1

GENERAL PROVISIONS

Section 3.101 [Short Title]

This Article shall be known and may be cited as Uniform Consumer Credit Code—Regulation of Agreements and Practices.

Section 3.102 [Scope]

Part 2 of this Article applies to disclosure with respect to consumer credit transactions. The provision on compliance with the Federal Truth in Lending Act (Section 3.201) applies to a sale of an interest in land or a loan secured by an interest in land, without regard to the rate of finance charge, if the sale or loan is otherwise a consumer credit sale or consumer loan. Parts 3 and 4 of this Article apply, respectively, to limitations on agreements and practices, and limitations on consumers' liabilities with respect to certain consumer credit transactions. Part 5 applies to home solicitation sales.

COMMENT

This Act does not apply to real property credit transactions in which the finance charge does not exceed 12% because these transactions are not consumer credit sales or consumer loans pursuant to Sections 1.301(12) and 1.-301(15). In order to make coverage of this Act coterminous for disclosure purposes with that of the Federal Truth in Lending Act which applies to all consumer credit transactions in real property, this section expressly provides that the provision on compliance with Truth in Lending applies to real property consumer credit transactions without regard to the rate of finance charge.

PART 2

DISCLOSURE

Section 3.201 [Compliance with Federal Truth in Lending Act]

(1) A person upon whom the Federal Truth in Lending Act imposes duties or obligations shall make or give to the consumer the disclosures, information, and notices required of him by that Act and in all respects comply with that Act. To the extent the Federal Truth in Lending Act does not impose duties or obligations upon a person in a credit transaction, except a consumer lease, that is a consumer credit transaction under this Act, the person shall make or give to the consumer disclosures, information, and notices in accordance with the Federal Truth in Lending Act with respect to the credit transaction.

(2) The Federal Truth in Lending Act is deemed to apply to a credit transaction which is a consumer credit transaction under this Act, notwithstanding its inclusion in a class of transactions within this State which, by regulation of the Board of Governors of the Federal Reserve System, is exempt from the Federal Truth in Lending Act.

COMMENT

This section incorporates the Federal Truth in Lending Act, defined by Section 1.302 as including Regulation Z, as the law of the adopting State. Section 6.-104(2) empowers the Administrator to enforce this body of law. The purpose is to attain the dual administrative enforcement of Truth in Lending as recommended by the Report of the National Commission on Consumer Finance p. 60 (1972). The second sentence of subsection (1) and subsection (2) impose on creditors in all transactions covered by this Act the duty to disclose as though the Federal Truth in Lending Act applied even though the latter Act might not actually apply to the transaction.

Section 3.202 [Consumer Leases]

(1) With respect to a consumer lease the lessor shall give to the lessee the following information:

(a) brief description or identification of the goods;

(b) amount of any payment required at the inception of the lease;

(c) amount paid or payable for official fees, registration, certificate of title, or license fees or taxes;

(d) amount of other charges not included in the periodic payments and a brief description of the charges;

(e) brief description of insurance to be provided or paid for by the lessor, including the types and amounts of the coverages;

(f) number of periodic payments, the amount of each payment, the due date of the first payment, the due dates of subsequent payments or interval between payments, and the total amount payable by the lessee;

(g) statement of the conditions under which the lessee may terminate the lease before the end of the term; and

(h) statement of the liabilities the lease imposes upon the lessee at the end of the term.

(2) The disclosures required by this section:

(a) shall be made clearly and conspicuously in writing, a copy of which shall be delivered to the lessee;

(b) may be supplemented by additional information or explanations supplied by the lessor, but none shall be stated, utilized, or placed so as to mislead or confuse the lessee or contradict, obscure, or detract attention from the information required to be disclosed by this section;

(c) need be made only to the extent applicable;

(d) shall be made on the assumption that all scheduled payments will be made when due and will comply with this section although rendered inaccurate by an act, occurrence, or agreement after the required disclosure; and

(e) shall be made before the lease transaction is consummated, but may be made in the lease to be signed by the lessee.

COMMENT

This Act recognizes the consumer lease to be an increasingly popular alternative to consumer credit sales as a method of distributing consumer goods on a periodic payment basis. See Comment to Section 1.301(14). The consumer lessee is given full disclosure of all charges imposed as well as information concerning the amounts, number, and schedule of payments. The lessor must also set out the terms under which the lessee may terminate the lease prior to the end of its term and any liabilities the lessee may incur at the end of the term of the lease. See Section 3.401. Subsection (2) makes the time and manner of disclosure for consumer leases consistent with the requirements of the Federal Truth in Lending Act.

Section 3.203 [Notice to Consumer]

The creditor shall give to the consumer a copy of any writing evidencing a consumer credit transaction, except one pursuant to open-end credit, if the writing requires or provides for the signature of the consumer. The writing evidencing the consumer's obligation to pay the debt shall contain a clear and conspicuous notice informing the consumer that he should not sign it before reading it, that he is entitled to a copy of it, and, except in case of a consumer lease, that he is entitled to prepay the unpaid balance at any time without penalty and may be entitled to receive a refund of unearned charges in accordance with law. The following notice if clear and conspicuous complies with this section:

NOTICE TO CONSUMER:

1. Do not sign this paper before you read it.
2. You are entitled to a copy of this paper.
3. You may prepay the unpaid balance at any time without penalty and may be entitled to receive a refund of unearned charges in accordance with law.

COMMENT

Under this section the consumer must receive a copy of the credit agreement in closed-end transactions and that agreement must contain a conspicuous legend cautioning the consumer to read before he signs and notifying him of his rights to a copy and to prepayment. These requirements are not made for open-end credit transactions. Some of the information in the notice is inapplicable to open-end credit, *i. e.* the right to prepay. Moreover, the consumer's obligation to pay in open-end credit may be evidenced by sales slips or the like, and it is operationally infeasible to require statutory legends on these informal writings. Then, too, Truth in Lending assures that the consumer will receive a copy of the terms under which the open-end credit account will operate and will receive periodic statements. Regulation Z Section 226.7(a) and (b).

Section 3.204 [Notice of Assignment]

A consumer may pay the original creditor until he receives notification of assignment of rights to payment pursuant to a consumer credit transaction and that payment is to be made to the assignee. A notification which does not reasonably identify the rights assigned is ineffective. If requested by the consumer, the assignee shall seasonably furnish reasonable proof that the assignment has been made and unless he does so the consumer may pay the original creditor.

COMMENT

The consumer is protected in paying the original creditor until he receives notice of an assignment. This section is derived from UCC Section 9—318(3) and overrides the provisions of UCC Section 3—603(1) in connection with a consumer loan evidenced by a negotiable instrument.

Section 3.205 [Change in Terms of Open-End Credit Accounts]

(1) Whether or not a change is authorized by prior agreement, a creditor may change the terms of an open-end credit account applying to any balance incurred before or after the effective date of the change. If the change increases the rate of the finance charge or of additional charges, alters the method of determining the balance upon which charges are made so that increased charges may result, or imposes or increases minimum charges, the change is effective with respect to a balance incurred before the effective date of the change only if the consumer after receiving disclosure of the change agrees to it in writing or the creditor delivers or mails to the consumer two written disclosures of the change, the first at least three months before the effective date of the change and the second at a later time before the effective date of the change.

(2) A disclosure provided for in subsection (1) is mailed to the consumer when mailed to him at his address used by the creditor for mailing him periodic billing statements.

(3) If a creditor attempts to change the terms of an open-end credit account as provided in subsection (1) without complying with this section, any additional cost or charge to the consumer resulting from the change is an excess charge and is subject to the remedies available to the consumer (Section 5.201) and to the Administrator (Section 6.113).

COMMENT

1. New developments in consumer credit practices may require changes in open-end credit accounts from time to time. A national department store or commercial bank issuing credit cards may have hundreds of thousands of cardholders. Insurmountable difficulties would confront such creditors were it necessary for them to obtain from each consumer has signed consent to a change in terms. Experience indicates that only a minority of customers take the trouble to return an express approval or disapproval of a change in terms. Nevertheless, merchants and banks should not be permitted to take advantage of customers by changes which are unfair, unanticipated, or inadequately communicated. This provision is designed to allow creditors to change the terms of their open-end accounts in a manner which is feasible from their standpoint but which safeguards the interests of their customers.

2. Truth in Lending requires 15-days notice of certain changes in an open-end credit account (Regulation Z Section 226.7(e)), and if the change either does not increase credit costs or, if costs are increased, affects only balances incurred after the date of the change, the creditor need only give the 15-day Truth in Lending notice. However, under this section if the change increases credit costs for consumers and applies to balances already incurred, the creditor must either obtain the consumer's written consent to the change or comply with the notice provisions of this section, as well as comply with Truth in Lending.

Section 3.206 [Receipts; Statements of Account; Evidence of Payment]

(1) The creditor shall deliver or mail to the consumer, without request, a written receipt for each payment by coin or currency on an obligation pursuant to a consumer credit transaction. A periodic statement showing a payment received by mail complies with this subsection.

(2) Upon written request of a consumer, the person to whom an obligation is owed pursuant to a consumer credit transaction, except one pursuant to open-end credit, shall provide a written statement of the dates and amounts of payments made within the 12 months preceding the month in which the request is received and the total amount unpaid as of the end of the period covered by the statement. The statement shall be provided without charge once during each year of the term of the obligation. If additional statements are requested the creditor may charge not in excess of [$______] for each additional statement.

(3) After a consumer has fulfilled all obligations with respect to a consumer credit transaction, except one pursuant to open-end credit, the person to whom the obligation was owed, upon request of the consumer, shall deliver or mail to the consumer written evidence acknowledging payment in full of all obligations with respect to the transaction.

COMMENT

Subsection (1) assures consumers of receipts for payments made in money but imposes no duty on creditors to give receipts for payments made by check, money order, or the like. Sending periodic statements pursuant to open-end credit (Regulation Z Section 228.-7(b)) or closed-end credit (Regulation Z Section 228.8(n) note 13) showing payments made relieves the creditor of any further duty to send receipts.

Subsection (2) allows consumers to obtain a statement of account in closed-end transactions. The consumer's receipt of periodic statements serves this need in open-end credit accounts. Subsection (3) allows the consumer to obtain evidence of satisfaction upon payment in full of closed-end credit obligations. Again, this requirement is unnecessary in open-end credit owing to the creditor's duty to reflect payments in periodic statements.

Section 3.207 [Form of Insurance Premium Loan Agreement]

An agreement pursuant to which an insurance premium loan is made shall contain the names of the insurance agent or broker negotiating each policy or contract and of the insurer issuing each policy or contract, the number and inception date of, and premium for, each policy or contract, the date on which the term of the loan begins, and a clear and conspicuous notice that each policy or contract may be cancelled if payment is not made in accordance with the agreement. If a policy or contract has not been issued by the time the agreement is signed, the agreement may provide that the insurance agent or broker may insert the appropriate information in the agreement and, if he does so, shall furnish the information promptly in writing to the insured.

COMMENT

This section requires that in insurance premium financing transactions the consumer be given pertinent information regarding the insurance contract and the fact that it may be cancelled upon his default. If the required information is unavailable at the time the agreement is entered into because the policy has not been issued, the agent must furnish the information promptly when the policy is issued.

Section 3.208 [Notice to Co-Signers and Similar Parties]

(1) A natural person, other than the spouse of the consumer, is not obligated as a co-signer, co-maker, guarantor, indorser, surety, or similar party with respect to a consumer credit transaction, unless before or contemporaneously with signing any separate agreement of obligation or any writing setting forth the terms of the debtor's agreement, the person receives a separate written notice that contains a completed identification of the debt he may have to pay and reasonably informs him of his obligation with respect to it.

(2) A clear and conspicuous notice in substantially the following form complies with this section:

NOTICE

You agree to pay the debt identified below although you may not personally receive any property, services, or money. You may be sued for payment although the person who receives the property, services, or money is able to pay. This notice is not the contract that obligates you to pay the debt. Read the contract for the exact terms of your obligation.

IDENTIFICATION OF DEBT YOU MAY HAVE TO PAY

____

(Name of Debtor)

____

(Name of Creditor)

____

(Date)

____

(Kind of Debt)

I have received a copy of this notice.

____

(Date)

____

(Signed)

(3) The notice required by this section need not be given to a seller, lessor, or lender who is obligated to an assignee of his rights.

(4) A person entitled to notice under this section shall also be given a copy of any writing setting forth the terms of the debtor's agreement and of any separate agreement of obligation signed by the person entitled to the notice.

COMMENT

The Report of the National Commission on Consumer Finance pp. 39–40 (1972) expresses concern that persons who assist consumers in obtaining credit by lending their signatures as sureties, or otherwise, may not understand the consequences of their act. This section responds to the Report's recommendation by requiring that the accommodation party be given a separate notice informing him of his potential liabilities as a condition of his being bound on his agreement; he must as well be given a copy of the agreement he is guaranteeing. Creditors who incur the liabilities of a transferor or indorser in assigning consumer paper are not entitled to the notice provided by this section. (Subsection (3)).

Section 3.209 [Advertising]

(1) A seller, lessor, or lender may not advertise, print, display, publish, distribute, broadcast, or cause to be advertised, printed, displayed, published, distributed, or broadcast in any manner any statement or representation with regard to the rates, terms, or conditions of credit with respect to a consumer credit transaction that is false, misleading, or deceptive.

(2) Advertising that complies with the Federal Truth in Lending Act does not violate this section.

(3) This section does not apply to the owner or personnel, as such, of any medium in which an advertisement appears or through which it is disseminated.

COMMENT

This section supplements the provisions on advertising appearing in the Truth in Lending Act, 15 U.S.C. §§ 1661–1665. It should be noted that the exemption granted to States by the Board of Governors of the Federal Reserve System pursuant to 15 U.S.C. § 1633 does not extend to advertising. Hence, even in States that obtain exemption from the Federal Truth in Lending Act, the provisions on advertising in the Federal Act will co-exist with this section in the enacting State.

PART 3

LIMITATIONS ON AGREEMENTS AND PRACTICES

Section 3.301 [Security in Sales and Leases]

(1) With respect to a consumer credit sale, a seller may take a security interest in the property sold. In addition, a seller may take a security interest in goods upon which services are performed or in which goods sold are installed or to which they are annexed, or in land to which the goods are affixed or which is maintained, repaired or improved as a result of the sale of the goods or services, if in the case of a security interest in land the debt secured is $1,000 or more, or, in the case of a security interest in goods the debt secured is $300 or more. The seller may also take a security interest in property to secure the debt arising from a consumer credit sale primarily for an agricultural purpose. Except as provided with respect to cross-collateral (Section 3.302) a seller may not otherwise take a security interest in property to secure the debt arising from a consumer credit sale.

(2) With respect to a consumer lease, except one primarily for an agricultural purpose, a lessor may not take a security interest in property to secure the debt arising from the lease. This subsection does not apply to a security deposit for a consumer lease.

(3) A security interest taken in violation of this section is void.

(4) The amounts of $1,000 and $300 in subsection (1) are subject to change pursuant to the provisions on adjustment of dollar amounts (Section 1.106).

COMMENT

This section limits sellers and lessors with respect to the manner in which they may secure the obligation arising from a consumer credit sale (Section 1.301(12)) or consumer lease (Section 1.301(14)). See Section 5.116 for limitations on the creditor's right to realize on collateral exempt under the law of this State.

1. Sales of goods. A seller may take a security interest in the goods sold but not in other goods or land unless the goods sold become closely connected with the goods or land in which the security interest is taken. Under this section an appliance dealer may retain a security interest in a washing machine sold

but may not take a security interest in other appliances to secure the sale obligation unless he complies with Section 3.302. Except as provided in Section 3.302, a seller of goods may take additional security for the sale obligation in other goods or land only if the debt secured is substantial—$300 in the case of a security interest in goods, $1,000 in the case of a security interest in land—and then only if the goods or land in which the additional security interest is taken are goods in which the goods sold are installed or to which they are annexed or land to which the goods sold are annexed or which is maintained, repaired, or improved by the goods sold.

2. Sales of services. The seller may not take a security interest in goods or land to secure an obligation arising out of the sale of services unless the services are performed on the goods or are used to maintain, repair, or improve the land. Even then, the debt secured must be $300 in the case of a security interest in goods and $1,000 in the case of a security interest in land. Thus a seller of dancing lessons may not take a security interest in goods or lands, and a carpenter or painter may take a security interest in a residence only if the debt arising from the sale of services is $1,000 or more.

3. Sales of land. The seller can retain a security interest only in the land sold and not in other goods or land. It should be noted, however, that this section applies only to consumer credit sales and a sale of an interest in land in which the finance charge is 12% or less is not a consumer credit sale. Section 1.301(12).

4. Consumer leases. A lessor may not secure the lease obligation by taking a security interest in property.

5. Sales for agricultural purposes. Farmers sometimes secure the unpaid balance of a sale obligation by giving security interests in their land or farm equipment. In order not to disturb this practice, an exception in the application of this section is made for sales and leases for agricultural purposes.

Section 3.302 [Cross-Collateral]

(1) In addition to contracting for a security interest pursuant to the provisions on security in sales and leases (Section 3.301), a seller in a consumer credit sale may secure the debt arising from the sale by contracting for a security interest in other property if as a result of a prior sale the seller has an existing security interest in the other property. The seller may also contract for a security interest in the property sold in the subsequent sale as security for the previous debt.

(2) If the seller contracts for a security interest in other property pursuant to this section, the rate of finance charge thereafter on the aggregate unpaid balances so secured may not exceed that permitted if the balances so secured were consolidat-

ed pursuant to the provisions on finance charge on consolidation (subsection (2) of Section 2.505). The seller has a reasonable time after so contracting in which to make any adjustments required by this section.

COMMENT

1. A seller who sells goods on credit to a buyer in more than one sale may secure the debts arising from each sale by a cross-security interest in the other goods sold so long as the seller has an existing security interest in the other goods. Section 3.303 specifies when a seller loses his security interest in goods in a cross-collateral situation.

2. Subsection (1) allows cross-collateral to be taken either for separate debts or for consolidated debts, but subsection (2) limits the rate of the finance charge that a seller may charge in the separate debt case to that chargeable had the debts been consolidated pursuant to Section 2.505(2). To illustrate, if a buyer who owes seller a $275 balance from one sale makes a subsequent $250 purchase, the seller may consolidate these debts under Section 2.505(2) so that the finance charge would be calculated on the sum of the refinanced balance of the first sale, *e. g.*, $260, and the amount financed under the second sale, $250, or a total of $510. Under Section 2.201, the seller may then charge a maximum rate of 36% on the first $300 and 21% on the next $210. However, if the debts were kept separate, the seller might charge the maximum of 36% on both the $275 and $250 balances. In effect subsection (2) prevents the seller from taking the advantages of cross-collateral without also offering the buyer the lower rates that would have resulted had the debts been consolidated pursuant to Section 2.505(2).

Section 3.303 [Debt Secured by Cross-Collateral]

(1) If debts arising from two or more consumer credit sales, except sales primarily for an agricultural purpose or pursuant to open-end credit, are secured by cross-collateral (Section 3.302) or consolidated into one debt payable on a single schedule of payments, and the debt is secured by security interests taken with respect to one or more of the sales, payments received by the seller after the taking of cross-collateral or the consolidation are deemed, for the purpose of determining the amount of the debt secured by the various security interests, to have been applied first to the payment of the debts arising from the sales first made. To the extent debts are paid according to this section, security interests in items of property terminate as the debt originally incurred with respect to each item is paid.

(2) Payments received by the seller upon an open-end credit account are deemed, for the purpose of determining the amount of the debt secured by the various security interests, to have been applied first to the payment of finance charges in the order of their entry to the account and then to the payment of debts in the order in which the entries to the account showing the debts were made.

(3) If the debts consolidated arose from two or more sales made on the same day, payments received by the seller are deemed, for the purpose of determining the amount of the debt secured by the various security interests, to have been applied first to the payment of the smallest debt.

COMMENT

1. When a seller consolidates debts arising from sales and secures the consolidated debt by security interests in the goods sold in these sales or when a seller secures separate debts by cross-collateral (Section 3.302), this section prevents the seller from retaining a security interest in all of the goods until the buyer's entire debt is paid. The basis of the section is that a security interest in goods terminates when the debt incurred in the sale of the goods is paid. For the purpose of determining when this debt is paid, subsection (1) allocates the buyer's payments first to the debts first incurred. Thus if the seller consolidates debts of $100, $200, and $300 arising from sales made in that order, the security interest in the goods purchased pursuant to the $100 sale terminates when $100 of the consolidated debt is paid. If the seller does not consolidate these debts but secures them by cross-collateral, he must allocate all of the buyer's payments to the $100 debt until it is paid off, and so forth. Subsection (2) applies this first-payments-against-first debts rule to open-end accounts.

2. Subsection (3) applies to the case in which the buyer purchases a $750 TV in one department at 9:30 a. m. and a $150 typewriter in another department at 10:00 a. m. Subsequently the debts are consolidated. This subsection relieves the seller of having to keep records of the exact hour a sale is made. It is derived from Regulation Z Section 226.8(h).

Section 3.304 [Use of Multiple Agreements]

(1) A creditor may not use multiple agreements with respect to a single consumer credit transaction with intent to obtain a higher finance charge than otherwise would be permitted by the provisions of the Article on Finance Charges and Related Provisions (Article 2).

(2) The excess amount of finance charge resulting from a violation of subsection (1) is an excess charge for the purposes of the provisions on rights of parties (Section 5.201) and the provisions on civil actions by Administrator (Section 6.113).

COMMENT

The graduated rate ceiling structure of this Act (Sections 2.-201 and 2.401) allows a creditor to charge higher rates on smaller balances. In order to achieve maximum rates a seller might arbitrarily divide a transaction into two or more agreements in order that the amount financed under each is within the $300 amount on which the highest rate can be charged. If he does so the excess amount of finance charge provided for is made by subsection (2) an excess charge for purposes of the provisions on remedies by consumers and the Administrator. A supervised lender would violate this provision if he directed a consumer seeking a $500 loan to sign one note for $250 and to have his wife sign another for $250. On the other hand, a supervised lender would not be in violation of this provision if a husband borrowed $250 at one time and his wife on a voluntary separate loan application borrowed $250 at some other time.

Section 3.305 [No Assignment of Earnings]

(1) A creditor may not take an assignment of earnings of the consumer for payment or as security for payment of a debt arising out of a consumer credit transaction. An assignment of earnings in violation of this section is unenforceable by the assignee of the earnings and revocable by the consumer. This section does not prohibit a consumer from authorizing deductions from his earnings in favor of his creditor if the authorization is revocable, the consumer is given a complete copy of the writing evidencing the authorization at the time he signs it, and the writing contains on its face a conspicuous notice of the consumer's right to revoke the authorization.

(2) A sale of unpaid earnings made in consideration of the payment of money to or for the account of the seller of the earnings is deemed to be a loan to him secured by an assignment of earnings.

COMMENT

This Act recognizes the potential for hardship for a consumer and his dependents which may result from a disruption of the steady flow of family income. Just as Section 5.104 prevents a creditor from attaching unpaid earnings of a consumer before he obtains judgment, this provision precludes a creditor from reaching the consumer's earnings pursuant to an irrevocable wage assignment obtained from the consumer. The purpose of both sections is to afford the consumer an opportunity to have his debt determined by a court before his unpaid earnings are taken against his will by a creditor. This provision prohibits a creditor from taking either an assignment of earnings as payment or as security for payment for a debt or a sale of earnings in payment of the price or rental. A revocable payroll deduction authorization in favor of a creditor is not forbidden by this section so long as the requisite notice is given to the consumer of his right to revoke.

Section 3.306 [Authorization to Confess Judgment Prohibited]

A consumer may not authorize any person to confess judgment on a claim arising out of a consumer credit transaction. An authorization in violation of this section is void.

COMMENT

This section reflects the view of the great majority of States in prohibiting authorizations to confess judgment. It is consistent with the policy of the Act of assuring the consumer a right to a judicial hearing before judgment is entered against him or his rights are otherwise affected. See Sections 3.305 and 5.104. This section follows a recommendation of the National Commission on Consumer Finance (NCCF Report, p. 26 (1972)). It does not prohibit the consumer himself from confessing judgment pursuant to the laws of this State.

Section 3.307 [Certain Negotiable Instruments Prohibited]

With respect to a consumer credit sale or consumer lease, [except a sale or lease primarily for an agricultural purpose,] the creditor may not take a negotiable instrument other than a check dated not later than ten days after its issuance as evidence of the obligation of the consumer.

COMMENT

This section, together with Sections 3.403, 3.404, and 3.405, states a major tenet of this Act: that the holder in due course doctrine should be abrogated in consumer cases. Whatever beneficial effects this doctrine may have in promoting the currency of paper is greatly outweighed by the harshness of its consequences in denying consumers the right to raise valid defenses arising out of credit transactions. The first step in abolition of the doctrine is the prohibition found in this section of the use of negotiable instruments in consumer credit sales and consumer leases. The presence of the bracketed language recognizes the strong tradition of the use of negotiable instruments in agricultural transactions in some States.

Section 3.308 [Balloon Payments]

(1) Except as provided in subsection (2), if any scheduled payment of a consumer credit transaction is more than twice as large as the average of earlier scheduled payments, the consumer has the right to refinance, without penalty, the amount of that payment at the time it is due. The terms of the refinancing shall be no less favorable to the consumer than the terms of the original transaction.

(2) This section does not apply to:

(a) a consumer lease;

(b) a transaction pursuant to open-end credit;

(c) a transaction primarily for an agricultural purpose;

(d) a transaction to the extent that the payment schedule is adjusted to the seasonal or irregular income or scheduled payments or obligations of the consumer; or

(e) a transaction of a class defined by rule of the Administrator as not requiring for the protection of the consumer his right to refinance as provided in this section.

COMMENT

1. Balloon payments may have legitimate uses, but they may also be used to induce a consumer to enter into a burdensome contract by offering him invitingly small instalment payments until the end of the contract when the consumer is confronted with a balloon payment too large to pay. See Section 2.308 requiring a regular schedule of payments in supervised loans not in excess of $1,000. This section meets the threat of misuse of balloon payments by giving the consumer the right to compel refinancing of the amount of the balloon payment at the time it is due without penalty under terms no less favorable than those of the original transaction. Under the refinancing the size of the instalment payments may not exceed the average scheduled payments excluding the balloon payment and the rate of the finance charge may not exceed that under the original agreement.

2. Subsection (2) excludes use of the option to refinance in cases in which balloon payments may be beneficial to the consumer, *e. g.*, paragraph (d) disallows the refinancing option when the payments were made irregular to meet the requirements of an irregular income flow on the part of the consumer or to mesh with a changing schedule of payments on the consumer's other obligations. Paragraph (a) recognizes that balloon payments in consumer leases are treated in Section 3.-401. Open-end credit is excluded by paragraph (b) because payments are necessarily irregular in open-end transactions. There are so many instances in which irreg-

ular payments are mutually beneficial in agricultural financing that it was thought desirable to make a blanket exception for agricultural transactions in paragraph (c). Since the purpose of this section is to protect consumers against deceptive or unfair use of irregular payments and not to inhibit their use in cases in which they are to the advantage of both parties, paragraph (e) offers a safety valve provision authorizing the Administrator to exempt transactions if he believes the interests of all would be best served by doing so.

Section 3.309 [Referral Sales and Leases]

With respect to a consumer credit sale or consumer lease, the seller or lessor may not give or offer to give a rebate or discount or otherwise pay or offer to pay value to the consumer as an inducement for a sale or lease for the consumer giving to the seller or lessor the names of prospective buyers or lessees, or otherwise aiding the seller or lessor in making a sale or lease to another person, if the earning of the rebate, discount or other value is contingent upon the occurrence of an event after the time the consumer agrees to buy or lease. If a consumer is induced by a violation of this section to enter into a consumer credit sale or consumer lease, the agreement is unenforceable by the seller or lessor and the consumer, at his option, may rescind the agreement or retain the property delivered and the benefit of any services performed, without any obligation to pay for them. A sale or lease that would be a referral sale or lease if credit were extended by the seller or lessor is nonetheless so because the property or services are paid for in whole or in part by use of a credit card or by a consumer loan with respect to which the lender is subject to claims and defenses arising from the sale or lease (Section 3.405), and the consumer has the same rights against the card issuer or lender that he has against the seller or lessor under this section.

COMMENT

1. The typical referral sale scheme which would be barred by this section is one in which the seller, before closing the sale, offers to reduce the price by $25 for every name of a person the buyer supplies who will agree to buy from the seller. The seller may be able to make an inflated price tag much more palatable to a buyer if he can convince the buyer that the referral plan will greatly reduce the amount he will actually have to pay. The buyer may not realize until later that his friends whose names he submitted are not as gullible as he and that he is bound to pay the original balance of the contract price.

2. The evil this section is aimed at is the raising of expectations in a buyer of benefits to accrue to him from events which are to occur in the future. This provision has no effect on a seller's agreement to reduce at the time of the sale the price of an item in exchange for the buyer's giving the seller a list of prospective purchasers or assisting in other ways if the price reduction is not contingent on whether the purchasers do in fact buy or on whether other events occur in the future.

3. The misuse of the referral sale scheme has been so pervasive in some segments of vendor credit that this provision, in an effort to halt these practices, not only makes agreements in violation of this section unenforceable but also allows the buyer to retain the goods sold or the benefit of services rendered with no obligation to pay for them. Alternatively, the buyer may rescind the agreement, return the goods, and recover any payment. Use of a referral scheme subjects the offending seller or lessor to a penalty under Section 5.201. Creditors cannot evade this section by the use of credit cards or consumer loans.

PART 4

LIMITATIONS ON CONSUMERS' LIABILITIES

Section 3.401 [Restriction on Liability in Consumer Lease]

The obligation of a lessee upon expiration of a consumer lease [, except one primarily for an agricultural purpose,] may not exceed twice the average payment allocable to a monthly period under the lease. This limitation does not apply to charges for damages to the leased property or for other default.

COMMENT

This section is designed to protect consumer lessees against abuses associated with what are described in some areas of the country as "open-end" leases. Under such an agreement the parties contract that at the expiration of the lease the article leased, usually an automobile, will have a certain depreciated value and will be sold. If it brings less than the agreed depreciated value, the lessee is liable for the difference; if it brings more, the lessee is entitled to the surplus. Under such an agreement, the lessee will have no understanding of how much the lease might cost him unless he can accurately predict what the second hand market will be at the expiration of lease. Moreover, if the lessor sets an unrealistically high depreciated value the contingent liability of the lessee will increase accordingly, and the lessor can offer deceptively low rental payments to a gullible customer.

Under this section the liability, contingent or otherwise, of the lessee at the end of the term of the lease is limited to twice the average monthly rental payment. This limitation not only avoids the possibility of a large contingent liability on the part of the lessee at the end of the term but also gives the lessee a basis for comprehending how much the lease will actually cost him.

Section 3.402 [Limitation on Default Charges]

Except for reasonable expenses incurred in realizing on a security interest, the agreement with respect to a consumer credit transaction other than a consumer lease may not provide for any charges as a result of default by the consumer except those authorized by this Act. A provision in violation of this section is unenforceable.

COMMENT

This Act limits the credit related charges a creditor may impose on a consumer not only at the outset of the contract but also at the default stage. Except for delinquency charges (Section 2.502) [, attorney's fees (Section 2.507),] and expenses arising from realizing on collateral (UCC Section 9—504), the creditor may impose no collection or default charges on a consumer.

[The bracketed language in this Comment should be omitted if Alternative A of Section 2.507 is selected.]

Section 3.403 [Card Issuer Subject to Claims and Defenses]

(1) This section neither limits the liability of nor imposes liability on a card issuer as a manufacturer, supplier, seller, or lessor of property or services sold or leased pursuant to the credit card. This section may subject a card issuer to claims and defenses of a cardholder against a seller or lessor arising from sales or leases made pursuant to the credit card.

(2) A card issuer is subject to claims and defenses of a cardholder against the seller or lessor arising from the sale or lease of property or services by a seller or lessor licensed, franchised, or permitted by the card issuer or a person related to the card issuer to do business under the trade name or designation of the card issuer or a person related to the card issuer, to the extent of the original amount owing to the card issuer with respect to the sale or lease of the property or services as to which the claim or defense arose.

(3) Except as otherwise provided in this section, a card issuer, including a lender credit card issuer, is subject to all claims and defenses of a cardholder against the seller or lessor arising from the sale or lease of property or services pursuant to the credit card:

(a) if the original amount owing to the card issuer with respect to the sale or lease of the property or services as to which the claim or defense arose exceeds $50;

(b) if the residence of the cardholder and the place where the sale or lease occurred are [in the same state or] within 100 miles of each other;

(c) if the cardholder has made a good faith attempt to obtain satisfaction from the seller or lessor with respect to the claim or defense; and

(d) to the extent of the amount owing to the card issuer with respect to the sale or lease of the property or services as to which the claim or defense arose at the time the card issuer has notice of the claim or defense. Notice of the claim or defense may be given before the attempt specified in paragraph (c). Oral notice is effective unless the card issuer requests written confirmation when or promptly after oral notice is given and the cardholder fails to give the card issuer written confirmation within the period of time, not less than 14 days, stated to the cardholder when written confirmation is requested.

(4) For the purpose of determining the amount owing to the card issuer with respect to a sale or lease upon an open-end credit account, payments received for the account are deemed to have been applied first to the payment of finance charges in the order of their entry to the account and then to the payment of debts in the order in which the entries of the debts are made to the account.

(5) An agreement may not limit or waive the claims or defenses of a cardholder under this section.

COMMENT

1. The policies stated in Sections 3.307 and 3.404 of abolition of the holder in due course doctrine could be thwarted if the parties could deprive consumers of their claims and defenses merely by recasting assigned paper transactions into credit card transactions. Thus subsection (3) subjects credit card issuers to consumer claims and defenses in those transactions in which the credit card is more likely to be used as a true credit device (sales or leases in excess of $50) and in which the great volume of credit card use takes place (sales or leases [within the consumer's state of residence or] within 100 miles of the residence). For a discussion of the amount of the debt owing against which the claim or defense can be asserted, see Comment 2 to Section 3.404.

2. The first sentence of subsection (1) recognizes that some credit card issuers (*e. g.*, the major retail chains) are themselves the sellers or lessors of products or services, and their liability as sellers or lessors is in no way affected by their status as credit card issuers. Subsection (2) provides that when the card issuer (*e. g.*, oil distributors), allows others to sell products while operating under the issuer's name, the card issuer should be liable to the full amount of the credit extended in the sale as the financer of the transaction but should bear no further liability for products defects or the like merely because the sale was made pursuant to its credit card. If such a card issuer was in fact the manufacturer or processor of the defective prod-

ucts sold pursuant to its credit card by its franchised dealer, then the case would fall within the first sentence of subsection (1) and the presence of the credit card would be irrelevant to the manufacturer's or processor's liability. Subsection (3) imposes liability on the card issuer as described in Comment 1 because of the card issuer's status as the financer of the sale or lease transaction made pursuant to its card. See the second sentence of subsection (1).

Section 3.404 [Assignee Subject to Claims and Defenses]

(1) With respect to a consumer credit sale or consumer lease [, except one primarily for an agricultural purpose], an assignee of the rights of the seller or lessor is subject to all claims and defenses of the consumer against the seller or lessor arising from the sale or lease of property or services, notwithstanding that the assignee is a holder in due course of a negotiable instrument issued in violation of the provisions prohibiting certain negotiable instruments (Section 3.307).

(2) A claim or defense of a consumer specified in subsection (1) may be asserted against the assignee under this section only if the consumer has made a good faith attempt to obtain satisfaction from the seller or lessor with respect to the claim or defense and then only to the extent of the amount owing to the assignee with respect to the sale or lease of the property or services as to which the claim or defense arose at the time the assignee has notice of the claim or defense. Notice of the claim or defense may be given before the attempt specified in this subsection. Oral notice is effective unless the assignee requests written confirmation when or promptly after oral notice is given and the consumer fails to give the assignee written confirmation within the period of time, not less than 14 days, stated to the consumer when written confirmation is requested.

(3) For the purpose of determining the amount owing to the assignee with respect to the sale or lease:

(a) payments received by the assignee after the consolidation of two or more consumer credit sales, except pursuant to open-end credit, are deemed to have been applied first to the payment of the sales first made; if the sales consolidated arose from sales made on the same day, payments are deemed to have been applied first to the smallest sale; and

(b) payments received for an open-end credit account are deemed to have been applied first to the payment of finance charges in the order of their entry to the account and then to the payment of debts in the order in which the entries of the debts are made to the account.

(4) An agreement may not limit or waive the claims or defenses of a consumer under this section.

COMMENT

1. This section codifies a growing body of case law under UCC Section 9—206 to the effect that assignees take consumer paper subject to consumer claims and defenses. This section explicitly provides for preservation of consumer defenses even though the assignee is a holder in due course (subsection (1)) or the consumer has purported to waive his claims and defenses as against the assignee (subsection (4)). The policy justifications for the section are to protect the consumer from the harshness of the holder in due course doctrine as well as to encourage financial institutions taking assignments of consumer paper to use discretion in dealing with sellers and lessors whose transactions give rise to an unusual percentage of consumer complaints. See Section 3.307.

2. The consumer, upon making a good faith attempt to obtain satisfaction from his seller or lessor, can assert his claim or defense against the assignee to the extent of the amount still owing to the assignee at the time the assignee learns of the claim or defense. If the assignee knows of the defense before any payments are made to him, the consumer can raise his claim or defense to the full amount of the assigned debt. Orderly procedures will necessitate some written record on the part of the assignee of the consumer's notification regarding his claim or defense, but the consumer ought to be able to rely on having given oral notification unless the assignee requests written confirmation. Hence, the assignee has the option of making his own written record upon receiving oral notice from the consumer or of requesting written notice from the consumer and allowing 14 days for the consumer to send his written confirmation. Subsection (3) uses the same tests for determining the amount owing on a debt as are used in Section 3.303.

Section 3.405 [Lender Subject to Claims and Defenses Arising from Sales and Leases]

(1) A lender, except the issuer of a lender credit card, who, with respect to a particular transaction, makes a consumer loan to enable a consumer to buy or lease from a particular seller or lessor property or services [, except primarily for an agricultural purpose,] is subject to all claims and defenses of the consumer

against the seller or lessor arising from that sale or lease of the property or services if:

(a) the lender knows that the seller or lessor arranged for the extension of credit by the lender for a commission, brokerage, or referral fee;

(b) the lender is a person related to the seller or lessor, unless the relationship is remote or is not a factor in the transaction;

(c) the seller or lessor guarantees the loan or otherwise assumes the risk of loss by the lender upon the loan;

(d) the lender directly supplies the seller or lessor with the contract document used by the consumer to evidence the loan, and the seller or lessor has knowledge of the credit terms and participates in preparation of the document;

(e) the loan is conditioned upon the consumer's purchase or lease of the property or services from the particular seller or lessor, but the lender's payment of proceeds of the loan to the seller or lessor does not in itself establish that the loan was so conditioned; or

(f) the lender, before he makes the consumer loan, has knowledge or, from his course of dealing with the particular seller or lessor or his records, notice of substantial complaints by other buyers or lessees of the particular seller's or lessor's failure or refusal to perform his contracts with them and of the particular seller's or lessor's failure to remedy his defaults within a reasonable time after notice to him of the complaints.

(2) A claim or defense of a consumer specified in subsection (1) may be asserted against the lender under this section only if the consumer has made a good faith attempt to obtain satisfaction from the seller or lessor with respect to the claim or defense and then only to the extent of the amount owing to the lender with respect to the sale or lease of the property or services as to which the claim or defense arose at the time the lender has notice of the claim or defense. Notice of the claim or defense may be given before the attempt specified in this subsection. Oral notice is effective unless the lender requests written confirmation when or promptly after oral notice is given and the consumer fails to give the lender written confirmation within the period of time, not less than 14 days, stated to the consumer when written confirmation is requested.

(3) For the purpose of determining the amount owing to the lender with respect to the sale or lease:

(a) payments received by the lender after consolidation of two or more consumer loans, except pursuant to open-end credit, are deemed to have been applied first to the payment of the loans first made; if the loans consolidated arose from loans made on the same day, payments are deemed to have been applied first to the smallest loan; and

(b) payments received for an open-end credit account are deemed to have been applied first to the payment of finance charges in the order of their entry to the account and then to the payment of debts in the order in which the entries of the debts are made to the account.

(4) An agreement may not limit or waive the claims or defenses of a consumer under this section.

COMMENT

1. This section extends this Act's policy of preserving consumer claims and defenses to direct loan cases in those situations in which the relationship between the seller or lessor and the lender justifies allowing the consumer to raise claims or defenses against the lender. The requisite relationship exists when the seller or lessor arranges for the extension of credit in paragraphs (a) and (d) of subsection (1) within the meaning of Regulation Z Section 226.2(f), is related to the lender in paragraph (b), or guarantees the loan in paragraph (c), and in cases in which the lender conditions the loan on the purchase or lease from a particular seller or lessor in paragraph (e), or knows before he makes the loan of a history of consumer complaints about the seller or lessor in paragraph (f).

2. For a discussion of the amount of the debt owing against which the claim or defense can be asserted under subsections (2) and (3), see Comment 2 to Section 3.404.

PART 5

HOME SOLICITATION SALES

Section 3.501 [Definition: "Home Solicitation Sale"]

"Home solicitation sale" means a consumer credit sale of goods or services, except primarily for an agricultural purpose, in which the seller or a person acting for him personally solicits the sale, and the buyer's agreement or offer to purchase is given to the seller or a person acting for him, at a residence. It does not include a sale made pursuant to a pre-existing open-end credit account with the seller or pursuant to prior negotiations between the parties at a business establishment at a fixed location where goods or services are offered or exhibited for sale, a transaction conducted and consummated entirely by mail or telephone, or a sale which is subject to the provisions of the Federal Truth in Lending Act on the consumer's right to rescind certain transactions. A sale that would be a home solicitation sale if credit were extended by the seller is nonetheless so because the goods or services are paid for in whole or in part by use of a credit card or by a consumer loan with respect to which the lender is subject to claims and defenses arising from the sale (Section 3.405), and the buyer has the same rights against the card issuer or lender that he has against the seller under this Part.

COMMENT

1. The Act singles out for special treatment consumer credit sales in which the buyer's order is given to the seller at a residence. An underlying consideration for Part 5 is the belief that in a significant proportion of such sales the consumer is induced to sign a sales contract by high pressure techniques. The Act recognizes that many buyers in such cases may be unwilling parties to the transaction and gives to them a limited right to cancel the sale. Section 3.502. The right of cancellation applies to "home solicitation sales."

2. The definition of "home solicitation sales" differentiates between those types of transactions which have been the subject of particular abuse and those which have not. Although high pressure salesmanship can be practiced anywhere, the underlying theory of Section 3.501 is that the sale in the home is particularly susceptible to such methods. Two elements are required to bring a transaction within the definition. First, there must be personal solicitation at a residence. Second, the act of the buyer in binding himself by agreeing or offering

to purchase, must also take place at a residence. The phrase "at a residence" rather than "in a residence" is used to prevent avoidance of the Act by the expedient of having the buyer sign the contract outside of, but in the immediate vicinity of, the home.

3. Sellers who sell by means of solicitation in the home can avoid the application of Part 5 [Section 3.501 et seq.] by having the contract or offer to purchase signed by the buyer at the office of the seller or at some place other than a residence. If the buyer must go to the seller's office or some other place to sign the contract or offer there is less likelihood that he is acting because of undue pressure by the seller. Similarly, where the buyer has already established a prior relationship with the seller by having a pre-existing open-end account or by having previously negotiated with the seller with respect to the sale at the seller's business establishment the likelihood of coercion of the buyer is substantially less. This Part does not apply in these cases.

4. Sellers may not avoid operation of this Part by permitting consumers to buy by using credit cards or by using loan proceeds provided by the seller or obtained through loans arranged by the seller or with respect to which the seller and lender share one of the other relationships described by Section 3.405.

5. A seller subject to this Part may also be subject to the FTC Regulation on Cooling Off Period for Door-to-Door Sales. In the event of direct inconsistency between that Regulation and this Act, that Regulation prevails. Subsection (2) of Section 3.503 provides that the seller complies with this Act if he uses the notice of cancellation prescribed by that Regulation. With regard to other areas in which FTC Regulation overlaps with this Act, the Administrator by rule (Section 6.104(1)(e)) may prescribe the compliance required by the seller under this Act in relation to that Regulation.

Section 3.502 [Buyer's Right to Cancel]

(1) Except as provided in subsection (5), in addition to any right otherwise to revoke an offer, the buyer may cancel a home solicitation sale until midnight of the third business day after the day on which the buyer signs an agreement or offer to purchase which complies with this Part.

(2) Cancellation occurs when the buyer gives written notice of cancellation to the seller at the address stated in the agreement or offer to purchase.

(3) Notice of cancellation, if given by mail, is given when it is properly addressed with postage prepaid and deposited in a mailbox.

(4) Notice of cancellation given by the buyer need not take a particular form and is sufficient if it indicates by any form of written expression the intention of the buyer not to be bound by the home solicitation sale.

(5) The buyer may not cancel a home solicitation sale if, by a separate dated and signed statement that is not as to its material provisions a printed form and describes an emergency requiring immediate remedy, the buyer requests the seller to provide goods or services without delay in order to safeguard the health, safety, or welfare of natural persons or to prevent damage to property the buyer owns or for which he is responsible, and

(a) the seller in good faith makes a substantial beginning of performance of the contract before the buyer gives notice of cancellation, and

(b) in the case of goods, they cannot be returned to the seller in substantially as good condition as when received by the buyer.

COMMENT

1. The buyer has a right to cancel a home solicitation sale pursuant to this section. The notice of cancellation must be in writing, given to the seller at the address stated in the agreement signed by the buyer, and given prior to midnight of the third busines day after the day the buyer signs an agreement or offer to purchase which complies with Section 3.503. These are the only formal requirements of the Act with respect to the buyer's cancellation.

2. Although the Act does not require that a notice of cancellation be mailed it is assumed that this will be the normal method of cancellation. Notice of cancellation is given at the time of mailing. The risk of non-receipt of a mailed notice of cancellation is placed on the seller, but the buyer has the burden of proving that the notice was properly mailed.

3. Goods and services are frequently sold on credit to a buyer at his home because of an emergency. Common examples are emergency repairs to broken water pipes, furnaces, appliances and the like. Since such transactions may come within the definition of home solicitation sales, sellers may be reluctant to perform services or deliver goods before expiration of the 3-day cancellation period. Application of the right of cancellation to emergency situations would have the undesirable effect of seriously deterring credit sellers from performing in time to deal with emergencies. Subsection (5) therefore provides that the buyer may not cancel a sale if the stated conditions are met. A portion of subsection (5) is derived from Regulation Z Section 226.9(e).

4. The right to cancel provided by Section 3.502 is not ex-

clusive. It in no way affects the right that the buyer may have independent of the Act to revoke an offer to purchase which has not been accepted by the seller, or to rescind because of fraud, duress, breach of warranty, or other causes, or under the Federal Truth in Lending Act.

Section 3.503 [Form of Agreement or Offer; Statement of Buyer's Rights]

(1) In a home solicitation sale, unless the buyer requests the seller to provide goods or services without delay in an emergency (subsection (5) of Section 3.502), the seller shall present to the buyer and obtain his signature to a written agreement or offer to purchase that designates as the date of the transaction the date on which the buyer actually signs and contains a statement of the buyer's rights that complies with subsection (2). A copy of any writing required by this subsection to be signed by the buyer, completed at least as to the date of the transaction and the name and mailing address of the seller, shall be given to the buyer at the time he signs the writing.

(2) The statement shall either:

(a) comply with any notice of cancellation or similar requirement of any trade regulation rule of the Federal Trade Commission which by its terms applies to the home solicitation sale; or

(b) appear under the conspicuous caption: "BUYER'S RIGHT TO CANCEL," and read as follows: "If you decide you do not want the goods or services, you may cancel this agreement by mailing a notice to the seller. The notice must say that you do not want the goods or services and must be mailed before midnight of the third business day after you sign this agreement. The notice must be mailed to: ______________________________."

(insert name & mailing address of seller)

(3) Until the seller has complied with this section the buyer may cancel the home solicitation sale by notifying the seller in any manner and by any means of his intention to cancel.

COMMENT

The 3-day period for cancellation does not begin to run until the buyer signs a written agreement or offer to purchase complying with this section. To comply, the agreement or offer must contain the date on which the buyer actually signs it and the caption and completed statement required by subsection (2). A notice of cancellation complying with the Federal Trade Commission Rule on "door-to-door sales" complies with this section.

Section 3.504 [Restoration of Down Payment]

(1) Within ten days after a notice of cancellation has been received by the seller or an offer to purchase has been otherwise revoked, the seller shall tender to the buyer any payments made by the buyer, any note or other evidence of indebtedness, and any goods traded in. A provision permitting the seller to keep all or any part of any goods traded in, payment, note, or evidence of indebtedness is in violation of this section and unenforceable.

(2) If the down payment includes goods traded in, the goods shall be tendered in substantially as good condition as when received by the seller. If the seller fails to tender the goods as provided by this section, the buyer may elect to recover an amount equal to the trade-in allowance stated in the agreement.

(3) Until the seller has complied with the obligations imposed by this section the buyer may retain possession of goods delivered to him by the seller and has a lien on the goods in his possession or control for any recovery to which he is entitled.

COMMENT

1. The 10-day period during which the seller must tender to the buyer any payments, any evidence of indebtedness, and any goods traded in runs from the time the notice of cancellation has been received by the seller.

2. If the seller took a trade-in as part of a home solicitation sale which has been cancelled he must tender the goods traded in. The risk of loss or damage to the goods rests with the seller. If he cannot tender the goods in substantially as good condition as when received, the buyer may elect to take in cash the trade-in allowance fixed by the parties in the contract. This provision is designed to protect the buyer where goods traded in have not been tendered or have been damaged. In such case he is given an election to sue either for return of the goods or for the trade-in allowance.

3. As a means of assuring compliance by the seller, subsection (3) provides that the buyer may retain possession of any goods delivered to him by the seller with respect to a sale cancelled under Section 3.502 until the seller complies with his obligations under this section. While in possession of the goods the buyer has a lien as security for his claim against the seller.

Section 3.505 [Duty of Buyer; No Compensation for Services Before Cancellation]

(1) Except as provided by the provisions on retention of goods by the buyer (subsection (3) of Section 3.504), and allowing for ordinary wear and tear or consumption of the goods contemplated by the transaction, within a reasonable time after a home solicitation sale has been cancelled or an offer to purchase revoked, the buyer upon demand shall tender to the seller any goods delivered by the seller pursuant to the sale, but he is not obligated to tender at any place other than his residence. If the seller fails to demand possession of goods within a reasonable time after cancellation or revocation, the goods become the property of the buyer without obligation to pay for them. For the purpose of this section, a reasonable time is presumed to be 40 days.

(2) The buyer shall take reasonable care of the goods in his possession before cancellation or revocation and for a reasonable time thereafter, during which time the goods are otherwise at the seller's risk.

(3) If a home solicitation sale is cancelled, the seller is not entitled to compensation for any services he performed pursuant to it.

COMMENT

1. Subsections (1) and (2) state the obligations of the buyer in the case of a cancelled home solicitation sale. To protect the buyer from the seller who may seek to impose an obligation on the buyer by unreasonable delays in demanding delivery of the goods the seller must demand possession within a reasonable time and 40 days is presumed to be a reasonable time. Goods not demanded within a reasonable time become the property of the buyer without obligation to pay for them.

2. To protect the seller the section imposes on the buyer a duty to take reasonable care of the goods while they are in his possession. Except for this duty of care, under subsection (2) the goods delivered under a home solicitation sale are at the seller's risk both prior to and after cancellation by the buyer; a buyer may cancel a sale after destruction of the goods without his fault if the destruction occurred during the cancellation period.

3. With respect to home solicitation sales involving the sale of services it is not possible to restore the parties to their original positions if services have been performed prior to cancellation. Subsection (3) discourages a seller from performing any services during the cancellation period by requiring him to act entirely at his own risk. He is entitled to no compensation for any services performed during this period if the contract is cancelled.

ARTICLE 4

INSURANCE

PART 1

INSURANCE IN GENERAL

Section 4.101 [Short Title]

This Article shall be known and may be cited as Uniform Consumer Credit Code—Insurance.

COMMENT

The provisions of this Article are derived in large part from Article 4 of the U3C 1968 Text. However, a number of changes both in style and in substance have been made. The style changes are not intended to change the meaning of the provisions in which they appear.

Section 4.102 [Scope [; Relation to Credit Insurance Act; Applicability to Parties]]

[(1)] This Article applies to insurance provided or to be provided in relation to a consumer credit transaction.

[(2) This Article supplements and does not repeal the Credit Insurance Act but to the extent of inconsistency between this Act and the Credit Insurance Act this Act controls. The provisions of this Act concerning administrative controls, liabilities, and penalties do not apply to persons acting as insurers, and the similar provisions of the Credit Insurance Act do not apply to creditors and debtors.]

COMMENT

1. A number of provisions of this Article are derived from the NAIC Model Act, prepared by the National Association of Insurance Commissioners, "to provide for the regulation of credit life insurance and credit accident and health insurance." In jurisdictions where the NAIC Model Act has been adopted there are many local variations in the text; and in some states where it has not been adopted parallel provisions appear in its insurance law or in

insurance department regulations issued under enabling legislation. In view of these diversities this Act does not refer to the NAIC Model Act as such, but reference is made to any local version of it by the expression "Credit Insurance Act." Section 4.103(2).

The scope of this Article is broader than that of the NAIC Model Act.

2. If the enacting State has enacted the NAIC Model Act or a similar statute, complete Section 4.102 as follows:

a. Remove brackets after "Scope" and before period in section heading of Section 4.102; and

b. Remove brackets before and after "(1)" and subsection (2) of Section 4.102.

3. If the enacting State has not enacted the NAIC Model Act or a similar statute, complete Section 4.102 as follows:

a. Revise section heading to read

Section 4.102 [Scope]

b. Delete "[(1)]" in line 3; and

c. Delete all of subsection (2).

Section 4.103 [Definition[s]: "Consumer Credit Insurance" [; "Credit Insurance Act"]]

In this Act:

[(1)] "Consumer credit insurance" means insurance, except insurance on property, by which the satisfaction of debt in whole or in part is a benefit provided, but does not include

(a) insurance provided in relation to a consumer credit transaction in which a payment is scheduled more than ten years after the extension of credit;

(b) insurance issued by an insurer as an isolated transaction not related to an agreement or plan for insuring consumers of or from the creditor; or

(c) insurance indemnifying the creditor against loss due to the consumer's default.

[(2) "Credit Insurance Act" means [NAIC Model Act, or any similar statute].]

COMMENT

1. The usual forms of consumer credit insurance provide benefits conditioned on the death or disability of the consumer, the contracts being described as credit life insurance and credit accident and health insurance. The insured event might also be loss of earnings in other ways, as by loss of employment. A type of insurance not embraced in the term "consumer credit insurance"

is that procured by a creditor to guard against the uncollectibility of his accounts. Insurance of this type, although historically and properly called "credit insurance," is conditioned on the non-payment of debt, and does not serve any interest of consumers of the insured person. This is true also of insurance indemnifying the creditor against loss due to non-filing of instruments. By contrast, the benefit of consumer credit insurance runs to consumers as well as creditors; any payment made to the creditor by the insurer under the policy satisfies the consumer's obligation to the extent of the payment.

2. The definition of "consumer credit insurance" excludes insurance related to long-term credit, following a similar but broader exclusion from the scope of the NAIC Model Act.

3. Exceptionally, there are occasions when credit life insurance or the like is appropriate but cannot be provided under a general arrangement for insuring consumers of the creditor. On these occasions the consumer may be expected to bargain actively about the insurance feature of the credit transaction. Therefore insurance issued as an isolated transaction is excluded from the definition of consumer credit insurance. It is also excluded from the scope of the NAIC Model Act.

4. If the enacting State has enacted the NAIC Model Act or a similar statute, complete Section 4.103 as follows:

a. Remove inner brackets in section heading of Section 4.103;

b. Remove brackets before and after "(1)" in line 4 of Section 4.103;

c. Remove brackets before and after subsection (2) of Section 4.103; and

d. Describe in subsection (2) the NAIC Model Act, or any similar statute.

5. If the enacting State has not enacted the NAIC Model Act or a similar statute, complete Section 4.103 as follows:

a. Revise section heading to read

   Section 4.103 [*Definition: "Consumer Credit Insurance"*];

b. Delete "[(1)]" in line 4 of Section 4.103; and

c. Delete all of subsection (2) of Section 4.103.

Section 4.104 [Creditor's Provision of and Charge for Insurance; Excess Amount of Charge]

(1) Except as otherwise provided in this Article and subject to the provisions on additional charges (Section 2.501) and maximum finance charges (Parts 2 and 4 of Article 2), a creditor may agree to provide insurance, and may contract for and receive a charge for insurance separate from and in addition to other charges. A creditor need not make a separate charge for insurance provided or required by him. This Act does not au-

thorize the issuance of the insurance prohibited under any statute, or rule thereunder, governing the business of insurance.

(2) The excess amount of a charge for insurance provided for in agreements in violation of this Article is an excess charge for purposes of the provisions of the Article on Remedies and Penalties (Article 5) as to effect of violations on rights of parties (Section 5.201) and of the provisions of the Article on Administration (Article 6) as to civil actions by the Administrator (Section 6.113).

COMMENT

1. Subsection (1) broadly authorizes creditors to contract for and receive payments for providing insurance in the whole range of transactions within the scope of this Article. Section 4.102. A creditor may provide insurance without making a separate charge in addition to the finance charge. If, however, the creditor requires insurance in connection with a consumer credit sale or consumer loan, the fact that he includes the cost of providing it in the finance charge, giving the insurance "free," will not necessarily exclude him from restrictions under the other insurance laws or this Article.

Limitations are placed on the making of an additional or separate charge for insurance in Section 2.501, and the authorization of this section is subject to those provisions. In addition, such a charge must be limited as provided in this Article. Section 4.107.

2. This Act does not purport to define "separate charge" for insurance. The question has been raised whether there is a separate charge for insurance when a creditor's finance charge varies depending upon whether or not consumer credit insurance is provided. This Act does not resolve that question.

Section 4.105 [Conditions Applying to Insurance to be Provided by Creditor]

If a creditor agrees with a consumer to provide insurance:

(1) the insurance shall be evidenced by an individual policy or certificate of insurance delivered to the consumer, or mailed to him at his address as stated by him, within 30 days after the term of the insurance commences under the agreement between the creditor and consumer, or the creditor shall promptly notify the consumer of any failure or delay in providing the insurance; and

(2) the creditor shall pay to the consumer or his estate all proceeds of consumer credit or property insurance received by the creditor in excess of the amount to which the creditor is entitled within ten days after receipt by the creditor of the proceeds.

Section 4.106 [Unconscionability]

(1) In applying the provisions of this Act on unconscionability (Sections 5.108 and 6.111) to a separate charge for insurance, consideration shall be given, among other factors, to:

(a) potential benefits to the consumer including the satisfaction of his obligations;

(b) the creditor's need for the protection provided by the insurance; and

(c) the relation between the amount and terms of credit granted and the insurance benefits provided.

(2) If consumer credit insurance otherwise complies with this Article and other applicable law, neither the amount nor the term of the insurance nor the amount of a charge therefor is in itself unconscionable.

COMMENT

It may be shown that an agreement about insurance, like other terms of a consumer credit contract, is unconscionable, and the effects are those specified in Sections 5.108 and 6.111. However, it is the intent of this section that the issue be judged in relation to the particular risks insured. The section lists only some of the factors to be considered, and indicates that a balancing of benefits, needs, and costs is required. In general, the creditor's need for insurance protection and the consumer's potential benefit are more patent in connection with extensions of credit that are substantial as to amounts and periods; the expense of providing exceptional coverage is suspect in relation to relatively small extensions of credit. The relation between the credit terms and the insurance terms must be taken into account in applying this section.

Section 4.107 [Maximum Charge by Creditor for Insurance]

(1) Except as provided in subsection (2), if a creditor contracts for or receives a separate charge for insurance, the amount charged to the consumer for the insurance may not exceed the premium to be charged by the insurer, as computed at the time the charge to the consumer is determined, conforming to any rate filings required by law and made by the insurer with the [Commissioner] of Insurance.

(2) A creditor who provides consumer credit insurance in relation to open-end credit may calculate the charge to the consumer in each billing cycle by applying the current premium rate to the balance in the manner permitted with respect to fi-

nance charges by the provisions on finance charge for consumer credit sales pursuant to open-end credit (Section 2.202).

COMMENT

Subsection (1) generally limits the creditor's charge to the consumer for insurance to the premiums to be charged by the insurer. Subsection (2), applying to both open-end sales and loan credit, authorizes convenient methods of calculating charges that might not be permitted if subsection (1) were applied inflexibly.

Section 4.108 [Refund Required; Amount]

(1) Upon prepayment in full of a consumer credit transaction other than a consumer lease by the proceeds of consumer credit insurance, the consumer or his estate is entitled to a refund of any portion of a separate charge for insurance which by reason of prepayment is retained by the creditor or returned to him by the insurer, unless the charge was computed from time to time on the basis of the balances of the consumer's account.

(2) This Article does not require a creditor to grant a refund to the consumer if all refunds due to him under this Article amount to less than $1 and, except as provided in subsection (1), does not require the creditor to account to the consumer for any portion of a separate charge for insurance because:

(a) the insurance is terminated by performance of the insurer's obligation;

(b) the creditor pays or accounts for premiums to the insurer in amounts and at times determined by the agreement between them; or

(c) the creditor receives directly or indirectly under any policy of insurance a gain or advantage not prohibited by law.

(3) Except as provided in subsection (2), the creditor shall promptly make or cause to be made an appropriate refund to the consumer with respect to any separate charge made to him for insurance if:

(a) the insurance is not provided or is provided for a shorter term than that for which the charge to the consumer for insurance was computed; or

(b) the insurance terminates before the end of the term for which it was written because of prepayment in full or otherwise.

(4) A refund required by subsection (3) is appropriate as to amount if it is computed according to a method prescribed or approved by the [Commissioner] of Insurance or a formula filed by the insurer with the [Commissioner] of Insurance at least 30 days before the consumer's right to a refund becomes determinable, unless the method or formula is employed after the [Commissioner] of Insurance notifies the insurer that he disapproves it.

COMMENT

1. Subsection (1) concerns a premium for consumer credit insurance, or any part of it, that is not treated by the insurer as earned, even though the insurer has paid benefits for which the premium charge was made. If the premium was the subject of a separate charge to the consumer, a refund must be made. Making the refund is not practicable, however, and is not required, if the charge has been computed on the consumer's outstanding balances. Subsection (2)(a) recognizes that the insurer may, upon performance of its obligation, properly treat the premium as earned.

2. Subsection (2)(c) permits a creditor to derive from consumer credit insurance gains and advantages not prohibited by law such as dividends and refunds resulting from favorable mortality or morbidity experience with respect to insured consumers, and is predicated on the following conclusions: (1) although the gains and advantages may be large to the creditor, they are relatively insignificant to each insured consumer and the calculating, clerical, and mailing costs of returning them to insured consumers would be unreasonably disproportionate to the amounts involved, and (2) the requirement of Article 4 that premiums for consumer credit insurance be reasonable in relation to benefits (Section 4.-203), if properly enforced by the State Insurance [Commissioner], will preclude the possibility of the use of consumer credit insurance as a device by creditors for concealing hidden charges from consumers.

3. Subsection (4) commits to the State Insurance [Commissioner] the responsibility for approval of methods and formulas for computing refunds that are required by the circumstances stated in subsection (3).

4. A consumer is entitled to a refund rather than a credit in the event of a required rebate of any separate charge for insurance. This precludes a creditor from holding a rebate until the contract is sufficiently paid down to have it constitute a prepayment in full which, particularly in long term contracts such as to finance a mobile home, gives the creditor free use of the consumer's money for a substantial period of time.

Section 4.109 [Existing Insurance; Choice of Insurer]

If a creditor requires insurance, upon notice to him the consumer has the option of providing the required insurance through an existing policy of insurance owned or controlled by the consumer, or through a policy to be obtained and paid for by the consumer, but the creditor for reasonable cause may decline the insurance provided by the consumer.

COMMENT

This section is directed against the practice of "tying" the grant of credit to the purchase of insurance from a particular insurer, through a particular agent, or the like, a practice prohibited by many existing statutes including the NAIC Model Act.

Section 4.110 [Charge for Insurance in Connection with a Deferral, Refinancing, or Consolidation; Duplicate Charges]

(1) A creditor may not contract for or receive a separate charge for insurance in connection with a deferral (Section 2.503), a refinancing (Section 2.504), or a consolidation (Section 2.505), unless:

(a) the consumer agrees at or before the time of the deferral, refinancing, or consolidation that the charge may be made;

(b) the consumer is or is to be provided with insurance for an amount or a term, or insurance of a kind, in addition to that to which he would have been entitled had there been no deferral, refinancing, or consolidation;

(c) the consumer receives a refund or credit on account of any unexpired term of existing insurance in the amount required if the insurance were terminated (Section 4.108); and

(d) the charge does not exceed the amount permitted by this Article (Section 4.107).

(2) A creditor may not contract for or receive a separate charge for insurance which duplicates insurance with respect to which the creditor has previously contracted for or received a separate charge.

COMMENT

A separate charge for insurance in connection with a deferral, a refinancing, or a consolidation, is permitted only if it has been agreed to by the consumer and bears an appropriate relation to the premium. Section 4.107. No new charge may be made for a coverage to which the consumer is already entitled. Actual termination of existing insurance is not required. Subsection (1)(b) recognizes that augmenting existing insurance coverage for a new separate charge is appropriate, but that "pyramiding" charges is not. Subsection (2) explicitly prohibits pyramiding.

Section 4.111 [Cooperation Between Administrator and [Commissioner] of Insurance]

The Administrator and the [Commissioner] of Insurance shall consult and assist one another in maintaining compliance with this Article. They may jointly pursue investigations, prosecute suits, and take other official action they deem appropriate if either of them is otherwise empowered to take the action. If the Administrator is informed of a violation or suspected violation by an insurer of this Article, or of the insurance laws, rules, and regulations of this State, he shall inform the [Commissioner] of Insurance of the circumstances.

COMMENT

Coordination of activities of creditors and insurers is essential to the provision of insurance related to consumer credit transactions. Accordingly, the public interest requires that the officials charged with supervising credit practices and those concerned with related insurance practices coordinate their efforts. This section encourages and empowers them to consult and work together in promoting compliance with this Article with efficiency and economy.

Section 4.112 [Administrative Action of [Commissioner] of Insurance]

[(1) To the extent that his responsibility under this Article requires, the [Commissioner] of Insurance shall adopt rules with respect to insurers, and with respect to refunds (Section 4.-108), forms, schedules of premium rates and charges (Section 4.203), and his approval or disapproval thereof and, in case of violation, may make an order for compliance.

(2)] [The State administrative procedure act] [Each provision of the Part on Administrative Procedure and Judicial Review (Part 4) of the Article on Administration (Article 6) that applies to and governs administrative action taken by the Administrator also] applies to and governs all administrative action taken by the [Commissioner] of Insurance pursuant to this section.

COMMENT

1. Subsection (1) may be omitted in an enacting State in which the NAIC Model Act or a statute giving the [Commissioner] of Insurance the powers and duties provided for in subsection (1) is in force. If subsection (1) is omitted "(2)" at the beginning of subsection (2) should also be omitted.

2. If the enacting State has an adequate State administrative procedure act applying to and governing administrative action taken by the [Commissioner] of Insurance, reference should be made to it in subsection (2), otherwise Part 4 of Article 6 [Section 6.401 et seq.] should be enacted and referred to in subsection (2). The bracketed language in subsection (2) should be retained or deleted dependent upon which course is followed. See Comment to Section 6.401.

PART 2

CONSUMER CREDIT INSURANCE

Section 4.201 [Term of Insurance]

(1) Consumer credit insurance provided by a creditor may be subject to the furnishing of evidence of insurability satisfactory to the insurer. Whether or not the evidence is required, the term of the insurance shall commence no later than when the consumer becomes obligated to the creditor or when the consumer applies for the insurance, whichever is later, except as follows:

(a) if any required evidence of insurability is not furnished until more than 30 days after the term otherwise would commence, the term may commence on the date the insurer determines the evidence to be satisfactory; or

(b) if the creditor provides insurance not previously provided covering debts previously created, the term may commence on the effective date of the policy.

(2) The originally scheduled term of consumer credit insurance shall extend at least until the due date of the last scheduled payment of the debt, except as follows:

(a) if the insurance relates to an open-end credit account, the term need extend only until payment of the debt under the account and may be sooner terminated after at least 30 days' notice to the consumer; or

(b) if the consumer is informed in writing that the insurance will be written for a specified shorter time, the term need extend only until the end of the specified time.

(3) The term of consumer credit insurance may not extend more than 15 days after the originally scheduled due date of the last scheduled payment of the debt, unless it is extended without additional cost to the consumer or as an incident to a deferral, refinancing, or consolidation.

COMMENT

1. Normally, the term of consumer credit insurance provided by a creditor should be the same as the term of the debt.

2. Subsection (1) permits postponement of the effective date of consumer credit insurance coverage until after the debt is incurred:

(1) under the preamble to subsection (1), when the consumer delays his application for the

insurance—coverage does not become effective at least until the consumer applies for the insurance,

(2) under subsection (1)(a), when the insurer requires the consumer to furnish evidence of insurability satisfactory to the insurer and the consumer does not furnish the evidence "until more than 30 days after the term otherwise would commence"—coverage does not become effective until the insurer determines the evidence of insurability to be satisfactory;

(3) under subsection (1)(b), when the creditor newly provides insurance with respect to debt previously created—coverage does not become effective at least until the effective date of the policy.

3. However, under subsection (1), if evidence of insurability satisfactory to the insurer is required, and is furnished within "30 days after the term otherwise would commence," coverage becomes effective when the term of the insurance otherwise would commence, e. g., the life of a consumer who less than 30 days after becoming obligated to a creditor furnishes evidence of insurability satisfactory to the insurer under a group policy insuring the lives of the creditor's consumers furnishing such evidence and who then dies is insured under the policy.

4. Subsection (2) specifies the circumstances when the term of consumer credit insurance need not extend to the due date of the last scheduled instalment of the debt.

5. Subsection (3) limits, subject to stated exceptions, the term of consumer credit insurance to 15 days after the scheduled due date of the last instalment of the debt.

Section 4.202 [Amount of Insurance]

(1) Except as provided in subsection (2):

(a) in the case of consumer credit insurance providing life coverage, the amount of insurance may not initially exceed the debt and, if the debt is payable in instalments, may not exceed at any time the greater of the scheduled or actual amount of the debt; or

(b) in the case of any other consumer credit insurance, the total amount of periodic benefits payable may not exceed the total of scheduled unpaid instalments of the debt, and the amount of any periodic benefit may not exceed the original amount of debt divided by the number of periodic instalments in which it is payable.

(2) If consumer credit insurance is provided in connection with an open-end credit account, the amounts payable as insurance benefits may be reasonably commensurate with the amount

of debt as it exists from time to time. If consumer credit insurance is provided in connection with a commitment to grant credit in the future, the amounts payable as insurance benefits may be reasonably commensurate with the total from time to time of the amount of debt and the amount of the commitment. If the debt or the commitment is primarily for an agricultural purpose and there is no regular schedule of payments, the amounts payable as insurance benefits may equal the total of the initial amount of debt and the amount of the commitment.

COMMENT

1. Subsection (1) provides generally applicable limitations on the amounts of consumer credit insurance and benefits.

2. Subsection (2) provides necessarily more flexible limitations on the amounts of consumer credit insurance benefits in connection with open-end credit accounts, credit commitments, and debt and credit commitments for an agricultural purpose.

3. Experience has demonstrated that limitations of these kinds are essential to the effectiveness of the requirement of Section 4.-203(2) that premium rates be not unreasonable in relation to the benefits provided by consumer credit insurance.

Section 4.203 [Filing and Approval of Rates and Forms]

(1) A creditor may not use a form or a schedule of premium rates or charges, the filing of which is required by this section, if the [Commissioner] of Insurance has disapproved the form or schedule and has notified the insurer of his disapproval. A creditor may not use a form or schedule unless:

(a) the form or schedule has been on file with the [Commissioner] of Insurance for 30 days, or has earlier been approved by him; and

(b) the insurer has complied with this section with respect to the insurance.

(2) Except as provided in subsection (3), all policies, certificates of insurance, notices of proposed insurance, applications for insurance, endorsements, and riders relating to consumer credit insurance delivered or issued for delivery in this State, and the schedules of premium rates or charges pertaining thereto, shall be filed by the insurer with the [Commissioner] of Insurance. Within 30 days after the filing of any form or schedule, he shall disapprove it if the premium rates or charges are unreasonable in relation to the benefits provided under the form, or if the form contains provisions which are unjust, unfair, ineq-

uitable, or deceptive, encourage misrepresentation of the coverage, or are contrary to any provision of the [Insurance Code] or of any rule or regulation promulgated thereunder.

(3) If a group policy of consumer credit insurance has been delivered in another state, the forms to be filed by the insurer with the [Commissioner] of Insurance are the group certificates and notices of proposed insurance. He shall approve them if:

(a) they provide the information that would be required if the group policy were delivered in this State; and

(b) the applicable premium rates or charges do not exceed those established by his rules or regulations.

COMMENT

1. Subsections (1) and (2) reaffirm and broaden the powers of the [Commissioner] of Insurance under the NAIC Model Act as to forms and schedules of premium rates or charges relating to consumer credit insurance. Unlike the NAIC Model Act which is directed primarily to insurers, this section is directed to both creditors and insurers. Moreover, in its formulation as to the relationship of premium rates and charges to the benefits provided, subsection (2) follows New York Insurance Law Section 154.7. That provision, as construed by the New York Court of Appeals in Old Republic Life Insurance Company v. Wikler, 9 N.Y.2d 524, 215 N.Y.S.2d 481, 175 N.E.2d 147 (1961), gives the New York Superintendent of Insurance ample power as to premium rates for credit life and accident and health insurance. Doubt, whether reasonable or not, has been expressed whether equivalent power is conferred by the corresponding formulation of Section 7B of the NAIC Model Act.

2. Subsection (3) facilitates insuring, as a group, the consumers of a creditor operating across state lines.

PART 3

PROPERTY AND LIABILITY INSURANCE

Section 4.301 [Property Insurance]

(1) A creditor may not contract for or receive a separate charge for insurance against loss of or damage to property, unless:

(a) the insurance covers a substantial risk of loss of or damage to property related to the credit transaction;

(b) the amount, terms, and conditions of the insurance are reasonable in relation to the character and value of the property insured or to be insured; and

(c) the term of the insurance is reasonable in relation to the terms of credit.

(2) The term of the insurance is reasonable if it is customary and does not extend substantially beyond a scheduled maturity.

(3) With respect to a transaction, except pursuant to open-end credit, a creditor may not contract for or receive a separate charge for insurance against loss of or damage to property, unless the amount financed exclusive of charges for the insurance is $300 or more and the value of the property is $300 or more.

(4) With respect to a transaction pursuant to open-end credit, the Administrator may adopt rules consistent with the principles set out in subsections (1) and (2) prescribing whether, and the conditions under which, a creditor may contract for or receive a separate charge for insurance against loss of or damage to property.

(5) The amounts of $300 in subsection (3) are subject to change pursuant to the provisions on adjustment of dollar amounts (Section 1.106).

COMMENT

1. Subsection (1) imposes restrictions on property insurance similar to those provided by a number of retail instalment sales acts.

2. Subsection (2) permits reasonable flexibility so that the expiration of the term of property insurance need not coincide exactly with the scheduled maturity of the debt.

3. With respect to transactions other than pursuant to open-end credit, subsection (3) prohibits a separate charge for property insurance when either

the amount of debt or the value of the property to be insured is relatively small.

4. With respect to transactions pursuant to open-end credit, fixed restrictions are not uniformly workable, *e. g.*, in the case of loans pursuant to open-end credit the value of the collateral could be much greater than the balance of the account while in the case of sales pursuant to open-end credit the balance of the account could include debt owing for services or consumables and be much larger than the value of the property securing the debt. However, neither is it desirable to exclude such transactions from restriction. Subsection (4) permits the Administrator to adopt rules consistent with the basic protective provisions of subsections (1) and (2) that will allow insurance charges to be made in appropriate circumstances in open-end credit transactions.

Section 4.302 [Insurance on Creditor's Interest Only]

If a creditor contracts for or receives a separate charge for insurance against loss of or damage to property, the risk of loss or damage not willfully caused by the consumer is on the consumer only to the extent of any deficiency in the effective coverage of the insurance, even though the insurance covers only the interest of the creditor.

COMMENT

This section prohibits a separate charge to the consumer for property insurance covering the creditor's interest in property unless the consumer also receives the benefit of the insurance to the extent he does not willfully cause the loss or damage, risk of which is insured. "Single interest" property insurance for which the creditor makes a separate charge to the consumer may not provide for subrogation of the insurer to the rights of the creditor as to any loss or damage not willfully caused by the consumer. See also Section 2.501(2).

Section 4.303 [Liability Insurance]

A creditor may not contract for or receive a separate charge for insurance against liability unless the insurance covers a substantial risk of liability arising out of the ownership or use of property related to the credit transaction.

COMMENT

This section imposes restrictions with respect to liability insurance comparable to those imposed with respect to property insurance by subsection (1) of Section 4.301.

Section 4.304 [Cancellation by Creditor]

This section does not apply to an insurance premium loan. A creditor may request cancellation of a policy of property or liability insurance only after the consumer's default or in accordance with a written authorization by the consumer. In either case the cancellation does not take effect until written notice is delivered to the consumer or mailed to him at his address as stated by him. The notice shall state that the policy may be cancelled on a date not less than ten days after the notice is delivered, or, if the notice is mailed, not less than 13 days after it is mailed. A cancellation may not take effect until those times.

COMMENT

This section requires advance written notice, by either the creditor or the insurer, of the prospective cancellation of property or liability insurance provided in connection with a consumer credit transaction. It is not applicable to lenders engaged in insurance premium financing. See Sections 5.110 and 5.111.

ARTICLE 5

REMEDIES AND PENALTIES

PART 1

LIMITATIONS ON CREDITORS' REMEDIES

Section 5.101 [Short Title]

This Article shall be known and may be cited as Uniform Consumer Credit Code—Remedies and Penalties.

Section 5.102 [Scope]

This Part applies to actions or other proceedings to enforce rights arising from consumer credit transactions, to extortionate extensions of credit (Section 5.107), and to unconscionability (Section 5.108).

COMMENT

Section 1.201 states the territorial applicability of this Act. Section 1.109 provides for the applicability of this Act by written agreement.

Section 5.103 [Restrictions on Deficiency Judgments]

(1) This section applies to a deficiency on a consumer credit sale of goods or services and on a consumer loan in which the lender is subject to claims and defenses arising from sales and leases (Section 3.405). A consumer is not liable for a deficiency unless the creditor has disposed of the goods in good faith and in a commercially reasonable manner.

(2) If the seller repossesses or voluntarily accepts surrender of goods that were the subject of the sale and in which he has a security interest, the consumer is not personally liable to the seller for the unpaid balance of the debt arising from the sale of a commercial unit of goods of which the cash sale price was $1,750 or less, and the seller is not obligated to resell the collateral unless the consumer has paid 60 per cent or more of the cash price and has not signed after default a statement renouncing his rights in the collateral.

(3) If the seller repossesses or voluntarily accepts surrender of goods that were not the subject of the sale but in which he

has a security interest to secure a debt arising from a sale of goods or services or a combined sale of goods and services and the cash price of the sale was $1,750 or less, the consumer is not personally liable to the seller for the unpaid balance of the debt arising from the sale, and the seller's duty to dispose of the collateral is governed by the provisions on disposition of collateral (Part 5 of Article 9) of the Uniform Commercial Code.

(4) If the lender takes possession or voluntarily accepts surrender of goods in which he has a purchase money security interest to secure a debt arising from a consumer loan in which the lender is subject to claims and defenses arising from sales and leases (Section 3.405) and the net proceeds of the loan paid to or for the benefit of the consumer were $1,750 or less, the consumer is not personally liable to the lender for the unpaid balance of the debt arising from that loan and the lender's duty to dispose of the collateral is governed by the provisions on disposition of collateral (Part 5 of Article 9) of the Uniform Commercial Code.

(5) For the purpose of determining the unpaid balance of consolidated debts or debts pursuant to open-end credit, the allocation of payments to a debt shall be determined in the same manner as provided for determining the amount of debt secured by various security interests (Section 3.303).

(6) The consumer may be held liable in damages to the creditor if the consumer has wrongfully damaged the collateral or if, after default and demand, the consumer has wrongfully failed to make the collateral available to the creditor.

(7) If the creditor elects to bring an action against the consumer for a debt arising from a consumer credit sale of goods or services or from a consumer loan in which the lender is subject to claims and defenses arising from sales and leases (Section 3.-405), when under this section he would not be entitled to a deficiency judgment if he took possession of the collateral, and obtains judgment:

(a) he may not take possession of the collateral, and

(b) the collateral is not subject to levy or sale on execution or similar proceedings pursuant to the judgment.

(8) The amounts of $1,750 in subsections (2), (3) and (4) are subject to change pursuant to the provisions on adjustment of dollar amounts (Section 1.106).

COMMENT

1. Where there has been a default with respect to a secured consumer credit transaction, the rights of the creditor and consumer are controlled by Part 5 (Default) of UCC Article 9 [U.C.C. § 9–501 et seq.], except to the extent that such rights are changed by this Act. Under the UCC the creditor has the right to take possession of the collateral on default subject to applicable constitutional limitations (compare Fuentes v. Shevin, 407 U.S. 67, 32 L.Ed.2d 556 (1972) and Mitchell v. W. T. Grant Co., 94 S.Ct. 1895, 416 U.S. 600, 40 L.Ed. 2d 406 (1974) with Adams v. Egley, 338 F.Supp. 614 (S.D.Cal. 1972), rev'd sub nom. Adams v. Southern California First National Bank, 492 F.2d 324 (9th Cir. 1974)), and may proceed without judicial process. UCC Section 9–503. The creditor may sell, lease or otherwise dispose of the collateral in public or private proceedings, and may buy at his own sale. The consumer is entitled to reasonable notification of the time and place of any public sale and reasonable notification of the time after which the collateral will be disposed of privately. UCC Section 9–504(1) and (3). Proceeds are applied first to the expenses of repossession and disposition and then to satisfaction of the indebtedness. Any excess is paid to the consumer and the consumer is liable for any deficiency. UCC Section 9–504(1) and (2). If the consumer has paid 60 per cent of the cash price in the case of a sale or 60 per cent of the principal in the case of a loan, and has not signed after default a statement renouncing his rights, the creditor must dispose of the collateral. If the creditor fails to dispose of the collateral within 90 days after repossession the consumer may recover in conversion or alternatively under UCC Section 9–507(1). In all other cases the creditor may retain the collateral in satisfaction of the debt, if the consumer does not object after receipt of notification. UCC Section 9–505. The consumer has a right to redeem the collateral at any time before disposition of the collateral or satisfaction of the obligation, by tendering fulfillment of all obligations secured by the collateral as well as expenses of the creditor. UCC Section 9–506.

2. The provisions of the UCC outlined above are modified to some extent by this section with respect to proceedings to enforce rights arising from consumer credit sales and consumer loans in which the lender is subject to claims and defenses arising from sales and leases (Section 3.405). For both types of transactions, this section adopts the position of that line of cases under the UCC that directly or indirectly deny the creditor a deficiency if the creditor has not disposed of the collateral in good faith and in a commercially reasonable manner. See, *e. g.*, Atlas Thrift Co. v. Horan, 27 Cal.App.3d 999, 104 Cal.Rptr. 315 (Cal.Ct.App.3d Dist.1972).

3. With respect to a consumer credit sale of a commercial unit of goods of which the cash price is $1750 or less, a seller who repossesses or voluntarily accepts

surrender of the goods sold in which he has a security interest may not obtain a deficiency judgment against the consumer if the proceeds on disposition of the goods are insufficient to pay the indebtedness and the expenses of the seller. The seller need not resell the goods unless the consumer has paid 60 per cent or more of the cash price and has not signed after default a statement renouncing his rights in the collateral. In cases of sales of $1750 or less, this section gives to the seller the option of either suing for the unpaid balance or repossessing, but he may not do both. The amount of $1750 in all subsections of this section in which it appears is derived from the Report of the National Commission on Consumer Finance. The concept of "commercial unit" is borrowed from UCC Section 2–105(6) and is employed to preclude the argument that subsection (2) is inapplicable to a consumer credit sale of a stove, a refrigerator, a washer, a dryer and a TV set for a total cash price of more than $1750 when each of these "commercial units" does not separately cost more than $1750.

4. The seller may have a security interest in collateral other than goods sold in the consumer credit sale. The Act allows the seller to take a security interest in collateral other than goods sold in some sales of services, in consumer credit sales primarily for agricultural purposes, and in cross-collateral transactions in which a seller makes more than one sale to one consumer and takes a security interest in goods sold in one sale to secure debt arising from other sales. Sections 3.301 and 3.302. In these cases, if the cash price of the sale is $1750 or less, the seller who repossesses or voluntarily accepts surrender of collateral may not obtain a deficiency judgment against the consumer. The rights of the consumer with respect to compulsory disposition of collateral which was not the subject of the sale and recovery of any surplus on disposition are defined in UCC Sections 9–504 and 9–505.

5. If a lender makes a consumer loan in which the net proceeds paid to or for the benefit of the consumer are $1750 or less to enable the consumer to purchase goods under circumstances where the lender is subject to claims and defenses arising from the sale of the goods (Section 3.405) and pursuant to a security interest acquired in the goods repossesses or voluntarily accepts surrender of the goods, the lender may not obtain a deficiency judgment against the consumer if the proceeds on disposition of the goods are insufficient to pay the indebtedness and the expenses of the lender with respect to that loan. Subsection (4) is limited to the described type of transaction as only this type of transaction is an alternative to a consumer credit sale in which the seller in financing the purchase would be limited by this section. The rights of the consumer with respect to compulsory disposition of the collateral and recovery of any surplus on disposition are defined in UCC Sections 9–504 and 9–505.

6. Subsection (6) is designed to protect creditors against consumers who wrongfully damage collateral or who wrongfully refuse to surrender collateral. In addition to the right of the creditor to repossess the collateral, the subsection gives to the creditor a right of action for damages for the loss of value of the collateral resulting from wrongful injury to the goods or, in the case of wrongful refusal to surrender the collateral, for any loss suffered by the creditor because of his inability to repossess.

7. Subsection (7) prohibits a creditor not entitled to a deficiency judgment under this section from achieving substantially the same result by first obtaining judgment for the debt and then levying on the collateral on execution.

Section 5.104 [No Garnishment Before Judgment]

Before entry of judgment in an action against a consumer for debt arising from a consumer credit transaction, the creditor may not attach unpaid earnings of the consumer by garnishment or like proceedings.

COMMENT

This section, within the scope of this Act, carries out the mandate of the Supreme Court in the landmark decision of Sniadach v. Family Finance Corp., 89 S.Ct. 1820, 395 U.S. 337, 23 L.Ed.2d 349 (1969) and further adopts the recommendation of the Report of the National Commission on Consumer Finance that prejudgment garnishment, even of nonresident consumers, should be abolished.

Section 5.105 [Limitation on Garnishment]

(1) For purposes of this Part:

(a) "disposable earnings" means that part of the earnings of an individual remaining after the deduction from those earnings of amounts required by law to be withheld; and

(b) "garnishment" means any legal or equitable procedure through which earnings of an individual are required to be withheld for payment of a debt.

(2) The maximum part of the aggregate disposable earnings of an individual for any workweek which is subjected to garnishment to enforce payment of a judgment arising from a consumer credit transaction may not exceed the lesser of:

(a) 25 per cent of his disposable earnings for that week, or

(b) the amount by which his disposable earnings for that week exceed 40 times the Federal minimum hourly wage prescribed by Section 6(a)(1) of the Fair Labor Standards Act of 1938, U.S.C. tit. 29, § 206(a)(1), in effect at the time the earnings are payable.

In case of earnings for a pay period other than a week, the Administrator shall prescribe by rule a multiple of the Federal minimum hourly wage equivalent in effect to that set forth in paragraph (b).

(3) No court may make, execute, or enforce an order or process in violation of this section.

(4) At any time after entry of a judgment in favor of a creditor in an action against a consumer for debt arising from a consumer credit transaction, the consumer may file with the court his verified application for an order exempting from garnishment pursuant to that judgment, for an appropriate period of time, a greater portion or all of his aggregate disposable earnings for a workweek or other applicable pay period than is provided for in subsection (2). He shall designate in the application the portion of his earnings not exempt from garnishment under this section and other law, the period of time for which the additional exemption is sought, describe the judgment with respect to which the application is made, and state that the designated portion as well as his earnings that are exempt by law are necessary for the maintenance of him or a family supported wholly or partly by the earnings. Upon filing a sufficient application under this subsection, the court may issue any temporary order necessary under the circumstances to stay enforcement of the judgment by garnishment, shall set a hearing on the application not less than [five] nor more than [ten] days after the date of filing of the application, and shall cause notice of the application and the hearing date to be served on the judgment creditor or his attorney of record. At the hearing, if it appears to the court that all or any portion of the earnings sought to be additionally exempt are necessary for the maintenance of the consumer or a family supported wholly or partly by the earnings of the consumer for all or any part of the time requested in the application, the court shall issue an order granting the application to that extent; otherwise it shall deny the application. The order is subject to modification or vacation upon further application of any party to it upon a showing of changed circumstances after a hearing upon notice to all interested parties.

COMMENT

1. This section is derived from the CCPA (15 U.S.C. § 1601 et seq., specifically §§ 1672, 1673). The exemption has been increased from thirty times the minimum hourly wage to forty in the belief that the higher figure is justified in consumer credit transactions, a belief substantiated by the recommendation of the Report of the National Commission on Consumer Finance.

2. Section 5.104 prohibits all garnishment before judgment for collection of consumer debt. This section limits the use of garnishment after judgment for collection of consumer debt. It complements rather than displaces local garnishment laws and applies only to garnishment and like proceedings directed toward one other than the consumer, *e. g.*, an employer. The consumer's interests are adequately protected in proceedings supplementary to judgment in which the consumer is personally before the court and the court is therefore able to take his and his dependents' needs into consideration in granting an order against him for payment of a judgment on a consumer debt.

3. Subsection (2) is designed to assure the consumer that under normal circumstances he will retain enough of his earnings to be able to support himself and his dependents by exempting a portion of his earnings from garnishment to enforce judgments for consumer debts. The exemption is based on the concept of "disposable earnings" rather than gross earnings. Disposable earnings are defined to include only those earnings which the consumer can spend after deductions required by law. If the law requires a portion of the consumer's wages to be withheld from him, the consumer has no power of disposition with respect to that portion, and that portion is therefore not included in disposable wages. Thus, amounts required to be withheld for social security or income taxes, amounts withheld pursuant to compulsory retirement, health insurance or similar plans imposed by law and amounts withheld because of a garnishment or levy by another creditor are excluded from "disposable earnings." However, if amounts are withheld from the consumer's earnings by the employer pursuant to a request by the employee or pursuant to a contract made by the employee or on his behalf by a labor union or similar organization, the amounts withheld are included in "disposable earnings" since the deduction is not required by law.

4. Subsection (2) sets limits on the maximum amount of disposable earnings that a creditor in a consumer credit transaction may reach by garnishment. There is a double test. The creditor may not garnish more than (a) 25 per cent of disposable earnings for any workweek or (b) the amount by which disposable earnings exceed 40 times the Federal minimum hourly wage, whichever is less.

Example: Assume that the Federal minimum hourly wage is $2.00. An unmarried consumer who has no dependents and therefore claims one withholding exemption earns $3.10 an hour. Wages are paid for a weekly pay period. During that period the consumer worked 38 hours. His gross wages were $117.80. His employer withholds Federal income taxes of $16.60, social security taxes of $6.89, union dues of $1.25 pursuant to a contract with the union, and $5.00 for a Christmas savings plan of which the consumer is a member. Net wages paid to the employee are $88.06. "Disposable earnings" are $94.31; 25 per cent of disposable earnings is $23.57; 40 times the minimum hourly wage of $2.-00 is $80.00; the excess of disposable earnings over $80.00 is $14.31. Under subsection (2), the creditor may garnish no more than $14.31, the lesser of $23.57 and $14.31.

5. Under unusual circumstances such as illness, an abnormally large number of dependents, or similar conditions, some or all of the amount of disposable earnings subject to garnishment by subsection (2) may be necessary for the support of the consumer or his family for a brief or an extended period of time. Subsection (4) affords the consumer in that instance an opportunity to be heard and introduce evidence, and in the event undue hardship is proved to the satisfaction of the court, the amount of the garnishment may be reduced or the garnishment removed. In this respect, subsection (4) follows a recommendation of the Report of the National Commission on Consumer Finance.

6. This section is not meant to displace other provisions of state law which may provide additional protection to the consumer. For example, if state law exempts 90 per cent of earnings, only $11.78 or 10 per cent of earnings of $117.80 may be collected under the garnishment in the example above.

7. There is no private right of action for monetary relief vested by this Act in the consumer for violation of this section; enforcement is expected to come primarily through the restriction imposed on the court in subsection (3) and appropriate action by the Administrator (Article 6, Part 1). However, this should not be construed as precluding an individual consumer from obtaining appropriate injunctive or other non-monetary relief for violation of the section, or from obtaining monetary relief consistent with Section 1.103 against a creditor for wrongful seizure of exempt earnings. See, *e. g.*, Albrecht v. Treitschke, 17 Neb. 205, 22 N.W. 418 (1885).

Section 5.106 [No Discharge From Employment for Garnishment]

An employer may not discharge an employee for the reason that a creditor of the employee has subjected or attempted to subject unpaid earnings of the employee to garnishment or like proceedings directed to the employer for the purpose of paying a judgment arising from a consumer credit transaction.

COMMENT

1. The employee's remedy for violation of this section is found in Section 5.201(5).

2. This section is derived from the CCPA (15 U.S.C., § 1601 et seq., specifically § 1674), but it prohibits an employer from discharging an employee by reason of any garnishment (whether one or more) under a judgment arising from a consumer credit transaction.

Section 5.107 [Extortionate Extensions of Credit]

(1) If it is the understanding of the creditor and the consumer at the time an extension of credit is made that delay in making repayment or failure to make repayment could result in the use of violence or other criminal means to cause harm to the person, reputation, or property of any person, the repayment of the extension of credit is unenforceable through civil judicial processes against the consumer.

(2) If it is shown that an extension of credit was made at an annual rate exceeding 45 per cent calculated according to the actuarial method and that the creditor then had a reputation for the use or threat of use of violence or other criminal means to cause harm to the person, reputation, or property of any person to collect extensions of credit or to punish the non-repayment thereof, there is prima facie evidence that the extension of credit was unenforceable under subsection (1).

COMMENT

1. This section is derived from 18 U.S.C. § 892, as added by Title II of the CCPA.

2. This section is intended to facilitate federal prosecutions with respect to making extortionate extensions of credit by providing one of the elements required for a prima facie case under the CCPA provision referred to above, viz., that the repayment of the extension of credit would be unenforceable through civil judicial processes against the consumer.

Section 5.108 [Unconscionability; Inducement by Unconscionable Conduct; Unconscionable Debt Collection]

(1) With respect to a transaction that is, gives rise to, or leads the debtor to believe will give rise to, a consumer credit transaction, if the court as a matter of law finds:

(a) the agreement or transaction to have been unconscionable at the time it was made, or to have been induced by unconscionable conduct, the court may refuse to enforce the agreement; or

(b) any term or part of the agreement or transaction to have been unconscionable at the time it was made, the court may refuse to enforce the agreement, enforce the remainder of the agreement without the unconscionable term or part, or so limit the application of any unconscionable term or part as to avoid any unconscionable result.

(2) With respect to a consumer credit transaction, if the court as a matter of law finds that a person has engaged in, is engaging in, or is likely to engage in unconscionable conduct in collecting a debt arising from that transaction, the court may grant an injunction and award the consumer any actual damages he has sustained.

(3) If it is claimed or appears to the court that the agreement or transaction or any term or part thereof may be unconscionable, or that a person has engaged in, is engaging in, or is likely to engage in unconscionable conduct in collecting a debt, the parties shall be afforded a reasonable opportunity to present evidence as to the setting, purpose, and effect of the agreement or transaction or term or part thereof, or of the conduct, to aid the court in making the determination.

(4) In applying subsection (1), consideration shall be given to each of the following factors, among others, as applicable:

(a) belief by the seller, lessor, or lender at the time a transaction is entered into that there is no reasonable probability of payment in full of the obligation by the consumer or debtor;

(b) in the case of a consumer credit sale or consumer lease, knowledge by the seller or lessor at the time of the sale or lease of the inability of the consumer to receive substantial benefits from the property or services sold or leased;

(c) in the case of a consumer credit sale or consumer lease, gross disparity between the price of the property or services sold or leased and the value of the property or services measured by the price at which similar property or services are readily obtainable in credit transactions by like consumers;

(d) the fact that the creditor contracted for or received separate charges for insurance with respect to a consumer credit sale or consumer loan with the effect of making the sale or loan, considered as a whole, unconscionable; and

(e) the fact that the seller, lessor, or lender has knowingly taken advantage of the inability of the consumer or debtor reasonably to protect his interests by reason of physical or mental infirmities, ignorance, illiteracy, inability to understand the language of the agreement, or similar factors.

(5) In applying subsection (2), consideration shall be given to each of the following factors, among others, as applicable:

(a) using or threatening to use force, violence, or criminal prosecution against the consumer or members of his family;

(b) communicating with the consumer or a member of his family at frequent intervals or at unusual hours or under other circumstances so that it is a reasonable inference that the primary purpose of the communication was to harass the consumer;

(c) using fraudulent, deceptive, or misleading representations such as a communication which simulates legal process or which gives the appearance of being authorized, issued, or approved by a government, governmental agency, or attorney at law when it is not, or threatening or attempting to enforce a right with knowledge or reason to know that the right does not exist;

(d) causing or threatening to cause injury to the consumer's reputation or economic status by disclosing information affecting the consumer's reputation for credit-worthiness with knowledge or reason to know that the information is false; communicating with the consumer's employer before obtaining a final judgment against the consumer, except as permitted by statute or to verify the consumer's employment; disclosing to a person, with knowledge or reason to know that the person does not have a legitimate business need for the information, or in any way prohibited by statute, information affecting the consumer's credit or other reputation; or disclosing information concerning the existence of a debt known to be disputed by the consumer without disclosing that fact; and

(e) engaging in conduct with knowledge that like conduct has been restrained or enjoined by a court in a civil action by the Administrator against any person pursuant to the provisions on injunctions against fraudulent or unconscionable agreements or conduct (Section 6.111).

(6) If in an action in which unconscionability is claimed the court finds unconscionability pursuant to subsection (1) or (2), the court shall award reasonable fees to the attorney for the consumer or debtor. If the court does not find unconscionability and the consumer or debtor claiming unconscionability has brought or maintained an action he knew to be groundless, the court shall award reasonable fees to the attorney for the party against whom the claim is made. In determining attorney's fees, the amount of the recovery on behalf of the consumer is not controlling.

(7) The remedies of this section are in addition to remedies otherwise available for the same conduct under law other than this Act, but double recovery of actual damages may not be had.

(8) For the purpose of this section, a charge or practice expressly permitted by this Act is not in itself unconscionable.

COMMENT

1. Subsections (1) and (3) are derived in significant part from UCC Section 2–302. Subsection (1), as does UCC Section 2–302, provides that a court can refuse to enforce or can adjust an agreement or part of an agreement that was unconscionable on its face at the time it was made. However, many agreements are not in and of themselves unconscionable according to their terms, but they would never have been entered into by a consumer if unconscionable means had not been employed to induce the consumer to agree to the contract. It would be a frustration of the policy against unconscionable contracts for a creditor to be able to utilize unconscionable acts or practices to obtain an agreement. Consequently subsection (1) also gives to the court the power to refuse to enforce an agreement if it finds as a matter of law that it was induced by unconscionable conduct. Finally, subsection (1) includes provisions for court determination of unconscionability in a transaction that a consumer is led to believe will give rise to a consumer credit transaction so that, for example, a seller cannot bind the consumer to a short term sale contract payable in a lump sum on the assurance the seller will secure financing for the consumer, and then inform the consumer financing is unavailable and keep the downpayment or goods traded in as a penalty for non-payment.

In subsection (3) the omission of the adjective "commercial" found in UCC Section 2–302 from the provision concerning the presentation of evidence as to the conduct's or contract's "setting, purpose, and effect" is deliberate. Unlike the UCC, this section is concerned only with transactions involving consumers, and the relevant standard of conduct for purposes of this section is not that which might be acceptable as between knowledgeable merchants but rather that which measures acceptable conduct on the part of a businessman toward a consumer.

2. Subsection (2) provides a consumer remedy for unconscionable conduct in the collection of consumer credit debts. In recent years, there has been much legislative activity in this area. In subjecting this type of creditor conduct to the concept of unconscionability, this section provides a more flexible device for halting multifarious activities than the specific and somewhat rigid treatment contained in other legislation, and follows the lead of Section 6.111 of this Act which affords the Administrator the means to deal with this type of practice. Indeed this section considered as a whole confers on the consumer the ability to obtain relief in basically the same situations the Administrator is authorized to seek relief under Section 6.111, although not necessarily under the same conditions, *e. g.*, no course of conduct is required. The section is not exclusive, however; subsection (7) stipulates that the remedies of this section are in addition to remedies otherwise available for the same conduct under law other than this Act so as to preserve, for example, the developing remedy for abusive debt collection in tort.

3. This section is intended to make it possible for the courts to police conduct which is, and contracts or clauses which are found to be unconscionable. The basic test is whether, in the light of the background and setting of the market, the needs of the particular trade or case, and the condition of the particular parties to the conduct or contract, the conduct involved is, or the contract or clauses involved are so one-sided as to be unconscionable under the circumstances existing at the time the conduct occurs or is threatened or at the time of the making of the contract. The principle is one of the prevention of oppression and unfair surprise and not the disturbance of reasonable allocation of risks or reasonable advantage because of superior bargaining power or position. The particular facts involved in each case are of utmost importance since certain conduct, contracts or contractual provisions may be unconscionable in some situations but not in others. The following cases illustrate prior application of the doctrine of unconscionability: Williams v. Walker-Thomas Furn. Co., 350 F.2d 445, 121 U.S.App.D.C. 315 (1965); American Home Improvement, Inc. v. MacIver, 105 N.H. 435, 201 A.2d 886 (1964); Ellsworth Dobbs, Inc. v. Johnson, 50 N.J. 528, 236 A.2d 843 (1967); Unico v. Owen, 50 N.J. 101, 232 A.2d 405 (1967); Henningsen v. Bloomfield Motors, Inc., 32 N.J. 358, 161 A.2d 69 (1960); Frostifresh Corp. v. Reynoso, 54 Misc. 2d 119, 281 N.Y.S.2d 964 (Sup. Ct., App.Term, 2d Dept. 1967), rev'g in part 52 Misc.2d 26, 274 N.Y.S.2d 757 (Nassau Co. 1966).

4. Subsections (4) and (5) list a number of specific factors to be considered on the issue of unconscionability. It is impossible to anticipate all of the factors and considerations which may support a conclusion of uncon-

scionability in a given instance so the listing is not exclusive. The following are illustrative of individual transactions which would entitle a consumer to relief under this section:

Under subsection (4)(a), a sale of goods to a low income consumer without expectation of payment but with the expectation of repossessing the goods sold and reselling them at a profit;

Under subsection (4)(b), a sale to a Spanish speaking laborer-bachelor of an English language encyclopedia set, or the sale of two expensive vacuum cleaners to two poor families sharing the same apartment and one rug;

Under subsection (4)(c), a home solicitation sale of a set of cookware or flatware to a housewife for $375 in an area where a set of comparable quality is readily available on credit in stores for $125 or less;

Under subsection (4)(e), a sale of goods on terms known by the seller to be disadvantageous to the consumer where the written agreement is in English, the consumer is literate only in Spanish, the transaction was negotiated orally in Spanish by the seller's salesman, and the written agreement was neither translated nor explained to the consumer, but the mere fact a consumer has little education and cannot read or write and must sign with an "X" is not itself determinative of unconscionability;

Under subsection (5)(a) and (c), threatening that the creditor will have the consumer thrown in jail and her welfare checks stopped if the debt is not paid.

5. Since the remedies of this section are non-monetary in nature except for the ability to recover actual damages for unconscionable debt collection, subsection (6) authorizes an award of reasonable attorneys fees to the successful consumer or debtor. However, to discourage litigation seeking exculpation from merely bad bargains, provision is also made for recovery by a creditor if the court does not find unconscionability and the consumer's or debtor's action was known by the consumer or debtor to be groundless.

6. Subsection (8) prohibits a finding that a charge or practice expressly permitted by this Act is in itself unconscionable. However, even though a practice or charge is authorized by this Act, the totality of a particular creditor's conduct may show that the practice or charge is part of unconscionable conduct. Therefore, in determining unconscionability, the creditor's total conduct, including that part of his conduct which is in accordance with the provisions of this Act, may be considered.

Section 5.109 [Default]

An agreement of the parties to a consumer credit transaction with respect to default on the part of the consumer is enforceable only to the extent that:

(1) the consumer fails to make a payment as required by agreement; or

(2) the prospect of payment, performance, or realization of collateral is significantly impaired; the burden of establishing the prospect of significant impairment is on the creditor.

COMMENT

1. One of the vital terms of every consumer credit agreement is that which sets forth the criteria which will constitute default. By its nature it is not a term that is agreed to by the parties but rather one that is dictated by the creditor. It is appropriate, therefore, that its content and implications be confined by the law so as to prevent abuse. This section is intended to accomplish that.

2. The section recognizes that there are two entirely distinct sets of circumstances which might constitute default on an instalment obligation. First and most common is the failure to pay an instalment as required. A default of this type is susceptible of being cured by the consumer without impairing a continuing contractual relationship. See Section 5.110. A second type of default relates to behavior of the consumer which endangers the prospect of a continuing relationship. It may be insolvency, illegal activity, or an impending removal of assets from the jurisdiction. There must, however, be circumstances present which significantly impair the relationship. The burden of proof is on the creditor to justify his action on a claim of default of this type.

Section 5.110 [Notice of Consumer's Right to Cure]

(1) With respect to a consumer credit transaction, after a consumer has been in default for ten days for failure to make a required payment and has not voluntarily surrendered possession of goods that are collateral, a creditor may give the consumer the notice described in this section. A creditor gives notice to the consumer under this section when he delivers the notice to the consumer or mails the notice to him at his residence (subsection (6) of Section 1.201).

(2) Except as provided in subsection (3), the notice shall be in writing and conspicuously state: the name, address, and telephone number of the creditor to whom payment is to be made, a brief identification of the credit transaction, the consumer's

right to cure the default, and the amount of payment and date by which payment must be made to cure the default. A notice in substantially the following form complies with this subsection:

(name, address, and telephone number of creditor)

(account number, if any)

(brief identification of credit transaction)

(date) is the LAST DAY FOR PAYMENT

(amount) is the AMOUNT NOW DUE

You are late in making your payment(s). If you pay the AMOUNT NOW DUE (above) by the LAST DAY FOR PAYMENT (above), you may continue with the contract as though you were not late. If you do not pay by that date, we may exercise our rights under the law.

If you are late again in making your payments, we may exercise our rights without sending you another notice like this one. If you have questions, write or telephone the creditor promptly.

(3) If the consumer credit transaction is an insurance premium loan, the notice shall conform to the requirements of subsection (2) and a notice in substantially the form specified in that subsection complies with this subsection, except for the following:

(a) in lieu of a brief identification of the credit transaction, the notice shall identify the transaction as an insurance premium loan and each insurance policy or contract that may be cancelled;

(b) in lieu of the statement in the form of notice specified in subsection (2) that the creditor may exercise his rights under the law, the statement that each policy or contract identified in the notice may be cancelled; and

(c) the last paragraph of the form of notice specified in subsection (2) shall be omitted.

COMMENT

1. This section must be read in conjunction with the preceding section (Section 5.109—Default) and the following section (Section 5.111—Cure of Default). Section 5.109 delineates the legal criteria for default and recognizes that a default consisting of the failure

to make a payment as required by the agreement is susceptible of being cured by the consumer without impairing a continuing contractual relationship. This section then provides for a notice which may be sent to the consumer in the case of a failure in payment. The notice may be given at any time after the payment is more than ten days late. This is the same point at which the creditor may be entitled to assess a delinquency charge under Section 2.502. The notice is calculated to give the consumer enough information to understand his predicament and to encourage him to take appropriate steps to alleviate it. However, if the default is coupled with a voluntary surrender of possession of goods that are collateral for the debt, it is considered that the consumer regards a continuing relationship at an end, and no notice is provided for.

2. With respect to an insurance premium loan, the consumer should be adequately forewarned of cancellation of his insurance by the creditor. Subsection (3) of this section provides for a particularized notice in this type of transaction.

3. The forms of notice specified in this section are not mandatory. However, Section 5.111 provides that a default consisting of a failure to make a required payment may be cured by the consumer if he makes that payment before the expiration of the minimum period prescribed after written notice of his default and that prior to this time the creditor may not proceed against goods that are collateral or accelerate the maturity of the unpaid debt. This provision prevents the practice of some unscrupulous creditors who repossess collateral when a payment is only a day or two late. It also gives the average consumer the opportunity to rehabilitate his account, bring a billing error to the attention of or present a breach of warranty claim to the creditor, or negotiate a refinancing or deferral arrangement that may be required by a change in his financial circumstances.

4. Section 5.111 imposes no limitation on the creditor's right to proceed against a consumer or goods that are collateral with respect to successive defaults on the same obligation other than an insurance premium loan or if the consumer has voluntarily surrendered possession, and particularly deals with the somewhat different nature of an insurance premium loan transaction.

Section 5.111 [Cure of Default]

(1) With respect to a consumer credit transaction, except as provided in subsection (2), after a default consisting only of the consumer's failure to make a required payment, a creditor, because of that default, may neither accelerate maturity of the unpaid balance of the obligation, nor take possession of or otherwise enforce a security interest in goods that are collateral until

20 days after a notice of the consumer's right to cure (Section 5.110) is given, nor, with respect to an insurance premium loan, give notice of cancellation as provided in subsection (4) until 13 days after a notice of the consumer's right to cure (Section 5.-110) is given. Until expiration of the minimum applicable period after the notice is given, the consumer may cure all defaults consisting of a failure to make the required payment by tendering the amount of all unpaid sums due at the time of the tender, without acceleration, plus any unpaid delinquency or deferral charges. Cure restores the consumer to his rights under the agreement as though the defaults had not occurred.

(2) With respect to defaults on the same obligation other than an insurance premium loan and subject to subsection (1), after a creditor has once given a notice of consumer's right to cure (Section 5.110), this section gives the consumer no right to cure and imposes no limitation on the creditor's right to proceed against the consumer or goods that are collateral. For the purpose of this section, in open-end credit, the obligation is the unpaid balance of the account and there is no right to cure and no limitation on the creditor's rights with respect to a default that occurs within 12 months after an earlier default as to which a creditor has given a notice of consumer's right to cure (Section 5.110).

(3) This section and the provisions on waiver, agreements to forego rights, and settlement of claims (Section 1.107) do not prohibit a consumer from voluntarily surrendering possession of goods which are collateral and the creditor from thereafter accelerating maturity of the obligation and enforcing the obligation and his security interest in the goods at any time after default.

(4) If a default on an insurance premium loan is not cured, the lender may give notice of cancellation of each insurance policy or contract to be cancelled. If given, the notice of cancellation shall be in writing and given to the insurer who issued the policy or contract and to the insured. The insurer, within two business days after receipt of the notice of cancellation together with a copy of the insurance premium loan agreement if not previously given to him, shall give any notice of cancellation required by the policy, contract, or law and, within ten business days after the effective date of the cancellation, pay to the lender any premium unearned on the policy or contract as of that effective date. Within ten business days after receipt of the unearned premium, the lender shall pay to the consumer indebted

upon the insurance premium loan any excess of the unearned premium received over the amount owing by the consumer upon the insurance premium loan.

COMMENT

See Comment to Section 5.110. Note subsection (2) of this section answers the question of what constitutes the obligation in open-end credit and specifies the applicable period in open-end credit with respect to notice of the consumer's right to cure under Section 5.110.

Section 5.112 [Creditor's Right to Take Possession After Default]

Upon default by a consumer with respect to a consumer credit transaction, unless the consumer voluntarily surrenders possession of the collateral to the creditor, the creditor may take possession of the collateral without judicial process only if possession can be taken without entry into a dwelling and without the use of force or other breach of the peace.

COMMENT

1. Under Section 9—503 of the UCC a secured creditor has the right to take possession of collateral without resorting to legal process if he can do so without a breach of the peace. This raises delicate problems when it comes to repossessing furniture or other property that is within a home or apartment. The disputes that result from such a situation are rarely the type that get to the appellate courts for resolution. It is necessary, therefore, to make it clear that dwellings cannot be entered absent the consent of the occupants except under the supervision of the court. This section is subject to the limitations imposed by preceding sections (Sections 5.109, 5.110 and 5.111).

2. There are currently several disputed issues pertaining to the proper procedures to be utilized by a creditor in proceeding against collateral. Whether a creditor, absent consent of the consumer, is entitled to use self-help at all is under question. And, when possession is sought by legal process, the issues remain as to whether a hearing is to be held prior to the issuance of process in only some cases, what type of hearing is required to meet constitutional requirements, and whether the right to a hearing can be waived. See Comment 1 to Section 5.103. These issues seem best resolved in the courts and therefore no attempt to resolve them in this Act is made.

Section 5.113 [Venue]

An action by a creditor against a consumer arising from a consumer credit transaction shall be brought in the [county] of the consumer's residence (subsection (6) of Section 1.201), unless an action is brought to enforce an interest in land securing the consumer's obligation, in which case the action may be brought in the [county] in which the land or a part thereof is located. If the [county] of the consumer's residence has changed, the consumer upon motion may have the action removed to the [county] of his current residence. If the residence of the consumer is not within this State, the action may be brought in the [county] in which the sale, lease, or loan was made. If the initial papers offered for filing in the action on their face show noncompliance with this section, the [clerk] shall not accept them.

COMMENT

One of the common abuses in consumer credit is the bringing of an action against the consumer in a county or district other than that of his residence. Although courts universally condemn this practice, general venue provisions that allow an action to be brought where either the plaintiff or the defendant resides facilitate it. This section requires an action by a creditor arising from a consumer credit transaction to be brought where the consumer resides except in a case involving an interest in land. This is a venue provision only and does not disturb existing requirements for service of legal process.

Section 5.114 [Complaint; Proof]

(1) In an action brought by a creditor against a consumer arising from a consumer credit transaction, the complaint shall allege the facts of the consumer's default, the amount to which the creditor is entitled, and an indication of how that amount was determined.

(2) A default judgment may not be entered in the action in favor of the creditor unless the complaint is verified by the creditor or sworn testimony, by affidavit or otherwise, is adduced showing that the creditor is entitled to the relief demanded.

COMMENT

Studies that have been performed of consumers who have legal action brought against them show a high rate of judgments taken by default, in excess of 90 per cent in some urban areas. Modern rules of procedure that require a complaint to contain only the barest of facts contemplate contested litigation. In the event judgment is taken by default there is not enough information in the pleadings to enable the court to enter an accurate award. This section provides that the minimum amount of information necessary to compute the award shall be brought to the attention of the court.

Section 5.115 [Stay of Enforcement of or Relief from Default Judgment]

At any time after entry of a default judgment in favor of a creditor and against a consumer in an action arising from a consumer credit transaction, the court which rendered the judgment, for cause including lack of jurisdiction to render the judgment, and upon motion of a party or its own motion, with notice as the court may direct, may stay enforcement of or relieve the consumer from the judgment by order upon just and equitable conditions.

COMMENT

The high rate of judgments by default arising out of consumer credit transactions suggests a need for broad judicial discretion to open or void such judgments and re-examine the claims upon which they were rendered in appropriate cases where cause exists. Particularly, the systematic practice by some process servers (usually private process servers) of filing an affidavit of service on the consumer when, in fact, the summons has never been served but stuffed in a "sewer" or elsewhere, cannot furnish the basis for a judgment. However, such discretion is generally associated with courts of general jurisdiction and most actions arising from consumer credit transactions fall within the purview of limited jurisdiction courts. This section is intended to confer that discretion upon any court with jurisdiction to entertain actions arising from consumer credit transactions.

Section 5.116 [Limitation on Enforcement of Security for Supervised Loan]

(1) Except as to a purchase money security interest, this section applies to a security interest in an item of goods other than a motor vehicle which (a) is possessed by a consumer, (b) is being used by him or a member of a family wholly or partly supported by him, (c) is or may be claimed to be exempt from execution on a money judgment under the laws of this State, and (d) is collateral for a supervised loan.

(2) Unless the consumer, after written notice to him of his rights under this section, voluntarily surrenders to the lender possession of any item of goods to which this section applies, the lender, without an order or process of the [ ] court, may

not take possession of the item or otherwise enforce the security interest according to its terms. The notice to the consumer shall conform to any rule adopted by the Administrator.

(3) The court may order or authorize process respecting an item of goods to which this section applies only after a hearing upon notice to the consumer of the hearing and his rights at it. The notice shall be as directed by the court. The order or authorization may prescribe appropriate conditions as to payments upon the debt secured or otherwise. The court may not order or authorize process respecting the item if it finds upon the hearing both that the consumer lacks the means to pay all or part of the debt secured and that continued possession and use of the item is necessary to avoid undue hardship for the consumer or a member of a family wholly or partly supported by him.

(4) The court, upon application of the lender or the consumer and notice to the other, and after a hearing and a finding of changed circumstances, may vacate or modify an order or authorization pursuant to this section.

COMMENT

1. This section responds to the recommendation of the National Commission on Consumer Finance that security interests in household goods should not be allowed in any loan or consolidation transaction if the goods were not acquired by the use of that credit because in the event of default the right to repossess or threat to repossess these goods have far too disruptive an impact on the family life of the debtor to be in the public interest. However, since the section more appropriately directs itself to a limitation on the right to enforce a security interest rather than to the right to contract for one, the purview of it extends beyond household goods to goods that this State has determined are entitled to exemption in accordance with the policy that a debtor should not be deprived of the necessities of life by his creditors if he is unable to pay his debts.

2. For the safeguards contemplated by this section to function, the consumer must be aware of his rights. Subsection (2) requires a notice to him and authorizes the Administrator to determine by rule what sort of notice should be given of those rights, when it should be given, and how the consumer should be able to waive his rights or claim the exemption. Subsection (3) provides for additional notice of rights to the consumer in the notice of the hearing and vests in the court the necessary discretion to fashion its order in conformity with the particular circumstances brought out at the hearing.

PART 2

CONSUMERS' REMEDIES

Section 5.201 [Effect of Violations on Rights of Parties]

(1) If a creditor has violated any provision of this Act applying to collection of an excess charge or amount or enforcement of rights (subsections (2) and (4) of Section 1.201), authority to make supervised loans (Section 2.301), restrictions on interests in land as security (Section 2.307), limitations on the schedule of payments on loan terms for supervised loans (Section 2.308), attorney's fees (Section 2.507), charges for other credit transactions (Section 2.601), disclosure with respect to consumer leases (Section 3.202), notice to consumers (Section 3.203), receipts, statements of account, and evidences of payment (Section 3.206), form of insurance premium loan agreement (Section 3.207), notice to co-signers and similar parties (Section 3.208), security in sales and leases (Section 3.301), no assignments of earnings (Section 3.305), authorizations to confess judgment (Section 3.306), certain negotiable instruments prohibited (Section 3.307), referral sales and leases (Section 3.309), limitations on default charges (Section 3.402), card issuer subject to claims and defenses (subsection (5) of Section 3.403), assignees subject to claims and defenses (subsection (4) of Section 3.404), lenders subject to claims and defenses arising from sales and leases (subsection (4) of Section 3.405), limitation on enforcement of security for supervised loan (Section 5.116), or assurance of discontinuance (Section 6.109), the consumer has a [claim for relief] [cause of action] to recover actual damages and also a right in an action other than a class action, to recover from the person violating this Act a penalty in an amount determined by the court not less than $100 nor more than $1,000. With respect to violations arising from sales or loans made pursuant to open-end credit, no action pursuant to this subsection may be brought more than two years after the violations occurred. With respect to violations arising from other consumer credit transactions, no action pursuant to this subsection may be brought more than one year after the scheduled or accelerated maturity of the debt.

(2) A consumer is not obligated to pay a charge in excess of that allowed by this Act and has a right of refund of any excess charge paid. A refund may not be made by reducing the consumer's obligation by the amount of the excess charge, unless

the creditor has notified the consumer that the consumer may request a refund and the consumer has not so requested within 30 days thereafter. If the consumer has paid an amount in excess of the lawful obligation under the agreement, the consumer may recover the excess amount from the person who made the excess charge or from an assignee of that person's rights who undertakes direct collection of payments from or enforcement of rights against consumers arising from the debt.

(3) If a creditor has contracted for or received a charge in excess of that allowed by this Act, or if a consumer is entitled to a refund and a person liable to the consumer refuses to make a refund within a reasonable time after demand, the consumer may recover from the creditor or the person liable in an action other than a class action a penalty in an amount determined by the court not less than $100 nor more than $1,000. With respect to excess charges arising from sales or loans made pursuant to open-end credit, no action pursuant to this subsection may be brought more than two years after the violation or passage of a reasonable time for refund occurs. With respect to excess charges arising from other consumer credit transactions no action pursuant to this subsection may be brought more than one year after the scheduled or accelerated maturity of the debt. For purposes of this subsection, a reasonable time is presumed to be 30 days.

(4) Except as otherwise provided, a violation of this Act does not impair rights on a debt.

(5) If an employer discharges an employee in violation of the provisions prohibiting discharge (Section 5.106), the employee within [ ] days may bring a civil action for recovery of wages lost as a result of the violation and for an order requiring reinstatement of the employee. Damages recoverable shall not exceed lost wages for six weeks.

(6) A creditor is not liable for a penalty under subsection (1) or (3) if he notifies the consumer of a violation before the creditor receives from the consumer written notice of the violation or the consumer has brought an action under this section, and the creditor corrects the violation within 45 days after notifying the consumer. If the violation consists of a prohibited agreement, giving the consumer a corrected copy of the writing containing the violation is sufficient notification and correction. If the violation consists of an excess charge, correction shall be made by an adjustment or refund. The Administrator and any official or agency of this State having supervisory authority over a super-

vised financial organization shall give prompt notice to a creditor of any violation discovered pursuant to an examination or investigation of the transactions, business, records, and acts of the creditor (Sections 2.305, 6.105 and 6.106).

(7) A creditor may not be held liable in an action brought under this section for a violation of this Act if the creditor shows by a preponderance of evidence that the violation was not intentional and resulted from a bona fide error notwithstanding the maintenance of procedures reasonably adapted to avoid the error.

(8) In an action in which it is found that a creditor has violated this Act, the court shall award to the consumer the costs of the action and to his attorneys their reasonable fees. In determining attorney's fees, the amount of the recovery on behalf of the consumer is not controlling.

COMMENT

1. Rights that are accompanied by inadequate remedies or no remedy at all and limitations on agreements and practices that do not provide for sufficient penalties or for any penalty at all are generally ineffective to accomplish the desired result. They become little more than exhortatory, easily ignored, and meaningless proclamations. In order to protect rights created and to deter provisions of agreements and practices proscribed by legislation, suitable remedies and penalties must exist. Since an aggrieved party is one of the persons best able to enforce violations of rights and limitations, this section sets forth a right of action in the consumer in the event of violation by the creditor of each section of this Act that does not include its own provision for infraction and better to deter such practices, even of some that do, as in the case of referral sales and leases (Section 3.309).

2. Subsection (1) lists 22 provisions of this Act for the contravention of which actual damages and a penalty could be recovered. The formula used for the penalty is derived from the CCPA (15 U.S.C. § 1601 et seq.) with a minimum and a maximum recovery. Within this range a court may apportion penalties according to the seriousness of the offense and the overall circumstances of each violation. The penalty is designed not only to provide a deterrent to potential violators but also an incentive to a consumer to bring an action when a violation has occurred. Consequently, penalties may not be recovered in a class action, although actual damages may be if the enacting State's rules of civil procedure permits.

3. Subsections (2) and (3) set forth the rights of the consumer with respect to excess charges by the creditor. A refund rather than a credit of an excess charge

must be made if requested by the consumer to prevent the creditor from holding a refund due until the contract is sufficiently paid down to have it credited as a prepayment in full. Subsection (3) imposes the same penalty on those who make excess charges or refuse to make refunds to which a consumer is entitled as that for violators of provisions listed in subsection (1). This provision is necessary because if the only rights the consumer had were those provided in subsection (2), it would be worth the creditor's gamble to make excess charges. The only thing that could be lost would be the illegal charge itself, and even that would be unlikely in view of the small percentage of consumers who would seek recovery.

4. Subsection (5) describes the rights of an employee who has been discharged in violation of Section 5.106.

5. Violations may occur for a variety of reasons, not all of them necessarily pernicious. Subsection (6) provides that if the creditor becomes aware of a violation, voluntarily notifies the consumer of the violation, and corrects the violation within 45 days after notification, he is not subject to a penalty. Such a provision encourages the autonomous correction of errors and violations. Voluntariness is considered to cease, however, either upon the commencement of an action against the creditor or upon his receipt of written notification from the consumer of the violation. Consistent with the idea that many errors and violations will be rectified upon knowledge without resort to sanctions, subsection (6) also provides that violations discovered pursuant to administrative examination or investigation shall promptly be brought to the attention of the creditor. Probably the most common type of creditor violation results from clerical mistake. No policy would be served in imposing liability for violations due to unintentional bona fide errors which occur notwithstanding the maintenance of procedures reasonably adapted to avoid them, and subsection (7) provides a creditor with an affirmative defense in such cases. Moreover, acts done or omitted in conformity with a rule, interpretation or declaratory ruling of the Administrator ought to result in no liability under this Act, except for refund of an excess charge. This Act so provides, as well as affording ample opportunity for creditor and consumer participation in the formulation and correction of rules. See Sections 6.104(4) and 6.107.

6. Subsection (8) directs the court to award to the consumer the costs of the action and to his attorney his reasonable fees in any action where it is found that a creditor has violated this Act. The direction to award attorney's fees should enable consumers to find attorneys to prosecute their cases, an essential element if the consumers' rights provided by this section are to be enforced, as an attorney is assured of adequate compensation. This is so whether or not the case goes to trial since any settlement offer

will have to take the attorney's compensation into account.

7. This Act provides for other remedies in addition to those set forth in this section. For example, the consumer has a defense to the enforcement of a transaction which violates Section 5.107 on extortionate extensions of credit. Section 5.108 gives a consumer or debtor a remedy in certain cases of unconscionability. [Optional Section 5.203, if enacted, sets forth the rights of a person with respect to transactions in which the creditor has violated the provisions on compliance with the Federal Truth in Lending Act. Section 3.201.] The consumer also has a right to cancel a home solicitation sale. Part 5 of Article 3 (Sections 3.501 et seq.).

In addition to the foregoing individual consumers' remedies the Act provides for actions by the Administrator for the benefit of consumers. The Administrator may issue cease and desist orders with respect to violations of the Act or may bring civil actions to restrain violations of the Act. Sections 6.108 and 6.110. The Administrator may also bring a civil action against a creditor to recover actual damages sustained and excess charges paid by one or more consumers who have a right to recover explicitly granted by this Act, but not for penalties, and amounts recovered shall be paid to each consumer or set off against his obligation. Section 6.113. Section 6.111 provides for civil actions by the Administrator for injunctions against a course of making unconscionable agreements or of fraudulent or unconscionable conduct.

Finally, in addition to the individual consumers' remedies and remedies of the Administrator described above, the consumer may have other remedies based on general principles of law or equity, or based on the provisions of other applicable law. See Sections 1.103 and 6.115. Also, damages or penalties to which a consumer is entitled may be set off against the consumer's obligation, and may be raised as a defense to an action on the obligation without regard to the time limitations prescribed by this section. See Section 5.202.

Section 5.202 [Damages or Penalties as Set-Off to Obligation]

Damages or penalties to which a consumer is entitled pursuant to this Part may be set off against the consumer's obligation, and may be raised as a defense to an action on the obligation without regard to the time limitations prescribed by this Part.

[Section 5.203 [Civil Liability for Violation of Disclosure Provisions]

(1) Except as otherwise provided in this section, a creditor who, in violation of the provisions of the Federal Truth in Lend-

ing Act other than its provisions concerning advertising of credit terms, fails to disclose information to a person entitled to it under this Act is liable to that person in an amount equal to the sum of:

(a) twice the amount of the finance charge in connection with the transaction, but the liability under this paragraph shall be not less than $100 or exceed $1,000; and

(b) in the case of a successful action to enforce the liability under paragraph (a), the costs of the action together with reasonable attorney's fees as determined by the court.

(2) A creditor has no liability under this section, if within 15 days after discovering an error, and before the institution of an action under this section or the receipt of written notice of the error, the creditor notifies the person concerned of the error and makes adjustments in the appropriate account as necessary to assure that the person will not be required to pay a finance charge in excess of the amount or percentage rate actually disclosed. The Administrator and any official or agency of this State having supervisory authority over a supervised financial organization shall give prompt notice to a creditor of any error discovered pursuant to an examination or investigation of the transactions, business, records, and acts of the creditor (Sections 2.305, 6.105 and 6.106).

(3) A creditor may not be held liable in any action brought under this section for a violation of this Act if the creditor shows by a preponderance of evidence that the violation was not intentional and resulted from a bona fide error notwithstanding the maintenance of procedures reasonably adapted to avoid the error.

(4) Any action which may be brought under this section against the original creditor in a credit transaction involving a security interest in land may be maintained against any subsequent assignee of the original creditor, if the assignee, its subsidiaries, or affiliates were in a continuing business relationship with the original creditor at the time the credit was extended or at the time of the assignment, unless the assignment was involuntary, or the assignee shows by a preponderance of evidence that it did not have reasonable grounds to believe that the original creditor was engaged in violations of this Act and that it maintained procedures reasonably adapted to apprise it of the existence of the violations.

(5) An obligor or consumer has all rights under this Act that he has under the Federal Truth in Lending Act concerning a right of rescission as to certain transactions. A creditor or other person has all liabilities and defenses under this section that he has under the Federal Truth in Lending Act.

(6) In this section, creditor includes a person who in the ordinary course of business regularly extends or arranges for the extension of credit, or offers to arrange for the extension of credit, and the seller of an interest in land and the lender who makes a loan secured by an interest in land if, but for the rate of the finance charge made in the transaction, the sale or loan would be a consumer credit sale or consumer loan.

(7) An action may not be brought under this section more than one year after the date of the occurrence of the violation.

(8) The liability of a creditor under this section is in lieu of and not in addition to his liability under the Federal Truth in Lending Act. An action by a person with respect to a violation may not be maintained pursuant to this section if a final judgment has been rendered for or against that person with respect to the same violation pursuant to the Federal Truth in Lending Act. If a final judgment has been rendered in favor of a person pursuant to this section and thereafter a final judgment with respect to the same violation is rendered in favor of the same person pursuant to the Federal Truth in Lending Act, a creditor liable under both judgments has a [claim for relief] [cause of action] against that person for appropriate relief to the extent necessary to avoid double liability with respect to the same violation.

(9) The Administrator shall adopt rules to keep this section in harmony with the Federal Truth in Lending Act. These rules supersede any provisions of this section which are inconsistent with the Federal Truth in Lending Act.]

COMMENT

1. This section is derived from the CCPA (15 U.S.C. § 1601 et seq., specifically, § 1640). It is intended to allow fulfillment of the demand of that statute that under state law classes of credit transactions be subject to requirements substantially similar to those imposed by the CCPA and that adequate provision for enforcement exist if the state enacting this Act wishes to apply for an exemption from the CCPA.

2. Subsections (1) through (4), consequently, are modeled exactly on the Federal provisions, except for the additional requirement of administrative notification to creditors of errors discovered through examinations or in-

vestigations, and subsection (9) directs the Administrator by rule to conform this section to any modifications from time to time of the Federal statute. If the Federal provisions on which this section is modeled are amended before enactment of this Act, this section should be conformed.

3. Subsection (5) is similar to subsection (9) in that it seeks to allow conformity of rights and liabilities under this section with those under the Federal Act, including the provision on a right of rescission as to certain transactions, as they may be formulated by case law interpretation.

4. Subsection (6) broadens the definition of "creditor" for purposes of this section beyond that applicable elsewhere in this Act (subsection (18) of Section 1.301) to again assure conformity.

5. Finally, subsection (8) mitigates against double creditor liability if a creditor is sued both under this section and under the CCPA.

6. If the enacting State wishes to apply for an exemption from the Federal Truth in Lending Act, the brackets before and after Sections 5.203 and 5.302 should be deleted and those sections enacted, the brackets before and after those sections in the Table of Articles, Parts, and Sections should be deleted, and the brackets in subsection (5) of Section 1.202 preceding and following the references to Sections 5.-203 and 5.302 deleted.

Otherwise,

a. Omit Sections 5.203 and 5.-302 and the references to them in the Table of Articles, Parts, and Sections, and

b. In subsection (5) of Section 1.202, delete the brackets and the language enclosed within them.

PART 3

CRIMINAL PENALTIES

Section 5.301 [Willful and Knowing Violations]

(1) A supervised lender who willfully and knowingly makes charges in excess of those permitted by the Article on Finance Charges and Related Provisions (Article 2) applying to supervised loans (Part 4) is guilty of a misdemeanor and upon conviction may be [sentenced to pay a fine not exceeding $ [ ], or to imprisonment not exceeding one year, or both].

(2) A person who, in violation of the provisions of this Act applying to authority to make supervised loans (Section 2.301), willfully and knowingly engages without a license in the business of making supervised loans, or of taking assignments of and undertaking direct collection of payments from and enforcement of rights against consumers arising from supervised loans, is guilty of a misdemeanor and upon conviction may be [sentenced to pay a fine not exceeding $ [ ], or to imprisonment not exceeding one year, or both].

(3) A person who willfully and knowingly engages in the business of entering into consumer credit transactions, or of taking assignments of rights against consumers arising therefrom and undertaking direct collection of payments or enforcement of these rights, without complying with the provisions of this Act concerning notification (Section 6.202) or payment of fees (Section 6.203), is guilty of a misdemeanor and upon conviction may be [sentenced to pay a fine not exceeding $100].

[Section 5.302 [Disclosure Violations]

(1) A person is guilty of a [misdemeanor] and upon conviction may be sentenced to pay a fine not exceeding $5,000, or to imprisonment not exceeding one year, or both, if he willfully and knowingly:

(a) gives false or inaccurate information or fails to provide information which he is required to disclose under the Federal Truth in Lending Act;

(b) uses any rate table or chart, the use of which is authorized by the provisions of the Federal Truth in Lending Act, in a manner which consistently understates the annual percentage rate determined according to those provisions; or

(c) otherwise fails to comply with any requirement of the provisions on disclosure of the Federal Truth in Lending Act.

(2) The criminal liability of a person under this section is in lieu of and not in addition to his criminal liability under the Federal Truth in Lending Act; no prosecution of a person with respect to the same violation may be maintained pursuant to both this section and the Federal Truth in Lending Act.]

COMMENT

This section is derived from the CCPA (15 U.S.C. § 1601 et seq., specifically, § 1611). See Comment to Section 5.203.

ARTICLE 6

ADMINISTRATION

PART 1

POWERS AND FUNCTIONS OF ADMINISTRATOR

Section 6.101 [Short Title]

This Article shall be known and may be cited as Uniform Consumer Credit Code—Administration.

Section 6.102 [Applicability and Scope]

This Part applies to persons who in this State:

(a) enter into, solicit, or participate in consumer credit transactions; or lead a debtor to believe that a transaction will give rise to a consumer credit transaction;

(b) directly collect payments from or enforce rights against consumers arising from consumer credit transactions, wherever they are entered into; or

(c) enter into a sale of an interest in land or a loan secured by an interest in land if, but for the rate of the finance charge, the sale or loan would be a consumer credit sale or consumer loan, but only for the purpose of authorizing the Administrator to enforce the provisions on compliance with the Federal Truth in Lending Act (Section 3.-201).

COMMENT

Except for this Part and Part 2 of this Article, Section 1.201 states the territorial application of this Act. This Part has a broader territorial application than some other provisions, but this section is not intended to extend the territorial application of other provisions beyond the limits specified in Section 1.201. The scope of this Part is also broader than that of some other provisions. Compare, *e. g.*, subsection (3) of this section and Section 1.-301(12)(b)(ii) and (15)(b)(ii).

Section 6.103 [Administrator]

"Administrator" means [ ].

COMMENT

In order to obtain the administration essential to the effectiveness of this Act, the National Conference recommends centralizing all powers of administration in a single official or agency. In recognition of the fact that in some States a single official or agency either is not constitutionally possible or may not be politically feasible, the Act does not attempt to identify the Administrator. The Administrator may be a single State official or department, two or more State officials or departments, or a Commission. For example in a State in which a single official (*e. g.*, Superintendent or Commissioner of Banks, Banking or Financial Institutions) or a single department (*e. g.*, Banking Department, Commerce Department or Department of Financial Institutions) presently supervises both banks and other financial institutions such as consumer finance companies and sales finance companies, it may be desirable to designate that official or department as the single Administrator. If two or more State officials or departments are to share the powers of the Administrator, the National Conference recommends that a Commission including those officials or departments be designated as Administrator, and that, unless a statutory division of areas of power and authority is provided for, the Commission be given power to prescribe the areas in which the officials or departments who are members of the Commission shall exercise the power and authority of the Administrator.

Section 6.104 [Powers of Administrator; Reliance on Rules; Duty to Report]

(1) In addition to other powers granted by this Act, the Administrator within the limitations provided by law may:

(a) receive and act on complaints, take action designed to obtain voluntary compliance with this Act, or commence proceedings on his own initiative;

(b) counsel persons and groups on their rights and duties under this Act;

(c) establish programs for the education of consumers with respect to credit practices and problems;

(d) make studies appropriate to effectuate the purposes and policies of this Act and make the results available to the public; [and]

(e) adopt, amend, and repeal rules to carry out the specific provisions of this Act, but not with respect to unconscionable agreements or fraudulent or unconscionable conduct [;

(f) maintain offices within this State; and]

[(g) appoint any necessary attorneys, hearing examiners, clerks, and other employees and agents and fix their compensation, and authorize attorneys appointed under this section to appear for and represent the Administrator in court].

(2) In addition to other powers granted by this Act, the Administrator shall enforce the Federal Truth in Lending Act, except to the extent otherwise provided by law.

(3) To keep the Administrator's rules in harmony with the rules of administrators in other jurisdictions that enact substantially the Uniform Consumer Credit Code, the Administrator, so far as is consistent with the purposes, policies, and provisions of this Act, shall:

(a) before adopting, amending, and repealing rules, advise and consult with administrators in other jurisdictions that enact substantially the Uniform Consumer Credit Code; and

(b) in adopting, amending, and repealing rules, take into consideration the rules of administrators in other jurisdictions that enact substantially the Uniform Consumer Credit Code.

(4) Except for refund of an excess charge, no liability is imposed under this Act for an act done or omitted in conformity with a rule, interpretation, or declaratory ruling of the Administrator, notwithstanding that after the act or omission the rule, interpretation, or ruling is amended or repealed or is determined by judicial or other authority to be invalid for any reason.

(5) The Administrator shall report [annually on or before January 1] to the [Governor and Legislature] on the operation of his office, the use of consumer credit in this State, and the problems of persons of small means obtaining credit from persons regularly engaged in extending sales or loan credit. For the purpose of making the report, the Administrator may conduct research and make appropriate studies. The report shall include a description of the examination and investigation procedures and policies of his office, a statement of policies followed in deciding whether to investigate or examine the offices of credit suppliers subject to this Act, a statement of the number and percentages of offices which are periodically investigated or examined, a statement of the types of consumer credit problems of both creditors and consumers which have come to his atten-

tion through his examinations and investigations and the disposition of them under existing law, a statement of the extent to which rules of the Administrator pursuant to this Act are not in harmony with the rules of administrators in other jurisdictions that enact substantially the Uniform Consumer Credit Code and the reasons for these variations, and a general statement of the activities of his office and of others to promote the purposes of this Act. The report may not identify the creditors against whom action is taken by the Administrator.

COMMENT

1. The Administrator is given broad power to make studies relative to the proper working of this Act, to provide educational services for consumers, and to advise persons and groups as to their rights and obligations under this Act. The various disclosure rules, rate limitations, and other provisions of the Act designed to protect the consumer cannot be fully effective unless consumers are aware of and understand their rights under the Act. Therefore, an essential part of the Administrator's total responsibility is providing consumer education.

The Administrator also is given the power to receive and act on complaints. Consumer complaints can be expected to be an important basis for the invocation of the Administrator's investigatory powers (Section 6.106). The ability to file a complaint in addition may be a significant adjunct to the consumer's private right of action for violations (Section 5.201) or for unconscionability (Section 5.108) and, in appropriate cases, even an alternative to it. Appropriate cases might involve situations where, in the context of a single case, a violation will be difficult to establish, where the complaint involves an untested provision of the Act, or where the amount at stake individually is not sufficient under the circumstances to prompt private action to cure a violation. Since the Administrator is not under a duty to act in any particular instance, he may act only in those cases where he believes it desirable to do so pursuant to policy considerations established by him. In acting, the Administrator may seek voluntary compliance or invoke the remedies provided in this Part.

This Act in numerous places specifically directs the Administrator to adopt rules as a more reasonable approach than providing long and complex statutory provisions that are likely to prove too inflexible in practice. However, little foresight is required to recognize that the need will arise for rules to carry out many other specific provisions of the Act. For example, this Act contains a provision restricting a separate charge for property insurance where the value of the property is less than $300 (subsection (3) of Section 4.301). To make this provision workable, the Administrator should adopt a rule specifying reasonable means for establishing an appropriate standard of value consistent with operational needs of creditors and the policy of the provision. Almost any provision also may need to be the subject of an interpretive rule, and procedural rules will be required in many instances to satisfy the requirements of administrative procedure statutes. Subsection (1)(e) grants the Administrator authority to adopt, amend, and repeal rules in these circumstances.

2. Subsection (2) requires the Administrator to enforce the Federal Truth in Lending Act, including, as defined in Section 1.-302, regulations pursuant to that Act made part of this Act by Section 3.201.

3. The direction to the Administrator in subsection (3) to keep his rules in harmony with the rules of administrators in other jurisdictions that enact substantially the Uniform Consumer Credit Code is derived from the Uniform Narcotic Drug Act Section 1 (14) (Alt.).

4. Under subsection (4), a person who acts in accordance with rules, interpretations, or declaratory rulings of the Administrator incurs no liability with respect to such conduct even if the rules, interpretations, or declaratory rulings are later amended, repealed or declared to be invalid, except that if a rule, interpretation, or ruling relating to charges is declared invalid, any excess charge made under the supposed authority of the invalid rule, interpretation or ruling may be covered by the consumers affected or by the Administrator for the consumers.

Section 6.105 [Administrative Powers with Respect to Supervised Financial Organizations]

(1) With respect to supervised financial organizations, the powers of examination and investigation (Sections 2.305 and 6.-106) and administrative enforcement (Section 6.108) shall be exercised by the official or agency to whose supervision the organization is subject. All other powers of the Administrator under this Act may be exercised by him with respect to a supervised financial organization.

(2) If the Administrator receives a complaint or other information concerning noncompliance with this Act by a supervised financial organization, he shall inform the official or agency having supervisory authority over the organization concerned. The Administrator may request information about supervised financial organizations from the officials or agencies supervising them.

(3) The Administrator and any official or agency of this State having supervisory authority over a supervised financial

organization shall consult and assist one another in maintaining compliance with this Act. They may jointly pursue investigations, prosecute actions, and take other official action, as they deem appropriate, if either of them otherwise is empowered to take the action.

COMMENT

1. "Supervised financial organizations" are by definition subject to supervision by an official or agency of this State or the United States. Section 1.-301(41). The powers of administration and investigation and administrative enforcement under this Act are delegated to that official or agency rather than to the Administrator, unless he is also the supervising official or agency. All other powers of the Administrator, including rule making and initiation of judicial action, may be exercised by him with respect to supervised financial organizations.

2. Subsections (2) and (3) provide for exchange of information and for cooperation between the Administrator under this Act and the supervisory authorities of supervised financial institutions. Subsection (3) goes further and requires the Administrator and the State agency having supervision over supervised financial organizations to consult with and assist each other in carrying out their duties under this Act.

Section 6.106 [Investigatory Powers]

(1) If the Administrator has cause to believe that a person has engaged in conduct or committed an act that is subject to action by the Administrator, he may make an investigation to determine whether the person has engaged in the conduct or committed the act. To the extent necessary for this purpose, he may administer oaths or affirmations, and, upon his own motion or upon request of any party, subpoena witnesses, compel their attendance, adduce evidence, and require the production of, or testimony as to, any matter relevant to the investigation, including the existence, description, nature, custody, condition, and location of any books, documents, or other tangible things and the identity and location of persons having knowledge of relevant facts, or any other matter reasonably calculated to lead to the discovery of admissible evidence.

(2) If the person's records are located outside this State, the person at his option shall make them available to the Administrator at a convenient location within this State or pay the reasonable and necessary expenses for the Administrator or his representative to examine them where they are located. The Ad-

ministrator may designate representatives, including comparable officials of the State in which the records are located, to inspect them on his behalf.

(3) Upon application by the Administrator showing failure without lawful excuse to obey a subpoena or to give testimony, and upon reasonable notice to all persons affected thereby, the [ ] court shall grant an order compelling compliance.

(4) The Administrator may not make public the name or identity of a person whose acts or conduct he investigates under this section or the facts disclosed in the investigation, but this subsection does not apply to disclosures in actions or enforcement proceedings pursuant to this Act.

COMMENT

1. Administrator under this section includes the official or agency referred to in Section 6.-105(1).

2. The Administrator may commence an investigation under this section if he has cause to believe that a violation of law or regulations or other act or conduct has occurred which would subject the person committing or engaging in it to action by the Administrator. The Administrator, therefore, may commence an investigation when he has met the usual administrative standards; political, judicial and other governmental processes provide ample protection against arbitrary use of the power. Action by the Administrator includes both administrative enforcement and enforcement by civil action.

Section 6.107 [Application of [Administrative Procedure Act] [Part on Administrative Procedure and Judicial Review]]

Except as otherwise provided, the [State Administrative Procedure Act] [Part on Administrative Procedure and Judicial Review (Part 4) of this Article] applies to and governs all administrative action taken by the Administrator pursuant to this Article.

COMMENT

If the enacting State has an adequate State administrative procedure act reference should be made to it in this section. Otherwise Part 4 of Article 6 [Section 6.401 et seq.] should be enacted and referred to here. Brackets and bracketed language in this section and its caption should be retained or deleted dependent upon which course is followed. See Comment to Section 6.401.

Section 6.108 [Administrative Enforcement Orders]

(1) After notice and hearing the Administrator may order a creditor or a person acting in his behalf to cease and desist from violating this Act. A respondent aggrieved by an order of the Administrator may obtain judicial review of the order and the Administrator may obtain an order of the court for enforcement of his order in the [ ] court. The proceeding for review or enforcement is initiated by filing a petition in the court. Copies of the petition shall be served upon all parties of record.

(2) Within 30 days after service of the petition for review upon the Administrator, or within any further time the court allows, the Administrator shall transmit to the court the original or a certified copy of the entire record upon which the order is based, including any transcript of testimony, which need not be printed. By stipulation of all parties to the review proceeding, the record may be shortened. After hearing, the court may (a) reverse or modify the order if the findings of fact of the Administrator are clearly erroneous in view of the reliable, probative, and substantial evidence on the whole record, (b) grant any temporary relief or restraining order it deems just, and (c) enter an order enforcing, modifying, and enforcing as modified, or setting aside in whole or in part the order of the Administrator, or remanding the case to the Administrator for further proceedings.

(3) An objection not urged at the hearing shall not be considered by the court unless the failure to urge the objection is excused for good cause shown. A party may move the court to remand the case to the Administrator in the interest of justice for the purpose of adducing additional specified and material evidence and seeking findings thereon upon good cause shown for the failure to adduce this evidence before the Administrator.

(4) The jurisdiction of the court shall be exclusive and its final judgment or decree is subject to review by the [ ] court in the same manner and form and with the same effect as in appeals from a final judgment or decree in a [special proceeding]. The Administrator's copy of the testimony shall be available at reasonable times to all parties for examination without cost.

(5) A proceeding for review under this section shall be initiated within 30 days after a copy of the order of the Administrator is received. If no proceeding is so initiated, the Administrator may obtain an order of the court for enforcement of his order upon showing that his order was issued in compliance with

this section, that no proceeding for review was initiated within 30 days after a copy of the order was received, and that the respondent is subject to the jurisdiction of the court.

(6) With respect to unconscionable agreements or fraudulent or unconscionable conduct by the respondent, the Administrator may not issue an order pursuant to this section but may bring a civil action for an injunction (Section 6.111).

COMMENT

1. A cease and desist order issued under this section is not enforceable against the respondent until a judicial enforcement order is secured by the Administrator. However, unless the respondent files a petition for judicial review of the cease and desist order within 30 days after he receives a copy of the order, it becomes final and the Administrator may obtain enforcement of it without having to support his findings with substantial evidence. The Administrator in such a case need show only issuance of the order in compliance with this section, failure of the respondent to seek review within 30 days, and jurisdiction of the court. Any issues other than those mentioned above must be raised by the filing of a petition for review within the proper time.

2. The Administrator may not issue cease and desist orders under this section as to conduct which violates only the unconscionability or fraudulent conduct rules set out in Section 6.111.

Section 6.109 [Assurance of Discontinuance]

If it is claimed that a person has engaged in conduct which could be subject to an order by the Administrator (Sections 2.303 and 6.108) or by a court (Sections 6.110, 6.111, and 6.112), the Administrator may accept an assurance in writing that the person will not engage in the same or similar conduct in the future. The assurance may include any of the following: stipulations for the voluntary payment by the creditor of the costs of investigation or of an amount to be held in escrow as restitution to debtors aggrieved by past or future conduct of the creditor or to cover costs of future investigation, or admissions of past specific acts by the creditor or that those acts violated this Act or other statutes. A violation of an assurance of discontinuance is a violation of this Act.

COMMENT

This section provides a method for resolving controversies without formal proceedings that involve conduct which is alleged to contravene the provisions of this Act. Considerable flexibility is granted to the Administrator in formulating the terms of any assurance entered into. If a creditor violates an assurance concluded with the Administrator, that itself constitutes a violation of this Act, for which the Administrator may invoke the remedies given him in this Part and an affected consumer may have a private right of action (Section 5.-201).

Section 6.110 [Injunctions Against Violations of Act]

The Administrator may bring a civil action to restrain any person from violating this Act and for other appropriate relief including but not limited to the following: to prevent a person from using or employing practices prohibited by this Act, to reform contracts to conform to this Act and to rescind contracts into which a creditor has induced a consumer to enter by conduct violating this Act, even though a consumer is not a party to the action. An action under this section may be joined with an action under the provisions on civil actions by Administrator (Section 6.113).

COMMENT

The Administrator has an option of proceeding either under this section or under Section 6.-108. In an action under this section the Administrator, in addition to relief appropriate under other law of this State, may seek relief under Sections 6.112 and 6.-113.

Section 6.111 [Injunctions Against Unconscionable Agreements and Fraudulent or Unconscionable Conduct Including Debt Collection]

(1) The Administrator may bring a civil action to restrain a person to whom this Part applies from engaging in a course of:

(a) making or enforcing unconscionable terms or provisions of consumer credit transactions;

(b) fraudulent or unconscionable conduct in inducing consumers to enter into consumer credit transactions;

(c) conduct of any of the types specified in paragraph (a) or (b) with respect to transactions that give rise to or that lead persons to believe will give rise to consumer credit transactions; or

(d) fraudulent or unconscionable conduct in the collection of debts arising from consumer credit transactions.

(2) In an action brought pursuant to this section the court may grant relief only if it finds:

(a) that the respondent has made unconscionable agreements or has engaged or is likely to engage in a course of fraudulent or unconscionable conduct;

(b) that the respondent's agreements have caused or are likely to cause or the conduct of the respondent has caused or is likely to cause injury to consumers or debtors; and

(c) that the respondent has been able to cause or will be able to cause the injury primarily because the transactions involved are credit transactions.

(3) In applying subsection (1)(a), (b), and (c), consideration shall be given to each of the factors specified in the provisions on unconscionability with respect to a transaction that is, gives rise to, or that a person leads the debtor to believe will give rise to, a consumer credit transaction (subsection (4) of Section 5.108), among others.

(4) In applying subsection (1)(d), consideration shall be given to each of the factors specified in the provisions on unconscionability with respect to the collection of debts arising from consumer credit transactions (subsection (5) of Section 5.108), among others.

(5) In an action brought pursuant to this section, a charge or practice expressly permitted by this Act is not in itself unconscionable.

COMMENT

1. Section 5.108 provides a private remedy for unconscionable conduct. This section, in addition, permits the Administrator to bring suit to enjoin a person to whom this Part applies from engaging in a course of conduct specified in subsection (1)(a), (b), (c), or (d). These subsections cover three different areas of unconscionable conduct: (1) unconscionable contract terms, (2) fraudulent or unconscionable conduct in inducing persons to enter into transactions, and (3) fraudulent or unconscionable conduct in the collection of consumer credit debts.

2. One purpose of this section is to afford the Administrator a means of dealing with new patterns of fraudulent or unconscionable conduct unforeseen and, perhaps, unforeseeable at the writing of this Act. Another is to give him a more flexible remedy for halting reprehensible creditor practices that have been specifically and somewhat rigidly treated in previous consumer credit legislation. For instance, this Act has no specific prohibition against the creditor's allowing the consumer to sign a credit agreement containing blanks. In some situations there may be legitimate reasons for a contract to contain blanks at the time of signing. However, if the creditor deliberately leaves blanks to be

filled in after the consumer's signature and without his consent, the Administrator may seek to restrain the practice as fraudulent or unconscionable conduct under this section.

3. Subsections (3) and (4) refer to a number of specific factors to be considered on the issue of unconscionability which are listed in Section 5.108. The illustrative individual transactions described in the Comment to Section 5.108, if engaged in by a person to whom this Part applies as a course of conduct, would entitle the Administrator to injunctive relief under this section.

4. Subsection (5) prohibits a finding that a charge or practice expressly permitted by this Act is in itself unconscionable. However, even though a practice or charge is authorized by this Act, the totality of a particular creditor's conduct may show that the practice or charge is part of an unconscionable course of conduct. Therefore, in determining unconscionability, the creditor's total conduct, including that part of his conduct which is in accordance with the provisions of this Act, may be considered.

5. For cases illustrating the prior application of the doctrine of unconscionability in private actions, see Comment to Section 5.-108. This doctrine was applied in an action by a public official in State by Lefkowitz v. ITM, Inc., 52 Misc.2d 39, 275 N.Y.S. 2d 303 (Sup.Ct.1966).

Section 6.112 [Temporary Relief]

With respect to an action brought to enjoin violations of the Act (Section 6.110) or unconscionable agreements or fraudulent or unconscionable conduct (Section 6.111), the Administrator may apply to the court for appropriate temporary relief against a defendant, pending final determination of the action. The court may grant appropriate temporary relief.

COMMENT

This section permits the Administrator to seek appropriate temporary relief in connection with actions brought pursuant to Sections 6.110 and 6.111, but leaves to other State law the determination of the circumstances in which it will be granted.

Section 6.113 [Civil Actions by Administrator]

(1) After demand, the Administrator may bring a civil action against a creditor to recover actual damages sustained and excess charges paid by one or more consumers who have a right to recover explicitly granted by this Act. In a civil action under this subsection, penalties may not be recovered by the Administrator. The court shall order amounts recovered under this subsection to be paid to each consumer or set off against his ob-

ligation. A consumer's action, except a class action, takes precedence over a prior or subsequent action by the Administrator with respect to the claim of that consumer. A consumer's class action takes precedence over a subsequent action by the Administrator with respect to claims common to both actions, but the Administrator may intervene. An Administrator's action on behalf of a class of consumers takes precedence over a consumer's subsequent class action with respect to claims common to both actions. Whenever an action takes precedence over another action under this subsection, the latter action may be stayed to the extent appropriate while the precedent action is pending and dismissed if the precedent action is dismissed with prejudice or results in a final judgment granting or denying the claim asserted in the precedent action. A defense available to a creditor in a civil action brought by a consumer is available to him in a civil action brought under this subsection.

(2) The Administrator may bring a civil action against a creditor or a person acting in his behalf to recover a civil penalty of no more than $5,000 for repeatedly and intentionally violating this Act. A civil penalty pursuant to this subsection may not be imposed for a violation of this Act occurring more than two years before the action is brought or for making unconscionable agreements or engaging in a course of fraudulent or unconscionable conduct.

(3) The Administrator may bring a civil action against a creditor for failure to file notification in accordance with the provisions on notification (Section 6.202) or to pay fees in accordance with the provisions on fees (Section 6.203) to recover the fees the defendant has failed to pay and a civil penalty in an amount determined by the court not exceeding the greater of three times the amount of fees the defendant has failed to pay or $1,000.

COMMENT

1. This Act explicitly grants a right of action to a consumer to recover actual damages and a penalty for the violation of numerous of its provisions. See Section 5.201. In addition, subsection (1) of this section allows the Administrator, after demand, to bring a civil action on behalf of one or more individual consumers in such cases, except for the recovery of penalties, in contemplation that in some number of these cases the Administrator may be the only person with the necessary informational or monetary resources properly to prosecute an action, may be the only person who can adequately represent a group of consumers,

or for other reasons may be an appropriate person to litigate the question involved. If a consumer brings an action on behalf of himself, his action takes precedence, whether prior or subsequent to the action of the Administrator. If the consumer brings a class action (the ability to do so depends on other law of this State), it takes precedence if it is brought before an action by the Administrator with respect to claims common to both actions, but the Administrator is given the authority to intervene. If the Administrator's action on behalf of a class of consumers is brought prior to that of the consumer, the Administrator's action takes precedence with respect to claims common to both actions.

2. Whether the Administrator's action is on behalf of a single consumer or a class of consumers, it is subject to the same limitations as if brought by the consumer or consumers. For example, if a defense of the running of the statute of limitations would be available to a creditor in an action brought pursuant to Section 5.201 it is available to the creditor to the same extent in an action brought under subsection (1) by the Administrator, and under this subsection the Administrator may recover excess charges from an assignee only where the assignee has undertaken direct collection or enforcement. See Section 5.201(1) and (2).

3. An action for a civil penalty under subsection (2) of this section may be in lieu of or in addition to an action under subsection (1). The civil penalty under subsection (2) may be recovered for any violation of the Act, but not for unconscionable or fraudulent conduct subject to action under Section 5.108 or under Section 6.111. The amount of the penalty to be imposed under subsection (2) is in the discretion of the court, but a penalty may be imposed only if it is found that the defendant has engaged in a course of repeated and intentional violations of the Act. Since this subsection confers a right of recovery on the Administrator in his own behalf, it prescribes its own statute of limitations. An unintentional and bona fide error defense is inapplicable since recovery can only be had for repeated and intentional violations, and if a creditor voluntarily notifies consumers of and corrects violations, his conduct should be taken into account with respect to whether an action under this subsection is appropriate or in connection with the penalty imposed.

4. Failure to file notification or to pay fees in accordance with the provisions of Sections 6.202 and 6.203 is a violation of this Act. However, the remedy of subsection (2) is inappropriate for a variety of reasons among which is it does not permit recovery of the unpaid fees as well as a penalty for the violation. Subsection (3) creates a more specific remedy for this type of violation. The amount of the penalty to be imposed is in the discretion of the court subject to a basic limitation of three times the unpaid fees. Since this amount of penalty may be of little consequence where small

amounts are owed, the court may impose a penalty in excess of three times the unpaid fees up to $1,000.

Section 6.114 [Jury Trial]

The Administrator has no right to trial by jury in an action brought by him under this Act.

Section 6.115 [Consumer's Remedies not Affected]

The grant of powers to the Administrator in this Article does not affect remedies available to consumers under this Act or under other principles of law or equity.

COMMENT

1. It is not the intention of the grant of powers to the Administrator or of any of the other provisions of this Act dealing with consumers' remedies to diminish in any way the availability of consumers' remedies under other principles of law or equity or to impede the development of judicially created law in this area. For example, the individual consumer has a cause of action under Section 5.201(2) and (3) to recover any charges in excess of those permitted in the Act and to recover a penalty in certain cases, and the Administrator may also bring an action under Section 6.113 to recover excess charges on behalf of consumers. Whether or not an action to recover excess charges by a class of private parties would lie depends upon the State law with respect to class actions. This Act does not specifically authorize such class actions nor does it preclude them. See also Section 5.105, Comment 7.

2. Various other consumers' remedies provided by other applicable law are not affected by this Act. Examples include the UCC provisions concerning the buyer's revocation of acceptance of goods delivered (UCC Section 2–608), the buyer's right to cancel the contract and to take a security interest in the goods delivered (UCC Section 2–711), the buyer's right to incidental and consequential damages (UCC Section 2–715), and the buyer's remedies for fraud (UCC Section 2–721). So, too, the limitations on contract provided for in the UCC in regard to penalties, liquidated damages, and limitation of remedies (UCC Sections 2–718 and 2–719) continue to apply to transactions governed by this Act.

[Section 6.116 [Venue]

The Administrator may bring actions or proceedings in a court in a [county] in which an act on which the action or proceeding is based occurred or in a [county] in which respondent resides or transacts business.]

COMMENT

This section is bracketed since it may be unnecessary in some States because of adequate venue rules in those States.

PART 2

NOTIFICATION AND FEES

Section 6.201 [Applicability]

This Part applies to a creditor engaged in entering into consumer credit transactions in this State and to a creditor having an office or place of business in this State who takes assignments and undertakes direct collection of payments from or enforcement of rights against consumers arising from these transactions.

COMMENT

1. All creditors engaged in entering into consumer credit transactions in this State must file notification under Section 6.202. As to when a creditor enters into a consumer credit transaction in this State see Section 1.201 on territorial application.

2. Assignees of consumer obligations must file notification under Section 6.202 only if all of the three following elements are present: (1) the assigned obligations arose out of consumer credit transactions entered into in this State, (2) the assignee has an office or place of business in this State, and (3) the assignee undertakes direct collection of payments from the consumers or direct enforcement of obligations against consumers. An assignee having no office or place of business within this State is not required to file notification even though he is engaged in direct collection or direct enforcement of consumer accounts in this State.

3. The direct collection provision excludes from the notification requirements the assignee "in bulk" or "for security" who leaves the collection of the obligation to the assignor and so has no relationship with the consumers with whom this Act is primarily concerned. If an assignee for some reason, such as the default or bankruptcy of the assignor, takes over the direct collection or direct enforcement of obligations against consumers, he must at that time file notification.

4. Under Sections 1.301(12)(b)(i) and (14)(a)(iv) a transaction pursuant to a lender credit card is excluded from the definitions of consumer credit sale and consumer lease and is classified as a loan made by the issuer of the card. Section 1.301(25). However, a transaction pursuant to a seller credit card may be a consumer credit sale or consumer lease. Consequently, a seller or lessor engaged in such transactions must file notification under Section 6.202.

Section 6.202 [Notification]

(1) Persons subject to this Part shall file notification with the Administrator within 30 days after commencing business in this State, and, thereafter, on or before January 31 of each year. The notification shall state:

(a) name of the person;

(b) name in which business is transacted if different from (a);

(c) address of principal office, which may be outside this State;

(d) address of all offices or retail stores, if any, in this State at which consumer credit transactions are entered into, or in case of a person taking assignments of obligations, the offices or places of business within this State at which business is transacted;

(e) if consumer credit transactions are entered into otherwise than at an office or retail store in this State, a brief description of the manner in which they are entered into;

(f) address of designated agent upon whom service of process may be made in this State; and

(g) whether supervised loans are made.

(2) If information in a notification becomes inaccurate after filing, no further notification is required until the following January 31.

COMMENT

1. The basic rule is that notification must be filed within 30 days after commencing in this State business which is subject to this Act. In the case of an assignee who did not take the assignment with the intention of engaging in direct collection or enforcement but who at some later time finds it necessary to do so, notification is required 30 days after undertaking direct collection or enforcement.

2. Subsection (1)(e) requires a brief description of the manner of selling, leasing, or lending under which the creditor receives the consumer's offer at a place other than at an office or retail store, *e. g.*, door to door selling, product parties.

3. Once a person has filed notification, he need file only once a year even though he changes his business name or opens additional places of business or makes other changes during the year.

Section 6.203 [Fees]

(1) A person required to file notification shall pay to the [Administrator] an annual fee of $10. The fee shall be paid

with the filing of the first notification and on or before January 31 of each year thereafter.

(2) Except as provided in subsection (4), a person required to file notification who is a seller, lessor, or lender shall pay at the time and in the manner stated in subsection (1) an additional fee of [$10] for each $100,000 or part thereof exceeding [$10,000], of the average unpaid balances, including unpaid scheduled periodic payments under consumer leases, of obligations arising from consumer credit transactions entered into by him in this State and held on the last day of each calendar month during the preceding calendar year and held either by the seller, lessor, or lender or by his immediate or remote assignee who has not filed notification. The unpaid balances of assigned obligations held by an assignee who has not filed notification are presumed to be the unpaid balances of the assigned obligations at the time of their assignment by the seller, lessor, or lender.

(3) Except as provided in subsection (4), a person required to file notification who is an assignee shall pay at the time and in the manner stated in subsection (1) an additional fee of [$10] for each $100,000, or part thereof exceeding [$10,000], of the average unpaid balances, including unpaid scheduled periodic payments payable by lessees, of obligations arising from consumer credit transactions entered into in this State taken by him by assignment and held by him by assignment and held by him on the last day of each calendar month during the preceding calendar year.

(4) A supervised financial organization is exempt from 50 per cent of the fees prescribed by subsections (2) and (3) to take account of its obligation to pay other fees or charges to officials or agencies to whose supervision it is also subject.

(5) To the extent that a seller, lessor, or lender, or his immediate or remote assignee is obligated to pay and pays fees to another state or official thereof pursuant to provisions similar but not necessarily identical to subsections (2) and (3), he is entitled to an exemption from the fees prescribed by subsections (2) and (3).

(6) The [Administrator] may collect a charge not exceeding [$25] from each person required to pay fees under this section with respect to fees not paid in full within 90 days after they are due.

COMMENT

1. Any person required to file notification under this Part must pay an annual fee of $10. Subsection (1) provides for payment of an annual fee with the first filing of a notification, to assure income for the first year of operations under this Act, and thereafter on or before January 31 of each year.

2. In addition, except as otherwise provided in this section, such a person who is a seller, lessor, or lender must pay an additional fee of [$10] for each $100,000, or part thereof exceeding [$10,000], of the average unpaid balances, including unpaid scheduled periodic payments under consumer leases, of obligations arising from consumer credit transactions entered into by him in this State and held on the last day of each calendar month during the preceding calendar year and held by him. An assignee must pay an additional fee of [$10] for each $100,000, or part thereof exceeding [$10,000], of the average unpaid balances of obligations arising from consumer credit transactions entered into in this State taken by him by assignment and held by him by assignment and held by him on the last day of each calendar month during the preceding calendar year. The exclusion of the first [$10,000] of consumer credit receivables is designed to enable a merchant who sells most of his closed-end paper to ordinarily avoid paying additional fees and the similar exclusion with respect to assignees is to maintain consistency. Average outstandings on the last day of each month during the year has been chosen as a convenient basis for calculating additional fees since creditors normally maintain records of these figures and they are easily audited by the Administrator. The additional fee per $100,000 or part thereof of receivables should be set by the enacting State at that figure which will produce for it, under its particular circumstances, funds sufficient for the adequate administration of this Act.

3. To illustrate the operation of this section and using a $10 additional fee and a $10,000 exclusion assume that a seller had average consumer credit sale unpaid balances during the preceding year of $975,000 of which he assigned immediately after the sales involved $325,000 to a sales finance company which had filed notification. The sum on which the seller must compute the additional fee in excess of the $10 annual fee is $975,000 less $325,000, or $650,000. Therefore, the seller's total fee will be an annual fee of $10 plus $70 of additional fee, or $80. The sales finance company's fee in addition to the $10 annual fee will be based on the average unpaid balances of the assigned accounts. Therefore, the sales finance company's total fee will be a $10 annual fee plus $40, or $50.

4. A seller, lessor or lender entering into consumer credit transactions in this State cannot escape liability for the fees imposed by subsection (2) by assigning the resulting obligations to an out-of-state assignee who

has not filed notification. Subsection (2) imposes a liability for the fees on the seller, lessor or lender if his immediate or remote assignee has not filed notification, and a presumption is created on the basis of which the fees can be computed.

5. All creditors extending consumer credit in a state enacting this Act are governed by it and should share in financing the cost of its administration. However, since supervised financial organizations are subject to examination, investigation, and administrative enforcement by officials or agencies to whose supervision they are subject other than the Administrator (Section 6.105) and pay fees or charges to those officials or agencies, subsection (4) creates an exemption from 50 per cent of the additional fees otherwise payable by such creditors.

6. It is conceivable that an obligation can exist to pay additional fees under this Act on consumer credit paper and also to pay similar fees to another state on the same consumer credit paper. To the extent of the obligation to pay and payment of fees to the other state or official thereof, subsection (5) permits an exemption from the additional fees payable under this section.

PART 3

COUNCIL OF ADVISORS ON CONSUMER CREDIT

Section 6.301 [Council of Advisors on Consumer Credit]

(1) The Council of Advisors on Consumer Credit is created consisting of [sixteen] members appointed by the Governor. The Governor shall designate one of the Advisors as Chairman. In appointing members of the Council, the Governor shall seek to achieve a fair representation from the various segments of the consumer credit industry and the public.

(2) The term of office of each member of the Council is [four] years. Of those members first appointed, [four] shall be appointed for a term of [one] year, [four] for a term of [two] years, [four] for a term of [three] years, and [four] for a term of [four] years. A member chosen to fill a vacancy arising otherwise than by expiration of term shall be appointed for the unexpired term of the member whom he is to succeed. A member of the Council is eligible for reappointment.

(3) Members of the Council shall serve without compensation, but are entitled to reimbursement of expenses reasonably incurred in the performance of their duties.

Section 6.302 [Function of Council; Conflict of Interest]

The Council shall advise and consult with the Administrator concerning the exercise of his powers under this Act and may make recommendations to him. Members of the Council may assist the Administrator in obtaining compliance with this Act. Since it is an objective of this Part to obtain competent representatives of creditors and the public to serve on the Council and to assist and cooperate with the Administrator in achieving the objectives of this Act, service on the Council does not in itself constitute a conflict of interest regardless of the occupations or associations of the members.

Section 6.303 [Meetings]

The Council and the Administrator shall meet together at a time and place designated by the Chairman at least twice each year. The Council may hold additional meetings when called by the Chairman.

[PART 4]

[ADMINISTRATIVE PROCEDURE AND JUDICIAL REVIEW]

[Section 6.401 [Applicability and Scope]

This Part applies to the Administrator, prescribes the procedures to be observed by him in exercising his powers under this Act, and supplements the provisions of the Part on Powers and Functions of Administrator (Part 1) of this Article and of the Part on Supervised Lenders (Part 3) of the Article on Finance Charges and Related Provisions (Article 2).]

COMMENT

This Part is patterned after the Uniform Law Commissioners' Revised Model State Administrative Procedure Act, hereinafter referred to as the Revised Model Act. It is intended for adoption only in those states which have not enacted an adequate administrative procedure act which would apply to the actions of the Administrator under this Act. States which have acts covering only a part of the matter dealt with in this Part may find it desirable to adopt portions of this Part. States which presently have administrative procedure acts which depart markedly from the Revised Model Act may find it desirable to adopt this Part or some of its sections to apply to actions of the Administrator. See Sections 2.306, 4.112, and 6.-107.

[Section 6.402 [Definitions in Part: "Contested Case"; "License"; "Licensing"; "Party"; "Rule"]

In this Part:

(1) "Contested case" means a proceeding, including but not restricted to one pursuant to the provisions on administrative enforcement orders (subsection (1) of Section 6.108) and licensing, in which the legal rights, duties, or privileges of a party are required by law to be determined by the Administrator after an opportunity for hearing.

(2) "License" means a license authorizing a person to make supervised loans pursuant to the provisions on authority to make supervised loans (Section 2.301).

(3) "Licensing" includes the Administrator's process respecting the grant, denial, revocation, suspension, annulment, withdrawal, or amendment of a license.

(4) "Party" means the Administrator and each person named or admitted as a party, or who is aggrieved by action taken and seeks to be admitted as a party.

(5) "Rule" means each rule specifically authorized by this Act that applies generally and implements, interprets, or prescribes law or policy, or each statement by the Administrator that applies generally and describes the Administrator's procedure or practice requirements or the organization of his office. The term includes the amendment or repeal of a prior rule but does not include:

(a) statements concerning only the internal management of the Administrator's office and not affecting private rights or procedures available to the public; [or]

(b) declaratory rulings issued pursuant to the provisions on declaratory rulings by Administrator (Section 6.409) [; or

(c) intra-office memoranda].]

COMMENT

These definitions are derived from Section 1 of the Revised Model Act.

[Section 6.403 [Public Information; Adoption of Rules; Availability of Rules and Orders]

(1) In addition to other rule-making requirements imposed by law, the Administrator shall:

(a) adopt as a rule a description of the organization of his office, stating the general course and method of the operations of his office and the methods whereby the public may obtain information or make submissions or requests;

(b) adopt rules of practice setting forth the nature and requirements of all formal and informal procedures available, including a description of all forms and instructions used by the Administrator or his office;

(c) make available for public inspection all rules and all other written statements of policy or interpretations formulated, adopted, or used by the Administrator in the discharge of his functions; and

(d) make available for public inspection all final orders, decisions, and opinions.

(2) A rule, order, or decision of the Administrator is not valid or effective against any person or party, nor may it be in-

voked by the Administrator for any person, until it has been made available for public inspection as herein required. This provision does not apply in favor of any person or party who has actual knowledge thereof.]

COMMENT

This section is derived from Section 2 of the Revised Model Act.

[Section 6.404 [Procedure for Adoption of Rules]

(1) Prior to the adoption, amendment, or repeal of any rule, the Administrator shall:

(a) give at least 30 days' notice of his intended action. The notice shall include a statement of either the terms or substance of the intended action or a description of the subjects and issues involved, and the time, place, and manner in which interested persons may present their views thereon. The notice shall be mailed to all persons who have made timely request of the Administrator for advance notice of his rule-making proceedings and be published in [here insert the medium of publication appropriate for the adopting State];

(b) afford all interested persons reasonable opportunity to submit data, views, or arguments, orally or in writing. In case of substantive rules, opportunity for oral hearing shall be granted if requested by 25 persons, a governmental subdivision or agency, or an association having not fewer than 25 members. The Administrator shall consider fully all written and oral submissions respecting the proposed rule. Upon adoption of a rule the Administrator, if requested to do so by an interested person before adoption or within 30 days thereafter, shall issue a concise statement of the principal reasons for and against its adoption, incorporating therein his reasons for overruling the considerations urged against its adoption.

(2) A rule is not valid unless adopted in substantial compliance with this section. A proceeding to contest any rule on the ground of non-compliance with the procedural requirements of this section shall be commenced within two years from the effective date of the rule.]

COMMENT

This section is derived from Section 3 of the Revised Model Act.

[Section 6.405 [Filing and Taking Effect of Rules]

(1) The Administrator shall file in the office of the [Secretary of State] a certified copy of each rule adopted by him. The [Secretary of State] shall keep a permanent register of the rules open to public inspection.

(2) Each rule hereafter adopted is effective 20 days after filing, except that a later effective date may be specified in the rule.]

COMMENT

This section is derived from Section 4 of the Revised Model Act.

[Section 6.406 [Publication of Rules]

(1) The [Secretary of State] shall compile, index, and publish all effective rules adopted by the Administrator. Compilations shall be supplemented or revised as often as necessary.

(2) Compilations shall be made available upon request to [agencies and officials of this State] free of charge and to other persons at prices fixed by the [Secretary of State] to cover mailing and publication costs.]

COMMENT

This section is derived from Section 5 of the Revised Model Act.

[Section 6.407 [Petition for Adoption of Rules]

An interested person may petition the Administrator requesting the adoption, amendment, or repeal of a rule. The Administrator shall prescribe by rule the form for petitions and the procedure for their submission, consideration, and disposition. Within 30 days after submission of a petition, the Administrator either shall deny the petition in writing (stating his reasons for the denials) or initiate rule-making proceedings in accordance with the provisions on procedure for adoption of rules (Section 6.404).]

COMMENT

This section is derived from Section 6 of the Revised Model Act.

[Section 6.408 [Declaratory Judgment on Validity or Applicability of Rules]

The validity or applicability of a rule may be determined in an action for declaratory judgment in the [ ] court if it is alleged that the rule, or its threatened application, interferes with or impairs, or threatens to interfere with or impair, the legal rights or privileges of the plaintiff. The Administrator shall be made a party to the action. A declaratory judgment may be rendered whether or not the plaintiff has requested the Administrator to pass upon the validity or applicability of the rule in question.]

COMMENT

This section is derived from Section 7 of the Revised Model Act.

[Section 6.409 [Declaratory Rulings by Administrator]

The Administrator shall provide by rule for the filing and prompt disposition of petitions for declaratory rulings as to the applicability of any statutory provision or of any rule of the Administrator. Rulings disposing of petitions have the same status as decisions or orders in contested cases.]

COMMENT

This section is derived from Section 8 of the Revised Model Act.

[Section 6.410 [Contested Cases; Notice; Hearing; Records]

(1) In a contested case, all parties shall be afforded an opportunity for hearing after reasonable notice.

(2) The notice shall include:

(a) a statement of the time, place, and nature of the hearing;

(b) a statement of the legal authority and jurisdiction under which the hearing is to be held;

(c) a reference to the particular provisions of the statutes and rules involved; and

(d) a short and plain statement of the matters asserted. If the Administrator or other party is unable to state the matters in detail at the time the notice is served, the initial notice may be limited to a statement of the issues involved. Thereafter upon application a more definite and detailed statement shall be furnished.

(3) Opportunity shall be afforded all parties to respond and present evidence and argument on all issues involved.

(4) Unless precluded by law, informal disposition may be made of a contested case by stipulation, agreed settlement, consent order, or default.

(5) The record in a contested case shall include:

(a) pleadings, motions, and intermediate rulings;

(b) evidence received or considered;

(c) a statement of matters officially noticed;

(d) questions and offers of proof, objections, and rulings thereon;

(e) proposed findings and exceptions;

(f) any decision, opinion, or report by the officer presiding at the hearing; and

(g) staff memoranda or data submitted to the hearing officer or members of the office of the Administrator in connection with their consideration of the case.

(6) Oral proceedings or any part thereof shall be transcribed on request of any party [, but at his expense].

(7) Findings of fact shall be based exclusively on the evidence and on matters officially noticed.]

COMMENT

This section is derived from Section 9 of the Revised Model Act.

[Section 6.411 [Rules of Evidence; Official Notice]

In contested cases:

(1) irrelevant, immaterial, or unduly repetitious evidence shall be excluded. The rules of evidence as applied in [non-jury] civil cases in the [ ] court of this State shall be followed. If necessary to ascertain facts not reasonably susceptible of proof under those rules, evidence not admissible thereunder may be admitted (except where precluded by statute) if it is of a type commonly relied upon by reasonably prudent men in the conduct of their affairs. The Administrator shall give effect to the rules of privilege recognized by law. Objections to eviden-

tiary offers may be made and shall be noted in the record. Subject to these requirements, if a hearing will be expedited and the interests of the parties will not be prejudiced substantially, any part of the evidence may be received in written form;

[(2) documentary evidence may be received in the form of copies or excerpts, if the original is not readily available. Upon request, parties shall be given an opportunity to compare the copy with the original;]

(3) a party may conduct cross-examinations required for a full and true disclosure of the facts;

(4) notice may be taken of judicially cognizable facts. In addition, notice may be taken of generally recognized technical or scientific facts within the Administrator's specialized knowledge. Parties shall be notified either before or during the hearing, or by reference in preliminary reports or otherwise, of the material noticed, including any staff memoranda or data, and they shall be afforded an opportunity to contest the material so noticed. The Administrator's experience, technical competence, and specialized knowledge may be utilized in the evaluation of the evidence.]

COMMENT

This section is derived from Section 10 of the Revised Model Act.

[Section 6.412 [Decisions and Orders]

A final decision or order adverse to a party in a contested case shall be in writing or stated in the record. A final decision shall include findings of fact and conclusions of law, separately stated. Findings of fact, if set forth in statutory language, shall be accompanied by a concise and explicit statement of the underlying facts supporting the findings. If, in accordance with rules of the Administrator, a party submitteed proposed findings of fact, the decision shall include a ruling upon each proposed finding. Parties shall be notified either personally or by mail of any decision or order. Upon request a copy of the decision or order shall be delivered or mailed forthwith to each party and to his attorney of record.]

COMMENT

This section is derived from Section 12 of the Revised Model Act.

[Section 6.413 [Licenses]

(1) Whenever the grant or denial of a license is required to be preceded by notice and opportunity for hearing, the provisions of this Part concerning contested cases apply.

(2) A revocation, suspension, annulment, or withdrawal of a license is unlawful unless the Administrator, before instituting proceedings, gives notice by mail to the licensee of facts or conduct which warrant the intended action, and the licensee was afforded an opportunity to show compliance with all lawful requirements for retention of the license.]

COMMENT

This section is derived from Section 14 of the Revised Model Act.

[Section 6.414 [Judicial Review of Contested Cases]

(1) A person who has exhausted all administrative remedies available before the Administrator and is aggrieved by a final decision in a contested case is entitled to judicial review under this Part. This section does not limit utilization of or the scope of judicial review available under other means of review, redress, relief, or trial de novo provided by law. A preliminary, procedural, or intermediate action or ruling of the Administrator is immediately reviewable if review of the final decision of the Administrator would not provide an adequate remedy.

(2) Proceedings for review are instituted by filing a petition in the [ ] court within [30] days after [mailing notice of] the final decision of the Administrator or, if a rehearing is requested, within [30] days after the decision thereon. Copies of the petition shall be served upon the Administrator and all parties of record.

(3) The filing of the petition does not itself stay enforcement of the decision of the Administrator. The Administrator may grant, or the reviewing court may order, a stay upon appropriate terms.

(4) Within [30] days after service of the petition, or within further time allowed by the court, the Administrator shall transmit to the reviewing court the original or a certified copy of the entire record of the proceeding under review. By stipulation of all parties to the review proceedings, the record may be shortened. A party unreasonably refusing to stipulate to limit the

record may be taxed by the court for the additional costs. The court may require or permit subsequent corrections or additions to the record.

(5) If, before the date set for hearing, application is made to the court for leave to present additional evidence, and it is shown to the satisfaction of the court that the additional evidence is material and there were good reasons for failure to present it in the proceeding before the Administrator, the court may order that the additional evidence be taken before the Administrator upon conditions determined by the court. The Administrator may modify his findings and decision by reason of the additional evidence and shall file that evidence and any modifications, new findings, or decisions with the reviewing court.

(6) The review shall be confined to the record and be conducted by the court without a jury. In cases of alleged irregularities in procedure before the Administrator, not shown in the record, proof thereon may be taken in the court. The court, upon request, shall hear oral argument and receive written briefs.

(7) The court may not substitute its judgment for that of the Administrator as to the weight of the evidence on questions of fact. The court may affirm the decision of the Administrator or remand the case for further proceedings. The court may reverse or modify the decision if substantial rights of the appellant have been prejudiced because the administrative findings, inferences, conclusions, or decisions are:

(a) in violation of constitutional or statutory provisions;

(b) in excess of the statutory authority of the Administrator;

(c) made upon unlawful procedure;

(d) affected by other error of law;

(e) clearly erroneous in view of the reliable, probative, and substantial evidence on the whole record; or

(f) arbitrary or capricious or characterized by abuse of discretion or clearly unwarranted exercise of discretion.]

COMMENT

This section is derived from Section 15 of the Revised Model Act.

[Section 6.415 [Appeals]

An aggrieved party may obtain a review of any final judgment of the [ ] court under this Part by appeal to the [ ] court. The appeal shall be taken as in other civil cases.]

COMMENT

This section is derived from Section 16 of the Revised Model Act.

ARTICLE 7

Reserved for Future Use

ARTICLE 8

Reserved for Future Use

ARTICLE 9

EFFECTIVE DATE AND REPEALER

Section 9.101 [Time of Taking Effect; Provisions for Transition]

(1) Except as otherwise provided in this section, this Act takes effect at 12:01 a. m. on [ ].

(2) To the extent appropriate to permit the Administrator to prepare for operation of this Act when it takes effect and to act on applications for licenses to make supervised loans under this Act (subsection (1) of Section 2.302), the Part on Supervised Lenders (Part 3) of the Article on Finance Charges and Related Provisions (Article 2), and the Article on Administration (Article 6) take effect [ ].

Note: Insert in lieu of brackets at the end of subsection (2) either "immediately" or the earliest time possible under the constitutional or statutory requirements of the enacting State.

(3) Transactions entered into before this Act takes effect and the rights, duties, and interests flowing from them thereafter may be terminated, completed, consummated, or enforced as required or permitted by any statute, rule of law, or other law amended, repealed, or modified by this Act as though the repeal, amendment, or modification had not occurred; but this Act applies to:

(a) refinancings, consolidations, and deferrals made after this Act takes effect as to sales, leases, and loans whenever entered into;

(b) sales or loans entered into after this Act takes effect pursuant to open-end credit entered into, arranged, or contracted for before this Act takes effect; and

(c) all credit transactions entered into before this Act takes effect insofar as the Article on Remedies and Penalties (Article 5) limits the remedies of creditors.

Section 9.102 [Continuation of Licensing]

All persons licensed or otherwise authorized under [list statutes] on the effective date of this Act are licensed to make supervised loans under this Act pursuant to the Part on Supervised Lenders (Part 3) of the Article on Finance Charges and Related Provisions (Article 2), and that Part applies to the persons so previously licensed or authorized. The Administrator may, but is not required to, deliver evidence of licensing to the persons so previously licensed or authorized.

COMMENT

This section provides automatic licensing under Article 2, Part 3 (Section 2.301 et seq.) for all lenders previously licensed under the State's licensed lender statutes prior to the effective date. No application or administrative action is required and the formal license under the prior statute, which will be repealed, will be a license under Part 3 of Article 2. The Administrator, at such time as his new duties under the Code permit him an opportunity, may substitute new licenses for those in the lenders' possession, but this is entirely a ministerial act.

Section 9.103 [Specific Repealer and Amendments]

(1) The following acts and parts of acts are repealed:

(a)

(b)

(c) [and so on]

(2) The following acts and parts of acts are amended:

(a)

(b)

(c) [and so on]

Note re Repealer and Amendatory Provisions

This Act is a comprehensive statute designed to regulate most aspects of consumer credit, maximum charges that may be made for consumer credit and rates of interest generally. Consumer credit covered includes sales credit related to the sale to consumers of goods or services, consumer loan credit, some credit related to the sale or financing of homes and some agricultural credit. All States have one or more acts regulating consumer credit and rates of interest and in many States additional provisions performing the same function appear in various other acts. To accommodate existing law to this Act, each State enacting this Act will need to repeal one or more existing acts or particular provisions in acts and may have to amend one or more other acts. The purpose of this Note is to suggest to the statutory revisor or other person preparing this Act for introduction into a particular State Legislature the acts which should be repealed or amended. To produce the uniformity which the Commissioners believe desirable, acts should be repealed or amended as recommended in this Note.

Acts to be Totally or Substantially Repealed

Subject to other specific suggestions of this Note, certain existing acts devoted primarily to regulating consumer credit should be repealed in their entirety. The revisor or draftsman should insert in this section the appropriate statutes or provisions to be repealed. To help guide the search for these acts or provisions, a list of some of the common popular names of these acts follow, although there may be others in any particular jurisdiction:

Small loan acts, personal loan acts, consumer loan acts, acts licensing personal loan lenders, sales finance companies, consumer finance companies, and industrial loan acts.

Instalment loan laws.

Retail instalment sales acts, motor vehicle instalment sales acts, all goods acts.

Revolving sales credit acts, revolving loan acts.

Truth in Lending acts.

Home solicitation sales acts.

Home improvement sales and loan acts.

Insurance premium financing acts.

Acts Permitting Maximum Charges for Credit and General Usury Acts

Repeal of the above listed consumer credit regulatory acts will automatically repeal provisions in these acts permitting maximum charges for the types of credit dealt with in the acts. In addition, all general usury statutes and all other provisions in acts permitting maximum charges for loans, forbearance, or the extension of credit should be repealed, excepting only provisions, if any, for maximum charges to be made by pawnbrokers.

Statutes providing for a "legal rate" of interest, that is, the rate to be applied for judgments, notes and other cases where there is no agreed rate or no agreement is possible (as in a judgment) should not be repealed. If these statutes are so intertwined with maximum contract rates, *e. g.*, usury provisions, that it is difficult to separate the two types of provisions, total repeal of the usury and legal rate statute plus the addition of the following provision in this Act or elsewhere in the State statutes may be in order:

"If there is no agreement or provision of law for a different rate, the interest of money shall be at the rate of [six] per cent per annum."

Provisions of Existing Statutes Affecting Powers of Organizations

In some States provisions relating to rates of interest are intertwined with provisions relating to powers of particular types of organizations, *e. g.*, licensed lenders, consumer finance companies, commercial and industrial banks and trust companies, and thrift institutions such as credit unions, savings banks, and savings and loan associations whether or not organized for profit. In these cases statutory provisions should be repealed, preserved or amended according to Section 1.108 of this Act. See Comment to Section 1.108.

Uniform Commercial Code

The Official Text of Uniform Commercial Code Section 9–203 and the Note which follows it read in part as follows:

> "A transaction, although subject to this Article, is also subject to . . . . . . *, and in the case of conflict between the provisions of this Article and any such statute, the provisions of such statute control. Failure to comply with any applicable statute has only the effect which is specified therein.
>
> **Note:** At * . . . insert reference to any local statute regulating small loans, retail installment sales and the like"

If a State which enacted the UCC followed the instructions in the Note and inserted at the asterisk in UCC Section 9–203 references to local statutes regulating small loans, retail instalment sales and the like, UCC Section 9–203 should be amended to substitute a reference to the Uniform Consumer Credit Code in lieu of those listed statutes. No other provisions of the UCC need be amended if it was enacted without variation from uniform language.

UNIFORM CONSUMER SALES PRACTICES ACT

NATIONAL CONFERENCE OF COMMISSIONERS ON UNIFORM STATE LAWS

APPROVED BY THE AMERICAN BAR ASSOCIATION

Table of Contents

UNIFORM CONSUMER SALES PRACTICES ACT

§ 1. [Purposes, Rules of Construction]

This Act shall be construed liberally to promote the following policies:

(1) to simplify, clarify, and modernize the law governing consumer sales practices;

(2) to protect consumers from suppliers who commit deceptive and unconscionable sales practices;

(3) to encourage the development of fair consumer sales practices;

(4) to make state regulation of consumer sales practices not inconsistent with the policies of the Federal Trade Commission Act relating to consumer protection; and

(5) to make uniform the law, including the administrative rules, with respect to the subject of this Act among those states which enact it.

Comment

This section provides general interpretative guidelines. As stated in § 1(4), Federal Trade Commission decisions, rules, and guides are germane to the interpretation of the Act.

§ 2. [Definitions]

As used in this Act:

(1) "consumer transaction" means a sale, lease, assignment, award by chance, or other disposition of an item of goods, a service, or an intangible [except securities] to an individual for purposes that are primarily personal, family, or household, or that relate to a business opportunity that requires both his expenditure of money or property and his personal services on a continuing basis and in which he has not been previously engaged, or a solicitation by a supplier with respect to any of these dispositions;

Comment

A consumer transaction typically involves a natural person who obtains or is solicited to obtain an item of goods, a service, or an intangible primarily for personal, family, or household purposes. Also included are certain analogous transactions in which a natural person obtains or is solicited to obtain a business opportunity in which he has not been previously engaged. In view of the extensive state regulation of securities transactions, their inclusion is left optional. On the assumption that land transactions frequently are, and should be, regulated by specialized legislation, they are excluded altogether.

(2) "Enforcing Authority" means [appropriate official or officials];

Comment

In order to obtain effective administration, the National Conference recommends centralizing all powers granted by the Uniform Consumer Sales Practices Act in a single official. In some states a single official, typically the Attorney General, already has been granted substantial power with respect to consumer sales practices. In these states, the Attorney General is the logical choice for designation as Enforcing Authority. Because the Enforcing Authority may frequently find it necessary to engage in litigation, the Attorney General also is likely choice for Enforcing Authority in states which have not previously subjected consumer sales practices to extensive regulation. Moreover, if an enacting state creates a new agency to administer the Act, that state should carefully review each provision of the Act and provide a statutory framework which will ensure an effective working relationship between the new agency and the Attorney General.

(3) "final judgment" means a judgment, including any supporting opinion, that determines the rights of the parties and concerning which appellate remedies have been exhausted or the time for appeal has expired;

Comment

This definition pertains to one of the preconditions of class action damage liability in §§ 9(b) (1) and 11(d) (1). The Enforcing Authority is required to maintain a public file of these judgments and to make them available for public dissemination, § 5(a) (3), (5).

(4) "person" means an individual, corporation, government, governmental subdivision or agency, business trust, estate, trust, partnership, association, cooperative, or any other legal entity;

Comment

This definition is derived from the *Uniform Statutory Construction Act* § 26(4) (1965).

(5) "supplier" means a seller, lessor, assignor, or other person who regularly solicits, engages in, or enforces consumer transactions, whether or not he deals directly with the consumer;

Comment

In addition to manufacturers, wholesalers, and dealers, debt collection agencies and advertising agencies fall within this definition. Section 14 should be consulted in order to ascertain the conduct by suppliers which is exempt from the Act.

§ 3. [Deceptive Consumer Sales Practices]

(a) A deceptive act or practice by a supplier in connection with a consumer transaction violates this Act whether it occurs before, during, or after the transaction.

Comment

This subsection forbids deceptive advertising, deceptive statements made when goods are delivered, and deceptive statements made in connection with debt collection. A deceptive act or practice has the likelihood of inducing a state of mind in a consumer that is not in accord with the facts. It is immaterial whether this capacity to mislead arises from a verbal, written, or graphic misrepresentation or a nondisclosure by a supplier.

(b) Without limiting the scope of subsection (a), the act or practice of a supplier in indicating any of the following is deceptive:

Comment

The acts and practices listed in this subsection are treated as *per se* deceptive. They merely illustrate the acts and practices which violate § 3(a).

(1) that the subject of a consumer transaction has sponsorship, approval, performance characteristics, accessories, uses, or benefits it does not have;

Comment

This subsection forbids such conduct as misrepresenting the durability or components of a product, or the efficacy of a service.

(2) that the subject of a consumer transaction is of a particular standard, quality, grade, style, or model, if it is not;

Comment

This subsection forbids such conduct as misrepresenting that a superseded style or model is the latest style or model of a product, or that a particular product, service, or intangible is the equivalent of another product, service, or intangible; for example, misrepresenting that a two-ply tire is the equivalent of a four-ply tire.

(3) that the subject of a consumer transaction is new, or unused, if it is not, or that the subject of a consumer transaction has been used to an extent that is materially different from the fact;

Comment

This subsection forbids such conduct as misrepresenting that returned goods which were used by the original purchaser are unused. However, it does not preclude the description of returned goods as either new or unused, if that is in fact the case.

(4) that the subject of a consumer transaction is available to the consumer for a reason that does not exist;

Comment

This subsection forbids such conduct as spurious "fire" or "lost our lease" sales.

(5) that the subject of a consumer transaction has been supplied in accordance with a previous representation, if it has not;

Comment

This subsection forbids such conduct as misrepresenting that different goods, services, or intangibles are those previously advertised or purchased.

(6) that the subject of a consumer transaction will be supplied in greater quantity than the supplier intends;

Comment

This subsection forbids "bait advertising," a practice by which a supplier seeks to attract customers through advertising bargains which he does not intend to sell in more than nominal amounts. In order to induce acquisition of unadvertised items on which there is a greater mark-up, acquisition of the "bait" is discouraged through various artifices, including disparagement and exhaustion of an undisclosed miniscule stock. A supplier who is willing to sell all of the advertised items that he has in stock can avoid violating this subsection by disclosing that he has only "limited quantities" available. However, in the absence of such a willingness and disclosure, the existence of a violation should be determined on the basis of such objective factors as the representations made, and, in view of the expectable public demand, the reasonableness of the quantity of the advertised goods, services, or intangibles available.

(7) that replacement or repair is needed, if it is not;

Comment

This subsection forbids such conduct as misrepresenting that a television picture tube must be replaced or that a roof needs repair.

(8) that a specific price advantage exists, if it does not;

Comment

This subsection forbids such conduct as misrepresenting the amount of a price reduction, a previous price, or the actual price that is paid by a consumer. However, general pricing claims or descriptions, such as "good prices," are not proscribed.

(9) that the supplier has a sponsorship, approval, or affiliation he does not have;

Comment

This subsection forbids such conduct as misrepresenting that a supplier is an authorized dealer, or that a supplier has received a favorable rating from an organization like Underwriters' Laboratories.

(10) that a consumer transaction involves or does not involve a warranty, a disclaimer of warranties, particular warranty terms, or other rights, remedies, or obligations if the indication is false; or

Comment

This subsection forbids misrepresentation of the rights, remedies, or obligations of either a supplier or a consumer. The prohibition includes such conduct as misrepresenting that a consumer is obligated to pay for unsolicited goods or services, that a warranty is unconditional, that a consumer is not entitled to the return of a downpayment, or that a supplier can garnish exempt wages.

(11) that the consumer will receive a rebate, discount, or other benefit as an inducement for entering into a consumer transaction in return for giving the supplier the names of prospective consumers or otherwise helping the supplier to enter into other consumer transactions, if receipt of the benefit is contingent on an event occurring after the consumer enters into the transaction.

Comment

This subsection forbids referral commission arrangements in which a consumer is to receive future commissions based upon events which occur after the time at which he enters into a related consumer transaction.

§ 4. [Unconscionable Consumer Sales Practices]

(a) An unconscionable act or practice by a supplier in connection with a consumer transaction violates this Act whether it occurs before, during, or after the transaction.

(b) The unconscionability of an act or practice is a question of law for the court. If it is claimed or appears to the court that an act or practice may be unconscionable, the parties shall be given a reasonable opportunity to present evidence as to its setting, purpose, and effect to aid the court in making its determination.

Comment

These subsections forbid unconscionable advertising techniques, unconscionable contract terms, and unconscionable debt collection practices. As under *Uniform Commercial Code* § 2—302 (1962 Official Text with Comments), unconscionability is a question of law for the court. Unconscionability typically involves conduct by which a supplier seeks to induce or to require a consumer to assume risks which materially exceed the benefits to him of a related consumer transaction.

(c) In determining whether an act or practice is unconscionable, the court shall consider circumstances such as the following of which the supplier knew or had reason to know:

Comment

"Knowledge or reason to know" often will be established by a supplier's course of conduct. Although probative, this scienter is not invariably required in order to establish unconscionability under § 4(a).

(1) that he took advantage of the inability of the consumer reasonably to protect his interests because of his physical infirmity, ignorance, illiteracy, inability to understand the language of an agreement, or similar factors;

Comment

This subsection includes such conduct as selling an English-language encyclopedia set for personal use to a Spanish-American bachelor laborer who does not read English, or using legal verbiage in a manner which can not be readily comprehended by a low-income consumer who both reads and speaks English.

(2) that when the consumer transaction was entered into the price grossly exceeded the price at which similar property or services were readily obtainable in similar transaction by like consumers;

Comment

This subsection includes such conduct as a home solicitation sale of a set of cookware to a housewife for $375 in an area where a set of comparable quality is readily available to such a housewife for $125 or less.

(3) that when the consumer transaction was entered into the consumer was unable to receive a substantial benefit from the subject of the transaction;

Comment

This subsection includes such conduct as the sale of two expensive vacuum cleaners to two poor families whom the salesman knows, or has reason to know, share the same apartment and the same rug.

(4) that when the consumer transaction was entered into there was no reasonable probability of payment of the obligation in full by the consumer;

Comment

This subsection includes such conduct as the sale of goods, services, or intangibles to a low-income consumer whom the salesman knows, or has reason to know, does not have sufficient income to make the stipulated payments.

(5) that the transaction he induced the consumer to enter into was excessively one-sided in favor of the supplier; or

Comment

This subsection includes such conduct as requiring a consumer to sign a one-sided adhesion contract which contains a penalty clause, an acceleration clause, a confession-of-judgment clause, a disclaimer of all warranties, and a clause permitting the supplier, but not the consumer, to cancel the contract at will. As indicated by this illustration, this subsection applies to contract terms which result in an excessively one-sided consumer transaction even though some or all of the contract terms are lawful in and of themselves. The exemption from the Act by subsection 14(a) (1) of acts or practices required or specifically permitted by or under federal or state law should accordingly be reconciled with this subsection by exempting only required or specifically permitted aggregations of contract terms and required or specifically permitted contract terms.

(6) that he made a misleading statement of opinion on which the consumer was likely to rely to his detriment.

Comment

This subsection applies to misleading subjective expressions of opinion on which a supplier should reasonably expect a consumer to rely to his detriment. For example, a violation of this subsection would occur if a prospective purchaser asked a supplier what the useful life of a paint job was and the supplier, with reason to know that repainting would be necessary within two years, responded, "in my opinion the paint will wear like iron." Overt factual misstatements expressed in the form of opinion are dealt with by § 3's proscription of deceptive consumer sales practices. For example, a violation of § 3 would occur if a prospective purchaser asked a supplier what the useful life of a two-year paint job was and the supplier responded, "in my opinion repainting will not be necessary for five years."

§ 4A. [Jurisdiction and Service of Process]

[(a) The [————] court of this State [may exercise] [has] jurisdiction over any supplier as to any act or practice in this State governed by this Act or as to any claim arising from a consumer transaction subject to this Act.]

Comment

This optional subsection grants the courts of an enacting state jurisdiction with respect to violations of the Act. It may be omitted in states where an express statutory grant of judicial jurisdiction is unnecessary.

[(b) In addition to any other method provided by [rule or] statute, personal jurisdiction over a supplier may be acquired in a civil action or proceeding instituted in the [————] court by the service of process in the following manner. If a supplier engages in any act or practice in this State governed by this Act, or engages in a consumer transaction subject to this Act, he may designate an agent upon whom service of process may be made in this State. The agent must be a resident of or a corporation authorized to do business in this State. The designation must be in writing and filed with the [Secretary of State]. If no designation is made and filed, or if process cannot be served in this State upon the designated agent, whether or not the supplier is a resident of this State or is authorized to do business in this State, process may be served upon the [Secretary of State], but service upon him is not effective unless the plaintiff promptly mails a copy of the process and pleadings by registered or certified mail to the defendant at his last reasonably ascertainable address. An affidavit of compliance with this section must be filed with the clerk of the court on or before the return day of the process, if any, or within any future time the court allows.]

Comment

This optional subsection provides a method for obtaining personal jurisdiction over out-of-state suppliers who have violated the Act. It may be omitted in states with comparable "long-arm" statutes.

§ 5. [Duties of the Enforcing Authority]

(a) The Enforcing Authority shall:

(1) enforce this Act throughout the State;

(2) cooperate with state and local officials, officials of other states, and officials of the Federal government in the administration of comparable statutes;

(3) inform consumers and suppliers on a continuing basis of the provisions of this Act and of acts or practices that violate this Act, including mailing information concerning final judgments to persons who request it, for which he may charge a reasonable fee to cover the expense;

(4) receive and act on complaints;

(5) maintain a public file of (i) final judgments rendered under this Act that have been either reported officially or made available for public dissemination under Section 5(a) (3), (ii) final consent judgments, and (iii), to the extent the Enforcing Authority considers appropriate, assurances of voluntary compliance; and

(6) report [annually on or before January 1] to the [Governor and Legislature] on the operations of his office and on the acts or practices occurring in this State that violate this Act.

(b) The Enforcing Authority's report shall include a statement of the investigatory and enforcement procedures and policies of his office, of the number of investigations and enforcement proceedings instituted and of their disposition, and of the other activities of his office and of other persons to carry out the purposes of this Act.

(c) In carrying out his duties, the Enforcing Authority may not publicly disclose the identity of a person investigated unless his identity has become a matter of public record in an enforcement proceeding or he has consented to public disclosure.

Comment

This section emphasizes that the Enforcing Authority's informational and educational duties are as important as his enforcement duties. The identity of persons investigated but not otherwise proceeded against must be kept confidential, § 5(c). However, § 5(c) does not preclude the confidential dissemination of information to other enforcement authorities, § 5(a) (2), or public disclosure of information in the file maintained under § 5(a) (5).

§ 6. [General Powers of the Enforcing Authority]

(a) The Enforcing Authority may conduct research, hold public hearings, make inquiries, and publish studies relating to consumer sales acts or practices.

Comment

This subsection illustrates the consumer education techniques which may be employed by the Enforcing Authority.

(b) The Enforcing Authority shall adopt substantive rules that prohibit with specificity acts or practices that violate Section 3 and appropriate procedural rules.

Comment

This subsection requires the Enforcing Authority to adopt specific substantive rules prohibiting deceptive consumer sales acts and practices. This substantive rule-making power must be exercised within the legislative standards provided by § 3. Adoption of appropriate procedural rules also is required.

§ 7. [Rule-making Requirements]

Alternative A

[The [State Administrative Procedure Act] applies to administrative action taken by the Enforcing Authority under this Act.]

Comment

Alternative A may be enacted in states that have administrative procedure acts. If a state does not have an administrative procedure act, Alternative B should be selected. The provisions in Alternative B and the accompanying optional §§ 7A–7E are derived from *Uniform Consumer Credit Code* §§ 6.403–408 (1969 Official Text with Comments).

Alternative B

[(a) In addition to complying with other rule-making requirements imposed by this Act, the Enforcing Authority shall:

(1) adopt as a rule a description of the organization of his office, stating the general course and method of operation of his office and methods whereby the public may obtain information or make submissions or requests;

(2) adopt rules of practice setting forth the nature and requirements of all formal and informal procedures available, including a description of the forms and instructions used by the Enforcing Authority or his office; and

(3) make available for public inspection all rules, written statements of policy, and interpretations formulated, adopted, or used by the Enforcing Authority in discharging his functions.

(b) A rule of the Enforcing Authority is invalid, and may not be invoked by the Enforcing Authority for any purpose, until it has been made available for public inspection under subsection (a). This provision does not apply to a person who has knowledge of a rule before engaging in an act or practice that violates this Act.]

§ 7A. [Rule-making Procedure]

(a) Before adopting, amending, or repealing a rule, the Enforcing Authority shall give at least [30] days' notice of his intended action. The notice shall include a statement of the terms or substance of the intended action or a description of the subjects and issues involved, and the time when, the place where, and the manner in which interested persons may present their views. The notice, for which the Enforcing Authority may charge a reasonable fee to cover the expense, shall be mailed to all persons who request it. It shall be published in [insert the appropriate medium of publication].

(b) The Enforcing Authority shall also offer all interested persons reasonable opportunity to submit data or recommendations orally or in writing. In the case of substantive rules, opportunity for oral hearing shall be granted if requested by 25 persons, a governmental subdivision or agency, or an association having at least 25 members. The Enforcing Authority shall consider all written and oral submissions respecting the proposed rule-making proceedings. Upon adoption of a rule, the Enforcing Authority, if requested to do so by an interested person not later than 30 days after adoption, shall issue a concise statement of the principal reasons for its adoption including the reasons for overruling any considerations urged against its adoption.

(c) A rule is invalid unless it is adopted in substantial compliance with this section. A proceeding to contest a rule on the ground of noncompliance with the procedural requirements of this section must be begun within 2 years after the effective date of the rule.]

§ 7B. [Filing and Taking Effect of Rules]

(a) The Enforcing Authority shall file in the office of the [Secretary of State] a certified copy of each rule adopted by him. The [Secretary of State] shall keep open to public inspection a permanent register of the rules.

(b) Each rule is effective [20] days after it is filed, unless a later date is specified in the rule.]

§ 7C. [Publication of Rules]

(a) The [Secretary of State] shall compile, index, and publish all rules adopted by the Enforcing Authority.

(b) Upon request, the [Secretary of State] shall make the compilations required by subsection (a) available free of charge to [agencies and officials of this State] and to other persons at a reasonable fee to cover the expense.]

§ 7D. [Petition for Adoption of Rules]

An interested person may petition the Enforcing Authority to adopt, amend, or repeal a rule. The Enforcing Authority shall prescribe by rule the form for such a petition and the procedure for its submission, consideration, and disposition. Within 30 days after submission, the Enforcing Authority shall either deny the petition in writing (stating his reasons for the denial) or initiate rule-making proceedings.]

§ 7E. [Declaratory Judgment on Validity or Applicability of Rules]

The validity or applicability of a rule may be determined in an action for a declaratory judgment in the [appropriate] court, if it is alleged that the rule, or its threatened application, interferes with or impairs, or threatens to interfere with or impair, the rights or privileges of the plaintiff. The Enforcing Authority shall be made a party to the action. The court may render a declaratory judgment whether or not the plaintiff has previously requested the Enforcing Authority to determine the validity or applicability of the rule.]

§ 7F. [Validity of Rules]

A rule of the Enforcing Authority may be invalidated only if it:

(1) violates a constitutional or statutory provision;

(2) exceeds the statutory authority of the Enforcing Authority; or

(3) is arbitrary, capricious, or otherwise clearly unreasonable in view of the whole record of the review proceeding.]

§ 8. [Investigatory Powers of the Enforcing Authority]

(a) If, by his own inquiries or as a result of complaints, the Enforcing Authority has reason to believe that a person has engaged in, is engaging in, or is about to engage in an act or practice that violates this Act, he may administer oaths and affirmations, subpoena witnesses or matter, and collect evidence.

(b) If matter that the Enforcing Authority subpoenas is located outside this State, the person subpoenaed may either make it available to the Enforcing Authority at a convenient location within the State or pay the reasonable and necessary expenses for the Enforcing Authority or his representative to examine the matter at the place where it is located. The Enforcing Authority may designate representatives, including officials of the state in which the matter is located, to inspect the matter on his behalf, and he may respond to similar requests from officials of other states.

(c) Upon failure of a person without lawful excuse to obey a subpoena and upon reasonable notice to all persons affected, the Enforcing Authority may apply to the [———] court for an order compelling compliance.

(d) [After consultation with the Attorney General,] the Enforcing Authority may request that an individual who refuses to comply with a subpoena on the ground that testimony or matter may incriminate him be ordered by the court to provide the testimony or matter. Except in a prosecution for [perjury] [false swearing], an individual who complies with a court order to provide testimony or matter after asserting a privilege against self-incrimination to which he is entitled by law, may not be subjected to a criminal proceeding or to a civil penalty with respect to the transaction concerning which he is required to testify or produce relevant matter. This subsection does not apply to damages recoverable under Section 11(b) or to civil sanctions imposed under Section 9(a) (2).

Comment

If he has reason to believe that this Act has been, is, or is about to be violated, this section authorizes the Enforcing Authority to investigate whether legal proceedings should be instituted. If necessary, the Enforcing Authority may request a court order requiring compliance with his investigative directives. The identity of persons investigated but not otherwise proceeded against must be kept confidential under § 5(c). Investigative proceedings may be terminated by acceptance of a written assurance of voluntary compliance with the Act from a supplier, § 9(c). An assurance is not evidence of a prior violation of this Act, but subsequent failure to comply with the terms of a valid assurance is prima facie evidence of a violation of the Act, § 9(c). In the event that a state elects not to designate the Attorney General as Enforcing Authority, the optional reference to the Attorney General in subsection 8(d) should be enacted in order to insure that immunity from prosecution will not be granted without prior consultation with the Attorney General.

§ 9. [Remedies of the Enforcing Authority]

(a) The Enforcing Authority may bring an action:

(1) to obtain a declaratory judgment that an act or practice violates this Act; or

(2) to enjoin, in accordance with the principles of equity, a supplier who has violated, is violating, or is otherwise likely to violate this Act;

(3) to recover actual damages, or obtain relief under subsection (b) (2), on behalf of consumers who complained to the Enforcing Authority before he instituted enforcement proceedings under this Act.

Comment

In addition to declaratory and injunctive relief, this subsection empowers the Enforcing Authority to recover actual damages and other corrective relief on behalf of individual consumers who complain to his office prior to the institution of enforcement proceedings. With the exception of § 9(b) (2), proceedings by the Enforcing Authority to obtain relief for these individual consumers are not subject to the provisions of § 9(b).

(b)

(1) The Enforcing Authority may bring a class action on behalf of consumers for the actual damages caused by an act or practice specified as violating this Act in a rule adopted by the Enforcing Authority under Section 6(b) before the consumer transactions on which the action is based, or declared to violate Section 3 or 4 by final judgment of [insert the appropriate court or courts of general jurisdiction and appellate courts] of this State that was either reported officially or made available for public dissemination under Section 5(a) (3) by the Enforcing Authority [10] days before the consumer transactions on which the action is based, or, with respect to a supplier who agreed to it, was prohibited specifically by the terms of a consent judgment that became final before the consumer transactions on which the action is based.

(2) On motion of the Enforcing Authority and without bond in an action under this subsection, the court may make appropriate orders, including appointment of a master or receiver or sequestration of assets, to reimburse consumers found to have been damaged, or to carry out a transaction in accordance with consumers' reasonable expectations, or to strike or limit the application of unconscionable clauses of contracts to avoid an unconscionable result, or to grant other appropriate relief. The court may assess the expenses of a master or receiver against a supplier.

(3) If a supplier shows by a preponderance of the evidence that a violation of this Act resulted from a bona fide error notwithstanding the maintenance of procedures reasonably adapted to avoid the error, recovery under Section 9(b) is limited to the amount, if any, by which the supplier was unjustly enriched by the violation.

(4) If an act or practice that violates this Act unjustly enriches a supplier and damages can be computed with reasonable certainty, damages recoverable on behalf of consumers who cannot be located with due diligence [shall escheat to the State] [shall be allocated under the Uniform Disposition of Unclaimed Property Act].

(5) No action may be brought by the Enforcing Authority under this subsection more than 2 years after the occurrence of a violation of this Act, or more than one year after the last payment in a consumer transaction involved in a violation of this Act, whichever is later.

Comment

This subsection requires that a supplier have notice of potential class action damage liability through the occurrence of one or more preconditions. As soon as one or more of the preconditions has been satisfied, the Enforcing Authority may bring class actions for damages on behalf of individual consumers with respect to consumer transactions which took place after the occurrence of the precondition, § 9(b) (1). However, a supplier who can establish that a violation resulted from a bona fide error notwithstanding the maintenance of procedures reasonably adapted to avoid the violation limits his liability to the amount by which he was unjustly enriched, § 9(b) (3). With respect to consumer transactions in which a consumer becomes obligated to pay someone other than the supplier with whom he engaged in the transaction, the statute of limitations against that supplier nonetheless runs until one year following the last scheduled payment arising in the consumer transaction, § 9(b) (5).

(c) The Enforcing Authority may terminate an investigation or an action other than a class action upon acceptance of a supplier's written assurance of voluntary compliance with this Act. Acceptance of an assurance may be conditioned on a commitment to reimburse consumers or take other appropriate corrective action. An assurance is not evidence of a prior violation of this Act. However, unless an assurance has been rescinded by agreement of the parties or voided by a court for good cause, subsequent failure to comply with the terms of an assurance is prima facie evidence of a violation of this Act.

Comment

Except with respect to class actions which are dealt with in §§ 12 and 13, this subsection authorizes the Enforcing Authority to terminate investigative and enforcement proceedings upon acceptance of a written assurance of voluntary compliance with the Act from a supplier. Unless an assurance has been abrogated by the parties or a court, subsequent failure to comply with the terms of an assurance is prima facie evidence of a violation of this Act. Moreover, if the parties have agreed that an assurance shall be filed with a court as a consent judgment, a failure to comply with its terms by a supplier who has agreed to it provides notice of potential class action damage liability, §§ 9(b) (1), 11(d) (1). The Enforcing Authority may include assurances, and must include consent judgments, in the public file maintained under § 5(a) (5).

§ 10. [Coordination with Other Supervision]

(a) If the Enforcing Authority receives a complaint or other information relating to noncompliance with this Act by a supplier who is subject to other supervision in this State, the Enforcing Authority shall inform the official or agency having that supervision. The Enforcing Authority may request information about such suppliers from the official or agency.

(b) The Enforcing Authority and any other official or agency in this State having supervisory authority over a supplier shall consult and assist each other in maintaining compliance with this Act. Within the scope of their authority, they may jointly or separately make investigations, prosecute suits, and take other official action they consider appropriate.

Comment

This Section coordinates the Enforcing Authority's powers with other administrative supervision of suppliers. Similar provisions appear in Uniform Consumer Credit Code § 6.105(2) and (3) (1969 Official Text with Comments). Conduct that is required or specifically permitted by other regulatory authorities is exempted from the Act by subsection 14(a) (1).

§ 11. [Private Remedies]

(a) Whether he seeks or is entitled to damages or has an adequate remedy at law, a consumer may bring an action to:

(1) obtain a declaratory judgment that an act or practice violates this Act; or

(2) enjoin, in accordance with the principles of equity, a supplier who has violated, is violating, or is otherwise likely to violate this Act.

Comment

This subsection permits a consumer to obtain appropriate declaratory and injunctive relief regardless whether he recovers or has standing to recover damages.

(b) Except in a class action, a consumer who suffers loss as a result of a violation of this Act may recover actual damages or [$100], whichever is greater.

Comment

In order to make an individual damage remedy meaningful, this subsection allows a consumer who has incurred actual damage to recover minimum damages of [$100].

(c) Whether a consumer seeks or is entitled to recover damages or has an adequate remedy at law, he may bring a class action for declaratory judgment, an injunction, and appropriate ancillary relief, except damages, against an act or practice that violates this Act.

Comment

This subsection authorizes a consumer to bring a class action for declaratory or injunctive relief regardless whether he recovers or has standing to recover damages.

(d)

(1) A consumer who suffers loss as a result of a violation of this Act may bring a class action for the actual damages caused by an act or practice (i) specified as violating this Act in a rule adopted by the Enforcing Authority under Section 6(b) before the consumer transactions on which the action is based, or (ii) declared to violate Section 3 or 4 by a final judgment of [insert the appropriate court or courts of general jurisdiction and appellate courts] of this State that was either reported officially or made available for public dissemination under Section 5(a) (3) by the Enforcing Authority [10] days before the consumer transaction on which the action is based, or (iii) with respect to a supplier who agreed to it, was prohibited specifically by the terms of a consent judgment which became final before the consumer transactions on which the action is based.

(2) If a supplier shows by a preponderance of the evidence that a violation of this Act resulted from a bona fide error notwithstanding the maintenance of procedures reasonably adapted to avoid the error, recovery under this section is limited to the amount, if any, by which the supplier was unjustly enriched by the violation.

(3) If an act or practice that violates this Act unjustly enriches a supplier and the damages can be computed with reasonable certainty, damages recoverable on behalf of consumers who cannot be located with due diligence [shall escheat to the State] [shall be allocated under the Uniform Disposition of Unclaimed Property Act].

Comment

This subsection requires that a supplier have notice of potential class action damage liability through the occurrence of one or more preconditions. As soon as one or more of the preconditions has been satisfied, a consumer may bring a class action for damages on behalf of individual consumers with respect to consumer transactions which took place after the occurrence of the precondition, § 11(d) (1). However, a supplier who can show that a violation resulted from a bona fide error notwithstanding the maintenance of procedures reasonably adapted to avoid the violation limits his liability to the amount by which he was unjustly enriched, § 11(d) (2).

(e) Except for services performed by the Enforcing Authority, the court may award to the prevailing party a reasonable attorney's fee limited to the work reasonably performed if:

(1) the consumer complaining of the act or practice that violates this Act has brought or maintained an action he knew to be groundless; or a supplier has committed an act or practice that violates this Act; and

(2) an action under this section has been terminated by a judgment or required by the court to be settled under Section 13(a).

Comment

This subsection authorizes the court to award a reasonable attorney's fee to certain prevailing parties in litigation under § 11. If a consumer has brought or maintained an action which he knew to be groundless, a reasonable attorney's fee can be awarded to a supplier. On the other hand, if a supplier either has been found to have violated the Act or has avoided this finding by invoking the forced settlement provisions of § 13, a reasonable attorney's fee can be awarded to a consumer.

(f) Except for consent judgments entered before testimony is taken, a final judgment in favor of the Enforcing Authority under Section 9 is admissible as prima facie evidence of the facts on which it is based in later proceedings under this section against the same person or a person in privity with him.

Comment

This subsection is comparable to 15 U.S.C. § 16(a) (1970), which makes final judgments in government antitrust proceedings admissible in subsequent actions by private parties. The subsection is not intended to forestall the application of principles of collateral estoppel which preclude a supplier from relitigating the facts established in an action by the Enforcing Authority.

(g) When a judgment under this section becomes final, the prevailing party shall mail a copy to the Enforcing Authority for inclusion in the public file maintained under Section 5(a)(5).

Comment

This subsection requires private litigants under the Act to assist the Enforcing Authority in providing notice of potential class action damage liability.

(h) An action under this section must be brought within 2 years after occurrence of a violation of this Act, within one year after the last payment in a consumer transaction involved in a violation of this Act, or within one year after the termination of proceedings by the Enforcing Authority with respect to a violation of this Act, whichever is later. However, when a supplier sues a consumer, he may assert as a counterclaim any claim under this Act arising out of the transaction on which suit is brought.

Comment

With respect to consumer transactions in which a consumer becomes obligated to pay someone other than the supplier with whom he engaged in the transaction, the statute of limitations against that supplier nonetheless runs until one year following the last scheduled payment arising in the consumer transaction.

§ 12. [Class Actions]

(a) An action may be maintained as a class action under this Act only if:

(1) the class is so numerous that joinder of all members is impracticable;

(2) there are questions of law or fact common to the class;

(3) the claims or defenses of the representative parties are typical of the claims or defenses of the class;

(4) the representative parties will fairly and adequately protect the interests of the class; and

(5) either:

(A) the prosecution of separate actions by or against individual members of the class would create a risk of:

(i) inconsistent or varying adjudications with respect to individual members of the class which would establish incompatible standards of conduct for the party opposing the class; or

(ii) adjudications with respect to individual members of the class which would as a practical matter be dispositive of the interests of the other members not parties to the adjudications or substantially impair or impede their ability to protect their interests; or

(B) the party opposing the class has acted or refused to act on grounds generally applicable to the class, thereby making appropriate final injunctive relief or corresponding declaratory relief with respect to the class as a whole; or

(C) the court finds that the questions of law or fact common to the members of the class predominate over any questions affecting only individual members, and that a class action is superior to other available methods for the fair and efficient adjudication of the controversy.

(b) The matters pertinent to the findings under subsection (a) (5) (C) include:

(1) the interest of members of the class in individually controlling the prosecution or defense of separate actions;

(2) the extent and nature of any litigation concerning the controversy already commenced by or against members of the class;

(3) the desirability or undesirability of concentrating the litigation of the claims in the particular forum; and

(4) the difficulties likely to be encountered in the management of a class action.

(c) As soon as practicable after the commencement of an action brought as a class action, the court shall determine by order whether it is to be so maintained. An order under this subsection may be conditional, and may be amended before the decision on the merits.

(d) In a class action maintained under subsection (a) (5) (C) the court may direct to the members of the class the best notice practicable under the circumstances, including individual notice to all members who can be identified through reasonable effort. The notice shall advise each member that:

(1) the court will exclude him from the class, if he so requests by a specified date;

(2) the judgment, whether favorable or not, will include all members who do not request exclusion; and

(3) any member who does not request exclusion may, if he desires, enter an appearance through his counsel.

(e) When appropriate, an action may be brought or maintained as a class action with respect to particular issues, or a class may be divided into subclasses and each subclass treated as a class.

(f) In the conduct of a class action the court may make appropriate orders:

(1) determining the course of proceedings or prescribing measures to prevent undue repetition or complication in the presentation of evidence or argument;

(2) requiring, for the protection of the members of the class or otherwise for the fair conduct of the action, that notice be given in the manner the court directs to some or all of the members or to the Enforcing Authority of any step in the action, or of the proposed extent of the judgment, or of the opportunity of members to signify whether they consider the representation fair and adequate, to intervene and present claims or defenses, or otherwise to come into the action;

(3) imposing conditions on the representative parties or on intervenors;

(4) requiring that the pleadings be amended to eliminate allegations as to representation of absent persons, and that the action proceed accordingly; or

(5) dealing with similar procedural matters.

(g) A class action shall not be dismissed or compromised without approval of the court. Notice of the proposed dismissal or compromise shall be given to all members of the class in such manner as the court directs.

(h) The judgment in an action maintained as a class action under subsection (a) (5) (A) or (B), whether or not favorable to the class, shall describe those whom the court finds to be members of the class. The judgment in a class action maintained under subsection (a) (5) (C), whether or not favorable to the class, shall specify or describe those to whom the notice provided in subsection (d) was directed, and who have not requested exclusion, and whom the court finds to be members of the class.

Comment

In order to facilitate its administration, this section is modeled closely on Federal Rule of Civil Procedure 23. The principal substantive deviation from the federal approach appears in § 12(d). Unlike its federal counterpart, § 12(d) allows a court discretion with respect to providing class members notice of an opportunity to exclude themselves from class actions based on the existence of common questions of law or fact. On the other hand, like the federal rule, § 12 permits actions against a class of defendants as well as actions on behalf of a plaintiff-class.

§ 13. [Special Provisions Relating to Class Actions]

(a) (1) A defendant in a class action may file a written offer of settlement. If it is not accepted within a reasonable time by a plaintiff class representative, the defendant may file an affidavit reciting the rejection. The court may determine that the offer has enough merit to present to the members of the class. If it so determines, it shall order a hearing to determine whether the offer should be approved. It shall give the best notice of the hearing that is practicable under the circumstances, including notice to each member who can be identified through reasonable effort. The notice shall specify the terms of the offer and a reasonable period within which members of the class who request it are entitled to be excluded from the class. The statute of limitations for those who are excluded pursuant to this subsection is tolled for the period the class action has been pending, plus an additional year.

(2) If a member who has previously lost an opportunity to be excluded from the class is excluded at his request in response to notice of the offer of settlement during the period specified under paragraph (1), he may not thereafter participate in a class action respecting the same consumer transaction, unless the court later disapproves the offer of settlement or approves a settlement materially different from that proposed in the original offer of settlement. After the expiration of the period specified under paragraph (1), a member of the class is not entitled to be excluded from it.

(3) If the court later approves the offer of settlement, including changes, if any, required by the court in the interest of a just settlement of the action, it shall enter a judgment, which is binding on all persons who are then members of the class. If the court disapproves the offer or approves a settlement materially different from that proposed in the original offer, notice shall be given to a person who was excluded from the action at his request in response to notice of the offer under paragraph (1) that he is entitled to rejoin the class, and, in the case of approval, participate in the settlement.

Comment

This section permits a court in its discretion to require settlement of actions that have been brought on behalf of a plaintiff-class. In order to do so, the court must notify individual class members of an opportunity to exclude themselves from the settlement proceedings. As long as they have not had a prior opportunity to exclude themselves from a class action under § 12, persons who exclude themselves from a class action under § 13(a) thereafter can maintain either class or individual actions with respect to the same consumer transaction. However, with the two exceptions noted in § 13(a) (2) & (3), persons who have had a prior opportunity to exclude themselves under § 12 and later exclude themselves under § 13(a) thereafter can maintain only individual actions with respect to the same consumer transaction. If the court determines that a supplier has avoided a finding that he violated this Act by resort to § 13, the court may award a reasonable attorney's fee to the representative of the consumer class, § 11(e).

(b) On the commencement of a class action under Section 11, the class representative shall mail by certified mail with return receipt requested or personally serve a copy of the complaint on the Enforcing Authority. Within 30 days after the receipt of a copy of the complaint, but not thereafter, the Enforcing Authority may intervene in the class action.

Comment

This subsection allows the Enforcing Authority a limited time within which to intervene in private class actions. The period within which intervention must take place does not begin to run until the Enforcing Authority has received a copy of the complaint in a private class action.

§ 14. [Application]

(a) This Act does not apply to:

(1) an act or practice required or specifically permitted by or under Federal law, or by or under State law;

Comment

This subsection harmonizes the Act with other federal and state regulation. Section 10 also requires the Enforcing Authority to cooperate with other officials in an enacting state who have authority over suppliers.

(2) a publisher, broadcaster, printer, or other person engaged in the dissemination of information or the reproduction of printed or pictorial matter insofar as the information or matter has been disseminated or reproduced on behalf of others without actual knowledge that it violated this Act;

Comment

This subsection exempts disseminators of information unless they commit a violation of this Act on behalf of others with actual knowledge that they are violating the Act or unless they commit a violation on their own behalf.

(3) (a) claim for personal injury or death or a claim for damage to property other than the property that is the subject of the consumer transaction; or

Comment

This subsection has primary application to product liability claims. To the extent that joinder is appropriate, it does not bar the joinder of a product liability claim with a related claim for violation of this Act, § 15.

(4) the credit terms of a transaction otherwise subject to this Act.

Comment

This subsection exempts only the credit terms of a consumer transaction. For example, advertising and contractual provisions with respect to the finance charge in a consumer transaction would be exempt, but advertising and contractual provisions with respect to the nature or quality of the subject of a consumer transaction would not be exempt.

(b) A person alleged to have violated this Act has the burden of showing the applicability of this Section.

Comment

This subsection allocates to a supplier the burden of establishing that his conduct is exempt from the Act.

§ 15. [Effect on Other Remedies]

The remedies of this Act are in addition to remedies otherwise available for the same conduct under state or local law, except that a class action relating to a transaction governed by this Act may be brought only as prescribed by this Act.

Comment

With the exception of class action provisions, this section makes clear that the Act does not preempt state and local remedies that are not explicitly repealed by § 18.

§ 16. [Short Title]

This Act may be cited as the Uniform Consumer Sales Practices Act.

§ 17. [Severability]

If any provision of this Act or the application thereof to any person or circumstance is held invalid, the invalidity does not affect other provisions or applications of this Act which can be given effect without the invalid provision or application, and to this end the provisions of this Act are severable.

§ 18. [Specific Repealer and Amendments]

(a) The following acts and parts of acts are repealed:

(1)

(2)

(3)

(b) The following acts and parts of acts are amended:

(1)

(2)

(3)

§ 19. [Time of Taking Effect]

This Act shall take effect on [ ].

UNIFORM FRAUDULENT CONVEYANCE ACT

Sec. 1. **Definition of Terms.** In this act "Assets" of a debtor means property not exempt from liability for his debts. To the extent that any property is liable for any debts of the debtor, such property shall be included in his assets.

"Conveyance" includes every payment of money, assignment, release, transfer, lease, mortgage or pledge of tangible or intangible property, and also the creation of any lien or incumbrance.

"Creditor" is a person having any claim, whether matured or unmatured, liquidated or unliquidated, absolute, fixed or contingent.

"Debt" includes any legal liability, whether matured or unmatured, liquidated or unliquidated, absolute, fixed or contingent.

Sec. 2. **Insolvency.** (1) A person is insolvent when the present fair salable value of his assets is less than the amount that will be required to pay his probable liability on his existing debts as they become absolute and matured.

(2) In determining whether a partnership is insolvent there shall be added to the partnership property the present fair salable value of the separate assets of each general partner in excess of the amount probably sufficient to meet the claims of his separate creditors, and also the amount of any unpaid subscription to the partnership of each limited partner, provided the present fair salable value of the assets of such limited partner is probably sufficient to pay his debts, including such unpaid subscription.

Sec. 3. **Fair Consideration.** Fair consideration is given for property, or obligation,

(a) When in exchange for such property, or obligation, as a fair equivalent therefor, and in good faith, property is conveyed or an antecedent debt is satisfied, or

(b) When such property, or obligation is received in good faith to secure a present advance or antecedent debt in amount not disproportionately small as compared with the value of the property, or obligation obtained.

Sec. 4. **Conveyances by Insolvent.** Every conveyance made and every obligation incurred by a person who is or will be thereby rendered insolvent is fraudulent as to creditors without regard to his actual intent if the conveyance is made or the obligation is incurred without a fair consideration.

Sec. 5. **Conveyances by Persons in Business.** Every conveyance made without fair consideration when the person making it is engaged or is about to engage in a business or transaction for which the property remaining in his hands after the conveyance is an unreasonably small capital, is fraudulent as to creditors and as to other persons who become creditors during the continuance of such business or transaction without regard to his actual intent.

Sec. 6. **Conveyances by a Person About to Incur Debts.** Every conveyance made and every obligation incurred without fair consideration when the person making the conveyance or entering into the obligation intends or believes that he will incur debts beyond his ability to pay as they mature, is fraudulent as to both present and future creditors.

Sec. 7. **Conveyance Made With Intent to Defraud.** Every conveyance made and every obligation incurred with actual intent, as distinguished from intent presumed in law, to hinder, delay, or defraud either present or future creditors, is fraudulent as to both present and future creditors.

Sec. 8. **Conveyance of Partnership Property.** Every conveyance of partnership property and every partnership obligation incurred when the partnership is or will be thereby rendered insolvent, is fraudulent as to partnership creditors, if the conveyance is made or obligation is incurred,

(a) To a partner, whether with or without a promise by him to pay partnership debts, or

(b) To a person not a partner without fair consideration to the partnership as distinguished from consideration to the individual partners.

Sec. 9. **Rights of Creditors Whose Claims Have Matured.** (1) Where a conveyance or obligation is fraudulent as to a creditor, such creditor, when his claim has matured, may, as against any person except a purchaser for fair consideration without knowledge of the fraud at the time of the purchase, or one who has derived title immediately or mediately from such a purchaser,

(a) Have the conveyance set aside or obligation annulled to the extent necessary to satisfy his claim, or

(b) Disregard the conveyance and attach or levy execution upon the property conveyed.

(2) A purchaser who without actual fraudulent intent has given less than a fair consideration for the conveyance or obligation, may retain the property or obligation as security for repayment.

Sec. 10. **Rights of Creditors Whose Claims Have Not Matured.** Where a conveyance made or obligation incurred is fraudulent as to a creditor whose claim has not matured he may proceed in a court of competent jurisdiction against any person against whom he could have proceeded had his claim matured, and the court may,

(a) Restrain the defendant from disposing of his property,

(b) Appoint a receiver to take charge of the property,

(c) Set aside the conveyance or annul the obligation, or

(d) Make any order which the circumstances of the case may require.

Sec. 11. **Cases Not Provided for in Act.** In any case not provided for in this act the rules of law and equity including the law merchant, and in particular the rules relating to the law of principal and agent, and the effect of fraud, misrepresentation, duress or coercion, mistake, bankruptcy or other invalidating cause shall govern.

Sec. 12. **Construction of Act.** This act shall be so interpreted and construed as to effectuate its general purpose to make uniform the law of those states which enact it.

Sec. 13. **Name of Act.** This act may be cited as the Uniform Fraudulent Conveyance Act.

Sec. 14. **Inconsistent Legislation Repealed.** Sections..... are hereby repealed, and all acts or parts of acts inconsistent with this Act are hereby repealed.

*

UNIFORM MOTOR VEHICLE CERTIFICATE OF TITLE AND ANTI-THEFT ACT

AN ACT CONCERNING VEHICLES AND TO MAKE UNIFORM THE LAW WITH REFERENCE THERETO

1955 ACT

PART 1.—DEFINITIONS AND EXCLUSIONS

Sec.

PART 2.—CERTIFICATES OF TITLE

PART 3.—OFFENSES AND ANTI-THEFT PROVISIONS

[Omitted]

PART 4.—INTERPRETATION, SHORT TITLE, SEVERABILITY, REPEALER AND EFFECTIVE DATE

[Omitted]

ALTERNATE A—FOR STATES HAVING NO CERTIFICATE OF TITLE ACT

PART 5.—PREVIOUSLY REGISTERED VEHICLES

[Omitted]

ALTERNATE B—FOR STATES HAVING A CERTIFICATE OF TITLE ACT BUT NOT REQUIRING ENDORSEMENT OF SECURITY INTERESTS ON CERTIFICATES

PART 5.—PREVIOUSLY CERTIFICATED VEHICLES

[Omitted]

PART 1—DEFINITIONS AND EXCLUSIONS

§ 1. [Definitions]

Except when the context otherwise requires, as used in this act:

(a) "Dealer" means a person engaged in the business of buying, selling, or exchanging vehicles who has an established place of business in this state [and to whom current dealer registration plates have been issued by the Department].

(b) "Department" means the [Department of Motor Vehicles] of this state. [The term includes a [County Clerk] when authorized by the Department to receive a document [or article] on its behalf.]

(c) "Identifying number" means the numbers, and letters if any, on a vehicle designated by the Department for the purpose of identifying the vehicle.

(d) "Implement of husbandry" means a vehicle designed and adapted exclusively for agricultural, horticultural or livestock raising operations or for lifting or carrying an implement of husbandry and in either case not subject to registration if used upon the highways.

(e) "Lienholder" means a person holding a security interest in a vehicle.

(f) To "mail" means to deposit in the United States mail properly addressed and with postage prepaid.

(g) "Owner" means a person, other than a lienholder, having the property in or title to a vehicle. The term includes a person entitled to the use and possession of a vehicle subject to a security interest in another person, but excludes a lessee under a lease not intended as security.

(h) "Person" means a natural person, firm, co-partnership, association or corporation.

[(i) "Pole trailer" means a vehicle without motive power designed to be drawn by another vehicle and attached to the towing vehicle by means of a reach, or pole, or by being boomed or otherwise secured to the towing vehicle, and ordinarily used for transporting long or irregularly shaped loads such as logs, poles, pipes, or structural members capable, generally, of sustaining themselves as beams between the supporting connections.]

(j) "Security agreement" means a written agreement which reserves or creates a security interest.

(k) "Security interest" means an interest in a vehicle reserved or created by agreement and which secures payment or performance of an obligation. The term includes the interest of a lessor under a lease intended as security. A security interest is "perfected" when it is valid against third parties generally, subject only to specific statutory exceptions.

(*l*) "Special mobile equipment" means a vehicle not designed for the transportation of persons or property upon a highway and only incidentally operated or moved over a highway, including but not limited to: ditch digging apparatus, well boring apparatus and road construction and maintenance machinery such as asphalt spreaders, bituminous mixers, bucket loaders, tractors other than truck tractors, ditchers, levelling graders, finishing machines, motor graders, road rollers, scarifiers, earth moving carry-alls and scrapers, power shovels and drag lines, and self-propelled cranes and earth moving equipment. The term does not include house trailers, dump trucks, truck mounted transit mixers, cranes or shovels, or other vehicles designed for the transportation of persons or property to which machinery has been attached.

(m) "State" means a state, territory or possession of the United States, the District of Columbia, the Commonwealth of Puerto Rico, or a province of the Dominion of Canada.

(n) "Vehicle" means a device in, upon, or by which a person or property is or may be transported or drawn upon a highway, except a device moved by human power or used exclusively upon stationary rails or tracks.

§ 2. [Exclusions]

(a) No certificate of title need be obtained for:

(1) A vehicle owned by the United States unless it is registered in this state;

(2) A vehicle owned by a manufacturer or dealer and held for sale, even though incidentally moved on the highway or used for purposes of testing or demonstration; or a vehicle used by a manufacturer solely for testing;

(3) A vehicle owned by a non-resident of this state and not required by law to be registered in this state;

(4) A vehicle regularly engaged in the interstate transportation of persons or property for which a currently effective certificate of title has been issued in another state;

(5) A vehicle moved solely by animal power;

(6) An implement of husbandry;

(7) Special mobile equipment;

[(8) A self-propelled wheel chair or invalid tricycle;]

[(9) A pole trailer.]

(b) Part 3 of this act does not apply to:

(1) A vehicle moved solely by animal power;

(2) An implement of husbandry;

(3) Special mobile equipment;

(4) A self-propelled wheel chair or invalid tricycle.

§ 3. [Excepted Liens and Security Interests [; Buyer From Manufacturer or Dealer]]

This act does not apply to or affect:

(a) A lien given by statute or rule of law to a supplier of services or materials for the vehicle;

(b) A lien given by statute to the United States, this state, or any political subdivision of this state;

(c) A security interest in a vehicle created by a manufacturer or dealer who holds the vehicle for sale [, but a buyer in the ordinary course of trade from the manufacturer or dealer takes free of the security interest].

PART 2—CERTIFICATES OF TITLE

§ 4. [Certificate of Title Required]

(a) Except as provided in Section 2, every owner of a vehicle which is in this state and for which no certificate of title has been issued by the Department shall make application to the Department for a certificate of title of the vehicle.

(b) The Department shall not register or renew the registration of a vehicle unless an application for a certificate of title has been delivered to the Department.

§ 5. [Optional Certificates of Title]

The owner of an implement of husbandry or special mobile equipment may apply for and obtain a certificate of title on it. All of the provisions of this Part are applicable to a certificate of title so issued, except that a person who receives a transfer of an interest in the vehicle without knowledge of the certificate of title is not prejudiced by reason of the existence of the certificate, and the perfection of a security interest under this act is not effective until the lienholder has complied with the provisions of applicable law which otherwise relate to the perfection of security interests in personal property.

§ 6. [Application for First Certificate of Title]

(a) The application for the first certificate of title of a vehicle in this state shall be made by the owner to the Department on the form it prescribes and shall contain:

(1) The name, residence and mail address of the owner;

(2) A description of the vehicle including, so far as the following data exists: its make, model, identifying number, type of body, the number of cylinders, and whether new or used;

(3) The date of purchase by applicant, the name and address of the person from whom the vehicle was acquired and the names and addresses of any lienholders in the order of their priority and the dates of their security agreements; and

(4) Any further information the Department reasonably requires to identify the vehicle and to enable it to determine whether the owner is entitled to a certificate of title and the existence or non-existence of security interests in the vehicle.

(b) If the application refers to a vehicle purchased from a dealer, it shall contain the name and address of any lienholder holding a security interest created or reserved at the time of the sale and the date of his security agreement and be signed by the dealer as well as the owner, and the dealer shall promptly mail or deliver the application to the Department.

(c) If the application refers to a vehicle last previously registered in another state or country, the application shall contain or be accompanied by:

(1) Any certificate of title issued by the other state or country;

(2) Any other information and documents the Department reasonably requires to establish the ownership of the vehicle and the existence or non-existence of security interests in it; and

(3) The certificate of a person authorized by the Department that the identifying number of the vehicle has been inspected and found to conform to the description given in the application, or any other proof of the identity of the vehicle the Department reasonably requires.

§ 7. [Examination of Records]

The Department, upon receiving application for a first certificate of title, shall check the identifying number of the vehicle shown in the application against the records of vehicles required to be maintained by Section 8 and against the record of stolen and converted vehicles required to be maintained by Section 35.

§ 8. [Issuance and Records]

(a) The Department shall file each application received and, when satisfied as to its genuineness and regularity and that the applicant is entitled to the issuance of a certificate of title, shall issue a certificate of title of the vehicle.

(b) The Department shall maintain a record of all certificates of title issued by it:

(1) Under a distinctive title number assigned to the vehicle;

(2) Under the identifying number of the vehicle;

[(3) Alphabetically, under the name of the owner;]

and, in the discretion of the Department, in any other method it determines.

§ 9. [Contents and Effect]

(a) Each certificate of title issued by the Department shall contain:

(1) The date issued;

(2) The name and address of the owner;

(3) The names and addresses of any lienholders, in the order of priority as shown on the application or, if the application is based on a certificate of title, as shown on the certificate;

(4) The title number assigned to the vehicle;

(5) A description of the vehicle including, so far as the following data exists: its make, model, identifying number, type of body, number of cylinders, whether new or used, and, if a new vehicle, the date of the first sale of the vehicle for use; and

(6) Any other data the Department prescribes.

(b) Unless a bond is filed as provided in Section 11(b), a distinctive certificate of title shall be issued for a vehicle last previously registered in another state or country the laws of which do not require that lienholders be named on a certificate of title to perfect their security interests. The certificate shall contain the legend "This vehicle may be subject to an undisclosed lien" and may contain any other information the Department prescribes. If no notice of a security interest in the vehicle is received by the Department within four (4) months from the issuance of the distinctive certificate of title, it shall, upon application and surrender of the distinctive certificate, issue a certificate of title in ordinary form.

(c) The certificate of title shall contain forms for assignment and warranty of title by the owner, and for assignment and warranty of title by a dealer, and may contain forms for applications for a certificate of title by a transferee, the naming of a lienholder and the assignment or release of the security interest of a lienholder.

(d) A certificate of title issued by the Department is prima facie evidence of the facts appearing on it.

(e) A certificate of title for a vehicle is not subject to garnishment, attachment, execution or other judicial process, but this Sub-section does not prevent a lawful levy upon the vehicle.

§ 10. [Delivery]

The certificate of title shall be mailed to the first lienholder named in it or, if none, to the owner.

§ 11. [Registration Without Certificate of Title; Bond]

If the Department is not satisfied as to the ownership of the vehicle or that there are no undisclosed security interests in it, the Department may register the vehicle but shall either:

(a) Withhold issuance of a certificate of title until the applicant presents documents reasonably sufficient to satisfy the Department as to the applicant's ownership of the vehicle and that there are no undisclosed security interests in it; or

(b) As a condition of issuing a certificate of title, require the applicant to file with the Department a bond in the form prescribed by the Department and executed by the applicant, and either accompanied by the deposit of cash with the Department or also executed by a person authorized to conduct a surety business in this state. The bond shall be in an amount equal to one and one-half times the value of the vehicle as determined by the Department and conditioned to indemnify any prior owner and lienholder and any subsequent purchaser of the vehicle or person acquiring any security interest in it, and their respective successors in interest, against any expense, loss or damage, including reasonable attorney's fees, by reason of the issuance of the certificate of title of the vehicle or on account of any defect in or undisclosed security interest upon the right, title and interest of the applicant in and to the vehicle. Any such interested person has a right of action to recover on the bond for any breach of its conditions, but the aggregate liability of the surety to all persons shall not exceed the amount of the bond. The bond, and any deposit accompanying it, shall be returned at the end of three (3) years or prior thereto if the vehicle is no longer registered in this state and the currently valid certificate of title is surrendered to the Department, unless the Department has been notified of the pendency of an action to recover on the bond.

§ 12. [Refusing Certificate of Title]

The Department shall refuse issuance of a certificate of title if any required fee is not paid or if it has reasonable grounds to believe that:

(a) The applicant is not the owner of the vehicle;

(b) The application contains a false or fraudulent statement; or

(c) The applicant fails to furnish required information or documents or any additional information the Department reasonably requires.

§ 13. [Lost, Stolen or Mutilated Certificates]

(a) If a certificate of title is lost, stolen, mutilated or destroyed or becomes illegible, the first lienholder or, if none, the owner or legal representative of the owner named in the certificate, as shown by the records of the Department, shall promptly make application for and may obtain a duplicate upon furnishing information satisfactory to the Department. The duplicate certificate of title shall contain the legend "This is a duplicate certificate and may be subject to the rights of a person under the original certificate." It shall be mailed to the first lienholder named in it or, if none, to the owner.

(b) The Department shall not issue a new certificate of title to a transferee upon application made on a duplicate until fifteen (15) days after receipt of the application.

(c) A person recovering an original certificate of title for which a duplicate has been issued shall promptly surrender the original certificate to the Department.

§ 14. [Transfer]

(a) If an owner transfers his interest in a vehicle, other than by the creation of a security interest, he shall, at the time of the delivery of the vehicle, execute an assignment and warranty of title to the transferee in the space provided therefor on the certificate or as the Department prescribes, and cause the certificate and assignment to be mailed or delivered to the transferee or to the Department.

(b) Except as provided in Section 15, the transferee shall, promptly after delivery to him of the vehicle, execute the application for a new certificate of title in the space provided therefor on the certificate or as the Department prescribes, and cause the certificate and application to be mailed or delivered to the Department.

(c) Upon request of the owner or transferee, a lienholder in possession of the certificate of title shall, unless the transfer was a breach of his security agreement, either deliver the certificate to the transferee for delivery to the Department or, upon receipt from the transferee of the owner's assignment, the transferee's application for a new certificate [, the registration card] [, license plates] and the required fee, mail or deliver them to the Department. The delivery of the certificate does not affect the rights of the lienholder under his security agreement.

(d) If a security interest is reserved or created at the time of the transfer, the certificate of title shall be retained by or delivered to the person who becomes the lienholder, and the parties shall comply with the provisions of Section 21.

(e) Except as provided in Section 15 and as between the parties, a transfer by an owner is not effective until the provisions of this Section [and Section 17] have been complied with [; however, an owner who has delivered possession of the vehicle of the transferee and has complied with the provisions of this Section [and Section 17] requiring action by him is not liable as owner for any damages thereafter resulting from operation of the vehicle].

§ 15. [Transfer to or from Dealer; Records]

(a) If a dealer buys a vehicle and holds it for resale and procures the certificate of title from the owner or the lienholder within ten (10) days after delivery to him of the vehicle, he need not send the certificate to the Department but, upon transferring the vehicle to another person other than by the creation of a security interest, shall promptly execute the assignment and warranty of title by a dealer, showing the names and addresses of the transferee and of any lienholder holding a security interest created or reserved at the time of the resale and the date of his security agreement, in the spaces provided therefor on the certificate or as the Department prescribes, and mail or deliver the certificate to the Department with the transferee's application for a new certificate.

(b) Every dealer shall maintain for five (5) years a record in the form the Department prescribes of every vehicle bought, sold or exchanged by him, or received by him for sale or exchange, which shall be open to inspection by a representative of the Department or peace officer during reasonable business hours.

§ 16. [Transfer by Operation of Law]

(a) If the interest of an owner in a vehicle passes to another other than by voluntary transfer, the transferee shall, except as provided in Sub-section (b), promptly mail or deliver to the Department the last certificate of title, if available, proof of the transfer, and his application for a new certificate in the form the Department prescribes.

(b) If the interest of the owner is terminated or the vehicle is sold under a security agreement by a lienholder named in the certificate of title, the transferee shall promptly mail or deliver to the Department the last certificate of title, his application for a new certificate in the form the Department prescribes, and an affidavit made by or on behalf of the lienholder that the vehicle was repossessed and that the interest of the owner was lawfully terminated or sold pursuant to the terms of the security agreement. If the lienholder succeeds to the interest of the owner and holds the vehicle for resale, he need not secure a new certificate of title but, upon transfer to another person, shall promptly mail or deliver to the transferee or to the Department the certificate, affidavit and other documents [and articles] required to be sent to the Department by the transferee.

(c) A person holding a certificate of title whose interest in the vehicle has been extinguished or transferred other than by voluntary transfer shall mail or deliver the certificate to the Department upon request of the Department. The delivery of the certificate pursuant to the request of the Department does not affect the rights of the person surrendering the certificate, and the action of the Department in issuing a new certificate of title as provided herein is not conclusive upon the rights of an owner or lienholder named in the old certificate.

§ 17. [Fees [; Registration Cards] [; License Plates]]

(a) An application for a certificate of title shall be accompanied by [the registration card] [,] [license plates] [and] the required fee when mailed or delivered to the Department.

(b) An application for the naming of a lienholder or his assignee on a certificate of title shall be accompanied by [the registration card and] the required fee when mailed or delivered to the Department.

[(c) A transferor of a vehicle, other than a dealer transferring a new vehicle, shall deliver to the transferee at the time of the delivery of possession of the vehicle [the registration card] [and] [license plates] for the vehicle.]

§ 18. [When Department to Issue New Certificate]

(a) The Department, upon receipt of a properly assigned certificate of title, with an application for a new certificate of title, the required fee and any other documents [and articles] required by law, shall issue a new certificate of title in the name of the transferee as owner and mail it to the first lienholder named in it or, if none, to the owner.

(b) The Department, upon receipt of an application for a new certificate of title by a transferee other than by voluntary transfer, with proof of the transfer, the required fee and any other documents [and articles] required by law, shall issue a new certificate of title in the name of the transferee as owner. If the outstanding certificate of title is not delivered to it, the Department shall make demand therefor from the holder thereof.

(c) The Department shall file and retain for [five (5)] years every surrendered certificate of title, the file to be maintained so as to permit the tracing of title of the vehicle designated therein.

§ 19. [Scrapping, Dismantling or Destroying Vehicle]

An owner who scraps, dismantles or destroys a vehicle and a person who purchases a vehicle as scrap or to be dismantled or destroyed shall immediately cause the certificate of title to be mailed or delivered to the Department for cancellation. A certificate of title of the vehicle shall not again be issued except upon application containing the information the Department requires, accompanied by a certificate of inspection in the form and content specified in Section 6(c) (3).

§ 20. [Perfection of Security Interests]

(a) Unless excepted by Section 3, a security interest in a vehicle of a type for which a certificate of title is required is not valid against creditors of the owner or subsequent transferees or lienholders of the vehicle unless perfected as provided in this act.

(b) A security interest is perfected by the delivery to the Department of the existing certificate of title, if any, an application for a certificate of title containing the name and address of the lienholder and the date of his security agreement and the required fee [and registration card]. It is perfected as of the time of its creation if the delivery is completed within ten (10) days thereafter, otherwise, as of the time of the delivery.

(c) If a vehicle is subject to a security interest when brought into this state, the validity of the security interest is determined by the law of the jurisdiction where the vehicle was when the security interest attached, subject to the following:

(1) If the parties understood at the time the security interest attached that the vehicle would be kept in this state

and it was brought into this state within thirty (30) days thereafter for purposes other than transportation through this state, the validity of the security interest in this state is determined by the law of this state.

(2) If the security interest was perfected under the law of the jurisdiction where the vehicle was when the security interest attached, the following rules apply:

(A) If the name of the lienholder is shown on an existing certificate of title issued by that jurisdiction, his security interest continues perfected in this state.

(B) If the name of the lienholder is not shown on an existing certificate of title issued by that jurisdiction, the security interest continues perfected in this state for four (4) months after a first certificate of title of the vehicle is issued in this state, and also, thereafter if, within the four (4) month period, it is perfected in this state. The security interest may also be perfected in this state after the expiration of the four (4) month period; in that case perfection dates from the time of perfection in this state.

(3) If the security interest was not perfected under the law of the jurisdiction where the vehicle was when the security interest attached, it may be perfected in this state; in that case, perfection dates from the time of perfection in this state.

(4) A security interest may be perfected under paragraph (2) (B) or paragraph (3) of this Sub-section either as provided in Sub-section (b) or by the lienholder delivering to the Department a notice of security interest in the form the Department prescribes and the required fee.

§ 21. [Security Interest]

If an owner creates a security interest in a vehicle:

(a) The owner shall immediately execute the application, in the space provided therefor on the certificate of title or on a separate form the Department prescribes, to name the lienholder on the certificate, showing the name and address of the lienholder and the date of his security agreement, and cause the certificate, application and the required fee [and registration card] to be delivered to the lienholder.

(b) The lienholder shall immediately cause the certificate, application and the required fee [and registration card] to be mailed or delivered to the Department.

(c) Upon request of the owner or subordinate lienholder, a lienholder in possession of the certificate of title shall either mail or deliver the certificate to the subordinate lienholder for delivery to the Department or, upon receipt from the subordinate lienholder of the owner's application and the required fee [and registration card], mail or deliver them to the Department with the certificate. The delivery of the certificate does not affect the rights of the first lienholder under his security agreement.

(d) Upon receipt of the certificate of title, application and the required fee [and registration card], the Department shall either endorse on the certificate or issue a new certificate containing the name and address of the new lienholder, and mail the certificate to the first lienholder named in it.

§ 22. [Assignment by Lienholder]

(a) A lienholder may assign, absolutely or otherwise, his security interest in the vehicle to a person other than the owner without affecting the interest of the owner or the validity of the security interest, but any person without notice of the assignment is protected in dealing with the lienholder as the holder of the security interest and the lienholder remains liable for any obligations as lienholder until the assignee is named as lienholder on the certificate.

(b) The assignee may, but need not to perfect the assignment, have the certificate of title endorsed or issued with the assignee named as lienholder, upon delivering to the Department the certificate and an assignment by the lienholder named in the certificate in the form the Department prescribes.

§ 23. [Release of Security Interest]

(a) Upon the satisfaction of a security interest in a vehicle for which the certificate of title is in the possession of the lienholder, he shall, within ten (10) days after demand and, in any event, within thirty (30) days, execute a release of his security interest, in the space provided therefor on the certificate or as the Department prescribes, and mail or deliver the certificate and release to the next lienholder named therein, or, if none, to the owner or any person who delivers to the lienholder an authorization from the owner to receive the certificate. The owner, other than a dealer holding the vehicle for resale, shall promptly cause the certificate and release to be mailed or delivered to the Department, which shall release the lienholder's rights on the certificate or issue a new certificate.

(b) Upon the satisfaction of a security interest in a vehicle for which the certificate of title is in the possession of a prior lienholder, the lienholder whose security interest is satisfied shall within ten (10) days after demand and, in any event, within thirty (30) days execute a release in the form the Department prescribes and deliver the release to the owner or any person who delivers to the lienholder an authorization from the owner to receive it. The lienholder in possession of the certificate of title shall either deliver the certificate to the owner, or the person authorized by him, for delivery to the Department, or, upon receipt of the release [and registration card], mail or deliver it [them] with the certificate to the Department, which shall release the subordinate lienholder's rights on the certificate or issue a new certificate.

§ 24. [Duty of Lienholder]

A lienholder named in a certificate of title shall, upon written request of the owner or of another lienholder named on the certificate, disclose any pertinent information as to his security agreement and the indebtedness secured by it.

§ 25. [Exclusiveness of Procedure]

The method provided in this act of perfecting and giving notice of security interests subject to this act is exclusive. Security interests subject to this act are hereby exempted from the provisions of law which otherwise require or relate to the [[recording] [filing] of instruments creating or evidencing security interests. . . .]

§ 26. [Supension or Revocation of Certificates]

(a) The Department shall suspend or revoke a certificate of title, upon notice and reasonable opportunity to be heard in accordance with Section 29, when authorized by any other provision of law or if it finds:

(1) The certificate of title was fraudulently procured or erroneously issued, or

(2) The vehicle has been scrapped, dismantled or destroyed.

(b) Suspension or revocation of a certificate of title does not, in itself, affect the validity of a security interest noted on it.

(c) When the Department suspends or revokes a certificate of title, the owner or person in possession of it shall, immediately upon receiving notice of the suspension or revocation, mail or deliver the certificate to the Department.

(d) The Department may seize and impound any certificate of title which has been suspended or revoked.

§ 27. [Fees]

(a) The Department shall be paid the following fees:

(1) For filing an application for a first certificate of title, $.....;

(2) For each security interest noted upon a certificate of title, $.....;

(3) For a certificate of title after a transfer, $.....;

(4) For each assignment of a security interest noted upon a certificate of title, $.....;

(5) For a duplicate certificate of title, $.....;

(6) For an ordinary certificate of title issued upon surrender of a distinctive certificate, $.....;

(7) For filing a notice of security interest, $.....; and

(8) For a certificate of search of its records for each name or identifying number searched against, $......

(b) If an application, certificate of title or other document [or article] required to be mailed or delivered to the Department under any provision of this act is not delivered to the Department within ten (10) days from the time it is required to be mailed or delivered, the Department shall collect, as a penalty, an amount equal to the fee required for the transaction.

§ 28. [Powers of Department]

(a) The Department shall prescribe and provide suitable forms of applications, certificates of title, notices of security interests, and all other notices and forms necessary to carry out the provisions of this act.

(b) The Department may:

(1) Make necessary investigations to procure information required to carry out the provisions of this act;

(2) Adopt and enforce reasonable rules and regulations to carry out the provisions of this act;

(3) Assign a new identifying number to a vehicle if it has none, or its identifying number is destroyed or obliter-

ated, or its motor is changed, and shall either issue a new certificate of title showing the new identifying number or make an appropriate indorsement on the original certificate.

§ 29. [Hearings]

A person aggrieved by an act or omission to act of the Department under this act is entitled, upon request, to a hearing in accordance with [the Administrative Procedure Act of this state] [law].

§ 30. [Court Review]

A person aggrieved by an act or omission to act of the Department under this act is also entitled to a review thereof by the [ ] Court in accordance with [the Administrative Procedure Act of this State] [law].

*

CONSUMER CREDIT PROTECTION ACT

Selected Sections

Public Law 90–321; 82 Stat. 146
as amended by

Public Law 91–508; 84 Stat. 1126
and by

Public Law 93–495; 88 Stat. 1500

Public Law 94–240; 90 Stat. 257
and as added by

Public Law 95–109; 91 Stat. 874

TABLE OF CONTENTS

TITLE I—CONSUMER CREDIT COST DISCLOSURE

(TRUTH IN LENDING)

Title I is commonly referred to as "Truth in Lending."

CHAPTER 1—GENERAL PROVISIONS

CHAPTER 2—CREDIT TRANSACTIONS

CHAPTER 3—CREDIT ADVERTISING

CHAPTER 4—CREDIT BILLING

CHAPTER 5—CONSUMER LEASES

TITLE III—RESTRICTION ON GARNISHMENT

TITLE V—GENERAL PROVISIONS

TITLE VI—CONSUMER CREDIT REPORTING

TITLE VII—EQUAL CREDIT OPPORTUNITY

TITLE VIII—DEBT COLLECTION PRACTICES

CONSUMER CREDIT PROTECTION ACT

§ 1. Short title of entire Act

This Act may be cited as the Consumer Credit Protection Act.

TITLE I—CONSUMER CREDIT COST DISCLOSURE

CHAPTER 1—GENERAL PROVISIONS

§ 101. Short title

This title may be cited as the Truth in Lending Act.

§ 102. Findings and declaration of purpose

(a) The Congress finds that economic stabilization would be enhanced and the competition among the various financial institutions and other firms engaged in the extension of consumer credit would be strengthened by the informed use of credit. The informed use of credit results from an awareness of the cost thereof by consumers. It is the purpose of this title to assure a meaningful disclosure of credit terms so that the consumer will be able to compare more readily the various credit terms available to him and avoid the uninformed use of credit, and to protect the consumer against inaccurate and unfair credit billing and credit card practices.

(b) The Congress also finds that there has been a recent trend toward leasing automobiles and other durable goods for consumer use as an alternative to installment credit sales and that these leases have been offered without adequate cost disclosures. It is the purpose of this title to assure a meaningful disclosure of the terms of leases of personal property for personal, family, or household purposes so as to enable the lessee to compare more readily the various lease terms available to him, limit balloon payments in consumer leasing, enable comparison of lease terms with credit terms where appropriate, and to assure meaningful and accurate disclosures of lease terms in advertisements.

§ 103. Definitions and rules of construction

(a) The definitions and rules of construction set forth in this section are applicable for the purposes of this title.

(b) The term "Board" refers to the Board of Governors of the Federal Reserve System.

(c) The term "organization" means a corporation, government or governmental subdivision or agency, trust, estate, partnership, cooperative, or association.

(d) The term "person" means a natural person or an organization.

(e) The term "credit" means the right granted by a creditor to a debtor to defer payment of debt or to incur debt and defer its payment.

(f) The term "creditor" refers only to creditors who regularly extend, or arrange for the extension of, credit which is payable by agreement in more than four installments or for which the payment of a finance charge is or may be required, whether in connection with loans, sales of property or services, or otherwise. For the purposes of the requirements imposed under Chapter 4 and sections 127(a)(6), 127(a)(7), 127(a)(8), 127(b)(1), 127(b)(2), 127 (b)(3), 127(b)(9), and 127(b)(11) of Chapter 2 of this Title, the term "creditor" shall also include card issuers whether or not the amount due is payable by agreement in more than four installments or the payment of a finance charge is or may be required, and the Board shall, by regulation, apply these requirements to such card issuers to the extent appropriate, even though the requirements are by their terms applicable only to creditors offering open end credit plans. The provisions of this subchapter apply to any such creditor, irrespective of his or its status as a natural person or any type of organization.

(g) The term "credit sale" refers to any sale with respect to which credit is extended or arranged by the seller. The term includes any contract in the form of a bailment or lease if the bailee or lessee contracts to pay as compensation for use a sum substantially equivalent to or in excess of the aggregate value of the property and services involved and it is agreed that the bailee or lessee will become, or for no other or a nominal consideration has the option to become, the owner of the property upon full compliance with his obligations under the contract.

(h) The adjective "consumer", used with reference to a credit transaction, characterizes the transaction as one in which the party to whom credit is offered or extended is a natural person, and the money, property, or services which are the subject of the transaction are primarily for personal, family, household, or agricultural purposes.

(i) The term "open end credit plan" refers to a plan prescribing the terms of credit transactions which may be made thereunder from time to time and under the terms of which a finance charge may be computed on the outstanding unpaid balance from time to time thereunder.

(j) The term "adequate notice", as used in section 133, means a printed notice to a cardholder which sets forth the pertinent facts clearly and conspicuously so that a person against whom it is to operate could reasonably be expected to have noticed it and understood its meaning. Such notice may be given to a cardholder by printing the notice on any credit card, or on each periodic statement of account, issued to the cardholder, or by any other means reasonably assuring the receipt thereof by the cardholder.

(k) The term "credit card" means any card, plate, coupon book or other credit device existing for the purpose of obtaining money, property, labor, or services on credit.

(l) The term "accepted credit card" means any credit card which the cardholder has requested and received or has signed or has used, or authorized another to use, for the purpose of obtaining money, property, labor, or services on credit.

(m) The term "cardholder" means any person to whom a credit card is issued or any person who has agreed with the card issuer to pay obligations arising from the issuance of a credit card to another person.

(n) The term "card issuer" means any person who issues a credit card, or the agent of such person with respect to such card.

(o) The term "unauthorized use", as used in section 133, means a use of a credit card by a person other than the cardholder who does not have actual, implied, or apparent authority for such use and from which the cardholder receives no benefit.

(p) The term "discount" as used in section 161 of this title means a reduction made from the regular price. The term "discount" as used in section 161 of this title shall not mean a surcharge.

(q) The term "surcharge" as used in section 103 and section 161 of this title means any means of increasing the regular price to a cardholder which is not imposed upon customers paying by cash, check, or similar means.

(r) The term "State" refers to any State, the Commonwealth of Puerto Rico, the District of Columbia, and any territory or possession of the United States.

(s) Any reference to any requirement imposed under this title or any provision thereof includes reference to the regulations of the Board under this title or the provision thereof in question.

(t) The disclosure of an amount or percentage which is greater than the amount or percentage required to be disclosed under this title does not in itself constitute a violation of this title.

§ 104. Exempted transactions

This title does not apply to the following:

(1) Credit transactions involving extensions of credit for business or commercial purposes, or to governments or governmental agencies or instrumentalities, or to organizations.

(2) Transactions in securities or commodities accounts by a broker-dealer registered with the Securities and Exchange Commission.

(3) Credit transactions, other than real property transactions, in which the total amount to be financed exceeds $25,000.

(4) Transactions under public utility tariffs, if the Board determines that a State regulatory body regulates the charges for the public utility services involved, the charges for delayed payment, and any discount allowed for early payment.

(5) Credit transactions primarily for agricultural purposes in which the total amount to be financed exceeds $25,000.

§ 105. Regulations

The Board shall prescribe regulations to carry out the purposes of this title. These regulations may contain such classifications, differentiations, or other provisions, and may provide for such adjustments and exceptions for any class of transactions, as in the judgment of the Board are necessary or proper to effectuate the purposes of this title, to prevent circumvention or evasion thereof, or to facilitate compliance therewith.

§ 106. Determination of finance charge

(a) Except as otherwise provided in this section, the amount of the finance charge in connection with any consumer credit transaction shall be determined as the sum of all charges, payable directly or indirectly by the person to whom the credit is extended, and imposed directly or indirectly by the creditor as an incident to the extension of credit, including any of the following types of charges which are applicable:

(1) Interest, time price differential, and any amount payable under a point, discount, or other system of additional charges.

(2) Service or carrying charge.

(3) Loan fee, finder's fee, or similar charge.

(4) Fee for an investigation or credit report.

(5) Premium or other charge for any guarantee or insurance protecting the creditor against the obligor's default or other credit loss.

(b) Charges or premiums for credit life, accident, or health insurance written in connection with any consumer credit transaction shall be included in the finance charge unless

(1) the coverage of the debtor by the insurance is not a factor in the approval by the creditor of the extension of credit, and this fact is clearly disclosed in writing to the person applying for or obtaining the extension of credit; and

(2) in order to obtain the insurance in connection with the extension of credit, the person to whom the credit is extended must give specific affirmative written indication of his desire to do so after written disclosure to him of the cost thereof.

(c) Charges or premiums for insurance, written in connection with any consumer credit transaction, against loss of or damage to property or against liability arising out of the ownership or use of property, shall be included in the finance charge unless a clear and specific statement in writing is furnished by the credtor to the person to whom the credit is extended, setting forth the cost of the insurance if obtained from or through the creditor, and stating that the person to whom the credit is extended may choose the person through which the insurance is to be obtained.

(d) If any of the following items is itemized and disclosed in accordance with the regulations of the Board in connection with any transaction, then the creditor need not include that item in the computation of the finance charge with respect to that transaction:

(1) Fees and charges prescribed by law which actually are or will be paid to public officials for determining the existence of or for perfecting or releasing or satisfying any security related to the credit transaction.

(2) The premium payable for any insurance in lieu of perfecting any security interest otherwise required by the creditor in connection with the transaction, if the premium does not exceed the fees and

charges described in paragraph (1) which would otherwise be payable.

(3) Taxes.

(4) Any other type of charge which is not for credit and the exclusion of which from the finance charge is approved by the Board by regulation.

(e) The following items, when charged in connection with any extension of credit secured by an interest in real property, shall not be included in the computation of the finance charge with respect to that transaction:

(1) Fees or premiums for title examination, title insurance, or similar purposes.

(2) Fees for preparation of a deed, settlement statement, or other documents.

(3) Escrows for future payments of taxes and insurance.

(4) Fees for notarizing deeds and other documents.

(5) Appraisal fees.

(6) Credit reports.

§ 107. Determination of annual percentage rate

(a) The annual percentage rate applicable to any extension of consumer credit shall be determined, in accordance with the regulations of the Board,

(1) in the case of any extension of credit other than under an open end credit plan, as

(A) that nominal annual percentage rate which will yield a sum equal to the amount of the finance charge when it is applied to the unpaid balances of the amount financed, calculated according to the actuarial method of allocating payments made on a debt between the amount financed and the amount of the finance charge, pursuant to which a payment is applied first to the accumulated finance charge and the balance is applied to the unpaid amount financed; or

(B) the rate determined by any method prescribed by the Board as a method which materially simplifies computation while retaining reasonable accuracy as compared with the rate determined under subparagraph (A).

(2) in the case of any extension of credit under an open end credit plan, as the quotient (expressed as a percentage) of the total finance charge for the period to which it relates divided by the amount upon which the finance charge for that period is based, multiplied by the number of such periods in a year.

(b) Where a creditor imposes the same finance charge for balances within a specified range, the annual percentage rate shall be computed on the median balance within the range, except that if the Board determines that a rate so computed would not be meaningful, or would be materially misleading, the annual percentage rate shall be computed on such other basis as the Board may by regulation require.

(c) The annual percentage rate may be rounded to the nearest quarter of 1 per centum for credit transactions payable in substantially equal installments when a creditor determines the total finance charge on the basis of a single add-on, discount, periodic, or other rate, and the rate is converted into an annual percentage rate under procedures prescribed by the Board.

(d) The Board may authorize the use of rate tables or charts which may provide for the disclosure of annual percentage rates which vary from the rate determined in accordance with subsection (a)(1)(A) by not more than such tolerances as the Board may allow. The Board may not allow a tolerance greater than 8 per centum of that rate except to simplify compliance where irregular payments are involved.

(e) In the case of creditors determining the annual percentage rate in a manner other than as described in subsection (c) or (d), the Board may authorize other reasonable tolerances.

(f) Prior to January 1, 1971, any rate required under this title to be disclosed as a percentage rate may, at the option of the creditor, be expressed in the form of the corresponding ratio of dollars per hundred dollars.

§ 108. Administrative enforcement

(a) Compliance with the requirements imposed under this title shall be enforced under

(1) section 8 of the Federal Deposit Insurance Act, in the case of

(A) national banks, by the Comptroller of the Currency.

(B) member banks of the Federal Reserve System (other than national banks), by the Board.

(C) banks insured by the Federal Deposit Insurance Corporation (other than members of the Federal Reserve System), by the Board of Directors of the Federal Deposit Insurance Corporation.

(2) section 5(d) of the Home Owners' Loan Act of 1933, section 407 of the National Housing Act, and sections 6(i) and 17 of the Federal Home Loan Bank Act, by the Federal Home Loan Bank Board (acting directly or through the Federal Savings and Loan Insurance Corporation), in the case of any institution subject to any of those provisions.

(3) the Federal Credit Union Act, by the Director of the Bureau of Federal Credit Unions with respect to any Federal credit union.

(4) the Federal Aviation Act of 1958, by the Civil Aeronautics Board with respect to any air carrier or foreign air carrier subject to that Act.

(5) the Packers and Stockyards Act, 1921 (except as provided in section 406 of that Act), by the Secretary of Agriculture with respect to any activities subject to that Act.

(6) the Farm Credit Act of 1971, by the Farm Credit Administration with respect to any Federal land bank, Federal land bank association, Federal intermediate credit bank, or production credit association.

(b) For the purpose of the exercise by any agency referred to in subsection (a) of its powers under any Act referred to in that subsection, a violation of any requirement imposed under this title shall be deemed to be a violation of a requirement imposed under that Act. In addition to its powers under any provision of law specifically referred to in subsection (a), each of the agencies referred to in that subsection may exercise, for the purpose of enforcing compliance with any requirement imposed under this title, any other authority conferred on it by law.

(c) Except to the extent that enforcement of the requirements imposed under this title is specifically committed to some other Government agency under subsection (a), the Federal Trade Commission shall enforce such requirements. For the purpose of the exercise by the Federal Trade Commission of its functions and powers under the Federal Trade Commission Act, a violation of any requirement imposed under this title shall be deemed a violation of a requirement imposed under that Act. All of the functions and powers of the Federal Trade Commission under the Federal Trade Commission Act are available to the Commission to enforce compliance by any person with the requirements imposed under this title, irrespective of whether that person is engaged in commerce or meets any other jurisdictional tests in the Federal Trade Commission Act.

(d) The authority of the Board to issue regulations under this title does not impair the authority of any other agency designated in this section to make rules respecting its own procedures in enforcing compliance with requirements imposed under this title.

§ 109. Views of other agencies

In the exercise of its functions under this title, the Board may obtain upon request the views of any other Federal agency which, in the judgment of the Board, exercises regulatory or supervisory functions with respect to any class of creditors subject to this title.

§ 110. Repealed. Pub.L. 94–239, § 3(b)(1), Mar. 23, 1976, 90 Stat. 253

§ 111. Effect on other laws

(a) This title does not annul, alter, or affect, or exempt any creditor from complying with, the laws of any State relating to the disclosure of information in connection with credit transactions, except to the extent that those laws are inconsistent with the provisions of this title or regulations thereunder, and then only to the extent of the inconsistency.

(b) This title does not otherwise annul, alter or affect in any manner the meaning, scope or applicability of the laws of any State, including, but not limited to, laws relating to the types, amounts or rates of charges, or any element or elements of charges, permissible under such laws in connection with the extension or use of credit, nor does this title extend the applicability of those laws to any class of persons or transactions to which they would not otherwise apply.

(c) In any action or proceeding in any court involving a consumer credit sale, the disclosure of the annual percentage rate as required under this title in connection with that sale may not be received as evidence that the sale was a loan or any type of transaction other than a credit sale.

(d) Except as specified in sections 125, 130, and 166, this title and the regulations issued thereunder do not affect the validity or enforceability of any contract or obligation under State or Federal law.

§ 112. Criminal liability for willful and knowing violation

Whoever willfully and knowingly

(1) gives false or inaccurate information or fails to provide information which he is required to disclose under the provisions of this title or any regulation issued thereunder,

(2) uses any chart or table authorized by the Board under section 107 in such a manner as to consistently understate the annual percentage rate determined under section 107(a)(1)(A), or

(3) otherwise fails to comply with any requirement imposed under this title,

shall be fined not more than $5,000 or imprisoned not more than one year, or both.

§ 113. Penalties inapplicable to governmental agencies

No civil or criminal penalty provided under this title for any violation thereof may be imposed upon the United States or any agency thereof, or upon any State or political subdivision thereof, or any agency of any State or political subdivision.

§ 114. Reports by Board and Attorney General

Not later than January 3 of each year after 1969, the Board and the Attorney General shall, respectively, make reports to the Congress concerning the administration of their functions under this title, including such recommendations as the Board and the Attorney General, respectively, deem necessary or appropriate. In addition, each report of the Board shall include its assessment of the extent to which compliance with the requirements imposed under this title is being achieved.

§ 115. Liability of assignees

Except as otherwise specifically provided in this title, any civil action for a violation of this title which may be brought against the original creditor in any credit transaction may be maintained against any subsequent assignee of the original creditor where the violation from which the alleged liability arose is apparent on the face of the instrument assigned unless the assignment is involuntary.

CHAPTER 2—CREDIT TRANSACTIONS

§ 121. General requirement of disclosure

(a) Each creditor shall disclose clearly and conspicuously, in accordance with the regulations of the Board, to each person to whom consumer credit is extended, the information required under this chapter or chapter 4.

(b) If there is more than one obligor, a creditor need not furnish a statement of information required under this chapter or chapter 4 to more than one of them.

(c) Repealed. Pub.L. 94–205, § 11, Jan. 2, 1976, 89 Stat. 1159.

§ 122. Form of disclosure; additional information

(a) Regulations of the Board need not require that disclosures pursuant to this chapter be made in the order set forth in this chapter, and may permit the use of terminology different from that employed in this chapter or chapter 4 if it conveys substantially the same meaning.

(b) Any creditor may supply additional information or explanations with any disclosures required under this chapter or chapter 4.

§ 123. Exemption for State-regulated transactions

The Board shall by regulation exempt from the requirements of this chapter any class of credit transactions within any State if it determines that under the law of that State that class of transactions is subject to requirements substantially similar to those imposed under this chapter, and that there is adequate provision for enforcement.

§ 124. Effect of subsequent occurrence

If information disclosed in accordance with this chapter is subsequently rendered inaccurate as the result of any act, occurrence, or agreement subsequent to the delivery of the required disclosures, the inaccuracy resulting therefrom does not constitute a violation of this chapter.

§ 125. Right of rescission as to certain transactions

(a) Except as otherwise provided in this section, in the case of any consumer credit transaction in which a security interest, including any such interest arising by operation of law, is or will be retained or acquired in any real property which is used or is expected to be used as the residence of the person to whom credit is extended, the obligor shall have the right to rescind the transaction until midnight of the third business day following the consummation of the transaction or the delivery of the disclosures required under this section and all other material disclosures required under this chapter, whichever is later, by notifying the creditor, in accordance with regulations of the Board, of his intention to do so. The creditor shall clearly and conspicuously disclose, in accordance with regulations of the Board, to any obligor in a transaction subject to this section the rights of the obligor under this section. The creditor shall also provide, in accordance with regulations of the Board, an adequate opportunity to the obligor to exercise his right to rescind any transaction subject to this section.

(b) When an obligor exercises his right to rescind under subsection (a), he is not liable for any finance or other charge, and any security interest given by the obligor, including any such interest arising by operation of law, becomes void upon such a rescission. Within 10 days after receipt of a notice of rescission, the creditor shall return to the obligor any money or property given as earnest money, downpayment, or otherwise, and shall take any action necessary or appropriate to reflect the termination of any security interest created under the transaction. If the creditor has delivered any property to the obligor, the obligor may retain possession of it. Upon the performance of the creditor's obligations under this section, the obligor shall tender the property to the creditor, except that if return of the property in kind would be impracticable or inequitable, the obligor shall tender its reasonable value. Tender shall be made at the location of the property or at the residence of the obligor, at the option of the obligor. If the creditor does not take possession of the property within ten days after tender by the obligor, ownership of the property vests in the obligor without obligation on his part to pay for it.

(c) Notwithstanding any rule of evidence, written acknowledgment of receipt of any disclosures required under this title by a person to whom a statement is required to be given pursuant to this section does no more than create a rebuttable presumption of delivery thereof.

(d) The Board may, if it finds that such action is necessary in order to permit homeowners to meet bona fide personal financial emergencies, prescribe regulations authorizing the modification or waiver of any rights created under this section to the extent and under the circumstances set forth in those regulations.

(e) This section does not apply to the creation or retention of a first lien against a dwelling to finance the acquisition of that dwelling or to a consumer credit transaction in which an agency of a State is the creditor.

(f) An obligor's right of rescission shall expire three years after the date of consummation of the transaction or upon the sale of the property, whichever occurs earlier, notwithstanding the fact that the disclosures required under this section or any other material disclosures required under this chapter have not been delivered to the obligor.

§ 126. Content of periodic statements

If a creditor transmits periodic statements in connection with any extension of consumer credit other than under an open end consumer credit plan, then each of those statements shall set forth each of the following items:

(1) The annual percentage rate of the total finance charge.

(2) The date by which, or the period (if any) within which, payment must be made in order to avoid additional finance charges or other charges.

(3) Such of the items set forth in section 127(b) as the Board may by regulation require as appropriate to the terms and conditions under which the extension of credit in question is made.

§ 127. Open end consumer credit plans

(a) Before opening any account under an open end consumer credit plan, the creditor shall disclose to the person to whom credit is to be extended each of the following items, to the extent applicable:

(1) The conditions under which a finance charge may be imposed, including the time period (if any) within which any credit extended may be repaid without incurring a finance charge, except that the creditor may, at his election and without disclosure, impose no such finance charge if payment is received after the termination of such time period.

(2) The method of determining the balance upon which a finance charge will be imposed.

(3) The method of determining the amount of the finance charge, including any minimum or fixed amount imposed as a finance charge.

(4) Where one or more periodic rates may be used to compute the finance charge, each such rate, the range of balances to which it is applicable, and the corresponding nominal annual percentage rate determined by multiplying the periodic rate by the number of periods in a year.

(5) If the creditor so elects,

(A) the average effective annual percentage rate of return received from accounts under the plan for a representative period of time; or

(B) whenever circumstances are such that the computation of a rate under subparagraph (A) would not be feasible or practical, or would be misleading or meaningless, a projected rate of return to be received from accounts under the plan. The Board shall prescribe regulations, consistent with commonly accepted standards for accounting or statistical procedures, to carry out the purposes of this paragraph.

(6) The conditions under which any other charges may be imposed, and the method by which they will be determined.

(7) The conditions under which the creditor may retain or acquire any security interest in any property to secure the payment of any credit extended under the plan, and a description of the interest or interests which may be so retained or acquired.

(8) A statement, in a form prescribed by regulations of the Board of the protection provided by sections 161 and 170 to an obligor and the creditor's responsibilities under sections 162 and 170. With respect to each of two billing cycles per year, at semi-annual intervals, the creditor shall transmit such statement to each obligor to whom the creditor is required to transmit a statement pursuant to section 127(b) for such billing cycle.

(b) The creditor of any account under an open end consumer credit plan shall transmit to the obligor, for each billing cycle at the end of which there is an outstanding balance in that account or with respect to which a finance charge is imposed, a statement setting forth each of the following items to the extent applicable:

(1) The outstanding balance in the account at the beginning of the statement period.

(2) The amount and date of each extension of credit during the period and a brief identification on or accompanying the statement of each extension of credit in a form prescribed by regulations of the Board sufficient to enable the obligor to identify the transaction, or relate it to copies of sales vouchers or similar instruments previously furnished.

(3) The total amount credited to the account during the period.

(4) The amount of any finance charge added to the account during the period, itemized to show the amounts, if any, due to the application of percentage rates and the amount, if any, imposed as a minimum or fixed charge.

(5) Where one or more periodic rates may be used to compute the finance charge, each such rate, the range of balances to which it is applicable, and, unless the annual percentage rate (determined under section 107(a)(2)) is required to be disclosed pursuant to paragraph (6), the corresponding nominal annual percentage rate determined by multiplying the periodic rate by the number of periods in a year.

(6) Where the total finance charge exceeds 50 cents for a monthly or longer billing cycle, or the pro rata part of 50 cents for a billing cycle shorter than monthly, the total finance charge expressed as an annual percentage rate (determined under section 107(a)(2)), except that if the finance charge is the sum of two or more products of a rate times a portion of the balance, the creditor may, in lieu of disclosing a single rate for the total charge, disclose each such rate expressed as an annual percentage rate, and the part of the balance to which it is applicable.

(7) At the election of the creditor, the average effective annual percentage rate of return (or the projected rate) under the plan as prescribed in subsection (a)(5).

(8) The balance on which the finance charge was computed and a statement of how the balance was determined. If the balance is determined without first deducting all credits during the period, that fact and the amount of such payments shall also be disclosed.

(9) The outstanding balance in the account at the end of the period.

(10) The date by which or the period (if any) within which, payment must be made to avoid additional finance charges, except that the creditor may, at his election and without disclosure, impose no such additional finance charge if payment is received after such date or the termination of such period.

(11) The address to be used by the creditor for the purpose of receiving billing inquiries from the obligor.

(c) In the case of any existing account under an open end consumer credit plan having an outstanding balance of more than $1 at or after the close of the creditor's first full billing cycle under the plan after the effective date of subsection (a) or any amendments thereto, the items described in subsection (a), to the extent applicable and not previously disclosed, shall be disclosed in a notice mailed or delivered to the obligor not later than the time of mailing the next statement required by subsection (b).

§ 128. Sales not under open end credit plans

(a) In connection with each consumer credit sale not under an open end credit plan, the creditor shall disclose each of the following items which is applicable:

(1) The cash price of the property or service purchased.

(2) The sum of any amounts credited as downpayment (including any trade-in).

(3) The difference between the amount referred to in paragraph (1) and the amount referred to in paragraph (2).

(4) All other charges, individually itemized, which are included in the amount of the credit extended but which are not part of the finance charge.

(5) The total amount to be financed (the sum of the amount described in paragraph (3) plus the amount described in paragraph (4)).

(6) Except in the case of a sale of a dwelling, the amount of the finance charge, which may in whole or in part be designated as a time-price differential or any similar term to the extent applicable.

(7) The finance charge expressed as an annual percentage rate except in the case of a finance charge

(A) which does not exceed $5 and is applicable to an amount financed not exceeding $75, or

(B) which does not exceed $7.50 and is applicable to an amount financed exceeding $75.

A creditor may not divide a consumer credit sale into two or more sales to avoid the disclosure of an annual percentage rate pursuant to this paragraph.

(8) The number, amount, and due dates or periods of payments scheduled to repay the indebtedness.

(9) The default, delinquency, or similar charges payable in the event of late payments.

(10) A description of any security interest held or to be retained or acquired by the creditor in connection with the extension of credit, and a clear identification of the property to which the security interest relates.

(b) Except as otherwise provided in this chapter, the disclosures required under subsection (a) shall be made before the credit is extended, and may be made by disclosing the information in the contract or other evidence of indebtedness to be signed by the purchaser.

(c) If a creditor receives a purchase order by mail or telephone without personal solicitation, and the cash price and the deferred payment price and the terms of financing, including the annual percentage rate, are set forth in the creditor's catalog or other printed material distributed to the public, then the disclosures required under subsection (a) may be made at any time not later than the date the first payment is due.

(d) If a consumer credit sale is one of a series of consumer credit sales transactions made pursuant to an agreement providing for the addition of the deferred payment price of that sale to an existing outstanding balance, and the person to whom the credit is extended has approved in writing both the annual percentage rate or rates and the method of computing the finance charge or charges, and the creditor retains no security interest in any property as to which he has received payments aggregating the amount of the sales price including any finance charges attributable thereto, then the disclosure required under subsection (a) for the particular sale may be made at any time not later than the date the first payment for that sale is due. For the purposes of this subsection, in the case of items purchased on different dates, the first purchased shall be deemed first paid for, and in the case of items purchased on the same date, the lowest priced shall be deemed first paid for.

§ 129. Consumer loans not under open end credit plans

(a) Any creditor making a consumer loan or otherwise extending consumer credit in a transaction which is neither a consumer credit sale nor under an open end consumer credit plan shall disclose each of the following items, to the extent applicable:

(1) The amount of credit of which the obligor will have the actual use, or which is or will be paid to him or for his account or to another person on his behalf.

(2) All charges, individually itemized, which are included in the amount of credit extended but which are not part of the finance charge.

(3) The total amount to be financed (the sum of the amounts referred to in paragraph (1) plus the amounts referred to in paragraph (2)).

(4) Except in the case of a loan secured by a first lien on a dwelling and made to finance the purchase of that dwelling, the amount of the finance charge.

(5) The finance charge expressed as an annual percentage rate except in the case of a finance charge

(A) which does not exceed $5 and is applicable to an extension of consumer credit not exceeding $75, or

(B) which does not exceed $7.50 and is applicable to an extension of consumer credit exceeding $75.

A creditor may not divide an extension of credit into two or more transactions to avoid the disclosure of an annual percentage rate pursuant to this paragraph.

(6) The number, amount, and the due dates or periods of payments scheduled to repay the indebtedness.

(7) The default, delinquency, or similar charges payable in the event of late payments.

(8) A description of any security interest held or to be retained or acquired by the creditor in connection with the extension of credit, and a clear identification of the property to which the security interest relates.

(b) Except as otherwise provided in this chapter, the disclosures required by subsection (a) shall be made before the credit is extended, and may be made by disclosing the information in the note or other evidence of indebtedness to be signed by the obligor.

(c) If a creditor receives a request for an extension of credit by mail or telephone without personal solicitation and the terms of financing, including the annual percentage rate for representative amounts of credit, are set forth in the creditor's printed material distributed to the public, or in the contract of loan or other printed material delivered to the obligor, then the disclosures required under subsection (a) may be made at any time not later than the date the first payment is due.

§ 130. Civil liability

(a) Except as otherwise provided in this section, any creditor who fails to comply with any requirement imposed under this chapter or chapter 4 or 5 of this title with respect to any person is liable to such person in an amount equal to the sum of—

(1) any actual damage sustained by such person as a result of the failure;

(2)(A)(i) in the case of an individual action twice the amount of any finance charge in connection with the transaction, or (ii) in the case of an individual action relating to a consumer lease under chapter 5 of this title, 25 per centum of the total amount of monthly payments under the lease, except that the liability under this subparagraph shall not be less than $100 nor greater than $1,000; or

(B) in the case of a class action, such amount as the court may allow, except that as to each member of the class no minimum recovery shall be applicable, and the total recovery in such action shall not be more than the lesser of $500,000 or 1 per centum of the net worth of the creditor; and

(3) in the case of any successful action to enforce the foregoing liability, the costs of the action, together with a reasonable attorney's fee as determined by the court.

In determining the amount of award in any class action, the court shall consider, among other relevant factors, the amount of any actual damages awarded, the frequency and persistence of failures of compliance by the creditor, the resources of the creditor, the number of persons adversely affected, and the extent to which the creditor's failure of compliance was intentional.

(b) A creditor has no liability under this section for any failure to comply with any requirement imposed under this chapter or chapter 5, if within fifteen days after discovering an error, and prior to the institution of an action under this section or the receipt of written notice of the error, the creditor notifies the person concerned of the error and makes whatever adjustments in the appropriate account are necessary to insure that the person will not be required to pay a charge in excess of the amount or percentage rate actually disclosed.

(c) A creditor may not be held liable in any action brought under this section for a violation of this title if the creditor shows by a preponderance of evidence that the violation was not intentional and resulted from a bona fide error notwithstanding the maintenance of procedures reasonably adapted to avoid any such error.

(d) Any action which may be brought under this section against the original creditor in any credit transaction involving a security interest in real property may be maintained against any subsequent assignee of the original creditor where the assignee, its subsidiaries, or affiliates were in a continuing business relationship with the original creditor either at the time the credit was extended or at the time of the assignment, unless the assignment was involuntary, or the assignee shows by a preponderance of evidence that it did not have reasonable grounds to believe that the original creditor was engaged in violations of this chapter, and that it maintained procedures reasonably adapted to apprise it of the existence of any such violations.

(e) Any action under this section may be brought in any United States district court, or in any other court of competent jurisdiction, within one year from the date of the occurrence of the violation.

(f) No provision of this section or section 112 imposing any liability shall apply to any act done or omitted in good faith in conformity with any rule, regulation, or interpretation thereof by the Board, notwithstanding that after such act or omission has occurred, such rule, regulation, or interpretation is amended, rescinded, or determined by judicial or other authority to be invalid for any reason.

(g) The multiple failure to disclose to any person any information required under this chapter or chapter 4 or 5 of this title to be disclosed in connection with a single account under an open end consumer credit plan, other single consumer credit sale, consumer loan, consumer lease, or other extension of consumer credit, shall entitle the person to a single recovery under this section but continued failure to disclose after a recovery has been granted shall give rise to rights to additional recoveries.

(h) A person may not take any action to offset any amount for which a creditor is potentially liable to such person under subsection (a)(2) against any amount owing to such creditor by such person, unless the amount of the creditor's liability to such person has been determined by judgment of a court of competent jurisdiction in an action to which such person was a party.

§ 131. Written acknowledgment as proof of receipt

Except as provided in section 125(c) and except in the case of actions brought under section 130(d), in any action or proceeding by or against any subsequent assignee of the original creditor without knowledge to the contrary by the assignee when he acquires the obligation, written acknowledgment of receipt by a person to whom a statement is required to be given pursuant to this title shall be conclusive proof of the delivery thereof and, unless the violation is apparent on the face of the statement, of compliance with this chapter. This section does not affect the rights of the obligor in any action against the original creditor.

§ 132. Issuance of credit cards

No credit cards shall be issued except in response to a request or application therefor. This prohibition does not apply to the issuance of a credit card in renewal of, or in substitution for, an accepted credit card.

§ 133. Liability of holder of credit card

(a) A cardholder shall be liable for the unauthorized use of a credit card only if the card is an accepted credit card, the liability is not in excess of $50, the card issuer gives adequate notice to the cardholder of the potential liability, the card issuer has provided the cardholder with a self-addressed, prestamped notification to be mailed by the cardholder in the event of the loss or theft of the credit card, and the unauthorized use occurs before the cardholder has notified the card issuer that an unauthorized use of the credit card has occurred or may occur as the result of loss, theft, or otherwise. Notwithstanding the foregoing, no cardholder shall be liable for the unauthorized use of any credit card which was issued on or after the effective date of this section, and, after the expiration of twelve months following such effective date, no cardholder shall be liable for the unauthorized use of any credit card regardless of the date of its issuance, unless (1) the conditions of liability specified in the preceding sentence are met, and (2) the card issuer has provided a method whereby the user of such card can be identified as the person authorized to use it. For the purposes of this section, a cardholder notifies a card issuer by taking such steps as may be reasonably required in the ordinary course of business to provide the card issuer with the pertinent information whether or not any particular officer, employee, or agent of the card issuer does in fact receive such information.

(b) In any action by a card issuer to enforce liability for the use of a credit card, the burden of proof is upon the card issuer to show that the use was authorized or, if the use was unauthorized, then the burden of proof is upon the card issuer to show that the conditions of liability for the unauthorized use of a credit card, as set forth in subsection (a), have been met.

(c) Nothing in this section imposes liability upon a cardholder for the unauthorized use of a credit card in excess of his liability for such use under other applicable law or under any agreement with the card issuer.

(d) Except as provided in this section, a cardholder incurs no liability from the unauthorized use of a credit card.

§ 134. Fraudulent use of credit card

(a) Whoever knowingly in a transaction affecting interstate or foreign commerce, uses or attempts or conspires to use any counterfeit, fictitious, altered, forged, lost, stolen, or fraudulently obtained credit card to obtain money, goods, services, or anything else of value which within any one-year period has a value aggregating $1,000 or more; or

(b) Whoever, with unlawful or fraudulent intent, transports or attempts or conspires to transport in interstate or foreign commerce a counterfeit, fictitious, altered, forged, lost, stolen, or fraudulently obtained credit card knowing the same to be counterfeit, fictitious, altered, forged, lost, stolen, or fraudulently obtained; or

(c) Whoever, with unlawful or fraudulent intent, uses any instrumentality of interstate or foreign commerce to sell or transport a counterfeit, fictitious, altered, forged, lost, stolen, or fraudulently obtained credit card knowing the same to be counterfeit, fictitious, altered, forged, lost, stolen, or fraudulently obtained; or

(d) Whoever knowingly receives, conceals, uses, or transports money, goods, services, or anything else of value (except tickets for interstate or foreign transportation) which (1) within any one-year period has a value aggregating $1,000 or more, (2) has moved in or is part of, or which constitutes interstate or foreign commerce, and (3) has been obtained with a counterfeit, fictitious, altered, forged, lost, stolen, or fraudulently obtained credit card; or

(e) Whoever knowingly receives, conceals, uses, sells, or transports in interstate or foreign commerce one or more tickets for interstate or foreign transportation, which (1) within any one-year period have a value aggregating $500 or more, and (2) have been purchased or obtained with one or more counterfeit, fictitious, altered, forged, lost, stolen, or fraudulently obtained credit cards; or

(f) Whoever in a transaction affecting interstate or foreign commerce furnishes money, property, services, or anything else of value, which within any one-year period has a value aggregating $1,000 or more, through the use of any counterfeit, fictitious, altered, forged, lost, stolen, or fraudulently obtained credit card knowing the same to be counterfeit, fictitious, altered, lost, stolen, or fraudulently obtained—shall be fined not more than $10,000 or imprisoned not more than ten years, or both.

§ 135. Business credit cards

The exemption provided by section 104(1) does not apply to the provisions of sections 132, 133, and 134, except that a card issuer and a business or other organization which provides credit cards issued by the same card issuer to ten or more of its employees may by contract agree as to liability of the business or other organization with respect to unauthorized use of such credit cards without regard to the provisions of section 133, but in no case may such business or other organization or card issuer impose liability upon any employee with respect to unauthorized use of such a credit card except in accordance with and subject to the limitations of section 133.

CHAPTER 3—CREDIT ADVERTISING

§ 141. Catalogs and multiple-page advertisements

For the purposes of this chapter, a catalog or other multiple-page advertisement shall be considered a single advertisement if it clearly and conspicuously displays a credit terms table on which the information required to be stated under this chapter is clearly set forth.

§ 142. Advertising of downpayments and installments

No advertisement to aid, promote, or assist directly or indirectly any extension of consumer credit may state:

(1) that a specific periodic consumer credit amount or installment amount can be arranged, unless the creditor usually and customarily arranges credit payments or installments for that period and in that amount.

(2) that a specified downpayment is required in connection with any extension of consumer credit, unless the creditor usually and customarily arranges downpayments in that amount.

§ 143. Advertising of open end credit plans

No advertisement to aid, promote, or assist directly or indirectly the extension of consumer credit under an open end credit plan may set forth any of the specific terms of that plan or the appropriate rate determined under section 127(a)(5) unless it also clearly and conspicuously sets forth all of the following items:

(1) The time period, if any, within which any credit extended may be repaid without incurring a finance charge.

(2) The method of determining the balance upon which a finance charge will be imposed.

(3) The method of determining the amount of the finance charge, including any minimum or fixed amount imposed as a finance charge.

(4) Where periodic rates may be used to compute the finance charge, the period rates expressed as annual percentage rates.

(5) Such other or additional information for the advertising of open end credit plans as the Board may by regulation require to provide for adequate comparison of credit costs as between different types of open end credit plans.

§ 144. Advertising of credit other than open end plans

(a) Except as provided in subsection (b), this section applies to any advertisement to aid, promote, or assist directly or indirectly any consumer credit sale, loan, or other extension of credit subject to the provisions of this title, other than an open end credit plan.

(b) The provisions of this section do not apply to advertisements of residential real estate except to the extent that the Board may by regulation require.

(c) If any advertisement to which this section applies states the rate of a finance charge, the advertisement shall state the rate of that charge expressed as an annual percentage rate.

(d) If any advertisement to which this section applies states the amount of the downpayment, if any, the amount of any installment payment, the dollar amount of any finance charge, or the number of installments or the period of repayment, then the advertisement shall state all of the following items:

(1) The cash price or the amount of the loan as applicable.

(2) The downpayment, if any.

(3) The number, amount, and due dates or period of payments scheduled to repay the indebtedness if the credit is extended.

(4) The rate of the finance charge expressed as an annual percentage rate.

§ 145. Nonliability of media

There is no liability under this chapter on the part of any owner or personnel, as such, of any medium in which an advertisement appears or through which it is disseminated.

§ 146. More-than-four-installment rule

Any advertisement to aid, promote, or assist directly or indirectly the extension of consumer credit repayable in more than four installments shall, unless a finance charge is imposed, clearly and conspicuously state, in accordance with the regulations of the Board;

"THE COST OF CREDIT IS INCLUDED IN THE PRICE QUOTED FOR THE GOODS AND SERVICES."

CHAPTER 4—CREDIT BILLING

§ 161. Correction of billing errors

(a) If a creditor, within sixty days after having transmitted to an obligor a statement of the obligor's account in connection with an extension of consumer credit, receives at the address disclosed under section 127(b)(11) a written notice (other than notice on a payment stub or other payment medium supplied by the creditor if the creditor so stipulates with the disclosure required under section 127(a)(8)) from the obligor in which the obligor—

(1) sets forth or otherwise enables the creditor to identify the name and account number (if any) of the obligor,

(2) indicates the obligor's belief that the statement contains a billing error and the amount of such billing error, and

(3) sets forth the reasons for the obligor's belief (to the extent applicable) that the statement contains a billing error,

the creditor shall, unless the obligor has, after giving such written notice and before the expiration of the time limits herein specified, agreed that the statement was correct—

(A) not later than thirty days after the receipt of the notice, send a written acknowledgment thereof to the obligor, unless the action required in subparagraph (B) is taken within such thirty-day period, and

(B) not later than two complete billing cycles of the creditor (in no event later than ninety days) after the receipt of the notice and prior to taking any action to collect the amount, or any part thereof, indicated by the obligor under paragraph (2) either—

(i) make appropriate corrections in the account of the obligor, including the crediting of any finance charges on amounts erroneously billed, and transmit to the obligor a notification of such corrections and the creditor's explanation of any change in the amount indicated by the obligor under paragraph (2) and, if any such change is made and the obligor so requests, copies of documentary evidence of the obligor's indebtedness; or

(ii) send a written explanation or clarification to the obligor, after having conducted an investigation, setting forth to the extent applicable the reasons why the creditor believes the account of the obligor was correctly shown in the statement and, upon request of the obligor, provide copies of documentary evidence of the obligor's indebtedness. In the case of a billing error where the obligor alleges that the creditor's billing statement reflects goods not delivered to the obligor or his designee in accordance with the agreement made at the time of the transaction, a creditor may not construe such amount to be correctly shown unless he determines that such goods were actually delivered, mailed, or otherwise sent to the obligor and provides the obligor with a statement of such determination.

After complying with the provisions of this subsection with respect to an alleged billing error, a creditor has no further responsibility under this section if the obligor continues to make substantially the same allegation with respect to such error.

(b) For the purpose of this section, a "billing error" consists of any of the following:

(1) A reflection on a statement of an extension of credit which was not made to the obligor or, if made, was not in the amount reflected on such statement.

(2) A reflection on a statement of an extension of credit for which the obligor requests additional clarification including documentary evidence thereof.

(3) A reflection on a statement of goods or services not accepted by the obligor or his designee or not delivered to the obligor or his designee in accordance with the agreement made at the time of a transaction.

(4) The creditor's failure to reflect properly on a statement a payment made by the obligor or a credit issued to the obligor.

(5) A computation error or similar error of an accounting nature of the creditor on a statement.

(6) Any other error described in regulations of the Board.

(c) For the purposes of this section, "action to collect the amount, or any part thereof, indicated by an obligor under paragraph (2)" does not include the sending of statements of account to the obligor following written notice from the obligor as specified under subsection (a), if—

(1) the obligor's account is not restricted or closed because of the failure of the obligor to pay the amount indicated under paragraph (2) of subsection (a), and

(2) the creditor indicates the payment of such amount is not required pending the creditor's compliance with this section.

Nothing in this section shall be construed to prohibit any action by a creditor to collect any amount which has not been indicated by the obligor to contain a billing error.

(d) Pursuant to regulations of the Board, a creditor operating an open end consumer credit plan may not, prior to the sending of the written explanation or clarification required under paragraph (B)(ii), restrict or close an account with respect to which the obligor has indicated pursuant to subsection (a) that he believes such account to contain a billing error solely because of the obligor's failure to pay the amount indicated to be in error. Nothing in this subsection shall be deemed to prohibit a creditor from applying against the credit limit on the obligor's account the amount indicated to be in error.

(e) Any creditor who fails to comply with the requirements of this section or section 162 forfeits any right to collect from the obligor the amount indicated by the obligor under paragraph (2) of subsection (a) of this section, and any finance charges thereon, except that the amount required to be forfeited under this subsection may not exceed $50.

§ 162. Regulation of credit reports

(a) After receiving a notice from an obligor as provided in section 161(a), a creditor or his agent may not directly or indirectly threaten to report to any person adversely on the obligor's credit rating or credit standing because of the obligor's failure to pay the amount indicated by the obligor under section 161(a)(2), and such amount may not be reported as delinquent to any third party until the creditor has met the requirements of section 161 and has allowed the obligor the same number of days (not less than ten) thereafter to make payment as is provided under the credit agreement with the obligor for the payment of undisputed amounts.

(b) If a creditor receives a further written notice from an obligor that an amount is still in dispute within the time allowed for payment under subsection (a) of this section, a creditor may not report to any third party that the amount of the obligor is delinquent because the obligor has failed to pay an amount which he has indicated under section 161(a)(2), unless the creditor also reports that the amount is in dispute and, at the same time, notifies the obligor of the name and address of each party to whom the creditor is reporting information concerning the delinquency.

(c) A creditor shall report any subsequent resolution of any delinquencies reported pursuant to subsection (b) to the parties to whom such delinquencies were initially reported.

§ 163. Length of billing period

(a) If an open end consumer credit plan provides a time period within which an obligor may repay any portion of the credit extended without incurring an additional finance charge, such additional finance charge may not be imposed with respect to such portion of the credit extended for the billing cycle of which such period is a part unless a statement which includes the amount upon which the finance charge for that period is based was mailed at least fourteen days prior to the date specified in the statement by which payment must be made in order to avoid imposition of that finance charge.

(b) Subsection (a) does not apply in any case where a creditor has been prevented, delayed, or hindered in making timely mailing or delivery of such periodic statement within the time period specified in such subsection because of an act of God, war, natural disaster, strike, or other excusable or justifiable cause, as determined under regulations of the Board.

§ 164. Prompt crediting of payments

Payments received from an obligor under an open end consumer credit plan by the creditor shall be posted promptly to the obligor's account as specified in regulations of the Board. Such regulations shall prevent a finance charge from being imposed on any obligor if the creditor has received the obligor's payment in readily identifiable form in the amount, manner, location, and time indicated by the creditor to avoid the imposition thereof.

§ 165. Crediting excess payments

Whenever an obligor transmits funds to a creditor in excess of the total balance due on an open end consumer credit account, the creditor shall promptly (1) upon request of the obligor refund the amount of the overpayment, or (2) credit such amount to the obligor's account.

§ 166. Prompt notification of returns

With respect to any sales transaction where a credit card has been used to obtain credit, where the seller is a person other than the card issuer, and where the seller accepts or allows a return of the goods or forgiveness of a debit for services which were the subject of such sale, the seller shall promptly transmit to the credit card issuer, a credit statement with respect thereto and the credit card issuer shall credit the account of the obligor for the amount of the transaction.

§ 167. Use of cash discounts

(a)(1) With respect to credit card which may be used for extensions of credit in sales transactions in which the seller is a person other than the card issuer, the card issuer may not, by contract or otherwise, prohibit any such seller from offering a discount to a cardholder to induce the cardholder to pay by cash, check, or similar means rather than use a credit card.

(2) No seller in any sales transaction may impose a surcharge on a cardholder who elects to use a credit card in lieu of payment by cash, check, or similar means.

(b) With respect to any sales transaction, any discount not in excess of 5 per centum offered by the seller for the purpose of inducing payment by cash, check, or other means not involving the use of a credit card shall not constitute a finance charge as determined under section 106, if such discount is offered to all prospective buyers and its availability is disclosed to all prospective buyers clearly and conspicuously in accordance with regulations of the Board.

§ 168. Prohibition of tie-in services

Notwithstanding any agreement to the contrary, a card issuer may not require a seller, as a condition to participating in a credit card plan, to open an account with or procure any other service from the card issuer or its subsidiary or agent.

§ 169. Prohibition of offsets

(a) A card issuer may not take any action to offset a cardholder's indebtedness arising in connection with a consumer credit transaction under the relevant credit card plan against funds of the cardholder held on deposit with the card issuer unless—

(1) such action was previously authorized in writing by the cardholder in accordance with a credit plan whereby the cardholder agrees periodically to pay debts incurred in his open end credit account by permitting the card issuer periodically to deduct all or a portion of such debt from the cardholder's deposit account, and

(2) such action with respect to any outstanding disputed amount not be taken by the card issuer upon request of the cardholder.

In the case of any credit card account in existence on the effective date of this section, the previous written authorization referred to in clause (1) shall not be required until the date (after such effective date) when such account is renewed, but in no case later than one year after such effective date. Such written authorization shall be deemed to exist if the card issuer has previously notified the cardholder that the use of his credit card account will subject any funds which the card issuer holds in deposit accounts of such cardholder to offset against any amounts due and payable on his credit card account which have not been paid in accordance with the terms of the agreement between the card issuer and the cardholder.

(b) This section does not alter or affect the right under State law of a card issuer to attach or otherwise levy upon funds of a cardholder held on deposit with the card issuer if that remedy is constitutionally available to creditors generally.

§ 170. Rights of credit card customers

(a) Subject to the limitation contained in subsection (b), a card issuer who has issued a credit card to a cardholder pursuant to an open end consumer credit plan shall be subject to all claims (other than tort claims) and defenses arising out of any transaction in which the credit card is used as a method of payment or extension of credit if (1) the obligor has made a good faith attempt to obtain satisfactory resolution of a disagreement or problem relative to the transaction from the person honoring the credit card; (2) the amount of the initial transaction exceeds $50; and (3) the place where the initial transaction occurred was in the same State as the mailing address previously provided by the cardholder or was within 100 miles from such address, except that the limitations set forth in clauses (2) and (3) with respect to an obligor's right to assert claims and defenses against a card issuer shall not be applicable to any transaction in which the person honoring the credit card (A) is the same person as the card issuer, (B) is controlled by the card issuer, (C) is under direct or indirect common control with the card issuer, (D) is a franchised dealer in the card issuer's products or services, or (E) has obtained the order for such transaction through a mail solicitation made by or participated in by the card issuer in which the cardholder is solicited to enter into such transaction by using the credit card issued by the card issuer.

(b) The amount of claims or defenses asserted by the cardholder may not exceed the amount of credit outstanding with respect to such transaction at the time the cardholder first notifies the card issuer or the person honoring the credit card of such claim or defense. For the purpose of determining the amount of credit outstanding in the preceding sentence, payments and credits to the cardholder's account are deemed to have been applied, in the order indicated, to the payment of: (1) late charges in the order of their entry to the account; (2) finance charges in order of their entry to the account; and (3) debits to the account other than those set forth above, in the order in which each debit entry to the account was made.

§ 171. Relation to State laws

(a) This chapter does not annul, alter, or affect, or exempt any person subject to the provisions of this chapter from complying with, the laws of any State with respect to credit billing practices, except to the extent that those laws are inconsistent with any provision of this chapter, and then only to the extent of the inconsistency. The Board is authorized to determine whether such inconsistencies exist. The Board may not determine that any State law is inconsistent with any provision of this chapter if the Board determines that such law gives greater protection to the consumer.

(b) The Board shall by regulation exempt from the requirements of this chapter any class of credit transactions within any State if it determines that under the law of that State that class of transacions is subject to requirements substantially similar to those imposed under this chapter or that such law gives greater protection to the consumer, and that there is adequate provision for enforcement.

CHAPTER 5—CONSUMER LEASES

§ 181. Definitions

For purposes of this chapter—

(1) The term "consumer lease" means a contract in the form of a lease or bailment for the use of personal property by a natural person for a period of time exceeding four months, and for a total contractual obligation not exceeding $25,000, primarily for personal, family, or household purposes, whether or not the lessee has the option to purchase or otherwise become the owner of the property at the expiration of the lease, except that such term shall not include any credit sale as defined in section 103(g). Such term does not include a lease for agricultural, business, or commercial purposes, or to a government or governmental agency or instrumentality, or to an organization.

(2) The term "lessee" means a natural person who leases or is offered a consumer lease.

(3) The term "lessor" means a person who is regularly engaged in leasing, offering to lease, or arranging to lease under a consumer lease.

(4) The term "personal property" means any property which is not real property under the laws of the State where situated at the time offered or otherwise made available for lease.

(5) The terms "security" and "security interest" mean any interest in property which secures payment or performance of an obligation.

§ 182. Consumer lease disclosures

Each lessor shall give a lessee prior to the consummation of the lease a dated written statement on which the lessor and lessee are identified setting out accurately and in a clear and conspicuous manner the following information with respect to that lease, as applicable:

(1) A brief description or identification of the leased property;

(2) The amount of any payment by the lessee required at the inception of the lease;

(3) The amount paid or payable by the lessee for official fees, registration, certificate of title, or license fees or taxes;

(4) The amount of other charges payable by the lessee not included in the periodic payments, a description of the charges and that the lessee shall be liable for the differential, if any, between the anticipated fair market value of the leased property and its appraised actual value at the termination of the lease, if the lessee has such liability;

(5) A statement of the amount or method of determining the amount of any liabilities the lease imposes upon the lessee at the end of the term and whether or not the lessee has the option to purchase the leased property and at what price and time;

(6) A statement identifying all express warranties and guarantees made by the manufacturer or lessor with respect to the leased property, and identifying the party responsible for maintaining or servicing the leased property together with a description of the responsibility;

(7) A brief description of insurance provided or paid for by the lessor or required of the lessee, including the types and amounts of the coverage and costs;

(8) A description of any security interest held or to be retained by the lessor in connection with the lease and a clear identification of the property to which the security interest relates;

(9) The number, amount, and due dates or periods of payments under the lease and the total amount of such periodic payments;

(10) Where the lease provides that the lessee shall be liable for the anticipated fair market value of the property on expiration of the lease, the fair market value of the property at the

inception of the lease, the aggregate cost of the lease on expiration, and the differential between them; and

(11) A statement of the conditions under which the lessee or lessor may terminate the lease prior to the end of the term and the amount or method of determining any penalty or other charge for delinquency, default, late payments, or early termination.

The disclosures required under this section may be made in the lease contract to be signed by the lessee. The Board may provide by regulation that any portion of the information required to be disclosed under this section may be given in the form of estimates where the lessor is not in a position to know exact information.

§ 183. Lessee's liability on expiration or termination of lease

(a) Where the lessee's liability on expiration of a consumer lease is based on the estimated residual value of the property such estimated residual value shall be a reasonable approximation of the anticipated actual fair market value of the property on lease expiration. There shall be a rebuttable presumption that the estimated residual value is unreasonable to the extent that the estimated residual value exceeds the actual residual value by more than three times the average payment allocable to a monthly period under the lease. In addition, where the lessee has such liability on expiration of a consumer lease there shall be a rebuttable presumption that the lessor's estimated residual value is not in good faith to the extent that the estimated residual value exceeds the actual residual value by more than three times the average payment allocable to a monthly period under the lease and such lessor shall not collect from the lessee the amount of such excess liability on expiration of a consumer lease unless the lessor brings a successful action with respect to such excess liability. In all actions, the lessor shall pay the lessee's reasonable attorney's fees. The presumptions stated in this section shall not apply to the extent the excess of estimated over actual residual value is due to to physical damage to the property beyond reasonable wear and use, or to excessive use, and the lease may set standards for such wear and use if such standards are not unreasonable. Nothing in this subsection shall preclude the right of a willing lessee to make any mutually agreeable final adjustment with respect to such excess residual liability, provided such an agreement is reached after termination of the lease.

(b) Penalties or other charges for delinquency, default, or early termination may be specified in the lease but only at an amount which is reasonable in the light of the anticipated or actual harm caused by the delinquency, default, or early termination, the difficulties of proof of loss, and the inconvenience or nonfeasibility of otherwise obtaining an adequate remedy.

(c) If a lease has a residual value provision at the termination of the lease, the lessee may obtain at his expense, a professional appraisal of the leased property by an independent third party agreed to by both parties. Such appraisal shall be final and binding on the parties.

§ 184. Consumer lease advertising

(a) No advertisement to aid, promote, or assist directly or indirectly any consumer lease shall state the amount of any payment, the number of required payments, or that any or no downpayment or other payment is required at inception of the lease unless the advertisement also states clearly and conspicuously and in accordance with regulations issued by the Board each of the following items of information which is applicable:

(1) That the transaction advertised is a lease.

(2) The amount of any payment required at the inception of the lease or that no such payment is required if that is the case.

(3) The number, amounts, due dates or periods of scheduled payments, and the total of payments under the lease.

(4) That the lessee shall be liable for the differential, if any, between the anticipated fair market value of the leased property and its appraised actual value at the termination of the lease, if the lessee has such liability.

(5) A statement of the amount or method of determining the amount of any liabilities the lease imposes upon the lessee at the end of the term and whether or not the lessee has the option to purchase the leased property and at what price and time.

(b) There is no liability under this section on the part of any owner or personnel, as such, of any medium in which an advertisement appears or through which it is disseminated.

§ 185. Civil liability

(a) Any lessor who fails to comply with any requirement imposed under section 182 or 183 of this chapter with respect to any person is liable to such person as provided in section 130.

(b) Any lessor who fails to comply with any requirement imposed under section 184 of this chapter with respect to any person who suffers actual damage from the violation is liable to such person as provided in section 130. For the purposes of this section, the term creditor as used in sections 115, 130, and 131 shall include a lessor as defined in this chapter.

(c) Notwithstanding section 130(e), any action under this section may be brought in any United States district court or in any other court of competent jurisdiction. Such actions alleging a failure to disclose or otherwise comply with the requirements of this chapter shall be brought within one year of the termination of the lease agreement.

§ 186. Relation to State laws

(a) This chapter does not annul, alter, or affect, or exempt any person subject to the provisions of this chapter from complying with, the laws of any State with respect to consumer leases, except to the extent that those laws are inconsistent with any provision of this chapter, and then only to the extent of the inconsistency. The Board is authorized to determine whether such inconsistencies exist. The Board may not determine that any State law is inconsistent with any provision of this chapter if the Board determines that such law gives greater protection and benefit to the consumer.

(b) The Board shall by regulation exempt from the requirements of this chapter any class of lease transactions within any State if it determines that under the law of that State that class of transactions is subject to requirements substantially similar to those imposed under this chapter or that such law gives greater protection and benefit to the consumer, and that there is adequate provision for enforcement.

TITLE III—RESTRICTION ON GARNISHMENT

§ 301. Findings and purpose

(a) The Congress finds:

(1) The unrestricted garnishment of compensation due for personal services encourages the making of predatory extensions of credit. Such extensions of credit divert money into excessive credit payments and thereby hinder the production and flow of goods in interstate commerce.

(2) The application of garnishment as a creditors' remedy frequently results in loss of employment by the debtor, and the resulting disruption of employment, production, and consumption constitutes a substantial burden on interstate commerce.

(3) The great disparities among the laws of the several States relating to garnishment have, in effect, destroyed the uniformity of the bankruptcy laws and frustrated the purposes thereof in many areas of the country.

(b) On the basis of the findings stated in subsection (a) of this section, the Congress determines that the provisions of this title are necessary and proper for the purpose of carrying into execution the powers of the Congress to regulate commerce and to establish uniform bankruptcy laws.

§ 302. Definitions

For the purposes of this title:

(a) The term "earnings" means compensation paid or payable for personal services, whether denominated as wages, salary, commission, bonus, or otherwise, and includes periodic payments pursuant to a pension or retirement program.

(b) The term "disposable earnings" means that part of the earnings of any individual remaining after the deduction from those earnings of any amounts required by law to be withheld.

(c) The term "garnishment" means any legal or equitable procedure through which the earnings of any individual are required to be withheld for payment of any debt.

§ 303. Restriction on garnishment

(a) Except as provided in subsection (b) and in section 305, the maximum part of the aggregate disposable earnings of an individual for any workweek which is subjected to garnishment may not exceed

(1) 25 per centum of his disposable earnings for that week, or

(2) the amount by which his disposable earnings for that week exceed thirty times the Federal minimum hourly wage prescribed by section 6(a) (1) of the Fair Labor Standards Act of 1938 in effect at the time the earnings are payable,

whichever is less. In the case of earnings for any pay period other than a week, the Secretary of Labor shall by regulation prescribe a multiple of the Federal minimum hourly wage equivalent in effect to that set forth in paragraph (2).

(b) The restrictions of subsection (a) do not apply in the case of

(1) any order of any court for the support of any person.

(2) any order of any court of bankruptcy under chapter XIII of the Bankruptcy Act.

(3) any debt due for any State or Federal tax.

(c) No court of the United States or any State may make, execute, or enforce any order or process in violation of this section.

§ 304. Restriction on discharge from employment by reason of garnishment

(a) No employer may discharge any employee by reason of the fact that his earnings have been subjected to garnishment for any one indebtedness.

(b) Whoever willfully violates subsection (a) of this section shall be fined not more than $1,000, or imprisoned not more than one year, or both.

§ 305. Exemption for State-regulated garnishments

The Secretary of Labor may by regulation exempt from the provisions of section 303(a) garnishments issued under the laws of any State if he determines that the laws of that State provide restrictions on garnishment which are substantially similar to those provided in section 303(a).

§ 306. Enforcement by Secretary of Labor

The Secretary of Labor, acting through the Wage and Hour Division of the Department of Labor, shall enforce the provisions of this title.

§ 307. Effect on State laws

This title does not annul, alter, or affect, or exempt any person from complying with, the laws of any State

(1) prohibiting garnishments or providing for more limited garnishments than are allowed under this title, or

(2) prohibiting the discharge of any employee by reason of the fact that his earnings have been subjected to garnishment for more than one indebtedness.

TITLE V—GENERAL PROVISIONS

§ 501. Severability

If a provision enacted by this Act is held invalid, all valid provisions that are severable from the invalid provision remain in effect. If a provision enacted by this Act is held invalid in one or more of its applications, the provision remains in effect in all valid applications that are severable from the invalid application or applications.

§ 502. Captions and catchlines for reference only

Captions and catchlines are intended solely as aids to convenient reference, and no inference as to the legislative intent with respect to any provision enacted by this Act may be drawn from them.

§ 503. Grammatical usages

In this Act:

(1) The word "may" is used to indicate that an action either is authorized or is permitted.

(2) The word "shall" is used to indicate that an action is both authorized and required.

(3) The phrase "may not" is used to indicate that an action is both unauthorized and forbidden.

(4) Rules of law are stated in the indicative mood.

§ 504. Effective dates

(a) Except as otherwise specified, the provisions of this Act take effect upon enactment.

(b) Chapters 2 and 3 of title I take effect on July 1, 1969.

(c) Title III takes effect on July 1, 1970.

TITLE VI—CONSUMER CREDIT REPORTING

§ 601. Short title

"This title may be cited as the Fair Credit Reporting Act.

§ 602. Findings and purpose

(a) The Congress makes the following findings:

(1) The banking system is dependent upon fair and accurate credit reporting. Inaccurate credit reports directly impair the efficiency of the banking system, and unfair credit reporting methods undermine the public confidence which is essential to the continued functioning of the banking system.

(2) An elaborate mechanism has been developed for investigating and evaluating the credit worthiness, credit standing, credit capacity, character, and general reputation of consumers.

(3) Consumer reporting agencies have assumed a vital role in assembling and evaluating consumer credit and other information on consumers.

(4) There is a need to insure that consumer reporting agencies exercise their grave responsibilities with fairness, impartiality, and a respect for the consumer's right to privacy.

(b) It is the purpose of this title to require that consumer reporting agencies adopt reasonable procedures for meeting the needs of commerce for consumer credit, personnel, insurance, and other information in a manner which is fair and equitable to the consumer, with regard to the confidentiality, accuracy, relevancy, and proper utilization of such information in accordance with the requirements of this title.

"§ 603. Definitions and rules of construction

(a) Definitions and rules of construction set forth in this section are applicable for the purposes of this title.

(b) The term "person" means any individual, partnership, corporation, trust, estate, cooperative, association, government or governmental subdivision or agency, or other entity.

(c) The term "consumer" means an individual.

(d) The term "consumer report" means any written, oral, or other communication of any information by a consumer reporting agency bearing on a consumer's credit worthiness, credit standing, credit capacity, character, general reputation, personal characteristics, or mode of living which is used or expected to be used or collected in whole or in part for the purpose of serving as a factor in establishing the consumer's eligibility for (1) credit or insurance to be used primarily for personal, family, or household purposes, or (2) employment purposes, or (3) other purposes authorized under section 604. The term does not include (A) any report containing information solely as to transactions or experiences between the consumer and the person making the report; (B) any authorization or approval of a specific extension of credit directly or indirectly by the issuer of a credit card or similar device; or (C) any report in which a person who has been requested by a third party to make a specific extension of credit directly or indirectly to a consumer conveys his decision with respect to such request, if the third party advises the consumer of the name and address of the person to whom the request was made and such person makes the disclosures to the consumer required under section 615.

(e) The term "investigative consumer report" means a consumer report or portion thereof in which information on a consumer's character, general reputation, personal characteristics, or mode of living is obtained through personal interviews with neighbors, friends, or associates of the consumer reported on or with others with whom he is acquainted or who may have knowledge concerning any such items of information. However, such information shall not include specific factual information on a consumer's credit record obtained directly from a creditor of the consumer or from a consumer reporting agency when such information was obtained directly from a creditor of the consumer or from the consumer.

(f) The term "consumer reporting agency" means any person which, for monetary fees, dues, or on a cooperative nonprofit basis, regularly engages in whole or in part in the practice of assembling or evaluating consumer credit information or other information on consumers for the purpose of furnishing consumer reports to third parties, and which uses any means or facility of interstate commerce for the purpose of preparing or furnishing consumer reports.

(g) The term "file", when used in connection with information on any consumer, means all of the information on that consumer recorded and retained by a consumer reporting agency regardless of how the information is stored.

(h) The term "employment purposes" when used in connection with a consumer report means a report used for the purpose of evaluating a consumer for employment, promotion, reassignment or retention as an employee.

(i) The term "medical information" means information or records obtained, with the consent of the individual to whom it relates, from licensed physicians or medical practitioners, hospitals, clinics, or other medical or medically related facilities.

§ 604. Permissible purposes of reports

A consumer reporting agency may furnish a consumer report under the following circumstances and no other:

(1) In response to the order of a court having jurisdiction to issue such an order.

(2) In accordance with the written instructions of the consumer to whom it relates.

(3) To a person which it has reason to believe—

(A) intends to use the information in connection with a credit transaction involving the consumer on whom the information is to be furnished and involving the extension of credit to, or review or collection of an account of, the consumer; or

(B) intends to use the information for employment purposes; or

(C) intends to use the information in connection with the underwriting of insurance involving the consumer; or

(D) intends to use the information in connection with a determination of the consumer's eligibility for a license or other benefit granted by a governmental instrumentality required by law to consider an applicant's financial responsibility or status; or

(E) otherwise has a legitimate business need for the information in connection with a business transaction involving the consumer.

§ 605. Obsolete information

(a) Except as authorized under subsection (b), no consumer reporting agency may make any consumer report containing any of the following items of information:

(1) Bankruptcies which, from date of adjudication of the most recent bankruptcy, antedate the report by more than fourteen years.

(2) Suits and judgments which, from date of entry, antedate the report by more than seven years or until the governing statute of limitations has expired, whichever is the longer period.

(3) Paid tax liens which, from date of payment, antedate the report by more than seven years.

(4) Accounts placed for collection or charged to profit and loss which antedate the report by more than seven years.

(5) Records of arrest, indictment, or conviction of crime which, from date of disposition, release, or parole, antedate the report by more than seven years.

(6) Any other adverse item of information which antedates the report by more than seven years.

(b) The provisions of subsection (a) are not applicable in the case of any consumer credit report to be used in connection with—

(1) a credit transaction involving, or which may reasonably be expected to involve, a principal amount of $50,000 or more;

(2) the underwriting of life insurance involving, or which may reasonably be expected to involve, a face amount of $50,000 or more; or

(3) the employment of any individual at an annual salary which equals, or which may reasonably be expected to equal $20,000, or more.

§ 606. Disclosure of investigative consumer reports

(a) A person may not procure or cause to be prepared an investigative consumer report on any consumer unless—

(1) it is clearly and accurately disclosed to the consumer that an investigative consumer report including information as to his character, general reputation, personal characteristics, and mode of living, whichever are applicable, may be made, and such disclosure (A) is made in a writing mailed, or otherwise delivered, to the consumer, not later than three days after the date on which the report was first requested, and (B) includes a statement informing the consumer of his right to request the additional disclosures provided for under subsection (b) of this section; or

(2) the report is to be used for employment purposes for which the consumer has not specifically applied.

(b) Any person who procures or causes to be prepared an investigative consumer report on any consumer shall, upon written request made by the consumer within a reasonable period of time after the receipt by him of the disclosure required by subsection (a) (1), shall make a complete and accurate disclosure of the nature and scope of the investigation requested. This disclosure shall be made in a writing mailed, or otherwise delivered, to the consumer not later than five days after the date on which the request for such disclosure was received from the consumer or such report was first requested, whichever is the later.

(c) No person may be held liable for any violation of subsection (a) or (b) of this section if he shows by a preponderance of the evidence that at the time of the violation he maintained reasonable procedures to assure compliance with subsection (a) or (b).

§ 607. Compliance procedures

(a) Every consumer reporting agency shall maintain reasonable procedures designed to avoid violations of section 605 and to limit the furnishing of consumer reports to the purposes listed under section 604. These procedures shall require that prospective users of the information identify themselves, certify the purposes for which the information is sought, and certify that the information will be used for no other purpose. Every consumer reporting agency shall make a reasonable effort to verify the identity of a new prospective user and the uses certified by such prospective user prior to furnishing such user a consumer report. No consumer reporting agency may furnish a consumer report to any person if it has reasonable grounds for believing that the consumer report will not be used for a purpose listed in section 604.

(b) Whenever a consumer reporting agency prepares a consumer report it shall follow reasonable procedures to assure maximum possible accuracy of the information concerning the individual about whom the report relates.

§ 608. Disclosures to governmental agencies

Notwithstanding the provisions of section 604, a consumer reporting agency may furnish identifying information respecting any consumer, limited to his name, address, former addresses, places of employment, or former places of employment, to a governmental agency.

§ 609. Disclosures to consumers

(a) Every consumer reporting agency shall, upon request and proper identification of any consumer, clearly and accurately disclose to the consumer:

(1) The nature and substance of all information (except medical information) in its files on the consumer at the time of the request.

(2) The sources of the information; except that the sources of information acquired solely for use in preparing an investigative consumer report and actually used for no other purpose need not be disclosed: *Provided,* That in the event an action is brought under this title, such sources shall be available to the plaintiff under appropriate discovery procedures in the court in which the action is brought.

(3) The recipients of any consumer report on the consumer which it has furnished—

(A) for employment purposes within the two-year period preceding the request, and

(B) for any other purpose within the six-month period preceding the request.

(b) The requirements of subsection (a) respecting the disclosure of sources of information and the recipients of consumer reports do not apply to information received or consumer reports furnished prior to the effective date of this title except to the extent that the matter involved is contained in the files of the consumer reporting agency on that date.

§ 610. Conditions of disclosure to consumers

(a) A consumer reporting agency shall make the disclosures required under section 609 during normal business hours and on reasonable notice.

(b) The disclosures required under section 609 shall be made to the consumer—

(1) in person if he appears in person and furnishes proper identification; or

(2) by telephone if he has made a written request, with proper identification, for telephone disclosure and the toll charge, if any, for the telephone call is prepaid by or charged directly to the consumer.

(c) Any consumer reporting agency shall provide trained personnel to explain to the consumer any information furnished to him pursuant to section 609.

(d) The consumer shall be permitted to be accompanied by one other person of his choosing, who shall furnish reasonable identification. A consumer reporting agency may require the consumer to furnish a written statement granting permission to the consumer reporting agency to discuss the consumer's file in such person's presence.

(e) Except as provided in sections 616 and 617, no consumer may bring any action or proceeding in the nature of defamation, invasion of privacy, or negligence with respect to the reporting of information against any consumer reporting agency, any user of information, or any person who furnishes information to a consumer reporting agency, based on information disclosed pursuant to section 609, 610, or 615, except as to false information furnished with malice or willful intent to injure such consumer.

§ 611. Procedure in case of disputed accuracy

(a) If the completeness or accuracy of any item of information contained in his file is disputed by a consumer, and such dispute is directly conveyed to the consumer reporting agency by the consumer, the consumer reporting agency shall within a reasonable period of time reinvestigate and record the current status of that information unless it has reasonable grounds to believe that the dispute by the consumer is frivolous or irrelevant. If after such reinvestigation such information is found to be inaccurate or can no longer be verified, the consumer reporting agency shall promptly delete such information. The presence of contradictory information in the consumer's file does not in and of itself constitute reasonable grounds for believing the dispute is frivolous or irrelevant.

(b) If the reinvestigation does not resolve the dispute, the consumer may file a brief statement setting forth the nature of the dispute. The consumer reporting agency may limit such statements to not more than one hundred words if it provides the consumer with assistance in writing a clear summary of the dispute.

(c) Whenever a statement of a dispute is filed, unless there is reasonable grounds to believe that it is frivolous or irrelevant, the consumer reporting agency shall, in any subsequent consumer report containing the information in question, clearly note that it is disputed by the consumer and provide either the consumer's statement or a clear and accurate codification or summary thereof.

(d) Following any deletion of information which is found to be inaccurate or whose accuracy can no longer be verified or any notation as to disputed information, the consumer reporting agency shall, at the request of the consumer, furnish notification that the item has been deleted or the statement, codification or summary pursuant to subsection (b) or (c) to any person specifically designated by the consumer who has within two years prior thereto received a consumer report for employment purposes, or within six months prior thereto received a consumer report for any other purpose, which contained the deleted or disputed information. The consumer reporting agency shall clearly and conspicuously disclose to the consumer his rights to make such a request. Such disclosure shall be made at or prior to the time the information is deleted or the consumer's statement regarding the disputed information is received.

§ 612. Charges for certain disclosures

A consumer reporting agency shall make all disclosures pursuant to section 609 and furnish all consumer reports pursuant to section 611(d) without charge to the consumer if, within thirty days after receipt by such consumer of a notification pursuant to section 615 or notification from a debt collection agency affiliated with such consumer reporting agency stating that the consumer's credit rating may be or has been adversely affected, the consumer makes a request under section 609 or 611(d). Otherwise, the consumer reporting agency may impose a reasonable charge on the consumer for making disclosure to such consumer pursuant to section 609, the charge for which shall be indicated to the consumer prior to making disclosure; and for furnishing notifications, statements, summaries, or codifications to person designated by the consumer pursuant to section 611 (d), the charge for which shall be indicated to the consumer prior to furnishing such information and shall not exceed the charge that the consumer reporting agency would impose on each designated recipient for a consumer report except that no charge may be made for notifying such persons of the deletion of information which is found to be inaccurate or which can no longer be verified.

§ 613. Public record information for employment purposes

A consumer reporting agency which furnishes a consumer report for employment purposes and which for that purpose compiles and reports items of information on consumers which are matters of public record and are likely to have an adverse effect upon a consumer's ability to obtain employment shall—

(1) at the time such public record information is reported to the user of such consumer report, notify the consumer of the fact that public record information is being reported by the consumer reporting agency, together with the name and address of the person to whom such information is being reported; or

(2) maintain strict procedures designed to insure that whenever public record information which is likely to have an adverse effect on a consumer's ability to obtain employment is reported it is complete and up to date. For purposes of this paragraph, items of public record relating to arrests, indictments, convictions, suits, tax liens, and outstanding judgments shall be considered up to date if the current public record status of the item at the time of the report is reported.

§ 614. Restrictions on investigative consumer reports

Whenever a consumer reporting agency prepares an investigative consumer report, no adverse information in the consumer report (other than information which is a matter of public record) may be included in a subsequent consumer report unless such adverse information has been verified in the process of making such subsequent consumer report, or the adverse information was received within the three-month period preceding the date the subsequent report is furnished.

§ 615. Requirements on users of consumer reports

(a) Whenever credit or insurance for personal, family, or household purposes, or employment involving a consumer is denied or the charge for such credit or insurance is increased either wholly or partly because of information contained in a consumer report from a consumer reporting agency, the user of the consumer report shall so advise the consumer against whom such adverse action has been taken and supply the name and address of the consumer reporting agency making the report.

(b) Whenever credit for personal, family, or household purposes involving a consumer is denied or the charge for such credit is increased either wholly or partly because of information obtained from a person other than a consumer reporting agency bearing upon the consumer's credit worthiness, credit standing, credit capacity, character, general reputation, personal characteristics, or mode of living, the user of such information shall, within a reasonable period of time, upon the consumer's written request for the reasons for such adverse action received within sixty days after learning of such adverse action, disclose the nature of the information to the consumer. The user of such information shall clearly and accurately disclose to the consumer his right to make such written request at the time such adverse action is communicated to the consumer.

(c) No person shall be held liable for any violation of this section if he shows by a preponderance of the evidence that at the time of the alleged violation he maintained reasonable procedures to assure compliance with the provisions of subsections (a) and (b).

§ 616. Civil liability for willful noncompliance

Any consumer reporting agency or user of information which willfully fails to comply with any requirement imposed under this title with respect to any consumer is liable to that consumer in an amount equal to the sum of—

(1) any actual damages sustained by the consumer as a result of the failure;

(2) such amount of punitive damages as the court may allow; and

(3) in the case of any successful action to enforce any liability under this section, the costs of the action together with reasonable attorney's fees as determined by the court.

§ 617. Civil liability for negligent noncompliance

Any consumer reporting agency or user of information which is negligent in failing to comply with any requirement imposed under this title with respect to any consumer is liable to that consumer in an amount equal to the sum of—

(1) any actual damages sustained by the consumer as a result of the failure;

(2) in the case of any successful action to enforce any liability under this section, the costs of the action together with reasonable attorney's fees as determined by the court.

§ 618. Jurisdiction of courts; limitation of actions

"An action to enforce any liability created under this title may be brought in any appropriate United States district court without regard to the amount in controversy, or in any other court of competent jurisdiction, within two years from the date on which the liability arises, except that where a defendant has materially and willfully misrepresented any information required under this title to be disclosed to an individual and the information so misrepresented is material to the establishment of the defendant's liability to that individual under this title, the action may be brought at any time within two years after discovery by the individual of the misrepresentation.

§ 619. Obtaining information under false pretenses

Any person who knowingly and willfully obtains information on a consumer from a consumer reporting agency under false pretenses shall be fined not more than $5,000 or imprisoned not more than one year, or both.

§ 620. Unauthorized disclosures by officers or employees

Any officer or employee of a consumer reporting agency who knowingly and willfully provides information concerning an individual from the agency's files to a person not authorized to receive that information shall be fined not more than $5,000 or imprisoned not more than one year, or both.

§ 621. Administrative enforcement

[Omitted.]

§ 622. Relation to State laws

"This title does not annul, alter, affect, or exempt any person subject to the provisions of this title from complying with the laws of any State with respect to the collection, distribution, or use of any information on consumers, except to the extent that those laws are inconsistent with any provision of this title, and then only to the extent of the inconsistency.

TITLE VII—EQUAL CREDIT OPPORTUNITY

§ 701. Prohibited discrimination; reasons for adverse action *

(a) It shall be unlawful for any creditor to discriminate against any applicant, with respect to any aspect of a credit transaction—

(1) on the basis of race, color, religion, national origin, sex or marital status, or age (provided the applicant has the capacity to contract);

(2) because all or part of the applicant's income derives from any public assistance program; or

(3) because the applicant has in good faith exercised any right under the Consumer Credit Protection Act.

* Effective date for amendments to section 701 is March 23, 1977. All other amendments are effective upon enactment.

(b) It shall not constitute discrimination for purposes of this title for a creditor—

(1) to make an inquiry of marital status if such inquiry is for the purpose of ascertaining the creditor's rights and remedies applicable to the particular extension of credit and not to discriminate in a determination of creditworthiness;

(2) to make an inquiry of the applicant's age or of whether the applicant's income derives from any public assistance program if such inquiry is for the purpose of determining the amount and probable continuance of income levels, credit history, or other pertinent element of creditworthiness as provided in regulations of the Board;

(3) to use any empirically derived credit system which considers age if such system is demonstrably and statistically sound in accordance with regulations of the Board except that in the operation of such system the age of an elderly applicant may not be assigned a negative factor or value; or

(4) to make an inquiry or to consider the age of an elderly applicant is to be used by the creditor in the extension of credit in favor of such applicant.

(c) It is not a violation of this section for a creditor to refuse to extend credit offered pursuant to—

(1) any credit assistance program expressly authorized by law for an economically disadvantaged class of persons;

(2) any credit assistance program administered by a nonprofit organization for its members or an economically disadvantaged class of persons; or

(3) any special purpose credit program offered by a profitmaking organization to meet special social needs which meets standards prescribed in regulations by the Board;

if such refusal is required by or made pursuant to such program.

(d)(1) Within thirty days (or such longer reasonable time as specified in regulations of the Board for any class of credit transaction) after receipt of a completed application for credit, a creditor shall notify the applicant of its action on the application.

(2) Each applicant against whom adverse action is taken shall be entitled to a statement of reasons for such action from the creditor. A creditor satisfies this obligation by—

(A) providing statements of reasons in writing as a matter of course to applicants against whom adverse action is taken; or

(B) given written notification of adverse action which discloses (i) the applicant's right to a statement of reasons within thirty days after receipt by the creditor of a request made within sixty days after such notification, and (ii) the identity of the person or office from which such statement may be obtained. Such statement may be given orally if the written notification advises the applicant of his right to have the statement of reasons confirmed in writing on written request.

(3) A statement of reasons meets the requirements of this section only if it contains the specific reasons for the adverse action taken.

(4) Where a creditor has been requested by a third party to make a specific extension of credit directly or indirectly to an applicant, the notification and statement of reasons required by this subsection may be made directly by such creditor, or indirectly through the third party, provided in either case that the identity of the creditor is disclosed.

(5) The requirements of paragraph (2), (3), or (4) may be satisfied by verbal statements or notifications in the case of any creditor who did not act on more than 150 applications during the calendar year preceding the calendar year in which the adverse action is taken, as determined under regulations of the Board.

(6) For purposes of this subsection, the term "adverse action" means a denial or revocation of credit, a change in the terms of an existing credit arrangement, or a refusal to grant credit in substantially the amount or on substantially the terms requested. Such term does not include a refusal to extend additional credit under an existing credit arrangement where the applicant is delinquent or otherwise in default, or where such additional credit would exceed a previously established credit limit.

§ 702. Definitions

(a) The definitions and rules of construction set forth in this section are applicable for the purposes of this title.

(b) The term "applicant" means any person who applies to a creditor directly for an extension, renewal, or continuation of credit, or applies to a creditor indirectly by use of an existing credit plan for an amount exceeding a previously established credit limit.

(c) The term "Board" refers to the Board of Governors of the Federal Reserve System.

(d) The term "credit" means the right granted by a creditor to a debtor to defer payment of debt or to incur debt and defer its payment or to purchase property or services and defer payment therefor.

(e) The term "creditor" means any person who regularly extends, renews, or continues credit; any person who regularly arranges for the extension, renewal, or continuation of credit; or any assignee of an original creditor who participates in the decision to extend, renew, or continue credit.

(f) The term "person" means a natural person, a corporation, government or governmental subdivision or agency, trust, estate, partnership, cooperative, or association.

(g) Any reference to any requirement imposed under this title or any provision thereof includes reference to the regulations of the Board under this title or the provision thereof in question.

§ 703. Regulations

(a) The Board shall prescribe regulations to carry out the purposes of this title. These regulations may contain but are not limited to such classifications, differentiation, or other provision, and may provide for such adjustments and exceptions for any class of transactions, as in the judgment of the Board are necessary or proper to effectuate the purposes of this title, to prevent circumvention or evasion thereof, or to facilitate or substantiate compliance therewith. In particular, such regulations may exempt from one or more of the provisions of this title any class of transactions not primarily for personal, family, or household purposes, if the Board makes an express finding that the application of such provision or provisions would not contribute substantially to carrying out the purposes of this title. Such regulations shall be prescribed as soon as possible after the date of enactment of this Act, but in no event later than the effective date of this Act.

(b) The Board shall establish a Consumer Advisory Council to advise and consult with it in the exercise of its functions under the Consumer Credit Protection Act and to advise and consult with it concerning other consumer related matters it may place before the Council. In apppointing the members of the Council, the Board shall seek to achieve a fair representation of the interests of creditors and consumers. The Council shall meet from time to time at the call of the Board. Members of the Council who are not regular full-time employees of the United States shall, while attending meetings of such Council, be entitled to receive compensation at a rate fixed by the Board, but not exceeding $100 per day, including travel time. Such members may be allowed travel expenses, including transportation and subsistence, while away from their homes or regular place of business.

§ 704. Administrative enforcement

(a) Compliance with the requirements imposed under this title shall be enforced under:

(1) Section 8 of the Federal Deposit Insurance Act, in the case of—

(A) national banks, by the Comptroller of the Currency;

(B) member banks of the Federal Reserve System (other than national banks), by the Board;

(C) banks insured by the Federal Deposit Insurance Corporation (other than members of the Federal Reserve System), by the Board of Directors of the Federal Deposit Insurance Corporation.

(2) Section 5(d) of the Home Owners' Loan Act of 1933, section 407 of the National Housing Act, and sections 6(i) and 17 of the Federal Home Loan Bank Act, by the Federal Home Loan Bank Board (acting directly or through the Federal Savings and Loan Insurance Corporation), in the case of any institution subject to any of those provisions.

(3) The Federal Credit Union Act, by the Administrator of the National Credit Union Administration with respect to any Federal Credit Union.

(4) The Acts to regulate commerce, by the Interstate Commerce Commission with respect to any common carrier subject to those Acts.

(5) The Federal Aviation Act of 1958, by the Civil Aeronautics Board with respect to any air carrier or foreign air carrier subject to that Act.

(6) The Packers and Stockyards Act, 1921 (except as provided in section 406 of that Act), by the Secretary of Agriculture with respect to any activities subject to that Act.

(7) The Farm Credit Act of 1971, by the Farm Credit Administration with respect to any Federal land bank, Federal land bank association, Federal intermediate credit bank, and production credit association.

(8) The Securities Exchange Act of 1934, by the Securities and Exchange Commission with respect to brokers and dealers; and

(9) The Small Business Investment Act of 1958, by the Small Business Administration, with respect to small business investment companies.

(b) For the purpose of the exercise by any agency referred to in subsection (a) of its powers under any Act referred to in that subsection, a violation of any requirement imposed under this title shall be deemed to be a violation of a requirement imposed under that Act. In addition to its powers under any provision of law specifically referred to in subsection (a), each of the agencies referred to in that subsection may exercise for the purpose of enforcing compliance with any requirement imposed under this title, any other authority conferred on it by law. The exercise of the authorities of any of the agencies referred to in subsection (a) for the purpose of enforcing compliance with any requirement imposed under this title shall in no way preclude the exercise of such authorities for the purpose of enforcing compliance with any other provision of law not relating to the prohibition of discrimination on the basis of sex or marital status with respect to any aspect of a credit transaction.

(c) Except to the extent that enforcement of the requirements imposed under this title is specifically committed to some other Government agency under subsection (a), the Federal Trade Commission shall enforce such requirements. For the purpose of the exercise by the Federal Trade Commission of its functions and powers under the Federal Trade Commission Act, a violation of any requirement imposed under this title shall be deemed a violation of a requirement imposed under that Act. All of the functions and powers of the Federal Trade Commission under the Federal Trade Commission Act are available to the Commission to enforce compliance by any person with the requirements imposed under this title, irrespective of whether that person is engaged in commerce or meets any other jurisdictional tests in the Federal Trade Commission Act, including the power to enforce any Federal Reserve Board regulation promulgated under this title in the same manner as if the violation had been a violation of a Federal Trade Commission trade regulation rule.

(d) The authority of the Board to issue regulations under this title does not impair the authority of any other agency designated in this section to make rules respecting its own procedures in enforcing compliance with requirements imposed under this title.

§ 705. Relation to State laws

(a) A request for the signature of both parties to a marriage for the purpose of creating a valid lien, passing clear title, waiving inchoate rights to property, or assigning earnings, shall not constitute discrimination under this title: *Provided, however,* That this provision shall not be construed to permit a creditor to take sex or marital status into account in connection with the evaluation of creditworthiness of any applicant.

(b) Consideration or application of State property laws directly or indirectly affecting creditworthiness shall not constitute discrimination for purposes of this title.

(c) Any provision of State law which prohibits the separate extension of consumer credit to each party to a marriage shall not apply in any case where each party to a marriage voluntarily applies for separate credit from the same creditor: *Provided,* That in any case where such a State law is so preempted, each party to the marriage shall be solely responsible for the debt so contracted.

(d) When each party to a marriage separately and voluntarily applies for and obtains separate credit accounts with the same creditor, those accounts shall not be aggregated or otherwise combined for purposes of determining permissible finance charges or permissible loan ceilings under the laws of any State or of the United States.

(e) Where the same act or omission constitutes a violation of this title and of applicable State law, a person aggrieved by such conduct may bring a legal action to recover monetary damages either under this title or under such State law, but not both. This election of remedies shall not apply to court actions in which the relief sought does not include monetary damages or to administrative actions.

(f) This title does not annul, alter, or affect, or exempt any person subject to the provisions of this title from complying with, the laws of any State with respect to credit discrimination, except to the extent that those laws are inconsistent with any provision of this title, and then only to the extent of the inconsistency. The Board is authorized to determine whether such inconsistencies exist. The Board may not determine that any State law is inconsistent with any provision of this title if the Board determines that such law gives greater protection to the applicant.

(g) The Board shall by regulation exempt from the requirements of sections 701 and 702 of this title any class of credit transactions within any State if it determines that under the law of that State that class of transactions is subject to requirements substantially similar to those imposed under this title or that such law gives greater protection to the applicant, and that there is adequate provision for enforcement. Failure to comply with any requirement of such State law in any transaction so exempted shall constitute a violation of this title for the purposes of section 706.

§ 706. Civil liability

(a) Any creditor who fails to comply with any requirement imposed under this title shall be liable to the aggrieved applicant for any actual damages sustained by such applicant acting either in an individual capacity or as a member of a class.

(b) Any creditor, other than a government or governmental subdivision or agency, who fails to comply with any requirement imposed under this title shall be liable to the aggrieved applicant for punitive damages in an amount not greater than $10,000, in addition to any actual damages provided in subsection (a), except that in the case of a class action the total recovery under this subsection shall not exceed the lesser of $500,000 or 1 per centum of the net worth of the creditor. In determining the amount of such damages in any action, the court shall consider, among other relevant factors, the amount of any actual damages awarded, the frequency and persistence of failures of compliance by the creditor, the resources of the creditor, the number of persons adversely affected, and the extent to which the creditor's failure of compliance was intentional.

(c) Upon application by an an aggrieved applicant, the appropriate United States district court or any other court of competent jurisdiction may grant such equitable and declaratory relief as is necessary to enforce the requirements imposed under this title.

(d) In the case of any successful action under subsection (a), (b), or (c), the costs of the action, together with a reasonable attorney's fee as determined by the court, shall be added to any damages awarded by the court under such subsection.

(e) No provision of this title imposing any liability shall apply to any act done or omitted in good faith in conformity with any official rule, regulation, or interpretation thereof by the Board or in conformity with any interpretation or approval by an official or employee of the Federal Reserve System duly authorized by the Board to issue such interpretations or approvals under such procedures as the Board may prescribe therefor, notwithstanding that after such act or omission has occurred, such rule, regulation, interpretation, or approval is amended, rescinded, or determined by judicial or other authority to be invalid for any reason.

(f) Any action under this section may be brought in the appropriate United States district court without regard to the amount in controversy, or in any other court of competent jurisdiction. No such action shall be brought later than two years from the date of the occurrence of the violation, except that—

(1) whenever any agency having responsibility for administrative enforcement under section 704 commences an enforcement proceeding within two years from the date of the occurrence of the violation;

(2) whenever the Attorney General commences a civil action under this section within two years from the date of occurrence of the violation.

then any applicant who has been a victim of the discrimination which is the subject of such proceeding or civil action may bring an action under this section not later than one year after the commencement of that proceeding or action.

(g) The agencies having responsibility for administrative enforcement under section 704, if unable to obtain compliance with section 701, are authorized to refer the matter to the Attorney General with a recommendation that an appropriate civil action be instituted.

(h) When a matter is referred to the Attorney General pursuant to subsection (g), or whenever he has reason to believe that one or more creditors are engaged in a pattern or practice in violation of this title, the Attorney General may bring a civil action in any appropriate United States district court for such relief as may be appropriate, including injunctive relief.

(i) No person aggrieved by a violation of this title and by a violation of section 805 of the Civil Rights Act of 1968 shall recover under this title and section 812 of the Civil Rights Act of 1968, if such violation is based on the same transaction.

(j) Nothing in this title shall be construed to prohibit the discovery of a creditor's credit granting standards under appropriate discovery procedures in the court or agency in which an action or proceeding is brought.

§ 707. Annual reports to Congress

Not later than February 1 of each year after 1976, the Board and the Attorney General shall, respectively, make reports to the Congress concerning the administration of their functions under this title, including such recommendations as the Board and the Attorney General, respectively, deem necessary or appropriate. In addition, each report of the Board shall include its assessment of the extent to which compliance with the requirements of this title is being achieved, and a summary of the enforcement actions taken by each of the agencies assigned administrative enforcement responsibilities under section 704.

§ 708. Effective date

This title takes effect upon the expiration of one year after the date of its enactment. The amendment made by the Equal Credit Opportunity Act Amendments of 1976 shall take effect on the date of enactment thereof and shall apply to any violation occurring on or after such date, except that the amendments made to section 701 of the Equal Credit Opportunity Act shall take effect 12 months after the date of enactment.

§ 709. Short title

This title may be cited as the "Equal Credit Opportunity Act."

As amended March 23, 1976.

TITLE VIII—DEBT COLLECTION PRACTICES

§ 801. Short title

This title may be cited as the "Fair Debt Collection Practices Act".

§ 802. Findings and purpose

(a) There is abundant evidence of the use of abusive, deceptive, and unfair debt collection practices by many debt collectors. Abusive debt collection practices contribute to the number of personal bankruptcies, to marital instability, to the loss of jobs, and to invasions of individual privacy.

(b) Existing laws and procedures for redressing these injuries are inadequate to protect consumers.

(c) Means other than misrepresentation or other abusive debt collection practices are available for the effective collection of debts.

(d) Abusive debt collection practices are carried on to a substantial extent in interstate commerce and through means and instrumentalities of such commerce. Even where abusive debt collection practices are purely intrastate in character, they nevertheless directly affect interstate commerce.

(e) It is the purpose of this title to eliminate abusive debt collection practices by debt collectors, to insure that those debt collectors who refrain from using abusive debt collection practices are not competitively disadvantaged, and to promote consistent State action to protect consumers against debt collection abuses.

§ 803. Definitions

As used in this title—

(1) The term "Commission" means the Federal Trade Commission.

(2) The term "communication" means the conveying of information regarding a debt directly or indirectly to any person through any medium.

(3) The term "consumer" means any natural person obligated or allegedly obligated to pay any debt.

(4) The term "creditor" means any person who offers or extends credit creating a debt or to whom a debt is owed, but such term does not include any person to the extent that he receives an assignment or transfer of a debt in default solely for the purpose of facilitating collection of such debt for another.

(5) The term "debt" means any obligation or alleged obligation of a consumer to pay money arising out of a transaction in which the money, property, insurance, or services which are the subject of the transaction are primarily for personal, family, or household purposes, whether or not such obligation has been reduced to judgment.

(6) The term "debt collector" means any person who uses any instrumentality of interstate commerce or the mails in any business the principal purpose of which is the collection of any debts, or who regularly collects or attempts to collect, directly or indi-

rectly, debts owed or due or asserted to be owed or due another. Notwithstanding the exclusion provided by clause (G) of the last sentence of this paragraph, the term includes any creditor who, in the process of collecting his own debts, uses any name other than his own which would indicate that a third person is collecting or attempting to collect such debts. For the purpose of section 808(6), such term also includes any person who uses any instrumentality of interstate commerce or the mails in any business the principal purpose of which is the enforcement of security interests. The term does not include—

(A) any officer or employee of a creditor while, in the name of the creditor, collecting debts for such creditor;

(B) any person while acting as a debt collector for another person, both of whom are related by common ownership or affiliated by corporate control, if the person acting as a debt collector does so only for persons to whom it is so related or affiliated and if the principal business of such person is not the collection of debts;

(C) any officer or employee of the United States or any State to the extent that collecting or attempting to collect any debt is in the performance of his official duties;

(D) any person while serving or attempting to serve legal process on any other person in connection with the judicial enforcement of any debt;

(E) any nonprofit organization which, at the request of consumers, performs bona fide consumer credit counseling and assists consumers in the liquidation of their debts by receiving payments from such consumers and distributing such amounts to creditors;

(F) any attorney-at-law collecting a debt as an attorney on behalf of and in the name of a client; and

(G) any person collecting or attempting to collect any debt owed or due or asserted to be owed or due another to the extent such activity (i) is incidental to a bona fide fiduciary obligation or a bona fide escrow arrangement; (ii) concerns a debt which was originated by such person; (iii) concerns a debt which was not in default at the time it was obtained by such person; or (iv) concerns a debt obtained by such person as a secured party in a commercial credit transaction involving the creditor.

(7) The term "location information" means a consumer's place of abode and his telephone number at such place, or his place of employment.

(8) The term "State" means any State, territory, or possession of the United States, the District of Columbia, the Commonwealth of Puerto Rico, or any political subdivision of any of the foregoing.

§ 804. Acquisition of location information

Any debt collector communicating with any person other than the consumer for the purpose of acquiring location information about the consumer shall—

(1) identify himself, state that he is confirming or correcting location information concerning the consumer, and, only if expressly requested, identify his employer;

(2) not state that such consumer owes any debt;

(3) not communicate with any such person more than once unless requested to do so by such person or unless the debt collector reasonably believes that the earlier response of such person is erroneous or incomplete and that such person now has correct or complete location information;

(4) not communicate by post card;

(5) not use any language or symbol on any envelope or in the contents of any communication effected by the mails or telegram that indicates that the debt collector is in the debt collection business or that the communication relates to the collection of a debt; and

(6) after the debt collector knows the consumer is represented by an attorney with regard to the subject debt and has knowledge of, or can readily ascertain, such attorney's name and address, not communicate with any person other than that attorney, unless the attorney fails to respond within a reasonable period of time to communication from the debt collector.

§ 805. Communication in connection with debt collection

(a) Communication with the Consumer Generally.—Without the prior consent of the consumer given directly to the debt collector or the express permission of a court of competent jurisdiction, a debt collector may not communicate with a consumer in connection with the collection of any debt—

(1) at any unusual time or place or a time or place known or which should be known to be inconvenient to the consumer. In the absence of knowledge of circumstances to the contrary, a debt collector shall assume that the convenient time for communicating with a consumer is after 8 o'clock antimeridian and before 9 o'clock postmeridian, local time at the consumer's location;

(2) if the debt collector knows the consumer is represented by an attorney with respect to such debt and has knowledge of, or can readily ascertain, such attorney's name and address, unless the attorney fails to respond within a reasonable period of time to a communication from the debt collector or unless the attorney consents to direct communication with the consumer; or

(3) at the consumer's place of employment if the debt collector knows or has reason to know that the consumer's employer prohibits the consumer from receiving such communication.

(b) Communication with Third Parties.—Except as provided in section 804, without the prior consent of the consumer given directly to the debt collector, or the express permission of a court of competent jurisdiction, or as reasonably necessary to effectuate a postjudgment judicial remedy, a debt collector may not communicate, in connection with the collection of any debt, with any person other than the consumer, his attorney, a consumer reporting agency if otherwise permitted by law, the creditor, the attorney of the creditor, or the attorney of the debt collector.

(c) Ceasing Communication.—If a consumer notifies a debt collector in writing that the consumer refuses to pay a debt or that the consumer wishes the debt collector to cease further communication with the consumer, the debt collector shall not communicate further with the consumer with respect to such debt, except—

(1) to advise the consumer that the debt collector's further efforts are being terminated;

(2) to notify the consumer that the debt collector or creditor may invoke specified remedies which are ordinarily invoked by such debt collector or creditor; or

(3) where applicable, to notify the consumer that the debt collector or creditor intends to invoke a specified remedy.

If such notice from the consumer is made by mail, notification shall be complete upon receipt.

(d) For the purpose of this section, the term "consumer" includes the consumer's spouse, parent (if the consumer is a minor), guardian, executor, or administrator.

§ 806. Harassment or abuse

A debt collector may not engage in any conduct the natural consequence of which is to harass, oppress, or abuse any person in connection with the collection of a debt. Without limiting the general application of the foregoing, the following conduct is a violation of this section:

(1) The use or threat of use of violence or other criminal means to harm the physical person, reputation, or property of any person.

(2) The use of obscene or profane language or language the natural consequence of which is to abuse the hearer or reader.

(3) The publication of a list of consumers who allegedly refuse to pay debts, except to a consumer reporting agency or to persons meeting the requirements of section 603(f) or 604(3) of this Act.

(4) The advertisement for sale of any debt to coerce payment of the debt.

(5) Causing a telephone to ring or engaging any person in telephone conversation repeatedly or continuously with intent to annoy, abuse, or harass any person at the called number.

(6) Except as provided in section 804, the placement of telephone calls without meaningful disclosure of the caller's identity.

§ 807. False or misleading representations

A debt collector may not use any false, deceptive, or misleading representation or means in connection with the collection of any debt.

Without limiting the general application of the foregoing, the following conduct is a violation of this section:

(1) The false representation or implication that the debt collector is vouched for, bonded by, or affiliated with the United States or any State, including the use of any badge, uniform, or facsimile thereof.

(2) The false representation of—

(A) the character, amount, or legal status of any debt; or

(B) any services rendered or compensation which may be lawfully received by any debt collector for the collection of a debt.

(3) The false representation or implication that any individual is an attorney or that any communication is from an attorney.

(4) The representation or implication that nonpayment of any debt will result in the arrest or imprisonment of any person or the seizure, garnishment, attachment, or sale of any property or wages of any person unless such action is lawful and the debt collector or creditor intends to take such action.

(5) The threat to take any action that cannot legally be taken or that is not intended to be taken.

(6) The false representation or implication that a sale, referral, or other transfer of any interest in a debt shall cause the consumer to—

(A) lose any claim or defense to payment of the debt; or

(B) become subject to any practice prohibited by this title.

(7) The false representation or implication that the consumer committed any crime or other conduct in order to disgrace the consumer.

(8) Communicating or threatening to communicate to any person credit information which is known or which should be known to be false, including the failure to communicate that a disputed debt is disputed.

(9) The use or distribution of any written communication which simulates or is falsely represented to be a document authorized, issued, or approved by any court, official, or agency of the United States or any State, or which creates a false impression as to its source, authorization, or approval.

(10) The use of any false representation or deceptive means to collect or attempt to collect any debt or to obtain information concerning a consumer.

(11) Except as otherwise provided for communications to acquire location information under section 804, the failure to disclose clearly in all communications made to collect a debt or to obtain information about a consumer, that the debt collector is attempting to collect a debt and that any information obtained will be used for that purpose.

(12) The false representation or implication that accounts have been turned over to innocent purchasers for value.

(13) The false representation or implication that documents are legal process.

(14) The use of any business, company, or organization name other than the true name of the debt collector's business, company, or organization.

(15) The false representation or implication that documents are not legal process forms or do not require action by the consumer.

(16) The false representation or implication that a debt collector operates or is employed by a consumer reporting agency as defined by section 603(f) of this Act.

§ 808. Unfair practices

A debt collector may not use unfair or unconscionable means to collect or attempt to collect any debt. Without limiting the general application of the foregoing, the following conduct is a violation of this section:

(1) The collection of any amount (including any interest, fee, charge, or expense incidental to the principal obligation) unless such amount is expressly authorized by the agreement creating the debt or permitted by law.

(2) The acceptance by a debt collector from any person of a check or other payment instrument postdated by more than five days unless such person is notified in writing of the debt collector's intent to deposit such check or instrument not more than ten nor less than three business days prior to such deposit.

(3) The solicitation by a debt collector of any postdated check or other postdated payment instrument for the purpose of threatening or instituting criminal prosecution.

(4) Depositing or threatening to deposit any postdated check or other postdated payment instrument prior to the date on such check or instrument.

(5) Causing charges to be made to any person for communications by concealment of the true purpose of the communication. Such charges include, but are not limited to, collect telephone calls and telegram fees.

(6) Taking or threatening to take any nonjudicial action to effect dispossession or disablement of property if—

(A) there is no present right to possession of the property claimed as collateral through an enforceable security interest;

(B) there is no present intention to take possession of the property; or

(C) the property is exempt by law from such dispossession or disablement.

(7) Communicating with a consumer regarding a debt by post card.

(8) Using any language or symbol, other than the debt collector's address, on any envelope when communicating with a consumer by use of the mails or by telegram, except that a debt collector may use his business name if such name does not indicate that he is in the debt collection business.

§ 809. Validation of debts

(a) Within five days after the initial communication with a consumer in connection with the collection of any debt, a debt collector shall, unless the following information is contained in the initial communication or the consumer has paid the debt, send the consumer a written notice containing—

(1) the amount of the debt;

(2) the name of the creditor to whom the debt is owed;

(3) a statement that unless the consumer, within thirty days after receipt of the notice, disputes the validity of the debt, or any portion thereof, the debt will be assumed to be valid by the debt collector;

(4) a statement that if the consumer notifies the debt collector in writing within the thirty-day period that the debt, or any portion thereof, is disputed, the debt collector will obtain verification of the debt or a copy of a judgment against the consumer and a copy of such verification or judgment will be mailed to the consumer by the debt collector; and

(5) a statement that, upon the consumer's written request within the thirty-day period, the debt collector will provide the consumer with the name and address of the original creditor, if different from the current creditor.

(b) If the consumer notifies the debt collector in writing within the thirty-day period described in subsection (a) that the debt, or any portion thereof, is disputed, or that the consumer requests the name and address of the original creditor, the debt collector shall cease collection of the debt, or any disputed portion thereof, until the debt collector obtains verification of the debt or a copy of a judgment, or the name and address of the original creditor, and a copy of such verification or judgment, or name and address of the original creditor, is mailed to the consumer by the debt collector.

(c) The failure of a consumer to dispute the validity of a debt under this section may not be construed by any court as an admission of liability by the consumer.

§ 810. Multiple debts

If any consumer owes multiple debts and makes any single payment to any debt collector with respect to such debts, such debt collector may not apply such payment to any debt which is disputed by the consumer and, where applicable, shall apply such payment in accordance with the consumer's directions.

§ 811. Legal actions by debt collectors

(a) Any debt collector who brings any legal action on a debt against any consumer shall—

(1) in the case of an action to enforce an interest in real property securing the consumer's obligation, bring such action only in a judicial district or similar legal entity in which such real property is located; or

(2) in the case of an action not described in paragraph (1), bring such action only in the judicial district or similar legal entity—

(A) in which such consumer signed the contract sued upon; or

(B) in which such consumer resides at the commencement of the action.

(b) Nothing in this title shall be construed to authorize the bringing of legal actions by debt collectors.

§ 812. Furnishing certain deceptive forms

(a) It is unlawful to design, compile, and furnish any form knowing that such form would be used to create the false belief in a consumer that a person other than the creditor of such consumer is participating in the collection of or in an attempt to collect a debt such consumer allegedly owes such creditor, when in fact such person is not so participating.

(b) Any person who violates this section shall be liable to the same extent and in the same manner as a debt collector is liable under section 813 for failure to comply with a provision of this title.

§ 813. Civil liability

(a) Except as otherwise provided by this section, any debt collector who fails to comply with any provision of this title with respect to any person is liable to such person in an amount equal to the sum of—

(1) any actual damage sustained by such person as a result of such failure;

(2)(A) in the case of any action by an individual, such additional damages as the court may allow, but not exceeding $1,000; or

(B) in the case of a class action, (i) such amount for each named plaintiff as could be recovered under subparagraph (A), and (ii) such amount as the court may allow for all other class members, without regard to a minimum individual recovery, not to exceed the lesser of $500,000 or 1 per centum of the net worth of the debt collector; and

(3) in the case of any successful action to enforce the foregoing liability, the costs of the action, together with a reasonable attorney's fee as determined by the court. On a finding by the court that an action under this section was brought in bad faith and for the purpose of harassment, the court may award to the

defendant attorney's fees reasonable in relation to the work expended and costs.

(b) In determining the amount of liability in any action under subsection (a), the court shall consider, among other relevant factors—

(1) in any individual action under subsection (a)(2)(A), the frequency and persistence of noncompliance by the debt collector, the nature of such noncompliance, and the extent to which such noncompliance was intentional; or

(2) in any class action under subsection (a)(2)(B), the frequency and persistence of noncompliance by the debt collector, the nature of such noncompliance, the resources of the debt collector, the number of persons adversely affected, and the extent to which the debt collector's noncompliance was intentional.

(c) A debt collector may not be held liable in any action brought under this title if the debt collector shows by a preponderance of evidence that the violation was not intentional and resulted from a bona fide error notwithstanding the maintenance of procedures reasonably adapted to avoid any such error.

(d) An action to enforce any liability created by this title may be brought in any appropriate United States district court without regard to the amount in controversy, or in any other court of competent jurisdiction, within one year from the date on which the violation occurs.

(e) No provision of this section imposing any liability shall apply to any act done or omitted in good faith in conformity with any advisory opinion of the Commission, notwithstanding that after such act or omission has occurred, such opinion is amended, rescinded, or determined by judicial or other authority to be invalid for any reason.

§ 814. Administrative enforcement

(a) Compliance with this title shall be enforced by the Commission, except to the extent that enforcement of the requirements imposed under this title is specifically committed to another agency under subsection (b). For purpose of the exercise by the Commission of its functions and powers under the Federal Trade Commission Act, a violation of this title shall be deemed an unfair or deceptive act or practice in violation of that Act. All of the functions and powers of the Commission under the Federal Trade Commission Act are available to the Commission to enforce compliance by any person with this title, irrespective of whether that person is engaged in commerce or meets any other jurisdictional tests in the Federal Trade Commission Act, including the power to enforce the provisions of this title in the same manner as if the violation had been a violation of a Federal Trade Commission trade regulation rule.

(b) Compliance with any requirements imposed under this title shall be enforced under—

(1) section 8 of the Federal Deposit Insurance Act, in the case of—

(A) national banks, by the Comptroller of the Currency;

(B) member banks of the Federal Reserve System (other than national banks), by the Federal Reserve Board; and

(C) banks the deposits or accounts of which are insured by the Federal Deposit Insurance Corporation (other than members of the Federal Reserve System), by the Board of Directors of the Federal Deposit Insurance Corporation;

(2) section 5(d) of the Home Owners Loan Act of 1933, section 407 of the National Housing Act, and sections 6(i) and 17 of the Federal Home Loan Bank Act, by the Federal Home Loan Bank Board (acting directly or through the Federal Savings and Loan Insurance Corporation), in the case of any institution subject to any of those provisions;

(3) the Federal Credit Union Act, by the Administrator of the National Credit Union Administration with respect to any Federal credit union;

(4) the Acts to regulate commerce, by the Interstate Commerce Commission with respect to any common carrier subject to those Acts;

(5) the Federal Aviation Act of 1958, by the Civil Aeronautics Board with respect to any air carrier or any foreign air carrier subject to that Act; and

(6) the Packers and Stockyards Act, 1921 (except as provided in section 406 of that Act), by the Secretary of Agriculture with respect to any activities subject to that Act.

(c) For the purpose of the exercise by any agency referred to in subsection (b) of its powers under any Act referred to in that subsection, a violation of any requirement imposed under this title shall be deemed to be a violation of a requirement imposed under that Act. In addition to its powers under any provision of law specifically referred to in subsection (b), each of the agencies referred to in that subsection may exercise, for the purpose of enforcing compliance with any requirement imposed under this title any other authority conferred on it by law, except as provided in subsection (d).

(d) Neither the Commission nor any other agency referred to in subsection (b) may promulgate trade regulation rules or other regulations with respect to the collection of debts by debt collectors as defined in this title.

§ 815. Reports to Congress by the Commission

(a) Not later than one year after the effective date of this title and at one-year intervals thereafter, the Commission shall make reports to the Congress concerning the administration of its functions under this title, including such recommendations as the Commission deems necessary or appropriate. In addition, each report of the Commission shall include its assessment of the extent to which compliance with this title is being achieved and a summary of the enforcement actions taken by the Commission under section 814 of this title.

(b) In the exercise of its functions under this title, the Commission may obtain upon request the views of any other Federal agency which exercises enforcement functions under section 814 of this title.

§ 816. Relation to State laws

This title does not annul, alter, or affect, or exempt any person subject to the provisions of this title from complying with the laws of any State with respect to debt collection practices, except to the extent that those laws are inconsistent with any provision of this title, and then only to the extent of the inconsistency. For purposes of this section, a State law is not inconsistent with this title if the protection such law affords any consumer is greater than the protection provided by this title.

§ 817. Exemption for State regulation

The Commission shall by regulation exempt from the requirements of this title any class of debt collection practices within any State if the Commission determines that under the law of that State that class of debt collection practices is subject to requirements substantially similar to those imposed by this title, and that there is adequate provision for enforcement.

§ 818. Effective date

This title takes effect upon the expiration of six months after the date of its enactment, but section 809 shall apply only with respect to debts for which the initial attempt to collect occurs after such effective date.

Approved September 20, 1977.

TRUTH IN LENDING REGULATIONS †

(REGULATION Z)

TITLE 12.—BANKS AND BANKING

PART 226—TRUTH IN LENDING

As amended to August 31, 1978 ††

The provisions of Part 226 of Title 12 of the Code of Federal Regulations, set forth below, are commonly known as Regulation Z.

REGULATIONS

SECTION 226.1—AUTHORITY, SCOPE, PURPOSE, ETC.

* (a) **Authority, scope, and purpose.** (1) This Part comprises the regulations issued by the Board of Governors of the Federal Reserve System pursuant to Title I (Truth in Lending Act) and Title V (General Provisions) of the Consumer Credit Protection Act, as amended (15 U.S.C. § 1601 et seq.). Except as otherwise provided herein, this Part, within the context of its related provisions, applies to all persons who are creditors, as defined in paragraph (s) of § 226.2, and in the case of consumer leases, as defined in paragraph (mm) of § 226.2, to all persons who are lessors, as defined in paragraph (oo) of § 226.2.

(2) This Part implements the Act, the purpose of which is to assure that every customer who has need for consumer credit is given meaningful information with respect to the cost of that credit which, in most cases, must be expressed in the dollar amount of finance charge, and as an annual percentage rate computed on the unpaid balance of the amount financed. Other relevant credit information must also be disclosed so that the customer may readily compare the various credit terms available to him from different sources and avoid the uninformed use of credit. This Part also implements the provision of the Act under which a customer has a right in certain circumstances to cancel a credit transaction

† This text corresponds to the Code of Federal Regulations, Title 12, Chapter II, Part 226, cited as 12 CFR 226. The words "this Part," as used herein, mean Regulation Z.

‡ The asterisks indicate those regulatory amendments adopted since October 28, 1975.

* Amended 3/23/77.

which involves a lien on his residence. Advertising of consumer credit and consumer lease terms must comply with specific requirements, and certain credit terms may not be advertised unless the creditor usually and customarily extends such terms. This Part also contains prohibitions against the issuance of unsolicited credit cards and limits on the cardholder's liability for unauthorized use of a credit card. In addition, this Part is designed to assist the customer to resolve credit billing disputes in a fair and timely manner, to regulate certain billing and credit card practices, and to strengthen the legal rights of consumers. This Part is also designed to assure that lessees of personal property are given meaningful disclosures of lease terms, to delimit the ultimate liability of lessees in leasing personal property and to require meaningful and accurate disclosures of lease terms in advertisements. Neither the Act nor this Part is intended to control charges for consumer credit, or interfere with trade practices except to the extent that such practices may be inconsistent with the purpose of the Act.

** (b) **Administrative enforcement.** (1) As set forth more fully in section 108 of the Act, administrative enforcement of the Act and this Part with respect to certain creditors, credit card issuers and lessors is assigned to the Comptroller of the Currency, Board of Directors of the Federal Deposit Insurance Corporation, Federal Home Loan Bank Board (acting directly or through the Federal Savings and Loan Insurance Corporation), Administrator of the National Credit Union Administration, Civil Aeronautics Board, Secretary of Agriculture, Farm Credit Administration, and Board of Governors of the Federal Reserve System.

(2) Except to the extent that administrative enforcement is specifically committed to other authorities, compliance with the requirements imposed under the Act and this Part will be enforced by the Federal Trade Commission.

* (c) **Penalties and liabilities.** Section 112 of the Act provides criminal liability for willful and knowing failure to comply with any requirement imposed under the Act and this Part. Section 134 provides for criminal liability for certain fraudulent activities related to credit cards. Section 130 provides for civil liability in individual or class actions for any creditor or lessor who fails to comply with any requirement imposed under chapter 2, chapter 4 or chapter 5 of the Act and the corresponding provisions of this Part. Section 130 also provides creditors or lessors a defense against civil and criminal liability under sections 130 and 112 for any act done or omitted in good faith in conformity with the provisions of this Part or any interpretation thereof by the Board, or with any interpretations or approvals issued by a duly authorized official or employee of the Federal Reserve System, notwithstanding that after such act or omission has occurred, such rule, regulation, interpretation or approval is amended, rescinded or otherwise determined to be invalid for any reason. Section 130 further provides that a multiple failure to disclose in connection with a single account or single consumer lease shall permit but a single recovery. Section 115 provides for civil liability for an assignee of an original creditor or lessor where the original creditor or lessor has violated the disclosure requirements and such violation is apparent on the face of the instrument assigned, unless the assignment is involuntary. Section 185(b) provides for civil liability under section 130 for any lessor who fails to comply with any requirement imposed under section 184 to any person who suffers actual damage from the violation. Pursuant to section 108 of the Act, violations of the Act or this Part constitute violations of other Federal laws which may provide further penalties.

** (d) **Issuance of staff interpretations.** (1) Unofficial staff interpretations will be issued at the staff's discretion where the protection of section 130(F) of the Act is neither requested nor required, or where a rapid response is necessary.

(2)(i) Official staff interpretations will be issued at the discretion of designated officials. No such interpretation will be issued approving creditors' or lessors' forms or statements. Any request for an official staff interpretation of this Part must be in writing and addressed to the Director of the Division of Consumer Affairs, Board of Governors of the Federal Reserve System, Washington, D.C. 20551. The request must contain a complete state-

** Amended 3/23/77.

* Amended 7/30/76 and 3/23/77.

** Added 7/30/76; amended 4/24/78.

ment of all relevant facts concerning the credit or lease transaction or arrangement and must include copies of all pertinent documents.

(ii) Within 5 business days of receipt of the request, an acknowledgement will be sent to the person making the request. If, in the opinion of the designated officials, issuance of an official staff interpretation is appropriate, it will be published in the *Federal Register* to become effective 30 days after the publication date. If a request for public comment is received, the effective date will be suspended. The interpretation will then be republished in the *Federal Register* and the public given an opportunity to comment. Any official staff interpretation issued after opportunity for public comment shall become effective upon publication in the *Federal Register.*

(3) Any request for public comment on an official staff interpretation of this Part must be in writing and addressed to the Secretary, Board of Governors of the Federal Reserve System, Washington, D.C. 20551, and postmarked or received by the Secretary's office within 30 days of the interpretation's publication in the *Federal Register.* The request must contain a statement setting forth the reasons why the person making the request believes that public comment would be appropriate.

(4) Pursuant to section 130(f) of the Act, the Board has designated the Director and other officials of the Division of Consumer Affairs as officials "duly authorized" to issue, at their discretion, official staff interpretations of this Part.

SECTION 226.2—DEFINITIONS AND RULES OF CONSTRUCTION

For the purposes of this Part, unless the context indicates otherwise, the following definitions and rules of construction apply:

(a) **"Accepted credit card"** means any credit card which the cardholder has requested or applied for and received, or has signed, or has used, or has authorized another person to use for the purpose of obtaining money, property, labor, or services on credit. Any credit card issued in renewal of, or in substitution for, an accepted credit card becomes an accepted credit card when received by the cardholder whether such card is issued by the same or a successor card issuer.

(b) **"Act"** refers to the Truth in Lending Act (Title I of the Consumer Credit Protection Act).

(c) **"Adequate notice"** means a printed notice to a cardholder which sets forth the pertinent facts clearly and conspicuously so that a person against whom it is to operate could reasonably be expected to have noticed it and understood its meaning.

* (d) **"Advertisement"** means any commercial message in any newspaper, magazine, leaflet, flyer or catalog, on radio, television or public address system, in direct mail literature or other printed material on any interior or exterior sign or display, in any window display, in any point-of-transaction literature or price tag which is delivered or made available to a customer or prospective customer or lessee or prospective lessee in any manner whatsoever.

(e) **"Agricultural purpose"** means a purpose related to the production, harvest, exhibition, marketing, transportation, processing, or manufacture of agricultural products by a natural person who cultivates, plants, propagates, or nurtures those agricultural products. "Agricultural products" includes agricultural, horticultural, viticultural, and dairy products, livestock, wildlife, poultry, bees, forest products, fish and shellfish, and any products thereof, including processed and manufactured products, and any and all products raised or produced on farms and any processed or manufactured products thereof.

(f) **"Amount financed"** means the amount of credit of which the customer will have the actual use determined in accordance with paragraphs (c)(7) and (d)(1) of § 226.8.

(g) **"Annual percentage rate"** means the annual percentage rate of finance charge determined in accordance with § 226.5.

** (h) **"Arrange for the extension of credit or for lease of personal property"** means to provide or offer to provide consumer credit or a lease which is or will be extended by another person under a business or other relationship pursuant to which the person arranging such credit or lease

(1) Receives or will receive a fee, compensation, or other consideration for such service, or

(2) Has knowledge of the credit or lease terms and participates in the preparation of the contract

* Amended 3/23/77.

** Amended 3/23/77.

documents required in connection with the extension of credit or the lease.
It does not include honoring a credit card or similar device where no finance charge is imposed at the time of that transaction.

(i) **"Billing cycle"** means the time interval between regular periodic billing statement dates. Such intervals may be considered equal intervals of time unless a billing date varies more than 4 days from the regular date.

(j) **"Billing error"** means:

(1) A reflection on or with a periodic statement of an extension of credit which (i) was not made to the customer, or (ii) was made to a person who did not have actual, implied, or apparent authority of the customer to use the account and from which use the customer received no benefit, or (iii) if made, was misidentified, insufficiently identified, or was not in the amount indicated or on the date specified on or with the periodic statement, or

(2) A reflection on a periodic statement of an extension of credit or indebtedness for which the customer requests explanation or clarification, including requests for copies of documentary evidence of the indebtedness reflected thereon, or

(3) A reflection on a periodic statement of an extension of credit for property or services not accepted by the customer or his designee, or not delivered to the customer or his designee in accordance with any agreement made in connection with the transaction,[1] or

(4) Any failure to properly reflect, on a periodic statement, a payment or other credit to the customer's account, or

(5) A computational error or similar error of an accounting nature made by the creditor on a periodic statement, including errors in computing finance charges, late payment charges, or other charges, or

(6) A failure to mail or deliver a customer's periodic statement to his current designated address, if the creditor has received notification of any change of address at least 10 days prior to the closing date of the billing cycle for which the periodic statement was incorrectly mailed or delivered.

(k) **"Board"** refers to the Board of Governors of the Federal Reserve System.

(l) **"Card issuer"** means any person who issues a credit card, or the agent of such person with respect to such card.

(m) **"Cardholder"** means any person to whom a credit card is issued for personal, family, household, agricultural, business, or commercial purposes, or any person who has agreed with the card issuer to pay obligations arising from the issuance of a credit card to another person for such purposes.

(n) **"Cash price"** means the price at which the creditor offers, in the ordinary course of business, to sell for cash the property or services which are the subject of a consumer credit transaction. It may include the cash price of accessories or services related to the sale such as delivery, installation, alterations, modifications, and improvements, and may include taxes to the extent imposed on the cash sale, but shall not include any other charges of the types described in § 226.4.

(o) **"Comparative Index of Credit Cost"** means the relative measure of the cost of credit under an open end credit account, computed in accordance with § 226.11, and is the expression of the "average effective annual percentage rate of return" and the "projected rate of return" which appear in section 127(a)(5) of the Act.

(p) **"Consumer credit"** means credit offered or extended to a natural person, in which the money, property, or service which is the subject of the transaction is primarily for personal, family, household, or agricultural purposes. "Consumer loan" is one type of "consumer credit."

(q) **"Credit"** means the right granted by a creditor to a customer to defer payment of debt, incur debt and defer its payment, or purchase property or services and defer payment therefor. (See also paragraph (jj) of this section.)

(r) **"Credit card"** means any card, plate, coupon book, or other single credit device existing for the purpose of being used from time to time upon presentation to obtain money, property, labor, or services on credit.

(s) **"Creditor"** means a person who in the ordinary course of business regularly extends or arranges for the extension of consumer credit, or offers to extend or arrange for the extension of such credit, which is payable by agreement in

[1] The delivery of property or services different from that described in any agreement, the delivery of the wrong quantity, late delivery, or delivery to the wrong location shall be considered to be a billing error subject to this paragraph, but any dispute with respect to the quality of property in the physical possession of the customer or services performed for the customer shall not be considered to be a billing error under this paragraph.

more than four instalments, or for which the payment of a finance charge is or may be required, whether in connection with loans, sales of property or services, or otherwise. For purposes of the requirements of §§ 226.7(a)(6), (7), (8), and (9); 226.7(b)(1)(i), (ii), (iii), (ix), and (x); 226.7(b)(2); 226.7(c), (d), (f), (g), (h), and (i); 226.13; and 226.14, the term "creditor" shall also include card issuers, whether or not the payment of a finance charge is or may be required. For purposes of the requirements of §§ 226.4(i) and 226.13(k) the term "creditor" shall include any person who honors a credit card.

(t) **"Credit sale"** means any sale with respect to which consumer credit is extended or arranged by the seller. The term includes any contract in the form of a bailment or lease if the bailee or lessee contracts to pay as compensation for use a sum substantially equivalent to or in excess of the aggregate value of the property and services involved and it is agreed that the bailee or lessee will become, or for no other or for a nominal consideration has the option to become, the owner of the property upon full compliance with his obligations under the contract.

(u) **"Customer"** means (1) a cardholder or (2) a natural person to whom consumer credit is offered or to whom it is or will be extended, and includes a comaker, endorser, guarantor, or surety for such natural person who is or may be obligated to repay the extension of consumer credit.

(v) **"Dwelling"** means a residential-type structure which is real property and contains one or more family housing units, or a residential condominium unit wherever situated.

(w) **"Finance charge"** means the cost of credit determined in accordance with § 226.4.

(x) **"Open end credit"** means consumer credit extended on an account pursuant to a plan under which (1) the creditor may permit the customer to make purchases or obtain loans, from time to time, directly from the creditor or indirectly by use of a credit card, check, or other device, as the plan may provide; (2) the customer has the privilege of paying the balance in full or in instalments; and (3) a finance charge may be computed by the creditor from time to time on an outstanding unpaid balance. For purposes of the requirements of §§ 226.7(a)(6), (7), (8), and (9); 226.7(b)(1)(i), (ii), (iii), (ix), and (x); 226.7(b)(2); 226.7(c), (d), (f), (g), (h), and (i); 226.13(i), (j), and (k); and 226.14, the term includes consumer credit extended on an account by use of a credit card, whether or not a finance charge may be imposed. The term does not include negotiated advances under an open end real estate mortgage or a letter of credit.

(y) **"Organization"** means a corporation, trust, estate, partnership, cooperative, association, government, or governmental subdivision, agency, or instrumentality.

(z) **"Period"** means a day, week, month, or other subdivision of a year.

(aa) **"Periodic rate"** means a percentage rate of finance charge which is or may be imposed by a creditor against a balance for a period. (See also § 226.5(a)(3).)

(bb) **"Person"** means a natural person or an organization.

(cc) **"Proper written notification of a billing error"** is any written notification (other than notice on a payment medium or other material accompanying the periodic statement if the creditor so stipulates in the disclosure required by § 226.7(a)(9), (d), and (i)) received at the address disclosed under § 226.7(b)(1)(x) within 60 days of the first mailing or delivering to the customer's current designated address (as required in § 226.7(b)) of the periodic statement on which the disputed item(s) or amount(s) is reflected in which the customer

(1) Sets forth or otherwise enables the creditor to identify the name and account number (if any) of the customer,

(2) Indicates the customer's belief that the periodic statement contains a billing error and the suspected amount of such error, and

(3) Sets forth the reasons for such belief, to the extent applicable or known by the customer.

(dd) **"Real property"** means property which is real property under the law of the State in which it is located.

(ee) **"Real property transaction"** means an extension of credit in connection with which a security interest in real property is or will be retained or acquired.

(ff) **"Residence"** means any real property in which the customer resides or expects to reside. The term includes a parcel of land on which the customer resides or expects to reside.

(gg) **"Security interest"** and **"security"** means any interest in property which secures payment or performance of an obligation. The terms include, but are not limited to, security interests under the Uniform Commercial Code, real property mortgages, deeds of trust, and other consensual or confessed liens whether or not recorded, mechanic's, materialmen's, artisan's, and other similar liens, vendor's liens in both real and personal property, the interest of a seller in a contract for the sale of real property, any lien on property arising by operation of law, and any interest in a lease when used to secure payment or performance of an obligation.

(hh) **"State"** means any State, the District of Columbia, the Commonwealth of Puerto Rico, and any territory or possession of the United States.

(ii) **"Unauthorized use"** means the use of a credit card by a person other than the cardholder

(1) who does not have actual, implied, or apparent authority for such use, and

(2) from which the cardholder receives no benefit.

* (jj) Unless the context indicates otherwise, "credit" shall be construed to mean "consumer credit," "loan" to mean "consumer loan," "transaction" to mean "consumer credit transaction," and "lease" to mean "consumer lease."

* (kk) A transaction shall be considered consummated at the time a contractual relationship is created between a creditor and a customer or a lessor and lessee irrespective of the time of performance of either party.

(ll) Captions and catchlines are intended solely as aids to convenient reference, and no inference as to the intent of any provision of this Part may be drawn from them.

** (mm) **"Consumer lease"** means a contract in the form of a bailment or lease for the use of personal property by a natural person primarily for personal, family or household purposes, for a period of time exceeding four months, for a total contractual obligation not exceeding $25,000, whether or not the lessee has the option to purchase or otherwise become the owner of the property at the expiration of the lease. It does not include a lease which meets the definition of a credit sale in § 226.2(t), nor does it include a lease for agricultural, business or commercial purposes or one made to an organization.

** (nn) **"Lessee"** means a natural person who leases under, or who is offered a consumer lease.

** (oo) **"Lessor"** means a person who in the ordinary course of business regularly leases, offers to lease or arranges for the leasing of personal property under a consumer lease.

** (pp) **"Personal property"** means any property which is not real property under the law of the State where it is located at the time it is offered or made available for lease.

** (qq) **"Realized value"** means (1) the price received by the lessor for the leased property at disposition, (2) the highest offer for disposition, or (3) the fair market value at the end of the lease term.

** (rr) **"Total lease obligation"** equals the total of (1) the scheduled periodic payments under the lease, (2) any nonrefundable cash payment required of the lessee or agreed upon by the lessor and lessee or any trade-in allowance made at consummation and (3) the estimated value of the leased property at the end of the lease term.

(ss) **"Value at consummation" equals the cost to the lessor of the leased property including, if applicable, any increase or markup by the lessor prior to consummation.

*** (tt) "**Regular price**" means (1) the tag or posted price charged for the property or service if a single price is tagged or posted; or (2) the price charged for the property or service when payment is made by use of an open end credit card account if either (a) no price is tagged or posted, or (b) two prices are tagged or posted, one of which is charged when payment is made by use of an open end credit card account and the other when payment is made by use of cash, check, or similar means. For purposes of this definition, payment by check, draft, or other negotiable instrument which may result in the debiting of a cardholder's open end account shall not be considered payment made by use of that account.

*** (uu) "**Discount**," as used in §§ 226.4(i) and 226.13(*l*), means a reduction made from the "regular price," as defined in § 226.2(tt).

*** (vv) "**Surcharge**," as used in § 226.4(i), means any amount added at the point of sale to the "regular price," as defined in § 226.2(tt), as a condition or consequence of payment being made by use of an open end credit card account. For purposes of this definition, payment by check, draft, or other negotiable instrument which may result in the debiting of a cardholder's open end account shall not be considered payment made by use of that account.

---

* Amended 3/23/77

** Added 3/23/77.

*** Added 7/21/77.

SECTION 226.3—EXEMPTED TRANSACTIONS

This Part does not apply to the following:

(a) **Business or governmental credit.** Extensions of credit to organizations, including governments, or for business or commercial purposes, other than agricultural purposes.

(b) **Certain transactions in security or commodities accounts.** Transactions in securities or commodities accounts with a broker-dealer registered with the Securities and Exchange Commission.

(c) **Non-real property credit over $25,000.** Credit transactions, other than real property transactions, in which the amount financed[1a] exceeds $25,000, or in which the transaction is pursuant to an express written commitment by the creditor to extend credit in excess of $25,000.

(d) **Certain public utility bills.** Transactions under public utility tariffs involving services provided through pipe, wire, or other connected facilities, if the charges for such public utility services, the charges for delayed payment, and any discount allowed for early payment are filed with, reviewed by, or regulated by an agency of the Federal Government, a State, or a political subdivision thereof.

(e) **Agricultural credit transactions.** Credit transactions primarily for agricultural purposes, including real property transactions, in which the amount financed[1b] exceeds $25,000 or in which the transaction is pursuant to an express written commitment by the creditor to extend credit in excess of $25,000.

** (f) **Certain lease transactions.** Lease transactions of personal property which are incident to the lease of real property and which provide that (1) the lessee has no liability for the value of the property at the end of the lease term except for abnormal wear and tear, and (2) the lessee has no option to purchase the leased property.

[1a] For this purpose, the amount financed is the amount which is required to be disclosed under § 226.8(c)(7), or (d)(1), as applicable, or would be so required if the transaction were subject to this Part.

[1b] For this purpose, the amount financed is the amount which is required to be disclosed under § 226.8(c)(7), or (d)(1), as applicable, or would be so required if the transaction were subject to this Part.

** Added 3/23/77.

SECTION 226.4—DETERMINATION OF FINANCE CHARGE

(a) **General rule.** Except as otherwise provided in this section, the amount of the finance charge in connection with any transaction shall be determined as the sum of all charges, payable directly or indirectly by the customer, and imposed directly or indirectly by the creditor as an incident to or as a condition of the extension of credit, whether paid or payable by the customer, the seller, or any other person on behalf of the customer to the creditor or to a third party, including any of the following types of charges:

(1) Interest, time price differential, and any amount payable under a discount or other system of additional charges.

(2) Service, transaction, activity, or carrying charge.[2]

(3) Loan fee, points, finder's fee, or similar charge.

(4) Fee for an appraisal, investigation, or credit report.

(5) Charges or premiums for credit life, accident, health, or loss of income insurance, written in connection with[3] any credit transaction unless

(i) the insurance coverage is not required by the creditor and this fact is clearly and conspicuously disclosed in writing to the customer; and

(ii) any customer desiring such insurance coverage gives specifically dated and separately signed affirmative written indication of such desire after receiving written disclosure to him of the cost of such insurance.

(6) Charges or premiums for insurance, written in connection with[4] any credit transaction,

[2] These charges include any charges imposed by the creditor in connection with a checking account to the extent that such charges exceed any charges the customer is required to pay in connection with such an account when it is not being used to extend credit.

[3] A policy of insurance owned by the customer, which is assigned to the creditor or otherwise made payable to the creditor to satisfy a requirement imposed by the creditor, is not insurance "written in connection with" a credit transaction if the policy was not purchased by the customer for the purpose of being used in connection with that extension of credit.

[4] A policy of insurance owned by the customer, which is assigned to the creditor or otherwise made payable to the creditor to satisfy a requirement imposed by the creditor, is not insurance "written in connection with" a credit transaction if the policy was not purchased by the customer for the purpose of being used in connection with that extension of credit.

against loss of or damage to property or against liability arising out of the ownership or use of property, unless a clear, conspicuous, and specific statement in writing is furnished by the creditor to the customer setting forth the cost of the insurance if obtained from or through the creditor and stating that the customer may choose the person through which the insurance is to be obtained.[5]

(7) Premium or other charge for any other guarantee or insurance protecting the creditor against the customer's default or other credit loss.

(8) Any charge imposed by a creditor upon another creditor for purchasing or accepting an obligation of a customer if the customer is required to pay any part of that charge in cash, as an addition to the obligation, or as a deduction from the proceeds of the obligation.

(b) **Itemized charges excludable.** If itemized and disclosed to the customer, any charges of the following types need not be included in the finance charge:

(1) Fees and charges prescribed by law which actually are or will be paid to public officials for determining the existence of or for perfecting or releasing or satisfying any security related to the credit transaction.

(2) The premium payable for any insurance in lieu of perfecting any security interest otherwise required by the creditor in connection with the transaction, if the premium does not exceed the fees and charges described in subparagraph (1) of this paragraph which would otherwise be payable.

(3) Taxes not included in the cash price.

(4) License, certificate of title, and registration fees imposed by law.

(c) **Late payment, delinquency, default, and reinstatement charges.** A late payment, delinquency, default, reinstatement, or other such charge is not a finance charge if imposed for actual unanticipated late payment, delinquency, default or other such occurrence.

(d) **Overdraft charges.** A charge imposed by a bank for paying checks which overdraw or increase an overdraft in a checking account is not a finance charge unless the payment of such checks and the imposition of such finance charge were previously agreed upon in writing.

(e) **Excludable charges, real property transactions.** The following charges in connection with any real property transaction, provided they are bona fide, reasonable in amount, and not for the purpose of circumvention or evasion of this Part, shall not be included in the finance charge with respect to that transaction:

(1) Fees or premiums for title examination, abstract of title, title insurance, or similar purposes and for required related property surveys.

(2) Fees for preparation of deeds, settlement statements, or other documents.

(3) Amounts required to be placed or paid into an escrow or trustee account for future payments of taxes, insurance, and water, sewer, and land rents.

(4) Fees for notarizing deeds and other documents.

(5) Appraisal fees.

(6) Credit reports.

(f) **Prohibited offsets.** Interest, dividends, or other income received or to be received by the customer on deposits or on investments in real or personal property in which a creditor holds a security interest shall not be deducted from the amount of the finance charge or taken into consideration in computing the annual percentage rate.

(g) **Demand obligations.** Obligations other than those debited to an open end credit account which are payable on demand shall be considered to have a maturity of one-half year for the purpose of computing the amount of the finance charge and the annual percentage rate, except that where such an obligation is alternatively payable upon a stated maturity, the stated maturity shall be used for the purpose of such computations.

(h) **Computation of insurance premiums.** If any insurance premium is required to be included as a part of the finance charge, the amount to be included shall be the premium for coverage extending over the period of time the creditor will require the customer to maintain such insurance. For this purpose, rates and classifications applicable at the time the credit is extended shall be applied over the full time during which coverage is required, unless the creditor knows or has reason to know that other rates or classifications will be applicable, in which case such other rates or classifications shall be used to the extent appropriate.

---

[5] A creditor's reservation or exercise of the right to refuse to accept an insurer offered by the customer, for reasonable cause, does not require inclusion of the premium in the finance charge.

*(i) **Discounts for payments in cash.** (1) Notwithstanding any other provision of this section, a discount which a creditor offers, allows, or otherwise makes available for the purpose of inducing payments for a purchase by cash, check, or similar means rather than by use of an open end credit card account, whether or not a credit card is physically used,[5a] is not a finance charge, Provides that:

(i) Such discount does not exceed 5 per cent when computed or expressed as a percentage of the regular price of the property or services which are the subject of the transaction,

(ii) Such discount is available to all prospective buyers, whether or not they are cardholders, and such fact is clearly and conspicuously disclosed by a sign or display posted at or near each public entrance to the seller's place of business wherein such discount is offered, and at all locations within the place of business where a purchase may be paid for, and

(iii) If an offer of property or services is advertised in any medium or if offers are invited or accepted through the mail, over the telephone, or by means other than personal contact between the customer and the creditor offering such a discount, and if customers are allowed to pay by use of a credit card or its underlying account and such fact is disclosed in the advertisement, telephone contact, or in other correspondence, the availability of such a discount must be clearly and conspicuously disclosed in any advertisement for such offerings and, in any case, before the transaction has been completed by use of the credit card or its underlying account. If a price other than the regular price, as defined in § 226.2(tt), is disclosed in an advertisement, telephone contact, or other correspondence promoting goods or services for which such a discount is offered, then the advertisement, telephone contact, or other correspondence shall also indicate that such price is not available to credit card purchasers.

(2) With respect to any such discount which is greater than 5 per cent, the total amount of such discount shall constitute a finance charge under § 226.4(a) to be disclosed in accordance with § 226.7(e).

(3) The availability of any discount may be limited by the creditor offering such discount to certain types of property or services or to certain outlets maintained by that creditor provided that such limitations are clearly and conspicuously disclosed.

(4) No creditor in any sales transaction may impose a surcharge. This paragraph shall cease to be effective on February 27, 1979.

(5) Notwithstanding any other provisions of this Part, any discount which, pursuant to paragraph (1), is not a finance charge for purposes of this Part shall not be considered a finance charge or other charge for credit under the laws of any State relating to:

(i) usury; or

(ii) disclosure of information in connection with credit extensions; or

(iii) the types, amounts, or rates of charges, or the element or elements of charges permissible in connection with the extension or use of credit.

SECTION 226.5—DETERMINATION OF ANNUAL PERCENTAGE RATE

(a) **General rule—open end credit accounts.** The annual percentage rates for open end credit accounts shall be computed so as to permit disclosure with an accuracy at least to the nearest quarter of 1 per cent. Such rate or rates shall be determined in accordance with § 226.7(a)(4) for purposes of disclosure before opening an account, § 226.10(c)(4) for purposes of advertising, and in the following manner for purposes of disclosure on periodic statements:

(1) Where the finance charge is exclusively the product of the application of one or more periodic rates

(i) by multiplying each periodic rate by the number of periods in a year; or

* Amended 7/21/77.

5a For purposes of this section, payment by check, draft, or other negotiable instrument which may result in the debiting of a cardholder's open end account shall not be considered payment made by use of that account.

(ii) at the creditor's option, if the finance charge is the result of the application of two or more periodic rates, by dividing the total finance charge for the billing cycle by the sum of the balances to which the periodic rates were applied and multiplying the quotient (expressed as a percentage) by the number of billing cycles in a year.

(2) Where the creditor imposes all periodic finance charges in amounts based on specified ranges or brackets of balances, the periodic rate shall be determined by dividing the amount of the finance charge for the period by the amount of the median balance within the range or bracket of balances to which it is applicable, and the annual percentage rate shall be determined by multiplying that periodic rate (expressed as a percentage) by the number of periods in a year. Such ranges or brackets of balances shall be subject to the limitations prescribed in subdivision (iv) of paragraph (c)(2) of this section.

(3) Where the finance charge imposed during the billing cycle is or includes

(i) any minimum, fixed, or other charge not due to the application of a periodic rate, other than a charge with respect to any specific transaction during the billing cycle, by dividing the total finance charge for the billing cycle by the amount of the balance(s) to which applicable and multiplying the quotient (expressed as a percentage) by the number of billing cycles in a year; or

(ii) any charge with respect to any specific transaction during the billing cycle (even if the total finance charge also includes any other minimum, fixed, or other charge not due to the application of a periodic rate), by dividing the total finance charge imposed during the billing cycle by the total of all balances and other amounts on which any finance charge was imposed during the billing cycle without duplication and multiplying the quotient (expressed as a percentage) by the number of billing cycles in a year,[5b] except that the annual percentage rate shall not be less than the largest rate determined by multiplying each periodic rate imposed during the billing cycle by the number of periods in a year; or

(iii) any minimum, fixed, or other charge not due to the application of a periodic rate and the total finance charge imposed during the billing cycle does not exceed 50 cents for a monthly or longer billing cycle, or the pro rata part of 50

[5b] In determining the denominator of the fraction under § 226.5(a)(3)(ii) no amount will be used more than once when adding the sum of the balances to which periodic rates apply to the sum of the amounts financed to which specific transaction charges apply. In every case the full amount of transactions to which specific transaction charges apply shall be included in the denominator. Other balances or parts of balances shall be included according to the manner of determining the balance to which a periodic rate is applied, as illustrated in the following examples of accounts on monthly billing cycles:

1. Previous balance—none.

A specific transaction of $100 occurs on first day of the billing cycle. The average daily balance is $100. A specific transaction charge of 3% is applicable to the specific transaction. The periodic rate is 1½% applicable to the average daily balance. The numerator is the amount of the finance charge, which is $4.50. The denominator is the amount of the transaction (which is $100), plus the amount by which the balance to which the periodic rate applies exceeds the amount of specific transactions (such excess in this case is 0), totaling $100.

The annual percentage rate is the quotient (which is 4.5%) multiplied by 12 (the number of months in a year), *i.e.*, 54%.

2. Previous balance—$100.

A specific transaction of $100 occurs at midpoint of the billing cycle. The average daily balance is $150. A specific transaction charge of 3% is applicable to the specific transaction. The periodic rate is 1½% applicable to the average daily balance. The numerator is the amount of finance charge which is $5.25. The denominator is the amount of the transaction (which is $100), plus the amount by which the balance to which the periodic rate applies exceeds the amounts of specific transactions (such excess in this case is $50), totaling $150.

As explained in example 1, the annual percentage rate is 3.5% × 12 = 42%.

3. If, in example 2, the periodic rate applies only to the previous balance, the numerator is $4.50 and the denominator is $200 (the amount of the transaction, $100, plus the balance to which only the periodic rate is applicable, the $100 previous balance). As explained in example 1, the annual percentage rate is 2.25% × 12 = 27%.

4. If, in example 2, the periodic rate applies only to an adjusted balance (previous balance less payments and credits) and the customer made a payment of $50 at midpoint of billing cycle, the numerator is $3.75 and the denominator is $150 (the amount of the transaction, $100, plus the balance to which only the periodic rate is applicable, the $50 adjusted balance). As explained in example 1, the annual percentage rate is 2.5% × 12 = 30%.

5. Previous balance—$100.

A specific transaction (check) of $100 occurs at the midpoint of the billing cycle. The average daily balance is $150. The specific transaction charge is 25 cents per check. The periodic rate is 1½% applied to the average daily balance. The numerator is the amount of the finance charge, which is $2.50 and includes the 25 cents check charge and the $2.25 resulting from the application of the periodic rate. The denominator is the full amount of the specific transaction (which is $100) plus the amount by which the average daily balance exceeds the amount of the specific transaction (which in this case is $50), totaling $150. As explained in example 1, the annual percentage rate would be 1⅔% × 12 = 20%.

cents for a billing cycle shorter than monthly, at the creditor's option, by multiplying each applicable periodic rate by the number of periods in a year, notwithstanding the provisions of subdivisions (i) and (ii) of this subparagraph.

(b) **General rule—other credit.** Except as otherwise provided in this section, the annual percentage rate applicable to any extension of credit, other than open end credit, shall be that nominal annual percentage rate determined as follows:

(1) In accordance with the actuarial method of computation so that it may be disclosed with an accuracy at least to the nearest quarter of 1 per cent. The mathematical equation and technical instructions for determining the annual percentage rate in accordance with the requirements of this paragraph are set forth in Supplement I to Regulation Z which is incorporated in this Part by reference. Supplement I to Regulation Z may be obtained from any Federal Reserve Bank or from the Board in Washington, D.C., 20551, upon written request.

(2) At the option of the creditor, by application of the United States Rule so that it may be disclosed with an accuracy at least to the nearest quarter of 1 per cent. Under this rule, the finance charge is computed on the unpaid balance for the actual time the balance remains unpaid and if the amount of a payment is insufficient to pay the accumulated finance charge, the unpaid accumulated finance charge continues to accumulate to be paid from the proceeds of subsequent payments and is not added to the amount financed.

(c) **Charts and tables.** (1) The Regulation Z Annual Percentage Rate Tables produced by the Board may be used to determine the annual percentage rate, and any such rate determined from these tables in accordance with instructions contained therein will comply with the requirements of this section. Volume I contains table FRB—100-M covering 1 to 60 monthly payments, table FRB—200-M covering 61 to 120 monthly payments, table FRB—300-M covering 121 to 480 monthly payments, and table FRB—100-W covering 1 to 104 weekly payments. Volume I also contains instructions for use of the tables in regular transactions and most irregular transactions which involve only odd first and final payments and odd first payment periods. Volume II contains factor tables and instructions for their use in connection with the tables in Volume I in the computation of annual percentage rates in any type of irregular payment or payment period transaction and in transactions involving multiple advances. Each volume is available from the Board in Washington, D.C., 20551, and the Federal Reserve Banks.

(2) Any chart or table other than the Board's Regulation Z Annual Percentage Rate Tables also may be utilized for the purpose of determining the annual percentage rate provided:

(i) It is prepared in accordance with the general rule set forth in paragraph (b)(1) or (2) of this section;

(ii) It bears the name and address of the person responsible for its production, an identification number assigned to it by that person which shall be the same for each chart or table so produced with like numerical content and configuration and, if prepared for use in connection with irregular transactions, an identification of the method of computation ("Actuarial" or "U.S. Rule");

(iii) Except as provided in subdivision (iv) of this subparagraph, it permits determination of the annual percentage rate to the nearest one-quarter of 1 per cent for the range of rates covered by the chart or table; and

(iv) If applicable to ranges or brackets of balances, it discloses the amount of the finance charge and the annual percentage rate on the median balance within each range or bracket of balances where a creditor imposes the same finance charge for all balances within a specified range or bracket of balances, and provided further that if the annual percentage rate determined on the median balance understates the annual percentage rate determined on the lowest balance in that range or bracket by more than 8 per cent of the rate on the lowest balance, then the annual percentage rate for that range or bracket shall be computed upon any balance lower than the median balance within that range so that any understatement will not exceed 8 per cent of the rate on the lowest balance within that range or bracket of balances.

(3) In the event an error in disclosure of the amount of a finance charge or an annual percentage rate occurs because of a corresponding error in a chart or table acquired or produced in good faith by the creditor, that error in disclosure shall not, in itself, be considered a violation of this Part provided that upon discovery of the error, that creditor makes no further disclosure based on that chart or table and promptly notifies the Board or a Federal Reserve Bank in writing of the error and identifies the inaccurate chart or table by giving the name and address of the per-

son responsible for its production and its identification number.

(d) **Minor irregularities.** In determining the annual percentage rate a creditor may, at his option, consider the payment irregularities set forth in this paragraph as if they were regular in amount or time, as applicable, provided that the transaction to which they relate is otherwise payable in equal instalments scheduled at equal intervals.

(1) If the period from the date on which the finance charge begins to accrue and the date the final payment is due is not less than 3 months in the case of weekly payments, 6 months in the case of biweekly or semimonthly payments, or 1 year in the case of monthly payments, either or both of the following:

(i) The amount of 1 payment other than any downpayment is not more than 50 per cent greater nor 50 per cent less than the amount of a regular payment; or

(ii) The interval between the date on which the finance charge begins to accrue and the date the first payment is due is not less than 5 days for an obligation otherwise payable in weekly instalments, not less than 10 days for an obligation otherwise payable in biweekly or semimonthly instalments, or not less than 20 days for an obligation otherwise payable in monthly instalments.

(2) If the period from the date on which the finance charge begins to accrue and the date the final payment is due is less than 3 months in the case of weekly payments, 6 months in the case of biweekly or semimonthly payments, or 1 year in the case of monthly payments, either or both of the following:

(i) The amount of 1 payment other than any downpayment is not more than 25 per cent greater nor 25 per cent less than the amount of a regular payment; or

(ii) The interval between the date on which the finance charge begins to accrue and the date the first payment is due is not less than 6 days for an obligation otherwise payable in weekly instalments, not less than 12 days for an obligation otherwise payable in biweekly or semimonthly instalments, or not less than 25 days for an obligation otherwise payable in monthly instalments.

(e) **Approximation of annual percentage rate—other credit.** In an exceptional instance when circumstances may leave a creditor with no alternative but to determine an annual percentage rate applicable to an extension of credit other than open end credit by a method other than those prescribed in paragraphs (b) or (c) of this section, the creditor may utilize the constant ratio method of computation provided such use is limited to the exceptional instance and is not for the purpose of circumvention or evasion of the requirements of this Part. Any provision of State law authorizing or requiring the use of the constant ratio method or any method of computing a percentage rate other than those prescribed in paragraphs (b) and (c) of this section does not justify failure of the creditor to comply with the provisions of those paragraphs, as applicable.

SECTION 226.6—GENERAL DISCLOSURE REQUIREMENTS

*(a) **Disclosures; general rule.** The disclosures required to be given by this Part shall be made clearly, conspicuously, in meaningful sequence, in accordance with the further requirements of this section, and at the time and in the terminology prescribed in applicable sections. Except with respect to the requirements of § 226.10, where the terms "finance charge" and "anual percentage rate" are required to be used, they shall be printed more conspicuously than other terminology required by this Part and all numerical amounts and percentages shall be stated in figures and shall be printed in not less than the equivalent of 10 point type, .075 inch computer type, or elite size typewritten numerals, or shall be legibly handwritten.

All disclosures required to be given by this Part shall be made in the English language except in the Commonwealth of Puerto Rico where disclosures may be made in the Spanish language with English language disclosures provided upon the customer's request, either in substitution for the Spanish disclosures or as additional information in accordance with § 226.6(c).

(b) **Inconsistent State requirements.** (1) With respect to the requirements of this Part, State law is inconsistent with the requirements of the Act and this Part, within the meaning of section 111(a) of the Act to the extent that it:

(i) Requires a creditor to make disclosures or take actions different from the requirements of this Part with respect to form, content, terminology, or time of delivery;

---

* Amended 4/11/77.

(ii) Requires disclosure of the amount of the finance charge determined in any manner other than that prescribed in § 226.4; or

(iii) Requires disclosure of the annual percentage rate of the finance charge determined in any manner other than that prescribed in § 226.5.

(2)(i) A State law with respect to credit billing practices which is similar in nature, purpose, scope, intent, effect, or requisites to the provisions of sections 161 or 162, or both, of the Act is inconsistent with the Act and this Part within the meaning of section 171(a) of the Act, and is preempted, if it provides procedures or imposes rights or responsibilites upon either customers or creditors which are different from those required by sections 161 or 162, or both, of the Act and their implementing provisions in this Part; except that, any such State law which allows a customer to make inquiry concerning an open end credit account and imposes upon the creditor an obligation to respond to such an inquiry after the time allowed in this Part for the customer to submit a proper written notification of a billing error shall not be preempted as to any situation in which the time period for making a proper written notification of a billing error as provided in this Part has expired.

(ii) A State law which is similar in nature, purpose, scope, intent, effect, or requisites to a section of chapter 4 of the Act other than sections 161 or 162 is not inconsistent with the Act or this Part within the meaning of section 171(a) of the Act if the creditor can comply with the State law without violating this Part. If the creditor cannot comply with a State law without violating a provision of this Part which implements a section of chapter 4 of the Act other than sections 161 or 162, such State law is inconsistent with the requirements of the Act and this Part within the meaning of section 171(a) of the Act and is preempted.

(iii) A State law which requires disclosure or notification to customers of provisions of State law which are inconsistent with chapter 4 of the Act and its implementing provisions in this Part within the meaning of section 171(a) of the Act is inconsistent with the Act and this Part within the meaning of sections 111(a) and 171(a) of the Act, and the creditor shall not make such a disclosure or provide such a notice. When a creditor gives written notice to a customer of the customer's rights under any provision of State law which would permit a customer to inquire concerning an open end credit account after the time period allowed in this Part for submission of a proper written notification of a billing error has expired, the creditor shall clearly and conspicuously set forth in the notice that reliance upon the longer time period available under State law may result in the customer losing important rights which could be preserved by acting more promptly under Federal law and that the State law provisions only become operative upon the expiration of the time period provided by this Part for submitting a proper written notification of a billing error. If such a disclosure is made on the same side of a sheet of paper as the disclosures required by § 226.7(a), (d), and (i) of this Part, such State disclosures shall appear separately and below the disclosures required by § 226.7(a), (d), and (i) of this Part; the disclosures required by § 226.7(a), (d), and (i) shall be clearly and conspicuously identified by a heading indicating they are made in compliance with Federal law and the disclosures of State law shall appear separately and below a conspicuous demarcation line.

(iv) A State, through its Governor, Attorney General, or other appropriate official having primary enforcement or interpretive responsibilities for its credit billing practices law, may apply to the Board for a determination that the State law offers greater protection to customers than a comparable provision(s) of chapter 4 of the Act and its implementing provision(s) in this Part, or is otherwise not inconsistent with chapter 4 of the Act and this Part, or for a determination with respect to any issues not clearly covered by § 226.6(b)(2)(i), (ii), and (iii) as to the consistency or inconsistency of a State law with chapter 4 of the Act or its implementing provisions in this Part.

* (3)(i) A State law which is similar in nature, purpose, scope, intent, effect or requisites to a section of chapter 5 of the Act is not inconsistent with the Act or this Part within the meaning of section 186(a) of the Act if the lessor can comply with the State law without violating this Part. If a lessor cannot comply with a State law without violating a provision of this Part which implements a section of chapter 5 of the Act, such State law is inconsistent with the requirements of the Act and this Part within the meaning of section 186(a) of the Act and is preempted.

(ii) A State, through its Governor, Attorney General, or other appropriate official having prim-

* Added 3/23/77.

ary enforcement or interpretative responsibilities for its consumer leasing law, may apply to the Board for a determination that the State law offers greater protection and benefit to lessees than a comparable provision(s) of chapter 5 of the Act and its implementing provision(s) in this Part, or is otherwise not inconsistent with chapter 5 of the Act and this Part, or for a determination with respect to any issues not clearly covered by § 226.6(b)(3)(i) as to the consistency or inconsistency of a State law with chapter 5 of the Act or its implementing provisions in this Part.

** (c) **Additional information.** At the creditor's or lessor's option, additional information or explanations may be supplied with any disclosure required by this Part, but none shall be stated, utilized, or placed so as to mislead or confuse the customer or lessee or contradict, obscure, or detract attention from the information required by this Part to be disclosed. Any creditor or lessor who elects to make disclosures specified in any provision of State law which, under paragraph (b) of this section, is inconsistent with the requirements of the Act and this Part may

(1) Make such inconsistent disclosures on a separate paper apart from the disclosures made pursuant to this Part, or

(2) Make such inconsistent disclosures on the same statement on which disclosures required by this Part are made; provided:

(i) All disclosures required by this Part appear separately and above any other disclosures,

(ii) Disclosures required by this Part are identified by a clear and conspicuous heading indicating that they are made in compliance with Federal law, and

(iii) All inconsistent disclosures appear separately and below a conspicuous demarcation line, and are identified by a clear and conspicuous heading indicating that the statements made thereafter are inconsistent with the disclosure requirements of the Federal Truth in Lending Act or the Federal Consumer Leasing Act.

** (d) **Multiple creditors or lessors; joint disclosure.** If there is more than one creditor or lessor in a transaction, each creditor or lessor shall be clearly identified and shall be responsible for making only those disclosures required by this Part which are within his knowledge and the purview of his relationship with the customer or lessee. If two or more creditors or lessors make a joint disclosure, each creditor or lessor shall be clearly identified. The disclosures required under paragraphs (b) and (c) of § 226.8 shall be made by the seller if he extends or arranges for the extension of credit. Otherwise disclosures shall be made as required under paragraphs (b) and (d) of § 226.8 or paragraph (b) of § 226.15.

** (e) **Multiple customers or lessees; disclosure to one.** In any transaction other than a credit transaction which may be rescinded under the provisions of § 226.9, if there is more than one customer or lessee, the creditor or lessor need furnish a statement of disclosures required by this Part to only one of them other than an endorser, comaker, guarantor, or a similar party.

* (f) **Unknown information estimate.** If at the time disclosures must be made, an amount or other item of information required to be disclosed, or needed to determine a required disclosure, is unknown or not available to the creditor or lessor and the creditor or lessor has made a reasonable effort to ascertain it, the creditor or lessor may use an estimated amount or an approximation of the information, provided the estimate or approximation is clearly identified as such, is reasonable, is based on the best information available to the creditor or lessor and is not used for the purpose of circumventing or evading the disclosure requirements of this Part.
Notwithstanding the requirement of this paragraph that the estimate be based on the best information available, a lessor is not precluded in a purchase option lease from understating the estimated value of the leased property at the end of the term in computing the total lease obligation as required in § 226.15(b)(15)(i).

* (g) **Effect of subsequent occurrence.** If information disclosed in accordance with this Part is subsequently rendered inaccurate as the result of any act, occurrence, or agreement subsequent to the delivery of the required disclosures, the inaccuracy resulting therefrom does not constitute a violation of this Part.[6]

** Amended 3/23/77.

* Amended 3/23/77 and 5/30/78.

[6] Such acts, occurrences, or agreements include the failure of the customer or lessee to perform his obligations under the contract and such actions by the creditor or lessor as may be proper to protect his interests in such circumstances. Such failure may result in the liability of the customer or lessee to pay delinquency charges, collection costs, or expenses of the creditor or lessor for perfection or acquisition of any security interest or amounts advanced by the creditor or lessor on behalf of the customer or lessee in connection with insurance, repairs to or preservation of collateral or leased property.

(h) **Overstatement.** The disclosure of the amount of the finance charge or a percentage which is greater than the amount of the finance charge or percentage required to be disclosed under this Part does not in itself constitute a violation of this Part: *Provided,* That the overstatement is not for the purpose of circumvention or evasion of disclosure requirements.

*(i) **Preservation and inspection of evidence of compliance.**

(1) Evidence of compliance with the requirements imposed under this Part, other than advertising requirements under section 226.10, shall be preserved by the creditor or lessor for a period of not less than 2 years after the date such disclosure is required to be made.

(2) With respect to a creditor or lessor subject to the administrative enforcement jurisdiction of the Comptroller of the Currency, Board of Directors of the Federal Deposit Insurance Corporation, Federal Home Loan Bank Board (acting directly or through the Federal Savings and Loan Insurance Corporation), Administrator of the National Credit Union Administration or Board of Governors of the Federal Reserve System, all evidence of compliance with the requirements imposed under this Part, dating from July 1, 1969, other than advertising requirements under section 226.10, shall be retained until

(A) the administrative authority for that creditor or lessor completes one examination for compliance with the requirements imposed under this Part subsequent to adoption of a statement of enforcement policy, [6a] and

(B) a period of not less than 2 years has elapsed from the date that disclosure was required to be made.

(3) Each creditor or lessor shall, when directed by the appropriate administrative enforcement authority designated in section 108 of the Act, permit that authority or its duly authorized representative to inspect its relevant records and evidence of compliance with this Part.

* Amended 3/23/77 and 5/30/78.

6a "Statement of enforcement policy" refers to a final statement based on the Joint Notice of Proposed Statement of Enforcement Policy published at 42 Fed. Reg. 55786 (1977).

(j) **Leap year.** Any variance in the amount of any finance charge, payment, percentage rate, or other term required under this Part to be disclosed, or stated in any advertisement, which occurs by reason of the addition of February 29 in each leap year, may be disregarded, and such term may be disclosed or stated without regard to such variance.

(k) **Transition period.** Any creditor who can demonstrate that he has taken bona fide steps, prior to October 28, 1975, to obtain printed forms which are necessary to comply with the requirements of this Part may, until such forms are received but in no event later than April 30, 1976, utilize existing supplies of printed forms for the purpose of complying with the disclosure requirements of this Part, provided that such forms are altered or supplemented as necessary to assure that all of the items of information the creditor is required to disclose to the customer are set forth clearly and conspicuously in every case except:

(1) Where a creditor has, prior to October 28, 1975, prepared the § 226.7(a) disclosures without the notice and statement required by § 226.7(a)(9) and dispersed them to remote locations, as in the case of mail order catalogs, the statement required by § 226.7(a)(9) may be made separately from the other § 226.7(a) disclosures until April 30, 1976, so long as the § 226.7(a)(9) statement is mailed or delivered to the customer no later than the date the first payment is due. For the purpose of this paragraph the creditor may disregard the required notice in § 226.7(a)(9) until April 30, 1976;

(2) Where a creditor's forms must be adapted to comply with the disclosure requirements of § 226.7(b)(1)(x), the creditor need not supplement or alter his forms if there is only one address listed on or with the periodic statement. In the case where a creditor has more than one address listed on or with the periodic statement and the creditor has not complied with the requirements of § 226.7(b)(1)(x), the creditor must accept as properly received any proper written notification of a billing error at any of the addresses listed on or with the periodic statement. New forms which comply with the requirements of § 226.7(b)(1)(x) must be in use no later than April 30, 1976;

(3) Where a creditor's forms must be adapted to comply with the disclosure requirements of § 226.7(g), the creditor need not supplement or alter his forms; however, complying forms must be in use no later than April 30, 1976;

(4) Where a creditor is disclosing inconsistent State law provisions within the meaning of section

171(a) of the Act and § 226.6(b)(2) of this Part or is making disclosures not in compliance with § 226.6(b)(2)(iii) on or with the disclosure required by this Part, the creditor need not alter or supplement his forms; however, complying forms must be in use no later than April 30, 1976; and

(5) Where, because of operational limitations, a creditor is unable to comply with the disclosure requirements in § 226.7(b)(1)(i) and (ix), which require appropriate identification of credit balances, or with the disclosure requirement in § 226.7(b)(1)(iii), which requires the dates of payments and credits, the creditor need not supplement or alter his forms; however, complying forms and procedures must be in use no later than April 30, 1976.

SECTION 226.7—OPEN END CREDIT ACCOUNTS—SPECIFIC DISCLOSURES

(a) **Opening new account.** Before the first transaction is made on any open end credit account, the creditor shall disclose to the customer in a single written statement, which the customer may retain, in terminology consistent with the requirements of paragraph (b) of this section, each of the following items, to the extent applicable:

(1) The conditions under which a finance charge may be imposed, including an explanation of the time period, if any, within which any credit extended may be paid without incurring a finance charge, except that the creditor may, at his option and without disclosure, refrain from imposing such finance charge even though payment is received after the termination of such time period.

(2) The method of determining the balance upon which a finance charge may be imposed.

(3) The method of determining the amount of the finance charge, including the method of determining any minimum, fixed, check service, transaction, activity, or similar charge, which may be imposed as a finance charge.

(4) Where one or more periodic rates may be used to compute the finance charge, each such rate, the range of balances to which it is applicable, and the corresponding annual percentage rate determined by multiplying the periodic rate by the number of periods in a year.[6b]

(5) If the creditor so elects, the Comparative Index of Credit Cost in accordance with § 226.11.

(6) The conditions under which any other charges may be imposed, and the method by which they will be determined.

(7) The conditions under which the creditor may retain or acquire any security interest in any property to secure the payment of any credit extended on the account, and a description or identification of the type of the interest or interests which may be so retained or acquired.

(8) The minimum periodic payment required.

(9) The following notice: "NOTICE: See accompanying statement for important information regarding your rights to dispute billing errors" and a separate statement containing substantially the following text,[7] as applicable, written clearly and conspicuously, shall accompany the statement required by paragraph (a) of this section; or the following text without the preceding notice may be included on the statement required by paragraph (a) of this section if disclosed clearly and conspicuously; or the following text may be included on the reverse side of the statement required by paragraph (a) of this section with the following notice on the face of the statement:

"NOTICE: See reverse side for important information regarding your rights to dispute billing errors.":

In Case of Errors or Inquiries About Your Bill

The Federal Truth in Lending Act requires prompt correction of billing mistakes.

1. If you want to preserve your rights under the Act, here's what to do if you think your bill is wrong or if you need more information about an item on your bill:

a. Do not write on the bill. On a separate sheet of paper write [Alternate: *Write on the bill or other sheet of paper*] *(you may telephone your*

[6b] A creditor imposing minimum charges is not required to adjust the disclosure of the range of balances to which each periodic rate would apply in order to reflect the range of the balances below which the minimum charge applies. If a creditor does not impose a finance charge when the outstanding balance is less than a certain amount, the creditor is not required to disclose that fact or the balance below which no such charge will be imposed.

[7] Wherever the word "creditor" appears or is referred to in the statement, the creditor may substitute appropriate references, such as "company," "bank," "we" or a specific name.

inquiry but doing so will not preserve your rights under this law) the following:

i. Your name and account number (if any).

ii. A description of the error and an explanation (to the extent you can explain) why you believe it is an error.

If you only need more information, explain the item you are not sure about and, if you wish, ask for evidence of the charge such as a copy of the charge slip. Do not send in your copy of a sales slip or other document unless you have a duplicate copy for your records.

iii. The dollar amount of the suspected error.

iv. Any other information (such as your address) which you think will help the creditor to identify you or the reason for your complaint or inquiry.

b. Send your billing error notice to the address on your bill which is listed after the words: "Send Inquiries To:" or similar wording. [Alternate: *Send your billing error notice to: (creditor's name and address)*].

Mail it as soon as you can, but in any case, early enough to reach the creditor within 60 days after the bill was mailed to you. If you have authorized your bank to automatically pay from your checking or savings account any credit card bills from that bank, you can stop or reverse payment on any amount you think is wrong by mailing your notice so the creditor receives it within 16 days after the bill was sent to you. However, you do not have to meet this 16-day deadline to get the creditor to investigate your billing error claim.

2. The creditor must acknowledge all letters pointing out possible errors within 30 days of receipt, unless the creditor is able to correct your bill during that 30 days. Within 90 days after receiving your letter, the creditor must either correct the error or explain why the creditor believes the bill was correct. Once the creditor has explained the bill, the creditor has no further obligation to you even though you still believe that there is an error, except as provided in paragraph 5 below.

3. After the creditor has been notified, neither the creditor nor an attorney nor a collection agency may send you collection letters or take other collection action with respect to the amount in dispute; but periodic statements may be sent to you, and the disputed amount can be applied against your credit limit. You cannot be threatened with damage to your credit rating or sued for the amount in question, nor can the disputed amount be reported to a credit bureau or to other creditors as delinquent until the creditor has answered your inquiry. However, you remain obligated to pay the parts of your bill not in dispute.

4. If it is determined that the creditor has made a mistake on your bill, you will not have to pay any finance charges on any disputed amount. If it turns out that the creditor has not made an error, you may have to pay finance charges on the amount in dispute, and you will have to make up any missed minimum or required payments on the disputed amount. Unless you have agreed that your bill was correct, the creditor must send you a written notification of what you owe; and if it is determined that the creditor did make a mistake in billing the disputed amount, you must be given the time to pay which you normally are given to pay undisputed amounts before any more finance charges or late payment charges on the disputed amount can be charged to you.

5. If the creditor's explanation does not satisfy you and you notify the creditor **in writing** *within* **10** *days after you receive his explanation that you still refuse to pay the disputed amount, the creditor may report you to credit bureaus and other creditors and may pursue regular collection procedures. But the creditor must also report that you think you do not owe the money, and the creditor must let you know to whom such reports were made. Once the matter has been settled between you and the creditor, the creditor must notify those to whom the creditor reported you as delinquent of the subsequent resolution.*

6. If the creditor does not follow these rules, the creditor is not allowed to collect the first $50 of the disputed amount and finance charges, even if the bill turns out to be correct.

7. If you have a problem with property or services purchased with a credit card, you may have the right not to pay the remaining amount due on them, if you first try in good faith to return them or give the merchant a chance to correct the problem. There are two limitations on this right:

a. You must have bought them in your home State or if not within your home State within 100 miles of your current mailing address; and

b. The purchase price must have been more than $50.

However, these limitations do not apply if the merchant is owned or operated by the creditor, or if the creditor mailed you the advertisement for the property or services.

*(b) **Periodic statements required.** (1) Except in the case of an account which the creditor deems to be uncollectible or with respect to which delinquency collection procedures have been instituted, the creditor of any open end credit account shall mail or deliver to the customer,* for each billing cycle at the end of which there is an outstanding undisputed debit or credit balance in excess of $1 in that account or with respect to which a finance charge is imposed, a statement or statements which the customer may retain, setting forth in accordance with paragraph (c) of this section each of the following items to the extent applicable:

(i) The outstanding balance in the account at the beginning of the billing cycle, using the term "previous balance," and in the case of a credit balance, an appropriate identification as such.

(ii) The information required by § 226.7(k).

(iii) The amounts and dates of crediting to the account during the billing cycle for payments, using the term "payments," and for other credits including returns, rebates of finance charges, and adjustments, using the term "credits," and unless previously furnished a brief identification[8] of each of the items included in such other credits, except that the date of crediting to the customer's account need not be provided if a delay in crediting does not result in the imposition of any finance charges, late payment charges, or other charges for that billing cycle or a later billing cycle.

(iv) The amount of any finance charge, using the term "finance charge," debited to the account during the billing cycle, itemized and identified to show the amounts, if any, due to the application of periodic rates and the amount of any other charge included in the finance charge, such as a minimum, fixed, check service, transaction, activity, or similar charge,[9] using appropriate descriptive terminology.

(v) Each periodic rate, using the term "periodic rate" (or "rates"), that may be used to compute the finance charge (whether or not applied during the billing cycle), the range of balances to which it is applicable, and the corresponding annual percentage rate determined by multiplying the periodic rate by the number of periods in a year. The words "corresponding annual percentage rate," "corresponding nominal annual percentage rate," "nominal annual percentage rate," or "annual percentage rate" (or "rates") may be used to describe the corresponding annual percentage rate. The requirements of § 226.6(a) of this Part with respect to disclosing the term "annual percentage rate" more conspicuously than other required terminology shall not be applicable to the disclosure made under this paragraph, although such term (or words incorporating such term) may, at the creditor's option, be shown as conspicuously as the terminology required under (b)(1)(vi) of this paragraph. Where a minimum charge may be applicable to the account, the amount of such minimum charge shall be disclosed.[9a]

(vi) When a finance charge is imposed during the billing cycle, the annual percentage rate or rates determined under § 226.5(a) using the term "annual percentage rate" (or "rates").

(vii) If the creditor so elects, the Comparative Index of Credit Cost in accordance with § 226.11.

(viii) The balance on which the finance charge was computed, and a statement of how that balance was determined. If the balance is determined without first deducting all credits during the billing cycle, that fact and the amount of such credits shall also be disclosed.

(ix) The closing date of the billing cycle and the outstanding balance in the account on that date, using the term "new balance," and in the case of a credit balance, appropriately identified as such, accompanied by the statement of the date by which, or the period within which, if any, payment must be made to avoid additional finance charges, except that the creditor may, at his option and without disclosure, impose no such

* Amended 8/27/76.

[8] Identification may be made on an accompanying slip or by symbol relating to an identification list printed on the statement.

[9] These charges include any charges imposed by the creditor for the issuance, payment, or handling of checks, for account maintenance or otherwise, to the extent that such charges exceed any similar charges the customer is required to pay when an account is not being used to extend credit.

[9a] A creditor imposing minimum charges is not required to adjust the disclosure of the range of balances to which each periodic rate would apply in order to reflect the range of the balances below which the minimum charge applies. If a creditor does not impose a finance charge when the outstanding balance is less than a certain amount, the creditor is not required to disclose that fact or the balance below which no such charge will be imposed.

additional finance charges if payment is received after such date or termination of such period.

(x) An address to be used by the creditor for the purpose of receiving billing inquiries from customers. Such address shall be preceded by the caption "Send Inquiries To:", or other similar language indicating that the address is the proper location to send such inquiries.

(2) If the terms of the open end credit plan provide a time period within which the customer may repay any portion of the new balance without incurring an additional finance charge, late payment charge, or other charge, no such charge may be imposed with respect to any portion of such new balance unless the periodic statement disclosing the new balance is mailed or delivered to the customer at least 14 days prior to the date specified in the statement as being the date by which payment of the new balance must be made in order to avoid the imposition of that finance charge or late payment charge, except that such time limitation shall not apply in any case where the creditor has been prevented, delayed, or hindered in mailing or delivering the periodic statement within such time limit because of an act of God, war, civil disorder, natural disaster, or strike.

*(c) **Location of disclosures.** The disclosures required by paragraph (b) of this section shall be made on the face of the periodic statement, except that, at the creditor's option:

(1) The information required to be disclosed under paragraph (b)(1)(ii) of this section and itemization of the amounts and dates required to be disclosed under paragraph (b)(1)(iii) of this section and of the amount of any finance charge required to be disclosed under paragraph (b)(1)(iv) of this section may be made on the reverse side of the periodic statement or on a separate accompanying statement(s), provided that the totals of the respective debits and credits under each of those paragraphs are disclosed on the face of the periodic statement.

(2) The disclosures required under paragraph (b)(1)(v) and (b)(1)(viii) of this section, except the disclosure of the balance on which the finance charge was computed, may be made on the reverse side of the periodic statement or on the face of a single supplemental statement which shall accompany the periodic statement.

(3) The disclosure required by paragraph (b)(1)(x) of this section may be made on the reverse side of the periodic statement.

(4) If the creditor exercises any of the options provided under this paragraph, the face of the periodic statement shall contain one of the following notices, as applicable: "NOTICE: See reverse side for important information" or "NOTICE: See accompanying statement(s) for important information" or "NOTICE: See reverse side and accompanying statement(s) for important information," and the disclosures shall not be separated so as to confuse or mislead the customer or to obscure or detract attention from the information required to be disclosed.

(d) **Semiannual statement required.** (1) The creditor shall mail or deliver during two billing cycles per year to each customer entitled to receive a periodic statement under § 226.7(b) for such billing cycle, the statement required by § 226.7(a)(9), written clearly and conspicuously either on one or both sides of a separate page or on one or both sides of the periodic statement required by paragraph (b) of this section.

(2) The timing of the mailing or delivery of such semiannual statements shall be not less than 5 nor more than 7 months after the month in which the last preceding such statement was mailed or delivered, Provided that:

(i) The creditor shall select at least 2 billing cycles in any 12 month calendar period for the mailing or delivery of such statements; and

(ii) The first semiannual statement to any new customer may be mailed or delivered to that customer during the next regularly scheduled mailing or delivery of semiannual statements in which he is entitled to receive a semiannual statement under paragraph (d)(1) of this section.

(3) If the creditor chooses to alter the cycle of mailing or delivering semiannual statements, the creditor may mail or deliver the semiannual statement less than 5 months after the last preceding such statement was mailed or delivered, provided that the creditor mails or delivers at least 3 such statements in the next 12 months computed from the month in which the last preceding semiannual statement was mailed or delivered.

(4) Nothing in this section shall be construed to prohibit a creditor from mailing or delivering the statement required by this section more frequently than semiannually.

(5) As an alternative to the requirements of paragraph (d)(1) of this section, the creditor

* Amended 8/27/76.

may mail or deliver, on or with each periodic statement required under paragraph (b)(1) of this section, substantially the following statement and, if applicable, the periodic statement must contain one of the notices provided for in paragraph (c)(4) of this section, provided that the creditor must promptly but in no event later than 30 days, mail or deliver to a customer the statement required by § 226.7(a)(9) at any time upon a customer's request and also upon receipt of each billing error notice mailed or delivered to the creditor by a customer:

IN CASE OF ERRORS OR INQUIRIES
ABOUT YOUR BILL

Send your inquiry in writing [at creditor's option: *on a separate sheet*] *so that the creditor receives it within 60 days after the bill was mailed to you. Your written inquiry must include:*

1. Your name and account number (if any);

2. A description of the error and why (to the extent you can explain) you believe it is an error; and

3. The dollar amount of the suspected error.

If you have authorized your creditor to automatically pay your bill from your checking or savings account, you can stop or reverse payment on any amount you think is wrong by mailing your notice so that the creditor receives it within 16 days after the bill was sent to you.

You remain obligated to pay the parts of your bill not in dispute, but you do not have to pay any amount in dispute during the time the creditor is resolving the dispute. During that same time, the creditor may not take any action to collect disputed amounts or report disputed amounts as delinquent.

If you have a problem with property or services purchased with a credit card, you may have the right not to pay the remaining amount due on them if you first try in good faith to return them or give the merchant a chance to correct the problem. There are two limitations on this right:

1. You must have bought them in your home State or, if not within your home State, within 100 miles of your current mailing address; and

2. The purchase price must have been more than $50.

However, these limitations do not apply if the merchant is owned or operated by the creditor, or if the creditor mailed you the advertisement for the property or services.

This is a summary of your rights; a full statement of your rights and the creditor's responsibilities under the Federal Fair Credit Billing Act will be sent to you both upon request and in response to a billing error notice.

(e) **Finance charge imposed at the time of transaction.** (1) Any creditor, other than the creditor of the open end credit account, who imposes a finance charge not excepted by § 226.4(i) *Discounts for payments in cash,* at the time of honoring a customer's credit card, shall make the disclosures required under paragraphs (b)(2) and (d) of § 226.8 *Credit other than open end—specific disclosures,* at the time of that transaction, and the annual percentage rate to be disclosed shall be determined by dividing the amount of the finance charge by the amount financed and multiplying the quotient (expressed as a percentage) by 12.

(2) The creditor of the open end credit account shall not separately consider any charge imposed under this paragraph for purposes of the disclosure requirements of paragraphs (a) and (b) of this section.

(f) **Change in terms.** Not later than 15 days prior to the beginning date of the billing cycle in which any change is to be made in the terms previously disclosed to the customer of an open end credit account, the creditor shall mail or deliver a written disclosure of such change to each customer required to be furnished a statement under paragraph (b) of this section. Such disclosure shall be mailed or delivered to each other customer who subsequently activates his account not later than the date of mailing or delivery of the next required billing statement on his account. However, if the periodic rate or rates, or any minimum, fixed, check service, transaction, activity, or similar charge is increased, the creditor shall mail or deliver a written disclosure of such increase to each customer at least 15 days prior to the beginning date of the billing cycle in which the increase is imposed on his account. No notice is necessary if the only change is a reduction in the minimum periodic payment, periodic rate or rates, or in any minimum, fixed, check service, transaction, activity, or similar charge applicable to the account.

(g) **Prompt crediting of payments.** Regardless of the date of actual posting of a payment to an account, such payment shall be credited to the customer's account as of the date such payment is received by the creditor, and no finance charge, late payment charge, or other charge shall be imposed with respect to the amount of such payment which is properly received by the creditor on or before the time indicated by the creditor as necessary to avoid imposition thereof, Provided that:

(1) If a creditor fails to post the customer's payment in time to avoid the imposition of finance charges, late payment charges, or other charges, the creditor shall adjust the customer's account so that the finance charges, late payment charges, or other charges are credited to the account during the customer's next billing cycle.

(2) For the purposes of paragraph (g) of this section the creditor may specify on the periodic statement or on accompanying material that need not be retained by the customer, reasonable requirements with respect to the form, amount, manner, location, and time for receipt of payments, except that:

(i) If no particular hour of the day has been clearly specified by the creditor as the time by which payment must be received by the creditor in order to obtain crediting to the customer's account as of that date, payments received prior to the close of business on that day must be credited as of that date;

(ii) If no location(s) has been clearly specified as the location(s) at which payment may be made, then payment at any location where the creditor conducts business shall be credited as of the date such payment is presented; and

(iii) If no particular manner of payment has been clearly specified, then payment by check, cash, money order, bank draft or other similar instrument in properly negotiable form shall constitute proper manner of payment.

(3) If the creditor accepts payment at locations other than those specified under paragraph (g)(2)(ii) of this section, the creditor shall credit the customer's account promptly (in no case later than 5 days from the date of receipt), provided that the possibility of such delay is clearly disclosed to the customer on the periodic statement or on accompanying material that need not be retained by the customer.

(4) Payments need not be credited as of the date of receipt (but in any case must be credited promptly) if a delay in crediting does not result in the imposition of any finance charges, late payment charges, or other charges for that billing cycle or a later billing cycle.

(5) If, because of operational limitations, the creditor is unable to credit a payment made on an average daily balance or daily balance account as of the date of receipt and there was a "previous balance" in the account for the billing cycle in which such payment was received, or the account is one in which the terms do not provide a time period within which the customer may repay any portion of the new balance without incurring an additional finance charge, late payment charge, or other charge, a creditor may credit such payment promptly (in no case later than 5 days from the date of receipt) until October 28, 1976.

(h) **Crediting and refunding excess payments.** (1) Whenever a customer mails or delivers payment to the creditor in excess of the new balance (as provided in § 226.7(b)(1)(ix)) to which the payment is to be applied, the creditor shall:

(i) Credit the customer's account with the total amount of the payment as specified in paragraph (g) of this section, or

(ii) Credit the customer's account with an amount equal to the total new balance as specified in paragraph (g) of this section and promptly (in no case later than 5 business days from the creditor's receipt of the payment) refund the excess amount.

(2) Notwithstanding the provisions of paragraph (h)(1) of this section, if the customer requests in writing a refund of any excess payments, a creditor shall refund any such excess payments, of $1 or more, promptly (in no case later than 5 business days from receipt of the customer's request).

(3) After crediting a customer's account with the total amount of a payment under paragraph (h)(1)(i) of this section, a creditor may refund any excess payment of any amount, whether or not requested by the customer.

(i) **Open end credit accounts existing on October 28, 1975.** In the case of any open end credit account in existence and in which a balance of more than $1 is outstanding at or after the closing date of the creditor's first full billing cycle after October 28, 1975, and which account is deemed to be collectible and with respect to which delinquency collection procedures have not been instituted, the items described in paragraph (a) of this section, to the extent applicable and not previously required to be disclosed to the customer, shall be disclosed in the form prescribed in paragraph (a) of this section, and mailed or delivered to the customer not later than the time of mailing or delivery of the periodic statement required under paragraph (b) of this section for that billing cycle.

* (j) **Supplemental credit devices for use in open end credit accounts.** If, subsequent to 30 days after delivering the disclosures required under paragraph (a) of this section, a creditor of an open end credit account mails or delivers, other than as a renewal or resupply, a blank check, payee designated check, blank draft or order or other similar credit device other than a credit card, to an existing customer or cardholder for use in connection with such account, such device shall be accompanied by a single written statement setting forth clearly and conspicuously those disclosures of paragraph (a) of this section which specifically relate to the use of such device. Such disclosure statement shall either be limited to the disclosures of paragraphs (a)(1), (2), (3), and (4) of this section or contain all disclosures required of such paragraph with the pertinent disclosures clearly and conspicuously referenced on or accompanying that disclosure statement. Such disclosure statement shall not appear on any promotional material mailed or delivered at the same time. The requirements of this paragraph shall not be applicable to checks to be used in conjunction with a checking account even though such checks may also activate a cash advance under an open end credit account.

** (k) **Identification of transactions.** (1) Each extension of credit for which an actual copy of the document evidencing the credit transaction (which does not include a so-called "facsimile draft") accompanies the periodic statement on which the transaction is first reflected shall be identified by disclosing on the periodic statement, or on accompanying statement(s) or document(s), the amount of the transaction and, at the creditor's option, either the date of the transaction or the date the transaction is debited to the customer's account.

(2) Each extension of credit for which an actual copy of the document evidencing the credit transaction does not accompany the periodic statement shall be identified by disclosing on or with the periodic statement on which that credit transaction is first reflected at least:

(i) For transactions in which the creditor and the seller are the same person or related persons,[9b] the amount of the transaction, the date on which the transaction took place,[9c] and a brief identification[9d] of any property or services purchased or an identifying number or symbol reasonably unique for that transaction with that creditor which appears on the document evidencing the transaction given to the customer; provided, that, if the creditor discloses such an identifying number or symbol, the absence of the identification of the property or services otherwise required must be treated as a billing error under §§ 226.2(j) and 226.14 and as an erroneous billing under § 226.14 (b) if the customer submits a proper written notice of a billing error relating to such absence, and the creditor must provide documentary evidence of the transaction to the customer free of charge whether or not the customer requests it.

(ii) For transactions in which the seller and the creditor are not the same person or related persons, the amount of the transaction, the date on which the transaction took place, and the seller's name and the address (city and State or foreign country, using understandable and generally accepted abbreviations if the creditor desires) where the transaction took place.

(3) Notwithstanding the provisions of §§ 226.7 (k)(1) and 226.7(k)(2), transactions involving nonsale credit, such as a cash advance or an overdraft or other checking plan transactions, shall be identified on or with the periodic statement upon which the transaction is first reflected by providing at least:

(i) An actual copy of the document evidencing the transaction which shows the amount of the transaction and either the date of the trans-

* Added 1/1/76.

** Added 8/27/76.

[9b] For purposes of § 226.7(k) a person is not related to the creditor simply because the person and the creditor have an agreement or contract pursuant to which the person is authorized to honor the creditor's credit card under the terms specified in the agreement or contract. Franchised or licensed sellers of a creditor's product shall be considered to be related to the creditor for purposes of § 226.7(k). Sellers who assign or sell open end customer sales accounts to a creditor or arrange for such credit under an open end credit plan which allows the customer to use the credit only in transactions with that seller shall be considered related to the creditor for purposes of § 226.7(k).

[9c] With respect to transactions which are not billed in full on any single statement but for which precomputed instalments are billed periodically, the date the transaction takes place for purposes of § 226.7(k) shall be deemed to be the date on which the amount is debited to the customer's account.

[9d] For purposes of § 226.7(k), designations such as "merchandise" or "miscellaneous" shall not be considered sufficient identification of property or services, but a reference to a department in a sales establishment which accurately conveys the identification of the type(s) of property or services which are available in such department shall be sufficient under this paragraph. Identification may be made on an accompanying slip or by symbol relating to an identification list printed on the statement.

action, the date the transaction was debited to the customer's account, or the date placed on the document or instrument by the customer (if the customer signed the document or instrument); or

*(ii) A description of the transaction, which characterizes it as a cash advance, loan, overdraft loan, or other designation as appropriate, and which includes the amount of the transaction and the date of the transaction[9e] or the date which appears on the document or instrument evidencing the transaction (if the customer signed the document or instrument), or the date of debiting the amount to the account, provided that if only the debiting date is disclosed and the customer submits a proper written notification of a billing error related to the transaction, the creditor shall treat such inquiry as a billing error under sections 226.2(j) and 226.14, and as an erroneous billing under section 226.-14(b), and shall supply documentary evidence of the transaction whether or not the customer requests it, within the time period allowed under section 226.14 for resolution of a billing error without charge to the customer. If the date of debiting is disclosed, it must be reasonably identified as such on the periodic statement.

(4) If, despite the maintenance of procedures reasonably adapted to procure the information required by §§ 226.7(k)(1), (2), and (3) such information is unavailable to the creditor, the date of debiting the amount to the account shall be substituted for the date otherwise required (except that the date of debiting need not be provided if an actual copy of the document evidencing the transaction is provided with the periodic statement) and the creditor shall disclose as much of the other required information as is available and omit any information which is not available, provided, that, if the customer submits a proper written notification of a billing error relating to the absence of the primarily required date or other information, such absence shall be treated as a billing error under §§ 226.2(j) and 226.14 and as an erroneous billing under § 226.14(b) and, unless previously furnished with a periodic statement, documentary evidence of the transaction must be furnished whether or not the customer requests it, within the time period allowed in § 226.14 for resolution of a billing error, without charge to the customer.

(5) In any case in which a transaction occurs other than in a State:

(i) The creditor may disclose the date of debiting the amount of the transaction to the open end credit account in place of any other date required elsewhere in § 226.7(k); and

(ii) The provisions of § 226.7(k)(4) shall apply and the creditor need not maintain procedures reasonably adapted to procure the information otherwise required by § 226.7(k).

(6) In complying with the disclosure requirements of §§ 226.7(k)(1), (2), (3), or (4):

(i) The creditor may rely upon and disclose the information supplied by the seller with respect to the date and amount of transactions for which the creditor and the seller are not the same person or related persons.

(ii) With regard to disclosing the seller's address where the transaction took place for purposes of § 226.7(k)(2)(ii), the creditor may omit the address or provide an address or other suitable designation which, in the creditor's opinion, will assist the customer in identifying the transaction or in relating the transaction, as reflected, to a document(s) evidencing the transaction previously furnished when no meaningful address is readily available because the transaction took place at a location which is not fixed (for example, aboard a public conveyance), or in the customer's home (in which case "customer's home" or a similar description is sufficient) or because the transaction was the result of a mail or telephone order (in which case "telephone order," "mail order," or similar description is sufficient); provided that any such disclosure made or omitted shall not be for the purpose of circumvention or evasion of this Part.

(iii) With regard to disclosing the seller's name for purposes of § 226.7(k)(2)(ii), disclosure of a seller's name which appears on the document evidencing the transaction (or a more complete spelling of such a name if the name is alphabetically abbreviated on the document evidencing the transaction) is sufficient for purposes of § 226.7 (k)(2)(ii).

(7)(i) As an alternative to the provisions of §§ 226.7(k)(1) through 226.7(k)(5), from October 28, 1976, until October 28, 1977: (A) the creditor may disclose the date of debiting the

* Amended 3/28/78.

[9e] In cases in which an amount is debited to a customer's open end credit account under an overdraft checking plan, the date of debiting the open end credit account shall be considered the date of the transaction for purposes of this paragraph.

amount of the transaction to the customer's account for the date of the transaction or the date placed on the document evidencing a credit transaction if, due to operational limitations, either such date is unavailable to the creditor for purposes of billing; and the creditor may disclose an identifying number or symbol which appears on the document evidencing the credit transaction given to or used by the customer at the time of or in connection with the credit transaction in place of the seller's name and address or description of the property or services purchased if, due to operational limitations, such information is unavailable to the creditor for purposes of billing; or (B) the creditor may identify the transaction by disclosing such information as is reasonably available and treating the absence of the information required by §§ 226.7(k)(1), (2), or (3), as applicable, as a billing error, as provided in §§ 226.2(j) and 226.14. If a customer submits a proper written notification of a billing error relating to the absence of such information and the information was, in fact, not disclosed as required by §§ 226.7 (k)(1), (2), or (3), as applicable, the transaction shall be treated as an erroneous billing under § 226.14(b) and documentary evidence of the transaction must be furnished whether or not the customer requests it (despite the provisions of §§ 226.2(j) and 226.14(a)(2)), within the time period allowed in § 226.14 for resolution of a billing error, without charge to the customer.

(ii) The effective date of §§ 226.7(k)(1) through 226.7(k)(7)(i), inclusive, is October 28, 1976. Until October 28, 1976, the creditor shall disclose the date of each extension of credit or the date such extension of credit is debited to the account during the billing cycle, the amount of such extension of credit and, unless previously furnished, a brief identification[9f] of any goods or services purchased or the extension of credit.

SECTION 226.8—CREDIT OTHER THAN OPEN END—SPECIFIC DISCLOSURES

*(a) **General rule.** Any creditor when extending credit other than open end credit shall, in accordance with § 226.6 and to the extent applicable, make the disclosures required by this section with respect to any transaction consummated on or after July 1, 1969. Except as otherwise provided in this section, such disclosures shall be made before the transaction is consummated. At the time disclosures are made, the creditor shall furnish the customer with a duplicate of the instrument or a statement by which the required disclosures are made and on which the creditor is identified. All of the disclosures shall be made together on either

(1) The note or other instrument evidencing the obligation on the same side of the page and above or adjacent to the place for the customer's signature; or

(2) One side of a separate statement which identifies the transaction.

** Notwithstanding the provisions of paragraphs (1) and (2) of this subsection, a creditor may, in any transaction in which the payments scheduled to repay the indebtedness vary, satisfy the requirements of section 226.8 (b)(3) with respect to the number, amount, and due dates or periods of payments by disclosing the required information on the reverse of the disclosure statement or on a separate page(s), provided that the following notice appears with the other required disclosures: "NOTICE: See [reverse side] [accompanying statement] for the schedule of payments."

*(b) **Disclosures in sale and nonsale credit.** In any transaction subject to this section, the following items, as applicable, shall be disclosed:

(1) The date on which the finance charge begins to accrue if different from the date of the transaction.

(2) The finance charge expressed as an annual percentage rate, using the term "annual percentage rate," except in the case of a finance charge

(i) which does not exceed $5 and is applicable to an amount financed not exceeding $75, or

(ii) which does not exceed $7.50 and is applicable to an amount financed exceeding $75. A creditor may not divide an extension of credit into two or more transactions to avoid the disclosure of an annual percentage rate, nor may any other percentage rate be disclosed if none is stated in reliance upon subdivisions (i) or (ii) of this subparagraph.

(3) The number, amount, and due dates or periods of payments scheduled to repay the in-

[9f] Identification may be made on an accompanying slip or by symbol relating to an identification list printed on the statement.

* Amended 1/21/76.

** Amended 8/31/78.

* Amended 10/10/77.

debtedness and, except in the case of a loan secured by a first lien or equivalent security interest on a dwelling made to finance the purchase of that dwelling and except in the case of a sale of a dwelling, the sum of such payments using the term "total of payments." [10] If any payment is more than twice the amount of an otherwise regularly scheduled equal payment, the creditor shall identify the amount of such payment by the term "balloon payment" and shall state the conditions, if any, under which that payment may be refinanced if not paid when due.

(4) The amount, or method of computing the amount, of any default, delinquency, or similar charges payable in the event of late payments.

(5) A description or identification of the type of any security interest held or to be retained or acquired by the creditor in connection with the extension of credit, and a clear identification of the property to which the security interest relates or, if such property is not identifiable, an explanation of the manner in which the creditor retains or may acquire a security interest in such property which the creditor is unable to identify. In any such case where a clear identification of such property cannot properly be made on the disclosure statement due to the length of such identification, the note, other instrument evidencing the obligation, or separate disclosure statement shall contain reference to a separate pledge agreement, or a financing statement, mortgage, deed of trust, or similar document evidencing the security interest, a copy of which shall be furnished to the customer by the creditor as promptly as practicable. If after-acquired property will be subject to the security interest, or if other or future indebtedness is or may be secured by any such property, this fact shall be clearly set forth in conjunction with the description or identification of the type of security interest held, retained or acquired.

(6) A description of any penalty charge that may be imposed by the creditor or his assignee for prepayment of the principal of the obligation (such as a real estate mortgage) with an explanation of the method of computation of such penalty and the conditions under which it may be imposed.

(7) Identification of the method of computing any unearned portion of the finance charge in the event of prepayment in full of an obligation which includes precomputed finance charges and a statement of the amount or method of computation of any charge that may be deducted from the amount of any rebate of such unearned finance charge that will be credited to an obligation or refunded to the customer. If the credit contract does not provide for any rebate of unearned finance charges upon prepayment in full, this fact shall be disclosed.

(8) If the annual percentage rate is disclosed under § 226.8(b)(2) is prospectively subject to increase, [10a] the following additional disclosures shall be made:

(i) the fact that the annual percentage rate is subject to increase and the conditions under which such rate may increase, including: (A) identification of the index, if any, with respect to which such increase in annual percentage rate is tied; and (B) any limitation on such increase;

(ii) the manner(s) (such as an increase in payment amounts, number of scheduled periodic payments, or in the amount due at maturity) in which any increase in the annual percentage rate may be effected;

(iii) if the obligation is repayable in substantially equal instalments at substantially equal intervals (including those obligations providing for "balloon" payments) and the increase could be effected by an increase in the periodic payment amount, a statement of the estimated increase in the amount of the payment caused by a hypothetical immediate increase of one quarter of one percentage point, based upon the number of scheduled periodic payments and original amount financed disclosed at consummation;

(iv) if the obligation is repayable in substantially equal instalments at substantially equal intervals (including those obligations providing for "balloon" payments) and the increase could be effected by an increase in the number of periodic payments, a statement of the estimated increase in the number of periodic payments caused by a hypothetical immediate increase of one quarter of one percentage point, based upon the periodic payment amount and the original amount financed disclosed at consummation.

Any increase in the annual percentage rate within the conditions or limitations disclosed in accordance

[10] The disclosures required by this sentence need not be made with respect to interim student loans made pursuant to federally insured student loan programs under Public Law 89–329, Title IV Part B of the Higher Education Act of 1965, as amended.

[10a] For this purpose, the phrase "prospectively subject to increase" does not apply to increases in the annual percentage rate upon such occurrences as default, acceleration, late payment, assumption or transfer of property.

with this paragraph is a subsequent occurrence under § 226.6(g) and is not a refinancing under § 226.8(j).

The disclosures required under § 226.8(b)(8)(iii) and (iv) need be made only in transactions in which a security interest is taken in real property used or expected to be used as the customer's dwelling, and they need not be made in transactions primarily for agricultural purposes, transactions in which the obligation is repayable in substantially equal instalments which do not include repayments of principal, or transactions in which disclosures are made pursuant to § 226.814.

(c) **Credit sales.** In the case of a credit sale, in addition to the items required to be disclosed under paragraph (b) of this section, the following items, as applicable, shall be disclosed:

(1) The cash price of the property or service purchased, using the term "cash price."

(2) The amount of the downpayment itemized, as applicable, as downpayment in money, using the term "cash downpayment," downpayment in property, using the term "trade-in," and the sum, using the term "total downpayment."

(3) The difference between the amounts described in subparagraphs (1) and (2) of this paragraph, using the term "unpaid balance of cash price."

(4) All other charges, individually itemized, which are included in the amount financed but which are not part of the finance charge.

(5) The sum of the amounts determined under subparagraphs (3) and (4) of this paragraph, using the term "unpaid balance."

(6) Any amounts required to be deducted under paragraph (e) of this section using, as applicable, the terms "prepaid finance charge" and "required deposit balance," and, if both are applicable, the total of such items using the term "total prepaid finance charge and required deposit balance."

(7) The difference between the amounts determined under subparagraphs (5) and (6) of this paragraph, using the term "amount financed."

(8) Except in the case of a sale of a dwelling:

*(i) The total amount of the finance charge, using the term "finance charge," and where the total charge consists of two or more types of charges, a description of the amount of each type, and

(ii) The sum of the amounts determined under subparagraphs (1), (4), and (8)(i) of this paragraph, using the term "deferred payment price."

(d) **Loans and other nonsale credit.** In the case of a loan or extension of credit which is not a credit sale, in addition to the items required to be disclosed under paragraph (b) of this section, the following items, as applicable, shall be disclosed:

(1) The amount of credit, excluding items set forth in paragraph (e) of this section, which will be paid to the customer or for his account or to another person on his behalf, including all charges, individually itemized, which are included in the amount of credit extended but which are not part of the finance charge, using the term "amount financed."

(2) Any amount referred to in paragraph (e) of this section required to be excluded from the amount in subparagraph (1) of this paragraph, using, as applicable, the terms "prepaid finance charge" and "required deposit balance," and, if both are applicable, the total of such items using the term "total prepaid finance charge and required deposit balance."

** (3) Except in the case of a loan secured by a first lien or equivalent security interest on a dwelling and made to finance the purchase of that dwelling, the total amount of the finance charge,[11] using the term "finance charge," and where the total charge consists of two or more types of charges, a description of the amount of each type.

(e) **Finance charge payable separately or withheld; required deposit balances.** The following amounts shall be disclosed and deducted in a credit sale in accordance with paragraph (c)(6) of this section, and in other extensions of credit shall be excluded from the amount disclosed under paragraph (d)(1) of this section, and shall be disclosed in accordance with paragraph (d)(2) of this section:

(1) Any finance charge paid separately, in cash or otherwise, directly or indirectly to the creditor or with the creditor's knowledge to another person, or withheld by the creditor from the proceeds of the credit extended.[12]

* Amended 8/6/76.

[11] The disclosure required by this subparagraph need not be made with respect to interim student loans made pursuant to federally insured student loan programs under Public Law 89-329, Title IV Part B of the Higher Education Act of 1965, as amended.

[12] Finance charges deducted or excluded as provided by this paragraph shall, nevertheless, be included in determining the finance charge under § 226.4.

(2) Any deposit balance or any investment which the creditor requires the customer to make, maintain, or increase in a specified amount or proportion as a condition to the extension of credit except:

(i) An escrow account under paragraph (e)(3) of § 226.4,

(ii) A deposit balance which will be wholly applied toward satisfaction of the customer's obligation in the transaction,

(iii) A deposit balance or investment which was in existence prior to the extension of credit and which is offered by the customer as security for that extension of credit, and

(iv) A deposit balance or investment which was acquired or established from the proceeds of an extension of credit made for that purpose upon written request of the customer.

(f) **First lien to finance construction of dwelling.** In any case where a first lien or equivalent security interest in real property is retained or acquired by a creditor in connection with the financing of the initial construction of a dwelling, or in connection with a loan to satisfy that construction loan and provide permanent financing of that dwelling, whether or not the customer previously owned the land on which that dwelling is to be constructed, such security interest shall be considered a first lien against that dwelling to finance the purchase of that dwelling.

(g) **Orders by mail or telephone.** If a creditor receives a purchase order or a request for an extension of credit by mail, telephone, or written communication without personal solicitation, the disclosures required under this section may be made any time not later than the date the first payment is due, provided:

(1) In the case of credit sales, the cash price, the downpayment, the finance charge, the deferred payment price, the annual percentage rate, and the number, frequency, and amount of payments are set forth in or are determinable from the creditor's catalog or other printed material distributed to the public; or

(2) In the case of loans or other extensions of credit, the amount of the loan, the finance charge, the total scheduled payments, the number, frequency, and amount of payments, and the annual percentage rate for representative amounts or ranges of credit are set forth in or are determinable from the creditor's printed material distributed to the public, in the contract of loan, or in other printed material delivered or made available to the customer.

(h) **Series of sales.** If a credit sale is one of a series of transactions made pursuant to an agreement providing for the addition of the amount financed plus the finance charge for the current sale to an existing outstanding balance, then the disclosures required under this section for the current sale may be made at any time not later than the date the first payment for that sale is due, provided:

(1) The customer has approved in writing both the annual percentage rate or rates and the method of treating any unearned finance charge on an existing outstanding balance in computing the finance charge or charges; and

(2) The creditor retains no security interest in any property as to which he has received payments aggregating the amount of the sale price including any finance charges attributable thereto. For the purposes of this subparagraph, in the case of items purchased on different dates, the first purchased shall be deemed first paid for, and in the case of items purchased on the same date, the lowest priced shall be deemed first paid for.

(i) **Advances under loan commitments.** If a loan is one of a series of advances made pursuant to a written agreement under which a creditor is or may be committed to extend credit to a customer up to a specified amount, and the customer has approved in writing the annual percentage rate or rates, the method of computing the finance charge or charges, and any other terms, the agreement shall be considered a single transaction, and the disclosures required under this section at the creditor's option need be made only at the time the agreement is executed.

(j) **Refinancing, consolidating, or increasing.** If any existing extension of credit is refinanced, or two or more existing extensions of credit are consolidated, or an existing obligation is increased, such transaction shall be considered a new transaction subject to the disclosure requirements of this Part. For the purpose of such disclosure, any unearned portion of the finance charge which is not credited to the existing obligation shall be added to the new finance charge and shall not be included in the new amount financed. Any increase in an existing obligation to reimburse the creditor for undertaking the customer's obligation in perfecting, protecting or preserving the security shall not be considered a new transaction subject to this Part. Any advance for agricultural purposes made under an open end real estate mortgage or similar lien shall not be considered a new transaction subject to the disclosure requirements of this section, provided:

(1) The maturity of the advance does not exceed 2 years;

(2) No increase is made in the annual percentage rate previously disclosed; and

(3) All disclosures required by this Part were made at the time the security interest was acquired by the creditor or at any time prior to the first advance made on or following the effective date of this Part.

(k) **Assumption of an obligation.** Any creditor who accepts a subsequent customer as an obligor under an existing obligation shall make the disclosures required by this Part to that customer before he becomes so obligated. If the obligation so assumed is secured by a first lien or equivalent security interest on a dwelling, and the assumption is made for the subsequent customer to acquire that dwelling, that obligation shall be considered a loan made to finance the purchase of that dwelling.

(l) **Deferrals or extensions.** In the case of an obligation other than an obligation upon which the amount of the finance charge is determined by the application of a percentage rate to the unpaid balance, if the creditor imposes a charge or fee for deferral or extension, the creditor shall disclose to the customer

(1) The amount deferred or extended;

(2) The date to which, or the time period for which payment is deferred or extended; and

(3) The amount of the charge or fee for the deferral or extension.

(m) **Series of single payment obligations.** Any extension of credit involving a series of single payment obligations shall be considered a single transaction subject to the disclosure requirements of this Part.

(n) **Periodic statements.** (1) If a creditor transmits a periodic billing statement [13] other than a delinquency notice, payment coupon book, or payment passbook, or a statement, billing, or advice relating exclusively to amounts to be paid by the customer as escrows for payment of taxes, insurance, and water, sewer, and land rents, it shall be in a form which the customer may retain and shall set forth:

(i) The annual percentage rate or rates unless exempted by § 226.8(b)(2), and

(ii) The date by which, or the period, if any, within which payment must be made in order to avoid late payment or delinquency charges.

(2) If the creditor is required to send a periodic statement under paragraph (q) of this section, the requirements of § 226.7(b)(1)(i), (ii), (iii), (ix), and (x), and § 226.7(b)(2) shall be met, as applicable, in addition to the disclosures required by this paragraph.

(o) **Discount for prompt payment of sales transactions.** (1) For the purposes of this paragraph, a "transaction subject to § 226.8(o)" is a credit sale transaction which is not exempt under § 226.3 and which is subject to a discount for payment on or before a specified date (e.g., 2% discount if paid within 10 days) or to a charge for delaying payment after a specified date (e.g. $98 cash, $100 if paid in 30 days). Both such a discount and such a charge are referred to in this paragraph as a "discount." In the case of any transaction subject to § 226.8(o), notwithstanding the provisions of the last sentence of paragraph (a) of this section, the creditor shall disclose on the invoice or other evidence of such sale, as applicable:

(i) The date of the sale or invoice.

(ii) The rate of discount, the date by which or period within which the discount may be taken, and the date by which or period within which the full amount of the obligation is due and payable. (For example, "2%/10 days, net 30 days"; or "$1 per ton/10 days, net 30 days.")

(iii) The information required under § 226.8 (b)(4) and (5).

(iv) The amount of the discount, designated as a "finance charge," using that term.

(v) If the discount shown for prompt payment exceeds 5% of the obligation to which the discount relates, the "annual percentage rate," using that term, computed in accordance with subparagraph (2) of this paragraph, but subject to the exceptions provided under § 226.8(b)(2).

(2) For the purposes of subparagraph (1)(v) of this paragraph, the annual percentage rate shall be determined by dividing the amount of the finance charge by the least amount payable in

[13] Any statement, notice, or reminder of payment due on any transaction payable in instalments which is mailed or delivered periodically to the customer in advance of the due date of the instalment shall be a periodic billing statement for the purpose of this paragraph.

satisfaction of the obligation and multiplying the quotient (expressed as a percentage) by a fraction in which the numerator is 12, and the denominator is the number of whole months (but not less than 1) between the first day of the monthly billing cycle in which the transaction is consummated and the first day of the monthly billing cycle in which the obligation becomes due.[13a]

(3) In a transaction with multiple discount rates (e.g., 6%/10 days, 4%/20 days, net 30 days), the largest discount shall be used for purposes of disclosing the amount of the finance charge under subparagraph (1)(iv) of this paragraph and the annual percentage rate under subparagraph (1)(v) of this paragraph.[13b]

(4) In order to determine the applicability of subparagraph (1)(v) of this paragraph and to facilitate disclosure of an annual percentage rate, if the amount of the discount for prompt payment is related, pursuant to usual business practice, to weight, quantity, or other physical measure (e.g., $1 per ton or 1¢ per gallon) rather than expressed as a percentage of discount, that discount may be converted to an approximate discount rate and, under subparagraph (2) of this paragraph, a reasonably accurate approximation of the annual percentage rate by using approximate or projected prices per physical unit determined on the basis of past experience, current information, or projected analysis.[13c]

(5) If by its terms a transaction subject to § 226.8(o) is payable in a single payment and no finance charge other than a discount is or may be imposed, and such discount is not utilized for the purpose of circumvention or evasion of disclosure requirements, the disclosure required by subparagraph (1) of this paragraph shall constitute compliance with the requirements of § 226.8 and under § 226.9(a) shall constitute "all other material disclosures required under this Part."

(6) If a transaction subject to § 226.8(o) is debited to an open end credit account, disclosures shall be made as specified in paragraph (1) of this section and also as specified in § 226.7. The full amount of the obligation including the amount of the discount may be debited to the open end credit account, under § 226.7(b)(1)(ii), and the amount of any finance charge representing the discount need not be added to any other finance charge for the purpose of computing and disclosing the total amount of finance charge and the annual percentage rate under § 226.5(a) and § 226.7.[13d]

(7) If a transaction subject to § 226.8(o) is not debited to an open end credit account, but either is subject to an additional finance charge or is payable by its terms in more than one payment, disclosures shall be made as specified in subparagraph (1) of this paragraph and also as specified in paragraphs (b) and (c) of this section. In such a case, if the transaction is payable in more than one payment, the amount of the discount shall be deducted for the purpose of computing and disclosing the cash price under paragraph (c)(1) of this section and shall be added to any other finance charge for the purpose of computing and disclosing the amount of the finance charge under paragraph (c)(8)(i) of this section and the annual percentage rate under paragraph (b)(2) of this section.[13e] If the transaction is payable in a single payment, the discount may be disregarded in computing and disclosing such cash price, finance charge, and annual percentage rate.[13f]

[13a] For example, a $1,000 purchase of feed subject to terms of 6%/10 days, net 30 days (or 6%/10 days, net E.O.M.; or 6%/10 days, net 10th of the following month; or 6%/20 days, net 30 days; or 6%/30 days, net 30 days; or 6% discount for cash, net 30 days) results in a finance charge of $60, a least amount payable of $940, and an annual percentage rate of 76.56%, which may be rounded to 76.50% or 76½%. Terms of 6%/20 days, net September 29 applied to an April purchase, assuming a calendar month billing cycle, result in an annual percentage rate of 15.31% (i.e., 6/94 × 12/5) which may be rounded to 15.25% or 15¼%. In this example the 29 days in September are ignored and the denominator (5) is determined by the number of whole months in the period.

[13b] For example, terms of 6%/10 days, 4%/20 days, net 30 days would be treated like terms of 6%/10 days, net 30 days, which would represent an annual percentage rate of 76½%.

[13c] For example, if terms of $3 discount per ton/10 days, net 30 days are offered on fertilizer that is expected to sell in a range of about $48 to $52 per ton, the annual percentage rate could be approximated for preprinting as if it were 6% (i.e., $3 on $50)/10 days, net 30 days, that is, 76½%.

[13d] For example, if a $1,000 sale on terms of 2%/10 days, net 30 days, is debited to an open end account on which 1% per month is charged, the periodic statement under § 226.7(b) (assuming no other transactions in the account) would show a previous balance of $1,000, a finance charge of $10, and an annual percentage rate of 12%.

[13e] For example, if a $1,000 sale on terms of 2%/10 days, net 30 days is subject to an add-on finance charge of $100 and is payable in instalments, the disclosures under § 226.8(b) and (c) would include a cash price of $980 and a finance charge of $120.

[13f] For example, if a $1,000 sale on August 2 not under an open end account is subject to terms of 2%/10 days, net 30 days, thereafter 8% per annum until De-

(8) Notwithstanding the provisions of the second sentence of paragraph (a) of this section, the disclosures required under subparagraph (1) of this paragraph made on the invoice or other evidence of the sale may be delivered subsequent to consummation of the transaction.

(9) Amended paragraph (o) of § 226.8 shall become effective August 11, 1969, but until March 1, 1970, any creditor may at his option use any printed forms which were prepared before such effective date in accordance with paragraph (o) of § 226.8 in effect at the time of such preparation.

(p) **Agricultural credit—information not determinable.** (1) In any transaction subject to this section, if the amount or date of any advance or payment in connection with an extension of credit for agricultural purposes under a written agreement is to be determined by production, seasonal needs, or similar operational factors, and is not determinable at the time of execution of the agreement, disclosures may be made at the creditor's option in accordance with this paragraph, provided the use of this paragraph is not for the purpose of circumvention or evasion of this Part.

(2) If a creditor elects to make disclosures under this paragraph, he shall disclose the following items in accordance with § 226.8(a), which shall constitute compliance with the requirements of § 226.8, and under § 226.9(a) shall constitute "all other material disclosures required under this Part":

(i) The method of computing the amount of the finance charge including an identification of each component thereof in accordance with § 226.4;

(ii) Any item required to be disclosed under § 226.8(b)(3) which is determinable at the time the disclosures are required to be made under this paragraph;

(iii) The disclosures, as applicable, required under § 226.8(b)(4), (5), (6), and (7) and the items described in § 226.8(e)(1) and (2); and

(iv) The disclosures, as applicable, required under § 226.8(o)(1), (2), (3), (4), (5), (8), and (9).

(3) Disclosures made pursuant to subparagraph (2)(i), (ii), and (iii) of this paragraph need be made only on the agreement or on a separate statement as specified in § 226.8(a).

cember 1, the disclosures under § 226.8(b) and (c) would include a cash price of $1,000, a finance charge of $19.95, and an annual percentage rate of 8.00%.

(4) If a creditor making disclosures pursuant to this paragraph transmits a periodic billing statement of the type described in paragraph (n) of § 226.8, such statement shall be in a form which the customer may retain and shall set forth the date by which, or the period, if any, within which payment must be made in order to avoid late payment or delinquency charges.

(q) **Credit card accounts.** In addition to the requirements of this section, consumer credit other than open end which is extended on an account by use of a credit card shall also be subject to the requirements of §§ 226.7(a)(6), (7), (8), and (9); 226.7(b)(1)(i), (ii), (iii), (ix), and (x); 226.7(b)(2); 226.7(c), (d), (g), (h), and (i); 226.13(i), (j), and (k); and 226.14.

SECTION 226.9—RIGHT TO RESCIND CERTAIN TRANSACTIONS

(a) **General rule.** Except as otherwise provided in this section, in the case of any credit transaction in which a security interest is or will be retained or acquired in any real property which is used or is expected to be used as the principal residence of the customer, the customer shall have the right to rescind that transaction until midnight of the third business day[14] following the date of consummation of that transaction or the date of delivery of the disclosures required under this section and all other material disclosures required under this Part, whichever is later, by notifying the creditor by mail, telegram, or other writing of his intention to do so. Notification by mail shall be considered given at the time mailed; notification by telegram shall be considered given at the time filed for transmission; and notification by other writing shall be considered given at the time delivered to the creditor's designated place of business.

(b) **Notice of opportunity to rescind.** Whenever a customer has the right to rescind a transaction under paragraph (a) of this section, the creditor shall give notice of that fact to the customer by furnishing the customer with two copies of the notice set out below, one of which may be used by the customer to cancel the transaction.

[14] For the purpose of this section, a business day is any calendar day except Sunday and those legal public holidays specified in Section 6103(a) of Title 5 of the United States Code (New Year's Day, Washington's Birthday, Memorial Day, Independence Day, Labor Day, Columbus Day, Veterans Day, Thanksgiving Day and Christmas Day).

Such notice shall be printed in capital and lower case letters of not less than 12 point bold-faced type on one side of a separate statement which identifies the transaction to which it relates. Such statement shall also set forth the entire paragraph (d) of this section, "Effect of rescission." If such paragraph appears on the reverse side of the statement, the face of the statement shall state: "See reverse side for important information about your right of rescission." Before furnishing copies of the notice to the customer, the creditor shall complete both copies with the name of the creditor, the address of the creditor's place of business, the date of consummation of the transaction, and the date, not earlier than the third business day following the date of the transaction, by which the customer may give notice of cancellation. Where the real property on which the security interest may arise does not include a dwelling, the creditor may substitute the words "the property you are purchasing" for "your home," or "lot" for "home," where these words appear in the notice.

Notice to customer required by Federal law:

You have entered into a transaction on (date) **which may result in a lien, mortgage, or other security interest on your home. You have a legal right under Federal law to cancel this transaction, if you desire to do so, without any penalty or obligation within three business days from the above date or any later date on which all material disclosures required under the Truth in Lending Act have been given to you. If you so cancel the transaction, any lien, mortgage, or other security interest on your home arising from this transaction is automatically void. You are also entitled to receive a refund of any downpayment or other consideration if you cancel. If you decide to cancel this transaction, you may do so by notifying**

(Name of creditor)

at (Address of creditor's place of business) **by mail or telegram sent not later than midnight of** (date) **You may also use any other form of written notice identifying the transaction if it is delivered to the above address not later than that time. This notice may be used for that purpose by dating and signing below.**

I hereby cancel this transaction.

(date) (customer's signature)

(c) **Delay of performance.** Except as provided in paragraph (e) of this section, the creditor in any transaction subject to this section, other than an extension of credit primarily for agricultural purposes, shall not perform, or cause or permit the performance of, any of the following actions until after the rescission period has expired and he has reasonably satisfied himself that the customer has not exercised his right of rescission:

(1) Disburse any money other than in escrow;

(2) Make any physical changes in the property of the customer;

(3) Perform any work or service for the customer; or

(4) Make any deliveries to the residence of the customer if the creditor has retained or will acquire a security interest other than one arising by operation of law.

(d) **Effect of rescission.** When a customer exercises his right to rescind under paragraph (a) of this section, he is not liable for any finance or other charge, and any security interest becomes void upon such a rescission. Within 10 days after receipt of a notice of rescission, the creditor shall return to the customer any money or property given as earnest money, downpayment, or otherwise, and shall take any action necessary or appropriate to reflect the termination of any security interest created under the transaction. If the creditor has delivered any property to the customer, the customer may retain possession of it. Upon the performance of the creditor's obligations under this section, the customer shall tender the property to the creditor, except that if return of the property in kind would be impracticable or inequitable, the customer shall tender its reasonable value. Tender shall be made at the location of the property or at the residence of the customer, at the option of the customer. If the creditor does not take possession of the property within 10 days after tender by the customer, ownership of the property vests in the customer without obligation on his part to pay for it.

(e) **Waiver of right of rescission.** A customer may modify or waive his right to rescind a transaction subject to the provisions of this section provided:

(1) The extension of credit is needed in order to meet a bona fide immediate personal financial emergency of the customer;

(2) The customer has determined that a delay of 3 business days in performance of the credi-

tor's obligation under the transaction will jeopardize the welfare, health or safety of natural persons or endanger property which the customer owns or for which he is responsible; and

(3) The customer furnishes the creditor with a separate dated and signed personal statement describing the situation requiring immediate remedy and modifying or waiving his right of rescission. The use of printed forms for this purpose is prohibited.

(f) **Joint ownership.** For the purpose of this section, "customer" shall include two or more customers where joint ownership is involved, and the following shall apply:

(1) The right of rescission of the transaction may be exercised by any one of them, in which case the effect of rescission in accordance with paragraph (d) of this section applies to all of them; and

(2) Any waiver of the right of rescission provided in paragraph (e) of this section is invalid unless signed by all of them.

(g) **Exceptions to general rule.** This section does not apply to:

(1) The creation, retention, or assumption of a first lien or equivalent security interest to finance the acquisition of a dwelling in which the customer resides or expects to reside.

(2) A security interest which is a first lien retained or acquired by a creditor in connection with the financing of the initial construction of the residence of the customer, or in connection with a loan committed prior to completion of the construction of that residence to satisfy that construction loan and provide permanent financing of that residence, whether or not the customer previously owned the land on which that residence is to be constructed.

(3) Any lien by reason of its subordination at any time subsequent to its creation, if that lien was exempt from the provisions of this section when it was originally created.

(4) Any advance for agricultural purposes made pursuant to either:

(i) Paragraph (j) of § 226.8 under an open end real estate mortgage or similar lien, provided the disclosure required under paragraph (b) of this section was made at the time the security interest was acquired by the creditor or at any time prior to the first advance made on or following the effective date of this Part, or

(ii) Paragraph (p) of § 226.8 under a written agreement, provided the disclosure required under paragraph (b) of this section was made at the time the written agreement was executed by the customer.

(5) Any transaction in which an agency of a State is the creditor.

**(6) Individual transactions under an open end credit account; provided:

(i) That the creditor and the seller are not the same or related persons.[14a]

(ii) That the creditor provides the disclosure required by section 226.9(b) at the time the disclosures required under section 226.7 (a) are required to be made, or, if the security interest is not retained or acquired at the time the section 226.7(a) disclosures are required to be made, at the time the security interest is retained or acquired.

(iii) That the creditor does not change the terms of a customer's account within the meaning of section 226.7(f) or increase the customer's line of credit without affording the customer the opportunity to refuse the change in terms or the increase. If the customer refuses the change in terms, the creditor need not extend any further credit on the account; however, the customer shall have the right to repay any existing obligation on the account under the then existing terms of the account. At the time a disclosure of a change in terms under section 226.7(f) is required to be made or prior to an increase in the customer's line of credit, the creditor shall provide the customer with two copies of a disclosure setting forth, as applicable: the fact that the creditor intends to change the terms or increase the line of credit of the customer's account; the fact that the account is secured by the customer's real property; and the fact that the customer may refuse the change in terms and repay any existing obligation under the then existing terms of the account, or refuse the increase in the line of credit, by giving the creditor written notice within three business days of the date of the disclosure.

(iv) That at least once each calendar year the creditor furnishes to the customer a dis-

---

** Amended 8/3/78.

14a For purposes of section 226.9(g)(6) a person is related to a creditor if that person would be deemed related to the creditor under footnote 9b to section 226.7(k).

closure of the fact that the customer's account is secured by the customer's real property and that failure to pay any outstanding balance in accordance with the terms of the account could result in the loss of the customer's real property.

(v) That each disclosure provided pursuant hereto is made on one side of a statement separate from any other documents, that the disclosure sets forth the name of the creditor and, in the case of the disclosures required by subparagraph (iii) hereof, the creditor's address, the date on which the disclosure is furnished to the customer, the date by which the customer should give notice of refusal of the increase in the line of credit or the change in terms of the account, and the fact that one copy of the disclosure can be used for that purpose.

(h) **Time limit for unexpired right of rescission.** In the event the creditor fails to deliver to the customer the disclosures required by this section or the other material disclosures required by this Part, a customer's right to rescind a transaction pursuant to this section shall expire the earlier of (1) three years after the date of consummation of the transaction, or (2) the date the customer transfers all his interest, both equitable and legal, in the property.

SECTION 226.10—ADVERTISING CREDIT AND LEASE TERMS

* (a) **General rule.**

(1) No advertisement to aid, promote, or assist directly or indirectly any extension of credit may state

(i) That a specific amount of credit or instalment amount can be arranged unless the creditor usually and customarily arranges or will arrange credit amounts or instalments for that period and in that amount; or

(ii) That no downpayment or that a specified downpayment will be accepted in connection with any extension of credit, unless the creditor usually and customarily accepts or will accept downpayments in that amount.

(2) No advertisement to aid, promote, or assist directly or indirectly any consumer lease may state that a specific lease of any property at specific amounts or terms is available unless the lessor usually and customarily leases or will lease such property at those amounts or terms.

* (b) **Catalogs and multi-page advertisements.** If a catalog or other multiple-page advertisement sets forth or gives information in sufficient detail to permit determination of the disclosures required by this section in a table or schedule of credit or lease terms, such catalog or multiple-page advertisement shall be considered a single advertisement provided:

(1) The table or schedule and the disclosures made therein are set forth clearly and conspicuously; and

(2) Any statement of credit or lease terms appearing in any place other than in that table or schedule of credit or lease terms clearly and conspicuously refers to the page or pages on which that table or schedule appears, unless that statement discloses all of the credit or lease terms required to be stated under this section. For the purpose of this subparagraph, cash price is not a credit term.

(c) **Advertising of open end credit.** No advertisement to aid, promote, or assist directly or indirectly the extension of open end credit may set forth any of the terms described in paragraph (a) of § 226.7, the Comparative Index of Credit Cost, or that a specified downpayment or periodic payment is required (either in dollars or as a percentage), the period of repayment or any of the following items, unless it also clearly and conspicuously sets forth all the following items in terminology prescribed under paragraph (b) of § 226.7:

(1) An explanation of the time period, if any, within which any credit extended may be paid without incurring a finance charge;

(2) The method of determining the balance upon which a finance charge may be imposed;

(3) The method of determining the amount of the finance charge, including the determination of any minimum, fixed, check service, transaction, activity, or similar charge, which may be imposed as a finance charge; and

(4) Where one or more periodic rates may be used to compute the finance charge, each corresponding annual percentage rate determined by multiplying the periodic rate by the number of periods in a year and, where there is more than one corresponding annual percentage rate, the range of balances to which each is applicable.[15]

---

* Amended 3/23/77.

[15] A creditor imposing minimum charges is not required to adjust the disclosure of the range of balances to

(d) **Advertising of credit other than open end.** No advertisement to aid, promote, or assist directly or indirectly any credit sale including the sale of residential real estate, loan, or other extension of credit, other than open end credit, subject to the provisions of this Part, shall state

(1) The rate of the finance charge except as an "annual percentage rate," using that term. No other rate of finance charge may be stated, except that:

(i) Where the total finance charge includes, as a component, interest computed at a simple annual rate, the simple annual rate may be stated in conjunction with, but not more conspicuously than, the annual percentage rate, or

(ii) Where the finance charge is computed solely by the application of a periodic rate to an unpaid balance, the periodic rate may be stated in conjunction with, but not more conspicuously than, the annual percentage rate.

(2) That no downpayment is required, or the amount of the downpayment or of any instalment payment required (either in dollars or as a percentage), the dollar amount of any finance charge, the number of instalments or the period of repayment, or that there is no charge for credit, unless it also clearly and conspicuously sets forth all of the following items in terminology prescribed under § 226.8:

(i) The cash price or the amount of the loan, as applicable.

(ii) In a credit sale, the amount of the downpayment required or that no downpayment is required, as applicable.

(iii) The number, amount, and due dates or period of payments scheduled to repay the indebtedness if the credit is extended.

(iv) The amount of the finance charge expressed as an annual percentage rate. The exemptions from disclosure of an annual percentage rate permitted in paragraph (b)(2) of § 226.8 shall not apply to this subdivision.

(v) Except in the case of the sale of a dwelling or a loan secured by a first lien on a dwelling to purchase that dwelling, the deferred payment price in a credit sale, or the total of payments in a loan or other extension of credit which is not a credit sale, as applicable.

(e) **Advertising of FHA Section 235 financing.** Any advertisement to aid, promote, or assist directly or indirectly the sale of residential real estate under Title II, Section 235, of the National Housing Act (12 U.S.C. 1715z) shall clearly identify those credit terms which apply to the assistance program and, except as provided in this paragraph, comply with the provisions of paragraph (d) of this section. No such advertisement shall state:

(1) The amount of any payment scheduled to repay the indebtedness without stating the family size and income level applicable to that amount.

(2) Any rate of a finance charge, or the amount of the finance charge, expressed as an annual percentage rate based on the assistance. The annual percentage rate exclusive of the assistance may be stated, but is not required.

(f) **Credit payable in more than four instalments; no identified finance charge.** Any advertisement to aid, promote, or assist directly or indirectly an extension of consumer credit repayable by agreement in more than four instalments shall, unless a specific finance charge is or may be imposed, state clearly and conspicuously: "The cost of credit is included in the price quoted for the goods and services."

* (g) **Advertising of consumer leases.** No advertisement to aid, promote, or assist directly or indirectly any consumer lease shall state the amount of any payment, the number of required payments, or that any or no downpayment or other payment is required at consummation of the lease unless the advertisement also states clearly and conspicuously each of the following items of information as applicable:

(1) That the transaction advertised is a lease.

(2) The total amount of any payment such as a security deposit or capitalized cost reduction required at the consummation of the lease, or that no such payments are required.

(3) The number, amounts, due dates or periods of scheduled payments, and the total of such payments under the lease.

(4) A statement of whether or not the lessee has the option to purchase the lease property and at what price and time. The method of determining the price may be substituted for disclosure of the price.

---

which each rate would apply in order to reflect the range of the balances below which the minimum charge applies. If a creditor does not impose a finance charge when the outstanding balance is less than a certain amount, the creditor is not required to disclose that fact or the balance below which no such charge will be imposed.

* Added 3/23/77.

(5) A statement of the amount or method of determining the amount of any liabilities the lease imposes upon the lessee at the end of the term and a statement that the lessee shall be liable for the difference, if any, between the estimated value of the lease property and its realized value at the end of the lease term, if the lessee has such liability.

* (h) **Multiple item leases; merchandise tags.** If a merchandise tag for an item normally included in a multiple item lease sets forth information which would require additional disclosures under § 226.10(g), such merchandise tag need not contain such additional disclosures, provided it clearly and conspicuously refers to a sign or display which is prominently posted in the lessor's showroom. Such sign or display shall contain a table or schedule of those items of information to be disclosed under § 226.10(g).

SECTION 226.11—COMPARATIVE INDEX OF CREDIT COST FOR OPEN END CREDIT

(a) **General rule.** Any creditor who elects to disclose the Comparative Index of Credit Cost on open end credit accounts

(1) Shall compute the Comparative Index of Credit Cost in accordance with paragraph (b) of this section;

(2) Shall recompute the Comparative Index of Credit Cost in accordance with paragraph (b) of this section based upon any new open end credit account terms to be adopted and shall disclose the new Comparative Index of Credit Cost in accordance with paragraph (c)(2) of this section concurrently with the notice required under paragraph (f) of § 226.7;

(3) Shall, when making such disclosure under the provisions of paragraphs (a)(5) and (b)(1)(vii) of § 226.7, make the disclosure to all open end credit account customers; and

(4) Shall not utilize such disclosure so as to mislead or confuse the customer or contradict, obscure, or detract attention from the required disclosures.

(b) **Computation of Comparative Index of Credit Cost.** The Comparative Index of Credit Cost for each open end credit plan shall be computed by applying the creditor's terms of that plan to the following hypothetical factors:

(1) A single transaction in the amount of $100 is debited on the first day of a billing cycle to an open end credit account having no previous balance.

(2) The creditor imposes all finance charges including periodic, fixed, minimum or other charges applicable to such account in amounts and on dates consistent with his policy of imposing such charges upon open end credit accounts.

(3) The exact amount of the required minimum periodic payment is paid on the last day of each subsequent and successive billing cycle until the amount of the single transaction, together with applicable finance charges, is paid in full.

(4) The Comparative Index of Credit Cost shall be expressed and disclosed as a percentage accurate to the nearest quarter of 1 per cent and shall be determined by dividing the total amount of the finance charges imposed by the sum of the daily balances and multiplying the quotient so obtained (expressed as a percentage) by 365.

(c) **Form of disclosure.** Any creditor who elects to disclose the Comparative Index of Credit Cost shall:

(1) Make the disclosure in the form of the following statement: "Our Comparative Index of Credit Cost under the terms of our open end credit account plan is __% per year, computed on the basis of a single transaction of $100 debited on the first day of a billing cycle to an account having no previous balance, and paid in required minimum consecutive instalments on the last day of each succeeding billing cycle until the transaction and all finance charges are paid in full. The actual percentage cost of credit on your account may be higher or lower depending on the dates and amounts of charges and payments."

(2) Disclose any newly computed Comparative Index of Credit Cost in the form of the statement prescribed in subparagraph (1) of this paragraph, except that the statement shall be preceded by the words "Effective as of ____(date)____," and the words "will be" shall be substituted for the word "is" in the second line of the statement.

SECTION 226.12—EXEMPTION OF CERTAIN STATE REGULATED TRANSACTIONS

* (a) **Exemption for State regulated transactions.** In accordance with the provisions of Supplements

* Added 3/23/77.

* Amended 3/23/77.

II, IV, V, and VI to Regulation Z, any State may make application to the Board for exemption of any class of transactions within the State from the requirements of chapters 2, 4 or 5 of the Act and the corresponding provisions of this Part, Provided that:

(1) The Board determines that under the law of that State, that class of transactions is subject to requirements substantially similar to those imposed under chapter 2 or chapter 4 of the Act, or both, or under chapter 5, and the corresponding provisions of this Part; or in the case of chapter 4, the consumer is afforded greater protection than is afforded under chapter 4 of the Act, or in the case of chapter 5, the lessee is afforded greater protection and benefit than is afforded under chapter 5 of the Act, and

(2) There is adequate provision for enforcement.

** (b) **Procedures and criteria.** The procedures and criteria under which any State may apply for the determination provided for in paragraph (a) of this section are set forth in Supplement II to Regulation Z with respect to disclosure and rescission requirements (sections 121-131 of chapter 2), Supplement IV with respect to the prohibition of the issuance of unsolicited credit cards and the liability of the cardholder for unauthorized use of a credit card (sections 132-133 of chapter 2), in Supplement V with respect to fair credit billing requirements (sections 161-171 of chapter 4) and in Supplement VI with respect to consumer leasing (sections 181-186 of chapter 5).

(c) **Civil liability.** In order to assure that the concurrent jurisdiction of Federal and State courts created in section 130(e) of the Act shall continue to have substantive provisions to which such jurisdiction shall apply, and generally to aid in implementing the Act with respect to any class of transactions exempted pursuant to paragraph (a) of this section and Supplement II, the Board pursuant to sections 105 and 123 hereby prescribes that:

(1) No such exemptions shall be deemed to extend to the civil liability provisions of sections 130 and 131; and

(2) After an exemption has been granted, the disclosure requirements of the applicable State law shall constitute the disclosure requirements of this Act, except to the extent that such State law imposes disclosure requirements not imposed by this Act. Information required under such State law with the exception of those provisions which impose disclosure requirements not imposed by this Act shall, accordingly, constitute the "information required under this chapter" (chapter 2 of the Act) for the purpose of section 130(a).

(d) **Exemptions granted.** Exemptions granted by the Board to particular classes of credit transactions within specified States are set forth in Supplement III to Regulation Z.

SECTION 226.13—CREDIT CARD TRANSACTIONS—SPECIAL REQUIREMENTS

(a) **Issuance of credit cards.** Regardless of whether a credit card is to be used for personal, family, household, agricultural, business, or commercial purposes, no credit card shall be issued to any person except:

(1) In response to a request or application therefor, or

(2) As a renewal of, or in substitution for, an accepted credit card whether such card is issued by the same or a successor card issuer.

(b) **Conditions of liability of cardholder.** A cardholder shall be liable for unauthorized use of each credit card issued only if

(1) The credit card is an accepted credit card;

(2) Such liability does not exceed the lesser of $50 or the amount of money, property, labor, or services obtained by such use prior to notification of the card issuer pursuant to paragraph (e) of this section;

(3) The card issuer has given adequate notice to the cardholder of his potential liability on the credit card or within 2 years preceding the unauthorized use; and

(4) The card issuer has provided the cardholder with an addressed notification requiring no postage to be paid by the cardholder which may be mailed by the cardholder in the event of the loss, theft, or possible unauthorized use of the credit card.

(c) **Other conditions of liability.** In addition to the conditions of liability in paragraph (b) of this section, no cardholder shall be liable for the unauthorized use of any credit card which was issued after January 24, 1971, and, regardless of the date of its issuance, after January 24, 1972, no cardholder shall be liable for the unauthorized use of any credit card, unless the card issuer has

** Amended 3/23/77.

provided a method whereby the user of such card can be identified as the person authorized to use it, such as by signature, photograph, or fingerprint on the credit card or by electronic or mechanical confirmation.

(d) **Notice to cardholder.** The notice to cardholder pursuant to paragraph (b)(3) of this section may be given by printing the notice on the credit card, or by any other means reasonably assuring the receipt thereof by the cardholder. An acceptable form of notice must state that liability shall not exceed $50 (or any lesser amount), that notice of loss, theft, or possible unauthorized use may be given orally or in writing, and the name and address of the party to receive the notice. It may include any additional information which is not inconsistent with the provisions of this section. An example of an acceptable notice is as follows:

"You may be liable for the unauthorized use of your credit card [*or other term which describes the credit device*]. You will not be liable for unauthorized use which occurs after you notify [*name of card issuer or his designee*] at [*address*] orally or in writing of loss, theft, or possible unauthorized use. In any case liability shall not exceed [*insert $50 or any lesser amount under other applicable law or under any agreement with the cardholder*]."

(e) **Notice to card issuer.** For the purposes of this section, a cardholder notifies a card issuer by taking such steps as may be reasonably required in the ordinary course of business to provide the card issuer with the pertinent information with respect to loss, theft, or possible unauthorized use of any credit card, whether or not any particular officer, employee, or agent of the card issuer does, in fact, receive such notice or information. Irrespective of the form of notice provided under paragraph (b)(4) of this section, at the option of the cardholder, notice may be given to the card issuer or his designee in person or by telephone or by letter, telegram, radiogram, cablegram, or other written communication which sets forth the pertinent information. Notice by mail, telegram, radiogram, cablegram, or other written communication shall be considered given at the time of receipt or, whether or not received, at the expiration of the time ordinarily required for transmission, whichever is earlier.

(f) **Action to enforce liability.** In any action by a card issuer to enforce liability for the use of a credit card, the burden of proof is upon the card issuer to show that the use was authorized or, if the use was unauthorized, then the burden of proof is upon the card issuer to show that the conditions of liability for the unauthorized use of a credit card, as set forth in paragraphs (b) and (c) of this section, have been met.

(g) **Effect on other applicable law or agreement.** Nothing in this section imposes liability upon a cardholder for the unauthorized use of a credit card in excess of his liability for such use under other applicable law or under any agreement with the card issuer.

(h) **Business use of credit cards.** If 10 or more credit cards are issued by one card issuer for use by the employees of a single business or other organization, nothing in this section prohibits the card issuer from agreeing by contract with such business or other organization as to liability for unauthorized use of any such credit cards without regard to the provisions of this section, but in no case may any business or other organization or card issuer impose liability on any employee of such business or other organization with respect to unauthorized use of such credit card except in accordance with and subject to the other liability limitations of this section.

(i) **Right of cardholder to assert claims or defenses against card issuer.** (1) When a person who provides property or services fails to satisfactorily resolve a dispute as to property or services purchased by use of a credit card in connection with a consumer credit transaction, the cardholder may assert all claims (other than tort claims) and defenses arising out of the transaction and relating to such failure against the card issuer, and the cardholder may withhold payment up to the amount of credit outstanding with respect to the property or services which gave rise to the dispute and any finance charges, late payment charges, or other charges imposed on that amount if:

(i) The cardholder has made a good faith attempt to obtain satisfactory resolution of the disagreement or problem relating to the transaction from the person honoring the credit card;

(ii) The amount of credit extended by the card issuer to the cardholder to obtain the property or services which resulted in the assertion of the claim(s) or defense(s) by the cardholder exceeds $50; and

(iii) The initial transaction which gave rise to the assertion of the claim(s) or defense(s) by the cardholder occurred in the same State as the cardholder's current designated address or, if not within the State of the cardholder's address, within 100 miles from such address, except that the limitations stated in paragraphs (ii) and (iii) of this section shall not apply when the person honoring the credit card:

(A) Is the same person as the card issuer, or

(B) Is controlled, directly or indirectly, by the card issuer, or

(C) Is under the direct or indirect control of a third person who also directly or indirectly controls the card issuer, or

(D) Controls, directly or indirectly, the card issuer, or

(E) Is a franchised dealer in the card issuer's products or services, or

(F) Has obtained the order for the transaction, relative to which the claim(s) or defense(s) is asserted, through a mail solicitation made by or participated in by the card issuer, in which the cardholder is solicited to enter into such transaction by using the credit card issued by the card issuer.

Simply honoring or indicating that a person honors a particular credit card is not any of the relationships described in paragraphs (A) through (F) for the purpose of removing the dollar and distance limitations.

(2) The amount of the claim(s) or defense(s) assertable by the cardholder under this section may not exceed the amount of credit outstanding with respect to the transaction which gave rise to the assertion of the claim(s) or defense(s) at the time the cardholder first notifies the card issuer or the person honoring the credit card for such transaction of the existence of such claim(s) or defense(s). For purposes of determining the amount of credit outstanding with respect to such transactions as provided in the preceding sentence, payments and other credits to the cardholder's account will be deemed to have been applied in the order indicated to the payment of:

(i) Late charges in the order of entry to the account,

(ii) Finance charges in the order of entry to the account,

(iii) Any other debits in the order in which each debit entry was made to the account, and

(iv) When more than one item is included in a single extension of credit, credits are to be distributed pro rata according to prices and applicable taxes.

(3) This section does not apply to cash advances obtained with a credit card when the advance is unrelated to any specific credit sale item.

*(4) If the cardholder refuses to pay the amount of credit outstanding with respect to the property or services which gave rise to the claim(s) or defense(s) under this section, the creditor may not report to any person that particular amount as delinquent until the dispute is settled or judgment is rendered.[15a]

(j) **Prohibition of offsets by card issuer.** (1) A card issuer may not take any action to offset a cardholder's indebtedness arising in connection with a consumer credit transaction under the relevant credit card plan against funds of the cardholder held on deposit with the card issuer unless a court order[16] is obtained.

(2) The prohibition in paragraph (j)(1) of this section does not apply to credit card plans in which the cardholder authorizes the card issuer as a method of payment to periodically deduct all or a portion of the cardholder's credit card debt from his deposit account with the card issuer (subject to the limitations in § 226.14(c)), Provided that:

(i) Such automatic debit was previously authorized in writing by the cardholder, or

(ii) With respect to such automatic debit accounts in existence on October 28, 1975, the card issuer has given notice of the provisions of paragraph (j) of this section to such accounts prior to renewal of the authorization (in no case later than October 28, 1976).

(k) **Prompt notification of returns.** (1) When any creditor other than the card issuer accepts the return of property or forgives a debt for services which is to be reflected as a credit to the customer's open end credit card account, he shall promptly (in no case later than 7 business days from the date the return is accepted) transmit a statement with respect thereto to the card issuer through the normal channels established by the card issuer for the transmittal of such statements.

(2) Upon receipt of a credit statement, the card issuer shall credit the customer's account promptly (in no case later than 3 business days

* Amended 8/27/76.

[15a] Nothing in this paragraph prohibits a creditor from reporting the disputed amount or account as being in dispute.

[16] This paragraph does not alter or affect the right of a card issuer acting under State law to attach or otherwise levy upon funds of a cardholder held on deposit with the card issuer if that remedy is constitutionally available to creditors generally.

from receipt of the refund statement) with the amount of the refund.

(3) If it is a creditor's (other than a card issuer) policy to give cash refunds to cash customers, he must also give credit or cash refunds to credit card customers, unless he clearly and conspicuously discloses that he does not give credit or cash refunds for returns at the time the transaction is consummated. Nothing in this section shall be construed to require that a creditor give refunds for returns nor shall it be construed to prohibit refunds in kind.

*(l) **Prohibited acts of card issuers.** (1) No card issuer may, by contract or otherwise:

(i) Prohibit any person from offering any discounts to all customers of such person, including cardholder customers, to induce such customers to pay by cash, check, or similar means rather than by use of a credit card or its underlying account for the purchase of property or services, or

(ii) Require any person who honors the card issuer's credit card to open or maintain a deposit account or procure any other service not essential to the operation of the credit card plan from the card issuer, its subsidiary, agent, or any other person, as a condition of participation in a credit card plan.

(2) Within 30 days of the effective date of these regulations, any card issuer with existing contracts which include either one or both of the restrictive clauses prohibited in paragraph (1) shall inform all parties to the contract that such provisions are inapplicable and no longer enforceable.

SECTION 226.14—BILLING ERRORS—RESOLUTION PROCEDURE

(a) **Correction of billing errors.** After the creditor receives proper written notification of a billing error, unless the customer has subsequently agreed that the periodic statement is correct, the creditor shall:

(1) Not later than 30 days after receipt of such notification, mail or deliver written acknowledgment thereof to the customer's current designated address, unless the appropriate actions in paragraph (2) of this section are taken within such 30 day period; and

(2) Resolve the dispute not later than 2 complete billing cycles (in no event more than 90 days) from the date of receipt of the notice of billing error and prior to any action by the creditor to collect[17] any portion of the amount(s) indicated by the customer as being a billing error or any finance charges, late payment charges, or other charges computed on such disputed amount(s) by:

(i) Correcting the customer's account in the full amount indicated by the customer to have been erroneously billed in accordance with paragraph (b)(2) of this section and mailing or delivering to the customer a written notification of corrections;[18] or

(ii) Correcting the customer's account by a differing amount from that indicated by the customer as being erroneously billed in accordance with paragraph (b)(2) of this section and mailing or delivering to the customer an explanation of the change(s), accompanied by copies of documentary evidence of the customer's indebtedness if such evidence is requested by the customer; or

(iii) Mailing or delivering a written explanation or clarification to the customer, after having conducted a reasonable investigation, setting forth, to the extent applicable, the reasons why the creditor believes the amount(s) was correctly shown on the periodic statement and, if the customer so requests, furnishing copies of documentary evidence of the customer's indebtedness with respect to the alleged billing error(s). In any case where the customer alleges that the periodic statement reflects property or services not delivered to the customer or his designee in accordance with any agreement made in connection with the transaction giving rise to the disputed amount, a creditor may not construe such amount to be correctly shown on the periodic statement unless the creditor determines, upon reasonable investigation, that such property or services were actually delivered, mailed, or otherwise sent to the customer or his designee and provides the customer with a written statement explaining such determination. In any case where

* Amended 7/21/77.

[17] If, despite the establishment by the creditor of procedures reasonably adapted to assure compliance with this paragraph, the creditor or his agent, within 2 business days after receiving proper written notification of a billing error pursuant to this section, inadvertently takes action to collect in contravention of this paragraph, such inadvertent action to collect will not be considered in violation of this paragraph.

[18] A notice on a subsequent billing statement clearly identifying any amount credited to the customer's account in response to a proper written notification of a billing error is one type of a proper transmittal of a written notification of corrections.

the customer alleges that an amount of a transaction reflected on the periodic statement is incorrect because the person honoring the credit card has made an incorrect report to the card issuer of the amount which should have been charged, the card issuer may not construe such amount to be correctly reflected on the periodic statement unless the creditor determines, upon reasonable investigation, that the correct amount is shown on the periodic statement and provides the customer with a written statement explaining such determination.

After complying with the provisions of this section with respect to an alleged billing error, a creditor has no further responsibility under this section if the customer continues to make substantially the same allegation with respect to such error.

(b) **Minimum periodic payments and finance charges on disputed amounts.** (1) When a minimum periodic payment is permitted, the customer may withhold that portion of the minimum periodic payment which the customer believes is related to the amount in dispute. When the disputed amount is only a part of the total amount of an item, the customer remains obligated to pay the amount not in dispute, and any minimum periodic payment and finance charges, late payment charges, or other charges may be collected on the undisputed amount. If, at the completion of the error resolution procedure, it is determined that the customer owes some or all of the disputed amount, the creditor may require payment of any minimum periodic payment amounts which the customer did not pay because of the dispute. The creditor may not, however, accelerate the customer's entire debt solely because the customer has exercised rights provided by the Act or this Part.

(2) With respect to an erroneous billing, the creditor must credit the customer's account in any amount the customer does not owe, plus any finance charges, late payment charges, or other charges imposed as a result of the erroneous billing. An erroneous billing by a creditor includes, but is not limited to, a misidentification, insufficient identification, or incorrect date of a transaction; a mailing of the periodic statement to other than the current designated address; improper crediting of payments or other credits; computation errors; or a billing for property or services not accepted or delivered in accordance with any agreement; as well as mistakes in dollar amounts.

(3) After or upon completion of the dispute resolution procedure prescribed by § 226.14(a):

(i) If the initial periodic statement is determined to be without error with regard to the disputed item, the creditor shall promptly mail or deliver to the customer written notification of the amount owed with regard to the disputed item, unless such notification is not required by paragraph (a) of this section, or

(ii) If the initial periodic statement is determined to be in error with regard to the disputed item and the creditor normally allows a period for the customer to pay such an item without incurring additional finance charges, late payment charges, or other charges, the creditor shall mail or deliver to the customer written notification of the total amount which the customer owes with regard to the disputed item and shall allow the customer the same number of days thereafter as he customarily or by credit agreement allows, whichever is longer (in no case less than 10 days), for the customer to pay undisputed amounts in accordance with § 226.7(b)(2), or

(iii) If the initial periodic statement is determined to be in error with regard to the disputed item and the creditor normally does not allow a period for the customer to pay such an item without incurring additional finance charges, late payment charges, or other charges, the creditor shall promptly mail or deliver to the customer a notice of the total amount which the customer owes with regard to the disputed item.

(4) Nothing in this section shall be construed to prohibit the mailing or delivery of periodic statements, which include disputed amounts, to the customer, provided that the creditor indicates on the face of the periodic statement that payment of the amount in dispute is not required pending the creditor's compliance with the provisions of this section.

(5) Nothing in this section shall prohibit any action by a creditor to collect any amount which has not been indicated by the customer to contain a billing error.

(c) **Automatic debit of disputed amounts.** (1) In the case of credit card plans where the cardholder has agreed to permit the card issuer to periodically pay the cardholder's indebtedness by deducting the appropriate amount from the cardholder's deposit account held by the card issuer, if the card issuer receives a proper written notification of a billing error within 16 days from the date of mailing or delivery of the periodic statement on which the suspected billing error first appears, the card issuer shall:

(i) Prevent the automatic debiting of any disputed amounts if receipt of such notification precedes the automatic debiting of the cardholder's account, or

(ii) Promptly (in no case more than 2 business days after receipt of the notice) restore to the cardholder's deposit account any portion of the disputed amount which was previously deducted, if receipt of such notification follows the automatic debiting of the cardholder's account for any disputed amounts.

(2) Nothing in this paragraph shall limit the cardholder's right to dispute an amount he believes to be in error within 60 days of the mailing or delivery of the erroneous periodic statement, as otherwise provided in this section.

(d) **Closing of accounts.** A creditor may not, prior to complying with the requirements of paragraphs (a) and (b) of this section, restrict or close an account with respect to which the customer has indicated a belief that such account contains a billing error solely because of the customer's refusal or failure to pay the amount indicated to be in error. This paragraph does not prohibit the creditor from applying any such amount to the customer's credit limitations.

(e) **Credit reports on amounts in dispute.** (1) After receiving a proper written notification of a billing error pursuant to this section, neither the creditor nor his agent may directly or indirectly threaten to report adversely to any person on the customer's credit standing or credit rating because of the customer's failure to pay the amount specified in such notification as being a billing error, or any finance charges, late payment charges, or other charges imposed thereon, nor shall such amount be reported as delinquent[19] to any third person unless such amount remains unpaid after the creditor has complied with all the requirements of this section and has allowed that customer the same number of days thereafter to pay as he customarily or by credit agreement allows, whichever is longer (in no case less than 10 days), for the customer to pay undisputed amounts so as to avoid the imposition of additional finance charges, late payment charges, or other charges. If, despite establishment by the creditor of procedures reasonably adapted to assure compliance with this paragraph, the creditor or his agent, within 2 business days after receiving proper written notification of a billing error pursuant to this section, inadvertently takes action in contravention of this paragraph, such inadvertent action will not be considered in violation of this paragraph.

(2) If, within the time limit allowed for payment in paragraph (e)(1) of this section, the creditor receives a further written notification from the customer that any portion of a billing error resolved under paragraph (a) of this section is still in dispute, the creditor may not report to any third party that such disputed amount is delinquent unless the creditor also reports that the amount or account is in dispute and, at the same time, notifies the customer in writing of the name and address of each party to whom the creditor is reporting information concerning the disputed amount. If, pursuant to this paragraph, a creditor has reported a disputed amount as being delinquent to any third person, the creditor shall report promptly in writing[20] to any such person subsequent resolution of the reported delinquency.

(3) If a creditor has reported an amount as being delinquent to any third person who is in the business of collecting and disseminating information relating to the creditworthiness of customers, and such amount is subsequently disputed by the customer in accordance with the requirements of § 226.2(cc), the creditor shall, within one billing cycle after receipt of proper written notification of the billing error, mail or deliver a written notice[21] to each such third person to whom the delinquency was reported that the amount is in dispute.

(f) **Forfeiture penalty.** (1) Any creditor who fails to comply with the requirements of this section forfeits any right to collect from the customer the amount indicated by the customer to be a billing error, whether or not such amount is in fact in error, and any finance charges, late payment charges, or other charges imposed thereon, provided that the amount so forfeited under this section shall not exceed $50 for each item or transaction on a periodic statement indicated by the customer to be a billing error. In no case shall a creditor forfeit any amount for an error in a total figure or subtotal figure reflected on a

[19] Nothing in this paragraph prohibits a creditor from reporting the disputed amount or account as being in dispute.

[20] "In writing" shall include transmission by computer communication.

[21] "Written notice" shall include computer communication.

statement which is caused solely by an error in another item which is the subject of a dispute, nor shall a creditor suffer any forfeit more than once for any item or transaction which may appear on a periodic statement.

(2) Nothing in this subsection shall be construed to limit a customer's right to recover under section 130 of the Act.

(g) **Exceptions to general rule.** This section does not apply to credit other than open end, whether or not a periodic statement is mailed or delivered, unless it is consumer credit extended on an account by use of a credit card.

* SECTION 226.15—CONSUMER LEASING

(a) **General requirements.** Any lessor shall, in accordance with § 226.6 and to the extent applicable, make the disclosures required by paragraph (b) of this section with respect to any consumer lease. Such disclosures shall be made prior to the consummation of the lease on a dated written statement which identifies the lessor and the lessee, and a copy of such statement shall be given to the lessee at that time. All of the disclosures shall be made together on either

(1) The contract or other instrument evidencing the lease on the same page and above the place for the lessee's signature; or

(2) A separate statement which identifies the lease transaction.

In any lease of multiple items, the description required by § 226.15(b)(1) may be provided on a separate statement or statements which are incorporated by reference in the disclosure statement required by § 226.15(a).

(b) **Specific disclosure requirements.** In any lease subject to this section the following items, as applicable, shall be disclosed:

(1) A brief description of the leased property, sufficient to identify the property to the lessee and lessor.

(2) The total amount of any payment, such as a refundable security deposit paid by cash, check or similar means, advance payment, capitalized cost reduction or any trade-in allowance, appropriately identified, to be paid by the lessee at consummation of the lease.

(3) The number, amount and due dates or periods of payments scheduled under the lease and the total amount of such periodic payments.

(4) The total amount paid or payable by the lessee during the lease term for official fees, registration, certificate of title, license fees or taxes.

(5) The total amount of all other charges, individually itemized, payable by the lessee to the lessor, which are not included in the periodic payments. This total includes the amount of any liabilities the lease imposes upon the lessee at the end of the term, but excludes the potential difference between the estimated and realized values, required to be disclosed under § 226.15(b)(13).

(6) A brief identification of insurance in connection with the lease including (i) if provided or paid for by the lessor, the types and amounts of coverages and cost to the lessee, or (ii) if not provided or paid for by the lessor, the types and amounts of coverages required of the lessee.

(7) A statement identifying any express warranties or guarantees available to the lessee made by the lessor or manufacturer with respect to the leased property.

(8) An identification of the party responsible for maintaining or servicing the leased property together with a brief description of the responsibility, and a statement of reasonable standards for wear and use, if the lessor sets such standards.

(9) A description of any security interest, other than a security deposit disclosed under § 226.15(b)(2), held or to be retained by the lessor in connection with the lease and a clear identification of the property to which the security interest relates.

(10) The amount or method of determining the amount of any penalty or other charge for delinquency, default or late payments.

(11) A statement of whether or not the lessee has the option to purchase the leased property and, if at the end of the lease term, at what price, and, if prior to the end of the lease term, at what time and the price or method of determining the price.

(12) A statement of the conditions under which the lessee or lessor may terminate the lease prior to the end of the lease term and the amount or method of determining the amount of any penalty or other charge for early termination.

(13) A statement that the lessee shall be liable for the difference between the estimated value of the property and its realized value at early termination or the end of the lease term, if such liability exists.

(14) Where the lessee's liability at early termination or at the end of the lease term is based on

* Added 3/23/77.

the estimated value of the leased property, a statement that the lessee may obtain at the end of the lease term or at early termination, at the lessee's expense, a professional appraisal of the value which could be realized at sale of the leased property by an independent third party agreed to by the lessee and the lessor, which appraisal shall be final and binding on the parties.

(15) Where the lessee's liability at the end of the lease term is based upon the estimated value of the leased property:

(i) The value of the property at consummation of the lease, the itemized total lease obligation at the end of the lease term and the difference between them.

(ii) That there is a rebuttable presumption that the estimated value of the leased property at the end of the lease term is unreasonable and not in good faith to the extent that it exceeds the realized value by more than three times the average payment allocable to a monthly period, and that the lessor cannot collect the amount of such excess liability unless the lessor brings a successful action in court in which the lessor pays the lessee's attorney's fees, and that this provision regarding the presumption and attorney's fees does not apply to the extent the excess of estimated value over realized value is due to unreasonable wear or use, or excessive use.

(iii) A statement that the requirements of § 226.15(b)(15)(ii) do not preclude the right of a willing lessee to make any mutually agreeable final adjustment regarding such excess liability.

(c) **Renegotiations or extensions.** If any existing lease is renegotiated or extended, such renegotiation or extension shall be considered a new lease subject to the disclosure requirements of this Part, except that the requirements of this paragraph shall not apply to (1) a lease of multiple items where a new item(s) is provided or a previously leased item(s) is returned, and the average payment allocable to a monthly period is not changed by more than 25 per cent, or (2) a lease which is extended for not more than six months on a month-to-month basis or otherwise.

*

EQUAL CREDIT OPPORTUNITY REGULATIONS (REGULATION B)

TITLE 12.—BANKS AND BANKING

PART 202—EQUAL CREDIT OPPORTUNITY

Effective March 23, 1977

REGULATIONS

Sec.

SECTION 202.1—AUTHORITY, SCOPE, ENFORCEMENT, PENALTIES AND LIABILITIES, INTERPRETATIONS

(a) **Authority and scope.** This Part [1] comprises the regulations issued by the Board of Governors of the Federal Reserve System pursuant to Title VII (Equal Credit Opportunity Act) of the Consumer Credit Protection Act, as amended (15 U.S.C. § 1601 *et seq.*). Except as otherwise provided herein, this Part applies to all persons who are creditors, as defined in section 202.2(*l*).

(b) **Administrative enforcement.** (1) As set forth more fully in section 704 of the Act, administrative enforcement of the Act and this Part regarding certain creditors is assigned to the Comptroller of the Currency, Board of Governors of the Federal Reserve System, Board of Directors of the Federal Deposit Insurance Corporation, Federal Home Loan Bank Board (acting directly or through the Federal Savings and Loan Insurance Corporation), Administrator of the National Credit Union Administration, Interstate Commerce Commission, Civil Aeronautics Board, Secretary of Agriculture, Farm Credit Administration, Securities and Exchange Commission, and Small Business Administration.

(2) Except to the extent that administrative enforcement is specifically committed to other authorities, compliance with the requirements imposed under the Act and this Part will be enforced by the Federal Trade Commission.

(c) **Penalties and liabilities.** (1) Sections 706(a) and (b) of the Act provide that any creditor who fails to comply with any requirement imposed under the Act or, pursuant to section 702(g), this Part is subject to civil liability for actual and punitive damages in individual or class actions. Pursuant to section 704 of the Act, violations of the Act or, pursuant to section 702(g), this Part constitute violations of other

[1] As used herein, the words "this Part" mean Regulation B, 12 CFR 202.

Federal laws that may provide further penalties. Liability for punitive damages is restricted by section 706(b) to non-governmental entities and is limited to $10,000 in individual actions and the lesser of $500,000 or one percent of the creditor's net worth in class actions. Section 706(c) provides for equitable and declaratory relief. Section 706(d) authorizes the awarding of costs and reasonable attorney's fees to an aggrieved applicant in a successful action.

(2) Section 706(e) relieves a creditor from civil liability resulting from any act done or omitted in good faith in conformity with any rule, regulation, or interpretation by the Board of Governors of the Federal Reserve System, or with any interpretations or approvals issued by a duly authorized official or employee of the Federal Reserve System, notwithstanding that after such act or omission has occurred, such rule, regulation, interpretation, or approval is amended, rescinded, or otherwise determined to be invalid for any reason.

(3) As provided in section 706(f), a civil action under the Act or this Part may be brought in the appropriate United States district court without regard to the amount in controversy or in any other court of competent jurisdiction within two years after the date of the occurrence of the violation or within one year after the commencement of an administrative enforcement proceeding or a civil action brought by the Attorney General within two years after the alleged violation.

(4) Sections 706(g) and (h) provide that, if the agencies responsible for administrative enforcement are unable to obtain compliance with the Act or, pursuant to section 702(g), this Part, they may refer the matter to the Attorney General. On such referral, or whenever the Attorney General has reason to believe that one or more creditors are engaged in a pattern or practice in violation of the Act or this Part, the Attorney General may bring a civil action.

*(d) **Issuance of staff interpretations.** (1) Unofficial staff interpretations will be issued at the staff's discretion where the protection of section 706(e) of the Act is neither requested nor required, or where a rapid response is necessary.

(2)(i) Official staff interpretations will be issued at the discretion of designated officials. No such interpretation will be issued approving creditors' or lessors' forms or statements. Any request for an official staff interpretation of this Part must be in writing and addressed to the Director of the Division of Consumer Affairs, Board of Governors of the Federal Reserve System, Washington, D.C. 20551. The request must contain a complete statement of all relevant facts concerning the credit or lease transaction or arrangement and must include copies of all pertinent documents.

(ii) Within 5 business days of receipt of the request, an acknowledgement will be sent to the person making the request. If, in the opinion of the designated officials, issuance of an official staff interpretation is appropriate, it will be published in the *Federal Register* to become effective 30 days after the publication date. If a request for public comment is received, the effective date will be suspended. The interpretation will then be republished in the *Federal Register* and the public given an opportunity to comment. Any official staff interpretation issued after opportunity for public comment shall become effective upon publication in the *Federal Register.*

(3) Any request for public comment on an official staff interpretation of this Part must be in writing and addressed to the Secretary, Board of Governors of the Federal Reserve System, Washington, D.C. 20551, and postmarked or received by the Secretary's office within 30 days of the interpretation's publication in the *Federal Register.* The request must contain a statement setting forth the reasons why the person making the request believes that public comment would be appropriate.

(4) Pursuant to section 130(f) of the Act, the Board has designated the Director and other officials of the Division of Consumer Affairs as officials "duly authorized" to issue, at their discretion, official staff interpretations of this Part.

* Amended 4/24/78.

SECTION 202.2—DEFINITIONS AND RULES OF CONSTRUCTION

For the purposes of this Part, unless the context indicates otherwise, the following definitions and rules of construction shall apply: [2]

(a) **Account** means an extension of credit. When employed in relation to an account, the word **use** refers only to open end credit.

(b) **Act** means the Equal Credit Opportunity Act (Title VII of the Consumer Credit Protection Act).

*(c) **Adverse action.** (1) For the purposes of notification of action taken, statement of reasons for denial, and record retention, the term means:

(i) a refusal to grant credit in substantially the amount or on substantially the terms requested in an application unless the creditor offers to grant credit other than in substantially the amount or on substantially the terms requested by the applicant and the applicant uses or expressly accepts the credit offered; or

(ii) a termination of an account or an unfavorable change in the terms of an account that does not affect all or a substantial portion of a classification of a creditor's accounts; or

(iii) a refusal to increase the amount of credit available to an applicant when the applicant requests an increase in accordance with procedures established by the creditor for the type of credit involved.

(2) The term does not include:

(i) a change in the terms of an account expressly agreed to by an applicant; or

(ii) any action or forbearance relating to an account taken in connection with inactivity, default, or delinquency as to that account; or

(iii) a refusal or failure to authorize an account transaction at a point of sale or loan, except when the refusal is a termination or an unfavorable change in the terms of an account that does not affect all or a substantial portion of a classification of the creditor's accounts or when the refusal is a denial of an application to increase the amount of credit available under the account; or

(iv) a refusal to extend credit because applicable law prohibits the creditor from extending the credit requested; or

(v) a refusal to extend credit because the creditor does not offer the type of credit or credit plan requested.

(3) An action that falls within the definition of both subsections (c)(1) and (c)(2) shall be governed by the provisions of subsection (c)(2).

(d) **Age** refers only to natural persons and means the number of fully elapsed years from the date of an applicant's birth.

(e) **Applicant** means any person who requests or who has received an extension of credit from a creditor, and includes any person who is or may be contractually liable regarding an extension of credit other than a guarantor, surety, endorser, or similar party.

(f) **Application** means an oral or written request for an extension of credit that is made in accordance with procedures established by a creditor for the type of credit requested. The term does not include the use of an account or line of credit to obtain an amount of credit that does not exceed a previously established credit limit. A **completed application for credit** means an application in connection with which a creditor has received all the information that the creditor regularly obtains and considers in evaluating applications for the amount and type of credit requested (including, but not limited to, credit reports, any additional information requested from the applicant, and any approvals or reports by governmental agencies or other persons that are necessary to guarantee, insure, or provide security for the credit or collateral); provided, however, that the creditor has exercised reasonable diligence in obtaining such information. Where an application is incomplete respecting matters that the applicant can complete, a creditor shall make a reasonable effort to notify the applicant of the incompleteness and shall allow the applicant a reasonable opportunity to complete the application.

(g) **Board** means the Board of Governors of the Federal Reserve System.

(h) **Consumer credit** means credit extended to a natural person in which the money, property, or service that is the subject of the transaction is

[2] Note that some of the definitions in this Part are not identical to those in 12 CFR 226 (Regulation Z).

* Amended 3/16/78.

primarily for personal, family, or household purposes.

(i) **Contractually liable** means expressly obligated to repay all debts arising on an account by reason of an agreement to that effect.

(j) **Credit** means the right granted by a creditor to an applicant to defer payment of a debt, incur debt and defer its payment, or purchase property or services and defer payment therefor.

(k) **Credit card** means any card, plate, coupon book, or other single credit device existing for the purpose of being used from time to time upon presentation to obtain money, property, or services on credit.

(*l*) **Creditor** means a person who, in the ordinary course of business, regularly participates in the decision of whether or not to extend credit. The term includes an assignee, transferee, or subrogee of an original creditor who so participates; but an assignee, transferee, subrogee, or other creditor is not a creditor regarding any violation of the Act or this Part committed by the original or another creditor unless the assignee, transferee, subrogee, or other creditor knew or had reasonable notice of the act, policy, or practice that constituted the violation before its involvement with the credit transaction. The term does not include a person whose only participation in a credit transaction involves honoring a credit card.

(m) **Credit transaction** means every aspect of an applicant's dealings with a creditor regarding an application for, or an existing extension of, credit including, but not limited to, information requirements; investigation procedures; standards of creditworthiness; terms of credit; furnishing of credit information; revocation, alteration, or termination of credit; and collection procedures.

(n) **Discriminate against an applicant** means to treat an applicant less favorably than other applicants.

(o) **Elderly** means an age of 62 or older.

(p) **Empirically derived credit system.** (1) The term means a credit scoring system that evaluates an applicant's creditworthiness primarily by allocating points (or by using a comparable basis for assigning weights) to key attributes describing the applicant and other aspects of the transaction. In such a system, the points (or weights) assigned to each attribute, and hence the entire score:

(i) are derived from an empirical comparison of sample groups or the population of creditworthy and non-creditworthy applicants of a creditor who applied for credit within a reasonable preceding period of time; and

(ii) determine, alone or in conjunction with an evaluation of additional information about the applicant, whether an applicant is deemed creditworthy.

(2) **A demonstrably and statistically sound, empirically derived credit system** is a system:

(i) in which the data used to develop the system, if not the complete population consisting of all applicants, are obtained from the applicant file by using appropriate sampling principles;

(ii) which is developed for the purpose of predicting the creditworthiness of applicants with respect to the legitimate business interests of the creditor utilizing the system, including, but not limited to, minimizing bad debt losses and operating expenses in accordance with the creditor's business judgment;

(iii) which, upon validation using appropriate statistical principles, separates creditworthy and non-creditworthy applicants at a statistically significant rate; and

(iv) which is periodically revalidated as to its predictive ability by the use of appropriate statistical principles and is adjusted as necessary to maintain its predictive ability.

(3) A creditor may use a demonstrably and statistically sound, empirically derived credit system obtained from another person or may obtain credit experience from which such a system may be developed. Any such system must satisfy the tests set forth in subsections (1) and (2); provided that, if a creditor is unable during the development process to validate the system based on its own credit experience in accordance with subsection (2)(iii), then the system must be validated when sufficient credit experience becomes available. A system that fails this validity test shall henceforth be deemed not to be a demonstrably and statistically sound, empirically derived credit system for that creditor.

(q) **Extend credit** and **extension of credit** mean the granting of credit in any form and include, but are not limited to, credit granted in addition to any existing credit or credit limit; credit granted pursuant to an open end credit plan; the refinancing or other renewal of credit, including the issuance of a new credit card in place of an expiring credit card or in substitution for an existing credit card; the consolidation of two or more obligations; or the continuance of existing credit without any special effort to collect at or after maturity.

(r) **Good faith** means honesty in fact in the conduct or transaction.

(s) **Inadvertent error** means a mechanical, electronic, or clerical error that a creditor demonstrates was not intentional and occurred notwithstanding the maintenance of procedures reasonably adapted to avoid any such error.

(t) **Judgmental system of evaluating applicants** means any system for evaluating the creditworthiness of an applicant other than a demonstrably and statistically sound, empirically derived credit system.

(u) **Marital status** means the state of being unmarried, married, or separated, as defined by applicable State law. For the purposes of this Part, the term "unmarried" includes persons who are single, divorced, or widowed.

(v) **Negative factor or value,** in relation to the age of elderly applicants, means utilizing a factor, value, or weight that is less favorable regarding elderly applicants than the creditor's experience warrants or is less favorable than the factor, value, or weight assigned to the class of applicants that are not classified as elderly applicants and are most favored by a creditor on the basis of age.

(w) **Open end credit** means credit extended pursuant to a plan under which a creditor may permit an applicant to make purchases or obtain loans from time to time directly from the creditor or indirectly by use of a credit card, check, or other device as the plan may provide. The term does not include negotiated advances under an open end real estate mortgage or a letter of credit.

(x) **Person** means a natural person, corporation, government or governmental subdivision or agency, trust, estate, partnership, cooperative, or association.

(y) **Pertinent element of creditworthiness,** in relation to a judgmental system of evaluating applicants, means any information about applicants that a creditor obtains and considers and that has a demonstrable relationship to a determination of creditworthiness.

(z) **Prohibited basis** means race, color, religion, national origin, sex, marital status, or age (provided that the applicant has the capacity to enter into a binding contract); the fact that all or part of the applicant's income derives from any public assistance program, or the fact that the applicant has in good faith exercised any right under the Consumer Credit Protection Act [3] or any State law upon which an exemption has been granted by the Board.

(aa) **Public assistance program** means any Federal, State, or local governmental assistance program that provides a continuing, periodic income supplement, whether premised on entitlement or need. The term includes, but is not limited to, Aid to Families with Dependent Children, food stamps, rent and mortgage supplement or assistance programs, Social Security and Supplemental Security Income, and unemployment compensation.

(bb) **State** means any State, the District of Columbia, the Commonwealth of Puerto Rico, or any territory or possession of the United States.

(cc) Captions and catchlines are intended solely as aids to convenient reference, and no inference as to the substance of any provision of this Part may be drawn from them.

(dd) Footnotes shall have the same legal effect as the text of the regulation, whether they are explanatory or illustrative in nature.

---

[3] The first clause of the definition is not limited to characteristics of the applicant. Therefore, "prohibited basis" as used in this Part refers not only to the race, color, religion, national origin, sex, marital status, or age of an applicant (or of partners or officers of an applicant), but refers also to the characteristics of individuals with whom an applicant deals. This means, for example, that, under the general rule stated in section 202.4, a creditor may not discriminate against a non-Jewish applicant because of that person's business dealings with Jews, or discriminate against an applicant because of the characteristics of persons to whom the extension of credit relates (e.g., the prospective tenants in an apartment complex to be constructed with the proceeds of the credit requested), or because of the characteristics of other individuals residing in the neighborhood where the property offered as collateral is located. A creditor may take into account, however, any applicable law, regulation, or executive order restricting dealings with citizens or governments of other countries or imposing limitations regarding credit extended for their use.

The second clause is limited to an applicant's receipt of public assistance income and to an applicant's good faith exercise of rights under the Consumer Credit Protection Act or applicable State law.

SECTION 202.3—SPECIAL TREATMENT FOR CERTAIN CLASSES OF TRANSACTIONS

(a) **Classes of transactions afforded special treatment.** Pursuant to section 703(a) of the Act, the following classes of transactions are afforded specialized treatment:

(1) extensions of credit relating to transactions under public utility tariffs involving services provided through pipe, wire, or other connected facilities if the charges for such public utility services, the charges for delayed payment, and any discount allowed for early payment are filed with, or reviewed or regulated by, an agency of the Federal government, a State, or a political subdivision thereof;

(2) extensions of credit subject to regulation under section 7 of the Securities Exchange Act of 1934 or extensions of credit by a broker or dealer subject to regulation as a broker or dealer under the Securities Exchange Act of 1934;

(3) extensions of incidental consumer credit, other than of the types described in subsections (a)(1) and (2):

(i) that are not made pursuant to the terms of a credit card account;

(ii) on which no finance charge as defined in section 226.4 of this Title (Regulation Z, 12 CFR 226.4) is or may be imposed; and

(iii) that are not payable by agreement in more than four instalments;

(4) extensions of credit primarily for business or commercial purposes, including extensions of credit primarily for agricultural purposes, but excluding extensions of credit of the types described in subsections (a)(1) and (2); and

(5) extensions of credit made to governments or governmental subdivisions, agencies, or instrumentalities.

(b) **Public utilities credit.** The following provisions of this Part shall not apply to extensions of credit of the type described in subsection (a)(1):

(1) section 202.5(d)(1) concerning information about marital status;

(2) section 202.10 relating to furnishing of credit information; and

(3) section 202.12(b) relating to record retention.

(c) **Securities credit.** The following provisions of this Part shall not apply to extensions of credit of the type described in subsection (a)(2):

(1) section 202.5(c) concerning information about a spouse or former spouse;

(2) section 202.5(d)(1) concerning information about marital status;

(3) section 202.5(d)(3) concerning information about the sex of an applicant;

(4) section 202.7(b) relating to designation of name, but only to the extent necessary to prevent violation of rules regarding an account in which a broker or dealer has an interest, or rules necessitating the aggregation of accounts of spouses for the purpose of determining controlling interests, beneficial interests, beneficial ownership, or purchase limitations and restrictions;

(5) section 202.7(c) relating to action concerning open end accounts, but only to the extent the action taken is on the basis of a change of name or marital status;

(6) section 202.7(d) relating to signature of a spouse or other person;

(7) section 202.10 relating to furnishing of credit information; and

(8) section 202.12(b) relating to record retention.

(d) **Incidental credit.** The following provisions of this Part shall not apply to extensions of credit of the type described in subsection (a)(3):

(1) section 202.5(c) concerning information about a spouse or former spouse;

(2) section 202.5(d)(1) concerning information about marital status;

(3) section 202.5(d)(2) concerning information about income derived from alimony, child support, or separate maintenance payments;

(4) section 202.5(d)(3) concerning information about the sex of an applicant to the extent necessary for medical records or similar purposes;

(5) section 202.7(d) relating to signature of a spouse or other person;

(6) section 202.9 relating to notifications;

(7) section 202.10 relating to furnishing of credit information; and

(8) section 202.12(b) relating to record retention.

(e) **Business credit.** The following provisions of this Part shall not apply to extensions of credit of the type described in subsection (a)(4):

(1) section 202.5(d)(1) concerning information about marital status;

(2) section 202.9 relating to notifications, unless an applicant, within 30 days after oral or written

notification that adverse action has been taken, requests in writing the reasons for such action;

(3) section 202.10 relating to furnishing of credit information; and

(4) section 202.12(b) relating to record retention, unless an applicant, within 90 days after adverse action has been taken, requests in writing that the records relating to the application be retained.

(f) **Governmental credit.** Except for section 202.1 relating to authority, scope, enforcement, penalties and liabilities, and interpretations, section 202.2 relating to definitions and rules of construction, this section, section 202.4 relating to the general rule prohibiting discrimination, section 202.6(a) relating to the use of information, section 202.11 relating to State laws, and section 202.12(a) relating to the retention of prohibited information, the provisions of this Part shall not apply to extensions of credit of the type described in subsection (a)(5).

SECTION 202.4—GENERAL RULE PROHIBITING DISCRIMINATION

A creditor shall not discriminate against an applicant on a prohibited basis regarding any aspect of a credit transaction.

SECTION 202.5—RULES CONCERNING APPLICATIONS

(a) **Discouraging applications.** A creditor shall not make any oral or written statement, in advertising or otherwise, to applicants or prospective applicants that would discourage on a prohibited basis a reasonable person from making or pursuing an application.

(b) **General rules concerning requests for information.** (1) Except as otherwise provided in this section, a creditor may request any information in connection with an application.[4]

(2) Notwithstanding any other provision of this section, a creditor shall request an applicant's race/national origin, sex, and marital status as required in section 202.13 (information for monitoring purposes). In addition, a creditor may obtain such information as may be required by a regulation, order, or agreement issued by, or entered into with, a court or an enforcement agency (including the Attorney General or a similar State official) to monitor or enforce compliance with the Act, this Part, or other Federal or State statute or regulation.

(3) The provisions of this section limiting permissible information requests are subject to the provisions of section 202.7(e) regarding insurance and sections 202.8(c) and (d) regarding special purpose credit programs.

(c) **Information about a spouse or former spouse.** (1) Except as permitted in this subsection, a creditor may not request any information concerning the spouse or former spouse of an applicant.

(2) A creditor may request any information concerning an applicant's spouse (or former spouse under (v) below) that may be requested about the applicant if:

(i) the spouse will be permitted to use the account; or

(ii) the spouse will be contractually liable upon the account; or

(iii) the applicant is relying on the spouse's income as a basis for repayment of the credit requested; or

(iv) the applicant resides in a community property State or property upon which the applicant is relying as a basis for repayment of the credit requested is located in such a State; or

(v) the applicant is relying on alimony, child support, or separate maintenance payments from a spouse or former spouse as a basis for repayment of the credit requested.

(3) A creditor may request an applicant to list any account upon which the applicant is liable and to provide the name and address in which such account is carried. A creditor may also ask the names in which an applicant has previously received credit.

(d) **Information a creditor may not request.** (1) If an applicant applies for an individual, unsecured account, a creditor shall not request the applicant's marital status, unless the applicant resides in a community property State or prop-

[4] This subsection is not intended to limit or abrogate any Federal or State law regarding privacy, privileged information, credit reporting limitations, or similar restrictions on obtainable information. Furthermore, permission to request information should not be confused with how it may be utilized, which is governed by section 202.6 (rules concerning evaluation of applications).

erty upon which the applicant is relying as a basis for repayment of the credit requested is located in such a State.[5] Where an application is for other than individual, unsecured credit, a creditor may request an applicant's marital status. Only the terms "married," "unmarried," and "separated" shall be used, and a creditor may explain that the category "unmarried" includes single, divorced, and widowed persons.

(2) A creditor shall not inquire whether any income stated in an application is derived from alimony, child support, or separate maintenance payments, unless the creditor appropriately discloses to the applicant that such income need not be revealed if the applicant does not desire the creditor to consider such income in determining the applicant's creditworthiness. Since a general inquiry about income, without further specification, may lead an applicant to list alimony, child support, or separate maintenance payments, a creditor shall provide an appropriate notice to an applicant before inquiring about the source of an applicant's income, unless the terms of the inquiry (such as an inquiry about salary, wages, investment income, or similarly specified income) tend to preclude the unintentional disclosure of alimony, child support, or separate maintenance payments.

(3) A creditor shall not request the sex of an applicant. An applicant may be requested to designate a title on an application form (such as Ms., Miss, Mr., or Mrs.) if the form appropriately discloses that the designation of such a title is optional. An application form shall otherwise use only terms that are neutral as to sex.

(4) A creditor shall not request information about birth control practices, intentions concerning the bearing or rearing of children, or capability to bear children. This does not preclude a creditor from inquiring about the number and ages of an applicant's dependents or about dependent-related financial obligations or expenditures, provided such information is requested without regard to sex, marital status, or any other prohibited basis.

(5) A creditor shall not request the race, color, religion, or national origin of an applicant or any other person in connection with a credit transaction. A creditor may inquire, however, as to an applicant's permanent residence and immigration status.

(e) **Application forms.** A creditor need not use written applications. If a creditor chooses to use written forms, it may design its own,[6] use forms prepared by another person, or use the appropriate model application forms contained in Appendix B. If a creditor chooses to use an Appendix B form, it may change the form:

(1) by asking for additional information not prohibited by this section;

(2) by deleting any information request; or

(3) by rearranging the format without modifying the substance of the inquiries; provided that in each of these three instances the appropriate notices regarding the optional nature of courtesy titles, the option to disclose alimony, child support, or separate maintenance, and the limitation concerning marital status inquiries are included in the appropriate places if the items to which they relate appear on the creditor's form. If a creditor uses an appropriate Appendix B model form or to the extent that it modifies such a form in accordance with the provisions of clauses (2) or (3) of the preceding sentence or the instructions to Appendix B, that creditor shall be deemed to be acting in compliance with the provisions of subsections (c) and (d).

SECTION 202.6—RULES CONCERNING EVALUATION OF APPLICATIONS

(a) **General rule concerning use of information.** Except as otherwise provided in the Act and this Part, a creditor may consider in evaluating an application any information that the creditor obtains,

[5] This provision does not preclude requesting relevant information that may indirectly disclose marital status, such as asking about liability to pay alimony, child support, or separate maintenance; the source of income to be used as a basis for the repayment of the credit requested, which may disclose that it is a spouse's income; whether any obligation disclosed by the applicant has a co-obligor, which may disclose that the co-obligor is a spouse or former spouse; or the ownership of assets, which may disclose the interest of a spouse, when such assets are relied upon in extending the credit. Such inquiries are allowed by the general rule of subsection (b)(1).

[6] A creditor also may continue to use any application form that complies with the requirements of the October 28, 1975 version of Regulation B until its present stock of those forms is exhausted or until March 23, 1978, whichever occurs first. The provisions of this Part shall not determine and are not evidence of the meaning of the requirements of the previous version of Regulation B.

so long as the information is not used to discriminate against an applicant on a prohibited basis.[7]

(b) **Specific rules concerning use of information.** (1) Except as provided in the Act and this Part, a creditor shall not take a prohibited basis into account in any system of evaluating the creditworthiness of applicants.[8]

(2)(i) Except as permitted in this subsection, a creditor shall not take into account an applicant's age (provided that the applicant has the capacity to enter into a binding contract) or whether an applicant's income derives from any public assistance program.

(ii) In a demonstrably and statistically sound, empirically derived credit system, a creditor may use an applicant's age as a predictive variable, provided that the age of an elderly applicant is not assigned a negative factor or value.

(iii) In a judgmental system of evaluating creditworthiness, a creditor may consider an applicant's age or whether an applicant's income derives from any public assistance program only for the purpose of determining a pertinent element of creditworthiness.[9]

(iv) In any system of evaluating creditworthiness, a creditor may consider the age of an elderly applicant when such age is to be used to favor the elderly applicant in extending credit.

(3) A creditor shall not use, in evaluating the creditworthiness of an applicant, assumptions or aggregate statistics relating to the likelihood that any group of persons will bear or rear children or, for that reason, will receive diminished or interrupted income in the future.

(4) A creditor shall not take into account the existence of a telephone listing in the name of an applicant for consumer credit. A creditor may take into account the existence of a telephone in the residence of such an applicant.

(5) A creditor shall not discount or exclude from consideration the income of an applicant or the spouse of the applicant because of a prohibited basis or because the income is derived from part-time employment, or from an annuity, pension, or other retirement benefit; but a creditor may consider the amount and probable continuance of any income in evaluating an applicant's creditworthiness. Where an applicant relies on alimony, child support, or separate maintenance payments in applying for credit, a creditor shall consider such payments as income to the extent that they are likely to be consistently made. Factors that a creditor may consider in determining the likelihood of consistent payments include, but are not limited to, whether the payments are received pursuant to a written agreement or court decree; the length of time that the payments have been received; the regularity of receipt; the availability of procedures to compel payment; and the creditworthiness of the payor, including the credit history of the payor where available to the creditor under the Fair Credit Reporting Act or other applicable laws.

(6) To the extent that a creditor considers credit history in evaluating the creditworthiness of similarly qualified applicants for a similar type and amount of credit, in evaluating an applicant's creditworthiness, a creditor shall consider (unless

---

[7] The legislative history of the Act indicates that the Congress intended an "effects test" concept, as outlined in the employment field by the Supreme Court in the cases of *Griggs* v. *Duke Power Co.,* 401 U.S. 424 (1971), and *Albemarle Paper Co.* v. *Moody,* 422 U.S. 405 (1975), to be applicable to a creditor's determination of creditworthiness. See Senate Report to accompany H.R. 6516, No. 94-589, pp. 4-5; House Report to accompany H.R. 6516, No. 94-210, p. 5.

[8] This provision does not prevent a creditor from considering the marital status of an applicant or the source of an applicant's income for the purpose of ascertaining the creditor's rights and remedies applicable to the particular extension of credit and not to discriminate in a determination of creditworthiness. Furthermore, a prohibited basis may be considered in accordance with section 202.8 (special purpose credit programs).

[9] Concerning income derived from a public assistance program, a creditor may consider, for example, the length of time an applicant has been receiving such income; whether an applicant intends to continue to reside in the jurisdiction in relation to residency requirements for benefits; and the status of an applicant's dependents to ascertain whether benefits that the applicant is presently receiving will continue.

Concerning age, a creditor may consider, for example, the occupation and length of time to retirement of an applicant to ascertain whether the applicant's income (including retirement income, as applicable) will support the extension of credit until its maturity; or the adequacy of any security offered if the duration of the credit extension will exceed the life expectancy of the applicant. An elderly applicant might not qualify for a five-percent down, 30-year mortgage loan because the duration of the loan exceeds the applicant's life expectancy and the cost of realizing on the collateral might exceed the applicant's equity. The same applicant might qualify with a larger downpayment and a shorter loan maturity. A creditor could also consider an applicant's age, for example, to assess the significance of the applicant's length of employment or residence (a young applicant may have just entered the job market; an elderly applicant may recently have retired and moved from a long-time residence).

the failure to consider results from an inadvertent error):

(i) the credit history, when available, of accounts designated as accounts that the applicant and a spouse are permitted to use or for which both are contractually liable;

(ii) on the applicant's request, any information that the applicant may present tending to indicate that the credit history being considered by the creditor does not accurately reflect the applicant's creditworthiness; and

(iii) on the applicant's request, the credit history, when available, of any account reported in the name of the applicant's spouse or former spouse that the applicant can demonstrate accurately reflects the applicant's creditworthiness.

(7) A creditor may consider whether an applicant is a permanent resident of the United States, the applicant's immigration status, and such additional information as may be necessary to ascertain its rights and remedies regarding repayment.

(c) **State property laws.** A creditor's consideration or application of State property laws directly or indirectly affecting creditworthiness shall not constitute unlawful discrimination for the purposes of the Act or this Part.

SECTION 202.7—RULES CONCERNING EXTENSIONS OF CREDIT

(a) **Individual accounts.** A creditor shall not refuse to grant an individual account to a creditworthy applicant on the basis of sex, marital status, or any other prohibited basis.

(b) **Designation of name.** A creditor shall not prohibit an applicant from opening or maintaining an account in a birth-given first name and a surname that is the applicant's birth-given surname, the spouse's surname, or a combined surname.

(c) **Action concerning existing open end accounts.** (1) In the absence of evidence of inability or unwillingness to repay, a creditor shall not take any of the following actions regarding an applicant who is contractually liable on an existing open end account on the basis of the applicant's reaching a certain age or retiring, or on the basis of a change in the applicant's name or marital status:

(i) require a reapplication; or

(ii) change the terms of the account; or

(iii) terminate the account.

(2) A creditor may require a reapplication regarding an open end account on the basis of a change in an applicant's marital status where the credit granted was based on income earned by the applicant's spouse if the applicant's income alone at the time of the original application would not support the amount of credit currently extended.

(d) **Signature of spouse or other person.** (1) Except as provided in this subsection, a creditor shall not require the signature of an applicant's spouse or other person, other than a joint applicant, on any credit instrument if the applicant qualifies under the creditor's standards of creditworthiness for the amount and terms of the credit requested.

(2) If an applicant requests unsecured credit and relies in part upon property to establish creditworthiness, a creditor may consider State law; the form of ownership of the property; its susceptibility to attachment, execution, severance, and partition; and other factors that may affect the value to the creditor of the applicant's interest in the property. If necessary to satisfy the creditor's standards of creditworthiness, the creditor may require the signature of the applicant's spouse or other person on any instrument necessary, or reasonably believed by the creditor to be necessary, under applicable State law to make the property relied upon available to satisfy the debt in the event of default.

(3) If a married applicant requests unsecured credit and resides in a community property State or if the property upon which the applicant is relying is located in such a State, a creditor may require the signature of the spouse on any instrument necessary, or reasonably believed by the creditor to be necessary, under applicable State law to make the community property available to satisfy the debt in the event of default if:

(i) applicable State law denies the applicant power to manage or control sufficient community property to qualify for the amount of credit requested under the creditor's standards of creditworthiness; and

(ii) the applicant does not have sufficient separate property to qualify for the amount of credit requested without regard to community property.

(4) If an applicant requests secured credit, a creditor may require the signature of the applicant's spouse or other person on any instrument necessary, or reasonably believed by the creditor

to be necessary, under applicable State law to make the property being offered as security available to satisfy the debt in the event of default, for example, any instrument to create a valid lien, pass clear title, waive inchoate rights, or assign earnings.

(5) If, under a creditor's standards of creditworthiness, the personal liability of an additional party is necessary to support the extension of the credit requested,[10] a creditor may request that the applicant obtain a co-signer, guarantor, or the like. The applicant's spouse may serve as an additional party, but a creditor shall not require that the spouse be the additional party. For the purposes of subsection (d), a creditor shall not impose requirements upon an additional party that the creditor may not impose upon an applicant.

(e) **Insurance.** Differentiation in the availability, rates, and terms on which credit-related casualty insurance or credit life, health, accident, or disability insurance is offered or provided to an applicant shall not constitute a violation of the Act or this Part; but a creditor shall not refuse to extend credit and shall not terminate an account because credit life, health, accident, or disability insurance is not available on the basis of the applicant's age. Notwithstanding any other provision of this Part, information about the age, sex, or marital status of an applicant may be requested in an application for insurance.

SECTION 202.8—SPECIAL PURPOSE CREDIT PROGRAMS

(a) **Standards for programs.** Subject to the provisions of subsection (b), the Act and this Part are not violated if a creditor refuses to extend credit to an applicant solely because the applicant does not qualify under the special requirements that define eligibility for the following types of special purpose credit programs:

(1) any credit assistance program expressly authorized by Federal or State law for the benefit of an economically disadvantaged class of persons; or

(2) any credit assistance program offered by a not-for-profit organization, as defined under section 501(c) of the Internal Revenue Code of 1954, as amended, for the benefit of its members or for the benefit of an economically disadvantaged class of persons; or

(3) any special purpose credit program offered by a for-profit organization or in which such an organization participates to meet special social needs, provided that:

(i) the program is established and administered pursuant to a written plan that (A) identifies the class or classes of persons that the program is designed to benefit and (B) sets forth the procedures and standards for extending credit pursuant to the program; and

(ii) the program is established and administered to extend credit to a class of persons who, pursuant to the customary standards of creditworthiness used by the organization extending the credit, either probably would not receive such credit or probably would receive it on less favorable terms than are ordinarily available to other applicants applying to the organization for a similar type and amount of credit.

(b) **Applicability of other rules.** (1) All of the provisions of this Part shall apply to each of the special purpose credit programs described in subsection (a) to the extent that those provisions are not inconsistent with the provisions of this section.

(2) A program described in subsections (a)(2) or (a)(3) shall qualify as a special purpose credit program under subsection (a) only if it was established and is administered so as not to discriminate against an applicant on the basis of race, color, religion, national origin, sex, marital status, age (provided that the applicant has the capacity to enter into a binding contract), income derived from a public assistance program, or good faith exercise of any right under the Consumer Credit Protection Act or any State law upon which an exemption has been granted therefrom by the Board; except that all program participants may be required to share one or more of those characteristics so long as the program was not established and is not administered with the purpose of evading the requirements of the Act or this Part.

(c) **Special rule concerning requests and use of information.** If all participants in a special purpose credit program described in subsection (a) are or will be required to possess one or more common characteristics relating to race, color, religion, national origin, sex, marital status, age, or receipt of income from a public assistance program and if

[10] If an applicant requests individual credit relying on the separate income of another person, a creditor may require the signature of the other person to make the income available to pay the debt.

the special purpose credit program otherwise satisfies the requirements of subsection (a), then, notwithstanding the prohibitions of sections 202.5 and 202.6, the creditor may request of an applicant and may consider, in determining eligibility for such program, information regarding the common characteristics required for eligibility. In such circumstances, the solicitation and consideration of that information shall not constitute unlawful discrimination for the purposes of the Act or this Part.

(d) **Special rule in the case of financial need.** If financial need is or will be one of the criteria for the extension of credit under a special purpose credit program described in subsection (a), then, notwithstanding the prohibitions of sections 202.5 and 202.6, the creditor may request and consider, in determining eligibility for such program, information regarding an applicant's marital status, income from alimony, child support, or separate maintenance, and the spouse's financial resources. In addition, notwithstanding the prohibitions of section 202.7(d), a creditor may obtain the signature of an applicant's spouse or other person on an application or credit instrument relating to a special purpose program if required by Federal or State law. In such circumstances, the solicitation and consideration of that information and the obtaining of a required signature shall not constitute unlawful discrimination for the purposes of the Act or this Part.

SECTION 202.9—NOTIFICATIONS

(a) **Notification of action taken, ECOA notice, and statement of specific reasons.**

(1) **Notification of action taken.** A creditor shall notify an applicant of action taken within:

(i) 30 days after receiving a completed application concerning the creditor's approval of, or adverse action regarding, the application (notification of approval may be express or by implication, where, for example, the applicant receives a credit card, money, property, or services in accordance with the application);

(ii) 30 days after taking adverse action on an uncompleted application;

(iii) 30 days after taking adverse action regarding an existing account; and

(iv) 90 days after the creditor has notified the applicant of an offer to grant credit other than in substantially the amount or on substantially the terms requested by the applicant if the applicant during those 90 days has not expressly accepted or used the credit offered.

(2) **Content of notification.** Any notification given to an applicant against whom adverse action is taken shall be in writing and shall contain: a statement of the action taken; a statement of the provisions of section 701(a) of the Act; the name and address of the Federal agency that administers compliance concerning the creditor giving the notification; and

(i) a statement of specific reasons for the action taken; or

(ii) a disclosure of the applicant's right to a statement of reasons within 30 days after receipt by the creditor of a request made within 60 days of such notification, the disclosure to include the name, address, and telephone number of the person or office from which the statement of reasons can be obtained. If the creditor chooses to provide the statement of reasons orally, the notification shall also include a disclosure of the applicant's right to have any oral statement of reasons confirmed in writing within 30 days after a written request for confirmation is received by the creditor.

(3) **Multiple applicants.** If there is more than one applicant, the notification need only be given to one of them, but must be given to the primary applicant where one is readily apparent.

(4) **Multiple creditors.** If a transaction involves more than one creditor and the applicant expressly accepts or uses the credit offered, this section does not require notification of adverse action by any creditor. If a transaction involves more than one creditor and either no credit is offered or the applicant does not expressly accept or use any credit offered, then each creditor taking adverse action must comply with this section. The required notification may be provided indirectly through a third party, which may be one of the creditors, provided that the identity of each creditor taking adverse action is disclosed. Whenever the notification is to be provided through a third party, a creditor shall not be liable for any act or omission of the third party that constitutes a violation of this section if the creditor accurately and in a timely manner provided the third party with the information necessary for the notification and was maintaining procedures reasonably adapted to avoid any such violation.

(b) **Form of ECOA notice and statement of specific reasons.**

(1) **ECOA notice.** A creditor satisfies the requirements of subsection (a)(2) regarding a statement of the provisions of section 701(a) of the Act and the name and address of the appropriate Federal enforcement agency if it provides the following notice, or one that is substantially similar:

The Federal Equal Credit Opportunity Act prohibits creditors from discriminating against credit applicants on the basis of race, color, religion, national origin, sex, marital status, age (provided that the applicant has the capacity to enter into a binding contract); because all or part of the applicant's income derives from any public assistance program; or because the applicant has in good faith exercised any right under the Consumer Credit Protection Act. The Federal agency that administers compliance with this law concerning this creditor is (name and address as specified by the appropriate agency listed in Appendix A).

The sample notice printed above may be modified immediately following the required references to the Federal Act and enforcement agency to include references to any similar State statute or regulation and to a State enforcement agency.

(2) **Statement of specific reasons.** A statement of reasons for adverse action shall be sufficient if it is specific and indicates the principal reason(s) for the adverse action. A creditor may formulate its own statement of reasons in checklist or letter form or may use all or a portion of the sample form printed below, which, if properly completed, satisfies the requirements of subsection (a)(2)(i). Statements that the adverse action was based on the creditor's internal standards or policies or that the applicant failed to achieve the qualifying score on the creditor's credit scoring system are insufficient.

STATEMENT OF CREDIT DENIAL, TERMINATION, OR CHANGE

DATE ____________

Applicant's Name: ____________

Applicant's Address: ____________

____

Description of Account, Transaction, or Requested Credit: ____________

____

Description of Adverse Action Taken:

____

____

PRINCIPAL REASON(S) FOR ADVERSE ACTION CONCERNING CREDIT

____ Credit application incomplete
____ Insufficient credit references
____ Unable to verify credit references
____ Temporary or irregular employment
____ Unable to verify employment
____ Length of employment
____ Insufficient income
____ Excessive obligations
____ Unable to verify income
____ Inadequate collateral
____ Too short a period of residence
____ Temporary residence
____ Unable to verify residence
____ No credit file
____ Insufficient credit file
____ Delinquent credit obligations
____ Garnishment, attachment, foreclosure, repossession, or suit
____ Bankruptcy
____ We do not grant credit to any applicant on the terms and conditions you request.
____ Other, specify: ____________

____

DISCLOSURE OF USE OF INFORMATION OBTAINED FROM AN OUTSIDE SOURCE

____ Disclosure inapplicable
____ Information obtained in a report from a consumer reporting agency
Name: ____________

____

Street address: ____________

____

Telephone number: ____________

____ Information obtained from an outside source other than a consumer reporting agency. Under the Fair Credit Reporting Act, you have the right to make a written request, within 60 days of receipt of this notice, for disclosure of the nature of the adverse information.

Creditor's name: ____________

Creditor's address: ____________

____

Creditor's telephone number: ____________

[Add ECOA Notice]

(3) **Other information.** The notification required by subsection (a)(1) may include other

information so long as it does not detract from the required content. This notification also may be combined with any disclosures required under other titles of the Consumer Credit Protection Act or any other law, provided that all requirements for clarity and placement are satisfied; and it may appear on either or both sides of the paper if there is a clear reference on the front to any information on the back.

(c) **Oral notifications.** The applicable requirements of this section are satisfied by oral notifications (including statements of specific reasons) in the case of any creditor that did not receive more than 150 applications during the calendar year immediately preceding the calendar year in which the notification of adverse action is to be given to a particular applicant.

(d) **Withdrawn applications.** Where an applicant submits an application and the parties contemplate that the applicant will inquire about its status, if the creditor approves the application and the applicant has not inquired within 30 days after applying, then the creditor may treat the application as withdrawn and need not comply with subsection (a)(1).

(e) **Failure of compliance.** A failure to comply with this section shall not constitute a violation when caused by an inadvertent error; provided that, on discovering the error, the creditor corrects it as soon as possible and commences compliance with the requirements of this section.

(f) **Notification.** A creditor notifies an applicant when a writing addressed to the applicant is delivered or mailed to the applicant's last known address or, in the case of an oral notification, when the creditor communicates with the applicant.

SECTION 202.10—FURNISHING OF CREDIT INFORMATION

(a) **Accounts established on or after June 1, 1977.** (1) For every account established on or after June 1, 1977, a creditor that furnishes credit information shall:

(i) determine whether an account offered by the creditor is one that an applicant's spouse is permitted to use or upon which the spouses are contractually liable other than as guarantors, sureties, endorsers, or similar parties; and

(ii) designate any such account to reflect the fact of participation of both spouses.[11]

(2) Except as provided in subsection (3), if a creditor furnishes credit information concerning an account designated under this section (or designated prior to the effective date of this Part) to a consumer reporting agency, it shall furnish the information in a manner that will enable the agency to provide access to the information in the name of each spouse.

(3) If a creditor furnishes credit information concerning an account designated under this section (or designated prior to the effective date of this Part) in response to an inquiry regarding a particular applicant, it shall furnish the information in the name of the spouse about whom such information is requested.[12]

(b) **Accounts established prior to June 1, 1977.** For every account established prior to and in existence on June 1, 1977, a creditor that furnishes credit information shall either:

(1) not later than June 1, 1977

(i) determine whether the account is one that an applicant's spouse, if any, is permitted to use or upon which the spouses are contractually liable other than as guarantors, sureties, endorsers, or similar parties;

(ii) designate any such account to reflect the fact of participation of both spouses;[13] and

(iii) comply with the reporting requirements of subsections (a)(2) and (a)(3); or

(2) mail or deliver to all applicants, or all married applicants, in whose name an account is carried on the creditor's records one copy of the notice set forth below.[14] The notice may be mailed with a billing statement or other mailing. All such notices shall be mailed or delivered by October 1, 1977. As to open end accounts, this requirement may be satisfied by mailing one notice at any time prior to October 2, 1977, regarding each account

---

[11] A creditor need not distinguish between participation as a user or as a contractually liable party.

[12] If a creditor learns that new parties have undertaken payment on an account, then the subsequent history of the account shall be furnished in the names of the new parties and need not continue to be furnished in the names of the former parties.

[13] See footnote 11.

[14] A creditor may delete the references to the "use" of an account when providing notices regarding closed end accounts.

for which a billing statement is sent between June 1 and October 1, 1977. The notice may be supplemented as necessary to permit identification of the account by the creditor or by a consumer reporting agency. A creditor need only send notices relating to those accounts on which it lacks the information necessary to make the proper designation regarding participation or contractual liability.

NOTICE

CREDIT HISTORY FOR MARRIED PERSONS

The Federal Equal Credit Opportunity Act prohibits credit discrimination on the basis of race, color, religion, national origin, sex, marital status, age (provided that a person has the capacity to enter into a binding contract); because all or part of a person's income derives from any public assistance program; or because a person in good faith has exercised any right under the Federal Consumer Credit Protection Act. Regulations under the Act give married persons the right to have credit information included in credit reports in the name of both the wife and the husband if both use or are responsible for the account. This right was created, in part, to insure that credit histories will be available to women who become divorced or widowed.

If your account with us is one that both husband and wife signed for or is an account that is being used by one of you who did not sign, then you are entitled to have us report credit information relating to the account in both your names. If you choose to have credit information concerning your account with us reported in both your names, please complete and sign the statement below and return it to us.

Federal regulations provide that signing your name below will not change your or your spouse's legal liability on the account. Your signature will only request that credit information be reported in both your names.

If you do not complete and return the form below, we will continue to report your credit history in the same way that we do now.

When you furnish credit information on this account, please report all information concerning the account in both our names.

______________	______________
Account number	Print or type name
	______________
	Print or type name
	______________
	Signature of either spouse

(c) **Requests to change manner in which information is reported.** Within 90 days after receipt of a properly completed request to change the manner in which information is reported to consumer reporting agencies and others regarding an account described in subsection (b), a creditor shall designate the account to reflect the fact of participation of both spouses.[15] When furnishing information concerning any such account, the creditor shall comply with the reporting requirements of subsections (a)(2) and (a)(3). The signature of an applicant or the applicant's spouse on a request to change the manner in which information concerning an account is furnished shall not alter the legal liability of either spouse upon the account or require the creditor to change the name in which the account is carried.

(d) **Inadvertent errors.** A failure to comply with this section shall not constitute a violation when caused by an inadvertent error; provided that, on discovering the error, the creditor corrects it as soon as possible and commences compliance with the requirements of this section.

SECTION 202.11—RELATION TO STATE LAW

(a) **Inconsistent State laws.** Except as otherwise provided in this section, this Part alters, affects, or preempts only those State laws that are inconsistent with this Part and then only to the extent of the inconsistency. A State law is not inconsistent with this Part if it is more protective of an applicant.

(b) **Preempted provisions of State law.** (1) State law is deemed to be inconsistent with the requirements of the Act and this Part and less protective of an applicant within the meaning of section 705(f) of the Act to the extent that such law:

(i) requires or permits a practice or act prohibited by the Act or this Part;

---

[15] See footnote 11.

(ii) prohibits the individual extension of consumer credit to both parties to a marriage if each spouse individually and voluntarily applies for such credit;

(iii) prohibits inquiries or collection of data required to comply with the Act or this Part;

(iv) prohibits asking age or considering age in a demonstrably and statistically sound, empirically derived credit system, to determine a pertinent element of creditworthiness, or to favor an elderly applicant; or

(v) prohibits inquiries necessary to establish or administer a special purpose credit program as defined by section 202.8.

(2) A determination as to whether a State law is inconsistent with the requirements of the Act and this Part will be made only in response to a request for a formal Board interpretation. All requests for such interpretations, in addition to meeting the requirements of section 202.1(d), shall comply with the applicable provisions of subsections (b)(1) and (2) of Supplement I to this Part. A determination shall be based on the factors enumerated in this subsection and, as applicable, subsection (c) of Supplement I. Notice of the interpretation shall be provided as specified in subsection (e)(1) of Supplement I, but the interpretation shall be effective in accordance with section 202.1. The interpretation shall be subject to revocation or modification at any time, as provided in subsection (g)(4) of Supplement I.

(c) **Finance charges and loan ceilings.** If married applicants voluntarily apply for and obtain individual accounts with the same creditor, the accounts shall not be aggregated or otherwise combined for purposes of determining permissible finance charges or permissible loan ceilings under any Federal or State law. Permissible loan ceiling laws shall be construed to permit each spouse to become individually liable up to the amount of the loan ceilings, less the amount for which the applicant is jointly liable.[16]

(d) **State and Federal laws not affected.** This section does not alter or annul any provision of State property laws, laws relating to the disposition of decedents' estates, or Federal or State banking regulations directed only toward insuring the solvency of financial institutions.

(e) **Exemption for State regulated transactions.** (1) In accordance with the provisions of Supplement I to this Part, any State may apply to the Board for an exemption from the requirements of sections 701 and 702 of the Act and the corresponding provisions of this Part for any class of credit transactions within the State. The Board will grant such an exemption if:

(i) the Board determines that, under the law of that State, that class of credit transactions is subject to requirements substantially similar to those imposed under sections 701 and 702 of the Act and the corresponding provisions of this Part, or that applicants are afforded greater protection than is afforded under sections 701 and 702 of the Act and the corresponding provisions of this Part; and

(ii) there is adequate provision for State enforcement.

(2) In order to assure that the concurrent jurisdiction of Federal and State courts created in section 706(f) of the Act will continue to have substantive provisions to which such jurisdiction shall apply; to allow Federal enforcement agencies to retain their authority regarding any class of credit transactions exempted pursuant to subsection (e)(1) and Supplement I; and, generally, to aid in implementing the Act:

(i) no such exemption shall be deemed to extend to the civil liability provisions of sections 706 or the administrative enforcement provisions of section 704 of the Act; and

(ii) after an exemption has been granted, the requirements of the applicable State law shall constitute the requirements of the Act and this Part, except to the extent such State law imposes requirements not imposed by the Act or this Part.

(3) Exemptions granted by the Board to particular classes of credit transactions within specified States will be set forth in Supplement II to this Part.

SECTION 202.12—RECORD RETENTION

(a) **Retention of prohibited information.** Retention in a creditor's files of any information, the use of which in evaluating applications is prohibited by the Act or this Part, shall not constitute

[16] For example, in a State with a permissible loan ceiling of $1,000, if a married couple were jointly liable for unpaid debt in the amount of $250, each spouse could subsequently become individually liable for $750.

a violation of the Act or this Part where such information was obtained:

(1) from any source prior to March 23, 1977;[17] or

(2) at any time from consumer reporting agencies; or

(3) at any time from an applicant or others without the specific request of the creditor; or

(4) at any time as required to monitor compliance with the Act and this Part or other Federal or State statutes or regulations.

(b) **Preservation of records.** (1) For 25 months after the date that a creditor notifies an applicant of action taken on an application, the creditor shall retain as to that application in original form or a copy thereof:[18]

(i) any application form that it receives, any information required to be obtained concerning characteristics of an applicant to monitor compliance with the Act and this Part or other similar law, and any other written or recorded information used in evaluating the application and not returned to the applicant at the applicant's request;

(ii) a copy of the following documents if furnished to the applicant in written form (or, if furnished orally, any notation or memorandum with respect thereto made by the creditor):

(A) the notification of action taken; and

(B) the statement of specific reasons for adverse action; and

(iii) any written statement submitted by the applicant alleging a violation of the Act or this Part.

(2) For 25 months after the date that a creditor notifies an applicant of adverse action regarding an account, other than in connection with an application, the creditor shall retain as to that account, in original form or a copy thereof:[19]

(i) any written or recorded information concerning such adverse action; and

(ii) any written statement submitted by the applicant alleging a violation of the Act or this Part.

(3) In addition to the requirements of subsections (b)(1) and (2), any creditor that has actual notice that it is under investigation or is subject to an enforcement proceeding for an alleged violation of the Act or this Part by an enforcement agency charged with monitoring that creditor's compliance with the Act and this Part, or that has been served with notice of an action filed pursuant to section 706 of the Act and sections 202.1(b) or (c) of this Part, shall retain the information required in subsections (b)(1) and (2) until final disposition of the matter, unless an earlier time is allowed by order of the agency or court.

(4) In any transaction involving more than one creditor, any creditor not required to comply with section 202.9 (notifications) shall retain for the time period specified in subsection (b) all written or recorded information in its possession concerning the applicant, including a notation of action taken in connection with any adverse action.

(c) **Failure of compliance.** A failure to comply with this section shall not constitute a violation when caused by an inadvertent error.

SECTION 202.13—INFORMATION FOR MONITORING PURPOSES

(a) **Scope and information requested.** (1) For the purpose of monitoring compliance with the provisions of the Act and this Part, any creditor that receives an application for consumer credit relating to the purchase of residential real property, where the extension of credit is to be secured by a lien on such property, shall request as part of any written application for such credit the following information regarding the applicant and joint applicant (if any):

(i) race/national origin, using the categories American Indian or Alaskan Native; Asian or Pacific Islander; Black; White; Hispanic; Other (Specify);

(ii) sex;

(iii) marital status, using the categories married, unmarried, and separated; and

(iv) age.

(2) "Residential real property" means improved real property used or intended to be used for residential purposes, including single family

[17] Pursuant to the October 28, 1975 version of Regulation B, the applicable date for sex and marital status information is June 30, 1976.

[18] "A copy thereof" includes carbon copies, photocopies, microfilm or microfiche copies, or copies produced by any accurate information retrieval system. A creditor who uses a computerized or mechanized system need not keep a written copy of a document if it can regenerate the precise text of the document upon request.

[19] See footnote 18.

homes, dwellings for from two to four families, and individual units of condominiums and cooperatives.

(b) **Method of obtaining information.** Questions regarding race/national origin, sex, marital status, and age may be listed, at the creditor's option, either on the application form or on a separate form that refers to the application.

(c) **Disclosure to applicant and joint applicant.** The applicant and joint applicant (if any) shall be informed that the information regarding race/national origin, sex, marital status, and age is being requested by the Federal government for the purpose of monitoring compliance with Federal anti-discrimination statutes and that those statutes prohibit creditors from discriminating against applicants on those bases. The applicant and joint applicant shall be asked, but not required, to supply the requested information. If the applicant or joint applicant chooses not to provide the information or any part of it, that fact shall be noted on the form on which the information is obtained.

(d) **Substitute monitoring program.** Any monitoring program required by an agency charged with administrative enforcement under section 704 of the Act may be substituted for the requirements contained in subsections (a), (b), and (c).

MAGNUSON–MOSS WARRANTY—FEDERAL TRADE COMMISSION IMPROVEMENT ACT

Selected Sections

PUBLIC LAW 93–637; 88 STAT. 2183

TITLE I—CONSUMER PRODUCT WARRANTIES

TABLE OF CONTENTS

Sec.

§ 101. Definitions

For the purposes of this title:

(1) The term "consumer product" means any tangible personal property which is distributed in commerce and which is normally used for personal, family, or household purposes (including any such property intended to be attached to or installed in any real property without regard to whether it is so attached or installed).

(2) The term "Commission" means the Federal Trade Commission.

(3) The term "consumer" means a buyer (other than for purposes of resale) of any consumer product, any person to whom such product is transferred during the duration of an implied or written warranty (or service contract) applicable to the product, and any other person who is entitled by the terms of such warranty (or service contract) or under applicable State law to enforce against the warrantor (or service contractor) the obligations of the warranty (or service contract).

(4) The term "supplier" means any person engaged in the business of making a consumer product directly or indirectly available to consumers.

(5) The term "warrantor" means any supplier or other person who gives or offers to give a written warranty or who is or may be obligated under an implied warranty.

(6) The term "written warranty" means—

(A) any written affirmation of fact or written promise made in connection with the sale of a consumer product by a supplier to a buyer which relates to the nature of the material or workmanship and affirms or promises that such material or workmanship is defect free or will meet a specified level of performance over a specified period of time, or

(B) any undertaking in writing in connection with the sale by a supplier of a consumer product to refund, repair, replace, or take other remedial action with respect to such product in the event that such product fails to meet the specifications set forth in the undertaking,

which written affirmation, promise, or undertaking becomes part of the basis of the bargain between a supplier and a buyer for purposes other than resale of such product.

(7) The term "implied warranty" means an implied warranty arising under State law (as modified by sections 108 and 104 (a)) in connection with the sale by a supplier of a consumer product.

(8) The term "service contract" means a contract in writing to perform, over a fixed period of time or for a specified duration, services relating to the maintenance or repair (or both) of a consumer product.

(9) The term "reasonable and necessary maintenance" consists of those operations (A) which the consumer reasonably can be expected to perform or have performed and (B) which are necessary to keep any consumer product performing its intended function and operating at a reasonable level of performance.

(10) The term "remedy" means whichever of the following actions the warrantor elects:

(A) repair,

(B) replacement, or

(C) refund;

except that the warrantor may not elect refund unless (i) the warrantor is unable to provide replacement and repair is not commercially practicable or cannot be timely made, or (ii) the consumer is willing to accept such refund.

(11) The term "replacement" means furnishing a new consumer product which is identical or reasonably equivalent to the warranted consumer product.

(12) The term "refund" means refunding the actual purchase price (less reasonable depreciation based on actual use where permitted by rules of the Commission).

(13) The term "distributed in commerce" means sold in commerce, introduced or delivered for introduction into commerce, or held for sale or distribution after introduction into commerce.

(14) The term "commerce" means trade, traffic, commerce, or transportation—

(A) between a place in a State and any place outside thereof, or

(B) which affects trade, traffic, commerce, or transportation described in subparagraph (A).

(15) The term "State" means a State, the District of Columbia, the Commonwealth of Puerto Rico, the Virgin Islands, Guam, the Canal Zone, or American Samoa. The term "State law" includes a law of the United States applicable only to the District of Columbia or only to a territory or possession of the United States; and the term "Federal law" excludes any State law.

§ 102. Warranty provisions

(a) In order to improve the adequacy of information available to consumers, prevent deception, and improve competition in the marketing of consumer products, any warrantor warranting a consumer product to a consumer by means of a written warranty shall, to the extent required by rules of the Commission, fully and conspicuously disclose in simple and readily understood language the terms and conditions of such warranty. Such rules may require inclusion in the written warranty of any of the following items among others:

(1) The clear identification of the names and addresses of the warrantors.

(2) The identity of the party or parties to whom the warranty is extended.

(3) The products or parts covered.

(4) A statement of what the warrantor will do in the event of a defect, malfunction, or failure to conform with such written warranty—at whose expense—and for what period of time.

(5) A statement of what the consumer must do and expenses he must bear.

(6) Exceptions and exclusions from the terms of the warranty.

(7) The step-by-step procedure which the consumer should take in order to obtain performance of any obligation under the warranty, including the identification of any person or class of persons authorized to perform the obligations set forth in the warranty.

(8) Information respecting the availability of any informal dispute settlement procedure offered by the warrantor and a recital, where the warranty so provides, that the purchaser may be required to resort to such procedure before pursuing any legal remedies in the courts.

(9) A brief, general description of the legal remedies available to the consumer.

(10) The time at which the warrantor will perform any obligations under the warranty.

(11) The period of time within which, after notice of a defect, malfunction, or failure to conform with the warranty, the warrantor will perform any obligations under the warranty.

(12) The characteristics or properties of the products, or parts thereof, that are not covered by the warranty.

(13) The elements of the warranty in words or phrases which would not mislead a reasonable, average consumer as to the nature or scope of the warranty.

(b)(1)(A) The Commission shall prescribe rules requiring that the terms of any written warranty on a consumer product be made available to the consumer (or prospective consumer) prior to the sale of the product to him.

(B) The Commission may prescribe rules for determining the manner and form in which information with respect to any written warranty of a consumer product shall be clearly and conspicuously presented or displayed so as not to mislead the reasonable, average consumer, when such information is contained in advertising, labeling, point-of-sale material, or other representations in writing.

(2) Nothing in this title (other than paragraph (3) of this subsection) shall be deemed to authorize the Commission to prescribe the duration of written warranties given or to require that a consumer product or any of its components be warranted.

(3) The Commission may prescribe rules for extending the period of time a written warranty or service contract is in effect to correspond with any period of time in excess of a reasonable period (not less than 10 days) during which the consumer is deprived of the use of such consumer product by reason of failure of the product to conform with the written warranty or by reason of the failure of the warrantor (or service contractor) to carry out such warranty (or service contract) within the period specified in the warranty (or service contract).

(c) No warrantor of a consumer product may condition his written or implied warranty of such product on the consumer's using, in connection with such product, any article or service (other than article or service provided without charge under the terms of the warranty) which is identified by brand, trade, or corporate name; except that the prohibition of this subsection may be waived by the Commission if—

(1) the warrantor satisfies the Commission that the warranted product will function properly only if the article or service so identified is used in connection with the warranted product, and

(2) the Commission finds that such a waiver is in the public interest.

The Commission shall identify in the Federal Register, and permit public comment on, all applications for waiver of the prohibition of this subsection, and shall publish in the Federal Register its disposition of any such application, including the reasons therefor.

(d) The Commission may by rule devise detailed substantive warranty provisions which warrantors may incorporate by reference in their warranties.

(e) The provisions of this section apply only to warranties which pertain to consumer products actually costing the consumer more than $5.

§ 103. Designation of warranties

(a) Any warrantor warranting a consumer product by means of a written warranty shall clearly and conspicuously designate such warranty in the following manner, unless exempted from doing so by the Commission pursuant to subsection (c) of this section:

(1) If the written warranty meets the Federal minimum standards for warranty set forth in section 104 of this Act, then it shall be conspicuously designated a "full (statement of duration) warranty".

(2) If the written warranty does not meet the Federal minimum standards for warranty set forth in section 104 of this Act, then it shall be conspicuously designated a "limited warranty".

(b) Sections 102, 103, and 104 shall not apply to statements or representations which are similar to expressions of general policy concerning customer satisfaction and which are not subject to any specific limitations.

(c) In addition to exercising the authority pertaining to disclosure granted in section 102 of this Act, the Commission may by rule determine when a written warranty does not have to be designated either "full (statement of duration)" or "limited" in accordance with this section.

(d) The provisions of subsections (a) and (c) of this section apply only to warranties which pertain to consumer products actually costing the consumer more than $10 and which are not designated "full (statement of duration) warranties".

§ 104. Federal minimum standards for warranty

(a) In order for a warrantor warranting a consumer product by means of a written warranty to meet the Federal minimum standards for warranty—

(1) such warrantor must as a minimum remedy such consumer product within a reasonable time and without charge, in the case of a defect, malfunction, or failure to conform with such written warranty;

(2) notwithstanding section 108(b), such warrantor may not impose any limitation on the duration of any implied warranty on the product;

(3) such warrantor may not exclude or limit consequential damages for breach of any written or implied warranty on such product, unless such exclusion or limitation conspicuously appears on the face of the warranty; and

(4) if the product (or a component part thereof) contains a defect or malfunction after a reasonable number of attempts by the warrantor to remedy defects or malfunctions in such product, such warrantor must permit the consumer to elect either a refund for, or replacement without charge of, such product or part (as the case may be). The Commission may by rule specify for purposes of this paragraph, what constitutes a reasonable number of attempts to remedy particular kinds of defects or malfunctions under different circumstances. If the warrantor replaces a component part of a consumer product, such replace-

ment shall include installing the part in the product without charge.

(b)(1) In fulfilling the duties under subsection (a) respecting a written warranty, the warrantor shall not impose any duty other than notification upon any consumer as a condition of securing remedy of any consumer product which malfunctions, is defective, or does not conform to the written warranty, unless the warrantor has demonstrated in a rulemaking proceeding, or can demonstrate in an administrative or judicial enforcement proceeding (including private enforcement), or in an informal dispute settlement proceeding, that such a duty is reasonable.

(2) Notwithstanding paragraph (1), a warrantor may require, as a condition to replacement of, or refund for, any consumer product under subsection (a), that such consumer product shall be made available to the warrantor free and clear of liens and other encumbrances, except as otherwise provided by rule or order of the Commission in cases in which such a requirement would not be practicable.

(3) The Commission may, by rule define in detail the duties set forth in section 104(a) of this Act and the applicability of such duties to warrantors of different categories of consumer products with "full (statement of duration)" warranties.

(4) The duties under subsection (a) extend from the warrantor to each person who is a consumer with respect to the consumer product.

(c) The performance of the duties under subsection (a) of this section shall not be required of the warrantor if he can show that the defect, malfunction, of failure of any warranted consumer product to conform with a written warranty, was caused by damage (not resulting from defect or malfunction) while in the possession of the consumer, or unreasonable use (including failure to provide reasonable and necessary maintenance).

(d) For purposes of this section and of section 102(c), the term "without charge" means that the warrantor may not assess the consumer for any costs the warrantor or his representatives incur in connection with the required remedy of a warranted consumer product. An obligation under subsection (a)(1)(A) to remedy without charge does not necessarily require the warrantor to compensate the consumer for incidental expenses; however, if any incidental expenses are incurred because the remedy is not made within a reasonable time or because the warrantor imposed an unreasonable duty upon the consumer as a condition of securing remedy, then the consumer shall be entitled to recover reasonable incidental expenses which are so incurred in any action against the warrantor.

(e) If a supplier designates a warranty applicable to a consumer product as a "full (statement of duration)" warranty, then the warranty on such product shall, for purposes of any action under section 110(d) or under any State law, be deemed to incorporate at least the minimum requirements of this section and rules prescribed under this section.

§ 105. Full and limited warranting of a consumer product

Nothing in this title shall prohibit the selling of a consumer product which has both full and limited warranties if such warranties are clearly and conspicuously differentiated.

§ 106. Service contracts

(a) The Commission may prescribe by rule the manner and form in which the terms and conditions of service contracts shall be fully, clearly, and conspicuously disclosed.

(b) Nothing in this title shall be construed to prevent a supplier or warrantor from entering into a service contract with the consumer in addition to or in lieu of a written warranty if such contract fully, clearly, and conspicuously discloses its terms and conditions in simple and readily understood language.

§ 107. Designation of representatives

Nothing in this title shall be construed to prevent any warrantor from designating representatives to perform duties under the written or implied warranty: *Provided,* That such warrantor shall make reasonable arrangements for compensation of such designated representatives, but no such designation shall relieve the warrantor of his direct responsibilities to the consumer or make the representative a cowarrantor.

§ 108. Limitation on disclaimer of implied warranties

(a) No supplier may disclaim or modify (except as provided in subsection (b)) any implied warranty to a consumer with respect to such consumer product if (1) such supplier makes any written warranty to the consumer with respect to such consumer product, or (2) at the time of sale, or within 90 days thereafter, such supplier enters into a service contract with the consumer which applies to such consumer product.

(b) For purposes of this title (other than section 104(a)(2)), implied warranties may be limited in duration to the duration of a written warranty of reasonable duration, if such limitation is conscionable and is set forth in clear and unmistakable language and prominently displayed on the face of the warranty.

(c) A disclaimer, modification, or limitation made in violation of this section shall be ineffective for purposes of this title and State law.

§ 109. Commission rules

(a) Any rule prescribed under this title shall be prescribed in accordance with section 553 of title 5, United States Code; except that the Commission shall give interested persons an opportunity for oral presentations of data, views, and arguments, in addition to written submissions. A transcript shall be kept of any oral presentation. Any such rule shall be subject to judicial review under section 18(e) of the Federal Trade Commission Act (as amended by section 202 of this Act) in the same manner as rules prescribed under section 18(a)(1)(B) of such Act, except that section 18(e) (3)(B) of such Act shall not apply.

(b) The Commission shall initiate within one year after the date of enactment of this Act a rulemaking proceeding dealing with warranties and warranty practices in connection with the sale of used motor vehicles; and, to the extent necessary to supplement the protections offered the consumer by this title, shall prescribe rules dealing with such warranties and practices. In prescribing rules under this subsection, the Commission may exercise any authority it may have under this title, or other law, and in addition it may require disclosure that a used motor vehicle is sold without any warranty and specify the form and content of such disclosure.

§ 110. Remedies

(a)(1) Congress hereby declares it to be its policy to encourage warrantors to establish procedures whereby consumer disputes are fairly and expeditiously settled through informal dispute settlement mechanisms.

(2) The Commission shall prescribe rules setting forth minimum requirements for any informal dispute settlement procedure which is incorporated into the terms of a written warranty to which any provision of this title applies. Such rules shall provide for participation in such procedure by independent or governmental entities.

(3) One or more warrantors may establish an informal dispute settlement procedure which meets the requirements of the Commission's rules under paragraph (2). If—

(A) a warrantor establishes such a procedure,

(B) such procedure, and its implementation, meets the requirements of such rules, and

(C) he incorporates in a written warranty a requirement that the consumer resort to such procedure before pursuing any legal remedy under this section respecting such warranty,

then (i) the consumer may not commence a civil action (other than a class action) under subsection (d) of this section unless he initially resorts to such procedure; and (ii) a class of consumers may not proceed in a class action under subsection (d) except to the extent the court determines necessary to establish the representative capacity of the named plaintiffs, unless the named plaintiffs (upon notifying the defendant that they are named plaintiffs in a class action with respect to a warranty obligation) initially resort to such procedure. In the case of such a class action which is brought in a district court of the United States, the representative capacity of the named plaintiffs shall be established in the application of rule 23 of the Federal Rules of Civil Procedure. In any civil action arising out of a warranty obligation and relating to a matter considered in such a procedure, any decision in such procedure shall be admissible in evidence.

(4) The Commission on its own initiative may, or upon written complaint filed by any interested person shall, review the bona fide operation of any dispute settlement procedure resort to which is stated in a written warranty to be a prerequisite to pursuing a legal remedy under this section. If the Commission finds that such procedure or its implementation fails to comply with the requirements of the rules under paragraph (2), the Commission may take appro-

priate remedial action under any authority it may have under this title or any other provision of law.

(5) Until rules under paragraph (2) take effect, this subsection shall not affect the validity of any informal dispute settlement procedure respecting consumer warranties, but in any action under subsection (d), the court may invalidate any such procedure if it finds that such procedure is unfair.

(b) It shall be a violation of section 5(a)(1) of the Federal Trade Commission Act (15 U.S.C. 45(a)(1)) for any person to fail to comply with any requirement imposed on such person by this title (or a rule thereunder) or to violate any prohibition contained in this title (or a rule thereunder).

(c)(1) The district courts of the United States shall have jurisdiction of any action brought by the Attorney General (in his capacity as such), or by the Commission by any of its attorneys designated by it for such purpose, to restrain (A) any warrantor from making a deceptive warranty with respect to a consumer product, or (B) any person from failing to comply with any requirement imposed on such person by or pursuant to this title or from violating any prohibition contained in this title. Upon proper showing that, weighing the equities and considering the Commission's or Attorney General's likelihood of ultimate success, such action would be in the public interest and after notice to the defendant, a temporary restraining order or preliminary injunction may be granted without bond. In the case of an action brought by the Commission, if a complaint under section 5 of the Federal Trade Commission Act is not filed within such period (not exceeding 10 days) as may be specified by the court after the issuance of the temporary restraining order or preliminary injunction, the order or injunction shall be dissolved by the court and be of no further force and effect. Any suit shall be brought in the district in which such person resides or transacts business. Whenever it appears to the court that the ends of justice require that other persons should be parties in the action, the court may cause them to be summoned whether or not they reside in the district in which the court is held, and to that end process may be served in any district.

(2) For the purposes of this subsection, the term "deceptive warranty" means (A) a written warranty which (i) contains an affirmation, promise, description, or representation which is either false or fraudulent, or which, in light of all of the circumstances, would mislead a reasonable individual exercising due care; or (ii) fails to contain information which is necessary in light of all of the circumstances, to make the warranty not misleading to a reasonable individual exercising due care; or (B) a written warranty created by the use of such terms as "guaranty" or "warranty", if the terms and conditions of such warranty so limit its scope and application as to deceive a reasonable individual.

(d)(1) Subject to subsections (a)(3) and (e), a consumer who is damaged by the failure of a supplier, warrantor, or service contractor to comply with any obligation under this title, or under a written warranty, implied warranty, or service contract, may bring suit for damages and other legal and equitable relief—

(A) in any court of competent jurisdiction in any State or the District of Columbia; or

(B) in an appropriate district court of the United States, subject to paragraph (3) of this subsection.

(2) If a consumer finally prevails in any action brought under paragraph (1) of this subsection, he may be allowed by the court to recover as part of the judgment a sum equal to the aggregate amount of cost and expenses (including attorneys' fees based on actual time expended) determined by the court to have been reasonably incurred by the plaintiff for or in connection with the commencement and prosecution of such action, unless the court in its discretion shall determine that such an award of attorneys' fees would be inappropriate.

(3) No claim shall be cognizable in a suit brought under paragraph (1)(B) of this subsection—

(A) if the amount in controversy of any individual claim is less than the sum or value of $25;

(B) if the amount in controversy is less than the sum or value of $50,000 (exclusive of interests and costs) computed on the basis of all claims to be determined in this suit; or

(C) if the action is brought as a class action, and the number of named plaintiffs is less than one hundred.

(e) No action (other than a class action or an action respecting a warranty to which subsection (a)(3) applies) may be brought under subsection (d) for failure to comply with any obligation under any written or implied warranty or service contract, and a class of consumers may not proceed in a class action under such subsection with respect to such a failure except to the extent the court determines necessary to establish the representative capacity of the named plaintiffs, unless the person obligated under the warranty or service contract is afforded a reasonable opportunity to cure such failure to comply. In the case of such a class action (other than a class action respecting a warranty to which subsection (a)(3) applies) brought under subsection (d) for breach of any written or implied warranty or service contract, such reasonable opportunity will be afforded by the named plaintiffs and they shall at that time notify the defendant that they are acting on behalf of the class. In the case of such a class action which is brought in a district court of the United States, the representative capacity of the named plaintiffs shall be established in the application of rule 23 of the Federal Rules of Civil Procedure.

(f) For purposes of this section, only the warrantor actually making a written affirmation of fact, promise, or undertaking shall be deemed to have created a written warranty, and any rights arising thereunder may be enforced under this section only against such warrantor and no other person.

§ 111. Effect on other laws

(a)(1) Nothing contained in this title shall be construed to repeal, invalidate, or supersede the Federal Trade Commission Act (15 U.S.C. 41 et seq.) or any statute defined therein as an Antitrust Act.

(2) Nothing in this title shall be construed to repeal, invalidate, or supersede the Federal Seed Act (7 U.S.C. 1551–1611) and nothing in this title shall apply to seed for planting.

(b)(1) Nothing in this title shall invalidate or restrict any right or remedy of any consumer under State law or any other Federal law.

(2) Nothing in this title (other than sections 108 and 104(a)(2) and (4)) shall (A) affect the liability of, or impose liability on, any person for personal injury, or (B) supersede any provision of State law regarding consequential damages for injury to the person or other injury.

(c)(1) Except as provided in subsection (b) and in paragraph (2) of this subsection, a State requirement—

(A) which relates to labeling or disclosure with respect to written warranties or performance thereunder;

(B) which is within the scope of an applicable requirement of sections 102, 103, and 104 (and rules implementing such sections), and

(C) which is not identical to a requirement of section 102, 103, or 104 (or a rule thereunder),

shall not be applicable to written warranties complying with such sections (or rules thereunder).

(2) If, upon application of an appropriate State agency, the Commission determines (pursuant to rules issued in accordance with section 109) that any requirement of such State covering any transaction to which this title applies (A) affords protection to consumers greater than the requirements of this title and (B) does not unduly burden interstate commerce, then such State requirement shall be applicable (notwithstanding the provisions of paragraph (1) of this subsection) to the extent specified in such determination for so long as the State administers and enforces effectively any such greater requirement.

(d) This title (other than section 102(c)) shall be inapplicable to any written warranty the making or content of which is otherwise governed by Federal law. If only a portion of a written warranty is so governed by Federal law, the remaining portion shall be subject to this title.

§ 112. Effective date

(a) Except as provided in subsection (b) of this section, this title shall take effect 6 months after the date of its enactment but shall not apply to consumer products manufactured prior to such date.

(b) Section 102(a) shall take effect 6 months after the final publication of rules respecting such section; except that the Commission, for good cause shown, may postpone the applicability of such sections until one year after such final publication in order to permit any designated classes of suppliers to bring their written warranties into compliance with rules promulgated pursuant to this title.

(c) The Commission shall promulgate rules for initial implementation of this title as soon as possible after the date of enactment of this Act but in no event later than one year after such date.

*

MAGNUSON-MOSS WARRANTY ACT REGULATIONS

Selected Parts

TITLE 16—COMMERCIAL PRACTICES

PART 700—INTERPRETATIONS OF MAGNUSON-MOSS WARRANTY ACT

PART 701—DISCLOSURE OF WRITTEN CONSUMER PRODUCT WARRANTY TERMS AND CONDITIONS

PART 702—PRE-SALE AVAILABILITY OF WRITTEN WARRANTY TERMS

REGULATIONS

PART 700—INTERPRETATIONS OF MAGNUSON-MOSS WARRANTY ACT

PART 701—DISCLOSURE OF WRITTEN CONSUMER PRODUCT WARRANTY TERMS AND CONDITIONS

PART 702—PRE-SALE AVAILABILITY OF WRITTEN WARRANTY TERMS

PART 700—INTERPRETATIONS OF MAGNUSON-MOSS WARRANTY ACT

§ 700.1 Products covered.

(a) The Act applies to written warranties on tangible personal property which is normally used for personal, family, or household purposes. This definition includes property which is intended to be attached to or installed in any real property without regard to whether it is so attached or installed. This means that a product is a "consumer product" if the use of that type of product is not uncommon. The percentage of sales or the use to which a product is put by any individual buyer is not determinative. For example, products such as automobiles and typewriters which are used for both personal and commercial purposes come within the definition of consumer product. Where it is unclear whether a particular product is covered under the definition of consumer product, any ambiguity will be resolved in favor of coverage.

(b) Agricultural products such as farm machinery, structures and implements used in the business or occupation of farming are not covered by the Act where their personal, family, or household use is uncommon. However, those agricultural products normally used for personal or household gardening (for example, to produce goods for personal consumption, and not for resale) are consumer products under the Act.

(c) The definition of "Consumer product" limits the applicability of the Act to personal property, "including any such property intended to be attached to or installed in any real property without regard to whether it is so attached or installed." This provision brings under the Act separate items of equipment attached to real property, such as air conditioners, furnaces, and water heaters.

(d) The coverage of separate items of equipment attached to real property includes, but is not limited to, appliances and other thermal, mechanical, and electrical equipment. (It does not extend to the wiring, plumbing, ducts and other items which are integral component parts of the structure.) State law would classify many such products as fixtures to, and therefore a part of, realty. The statutory definition is designed to bring such products under the Act regardless of whether they may be considered fixtures under state law.

(e) The coverage of building materials which are not separate items of equipment is based on the nature of the purchase transaction. An analysis of the transaction will determine whether the goods are real or personal property. The numerous products which go into the construction of a consumer dwelling are all consumer products when sold "over the counter," as by hardware and building supply retailers. This is also true where a consumer contracts for the purchase of such materials in connection with the improvement, repair, or modification of a home (for example, paneling, dropped ceilings, siding, roofing, storm windows, remodeling). However, where such products are at the time of sale integrated into the structure of a dwelling they are not consumer products as they cannot be practically distinguished from realty. Thus, for example, the beams, wallboard, wiring, plumbing, windows, roofing, and other structural components of a dwelling are not consumer products when they are sold as part of real estate covered by a written warranty.

(f) In the case where a consumer contracts with a builder to construct a home, a substantial addition to a home, or other realty (such as a garage or an in-ground swimming pool) the building materials to be used are not consumer products. Although the materials are separately identifiable at the time the contract is made, it is the intention of the parties to contract for the construction of realty which will integrate the component materials. Of course, as noted above, any separate items of equipment to be attached to such realty are consumer products under the Act.

(g) Certain provisions of the Act apply only to products actually costing the consumer more than a specified amount. Section 103 applies to consumer products actually costing the consumer more than $10, excluding tax. The $10 minimum will be interpreted to include multiple-packaged items which may individually sell for less than $10, but which have been packaged in a manner that does not permit breaking the package to purchase an item or items at a price less than $10. Thus, a written warranty on a dozen items packaged and priced for sale at $12 must be designated, even though identical items may be offered in smaller quantities at under $10. This interpretation applies in the same manner to the minimum dollar limits in section 102 and rules promulgated under that section.

(h) Warranties on replacement parts and components used to repair consumer products are covered; warranties on services are not covered. Therefore, warranties which apply solely to a repairer's workmanship in performing repairs are not subject to the Act. Where a written agreement warrants both the parts provided to effect a repair and the workmanship in making that repair, the warranty must comply with the Act and the rules thereunder.

(i) The Act covers written warranties on consumer products "distributed in commerce" as that term is defined in section 101(3). Thus, by its terms the Act arguably applies to products exported to foreign jurisdictions. However, the public interest would not be served by the use of Commission resources to enforce the Act with respect to such products. Moreover, the legislative intent to apply the requirements of the Act to such products is not sufficiently clear to justify such an extraordinary result. The Commission does not contemplate the enforcement of the Act with respect to consumer products exported to foreign jurisdictions. Products exported for sale at military post exchanges remain subject to the same enforcement standards as products sold within the United States, its territories and possessions.

§ 700.2 Date of manufacture.

Section 112 of the Act provides that the Act shall apply only to those consumer products manufactured after July 4, 1975. When a consumer purchases repair of a consumer product the date of manufacture of any replacement parts used is the measuring date for determining coverage under the Act. The date of manufacture of the consumer product being repaired is in this instance not relevant. Where a consumer purchases or obtains on an exchange basis a rebuilt consumer product, the date that the rebuilding process is completed determines the Act's applicability.

§ 700.3 Written warranty.

(a) The Act imposes specific duties and liabilities on suppliers who offer written warranties on consumer products. Certain representations, such as energy efficiency ratings for electrical appliances, care labeling of wearing apparel, and other product information disclosures may be express warranties under the Uniform Commercial Code. However, these disclosures alone are not written warranties under this Act. Section 101(6) provides that a written affirmation of fact or a written promise of a specified level of performance must relate to a specified period of time in order to be considered a "written warranty."[1] A product information disclosure without a specified time period to which the disclosure relates is therefore not a written warranty. In addition, section 111(d) exempts from the Act (except section 102(c)) any written warranty the making or content of which is required by federal law. The Commission encourages the disclosure of product information which is not deceptive and which may benefit consumers, and will not construe the Act to impede information disclosure in product advertising or labeling.

(b) Certain terms, or conditions, of sale of a consumer product may not be "written warranties" as that term is defined in Section 101(6), and should not be offered or described in a manner that may deceive consumers as to their enforceability under the Act. For example, a seller of consumer products may give consumers an unconditional right to revoke acceptance of goods within a certain number of days after delivery without regard to defects or failure to meet a specified level of performance. Or a seller may permit consumers to return products for any reason for credit toward purchase of another item. Such terms of sale taken alone are not written warranties under the Act. Therefore, suppliers should avoid any characterization of such terms of sale as warranties. The use of such terms as "free trial period" and "trade-in credit policy" in this regard would be appropriate. Furthermore, such terms of sale should be stated separately from any written warranty. Of course, the offering and performance of such terms of sale remain subject to section 5 of the Federal Trade Commission Act, 15 U.S.C. 45.

[1] A "written warranty" is also created by a written affirmation of fact or a written promise that the product is defect free, or by a written undertaking of remedial action within the meaning of § 101(6)(B).

(c) The Magnuson-Moss Warranty Act generally applies to written warranties covering consumer products. Many consumer products are covered by warranties which are neither intended for, nor enforceable by, consumers. A common example is a warranty given by a component supplier to a manufacturer of consumer products. (The manufacturer may, in turn, warrant these components to consumers.) The component supplier's warranty is generally given solely to the product manufacturer, and is neither intended to be conveyed to the consumer nor brought to the consumer's attention in connection with the sale. Such warranties are not subject to the Act, since a written warranty under section 101(6) of the Act must become "part of the basis of the bargain between a supplier and a buyer for purposes other than resale." However, the Act applies to a component supplier's warranty in writing which is given to the consumer. An example is a supplier's written warranty to the consumer covering a refrigerator that is sold installed in a boat or recreational vehicle. The supplier of the refrigerator relies on the boat or vehicle assembler to convey the written agreement to the consumer. In this case, the supplier's written warranty is to a consumer, and is covered by the Act.

§ 700.4 Parties "actually making" a written warranty.

Section 110(f) of the Act provides that only the supplier "actually making" a written warranty is liable for purposes of FTC and private enforcement of the Act. A supplier who does no more than distribute or sell a consumer product covered by a written warranty offered by another person or business and which identifies that person or business as the warrantor is not liable for failure of the written warranty to comply with the Act or rules thereunder. However, other actions and written and oral representations of such a supplier in connection with the offer or sale of a warranted product may obligate that supplier under the Act. If under state law the supplier is deemed to have "adopted" the written affirmation of fact, promise, or undertaking, the supplier is also obligated under the Act. Suppliers are advised to consult state law to determine those actions and representations which may make them co-warrantors, and therefore obligated under the warranty of the other person or business.

§ 700.5 Expressions of general policy.

(a) Under section 103(b), statements or representations of general policy concerning customer satisfaction which are not subject to any specific limitation need not be designated as full or limited warranties, and are exempt from the requirements of sections 102, 103, and 104 of the Act and rules thereunder. However, such statements remain subject to the enforcement provisions of section 110 of the Act, and to section 5 of the Federal Trade Commission Act, 15 U.S.C. 45.

(b) The section 103(b) exemption applies only to general policies not, to those which are limited to specific consumer products manufactured or sold by the supplier offering such a policy. In addition, to qualify for an exemption under section 103(b) such policies may not be subject to any specific limitations. For example, policies which have an express limitation of duration or a limitation of the amount to be refunded are not exempted. This does not preclude the imposition of reasonable limitations based on the circumstances in each instance a consumer seeks to invoke such an agreement. For instance, a warrantor may refuse to honor such an expression of policy where a consumer has used a product for 10 years without previously expressing any dissatisfaction with the product. Such a refusal would not be a specific limitation under this provision.

§ 700.6 Designation of warranties.

(a) Section 103 of the Act provides that written warranties on consumer products manufactured after July 4, 1975, and actually costing the consumer more than $10, excluding tax, must be designated either "Full (statement of duration) Warranty" or "Limited Warranty". Warrantors may include a statement of duration in a limited warranty designation. The designation or designations should appear clearly and conspicuously as a caption, or prominent title, clearly separated from the text of the warranty. The full (statement of duration) warranty and limited warranty are the exclusive designations permitted under the Act, unless a specific exception is created by rule.

(b) Section 104(b)(4) states that "the duties under subsection (a) (of respect to the consumer product." Secsection 104) extend from the warrantor to each person who is a consumer with tion 101(3) defines a consumer as "a buyer (other than for purposes of resale) of any consumer product, any person to whom such product is transferred during the duration of an implied or written warranty (or service contract) applicable to the product * *." Therefore, a full warranty may not expressly restrict the warranty rights of a transferee during its stated duration. However, where the duration of a full warranty is defined solely in terms of first purchaser ownership there can be no violation of section 104(b)(4), since the duration of the warranty expires, by definition, at the time of transfer. No rights of a subsequent transferee are cut off as there is no transfer of ownership "during the duration of (any) warranty." Thus, these provisions do not preclude the offering of a full warranty with its duration determined exclusively by the period during which the first purchaser owns the product, or uses it in conjunction with another product. For example, an automotive battery or muffler warranty may be designated as "full warranty for as long as you own your car." Because this type of warranty leads the consumer to believe that proof of purchase is not needed so long as he or she owns the product a duty to furnish documentary proof may not be reasonably imposed on the consumer under this type of warranty. The burden is on the warrantor to prove that a particular claimant under this type of warranty is not the original purchaser or owner of the product. Warrantors or their designated agents may, however, ask consumers to state or affirm that they are the first purchaser of the product.

§ 700.7 Use of warranty registration cards.

(a) Under section 104(b)(1) of the Act a warrantor offering a full warranty may not impose on consumers any duty other than notification of a defect as a condition of securing remedy of the defect or malfunction, unless such additional duty can be demonstrated by the warrantor to be reasonable. Warrantors have in the past stipulated the return of a "warranty registration" or similar card. By "warranty registration card" the Commission means a card which must be returned by the consumer shortly after purchase of the product and which is stipulated or implied in the warranty to be a condition precedent to warranty coverage and performance.

(b) A requirement that the consumer return a warranty registration card or a similar notice as a condition of performance under a full warranty is an unreasonable duty. Thus, a provision such as, "This warranty is void unless the warranty registration card is returned to the warrantor" is not permissible in a full warranty, nor is it permissible to imply such a condition in a full warranty.

(c) This does not prohibit the use of such registration cards where a warrantor suggests use of the card as one possible means of proof of the date the product was purchased. For example, it is permissible to provide in a full warranty that a consumer may fill out and return a card to place on file proof of the date the product was purchased. Any such suggestion to the consumer must include notice that failure to return the card will not affect rights under the warranty, so long as the consumer can show in a reasonable manner the date the product was purchased. Nor does this interpretation prohibit a seller from obtaining from purchasers at the time of sale information requested by the warrantor.

§ 700.8 Warrantor's decision as final.

A warrantor shall not indicate in any written warranty or service contract either directly or indirectly that the decision of the warrantor, service contractor, or any designated third party is final or binding in any dispute concerning the warranty or service contract. Nor shall a warrantor or service contractor state that it alone shall determine what is a defect under the agreement. Such statements are deceptive since section 110(d) of the Act gives state and federal courts jurisdiction over suits for breach of warranty and service contract.

§ 700.9 Duty to install under a full warranty.

Under section 104(a)(1) of the Act, the remedy under a full warranty must be provided to the consumer without charge. If the warranted product has utility only when installed, a full warranty must provide such installation without charge regardless of whether or not the consumer originally paid for installation by the warrantor or his agent. However, this does not preclude the warrantor from imposing on the consumer a duty to remove, return, or reinstall where such duty can be demonstrated by the warrantor to meet the standard of reasonableness under section 104(b)(1).

§ 700.10 Section 102(c).

(a) Section 102(c) prohibits tying arrangements that condition coverage under a written warranty on the consumer's use of an article or service identified by brand, trade, or corporate name unless that article or service is provided without charge to the consumer.

(b) Under a limited warranty that provides only for replacement of defective parts and no portion of labor charges, section 102(c) prohibits a condition that the consumer use only service (labor) identified by the warrantor to install the replacement parts. A warrantor or his designated representative may not provide parts under the warranty in a manner which impedes or precludes the choice by the consumer of the person or business to perform necessary labor to install such parts.

(c) No warrantor may condition the continued validity of a warranty on the use of only authorized repair service and/or authorized replacement parts for non-warranty service and maintenance. For example, provisions such as, "This warranty is void if service is performed by anyone other than an authorized 'ABC' dealer and all replacement parts must be genuine 'ABC' parts," and the like, are prohibited where the service or parts are not covered by the warranty. These provisions violate the Act in two ways. First, they violate the section 102 (c) ban against tying arrangements. Second, such provisions are deceptive under section 110 of the Act, because a warrantor cannot, as a matter of law, avoid liability under a written warranty where a defect is unrelated to the use by a consumer of "unauthorized" articles or service. This does not preclude a warrantor from expressly excluding liability for defects or damage caused by such "unauthorized" articles or service; nor does it preclude the warrantor from denying liability where the warrantor can demonstrate that the defect or damage was so caused.

§ 700.11 Written warranty, service contract, and insurance distinguished for purposes of compliance under the Act.

(a) The Act recognizes two types of agreements which may provide similar coverage of consumer products, the written warranty, and the service contract. In addition, other agreements may meet the statutory definitions of either "written warranty" or "service contract," but are sold and regulated under state law as contracts of insurance. One example is the automobile breakdown insurance policies sold in many jurisdictions and regulated by the state as a form of casualty insurance. The McCarran-Ferguson Act, 15 U.S.C. 1011 et seq., precludes jurisdiction under federal law over "the business of insurance" to the extent an agreement is regulated by state law as insurance. Thus, such agreements are subject to the Magnuson-Moss Warranty Act only to the extent they are not regulated in a particular state as the business of insurance.

(b) "Written warranty" and "service contract" are defined in sections 101(6) and 101(8) of the Act, respectively. A written warranty must be "part of the basis of the bargain." This means that it must be conveyed at the time of sale of the consumer product and the consumer must not give any consideration beyond the purchase price of the consumer product in order to benefit from the agreement. It is not a requirement of the Act that an agreement obligate a supplier of the consumer product to a written warranty, but merely that it be part of the basis of the bargain between a supplier and a consumer. This contemplates written warranties by third-party non-suppliers.

(c) A service contract under the Act must meet the definitions of section 101(8). An agreement which would meet the definition of written warranty in section 101(6)(A) or (B) but for its failure to satisfy the basis of the bargain test is a service contract. For example, an agreement which calls for some consideration in addition to the purchase price of the consumer product, or which is entered into at some date after the purchase of the consumer product to which it applies, is a service contract. An agreement which relates only to the performance of maintenance and/or inspection services and which is not an undertaking, promise, or affirmation with respect to a specified level of performance, or that the product is free of defects in materials or workmanship, is a service contract. An agreement to perform periodic cleaning and inspection of a product over a specified period of time, even when offered at the time of sale and without charge to the consumer, is an example of such a service contract.

§ 700.12 Effective date of 16 CFR, Parts 701 and 702.

The Statement of Basis and Purpose of the final rules promulgated on December 31, 1975, provides that Parts 701 and 702 will become effective one year after the date of promulgation, December 31, 1976. The Commission intends this to mean that these rules apply only to written warranties on products manufactured after December 31, 1976.

PART 701—DISCLOSURE OF WRITTEN CONSUMER PRODUCT WARRANTY TERMS AND CONDITIONS

§ 701.1 Definitions

(a) "The Act" means the Magnuson-Moss Warranty Federal Trade Commission Improvement Act, 15 U.S.C. 2301, et seq.

(b) "Consumer product" means any tangible personal property which is distributed in commerce and which is normally used for personal, family, or household purposes (including any such property intended to be attached to or installed in any real property without regard to whether it is so attached or installed. Products which are purchased solely for commercial or industrial use are excluded solely for purposes of this Part.

(c) "Written warranty" means—(1) any written affirmation of fact or written promise made in connection with the sale of a consumer product by a supplier to a buyer which relates to the nature of the material or workmanship and affirms or promises that such material or workmanship is defect free or will meet a specified level of performance over a specified period of time, or

(2) any undertaking in writing in connection with the sale by a supplier of a consumer product to refund, repair, replace, or take other remedial action with respect to such product in the event that such product fails to meet the specifications set forth in the undertaking, which written affirmation, promise or undertaking becomes part of the basis of the bargain between a supplier and a buyer for purposes other than resale of such product.

(d) "Implied warranty" means an implied warranty arising under State law (as modified by secs. 104(a) and 108 of the Act) in connection with the sale by a supplier of a consumer product.

(e) "Remedy" means whichever of the following actions the warrantor elects:

(1) repair,

(2) replacement, or

(3) refund; except that the warrantor may not elect refund unless: (i) the warrantor is unable to provide replacement and repair is not commercially practicable or cannot be timely made, or

(ii) the consumer is willing to accept such refund.

(f) "Supplier" means any person engaged in the business of making a consumer product directly or indirectly available to consumers.

(g) "Warrantor" means any supplier or other person who gives or offers to give a written warranty.

(h) "Consumer" means a buyer (other than for purposes of resale or use in the ordinary course of the buyer's business) of any consumer product, any person to whom such product is transferred during the duration of an implied or written warranty applicable to the product, and any other such person who is entitled by the terms of such warranty or under applicable State law to enforce against the warrantor the obligations of the warranty.

(i) "On the face of the warranty" means—(1) where the warranty is a single sheet with printing on both sides of the sheet or where the warranty is comprised of more than one sheet, the page on which the warranty text begins;

(2) where the warranty is included as part of a larger document, such as a use and care manual, the page in such document on which the warranty text begins.

§ 701.2 Scope

The regulations in this part establish requirements for warrantors for disclosing the terms and conditions of written warranties on consumer products actually costing the consumer more than $15.00.

§ 701.3 Written warranty terms

(a) Any warrantor warranting to a consumer by means of a written warranty a consumer product actually costing the consumer more than $15.00 shall clearly and conspicuously disclose in a single document in simple and readily understood language, the following items of information: (1) The identity of the party or parties to whom the written warranty is extended, if the enforceability of the written warranty is limited to the original consumer purchaser or is otherwise limited to persons other than every consumer owner during the term of the warranty;

(2) A clear description and identification of products, or parts, or characteristics, or components or properties covered by and where necessary for clarification, excluded from the warrany;

(3) A statement of what the warrantor will do in the event of a defect, malfunction or failure to conform with the written warranty, including the items or services the warrantor will pay for or provide, and, where necessary for clarification, those which the warrantor will not pay for or provide;

(4) The point in time or event on which the warranty term commences, if different from the purchase date, and the time period or other measurement of warranty duration;

(5) A step-by-step explanation of the procedure which the consumer should follow in order to obtain performance of any warranty obligation, including the persons or class of persons authorized to perform warranty obligations. This includes the name(s) of the warrantor(s), together with: the mailing address(es) of the warrantor(s), and/or the name or title and the address of any employee or department of the warrantor responsible for the performance of warranty obligations, and/or a telephone number which consumers may use without charge to obtain information on warranty performance;

(6) Information respecting the availability of an informal dispute settlement mechanism elected by the warrantor in compliance with Part 703 of this subchapter;

(7) Any limitations on the duration of implied warranties, disclosed on the face of the warranty as provided in Section 108 of the Act, accompanied by the following statement:

Some states do not allow limitations on how long an implied warranty lasts, so the above limitation may not apply to you.

(8) Any exclusions of or limitations on relief such as incidental or consequential damages, accompanied by the following statement, which may be combined with the statement required in sub-paragraph (7) above:

Some states do not allow the exclusion or limitation of incidental or consequential damages, so the above limitation or exclusion may not apply to you.

(9) A statement in the following language:

This warranty gives you specific legal rights, and you may also have other rights which vary from state to state.

(b) Paragraph (a)(1)—(9) of this Section shall not be applicable with respect to statements of general policy on emblems, seals or insignias issued by third parties promising replacement or refund if a consumer product is defective, which statements contain no representation or assurance of the quality or performance characteristics of the product; provided that (1) the disclosures required by paragraph (a)(1)—(9) are published by such third parties in each issue of a publication with a general circulation, and (2) such disclosures are provided free of charge to any consumer upon written request.

§ 701.4 Owner registration cards

When a warrantor employs any card such as an owner's registration card, a warranty registration card, or the like, and the return of such card is a condition precedent to warranty coverage and performance, the warrantor shall disclose this fact in the warranty. If the return of such card reasonably appears to be a condition precedent to warranty coverage and performance, but is not such a condition, that fact shall be disclosed in the warranty.

PART 702—PRE-SALE AVAILABILITY OF WRITTEN WARRANTY TERMS

§ 702.1 Definitions

(a) "The Act" means the Magnuson-Moss Warranty Federal Trade Commission Improvement Act, 15 U.S.C. 2301, et seq.

(b) "Consumer product" means any tangible personal property which is distributed in commerce and which is normally used for personal, family, or household purposes (including any such property intended to be attached to or installed in any real property without regard to whether it is so attached or installed). Products which are purchased solely for commercial or industrial use are excluded solely for purposes of this Part.

(c) "Written warranty" means—(1) any written affirmation of fact or written promise made in connection with the sale of a consumer product by a supplier to a buyer which relates to the nature of the material or workmanship and affirms or promises that such material or workmanship is defect free or will meet a specified level of performance over a specified period of time, or

(2) any undertaking in writing in connection with the sale by a supplier of a consumer product to refund, repair, replace, or take other remedial action with respect to such product in the event that such product fails to meet the specifications set forth in the undertaking, which written affirmation, promise or undertaking becomes part of the basis of the bargain between a supplier and a buyer for purposes other than resale of such product.

(d) "Warrantor" means any supplier or other person who gives or offers to give a written warranty.

(e) "Seller" means any person who sells or offers for sale for purposes other than resale or use in the ordinary course of the buyer's business any consumer product.

(f) "Supplier" means any person engaged in the business of making a consumer product directly or indirectly available to consumers.

(g) "Binder" means a locking binder, notebook, or similar system which will provide the consumer with convenient access to copies of product warranties.

§ 702.2 Scope

The regulations in this part establish requirements for sellers and warrantors for making the terms of any written warranty on a consumer product available to the consumer prior to sale.

§ 702.3 Pre-sale availability of written warranty terms

The following requirements apply to consumer products actually costing the consumer more than $15.00: (a) *Duties of the seller.* Except as provided in paragraphs (c)–(d) of this section, the seller of a consumer product with a written warranty shall:

(1) make available for the prospective buyer's review, prior to sale, the text of such written warranty by the use of one or more of the following means:

(i) clearly and conspicuously displaying the text of the written warranty in close conjunction to each warranted product; and/or

(ii) maintaining a binder or series of binders which contain(s) copies of the warranties for the products sold in each department in which any consumer product with a written warranty is offered for sale. Such binder(s) shall be maintained in each such department, or in a location which provides the prospective buyer with ready access to such binder(s), and shall be prominently entitled "Warranties" or other similar title which clearly identifies the binder(s). Such binder(s) shall be indexed according to product or warrantor and shall be maintained up to date when new warranted products or models or new warranties for existing products are introduced into the store or department by substituting superseding warranties and by adding new warranties as appropriate. The seller shall either:

(A) display such binder(s) in a manner reasonably calculated to elicit the prospective buyer's attention; or

(B) make the binders available to prospective buyers on request, and place signs reasonably calculated to elicit the prospective buyer's attention in prominent locations in the store or department advising such prospective buyers of the availability of the binders, including instructions for obtaining access; and/or

(iii) displaying the package of any consumer product on which the text of the written warranty is disclosed, in a manner such that the warranty is clearly visible to prospective buyers at the point of sale; and/or

(iv) placing in close proximity to the warranted consumer product a notice which discloses the text of the written warranty, in a manner which clearly identifies to prospective buyers the product to which the notice applies;

(2) Not remove or obscure any warranty disclosure materials provided by a warrantor, except:

(i) where such removal is necessary for store window displays, fashion shows, or picture taking; or

(ii) where the seller otherwise, through means provided for in subparagraph (1) above, makes the terms of the warranty information available to the consumer.

(b) *Duties of the warrantor.* (1) A warrantor who gives a written warranty warranting to a consumer a consumer product actually costing the consumer more than $15.00 shall:

(i) Provide sellers with warranty materials necessary for such sellers to comply with the requirements set forth in paragraph (a) of this section, by the use of one or more by the following means:

(A) Providing a copy of the written warranty with every warranted consumer product; and/or

(B) Providing a tag, sign, sticker, label, decal or other attachment to the product, which contains the full text of the written warranty; and/or

(C) Printing on or otherwise attaching the text of the written warranty to the package, carton, or other container if that package, carton or other container is normally used for display purposes. If the warrantor elects this option a copy of the written warranty must also accompany the warranted product; and/or

(D) Providing a notice, sign, or poster disclosing the text of a consumer product warranty.

If the warrantor elects this option, a copy of the written warranty must also accompany each warranted product.

(ii) Provide catalog, mail order, and door-to-door sellers with copies of written warranties necessary for such sellers to comply with the requirements set forth in paragraphs (c) and (d) of this section.

(2) Sub-paragraph (1) of this paragraph (b) shall not be applicable with respect to statements of general policy on emblems, seals or insignias issued by third parties promising replacement or refund if a consumer product is defective, which statements contain no rep-

resentation or assurance of the quality or performance characteristics of the product; provided that (i) the disclosures required by 701.3(a)(1)–(9) are published by such third parties in each issue of a publication with a general circulation, and (ii) such disclosures are provided free of charge to any consumer upon written request.

(c) *Catalog and Mail Order Sales.* (1) For purposes of this paragraph:

(i) "Catalog or mail order sales", means any offer for sale, or any solicitation for an order for a consumer product with a written warranty, which includes instructions for ordering the product which do not require a personal visit to the seller's establishment.

(ii) "Close conjuction" means on the page containing the description of the warranted product, or on the page facing that page.

(2) Any seller who offers for sale to consumers consumer products with written warranties by means of a catalog or mail order solicitation shall:

(i) clearly and conspicuously disclose in such catalog or solicitation in close conjunction to the description of warranted product, or in an information section of the catalog or solicitation clearly referenced, including a page number, in close conjunction to the description of the warranted product, *either:*

(A) the full text of the written warranty; or

(B) that the written warranty can be obtained free upon specific written request, and the address where such warranty can be obtained. If this option is elected, such seller shall promptly provide a copy of any written warranty requested by the consumer.

(d) *Door-to-door sales.* (1) For purposes of this paragraph:

(i) "Door-to-door sale" means a sale of consumer products in which the seller or his representative personally solicits the sale, including those in response to or following an invitation by a buyer, and the buyer's agreement to offer to purchase is made at a place other than the place of business of the seller.

(ii) "Prospective buyer" means an individual solicited by a door-to-door seller to buy a consumer product who indicates sufficient interest in that consumer product or maintains sufficient contact with the seller for the seller reasonably to conclude that the person solicited is considering purchasing the product.

(2) Any seller who offers for sale to consumers consumer products with written warranties by means of door-to-door sales shall, prior to the consummation of the sale, disclose the fact that the sales representative has copies of the warranties for the warranted products being offered for sale, which may be inspected by the prospective buyer at any time during the sales presentation. Such disclosure shall be made orally and shall be included in any written materials shown to prospective buyers.

*

FEDERAL TRADE COMMISSION HOLDER–IN–DUE–COURSE REGULATIONS

TITLE 16—COMMERCIAL PRACTICES

PART 433—PRESERVATION OF CONSUMERS' CLAIMS AND DEFENSES

As promulgated on November 14, 1975

REGULATIONS

§ 433.1 Definitions

(a) *Person.* An individual, corporation, or any other business organization.

(b) *Consumer.* A natural person who seeks or acquires goods or services for personal, family, or household use.

(c) *Creditor.* A person who, in the ordinary course of business, lends purchase money or finances the sale of goods or services to consumers on a deferred payment basis; *Provided,* such person is not acting, for the purposes of a particular transaction, in the capacity of a credit card issuer.

(d) *Purchase money loan.* A cash advance which is received by a consumer in return for a "Finance Charge" within the meaning of the Truth in Lending Act and Regulation Z, which is applied, in whole or substantial part, to a purchase of goods or services from a seller who (1) refers consumers to the creditor or (2) is affiliated with the creditor by common control, contract, or business arrangement.

(e) *Financing a sale.* Extending credit to a consumer in connection with a "Credit Sale" within the meaning of the Truth in Lending Act and Regulation Z.

(f) *Contract.* Any oral or written agreement, formal or informal, between a creditor and a seller, which contemplates or provides for cooperative or concerted activity in connection with the sale of goods or services to consumers or the financing thereof.

(g) *Business arrangement.* Any understanding, procedure, course of dealing, or arrangement, formal or informal, between a creditor and a seller, in connection with the sale of goods or services to consumers or the financing thereof.

(h) *Credit card issuer.* A person who extends to cardholders the right to use a credit card in connection with purchases of goods or services.

(i) *Consumer credit contract.* Any instrument which evidences or embodies a debt arising from a "Purchase Money Loan" transaction or a "financed sale" as defined in paragraphs (d) and (e).

(j) *Seller.* A person who, in the ordinary course of business, sells or leases goods or services to consumers.

§ 433.2 Preservation of consumers' claims and defenses, unfair or deceptive acts or practices

In connection with any sale or lease of goods or services to consumers, in or affecting commerce as "commerce" is defined in the Federal Trade Commission Act, it is an unfair or deceptive act or practice within the meaning of Section 5 of that Act for a seller, directly or indirectly, to:

(a) Take or receive a consumer credit contract which fails to contain the following provision in at least ten point, bold face, type:

NOTICE

ANY HOLDER OF THIS CONSUMER CREDIT CONTRACT IS SUBJECT TO ALL CLAIMS AND DEFENSES

WHICH THE DEBTOR COULD ASSERT AGAINST THE SELLER OF GOODS OR SERVICES OBTAINED PURSUANT HERETO OR WITH THE PROCEEDS HEREOF. RECOVERY HEREUNDER BY THE DEBTOR SHALL NOT EXCEED AMOUNTS PAID BY THE DEBTOR HEREUNDER.

or, (b) Accept, as full or partial payment for such sale or lease, the proceeds of any purchase mony loan (as purchase money loan is defined herein), unless any consumer credit contract made in connection with such purchase money loan contains the following provision in at least ten point, bold face, type:

NOTICE

ANY HOLDER OF THIS CONSUMER CREDIT CONTRACT IS SUBJECT TO ALL CLAIMS AND DEFENSES WHICH THE DEBTOR COULD ASSERT AGAINST THE SELLER OF GOODS OR SERVICES OBTAINED WITH THE PROCEEDS HEREOF. RECOVERY HEREUNDER BY THE DEBTOR SHALL NOT EXCEED AMOUNTS PAID BY THE DEBTOR HEREUNDER.

§ 433.3 Exemption of sellers taking or receiving open end consumer credit contracts before September 15, 1977, from requirements of § 433.2(a).

(a) Any seller who has taken or received an open end consumer credit contract before October 31, 1977, shall be exempt from the requirements of 16 CFR Part 433 with respect to such contract provided the contract does not cut off consumers' claims and defenses.

(b) *Definitions.* The following definitions apply to this exemption:

(1) All pertinent definitions contained in 16 CFR 433.1.

(2) Open end consumer credit contract: a consumer credit contract pursuant to which "open end credit" is extended.

(3) "Open end credit": Consumer credit extended pursuant to a plan under which a creditor may permit an applicant to make purchases or make loans from time to time directly from the creditor or indirectly by use of a credit card, check or other device as the plan may provide. The term does not include negotiated advances under an open end real estate mortgage or a letter of credit.

(4) Contract which does not cut off consumers' claims and defenses: a consumer credit contract which does not constitute or contain a negotiable instrument, or contain any waiver, limitation, term, or condition which has the effect of limiting a consumer's right to assert against any holder of the contract all legally sufficient claims and defenses which the consumer could assert against the seller of goods or services purchased pursuant to the contract.

FEDERAL TRADE COMMISSION REGULATIONS FOR DOOR-TO-DOOR SALES

Cooling Off Period for Door-to-Door Sales

Federal Trade Commission Trade Regulation Rule, Title 16, Code of Federal Regulations, Ch. I, subch. D, part 429, promulgated October 18, 1972, effective June 7, 1974; 37 F.R. 22934, 38 F.R. 33766; as modified, November 1, 1973; 38 F.R. 30105.

§ 429.1 The Rule.

In connection with any door-to-door sale, it constitutes an unfair and deceptive act or practice for any seller to:

(a) Fail to furnish the buyer with a fully completed receipt or copy of any contract pertaining to such sale at the time of its execution, which is in the same language, e. g., Spanish, as that principally used in the oral sales presentation and which shows the date of the transaction and contains the name and address of the seller, and in immediate proximity to the space reserved in the contract for the signature of the buyer or on the front page of the receipt if a contract is not used and in boldface type of a minimum size of 10 points, a statement in substantially the following form:

"YOU, THE BUYER, MAY CANCEL THIS TRANSACTION AT ANY TIME PRIOR TO MIDNIGHT OF THE THIRD BUSINESS DAY AFTER THE DATE OF THIS TRANSACTION. SEE THE ATTACHED NOTICE OF CANCELLATION FORM FOR AN EXPLANATION OF THIS RIGHT."

(b) Fail to furnish each buyer, at the time he signs the door-to-door sales contract or otherwise agrees to buy consumer goods or services from the seller, a completed form in duplicate, captioned "NOTICE OF CANCELLATION", which shall be attached to the contract or receipt and easily detachable, and which shall contain in ten point bold face type the following information and statements in the same language, e. g., Spanish, as that used in the contract:

NOTICE OF CANCELLATION

(enter date of transaction)

____

(Date)

YOU MAY CANCEL THIS TRANSACTION, WITHOUT ANY PENALTY OR OBLIGATION, WITHIN THREE BUSINESS DAYS FROM THE ABOVE DATE.

IF YOU CANCEL, ANY PROPERTY TRADED IN, ANY PAYMENTS MADE BY YOU UNDER THE CONTRACT OR SALE, AND ANY NEGOTIABLE INSTRUMENT EXECUTED BY YOU WILL BE RETURNED WITHIN 10 BUSINESS DAYS FOLLOWING RECEIPT BY THE SELLER OF YOUR CANCELLATION NOTICE, AND ANY SECURITY INTEREST ARISING OUT OF THE TRANSACTION WILL BE CANCELED.

IF YOU CANCEL, YOU MUST MAKE AVAILABLE TO THE SELLER AT YOUR RESIDENCE, IN SUBSTANTIALLY AS GOOD CONDITION AS WHEN RECEIVED, ANY GOODS DELIVERED TO YOU UNDER THIS CONTRACT OR SALE; OR YOU MAY IF YOU WISH, COMPLY WITH THE INSTRUCTIONS OF THE SELLER REGARDING THE RETURN SHIPMENT OF THE GOODS AT THE SELLER'S EXPENSE AND RISK.

IF YOU DO MAKE THE GOODS AVAILABLE TO THE SELLER AND THE SELLER DOES NOT PICK THEM UP WITHIN 20

DAYS OF THE DATE OF YOUR NOTICE OF CANCELLATION, YOU MAY RETAIN OR DISPOSE OF THE GOODS WITHOUT ANY FURTHER OBLIGATION. IF YOU FAIL TO MAKE THE GOODS AVAILABLE TO THE SELLER, OR IF YOU AGREE TO RETURN THE GOODS TO THE SELLER AND FAIL TO DO SO, THEN YOU REMAIN LIABLE FOR PERFORMANCE OF ALL OBLIGATIONS UNDER THE CONTRACT.

TO CANCEL THIS TRANSACTION, MAIL OR DELIVER A SIGNED AND DATED COPY OF THIS CANCELLATION NOTICE OR ANY OTHER WRITTEN NOTICE, OR SEND A TELEGRAM, TO ____________________,

[Name of seller]

AT ____________________

[Address of seller's place of ________ business] NOT LATER THAN

MIDNIGHT OF ____________.

[Date]

I HEREBY CANCEL THIS TRANSACTION.

________ (Date) ________________ (Buyer's Signature)

(c) Fail, before furnishing copies of the "Notice of Cancellation" to the buyer, to complete both copies by entering the name of the seller, the address of the seller's place of business, the date of the transaction, and the date, not earlier than the third business day following the date of the transaction, by which the buyer may give notice of cancellation.

(d) Include in any door-to-door contract or receipt any confession of judgment or any waiver of any of the rights to which the buyer is entitled under this section including specifically his right to cancel the sale in accordance with the provisions of this section.

(e) Fail to inform each buyer orally, at the time he signs the contract or purchases the goods or services, of his right to cancel.

(f) Misrepresent in any manner the buyer's right to cancel.

(g) Fail or refuse to honor any valid notice of cancellation by a buyer and within 10 business days after the receipt of such notice, to (i) refund all payments made under the contract or sale; (ii) return any goods or property traded in, in substantially as good condition as when received by the seller; (iii) cancel and return any negotiable instrument executed by the buyer in connection with the contract or sale and take any action necessary or appropriate to terminate promptly any security interest created in the transaction.

(h) Negotiate, transfer, sell, or assign any note or other evidence of indebtedness to a finance company or other third party prior to midnight of the fifth business day following the day the contract was signed or the goods or services were purchased.

(i) Fail, within 10 business days of receipt of the buyer's notice of cancellation, to notify him whether the seller intends to repossess or to abandon any shipped or delivered goods.

Note 1: *Definitions.* For the purposes of the section the following definitions shall apply:

(a) *Door-to-door sale.* A sale, lease, or rental of consumer goods or services with a purchase price of $25 or more, whether under single or multiple contracts, in which the seller or his representative personally solicits the sale, including those in response to or following an invitation by the buyer, and the buyer's agreement or offer to purchase is made at a place other than the place of business of the seller. The term "door-to-door sale" does not include a transaction:

(1) Made pursuant to prior negotiations in the course of a visit by the buyer to a retail business establishment having a fixed permanent location where the goods are exhibited or the services are offered for sale on a continuing basis; or

(2) In which the consumer is accorded the right of rescission by the provisions of the Consumer Credit Protection Act (15 U.S.C. 1635) or regulations issued pursuant thereto; or

(3) In which the buyer has initiated the contact and the goods or services are needed to meet a bona fide immedi-

ate personal emergency of the buyer, and the buyer furnishes the seller with a separate dated and signed personal statement in the buyer's handwriting describing the situation requiring immediate remedy and expressly acknowledging and waiving the right to cancel the sale within 3 business days; or

(4) Conducted and consummated entirely by mail or telephone; and without any other contact between the buyer and the seller or its representative prior to delivery of the goods or performance of the services; or

(5) In which the buyer has initiated the contact and specifically requested the seller to visit his home for the purpose of repairing or performing maintenance upon the buyer's personal property. If in the course of such a visit, the seller sells the buyer the right to receive additional services or goods other than replacement parts necessarily used in performing the maintenance or in making the repairs, the sale of those additional goods or services would not fall within this exclusion; or

(6) Pertaining to the sale or rental of real property, to the sale of insurance or to the sale of securities or commodities by a broker-dealer registered with the Securities and Exchange Commission.

(b) *Consumer goods or services.* Goods or services purchased, leased, or rented primarily for personal, family, or household purposes, including courses of instruction or training regardless of the purpose for which they are taken.

(c) *Seller.* Any person, partnership, corporation, or association engaged in the door-to-door sale of consumer goods or services.

(d) *Place of business.* The main or permanent branch office of local address of a seller.

(e) *Purchase price.* The total price paid or to be paid for the consumer goods or services, including all interest and service charges.

(f) *Business day.* Any calendar day except Sunday, or the following business holidays: New Year's Day, Washington's Birthday, Memorial Day, Independence Day, Labor Day, Columbus Day, Veterans' Day, Thanksgiving Day, and Christmas Day.

Note 2: *Effect on State laws and municipal ordinances.* (a) The Commission is cognizant of the significant burden imposed upon door-to-door sellers by the various and often inconsistent State laws which provide the buyer with the right to cancel door-to-door sales transactions. However, it does not believe that this constitutes sufficient justification for preempting all of the provisions of such laws or of the ordinances of the political subdivisions of the various States. The record in the proceedings supports the view that the joint and coordinated efforts of both the Commission and State and local officials are required to insure that a consumer who has purchased from a door-to-door seller something he does not want, does not need, or cannot afford, is accorded a unilateral right to rescind, without penalty, his agreement to purchase the goods or services.

(b) This section will not be construed to annul, or exempt any seller from complying with the laws of any State, or with the ordinances of political subdivisions thereof, regulating door-to-door sales, except to the extent that such laws or ordinances, if they permit door-to-door selling, are directly inconsistent with the provisions of this section. Such laws or ordinances which do not accord the buyer, with respect to the particular transaction, a right to cancel a door-to-door sale which is substantially the same or greater than that provided in this section, or which permit the imposition of any fee or penalty on the buyer for the exercise of such right, or which do not provide for giving the buyer notice of his right to cancel the transaction in substantially the same form and manner provided for in this section, are among those which will be considered directly inconsistent.

*

BANKRUPTCY ACT OF 1898

Selected Sections

Title 11, United States Code

Sec. 1 (11 U.S.C. § 1) Meaning of words and phrases

The words and phrases used in this title and in proceedings pursuant hereto shall, unless the same be inconsistent with the context, be construed as follows:

(1) "A person against whom a petition has been filed" shall include a person who has filed a voluntary petition;

(2) "Adjudication" shall mean a determination, whether by decree or by operation of law, that a person is a bankrupt;

(3) "Appellate courts" shall include the United States courts of appeals and the Supreme Court of the United States;

(4) "Bankrupt" shall include a person against whom an involuntary petition or an application to revoke a discharge has been filed, or who has filed a voluntary petition, or who has been adjudged a bankrupt;

(5) "Bona-fide purchaser" shall include a bona-fide encumbrancer or pledgee and the transferee, immediate or mediate, of any of them; . . .

(8) "Corporation" shall include all bodies having any of the powers and privileges of private corporations not possessed by individuals or partnerships and shall include partnership associations organized under laws making the capital subscribed alone responsible for the debts of the association, joint-stock companies, unincorporated companies and associations, and any business conducted by a trustee or trustees wherein beneficial interest or ownership is evidenced by certificate or other written instrument;

(8a) "Council" shall mean the Judicial Council of the circuit;

(9) "Court" shall mean the judge or the referee of the court of bankruptcy in which the proceedings are pending;

(10) "Courts of bankruptcy" shall include the United States district courts and the district courts of the Territories and possessions to which this title is or may hereafter be applicable;

(11) "Creditor" shall include anyone who owns a debt, demand, or claim provable in bankruptcy, and may include his duly authorized agent, attorney, or proxy;

(12) "Date of adjudication" shall mean the date of the filing of any petition which operates as an adjudication, or the date of entry of a decree of adjudication, or if such decree is appealed from, then the date when such decree is finally confirmed or the appeal is dismissed;

(13) "Date of bankruptcy", "time of bankruptcy", "commencement of proceedings", or "bankruptcy", with reference to time, shall mean the date when the petition was filed;

(14) "Debt" shall include any debt, demand, or claim provable in bankruptcy; . . .

(15) "Discharge" shall mean the release of a bankrupt from all of his debts which are provable in bankruptcy, except such as are excepted by this title;

(16) "Document" shall include any book, deed, record, paper, or instrument in writing; . . .

(19) A person shall be deemed insolvent within the provisions of this title whenever the aggregate of his property, exclusive of any property which he may have conveyed, transferred, concealed, removed, or permitted to be concealed or removed, with intent to defraud, hinder, or delay his creditors, shall not at a fair valuation be sufficient in amount to pay his debts;

(20) "Judge" shall mean a judge of a court of bankruptcy, not including the referee;

(21) "Oath" shall include affirmation;

(22) "Officer" shall include clerk, marshal, receiver, custodian, referee, and trustee, and the imposing of a duty upon, or the forbidding of an act by, any officer shall include his successor and any person authorized by law to perform the duties of such officer;

(23) "Persons" shall include corporations, except where otherwise specified, and officers, partnerships, and women, and when used with reference to the commission of acts which are forbidden under this title shall include persons who are participants in the forbidden acts, and the agents, officers, and members of the board of directors or trustees or of other similar controlling bodies of corporations;

(24) "Petition" shall mean a document filed in a court of bankruptcy or with a clerk thereof initiating a proceeding under this title; . . .

(28) "Secured creditor" shall include a creditor who has security for his debt upon the property of the bankrupt of a nature to be assignable under this title or who owns such a debt for which some endorser, surety, or other person secondarily liable for the bankrupt has such security upon the bankrupt's assets;

(29) "States" shall include the Territories and possessions to which this title is or may hereafter be applicable, Alaska, and the District of Columbia;

(29a) "Statutory lien" shall mean a lien arising solely by force of statute upon specified circumstances or conditions, but shall not include any lien provided by or dependent upon an agreement to give security, whether or not such lien is also provided by or is also dependent upon statute and whether or not the agreement or lien is made fully effective by statute;

(30) "Transfer" shall include the sale and every other and different mode, direct or indirect, of disposing of or of parting with property or with an interest therein or with the possession thereof or of fixing a lien upon property or upon an interest therein, absolutely or conditionally, voluntarily or involuntarily, by or without judicial proceedings, as a conveyance, sale, assignment, payment, pledge, mortgage, lien, encumbrance, gift, security, or otherwise; the retention of a security title to property delivered to a debtor shall be deemed a transfer suffered by such debtor;

(31) "Trustee" shall include all of the trustees and "receiver" shall include all of the receivers of an estate; . . .

Sec. 60 (11 U.S.C. § 96) Preferred creditors

a. (1) A preference is a transfer, as defined in this title, of any of the property of a debtor to or for the benefit of a creditor for or on account of an antecedent debt, made or suffered by such debtor while insolvent and within four months before the filing by or against him of the petition initiating a proceeding under this title, the effect of which transfer will be to enable such creditor to obtain a greater percentage of his debt than some other creditor of the same class.

(2) For the purposes of subdivisions (a) and (b) of this section, a transfer of property other than real property shall be deemed to have been made or suffered at the time when it became so far perfected that no subsequent lien upon such property obtainable by legal or equitable proceedings on a simple contract could become superior to the rights of the transferee. A transfer of real property shall be deemed to have been made or suffered when it became so far perfected that no subsequent bona fide purchase from the debtor could create rights in such property superior to the rights of the transferee. If any transfer of real property is not so perfected against a bona fide purchase, or if any transfer of other property is not so perfected against such liens by legal or equitable proceedings prior to the filing of a petition initiating a proceeding under this title, it shall be deemed to have been made immediately before the filing of the petition.

(3) The provisions of paragraph (2) of this subsection shall apply whether or not there are or were creditors who might have obtained such liens upon the property other than real property transferred and whether or not there are or were persons who might have become bona fide purchasers of such real property.

(4) A lien obtainable by legal or equitable proceedings upon a simple contract within the meaning of paragraph (2) of this subsection is a lien arising in ordinary course of such proceedings upon the entry or docketing of a judgment or decree, or upon attachment, garnishment, execution, or like process, whether before, upon, or after judgment or decree and whether before or upon levy. It does not include liens which under applicable law are given a special priority over other liens which are prior in time.

(5) A lien obtainable by legal or equitable proceedings could become superior to the rights of a transferee or a purchase could create rights superior to the rights of a transferee within the meaning of paragraph (2) of this subsection, if such consequences would follow only from the lien or purchase itself, or from such lien or purchase followed by any step wholly within the control of the respective lien holder or purchaser, with or without the aid of ministerial action by public officials. Such a lien could not, however, become so superior and such a purchase could not create such superior rights for the purposes of paragraph (2) of this subsection through any acts subsequent to the obtaining of such a lien or subsequent to such a purchase which require the agreement or concurrence of any third party or which require any further judicial action, or ruling.

(6) The recognition of equitable liens where available means of perfecting legal liens have not been employed is declared to be contrary to the policy of this section. If a transfer is for security and if (A) appli-

cable law requires a signed and delivered writing, or a delivery of possession, or a filing or recording, or other like overt actions as a condition to its full validity against third persons other than a buyer in the ordinary course of trade claiming through or under the transferor and (B) such overt action has not been taken, and (C) such transfer results in the acquisition of only an equitable lien, then such transfer is not perfected within the meaning of paragraph (2) of this subsection. Notwithstanding the first sentence of paragraph (2) of this subsection, it shall not suffice to perfect a transfer which creates an equitable lien such as is described in the first sentence of this paragraph, that it is made for a valuable consideration and that both parties intend to perfect it and that they take action sufficient to effect a transfer as against liens by legal or equitable proceedings on a simple contract: *Provided, however,* That where the debtor's own interest is only equitable, he can perfect a transfer thereof by any means appropriate fully to transfer an interest of that character: *And provided further,* That nothing in this paragraph shall be construed to be contrary to the provisions of paragraph (7) of this subsection.

(7) Any provision in this subsection a to the contrary notwithstanding if the applicable law requires a transfer of property other than real property for or on account of a new and contemporaneous consideration to be perfected by recording, delivery, or otherwise, in order that no lien described in paragraph (2) of this subsection could become superior to the rights of the transferee therein, or if the applicable law requires a transfer of real property for such a consideration to be so perfected in order that no bona fide purchase from the debtor could create rights in such property superior to the rights of the transferee, the time of transfer shall be determined by the following rules:

I. Where (A) the applicable law specifes a stated period of time of not more than twenty-one days after the transfer within which recording, delivery, or some other act is required, and compliance therewith is had within such stated period of time; or where (B) the applicable law specifies no such stated period of time or where such stated period of time is more than twenty-one days, and compliance therewith is had within twenty-one days after the transfer, the transfer shall be deemed to be made or suffered at the time of the transfer.

II. Where compliance with the law applicable to the transfer is not had in accordance with the provisions of subparagraph I of this paragraph, the transfer shall be deemed to be made or suffered at the time of compliance therewith, and if such compliance is not had prior to the filing of the petition initiating a proceeding under this title, such transfer shall be deemed to have been made or suffered immediately before the filing of such petition.

(8) If no such requirement of applicable law specified in paragraph (7) of this subsection exists, a transfer wholly or in part, for or on account of a new and contemporaneous consideration shall, to the extent of such consideration and interest thereon and the other obligations of the transferor connected therewith, be deemed to be made or suffered at the time of the transfer. A transfer to secure a future loan, if such a loan is actually made, or a transfer which becomes security for a future loan, shall have the same effect as a transfer for or on account of a new and contemporaneous consideration.

b. Any such preference may be avoided by the trustee if the creditor receiving it or to be benefited thereby or his agent acting with reference thereto has, at the time when the transfer is made, reasonable cause to believe that the debtor is insolvent. Where the preference is voidable, the trustee may recover the property or, if it has been converted, its value from any person who has received or converted such property, except a bona-fide purchaser from or lienor of the debtor's transferee for a present fair equivalent value: *Provided, however,* That where such purchaser or lienor has given less than such value, he shall nevertheless have a lien upon such property, but only to the extent of the consideration actually given by him. Where a preference by way of lien or security title is voidable, the court may on due notice order such lien or title to be preserved for the benefit of the estate, in which event such lien or title shall pass to the trustee. For the purpose of any recovery or avoidance under this section, where plenary proceedings are necessary, any State court which would have had jurisdiction if bankruptcy had not intervened and any court of bankruptcy shall have concurrent jurisdiction.

c. If a creditor has been preferred, and afterward in good faith gives the debtor further credit without security of any kind for property which becomes a part of the debtor's estate, the amount of such new credit remaining unpaid at the time of the adjudication in bankruptcy may be set off against the amount which would otherwise be recoverable from him.

. . .

Sec. 64 (11 U.S.C. § 104) Debts which have priority.

a. The debts to have priority, in advance of the payment of dividends to creditors, and to be paid in full out of bankrupt estates, and the order of payment, shall be (1) the costs and expenses of administration, including the actual and necessary costs and expenses of preserving the estate subsequent to filing the petition; the fees for the referees' salary and expense fund; the filing fees paid by creditors in involuntary cases or by persons other than the bankrupts in voluntary cases; where property of the bankrupt, transferred or concealed by him either before or after the filing of the petition, is recovered for the benefit of the estate of the bankrupt by the efforts and at the cost and expense of one or more creditors, the reasonable costs and expenses of such recovery; the trustee's expenses in opposing the bankrupt's discharge or in connection with the criminal prosecution of an offense punishable under chapter 9 of title 18 of the United States Code, or an offense concerning the business or property of the bankrupt punishable under other laws, Federal or State; the fees and mileage payable to witnesses as now or hereafter provided by the laws of the United States, and one reasonable attorney's fee, for the professional services actually rendered, irrespective of the number of attorneys employed, to the bankrupt in voluntary and involuntary cases, and to the petitioning creditors in involuntary cases, and if the court adjudges the debtor bankrupt over the debtor's objection or pursuant to a voluntary petition filed by the debtor during the pendency of an involuntary proceeding, for the reasonable costs and expenses incurred, or the reasonable disbursements made, by them, including but not limited to compensation of accountants and appraisers employed by them, in such amount as the court may allow. Where an order is entered in a proceeding under any chapter of this Act directing that bankruptcy be proceeded with, the costs and expenses of administration incurred in the ensuing bankruptcy proceeding, including expenses necessarily incurred by a debtor in possession, receiver, or trustee in preparing the schedule and statement required to be filed by section 638, 778, or 883, shall have priority in advance of payment of the unpaid costs and expenses of administration, including the allowances provided for in such chapter, incurred in the superseded proceeding and in the suspended bankruptcy proceeding, if any; (2) wages and commissions, not to exceed $600 to each claimant, which have been earned within three months before the date of the commencement of the proceeding, due to workmen, servants, clerks, or traveling, or city salesmen on salary or commission basis, whole or part time, whether or not selling exclusively for the bankrupt; and for the purposes of this clause, the term 'traveling or city salesman' shall include all such salesmen, whether or not they are independent contractors selling the products or services of the bankrupt on a commission basis, with or without a drawing account or formal contract; (3) where the confirmation of an arrangement or wage earner plan or the bankrupt's discharge has been refused, revoked, or set aside upon the objection and through the efforts and at the cost and expense of one or more creditors, or, where through the efforts and at the cost and expense of one or more creditors, evidence shall have been adduced resulting in the conviction of any person of an offense under chapter 9 of title 18 of the United States Code, the reasonable costs and expenses of such creditors in obtaining such refusal, revocation, or setting aside, or in adducing such evidence; (4) taxes which became legally due and owing by the bankrupt to the United States or to any State or any subdivision thereof which are not released by a discharge in bankruptcy: *Provided, however,* That no priority over general unsecured claims shall pertain to taxes not included in the foregoing priority: *And provided further,* That no order shall be made for the payment of a tax assessed against any property of the bankrupt in excess of the value of the interest of the bankrupt estate therein as determined by the court; and (5) debts other than for taxes owing to any person, including the United States, who by the laws of the United States is entitled to priority, and rent owing to a landlord who is entitled to priority by applicable State law or who is entitled to priority by paragraph (2) of subdivision c of section 67 of this Act: *Provided, however,* That such priority for rent to a landlord shall be restricted to the rent which is legally due and owing for the actual use and occupancy of the premises affected, and which accrued within three months before the date of bankruptcy. . . .

Sec. 67 (11 U.S.C. § 107) Liens and fraudulent transfers

a. (1) Every lien against the property of a person obtained by attachment, judgment, levy, or other legal or equitable process or proceedings within four months before the filing of a petition initiating a proceeding under this title by or against such person shall be deemed null and void (a) if at the time when such lien was obtained such person was insolvent or (b) if such lien was sought and permitted in fraud of the provisions of this title: *Provided, however,* That if such person is not finally adjudged a bankrupt in any proceeding under this title and if no arrangement or plan is proposed and confirmed, such lien shall be deemed reinstated with the same effect as if it had not been nullified and voided.

(2) If any lien deemed null and void under the provisions of paragraph (1) of this subdivision, has been dissolved by the furnishing of a bond or other obligation, the surety on which has been indemnified directly or indirectly by the transfer of or the creation of a lien upon any of the nonexempt property of a person before the filing of a petition initiating a proceeding under this title by or against him, such indemnifying transfer or lien shall also be deemed null and void: *Provided, however,* That if such person is not finally adjudged a bankrupt in any proceeding under this title, and if no arrangement or plan is proposed and confirmed, such transfer or lien shall

be deemed reinstated with the same effect as if it had not been nullified and voided.

(3) The property affected by any lien deemed null and void under the provisions of paragraphs (1) and (2) of this subdivision a shall be discharged from such lien, and such property and any of the indemnifying property transferred to or for the benefit of a surety shall pass to the trustee or debtor, as the case may be, except that the court may on due notice order any such lien to be preserved for the benefit of the estate, and the court may direct such conveyance as may be proper or adequate to evidence the title thereto of the trustee or debtor, as the case may be: *Provided, however,* That the title of a bona-fide purchaser of such property shall be valid, but if such title is acquired otherwise than at a judicial sale held to enforce such lien, it shall be valid only to the extent of the present consideration paid for such property. . . .

b. The provisions of section 96 [60] of this title to the contrary notwithstanding and except as otherwise provided in subdivision (c) of this section, statutory liens in favor of employees, contractors, mechanics, or any other class of persons, and statutory liens for taxes and debts owing to the United States or to any State or any subdivision thereof, created or recognized by the laws of the United States or any State, may be valid against the trustee, even though arising or perfected while the debtor is insolvent and within four months prior to the filing of the petition initiating a proceeding under this title by or against him.

c. (1) The following liens shall be invalid against the trustee:

(A) every statutory lien which first becomes effective upon the insolvency of the debtor, or upon distribution or liquidation of his property, or upon execution against his property levied at the instance of one other than the lienor;

(B) every statutory lien which is not perfected or enforceable at the date of bankruptcy against one acquiring the rights of a bona fide purchaser from the debtor on that date, whether or not such purchaser exists: *Provided,* That where a statutory lien is not invalid at the date of bankruptcy agaisnt the trustee under subdivision (c) of section 110 [70] of this title and is required by applicable lien law to be perfected in order to be valid against a subsequent bona fide purchaser, such a lien may nevertheless be valid under this subdivision if perfected within the time permitted by and in accordance with the requirements of such law: *And provided further,* That if applicable lien law requires a lien valid against the trustee under section 110(c) [70(c)] of this title to be perfected by the seizure of property, it shall instead be perfected as permitted by this subdivision by filing notice thereof with the court;

(C) every statutory lien for rent and every lien of distress for rent, whether statutory or not. A right of distress for rent which creates a security interest in property shall be deemed a lien for the purposes of this subdivision.

(2) The court may, on due notice, order any of the aforesaid liens invalidated against the trustee to be preserved for the benefit of the estate and in that event the lien shall pass to the trustee. A lien not preserved for the benefit of the estate but invalidated against the trustee shall be invalid as against all liens indefeasible in bankruptcy, so as to have the effect of promoting liens indefeasible in bankruptcy which would otherwise be subordinate to such invalidated lien. Claims for wages, taxes, and rent secured by liens hereby invalidated or preserved shall be respectively

allowable with priority and restricted as are debts therefor entitled to priority under clauses (2), (4), and (5) of subdivision (a) of section 104 [64] of this title, even though not otherwise granted priority.

(3) Every tax lien on personal property not accompanied by possession shall be postponed in payment to the debts specified in clauses (1) and (2) of subdivision (a) of section 104 [64] of this title. Where such a tax lien is prior in right to liens indefeasible in bankruptcy, the court shall order payment from the proceeds derived from the sale of the personal property to which the tax lien attaches, less the actual cost of that sale, of an amount not in excess of the tax lien, to the debts specified in clauses (1) and (2) of subdivision (a) of section 104 [64] of this title. If the amount realized from the sale exceeds the total of such debts, after allowing for prior indefeasible liens and the cost of the sale, the excess up to the amount of the difference between the total paid to the debts specified in clauses (1) and (2) of subdivision (a) of section 104 [64] of this title and the amount of the tax lien, is to be paid to the holder of the tax lien.

(4) Where a penalty not allowable under subdivision (j) of section 93 [57] of this title is secured by a lien, the portion of the lien securing such penalty shall not be eligible for preservation under this subdivision.

(5) This subdivision shall not apply to liens enforced by sale before the filing of the petition, nor to liens against property set aside to the bankrupt as exempt, nor to liens against property abandoned by the trustee or unadministered in bankruptcy for any reason and shall not apply in proceedings under section 205[77] of this title, nor in proceedings under chapter 10 of this title unless an order has been entered directing that bankruptcy be proceeded with.

d. (1) For the purposes of, and exclusively applicable to, this subdivision: (a) "Property" of a debtor shall include only his nonexempt property; (b) "debt" is any legal liability, whether matured or unmatured, liquidated or unliquidated, absolute, fixed, or contingent; (c) "creditor" is a person in whose favor a debt exists; (d) a person is "insolvent" when the present fair salable value of his property is less than the amount required to pay his debts; and to determine whether a partnership is insolvent, there shall be added to the partnership property the present fair salable value of the separate property of each general partner in excess of the amount required to pay his separate debts, and also the amount realizable on any unpaid subscription to the partnership of each limited partner; and (e) consideration given for the property or obligation of a debtor is "fair" (1) when, in good faith, in exchange and as a fair equivalent therefor, property is transferred or an antecedent debt is satisfied, or (2) when such property or obligation is received in good faith to secure a present advance or antecedent debt in an amount not disproportionately small as compared with the value of the property or obligation obtained.

(2) Every transfer made and every obligation incurred by a debtor within one year prior to the filing of a petition initiating a proceeding under this title by or against him is fraudulent (a) as to creditors existing at the time of such transfer or obligation, if made or incurred without fair consideration by a debtor who is or will be thereby rendered insolvent, without regard to his actual intent; or (b) as to then existing creditors and as to other persons who become creditors during the continuance of a business or transaction, if made or incurred without fair consideration by a debtor who is engaged or is about to engage in such business or transaction, for which the property remaining in his hands is an unreasonably small capital, without regard to his actual intent; or (c) as to then existing and future

creditors, if made or incurred without fair consideration by a debtor who intends to incur or believes that he will incur debts beyond his ability to pay as they mature; or (d) as to then existing and future creditors, if made or incurred with actual intent as distinguished from intent presumed in law, to hinder, delay, or defraud either existing or future creditors.

(3) Every transfer made and every obligation incurred by a debtor who is or will thereby be rendered insolvent, within four months prior to the filing of a petition initiating a proceeding under this title by or against him is fraudulent, as to then existing and future creditors: (a) if made or incurred in contemplation of the filing of a petition initiating a proceeding under this title by or against the debtor or in contemplation of liquidation of all or the greater portion of the debtor's property, with intent to use the consideration obtained for such transfer or obligation to enable any creditor of such debtor to obtain a greater percentage of his debt than some other creditor of the same class, and (b) if the transferee or obligee of such transfer or obligation, at the time of such transfer or obligation, knew or believed that the debtor intended to make such use of such consideration. The remedies of the trustee for the avoidance of such transfer or obligation and of any ensuing preference shall be cumulative: *Provided, however,* That the trustee shall be entitled to only one satisfaction with respect thereto.

(4) Every transfer of partnership property and every partnership obligation incurred within one year prior to the filing of a petition initiating a proceeding under this title by or against the partnership, when the partnership is insolvent or will be thereby rendered insolvent, is fraudulent as to partnership creditors existing at the time of such transfer or obligation, without regard to actual intent if made or incurred (a) to a partner, whether with or without a promise by him to pay partnership debts, or (b) to a person not a partner without fair consideration to the partnership as distinguished from consideration to the individual partners.

(5) For the purposes of this subdivision, a transfer shall be deemed to have been made at the time when it became so far perfected that no bona fide purchaser from the debtor could thereafter have acquired any rights in the property so transferred superior to the rights of the transferee therein, but, if such transfer is not so perfected prior to the filing of the petition initiating a proceeding under this title, it shall be deemed to have been made immediately before the filing of such petition.

(6) A transfer made or an obligation incurred by a debtor adjudged a bankrupt under this title, which is fraudulent under this subdivision against creditors of such debtor having claims provable under this title, shall be null and void against the trustee, except as to a bona fide purchaser, lienor, or obligee for a present fair equivalent value: *Provided, however,* That the court may, on due notice, order such transfer or obligation to be preserved for the benefit of the estate and, in such event, the trustee shall succeed to and may enforce the rights of such transferee or obligee: *And provided further,* That such purchaser, lienor, or obligee, who without actual fraudulent intent has given a consideration less than fair, as defined in this subdivision, for such transfer, lien, or obligation may retain the property, lien, or obligation as security for repayment.

(7) Nothing contained in this subdivision d shall be construed to validate a transfer which is voidable under section 96[60] of this title.

e. For the purpose of any recovery or avoidance under this section, where plenary proceedings are necessary, any State court which would have had jurisdiction if bankruptcy had not intervened and any court of bankruptcy shall have concurrent jurisdiction. . . .

Sec. 68 (11 U.S.C. § 108) Set-offs and counterclaims

a. In all cases of mutual debts or mutual credits between the estate of a bankrupt and a creditor the account shall be stated and one debt shall be set off against the other, and the balance only shall be allowed or paid.

b. A set-off or counterclaim shall not be allowed in favor of any debtor of the bankrupt which (1) is not provable against the estate and allowable under subdivision g of section 93[57] of this title; or (2) was purchased by or transferred to him after the filing of the petition or within four months before such filing, with a view to such use and with knowledge or notice that such bankrupt was insolvent or had committed an act of bankruptcy.

Sec. 70 (U.S.C. § 110) Title to property

a. The trustee of the estate of a bankrupt and his successor or successors, if any, upon his or their appointment and qualification, shall in turn be vested by operation of law with the title of the bankrupt as of the date of the filing of the petition initiating a proceeding under this title, except insofar as it is to property which is held to be exempt, to all of the following kinds of property wherever located (1) documents relating to his property; (2) interests in patents, patent rights, copyrights, and trade-marks, and in applications therefor: *Provided,* That in case the trustee, within thirty days after appointment and qualification, does not notify the applicant for a patent, copyright, or trade-mark of his election to prosecute the application to allowance or rejection, the bankrupt may apply to the court for an order revesting him with the title thereto, which petition shall be granted unless for cause shown by the trustee the court grants further time to the trustee for making such election; and such applicant may, in any event, at any time petition the court to be revested with such title in case the trustee shall fail to prosecute such application with reasonable diligence; and the court, upon revesting the bankrupt with such title, shall direct the trustee to execute proper instruments of transfer to make the same effective in law and upon the records; (3) powers which he might have exercised for his own benefit, but not those which he might have exercised solely for some other person; (4) property transferred by him in fraud of his creditors; (5) property, including rights of action, which prior to the filing of the petition he could by any means have transferred or which might have been levied upon and sold under judicial process against him, or otherwise seized, impounded, or sequestered: *Provided,* That rights of action ex delicto for libel, slander, injuries to the person of the bankrupt or of a relative, whether or not resulting in death, seduction, and criminal conversation shall not vest in the trustee unless by the law of the State such rights of action are subject to attachment, execution, garnishment, sequestration, or other judicial process: *And provided further,* That when any bankrupt, who is a natural person, shall have any insurance policy which has a cash surrender value payable to himself, his estate, or personal representatives, he may, within thirty days after the cash surrender value has been ascertained and stated to the trustee by the company issuing the same, pay or secure to the trustee the sum so ascertained and stated, and continue to hold, own, and carry such policy free from the claims of the creditors participating in the distribution of his estate under the bankruptcy proceedings, otherwise the policy shall pass to the trustee as assets; (6) rights of action arising upon contracts, or usury, or the unlawful taking or detention of or injury to his property; (7) contingent remainders, executory devises and limitations, rights of entry for condition broken, rights or possibilities of reverter, and like interests in real property, which were nonassignable prior to bankruptcy and which, within six months thereafter, become assignable interests or estates or give rise to powers in the bankrupt to acquire assignable interests or estates; and (8) property held by an assignee for the benefit of creditors appointed under an assignment which constituted an act of bankruptcy, which property shall, for the purposes of this title, be deemed to be held by the assignee as the agent of the bankrupt and shall be subject to the summary jurisdiction of the court.

All property, wherever located, except insofar as it is property which is held to be exempt, which vests in the bankrupt within six months after bankruptcy by bequest, devise or inheritance shall vest in the trustee and his successor or successors, if any, upon his or their appointment and qualification, as of the date when it vested in the bankrupt, and shall be free and discharged from any transfer made or suffered by the bankrupt after bankruptcy.

All property, wherever located, except insofar as it is property which is held to be exempt, in which the bankrupt has at the date of bankruptcy an estate or interest by the entirety and which within six months after bankruptcy becomes transferable in whole or in part solely by the bankrupt shall, to the extent it becomes so transferable, vest in the trustee and his successor or successors, if any, upon his or their appointment and qualification, as of the date of bankruptcy.

The title of the trustee shall not be affected by the prior possession of a receiver or other officer of any court.

b. The trustee shall assume or reject an executory contract, including an unexpired lease of real property, within sixty days after the adjudication or within thirty days after the qualification of the trustee, whichever is later, but the court may for cause shown extend or reduce the time. Any such contract or lease not assumed or rejected within that time shall be deemed to be rejected. If a trustee is not appointed, any such contract or lease shall be deemed to be rejected within thirty days after the date of the order directing that a trustee be not appointed. A trustee shall file, within sixty days after adjudication or within thirty days after he has qualified, whichever is later, unless the court for cause shown extends or reduces the time, a statement under oath showing which, if any, of the contracts of the bankrupt are executory in whole or in part, including unexpired leases of real property, and which, if any, have been rejected by the trustee. Unless a lease of real property expressly otherwise provides, a rejection of the lease or of any covenant therein by the trustee of the lessor does not deprive the lessee of his estate. A general covenant or condition in a lease that it shall not be assigned shall not be construed to prevent the trustee from assuming the same at his election and subsequently assigning the same; but an express covenant that an assignment by operation of law or the bankruptcy of a specified party thereto or of either party shall terminate the lease or give the other party an election to terminate the same is enforcible. A trustee who elects to assume a contract or lease of the bankrupt and who subsequently, with the approval of the court and upon such terms and conditions as the court may fix after hearing upon notice to the other party to the contract or lease, assigns the contract or lease to a third person, is not liable for breaches occurring after the assignment.

c. The trustee may have the benefit of all defenses available to the bankrupt as against third persons, including statutes of limitation, statutes of frauds, usury, and other personal defenses; and a waiver of any such defense by the bankrupt after bankruptcy shall not bind the trustee. The trustee shall have as of the date of bankruptcy the rights and powers of: (1) a creditor who obtained a judgment against the bankrupt upon the date of bankruptcy, whether or not such a creditor exists, (2) a creditor who upon the date of bankruptcy obtained an execution returned unsatisfied against the bankrupt, whether or not such a creditor exists, and (3) a creditor who upon the date of bankruptcy obtained a lien by legal or equitable proceedings upon all property, whether or not coming into possession or control of the court, upon which a creditor of the bankrupt upon a simple contract could have obtained such a lien, whether or not such a creditor exists. If a transfer is valid in part against creditors whose rights and powers are conferred upon the trustee under this subdivision, it shall be valid to a like extent against the trustee. In cases where repugnancy or inconsistency exists with reference to the rights and powers in this subdivision conferred, the trustee may elect which rights and powers to exercise with reference to a particular party, a particular remedy, or a particular transaction, without prejudice to his right to maintain a different position with reference to a different party, a different remedy, or a different transaction.

d. After bankruptcy and either before adjudication or before a receiver takes possession of the property of the bankrupt, whichever first occurs—

(1) A transfer of any of the property of the bankrupt, other than real estate, made to a person acting in good faith shall be valid against the trustee if made for a present fair equivalent value or, if not made for a present fair equivalent value, then to the extent of the present consideration actually paid therefor, for which amount the transferee shall have a lien upon the property so transferred;

(2) A person indebted to the bankrupt or holding property of the bankrupt may, if acting in good faith, pay such indebtedness or deliver such property, or any part thereof, to the bankrupt or upon his order, with the same effect as if the bankruptcy were not pending;

(3) A person having actual knowledge of such pending bankruptcy shall be deemed not to act in good faith unless he has reasonable cause to believe that the petition in bankruptcy is not well founded;

(4) The provisions of paragraphs (1) and (2) of this subdivision shall not apply where a receiver or trustee appointed by a United States or State court is in possession of all or the greater portion of the non-exempt property of the bankrupt;

(5) A person asserting the validity of a transfer under this subdivision shall have the burden of proof. Except as otherwise provided in this subdivision and in subdivision g of section 44[21] of this title, no transfer by or in behalf of the bankrupt after the date of bankruptcy shall be valid against the trustee: *Provided, however,* That nothing in this title shall impair the negotiability of currency or negotiable instruments.

e. (1) A transfer made or suffered or obligation incurred by a debtor adjudged a bankrupt under this title which, under any Federal or State law applicable thereto, is fraudulent as against or voidable for any other reason by any creditor of the debtor, having a claim provable under this title, shall be null and void as against the trustee of such debtor.

(2) All property of the debtor affected by any such transfer shall be and remain a part of his assets and estate, discharged and released from such transfer and shall pass to, and every such transfer or obligation shall be avoided by, the trustee for the benefit of the estate: *Provided, however,* That the court may on due notice order such transfer or obligation to be preserved for the benefit of the estate and in such event the trustee shall succeed to and may enforce the rights of such transferee or obligee. The trustee shall reclaim and recover such property or collect its value from and avoid such transfer or obligation against whoever may hold or have received it, except a person as to whom the transfer or obligation specified in paragraph (1) of this subdivision is valid under applicable Federal or State laws.

(3) For the purpose of such recovery or of the avoidance of such transfer or obligation, where plenary proceedings are necessary, any State court which would have had jurisdiction if bankruptcy had not intervened and any court of bankruptcy shall have concurrent jurisdiction. . . .

1898 ACT CONVERSION TABLE

1898 Act Section	1978 Act Section
1	101
60	547, 550, 551, 552
64	507
67a	547, 550, 551
67b, c	545, 550, 551
68	553
70a	541
70c, e	544, 550, 551, 552
70d	549, 550

BANKRUPTCY REFORM ACT OF 1978

Selected Sections

Title 11, United States Code

---

§ 101. Definitions

In this title—

. . .

(2) "affiliate" means—

(A) entity that directly or indirectly owns, controls, or holds with power to vote, 20 percent or more of the outstanding voting securities of the debtor, other than an entity that holds such securities—

(i) in a fiduciary or agency capacity without sole discretionary power to vote such securities; or

(ii) solely to secure a debt, if such entity has not in fact exercised such power to vote;

(B) corporation 20 percent or more of whose outstanding voting securities are directly or indirectly owned, controlled, or held with power to vote, by the debtor, or by an entity that directly or indirectly owns, controls or holds with power to vote, 20 percent or more of the outstanding voting securities of the debtor, other than an entity that holds such securities—

(i) in a fiduciary or agency capacity without sole discretionary power to vote such securities; or

(ii) solely to secure a debt, if such entity has not in fact exercised such power to vote;

(C) person whose business is operated under a lease or operating agreement by a debtor, or person substantially all of whose property is operated under an operating agreement with the debtor; or

(D) entity that operates the business or all or substantially all of the property of the debtor under a lease or operating agreement;

. . .

(4) "claim" means—

(A) right to payment, whether or not such right is reduced to judgment, liquidated, unliquidated, fixed, contingent, matured, unmatured, disputed, undisputed, legal, equitable, secured, or unsecured; or

(B) right to an equitable remedy for breach of performance if such breach gives rise to a right to payment, whether or not such right to an equitable remedy is reduced to judgment, fixed, contingent, matured, unmatured, disputed, undisputed, secured, or unsecured;

. . .

(6) "community claim" means claim that arose before the commencement of the case concerning the debtor for which property of the kind specified in section 541(a)(2) of this title is liable, whether or not there is any such property at the time of the commencement of the case;

. . .

(8) "corporation"—

(A) includes—

(i) association having a power or privilege that a private corporation, but not an individual or a partnership, possesses;

(ii) partnership association organized under a law that makes only the capital subscribed responsible for the debts of such association;

(iii) joint-stock company;

(iv) unincorporated company or association; or

(v) business trust; but

(B) does not include limited partnership;

(9) "creditor" means—

(A) entity that has a claim against the debtor that arose at the time of or before the order for relief concerning the debtor;

(B) entity that has a claim against the estate of a kind specified in section 502(f), 502(g), 502(h) or 502(i) of this title; or

(C) entity that has a community claim;

. . .

(11) "debt" means liability on a claim;

(12) "debtor" means person or municipality concerning which a case under this title has been commenced;

. . .

(14) "entity" includes person, estate, trust, governmental unit;

. . .

(21) "governmental unit" means United States; State; Commonwealth; District; Territory; municipality; foreign state; department, agency, or instrumentality of the United States, a State, a Commonwealth, a District, a Territory, a municipality, or a foreign state; or other foreign or domestic government;

. . .

(25) "insider" includes—

(A) if the debtor is an individual—

(i) relative of the debtor or of a general partner of the debtor;

(ii) partnership in which the debtor is a general partner;

(iii) general partner of the debtor; or

(iv) corporation of which the debtor is a director, officer, or person in control;

(B) if the debtor is a corporation—

(i) director of the debtor;

(ii) officer of the debtor;

(iii) person in control of the debtor;

(iv) partnership in which the debtor is a general partner;

(v) general partner of the debtor; or

(vi) relative of a general partner, director, officer, or person in control of the debtor;

(C) if the debtor is a partnership—

(i) general partner in the debtor;

(ii) relative of a general partner in, general partner of, or person in control of the debtor;

(iii) partnership in which the debtor is a general partner;

(iv) general partner of the debtor; or

(v) person in control of the debtor;

(D) if the debtor is a municipality, elected official of the debtor or relative of an elected official of the debtor;

(E) affiliate, or insider of an affiliate as if such affiliate were the debtor; and

(F) managing agent of the debtor;

(26) "insolvent" means—

(A) with reference to an entity other than a partnership, financial condition such that the sum of such entity's debts is greater than all of such entity's property, at a fair valuation, exclusive of—

(i) property transferred, concealed, or removed with intent to hinder, delay, or defraud such entity's creditors; and

(ii) property that may be exempted from property of the estate under section 522 of this title; and

(B) with reference to a partnership, financial condition such that the sum of such partnership's debts is greater than the aggregate of, at a fair valuation—

(i) all of such partnership's property, exclusive of property of the kind specified in subpargaraph (A)(i) of this paragraph; and

(ii) the sum of the excess of the value of each general partner's separate property, exclusive of property of the kind specified in subparagraph (A)(ii) of this paragraph, over such partner's separate debts;

(27) "judicial lien" means lien obtained by judgment, levy, sequestration, or other legal or equitable process or proceeding;

(28) "lien" means charge against or interest in property to secure payment of a debt or performance of an obligation;

(29) "municipality" means political subdivision or public agency or instrumentality of a State;

(30) "person" includes individual, partnership, and corporation, but does not include governmental unit;

(31) "petition" means petition filed under section 301, 302, 303, or 304 of this title, as the case may be, commencing a case under this title;

(32) "purchaser" means transferee of a voluntary transfer, and includes immediate or mediate transferee of such a transferee;

. . .

(34) "relative" means individual related by affinity or consanguinity within the third degree as determined by the common law, or individual in a step or adoptive relationship within such third degree;

. . .

(36) "security agreement" means agreement that creates or provides for a security interest;

(37) "security interest" means lien created by an agreement;

(38) "statutory lien" means lien arising solely by force of a statute on specified circumstances or conditions, or lien of distress for rent, whether or not statutory, but does not include security interest or judicial lien, whether or not such interest or lien is provided by or is dependent on a statute and whether or not such interest or lien is made fully effective by statute;

. . .

(40) "transfer" means every mode, direct or indirect, absolute or conditional, voluntary or involuntary, of disposing of or parting with property or with an interest in property, including retention of title as a security interest.

. . .

§ 362. Automatic stay

(a) Except as provided in subsection (b) of this section, a petition filed under section 301, 302, or 303 of this title operates as a stay, applicable to all entities, of—

(1) the commencement or continuation, including the issuance or employment of process, of a judicial, administrative, or other proceeding against the debtor that was or could have been commenced before the commencement of the case under this title, or to recover a claim against the debtor that arose before the commencement of the case under this title;

(2) the enforcement, against the debtor or against property of the estate, of a judgment obtained before the commencement of the case under this title;

(3) any act to obtain possession of property of the estate or of property from the estate;

(4) any act to create, perfect, or enforce any lien against property of the estate;

(5) any act to create, perfect, or enforce against property of the debtor any lien to the extent that such lien secures a claim that arose before the commencement of the case under this title;

(6) any act to collect, assess, or recover a claim against the debtor that arose before the commencement of the case under this title;

(7) the setoff of any debt owing to the debtor that arose before the commencement of the case under this title against any claim against the debtor; and

(8) the commencement or continuation of a proceeding before the United States Tax Court concerning the debtor.

. . .

§ 506. Determination of secured status

(a) An allowed claim of a creditor secured by a lien on property in which the estate has an interest, or that is subject to setoff under section 553 of this title, is a secured claim to the extent of the value of such creditor's interest in the estate's interest in such property, or to the extent of the amount subject to setoff, as the case may be, and is an unsecured claim to the extent that the value of such creditor's interest or the amount so subject to setoff is less than the amount of such allowed claim. Such value shall be determined in light of the purpose of the valuation and of the proposed disposition or use of such property, and in conjunction with any hearing on such disposition or use or on a plan affecting such creditor's interest.

(b) To the extent that an allowed secured claim is secured by property the value of which, after any recovery under subsection (c) of this section, is greater than the amount of such claim, there shall be allowed to the holder of such claim, interest on such claim, and any reasonable fees, costs, or charges provided under the agreement under which such claim arose.

(c) The trustee may recover from property securing an allowed secured claim the reasonable, necessary costs and expenses of preserving, or disposing of, such property to the extent of any benefit to the holder of such claim.

(d) To the extent that a lien secures a claim against the debtor that is not an allowed secured claim, such lien is void, unless—

(1) a party in interest has not requested that the court determine and allow or disallow such claim under section 502 of this title; or

(2) such claim was disallowed only under section 502(e) of this title.

§ 507. Priorities

(a) The following expenses and claims have priority in the following order:

(1) First, administrative expenses allowed under section 503(b) of this title, and any fees and charges assessed against the estate under chapter 123 of title 28.

(2) Second, unsecured claims allowed under section 502(f) of this title.

(3) Third, allowed unsecured claims for wages, salaries, or commissions, including vacation, severance and sick leave pay—

(A) earned by an individual within 90 days before the date of the filing of the petition or the date of the cessation of the debtor's business, whichever occurs first; but only

(B) to the extent of $2,000 for each such individual.

(4) Fourth, allowed unsecured claims for contributions to employee benefit plans—

(A) arising from services rendered within 180 days before the date of the filing of the petition or the date of the cessation of the debtor's business, whichever occurs first; but only

(B) for each such plan, to the extent of—

(i) the number of employees covered by such plan multiplied by $2,000; less

(ii) the aggregate amount paid to such employees under paragraph (3) of this subsection, plus the aggregate amount paid by the estate on behalf of such employees to any other employee benefit plan.

(5) Fifth, allowed unsecured claims of individuals, to the extent of $900 for each such individual, arising from the deposit, before the commencement of the case, of money in connection with the purchase, lease, or rental of property, or the purchase of services, for the personal, family, or household use of such individuals, that were not delivered or provided.

(6) Sixth, allowed unsecured claims of governmental units, to the extent that such claims are for—

(A) a tax on or measured by income or gross receipts—

(i) for a taxable year ending on or before the date of the filing of the petition for which a return, if required, is last due, including extensions, after three years before the date of the filing of the petition;

(ii) assessed within 240 days, plus any time plus 30 days during which an offer in compromise with respect to such tax that was made within 240 days after such assessment was pending, before the date of the filing of the petition; or

(iii) other than a tax of a kind specified in section 523(a)(1)(B) or 523(a)(1)(C) of this title, not assessed before, but assessable, under applicable law or by agreement, after, the commencement of the case;

(B) a property tax assessed before the commencement of the case and last payable without penalty after one year before the date of the filing of the petition;

(C) a tax required to be collected or withheld and for which the debtor is liable in whatever capacity;

(D) an employment tax on a wage, salary, or commission of a kind specified in paragraph (3) of this subsection earned from the debtor before the date of the filing of the petition, whether or not actually paid before such date, for which a return is last due, under applicable law or under any extension, after three years before the date of the filing of the petition;

(E) an excise tax on—

(i) a transaction occurring before the date of the filing of the petition for which a return, if required, is last due, under applicable law or under any extension, after three years before the date of the filing of the petition; or

(ii) if a return is not required, a transaction occurring during the three years immediately preceding the date of the filing of the petition;

(F) a customs duty arising out of the importation of merchandise—

(i) entered for consumption within one year before the date of the filing of the petition;

(ii) covered by an entry liquidated or reliquidated within one year before the date of the filing of the petition; or

(iii) entered for consumption within four years before the date of the filing of the petition but unliquidated on such date, if the Secretary of the Treasury certifies that failure to liquidate such entry was due to an investigation pending on such date into assessment of antidumping or countervailing duties or fraud, or if information needed for the proper appraisement or classification of such merchandise was not available to the appropriate customs officer before such date; or

(G) a penalty related to a claim of a kind specified in this paragraph and in compensation for actual pecuniary loss.

. . .

§ 522. Exemptions

(a) In this section—

(1) "dependent" includes spouse, whether or not actually dependent; and

(2) "value" means fair market value as of the date of the filing of the petition.

(b) Notwithstanding section 541 of this title, an individual debtor may exempt from property of the estate either—

(1) property that is specified under subsection (d) of this section, unless the State law that is applicable to the debtor under paragraph (2)(A) of this subsection specifically does not so authorize; or, in the alternative,

(2)(A) any property that is exempt under Federal law, other than subsection (d) of this section, or State or local law that is applicable on the date of the filing of the petition at the place in which the debtor's domicile has been located for the 180 days immediately preceding the date of the filing of the petition, or for a longer portion of such 180-day period than in any other place; and

(B) any interest in property in which the debtor had, immediately before the commencement of the case, an interest as a tenant by the entirety or joint tenant to the extent that such interest as a tenant by the entirety or joint tenant is exempt from process under applicable nonbankruptcy law.

(c) Unless the case is dismissed, property exempted under this section is not liable during or after the case for any debt of the debtor that arose, or that is determined under section 502 of this title as if such claim had arisen before the commencement of the case, except—

(1) a debt of a kind specified in section 523(a)(1) or section 523(a)(5) of this title; or

(2) a lien that is—

(A) not avoided under section 544, 545, 547, 548, 549, or 724(a) of this title;

(B) not voided under section 506(d) of this title; or

(C)(i) a tax lien, notice of which is properly filed; and

(ii) avoided under section 545(2) of this title.

(d) The following property may be exempted under subsection (b)(1) of this section:

(1) The debtor's aggregate interest, not to exceed $7,500 in value, in real property or personal property that the debtor or a dependent of the debtor uses as a residence, in a cooperative that owns property that the debtor or a dependent of the debtor uses as a residence, or in a burial plot for the debtor or a dependent of the debtor.

(2) The debtor's interest, not to exceed $1,200 in value, in one motor vehicle.

(3) The debtor's interest, not to exceed $200 in value in any particular item, in household furnishings, household goods, wearing apparel, appliances, books, animals, crops, or musical instruments, that are held primarily for the personal, family, or household use of the debtor or a dependent of the debtor.

(4) The debtor's aggregate interest, not to exceed $500 in value, in jewelry held primarily for the personal, family, or household use of the debtor or a dependent of the debtor.

(5) The debtor's aggregate interest, not to exceed in value $400 plus any unused amount of the exemption provided under paragraph (1) of this subsection, in any property.

(6) The debtor's aggregate interest, not to exceed $750 in value, in any implements, professional books, or tools, of the trade of the debtor or the trade of a dependent of the debtor.

(7) Any unmatured life insurance contract owned by the debtor, other than a credit life insurance contract.

(8) The debtor's aggregate interest, not to exceed in value $4,000 less any amount of property of the estate transferred in the manner specified in section 542(d) of this title, in any accrued dividend or interest under, or loan value of, any unmatured life insurance contract owned by the debtor under which the insured is the debtor or an individual of whom the debtor is a dependent.

(9) Professionally prescribed health aids for the debtor or a dependent of the debtor.

(10) The debtor's right to receive—

(A) a social security benefit, unemployment compensation, or a local public assistance benefit;

(B) a veterans' benefit;

(C) a disability, illness, or unemployment benefit;

(D) alimony, support, or separate maintenance, to the extent reasonably necessary for the support of the debtor and any dependent of the debtor;

(E) a payment under a stock bonus, pension, profitsharing, annuity, or similar plan or contract on account of illness, disability, death, age, or length of service, to the extent reasonably necessary for the support of the debtor and any dependent of the debtor, unless—

(i) such plan or contract was established by or under the auspices of an insider that employed the debtor at the time the debtor's rights under such plan or contract arose;

(ii) such payment is on account of age or length of service; and

(iii) such plan or contract does not qualify under section 401(a), 403(a), 403(b), 408, or 409 of the Internal Revenue Code of 1954 (26 U.S.C. 401(a), 403(a), 403(b), 408, or 409).

(11) The debtor's right to receive, or property that is traceable to—

(A) an award under a crime victim's reparation law;

(B) a payment on account of the wrongful death of an individual of whom the debtor was a dependent, to the extent reasonably necessary for the support of the debtor and any dependent of the debtor;

(C) a payment under a life insurance contract that insured the life of an individual of whom the debtor was a dependent on the date of such individual's death, to the extent reasonably necessary for the support of the debtor and any dependent of the debtor;

(D) a payment, not to exceed $7,500, on account of personal bodily injury, not including pain and suffering or compensation for actual pecuniary loss, of the debtor or an individual of whom the debtor is a dependent; or

(E) a payment in compensation of loss of future earnings of the debtor or an individual of whom the debtor is or was a dependent, to the extent reasonably necessary for the support of the debtor and any dependent of the debtor.

(e) A waiver of exemptions executed in favor of a creditor that holds an unsecured claim against the debtor is unenforceable in a case under this title with respect to such claim against property that the debtor may exempt under subsection (b) of this section. A waiver by the debtor of a power under subsection (f) or (h) of this section to avoid a transfer, under subsection (g) or (i) of this section to exempt property, or under subsection (i) of this section to recover property or to preserve a transfer, is unenforceable in a case under this title.

(f) Notwithstanding any waiver of exemptions, the debtor may avoid the fixing of a lien on an interest of the debtor in property to the extent that such lien impairs an exemption to which the debtor would have been entitled under subsection (b) of this section, if such lien is—

(1) a judicial lien; or

(2) a nonpossessory, nonpurchase-money security interest in any—

(A) household furnishings, household goods, wearing apparel, appliances, books, animals, crops, musical instruments, or jewelry that are held primarily for the personal, family, or household use of the debtor or a dependent of the debtor;

(B) implements, professional books, or tools, of the trade of the debtor or the trade of a dependent of the debtor; or

(C) professionally prescribed health aids for the debtor or a dependent of the debtor.

(g) Notwithstanding sections 550 and 551 of this title, the debtor may exempt under subsection (b) of this section property that the trustee recovers under section 510(c)(2), 542, 543, 550, 551, or 553 of this title, to the extent that the debtor could have exempted such property under subsection (b) of this section if such property had not been transferred, if—

(1)(A) such transfer was not a voluntary transfer of such property by the debtor; and

(B) the debtor did not conceal such property; or

(2) the debtor could have avoided such transfer under subsection (f)(2) of this section.

(h) The debtor may avoid a transfer of property of the debtor or recover a setoff to the extent that the debtor could have exempted such property under subsection (g)(1) of this section if the trustee had avoided such transfer, if—

(1) such transfer is avoidable by the trustee under section 544, 545, 547, 548, 549, or 724(a) of this title or recoverable by the trustee under section 553 of this title; and

(2) the trustee does not attempt to avoid such transfer.

(i)(1) If the debtor avoids a transfer or recovers a setoff under subsection (f) or (h) of this section, the debtor may recover in the manner prescribed by, and subject to the limitations of section 550 of this title, the same as if the trustee had avoided such transfer, and may exempt any property so recovered under subsection (b) of this section.

(2) Notwithstanding section 551 of this title, a transfer avoided under section 544, 545, 547, 548, 549, or 724(a) of this title, under subsection (f) or (h) of this section, or property recovered under section 553 of this title, may be preserved for the benefit of the debtor to the extent that the debtor may exempt such property under subsection (g) of this section or paragraph (1) of this subsection.

(j) Notwithstanding subsections (g) and (i) of this section, the debtor may exempt a particular kind of property under subsections (g) and (i) of this section only to the extent that the debtor has exempted less property in value of such kind than that to which the debtor is entitled under subsection (b) of this section.

(k) Property that the debtor exempts under this section is not liable for payment of any administrative expense except—

(1) the aliquot share of the costs and expenses of avoiding a transfer of property that the debtor exempts under subsection (g) of this section, or of recovery of such property, that is attributable to the value of the portion of such property exempted in relation to the value of the property recovered; and

(2) any costs and expenses of avoiding a transfer under subsection (f) or (h) of this section, or of recovery of property under subsection (i)(1) of this section, that the debtor has not paid.

(*l*) The debtor shall file a list of property that the debtor claims as exempt under subsection (b) of this section. If the debtor does not file such a list, a dependent of the debtor may file such a list or may claim property as exempt from property of the estate on behalf of the debtor. Unless a party in interest objects, the property claimed as exempt on such list is exempt.

(m) This section shall apply separately with respect to each debtor in a joint case.

. . .

§ 541. Property of the estate

(a) The commencement of a case under section 301, 302, or 303 of this title creates an estate. Such estate is comprised of all the following property, wherever located:

(1) Except as provided in subsections (b) and (c)(2) of this section, all legal or equitable interests of the debtor in property as of the commencement of the case.

(2) All interests of the debtor and the debtor's spouse in community property as of the commencement of the case that is—

(A) under the sole, equal, or joint management and control of the debtor; or

(B) liable for an allowable claim against the debtor, or for both an allowable claim against the debtor and an allowable claim against the debtor's spouse, to the extent that such interest is so liable.

(3) Any interest in property that the trustee recovers under section 543, 550, 553, or 723 of this title.

(4) Any interest in the property preserved for the benefit of or ordered transferred to the estate under section 510(c) or 551 of this title.

(5) An interest in property that would have been property of the estate if such interest had been an interest of the debtor on the date of the filing of the petition, and that the debtor acquires or becomes entitled to acquire within 180 days after such date—

(A) by bequest, devise, or inheritance;

(B) as a result of a property settlement agreement with the debtor's spouse, or of an interlocutory or final divorce decree; or

(C) as a beneficiary of a life insurance policy or of a death benefit plan.

(6) Proceeds, product, offspring, rents, and profits of or from property of the estate, except such as are earnings from services performed by an individual debtor after the commencement of the case.

(7) Any interest in property that the estate acquires after the commencement of the case.

(b) Property of the estate does not include any power that the debtor may only exercise solely for the benefit of an entity other than the debtor.

(c)(1) Except as provided in paragraph (2) of this subsection, an interest of the debtor in property becomes property of the estate under subsection (a)(1), (a)(2), or (a)(5) of this section notwithstanding any provision—

(A) that restricts or conditions transfer of such interest by the debtor; or

(B) that is conditioned on the insolvency or financial condition of the debtor, on the commencement of a case under this title, or on the appointment of or the taking possession by a trustee in a case under this title or a custodian, and that effects or gives an option to effect a forfeiture, modification, or termination of the debtor's interest in property.

(2) A restriction on the transfer of a beneficial interest of the debtor in a trust that is enforceable under applicable nonbankruptcy law is enforceable in a case under this title.

(d) Property in which the debtor holds, as of the commencement of the case, only legal title and not an equitable interest, such as a mortgage secured by real property, or an interest in such a mortgage sold by the debtor but as to which the debtor retains legal title to service or supervise the servicing of such mortgage or interest, becomes property of the estate under subsection (a) of this section only to the extent of the debtor's legal title to such property, but not to the extent of any equitable interest in such property that the debtor does not hold.

(e) The estate shall have the benefit of any defense available to the debtor as against an entity other than the estate, including statutes of limitation, statutes of frauds, usury, and other personal defenses. A waiver of any such defense by the debtor after the commencement of the case does not bind the estate.

. . .

§ 544. Trustee as lien creditor and as successor to certain creditors and purchasers

(a) The trustee shall have, as of the commencement of the case, and without regard to any knowledge of the trustee or of any creditor, the rights and powers of, or may avoid any transfer of property of the debtor or any obligation incurred by the debtor that is voidable by—

(1) a creditor that extends credit to the debtor at the time of the commencement of the case, and that obtains, at such time and with respect to such credit, a judicial lien on all property on which a creditor on a simple contract could have obtained a judicial lien, whether or not such a creditor exists;

(2) a creditor that extends credit, to the debtor at the time of the commencement of the case, and obtains, at such time and with respect to such credit, an execution against the debtor that is returned unsatisfied at such time, whether or not such a creditor exists; and

(3) a bona fide purchaser of real property from the debtor, against whom applicable law permits such transfer to be perfected, that obtains the status of a bona fide purchaser at the time of the commencement of the case, whether or not such a purchaser exists.

(b) The trustee may avoid any transfer of an interest of the debtor in property or any obligation incurred by the debtor that is voidable under applicable law by a creditor holding an unsecured claim that is allowable under section 502 of this title or that is not allowable only under section 502(e) of this title.

§ 545. Statutory liens

The trustee may avoid the fixing of a statutory lien on property of the debtor to the extent that such lien—

(1) first becomes effective against the debtor—

(A) when a case under this title concerning the debtor is commenced;

(B) when an insolvency proceeding other than under this title concerning the debtor is commenced;

(C) when a custodian is appointed or takes possession;

(D) when the debtor becomes insolvent;

(E) when the debtor's financial condition fails to meet a specified standard; or

(F) at the time of an execution against property of the debtor levied at the instance of an entity other than the holder of such statutory lien;

(2) is not perfected or enforceable on the date of the filing of the petition against a bona fide purchaser that purchases such property on the date of the filing of the petition, whether or not such a purchaser exists;

(3) is for rent; or

(4) is a lien of distress for rent.

§ 546. Limitations on avoiding powers

(a) An action or proceeding under section 544, 545, 547, 548, or 553 of this title may not be commenced after the earlier of—

(1) two years after the appointment of a trustee under section 702, 1104, 1163, or 1302 of this title; and

(2) the time the case is closed or dismissed.

(b) The rights and powers of the trustee under section 544, 545, or 549 of this title are subject to any generally applicable law that permits perfection of an interest in property to be effective against an entity that acquires rights in such property before the date of such perfection. If such law requires seizure of such property or commencement of an action to accomplish such perfection, and such property has not been seized or such action has not been commenced before the date of the filing of the petition, such interest in such property shall be perfected by notice within the time fixed by such law for such seizure or commencement.

(c) The rights and powers of the trustee under sections 544(a), 545, 547, and 549 of this title are subject to any statutory right or common-law right of a seller, in the ordinary course of such seller's business, of goods to the debtor to reclaim such goods if the debtor has received such goods while insolvent, but—

(1) such a seller may not reclaim any such goods unless such seller demands in writing reclamation of such goods before ten days after receipt of such goods by the debtor; and

(2) the court may deny reclamation to a seller with such a right of reclamation that has made such a demand only if court—

(A) grants the claim of such a seller priority as an administrative expense; or

(B) secures such claim by a lien.

§ 547. Preferences

(a) In this section—

(1) "inventory" means personal property leased or furnished, held for sale or lease, or to be furnished under a contract for service, raw materials, work in process, or materials used or consumed in a business, including farm products such as crops or livestock, held for sale or lease;

(2) "new value" means money or money's worth in goods, services, or new credit, or release by a transferee of property previously transferred to such transferee in a transaction that is neither void nor voidable by the debtor or the trustee under any applicable law, but does not include an obligation substituted for an existing obligation;

(3) "receivable" means right to payment, whether or not such right has been earned by performance; and

(4) a debt for a tax is incurred on the day when such tax is last payable, including any extension, without penalty.

(b) Except as provided in subsection (c) of this section, the trustee may avoid any transfer of property of the debtor—

(1) to or for the benefit of a creditor;

(2) for or on account of an antecedent debt owed by the debtor before such transfer was made;

(3) made while the debtor was insolvent;

(4) made—

(A) on or within 90 days before the date of the filing of the petition; or

(B) between 90 days and one year before the date of the filing of the petition, if such creditor, at the time of such transfer—

(i) was an insider; and

(ii) had reasonable cause to believe the debtor was insolvent at the time of such transfer; and

(5) that enables such creditor to receive more than such creditor would receive if—

(A) the case were a case under chapter 7 of this title;

(B) the transfer had not been made; and

(C) such creditor received payment of such debt to the extent provided by the provisions of this title.

(c) The trustee may not avoid under this section a transfer—

(1) to the extent that such transfer was—

(A) intended by the debtor and the creditor to or for whose benefit such transfer was made to be a contemporaneous exchange for new value given to the debtor; and

(B) in fact a substantially contemporaneous exchange;

(2) to the extent that such transfer was—

(A) in payment of a debt incurred in the ordinary course of business or financial affairs of the debtor and the transferee;

(B) made not later than 45 days after such debt was incurred;

(C) made in the ordinary course of business or financial affairs of the debtor and the transferee; and

(D) made according to ordinary business terms;

(3) of a security interest in property acquired by the debtor—

(A) to the extent such security interest secures new value that was—

(i) given at or after the signing of a security agreement that contains a description of such property as collateral;

(ii) given by or on behalf of the secured party under such agreement;

(iii) given to enable the debtor to acquire such property; and

(iv) in fact used by the debtor to acquire such property; and

(B) that is perfected before 10 days after such security interest attaches;

(4) to or for the benefit of a creditor, to the extent that, after such transfer, such creditor gave new value to or for the benefit of the debtor—

(A) not secured by an otherwise unavoidable security interest; and

(B) on account of which new value the debtor did not make an otherwise unavoidable transfer to or for the benefit of such creditor;

(5) of a perfected security interest in inventory or a receivable or the proceeds of either, except to the extent that the aggregate of all such transfers to the transferee caused a reduction, as of the date of the filing of the petition and to the prejudice of other creditors holding unsecured claims, of any amount by which the debt secured by such security interest exceeded the value of all security interest for such debt on the later of—

(A)(i) with respect to a transfer to which subsection (b)(4)(A) of this section applies, 90 days before the date of the filing of the petition; or

(ii) with respect to a transfer to which subsection (b)(4)(B) of this section applies, one year before the date of the filing of the petition; and

(B) the date on which new value was first given under the security agreement creating such security interest; or

(6) that is the fixing of a statutory lien that is not avoidable under section 545 of this title.

(d) A trustee may avoid a transfer of property of the debtor transferred to secure reimbursement of a surety that furnished a bond or other obligation to dissolve a judicial lien that would have been avoidable by the trustee under subsection (b) of this section. The liability of such surety under such bond or obligation shall be discharged to the extent of the value of such property recovered by the trustee or the amount paid to the trustee.

(e)(1) For the purposes of this section—

(A) a transfer of real property other than fixtures, but including the interest of a seller or purchaser under a contract for the sale of real property, is perfected when a bona fide purchaser of such property from the debtor against whom applicable law permits such transfer to be perfected cannot acquire an interest that is superior to the interest of the transferee; and

(B) a transfer of a fixture or property other than real property is perfected when a creditor on a simple contract cannot acquire a judicial lien that is superior to the interest of the transferee.

(2) For the purposes of this section, except as provided in paragraph (3) of this subsection, a transfer is made—

(A) at the time such transfer takes effect between the transferor and the transferee, if such transfer is perfected at, or within 10 days after, such time;

(B) at the time such transfer is perfected, if such transfer is perfected after such 10 days; or

(C) immediately before the date of the filing of the petition, if such transfer is not perfected at the later of—

(i) the commencement of the case; and

(ii) 10 days after such transfer takes effect between the transferor and the transferee.

(3) For the purposes of this section, a transfer is not made until the debtor has acquired rights in the property transferred.

(f) For the purposes of this section, the debtor is presumed to have been insolvent on and during the 90 days immediately preceding the date of the filing of the petition.

§ 548. Fraudulent transfers and obligations

(a) The trustee may avoid any transfer of an interest of the debtor in property, or any obligation incurred by the debtor, that was made or incurred on or within one year before the date of the filing of the petition, if the debtor—

(1) made such transfer or incurred such obligation with actual intent to hinder, delay, or defraud any entity to which the debtor was or became, on or after the date that such transfer occurred or such obligation was incurred, indebted; or

(2)(A) received less than a reasonably equivalent value in exchange for such transfer or obligation; and

(B)(i) was insolvent on the date that such transfer was made or such obligation was incurred, or became insolvent as a result of such transfer or obligation;

(ii) was engaged in business, or was about to engage in business or a transaction, for which any property remaining with the debtor was an unreasonably small capital; or

(iii) intended to incur, or believed that the debtor would incur, debts that would be beyond the debtor's ability to pay as such debts matured.

(b) The trustee of a partnership debtor may avoid any transfer of an interest of the debtor in property, or any obligation incurred by the debtor, that was made or incurred on or within one year before the date of the filing of the petition, to a general partner in the debtor, if the debtor was insolvent on the date such transfer was made or such obligation was incurred, or became insolvent as a result of such transfer or obligation.

(c) Except to the extent that a transfer or obligation voidable under this section is voidable under section 544, 545, or 547 of this title, a transferee or obligee of such a transfer or obligation that takes for value and in good faith has a lien on any interest transferred, may retain any lien transferred, or may enforce any obligation incurred, as the case may be, to the extent that such transferee or obligee gave value to the debtor in exchange for such transfer or obligation.

(d)(1) For the purposes of this section, a transfer is made when such transfer becomes so far perfected that a bona fide purchaser from the debtor against whom such transfer could have been perfected cannot acquire an interest in the property transferred that is superior to the interest in such property of the transferee, but if such transfer is not so perfected before the commencement of the case, such transfer occurs immediately before the date of the filing of the petition.

(2) In this section—

(A) "value" means property, or satisfaction or securing of a present or antecedent debt of the debtor, but does not include an unperformed promise to furnish support to the debtor or to a relative of the debtor; and

(B) a commodity broker or forward contract merchant that receives a margin payment, as defined in section 761(15) of this title, takes for value.

§ 549. Postpetition transactions

(a) Except as provided in subsection (b) and (c) of this section, the trustee may avoid a transfer of property of the estate—

(1) that occurs after the commencement of the case; and

(2)(A) that is authorized under section 303(f) or 542(c) of this title; or

(B) that is not authorized under this title or by the court.

(b) In an involuntary case, a transfer that occurs after the commencement of such case but before the order for relief is valid against the trustee to the extent of any value, including services, but not including satisfaction or securing of a debt that arose before the commencement of the case, given after the commencement of the case in exchange for such transfer, notwithstanding any notice or knowledge of the case that the transferee has.

(c) The trustee may not avoid under subsection (a) of this section a transfer, to a good faith purchaser without knowledge of the commencement of the case and for present fair equivalent value or to a purchaser at a judicial sale, of real property located other than in the county in which the case is commenced, unless a copy of the petition was filed in the office where conveyances of real property in such county are recorded before such transfer was so far perfected that a bona fide purchaser of such property against whom applicable law permits such transfer to be perfected cannot acquire an interest that is superior to the interest of such good faith or judicial sale purchaser. A good faith purchaser, without knowledge of the commencement of the case and for less than present fair equivalent value, of real property located other than in the county in which the case is commenced, under a transfer that the trustee may avoid under this section, has a lien on the property transferred to the extent of any present value given, unless a copy of the petition was so filed before such transfer was so perfected.

(d) An action or proceeding under this section may not be commenced after the earlier of—

(1) two years after the date of the transfer sought to be avoided; and

(2) the time the case is closed or dismissed.

§ 550. Liability of transferee of avoided transfer

(a) Except as otherwise provided in this section, to the extent that a transfer is avoided under section 544, 545, 547, 548, 549, or 724(a) of this title, the trustee may recover, for the benefit of the estate, the property transferred, or, if the court so orders, the value of such property, from—

(1) the initial transferee of such transfer or the entity for whose benefit such transfer was made; or

(2) any immediate or mediate transferee of such initial transferee.

(b) The trustee may not recover under section (a)(2) of this section from—

(1) a transferee that takes for value, including satisfaction or securing of a present or antecedent debt, in good faith, and without knowledge of the voidability of the transfer avoided; or

(2) any immediate or mediate good faith transferee of such transferee.

(c) The trustee is entitled to only a single satisfaction under subsection (a) of this section.

(d)(1) A good faith transferee from whom the trustee may recover under subsection (a) of this section has a lien on the property recovered to secure the lesser of—

(A) the cost, to such transferee, of any improvement made after the transfer, less the amount of any profit realized by such transferee from such property; and

(B) any increase in value as a result of such improvement, of the property transferred.

(2) In this subsection, "improvement" includes—

(A) physical additions or changes to the property transferred;

(B) repairs to such property;

(C) payment of any tax on such property;

(D) payment of any debt secured by a lien on such property;

(E) discharge of any lien against such property that is superior or equal to the rights of the trustee; and

(F) preservation of such property.

(e) An action or proceeding under this section may not be commenced after the earlier of—

(1) one year after the avoidance of the transfer on account of which recovery under this section is sought; and

(2) the time the case is closed or dismissed.

§ 551. Automatic preservation of avoided transfer

Any transfer avoided under section 522, 544, 545, 547, 548, 549, or 724(a) of this title, or any lien void under section 506(d) of this title, is preserved for the benefit of the estate but only with respect to property of the estate.

§ 552. Postpetition effect of security interest

(a) Except as provided in subsection (b) of this section, property acquired by the estate or by the debtor after the commencement of the case is not subject to any lien resulting from any security agreement entered into by the debtor before the commencement of the case.

(b) Except as provided in sections 363, 506(c), 544, 545, 547, and 548 of this title, if the debtor and a secured party enter into a security agreement before the commencement of the case and if the security interest created by such security agreement extends to property of the debtor acquired before the commencement of the case and to proceeds, product, offspring, rents, or profits of such property, then such security interest extends to such proceeds, product, offspring, rents, or profits acquired by the estate after the commencement of the case to the extent provided by such security agreement and by applicable nonbankruptcy law, except to the extent that the court, after notice and a hearing and based on the equities of the case, orders otherwise.

§ 553. **Setoff**

(a) Except as otherwise provided in this section and in sections 362 and 363 of this title, this title does not affect any right of a creditor to offset a mutual debt owing by such creditor to the debtor that arose before the commencement of the case under this title against a claim of such creditor against the debtor that arose before the commencement of the case, except to the extent that—

(1) the claim of such creditor against the debtor is disallowed other than under section 502(b)(3) of this title;

(2) such claim was transferred, by an entity other than the debtor, to such creditor—

(A) after the commencement of the case; or

(B)(i) after 90 days before the date of the filing of the petition; and

(ii) while the debtor was insolvent; or

(3) the debt owed to the debtor by such creditor was incurred by such creditor—

(A) after 90 days before the date of the filing of the petition;

(B) while the debtor was insolvent; and

(C) for the purpose of obtaining a right of setoff against the debtor.

(b)(1) Except with respect to a setoff of a kind described in section 362(b)(6) or 365(h)(1) of this title, if a creditor offsets a mutual debt owing to the debtor against a claim against the debtor on or within 90 days before the date of the filing of the petition, then the trustee may recover from such creditor the amount so offset to the extent that any insufficiency on the date of such setoff is less than the insufficiency on the later of—

(A) 90 days before the date of the filing of the petition; and

(B) the first date during the 90 days immediately preceding the date of the filing of the petition on which there is an insufficiency.

(2) In this subsection, "insufficiency" means amount, if any, by which a claim against the debtor exceeds a mutual debt owing to the debtor by the holder of such claim.

(c) For the purposes of this section, the debtor is presumed to have been insolvent on and during the 90 days immediately preceding the date of the filing of the petition.

INTERNAL REVENUE CODE

Selected Sections

Title 26, United States Code

Subtitle F—Procedure and Administration

Chapter 64—Collection

Subchapter C—Lien for Taxes

---

§ 6321. Lien for taxes

If any person liable to pay any tax neglects or refuses to pay the same after demand, the amount (including any interest, additional amount, addition to tax, or assessable penalty, together with any costs that may accrue in addition thereto) shall be a lien in favor of the United States upon all property and rights to property, whether real or personal, belonging to such person.

§ 6322. Period of lien

Unless another date is specifically fixed by law, the lien imposed by section 6321 shall arise at the time the assessment is made and shall continue until the liability for the amount so assessed (or a judgment against the taxpayer arising out of such liability) is satisfied or becomes unenforceable by reason of lapse of time.

§ 6323. Validity and priority against certain persons

(a) Purchases,[1] holders of security interests, mechanic's lienors, and judgment lien creditors.—The lien imposed by section 6321 shall not be valid as against any purchaser, holder of a security interest, mechanic's lienor, or judgment lien creditor until notice thereof which meets the requirements of subsection (f) has been filed by the Secretary or his delegate.

(b) Protection for certain interests even though notice filed.—Even though notice of a lien imposed by section 6321 has been filed, such lien shall not be valid—

(1) Securities.—With respect to a security (as defined in subsection (h) (4))—

(A) as against a purchaser of such security who at the time of purchase did not have actual notice or knowledge of the existence of such lien; and

(B) as against a holder of a security interest in such security who, at the time such interest came into existence, did not have actual notice or knowledge of the existence of such lien.

[1] So in original. Probably should be "Purchasers."

(2) Motor vehicles.—With respect to a motor vehicle (as defined in subsection (h) (3)), as against a purchaser of such motor vehicle, if—

(A) at the time of the purchase such purchaser did not have actual notice or knowledge of the existence of such lien, and

(B) before the purchaser obtains such notice or knowledge, he has acquired possession of such motor vehicle and has not thereafter relinquished possession of such motor vehicle to the seller or his agent.

(3) Personal property purchased at retail.—With respect to tangible personal property purchased at retail, as against a purchaser in the ordinary couse of the seller's trade or business, unless at the time of such purchase such purchaser intends such purchase to (or knows such purchase will) hinder, evade, or defeat the collection of any tax under this title.

(4) Personal property purchased in casual sale.—With respect to household goods, personal effects, or other tangible personal property described in section 6334(a) purchased (not for resale) in a casual sale for less than $250, as against the purchaser, but only if such purchaser does not have actual notice or knowledge (A) of the existence of such lien, or (B) that this sale is one of a series of sales.

(5) Personal property subject to possessory lien.—With respect to tangible personal property subject to a lien under local law securing the reasonable price of the repair or improvement of such property, as against a holder of such a lien, if such holder is, and has been, continuously in possession of such property from the time such lien arose.

(6) Real property tax and special assessment liens.—With respect to real property, as against a holder of a lien upon such property, if such lien is entitled under local law to priority over security interests in such property which are prior in time, and such lien secures payment of—

(A) a tax of general application levied by any taxing authority based upon the value of such property;

(B) a special assessment imposed directly upon such property by any taxing authority, if such assessment is imposed for the purpose of defraying the cost of any public improvement; or

(C) charges for utilities or public services furnished to such property by the United States, a State or political subdivision thereof, or an instrumentality of any one or more of the foregoing.

(7) Residential property subject to a mechanic's lien for certain repairs and improvements.—With respect to real property subject to a lien for repair or improvement of a personal residence (containing not more than four dwelling units) occupied by the owner of such residence, as against a mechanic's lienor, but only if the contract price on the contract with the owner is not more than $1,000.

(8) Attorneys' liens.—With respect to a judgment or other amount in settlement of a claim or of a cause of action, as against an attorney who, under local law, holds a lien upon or a contract enforcible against such judgment or amount, to the extent of his reasonable compensation for obtaining such judgment or procuring such settlement, except that this paragraph shall not apply to any judgment or amount in settlement of a claim or of a cause of action against the United States to the extent that the United States offsets such judgment or amount against any liability of the taxpayer to the United States.

(9) Certain insurance contracts.—With respect to a life insurance, endowment, or annuity contract, as against the organization which is the insurer under such contract, at any time—

(A) before such organization had actual notice or knowledge of the existence of such lien;

(B) after such organization had such notice or knowledge, with respect to advances required to be made automatically to maintain such contract in force under an agreement entered into before such organization had such notice or knowledge; or

(C) after satisfaction of a levy pursuant to section 6332(b), unless and until the Secretary or his delegate delivers to such organization a notice, executed after the date of such satisfaction, of the existence of such lien.

(10) Passbook loans.—With respect to a savings deposit, share, or other account, evidenced by a passbook, with an institution described in section 581 or 591, to the extent of any loan made by such institution without actual notice or knowledge of the existence of such lien, as against such institution, if such loan is secured by such account and if such institution has been continuously in possession of such passbook from the time the loan is made.

(c) Protection for certain commercial transactions financing agreements, etc.—

(1) In general.—To the extent provided in this subsection, even though notice of a lien imposed by section 6321 has been filed, such lien shall not be valid with respect to a security interest which came into existence after tax lien filing but which—

(A) is in qualified property covered by the terms of a written agreement entered into before tax lien filing and constituting—

(i) a commercial transactions financing agreement,

(ii) a real property construction or improvement financing agreement, or

(iii) an obligatory disbursement agreement, and

(B) is protected under local law against a judgment lien arising, as of the time of tax lien filing, out of an unsecured obligation.

(2) Commercial transactions financing agreement.—For purposes of this subsection—

(A) Definition.—The term "commercial transactions financing agreement" means an agreement (entered into by a person in the course of his trade or business)—

(i) to make loans to the taxpayer to be secured by commercial financing security acquired by the taxpayer in the ordinary course of his trade or business, or

(ii) to purchase commercial financing security (other than inventory) acquired by the taxpayer in the ordinary course of his trade or business;

but such an agreement shall be treated as coming within the term only to the extent that such loan or purchase is made before the 46th day after the date of tax lien filing or (if earlier) before the lender or purchaser had actual notice or knowledge of such tax lien filing.

(B) Limitation on qualified property.—The term "qualified property", when used with respect to a commercial transactions financing agreement, includes only commercial financing security acquired by the taxpayer before the 46th day after the date of tax lien filing.

(C) Commercial financing security defined.—The term "commercial financing security" means (i) paper of a kind ordinarily arising in commercial transactions, (ii) accounts receivable, (iii) mortgages on real property, and (iv) inventory.

(D) Purchaser treated as acquiring security interest.—A person who satisfies subparagraph (A) by reason of clause (ii) thereof shall be treated as having acquired a security interest in commercial financing security.

(3) Real property construction or improvement financing agreement.—For purposes of this subsection—

(A) Definition.—The term "real property construction or improvement financing agreement" means an agreement to make cash disbursements to finance—

(i) the construction or improvement of real property,

(ii) a contract to construct or improve real property, or

(iii) the raising or harvesting of a farm crop or the raising of livestock or other animals.

For purposes of clause (iii), the furnishing of goods and services shall be treated as the disbursement of cash.

(B) Limitation on qualified property.—The term "qualified property", when used with respect to a real property construction or improvement financing agreement, includes only—

(i) in the case of subparagraph (A) (i), the real property with respect to which the construction or improvement has been or is to be made,

(ii) in the case of subparagraph (A) (ii), the proceeds of the contract described therein, and

(iii) in the case of subparagraph (A) (iii), property subject to the lien imposed by section 6321 at the time of tax lien filing and the crop or the livestock or other animals referred to in subparagraph (A) (iii).

(4) Obligatory disbursement agreement.—For purposes of this subsection—

(A) Definition.—The term "obligatory disbursement agreement" means an agreement (entered into by a person in the course of his trade or business) to make disbursements, but such an agreement shall be treated as coming within the term only to the extent of disbursements which are required to be made by reason of the intervention of the rights of a person other than the taxpayer.

(B) Limitation on qualified property.—The term "qualified property", when used with respect to an obligatory disbursement agreement, means property subject to the lien imposed by section 6321 at the time of tax lien filing and (to the extent that the acquisition is directly traceable to the disbursements referred to in subparagraph (A)) property acquired by the taxpayer after tax lien filing.

(C) Special rules for surety agreements.—Where the obligatory disbursement agreement is an agreement ensuring the performance of a contract between the taxpayer and another person—

(i) the term "qualified property" shall be treated as also including the proceeds of the contract the performance of which was ensured, and

(ii) if the contract the performance of which was ensured was a contract to construct or improve real property, to produce goods, or to furnish services, the term "qualified property" shall be treated as also including any tangible personal property used by the taxpayer in the performance of such ensured contract.

(d) 45-day period for making disbursements.—Even though notice of a lien imposed by section 6321 has been filed, such lien shall not be valid with respect to a security interest which came into existence after tax lien filing by reason of disbursements made before the 46th day after the date of tax lien filing, or (if earlier) before the person making such disbursements had actual notice or knowledge of tax lien filing, but only if such security interest—

(1) is in property (A) subject, at the time of tax lien filing, to the lien imposed by section 6321, and (B) covered by the terms of a written agreement entered into before tax lien filing, and

(2) is protected under local law against a judgment lien arising, as of the time of tax lien filing, out of an unsecured obligation.

(e) Priority of interest and expenses.—If the lien imposed by section 6321 is not valid as against a lien or security interest, the priority of such lien or security interest shall extend to—

(1) any interest or carrying charges upon the obligation secured,

(2) the reasonable charges and expenses of an indenture trustee or agent holding the security interest for the benefit of the holder of the security interest,

(3) the reasonable expenses, including reasonable compensation for attorneys, actually incurred in collecting or enforcing the obligation secured,

(4) the reasonable costs of insuring, preserving, or repairing the property to which the lien or security interest relates,

(5) the reasonable costs of insuring payment of the obligation secured, and

(6) amounts paid to satisfy any lien on the property to which the lien or security interest relates, but only if the lien so satisfied is entitled to priority over the lien imposed by section 6321,

to the extent that, under local law, any such item has the same priority as the lien or security interest to which it relates.

(f) Place for filing notice; form.—

(1) Place for filing.—The notice referred to in subsection (a) shall be filed—

(A) Under State laws.—

(i) Real property.—In the case of real property, in one office within the State (or the county, or other governmental subdivision), as designated by the laws of such State, in which the property subject to the lien is situated; and

(ii) Personal property.—In the case of personal property, whether tangible or intangible, in one office within the State (or the county, or other governmental subdivision), as designated by the laws of such State, in which the property subject to the lien is situated; or

(B) With clerk of district court.—In the office of the clerk of the United States district court for the judicial district in which the property subject to the lien is situated, whenever the State has not by law designated one office which meets the requirements of subparagraph (A); or

(C) With Recorder of Deeds of the District of Columbia.—In the office of the Recorder of Deeds of the District of Columbia, if the property subject to the lien is situated in the District of Columbia.

(2) Situs of property subject to lien.—For purposes of paragraph (1) and (4), property shall be deemed to be situated—

(A) Real property.—In the case of real property, at its physical location; or

(B) Personal property.—In the case of personal property, whether tangible or intangible, at the residence of the taxpayer at the time the notice of lien is filed.

For purposes of paragraph (2) (B), the residence of a corporation or partnership shall be deemed to be the place at which the principal executive office of the business is located, and the residence of a taxpayer whose residence is without the United States shall be deemed to be in the District of Columbia.

(3) Form.—The form and content of the notice referred to in subsection (a) shall be prescribed by the Secretary. Such notice shall be valid notwithstanding any other provision of law regarding the form or content of a notice of lien.

(4) Indexing required with respect to certain real property.—In the case of real property, if—

(A) under the laws of the State in which the real property is located, a deed is not valid as against a purchaser of the property who (at the time of purchase) does not have actual notice or knowledge of the existence of such deed unless the fact of filing of such deed has been entered and recorded in a public index at the place of filing in such a manner that a reasonable inspection of the index will reveal the existence of the deed, and

(B) there is maintained (at the applicable office under paragraph (1)) an adequate system for the public indexing of Federal tax liens,

then the notice of lien referred to in subsection (a) shall not be treated as meeting the filing requirements under paragraph (1) unless the fact of filing is entered and recorded in the index referred to in subparagraph (B) in such a manner that a reasonable inspection of the index will reveal the existence of the lien.

(g) Refiling of notice.—For purposes of this section—

(1) General rule.—Unless notice of lien is refiled in the manner prescribed in paragraph (2) during the required refiling period, such notice of lien shall be treated as filed on the date on which it is filed (in accordance with subsection (f)) after the expiration of such refiling period.

(2) Place for filing.—A notice of lien refiled during the required refiling period shall be effective only—

(A) if—

(i) such notice of lien is refiled in the office in which the prior notice of lien was filed, and

(ii) in the case of real property, the fact of refiling is entered and recorded in an index to the extent required by subsection (f)(4); and

(B) in any case in which, 90 days or more prior to the date of a refiling of notice of lien under subparagraph (A), the Secretary or his delegate received written information (in the manner prescribed in regulations issued by the Secretary or his delegate) concerning a change in the taxpayer's residence, if a notice of such lien is also filed in accordance with subsection (f) in the State in which such residence is located.

(3) Required refiling period.—In the case of any notice of lien, the term "required refiling period" means—

(A) the one-year period ending 30 days after the expiration of 6 years after the date of the assessment of the tax, and

(B) the one-year period ending with the expiration of 6 years after the close of the preceding required refiling period for such notice of lien.

(4) Transitional rule.—Notwithstanding paragraph (3), if the assessment of the tax was made before January 1, 1962, the first required refiling period shall be the calendar year 1967.

(h) Definitions.—For purposes of this section and section 6324—

(1) Security interest.—The term "security interest" means any interest in property acquired by contract for the purpose of securing payment or performance of an obligation or indemnifying against loss or liability. A security interest exists at any time (A), if, at such time, the property is in existence and the interest has become protected under local law against a subsequent judgment lien arising out of an unsecured obligation, and (B) to the extent that, at such time, the holder has parted with money or money's worth.

(2) Mechanic's lienor.—The term "mechanic's lienor" means any person who under local law has a lien on real property (or on the proceeds of a contract relating to real property) for services, labor, or materials furnished in connection with the construction or improvement of such property. For purposes of the preceding sentence, a person has a lien on the earliest date such lien becomes valid under local law against subsequent purchasers without actual notice, but not before he begins to furnish the services, labor, or materials.

(3) Motor vehicle.—The term "motor vehicle" means a self-propelled vehicle which is registered for highway use under the laws of any State or foreign country.

(4) Security.—The term "security" means any bond, debenture, note, or certificate or other evidence of indebtedness, issued by a corporation or a government or political subdivision thereof, with interest coupons or in registered form, share of stock, voting trust certificate, or any certificate of interest or participation in, certificate of deposit or receipt for, temporary or interim certificate for, or warrant or right to subscribe to or purchase, any of the foregoing; negotiable instrument; or money.

(5) Tax lien filing.—The term "tax lien filing" means the filing of notice (referred to in subsection (a)) of the lien imposed by section 6321.

(6) Purchaser.—The term "purchaser" means a person who, for adequate and full consideration in money or money's worth, acquires an interest (other than a lien or security interest) in property which is valid under local law against subsequent purchasers without actual notice. In applying the preceding sentence for purposes of subsection (a) of this section, and for purposes of section 6324—

(A) a lease of property,

(B) a written executory contract to purchase or lease property,

(C) an option to purchase or lease property or any interest therein, or

(D) an option to renew or extend a lease of property, which is not a lien or security interest shall be treated as an interest in property.

(i) Special rules.—

(1) Actual notice or knowledge.—For purposes of this subchapter, an organization shall be deemed for purposes of a particular transaction to have actual notice or knowledge of any fact from the time such fact is brought to the attention of the individual conducting such transaction, and in any event from the time such fact would have been brought to such individual's attention if the organization had exercised due diligence. An organization exercises due diligence if it maintains reasonable routines for communicating significant information to the person conducting the transaction and there is reasonable compliance with the routine. Due diligence does not require an individual acting for the organization to communicate information unless such communication is part of his regular duties or unless he has reason to know of the transaction and that the transaction would be materially affected by the information.

(2) Subrogation.—Where, under local law, one person is subrogated to the rights of another with respect to a lien or interest, such person shall be subrogated to such rights for purposes of any lien imposed by section 6321 or 6324.

(3) Repealed. Pub.L. 94–455, Title XII, § 1202(h)(2), Oct. 4, 1976, 90 Stat. 1688.

NOTE

(A) The amendments made [to sections 6323(f)(4) and 6323 (g)(2)(A)] by this subsection shall apply with respect to liens, other security interests, and other interests in real property acquired after the date of the enactment of this Act.

(B) If, after the date of the enactment of this Act, there is a change in the application (or nonapplication) of section 6323(f)(4) of the Internal Revenue Code of 1954 (as amended by paragraph (1)) with respect to any filing jurisdiction, such change shall apply only with respect to liens, other security interests, and other interests in real property acquired after the date of such change.

†

when there is a forged indorsement - absent negligence on the part of the owner of the check the loss should normally come to rest upon the first solvent party in the stream after the one who forged the instrument.

If an instrument is payable to bearer because it was issued that way or because it was indorsed in blank by a holder, the possessor is a holder + maybe a HDC - even if the instrument passed through a thief.

No party can ever be a holder of an order instrument stolen prior to indorsment by the owner 3-202(2)